History of Greene County, Pennsylvania

HISTORY

OF

GREENE COUNTY,

PENNSYLVANIA,

BY

SAMUEL P. BATES.

Hills, vales, woods, netted in silver mist,
Farms, granges, doubled up among the hills
And cattle grazing in the watered vales,
And cottage chimneys smoking from the woods,
And cottage gardens smelling everywhere,
Confused with smell of orchards See! I said,
And see! is God not with us on the earth?
—ELIZABETH BARRETT BROWNING

ILLUSTRATED

NELSON, RISHFORTH & CO.,
CHICAGO
1888.

PREFACE.

The section of country, of which Greene County occupies a central position, has more vitally interesting problems in its history, than any other portion of the United States. The nationality which should occupy. the great Mississippi Valley—Spanish, French, or English; the narrowed struggle between the French and the English, inaugurated by Marquette and LaSalle, in their pious ceremonials, and by Celeron in planting the leaden plates; the fierce military contest led by Washington, Braddock, and Forbes for possession of Fort Pitt and the final banishment of the French beyond the lakes; the long and wasting conflict with the natives in which isolated pioneers with their families were exposed in their scattered cabins in the forest, to the fiendish arts of the stealthy and heartless savage, who spared neither the helpless infant, the tender female, nor trembling age; the protracted controversy with Maryland over the possession of territory which both States claimed; the settlements of a Virginia company on Pennsylvania soil, and the claim of the former State to the whole boundless Northwest; the chances by which the final settlement of possession was invested, and the finding of the southwest corner of the State finally accomplished by astronomical observations at the instance of Thomas Jefferson; the subtle influences which swayed the location of the National road, and the Baltimore and Ohio railway—these were all questions which nearly touch the ultimate reaches of its history. It has been thought best accordingly, to give generous space in this volume to these vital subjects, which will ever command the attention of the thoughtful, will daily increase in interest to the oncoming generations, and by means of which we trace the philosophy of the vital events of history that are really useful.

In preparing these pages for publication it has been decided not to encumber the text with marginal notes, and references to authorities; but to name authors where their investigations have been used, and to make acknowledgements in a general way. It would be impossible to name all, but the following have been found especially useful and have been freely consulted: The Histories of the United States by Bancroft, Hildreth, Spencer, Bryant, and Lossing; Irving's Life of Washington; Life and Writings of William Penn; Colonial Records, and Pennsylvania archives; History of Pennsylvania Volunteers; the Western Annals, History of

Western Pennsylvania; Redstone Presbytery; McConnell's Map of Greene County; The Historical Atlas; the State Reports of Education from 1837 to 1887; and Crumrine's History of Washington County.

Especial acknowledgements are due to L. K. Evans, Esq., who, during the Centennial year of American Independence, published in the Waynesburg *Republican*, which he then edited, a series of articles running through an entire year of weekly issues, embracing investigations which he pushed with singular perseverance and marked success, covering much of the early history of the county. In a spirit of generosity and kindness, he not only placed at my disposal a complete set of these articles, but also a mass of manuscript which had been addressed to him by aged citizens in various sections of the county, bearing upon the subject of his investigations. From these sources matter has been freely drawn; and though it has not been possible, on account of the limits prescribed to this work, to use as much as might have been desired, in the interesting style in which it appears, yet in a condensed form it has been freely appropriated.

Probably no equal portion of any part of the United States has been the scene of so many cold-blooded and heartless murders by the Indians as this county; not because the pioneers here provoked the natives to revenge, nor because they were the special objects of hatred, but because they happened to be in the way of the savages in their march to and fro upon their war expeditions, and because this was their ancient hunting ground. The Indians never made this section their home, having no villages nor wigwams in all its limits; but from time immemorial had kept this as a sort of park or preserve for the breeding of their game. They may have felt aggrieved in seeing their favorite hunting grounds broken in upon, and the game scared away by the ring of the settler's ax, the echo of his gun, and his frequent burnings; but it is probable that this had less influence than the fact that their war-paths happened to cross here, and they found in their way subjects on whom they could glut their savage instincts. There are over one hundred well authenticated records in the State archives of murders committed within the limits of this small county alone.

Hoping that the work will prove useful to the citizens of the county, and especially to the rising generation, and will serve to stimulate to further inquiry into the subjects which it touches, it is respectively submitted to their considerate judgment.

S. P. B.

Waynesburg, Nov. 13, 1888

CONTENTS.

HISTORY OF GREENE COUNTY.

CONTENTS.

BIOGRAPHICAL SKETCHES.

CONTENTS.

xi

CONTENTS.

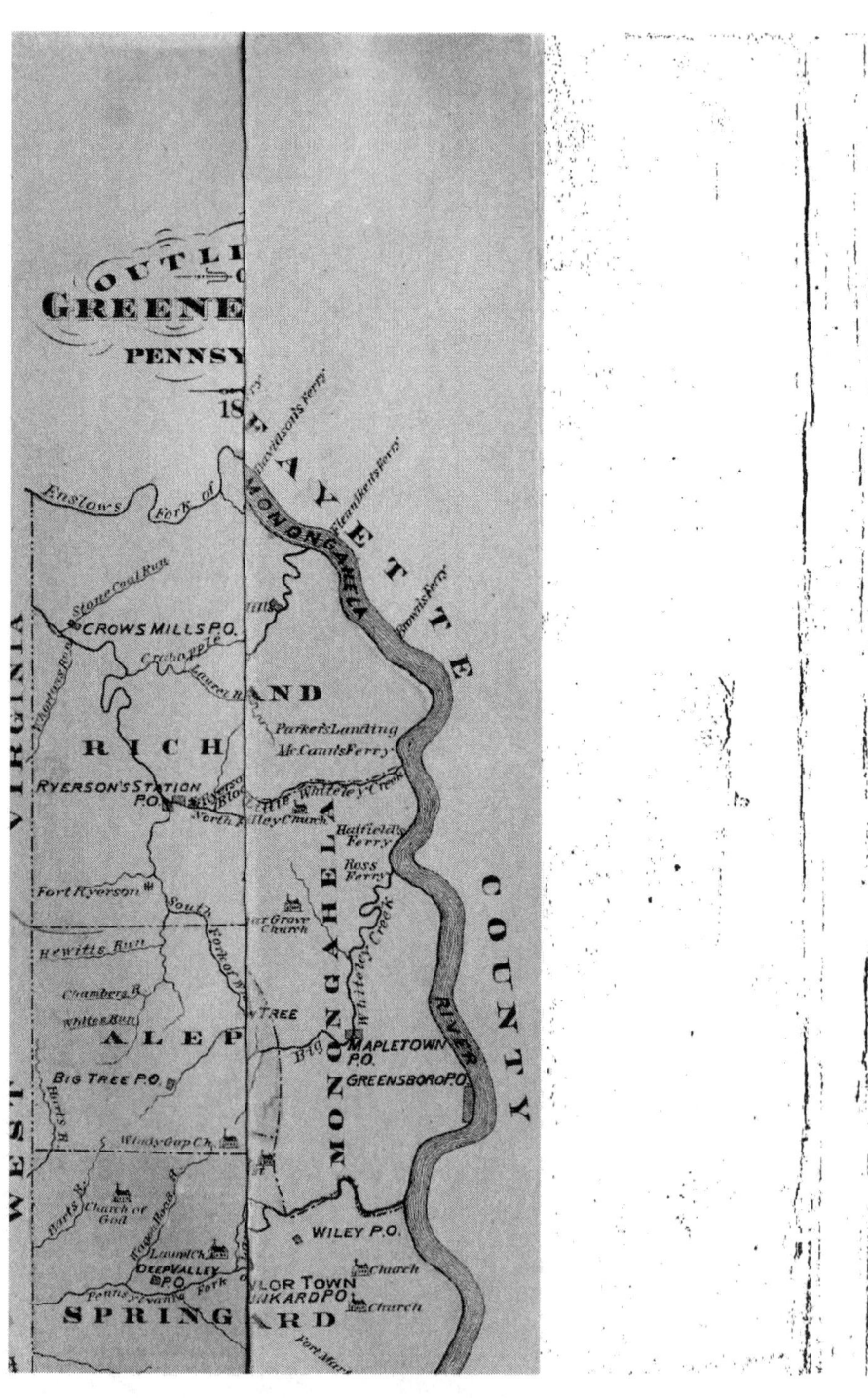

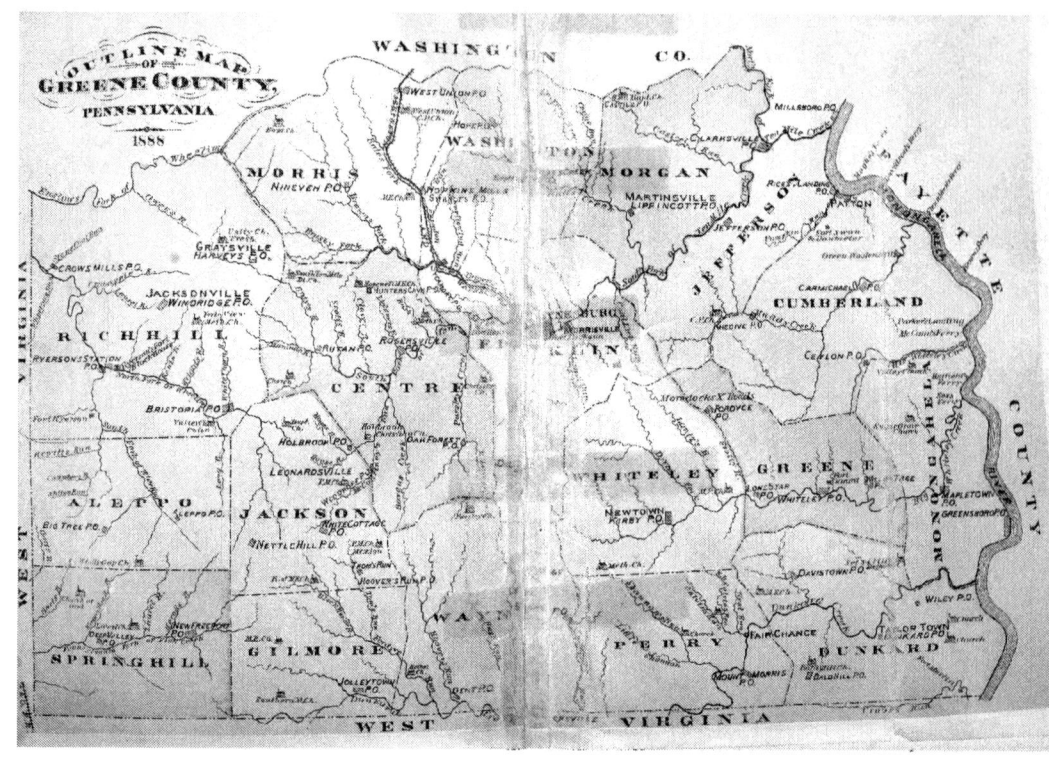

HISTORY OF GREENE COUNTY,

PENNSYLVANIA.

CHAPTER I.

PICTURESQUE BEAUTY OF GREENE COUNTY—WORDS OF ALEXANDER
CAMPBELL—ITS LOCATION—389,120 SQUARE ACRES—STREAMS,
DRAINING IT—WATER-SHED—TREND OF THE HILLS—FERTILITY
OF THE SOIL.—LIMESTONE—FORESTS—REMARKS UPON FORESTRY
—A GIRDLED FOREST—CONSEQUENCE OF WAR UPON THE FOR-
ESTS—JUDICIOUS PLANTING—THE SUGAR MAPLE—AS SEEN IN
SOUTHERN ITALY—QUESTIONS TOUCHING ITS EARLY OCCUPATION.

AN English nobleman of the last generation, schooled by travel in
many lands, in a book which he wrote descriptive of an extended
tour in the United States, deliberately declared that of all the lands
which had gladdened his vision by their picturesque beauty in any
part of the globe, none excelled those along the upper waters of the
Ohio and its tributary streams. Indeed, so fascinated were the early
French visitants, accustomed in their own land to scenes of enchanting natural beauty, that when they beheld the Ohio, they designated
it, and ever after called it in all their books and writings. *La Belle
Reviére.*

Of that portion of country, which, by its lines of beauty and
grace, has justly won these generous and just encomiums, to none
can they more fairly be applied, than to that territory included within
the limits of Greene County; for it will be remembered that the
French knew less of what is now designated the Ohio River, than
its two principal tributaries, to which they applied the one common
name. To the traveler who passes on over its network of highways,
winding among its crown of hills, or by the margin of its sparkling
streams, on every side are presented the elements of beauty; and the
artist who seeks for worthy subjects of his brush, cannot fail to find
them here. The monotony which plagues the traveler in a prairie
land, and in many portions of the Atlantic shores, is unknown to

1

him here. Scarcely one field in all its broad domain is like another.
Nor is there here the other extreme,—the bald and shaggy mountain
with its inaccessible summits, forbidding intercourse from its op
posing sides, given up to barrenness and sterility.
But everywhere is pleasing variety. In spring time the whole surface of the landscape is gladdened with the verdure of the fast spring-
ing wheat, and rich pasturage links the margins of the quick flowing
streams to the summits of the farthest hills. In summer time numberless flocks and herds lick up the morning dew of the valley, repose
at the heated noontide beneath ample shade, or slake their thirst at
the cool and abundant fountains, and find rest at night-fall on some
breezy knoll or sheltered nook. In autumn shocks of well ripened
grain gladden all the valleys, and along the hills are ridges of golden
corn. When winter comes with its hoary breath, and river, and creek,
and brooklet are bound in icy adamant, and the great clouds of snow-
flakes come whirling over hill-tops and down the valleys, wrapping
all the earth in a drapery of white, the sun, though with far-off
slanting rays, peers into happy homes, sheltered from the biting
blast by massive hills that rise up in giant form on every side, like
trusty sentinels to keep back and break the force of the blizzards that
come with their deathly embrace to torment the dwellers on the
western plains.
That I may not seem extravagant in my estimate of the beauties
of a Greene County landscape, or the fertility of its soil, I quote the
language of one who well knew of what he was writing, and was not
accustomed to speak in terms of exaggeration,—the Memoirs of Alexander Campbell. "As we follow the descending waters, the hills and
upland regions, which in reality preserve pretty much the same
level, seem gradually to become higher, so that by the time we approach the Ohio and Monongahela Rivers, their sides growing more
and more precipitous, rise to a height of four or five hundred feet.
These steep declivities inclose the fertile valleys, through which the
larger streams wind in graceful curves. Into these wide valleys
small rivulets pour their limpid waters, issuing at short intervals upon
each side from deep ravines formed by steep hillsides, which closely
approach each other, and down which the waters of the springs, with
which the upland is abundantly supplied, fall from rock to rock in
miniature cascades. Upon the upland not immediately bordering
upon the streams, the country is rolling, having the same general
elevation, above which, however, the summit of a hill occasionally
lifts itself, as though to afford to lovers of beautiful landscapes most
delightful views of a country covered for many miles with rich
pasturages, with grazing herds or flocks, fruitful grain-fields or orchards, gardens and farm-houses, while upon the steeper sides of the
valleys still remain some of the ancient forest growths of oak and

ash, walnut, hickory and maple. Frequently as the traveler passes along the roads upon the upland, he sees suddenly from some dividing ridge, charming valleys stretching away for miles with their green meadows, rich fields of corn, and sparkling streamlets. At other times, as he advances, he admires with delight in the distance, the ever varying line of the horizon, which on all sides is formed by the summits of remote ridges and elevations, sometimes, conical in form, but mostly defined by various arcs of circles, as regularly drawn as if a pair of compasses had traced the lines upon the sky. Everywhere around him he sees lands abounding in limestone, and all the necessary elements of fertility, and producing upon even the highest summits abundant crops of all the cereal grains To enhance the natural resources of this picturesque country, its hills conceal immense deposits of bituminous coal, which the descending streams here and there expose. * * * Such for nearly two hundred miles west of the Alleghanies, is the general character of this region especially of that portion of it lying along the Monongahela and Ohio, a region whose healthfulness is not surpassed by that of any country in the world."

We have thus far considered only the general aspects of the county. Its location and topographical features can be briefly stated. Greene County is situated in the extreme southwest corner of Pennsylvania, and is bounded on the north by Washington County, on the east by the Monongahela River which separates it from Fayette County, on the south by West Virginia, the western extremity of Mason and Dixon's line forming the dividing boundary, and on the west by West Virginia, known as the Panhandle, the western meridian line of five degrees measuring the length of the State constituting the line of demarkation. It contains within these limits three hundred and eighty-nine thousand, one hundred and twenty square acres (389,120) of surface, or about six hundred and eight square miles (608). Were it in the form of an absolute square it would be nearly twenty-five miles on each side, or a hundred miles in circuit; but as the length is to the breadth as five to three, the average length may be set down as thirty-two miles and breadth nineteen. The surface is drained by the Monongahela River, which unites with the Allegheny at Pittsburg and forms the Ohio proper, and by the Wheeling River which also falls into the Ohio, and forms part of the great Mississippi system. The water-shed which separates the waters of the Monongahela from the Wheeling system, commences at a point on the Washington County line a little north and east of the Baptist church, near the northern extremity of Morris Township, and pursues a southwesterly course cutting a small section of the eastern portion of Richhill Township, striking Jackson Township at a point near the intersection of Jackson with Centre, dividing Jackson from north to south very nearly at its center, cutting off the north-west corner of Gilmore, and the southwest corner of Springhill Townships, and passes on into West Virginia near the center of the southern boundary of the latter township, thus forming as it were, the back-bone of the county, and sending the waters on its eastern slope through innumerable and devious channels to the on-moving waters of the Monongahela, and those upon the western slope to the Wheeling.

Of the streams which drain the eastern slope, Ten Mile Creek is the most considerable, draining with its tributaries a full third of the entire territory; the second in magnitude, and nearly the equal of the former, though receiving a considerable portion of its volume from West Virginia, is Dunkard Creek. Of lesser magnitude are Muddy Creek, Little Whiteley and Whiteley. On the western slope are Enslow's and North Forks of Wheeling Creek and Pennsylvania Fork of Fish Creek.

Ten Mile Creek, which forms the northern boundary of Jefferson Township, and the northern limit of the county and is something less than four miles in length, is formed by the junction of the North and South Forks. The North Fork is for the most part in Washington County, draining its southeastern section. The South Fork which drains the central and northeastern portion of Greene County, has for its tributaries on the left bank, Casteel Run, Ruff's Creek, Wylies Run, Brown's Fork, Bates' Fork, Brushy Fork, Gray Run and Miranda Run, and upon the right bank, McCourtney's Run, Hargus Creek, Pursley Creek, Smith Creek, Laurel Run and Coal Lick Run. Pumpkin Run is the next stream south of Ten Mile Creek and empties into the Monongahela at the point where is located the village of Patton and Hughe's Ferry. Muddy Creek drains for the most part Cumberland Township, passes through the village of Carmichaels and enters the river where has been established Flenniken's Ferry. Whiteley Creek which is fed by Frosty, Lantz and Dyer's Runs from the north, drains Whiteley, Greene and Monongahela Townships, passes through the villages of Kirby, Lone Tree, Whiteley and Mapletown, and falls into the Monongahela River at Ross' Ferry. Dunkard Creek, which has for tributaries West's, Culvin's, Shannon's, Randolph's Robert's, Rush's Hoover's, Fordyce's, Tom's and Blockhouse Runs from the north, and numberless confluents from West Virginia from the south, has upon its banks the villages of Mt. Morris, Fair Chance and Taylortown and is the last of the considerable streams that flow into the Monongahela River on the south in Pennsylvania. The North Fork of Wheeling Creek, which drains the western slope of the county is fed upon the left bank by Whorton's, Hewitt's, Chamber's and White's Runs, and on the right bank by Stonecoal, Crabapple, Laurel, Kent's, Wright's and White Thorn Runs, and has the villages of Bristoria, Ryerson and Crow's Mills, located upon its banks. Fish Creek is fed by Hart's, Waggon-road, Laurel and Herod's Runs, and has the villages of Freeport and Deep Valley.

The general trend of the hills throughout the county of Greene is from northwest to southeast, and the roads which follow the valleys by which the hills are bordered, follow the same general direction, being for the most part parallel to each other and connected at intervals by cross roads leading over the hills, or through intersecting valleys. The only exception to this general law is the tract embracing the three western townships, comprising the valley of Wheeling Creek, where the course is from north to south or bearing somewhat from northeast to southwest. Every part of the surface is well watered by abundant springs and streams, and the soil is deep and fertile, being tillable even to the very summits of the highest hills. In many portions the hillsides, though very abrupt, are capable of being cultivated, and yield good returns for the labor bestowed. In the western section of the county are beds of limestone, which, on being reduced and applied to the soil, stimulates it to great fertility. When first visited by the white man, this whole stretch of country was covered with one vast forest, the trees of giant growth, consisting of white oak, red oak, black oak, and in many sections of sugar maple, chestnut, black walnut, hickory, butternut, ash, poplar, locust, cherry, ironwood, laurel and bay. In the rich bottoms, along the Monongahela River, in the southeastern section of the county, were, originally, vast tracts of pine and hemlock and spruce. These have been swept away for use in building, and the arts, until scarcely a vestige remains of the pristine forests, and few if any of a new growth have been permitted to spring up in their places. As a consequence, all the rough timber and sheeting boards used in building, are of the different varieties of oak. Poplar and hard-woods have now to be used as a finishing wood, or if pine is employed it has to be imported.

The observation may be permitted in this connection, though not strictly in place here, that the subject of forestry has been too much overlooked by the inhabitants of Greene County In a former generation the deep, dense forest was looked upon as the worst enemy of the settler, standing in the way of his improvements, and shutting out the sunlight from his vegetables and growing crops. Hence, to get the heavy growths out of his way, and prevent future growths was his greatest care. In what way this could be accomplished with the least labor and most speedily, was his chief concern. Hence the hardy axmen went forth at the first breaking of the rosy tinted morn, and we can realize as he attacks,

" ——some stately growth of oak or pine,
Which nods aloft and proudly spreads her shade,
The sun's defiance and the flock's defence:
How by strong strokes tough fibers yield at length,

Loud groans her last, and rushing from her height,
In cumbrous ruin thunders to the ground
The concious forest trembles at the shock,
And hill, and stream, and distant dale resound "

This is but the history of what was transpiring in every portion
of the county, day after day, and year after year, through all the
early generations   It was too laborious and troublesome to chop the
monster trunks into sections fit for handling, so, fire was brought
into requisition, and at convenient intervals burnings were made,
when the dissevered parts could then be swung around into piles and
the torch applied   All through the dry season vast volumes of smoke
would ascend heavenward, and at night the sky would be illumined
by the flames leaping upward and standing like beacon lights on
every hill-top and down every valley.   And when the settler was in
too much haste to cut and burn the cumbersome forest, he would rob
the innocent trees of their life by girdling the sap, thus cutting off
the health giving currents.   By this process the foliage was forever
broken, and the light and genial warmth of the sun was let in upon
the virgin mould of centuries, which was quickened into life as the
husbandman dropped his cherished seed.   But there stood the giant
forest still, torn and wrenched by lightning and storm, stretching
out its massive arms to heaven, bleached and whitened by sun and
shower, like the ghosts of their departed greatness, and as if implor-
ing mercy still.   One can scarcely pass one of these lifeless forests,
without a sigh of pity for the decaying monarchs
     But they subserve a purpose   The constant droppings from their
decaying limbs engender moisture, and give nourishment to the rich
pasturage which springs, like tufts of velvet, beneath them; and,
when at length they yield to the blows of the elements, and the cor-
oding tooth of time, they are reduced to ashes, and finally disappear
from sight.   They were sometimes fired while still standing, and
scarcely can a more sublime sight be imagined than a forest of lifeless
trees in full blaze   The ashes from a burned forest were sometimes gathered up and converted into potash, which always commanded ready sale in the eastern market, and was exchanged for salt
and other necessaries of life not produced in the vicinage
     But what will be the consequence of this indiscriminate war upon
the forests ?   In a few generations the hills, being entirely denuded
of shade, will be parched by the burning suns of summer, and the
streams will become less copious in the heated term and will eventually become entirely dry.   On the other hand, in the spring time, with
no forests to hold the moisture, and yield it up gradually through
the burning months when needed, the rains and melting snows will
descend in torrents, and flood the valleys   The fertility of the soil
will be soaked and drained out of it, the hillsides will be gashed and

seamed by the descending torrents, and thus all the hills, burned in summer and flooded in winter, will become barren. The tiller of the soil will wonder at the scantiness of his crops, and his flocks and herds will bleat and call in hopeless starvation.

Of late years an attempt has been made to excite an interest in forestry. Mr. Northup, in Connecticut, has secured some legislation upon the subject in that State and by lecturing before teachers' institutes, and on public occasions, has called attention to the subject, so that we have our forestry day in this State, to which the governor annually calls attention by a special proclamation But the manner in which it is acted upon, instead of resulting in a public good, will be a positive injury. In the appeals of Mr. Northup and others, the call is to have trees planted about school-houses and dwellings. Now what will be the consequence? In a few years, when the trees have become grown, there will be excessive shade and moisture. Moss will accumulate upon the roofs, the sunlight will be entirely shut out, and the children will be pale and sickly in consequence. The school-room will become unhealthy for lack of sunlight, and the dwelling will be damp and gloomy. One tree for a school ground not exceeding one acre, is ample shade. Excessive shade must always prove injurious to health, while sun light is a better medicine for failing strength than ever human ingenuity compounded.

But what is the remedy for the evil complained of? The forester should commence his work upon the far-off hill tops, and with diligent hand should crown them with forests most useful and valuable to man,—the fine maple, comely in shape, challenging the painter's most gaudy pigments for color, close-grained and unyielding in fiber for lumber; the walnut, cherry and ash, unrivalled for furniture and finishing; the chestnut, valuable for its nuts and for fencing, and pine and birch and hemlock, useful all. For holding moisture, and tempering the heats of summer, none are more useful than the evergreens. All the waste places, the ravines and rugged hill-sides, unsuitable for cultivation, should be planted. The sugar from a thousand good trees will bring to any farmer a bigger income than the whole produce of his farm in other ways. The price of a good black walnut log is almost fabulous. A white ash of twenty years' growth will yield a timber unsurpassed for carriages; and pine of fifteen years' growth will produce lumber which will be much sought for, and is year by year becoming more and more scarce. A good field of planted trees, or sprout land, should be fenced and protected from the browsing of cattle, as carefully as a field of corn. It may seem an unpalatable doctrine to preach, that the forests, which our fathers worked themselves lean to banish, should be protected, and nurtured, and brought back to their old places. But it is a true gospel, and if we look carefully at it in all its bearings, we shall receive it and recognize it as possessing saving grace.

Along the hills of southern Italy may be seen, to-day, an aspect which, in a few years, will be presented in the now fertile lands of Greene County. The Italian hills for centuries have been swept bare of forests As a consequence, the soil is parched in summer time, and has become bare and barren; the streams, which in other days were deep and ran in full volume to the sea, and were the theme of extravagant praises by the Latin poets, are now for months together entirely dry, not a gush of water gladdening their baked and parched beds Of the innumerable streams which fall into the Mediterranean on the western coast, from Genoa to the Straits of Messina, there are only a very few, like the Anio and the Tibor, that do not, in July and August, cease to flow, the husbandman being obliged to resort to artesian wells to feed his vegetables and growing crops.

We have now considered the general features of the territory known as Greene County. But before entering upon a more particular description of the settlement, and growth of its civil and religious institutions, it will be proper to consider several very interesting questions vitally touching its early occupation. The manner in which the original inhabitants became dispossessed of the inheritance of their fathers, and were driven towards the setting sun; why the dwellers in this valley are English, and not a French-speaking people, how it has transpired that we are the subjects of Pennsylvania rule, and not of Virginia or Maryland, and, finally, why we are not the constituent parts of a new State formed out of western Pennsylvania and portions of West Virginia and eastern Ohio,—these were living questions which plagued our fathers, and were not settled without desperate struggles, marked with slaughter, which may justly give to this county of Greene the title of the "dark and bloody ground."

CHAPTER II.

Why Called Indians—The Grandfathers, or Delawares—Shawnees—Six Nations or Iroquois, or Mingoes—The Tuscaroras
—Delawares Vassals—Indians' Shemitic Origin—Application of Bible Prophecy—The Indian Sui Generis—Characteristics—Indolent—Position of Woman—The Indian a Law
to Himself—His Occupations—Thievish—Patient of Toil
to Feed Revenge—View of Columbus—Amida's and Barlow's Experience—Penn's Testimony—Bancroft's View—The
Stealth Practiced in Hunting Served them in Seeking the
Victims of their Savage Cruelty—Brebeuf Describes an
Instance of their Barbarity which he Beheld—Cruelty a
Delight—Greene County the Scene of this Savage Barbarity.

WHEN Columbus, after having demonstrated the rotundity of the
earth in his scholar's cell, had verified the truth of his theory
by sailing westward in search of the farthest east, and had actually
reached and discovered the shores of the New World, he believed
that he had found the famed Cathay. Though he made several voyages, and lived a number of years, he still thought that it was the
Indies he had found, and died in ignorance of the grandeur of his
discovery. To the inhabitants whom he found in the new country
he gave the name of Indians, and, though wholly inappropriate in
view of the historical facts, it has clung to them through every vicis-
situde of fortune, and when the last of their race shall have disappeared forever from the earth, they will be recorded as Indians.

The natives who occupied the greater portion of that part of the
North American continent now designated Pennsylvania, were known
as the Lenni Lenape, the original people, or grandfathers. They
were by nature fierce and warlike, and there was a tradition among
them that the Lenapes, in ages quite remote, had emigrated from beyond the Mississippi, exterminating or driving out, as they came
eastward, a race far more civilized than themselves, numerous, and
skilled in the arts of peace. That this country was once the abode
of a more or less civilized people, accustomed to many of the comforts of enlightened communities, that they knew the use of tools,
and were numerous, is attested by remains, thickly studding western
Pennsylvania and the entire Ohio valley; but whether their extermi-

nation was the work of fiercer tribes than themselves, or whether they were swept off by epidemic diseases, or gradually wasted as the fate of a decaying nation, remains an unsolved problem. The three principal tribes of which the Lenapes were composed,—the Turtles or Unamis, the Turkeys or Unalachtgos, the Wolfs or Monseys,—occupied the eastern portion of Pennsylvania, and claimed the territory from the Hudson to the Potomac. They were known to the English as the Delawares. The Shawnees, a restless tribe which had come up from the south, had been received and assigned places of habitation on the Susquehanna, by the Delawares, and finally become a constituent part of the Delaware nation.

But the Indian nationality which more nearly concerns the section of country of which we are treating, is the Six Nations, or as they were designated by the French, the Iroquois. They called themselves Aquanuschioni or United Tribes, or in our own parlance, United States, and the Lenapes called them Mingoes. They originally consisted of five tribes, and hence were known as the Five Nations, viz: the Senecas, who were the most vigorous, stalwart and numerous; the Mohawks, who were the first in numbers and in rank, and to whom it was reserved to lead in war; the Onondagas, who guarded the council fire, and from among whom the Sachem or civil head of the confederacy was taken; the Oneidas, and the Cayugas. Near the beginning of the eighteenth century, the Tuscaroras, a large tribe from central North Carolina and Virginia, having been expelled from their former dwelling place, were adopted by the Five Nations, and thenceforward were known as the Six Nations. They occupied the country stretching from Lake Champlain to Lake Erie, and from Lake Ontario and the river St. Lawrence on the north, to the head waters of the Delaware, the Susquehanna and the Allegheny rivers on the south. It was a country well suited for defence in savage warfare, being guarded on three sides by great bodies of water. They were quick to learn the methods of civilized warfare, and securing fire-arms from the Dutch on the Hudson, they easily overcame neighboring hostile tribes whom they held in a condition of vassalage, exacting an annual tribute, but protected them, in return, in the possession of their rightful hunting grounds. The Lenapes, or Delawares, were held under subjection in this manner, which gave to the Six Nations semi-authority over the whole territory of the State of Pennsylvania, and reaching out into Ohio. This humiliating vassalage to which the Lenapes or Delawares were subjected, had been imposed upon them by conquest of the Iroquois; but the former claimed that it was assumed by them voluntarily, that "they had agreed to act as mediators and peace-makers among the other great nations, and to this end they had consented to lay aside entirely the implements of war, and to hold and to keep bright the chain of peace." It was the office, when tribes had weakened themselves by desperate conflict, for the women of those tribes, in order to save their kindred from utter extermination, to rush between the contending warriors and implore a cessation of slaughter. It became thus the office of women to be peace-makers. The Delawares claimed that they had assumed this office from principle; but the Iroquois declared that it was a matter of necessity, and applied the epithet "women" as a stigma, thus characterizing them as wanting in the quality of the braves. The pious Moravian missionary, Heckewelder, who spent much time among them, and knew their character well, believed that the Delawares were sincere in their claim, and from the fact that they had a great admiration for William Penn, with whom they associated much, and imbibed his sentiments of peace, it may be that they came to hold those principles, even if they had formerly been conquered in war, and been compelled to accept terms of dependence. Gen. Harrison, afterwards President of the United States, in a discourse on the aborigines of the valley of the Ohio, observes: "Even if Mr. Heckewelder has succeeded in making his readers believe that the Delawares, when they submitted to the degradation proposed to them by their enemies, were influenced, not by fear, but by the benevolent desire to put a stop to the calamities of war, he has established for them the reputation of being dupes This is not often the case with Indian sachems They are rarely cowards, but still more rarely are they deficient in sagacity or discernment to detect any attempt to impose upon them. I sincerely wish I could unite with the worthy German in removing this stigma from the Delawares. A long and intimate knowledge of them in peace and war, as enemies and friends, has left upon my mind the most favorable impressions of their character for bravery, generosity and fidelity to their engagements." But whatever may have been their original purposes, or their subsequent convictions, after their associations with Penn, they did demand complete independence of the Iroquois in 1756, and had their claims allowed.

Of the origin of the Indian race little is definitely known. The Indians themselves had no tradition and they had no writings, coins or monuments by which their history could be preserved. Ethnologists are, however, well assured that the race came originally from eastern Asia. Without reciting here the arguments which support this theory, it is sufficient for our present purpose to state, that it seems well attested that the race has dwelt upon this continent from a period long anterior to the Christian era, obtaining a foothold here within five hundred years from the dispersion of the race, and that their physical and mental peculiarities have become fixed by ages of subjection to climate and habits of life. Mr. Schoolcraft, who has written much upon Indian history, and has given much study and thought to the subject, adduces the following considerations as proof of the fulfillment of that prophecy of scripture recorded in the ninth chapter of Genesis: "And the sons of Noah that went forth of the Ark were Shem, Ham, and Japheth. God shall enlarge Japheth [Europeans] and he shall dwell in the tents of Shem [Indians] and Canaan [Negro] shall be his servant."

"Assuming," says Schoolcraft, "the Indian tribes to be of Shem-itic origin, which is generally conceded, they were met on this conti-nent in 1492, by the Japhet-ic race, after the two stocks had passed around the globe by directly different routes. Within a few years subsequent to this event, as is well attested the humane influence of an eminent Spanish ecclesiastic, led to the calling over from the coast of Africa, of the Ham-itic branch. As a mere historical question, and without mingling it in the slightest degree with any other, the result of three centuries of occupancy has been a series of movements in all the colonial stocks, south and north, by which Japhet has been immeasurably enlarged on the continent, while the called and not voluntary sons of Ham, have endured a servitude, in the wide stretching valleys of the tents of Shem."

The Indian, as he was found upon this continent when first vis-ited by the European, was very different in form, features, mental constitution, and habits from the latter, and apparently unalterably different from any other race. But while they were thus unlike other races, there was found to be a strong resemblance in all essen-tial elements in all the various tribes and nationalities of their own race. The color of the skin was of a reddish brown, their hair was black, straight, stiff, not plentiful, and the males had scarcely any beard; the jaw-bone was large, the cheek-bone high and prominent, and the forehead high, square and prominent above the eyes, show-ing a large development of the perceptive faculties; but narrow, and sloping backward at the top, showing defective reasoning powers. The person, unincumbered with the clothing common to a fashionable age in civilized countries, was erect, well developed, and in movement quick, lithe, and graceful.

Dr. Spencer, in his chapter on the characteristics of the Indians, has given the following graphic account of them: "Their intellect-ual faculties were more limited, and their moral sensibilities, from want of cultivation, less lively. They seemed to be characterized by an inflexibility of organization, which rendered them almost incapa-ble of receiving foreign ideas, or amalgamating with more civilized nations—constituting them, in short, a people that might be broken, but could not be bent. This peculiar organization, too, together with the circumstances in which they were placed, moulded the character of their domestic and social condition. Their dwellings were of the simplest and rudest character. On some pleasant spot by the banks of a river or near a sweet spring, they raised their groups of wigwams, constructed of the barks of trees, and easily taken down and removed to another spot. The abodes of the chiefs were sometimes more spacious, and constructed with care, but of the same materials. Their villages were sometimes surrounded by defensive palisades. Skins taken in the chase, served them for repose. Though principally dependent upon hunting and fishing, its uncertain supply had led them to cultivate around their dwellings some patches of maize; but their exertions were desultory, and they were often exposed to the severity of famine. Every family did everything necessary within itself; and interchange of articles of commerce was hardly at all known among them."

The Indian is by nature and habit indolent—as "lazy as he can be." To take up a tract of land, build himself a house with the conveniencies and privacies of civilized home life, clear away the heavy forests which incumber it, plough and cultivate the sodden acres, fence in the many fields, dig for himself a well, get and care for flocks and herds, and lay up for himself and family abundant supplies of the products of the soil, would have been to entail upon him insufferable misery, and rather than undertake the first stroke of such a life of toil, he would rather end it at once. He believed that the fish of the stream, the fowls of the air, the beasts of the field, and the land where he should stretch his wigwam, were as free and open to appropriation as the air we breathe, or the waters that run sparkling in abundance to the sea. They ridiculed the idea of fencing a field, and depriving any who desired the use of it. The strong dominated over the weak. The male assumed superiority over the female, and made her in reality his slave. His grunt was law to her, and if he started upon a journey she must trot after, bearing the infant, if she have one, and the burdens. If crops were to be planted, and cultivated, and gathered, it was by the sweat of her brow that it must be done. She must gather the fuel for the fire, weave the mat on which to set and sleep, fashion the basket and decorate it with fanciful colors. She was in short little less than the abject and degraded slave.

Of the more special occupations of the men Dr. Spencer has given the following interesting picture: "In cases of dispute and dissension, each Indian held to the right of retaliation, and relied on himself almost always to effect his revenge for injuries received. Blood for blood was the rule, and the relatives of the slain man were bound to obtain bloody revenge for his death. This principle gave rise, as a matter of course, to innumerable and bitter feuds, and wars of extermination, where that was possible. War, indeed, rather than peace, and the arts of peace, was the Indian's glory and delight; war, not conducted on the scale of more civilized, if not more Christian-like people; but war where individual skill, endurance, gallantry and

cruelty were prime requisites. For such a purpose as revenge the
Indian was capable of making vast sacrifices, and displayed a patience
and perseverance truly heroic; but when the excitement was over, he
sunk back into a listless, unoccupied, well-nigh useless savage. The
intervals of his more exciting pursuits the Indian filled up in the
decoration of his person with all the refinements of paints and feathers, with the manufacture of his arms—the club, the bow and arrows—and of canoes of bark, so light that they could easily be carried on the shoulder from stream to stream. His amusements were
the war dance and song, and athletic games, the narration of his exploits, and listening to the oratory of the chiefs. But, during long
periods of his existence, he remained in a state of torpor, gazing
listlessly upon the trees of the forest, and the clouds that sailed far
above his head; and this vacancy imprinted an habitual gravity and
even melancholy upon his aspect and general deportment."

The Indian was thievish to the last degree, indeed this seems to
have been as much a temper of his mind as indolence was of his
body. The disposition to take that which did not belong to him
may have in a measure resulted from his belief in the common property of water and air, and land, the beast and fowl that swarm upon
its surface, and the fish that dart in its streams. It seems to him no
sin to steal. Among the first colonies sent out from England to
colonize the American coast an Indian was discovered to have stolen
a silver cup. The punishment inflicted by the inconsiderate colonists of burning their villages, and destroying their growing crops,
provoked a revenge which resulted in the utter annihilation of the
colony and engendered a hatred which many subsequent colonists
felt the force of, and which inherited from generation to generation,
seems never to have been worn out of the savage mind.

The Indians of North America, as they were found upon the
arrival of Europeans, could not be said to have been under the government of law. If an Indian had suffered an injury or an insult,
he took it upon himself to avenge without the forms of proof to fix
the guilt, and if he was killed in the quarrel his nearest relatives
felt themselves obliged to take up the avengement. Thus from the
merest trifle the most deadly feuds arose by which the population
was visibly diminished. The warrior chiefs among them became
such by superior skill or cunning, and not by any rule of hereditary
decent, or majority of voices. Matters of public interest were discussed in public assemblies of the whole people, in which all were
free to join. Decisions were generally in favor of him who could
work most powerfully upon the feelings of his audience, either by
his native eloquence or by appeals to their superstition, by which
they were easily moved. The man who pretended to be the representative of the Great Spirit, had a great influence over them, and

in cases of sickness he was appealed to as a last resort. It has been observed above that the Indian was naturally lazy. To that assertion one exception should be made. To carry out his purpose of revenge the Indian was capable of making sacrifices, enduring hardships, and undergoing sufferings unsurpassed by the most daring of the human race. To gratify his thirst for revenge, he would make long and exhausting marches, with scant food, subsisting upon the bark of trees, the roots of the forest, and such random game as he might come upon, would lie in wait for his victims for hours and days enduring untold suffering.

It is curious to observe the impression which the natives made upon the first European visitants to these shores   Columbus in his report to Ferdinand and Isabella after his first voyage, said: " I swear to your majesties, that there is not a better people in the world than these, more affectionate, affable, or mild.   They love their neighbors as themselves; their language is the sweetest and the softest, and the most cheerful, for they always speak smiling, and although they go naked, let your majesties believe me, their customs are very becoming, and their king who is served with great majesty, has such engaging manners, that it gives great pleasure to see him, and also to consider the great retentive faculty of that people, and their desire of knowledge, which incites them to ask the causes of things."   If these were the real sentiments of Columbus, we are forced to believe that he had never seen an Indian in his war-paint and feathers, and that he had seen the Shylock who had money to lend, and not the Shylock who was exacting the penalty of the forfeited bond.

The adventurers whom Sir Walter Raleigh sent out for discovery and settlement, Amidas and Barlow, gave a graphic report of their impressions of the natives upon their return, which Hakluyt has preserved in his annals: "The soile is the most plentifull, sweete, fruitfull and wholesome, of all the worlde; there are above fourteene severall sweete smelling timber trees, and the most part of their underwoods are bayes and such like; they have such oakes that we have, but farre greater and better.   After they had been divers times aboard our shippes. myselfe, with seven more went twentie mile into the river that runneth towards the citie of Shicoak, which river they call Occam; and the evening following we came to an island, which they call Roanoke, distant from the harbor by which we entered seven leagues; and at the north end thereof was a village of nine houses, built of cedar, and fortified round about with sharpe trees to keep out their enimies, and the entrance into it made like a turnpike very artificially; when we came towards it, standing neere unto the waters' side, the wife of Granganimo, the king's brother, came running out to meete us very cheerfully and friendly; her husband was

not then in the village; some of her people shee commanded to drawe
our boate on shore, for the beating of the billoe, others she appointed
to carry us on their backes to the dry ground, and others to bring
our oares into the house for feare of stealing   When we were come
into the utter room, having five rooms in her house, she caused us to
sit down by a great fire, and after tooke off our choathes, and washed
them, and dried them againe, some of the women plucked off our
stockings, and washed them, some washed our feete in warm water,
and she herself tooke great paines to see all things ordered in the
best manner she could, making greate haste to dresse some meate for
us to eate.   After we had thus dried ourselves she brought us into
this inner roome, where shee set on the boord standing along the
house, some wheate like fermentie; sodden venison and roasted; fish,
sodden, boyled, and roasted; melons, rawe and sodden; rootes of
divers kinds; and divers fruits.   Their drink is commonly water,
but while the grape lasteth, they drinke wine, and for want of caskes
to keepe it, all the yere after they drink water, but it sodden with
ginger in it, and black sinnamon, and sometimes sassaphias, and
divers other wholesome, and medicinable hearbes and trees   We
were entertained with all love and kindnesse, and with as much
bountie, after their manner as they could possibly devise.   We
found the people most gentle, loving, and faithtull, voide of all guile
and treason, and such as live after the manner of the golden age
The people onely care to defend themselves from the cold in their
short winter, and to feed themselves with such meat as the soile
afforeth; their meat is very well sodden, and they make broth very
sweet and savorie, their vessels are earthen pots, very large, white,
and sweete; their dishes are wooden platters of sweet timber.   Within the place where they feede was their lodging, and within that
their idoll, which they worship, of whom they speak incredible things.
While we were at meate, there came in at the gates two or three
men with their bowes and arrowes from hunting, whom, when we
espied, we began to looke one towards another, and offered to reach
our weapons; but as soone as she espied our mistrust, she was very
much moved, and caused some of her men to runne out, and take
away their bowes and arrowes and breake them, and withall beate the
poore fellowes out of the gate againe.   When we departed in the
evening, and would not tarry all night, she was very sory, and gave
us into our boate our supper half dressed pottes and all, and brought
us to our boateside, in which we lay all night, removing the same a
prettie distance from the shore; she perceiving our jelousie, was
much grieved, and sent divers men and thirtie women, to sit all
night on the bank-side by us, and sent into our boates five mattes to
cover us from the raine, using very many wordes to entreate us to
rest in their houses; but because we were fewe men, and if we had

Yours Truly
J. M. Sayers

miscarried the voyage had beene in very great danger, we durst not adventure anything, although there was no cause of doubt, for a more kinde and loving people there cannot be found in the worlde, as far as we have hitherto had triall."

Though given here at some length, this passage from the records of the faithful Hakluyt is very valuable as picturing the life of the simple Indians, and their temper towards the early European voyagers, before their minds had been soured by injury and wrong which careless and brutal colonists subsequently visited upon them; and it may well be questioned whether, they would not have remained friendly and loving as here described had they received loving and Christian treatment in return. It is possible that such relations might have been preserved with the natives, that the tales of blood and savagery which form a dark page in the early history of Greene County would never have had occasion to be recorded. Certain it is that the redmen have had great provocation, and have received most inhuman and unchristian treatment at the hands of the pale face.

The relations of William Penn with the savages was different from those of any other European. He really believed them brethren in the true scripture sense, and treated them as such. Hence his view of the Indian character would naturally be more favorable to them than if regarded through prejudiced eyes. "For their persons," he says, "they are generally tall, straight, well built, and of singular proportion. They tread strong and clever, and mostly walk with a lofty chin. Their language is lofty, yet narrow; but, like the Hebrew, in signification, full If an European comes to see them, or calls for lodging at their house or wigwam, they give him the best place and first cut. If they come to visit us, they salute us with an 'Itah!' which is as much as to say 'Good be to you!' and set them down, which is mostly on the ground, close to their heels, their legs upright. It may be they speak not a word, but observe all passages. If you give them anything to eat or drink, well, for they will not ask; and be it little or much, if it be with kindness, they are well pleased; else they go away sullen, but say nothing."

"In liberality," he says, "they excel; nothing is too good for their friend; give them a fine gun, coat or other thing, it may pass twenty hands before it sticks; light of heart, strong affections, but soon spent. The most merry creatures that live, feast and dance perpetually; they never have much nor want much; wealth circulateth like the blood; all parts partake; and though none shall want what another hath, yet exact observers of property. Some kings have sold, others presented me with several parcels of land; the pay, or presents I made them were not hoarded by their particular owners; but the neighboring kings and their clans being present when the goods were brought out, the parties chiefly concerned consulted what,

2

and to whom, they would give them To every king then, by the hands of a person for that work appointed, is a proportion sent, so sorted and folded, and with that gravity that is admirable. Then the king subdivideth it, in like manner, among his dependants, they hardly leaving themselves an equal share with one of their subjects; and be it on such occasions as festivals, or at their common meals, the kings distribute and to themselves last. They care for little because they want little, and the reason is a little contents them. * * * We sweat and toil to live: their pleasure feeds them; I mean their hunting, fishing and fowling, and their table is spread everywhere They eat twice a day, morning and evening, their seats and table are the ground Since the Europeans came into these parts, they are grown great lovers of strong liquors, rum especially, and for it exchange the richest of their skins and furs. If they are heated with liquors, they are restless till they have enough to sleep, that is their cry, 'Some more and I will go to sleep,' but when drunk, one of the most wretched spectacles in the world "

Bancroft, in his elaborate chapter on the habits and customs of the Indians, says. "During the mild season there may have been little suffering. But thrift was wanting; the stores collected by the industry of the women was squandered in festivities. The hospitality of the Indian has rarely been questioned. The stranger enters his cabin, by day or by night, without asking leave, and is entertained as freely as a thrush or a black-bird that regales himself on the luxuries of the fruitful grove. He will take his own rest abroad, that he may give up his own skin, or mat of sedge, to his guest. Nor is the traveler questioned as to the purpose of his visit; he chooses his own time freely to deliver his message "

We may gather from the testimony of those who earliest encountered them, what were some of the most marked of the characteristics. Of the stealth of the Indian in creeping upon his victim unawares, and the laying in wait for him in some well-chosen ambuscade, we may look for the cause in the necessity he was under of practicing these qualities in the pursuit of his game. From childhood he was taught to move noiselessly through the forest lest by the breaking of a twig he put to flight the coveted game for lack of which he was perhaps starving. The same noiseless tread with which he approached the pool where sported the finny tribe, and came unnoticed upon the wild fowl, was practiced in seeking out the victims of his revenge, or putting to the torture his prisoners of war. Of the barbarity practiced upon the latter, in no part of the human race is it equalled. Biebeuf has described it in all its horrors, as recorded by Bancroft· "On the way to the cabins of his conquerors, the hands of an 'Iroquois prisoner were crushed between stones, his fingers torn off or mutilated, the joints of his arms scorched and gashed, while he himself preserved his tranquility, and sang the songs of his nation. Arriving at the homes of his conquerors, all the cabins regaled him, and a young girl was bestowed upon him, to be the wife of his captivity and the companion of his last loves * * * To the crowd of his guests he declared: 'My brothers, I am going to die; make merry around me with good heart; I am a man; I fear neither death nor your torments;' and he sang aloud. The feast being ended, he was conducted to the cabin of blood. They place him on a mat, and bind his hands; he rises and dances around the cabin, chanting his death song. At eight in the evening eleven fires had been kindled, and these are hedged in by files of spectators The young men selected to be the actors are exhorted to do well, for their deeds would be grateful to Areskoui, the powerful war god. A war chief strips the prisoner, shows him naked to the people, and assigns their office to the tormentors. Then ensued a scene the most horrible; torments lasted till after sunrise, when the wretched victim, bruised, gashed, mutilated, half roasted and scalped, was carried out of the village and hacked in pieces."

From the venerable sachem to the infant in arms, the aged mother to the tender maiden, by all the tribe was this torture of the captive beheld. It was an occasion of feasting and rejoicing. The greater. the power of endurance of the victim and the more fierce and terrible the torture invented the more exquisite the enjoyment of the spectators. To add a pang to the sufferer was a subject of congratulation to the one who inflicted it. Often the greatest refinement of cruelty was devised and inflicted by the women. And when the last pang had been endured and all was over they feasted upon the victim's flesh.

Further on in this work some account will be given of deeds of blood perpetrated by the savages in this county From the evidence which has now been adduced some conception of the primary character of the natives can be formed, and an idea entertained of those qualities of mind and heart which could prompt them to the midnight murdering and deeds of savagery which were to them a favorite trade.

CHAPTER III.

Original Settlement Upon the Continent by Europeans—Ponce de Leon in Florida—Vasquez de Ayllon Seizing Natives for Slaves—De Soto Discovers the Mississippi—Voyages of Verrazzani—Jaques Carter—Champlain in Canada—His Expedition Against the Iroquois—Marquette and Joliet Voyage to the Mississippi—Map of Country—Death of Marquette—Remarks of Hildreth and Charlevoix—La Salle Pushes Explorations on the Mississippi—Takes Formal Possession of the River and Lands it Drains—Possibilities of Greene County—England Colonizes—Early Attempts Abortive—Grants of James I—Settlement of Jamestown and Plymouth—The Dutch on the Delaware—By What Right Had European Possessions on This Continent—A Fruitful Country Unused—A Savage and Barbaric People Encumber It—Observations of Justice Story—Decision of Chief Justice Marshall—The Injustice Rankled in the Breasts of the Savages.

Aroused by the roseate accounts given by Columbus and the companions of his voyage of discovery in 1492, which was spread broadcast over Europe by the art of printing just then brought into use, the Sovereigns of three European nations, at that time most puissant, encouraged their subjects to make voyages of discovery and issued patents empowering them to take possession of such portions of the main land in the New World, and the contiguous islands of the sea, as they might visit and explore Spain, having through Ferdinand and Isabella, patronized the great discoverer, took the lead, assuming a preemption right to the continent, by virtue of discovery, and Cortes and Pizzaro did their work of slaughter and extermination upon weaker and inoffensive peoples, innocent of any crimes against their oppressors.

Juan Ponce de Leon, who had been a companion of Columbus, having heard of a miraculous fountain upon the mainland whose waters could impart life and perpetual youth, eager to bathe in the healing stream, sailed on the 3d of March, 1512, in quest of it. It was the season, when, in that far southern clime, the whole land was bursting into blossom, and, as he coasted along a great country presenting one mass of bloom, he thought indeed, he had found the land of perpetual life, and, accordingly, named it Florida. But the weather was tempestuous, and returning to the West Indies, he sought, and obtained from Charles V., of Spain, authority to take and govern the country; but upon his second expedition he found the natives hostile, and upon giving battle was mortally wounded and returned to the Islands to die.

Vasquez de Ayllon, in quest of slaves to work in the mines of Mexico, came upon this coast, and having enticed numbers of natives on board his vessels, perfidiously sailed away; but one of his ships was lost in a storm, and the natives, who survived, disdaining to work, refused to eat, and died miserably of starvation. Not satisfied with his experience, de Ayllon obtained authority from Charles V. to conquer and govern the country, and in 1525 again set sail with his colonists. But now he found his tactics reversed; for the natives were the enticers, and having invited the body of the visitants to a feast gave them to slaughter and destruction. Again in 1528, Pamphilo de Narvaez with Alvar de Vacca and four hundred colonists sailed for Tampa Bay; but after fruitless wanderings by sea and land in which the leader was lost, de Vacca made his escape with but four of his companions alive, having spent ten years in fruitless search for gold and booty. In his adventures he had traversed the whole southern border of what is now the United States, crossed the Mississippi, bent his steps onward to the Rocky Mountains, gladly performing the offices of a slave for sustenance and the poor boon of life, and arrived at last in Mexico, whence he returned to Spain. Undismayed by the ill-fortune of others, and thirsting for riches, which he might have for the seizing, Hernando de Soto, invested with the patent of power and the title of Governor General of Cuba and Florida, with about a thousand followers; in ten vessels, set sail in 1539 well armed, and provided with the implements of mining, even to bloodhounds for capturing slaves, and chains for securing them. The first night on shore he was attacked by the Indians lying in wait for him, and driven in disgrace to his ships. Returning to the land he commenced even wider search than de Vacca, and after three years of toilsome and fruitless wanderings, and incessant conflicts with Indians, having crossed the Mississippi and reached the great plains where grazed the countless herds of buffalo, finally, broken and dispirited at finding neither the wealth of gold which he sought, nor the empire which he coveted, he died, and the waters of the Mississippi roll perpetually above his bones. Having but one purpose, that of escape from this hated country, his surviving followers floated down the river, and retired to Spanish settlements in Mexico. Thus ended miserably the greatest expedition hitherto attempted upon the Florida coast. For a score or more of years religionists from Spain and France attempted permanent lodgement upon this territory, in which the town of St Augustine was founded, at present the oldest town in the United States. But instead of practicing the mild and gentle precepts of their Master, they were torn by mortal feuds, and a large proportion perished in their deadly and treacherous conflicts

Thus, of the vast sums of money expended and hardships endured, in which the greater portion of the southern half of our country was overrun, and perpetual and wasting warfare for a quarter of a century was prosecuted with the natives, nothing good or lasting was the result, though there was exhibited a resolution and unconquerable spirit by those proud cavaliers who went forth clad in their habiliaments of silk, rejoicing in their trailing plumes and glittering armor, truly worthy of a better cause They expected to find great nations overflowing with gold and precious treasures, whom they could easily overcome and despoil, where they might set up a kingdom Unhappily for them they found no such people; the gold they coveted existed only in their own heated imagination, and the empire which they hoped to fond vanished like the mists of the valley before the breath of a summer morn. Their cause was the cause of the gambler and the freebooter in every country and in every age, and the lesson is one which the race may well take to heart.

Of the great European nations, France was the next to send out colonies to take possession of, and settle the American continent. Moved by a knowledge of the misfortunes which had attended Spanish settlements far to the south, the French sought a far northern latitude, and though on the same parallel as Paris, was swept by blizzards, and bound in icy fetters such as were wholly unknown in sunny France. This very circumstance may have defeated the entire French plans of colonization, and changed the whole course of empire upon this continent For the French possessed, in an eminent degree, the spirit of colonization, and were eager to push plans of empire. Had the first adventurers seated themselves upon the Potomac or the James, or along the shores of the Carolinas, they would have found so genial a climate and similar to their own, that they would have gained so firm a foothold and so long in advance of the English, that they would probably not have been supplanted.

The state of navigation at this time was so crude, the vessels so small and imperfect in construction, that a voyage on the open ocean, across the Atlantic, was attended with deadly perils, and solemn religious services marked the departure of the venturesome voyagers as they went down upon the seas, a large proportion of whom never emerged from the waves. Fishermen from Brittany, in France, as early as 1504, had discovered the rich fishing grounds on the Banks of Newfoundland, and had visited and named Cape Breton, a name which it still retains. Francis I of France, a sovereign not un mindful of the growth of his kingdom, seeing the activity of neighboring nations in sending out their subjects for voyages of discovery and colonization, dispatched Juan Verrazzani, a Florentine navigator, in 1524, in a single vessel, the Dolphin, to discover and take possession, in the name of France, of lands in the famed New World. After "as sharp and terrible a tempest as ever sailors suffered," Verrazzani arrived upon the coast, touched at the Carolinas, at Long Island, at Newport, and skirted the coast to the fiftieth degree north, when he returned without making a settlement. Ten years later, in 1534, Jaques Cartier was dispatched by Chabot, Admiral of France, on an expedition to the Northwest, and arrived at the mouth of the St. Lawrence Returning to France with extravagant reports of the excellence of the country and the climate, he was dispatched on the following year with three large ships, and upon his arrival on St. Lawrence-day, gave that name to the Gulf which he had entered, and the river which drains the great lakes Ascending the river, he visited Hochelaza, now Montreal. and wintered at the Isle of Orleans. The cold was intense, in marked contrast to his former visit, which was in the heat of summer, and his followers, suffering from scurvy and the severity of the climate, clamored to be led back to France In 1540, Cartier was again sent out, and now with five ships, and Francis de la Roque as Governor of Canada. But strife ensuing, the attempt at colonization was abortive. This put an end to further attempts at settlement in this latitude for upwards of half a century.

In 1598, the great Sully, under Henry IV. of France, dispatched the Marquis de la Roche, of Brittany, to take possession of Canada and other countries "not possessed by any Christian Prince." The expedition, however, failed utterly, though the enterprise of private individuals in trading with the natives for rich furs had in the meantime proved successful. In 1603, Samuel Champlain was sent out, who carefully explored the river St. Lawrence, and selected the site of Quebec as a proper location for a fort At about the same time De Monts, a Huguenot of the King's household, was granted a commission to assume the sovereignty of Acadie, from the fortieth to the forty-sixth degree of north latitude, which meant from the latitude of Delaware Bay to the north pole,—a glorious empire if it could be held and peopled. But the trouble with all the European sovereigns in drawing patents for slices of the New World, was that they did what was charged upon the greedy countryman when offered tobacco —bit off more than he could chew. The expedition of De Monts, consisting of four ships, sailed in 1604, and the right of trade proving lucrative, the monopoly was revoked. But Champlain continued his explorations, embracing the St. John's River, Bay of Fundy and Island of St Croix. By the advice of Champlain, Quebec was founded in 1608 by a company of merchants from Dieppe and St. Molo. In the following year Champlain explored the lake which bears his name, and, that he might secure the good will of the natives of Canada, he accompanied the Algonquins on a hostile campaign against the Five Nations, or Iroquois. But this proved a fatal mistake; for it provoked the implacable hatred against the French of that powerful Indian confederacy which held in an iron grasp what is now the States of New York and Pennsylvania. Thus, by an inscrutable Providence, was France again cut off from taking that course of empire, which would doubtless have given that nation preponderance upon this continent. Champlain was devoted to his religion, regarding "the salvation of a soul of more consequence than the conquest of an empire." His chosen servants, the Franciscans, but later the Jesuits, assumed control of the missions to the Indians, and for a score of years threaded the mazes of the forest for new converts, pushing out along the great lakes by the northern shore, even to Huron, Michigan and Superior; but in all their efforts to reclaim the Iroquois meeting with little success, and suffering, at the hands of these savages, whippings, and torments, and death. With the tribes of the north and west, even to the Chippewas, Pottawatamies, Sacs and Foxes, and Illinois, they had better fortune, and with them made alliances against the Iroquois. From the Sioux they learned that there was a great river to the south, and this they were seized with a desire to explore.

In the spring of 1673, Jaques Marquette and M. Joliet, with attendants, embarked in two bark canoes at Mackinaw, and passing down the lake to Green Bay, entered the Fox River. Toilsomely ascending its current to its head waters, they bore with difficulty their canoes across the ridge which divides the waters of the great lakes from the gulf, and having reached the sources of the Wisconsin River, launched their frail boats upon its turbid waters, and floated onward upon the current, the stream studded with islands and the shores adorned with goodly trees and creeping vines, until, on the 17th of June, with "inexpressible joy and thankfulness to God for his mercies," they entered the Mississippi. Marquette was frequently warned by the natives not to expose himself to the dangers of the voyage, and to desist from the further prosecution of his journey; but the reply of the pious priest was characteristic: "I do not fear death, and I would esteem it a happiness to lose my life in the service of God."

Passing, in turn the Des Moines, the Missouri, with its turbid stream, the Ohio gently rolling, they proceeded as far south as the Arkansas. Here they were fiercely attacked by the natives. But Marquette boldly presented the pipe of peace, and called down the blessing of heaven upon his enemies, in return for which the old men received him, and called off their braves who were intent upon blood. But now the dangers seemed to thicken as they descended.

Geo. W. Wiseavver.

Fearing that they might hazard all by proceeding further, and being now satisfied that the river must empty into the Gulf of Mexico, having made a complete map of the portion thus far explored, Marquette determined to return and report his great discoveries to Talon, the intendant of France. With incredible exertion they forced their way against the current of the Mississippi, up the Illinois, across the portage, down the Fox by the same course that they had come, and reached Green Bay in safety. Though filled with satisfaction at the importance of his discovery, and extravagant in praise of the country which he had seen—" such grounds, meadows, woods, stags, buffaloes, deer, wildcats, bustards, swans, ducks, paroquetts, and even beavers," as he found on the Illinois River being nowhere equalled;—yet he apparently felt a more serene and heartfelt satissaction, in the fact that the natives had brought to him a dying infant to be baptized, which he did about a half an hour before it died, which he asserts God was thus pleased to save, than in all the far reaching consequences of his expedition. On the 18th of May, 1675, as he was passing up Lake Michigan with his boatmen upon the eastern shore, he proposed to land and perform mass. With pious and devoted steps leaving his attendants in the boat, he ascended the banks of a fast flowing stream to perform the rite. Not returning as he had indicated he would, his followers, recollecting that he had spoken of his death, went to seek him, and found him indeed dead. Hollowing a grave for him in the sand, they buried him on the very spot which his prayers had consecrated.

In commenting upon the devotion and loyalty of these pious men —Marquette, and his associates, Hildreth justly remarks, " Now and then he would make a voyage to Quebec in a canoe, with two or three savages, paddle in hand, exhausted with rowing, his feet naked, his breviary hanging about his neck, his shirt unwashed, his cassock half torn from his lean body, but with a face full of content, charmed with the life he led, and inspiring by his air and his words a strong desire to join him in his mission " And Charlevoix, in his annals, even more vividly describes the character of these devoted men. " A peculiar unction" he says, " attached to this savage mission, giving it a preference over many others far more brilliant and more fruitful. The reason no doubt was, that nature, finding nothing there to gratify the senses or to flatter vanity—stumbling blocks too common even to the holiest—grace worked without obstacle. The Lord, who never allows himself to be outdone, communicates himself without measure to those who sacrifice themselves without reserve; who, dead to all, detached entirely from themselves and the world, possess their souls in unalterable peace, perfectly established in that childlike spirituality which Jesus Christ has recommended to his disciples, as that which ought to be the most marked trait of their character.

* ~ * Such is the portrait of the missionaries of New France drawn by those who knew them best. I myself knew some of them in my youth, and I found them such as I have painted them, bending under the labor of a long apostleship, with bodies exhausted by fatigues and broken with age, but still preserving all the vigor of the apostolic spirit." It should be added to this picture of the labors of the priests, that of all the heathen in any part of the world to whom the gospel has been sent, none were more difficult to reach and indoctrinate in its mild and gentle spirit, than the North American Indians.

The report of the discovery of a great river to the west, draining boundless territory, and opening a highway to the gulf, aroused cupidity, and the desire to enlarge the dominion of France. Robert Cavalier de La Salle, who had already manifested remarkable enterprise in his explorations along the shores of Ontario and Erie, and in his mercantile enterprises with the natives, was seized with the desire to follow the course of the Mississippi to its mouth. Returning to France he sought and obtained from Colbert authority to proceed with his explorations, and take possession of the country in the name of France. Returning to Fort Frontenac with the Chevalier Tonti, and a picked band, he ascended to the rapids of Niagara, passed around the falls with his equipment, built a vessel of sixty tons which he named the Griffin, and began his voyage up the great lakes, now for the first time gladdened by so pretentious a craft, the forerunner of a commerce whose white wings has come to enliven all its ways.

Arrived at Green Bay, he sent back his craft for supplies with which to prosecute his voyage down the great valley of the prince of streams. Caught in one of those storms which lurk in the secret places of these lakes, the little vessel was lost on its return voyage. Waiting in vain for tidings of his supplies he crossed over to the Illinois River, and in the vicinity of the present town of Peoria, he erected a fort, which, in consonance with his own disappointed spirit, he named Creve-cœur, the Broken Heart. Leaving Tonti and the Recollect, Hennepin, to prosecute the explorations of the valley, La Salle set out with only three followers to make his way back through the sombre forests which skirt the lakes, to Fort Frontenac at the mouth of Lake Ontario. In the meantime Hennepin explored the Illinois and the Mississippi to the Falls of St. Anthony, accounts of which on his return to France he published. Gathering fresh supplies and men, La Salle started again upon his arduous and perilous voyage; but upon his arrival at Fort Crevecœur, upon the Illinois, he found it deserted and his forces scattered, Tonti, whom he had left in charge, having been forced to flee. Not dismayed, again he returned to Frontenac, having fallen in with Tonti at Macinaw. Again provided with the necessary supplies, but now with less cumbersome outfit, he started again, after having encountered discouragements that would have broken the spirit of a less resolute man, in August, 1681, and proceeded on his devious way. But now instead of the course which they had before pursued he moved up the Chicago River on sledges, and, having passed the portage, found Fort Crevecœur in good state of preservation Having here constructed a barge of sufficient dimensions for his party he commenced his voyage down the Mississippi, and reached the Gulf without serious incident. Overjoyed at finally having brought his projects to a successful consummation he took possession of the river, and all the vast territory which it drained,—large enough to constitute several empires like France,—with a formal pomp and ceremony which was sufficient, if it were to depend on pomp and ceremony, to have insured the possession of the country in all time to come. They thoroughly explored the channels which form the delta at the mouth of the stream, and having selected a place high and dry, and not liable to inundation, which they found by the elevation of the north star to be in latitude twenty-seven degrees north, they erected a column and a cross to which they affixed a signal bearing this inscription, "Louis le Grand, Roi de France et de Navarre, regne, le neuvieme, Avril, 1682." Then chanting the Te Deum, Exaudiat, and the Domine salvum fac Regem, and shouting Vive le Roi to a salvo of arms, La Salle, in a loud voice, read his process verbal, as though all the nations of the world were listening: "In the name of the most high, mighty, invincible, and victorious prince, Louis the Great, by the grace of God King of France, and Navarre, Fourteenth of the name, this ninth day of April, 1682, I, in virtue of the commission of his majesty, which I hold in my hand, and which may be seen by all whom it may concern, have taken, and now do take, in the name of his majesty and of his successors to the crown, possession of this country of Louisiana." And here follows a description of the rivers, and countries drained by them, which he claims; and that all this is by the free consent of the natives who inhabit these lands, a statement which would probably have been difficult of verification, and in his verbal process he inserts the name Colbert, the king's minister, in place of Mississippi. He claims besides that they are the first Europeans who have ascended or descended the stream, on the authority of the peoples who dwell there, a statement which would also be uncertain of verification, and thus ends his process, "hereby protesting against all those who may hereafter undertake to invade any or all of these countries, people or lands above described to the prejudice of the right of his majesty, acquired by the consent of the nations herein named. Of which, and of all that can be needed, I hereby take to witness those who hear me, and demand an act of the notary, as required by law." In addition to this, he caused to be buried at the foot of the cross a leaden plate with this inscription in Latin: "Ludovicus, magnus Reget. Nono Aprilis MDCLXXXII. Robertus Cavellier, cum Domino de Tonty Legato R. P. Zenobi Membré, Recollecto, et viginti Gallis primus hoc flumen, inde ab Ilineorum Pago, Enavigavit, ejusque ostium fecit pervivum, nono Aprilis, Anni MDCLXXXII."

By the terms of the law, recognized by all civilized nations, the nation whose subjects were the discoverers of the mouth of a river, could rightfully lay claim to all the territory drained by that river, and all its tributaries even to their remotest limits Had this claim been successfully vindicated, Louis-iana would have been bounded by the Alleghany Mountains on the east, the Rocky Mountains on the west, and would have embraced the bulk of the territory now the United States, and thus Pennsylvania would have been despoiled of a large proportion of its proud domain, and Greene County been a vicinage of France. But the claim of La Salle was not well founded, he not having been the original discoverer For de Soto, a hundred and forty years before, had discovered the river, and, through his followers, had traced it to its mouth, and had taken possession of the river in the name of the King of Spain, with even greater pomp and ceremony than La Salle, setting up the cross and' performing religious rites which the well known painting repeated on the greenbacks of our national currency has commemorated Had the claim of Spain been maintained by force, and followed by settlement, the people of Greene County would to-day be under the dominion of Spain, or of a Spanish speaking people. But if, by the failure of Spain, the French had been successful in establishing their claims, then the Bourbon lilies would have succeeded to power here, and French would have been the language. As we shall soon see, the chances by which it escaped that sway, were, for a time, quite evenly balanced between the French and the English.

La Salle returned to France with great expectations of empire for his country. With a fleet of thirty vessels, and people for a large colony, he set sail for the new possessions, four of which under his immediate command steered direct for the Gulf of Mexico, with the intention of entering the mouth of the Mississippi River; but he failed to find the entrance, and, after suffering untold hardships and privations on the coast of Texas by shipwreck, dissension among his followers, and the tireless hostility of the savages, his expedition came to an ignoble end, he himself fortunate in escaping with his life. May we not believe that Providence had other designs for this continent?

The third, and last of the European nations to engage in active colonization on the North American coast, was England. For, though Holland, Denmark, and other European nations sent out colonies. they all became subject to the English. Henry VII., who had turned a deaf ear to the appeals of Columbus, saw with envy what he thought were great advantages being secured to neighboring nations through the discoveries of the great navigator. He accordingly lent a ready ear to the Cabots, of Bristol, his chief port. As early as 1497 they set out to share in New World enterprise, and in their voyages explored the coast from Labrador to the Carolinas, and subsequently South America, giving name to the great river of the south, Rio de la Plata. Forbisher followed, and Sir Humphrey Gilbert, half-brother of Sir Walter Raleigh, who aided Gilbert with his fortune and his powerful influence at Court, but perished by shipwreck without effecting a foothold upon the virgin soil   Under the patronage of Raleigh, Amidas and Barlow in 1584 were sent, who made a lodgment on the shores of the Carolinas; but instead of observing seed-time and harvest, they wasted their energies in the vain search for gold, which they probably hoped to pick up in great nuggets, and their attempt at settlement came to naught.   Not discouraged Raleigh fitted out another expedition under Sir Richard Grenville, and exhausted his great fortune in the enterprise.   A lodgment was made at Roanoke, but the colony planted held a sickly existence for a short time, when, after incurring vast expense, it was forever abandoned.   Hendrick Hudson, under the patronage of London merchants, and subsequently of the Dutch, made voyages of discovery, and in 1609 entered Delaware Bay, and made a landing on the soil of what is Pennsylvania, entered New York Bay, and ascended the Hudson River, to which he gave his name, and took possession of all this country in the name of the Dutch, in whose employ he was then sailing.   As yet nothing permanent by way of settlement had been acheived.

But the English having explored most of the coast from Halifax in Nova Scotia, to Cape Fear in North Carolina, laid claim to all this stretch of the coast, and indefinitely westward.   In the reign of the feeble and timid James I., this immense country was divided into two parts, the one extending from New York Bay to Canada, known as North Virginia, which was granted for settlement to the Plymouth Company organized in the west of England, and the other reaching from the mouth of the Potomac southward to Cape Fear, was called South Virginia, and was bestowed upon the London Company composed of residents of that city.   It will thus be seen that a belt of some two hundred miles was left between the two grants so that they should have no liability to encroach upon each others settlements   The language of these grants by James was remarkable for every quality of style but clearness and perspicuity.   The London Company were to be limited between thirty-fourth and forty-first degrees of north latitude, and the Plymouth Company between the thirty-eighth and forty-fifth degrees. It will thus be seen that the two grants overlap each other by three degrees; but as neither company was to begin settlements within a hundred miles of the territory of the other, it practically left the limits as given above. Previous to the active operations inaugurated by these companies, frequent attempts had been made by the English at colonization; but hitherto, beyond a few fishing stations, and the fort which the Spanish continued to maintain at St. Augustine, no foothold had been gained by them along the whole stretch of the Atlantic, now occupied by the States of the Union. The London Company, in 1607, sent one hundred and five colonists in three small ships under command of Christopher Newport, to make a settlement in South Virginia. Among the number was Bartholomew Gosnold, who was the real organizer of the company, and the renowned Captain John Smith, by far the ablest. They entered Chesapeake Bay, giving the names Charles and Henry, the names of King James' two sons, to the opposite capes at the entrance, and having moved up the James River, they selected a spot upon its banks for a capital of the future empire, which in honor of the king, they called Jamestown. The seat here chosen became the seed of a new nation. The encounter with the powerful war chief Powhatan, and the romantic story of his gentle and lovely daughter Pocahontas, will ever lend a charm to the early history of Virginia.

The Plymouth Company having made fruitless attempts to get a foothold upon their territory, applied to the king for a new and more definite charter. Forty of "the wealthiest and most powerful men in the realm" associated themselves together under the name of the Council of Plymouth, which superceded the original Plymouth Company, and to them James granted a new charter embracing all the territory lying between the fortieth and the forty-eighth degrees of north latitude and stretching away to the Pacific—a boundless grant, little comprehended by the king and his ministers, they believing that the South Sea, as the Pacific was designated, which had been seen by Balboa from a high mountain upon the isthmus, was close at hand. In 1620, a band of English Puritans, who had been persecuted and harried for non-conformity to the English church, having escaped to Holland, and there heard flattering accounts of the New World, conceived the idea of setting up in the new country a home for freedom. Having obtained from the new Council of Plymouth authority to make a settlement upon their grant, and having received assurance that their non-conformity would be winked at, a company of forty-one men with their families, one hundred and one in all, "the winnowed remnants of the Pilgrims," embarked in the Mayflower, and after a perilous voyage of sixty-three days, landed on the shores of Massachusetts, at Plymouth Rock, and made a settlement which they called New Plymouth. Before leaving the ship they drew up, and the whole colony signed, a form of government, and elected John Carver governor. The elder Brewster had accompanied them as their spiritual guide, and here in a mid-winter of almost arctic fierceness, they suffered and endured; but sang the songs of freedom. By spring the governor and his wife and forty-one of their number were in their graves; but not dismayed they observed seed-time, and gathered in harvest; other pilgrims joined them; it became the seed of a state.

In the meantime, the Dutch had planted upon the Hudson and the Delaware by virtue of the discoveries of Hudson in 1609. And now in succession followed the planting of Maryland in 1634-5, Connecticut in 1632, Rhode Island in 1636, New Hampshire in 1631, Pennsylvania in 1682, the Carolinas in 1680, and Georgia in 1733.

But has it ever occurred to the reader when unfolding the charters conveying unlimited possession of vast sketches of the new found continent, by the great sovereigns of Europe, to ask by what right or by what legal authority they assumed to apportion out, and give away, and set up bounds in this land? Here was a people in possession of this country whose right to the soil could not be questioned. True, it was not so densely peopled as the continent of Europe; but the population was quite generally distributed, and they were organized into tribes and confederacies, and were in actual possession—a claim fortified by long occupancy. The European sovereigns were careful to insert in their charters, "not heretofore occupied by any Christian prince." But the Indians believed in a Great Spirit whom they worshipped.

The answer to this question, whether satisfactory or not, has been, that the civilized nations of Europe, on crossing the ocean, found here a vast country of untold resources lying untouched and unstirred, the Indians subsisting almost exclusively by hunting and fishing, the few spots used for cultivation being small in proportion to the whole and consequently their right to the soil as being unworthy of consideration. They found a people grossly ignorant, superstitious, idle, exhibiting the fiercest and most inhuman passions that vex the human breast, their greatest enjoyment, their supreme delight being the infliction upon their victims such refinements of torment, and perpetrations of savagery, as makes the heart sick to contemplate. Europeans have, therefore, held that they were justified in entering upon this practically unused soil, and dispossessing this scattered barbaric people.

Mr. Justice Story, in his familiar exposition of the constitution, in commenting upon this subject says: "As to countries in the possession of native inhabitants and tribes, at the time of the discovery, it seems difficult to perceive what ground of right any discovery could confer. It would seem strange to us, if, in the present times, the natives of the south sea islands, or of Cochin China, should, by making voyages to, and discovery of, the United States, on that account, set up a right to the soil within our boundaries. The truth is, that the European nations paid not the slightest regard to the rights of the native tribes. They treated them as mere barbarians and heathens, whom, if they were not at liberty to extirpate, they were entitled to deem mere temporary occupants of the soil. They might convert them to Christianity, and, if they refused conversion, they might drive them from the soil as unworthy to inhabit it   They affected to be governed by the desire to promote the cause of Christianity, and were aided in this ostensible object by the whole influence of the papal power. But their real object was to extend their own power and increase their own wealth, by acquiring the treasures, as well as the territory of the new world. Avarice and ambition were at the bottom of all their original enterprises "

This may be a just view of the moral and primary estimate of the case, yet the Supreme Court of the United States passed upon the question, Chief Justice Marshall delivering the opinion, holding that " the Indian title to the soil is not of such a character or validity as to interfere with the possession in fee, and disposal of the land as the State may see fit." In point of fact, every European nation, has, by its conduct, shown, that it had a perfect right to seize and occupy any part of the continent, and as much as it could by any possibility get its hands upon, could with perfect impunity steal and sell into slavery the natives, drive them out from their hunting grounds, burn and destroy their wigwams and scanty crops on the slightest pretext, and inflict upon them every species of injury which caprice or lust suggested   It is no wonder, therefore, that the Indians felt aggrieved, and that their savage instincts were whetted for their fell work of blood, and many of the massacres which were perpetrated within the limits of Greene County, which will form the subject of a future chapter, may be traced to a bitterness thus engendered. Generations of ill usage could be scarcely expected to bear other fruitage.

James Lindsey

CHAPTER IV.

The Dutch and Swedes upon the Delaware—The English Super-
cede them—In 1677 Came the English Quakers—William
Penn Interested in New Jersey—Admiral Penn—The Uncer-
tain Bounds—King Charles II. Grants Penn a Liberal
Domain—Charter of Pennsylvania—Liberal Terms—Spell-
ing—Penn had Meditated of a Free Commonweath—Re-
ceives his Grant in an Humble Spirit—Bitter Experiences
in the Life of Penn—Disinherited—Father Relents on his
Death-bed—Urges his Son Not to Wrong his Conscience—
Seeks a Deed of Quit-claim from James, and Buys the Lower
Counties—Perplexed in Devising a Form of Government—
Secures Freedom to the Subject—Published Abroad—Letter
Showing Abundance of Products—Penn Warns All to Con-
sider Well before Embarking the Privations they Must
Endure—Tender of Rights of the Natives—Sends a Notice
to them of his Purposes—All Alike Answerable to God—
Will Take no Land Except by Their Consent—Might have
Become Citizens—Four Hundred Years of Intercourse has
not Changed Their Nature—Show no Levity in Their Pres-
ence—"They Love Not to be Smiled On."

THE Colony of Pennsylvania was later in being permanently
settled than most of the others upon the sea-board. It is true
that the Dutch, who originally settled New York, had effected a
lodgment upon the Delaware, and maintained a fort there for
trading purposes, soon after its discovery by Hudson, in 1609, the
Dutch claiming all the territory which the Delaware and the Hudson
drain by reason of Hudson's discoveries. Dutch colonies increased
upon the Delaware, and made settlements on both sides of the river,
and Dutch governors were sent to rule there with justices of the
peace, constables, and all the appurtenances of civil government.
In 1638 came the Swedes, the representatives of the great monarch,
Gustavus Adolphus, and for several years there was divided authority
upon the Delaware, the Dutch and the Swedes contending for the
mastery. In 1664, upon the accession of Charles II. to the English
throne, came the English with a patent from the King covering all
the territory between the Connecticut and the Delaware Rivers, or in
short, all the territory occupied by the Dutch. Seeing themselves

3

likely to be overcome by force, the Dutch quietly surrendered, and the colony upon the Delaware passed under English rule. The list of taxables between the ages of sixteen and sixty, made in the year 1677, in the colony upon the Delaware, contained 443 names, which gives a population of 3,101. In this same year came three ship-loads of emigrants, for the most part English Quakers, who settled on either side of the Delaware, but the greater part in West Jersey. Some of this religious sect had preceded them, and in 1672 George Fox, the founder, had traveled through the Delaware country, " fording streams in his course, camping out at night, and visiting and counseling with his followers on the way " In 1664 Lord Berkeley and Sir George Carteret received from the Duke of York a grant of territory between the Delaware and the ocean, including the entire southern portion of New Jersey After ten years of troublesome attempts to settle their country, with little profit or satisfaction, Berkeley and Carteret sold New Jersey for a thousand pounds to John Fenwick, in trust for Edward Byllinge, both Quakers. - But the affairs of Byllinge were in confusion, and upon making an assignment, Gawin Lawrie, William Penn and Nicholas Lucas, became his assignees Upon settlement of his affairs Byllinge came into possession of West New Jersey, as his share of the province. In the discharge of his duty as trustee for Byllinge, William Penn, who was himself a convert to the doctrines of Fox, became greatly interested in the colonization of the Quakers in the New World, they having suffered grievous persecution for religious opinions' sake. In his devotion to their interests he had spent much time and labor in drawing up a body of laws for the government of the colony, devised in a spirit of unexampled liberality and freedom for the colonist.

We, who are accustomed to entire freedom in our modes of worship, can have little idea of the bitterness, and deadly animosity of the persecutions for religious opinion's sake, which prevailed in the reigns of bloody Mary and her successors Even as late as the accession of James II to the English throne, over fourteen hundred Quakers, the most learned and intelligent of that faith, mild and inoffensive, were languishing in the prisons of England, for no other crime than a sincere attempt to follow in the footsteps of their Divine Master, for Theeing and Thouing as they conceived He had done. To escape this hated and harassing persecution first turned the mind of Penn to the New World.

Penn had reason to expect favor at the hands of James II. His father, who was a true born Englishman, was an eminent admiral in the British navy, and had won great honor upon the seas for his country's flag. He had commanded the expedition which was sent to the West Indies by Cromwell, and had reduced the island of Jamaica to English rule. When James, then Duke of York, made his expedition against the Dutch, Admiral Penn commanded the fleet which descended upon the Dutch coast, and gained a great naval victory over the combined forces led by Van Opdam. For his gallantry in this campaign " he was knighted, and became a favorite at court, the King, and his brother the Duke, holding him in cherished remembrance." It was natural, therefore, that the son should seek favors at court for his distressed religious associates. Upon the death of Admiral Penn, the British government was indebted to him in the sum of sixteen thousand pounds, a part of it money actually advanced by the Admiral in fitting out the fleet which had gained the great victory. In lieu of this sum of money, which in those days was looked upon as a great fortune, the son, William, proposed to the King, Charles II., who had now come to the English throne, that he should grant him a province in America, "a tract of land in America, lying north of Maryland, bounded east by the Delaware River, on the west limited as Maryland, and northward to extend as far as plantable." These expressions, "as far as plantable," or, "as far up and northward as convenient," and the like, were favorite forms of expression, in cases where the country had been unexplored and no maps existed for the guidance of the royal secretaries, and were the cause of much uncertainty in interpreting the royal patents, and of long and wasting controversies over the just boundaries of the colonies, and were really the cause which made it possible for this County of Greene to have been subject to Virginia, or Maryland, or even to Massachusetts, or Connecticut.

King Charles, who had trouble enough in meeting the ordinary expenses of his throne without providing for an old score, lent a ready ear to the application of the son, and the idea of paying off a just debt, with a slice of that country which had cost him nothing, induced him to be liberal, and he gave Penn more than he had asked for. Already there were conflicting claims The Duke of York held the grant of the three counties of Delaware, and Lord Baltimore held a patent, the northern limit of which was left indefinite. The King himself manifested unusual solicitude in perfecting the title to his grant, and in many ways showed that he had at heart great friendship for Penn. All conflicting claims were patiently heard by the Lords, and that the best legal and judicial light upon the subject might be had the Attorney General Jones and Chief Justice North were called in. Finally, after careful deliberation, the Great Charter of Pennsylvania, conveying territory ample for an empire, holding unexampled resources upon its surface, and within its bosom, gladdened on every hand by lordly streams, and so diversified in surface as to present a scene of matchless beauty, was conveyed to Penn in these liberal, almost loving words: "Charles II, by the grace of

God, King of England, Scotland, France and Ireland, defender of the faith, etc, To all to whom these presents shall come greeting."

"Whereas our trustie and well beloved subject, William Penn, Esquire, sonn and heire of Sir William Penn, deceased, out of a commendable desire to enlarge our English Empire, and promote such usefull commodities as may bee of benefitt to us and our dominions, as alsoe to reduce the Savage Natives by gentle and just manners to the love of civill Societie and Christian Religion hath humbley besought leave of us to transport an ample colonie unto a certain countrey hereinafter described in the partes of America not yet cultivated and planted. And hath likewise humbley besought our Royall majestie to give, grant and confirme all the said countrey with certaine priviledges and jurisdiccons requisite for the good Government and saftie of the said Countrey and Colonie, to him and his heires forever Know yee, therefore, that wee, favoring the petition and good purpose of the said William Penn, and having regard to the memorie and meritts of his late father, in divers services, and particulerly to his conduct, courage and discretion under our dearest brother, James, Duke of Yorke, in the signall battell and victorie, fought and obteyned againste the Dutch fleete, commanded by Heer Van Opdam, in the year one thousand six hundred sixty-five, in consideration thereof of our special grace, certain knowledge and meere motion, Have given and granted, and by this our present Charter, for us, our heires and successors, Doe give and grant unto the said William Pen, his heires and assigns, all that tract or parte of land in America, with all the islands therein conteyned, as the same is bounded on the East by Delaware River, from twelve miles distance, Northwarde of New Castle Towne unto the three and fortieth degree of Northern latitude, if the said River doth extend so far Northwards, But if the said River shall not extend soe farre Northward, then by the said River soe farr as it doth extend, and from the head of the said River the Easterne bounds are to bee determined by a meridian line, to bee drawn from the head of the said River unto the said three and fortieth degree, the said lands to extend Westwards five degrees in longitude, to bee computed from the said Easterne Bounds, and the said lands to be bounded on the North by the beginning of the three and fortieth degree of Northern latitude, and on the South by a circle drawn at twelve miles, distance from New Castle Northwards, and Westwards unto the beginning of the fortieth degree of Northerne Latitude, and then by a straight line Westwards to the limit of Longitude above menconed.

"Wee doe also give and grant unto the said William Penn, his heires and assignes, the free and undisturbed use, and continuance in and passage into and out of all and singular, Ports, harbours, Bayes, waters, rivers, Isles and Inletts, belonging unto, or leading to and from the Country, or Islands aforesaid; and all the soyle, lands, fieldd, woods, underwoods, mountaines, hills, fenns, Isles, Lakes, Rivers, waters, rivuletts, Bays and Inletts, scituate or being within or belonging unto the Limitts and bounds aforesaid, together with the fishing of all sortes of fish, whales, sturgeons, and all Royall and other fishes in the sea, bayes, Inletts, waters, or Rivers within the premises, and the fish therein taken, and alsoe all veines, mines and quarries, as well discovered as not discovered, of Gold, Silver, Gemms and pretious Stones, and all other whatsoever stones, metals, or of any other thing or matter whatsoever found or to be found within the Countrey, Isles or Limitts aforesaid; and him the said William Penn, his heires and assignes, Wee doe, by this our Royall Charter, for us, our heires and successors, make, create and constitute the true and absolute proprietaries of the Countrey aforesaid, and of all other, the premises, saving always to us, our heires and successors, the faith and allegiance of the said William Penn, his heires and assignes, and of all other, the proprietaries, tenants and Inhabitants that are, or shall be within the territories and precincts aforesaid; and saving also unto us, our heirs and Successors, the Sovreignity of the aforesaid Countrey, To Have, hold and possesse and enjoy the said tract of Land, Countrey, Isles, Inletts and and other the premises, unto the said William Penn, his heires and assignes, to the only proper use and behoofe of the said William Penn, his heires and assignes forever."

Such is the introduction and deed of conveyance of the great charter by which Penn came into possession of that royal domain, Pennsylvania   But as it was to be in the nature of a sale, to make this deed of transfer binding according to the forms of law, there must be a consideration, the payment of which could be acknowledged or enforced, and the King, in a merry mood, exacted the payment thus, "yielding and paying therefor to us, our heires and successors, two Beaver Skins to bee delivered att our said Castle of Windsor, on the first day of January, in everey yeare."   The King also added a fifth of all gold and and silver which might be found.   But as that was an uncertain thing, and as in point of fact none ever was discovered, the sale of this great State was made, so far as this instrument shows, for two beaver skins, to be annually paid to the King.   And as a sequence to this condition the King says, " of our further grace certain knowledge and meer mocon have thought fitt to Erect the aforesaid Country Islands, into a province and Seigniorie, and do call itt Pensilvania, and soe from henceforth wee will have itt called, and forasmuch as wee have hereby made and ordeyned the aforesaid William Penn, his heirs and assignes, the true and absolute Proprietaries of all the lands and Dominions aforesaid."

Penn had proposed that his province be called New Wales, but the King objected to this. Penn then proposed Sylvania, as the country was reputed to be overshadowed by goodly forests. To this the King assented provided the prefix Penn should be attached. Penn vigorously opposed this as savoring of his personal vanity. But the King was inflexible, claiming this as an opportunity to honor his great father's name, and accordingly, when the charter was drawn, that name was inserted. Following the provisions quoted above are twenty-three sections providing for the government and internal regulation of the proposed colony, and adjusting with great particularity and much tedious circumlocution, the relations of the colony to the home government. It is not on this account thought best to quote the entire matter of the charter here, but any who may be curious to consult the document in its entirety will find the original, engrossed on parchment with an illuminated border, in the executive office at Harrisburg, and a true copy printed in the first volume of the Colonial Records, page seventeen. If anything is wanting to show the heartfelt consideration of the King for Penn, it is found in the twenty-third and last section, "And if, perchance, it should happen hereafter, any doubts or questions should arise concerning the true sense and meaning of any word, clause, or sentence, contained in this our present charter, We will ordaine, and command, that att all times and in all things such interpretacon be made thereof and allowed in any of our Courts whatsoever, as shall be adjudged most advantageous and favorable unto the said William Penn, his heires and assignes."

It will be noticed that the spelling of the royal secretary seems peculiar at this day, and that the capital letters and the alphabet generally are used with a freedom and originality which would have taxed the utmost stretch of ingenuity of so acknowledged an expert as Artemus Ward himself; but in the matter of composition it followed the legal forms prevalent in the courts of England of that day, and was drawn with a particularity and minuteness of detail scarcely paralleled in similar documents, apparently with a sincere desire to make the provisions so clear that there should be no chance for future dispute or misunderstanding, and the authority given to Penn as the proprietary was almost unlimited. In the matter of the boundaries the terms were such that there could be no possibility of mistake, the boundary lines being fixed by actual measurement and mathematical calculation, or by the observation of the heavenly bodies. The Delaware river formed its eastern limits, and all the others were lines of longitude and latitude. In this respect this portion of the charter was drawn with less equivocal terms than any other similar document. And yet the authorities of Pennsylvania had more difficulty in establishing its claims—for reasons which will hereafter be explained—than all the others together,

It was a joyful day for Penn when he received, at the hands of the King, the great charter, drawn with such liberality, conferring almost unlimited power, and with so many marks of the kindness of heart and personal favor of his sovereign. He had long meditated of a free commonwealth where it should be the study of the law-giver to form his codes with an eye to the greatest good and happiness of his subjects, and where the supreme delight of the subject would be to render implicit obedience to its requirements Plato's dream of an ideal republic, a land of just laws and happy men, "the dream of that city where all goodness should dwell, whether such has ever existed in the infinity of days gone by, or even now exists in the gardens of the Hesperides far from our sight and knowledge, or will perchance hereafter, which, though it be not on earth, must have a pattern of it laid up in heaven,"—such a dream was ever in the mind of Penn. The thought that he now had in a new country an almost unlimited stretch of land, where he could go and set up his republic, and form and govern it to his own sweet will. and in conformity to his cherished ideal, thrilled his soul and filled him with unspeakable delight. But he was not puffed up with vain glory. To his friend Turner he writes: "My true love in the Lord salutes thee, and dear friends that love the Lord's precious truth in those parts. Thine epistle I have, and, for my business here, know that after many waitings, watchings, solicitings and disputes in council, this day my country was confirmed to me under the great seal of England, with large powers and privileges, by the name of Pennsylvania, a name the king would give it in honor of my father. * * * Thou mayest communicate my grant to Friends, and expect shortly my proposals. It is a clear and just thing, and my God, that has given it me through many difficulties, will, I believe, bless and make it the seed of a nation." And may we not cherish the belief that the many and signal blessings which have come to this commonwealth in succeeding years, have come through the devout and pious spirit of the founder.'

He had seen the companions of his religious faith sorely treated throughout all England, and for them he now saw the prospect of a release from their tribulations. Penn himself had come up through bitter persecution and scorn on account of his religion. At the age of fifteen he entered Oxford University, and for the reason that he and some of his fellow-students practiced the faith of the Friends, they were admonished and finally expelled. Returning to his home in Ireland, where his father had large estates, his serious deportment gave great offence, the father fearing that his advancement at court would thereby be marred. Thinking to break the spirit of the son, the boy was whipped, and finally expelled from the family home. At Cork, where he was employed in the service of the Lord Lieutenant, he, in company with others, was apprehended at a religious meeting of Friends, and cast into prison While thus incarcerated he wrote to the Lord President of Munster, pleading for liberty of conscience. On being liberated he became more devoted than before, and so impressed was he with a sense of religious duty that he became a minister of the gospel Religious controversy at this time was sharp, and a pamphlet, which he wrote, gave so much offense to the Bishop of London that Penn was thrown into the Tower, where he languished for eight and a half months. But he was not idle, and one of the books which he wrote during his imprisonment,—" No Cross, No Crown,"—attained a wide circulation, and is still read with satisfaction by the faithful in all lands. Fearing that his motives might be misconceived, he made this distinct statement of his belief, " Let all know this, that I pretend to know no other name by which remission, atonement and salvation can be obtained but Jesus Christ, the Savior, who is the power and wisdom of God." Upon his release he continued to preach and exhort, was arrested with his associate Mead, and was tried at the Old Bailey. Penn plead his own cause with great boldness and power, and was acquitted; but the court imposed a fine for contempt in wearing his hat, and, for non-payment, was cast into Newgate with common felons At this time, 1670, the father, feeling his end approaching, sent money privately to pay the fine, and summoned the son to his bedside The meeting was deeply affecting. The father's heart was softened and completely broken, and, as would seem from his words, had become converted to the doctrines of the son, for he said to him with his parting breath, " Son William, I am weary of the world! I would not live over again my days, if I could command it with a wish; for the snares of life are greater than the fears of death. This troubles me, that I have offended a gracious God The thought of that has followed me to this day Oh! have a care of sin! It is that which is the sting both of life and death. Let nothing in this world tempt to wrong your conscience; so you will keep peace at home, which will be a feast to you in the day of trouble " Before his death he sent a friend to the Duke of York with a dying request, that the Duke would endeavor to protect his son from persecution, and use his influence with the King to the same end.

The King had previously given James, Duke of York, a charter for Long Island, with an indefinite western boundary, and, lest this might at some future day compromise his right to some portion of his territory, Penn induced the Duke to execute a deed for the same territory covered by the royal charter, and substantially in the same words used in describing its limits. But he was still not satisfied to have the shores of the only navigable river communicating with the ocean under the dominion of others, who might in time become

John S Fuller

hostile and interfere with the free navigation of the stream. He accordingly induced the Duke to make a grant to him of New Castle and New Castle County, and on the same day a grant of the territory stretching onward to the sea, covering the two counties of Kent and Sussex, the two grants together embracing what were designated the territories, or the three lower counties, what in after years became the State of Delaware; but by which acts became and long remained component parts of Pennsylvania. No such colony as Delaware ever existed. This gave Penn a considerable population, as in these three counties the Dutch and Swedes since 1609 had been settling.

Penn was now ready to settle his own colony and try his schemes of government. Lest there might be a misapprehension respecting his purpose in obtaining his charter, and unworthy persons with unworthy motives might be induced to emigrate, he declares repeatedly his own sentiments: "For my country I eyed the Lord in obtaining it; and more was I drawn inwards to look to Him, and to owe to His hand and power than to any other way. I have so obtained and desire to keep it, that I may not be unworthy of His love, but do that which may answer His kind providence and people."

In choosing a form of government he was much perplexed. He had thought the government of England all wrong, when it bore so heavily upon him and his friends, and he, doubtless, thought in his earlier years, that he could order one in righteousness; but when it was given him to draw a form that should regulate the affairs of the future state, he hesitated. "For particular frames and models, it will become me to say little. 'Tis true, men seem to agree in the end, to wit, happiness; but in the means, they differ, as to divine, so to this human felicity; and the cause is much the same, not always want of light and knowledge, but want of using them rightly. Men side with their passions against their reason, and their sinister interests have so strong a bias upon their minds that they lean to them against the things they know. I do not find a model in the world, that time, place, and some singular emergencies have not necessarily altered, nor is it easy to frame a civil government that shall serve all places alike. I know what is said of the several admirers of Monarchy, Aristocracy, and Democracy, which are the rule of one, of a few, and of many, and are the three common ideas of government, when men discourse on that subject. But I propose to solve the controversy with this small distinction, and it belongs to all three; any government is free to the people under it, whatever be the frame, where the laws rule, and the people are a party to those laws, and more than this is tyranny, oligarchy, and confusion."

" But when all is said, there is hardly one frame of government in the world so ill-designed by its first founders, that in good hands would not do well enough; and story tells us, the best in ill ones can do nothing that is great and good; witness the Jewish and the Roman states Governments, like clocks, go from the motion men give them, and as governments are made and moved by men, so by them are they ruined too. Wherefore governments rather depend upon men, than men upon governments Let men be good, and the government cannot be bad, if it be ill, they will cure it. But if men be bad, let the government be never so good, they will endeavor to warp and spoil to their turn "

"I know some say let us have good laws, and no matter for the men that execute them, but let them consider, that though good laws do well, good men do better; for good laws may want good men, and be abolished or invaded by ill men; but good men will never want good laws, nor suffer ill ones. 'Tis true, good laws have some awe upon ill ministers; but that is where they have not power to escape. or abolish them, and the people are generally wise and good; but a loose and depraved people, which is to the question, love laws and an administration like themselves. That, therefore, which makes a good constitution, must keep it, viz , men of wisdom and virtue, qualities that because they descend not with worldly inheritances, must be carefully propagated by a virtuous education of youth, for which after ages will owe more to the care and prudence of founders, and the successive magistracy, than to their parents for their private patrimonies."

These considerations, which stand as a preface to his frame of government, are given at some length here, in order to show the temper of mind and heart of Penn, as he entered upon his great work. He seems like one who stands before the door of a royal palace, and is loth to lay his hand upon the knob, whose turn shall give him entrance, for fear his tread should be unsanctified by the grace of Heaven, or lack favor in the eyes of his subjects For he says in closing his disquisition : "These considerations of the weight of government, and the nice and varied opinions about it, made it uneasy to me to think of publishing the ensuing frame and conditional laws, forseeing both the censures they will meet with· from men of differing humours and engagements, and the occasion they may give of discourse beyond my design. But next to the power of necessity, this induced me to a compliance, that we have (with reverence to God, and good conscience to men), to the best of our skill, contrived and composed the frame and laws of this government, to the great end of all government, viz : To support in reverence with the people, and to secure the people from the abuse of power; that they may be free by their just obedience, and the magistrates honorable for their just administration; for liberty without obedience is confusion, and obedience without liberty is slavery. To carry this evenness is partly owing to the constitution, and partly to the magistracy; where either of these fail, government will be subject to confusion; but where both are wanting, it must be totally subverted; then where both meet, the government is like to endure. Which I humbly pray and hope God will please to make the lot of this of Pennsylvania Amen."

In such temper, and with such a spirit did our great founder approach the work of drawing a frame of government and laws for his proposed community, insignificant in numbers at first; but destined at no distant day to embrace millions. It is not to be wondered at that he felt great solicitude, in view of the future possibilities With great care and tenderness for the rights and privileges of the individual, he drew the frame or constitution in twenty-four sections, and the body of laws in forty. And who can estimate the power for good to this people, of the system of government set up by this pious, God fearing man, every provision of which was a subject of his prayers, and tears, and the deep yearnings of a sanctified heart.

The town meeting works the destruction of thrones Penn's system was, in effect, at the outset, a free Democracy, where the individual was supreme. Had King Charles foreseen, when he gave his charter, what principles of freedom to the individual would be embodied in the government of the new colony, and would be nurtured in the breasts of the oncoming generations, if he had held the purpose of keeping this a constituent and obedient part of his kingdom, he would have witheld his assent to it, as elements were implanted therein antagonistic to arbitrary, kingly rule. But men sometimes contrive better than they know, and so did Charles.

When finished, the frame of government was published, and was sent out, accompanied with a description of the country, and especial care was taken that these should reach the members of the society of Friends. Many of the letters written home to friends in England by those who had settled in the country years before, were curious and amusing, and well calculated to excite a desire to emigrate Two years before this, Mahlon Stacy wrote an account of the country, which the people of our day would scarcely be able to match. "I have seen," he says, "orchards laden with fruit to admiration; their very limbs torn to pieces with weight, most delicious to the taste, and lovely to behold. I have seen an apple-tree. from a pippin-kernel, yield a barrel of curious cider, and peaches in such plenty that some people took their carts a peach-gathering. I could not but smile at the conceit of it; they are very delicious fruit, and hang almost like our onions, that are tied on ropes. I have seen and know, this summer, forty bushels of bold wheat of one bushel sown. From May to Michaelmas great store of very good wild fruit as strawberries, cranberries and hurtleberries, which are like our bilberries in England, only far sweeter; the cranberries, much like cherries for color and bigness, which may be kept till fruit comes again; an excellent sauce is made of them for venison, turkeys, and other great fowl, and they are better to make tarts of than either gooseberries or cherries, we have them brought to our houses by the Indians in great plenty. My brother Robert had as many cherries this year as would have loaded several carts   As for venison and fowls we have great plenty, we have brought home to our countries by the Indians, seven or eight fat bucks in a day.   We went into the river to catch herrings after the Indian fashion   We could have filled a three-bushel sack of as good large herrings as ever I saw   And as to beef and pork, here is a great plenty of it, and good sheep.   The common grass of the country feeds beef very fat.   Indeed, the country, take it as a wilderness, is a brave country."

If the denizens of England were to accept this description as a true picture of the productions and possibilities of the New World, they might well conclude with the writer that "for a wilderness" it was a "brave country," and we can well understand why they flocked to the new El Dorado.   But lest any might be tempted to go without sufficient consideration, Penn issued a pronunciamento, urging every one who contemplated removal thither to consider well the inconveniences of the voyage, and the labor and privation required of emigrants to a wilderness country, "that so none may move rashly or from a fickle, but from a solid mind, having above all things an eye to the providence of God in the disposing of themselves."

And that there should be no deception or misunderstanding in regard to the rights of property, Penn drew up "Certain Conditions and Concessions" before leaving England, which he circulated freely, touching the laying out of roads and highways, the plats of towns, the settling of communities on ten thousand acre tracts, so that friends and relatives might be together; declaring that the woods, rivers, quarries and mines are the exclusive property of those on whose purchases they were found; for the allotment to servants; that the Indians shall be treated justly; the Indians' furs should be sold in open market; that the Indian shall be treated as a citizen, and that no man shall leave the province without giving three weeks' public notice posted in the market-place, that all claims for indebtedness might be liquidated.   These and many other matters of like tenor form the subject of these remarkable concessions, all tending to show the solicitude of Penn for the interests of his colonists, and that none should say that he deceived or overreached them in the sale of his lands   He foresaw the liability that the natives would be under to be deceived and cheated by the crafty and designing, being entirely unskilled in judging of the values of things. He accordingly devotes a large proportion of the matter of these concessions to secure and defend the rights of the ignorant natives. If it was possible to make a human being conform to the rights and privileges of civilized society, and make him truly an enlightened citizen, Penn's treatment of the Indian was calculated to make him so. He treated the natives as his own people, as citizens in every important particular, and as destined to an immortal inheritance. He wrote to them: "There is a great God and power that hath made the world and all things therein, to whom you and I and all people owe their being and well-being; and to whom you and I must one day give an account for all that we do in the world. This great God hath written His law in our hearts, by which we are taught and commanded to love, and help, and do good to one another. Now the great God hath been pleased to make me concerned in your part of the world, and the king of the country where I live hath given me a great province therein; but I desire to enjoy it with your love and consent, that we may always live together as neighbors and friends; else what would the great God do to us, who hath made us not to devour and destroy one another, but to live soberly and kindly together in the world? Now I would have you well observe that I am very sensible of the un-kindness and injustice that have been too much exercised towards you by the people of these parts of the world, who have sought them-selves, and to make great advantages by you, rather than to be ex-amples of goodness and patience unto you, which I hear hath been a matter of trouble to you, and caused great grudging and animosities, sometimes to the shedding of blood, which hath made the great God angry. But I am not such a man, as is well known in my country. I have great love and regard toward you, and desire to gain your love and friendship by a kind, just and peaceable life, and the people I send are of the same mind, and shall in all things behave them-selves accordingly; and if in anything any shall offend you or your people, you shall have a full and speedy satisfaction for the same by an equal number of just men on both sides, that by no means you may have just occasion of being offended against them. I shall shortly come to you myself, at which time we may more largely and freely confer and discourse of these matters. In the meantime I have sent my commissioners to treat with you about land, and form a league of peace. Let me desire you to be kind to them and their people, and receive these tokens and presents which I have sent you as a testimony of my good will to you, and my resolution to live justly, peaceably and friendly with you." Such was the mild and gentle attitude in which Penn came to the natives.

Had the Indian character been capable of being broken and changed, so as to have adopted the careful and laborious habits which Europeans possess, the aborigines might have been assimilated and be-come a constituent part of the population. Such was the expectation of Penn. They could have become citizens, as every other foreign race have   But the Indian could no more be tamed than the wild partridge of the woods   Fishing and hunting were his occupation, and if any work or drudgery was to be done, it was shifted to the women, as being beneath the dignity of the free savage of the forest. Two hundred and fifty years of intercourse with European civilization and customs have not in the least changed his nature.   He is essentially the savage still, as he was on the day when Columbus first met him, four hundred years ago.

But this fact does not change the aspect in which we should view the pious and noble intents of Penn, and they must ever be regarded with admiration, as indicative of his loving and merciful purposes. He not only provided that they should be treated as human beings, on principles of justice and mercy, but he was particular to point out to his commissioners the manners which should be preserved in their presence· "Be tender of offending the Indians, and let them know that you come to sit down lovingly among them.   Let my letter and conditions be read in their tongue, that they may see we have their good in our eye   Be grave.   They love not to be smiled on."

CHAPTER V.

Markham First Governor—Sails for New York and is Accorded Permission to Assume Control on the Delaware—Purchase Land of the Indians—Seek a Site of a Great City—Penn Sails for America—Advice to Wife and Children on Leaving—Love of Rural Life—Thirty Passengers Die on the Voyage—Calls an Assembly and Enacts Laws—Civil and Religious Liberty—Visits Site of the New City—Satisfied With It—Visits Governor of New York and Friends in Long Island and Jersey—Discusses Boundary With Lord Baltimore—The Great Treaty—Method of the Indians—Terms of the Treaty—Speech of Penn—Legal Forms Observed—"Treaty Tree" Preserved—Walking Purchase—Consideration of Penn—Injustice of Later Governor—Rapid Increase —Penn Describes the New City—Distances From the Chief Cities—Latitude and Longitude—Designs River Bank for a Public Park—Disregarded—Names His City Philadelphia—Growth of the Colony—Compared With Other Colonies.

NOT being in readiness to go immediately to his province, Penn issued a commission bearing date March 6, 1681, to his cousin, William Markham, as Lieutenant Governor, and sent him forward with three ship-loads of settlers to take possession of his province. Markham sailed directly to New York, where he exhibited his commission to the acting governor of that province, who made a record of the fact, and gave Gov. Markham a letter addressed to the civil magistrates on the Delaware thanking them for their zeal and fidelity, and directing them to transfer their allegiance to the new Proprietary. Armed now with complete authority, Markham proceeded to the Delaware, where he was kindly received and all allegiance promptly accorded to him as the rightful governor. Markham was accompanied by four commissioners, who were first to establish friendly relations with the Indians and acquire land by purchase, and second to select and survey and lay out the plot of a great city. Penn had received a complete grant and deed of transfer of these lands, and had he followed the example of the other colonists he would have taken arbitrary possession without consulting the natives. But he held that their claims to rightful ownership by possession for immemorial time, must first be satisfied. Accordingly, following the pacific instructions of Penn, the commissioners found no difficulty in opening negotiations with the simple inhabitants of the forest, and in purchasing long reaches of land on the south and west bank of the Delaware and far beyond the Schuylkill

But it was not so easy to find a site for a great city to completely fill all the conditions which the founder had imposed It must be on a stream navigable, where many boats could ride in safety and of sufficient depth so that ships could come up to the wharf and load and unload without " boating and lightening of it " " The situation must be high, at least dry and sound, and not swampy, which is best known by digging up two or three earths and seeing the bottom." The site was to contain a block of 10,000 square acres in one square, and the streets to be regularly laid out " Let every house be placed, if the person pleases, in the middle of its plat, as to the breadthway of it, that so there may be ground on each side for gardens or orchards or fields, that it may be a green country town, which will never be burned, and always wholesome "

These instructions of Penn were most carefully observed, and for many weeks the commissioners searched for such a site as he had pictured, their investigations extending far up the Delaware They finally fixed upon the present site of Philadelphia, which was settled, and has grown as then surveyed It was between two navigable streams; it was dry, being one vast bed of sand and gravel and hence easily drained; and so high as not to be liable to overflow; it had ten thousand square acres; but there was not distance enough between the two rivers to allow it to be in a square block. However, as there was room for indefinite extension up and down the streams, this was not regarded as fatal to the choice. The streets were laid with exact regularity, crossing each other at right angles. Through the center, Market street extended from river to river, and so wide that originally, and until within the memory of many now living, long, low market houses, or sheds stretched along its middle, and at its center it was crossed by Broad street, a magnificent avenue. At their intersection a park was left, upon which the city has recently erected a structure of marble for the purposes of the city government, which, for beauty of architecture, convenience and solidity of structure is scarcely matched anywhere in the world

Having settled all things at home to his satisfaction, Penn prepared to depart for his new country But before departing he addressed farewell letters to his friends, and to his wife and children. From these we can gather what was really in his heart of hearts, what was his true character and the tenor of his inmost thoughts. To his fellow laborer, Stephen Crisp, he wrote, "Stephen, we know one another, and I need not say much to thee. * * * The Lord

Capt John Scott

will bless that ground (Pennsylvania). * * - * And truly, Stephen, · there is work enough, and here is room to work in. Surely God will come in for a share in this planting-work, and that leaven shall leaven the lump in time." As he was now about to depart on a voyage over the treacherous ocean, he wrote to his wife and children as though he might never return to them again. To his wife he said, "God knows and thou knowest it, I can say it was a match of .Providence's making, and God's image in us both was the first thing." In counselling her not to become involved in debt, he says, "My mind is rapt up in a saying of thy father's, 'I desire not riches, but to owe nothing;' and truly that is wealth, and more than enough to live is attended with many sorrowes." Of his children he says, "I had rather they were homely, than finely bred, as to outward behavior; yet I love sweetness mixed with gravity. Religion in the heart leads into this true civility. * * * For their learning be liberal. Spare no cost; for by such parsimony all is lost that is saved; but let it be useful knowledge, such as is consistent with truth and godliness, not cherishing a vain conversation or idle mind, but ingenuity mixed with industry is good for the body and mind too. I recommend the useful part of mathematics, as building houses or ships, measuring, surveying, dialing, navigation; but agriculture is especially in my eye—let my children be husbandmen and housewives; it is industrious, healthy, honest, and of good example; like Abraham and the holy ancients, who pleased God and obtained a good report. This leads to consider the works of God and nature of things that are good, and diverts the mind from being taken up with the vain arts and inventions of a luxurious world. * * * Of cities and towns of concourse beware; the world is apt to stick close to those who have lived and got wealth there; a country life and estate I like best for my children." To his children he said, "First love and fear the Lord, and delight to wait on the God of your father and mother. * * * Next be obedient to your dear mother, a woman whose virtue and good name is an honor to you; for she hath been exceeded by none in her time for her plainness, integrity, industry, humanity, virtue, good understanding; qualities not usual among women of her worldly condition and quality. * * * Betake yourselves to some honest, industrious course of life. * * * And if you marry, mind neither beauty nor riches, but the fear of the Lord, and a sweet and amiable disposition; and being married, be tender, affectionate and meek. * * * Be sure to live within compass; borrow not, neither be beholden to any. * * * Love not money nor the world; use them only, and they will serve you; but if you love them you serve them, which will debase your spirits as well as offend the Lord. * * * Be humble and gentle in your conversation; of few words, but always pertinent when you speak,

4

hearing out before you attempt to answer, and then speaking as if you would pursuade not impose. Affront none, neither revenge the affronts that are done to you; but forgive and you shall be forgiven of your heavenly father. In making friends consider well first; and when you are fixed be true. Watch against anger; neither speak nor act in it, for, like drunkenness, it makes a man a beast. Avoid flatterers, for they are thieves in disguise. * * * They lie to flatter, and flatter to cheat. * * * Be temperate in all things; in your diet, for that is physic by prevention; it keeps, nay, it makes people healthy, and their generation sound. * * * Avoid pride, avarice and luxury. Make your conversation with the most eminent for wisdom and piety, and shun all wicked men, as you hope for the blessing of God, and the comfort of your father's living and dying prayers. * * * Be no busy bodies. In your families remember, Abraham, Moses and Joshua, their integrity to the Lord. * * * Keep on the square for God sees you."

Of this remarkable letter, which is worthy to lay to heart and be made a frequent study by the rising generation, only a few brief extracts are given above, yet enough has been adduced to show the pious intent of the founder of our noble Commonwealth. In June, 1682, Penn set sail for America in the ship "Welcome," with some hundred passengers, of whom thirty died of small-pox on the voyage. He landed at New Castle, where he took formal possession of the country. At a public meeting called at the court-house he explained his object in coming, his plan of government, and renewed the commissions of the magistrates. Proceeding to Uplands, which he named Chester, he called an assembly composed of an equal number from the province and territories, (afterwards Delaware), and proceeded to enact a frame of government and a body of laws. The convention was in session but three days, as it was in harvest, and the farmers could not afford to spend much time; but in that brief period, which in these days would scarcely suffice for the speaker to make up his committees, the constitution was considered article by article, amended and adopted, and the laws in like manner, so that when they adjourned, after this brief session, it could be said that the great ship of State, Pennsylvania, was fairly launched, and the government, which, in this simple way, was there adopted in the town of Chester, has formed the basis of that system which has guided the State in safety through the more than two centuries of its growth, and brought it safely on in the voyage of empire, with its more than four millions of people.

Penn's first and chief care was to establish civil and religious liberty so firmly, that it should not be in the power of future rulers to alter or destroy it. As he himself declared, "For the matter of liberty and privilege, I purpose that which is extraordinary, and leave myself and successors no power of doing mischief, that the will of one man may not hinder the good of a whole country.". Having suffered sore persecution himself, as well as his religious associates, he cherished a bitter hatred of any system which could impose or even suffer such injustice, and accordingly he placed at the head of his Fundamentals this, in that age, remarkable provision: "In reverence to God, the Father of light and spirits, the author as well as object of all divine knowledge, faith and worship, I do for me and mine, declare and establish for the first fundamental of the government of my province, that every person, that doth and shall reside therein, shall have and enjoy the free possession of his or her faith and exercise of worship towards God, in such way and manner as every such person shall in conscience believe is most acceptable to God."

It would seem as if the new world was opened at a time when persecution in the old world was rife, that the oppressed people of all nations might have an asylum, where civil and religious liberty should forever be preserved. Having thus settled his form of government, and set it fairly in operation, be began to make journeys into the distant parts of his country. He first visited the site which had been selected for the new city, proceeding in a barge from Chester, and landed at the mouth of Dock Creek, now Dock street. Forests covered the site, conies burrowed in the bank, and wild animals dashed past him as Penn was pulled up the side The situation pleased him, and the country was even more inviting than he had been led to believe. "I am very well and much satisfied with my place and portion. * * * As to outward things we are satisfied; the land good, the air clear and sweet, the springs plentiful, and provision good and easy to come at, an innumerable quantity of wild-fowl and fish; in fine, here is what an Abraham, Isaac and Jacob would be well contented with, and service enough for God; for the fields are white for harvest. Oh how sweet is the quiet of these parts, freed from the anxious and troublesome solicitations, heresies and perplexities of woful Europe."

Penn understood well the proprieties of social life, as well as the advantage of politeness to good fellowship He took early occasion to visit New York, and pay his respects to the Governor and his associates there. But wherever he went, he never divested himself of his character as a laborer in the vineyard of the Lord. Accordingly, after having taken his leave of the Governor, he paid visits to the members of the society of Friends living on Long Island, and in east New Jersey, which had previously come into the possession of a company of which he was one, and everywhere did "service for the Lord." He also visited Lord Baltimore, in Maryland, that they might confer together upon the subject of the boundaries of the two colonies. As the weather became intensely cold, precluding the possibility of taking stellar observations or making the necessary surveys, it was agreed to adjourn the conference to the milder weather of the spring.

The founder took great care to secure the friendship and interest of the Indians in the new State. He accordingly took early occasion to summon a council of all the neighboring tribes, that he might make a formal treaty of peace with them, and secure a legally executed deed for their lands. The meeting was held beneath the shade of a giant elm at Kensington, ever after known and held in veneration as the "Treaty tree." The Indians from far and near had come, as it was an event that had been widely heralded, and the desire on the part of the natives to see and hear the great founder, who had addressed them the year before in such loving words, was doubtless intense. Penn came with his formal treaty all drawn up, and engrossed on parchment, as well as a deed for their lands. In his letter to friends in England he describes the manner of the Indians in council, which was doubtless the method observed on the occasion of concluding the great treaty. "I have had occasion," he says, "to be in council with them upon treaties for land, and to adjust the terms of trade. Their order is thus: the king sits in the middle of a half-moon, and has his council, the old and wise on each hand. Behind them, or at a little distance, sit the younger fry in the same figure. Having consulted and resolved their business, the king ordered one of them to speak to me. He stood up, came to me, and in the name of his king saluted me, then he took me by the hand, and told me that he was ordered by his king to speak to me, and that now it was not he but the king who spoke, because what he should say was the king's mind. Having thus introduced his matter, he fell to the bounds of the land they had agreed to dispose of, and the price, which now is little and dear, that which would have bought twenty miles, not buying now two. During the time that this person spoke, not a man of them was observed to whisper or smile, the old grave, the young reverent, in their deportment. They speak little but fervently, and with elegance. I have never seen more natural sagacity, considering them without the help (I was going to say, the spoil of tradition) and he will deserve the name of wise, who outwits them in any treaty about a thing they understand." Penn now responded to them in a like sober and reverent spirit, assuring them that the red man and the white man are equally the care of the Great Spirit, and that it is his desire to live in peace and good fellowship with them. "It is not our custom," he says, "to use hostile weapons against our fellow creatures, for which reason we have come unarmed." Penn now unrolls his parchment, and reads and explains the force of each article, all of which is interpreted into their own language,—though it should here be stated that Penn learned the Indian language, and was able to speak to them in their own tongue. "I will not do," he continued, "as the Marylanders did, call you children or brothers only; for parents are apt to whip their children too severely; and brothers sometimes will differ; neither will I compare the friendship between us to a chain, for the rain may rust it, or a tree may fall and break it; but I will consider you as the same flesh and blood as the Christians, and the same as if one man's body were to be divided into two parts." In response to this declaration the spokesman for the king again comes forward and makes great promises and declares that "the Indians and the English must live in love as long as the sun doth give its light." Another speaker now turns to the Indians and explains to them what had been said and done, and counsels them " to love the Christians, that many Governors had been in the river, but that no Governor had come himself to live and stay here before, and having now such an one that had treated them well they should never do him nor his any wrong," all of which was received by the entire assemblage with accents of approval.

Penn took special pains to have all his purchases of the Indians executed in due legal form, and recorded in the offices of his government, so that if any question concerning the conditions should arise there should be the exact evidence of the bargain at hand. The Indians themselves had no method of recording their agreements, but their memory of such transactions was remarkably exact and tenacious. They had some arbitrary way by which they were able to recall their knowledge of events. The Indian missionary and historian says, "They frequently assembled together in the woods, in some shady spot, as nearly as possible similar to those where they used to meet their brother Miquon (Penn), and there lay all his words and speeches, with those of his descendants on a blanket or clean piece of bark, and with great satisfaction go successively over the whole. * * *. This practice, which I have repeatedly witnessed, continued until 1780 (a period of a hundred years), when disturbances which took place put an end to it probably forever."

The venerable elm tree under which this noted conference was held was carefully guarded and preserved. Even while the city of Philadelphia was in possession of the enemy during the Revolutionary war, and firewood was scarce, the Treaty Tree, this venerable elm, was preserved from mutilation. The British General Simcoe stationed a guard over it. It stood till 1810, when it fell a victim to the storms; and was found to be 283 years old, showing that at the time of the treaty it was 155. The Penn Society of Philadelphia have marked the spot where it stood by erecting a durable monument.

Of Penn's purchases of the Indians two deeds are on record,

executed in 1683, one of them bearing the signature of the renowned chieftain Taminend. In one of these the method of measurement was unique. The terms were that the tract should embrace the territory between two rivers and "shall extend as far back as a man can walk in three days." It does not provide whether the days are to be from sun to sun, nor at what season of the year the walk is to be made, nor whether a day shall be reckoned at twenty-four hours, or whether the walk shall be executed by an experienced walker at the top of his bent, or be walked leisurely. But Penn, actuated by a sense of simple justice, construed entirely to the advantage of the Indians, that he might show them that he was actuated by none but the most exalted motives. Accordingly, Penn, himself, with a number of his friends, accompanied by a gay party of the natives, made the walk. They did not turn it into a race, but treated it as a pleasure party, proceeding leisurely, sitting down at intervals to "smoke their pipes, eat biscuit and cheese, and drink a bottle of wine." Commencing at the mouth of Neshaminy Creek they proceeded on up the shores of the Delaware. At the end of a day and a half they reached a spruce tree on the bank of Baker Creek, about thirty miles, when Penn, thinking that he had as much land as he would want for the present, agreed with the Indians to stop there and allow the remaining day and a half of space to be walked out at some future time. The execution of the balance of the contract was in marked contrast to the liberal interpretation of the founder. It was not made till 1733, when the then Governor offered a prize of 500 acres of land and £5 in money to the man who would make the greatest walk. There were three contestants, and one, Edward Marshall, won the prize, making a distance of eighty-six miles in the single day and a half, an unprecedented feat. The advantage taken by the Governor in this transaction gave great offense to the Indians. "It was the cause," says Jenney, "of the first dissatisfaction between them and the people of Pennsylvania; and it is remarkable that the first murder committed by them in the province, seventy-two years after the landing of Penn, was on this very ground which had been taken from them by fraud."

The excellence of the country, the gentleness of the government, and the loving society of Friends, caused a good report to go out to all parts of Europe, and thither came flocking emigrants from many lands, from London, Cheshire, Lancashire, Ireland, Scotland, Germany, and from Wales a company of the stock of Ancient Britons. For the most part they were of the Society of Friends, and were escaping from bitter persecution for their religion. They were, consequently, people of pure hearts, good elements for the building of a colony. On landing they would seek the shelter of a tree with their household goods, and there they would live till they could secure

their land and erect a rude shelter. Some betook themselves to the
river's bank and dug caves for temporary shelter. In one of these
caves the first child, John Key, was born in the new city, known
long after as Penny-pot, near Sassafras street. He lived to his
eighty-fifth year, dying in 1768. It will be seen that many privations had to be endured, and so great was the influx of settlers that
food was sometimes scarce. But they were patient, accustomed to
toil, and devoted in their worship, so that the colony had wonderful
prosperity and increase.

Penn's own impressions are conveyed in a letter to his friends in
England. "Philadelphia, the expectation of those who are concerned, is at last laid out to the great content of those here. The
situation is a neck of land, and lieth between two navigable rivers,
Delaware and Schuylkill, whereby it hath two fronts upon the water,
each a mile, and two from river to river. * * * This I will say
for the good providence of God, of all the places I have seen in the
world I remember not one better seated; so that it seems to me to
have been appointed for a town; whether we regard the rivers, or the
conveniency of the coves, docks and springs, the loftiness and sound-
ness of the land, and the air, held by the people of these parts to be
very good. I bless God I am fully satisfied with the country and
entertainment I got in it " By the course of the river the city is
120 miles from the ocean, but only sixty in direct line. It is eighty-
seven miles from New York, ninety-five from Baltimore, 136 from
Washington, 100 from Harrisburg, and 300 from Pittsburg, and is
in latitude north 39°, 56', 54", and in longitude west from Green-
wich 75°, 8', 45". The Delaware at this time was nearly a mile
wide opposite the city and navigable for ships of the greatest tonnage.
The tide here has a rise of about six feet and flows back to the falls
of Trenton, some thirty miles The tide in the Schuylkill flows
only about six miles above its confluence with the Delaware. The
purpose of Penn was that the land along the river bank should be a
public park, holding in his mind's eye its future adornment with
walks and fountains and statues, trees and sweet smelling shrubs
and flowers; for when pressed to allow warehouses to be built upon it
he resolutely declared, "The bank is a top common, from end to end;
the rest next to the water belongs to front-lot men no more than
back-lot men. The way bounds them " But Penn, at this early day,
in the simplicity of his nature had little conception of the necessities
which commerce would impose, when the city should grow to the
million of population, which it now has, so that the cherished design
of the founder has been disregarded, and great warehouses where a
vast tonnage is constantly moving, embracing the commerce from the
remotest corners of the globe, cumber all the bank. Penn had cherished the purpose of founding a great city from his earliest years,

and had adopted the name Philadelphia (brotherly love) before he had any reasonable prospect of coming to America. So that the name was not a matter of question.

The growth of the province was something wonderful, and caused Penn to say in a spirit of exultation unusual to him, " I must, without vanity say, I have led the greatest colony into America that ever any man did upon a private credit." Bancroft very justly observes, " There is nothing in the history of the human race like the confidence which the simple virtues and institutions of William Penn inspired. The progress of his province was more rapid than that of New England In August, 1683, Philadelphia consisted of three or four little cottages. The conies were yet undisturbed in their heredi tary burrows, the deer fearlessly bounded past blazed trees, unconscious of foreboded streets; the stranger that wandered from the river bank was lost in thickets of interminable forest; and two years afterward the place contained about six hundred houses, and the schoolmaster and the printing-press had begun their work. In three years from its foundation Philadelphia had gained more than New York had done in half a century. It was not long till Philadelphia led all the cities in America in population, though one of the latest founded By the census of 1800 Pennsylvania led all the other States in the number of white population, having 586.095; New York, 557,731; Virginia, 514,280; Massachusetts, 416,393; North Carolina, 337,764; Connecticut, 244,721; Maryland, 216,326; South Carolina, 196,255; New Jersey, 194,325; New Hampshire, 182,998; Kentucky, 179,873; Vermont, 153,908; Maine, 150,901: Georgia, 102,261; Tennessee, 91,709; Rhode Island, 65,438; Delaware, 49,852; Ohio, 45,028; Indiana, 5,343; Mississippi, 5,179.

John Clayton

CHAPTER VI.

Controversy with Lord Baltimore Opened—Charters Compared—Penn Visits Lord Baltimore—Baltimore Makes Excuses—Ambiguities in Both Charters—Baltimore Offers Disputed Lands for Sale and Drives Out Pennsylvania Owners—Summons to Quit—Response—Penn Offers to Purchase—Penn Carries the Controversy Before the Royal Commission—Letter to His Friends on Quitting His Colony—Found Officers Sour and Stern—New King Friendly, but Ministry Hostile to Dissenters—Claims Compromised—Elaborate Treaty of 1760—Line Described—Local Surveyors Appointed—Mason and Dixon Appointed—Native Surveyors' Work Found Correct—Sample of Work—Delaware Line Established—Extracts from Notes—"Visto" Cleared—Horizontal Measurement—Stone Pillars Set—Indians View Astronomical Observations with Awe—War Path in Greene County Survey Stops—Tedious Labors of Surveyors—Boundary Stones Cut in England—Cost of Survey for Pennsylvania, $171,000—End Not Yet.

THOUGH feeling a just pride in the prosperity and wonderful growth of his colony, Penn was not free from tribulations. Language could not be made more explicit than that employed to fix the boundaries of his province. That there might be no mistaking the place which it occupied upon the continent the stars were called to stand as sentinels, and science was invoked to fix the places which they marked. But the ink was scarcely dry upon the parchment which recorded the gift before the whisperings of counter claims were heard. Markham, who was sent forward by Penn as Lieutenant-Governor to take possession of the land and commence surveys upon it, had hardly shaken the salt spray from his locks before he was visited at Chester by Lord Baltimore from Maryland, who presented his claim to all that country.

On the 20th of June, 1632, just fifty years before Penn received his patent, the King had granted to Lord Baltimore a charter for Maryland, named for Henrietta Maria, daughter of Henry IV. and wife of Charles I., bounded by the ocean, the 40° of north latitude, the meridian of the western fountain of the Potomac, the river Potomac from its source to its mouth, and a line drawn east from Watkins Point to the Atlantic, the place of beginning This territory was given to him, his heirs and assigns, on the payment of a yearly rent of two Indian arrows. Lord Baltimore exhibited his claim to Governor Markham, and to satisfy the latter that his claim was valid, he made an observation of the heavens, which showed that the latitude of Chester was twelve miles south, of the 41° north to which he claimed. Had this claim been allowed, the whole of Delaware bay and river, the three lower counties, now the State of Delaware, the city of Philadelphia, York, Chambersburg, Gettysburg, indeed the whole tier of southern counties would have been cut off from Pennsylvania. As it will be seen the allowance of this claim would have swallowed all the settlements which had been made for three quarters of a century, and all the wonderful emigration and growth which had now set in, including the great city which Penn had founded with so much satisfaction, and cherished with his pains and his prayers, as well as the fairest section of his territory.

Markham, on his part, exhibited the Pennsylvania charter, which explicitly provides that the southern boundary shall be the " beginning of the 40th degree of northern latitude." But this would have included Baltimore, and even as far south as the city of Washington, embracing all the growth of the Maryland colony for half a century, and would have only left for Maryland a modicum of land west of the Potomac and south of the 40° north along either shore of the lower Chesepeake, about equal to the present State of Delaware This Lord Baltimore regarded an unendurable hardship, and as his charter ante dated that of Penn by fifty years, he held that the charter of the latter was invalidated, and that his own claim could be maintained

In this condition matters rested until the coming of Penn. As we have already seen the new proprietary made it his business to visit Lord Baltimore very soon after his arrival upon the Delaware, and for two days the claims of the two governors were talked over and canvassed. But as the weather became cold so as to preclude the possibility of taking observations to fix accurately the latitude and longitude of the place, it was agreed to postpone further consideration of the question for the present. A true picture of these two eminent men in this opening controversy would be one of great historical interest But we can well imagine that while the representative of Pennsylvania preserved throughout this conference a demeanor that was "childlike and bland," there was in the brain, which the broad-brim sheltered, and in the heart which the shad-bellied coat kept warm, an unalterable purpose not to yield the best portion of his heritage.

Early in the spring Penn invited Lord Baltimore to come to the Delaware for the settlement of their differences; but it was late in the season before he arrived. Penn proposed that the hearing be had before them in the nature of a legal investigation with the aid of counsel and in writing. But this was not agreeable to Baltimore, and now he complained of the sultryness of the weather. Before it was too cold, now it was too hot. Accordingly the conference again broke up without anything being accomplished. It was now plainly evident that Baltimore did not intend to come to any agreement with Penn, but would carry his cause before the royal tribunal in London.

Penn now well understood all the conditions of the controversy, and that there were grave difficulties to be encountered. In the first place his own charter was explicit and would give him, if allowed, three full degrees of latitude and five of longitude. On the other hand the charter of Baltimore made his northern boundary the fortieth degree, but whether the beginning or the ending was not stated. If the beginning, then Maryland would be crowded down nearly to the city of Washington, and Pennsylvania would embrace the city of Baltimore and the greater portion of what is now Maryland and part of Virginia. On the other hand, if the ending of the fortieth degree, then Philadelphia and all the southern tier of counties would have to be given up. By the usual interpretation of language the charter of Baltimore would only give him to the beginning of the fortieth degree. But he had boldly assumed the other interpretation, and had made nearly all his settlements above that line. Again it was provided in the charter of Lord Baltimore that the boundaries prescribed should not include any territory already settled. But it was well known that the settlements along the right bank of the Delaware, from the first visit of Hudson in 1609, long before the charter of Baltimore was given, had been made on the territory now claimed by him. On the other hand there were difficulties in construing one portion of the charter of Penn, doubtless caused by the ignorance of the royal secretaries, who drew it, of the geography of the country, there having been no accurate maps showing latitude made at this time. Consequently when they commenced to describe the southern boundary of Pennsylvania they said, "and on the south by a circle drawn at twelve miles distance from New Castle, Northwards and Westwards unto the beginning of the fortieth degree of Northern Latitude; and then by a straight line westwards to the limitt of Longitude above mentioned," that is to the Panhandle line, as now ascertained. But this circle which is here described at twelve miles distant from New Castle northwards and westwards, to reach the beginning of the fortieth, would not only have to be extended northward and westward, but southward, and the radius of twelve miles southward would by no means reach the beginning of the fortieth degree, and hence would have to be extended on an arbitrary line still further southward, not provided for in the charter. The royal secretaries seemed to have labored under the impression that New Castle town was about on the beginning of the fortieth parallel, whereas it was nearly two-thirds of a degree to the north of that line.

It must be confessed that there were many grave difficulties in the way of a satisfactory adjustment of these counter claims, and it is reported that Lord Baltimore, on his first visit to Markham, after having found by observation the true latitude of New Castle, and heard the provisions of Penn's charter read, dolefully but very pertinently asked: "If this be allowed, where then is my province?" Baltimore, from the very moment that he discovered what the claims of Penn were, had evidently resolved not to make any effort to come to an agreement with Penn, which is abundantly shown by his frivolous excuses for not proceeding to business in their several interviews; but had determined to pursue a bold policy in pushing the sale of lands on the disputed tract, constantly assuming that his interpretation was the true one, and even opening an aggressive policy, trusting to the maintenance of his claims before the officers of the crown in England.

Accordingly, Baltimore issued proposals for the sale of lands in the lower counties, now the State of Delaware, territory which Penn had secured by deed from the Duke of York, after receiving his charter from the King, offering cheaper rates than Penn had done. Penn had also learned that Lord Baltimore had sent a surveyor to take an observation and find the latitude of New Castle, had prepared an *ex parte* statement of his case and was actually, by his agents, pressing the cause to a decision before the Lords of the Committee of Plantations in England, without giving any notice to Penn. Believing in the strong point of possession, Baltimore was determined to pursue a vigorous policy. He accordingly drew up a summons to quit, and sent a messenger, Colonel Talbot, to Philadelphia to "demand of William Penn all that part of the land on the west side of the said river that lyeth to the southward of the fortieth degree of north latitude" Penn was absent at the time, and the summons was delivered to the acting Governor, Nicholas Moore. But upon his return the Proprietary made answer in strong but earnest terms, showing the grounds of his own claim and repelling any counter claim. The conduct of Baltimore alarmed him, for he saw plainly that if settlers from Maryland entered his province under claim of protection from its Governor, it would very soon lead to actual conflict for possession. What he feared came to pass sooner than he had anticipated; for in the spring of 1684, in time to put in their crops, a company from Maryland came in force into the lower counties, drove off the peaceable Pennsylvania settlers, and took possession of their farms. Taking the advice of his council, Penn sent a copy of his reply to the demand that Talbot had brought, which he ordered to be read to the intruders, and ordered William Welch, sheriff of the county, to reinstate the lawful owners. He then issued his proclamation reiterating and defending his claims, and warning all intruders to desist in future from such unlawful acts.

As has been previously observed, if Penn should tamely submit to the claim of Baltimore, his entire colony would have been swallowed up, and all his labor would have been lost. This result Baltimore seemed determined to effect. To the peaceful, quiet and loving disposition of Penn this contention was exceedingly distasteful. As for quantity of land, he freely declared that he would have had enough if he had retained only the two degrees which would have remained after allowing Baltimore all that he claimed. But he was unwilling to give up the rapidly growing city and colonies which he had founded, and more than all to yield possession of Delaware Bay and river, his only means of communication with the ocean. He foresaw that if the two shores of this noble stream were in the possession of hostile States, how easy it would be to make harrassing regulations governing its navigation. But Penn was a man of just and benevolent instincts, and he was willing to make reasonable concessions and compromises to secure peace and satisfy his neighbor in Maryland. Accordingly, at one of their interviews Penn asked Baltimore what he would ask per square mile for the territory south of the Delaware and reaching to the ocean, though he already had the deed for this same land from the Duke of York, secured by patent from the King, and Baltimore's own patent expressly provided that he could not claim territory already settled. But this generous offer to repurchase what he already owned, was rejected by the proprietor of Maryland.

Penn now saw but too plainly that there was no hope of coming to a peaceful and equitable composition of their differences in this country, and that if he would secure a decision in his interest he had no time to lose in repairing to London, and personally defending his rights before the royal commission. There is no question but that he came to this decision with unfeigned regret. His colony was prosperous, the settlers were happy and contented in their new homes, the country itself was all that he could wish and he no doubt fondly hoped to live and die in the midst of his people. But the demand for his return to England was imperative, and he prepared to obey it. He accordingly empowered the Provincial Council, of which Thomas Lloyd was president, to act in his stead, and on the 6th of June, 1684, sailed for England. From on board the vessel, before leaving the Delaware, he sent back an address to the council, in which he unbosoms himself freely· "Dear Friends:—My love and my life is to you and with you; and no water can quench it, nor distance wear it out, nor bring it to an end   I have been with you, cared over you, and served you with unfeigned love; and you are beloved of me and near to me beyond utterance.   *   *   *   Oh, that you would eye Him in all, through all, and above all the works of your hands; for to a blessed end are you brought hither.   *   *   * You are now come to a quiet land; provoke not the Lord to trouble it, and now that liberty and authority are with you, and in your hands, let the government be upon his shoulders, in all your spirits; that you may rule for Him, under whom the princes of this world will one day esteem it their honor to govern and serve in their places.   *   *   *   And thou Philadelphia, the virgin settlement of this province, named before thou wert born, what love, what service and travail has there been to bring thee forth, and preserve thee from such as would abuse and defile thee!"

Upon his arrival in England, on the 6th of October, he took an early opportunity to pay his respects to the King, and the Duke of York, "who received me," he says, "very graciously, as did the ministers very civilly. Yet I found things in general with another face than I left them—sour and stern, and resolved to hold the reins of power with a stiffer hand than before" In a letter to Lloyd, of the 16th of March, 1685, he says: "The King (Charles I.) is dead, and the Duke succeeds peaceably. He was well on the First-day night, being the first of February so called. About eight next morning, as he sat down to shave, his head twitched both ways or sides, and he gave a shriek and fell as dead, and so remained some hours. They opportunely blooded and cupped him, and plied his head with red hot frying-pans He returned and continued till sixth day noon, but mostly in great tortures He seemed very penitent, asking pardon of all, even the poorest subject he had wronged.   *   *   *   He was an able man for a divided and troubled kingdom. The present King was proclaimed about three o'clock that day "

The new king being a personal friend of Penn, he had hopes of favor at court, and did secure many indulgences for his oppressed Friends in the kingdom, but the ministry was bitterly hostile to dissenters, and he found his controversy with Lord ·Baltimore very difficult of management. Penn now pressed his controversy with Lord Baltimore to a final settlement, and in November, 1685, a decision was made in the English court, compromising the claims of the two Governors, and providing that the portion of territory between the Delaware and Chesapeake bays should be divided by a line through the centre, and that the portion bordering upon the Delaware should belong to Penn, and that upon the Chesapeake to Lord Baltimore.

This settled the dispute for the time; but upon attempting to measure and run the dividing line, the language of the act was so indefinite that the attempt was abandoned, and the old controversy was again renewed Not wishing to press his suit at once, while the memory of the decision already made was green, Lord Baltimore suffered the controversy to rest, and each party laid claim to the territory adjudged to him in theory by the royal decree, but without any division line.

On the 28th of April, 1707, the goverment of Maryland presented to the Queen an address asking that an order should be made requiring the authorities of the two colonies, Maryland and Pennsylvania, " to run the division lines and ascertain the boundaries between them, for the ease of the inhabitants, who have been much distressed by their uncertainty. It would appear that the controversy,—after William Penn in 1685 had secured the lands upon the right bank of the Delaware,—was left to work out its own cure, as a definite agreement was entered into in the life time of the founder that the authorities in neither colony should disturb the settlers in the other, and as the colonies were substantially located originally with a dividing line where the line was subsequently run, the portion of territory on this disputed belt which each was to give up settled itself, and only needed to be specifically defined, surveyed and marked. Repeated conferences were held, and lines run, but nothing satisfactory was accomplished until the 4th of July 1760, when Frederick, Lord Baron of Baltimore, and Thomas, and Richard Penn, sons of the founder, entered into an elaborate and formal treaty by which the limits of the two provinces were provided. The boundary lines were made mathematically exact, so that there could by no possibility be further controversy, provided surveyors were found who had the skill and the instruments necessary for determining them.

The line was to commence at Cape Henlopen on the Atlantic coast. This cape as originally located was placed on the point opposite Cape May at the entrance of Delaware Bay, and Cape Henrietta was fifteen miles down the coast. By an error in the map used by the parties, the names of these two capes had been interchanged, and Henlopen was placed fifteen miles down the coast. At this mistaken point, therefore, the division commenced. When this was discovered, a complaint was made before Lord Hardwick; but in a formal decree, promulgated in 1750, it was declared " that Cape Henlopen ought to be deemed and taken to be situated at the .place where the same is laid down and described in the maps or plans annexed to the said articles to be situated."

This point of beginning having been settled the dividing lines were to be substantially as follows: Commencing at Henlopen on the Atlantic, a due westerly line was to be run to the shores of the

Chesapeake Bay, found to be 69 miles 298 perches. At the middle of
this line a line was to be run in a direction northwesterly till it should
form a tangent to the circumference of a circle drawn with a radius
of twelve miles from the spire of the Court House in New Castle.
From this tangent point a line was to be run due north until it should
reach a meridian line 15 miles south of the most southern extremity
of Philadelphia, and the point thus reached, should be the northeast
corner of Maryland. If the due north line from the tangent point
should cut off a segment of a circle from the twelve mile circuit,
then the slice thus cut off should be adjudged a part of New Castle
County, and consequently should belong to Pennsylvania. The
corner-stone at the extremity of the due north line from the tangent
point was to be the beginning of the now famous Mason and Dixon's
line, and was to extend due west to the western limit of Maryland.

This settled the long dispute so far as it could be on paper, but
to execute its provisions in practice was more difficult. The primeval
forest covered the greater part of the line, stubborn mountains stood
in the way, and instruments were imperfect and liable to variation.
Commissioners were appointed to survey, and establish the lines in
1739, but a controversy having arisen, whether the measurement
should be horizontal or superficial, the commission broke up and nothing more was done till 1760, when local surveyors were appointed,
John Lukens and Archibald McLean on the part of Pennsylvania,
Thomas Garnett and Jonathan Hall for Maryland, who commenced
to lay off the lines as provided in the indenture of agreement entered
into by the proprietaries. Their first care was to clear away the
vistas or narrow openings eight yards wide through the forest.
Having ascertained the middle point of the Henlopen line they ran
an experimental line north until opposite New Castle, when they
measured the radius of twelve miles and fixed the tangent point.
There were so many perplexing conditions, that it required much
time to perfect their calculations and plant their bounds After these
surveyors had been three years at their work, the proprietaries in
England, thinking the reason of their long protracted labors
indicative of a lack of scientific knowledge on their part, or lack of
suitable instruments, employed, on the 4th of August, 1763, two
surveyors and mathematicians to go to America and conduct the
work. They brought with them the best instruments procurable at
that time—an excellent sector " six feet radius which magnified
twenty-five times, the property of Hon. Mr. Penn, the first which
ever had the plumb line passing over and bisecting a point at the
centre of the instrument " They obtained from the Royal Society a
brass standard measure, and standard chains. These surveyors were
none other than Charles Mason and Jeremiah Dixon, names forever
blazoned upon the political history of the United States, magnates at

Charles W. Tilton.

home, but no more skilled nor more accurate in their work, over mountains and valleys, through the tangled and interminable forests of the American continent, than our own fellow-citizens, McLean and Lukens, and Garnett and Hall, who had preceded them.

The daily field notes of Mason and Dixon commence November 15th, 1763; and the first entry is, "Arrived at Philadelphia;" 16th, "Attended meeting of the commissioners appointed to settle the bounds of Pennsylvania;" 22d to 28th, "Landed and set up instruments, and found they had received no damage;" December 5th, "Directed a carpenter to build an observatory near the point settled by the commissioners to be the south point of the city of Philadelphia," which was to be one of the initial points of the line. When the observatory was finished the instruments were mounted and observations taken to fix the latitude of the place. That the reader may observe the painstaking accuracy with which these surveyors conducted their work, there is subjoined a table of one night's observations:

1763	Stars Magnitude.		Right Ascensions.	Nearest point on ye Sector.	Revolutions and seconds on Micrometer.		Difference.	Apparent zenith distance.	Stars No. or So.
			h ' o	'	r ''	'	''	o ' ''	
Dec. 21.	α α	Cygni	20 34 4	30+	{8 8}	36 20	0 16.0	4 30 16.0	N. faint.
	v	Androm	1	15−	{7 8}	48+ 7	0 10.0	1 14 49.3	N.
	B	Persei	0	5+	{8 8}	33½ 7	0 26.3	0 5 26.3	N.
	S	Do.	7	5−	{6 7}	45½ 38	0 14.5	7 4 15.5	N.
		Capella	5	50	{7 10}	37½ 43	3 5.5	5 47 18.5	N.
	B	Aurige	4	55+	{11 8}	14½ 41½	2 25.2	4 57 9.2	N.
		Castor	7 19 7	35−	{8 6}	9— 14½	1 46.2	7 33 21.8	N.

Cha: Mason.
Jere: Dixon.

Nearly one whole year was spent in ascertaining the middle point of the Henlopen line across the peninsula, and running the line northward to find the tangent point on the twelve mile periphery from the steeple of New Castle Court House, and on the 13th of November, 1764, they make the following entry in their notes,

" From data in minute of ye 27th of August, we computed how far the true tangent line would be distant from the Post (shown us to be the tangent point), and found it would not pass one inch to the westward or eastward. On measuring the angle of our last line, with the direction from New Castle, it was so near a right angle that on a mean from our lines, the above mentioned post is the true tangent point." Thus it was shown that with all the difficulties our native surveyors had to contend with, the English surveyors found, after a year's careful labor, that the work of their predecessors was correct.

On the 18th of June, 1765, Mason and Dixon make this entry in their notes, " We set seven stones, viz: one at the tangent point, four in the periphery of the circle-round New Castle, one in the north line from tangent point, and one at the intersection of the north line (from ye Tangent Point) and the Parallel 15 Miles South of the Southermost Point of the City of Philadelphia, The Gent: Commissioners of both provinces present." On the 27th of October, 1765, the following entry was made, " Capt: Shelby again went with us to the summit of the mountain (when the air was very clear), and shewed us the Northernmost bend of the River Potowmack at the Conoloways; from which we judge the line will pass about two miles to the North of the said River. From hence we could see the Alleghany Mountains for many miles, and judge it by its appearance to be about 50 miles distance in the direction of the Line." On the 26th of September, 1766, the following important entry was made, " From any eminence in the Line, where 15 or 20 Miles of the Visto can be seen (of which there are many) the said line, or Visto, very apparently shews itself to form a parallel of Northern Latitude. The line in measured horizontal: the Hills and the Mountains with a $16\frac{1}{2}$ Feet Level. And beside the Mile Posts we have set Posts in the true Line (marked W on the west side) all along the Line opposite the Stationary Points, where the Sector and Transit Instruments stood. The said Posts stand in the middle of the Visto, which in general is about 8 yards wide. The number of Posts in the West Line is 303."

It will be understood that this " visto" or vista properly, was a straight east and west belt of eight yards in width, cleared by the axmen through the dense forest for the purpose of the survey. The view from these eminences to which they refer, must have been grand, the forest for the most part resting undisturbed, as it had been for ages, the two sides of the clearing seeming in the distance to approach each other and join, the silver current of the river showing here and there, and the noisy brook tumbling down the mountain side. In the spring-time, the surveyors were often awakened in the morning by the gobbling of the wild turkeys, and the rattle of their chain chimed melodiously with the distant drumming of the partridge.

On the 14th to 18th of July, 1767, they make the following entries: "At 168 miles, 78 chains is the top of the great dividing Ridge of the Alleghany Mountains. At 169 m 60 ch., crossed a small branch of the Little Yochio Geni. The head of Savage River south, distant about a mile This day (16th) we were joined by 14 Indians deputied by the chiefs of the Six Nations to go with us on the line. With them came Mr. Hugh Crawford, Interpreter. At 171 m. 5 ch., crossed a branch of ye Little Yochio Ceni, 171 m 63 ch., crossed do. the last time (in the whole 6 or 7 times)." August 17, " At this station, Mr. John Green, one of the Chiefs of the Mohock Nation, and his Nephew, left us, in order to return to their own country." August 31, " At 204 m. 11 ch., crossed a small run running southward. Here, by information, the Big Meadows are north, distant about 5 miles." " At 217 m. 13 ch. is the foot of the Laurel Hill, on the west side." "At 219 m. 22 ch. 25 lks. crossed the Cheat river obliquely." "At 222 m. 24 ch 12 lks. is the top of a very high Bank, at the foot of which is the River Manaungahela," September 27th, are the following notes: " About a mile and a half north of where the Sector stands, the Rivers Cheat and Manaungahela join. The mouth of Redstone creek, by information, bears due north from this station, distant 25 miles. Fort Pit is supposed to be due north distant about 50 miles." September 30, " At 222 m. 34 chains, 50 Links, the east bank of ye River Manaungahela at 222 m. 40 ch. 25 links the west bank, breadth about 5 chaines."

In all the work of the surveyors, the Indians had preserved an attitude of awe and superstitious dread. They could not understand what all this peering into the heavens, and always in the dead of the night (as all astronomical observations must be made at that time of night when the particular star desired came into view) portended. They looked with special distrust on those curious little tubes covered with glass, through which the surveyors stood patiently watching somebody in the far off heavens. The Six Nations, who were supreme in these parts, had given permission by treaty to run this line; but when they heard of the methods adopted, we may well imagine their speculations in the native council chambers, in the deep shadows of the wood, touching the purpose of these nightly vigils. They entertained a suspicion that the surveyors were holding communication with spirits in the skies, who were pointing out the track of their line. So much had their fears become wrought upon, that when Mason and Dixon had reached the summit of the Little Alleghany, the Six Nations gave notice upon the departure of their agents, that the survey must cease at that point. But, by the adroit representations of Sir William Johnson, the Six Nations were induced to allow the survey to proceed. No further interruption was experienced until they reached the bottom of a deep, dark valley on the border of a stream, marked Dunkard Creek, on their map, where they came upon an ancient Indian war-path winding through the dense forest; and here the representatives of the Six Nations declared that this was the limit of the ground which their commission covered, and refused to proceed further. In the language of the field notes, "This day the Chief of the Indians which joined us on the 16th of July, informed us that the above mentioned War Path was the extent of his commission from the Chiefs of the Six Nations, that he should go with us to the line, and that he would not proceed one step further."

For some days previous, the Indians had been giving intimations of trouble, and when arrived at the banks of the Manaungahela, "twenty-six of our Men left us," say the notes. "They would not pass the River for fear of the Shawnees and Delaware Indians. But we prevailed upon 15 ax men to proceed with us; and with them we continued the Line Westward" There would be no safety to the surveyors without the Indian escort, as they would be at the mercy of wandering bands of savages, who knew not the meaning of the word compassion or mercy; but who could dash the brains out of a helpless infant, and tear the scalp from the head of a trembling and defenceless female with as keen a relish as they ever sat down to a breakfast of hot turtle soup Therefore, there was no alternative; and although they were now within 36 miles of the end of the line, and in a few days more would have reached the limit, they were forced to desist: and here, on the margin of Dunkard Creek, on the line of this famous war-path, in Greene County, Mason and Dixon set up their last monumental stone, 233 m, 13 ch 68 links from the initial point of this now famous line which bears their name, and ended the survey. Returning to Philadelphia they made their final report to the commissioners, and received an honorable discharge on the 26th of December, 1767

The work of those surveyors was tedious and toilsome, being conducted in the primeval forest through which a continuous vista, twenty-five feet wide, had to be cleared as they went, and in which they were obliged to camp out in all weathers of a changeable climate. To keep on a due east and west line they were exclusively guided by the stars, and their rest at night must constantly be broken by these necessary vigils

By the terms of the agreement of 1732, and the order of the Lord High Chancellor Hardwick, every fifth mile of this line was to be marked by a stone monument engraved with the arms of the Proprietaries, and the intermediate miles by smaller stones marked by a P on the side facing Pennsylvania, and an M on the side facing

Maryland. These stones were some twelve inches square, and four feet long, and were cut and engraved in England, and sent over ready for setting. The fixing the exact location of these stones gave no little vexation to the surveyors. This formal marking, as directed, was observed till the line reached Sidelong Hill; but here, all wheel transportation ceasing for lack of roads, the further marking was by the "visto" "eight or nine yards wide," "and marks were set up on the tops of all the High Ridges and Mountains." Their entry on the 19th of November, 1767, was "Snow twelve or fourteen inches deep; made a pile of stones on the top of Savage Mountain, or the great dividing ridge of the Alleghany Mountains. West of this mountain to ye end of ye line, the Mile Posts are five feet in length, twelve inches square and set two feet in the ground, and round them are heaped Earth and Stone eight feet Diameter at bottom and two and one half feet high." At the end of their line in Greene County, at Dunkard Creek, they say, "we set up a Post marked W on the West side, and heaped round it earth, etc, three yards and a half in Diameter at Bottom, and five feet High—the heap nearly conical," making an extra large mound here, as if to emphasize it, and make a period to their work, until it should be resumed again, but which proved to be the final termination of their labors. Mason and Dixon were paid twenty one shillings per day for their labor, the entire expense to Pennsylvania being £34,200, or $171,000.

Nothing further was done towards completing the survey of this line until 1779, in the very midst of the Revolutionary war. So far as Maryland was concerned the controversy was at an end, as its western boundary terminates with the meridian marking the source of the Potomac River. But on the above mentioned date, Patrick Henry, then Governor of Virginia, addressed a letter to the Governor of Pennsylvania, and enclosed a resolution of the House of Delegates of that State respecting commissioners to be appointed for fixing the boundary between Virginia and Pennsylvania. But, as this opens an entirely new subject of controversy, involving the interpretation of the Virginia Charter, and the rights of the Ohio Land Company, the consideration of this topic will be reserved to the proper place in the narrative.

CHAPTER VII.

FRENCH CLAIM THE ENTIRE VALLEY OF THE MISSISSIPPI—THE PEACE
OF RYSWICK—THE PEACE OF UTRECHT—THE FIVE NATIONS SUB-
JECT TO THE ENGLISH—FRANCE STILL CONFIRMED IN POSSESSION
OF THE MISSISSIPPI VALLEY—CLAIM OF THE ENGLISH—THE PEACE
OF AIX-LA-CHAPELLE—UNPRINCIPLED TRADERS—OHIO COM-
PANY FORMED—THE BOY WASHINGTON—OHIO COMPANY TO,
LOCATE 200,000 ACRES—FRENCH JEALOUS—SEND CELERON TO
BURY PLATES—PASS OVER CHATAUNQUA LAKE—THE ROUTE BY
PRESQUE ISLE AND LE BOEUF SUBSEQUENTLY ADOPTED—INDIANS
ON THE WATCH—PLATE BURIED AT WARREN—INSCRIPTION UPON
PLATE—PLATE DUG UP AND CARRIED TO SIR WILLIAM JOHNSON
—GOVERNOR CLINTON COMMUNICATES CONTENTS TO LORDS OF
TRADE, AND TO GOVERNOR HAMILTON—SPEECH OF INDIAN CHIEF-
TAIN AND INTERPRETION OF INSCRIPTION—REPLY OF CHIEFTAIN
—CELERON PLANTS ANOTHER PLATE AT INDIAN GOD—ANOTHER AT
LOGSTOWN—EXPELS ENGLISH TRADERS—SENDS LETTER TO GOV-
ERNOR HAMILTON WARNING HIM—OTHER PLATES AT MOUTH OF
MUSKINGUM, GREAT KANAWHA, AND GREAT MIAMI—ASCENDS THE
MIAMI AND DOWN THE MAUMEE—PLATES FOUND—PROPRIETARY
DISTURBED—NOTES OF CROGHAN—BUILDING A FORT CONTEM-
PLATED.

A S has been previously observed, it was held as a principle of the
law of nations that the discovery of and occupancy of the mouth
of a river, entitles the discoverer to all the land drained by that
river and its tributaries, even to their remotest sources By reason
of the discoveries of Marquette and La Salle, and the formal possession taken of the Mississippi River by them under the French flag,
France laid claim to all the territory drained by this river.   Had
this claim been allowed all that portion of New York, Pennsylvania
and Virginia lying west of the water-shed formed by the Alleghany
Mountains, would have been given up to the French, and Greene
County would have been settled by a French speaking people, the
subjects of the French King.
In the early settlement of the North American continent by
Europeans, the French showed by far the greater spirit and enter-
prise, and in numbers were superior.   In 1688, France commenced

a wasting war against England and her allies, which was finally concluded by the treaty of Ryswick, by which France was confirmed in the possession of Hudson Bay, Canada and the valley of the Mississippi; but it was provided that neither party should interfere with the Indian allies of the other. Both parties laid claim to the Six Nations as allies. Jesuit priests were active in endeavoring to win these Indians over to the French, which induced the New York legislature, in 1700, to pass an act "to hang every popish priest that should come voluntarily into the province." In 1698, through the offices of Count Ponchartrain, D'Iberville was appointed governor, and his brother, De Bienville, intendant of Louisiana, and were sent with a colony direct to the mouth of the Mississippi, to make a settlement there.

Peace between France and England was of short duration, and in 1701 war broke out between them, which was waged along the border in America with sanguinary ferocity and cruelty. It was concluded by the peace of Utrecht, in 1713, by which England obtained control of the fisheries, Hudson Bay and its borders, Newfoundland and Nova Scotia, or Acadia, and it was expressly stipulated that "France should not molest the Five Nations, subject to the dominion of Great Britain, whose possessions embraced the whole of New York and Pennsylvania, though the French did not allow them that much territory. But the valley of the Mississippi still remained to the French, the English embassadors not being alive to the importance of this magnificent stretch of country. William Penn had advised that the St. Lawrence should be made the boundary line to the north and that the English claim should include the great valley of the continent It "will make a glorious country" said Penn The failure to fix definitely the bounds, caused another half century of bitter contention and bloody strife, in which the ignorant savages were used as agents by either party. In 1748, a four years' war was concluded between the old enemies, French and English, by the peace of Aix La-Chapelle, by which England was confirmed in her possessions in North America. But the boundaries were still indefinite.

France claimed the Mississippi valley in its entirety; that is, all the land drained by the tributaries of the great river. The British crown claimed the territory on the upper Ohio on the ground of a treaty executed at Lancaster, Pennsylvania, in 1744, at which the share paid by Virginia was £220 in goods, and that paid by Maryland £200 in gold. On this purchase the claim of the Iroquois as allies, and the claim of the settlements on the Atlantic coast of territory westward from ocean to ocean, rested the right of the English to this imperial valley. The fact is, however, that the party which could show most strength in men and money was destined to hold it. By the middle of the eighteenth century the English, in respect to force, had greatly the advantage As early as 1688 a census of French North America showed a population of 11,249, while the English population at this time was estimated at a quarter of a million. During the next half century both nationalities increased rapidly, but the English much the faster.

Previous to the treaty of Chapelle adventurous traders from Pennsylvania had explored the passes of the Alleghany Mountains, and pushed on to the borders of the Monongahela and the Ohio. By the good offices of the colonial governors of New York and Pennsylvania, the Six Nations had been kept in firm alliance with the English The French had sought to win them over to their power, and had distributed many showy presents. Thinking that the simple natives would never know the difference, the French had made a large gift of bright looking hatchets, but which, instead of being made of fine steel, were only soft iron The Indians soon discovered the difference, and were more incensed than ever against the French Lest the latter, who were active and vigilant, might gain an advantage on the Ohio, Conrad Weiser was sent out to Logstown, a few miles below Pittsburg on the Ohio, in 1748, with valuable and useful presents to win the favor of the natives It was seen, however, that the valuable trade with the Indians at this time was in the hands "of unprincipled men, half civilized, half savage, who, through the Iroquois, had from the earliest period penetrated to the lakes of Canada, and competed everywhere with the French for skins and furs " More with the purpose of controlling and legitimizing this trade than of effecting permanent settlements, it was proposed in the Virginia colony to form a great company which should hold lands on the Ohio, build forts for trading posts, import English goods, and establish regular traffic with the Indians. Accordingly, Thomas Lee, president of the council of Virginia, and twelve other Virginians, among whom was John Hanbury, a wealthy London merchant, formed in 1749 what was known as the "Ohio Company," and applied to the English government for a grant of land for this purpose. The request was favorably received, and the Legislature of Virginia was authorized to grant to the petitioners a half million acres of land within the bounds of that colony, "west of the Alleghanies, between the Monongahela and Kanawha rivers; though part of the land might be taken up north of the Ohio should it be deemed expedient."

It was at about this period, in March, 1748, that a boy of sixteen years set out from the abodes of civilization with his theodolite to survey wild lands in the mountains and valleys of the Virginia colony. In a letter to one of his young friends he says: "I have not slept above three or four nights in a bed, but after walking a good

Thomas Jerns

deal all day I have lain down before the fire upon a little straw or fodder, or a bear skin, whichever was to be had, with man, wife and children, like dogs and cats; and happy is he who gets the berth nearest the fire." This youth, thus early inured to hardship and toil, was none other than George Washington, destined to great labors for his country, and a life of patriotism and unbending devotion scarcely matched in the annals of mankind.

A condition of the grant of the " Ohio Company" was that two hundred thousand acres should be located at once. This was to be held for ten years free of rent, provided the company would put there one hundred families within seven years, and build a fort sufficient to protect the settlement. This the company prepared to do, and sent a ship to London for a cargo of goods suited to the Indian trade. Upon the death of Thomas Lee, the president of the Ohio Company, which soon took place, Lawrence Washington, a brother of George, was given the " chief management" of the company, a man of enlightened views and generous spirit.

But the organization of this company, and the preparations to take possession of the Ohio country, did not escape the vigilant eye of the French, and if they would hold the territory claimed by them they must move at once, or the enterprising English would be there, and would have such a foothold as would render it impossible to rout them.

Accordingly, early in 1749, the Marquis de la Galisonniere, Governor General of Canada, dispatched Céleron de Bienville with a party of some two hundred French and fifty Indians to take formal possession of the Ohio country, the Alleghany being designated by the French by that name. Father Bonnecamps acted as chaplain, mathematician and historian of the party. The expedition started on the 15th of June, 1749, from La Chine on the St. Lawrence. Passing up the river through the net work of islands and along the shore of Ontario to Niagara Falls, they commenced the labor of debarking and transporting their entire outfit around the cataract. In this work they were engaged for nearly a week; but by the 13th of July they were again afloat on the waters of Lake Erie. At a point nearest to Chautauqua Lake they landed and commenced transporting their boats and stores overland a distance of eight miles, and over a water-shed more than eight hundred feet above the waters of Lake Erie. The party was accompanied by the two sons of Joncaire (Jean Coeur) who had lived with the Indians in this locality, and knew every path and water course. To them Céleron looked for guidance in this novel voyage over land. When surveyors had marked the track, pioneers cut and cleared a road, over which the whole was transported to the shores of Chautauqua, where they again embarked, and passing down the Conewango Creek, the outlet of the lake, made their way to its confluence with the Allegheny River, near the town of Warren. Here they paused to commence the work of possessing the country.

It may be proper to observe in this connection that this experience of reaching the Chautauqua Lake with all their *impedimenta* over the high ridge was so toilsome that in future expeditions they abandoned this route and went by the way of Presque Isle (Erie) and Waterford, where they struck French Creek or the Venango River, down which they passed to the Allegheny River at Franklin. In the deposition of one Stephen Coffin before Colonel Johnson, of New York, he says: "From Niagara fort we set off by water, being April, and arrived at Chadakoin (Chautauqua) on Lake Erie, where they were ordered to fell timber and prepare it for building a fort there according to the Governor's instructions; but M. Morang, coming up with five hundred men and twenty Indians, put a stop to erecting a fort at that place, by reason of his not liking the situation, and the river of Chadakoins being too shallow to carry any craft with provisions to Belle Riviere The deponent says there arose a warm debate between Messieurs Babeer and Morang thereon, the first insisting on building the fort there agreeable to his instructions, otherwise on Morang's giving him an instrument in writing to satisfy the Governor in that point, which Morang did, and then Monsieur Mercie, who was both commissary and engineer, to go along said lake and look for a good situation, which he found in three days. They were then all ordered thither, they fell to work and built a square fort of chestnut logs, and called it Fort Le Presque Isle * * * As soon as the fort was finished they marched southward. cutting a wagon road through a fine level country twenty-one miles [15] to the river *aux Boeufs* [Waterford]" Thus, though the distance to Chautauqua Lake was not so great as to Waterford, the road to the latter was "through a fine level country" and not over a rugged ridge as at the former.

Céleron and his party had not left the shores of Chautauqua, where he had encamped, probably in the vicinity of Lakewood, before he discovered that his movements were being watched by the natives. Parties were sent out to intercept them and cultivate their friendship, but were unsuccessful. Having reached the Allegheny River at or near Warren, as we have seen, Céleron with religious ceremony took possession of the river and country, and buried a leaden plate, on the south bank of the Allegheny River, opposite a little island at the mouth of the Conewango, in token of French possession Upon this plate was the following inscription in French: "L'an 1749 dv regne de Lovis XV Roy de France novs Céloron commandant don de tachement envoie par monsieur le mis de la Galissonière commandant General de la nouvelle France povr retablir la tranquillte dans quelques villages sauvages de ces cantons avous euterre cette plaque a lentru de l' riviere Chinodahichetha le 18 Aoust pies de la riviere Oyo autrement Belle riviere pour monument du renovvelle-ment de possession que nous avous pris de la ditte riviere Oyo et de toutes celles qui y tombut et de toves les terres des deux cotes jusque aux sources des dittes rivies vinsi que out Jovy ou du Jovir les pre-cedents Roys de France et quils sisont maintenus par les armes et par les trattes specialement par ceux de Risvuick d' Utrecht et d' Aix-La-Chapelle."

In English, "In the year 1749, of the reign of Louis XIV., King of France, We Céleron, commander of a detachment sent by Monsieur the Marquis de la Galissonière, Governor General of New France, to re-establish tranquility in some Indian villages of these cantons, have buried this plate of lead at the confluence of the Ohio with the Chau-tauqua, this 29th day of July, near the river Ohio, otherwise Belle Rivière, as a monument of the renewal of the possession we have taken of the said river Ohio, and of all those which empty into it, and of all the lands on both sides as far as the sources of the said river, as enjoyed, or ought to have been enjoyed by the King of France preceding, and as they have there maintained themselves by arms and by treaties, especially those of Ryswick, Utrecht and Aix-la-Chapelle"

All the men and officers were drawn up in military order when the plate was buried, and Céleron proclaimed in a strong tone, "Vive le Roi!" and declared that possession of the country was now taken in behalf of the French. A plate with the lilies of France inscribed thereon was nailed to a tree near by. All this officious ceremony did not escape the keen eyes of the ever vigilant and superstitious natives, and scarcely were Céleron and his party well out of sight in their course down the Allegheny, before that leaden missive with the mysterious characters engraved thereon was pulled from its place of concealment, and fast runners were on their way to the home of the Iroquois chiefs, who immediately dispatched one of their number to take it to Sir William Johnson, at Albany. Mr. O. H. Marshall, in his admirable historical address on this subject, says: "The first of the leaden plates was brought to the attention of the public by Gov. George Clinton to the Lords of Trade in London, dated New York, December 19, 1750, in which he states that he would send to their Lordships in two or three weeks a plate of lead full of writing which some of the upper nations of Indians stole from Jean Coeur, the French interpreter at Niagara, on his way to the River Ohio, which river, and all the lands thereabouts, the French claim, as will appear by said writing. He further states 'that the lead plates gave the Indians so much uneasiness that they immediately dispatched some of the Cayuga chiefs to him with it, saying that their only reliance was on him, and earnestly begged he would communicate the contents to them, which he had done, much to their satisfaction and the interests of the English.' The Governor concludes by saying that 'the contents of the plate may be of great importance in clearing up the encroachments which the French have made on the British empire in America.' The plate was delivered to Colonel, afterward Sir William Johnson, on the 4th of December, 1750 (49), at his residence on the Mohawk, by a Cayuga sachem "

Governor Clinton also wrote to Governor Hamilton of Pennsylvania, as shown by the minutes of council, as follows· "* * * I send you a copy of an inscription on a leaden plate stolen from Jean Coeur, some months since, in the Senecas' country, as he was going to the river Ohio, which plainly demonstrates the French scheme by the exorbitant claims therein mentioned; also a copy of a Cayuga Sachem's speech to Colo Johnson, with his reply." The Cayuga sachem's speech was as follows: "Brother Corlear and War-ragh-i-ya-ghey! I am sent here by the Five Nations with a piece of writing which the Senecas, our brethren, got by some artifice from Jean Coeur, earnestly beseeching you will let us know what it means, and as we put all our confidence in you, our brother, we hope you will explain it ingeniously to us " (The speaker here delivered the square leaden plate and a wampum belt, and proceeded.) "I am ordered further to acquaint you that Jean Coeur, the French interpreter, when on his journey this last summer to Ohio River, spoke thus to the Five Nations and others in our alliance: 'Children.—Your Father, having, out of a tender regard for you, considered the great difficulties you labor under by carrying your goods, canoes, &c , over the great carrying place of Niagara, has desired me to acquaint you that, in order to ease you all of so much trouble for the future, he is resolved to build a house at the other end of said carrying place, which he will furnish with all necessaries requisite for your use.' * * * He also told us that he was on his way to the Ohio River, where he intended to stay three years; * * * that he was sent thither to build a house there; also at the carrying place between said river Ohio and Lake Erie (Presque Isle and Waterford), where all the western Indians should be supplied with whatever goods they may have occasion for, and not be at the trouble and loss of time of going so far to market as usual (meaning Oswego). After this he desired to know our opinion of the affair, and begged our consent to build in said places. He gave us a large belt of wampum, thereon desiring our answer, which we told him we would take some time to consider of "

Assuring the Indian chieftains of the unalterable friendship of the English towards their people, and the enmity and duplicity of the French, of which many examples were cited, Sir William Johnson said: "Their scheme now laid against you and yours, at a time when they are feeding you up with fine promises of serving you several shapes, is worse than all the rest, as will appear by their own writing on this plate." Here Johnson translated the French writing on the plate, commenting as he proceeded on the force and intent of the several parts, and explaining the purpose of the French in burying the plate. Proceeding he said, "This is an affair of the greatest importance to you, as nothing less than all your lands and best hunting places are aimed at, with a view of secluding you entirely from us and the rest of your brethren, viz: the Philadelphians, the Virginians, who can always supply you with the necessaries of life at a much lower rate than the French ever did or could, and under whose protection you are and ever will be safer, and better served in every respect, than under the French. These and a hundred other substantial reasons I could give you to convince you that the French are your implacable enemies; but, as I told you before, the very instrument you now brought me of their own writing is sufficient of itself to convince the world of their villainous designs; therefore I need not be at the trouble, so shall only desire that you and all the nations in alliance with you seriously consider your own interest and by no means submit to the impending danger which now threatens you, the only way to prevent which is to turn Jean Coeur away immediately from Ohio, and tell him that the French shall neither build there, nor at the carrying place of Niagara, nor have a foot of land more from you. Brethren, what I now say I expect and insist upon it being taken notice of and sent to the Indians of the Ohio, that they may immediately know the vile designs of the French."

Having presented a belt of wampum, by way of emphasis, and to convince the natives of the honesty and fidelity with which he spoke, the sachem replied: "Brother Corlear and War-ragh-i-ya-ghey, I have with great attention and surprise heard you repeat the substance of the devilish writing which I brought you, and also with pleasure noticed your just remarks thereon, which really agree with my own sentiments on it. I return you my most hearty thanks in the name of all the nations for your brotherly love and cordial advice, which I promise you sincerely, by this belt of wampum, shall be communicated immediately and verbatim to the Five Nations by myself, and, moreover, shall see it forwarded from the Senecas' castle with belts from each of our own nations to the Indians at Ohio, to strengthen your desire, as I am thoroughly satisfied you have our interest at heart."

Returning to Céleron and his party, whom we left upon the deep, rapid current of the Allegheny River, where they found rest at night beneath the sombre forest that skirted its bank, and floated by day leisurely upon its current, we see them passing Indian villages and the mouths of Oil Creek and Venango River (Les Bœufs), without making any considerable pause, though the latter point, now Franklin, was then a station of importance. But at the Indian God, some nine or ten miles below the latter point, they paused, and beneath the shadow of an immense boulder, on which had been cut rude figures held in superstitious awe by the natives, on the south bank, opposite a bald mountain, the second of these leaden plates were buried, accompanied with the usual formal ceremonies which was continued at each burial. Resuming their journey they passed Chartiers Town, a Shawneese village, now deserted, and passed the mouth of the Monongahela River without pausing; but at Logstown, some twelve miles below, an Indian town, now a place of importance as the council house of the sachems of surrounding tribes, they made a landing. Here the agents of the English colonies upon the Atlantic were accustomed to meet them and make their formal talks, smoke the pipe of peace, distribute the high piled presents, and ratify solemn treaties which were not to be broken so long as the sun and the moon go round the earth. Here, too, the traders brought their goods and bartered them for valuable skins and furs, and, shame to say it, here these conscienceless traders brought kegs of fire-water, and when the poor Indians were made drunken were cheated and abused Here Céleron buried another of his plates, and discovering a number of the English trading with the Indians his wrath was kindled. He expelled these intruders, as he called them, and made a speech to the assembled Indians of many tribes, telling them that all the country along the Beautiful River belonged to the French, and that they would supply the Indians with all the goods they needed. He forbade them to trade with the English, and said he was now on his way down the river to whip the Wyandots back to their homes. The absolute manner of Céleron, more than his words, gave offense to the Indians, who had not been accustomed to be spoken to in that way.

Determined to effect the purpose of his expedition he sent from this point the following curt letter to Governor Hamilton of Pennsylvania: "Sir: Having been sent with a detachment into these quarters by Monsieur the Marquis de la Galissioniere, commandant general of New France, to reconcile among themselves certain savage nations who are ever at variance on account of the war just terminated, I have been much surprised to find some traders of your government in a country to which England never had any pretensions. It even appears that the same opinion is entertained in New England, since in many of the villages I have passed through, the English who were trading there have mostly taken flight. Those whom I first fell in with, and by whom I write you, I have treated with all mildness possible, although I would have been justified in treating them as interlopers and men without responsibility, their enterprise being contrary to the preliminaries of peace signed five months ago. I hope, Sir, for the future you will carefully prohibit this trade, which is contrary to treaties, and give notice to your traders that they will expose themselves to great risks in returning to these countries, and that they must impute to themselves the misfortunes they may meet with. I know that our commandant-general would be very sorry to have recourse to violence, but he has orders not to permit foreign traders in his government."

Continuing his journey down the Ohio, Céleron and his party took formal possession of the country by burying plates at the mouth of the Muskingum River, another at the mouth of the Great Kanawha, and the sixth and last at the mouth of the Great Miami. Believing that he had now covered all the territory that was likely, for the present, to be claimed by the English, Céleron paused in his course, and toilsomely ascended the Miami till he reached the portage, where he burned his boats, and procuring ponies, crossed over to the Maumee, down which he moved to Lake Erie, by which and Ontario he returned to Fort Frontinac, arriving on the 6th of November.

These metal plates, planted with so much formality, regarded as symbols of French power, which they were to defend with force of arms, remained for a long time where they were originally planted with the exception of the first, which, as we have seen, was immediately disinterred and sent to Sir William Johnson. That buried at the mouth of the Muskingum was washed out by the changing of the banks in the flood-tides, and was discovered in 1798 by some boys who were bathing at low water in the summer time, and having no idea of its use, or the purport of the characters cut on its surface, they cut off a portion of it and run it into bullets. The remaining portion was sent to Governor DeWitt Clinton, of New York, and is still preserved at Boston, Mass. That which was buried at the mouth of the Kanawha was found in 1846 by a son of J. W. Beale, of Point Pleasant, Virginia. In playing along the river bank he saw the edge of it protruding from the sand a little below the surface, where it had been carried by the current. It was dug out and has been preserved in its original form.

As may be well imagined the intelligence of this expedition of Céleron in considerable force down the Ohio, with the design of taking formal possession of the territory which the river drained was viewed with concern by the Proprietaries of Pennsylvania, and especially by those in England interested in the colony of Virginia. They saw that if this claim was maintained by the French their territories would be vastly curtailed, and the claims of the Massachusetts and Virginia colonies from ocean to ocean would become abortive. The then proprietary of Pennsylvania wrote to Governor Hamilton in these terms, as preserved in the Colonial Records: " The account you give of a party of French having come to Allegheny and laid claim to that country, and the tribes of Indians with whom we have lately entered into treaty, a good deal alarms me; and I hear the party has returned to Canada, threatening to return with a great force next year. I have communicated the French commandant's letter and paper, with an account of the affair to the Duke of Bedford and Lord Halifax, and I think something should be done immediately, if it can be by consent of the Indians, to take possession This, I think, you should advise with the Council and Assembly about, as it is of great import to the trade of the Province to have a settlement there, and a house a little more secure than an Indian cabin. I make no doubt the Indians would consent to such a settlement; and if there is stone and lime in the neighborhood, I think a house of thick walls of stone, with small bastions, might be built at no very great expense, as it is little matter how rough it is inside; or a wall of that sort perhaps fifty feet square, with a small log house in the middle of it, might perhaps do better. The command of this might be given to the principal Indian trader, and he be obliged to keep four or six men at it, who might serve him in it, and the house be a magazine for goods. If something of this sort can be done, we shall be willing to be at the expense of four hundred pounds currency for the building of it, and of one hundred pounds a year for keeping some men with a few arms and some powder; this, with what the assembly might be induced to give, will in some measure protect the trade, and be a mark of possession However few the men are, they should wear an uniform dress, that though very small it may look fort like."

This recommendation looked to the building of a Fort on the Ohio, as was afterwards done at Fort Pitt, and was a wise provision, if the encroachments of the French were to be met by force. Governor Hamilton was a wise and politic man, and instead of moving officially in the matter he held several conferences with the Speaker and members of the House with a view to carrying into effect the proposal of the Proprietaries But the ruling sentiment of the Assembly was averse to assuming a warlike or force attitude, the Quaker element in the council and the provident members opposed to the spending of public money, being in the ascendant. As may be seen by the above communication, the Proprietaries had no religious scruples against warlike preparations, the sons of Penn having forsaken the religion of their father, John Penn, the grandson, and subsequently Governor, showing a vigorous war spirit against the Indians, and even going so far as to offer, without scruple, graduated bounties for their capture, scalping, or death

Accordingly, Governor Hamilton gave instructions to the State

John I. Worley.

agents, George Croghan and Andrew Montour, who had been sent
out to distribute presents to the Indians, and who made Logstown
their headquarters, to ascertain the temper of the natives towards the
building of such a fort as the letter of the Proprietary suggested.
In compliance with this instruction, Crogan dispatched a letter dated
on the 16th of December, 1750, couched in these words· "Sir,—
Yesterday Mr. Montour and I got to this town, where we found
thirty warriors of the Six Nations going to war against the Catawba
Indians.   They told us that they saw John Coeur about one hundred
and fifty miles up the river at an Indian town, where he intends to
build a fort if he can get liberty from the Ohio Indians.   He has five
canoes loaded with goods, and is very generous in making presents
to all the chiefs of the Indians he meets with.   He has sent two
messengers to this town, desiring the Indians here to go and meet
him, and clear the road for him, [that is, secure the consent of the
Indians to his coming], to come down the river; but they have so
little respect for his message that they have not thought it worth
while to send him an answer as yet."

It will be observed from this note, that the French recognized
the Indian friendship as an important factor in holding the country,
and that they were willing to spend money freely in furnishing
presents in order to buy it over to their cause.   Their agent, Jean
Coeur, was skilled in all the arts of Indian diplomacy, and had lived
much among them; but he was not successful in his first essays with
these Ohio Indians.   On the 20th of May, 1751, Croghan records in
his journal, "Forty warriors of the Six Nations came to Logstown,
from the head of the Ohio, with M. Jean Coeur, and one Frenchman
more in company."   On the following day he records that Jean
Coeur made a talk to the Indians, telling them that Onontio, Governor of New France, directed that they send away the English and
deal wholly with the French.   The words of Jean Coeur failed of
their effect upon the natives; for their chieftain made answer that he
would not send the English away, but would trade with them as long
as he lived, and that "if he had anything to say, and was the man he
pretended to be, he should say it to that man," pointing to Croghan.

On the 25th of May, Croghan again records: "I had a conference
with Monsieur Jean Coeur; he desired I would excuse him, and not
think hard of him for the speeches he made to the Indians, requesting them to turn the English traders away, and not to suffer them
to trade; for it was the Governors of Canada who ordered him, and
he was obliged to obey them, though he was very sensible which way
the Indians would receive them, for he was sure the French would
not accomplish their design with the Six Nations, without it could
be done by force, which he said he believed they would find to be as
6

difficult as the method they had just tried, and would meet with the like want of success."

It will be seen from the temper of this conversation that Jean Coeur was convinced that the Indians were not in a temper to be won over by fair words or showy French presents; but that force would be necessary, and in that they would fail. But he had been sent on this mission by his government, and it was necessary for him to carry out his instructions. Accordingly, having exhausted his diplomacy with the Indians, he sent the following missive to Governor Hamilton, and returned to Canada: "Sir,—Monsieur the Marquis de la Galissoniere, Governor of the whole of New France, having honored me with his orders to watch that the English make no treaty in the country of the Ohio, I have directed the traders of your Government to withdraw. You cannot be ignorant, sir, that all the lands of this region have always belonged to the King of France, and that the English have no right to come here to trade. My superior has commanded me to apprise you of what I have done, in order that you may not affect ignorance of the reasons of it; and he has given me this order, with so much the greater reason because it is now two years since Monsieur Céleron, by order of the Marquis of Galissoniere, then Commandant-general, warned many English who were trading with the Indians along the Ohio against so doing, and they promised him not to return to trade on the lands, as Monsieur Céleron wrote you."

CHAPTER VIII.

ACTIVITY OF THE "OHIO COMPANY"—EXPLORATIONS OF GIST—PREP-
ARATIONS OF THE FRENCH TO OCCUPY—ARMS SENT TO INDIANS—
HALF, KING WARNS THE FRENCH—INSOLENT REPLY—EARL
HOLDERNESS WARNS GOVERNORS OF THE COLONIES—WAR VESSEL
SENT TO VIRGINIA—WASHINGTON COMMISSIONED TO VISIT FRENCH
COMMANDER—PERILOUS JOURNEY—SELECTS SITE OF FORT PITT
—PROVISIONS SENT FROM NEW ORLEANS—"WHERE DOES THE
INDIAN'S LAND LIE?"—JEAN COEUR AT FRANKLIN—RECEIVED AT
LEBOEUF BY LEGARDEUR ST. PIERRE—ANSWER—POLITENESS OF
THE GENERAL—REFERS TO THE MARQUIS DUQUESNE—RETURN
OF WASHINGTON—TREACHEROUS INDIAN FIRES AT HIM—SUF-
FERING FROM THE COLD—MAKES HIS REPORT TO GOVERNOR
DINWIDDIE—JOURNAL WIDELY CIRCULATED—THE INTENTION OF
THE FRENCH TO HOLD THE OHIO VALLEY BY FORCE CLEARLY
MANIFEST.

THE goodly lands along the "Beautiful River," and its many tributaries, seemed now more attractive than ever, and the next few years
succeeding the planting of plates by Céleron, witnessed a vigorous
and sanguinary struggle for their occupancy. And now commences
the active operations of the Ohio Company, chartered by the Virginia Legislature by authority of the English government, previously
detailed, for the settlement and permanent occupancy of this coveted
country. How Virginia could lay claim to this section, so clearly
embraced in the charter of Penn, is difficult to comprehend; but the
grounds of the claim will be stated in a succeeding chapter.

Boldly assuming the right, the company sent out from Virginia,
in 1750, as its agent, Christopher Gist, with instructions to explore
the territory, and sound the temper of the Indians towards its settlement by the whites. During this and the following year, he
traversed the country on either bank of the Ohio, as far down as the
present site of the city of Louisville, going even further than Céleron
had done with his pewter plates, and making a far more extensive
and thorough exploration of the country. In 1752 he was present
at Logstown as commissioner with Colonel Fry in concluding the
treaty with the chiefs of the Six Nations, which secured rights of
settlement in this country. The French were ever watchful, and the
provisions of this treaty were not unknown to them as well as the
explorations of Gist.

The evidences of activity on the part of the French to seize and hold this country by force were not wanting. Early in May an expedition was sent out from Canada, prepared to assert their claims. The commanding officer at Oswego, sent the following intelligence to Col. Johnson, dated May 15, 1753· " Yesterday passed by here thirty odd French canoes, part of an army going to Belle Riviére, to make good their claim there. The army is reported to consist of six thousand French." On the 21st of May, as shown by the Colonial Records, " the Governor laid before the board several letters from Governor Clinton, inclosing accounts from Col. Johnson, and from the commanding officer at Oswego, that a large armament of French and Indians, had passed by that Fort, destinated as was suspected for Ohio, in order to take possession of that country, and to build forts on that river; whereupon he had dispatched messengers to the governors of Maryland and Virginia, and likewise Mr West was sent to Susquehanna, there to procure and send away two messengers, one by Potowmack, and the other by Juniata, to give the Indians notice of this and put them on their guard."

The forces of the French who were thus reported as on their way to the Ohio, though greatly exaggerated, were of considerable strength, learned by other sources to consist of " exactly twenty-four hundred men and eight pieces of brass cannon " This force completed and manned the forts at Presquils, Le Boeuf and Venango, and were preparing to descend the river in force in the following spring   On hearing of these aggressive movements of the French, the Virginia authorities became much alarmed and sent to the Indians on the Ohio, who were known to be unwavering in their friendship for the English, " one hundred small arms, powder, shot, and some clothing," to be distributed by their agents Gist, Montour and Trent. The rumors of fort building by the French, and of their threatening to come as an army with banners, greatly agitated the minds of the simple natives   Their chief, the old Half King, Tanacharison, who represented the Iroquois here, set out to meet the French at Venango and Le Boeuf, to remonstrate with them and to warn them away. But he was received with no consideration, "and was discharged home, and told that he was an old woman, and that all his nation was in their favor only him, and if he would not go home, he would be put in irons " So strongly had the imperious manner of the commandant worked upon the old chief, that upon his return he begged with tears in his eyes that the English would go off "for fear they should be hurt." To subsequent messages from the Half King, the commandant returned this message: " But this I will tell you, I am commanded to build four strong houses, viz: at Weningo, Monongalio Forks, Logs Town and Beaver Creek, and this I will do "

The Half King still persisting in his demands to leave the country, the commandant became offensive and scurrilous. "Now, my child, I have heard your speech; you spoke first, and it is my time to speak now. This wampum I do not know, which you have discharged me off the land with; but you need not put yourself to the trouble of speaking, for I will not hear you I am not afraid of flies or mosquitoes, for Indians are such as those; I tell you that down the river I will go, and build upon it, according to my command. If the river was blocked up, I have forces sufficient to burst it open, and tread under my feet all that stand in opposition; for my force is as the sand upon the sea shore; therefore here is your wampum, I sling it at you. Child you talk foolish; you say this land belongs to you, but there is not the black of my nail yours. I saw the land sooner than you did. It is my land, and I will have it, let who will stand up for, or say against it."

The systematic operations of the French in building a line of forts, and providing cannon and a strong military force at each, substantially on the same line that Céleron had formally taken possession of with his plates, finally aroused the attention of the British government, and the Secretary of State, Earl Holderness, addressed the governors of the several colonies urging that they be put in a state of defense. The communication to the governor of Virginia was considered of so much importance as to be sent by a government ship. It reached its destination in October, 1753, and the matter of the dispatch was of such pressing import, as to require the sending of a special messenger to the French commandant on this side of the great lakes, to remonstrate with him in an official capacity for intruding upon English territory, but probably more especially to ascertain precisely what had been done and with what forces the French were preparing to contest their claims

Robert Dinwiddie, then Lieutenant-governor of Virginia, made no delay in selecting a suitable person for this embassage, and his choice fell upon George Washington, the Adjutant General of the Northern Division of the Virginia militia, and only twenty-one years of age It should here be observed that Lawrence Washington, the brother of George, who was president and a leader of the Ohio Company, had died July 26, 1752, and that by his will a large share of his estates and interests had fallen to George. He consequently had a pecuniary interest in holding the lands of the Ohio Company, in addition to the patriotic one of discharging a public trust. It should also be observed that Dinwiddie was a large stockholder in the Ohio Company.

The youthful Washington made no delay in accepting the trust imposed on him, and though now the inclement season of the year, he quickly had his preparations completed for his departure. It appears from the following note to the Lords of Trade, that the governor had previously sent a messenger on a similar errand: "The person [Capt. William Trent] sent as a commissioner to the commandant of the French forces, neglected his duty, and went no further than Logstown, on the Ohio. He reports the French were then one hundred and fifty miles further up the river, and I believe was afraid to go to them." But there was no fear on the part of George Washington, though then but a mere boy, and he was soon on his way. That we may understand precisely the nature of his mission we present the commission and instructions which he received: "Whereas, I have received information of a body of French forces being assembled in a hostile manner on the river Ohio, intending by force of arms to erect certain forts on said river within this territory, and contrary to the dignity and peace of our sovereign, the King of Great Britain, These are, therefore, to require and direct you, the said George Washington, forthwith to repair to Logstown, on the said river Ohio, and, having there informed yourself where the French forces have posted themselves, thereupon, to proceed to such place, and, being there arrived, to present your credentials, together with my letter, to the chief commanding officer, and in the name of his Britanic Majesty, to demand an answer, thereto. On your arrival at Logstown, you are to address yourself to the Half King, to Monacatoocha, and the other Sachems of the Six Nations, acquainting them with your orders to visit and deliver my letter to the French commanding officer, and desiring the said chiefs to appoint you a sufficient number of their warriors to be your safeguard, as near the French as you may desire, and to await your further direction. You are diligently to inquire into the numbers and force of the French on the Ohio and the adjacent country, how they are likely to be assisted from Canada, and what are the difficulties and conveniences of that communication, and the time required for it. You are to take care to be truly informed what forts the French have erected, and where; how they are garrisoned and appointed, and what is their distance from each other, and from Logstown, and from the best intelligence you can procure, you are to learn what gave occasion to this expedition of the French; how they are likely to be supported, and what their pretensions are. When the commandant has given you the required, and necessary dispatches, you are to desire of him a proper guard to protect you as far on your return, as you may judge for your safety against any straggling Indians or hunters that may be ignorant of your character and molest you."

It will be observed that the ship bearing the royal dispatch reached Virginia in October. This letter of instructions was dated October 30th, 1753, and on the same day the youthful envoy left Williamsburg, reaching Fredericksburg on the 31st. Here he engaged his old "master of fence," one Jacob Van Braum, a soldier of fortune, as interpreter, though as Irving observes, "the veteran swordsman was but indifferently versed either in French or English" Purchasing horses and tents at Winchester, he bade good-bye to the abodes of civilization, and pushed on over mountain and across stream, through the wilderness, on his important and perilous mission. At Will's Creek, now Cumberland, he engaged Mr. Gist, who had been the agent of the Ohio Company in exploring all that region and negotiating with the natives, to pilot him on, and secured the services of John Davidson as Indian interpreter, and four frontiersmen. With this escort he set out on the 15th of November, but found his way impeded by storms of rain and snow. Passing Gist's cabin, now Mount Braddock, and John Frazier's place at the mouth of Turtle Creek on the Monongahela River, and finding the river swollen by recent rains, he placed his luggage in a canoe, thus relieving the horses, and himself rode on to the confluence of the Monongahela with the Ohio. "As I got down before the canoe" he writes in his journal, "I spent some time in viewing the rivers, and the land at the Fork, [now Pittsburg], which I think extremely well suited for a fort, as it has the absolute command of. both rivers. The land at the point is twenty or twenty-five feet above the common surface of the water, and a considerable bottom of flat, well timbered all around it, very convenient for building. The rivers are each a quarter of a mile or more across, and run here very nearly at right angles; Allegheny bearing northeast, and Monongahela southwest. The former of these two is a very rapid and swift running water, the other deep and still without any perceptible fall "

It had been proposed, by the agents of the Ohio Company, to build a fort two miles below the forks on the south side, where lived Shingiss, chief Sachem of the Delawares. But Washington says in his journal, "As I had taken a good deal of notice yesterday of the situation at the fork, my curiosity led me to examine this more particularly, and I think it greatly inferior, either for defence or advantages." The good judgment of Washington in preferring the forks for a fort was subsequently confirmed by the French engineers, who adopted the site at the forks At Logstown, which was twelve miles below the forks, Washington met ten Frenchmen, deserters from a party of one hundred, who had been sent up from New Orleans with eight canoe loads of provisions to this place, where they expected to meet a force from Lake Erie. This showed unmistakable evidence that the French were determined to take forcible possession of the country The wily chieftains asked Washington why he wanted to communicate with the French commandant, and being naturally suspicious that they had not fathomed all the purposes, and bearings of this mission, they delayed him by their maneuvres.

Indeed, an old Indian Sachem had previously propounded, to Mr. Gist, while surveying the lands south of the Ohio, this question, "The French claim all the land on one side of the Ohio, the English claim all the land on the other side—now where does the Indian's land lie ?" There was, undoubtedly, a suspicion in the minds of these dusky kings that the English as well as the French were preparing to occupy this delectable country. " Poor savages !" exclaims Mr. Irving, " Between their 'fathers', the French, and their 'brothers,' the English, they were in a fair way of being most lovingly shared out of the whole country."

Finally, after having been detained about a week by Indian diplomacy, Washington set out on the 30th of November, with an additional escort of three of the Indian chiefs, Half King, Jeskakake and White Thunder, and one of their best hunters. A toilsome journey of five days brought the party to Venango, at the mouth of the Venango River, or French Creek, where the French flag was floating upon a cabin which had been occupied by the same John Frazier visited on the Monongahela, where he had plied the trade of a gunsmith; but from which he had been driven by the French. Captain Jean Coeur was in command here, who said he was in command on the Ohio, but he advised Washington to present his credentials for an answer, to a general officer who had his headquarters at " the near fort " " He invited me to sup with them " the journal proceeds, "and treated us with the greatest complaisance The wine as they dosed themselves pretty plentifully with it soon banished the restraint which at first appeared in their conversation, and gave a license to their tongues to reveal their sentiments more freely. They told me that it was their absolute design to take possession of the Ohio, and by G—d they would do it, for that though they were sensible the English had two men for their one, yet they knew their motions were too slow and dilatory to prevent any undertaking of theirs " But the French had yet something to learn of the temper and steady endurance of the English in America Washington ascertained that there had been some " fifteen hundred men on this side of Ontario lake But upon the death of the General all were recalled to about six or seven hundred, who were left to garrison four forts, one on a little lake at the head waters of French Creek, now Waterford, another at Erie, fifteen miles away " Jean Coeur was adroit in his influence over the Indians, and used his best arts to win the chiefs, who had accompanied Washington, from their allegience to him, plying them with liquor, and refusing to receive back the wampum belt which the Half King offered as a token of his tribe's allegiance to the French. But after long parleying they finally got off on the 7th. Washington records in the journal: " We passed over much good land since we left Venango, and

James Barnes

through several very extensive and rich meadows, one of which, I believe, was nearly four miles in length, and considerably wide in some places." This passage undoubtedly refers to the valley where is now spread out the city of Meadville.

At the fort at LeBoeuf, now Waterford, Washington was courteously received by the General in command of all the forces south of the lakes. "The commander," proceeds the Journal under date of December 12, "is a knight of the military order of St. Louis and named Legardeur de St. Pierre. He is an elderly gentleman, and has much the air of a soldier. He was sent over to take the command immediately upon the death of the late general and arrived here about seven days before me." In the letter which Dinwiddie had entrusted to Washington, the claim of the English to all this Ohio territory was reiterated, and a demand made that the French should depart from it, and no more molest its peaceful occupancy. The answer of the Chevalier was courteous, but firm. He said that the question of the rightful occupancy of this territory was not one which he could properly argue, that he was an officer commanding a detachment of the French army in America, but that he would transmit the letter of the Governor to his General, the Marquis Du Quesne, "to whom it better belongs than to me to set forth the evidence and reality of the rights of the king my master upon the lands situated along the river Ohio, and to contest the pretensions of the King of Great Britain thereto. His answer shall be law to me. * * * As to the summons you send me to retire, I do not think myself obliged to obey it. Whatever may have been your instructions, I am here by virtue of the orders of my general; and I entreat you, sir, not to doubt one moment but that I am determined to conform myself to them with all the exactness and resolution which can be expected from the best officer."

Governor Dinwiddie had added to the business part of his communication the following request: "I persuade myself you will receive and entertain Major Washington with the candor and politeness natural to your nation, and it will give me the greatest satisfaction, if you can return him with an answer suitable to my wishes for a long and lasting peace between us." In his response the Chevalier added in reply to this clause: "I made it my particular care to receive Mr. Washington with a distinction suitable to your dignity, as well as his own quality and great merit. I flatter myself that he will do me this justice before you, sir, and that he will signify to you, in the manner I do myself, the profound respect with which I am, sir," etc.

His mission over, he sent his horses on in advance, and himself and party took to canoes in which they floated down French Creek to Fort Venango. Finding his horses jaded and reduced, he gave up his own saddle horse for transporting the baggage. Equipped in an Indian hunting dress he accompanied the train for three days. Finding the progress very slow, and the cold becoming every day more intense, he placed the train in charge of Van Braam, and taking his necessary papers, pulled off his clothes, and tied himself up in a watch-coat. Then with gun in hand, and pack on his back, he set out with Mr Gist, to make his way on foot back to the Ohio. Falling in with a party of French and Indians, he engaged one of them for a guide, who proved treacherous, leading them out of their way, and finally turned upon and fired at Washington, "not fifteen steps off" But he missed, or the great spirit guided the bullet aside Ridding themselves of him they traveled all night to escape pursuit. Being obliged to cross the Allegheny, with "one poor hatchet" they toil-somely made a raft "Before we were half way over," proceeds the journal, "we were jammed in the ice, in such a manner that we expected every moment our raft.to sink and ourselves to perish. I put out my setting pole to try to stop the raft that the ice might pass by, when the rapidity of the stream threw it with so much violence against the pole, that it jerked me out into ten feet water. Notwithstanding all our efforts we could not get to either shore, but were obliged, as we were near an island, to quit our raft and make to it. The cold was so extremely ·severe, that Mr. Gist had all his fingers and some of his toes frozen, and the water was shut up so hard that we found no difficulty in getting off the island on the ice in the morning."

Arrived at the Gist settlement, Washington bought a horse and saddle, and on the 6th of January, 1754, he records "we met seventeen horses loaded with materials and stores for a fort at the fork of the Ohio, and the day following some families going out to settle This day we arrived at Will's Creek, after as fatiguing a journey as it is possible to conceive, rendered so by excessive bad weather. From the first day of December to the fifteenth there was but one day on which it did not rain or snow incessantly, and throughout the whole journey we met with nothing but one continued series of cold, wet weather, which occasioned very uncomfortable lodgings, especially after we had left behind us our tent, which had been some screen from the inclemency of it. * * * I arrived at Williams-burg on the 16th, when I waited upon his Honor, the Governor, with the letter I had brought from the French commandant, and to give an account of the success of my proceedings This I beg leave to do by offering the foregoing narrative, as it contains the most remarkable occurrences which happened in my journey. I hope what has been said will be sufficient to make your Honor satisfied with my conduct; for that was my aim in undertaking the journey and chief study throughout the prosecution of it."

It must be confessed that this embassage, undertaken in the dead of winter, through an almost trackless wilderness infested by hostile savages, by a boy of twenty-one, was not only romantic, but arduous and dangerous in the extreme, and in its execution showed a discretion and persistent resolution remarkable for so youthful a person, and giving promise of great future usefulness.

The information which he obtained, and which was embodied in a modest way in his journal, was of great importance. The journal was published and widely circulated in this country and in England. It plainly disclosed the fact that the French, in building strong forts and providing cannon and a military force for garrisoning them, meant to hold this whole Ohio country by force of arms, and that if the English would foil them in this design they must lose no time in preparation to oppose force to force. The lateness of the season and the coming on of severe weather alone prevented the French from proceeding down the Allegheny and taking post on the Ohio, in the fall of 1753. The following spring would doubtless witness such a hostile movement. Which shall win? Thus far the French had shown much the greater military activity, and their strong points were selected by competent engineers detailed from the French army, who had superintended the erection of their strong forts. Arrived at the threshold of a great era, the near future will witness the decision, whether this fair land, in the midst of which is what is now the county of Greene, shall be peopled by the Frank, and be under the control of the lilies of France, or an English-speaking people shall spread over this broad domain—the whole Mississippi valley, the flower of the continent—whether the Catholic or the Protestant shall be the religion of its people

CHAPTER IX.

TROOPS SENT TO FORT PITT—FRENCH CAPTURE IT—THE SUMMONS—
WASHINGTON MOVES FORWARD—JUMONVILLE SKIRMISH—TAKES
POST AT THE GREAT MEADOWS—SURRENDER—CAMPAIGN WITH
FOUR OBJECTS—BRADDOCK TO MOVE AGAINST FORT DU QUESNE
—FRANKLIN FURNISHES WAGONS—BRADDOCK MOVES LEISURELY—
ORDER OF MARCH—OBSERVATION OF FRANKLIN—SICKNESS OF
WASHINGTON—INDIANS IN CAMP—BRIGHT LIGHTNING—INDICA-
TIONS OF A HOSTILE FORCE—MENACING INSCRIPTIONS—CROSS AND
RECROSS THE RIVER—A MILITARY PAGEANT—ARMY PUT IN
BATTLE ORDER—ENEMY COMMANDED BY BEAUJEU—THE WAR
WHOOP—INDIANS GAIN THE FLANK BY A WOODED RAVINE—
REGULARS THROWN INTO CONFUSION—BRADDOCK MORTALLY
WOUNDED—KILLED AND WOUNDED—WASHINGTON PRESERVED—
GREAT SPIRIT PROTECTED HIM—BRADDOCK BURIED—DUNBAR
COWED—ENEMY'S STRENGTH—WASHINGTON'S LOSSES—GAL-
LANTRY ADMIRED

CAPTAIN TRENT, who seems to have been much relied upon, was ordered by the Governor of Virginia to enlist a company of one hundred men and proceed without delay to the forks of Ohio and complete the fort there begun. Washington was empowered to raise a company of like number with which to collect supplies and forward to the working party at the fort. In the meantime Dinwiddie convened the Virginia Legislature and asked for money with which to conduct his military operations, and called upon the other colonies to join him. Lack of funds, want of royal authority to enter upon this warfare, and other excuses, kept the other colonies from engaging immediately; but the Virginia Legislature voted money, and the number of troops authorized was increased to 300, to be divided into six companies, of which Washington was offered the command. But on account of his youth he declined it, and Joshua Fry was made Colonel and Washington, Lieutenant-Colonel. On the 2d of April, 1754, Washington set out with two companies of 150 men for the fort on the Ohio, Colonel Fry with the artillery, which had just arrived from England, to follow. But before Washington had arrived at Will's Creek intelligence, was received that Captain Contraœur, acting under authority of the Governor General of New France, having embarked a thousand men with field-pieces, upon sixty batteaux and three hundred canoes, at the flood-tide in the Allegheny River, had dropped down and captured the meagre force working upon the fort at the forks, both Trent and Frazier, the two highest in command, being at the time absent. The garrison of about fifty men were allowed to depart with their working tools.

Though bloodless, this was an act of hostility. The war was begun which was to greatly modify the map of the world. "The seven years war," says Albach, "arose at the forks of the Ohio; it was waged in all quarters of the world; it made England a great imperial power; it drove the French from Asia and America, and dissipated their scheme of empire." Contracœur immediately proceeded with the building of the fort which the Virginians had begun. He had issued, before the surrender, what he was pleased to denominate a summons, in which he "sirs" every sentence, and orders the English out of the Ohio country in the most absolute and authoritative way. "Nothing," he says, "can surprise me more than to see you attempt a settlement upon the lands of the King, my master, which obliges me now, sir, to send you this gentleman, Chevalier Le Mercier, Captain of the Artillery of Canada, to know of you, sir, by virtue of what authority you are come to fortify yourself within the dominions of the King, my master. * * * Let it be as it will, sir, if you come out into this place charged with orders, I summon you in the name of the King, my master, by virtue of orders which I got from my General, to retreat peaceably with your troops from off the lands of the King and not to return, or else I will find myself obliged to fulfill my duty, and compel you to it. * * * I prevent you, sir, from asking one hour of delay."

Washington, though but a stripling, determined to move boldly forward, although his force was but a moiety of that of the French, and intrench upon the Redstone. To add to his perplexity, he received intelligence that a reinforcement of 800 men was on its way up the Mississippi to join Contracœur at the forks. Sending out messengers to the governors of Pennsylvania, Virginia, and Maryland, to ask for reinforcements, he pushed on to the Great Meadows, arriving on the 27th. Here he learned that a scouting party of the French was already in this neighborhood. Not delaying a moment, he started with forty picked men, and though the night was dark and the rain fell in torrents, he came up with the French before morning, encamped in a retreat shielded by rocks and a broken country. Order of attack was immediately formed, the English on the right, and the friendly Indians on the left. The French aroused, flew to arms, when a brisk firing commenced, which lasted for sometime, and the French, seeing no way of escape, surrendered. In this spirited skirmish, Jumonville, the commander, and ten of his men were slain, and twenty-two were taken prisoners. Washington's loss was one killed and two wounded. This was the young commander's first battle, and if we may judge of it by the measure of success it was the presage of a brilliant career. He naturally felt a degree of pride and exultation. In a letter to his brother he added a postscript in these words, "I fortunately escaped without any wounds; for the right wing, where I stood, was exposed to and received all the enemy's fire; and it was the part where the man was killed and the rest wounded. I heard the bullets whistle, and, believe me, there is something charming in the sound." When this was reported to the King, George II, he dryly remarked, "He would not say so, if he had been used to hear many."

At the Great Meadows a fort was marked out and partially fortified, which was designated Fort Necessity. Supplies were scarce and could be brought up with difficulty. Not satisfied to stop here, Washington pushed on to Gist's at the head waters of the Redstone, where some intrenchments were thrown up. But learning that the French were approaching in force, and seeing that no sufficient supply of provisions could be had, he was obliged to return to Fort Necessity, which he proceeded to strengthen. On the morning of the 3d of July, the French under Captain de Villiers, a brother-in-law of Jumonville, with a force 900 strong, commenced an attack upon the fort. Outnumbered nearly three to one Washington boldly accepted the wager of battle and all day long and until eight at night, made a gallant fight, when the French commander asked for a parley and demanded a surrender, which was refused; again the demand was made and again refused. Exhausted by the fatigues of the day and suffering for lack of provisions, Washington, on being offered the privilege of marching out with the honors of war, decided to accept the terms, and on the 4th of July, a day memorable in the future annals of the country, though of humiliation now, departed with drums beating and colors flying. In this engagement, of 300 under Washington's command, twelve had been killed and forty-three wounded. The loss in Captain Mackay's independent company of South Carolinians was not known, nor the loss of the French, which was believed to be much more serious.

Returning to Will's Creek, a strong work, designated Fort Cumberland, was constructed, which should be a rallying point. In the meantime Colonel Fry had died, and Colonel Innes, of North Carolina, had been promoted to chief command. The army which came under his orders was composed of the Virginia, North Carolina and Maryland militia, and independent companies of South Carolina, New York and Virginia, under the pay of the King, and officered by soldiers bearing his commission. And now succeeded months of negotiation carried on between London and Paris; but nothing was definitely settled, and in the early spring of 1755, it was decided in the British cabinet to prosecute an active campaign against the French in America, with four objects in view; to eject the French from Nova Scotia,'to drive them from Crown Point on Lake Champlain; to gain possession of Fort Niagara; and to recover the Ohio country. For the accomplishment of these purposes Major-General Edward Braddock, was dispatched to America with two regiments of the line,· Forty-fourth and Forty-eighth, commanded by Sir Peter Halket, and Colonel Dunbar, with directions to take the supreme command of all the forces. Two ships of war and several transports were in the Chesapeake. Alexandria was made the rallying point, and here the regulars encamped. Commodore Keppel furnished four heavy pieces of ordinance with a detail of tars to man the prolongs in passing the streams and the mountains. Before starting on his campaign, the general held a conference at Alexandria with the governors of the several colonies: Shirley of Massachusetts, Delaney of New York, Sharpe of Maryland, Dinwiddie of Virginia, Dobbs of North Carolina and Morris of Pennsylvania. This conference considered little more than the question of furnishing troops and supplies for the expeditions.

The force against Nova Scotia was earliest in the field, and was entirely successful, the country being reduced and placed under martial law, and two French men-of-war were captured by the English Admiral Boscawen. The force destined against the French on the Ohio, to be commanded by General Braddock in person, was slow in moving. Wagons and horses were not in readiness, and could not be procured. Two hundred wagons and two thousand horses must be had, or the general would not move, and when the expedition was on the point of failure for lack of them, Benjamin Franklin, then postmaster of Pennsylvania, appeared and assured the General that he would provide the desired transportation if authorized to do so; that authority was quickly and joyfully given, and the desired horses and wagons were soon forthcoming. It should be observed that Braddock had studied the military art as practiced in the open countries of Europe, where smooth, hard roads everywhere checkered the landscape, and he made his requisitions for baggage, artillery and amunition as though his expedition was to be made over such a country, instead of over one bristling with mountains and torrent streams, through a trackless wilderness. Had he gone in light marching order with amunition and provisions on pack-horses, he would have been better prepared to meet the obstacles which impeded his way. Instead, the *impedimenta* of his little force, of less than three thousand men, was greater than was taken by a full army corps of 20,000 men in many of the campaigns of the late war.

Before starting Braddock organized his force in two divisions. The first under Sir Peter Halket, was composed of the 44th regulars, Peyronie and Waggoner's Virginia companies, Dagworthy's Maryland company, Rutherford and Gates' New York companies, and Polson's pioneers The second, under Colonel Thomas Dunbar, consisted of the 48th regulars, Dermaries' South Carolinians, Stephens, Hogg, and Cock's Virginians, Dobb's North Carolinians, and Mercer's pioneers. The field officers under Halket and Dunbar were, Lieutenant-Colonels Burton and Gage, Majors Chapman and Sparks, Brigade Major, Francis Halket; Quartermaster, John Sinclair; Assistant. Quartermaster, General Matthew Leslie; Secretary to the General, Wm Shirley, and Aids-de-camp, Orme, Washington, and Morris.   Christopher Gist and his son Nathaniel went as guides, and the Indian agents Croghan and Montour, acted as interpreters. Orme's journal, which was about the only record of this ill-starred campaign which escaped destruction, records that the soldiers were required to be provided with "one new spare shirt, one new pair of stockings, and one new pair of shoes; and Osnabrig waist-coats and breeches were provided for them, as the excessive heat would have made the others insupportable; and the commanding officers of companies were desired to provide leather or bladders for the men's hats "

On the 9th of April, Sir Peter Halket, with six companies of the Forty-fourth, moved by way of Winchester for Fort Cumberland, at Will's Creek; leaving Lieut. Col. Gage with four companies to escort the artillery. By the advice of Sir John Sinclair, who had been sent forward in advance to Winchester and Fort Cumberland, to prepare the way for the march, the second division under Col. Dunbar, accompanied with the artillery and heavy trains, moved by way of Frederick, Maryland.   But though the roads were better approaching Frederick than by Winchester, there were absolutely none beyond there crossing the Alleghany Mountains, and accordingly this wing was obliged to recross the Potomac and gain the Winchester road They now marched on with all the "pride and circumstance" of glorious war. "At high noon," says the chronicler, "on the 10th of May, while Halket's command was encamped at the common destination, the Forty-eighth was startled by the passage of Braddock and his staff through their ranks, with a body of light horse, one galloping on each side of his traveling chariot, in haste to reach Fort Cumberland.   The troops saluted, the drums rolled out the Grenadier's March, and the cortege passed by An hour later they heard the booming of artillery which welcomed the General's arrival at Fort Cumberland, and a little later themselves encamped on the hillsides about the post." In place of this vain display, Braddock should by this time have been knocking at the gates of Fort Du Quesne.

But arrived at Fort Cumberland, he sat down one whole month of the very best campaigning season, preparing for the execution of

Jean Louis Guillaume Mestrezat

his plans after the methods of European warfare. His utter lack of appreciation of the kind of warfare he was to wage, is given in the Autobiography of Franklin: "In conversation with him one day, he was giving me some account of his intended progress. 'After taking Fort Du Quesne,' said he, 'I am to proceed to Niagara; and, having taken that, to Frontenac, if the season will allow time; and I suppose it will, for Du Quesne can hardly detain me above three or four days; and then I can see nothing that can obstruct my march to Niagara.' Having before resolved in my mind," continues Franklin, "the long line his army must make in their march by a very narrow road, to be cut for them through the woods and bushes, and also of what I had heard of a former defeat of fifteen hundred French, who invaded the Illinois country, I had conceived some doubts and some fears for the event of the campaign; but I ventured only to say, 'To be sure, sir, if you arrive well before Du Quesne with these fine troops, so well provided with artillery, the fort though completely fortified, and assisted with a very strong garrison, can probably make but a short resistance. The only danger I apprehend of obstruction to your march is from the ambuscades of the Indians, who by constant practice, are dexterous in laying and executing them; and the slender line, nearly four miles long, which your army must make may expose it to be attacked by surprise on its flanks, and to be cut like thread into several pieces, which, from their distance, cannot come up in time to support one another.'

"He smiled at my ignorance, and replied: 'These savages may indeed be a formidable enemy to raw American militia, but upon the King's regular and disciplined troops, sir, it is impossibe they should make an impression!' I was conscious of an impropriety in my disputing with a military man in matters of his profession"

It was June before the army was ready to set forward. The wagons and artillery were a great hindrance in crossing the mountains, and it was soon found necessary to send them back, especially the King's wagons which were very heavy. The horses became weakened by incessant pulling over rough and untraveled roads, and many died. The Little Meadows was not reached until the 18th of the month. Through the advice of Washington, the General decided to change the order of march, and with a force of his picked men, with as little incumbrance of trains as possible, to push forward. Accordingly, with a force of twelve hundred men, Braddock set out, leaving Colonel Dunbar with the balance of the command to bring on the heavy artillery and trains. At the camp, near the crossing of Castleman's River, on the 19th, Washington was taken violently ill. "Braddock," he said, in relating the circumstance afterward, "was both my General and my physician. I was attacked with a dangerous fever on the march, and he left a sergeant to take care of me, and

7

James' fever powders, with the directions how to give them, and a wagon to bring me on when I would be able, which was only the day before the defeat."

The army was attended on its march by a small body of Indians under command of Croghan. They had come into camp at Fort Cumberland, attended by their squaws "These," says Irving, "were even fonder than the men of loitering about the British camp. They were not destitute of attractions; for the young squaws resemble the gypsies, having seductive forms, small hands and feet, and soft voices. Among those who visited the camp was one who no doubt passed for an Indian princess. She was the daughter of the Sachem, White Thunder, and bore the dazling name of Bright Lightning. The charms of these wild-wood beauties were soon acknowledged." "The squaws," writes Secretary Peters, "bring in money plenty; the officers are scandalously fond of them! The jealousy of the warriors was aroused; some of them became furious. To prevent discord, the squaws were forbidden to come into the British camp. Finally it became necessary to send Bright Lightning with all the women and children back to Aughquick."

Washington was disappointed by the manner in which Braddock acted upon his advice to move rapidly with his best troops, and leave the heavy portion of the *impedimenta* to be moved more leisurely. Washington had given up his own horse for the uses of the trains, and traveled with his baggage half filling a portmanteau. But the officers of the line could not bring themselves to this simplicity. "Brought up," says Irving, "many of them in fashionable and luxurious life, or the loitering indulgence of country quarters, they were so encumbered with what they considered indispensable necessaries, that out of two hundred and twelve horses generally appropriated to their use, not more than a dozen could be spared by them for the public service." Nor was the progress even with these drawbacks at all in consonance with the wishes of Washington. "I found," he says, "that instead of pushing on with vigor, without regarding a little rough road, they were halting to level every mole-hill, and to erect bridges over every brook, by which means we were four days in getting twelve miles" He had been about a month in marching a hundred miles. Indeed, his movements were so sluggish as to cause impatience by his friends in Europe. "The Duke of Brunswick," who had planned the campaign, writes Horace Walpole, "is much dissatisfied at the slowness of General Braddock, who does not march as if he was at all impatient to be scalped."

Though still weak, Washington had come up with the advance; but on the 23d of June, at the great crossings of the Youghiogheny, he was unable to proceed. Here the General interposed his authority and forbade his young aid to go further, assigned him a guard, placed him under the care of his surgeon, Dr. Craig, with directions not to move until the surgeon should consider him sufficiently recovered to resume the march with safety, at the same time assuring him that he should be kept informed of the progress of the column, and the portents of a battle. He was, however, impatient at the restraint, and regarded with distress the departure of the army leaving him behind, fearful lest he might not be up in time for the impending battle, which, he assured his brother aid-de-camp, "he would not miss for five hundred pounds."

Indications of the presence of a hostile force of French and Indians hovering upon the flanks of the column hourly multiplied. On the 24th a deserted Indian camp of 170 braves was passed, where the trees had been stripped of bark, and taunting words in the French language, and scurrilous figures were painted thereon. On the following morning three men venturing beyond the sentinels were shot and scalped. These hostile parties were often seen, but they always managed to elude the parties sent out to capture them. In passing over a mountain quite steep and precipitous, the carriages had to be raised and lowered by means of halyards and pulleys by the assistance of the sailors. Such was the nature of the hurried march with his best troops which Braddock had consented to make. On the 26th, only four miles were marched, and the half was at another Indian camp, which the warriors had but just left, the brands of their camp-fire still burning. "It had a spring in the middle, and stood at the termination of the Indian path to the Monongahela. * * * The French had inscribed their names on some of the trees with insulting bravadoes, and the Indians had designated in triumph the scalps they had taken two days previously. A party was sent out with guides, to follow their tracks and fall on them in the night, but without success. In fact, it was the Indian boast, that throughout this march of Braddock, they saw him every day from the mountains, and expected to be able to shoot down his soldiers 'like pigeons'"

Still the column went toiling on, in one whole day making barely two miles, men and officers alike all unconscious of the fact that a pitfall was being prepared for them into which they would plunge to destruction, and laying no adequate plans to guard and shield themselves from such a fate.

On the 8th of July, Washington found himself sufficiently recovered to join the advance of the army, at its camp about two miles from the Monongahela and fifteen from Fort Du Quesne. Though they were now on the same side of the river as the fort, yet not far in advance, a precipitous bluff extended down close in upon the river bank, leaving little room for the march, and where a column would be exposed for a distance of two miles to sudden attack from the heights. Accordingly, it was determined to cross to the left bank of the river by a ford, move down five miles, recross to the right bank, and then move on to the attack of the fort According to orders, Gage, with two companies of grenadiers, the company of Capt. Gates, and two six pounders, before daylight on the morning of the 9th, crossed and recrossed the river, as planned, and took up a position favorable for covering the moving of the remainder of the column. A party of some fifty Indians rushed out upon them but were soon put to flight. Knowing the nature of the ground upon which they had now come, and realizing the hazards from a covert attack to which they were exposed, having come in such close proximity to the enemy, and doubtless recalling the buzz of the bullets and buck-shot about his ears in his fight at Fort Necessity, Washington ventured to suggest, that as the Virginia rangers were accustomed to Indian warfare that they be given the advance. But the proposition was received with a sharp rebuke by the General, believing, no doubt, that the young provincial aid was ignorant of the principles of high art in warfare, and indignant that any subordinate should pretend to advise him.

Braddock was now near enough to the fort to anticipate the battle at any moment. He accordingly prepared to make a fine show. At sunrise the main body under his immediate command, turned out in full uniform. Their arms had been brightened the night before, and at the beating of the general were charged with fresh cartridges. At the crossings of the stream, where it was supposed that the enemy would be on the watch to observe them, in order that they might make the greatest show of power and strength, they moved with fixed bayonets, colors gayly given to the breeze, the trumpet sounding, and the fife and drum marking the measured tread. "Washington," says Irving, "with his keen and youthful relish for military affairs, was delighted with their perfect order and equipment, so different from the rough bush-fighters to which he had been accustomed. Roused to new life, he forgot his recent ailments, and broke forth in expressions of enjoyment and admiration, as he rode in company with his fellow aids-de-camp, Orme and Morris. Often in after life, he used to speak of the effect upon him of the first sight of a well-disciplined European army marching in high confidence and bright array, on the eve of a battle."

Having now all crossed to the right bank, and being, as was supposed, within nine miles of the fort, the column was put in battle order, Gage, with his force preceded by the engineers and guides, and six light horsemen leading; St. Clair, with the working party flanked with soldiers, and the wagons and two six-pounders following; then the General with the main body, and the provincial troops bringing up the rear. Along the track they were to pursue was a plain for some distance, then rising ground flanked on either side by wooded ravines. At two o'clock the advance under Gage having crossed this plain was ascending the rise, the General himself having given the order to the main body to march, and being now under way, suddenly a heavy firing was heard at the head of the column, accompanied by unearthly yells. Colonel Burton was immediately ordered forward to the support of Gage, who had been attacked by an unseen foe lurking in ambush, but drawn out in most advantageous order for extending their attack upon the flanks of the advancing English. They were commanded by a Frenchman, Beaujeu, attired in a "gayly fringed hunting shirt," who led them on and directed the fight. The Indians observed no order, but, extending rapidly down the ravine on the flank of the column, poured in a murderous fire upon the regulars and pioneers, who stood out boldly presenting themselves as targets for the concealed foe, who used their rifles with deadly effect. The firing on both sides was brisk. The Indian was accustomed to see his foe dodge behind trees and seek cover wherever he could. He had never seen such fine sport before, where his victim stood up boldly, giving a fair chance to shoot him down. The Indian war-whoop was something appalling, and the regulars seemed to dread it more than the bullets. Gage ordered his men to fix bayonets and form for a charge up a hill whence was the heaviest fire; but all to no purpose. They were being surrounded by an unseen foe, which crept stealthily along the hills and ravines, keeping up a most deadly fire. A panic seized the pioneers and many of the soldiers. Braddock and his officers behaved in the most gallant manner, exposing themselves to the fire of their dusky foes in their attempts to reform the shattered ranks and advance them to the attack. Washington suggested that the Indian mode of skulking be resorted to. But Braddock would listen to no advice, being reported to have said upon the occasion, "What! a Virginia colonel teach a British general how to fight!" But that young Virginian counselled wisely in this dire necessity. For three long hours Braddock saw the work of slaughter go on, while he attempted to form his troops in platoons, in the open ground, and advance them upon the concealed foe. The provincial troops, in spite of the General, shielded themselves behind trees and did greater execution upon the foe than all the firing of the regulars. The latter were thrown into great confusion by this savage style of warfare, where no foe could be seen, and where they were only guided in directing their fire by the flashes and smoke from the rifles of the skulking enemy. They huddled together and fired at random, sometimes shooting down their own friends. The carnage on the part of the English was terrible, nearly one-half of all those who had marched forth in faultless uniforms, and whose bright armour had reflected the morning sunlight, before night-fall lay stark and stiff in death, or were suffering from ghastly wounds. The foe was largely made up of Indians, and only about half the number of the English, who were utterly defeated. Finally, General Braddock himself was mortally wounded, and immediately gave orders for the troops to fall back. Fortunately the Indians fell to plundering, and neglected to pursue the retreating army.

General Braddock had five horses shot under him before receiving his death wound. It has been currently reported that he was shot by Thomas Faucett, one of the independent rangers. Braddock had given orders that none of his soldiers should take shelter behind trees or cover. Faucett's brother had sheltered himself, when Braddock to enforce his order struck the refractory soldier to the earth with his sword. Seeing his brother fall, Faucett shot the General in the back, and thereafter the provincials fought as they pleased and did good execution. Sir Peter Halket was instantly killed, Shirley was shot through the head, Col. Burton, Sir John St. Clair, Col. Gage, Col. Orme, Major Sparks and Major Halket were wounded. Five captains were killed, and five wounded; fifteen lieutenants were killed and twenty-two wounded. The killed and wounded of the privates amounted to seven hundred and fourteen. Over four hundred were supposed to have been killed. The very large and unusual number killed outright can only be accounted for on the supposition that the badly wounded who were unable to get away were murdered by the Indians when they came upon the field, as all were stripped and scalped.

When the two aids, Orme and Sparks, were wounded all orders upon the field had to be carried by Washington, who was conspicuous upon every part, behaving in the most gallant manner. He had two horses shot under him and four bullet holes through his coat. In a letter to his brother he said: "As I have heard, since my arrival at this place, a circumstantial account of my death and dying speech, I take this opportunity of contradicting the first and of assuring you that I have not composed the latter. By the all-powerful dispensations of Providence I have been protected beyond all human probability or expectation; for I had four bullets through my coat, and two horses shot under me, and escaped unhurt, although death was leveling my companions on every side of me." Many of the remarkable stories told of eminent men are of doubtful authenticity; but the following is unquestionably true. Dr. Craig, the intimate friend of Washington, who had attended him in his sickness and was present in this battle, relates that some fifteen years afterward, "while traveling with Washington near the junction of the Great Kanawha and Ohio Rivers in exploring wild lands, they were met by a party of Indians with an interpreter, headed by a venerable chief. The old Sachem said he had come a long way to see Colonel Washington, for in the battle of the Monongahela he had singled him out as a conspicuous object, had fired his rifle at him fifteen times, and directed his young warriors to do the same, but not one could hit him. A superstitious dread seized him, and he was satisfied that the Great Spirit protected the young hero, and ceased firing at him." It is a singular circumstance that in all his campaignings Washington was never wounded.

Of the conduct of the regulars in this battle some diversity of opinion exists. Washington, in a letter to his mother, which he never suspected would be made public, and in which he would be expected to tell his real sentiments, says: "In short, the dastardly behavior of those they call regulars, exposed all others who were inclined to do their duty to almost certain death; and at last, in despite of all the efforts of the officers to the contrary, they ran as sheep pursued by dogs, and it was impossible to rally them."

Braddock, though mortally wounded, was still able to give orders. After having brought off the remnant of his force and recrossed the river, he posted his command in an advantageous position and put out sentinels, in the hope of still making a successful advance, when his reinforcements under Dunbar should come up; but before an hour had elapsed most of his men had stolen away, and fled towards Fort Cumberland. Indeed, the teamsters had, from the beginning of the battle, taken out the best horses from their teams, and rode away. Seeing that no stand could be made the retreat was continued, and Colonel Gage coming up with eighty men whom he had rallied gave some show of order. Washington was directed to proceed to Dunbar's camp, forty miles away, and order forward trains and supplies for bringing off the wounded. This was executed. At Gist's plantation he met Gage escorting Braddock and a portion of the wounded. At Dunbar's camp a halt of one day was made, when the retreat was resumed, and at the Great Meadows on the night of the 13th Braddock breathed his last. He had been heard to mutter, "Who would have thought it!" and "We shall better know how to deal with them another time," as if he still hoped to rally and fight. Lest the Indians should be watching and know of his death and burial place the ceremony of his interment took place just before dawn in the morning. The chaplain had been wounded, and Washington read the burial service over his grave. He was buried in the road-way, and the trains were driven over the grave, so that the savages should not discover his last resting-place. The grave is a few yards north of the present National Road, between the fifty-third and fifty-fourth mile-stone from Cumberland, and about a mile west of Fort Necessity, at the Great Meadows. "Whatever may have been his [Braddock's] faults and errors," says Irving, " he, in a manner, expiated them by the hardest lot that can befall a brave soldier, ambitious of renown—an unhonored grave in a strange land."

Dunbar seems to have been completely cowed by the misfortunes of the day, and the death of his general. He hastily burst all the cannon, burned the baggage and gun carriages, destroyed the ammunition and stores, and made a hasty retreat to Fort Cumberland. When all were got together he found he had fifteen hundred troops, a sufficient number to have gone forward and taken the fort. But the war-whoop of the savage seemed to be still ringing in his ears, and the fear of losing his scalp overshadowed all. He continued to fall back and did not seem quite at ease till he had reached Philadelphia, where the population could afford him entire security. The result of the campaign was humiliating to British arms, and Franklin observed in his autobiography, "The whole transaction gave us the first suspicion that our exalted ideas of British regular troops had not been well founded." Had Braddock moved in light marching order, using pack-horses for transportation, and taken only so much baggage as was necessary for a short campaign, or had he when attacked taken shelter and raked the ravines with his artillery, the fort would have been his with scarcely a struggle.

It has since been disclosed with how slender a force Braddock was defeated. "The true reason," says Irving, "why the enemy did not pursue the retreating army was not known until sometime afterwards, and added to the disgrace of the defeat. They were not the main force of the French, but a mere detachment, 72 regulars, 146 Canadians, and 637 Indians, 855 in all, led by Captain de Beaujeu. De Contrecœur, the commander of Fort Duquesne, had received information, through his scouts, that the English, three thousand strong, were within six leagues of his fort. Despairing of making any effectual defence against such a superior force, he was balancing in his mind whether to abandon his fort without awaiting their arrival, or to capitulate on honorable terms In this dilemma Beaujeu prevailed on him to let him sally forth with a detachment to form an ambush, and give check to the enemy. De Beaujeu was to have taken post at the river, and have disputed the passage at the ford For that purpose he was hurrying forward when discovered by the pioneers of Gage's advance party. He was a gallant officer and fell at the beginning of the fight. The whole number killed and wounded of French and Indians did not exceed seventy. Such was the scanty force which the imagination of the panic stricken army had magnified into a great host and from which they had fled in breathless terror, abandoning the whole frontier. No one could be more surprised than the French commander himself, when the ambuscading party returned in triumph with a long train of pack-horses laden with booty, the savages uncouthly clad in the garments

David Spragg

of the slain,—grenadier caps, officers' gold-laced coats, and glittering epaulettes,—flourishing swords and sabres, or firing off muskets, and uttering fiend-like yells of victory. But when De Contrecœur was informed of the utter rout and destruction of the much dreaded British army, his joy was complete. He ordered the guns of the fort to be fired in triumph, and sent out troops in pursuit of the fugitives."

Braddock lost all his papers, orders and correspondence, even to his own commission, his military chest containing £25,000 in money, and one hundred beeves. Washington lost his journal and the notes of his campaign to Fort Necessity of the year before. Indeed, with the exception of Orme's journal and a seaman's diary, no papers were saved. In a letter to his brother Augustine, Washington recounted his losses and privations in his several public services, in a repining strain. " I was employed to go a journey in the winter, when I believe few or none would have undertaken it, and what did I get by it?—my expenses borne. I was then appointed, with trifling pay, to conduct a handful of men to the Ohio. What did I get by that? Why, after putting myself to a considerable expense in equipping and providing necessaries for the campaign, I went out, was soundly beaten, and lost all! Came in and had my commission taken from me; or, in other words my command reduced, under a pretence of an order from home (England). I then went out a volunteer with General Braddock, and lost all my horses, and many other things. But this being a voluntary act, I ought not to have mentioned it; nor should I have done it, were it not to show that I have been on the losing order ever since I entered the service, which is now nearly two years."

Ah! George, this does look like a sad case to you now! You did lose a few horses with their trappings; you did suffer on a winter tramp through the forest and were fired at by the savage, and hurled into the icy current of the river. You did get entrapped at Fort Necessity, and on Braddock's field innumerable bullets were aimed at you, when pale with sickness you rode up and down that bloody ground. But, my young friend, did you ever cast up your gains in these campaignings? You did suffer some losses in horses and bridles and the like. But there was not a true breast in all America that did not swell with pride when it knew of the fidelity and resolution you displayed in the trusts imposed upon you, and the gallant manner in which you acted on that fatal field, when all around you seemed stricken with terror and dismay, and your General was bleeding with a mortal hurt. You did indeed lose some sleep, and disease preyed upon your system in consequence of exposure; but there was not an Englishman anywhere in the civilized world who was not touched with some share of your anguish when the story of

7*

your heroism was rehearsed; not a Christian in all the land who could not join with the President of Princeton College, the Rev. Samuel Davis, who referred in a sermon preached not long after the event to "that heroic youth, Colonel Washington, whom I cannot but hope Providence has hitherto preserved in so signal a manner for some important service to his country."

CHAPTER X.

Seven Years' War Opened—Indians Inspired by Defeat of Brad-
dock—Terrible War Upon Settlers—French Offer Re-
wards for Scalps—Line of Forts Along the Kittatinny Hills
—Franklin in Command—Armstrong at Kittanning—Lord
Loudon Unsuccessful—William Pitt Comes to Power—Aber-
crombie and Boscawen—Ticonderoga Held, but Frontenac
Lost by the French—General Forbes at Fort du Quesne—
Moravian Post Sent to the Indians—The Vicegerent of the
Lord—Indians Superstitious — Indian Methods—Fort du
Quesne Occupied—Amherst in·Command—Ticonderoga and
Crown Point and Niagara Taken—Wolf on the Plains of
Abraham—Quebec Defended — Montreal Captured—The
French Expelled From North America East of the Missis-
sippi—Pitt's Vigorous Policy Everywhere Crowned with
Success—But at a Cost of $560,000,000—English Speaking
and Not French.

THOUGH some advantages had been gained at Nova Scotia and at Fort William Henry in New York, yet the great disaster to Braddock, on whose success towering hopes had been formed, spread. gloom through the colonies and touched the pride of the British nation. Seeing that the claims of the French to the country west of the Alleghany Mountains as well as the northern frontiers of the colonies were likely to be vigorously pushed, the English government determined to assert counter claims with even greater vigor. Accordingly war was declared against France on the 17th of May, 1756, and General Abercrombie was sent to take active command in the field in place of Shirley, who had succeeded to the command on the fall of Braddock, and Lord London, who had been appointed Governor of Virginia, was placed in supreme command of all the armies in America. The plan of campaign of 1756 was a vigorous one.

Ten thousand men were to attack Crown Point, six thousand were to advance upon Niagara, three thousand were to constitute the column to move against Fort du Quesne, and two thousand were to descend from the Kennebec upon the French upon the Chaudiere River. But before any movement could be made, the French, under Montcalm, crossed Lake Ontario, captured Fort Ontario, killing the commander, Colonel Mercer, took fourteen hundred prisoners, a quantity of arms and stores, and several vessels, and having destroyed the forts, returned to Canada without serious loss. This threw the whole frontier of New York and the Six Nations, who had remained loyal to the English, open to the French.

Previous to the expedition of Braddock, the Indians along the upper Ohio, the Shawneese and Delawares, had been kept by frequent friendly messages from their Fathers, the Governors of the colonies, but more by high piled up presents, true to their allegiance to the English. Indeed so much confidence had the friendship of the tribes inspired that several families had settled along the valley of the Monongahela, in Pennsylvania But the coming of a detachment of the French army with their great guns, dressed in showy uniforms, the officers bedecked with gold lace and nodding plumes, and taking possession unopposed of the strong fort the English were building, changed all this.   They concluded that the French had established themselves permanently here, and consequently they were easily won over, and induced to fight with what they judged was the stronger party.   When Braddock came they were seized with fear at the appearance of strength, and were with great difficulty induced to go out with Beaujeu to offer fight.   But when they found how easily this great force of English was overcome, and what a harvest of scalps and booty they gathered with little loss to themselves, they were inspired with great contempt for the red coats, and a corresponding admiration for the French.   That battle aroused all the bloody instincts that are common to the savage breast.   So confident did the French become that they could hold the country by the aid of the natives, that instead of reinforcing the fort with additional troops, they actually sent away a portion of those who were there to Venango and other posts beyond.

When, therefore, Braddock's column retreated out of the Monongahela valley, the settlers, knowing their insecurity, fled to the nearest forts for safety.   The savages had now the taste of blood, and like wild beasts would not be satisfied until they were gorged.   Not two months from the time when the English retired, the warrior chieftain, Shingiss, with a band of warriors from the Delawares and Shawneese, had moved out to the Alleghanies and crossed the summits.   Being now upon the war-path, with stealthy step he came upon the unsuspecting settler, and his stony heart was untouched by the cries for pity. The tender infant and trembling age were mercilessly tomahawked and scalped, and their cabins burned.   On the 4th of October, wrote to Col Burd: "Last night came to the. Mill at Wolgomoth's, an Express going on to the Governor of Maryland with an account of the inhabitants being out on Patterson's Creek; and about the fort the express says, there is forty killed and taken, and that one whole family was burned to death in a house. The Indians destroyed all before them, firing Houses, Barnes, Stackyards and everything·that will burn" Governor Sharpe, of Maryland, writes a few days later to the Governor of Pennsylvania, "I have received several letters advising me that the Indians have since the 1st inst. (Oct) cut off a great many families who lived near Fort Cumberland, and on both sides of Potowmack some miles eastward of the fort.   It is supposed that near one hundred persons have been murdered, or carried away prisoners by these barbarians, who have burnt the houses, and ravaged all the plantations.   Parties of the enemy appear within sight of Fort Cumberland every day, and frequently in greater numbers than the garrison consists of   As I presume it will not be long before these people pay a visit to your borders, I take this opportunity of intimating what I think may be expected "

And now the torch of savage warfare lighted up all the border, and even penetrated far into the older settled portions of the country. Weiser, the Indian trader, sent word to Governor Morris of a massacre which had taken place on John Penn's Creek, which flows into the Susquehanna five miles above the confluence of the North and West branches "Several people have been found scalped and twenty-eight are missing; the people are in great consternation, and are coming down leaving their plantations and corn behind them." A party who had been to Shamokin to ascertain where the enemy had come from who had perpetrated the outrages on Penn's Creek, were fired on by lurking savages on their return, and four were killed and four drowned in attempting to cross the river.   Warned of their danger, the settlements for fifty miles along the river Susquehanna were abandoned. · "The people," says Governor Morris to the Governor of Virginia, " are mostly without arms, and struck with such a panick that they flee as fast as they can from their habitations."

The portents of Indian depredations now thickened on every side, and no doubt exaggerated reports of the coming of the French and Indians helped to swell the consternation.   The settlement at Great Cove, in Cumberland County, was attacked on Sunday morning, Nov. 2d, when six were killed and seventeen borne away into a captivity more terrible than death,   The town of Little Cove and Conoloways, on the following day were attacked, and the sheriff of the county, Mr. Potter, reported "that of ninety-three families which were settled in the two Coves and the Conoloways, forty-seven were either killed or taken and the rest deserted." Encouraged by their successes gained over defenseless' settlers whom they stole upon and murdered, the Indians pushed on into Berks County, and on the 18th of November the Governor informed the Mayor of Philadelphia, "that the Indians have fallen upon the settlements of Tulpehoscon; that they had slaughtered many of the inhabitants, and laid waste the country, and were moving towards the town of Reading, which is within sixty miles of this city. The Moravian settlement on the Lehigh was attacked, and their meeting-house, dwelling houses, barns, in which were hay, horses, and forty head of fat cattle, were destroyed.

The Indians had now compassed the whole frontier east of the mountains, stretching from the Delaware Water Gap to the Potomac waters, a distance of 150 miles, and a breadth of twenty to thirty miles. In a report to the Council made on the 29th of November, the Secretary said, the frontier "has been entirely deserted, the houses and improvements reduced to ashes, the cattle, horses, grain, goods, and effects of the inhabitants either destroyed, burned, or carried off by the Indians. All our accounts agree in this, that the French since the defeat of Gen. Braddock, have gained over to their interest the Delawares, Shawanees, and many other Indian nations formerly in our alliance, and on whom, through fear and their large promises of rewards for scalps, and assurances of reinstating them in the possession of the lands they have sold to the English, they have prevailed to take up arms against us, and to join heartily with them in the execution of the ground they have been long meditating, the possession of all the country between the river Ohio and the river Susquehanna, and to secure that possession by building a strong fort at Shamokin, which, by its so advantageous situation at the conflux of the two main branches of Susquehanna, one whereof interlocks with the waters of the Ohio, and the other heads in the center of the country of the Six Nations, will command and make the French entire masters of all that extensive, rich and fertile country, and of all the trade with the Indians, and from whence they can at pleasure enter and annoy our territories, and put an effectual stop to the future extension of our settlement on that quarter, not to mention the many other obvious mischiefs and fatal consequences that must attend their having a fort at Shamokin."

So deadly had the Indian incursions become and so threatening to the peace and safety of the colony, that the Governor, on the 14th of April, issued his proclamation declaring war against the Delawares, and offering a reward for Indian scalps and prisoners. In Virginia the enemy showed a like activity hovering about the fort at Mills Creek, and even pushing forward till they had actually reached and invested the town of Winchester. Whereupon the Governor called out the militia of the eleven contiguous counties   But the campaign undertaken was fruitless, for when the Indians perceived a competent force opposed to them, dispersed and disappeared, or lured their pursuers on to destruction.

To check the progress of these savage inroads upon the settlements troops were raised in Pennsylvania through the influence of Franklin, and a line of forts was erected along the Kittatinny Hills, extending from the Delaware to the Patomac, at a cost of £85,000; those on the east bank of the Susquehanna being Depui, Lehigh,. Allen, Everitt, Williams, Henry, Swatara, Hunter, Halifax and Augusta, and those on the west bank Louther, Morris, Franklin, Granville, Shirley, Lyttleton and Loudoun   Much difficulty was experienced in overcoming the scruples of the Quakers, but Franklin issued and circulated a dialogue answering the objections to a legalized militia, and at the earnest solicitation of the Governor, he was put in command of the troops raised   As soon, however, as he had the requisite force and saw the work of locating and building the forts well under way he retired to take his seat in the assembly, and Colonel Clapham was left in command.

In July, 1756, King Shingiss, with a hostile band, appeared before Fort Granville, now Lewistown, and finding it feebly manned, carried it by storm, killing some of its defenders, and carrying away captives a considerable number of inmates.   The home of this formidable chief was Kittanning, on the banks of the Allegheny River. Here he had quite a town, and here dwelt Captain Jacobs, chief of the Delawares.   The French supplied them with arms and ammunition and needed supplies, which were floated down the Venango and Allegheny Rivers.   At the time of this attack upon the fort at Lewistown, Colonel John Armstrong was in command of the Second regiment of Pennsylvania troops, stationed west of the Susquehanna, and it was determined to send him in pursuit of these dusky warriors. Cautiously pushing forward from the point of rendezvous at Fort Shirley, now Huntingdon County, with a force of some three hundred men, sending forward scouting parties to prevent discovery, he fortunately came in close upon the town without discovery.   From his official report dated at Fort Lyttleton (Bedford), September 14, he says   We lost much time "from the ignorance of our pilots, who neither knew the true situation of the town, nor the best paths that led thereto; by which means after crossing a number of hills and valleys our front reached the river Allegheny about one hundred perches below the main body of the town a little before the setting of the moon, to which place, rather than by pilots, we were guided by the beating of the drum, and the whooping of the warriors at their dances   It then became us to make the best use of our moonlight, but we were aware an Indian whistled in a very singular manner, about thirty perches from our front in the foot of a corn-field, upon which we immediately sat down, and after passing silence to the rear, I asked one Baker, a soldier, who was our best assistant, whether that was not a signal to their warriors of our approach He answered, "no;" and said it was the manner of a young fellow call-ing a squaw, after he had done his dance, who, accordingly kindled a fire, cleaned his gun, and shot it off before he went to sleep."

The night was warm and the Indians prepared to sleep in differ-ent parts of the corn field, building some light fires to drive away gnats. Sending a part of his force along the hills to the right to cut off retreat in that direction, he himself led the larger part below and opposite the corn field where he supposed the warriors lay. At break of day the attack was made, advancing rapidly through the corn and sending a detachment to advance upon the houses. "Cap-tain Jacobs then gave the warwhoop, and with sundry other Indians, as the English prisoners afterwards told us, cried, 'the white men were at last come, they would have scalps enough,' but at the same time ordered the squaws and children to flee to the woods." The fire in the corn field was brisk, and from the houses, which were built of logs and loopholed, the Indians did some execution without expos-ing themselves. Accordingly the order was given to fire the houses, and as the flames spread the Indians were summoned to surrender, but one of them said: "I am a man, and will not be a prisoner." He was told that he would be burned. To this he replied that he did not care for he would kill four or five before he died. "As the fire began to approach, and the smoke grew thick, one of the Indian fellows to show his manhood began to sing. A squaw in the same house, and at the same time, was heard to cry and make a noise; but for so doing was severely rebuked by the men; but, by and by, the fire being too hot for them, two Indian fellows and a squaw sprang out and made for the corn field, who were immediately shot down; then surrounding the houses, it was thought Captain Jacobs tumbled himself out at the garret or cockloft window at which he was shot—our prisoners offering to be qualified to the powder-horn and pouch, there taken off him, which they say he had lately got from a French officer, in exchange for Lieutenant Armstrong's boots, which he carried from Fort Greenville, where the Lieutenant was killed. The same prisoners say they are perfectly assured of his scalp, as no other Indians there wore their hair in the same manner. They also say they know the squaw's scalp by a particular bob, and also know the scalp of a young Indian called the King's Son. Be-fore this time, Captain Hugh Mucer, who early in the action was wounded in the arm, had been taken to the top of the hill above the town, to where a number of the men and some of the officers were gathered."

When all the houses had been fired Colonel Armstrong determined to take to the hills before destroying the corn and beating up the savages probably lurking there, for fear of being surrounded and cut off by reinforcements from Du Quesne, or French coming down the river, as Indians had been seen crossing the river from above. "During the burning of the houses," says Colonel Armstrong, "which were nearly thirty in number, we were agreeably entertained with a quick succession of charged guns gradually firing off, as they were reached by the fire, but more so with the vast explosion of sundry bags and large kegs of gun powder, where with almost every house abounded. The prisoners afterwards informed us that the Indians had frequently said they had a sufficient stock of ammunition for ten years, to war with the English. With the roof of Captain Jacob's house, when the powder blew up, was thrown the leg and thigh of an Indian, with a child of three or four years old, such a height that they appeared as nothing, and fell into the adjacent corn field. There was also a great quantity of goods burnt, which the Indians had received but ten days before from the French "

On the day before a party of twenty-four Indians had been sent out from Kittanning as the advance force that was to have followed, to destroy Fort Shirley, Cioghan's fort on the Juniata. This scouting party fell in with a party of Armstrong's men, under Lieutenant Hogg, who had been left in charge of the horses and baggage, and a sharp skirmish ensued causing loss on both sides, but in which the savages were eventually put to flight. Lieutenant Hogg was mortally wounded

Though there was not so much accomplished as could have been desired, owing to the ignorance of the guides, and the difficulty of approaching so alert and wily a foe, yet it must be regarded as a signal success, brought about by a display of bravery and skill rarely excelled in conducting campaigns against Indians. The place had to be found by ways entirely unknown to them; the log-houses were well provided with port-holes, from which the occupants could fire upon the troops approaching without exposing themselves, and the corn field gave cover to the skulking manner of savage warfare. In, the face of these difficulties Armstrong boldly advanced till he found the town, skillfully posted his little force so as to cut off retreat, and after a stubborn fight put the savages to the sword, burned their town, destroyed their supplies of ammunition and French goods, and brought off his force with but the loss of seventeen killed, thirteen wounded, and nineteen missing. The loss of the Indians was unknown, "but on a moderate computation, it is generally believed that there cannot be less than thirty or forty killed or mortally wounded." The blow was sorely felt by the Indians. It called a halt in their ravages, and reminded them that there were blows to take as well as

Jacob Hatfield M D

give. It caused them to ask themselves what they were gaining by their warfare upon the English, and what they were really receiving from the French beyond ammunition and guns with which to prosecute the war. They found themselves pushed forward to do the fighting while the French could lay back in their secure fortifications, and reap the advantages of their temerity.

Great was the rejoicing in Philadelphia at the result of this expedition; the councils voted thanks for the success attending the enterprise, and the sum of £150, for the purchase of presents for the officers and for the relief of the families of the killed. On the commander was bestowed a medal bearing on one side the words, " Kittanning destroyed by Colonel Armstrong, September, 1756," and on the other, " The gift of the corporation of Philadelphia "

The campaign of 1757 in America, was conducted on the part of the English with little judgment or vigor. The dilatory, brainless Lord Loudoun was in supreme command in America, and confined his principal operation to an attack upon Louisburg. But when arrived with a strong land force and a powerful fleet, being told that the enemy outnumbered him, he abandoned the enterprise and returned to New York without even showing a hostile front. In the meantime, the French under Montcalm, had struck a blow at Fort William Henry in northern New York, and compelled the garrison to surrender, three thousand strong. In marching off with the honors of war accorded them by Montcalm, the enraged Indians, not accustomed to see an enemy escape in that way, fell upon the retreating English and made a great slaughter, plundered their baggage, and pursued them to their shelter.

At this juncture of disgrace (29th of June, 1757,) William Pitt was called to the head of the British ministry. Mortified by the failures of his country, he planned to prosecute the war in America in his peerless way. The heartless Lord Loudoun was recalled and General Abercrombie was placed in command of the land, and Admiral Boscawen of a strong naval force. Twelve thousand additional regulars were dispatched to America, and the colonies were asked to raise twenty thousand more, Pitt promising in the name of Parliament to furnish arms and provisions, and to reimburse all the money expended in raising and clothing them. The word of Pitt was magical, fifteen thousand volunteering from New England alone. Louisburg, Ticonderoga, and Fort Du Quesne, were to be the points of attack in the campaign of 1758. Admiral Boscawen arrived at Halifax in May with forty vessels of war and twelve thousand men, under Generals Amherst and Wolfe. Louisburg was invested, and though a vigorous defence for fifty days was maintained, it was compelled to surrender with a loss of five thousand prisoners, a large quantity of

8

munitions of war, and the destruction of all the shipping in the harbor.

But not so well fared the advance upon Ticonderoga, which was made by General Abercrombie and the young Lord Howe. With seven thousand regulars, nine thousand provincials, and a heavy artillery train, an advance was made upon the fort defended by Montcalm with scarcely four thousand French. The attack was vigorously made, but Lord Howe was killed in a skirmish with a scouting party, and after four hours of severe fighting and the loss of two thousand men, Abercrombie, finding the work stronger than he had anticipated, fell back discomforted, and after sending out a force under Colonel Bradstreet, who captured Fort Frontenac, and subsequently built Fort Stanwix, where Rome, New York, now stands, and garrisoned Fort George, he retired with the main body to Albany The fall of Frontenac, with the loss of a thousand prisoners, ten armed vessels, fifty serviceable cannon, sixteen mortars, a large quantity of ammunition and stores, and valuable magazines of goods designed for trade with the Indians, was a heavy blow to the French, as it deprived them of their great store-house for supplies.

The campaign against Fort Du Quesne was entrusted to General John Forbes, with about nine thousand men, including the Virginia militia under Washington, stationed at Fort Cumberland Forbes was a sick man, and was detained on that account in Philadelphia, while Boquet, who was second, moved forward with his forces. Washington favored an advance by Braddock's road, but Boquet chose a line more direct, and further north. The labor of cutting an entirely new road through the trackless forest and over craggy steeps was toilsome.

In the meantime, that the Indians, who had thus far fought desperately for the French, might be weakened in their adherence, a messenger was sent to visit the tribes upon the Ohio, to show these dusky men of the forest how they were being used by their masters the French, for their own selfish purposes. The agent selected was a Moravian, Christian Post, a man who had spent much time among the Indians, and had married among them. He was a pious man speaking much in scripture phrase, and apparently sincerely believing that he was under the special care of divine Providence, and it is a singular fact confirmatory of his belief, that although he made two journeys back and forth conveying messages from the Governor and from General Forbes, through a country everywhere infested by hostile savages thirsting for scalps, he escaped unharmed, and was everywhere kindly received and his pious conversation treasured in their hearts. His broad brimmed hat was like a halo over him. In closing his journal after a safe return, he says, "The Lord has preserved me through all the dangers and difficulties I have ever been under. He directed me according to his will, by his holy spirit. I had no one to converse with but him He brought me under a thick, heavy, and a dark cloud, into the open air; for which I adore, praise, and worship the Lord my God, that I know has grasped me in his hands, and has forgiven me all my sins, and has sent and washed my heart with his most precious blood; that I now live not for myself, but for him that made me; and to do his holy will is my pleasure."

Such was the spirit in which he went, and it was this spirit which inclined the most warlike and hostile Indians to listen. They would share with him their last morsel, would conduct him on his way, and watch patiently over him through the long hours of the gloomy night, that no evil should befall him. They were, therefore, disposed to listen to his message, and when he showed them that they were being put forward by the French to fight their battles, and that the purpose of the French was to hold all this fine country, and if they were successful in driving off the English, they would then turn upon the poor Indians and drive them off, they began to realize the truth of his words

The following fragment of a conversation recorded in Post's first journal will illustrate the nature of his mission: "Now Brother (Post), we (Pisquetumen, Tom Hickman, and Shingiss), love you, but cannot help wondering why the English and French do not make up with one another, and tell one another not to fight on our land." Post replied to them, "Brother, if the English told the French so a thousand times, they never would go away. Brother, you know so long as the world has stood there has not been such a war. You know when the French lived on the other side the war was there, and here we lived in peace Consider how many thousand men are killed, and how many houses are burned since the French lived here; if they had not been here it would not have been so; you know we do not blame you, we blame the French; they are the cause of this war; therefore, we do not come to hurt you, but to chastise the French "

The effect which the words of the messenger had upon the Indians, may be judged by the following answer which was made to a messenger of the French who had come with wampum to summon them to the fort, by a party of chieftains who had assembled to confer with Post: "Give it (the wampum) to the French captain and let him go with his young men; he boasted much of his fighting; now let us see his fighting. We have often ventured our lives for him; and hardly a loaf of bread, when we came to him; and now he thinks we should jump to serve him."

The Indian is naturally a worshiper, a bundle of superstitions. Though possessed of savage instincts they were captivated by Post because he professed to be ever under the control of the great spirit, and spoke with such trust, as though he was upon earth a vicegerent

of the Lord.   Post himself says of them; "There is not a prouder,
or more high-minded people, in themselves, than the Indians. They
think themselves the wisest and prudentest men in the world; and
that they can overpower both the French and English when they
please.   The white people are in their eyes, nothing at all.   They
say that through their conjuring craft, they can do what they please,
and nothing can withstand them.   In their way of fighting, they
have this method, to see that they first shoot the officers and commanders, and then they say they shall be sure to have them.   They
also say, that if their conjurers run through the middle of our people no bullet can hurt them.   They say too that when they have
shot the commanders the soldiers will all be confused, and will not
know what to do.   They say of themselves, that every one of them
is like a king and captain, and fights for himself.   They say that
the English people are fools; they hold their guns half man high,
and then let them snap; we take sight and have them at a shot and
so do the French   They say the French load with a bullet, and six
swan shot.   We take care to have the first shot at our enemies and
then they are half dead before they begin to fight."

The efforts of the messenger had great influence with the savages.   In the midst of his conference with them, a Cayuga Chief
delivered a string in the name of the Six Nations, who had always
remained true to the English, with these words   "Cousing, hear
what I have to say; I see you are sorry, and the tears stand in your
eyes.   I would open your eyes, and clear your eyes from tears, so
that you may see, and hear what your uncles, the Six Nations have to
say.   We have established a friendship with your brethren, the
English.   We see that you are all over bloody, on your body.   I
clean the heart from dust, and your eyes from tears, and your bodies
from the blood, that you may hear and see your brethren, the English, and appear clean before them, and that you may speak from the
heart with them "

It is not strange that the grave Cayuga chief should say, remembering how the Ohio Indians had imbrued themselves in the
affair with Braddock and had murdered and massacred along the
whole frontier, "you are all over bloody, on your body," speaking in
that Indian figurative way which was their custom   It was by such
means as these we have here detailed, by messages taken among
them by this plain Moravian Christian in his plain garb, that the Indians were brought to realize the true position they were sustaining
to the French, and the ties which bound them were loosened, so that
when the English came in force their work was in a measure already
done

Colonel Boquet, who had prevailed upon General Forbes, the
commander of the expedition, and who had been left sick in Phila-

delphia, to allow him to cut a new road over the mountains wholly in Pennsylvania, had made so slow progress, that so late as September he was still with six thousand men not over the Alleghany Mountains. At Raystown, now Bedford, the General came up with the column, and was there joined by Washington from Fort Cumberland. Colonel Boquet, with 2,000 men had already advanced to Loyalhanna. That it might be known what was the condition of the country in front, and the temper of the foe, Major Grant, accompanied with Major Andrew Lewis, of the Virginia forces, and a detachment of eight hundred men, was sent forward on the 11th of September to reconnoiter. The third day out Grant arrived close in upon the fort without meeting any foe. Having left the baggage two miles to the rear, with his main force Grant approached under cover of darkness within a quarter of a mile, overlooking the fort. Early in the morning Major Lewis was sent with four hundred men to lay in ambush along the path by which they had come, and the remaining force with Grant lay along the hill facing the fort. Then sending out a company under Captain McDonald, with drums beating, in the hope of drawing on the enemy, he waited the result, hoping that the garrison was weak. But in this he was mistaken; for they followed the decoy in great numbers, and boldly attacked. The regulars stood up boldly and were shot down from the coverts. The Americans took to the woods and fought Indian style. Major Lewis joined in the fight. Major Grant showed the most intrepid bravery, exposing himself to the enemy's fire, but all to no purpose Many were drowned in attempting to cross the river. Seeing that he was outnumbered and hemmed in by the enemy standing on commanding ground, Grant retired to the baggage, where Captain Bullet had held his company, and as the enemy came on with assurance, his little force made a determined stand, doing good execution. Here Grant endeavored to rally his broken columns; but the terror of the scalping knife had seized them, and one by one they slipped away. Bullet finding his force dwindling finally gave the order to retire; but the resolute stand he had made enabled the main body to retire without molestation, and the hail of bullets he had poured into the faces of the foe left them no stomach to pursue. The loss in this engagement was two hundred and seventy-two killed, forty-two wounded, and many, including Grant, taken prisoners. The loss in killed was out of all proportion to the wounded, and the number engaged. The ambuscade could not have been well planned, or was badly executed. Grant was sent with his force to reconnoitre and ascertain the strength and disposition of the enemy. Instead he marched his forces full upon the fort and offered the challenge of battle. The enemy, by keeping quiet in their fort and simulating fear, gave the impression that they were weak, so that when they threw off the disguise, and rushed out in overwhelming numbers, they went to an easy victory.

Gathering confidence by their great slaughter and great rout of the English here, determined them to follow up their advantage, hoping to find the main body thrown into confusion and ready to retreat as the Braddock army had done under the timid Dunbar. Accordingly they came on rejoicing in their strength, twelve hundred French and two hundred Indians, led by De Vetri, and boldly attacked the camp of Boquet at Loyalhanna on the 12th of October. From eleven in the morning till three in the afternoon the battle was maintained with great fury, when the French, finding that the English were not likely to run, withdrew, but at night renewed the attack, hoping, between the terrors of the night and the wild whoop of the Indian brandishing his scalping knife, to start a stampede But Boquet was prepared, and, " when, in return for their melodious music," says the chronicler, " we gave them some shells from our mortars, it soon made them retreat" The loss in this engagement was twelve killed, seventeen wounded, and thirty-one prisoners. It will be observed that in this last engagement the French were compelled to do most of the fighting themselves, showing that the savages were beginning to tire of their adhesion to the French.

General Forbes now pushed forward with the main body of the army from Bedford to Loyalhanna, where he arrived about the first of November Here the wintry weather set in unusually early, and the summits were already white with snow A council of war was held, and it was decided that it was impracticable to prosecute the campaign further before the opening of the spring. But it having been learned from captives that the garrison at Du Quesne was weak, the Indians having mostly gone off on their autumn hunt preparatory for the winter, the decision of the council was reversed, and Forbes gave orders to push on with all possible despatch. Colonel Washington was sent forward with a detachment to open the road, in prosecuting which he had a slight skirmish with the enemy, and a small force sent out to his assistance under Colonel Mercer having been mistaken for the foe, was fired upon and several fell Having pushed forward Colonel Armstrong with a thousand men to aid Washington in opening the road, General Forbes followed with the main body, four thousand three hundred effective men, leaving a well-appointed force at Bedford and Loyalhanna When arrived within twelve miles of the fort a rumor was current that the French, either by accident or design, had blown up the fort, and all had been burned. This was soon confirmed by the arrival of Indian scouts, who had been near enough to see the ruins. A company of cavalry was dispatched with instructions to extinguish the flames and save all the property possible. The whole army now pushed forward with joyous step, and arrived on the 29th; but only the blackened chimneys of the quarters and the walls of the fort remained. It was found that a strong work had been built at the point between the two rivers, and a much larger one apparently unfinished some distance up the bank of the Allegheny. There were two magazines, one of which had been blown up, and in the other were found sixteen barrels of ammunition, gun-barrels, a quantity of carriage iron, and a wagon load of scalping knives. The cannon had all disappeared, probably had been taken down the Ohio. The garrison, which consisted of some five hundred French, had separated, a part having gone down the Ohio, a hundred had gone to Presque Isle by an Indian path, and the remainder, with the Governor de Lignery, moved up the Allegheny to Fort Venango, where he informed the natives that he would winter and go down in the spring and rout the English.

A somewhat more spirited account of this important event is given by Mr. Ormsby, a commissary in the army, as quoted in the Western Annals: "At Turtle Creek a council of war was held, the result of which was, that it was impracticable to proceed, all the provisions and forage being exhausted. On the General's being told of this, he swore a furious oath, that he would sleep in the fort or in a worse place the next night. It was a matter of indifference to the General where he died, as he was carried the whole distance from Philadelphia and back on a litter. About midnight a tremendous explosion was heard from the westward, on which Forbes swore that the French magazine was blown up, which revived our spirits. This conjecture of the 'head of iron' was soon confirmed by a deserter from Fort du Quesne, who said that the Indians, who had watched the English army, reported that they were as numerous as the trees in the woods. This so terrified the French that they set fire to their magazine and barracks, and pushed off, some up and some down the Ohio."

Forbes now saw himself in possession of the fort and the commanding ground, which, for four years, the English had been struggling for. Well knowing that he could not subsist his army and beasts here, he rapidly threw up an earthwork on the Monongahela bank, and, leaving Colonel Mercer in command with two hundred men, he retired with the army to Loyalhanna, where he built a blockhouse, which he stocked with stores and manned with a garrison, and then moved back across the mountains. He died in the following March. The *Gazette* said of him: "His services in America are well known. By a steady pursuit of well concerted measures, in defiance of disease and numberless obstructions, he brought to a happy issue a most extraordinary campaign, and made a willing sacrifice of his own life to what he valued more—the interests of his King and country."

The campaigns of the English in 1758 had proved very successful Louisburg, Frontenac and du Quesne were in their hands. Pitt was now become the master of the Parliament and nation. Elated by his successes in America, he formed the bold plan of not only holding the Ohio valley, but of conquering and possessing the whole of Canada. The Indians, too, had been shaken in their alegiance to the French, a great council-fire having been kindled at Easton in the summer of 1758, at which the Delawares, Shawneese, Nanticokes, Mohegans, Conoys, Monseys and Twigtwees sat, and pledged lasting friendship for the English. The terms of this treaty were carried by the Moravian, Post, to the tribes upon the Ohio, who still remained hostile, which he often refers to in his journal, and contributed largely to weaken their faith in the French cause.

The Secretary, Pitt, had kept his word with the colonists, and had fully reimbursed them for all their expenses, in the sum of over a million dollars. They were therefore ready to second him in his grand schemes of ending French dominion in America. His plan was a bold one General Amherst succeeded Abercrombie in chief command. Twenty thousand provincials and a strong detachment of land and naval forces of regulars stood ready to execute his orders. General Wolfe was sent up the St. Lawrence against Quebec Amherst himself was to move upon Lake Champlain and seize Montreal, and General Prideaux was to capture Fort Niagara Amherst took the field, and with eleven thousand men moved upon Fort Ticonderoga, which the French abandoned without a struggle. Amherst pursued to Crown Point, which the French likewise abandoned and fled to Isle Aux Noix in the Sorel River. Deterred from pursuing further by the heavy storms that now, October 11, began to prevail, he retired to Crown Point, where he built a fortress and placed his army in winter quarters

General Prideaux, with Sir William Johnson second in command, moved by transport from Oswego by Lake Ontario to Niagara, and laid seige to the fort. Prideaux was almost immediately killed by the bursting of a gun, and the command devolved upon Johnson. For three weeks the closely beleagured garrison of French held out, when on the 24th of July a force of three thousand French came to their relief But Johnson so met them that they were put to rout after a desperate and sanguinary engagement, and on the following day the garrison, some seven hundred men, surrendered. After having strongly garrisoned this fort, the last remaining link between Canada and the Ohio country, Johnson returned home.

General Wolfe with eight thousand troops, and a fleet under Admirals Holmes and Saunders, moved up the St. Lawrence, and landed on Orleans Island, a little below Quebec, on the 27th of June, Montcalm with a strong body of French regulars held the

N. H. Biddle

town, which in the upper part, comprising a local plateau some three hundred feet above the water, known as the Plains of Abraham, was fortified. By throwing hot shot from Point Levi, opposite the town, the English nearly destroyed the lower town, but could not reach the upper portion. An attempt to force the passage of the Montmorenci failed with a loss of five hundred men. For eight weeks all attempts to take the city proved fruitless. Meantime Wolfe had heard of the partial failure of Amherst, and the prospect seemed gloomy enough. Finally, by the advice of General Townsend, his faithful lieutenant, he determined to scale the rugged bluff which hems in the river, by secret paths. Accordingly, on the evening of the 12th of September, ascending the river with muffled oars to the mouth of a ravine, and following trusty guides, Wolfe brought his whole army with artillery by sunrise upon the Plains of Abraham, much to the surprise and discomfiture of the French, whose attention had been diverted by a noisy demonstration where a previous attempt had been made Montcalm' immediately drew up his entire force to meet the offered wager of battle Long and fiercely the battle raged, but everywhere the French were worsted. Both Generals were mortally wounded. When at length Wolfe heard the glad accents of victory, he asked to have his head raised, and when he beheld the French fleeing on all sides he exclaimed with his failing breath, " I die content "

The campaign of 1759, like the preceding, ended gloriously for the combined English and American arms, yet the French were not entirely dispossessed of power in Canada. Early in the spring of 1760, Vaudreuil, Governor General, sent Levi, successor to Montcalm, with six frigates and a strong force to retake Quebec. He was met three miles from the city by General Murray, and a very sanguinary battle was fought on April 28th, in which the English were defeated, Murray losing a thousand men and all his artillery. Levi now laid siege to the city, and just when its condition was becoming perilous from the lack of supplies, a British squadron with reinforcements and supplies appeared in the St. Lawrence. Whereupon Levi hastily raised the siege, and losing most of his shipping, fled to Montreal Vaudreuil now had but one stronghold left, that of Montreal, and here he gathered in all his forces and prepared to defend his " last ditch." Early in September, three English armies met before the city. First came Amherst on the 6th with ten thousand, accompanied by Johnson with a thousand of the Six Nations, and on the same day came Murray with four thousand from Quebec, and on the following day Col. Haviland with three thousand from Crown Point. Seeing that it would be useless to hold out against such a force, Vaudreuil capitulated, surrendering Montreal and the entire dominion of Canada into the hands of the English. This ended the war upon the land.   But upon the ocean, and among the West India Islands, it was prosecuted until 1763, when a treaty of peace was signed at Paris, February 10th, whereby France surrendered all her possessions in America east of the Mississippi and north of the latitude of the Iberville River, and Spain at the same time ceded to the English East and West Florida.

Thus was the Indian war, virtually commenced by planting the leaden plates by the French along the Allegheny and Ohio Rivers, and commonly designated in history as the *Seven Years' War*, brought to a successful close, by the vast plans of empire formed by the comprehensive mind of Pitt, though at a cost to the British nation of five hundred and sixty millions of dollars

And now was forever settled the question whether the population about to spread over the beautiful valleys bordering upon the Allegheny and Monongahela Rivers—La Belle Riviére,—should be an English or a French speaking people, should be Catholic or Protestant.

CHAPTER XI.

MIND OF INDIAN POISONED—THE RED AND WHITE MAN LIVE TOGETHER
—PONTIAC—HIS CONSPIRACY—GAME OF BAGGATIWA—GLADWIN
AT DETROIT—INDIAN GIRL DISCLOSES THE PLOT—PONTIAC FOILED
—CONCEALED MUSKETS—ATTACKS THE FORT—GLADWIN SECURES
SUPPLIES— PONTIAC'S ORDERS FOR SUPPLIES MADE ON BIRCH BARK—
DALZELL SENT FOR SUCCOR—BOLDLY OFFERS BATTLE—REPULSED,
DEATH—SETTLERS DRIVEN FROM THEIR HOMES—PITIABLE CON-
DITION—PRESQUE ISLE—LE BOEUF AND VENANGO FALL—FORT
PITT ATTACKED—COMMANDER SUMMONED TO SURRENDER—BO-
QUET SENT FOR RELIEF—BATTLE OF BUSHY RUN—WON BY
STRATEGY—RAISE THE SIEGE—BOQUET ENTERS—£100 OFFERED
FOR PONTIAC—COLONEL BRADSTREET—DECEIVED BY THE INDIANS
—BOQUET FIRM—DEMANDS PRISONERS AND HOSTAGES—IS STERN
—MAKES TERMS—CAPTIVES BROUGHT IN—NOT RECOGNIZED—
MANY PREFER TO STAY WITH THE INDIANS—LOVERS BRAVE ALL
FOR THEIR LOVES—SONG OF THE GERMAN MOTHER—PONTIAC
YIELDS—MISERABLE DEATH.

THE treaty of Paris put a period to the sanguinary campaigns
of the Seven Years' War, so far as treaty stipulations could. But
the Indians, who had confederated with the French, could not be
reached nor bound by stipulations made three thousand miles away
across the ocean, in which they had no voice.   Though some of the
tribes assembled and smoked the pipe of peace with the English, yet
they had grown suspicious.   The French had poisoned their minds
against the English, telling them that the desire to obtain the fine
lands was the motive which incited this deadly warfare, and that if
the French were finally beaten, then the English would turn upon the
natives, and drive them from all their pleasant hunting grounds.
Though the French in America had accepted the conditions of the
treaty, and were as a nation willing to be bound by it, yet there
were individuals in whose breasts the recollection of sore defeats still
rankled, and who saw in the hostility of the red men a means of
wreaking their vengeance   .
    The thoughtful Indians saw, or fancied they saw, that daily com-
ing to pass which the French had told them.   They asked themselves, not without reason, why the English were so intent to drive

the French from the Ohio valley, spending freely hundreds of millions of money, and sacrificing countless lives, if they did not expect to occupy these luxuriant valleys themselves; and when they saw the surveyor with his Jacob's staff and chain advancing as the armies retired, blazing his way through the forests, and setting up his monuments to mark the limits of the tracts, he was strongly confirmed in his suspicions. The English contemplated doing, so far as reclaiming the forests and settling the country, what was eventually done; but they indulged the hope that the red man and the pale-face could dwell together in peace and unity, as the white man and the African have done since. But that dream had a baseless fabric. Hunting, fishing and war were the occupations of the one, while the arts of peace on farm, in workshop and mill, were the delight of the other.

The mutterings of discontent were heard among the Indians during the seasons of 1760-1-2, and secret enterprises of dangerous consequence had been detected and broken up. Major Rogers, who with a small detachment had been sent to receive the surrender of the French posts along the great lakes of the Northwest, and raise the English colors, had met on his way the chief of the Ottawas, Pontiac, who dwelt on the Michigan Peninsula, who demanded from Rogers why he was entering upon the land of the Ottawas with a hostile band without his permission. Explanations ensued, the pipe of peace was smoked, and Rogers was allowed to proceed on his mission.

But ill concealed disaffection existed among all the tribes as they saw the emblem of the power of Britain floating from posts along all the lakes and the great river courses. Even the Six Nations, who had always remained the fast friends of the English, especially the Senacas, showed signs of hostility. These, with the Delawares and Shawnees, for two years had been holding secret communications with the tribes of the great Northwest, laboring to induce them to join in a war of extermination upon the English. "So spoke the Senacas," says Bancroft, "to the Delawares, and they to the Shawnees, and the Shawnees to the Miamis, and Wyandots, whose chiefs, slain in battle by the English, were still unavenged, until everywhere, from the Falls of Niagara and the piny declivities of the Alleghanies to the whitewood forests of the Mississippi, and the borders of Lake Superior, all the nations concerted to rise and put the English to death."

It was not easy to arouse the tribes to united action, many feeling themselves bound to the English by treaties, and some by real friendship. It was necessary to work upon their superstition. A chief of the Abenakis declared that the great Manitou had shown himself to him in a dream saying: "I am the Lord of Life; it is I who made all men; I wake for their safety. Therefore I give you warning, that if you suffer the Englishmen to dwell among you, their diseases and their poisons shall destroy you utterly, and you shall all die."

The leader in all these discontents was Pontiac. He was now about fifty years old. He had been taken a prisoner from the Catawbas, and had been adopted into the tribe of the Ottawas, instead of having been tortured and burned, and had by his cunning and skill risen to be chief, and was now asserting his authority over all the tribes of the north. Pontiac had been a leading warrior, a sort of lieutenant general in the battle of the Monongahela, in which General Braddock had been worsted and mortally wounded. Seeing what slaughter his people had then wrought he doubtless thought that it would be easy, if all the Indians could be united, to utterly exterminate the English, and reclaim their country. Accordingly he sent out his runners to all the tribes in the northwest, with the black wampum, the signal for war, and the red tomahawk, directing to prepare for war, and on a day agreed upon they were to rise, overpower the garrisons, and then lay waste and utterly exterminate the English settlers. That he might rouse the entire people he summoned the chiefs to a council, which was held at the river Ecorces on the 27th of April, 1763. Pontiac met them with the war-belt in his hand and spoke in his native and firey eloquence. He pointed to the British flags floating everywhere, to the chieftains slain unavenged. He said the blow must now be struck or their hunting grounds would be forever lost. The chiefs received his words with accents of approval, and separated to arouse their people and engage in the great conspiracy. The plan was skillfully laid. They were to fall upon the frontiers along all the settlements during harvest time, and destroy the corn and cattle, when they could fall upon all the outposts which should hold out and reduce them, pinched with hunger. The blow fell at the concerted signal and blood and devastation marked the course of the conspirators. So sudden and unexpected was the attack that of eleven forts only three of them were successfully defended, Venango, Le Boeuf, Presque Isle, La Bay, St. Joseph's, Miamis, Ouachtunon, Sandusky and Michilimackinac, falling into their hands, the garrisons being mercilessly slaughtered; Detroit, Niagara and Fort Pitt alone holding out.

Among the first to feel the blow was Michilimackinac. Major Etherington, who was in command, felt no alarm at the assembling of an unusual number of the tribes under their chief Menehwehna; though he had been warned of their hostility. But so confident was the Major of their pacific intentions that he threatened to send any one who should express a doubt of their friendly purposes a prisoner to Detroit. On the 4th of June, the Indians to the number of about four hundred began, as if in sport, to play a game of ball, called baggatiway. Two stakes are driven into the earth something like a mile apart, and the ball is placed on the ground midway between them. Dividing their party into two sides each strives to drive the ball by means of bats to the stake of the other. This game they commenced, and the strife became fierce and noisy. Presently the ball was sent, as if by accident, over the stockade into the fort when the whole company rushed pell mell into the fort. This maneuvre was repeated several times without exciting any suspicion Finally, having discovered all of the interior desired, they again sent the ball within, and when all had gained admission, suddenly turned upon the garrison, ninety in number, and murdered all but twenty, whom they led away to be made the subjects of torture or servitude.

For several reasons the fort at what is now Detroit was among the most important of all the fortified posts. Its location on the river which connects the upper with the lower lakes gives it the command of these great waterways, and along its margin ran the chief Indian war-path into the great Northwest. Attracted by the fertility of the soil, and the mildness of the climate, the French farmers had early settled here. "The lovely and cheerful region attracted settlers, alike white men and savages, and the French had so occupied the two banks of the river that their numbers were rated so high as twenty-five hundred souls. * * * * The French dwelt upon farms, which were about three or four acres wide upon the river, and eighty acres deep; indolent in the midst of plenty, graziers as well as tillers of the soil, and enriched by Indian traffic."

All this happiness and prosperity Pontiac regarded with an evil eye. To his mind all this country of right belonged to the red man. By the cutting down of the forest, and multiplying the sounds of civilization, the game, which was their chief resource for living, was frightened away The favored spots by the living springs and the fountains of sweet waters were grasped by the white man to make his continual abiding place, and would consequently be forever lost to the red man. If, by deep laid strategy, and unblushing deception, they could once seize upon all the strongholds and put the defenders to the slaughter they could then pursue their trade of blood upon the defenceless frontiers until the whole land would be cleared of the pale-face and his race exterminated

The fort was situated upon the banks of the river within the limits of the present city of Detroit. It consisted of a stockade twenty feet high, some two hundred yards in circumference and inclosing seventy or more houses. The garrison, under command of Colonel Gladwin, was composed of the remains of the eightieth regiment of the line, reduced now to about one hundred and twenty men and eight officers. Two six-pounder and one three-pounder guns and three useless mortars constituted the armament of the fort, and two gunboats lay in the stream. Against this, Pontiac, with a smile on his face, but treachery in his black heart, came in person with fifty of his warriors on the first of May. He announced his purpose to come in a more formal manner in a few days for the purpose of brightening the chain of friendship,—which usually meant that the chiefs were ready to receive high piled up presents,—and to renew pledges of lasting peace. As this was a ceremony of frequent occurrence Gladwin had no suspicion of treachery. Tribes of the Pottawatamies and Wyandots dwelt a few miles below the fort, and a short distance above on the eastern side, the Ottawas, Pontiac's own tribe. The day was drawing near when the universal uprising, which had been agreed upon in council, should take place. Pontiac had laid his scheme skillfully, and as he thought there could be no possibility of failure. He had already been admitted to the fort, and had spied out its strength and appointments and had bespoken admittance with his warriors. He had agreed with his confederates that when he should rise to speak he would hold in his hands a belt of wampum, white on one side and green on the other, and when he should turn the green side uppermost that should be the signal for the massacre of the garrison. But in savage as in civilized diplomacy,

> The best laid schemes of mice and men
> Gang oft a-gley.

A dusky maiden of the forest had formed an abiding friendship for Colonel Gladwin. She had often visited the fort, and had, with native art, executed pieces of her handy work for the use of the Colonel. She had received from his hands a curious elk skin, from which she had wrought with her usual skill a pair of moccasins, and on the night previous to the contemplated massacre she had visited the fort to bring the work, and return the unused portion of the skin. So pleased was Gladwin with her skill that he asked her to take the skin and make him another pair, and if any were then left she might appropriate it to her own use. Having paid her for her work she was supposed to have gone to her wigwam. But when the watchmen whose duty it was to clear the fort and shut the gates went at the evening signal gun, they found this maiden lingering in the inclosure and unwilling to depart. On being informed of this, Gladwin ordered her to be led to his presence, and in answer to the inquiry why she did not go away as had been her custom, she made the lame excuse that she did not like to take away the skin which the Colonel seemed to set so high a value on lest some injury or destruction might come to it. When asked why she had not made that objection before, seeing that she must now disclose her trouble, she ingenuously declared, "If I take it away, I shall never be able to return it to you." Inferring that something unusual was foretold in this answer, she was urged to explain her meaning. Whereupon she revealed the whole secret,—that Pontiac, and his chiefs were to come to the fort on the morrow, and while the dusky warrior was delivering his pretended speech of peace he was to present a white and green belt which on being turned in a peculiar way was to be the signal for the murder of the commandant and all the garrison. That the hostile intent might be entirely hidden beneath the garb of peace, the ingenious savages had cut off a piece from the barrels of their guns so that they could carry them concealed beneath their blankets. Having given the particulars of the conspiracy she departed.

Being thus put in possession of the horrible purpose Gladwin communicated the intelligence to his men, and sent word to all the traders to be on their guard. At night a cry as of defiance was heard and the garrison anticipated an immediate attack. The garrison fires were extinguished, and the men silently sought their places in readiness to meet the onset. But none came, and it was supposed the chiefs were acting their parts by their camp fires, which they were to play on the morrow.

At the appointed hour, Pontiac, came accompanied by thirty-six chiefs and a cloud of dusky warriors bearing his speech belt and the pipe of peace. Gladwin was prepared to receive him, his men all under arms, guns cleaned and freshly loaded, and officers with their swords. On entering the fort Pontiac started back uttering a cry of anguish, convinced that he had been betrayed, by the evidences of preparation about him ; but there was no way of retreat now. When the number agreed upon had been admitted the gates were closed. When arrived, at the council chamber, Pontiac complained that the garrison was all under arms, a thing unusual in an embassage of peace. Gladwin explained that the garrison were that morning holding a regimental drill. But Pontiac knew better than that. He commenced his speech with that air of dissimulation which he had the ability to command, and expressed the desire for peace and friendship with the English which he hoped would be as lasting as the coming and going of the night and morning. But when he advanced to present the belt the officers grasped their swords, and drew them partially from their scabbars. Seeing that his treachery was known, but not in the least disconcerted, he did not give the signal, he had agreed upon, and closed his speech in the most friendly and pacific tone.

When Colonel Gladwin came to reply he boldly charged the chieftain with his black hearted perfidy. But the latter protested his innocence, and expressed a sense of injury that he should be suspected of so base a crime; but when Gladwin advanced to the

W. S. Throckmorton. M.D.

nearest chieftain and pulling aside his blanket, disclosed the shortened gun with which each of them was secretly armed his discomfiture was complete. He was suffered to depart, but unwisely, has been the unanimous judgment of historians. Indeed, so little reliance has come to be placed on the words of an Indian, that it has been declared that "the only good Indian is a dead Indian." Hoping still to disarm the suspicions of the commandant, and gain admission to the fort through treachery, Pontiac came again on the following morning accompanied with only three of his chiefs and smoked the pipe of peace in the most innocent garb, and declared that his whole Ottawa nation desired to come on the following morning to smoke. But Gladwin declared that this was unnecessary, as he was willing to accept the word of the chiefs, and if they were so anxious to be at peace their own conduct would be the best pledge of their pacific intentions.

Seeing that his treacherous purposes were understood, and that he could not gain admission to the fort by any professions of friendship, he threw off the cloak of deceit under which he had intended to slaughter the garrison and possess the post, and attacked the fort with all his warriors. The few English who were outside were murdered, all communication was cut off, death was threatened any who should attempt to carry supplies to the garrison, and the keenest strategy was employed to tempt the troops to open combat. Carts loaded with combustibles were pushed up to the palisades in the attempt to burn them; but all to no purpose Gladwin was wary, and met every artifice of the wiley foe with a counter-check. In one part the savages attempted to gain entrance by chopping down the picket posts. In this Gladwin ordered his men to assist them by cutting on the inside. When these fell a rush was made by the Indians to enter; but a brass four-pounder, which had been charged with grape and canister and so planted as to command the breach, was discharged at the opportune moment, which effected great slaughter. Pontiac now settled down to a close seige. Unfortunately Gladwin had only supplies for three weeks. The savage chieftain, believing that he had learned something of civilized warfare, on the 10th of May, summoned the garrison to surrender. Gladwin asked for a parley, intimating through the offices of a French emissary, that he was willing to redress any grievances of the Indians, not suspecting that the attack on him was a part of a deep laid conspiracy reaching all the posts of the frontier. Pontiac consented and Major Campbell and Lieutenant McDougal were sent. Hostilities were suspended and Gladwin improved the opportunity to lay in ample supplies for the siege, when he ended the conference. But Major Campbell was retained as a prisoner and was subsequently murdered. The siege was now closely maintained, a species of hos-

9

tility which the Indians had never before exhibited an aptitude to
practice, but which the genius of their leader had acquired in his
fellowship with the French. He organized a system .of obtaining
supplies after the best European methods, scorning the make-shifts
of the freebooter; but giving his receipt for every thing taken, and
issuing his promissory notes, written on the bark of the papyrus
birch, and executed with the outline of an otter, which passed current among the French farmers, all of which he faithfully redeemed.
Lieutenant Cuyler, with a force of ninety-six men and supplies
for Gladwin, was dispatched from the fort at Niagara; but landing
at the mouth of the Detroit River, he was attacked in his camp at
midnight of the 28th of May, and utterly defeated, losing three of
his boats, two only escaping with Cuyler, who returned to Niagara

On the 29th of July, Captain Dalzell, taking advantage of the
darkness of the night, had reached the fort with a reinforcement of
some two hundred men.   Dalzell was full of fight, and with but one
day's rest insisted on marching out to offer battle   Gladwin knew
the numbers and temper of the Indians and their treacherous methods
better than the Captain, and counseled strongly against the adventure; but the latter was confident and the commandant yielded a
reluctant assent.   At the head of two hundred and forty-seven
chosen men, Dalzell bravely led out of the fort at a little past midnight of the 30th of July, accompanied by two barges in the river.
Unfortunately the French had notified Pontiac of the intended attack.
The course of Dalzell was along the river bank by Canadian cottages
and gardens   A mile and a half above the fort was a small creek,
since appropriately known as Bloody Run   Over this was a narrow
bridge and on the heights beyond were the entrenchments of the
foe, straggling fences and cabins, behind which they were in
waiting for the approach of Dalzell. Scarcely had the advance
crossed this bridge than the savages poured into their faces a
volley from their safe hiding places   A charge was ordered before
which the Indians vanished in the darkness, but soon reappeared in
the rear with the design of cutting off escape; and now the red men
had taken shelter behind houses and attacked in flank   This threw
the line into confusion and in disorder, a retreat along the river commenced.   Major Rogers with a squadron of provincials took position
in a house, which covered the retreat, and succeeded to check the
onrushing savages   Captain Grant with another party gained an
advantageous position for covering the retreat, when the forces were
finally brought within the shelter of the fort, but with the loss of
fifty-nine men, including the bold leader Dalzell

In the meantime one of the schooners had been dispatched to
Niagara for supplies. On its return the savages, who had learned
that it was manned by only ten men, planned to attack and capture

it. In canoes they approached in the darkness in great numbers and in face of a rapid musketry fire were boarding the vessel, when the commander gave the order to fire the magazine and blow up the ship, which the Indians hearing, leaped overboard and swam to shore to escape the explosion, when the vessel moved up under cover of the fort unmolested.

The peace of Paris had been concluded in April, yet the intelligence was tardy in reaching the frontiers, and when finally it was known, the hatred of the English and the hope of yet driving them away through Indian warfare was still kept alive. But the stubborn defence of Detroit finally convinced the more considerate of the French that it was their best policy to submit to the English authority. Accordingly Neyon informed Pontiac that no further assistance could be expected from the King of France, a tale of whose coming with a great army to annihilate the English having been persistently dinned into his ears, that peace had been concluded, that France had surrendered everything in America, and that the English were now the only rightful rulers. The sullen Pontiac received the tidings with disgust, broke the siege in no spirit of submission, and declared that he would return again in the spring and renew his warfare.

From the first the will of Pontiac ruled all the frontier, though absent in person. The war belt which he sent was a sufficient commission for stealthy murders and midnight scalpings and burnings along all the borders. On the receipt of news of the conclusion of peace, the settlers who had been driven from their cabins during the continuance of hostilities, supposing that the pacification would be made complete, hastened back to their settlements in the hope of getting their plantings and sewings made in season for crops that should be their support for the coming winter. But the decree of Pontiac disappointed all their hopes, and made this summer of 1763 the most bloody of all the seven. "About the first of June," it is recorded in the History of Western Pennsylvania, "the scalping parties perpetrated several murders in the vicinity of Fort Pitt. Upon receipt of this intelligence Governor Hamilton, with the assistance of the provincial commissioners, immediately reinforced the garrison at Augusta, and sent out small parties to protect the frontiers. As the first attack was not immediately followed up by the Indians, the government was willing to believe it to have been the effect of some private resentments, rather than a general combination for war. But such hopes were dissipated by inroads upon the settled parts of the province and the flight of the inhabitants to the interior. The whole country west of Shippensburg became the prey of the fierce barbarians. They set fire to houses, barns, corn, hay, and everything that was combustible. The wretched inhabitants whom they surprised at night, at their meals, or in the labors of the fields, were massacred with the utmost cruelty and barbarity; and those who fled were scarce more happy. Overwhelmed by sorrow, without shelter or means of transportation, their tardy flight was impeded by fainting women and weeping children. The inhabitants of Shippensburg and Carlisle, now become the barrier towns, opened their hearts and their houses to their afflicted brethren. In the towns, every stable and hovel was crowded with miserable refugees who, having lost their houses, their cattle and their harvest, were reduced from independence and happiness to beggary and despair. (On the 25th of July, 1763, there were in Shippensburg 1,384 of poor, distressed, back inhabitants, viz: men, 301; women, 345; children, 738; many of whom were obliged to lie in barns, stables, cellars, and under old leaky sheds, the dwelling houses being all crowded.) The streets were filled with people; the men, distracted by grief for their losses and the desire for revenge, more poignantly excited by the disconsolate females and bereaved children who wailed around them. In the woods, for some miles, on both sides of the Susquehanna River, many families with their cattle sought shelter, being unable to find it in towns."

While the scattered settlers fled for safety before the roving bands, the garrisons of the isolated forts far out beyond the farthest verge of the settlements were shut off from communication with their comrades whence succor could come, and were made the objects against which the best resources of the savages were directed. It was a new kind of warfare to them; but they had seen enough of siege work in the operations of the English against the French, to understand its nature, and to undertake it with all the relish inspired by a new thing. They had no artillery, but they could shoot fiery darts, mine with the zeal of a beaver, preserve constant vigils, and destroy by combustibles whatever was destructible that they could reach.

Presque Isle, next to Niagara and Detroit, was the most important post along the line of defenses, as it guarded the communication east and west, and being on water communication could be easily reached with supplies and reinforcements. On the 22d of June it was attacked. It had a garrison of twenty-four men and was easily defensible for any period. But the commander, Ensign Christy, after defending himself two days, in the most shameless manner capitulated, giving up all his men, who were no sooner in the hands of the savages than they were treacherously given over to the scalping knife, he himself being carried away a prisoner to Detroit reserved for future torments. The fort at Le Boeuf (Waterford), but a few miles away, on the head waters of the Venango River (French Creek), one of the tributaries of the Allegheny, had been attacked four days before. The fort was of combustible material, and at midnight the savages succeeded in firing it, when the garrison, seeing that the flames could not be stayed, secretly withdrew under cover of the darkness into the woods and made good their escape, the Indians believing them burned. On their way down the river they saw at Venango the ruins of the fort, the garrison there having all been massacred, not one escaping to tell the tale.

Fort Pitt (Pittsburg), which had been laid out and its construction pushed with so much energy, had never been finished, and the floods of spring which had eaten in upon the banks with great violence had opened it on three sides. Captain Ecuyer, who was in command, had with him a garrison of three hundred and thirty men. With energy and skill he had reared a rampart on the unprotected sides, had palisaded the interior work, and had constructed an engine for extinguishing fire should the foe succeed in firing the work.

On the 22d of June, the very day on which the attack had been made at Presque Isle, the dusky warriors made their appearance before Fort Pitt, and commenced the attack, investing it on all sides, killing one and wounding another. With prying eye they skulked around at night peering in on every side to discover if possible its weak part. Concluding, probably, that the work would be a difficult one to overcome, and judging that strategy would be surer of success than force, after midnight they asked for a parley. Turtle Heart, chief of the Delawares spoke: " Brothers," he said, "all your posts and strong places, from this backwards are burnt and cut off. This is the only one you have left in our country. We have prevailed with six different nations of Indians, that are ready to attack you, to forbear till we came and warned you to go home. They have further agreed to permit you and your people to pass safe to the inhabitants. Therefore, brother, we desire that you may set off to-morrow, as great numbers of Indians are coming here, and after two days we shall not be able to do anything with them for you." Their purpose in this exhortation was doubtless to get the garrison in their power and then massacre them as they had done at Presque Isle, which had induced General Amherst to observe, " I am surprised that any officer in his senses would enter into terms with such barbarians."

To this apparently innocent and reasonable appeal, Ecuyer sternly refused to listen, but reminded them that three English armies were on their way to chastise them, and that it was they who should be seeking safety. The fort was now closely invested and no intelligence could be sent through, either to or from the fort. Though suffering for lack of many things necessary for the comfort and successful defence of the fort, the gallant captain vigilantly held and guarded it, though wounded by an Indian arrow, the foe using most skillfully all their savage implements of warfare. Again and again was the demand for the surrender of the fort made. Shingiss and Big Wolf speaking for the Delawares and Shawnees said, "You know this is our country. You yourselves are the people that have disturbed the chain of friendship. All the nations over the lakes are soon to be on their way to the forks of the Ohio. Here is the wampum. If you return quietly home, to your wise men, this is the furthest they will go. If not, see what will be the consequence; so we desire you to remove off.". In his answer Ecuyer said, "You suffered the French to settle in the heart of your country; why would you turn us out of it now? I will not abandon this post; I have warriors, provisions, and ammunition in plenty to defend it three years against all the Indians in the woods. Go home to your towns, and take care of your women and children."

', The siege was now pushed with redoubled vigor, digging holes by night and running their trenches close up to the walls of the fort, and keeping up a galling fire of musketry and fiery arrows from their safe hiding places upon the defenders. This close investment was continued till the close of July; but on the 1st of August all had disappeared, a danger which Ecuyer had threatened now impending. General Amherst, who was still in command of the English army in America, when informed of the general Indian war which had broken out under the inspiration of the savage Pontiac, was without sufficient troops with which to meet the threatened danger, a large part of the British regulars having been sent to the West Indies. His energies were bent with what scattered forces he could gather up, to the relief of Detroit, Niagara and Fort Pitt. Fortunately Niagara was not attacked. For the relief of Fort Pitt Colonel Boquet was dispatched with the fragments of the Forty-seventh and Seventy-seventh regiments of Highlanders, comprising only 214 and 133 men respectively, and these greatly weakened by their severe service in the siege of Havanna. At Carlisle, he was to be furnished with supplies; but upon his arrival there, no supplies were collected, and eighteen days were consumed in gathering them. Plenty of grain stood ripe ready for the sickle, but the reapers were gone, and the mills were deserted. With scarcely five hundred men Boquet moved boldly forward on that bloody path which had been so often traversed before with such disastrous results, driving two hundred sheep, and half the number of kine, bearing ammunition, flour, and provisions carried upon pack-horses and in wagons drawn by oxen. Beyond the Alleghanies was Fort Ligonier, held by a small garrison under command of Lieutenant Blane. It was of the utmost importance that this should be held, as the stores of ammunition deposited there if allowed to fall into the hands of the Indians would afford them the means of prolonging the war. Besides, it furnished a rallying point for the force in advancing, and falling back if misfortune should overtake them. Accordingly, Boquet dispatched thirty picked men under a discreet officer to proceed by forced marches to gain the fort. This they successfully accomplished, carrying succor to the closely beleaguered post. A party of skilled woodsmen had previously been sent out from Fort Bedford, a point midway between Carlisle and Fort Pitt, one hundred miles from either point.

Boquet could get no information on the way, as roving bands of Indians picked off any one who ventured to pass from one point to the other, though the savages were kept constantly informed of every movement of the troops. Arrived with his main body at Ligonier, the Colonel determined to leave his wagons, and proceed only encumbered with pack-horses. By the road that he was to follow, was a dangerous defile of several miles in extent overhung by high craggy hills. This he was familiar with, and intended to pass it by a night march, hoping thus to surprise the foe and escape an attack by them on this difficult ground. At Bushy Run, a tributary of Brush Run and that of Turtle Creek, and twenty-one miles from Pittsburg, he had intended to halt for rest; but when arrived within a half mile of this point, on August 5th, he was suddenly attacked by an unseen foe, who came upon him unawares. A charge upon the attacking party sent them fleeing; but when pushed in one direction they appeared in another, and soon they attacked along the whole flank. A steady charge of the regulars sent them back, but only to appear again in another part, until they had the little force of Boquet completely surrounded by a continuous line, and were becoming every moment more daring and eager for the fight. They, no doubt, believed that they now had the whole force completely in their power, and would soon have the fighting men picked off from their hiding places. It must be acknowledged that the prospect seemed gloomy enough. Should this army be now sacrificed, the whole frontier would be thrown open to the attacks of the stealthy savages, and the tomahawk and the scalping-knife would bear undisputed sway, even to the very doors of Philadelphia.

But Boquet understood the methods of savage warfare better than Braddock, and Halket, and Dunbar, and was unmoved by the fierce whoop of the Red Man or his gleaming scalping knife. He could not advance in any direction and leave his pack-horses and his stores, as they would immediately fall into the hands of the foe. He, accordingly, formed his forces in a circle facing outwards, and drew up his trains in the center. Noticing that the Indians were becoming more and more eager for the fray, and every moment more venturesome, Boquet determined to give them a taste of their own tactics. At dawn of the second day of the action the enemy were early awake, and opened the battle with the most horrid and unearthly screechings. Having the advantage of elevated ground, and being somewhat concealed by the foliage of the trees and bushes, Boquet could maneuver his forces without disclosing his movements. Seeing that the savages were eager to rush forward whenever they saw the least disposition of the troops to yield, he determined to feign a retreat. He accordingly ordered the two companies occupying the advance to retire within the circle, and the lines again to close up, as if the whole force was commencing the retreat But before commencing this movement he had posted a force of light infantry in ambuscade, who, if the Indians should follow the retreating troops, would have them at their mercy   The stratagem succeeded precisely as had been anticipated.   The Indians, seeing the troops retreating, and the feeble lines closing in behind them, as if covering the retirement, rushed forward in wildest confusion and in great numbers   But when the grenadiers who had been posted on either side, saw then opportunity they advanced from their concealment, and charged with the greatest steadiness, shooting down the savages in great numbers, who returned the fire, but soon broke in confusion and disorderly flight But now the companies of light infantry which had been posted on the opposite side, rose up from their ambush and received the flying mass with fresh volleys.   Seized with terror at this unexpected disaster, and having lost many of their best fighting men and war chiefs, they became disheartened, and seeing the regulars giving close pursuit, they broke and fled in all directions.   All efforts of their surviving chiefs to rally and form them were unavailing.   They could no longer be controlled; but breaking up they fled singly and in parties to their homes, many of them not pausing till they had reached the country of the Muskingum

Boquet, though entirely successful in this, the battle of Bushy Run, had lost nearly a fourth of his whole army, fifty killed, sixty wounded and five missing, and nearly all his pack-horses, and therefore took every precaution to avoid a surprise and further loss.   He destroyed all his stores which he could not carry with him, that they might not fall into the enemy's hands, and moved forward in close order; but without further molestation, and in four days reached Fort Pitt, the enemy having been so thoroughly broken that they did not again show themselves before the fort.   The savages lost in this engagement sixty killed and many wounded in the pursuit.

As the tidings of the fall of post after post, along the whole frontier, came day after day to General Amherst, who had his head-quarters at New York, and of the savage attacks upon Detroit and Fort Pitt, his anger knew no bounds.   He recognized in Pontiac the chief of the conspiracy and the investigator of all their savage designs.   Before receiving news of the success of Boquet, he wrote to Gladwin, by the hand of Gardiner:—"The Senecas, and all these hostile tribes must be deemed our enemies, and used as such; not

as a generous enemy, but as the vilest race of beings that ever infested the earth, and whose riddance from it must be esteemed a meritorious act, for the good of mankind. You will, therefore, take no prisoners, but put to death all that fall into your hands of the nations who have so unjustly and cruelly committed depredations. I have thought proper to promise a reward of one hundred pounds to the man who shall kill Pontiac, the chief of the Ottawas—a cowardly villain."

Though the campaign of 1763 had been disastrous to English arms in America, yet its termination in the triumph of Bushy Run and relief of Fort Pitt, and the complete toil given to all the plans of Pontiac, which he personally conducted, gave the Indians a gloomy outlook for the future. Nevertheless, Pontiac returned in the spring of 1764 to the siege of Detroit. General Gage, who had succeeded Amherst in command in America, determined to push the campaign with a strong hand. Two expeditions were planned, one to advance under Colonel Bradstreet by Niagara, Presque Isle and Sandusky, and a second under Colonel Boquet by way of Fort Pitt and the country of the Muskingum. Sir William Johnson had always possessed great influence with the Indians, especially with the Six Nations, occupying the greater part of New York, and during the winter of 1763-64 had sent out messengers to all the tribes advising peace. Hence when Bradstreet reached Presque Isle, he was met by the chiefs, Shawnees and Delawares, and at Sandusky by the Ottawas, Wyandotts, and Miamis, who, under the garb of peace and friendship, desired to make a treaty of pacification. But, notwithstanding their promises, murders and massacres continued. At Detroit, he was met by the Ottawas, Ojibwas, Pottawattamies, Sacs, and Wyandotts, who likewise made treaties of peace; but they were unable either to control the young warriors, or they never meant to comply with the terms they had agreed to, and the whole campaign proved fruitless, Bradstreet returning to Niagara, and Gage issuing orders to annul all his treaties.

Not so with Boquet, who knew the Indian tactics better. With five hundred regulars and a thousand provincials he marched from Carlisle on the 5th of August, and arrived at Fort Pitt about the middle of September. He had received a message from Bradstreet on the way informing him that he had concluded treaties of peace with all the western tribes, and that it would be unnecessary to proceed further. But Boquet knew that the Colonel had been duped, and pushed forward with his army. At Fort Pitt Boquet learned that the messenger sent by him to Bradstreet had been murdered and his head set up upon a pole in the road. The chiefs of Delawares, Senecas, and Shawnees waited upon him on his arrival and advised peace, and that he proceed no further, alleging that their young men had committed the outrages charged without authority. Boquet boldly charged faithlessness, and that they should punish their young men if they disobeyed He boldly marched on down the Ohio into the very heart of the Indian country, and so stern were his words and so summary his threats, and the taste of his fighting had inspired such dread, that the tribes sent their chiefs to sue for peace. Boquet met them in the midst of his army, and in answer to their entreaties for peace charged them with constantly breaking their promises. " You have," said he, " promised at every former treaty, as you do now, to deliver up all your prisoners, and have received at every time presents, but have never complied with the engagements. I am now to tell you, therefore, that the English will no longer be imposed upon by your promises This army shall not leave your country until you have fully complied with every condition that is to precede a treaty with you. * * * If I find you faithfully execute the following preliminary conditions, I will not treat you with the severity you deserve I give you twelve days to deliver into my hands all the prisoners in your possession. without any exception. Englishmen, Frenchmen, women and children, whether adopted in your tribes, married or living amongst you under any denomination and pretense, whatsoever, together with all the negroes "

The stern tone of the brave Colonel had the desired effect They saw before them a man determined to enforce his commands surrounded by soldiers ready to execute vengeance. They became submissive and a part of them asked for peace, but the Colonel refused to take them by the hand until their promises were fulfilled, and the terms of peace fully agreed upon The chiefs were much grieved by this lack of confidence, and used their utmost endeavors to induce their people to bring forward their captives. By the 9th of November all the captives had been brought in and delivered up, to the number of two hundred and six,—Virginians, thirty-two males and fifty-eight females, and Pennsylvanians, forty-nine males and sixty-seven females This number did not include nearly a hundred in the hands of the Shawnees, who were to gather and deliver them up in the following spring.

When all had been accomplished, Keyashuta, chief of the Senecas, a tribe of the Delawares spoke: "Brother, the misfortune which has happened of one of your people being murdered, gives us the same sorrow it gives you. By this string of wampum (giving one) we wipe the tears from your eyes, and remove from your heart the resentment which this murder has raised against us * * * We have strictly complied with your desire, and now deliver you these three prisoners, which are the last of your flesh and blood that remain among us. * * * Brother, we cover the bones which have been buried, in such a manner, that they never more be remembered. We cover them again with leaves, that the place where they are buried, may never more be seen As we have been a long time astray, and the path between us and you stopped, we hope the path will be again cleared, and we now extend this belt of wampum between you and us, that we may again travel in peace to see our brothers as our ancestors formerly did * * * As we have now extended a belt representing the road between you and us, we beg that you will take fast hold of it, that the path may always be kept open between us."

In answer to these earnest sentiments of peace Colonel Boquet replied: "I bury the bones of the people who fell in the war, so that the place be no more seen (presents a belt). Your readiness in complying with every condition I have already required of you, convinces me that your intentions are upright, and I will now treat you as brethren (presents a belt). Brother you ask peace. The King, my master, and your father, has appointed me to make war upon you; but he has other servants who are employed in the work of peace, and his majesty has been pleased to empower Sir William Johnson to make peace with the Indians." Before departing, however, he required that the four hostages to be kept at Fort Pitt until peace was finally settled, should be delivered to him, and that the deputies to be sent to Sir William Johnson should be fully empowered to conclude the terms of peace, and that they should agree to abide by the terms thus concluded These conditions having been settled, Boquet shook hands with them in token of his satisfaction, which greatly rejoiced the hearts of the savages.

The Shawnees were the most resolute in their enmity and were the last to yield Boquet was ready to move against them; but on the 12th of November they met the Colonel in conference and said, Red Hawk speaking: "One year and a half ago we made peace with you at Fort Pitt, which was soon after broken; but that was neither your fault nor ours; but the whole blame is to be laid to the Ottawas (Pontiac's tribe), who are a foolish people, and are the cause of this war. When we now saw you coming this road, you advanced towards us with a tomahawk in your hand, but we, your younger brothers, take it out of your hand and send it up to God to dispose of it as he pleases, by which means we hope never to see it any more. And now, brethren, we beg leave that you, who are warriors, will take hold of this chain of friendship and receive it from us, who are always warriors, and let us think no more of war, but to take pity on our old men, women and children "

Boquet received the captives whom they brought, but sternly reminded them of their long holding back and tardiness in bringing in the prisoners. He demanded the rest of the captives, and that six of their chiefs should be delivered into his hands as hostages. When these terms had been agreed to he said: "I came here determined to strike you, with a tomahawk in my hand; but since you have submitted, it shall not fall upon your heads. I will let it drop, and it shall no more be seen. I bury the bones of all the people who have fallen in this war, and cover the place with leaves so that it shall no more be perceived."

The long captivity of many of those who were brought in had effaced from their recollection all memory of their former relatives and friends, and they preferred to remain with the savages, having come now to know no other way of life. The savages religiously observed their promises, bringing in all their captives even to the children who had been born to the women during their captivity. So wedded were many of the captives to the Indians that the Shawnees were obliged to bind many of them in order to bring them in. Some, after being delivered up, escaped and returned to their life in the woods. The Indians parted with their adopted families not without many tears. Many affecting scenes transpired when the captives were brought, and those who had lost friends and relatives recognized their own after long separation. The children who had been carried away in tender years and had grown up in savage life, knowing no other, could not recognize their own parents and timidly approached them. The Shawnees chief gave those who had recovered children or friends some good advice: "Father, we have brought your flesh and blood to you; they have all been united to us by adoption, and although we now deliver them up to you, we will always look upon them as our relations, whenever the Great Spirit is pleased that we may visit them. We have taken as much care of them as if they were our own flesh and blood. They are now become unacquainted with your customs and manners, and therefore we request you will use them tenderly and kindly, which will induce them to live contentedly with you."

Many of the Indians, who had given up captives whom they loved, followed the army back, that they might be with them as long as possible, bringing them corn, skins, horses, and articles which the captives had regarded as their own, hunting and bringing in game for them. A young Mingo had loved a young Virginia woman and made her his wife. In defiance of the dangers to life which he submitted himself to in going among the exasperated settlers, he persisted in following her back.

"A number of the restored prisoners were brought to Carlisle, and Colonel Boquet advertised for those who had lost children to come to this place and look for them. Among those that came was a German woman, a native of Rentlingen, in Wittemberg, Germany, who with her husband had emigrated to America prior to the French war, and settled in Lancaster County, Tulpehocken, where two of her daughters, Barbara and Regina, were abducted by the Indians   The mother was now unable to designate her children, even if they should be among the number of the recaptured.   With her brother, the distressed, aged woman lamented to Colonel Boquet her hopeless case, telling him how she used, years ago, to sing to her little daughters, hymns of which they were fond.   The Colonel requested her to sing one of the hymns, which she did in these words:

> Allein, und doch nicht ganz alleine
> Bin ich in meiner Einsamkeit,
> Dann wann ich gleich verlassen scheine,
> Vertreibt mir Jesus selbst die zeit:
> Ich bin bei ihm, und er bei mir,
> So kommt mir gar nichts einsam für,
>
> Alone, yet not alone am I,
> Though in this solitude so drear,
> I feel my Savior always nigh.
> He comes, my dreary hours to cheer—
> I'm with him and he with me
> Thus, I cannot solitary be—

And Regina, the only daughter present, rushed into the arms of the mother.   Barbara, the other daughter, was never restored."

Though Pontiac still persisted in his hostility in the Detroit country, yet he could have no prospect of success.   The French had held out in their hostility to the English even after the treaty of Paris had been concluded, and this enmity was especially persevered in by the more lawless and revengeful, yet the fruitlessness of this course was becoming day by day more apparent.   Official notice, by order of the French court, was given of relinquishment of all power in Canada.   De Neyon, the commandant at Fort Charters, "sent belts," says Bancroft, " and peace pipes, to all parts of the continent, exhorting the many nations of savages to bury the hatchet, and take the English by the hand for they would never see him more. * * * The courier who took the belt to the north offered peace to all the tribes wherever he passed; and to Detroit, where he arrived on the last day of October, 1764, he bore a letter of the nature of a proclamation, informing the inhabitants of the cession of Canada to England; another addressed to twenty-five nations by name, to all the Red Men, and particularly to Pontiac, chief of the Ottawas; a third to the commander, expressing a readiness to surrender to the English all the forts on the Ohio, and east of the Mississippi   The next morning Pontiac sent to Gladwin, that he accepted the peace which his father, the French, had sent him, and desired all that had passed might be forgot on both sides."

Thus ended the conspiracy of Pontiac, a warrior unexcelled by any of his race for vigor of intellect and dauntless courage.   His end was ignoble.   An English trader hired a Peoria Indian for a barrel of rum to murder him.   The place of his death was Cahokia, a small village a little below St. Louis   He had been a chief leader in the army of the French in the battle with Braddock, at Monongahela, and he was held in high repute by the French General Montcalm, and at the time of his death, Pontiac was dressed in a French uniform presented to him by that commander.

CHAPTER XII.

First Settlers—Lands Must be Acquired of Indians — King's Proclamation—Lands West of the Alleghanies — "Fair Play" Court—Two Roads Leading West—Proclamation of Governor Penn—Little Heed to Them—Sachems Complain —Settlers Placate the Local Tribes by Kindness—Gage to Penn and Reply—Law Passed Giving the Settlers to Death Who Do Not Move Off—Notice Given—Indians Interfere—Settlers Willing to Remove though Encouraged to Remain—Postscript to Report—Names of Settlers—Indian Conference at Fort Pitt—Murder of Indians—Satisfied by Presents—Indians Agree to Warn Off the Settlers—Finally Decline — Reasons—Plan to Secure the Removal by Indians in the Interest of Philadelphia Speculators—Hillsborough Attempts to Destroy Virginia Claim —Eagerness to Secure Blocks of these Western Lands by Speculators—Great Gathering at Fort Stanwix—Treaty Made—Lands Acquired—Pennsylvania Land Office Opened — Rush of Applicants — Case of Henry Taylor — Testimony—Dishonest Claimants.

HITHERTO no permanent settlements had been made in the limits of what is now known as Greene County.   Traders had for some years previous passed through all this section of country, and had tarrying posts, where the natives were met and bartered with for valuable skins and furs, furnishing them in return with traps, axes, knives, guns and ammunition.   But no permanent settlements, in which families had come and taken up the land they proposed to reclaim, and erected huts for shelter and a home, had been attempted.   Veech, in his Monongahela of Old, states that the Brown's, Wendell and his sons, Mannus and Adam, were among the earliest thus to come. They came in 1750, or perhaps a little earlier, and settled in Jacob's Creek valley in what is now Fayette County. Early in the '50's, Christopher Gist, whom we have previously mentioned, planted himself in the valley east of the Monongahela, and others followed into these pleasant regions. Though we have no definite information respecting the number of settlers up to this time, yet there must have been a considerable population gathered in during the period from 1760 to '70; for Mason and Dixon record in their field notes under date of September 30, 1767, "Sent to Redstone for more hands."

The colonial governments nominally held that settlers had no right to occupy any lands that had not been formally purchased of the Indians, and the purchase been confirmed by treaty stipulations None of the territory west of the Alleghany Mountains had been thus secured previous to 1768, though the Ohio company, which had been formed in Virginia in 1748, had stipulated for the settlement of 100 families within seven years. A treaty had been held at Lancaster, as before noted, on the 21st of June, 1744, at which representatives of Pennsylvania, Maryland and Virginia were present, and a vast tract west of the mountains was purchased and paid for in goods and gold. But the Indians who dwelt upon these lands repudiated the purchase, as did the Six Nations, and indeed the British government subsequently. But the Ohio Company proceeded to send settlers on the strength of this purchase, as did the government of Pennsylvania. However, when the seven years' war broke out in 1756, all settlements in this western country were abandoned. During the pendency of the operations under Colonel Boquet against the Indians in the Pontiac war, the King of Great Britain had issued his proclamation, in the hope of pacifying the Indians, forbidding settlements in these words: "Whereas, it is just and reasonable, and essential to our interest, and the security of our colonies, that the several nations or tribes of Indians with whom we are connected, and who live under our protection, should not be molested or disturbed in the possession of such parts of our dominions and territories as, not having been ceded to, or purchased by us, are reserved to them, or any of them, as their hunting grounds; we do, therefore, with the advice of our privy council, declare it to be our royal will and pleasure * * * that no Governor or Commander-in-chief of our other colonies or plantations in America, do presume for the present, and until our further pleasure be known, to grant warrants of survey, or pass patents for any lands beyond the heads or sources of any of the rivers which fall into the Atlantic Ocean from the west or northwest, or upon any lands whatever, which never having been ceded to, or purchased by us, are reserved to the said Indians * * * and we do hereby strictly forbid, on pain of our displeasure, all our loving subjects from making any purchases or settlements whatever or taking possession of any of the lands above reserved, without our special leave and license for that purpose first obtained. And we do further strictly enjoin and require all persons whatever, who have either wilfully or inadvertently seated themselves upon any lands within the countries above described, or upon any other lands * * * which are still reserved to the said Indians, *forthwith to remove themselves, from such settlements.*"

It will be seen by this royal proclamation, that all lands west of the sources of the rivers falling into the Atlantic Ocean were withheld from settlement, as not having been legally purchased of the Indians, and settlers who had taken lands there were summoned to vacate them. But the settlers paid little heed to this proclamation, and when the peace secured by Colonel Boquet was declared, in 1764, hardy settlers hastened back to the tracts which they had previously selected, and many more followed in their footsteps. As they could claim no protection from the government, entering upon their lands in direct violation of the royal proclamation, they became a law unto themselves. In a note to Smith's laws, Vol. II, he says· "In the meantime, in violation of all law, a set of hardy adventurers had from time to time seated themselves upon this doubtful territory. They made improvements, and formed a very considerable population. It is true so far as regards the rights to real property, they were not under the protection of the laws of the country; and were we to adopt the visionary theory of some philosophers, who have drawn their arguments from a supposed state of nature, we might be led to believe that the state of these people, would have been a state of continual warfare, and that in contests for property the weakest must give way to the strongest. To prevent the consequences, real or supposed, of this state of things, they formed a mutual compact among themselves. They annually elected a tribunal, in rotation of three of their settlers, whom they called Fair-play-men, who were to decide all controversies and set tle disputed boundaries. From their decision there was no appeal. There could be no resistance. The decree was enforced by the whole body, who started up in mass, at the mandate of the court and execution and eviction were as sudden and irresistible as the judgment Every new comer was obliged to apply to this powerful tribunal, and, upon his solemn engagement to submit in all respects to the law of the land, he was permitted to take possession of some vacant spot. Their decrees were however just; and when their settlements were recognized by law and "Fair-play" had ceased, their decisions were received in evidence and confirmed by judgments of courts." The "Fair-play" dominions were embraced in the purchase

G. W. Moss

which was made in 1768, of which the territory of Greene formed a part.

There were two roads leading through the rugged ranges of the Alleghany Mountains, which led from the settlements on the Delaware and the James to the country of the Monongahela; that opened by Wills' Creek (Cumberland) the Great Meadows, and Redstone (Brownsville) for the passage of Braddock's army, which became substantially the route of the national road of Jefferson's time, and that by Bedford, Ligonier and Royalhanna, opened for the passage of the army of General Forbes. Strictly, the English armies according to the royal proclamation above quoted, except the ever ready one of military necessity, had no right to cut these roads and march armies over them. Indeed, the Ohio Company, which claimed its authority from the crown, was acting in contravention to that proclamation, though they held that the treaty which their agents had concluded with the Indians, was their warrant. "During the summer of 1760," says Albach, " General Monkton, by a treaty at Fort Pitt, obtained leave to build posts within the wild lands, each post having ground enough about it to raise corn and vegetables for the use of the garrison Nor were the settlements of the Ohio Company 'and the forts the only inroads upon the hunting grounds of the savages. In 1757, by the books of the secretary of Virginia, three millions of acres had been granted west of the mountains. Indeed, in 1758, that State attempted by law to encourage settlements in the West"

So disastrous had been the wars with the Indians, and so bitter their hatred of the settlers, that government exercised care in preventing encroachments and in removing intruders upon unacquired territory. Governor Penn, in September, 1766, issued his proclamation warning " all his majesty's subjects of this or any other province or colony from making any settlements, or taking any possession of lands, by marking trees or otherwise, beyond the limits of the last Indian purchase, that of 1758, within this province, upon pain of the severest penalties of the law, and of being excluded from the privilege of securing such settlements should the lands where they shall be made be hereafter purchased of the Indians." A little earlier, in June of this year, Captain Mackay, with a squadron of English regulars was sent out from Fort Pitt to Redstone, to order the settlers away. Governor Farquier, of Virginia, issued a proclamation of a tenor similar to that of Governor Penn

But notwithstanding the loud words of royal and governor's proclamations, and the presence of the king's troops, it is probable that little heed was given to these commands by the hardy pioneers who had ventured forth in small parties and pressed into this beautiful and fruitful country, where they could get the best lands by

10

"squatting" on them, and driving a few stakes. They made fast friends of the Indians, whom they casually met, by gifts and kindnesses. But the great war Sachems looked with a jealous eye upon these encroachments, and made loud complaints to the colonial authorities So threatening had these protests become near the close of 1767, that General Gage, who had succeeded General Amherst in the command of the royal forces in America, wrote to Governor Penn, that Sir William Johnson, who was the most trusted medium between the English and the Indians, to whom the latter were accustomed freely to unbosom themselves, had advised him that there was danger of an immediate rupture, the chief ground of complaint being "the obstinacy of the people who persist to settle on their lands."

In his reply, Governor Penn very judiciously and candidly observes: "With respect to the inefficiency of the laws to secure the Indians in their persons and properties, I would beg leave to observe that the remote situation of their country, and the dispersed and vagrant manner in which the people live, will generally render the best laws that can be framed for those ends in a great measure ineffectual The civil officers, whose business it is to see that they are duly enforced, cannot exert their authority in so distant and extensive a wilderness In the execution thereof, of the present interesting matter, I am persuaded that, notwithstanding, all the Legislature can do, I shall find it necessary to apply the military aid, which you have so readily offered me in support of the civil power. Yet I fear that while the severity of the weather in the winter season continues, it will be found extremely difficult, if not impracticable, to oblige these lawless people to abandon their present habitations, and to remove with their families and effects into the interior part of the country, and I am of the opinion that it would be unadvisable to make any attempt of that kind before spring"

At the opening of the legislative session of 1768, the Governor called attention to these irregularities, and called upon the Assembly to pass such a law as will effectually remedy these provocations, and the first law of the session was one providing that if any person settled upon lands not purchased of the Indians by the proprietaries, shall refuse to remove for the space of thirty days after having been requested so to do, or if any person shall remove and then return, or shall settle on such lands after the notice of the provisions of this act have been duly proclaimed, any such persons on being duly convicted shall be put to death without benefit of clergy.

This statute having been duly enacted, it was printed with a proclamation of the Governor, and a committee consisting of John Steel, John Allison, Christopher Lemes and James Potter, were dispatched to the Monongahela country to distribute these documents and give the necessary notice.

This embassage was faithfully performed, the settlers being called together and the law and the message of the Governor being read to them, and the occasion of the action. Upon their return they made a report of their proceedings in which they say: " We arrived at the settlement on Redstone on the twenty-third day of March. The people having heard of our coming had appointed a meeting among themselves, on the twenty-fourth, to consult what measures they should take. We took the advantage of this meeting, read the act of assembly and proclamation, explaining the law, and giving the reason of it as well as we could, and used our endeavors to persuade them to comply, alleging to them that it was the most probable method, to entitle them to favor with the honorable proprietaries when the land was purchased. After lamenting their distressed condition, they told us the people were not fully collected; but as they expected, all would attend on the Sabbath following, then they would give us answer. They, however, affirmed that the Indians were very peaceable, and seemed sorry they were to be removed; and said they apprehended the English intended to make war upon the Indians, as they were moving off their people from their neighborhood. We labored to persuade them that they were imposed on by a few straggling Indians, that Sir William Johnson, who had informed our government, must be better acquainted with the mind of the Six Nations, and that they were displeased with the white people settling on their unpurchased lands. On the Sabbath a considerable number attended, and most of them told us they were resolved to move off, and would petition your honor for preference in obtaining their improvements when a purchase was made."

" While we were conversing, we were informed that a number of Indians had come to Indian Peters! We, judging it might be subservient to our main design that the Indians should be present while we were advising the people to obey the law, sent for them. They came, and after sermon delivered a speech, with a string of wampum to be transmitted to your Honor. The speech was: ' Ye are come, sent by the great men to tell these people to go away from the land, which you say is ours; and we are sent by our great men, and are glad we have met here this day. We tell you the white people must stop, and we stop them till the treaty, and when George Croghan and our great men will talk together we will tell them what to do! * * * After this the people were more confirmed that there was no danger of war. They dropped the design of petitioning, and said they would wait the issue of the treaty. Some, however, declared they would move off."

By a similar manner of procedure, the settlers on Cheat River, and Stewart's crossings of Youghiogheny were met, and copies of the law and proclamation were sent to Turkeyfoot, and other scattered settlers. In conclusion they say: "It is our opinion that some will move off, in obedience to the law, that the greater part will wait the treaty, and if they find the Indians indeed dissatisfied, we think that the whole can be persuaded to remove. The Indians coming to Redstone and delivering their speech greatly obstructed our design."

This closed the report of the commissioners; but a private letter of the chairman, John Steel, to the Governor, discloses the secret spring that may have been moving in this whole matter, and gives a smack of the milk that is in the cocoanut. He says: "Sir, there is one thing which, in preparing the extract of our journal, happened to be overlooked, viz : The people at Redstone alleged that the removing them from the unpurchased lands was a contrivance of the gentlemen and merchants of Philadelphia, that they might take rights for their improvements when a purchase was made In confirmation of this, they said that a gentleman of the name of Harris, and another called Wallace, with one Priggs, a pilot, spent a considerable time last August in viewing the lands and creeks thereabouts We promised to acquaint your honor with this " It was a most fortunate lapse of memory on the part of the commissioners that they forgot to put any mention of this little scheme into their report, as it might have been made public and defeated the underlying motive of their mission. Mr. Steel adds in this note, " I am of opinion from the appearance of the people and the best intelligence we could obtain, that there are but about an hundred and fifty families in the different settlements."

The commissioners appended the names of the men whom they met, and as this gives a clue to the earliest settlers in the country of the Monongahela they are given as one of the very early records of 1768: "John Wiseman, Henry Prisser, William Linn, William Colvin, John Vervalson, Abraham Tygard (Teagarden), Thomas Brown, Richard Rogers, John Delong, Peter Young, George Martin, Henry Swartz, Joseph McLeon, Jesse Martin, Adam Hatton, John Vervul, Jr., James Waller, Thomas Douter, Captain Coburn, Michael Hooter, Andrew Linn, Gabriel Conn, Thomas Down, Andrew Gudgeon (Gudgel), Phil Sute (Shute), James Crawford, John Peters, John Martin, Hans Cock, Daniel McCay, Josias Crawford, —— Province " At Gist's place were· "James Lyne, —— Blounfield (Brownfield), Eze Johnson, Thomas Guesse (Gist), Charles Linsey, James Wallace, Richard Harrison, Jet. Johnson, Henry Burken (Burkham), Lawrence Harrison, Ralph Hickenbottom, and at Turkeyfoot, Henry Abrahams, Eze Dewit, James Spence, Benjamin Jennings, John Cooper, John Enslow, Henry Enslow, Benjamin Pursley." It is probable that many of these names have a different form from the names borne by descendants of the same families; but there is no doubt that many of the inhabitants of the Monongahela country at the present day are the descendants of these people who had planted themselves here in the wilderness nearly a century and a quarter ago.

Preparations had been for some time in progress for holding a conference with the Indians at Fort Pitt   George Croghan, who was the deputy under Sir William Johnson, had the matter in charge, and had informed Governor John Penn that if he wished to be represented he should send delegates. The council convened on the 26th of April and lasted till the 9th of May, John Allen and Joseph Shippen, Jr, representing Pennsylvania   The records show that the Indians were very fully represented, twelve Sachems, six war chiefs, and two hundred and ninety braves, besides women and children (which accompanied all the tribes) of the Six Nations, thirteen Sachems, nine war chiefs, and three hundred and eleven braves of the Delawares; ten Sachems, eight war chiefs, and one hundred and forty braves of the Shawneese; five Sachems and one hundred and ninety-six braves of the Munsies; three Sachems and ninety warriors of the Mohickions; seven of the Wyandots; in all, eleven hundred, besides women and children

The first business considered was the atonement for the murder of Indians which had recently been perpetrated by the enraged settlers, who had taken it upon themselves to avenge the outrages which had been perpetrated by the red men in the way of murders, scalpings and burnings in the progress of the late wars—the victims in most cases being wholly innocent, whose only crime was that of having a red skin and being clothed in feathers and paint. Much palaver was had over this subject, the great chiefs airing their wild rhetoric of the woods very freely. The representative of the white men, Croghan, shrewdly admitted everything charged, bewailing their losses, and grieving over their wounded feelings. But he had come prepared to amend all, and when he brought out the " piled up" presents to the amount of over fourteen hundred pounds, the warrior braves regarded them with grunts of satisfaction, and freely forgave all.

The council was a long time in reaching the second subject of consideration, what should be the decision in regard to settlers on the lands not purchased of the rightful owners. There appear to have been no friends of the settlers admitted to the council, the agents of the Pennsylvania government, Allen and Shippen, being only intent on securing the execution of that barbarous statute which prescribed hanging if they did not summarily give up their homes. Tohonissawgorrawa, the sound of whose name was enough to inspire terror, at length was induced to enter a complaint addressed to

Brother Ouas (Penn) against the English for entering upon lands not yet bought, and demanding that they be removed. The answer made by the Pennsylvania commissioners disclosed the sole purpose which they had. They explained the provisions of the law recently passed, relating to this subject of removal, showed the result of the labors of the agents sent to deliver printed copies of the law and Governor's proclamation; but bewail the fact, that after the settlers had been persuaded to leave, there came certain Mingo Indians, who exhorted them to stay until the result of this treaty should be made known. Allen and Shippen now demanded that discreet chieftains should be sent to the settlers to order their immediate departure. After this is done say they: " If they shall refuse to remove by the time limited them, you may depend upon it the government will not fail to put the law into execution against them." The proposition of the Pennsylvania agents that the Indians should send some of their wise men to warn the settlers off, and undo the mischief done by the Mingo messengers was agreed to, and a delegation was named on the part of the Six Nations, who received formal written instructions, and John Frazer and John Thompson were designated to accompany them on their errand. It was understood that they were to proceed on this mission at once. But after waiting several days and vainly importuning them to set off, they finally came to the commissioners and said that " they had been seriously considering the business they were going to be sent on, and it now appeared to them so disagreeable that they could by no means consent to undertake it, and immediately returned the wampum which had been given them. * * * The driving of white people away from their settlements was a matter which no Indians could with any satisfaction be concerned in, and they thought it most proper for the English themselves to compel their own people to remove from the Indians' lands."

Though the settlers had no representative admitted to the great conclave to speak for them, yet it is very evident that they had some shrewd member present with the Indians counseling with them and inspiring their replies. For while these answers are in entire harmony with the native dignity of these men of the forest; yet we cannot but believe that the timely appearance of the Mingo braves at Redstone, and their plea for the sitting of the settlers for the present, and now the refusal to undertake the embassage which they had formally agreed to in council and their very cogent and dignified reasons therefor, were inspired by an agent of the settlers. And this view is greatly strengthened when we consider the following written statement, which Guyasutha delivered to the Pennsylvania commissioners: " I now find that not only the Indians appointed by us, but all our other young men, are very unwilling to carry a message from us to the white people, ordering them to remove from our lands. They say they would not choose to incur the ill-will of those people; for if they should be now removed they will hereafter return to their settlements when the English have purchased the country from us. And we shall be very unhappy if, by our conduct towards them at this time, we shall give them reason to dislike us, and treat us in an unkind manner when they again become our neighbors. We therefore hope, brethren, you will not be displeased at us, for not performing our agreement with you, for you may be assured we have good hearts towards all our brethren, the English."

The true secret of this whole attempt to remove the settlers west of Alleghanies was this: Since the surveys made by Mason and Dixon which had been stopped by the Indians at the great war path on Dunkard Creek, Greene County, and within some thirty-six miles of the western boundary of the State, the State authorities and the magnates of Philadelphia being now definitely apprised of the southern limits of the colony, beheld a large number of settlers, mostly Virginians, whom the Ohio Company had been instrumental in bringing there, seated upon some of the finest lands in this whole Monongahela Valley, and they desired them dispossessed by the Indians, so that when all this stretch of country west of the Alleghanies should be acquired by purchase, it would be open for occupancy by Pennsylvanians. But in this business the Indians showed themselves unwilling to draw the chestnuts from the embers to accommodate the prospective purchasers. The settlers themselves were entirely innocent of any evil designs, having come upon these lands in the belief that the Ohio Company, which had the authority and encouragement of the British government, had acquired a just title to them, and that they owed allegiance to the State of Virginia which assumed a rightful authority over them. Having selected their lands, and with great toil and hardship made clearings and cultivations, they felt a deep reluctance to give them up, and believed that they could not be rightfully dispossessed. Hence, these early Virginia settlers were anxious to cultivate a good understanding with the Indians, which tended to promote further settlements, and came to look with an evil eye on the government of Pennsylvania, which had authorized their hanging if they did not remove.

In all these negotiations the Indians intimated that they expected to sell these lands west of the Alleghanies to the English. For in their excuses for not ordering off the white people, as they had agreed to do, they used this expression, " when the English shall have purchased the country from us." Virginia was the only colony which laid claim to the country drained by the Ohio River. The New England States, except Connecticut, were entirely cut off; New York could only extend westward to the lakes, Pennsylvania had exact limits prescribed by charter on the west, even if that limit was allowed, although Virginia was claiming the portion west of the Alleghany Mountains   But Virginia laid claim to the entire Ohio Valley north as well as south   This claim Hillsborough, the English Secretary, determined to curtail, by confirming the Indians in their claims to all these lands, at least until the claim of Virginia was broken, and accordingly ordered his agent, Stuart, to continue the line which he had traced along the western limits of the Carolinas, from Chiswell's mine to the mouth of the Kanawha   This line was confirmed by treaty with the Cherokees at Hard Labor on the 14th of October, 1768.   By this procedure all of Kentucky, as well as the entire territory northwest of the Ohio, would be relieved of the claim of Virginia, and the Indians be confirmed in absolute owner-ship.

The English Secretary was moreover jealous of the encroach-ments of the Spanish at St Louis and New Orleans, who were bidding for the fur trade of the lakes, and the Western settlers   By establish-ing the native tribes in their rights he thought to cut off this trade through their country, and not only stop emigration to these Western lands, but clear off the few who had already made improvements Hence this savage law of the Pennsylvania Legislature, imposing death on these settlers if they did not leave, was well pleasing to him.

There was much contention at this time both in the colonies and at the English court to obtain grants of these Western lands   The Ohio Company, Mississippi Company and Walpole's grants, which will be referred to further on, were specimens of this grasping spirit. Franklin was in England urging these grants and was in correspondence with his compeers in this country.   Sir William Johnson was not without ambitious designs, and he had accordingly made arrange-ments for a grand conclave of Indians from far and near to be held at Fort Stanwix, now Rome, New York, in the mild October days of 1768.   The conference held at Fort Pitt, detailed above, earlier in the season, was but the forerunner of this grander meeting, and the munificent gifts there distributed were baits to lure the savages on.

Thomas Walker represented Virginia; Governor William Frank-lin, New Jersey; Governor Penn was present from Pennsylvania, but was obliged to leave before the business was completed.   Sir Will-iam Johnson represented New York and the English government, orders having been transmitted to him early in the spring to make the proposed purchase of lands and settle all difficulties with the In-dians.   The number of Indians present was extraordinary, being ac-cording to Bancroft a little short of three thousand   " Every art," he says, " was used to conciliate the chiefs of the Six Nations, and gifts were lavished on them with unusual generosity.   They in turn complied with the solicitations of the several agents.   The line that

Jacob Johns sen

was established began at the north, where Canada Creek joins Wood Creek; on leaving New York, it passed from the nearest fork of the West Branch of the Susquehanna to Kittanning on the Allegheny, whence it followed that river and the Ohio. At the mouth of the Kanawha it met the line of Stewart's treaty. Had it stopped here the Indian frontier would have been marked all the way from northern New York to Florida. But instead of following his instructions, Sir William Johnson pretended to recognize a right of the Six Nations to the largest part of Kentucky, and continued the line down the Ohio to the Tennessee River which was thus constituted the western boundary of Virginia." This was in contravention to the policy of Secretary Hillsborough, and again opened the extravagant claims of Virginia.

Thus was acquired, by the transactions of one day, the 5th of November, 1768, a day ever memorable in the annals of Western Pennsylvania, this hilarious carnival day of the Indians, a vast tract stretching away a thousand miles or more, enough for an empire of the largest proportions. It embraced in Pennsylvania the very farthest stretch from the Delaware River in the northeast to Greene County in the southwest, comprising the counties of Wayne, Susquehanna, Lackawanna, Luzerne, Wyoming, Sullivan, a part of Bradford, Columbia, Montour, Northumberland, Lycoming, Union, parts of Centre, Clinton, Clearfield, Indiana, Armstrong and Allegheny, and the counties entire of Cambria, Somerset, Westmoreland, Washington, Fayette and Greene. Thus was ended by one sweeping purchase a controversy with the Indians for possession of the soil along the waters of the Monongahela, which was beginning to threaten deadly feuds. We say ended; but not ended. The treaty was signed by the chiefs of the Six Nations, for themselves, their allies and defendants, the Shawnees, Delawares, Mingoes and others; but the Shawnees and Delaware deputies did not sign, and hence there was left open a plea for individual hostility, which for many years proved very grievous to the early settlers of Greene County, though the Six Nations claimed the right to themselves to make sale of all these lands by right of conquest of the natives which inhabited them, a right which the Delawares and Shawnees never dared to dispute.

The title of the government to all the lands along the Monongahela and upper Ohio being now thought to be complete, having a title deed for it from the Six Nations duly recorded, there was no reason why these lands should not be taken up under colonial authority. Virginia was laying claim to all this section of country, on what grounds we shall detail further on; but Pennsylvania having already extended its southern boundary as claimed by chartered right, very nearly to its western extremity, felt secure in extending the ægis of its power over these regions, though for the most part settled to this time by Virginians. Accordingly, early in the year 1769, public notice was given that the land office of the colony would be opened on the 3d of April for the sale of lands within the limits of the new purchase, at a price of five pounds sterling per one hundred acres, and a quit-rent of a penny per acre, the Proprietaries holding that as they had the land on condition of making of an annual payment of two beaver skins, they were obliged to impose an annual quit-rent to make a sale binding. A penny an acre, though seeming a mere nominal sum, if exacted on the whole territory of the State would bring a snug little income. By the rules of the office no one person was allowed to purchase more than three hundred acres.

As we have already seen numbers of hardy pioneers, previous to this date, had chosen lands, and made for themselves homes on the favorite spots throughout all this picturesque country southward from Fort Pitt, between the Ohio and Monongahela rivers, though they had acquired no recognized right to do so previous to the date named above. When the land office was opened on the morning of that day there was a great rush of applicants desiring to perfect a title to their lands. Among others who had settled on lands near the mouth of Ten Mile Creek, previous to 1768, was Abraham Teagarden, and among names of those who were granted patents for lands west of the Monongahela on this first day were those of Preston, Harrison, Fooks and Evans, and subsequently those of Hunter, McDowell, Drummond, Allman, Marshall, Indian Peter, Parkinson, Cox, Grimes and Taylor.

To illustrate the manner in which titles were acquired and conflicting claims were settled in those early times, the following extracts from the testimony in a suit for ejectment which was brought by the last named person, Henry Taylor, are here given, the case turning upon the question of priority of occupancy. Isaac Williams testified: " That in the year 1770 he saw Henry Taylor living in the forks of Chartiers Creek, he was improving that land that is now in dispute, and to make a settlement thereon; that he hired his brother, John Williams, to strengthen the improvements then claimed by said Taylor; that he knew the work to be done, as he hunted to get provision for the men while they were doing the work; that he also knew Taylor to pay his brother a rifle gun and some cash when he went away, and on his return paid the sum of eight pounds; that when they were doing the work he found a new cabin on the White Oak Ridge, appearing to have been built that winter; that on Taylor's finding that some person had been at work on his land he employed me to enquire, and if possible find out who it was, and to purchase their claim, which I found it to be Hugh Sidwell, and purchased the said White Oak cabin and all his claim for the sum of twenty shillings"

In answer to the question whether Bolzer Shilling did not make a practice of running about through the woods, marking and hazing trees and calling that his improvements, and that in great number," Williams answered, "He knew it well to be his constant practice" John Williams also testified "that he deadened some timber and cut and split five hundred rails on the Rich Hill tract, five hundred rails on the White Oak Ridge tract, that he built a good cabin and split five hundred rails on another tract, for which the said Taylor paid him before he left the settlement a rifle gun and four dollars cash, and the next spring when the said Taylor returned from Cecil County, Maryland, he paid me the remainder honorably, being eight pounds Pennsylvania money."

Frederick Lamb also testified, "That some time in the month of April, 1772, he came to Bolzer Shilling where he was doing some work on a certain tract of land where Richard Yates now dwells on; he had seen on a tree a small distance from them, with H. T. on it, which at the time he thought it had been Henry Taylor's claim, and he asked the said Bolzer, 'Was not this Henry Taylor's claim?' Bolzer answered 'Yes,' it is his claim, and that he was working there on purpose to affront said Taylor; and he wanted Taylor to come there on purpose to quarrel with him, and give Taylor a thrashing, and would black his eyes well.' He then told Bolzer that Henry Taylor was a civil man, and would not fight with him, and 'twas better to let alone. Then Bolzer said he would go up and let Van Sweringen have it, for Van was not ashamed of any mean action, and he knew Van to be rogue enough to cheat Taylor out of the land."

Better than pages of description this testimony of the early pioneers, informs us of the trials and hardships which the settlers had to endure in getting a foothold upon lands in this goodly country, in the face of disputed authority of the State, the jealousy of the natives, the quarrels of conflicting claimants, and the lying and cheating of dishonest bullies.

CHAPTER XIII.

TREATY OF 1784—CUMBERLAND COUNTY SEAT AT CARLISLE—BEDFORD
COUNTY—PITT AND SPRINGHILL TOWNSHIPS—ASSESSMENTS—
NAMES OF TAX PAYERS—WESTMORELAND COUNTY FORMED—
HANNASTOWN—ARTHUR ST. CLAIR—ROAD LAID OUT FROM
MOUTH OF FISHPOT RUN EASTWARD—IMPORTANT THOROUGHFARE
—CASE OF ELIZABETH SMITH—DELEGATES ASSUME ALL AU-
THORITY OVER THE COLONY—CONVENTION TO FORM A NEW
GOVERNMENT—FRANKLIN PRESIDENT—COMMITTEE OF SAFETY—
GOVERNOR JOHN PENN RELIEVED—THE FOUNDER REMEMBERED
GRATEFULLY—NEW CONSTITUTION, THOMAS WHARTON, PRESI-
DENT—ASSEMBLY LEGALIZED ALL ACTS OF PRECEDING COURTS
AND PROVIDED FOR COMPLETING UNSATISFIED CASES—REINSTATED
CIVIL OFFICERS—THREAD OF AUTHORITY WAS TAKEN UP BY
THE NEW PEOPLES' GOVERNMENT JUST AS DROPPED BY THAT ACT-
ING UNDER ROYAL AUTHORITY

ALL the territory of Pennsylvania to the north and west of the line of counties named in the last chapter, as having been acquired from the Indians by the treaty of Fort Stanwix of 1768, still remained in the hands of the Indians, over which the government of Pennsylvania could exercise no jurisdiction. All this stretch of country, embracing a full third of the State, covering all the broad northwest, remained to the Indians until after the close of the Revolutionary war, having been finally acquired by the treaty of Fort McIntosh concluded in 1784. No provision was made for the civil government of this territory, acquired by the purchase of 1768, until 1771.

Chester was one of the three original counties formed from the territory acquired from the Indians by Penn in 1682, and by subsequent treaties down to 1736. Lancaster was formed from a part of Chester in 1729. Cumberland was apportioned from a part of Lancaster in 1750. Up to 1771 all county business by settlers in all the western portion of the State had to be transacted at Carlisle, the present county seat of Cumberland County. For three years, from 1768 to 1771, the inhabitants of Greene County were obliged to go to Carlisle for the transaction of any county business. On the latter date, March 9th, the county of Bedford was erected out of portions of Cumberland, and was made to embrace the vast tract as described in the list, as beginning on the south where the Province line crosses the Tuscarora Mountain, the present eastern limit of Fulton County, and running along the summit of that mountain to the gap near the head of Path Valley, thence north to the Juniata River; thence with the Juniata to the mouth of Shaver's Creek; thence northeast to the line of Berks County; thence along the Berks County line to the western boundaries of the Province, thence southward by the western boundaries of the Province, to the southwest corner, and thence eastward by the southern boundary of the Province to the place of beginning As will be seen, this county organization embraced the territory included in the present County of Greene, and hence for a period, all county business was done at the town of Bedford, one hundred miles from Pittsburg. Though now having a legal county organization, and full protection guaranteed by the Province to all its inhabitants, yet the dream seems to have been indulged in by many of the early settlers that this territory between the Monongahela and Ohio rivers belonged to Virginia, and that its claim would ultimately be vindicated

The first court held at Bedford, was opened on the 16th of April, 1771, at which George Wilson reported as justice for the southwestern corner of the State, whose home was at the mouth of Georges Creek, Fayette County. William Crawford, who was the land agent of George Washington, who figured prominently afterward in the military annals of the country, after whom the county of Crawford was named, who was inhumanly burned by the Indians at Sandusky, and who had previously figured as a justice of Cumberland, was also a justice of Bedford, as was also Thomas Gist, son of Christopher Gist, the companion of Washington in his journey to Fort Le Boeuf, in 1753. Dorsey Pentecost, who afterwards was the second president Judge of Washington County, and a member of the first board of county commissioners of Bedford County, was also a justice In the division of the new county of Bedford into townships, the whole territory west of the Monongahela River, now embracing the counties of Greene, Washington and parts of Allegheny and Beaver, was embraced in two townships, Pitt and Springhill, bounded as follows: "Beginning at the mouth of the Kiskeminitas, and running down the Allegheny River to its junction with the Monongahela, then down the Ohio to the western limits of the Province, thence with the western boundary to the line of Springhill, thence with that line to the mouth of Redstone Creek, thence down the Monongahela to the mouth of Youghiogheny, thence with the line of Hempfield to the mouth of Brush Run, thence with the line of said township to the beginning." Springhill: "Beginning at the mouth of Redstone Creek, and running thence a due west course, to the western boundary of the Province, thence south with the Province line to the southern boundary of the Province, then east with that line to where it crosses the Youghiogheny to Laurel Hill, thence with the line of Tyrone to Gist's, and thence with that line to the beginning."

"The official assessment rolls," says Crumrine, in his history of Washington County, "for these townships for 1772, show that Pitt Township had fifty-two landholders, twenty tenants, and thirteen single freemen; Springhill (which embraced Greene County), three hundred and eight land-holders, eighty-nine tenants, and fifty-eight single freemen. * * * The assessment roll for 1772 of Springhill Township shows the following names among others: Thomas Brown (Ten-Mile), Jeremiah Beek, (Beck), William Brashear, William Crawford, (the Quaker, afterwards of East Bethlehem), Josiah Crawford, Oliver Crawford, John Casteel, Henry Enoch, John Garrard, Jr., Zachariah Goben, (Gaben), James Harrod, William Harrod, Levi Harrod, Thomas Hughes (Muddy Creek), Andrew Link, Jacob Link, John Moore, David Morgan, John Masterson, Daniel Moredock, James Moredock, John Swan, Robert Syre, Abraham Teagarden, George Teagarden, Henry Michael, Samuel Eckerly, John Hupp, William Teagarden and John Williams. Among the names from the Pitt Township list are Jacob Bausman, John Barr, John Campbell, Samuel Heath and John McDonald" But the large numbers embraced in the tax list of 1772, show how rapidly the country filled up when once the way was open. When we consider that the right to acquire land had only existed for four years, when this assessment was made, we must conclude that these lands had a special charm for the pioneer.

But the necessity of making a journey of a hundred miles, over rugged mountains, and by roads that were little more than bridle paths through the forest, in order to reach the county seat, proved too burdensome, and after the lapse of five years, February 26, 1773, a new county was organized on this side of the Alleghanies, embracing a part of the original county of Bedford, and designated Westmoreland. The act of incorporation defining its legal limits was in these words: "That all and singular the lands lying within the province of Pennsylvania, and being within the boundaries following, that is to say: beginning in the province line, where the most westerly branch, commonly called the South or Great branch of the Youghiogheny River crosses the same; then down the easterly side of the said branch and river to the Laurel Hill; thence along the ridge of the said hill, north-eastward so far as it can be traced, or till it runs into the Alleghany Hill; thence, along the ridge dividing the waters of Susquehanna and the Allegheny rivers to the purchase line, at the head of the Susquehanna, thence due west to the limits of the province and by the same to the place of beginning; shall be, and the same is hereby declared to be, erected into a county, henceforth to be called Westmoreland."

It will be seen by reference to any map of this part of the State, that the northern boundary " to the purchase line at the head of Susquehanna, thence due west to the limits of the province," embraces a considerable territory north of the Allegheny and Ohio rivers which had not yet been acquired by purchase of the Indians, the Fort Stanwix purchase being confined to lands east and south, or the left bank of these streams. But it is probable that this stretch of legal authority was made to accommodate persons who had fixed their eyes on some delectable spots on the right bank, as for example Allegheny City.

"By the provisions of the organic act," quoting Crumrine, "the courts of Westmoreland County were to be held at the house of Robert Hanna, until the Court House shall be built." Robert Hanna, one of the early pioneers in these then western wilds, had seated himself at a point near the site of Greensburg, the county seat of the present county of Westmoreland. Here he had opened a house for public entertainment, and around him had gathered the cabins of a number of the hardy settlers, the whole taking the pretentious name of Hanna's Town. This point was on the line of the new road opened by General Forbes in his expedition to Fort Pitt in 1758, and is on the line of the Pennsylvania Railroad.

The courts were held here for a number of years, and hence, it became a place of considerable importance, figuring extensively in the contentions that ensued to State authority over this territory. The commissions issued to justices of the peace for this county embraced many names that became prominent in the future history of the State and the nation: Arthur St. Clair, afterwards a prominent Major-General in the American army under Washington, and the leader of the unfortunate expedition against the Indians in 1789; William Crawford, the land agent of Washington, and the leader of an expedition against the western Indians; Alexander McClean, who completed the survey of Mason and Dixon's line, Alexander McKee, Robert Hanna, William Louchry, George Wilson, Eneas Mackay, Joseph Spear and James Caveat. In the following year, when the integrity of Pennsylvania territory was threatened by the encroachments of Virginia, led by Dr. Connolly, additional justices were commissioned, among whom were Alexander Ross, Van Swearingen, who lived just opposite Greenfield, on the left bank of the Monongahela River, and who became the first sheriff of Washington County, then embracing Greene; Andrew MacFarlane, Oliver Miller, and subsequently, in 1777, Edward Cook and James Marshel. William Crawford, having been first commissioned, was the presiding justice.

The machinery of legal business for the new county was set in motion with very little ceremony, as the following record of the Provincial Council for February 27, 1773, abundantly shows. "A law having passed yesterday for the erecting a part of the county of Bedford into a separate county, called Westmoreland, and Arthur St. Clair, Esq , the present prothonotary, &c., of Bedford, having requested the Governor to grant him the offices in the new county, in lieu of those he now holds in Bedford county, His Honor this day was pleased to appoint him to the several offices following, in the said county of Westmoreland, by three separate commissions, under the great seal of the Province, viz· Prothonotary, or principal clerk of the county court of Common pleas, Clerk, or Register of the Orphans' Court, and Recorder of Deeds."

St Clair thus became a sort of *fac totum* of the new courts. Having served in a similar capacity in Bedford County, he was well fitted to discharge the duties, and set the wheels of government in motion.   He seems to have been a man of talent and something of a scholar.   He was a Scotchman by birth, was educated at the University of Edinburgh, studied medicine with the celebrated William Hunter, of London, entered the military service in the Royal American regiment of foot, the Sixtieth of the line, came to this country with Admiral Boscawen and served under Gen. Amherst. He was with Wolfe at the reduction of Quebec on the plains of Abraham. In 1762 he resigned his commission in the British army, and settled first in Bedford, and later in the Ligonier valley   In 1770 he was appointed Surveyor of Cumberland County, was commissioned a justice of the courts, and was sent a member of the Supreme Executive Council   In the conflict between Virginia and Pennsylvania he ardently espoused the Pennsylvania side   At the breaking out of the Revolutionary war he entered the service, rose to the rank of a Major-General in the Continental army, and became the intimate friend and adviser of Washington.   At the close of the war he was made a member of the Council of Censors, served in the Continental Congress from 1785 to 1787, and in the latter year was made president of that august body. He was appointed Governor of the Northwestern territory in 1788, and two years later fixed the seat of government of the territory at the point where Cincinnati now is, which name he gave to the place in honor of that order of old soldiers styled the Society of the Cincinnati, of which he was president over the Pennsylvania chapter from 1783 to 1789. In an engagement with the Indians on the Wabash he was badly defeated in 1791.   In 1802, upon the admission of Ohio as a State into the Union, he declined election as Governor and retired to a log cabin in the Chestnut Ridge in Westmoreland County, ruined in fortune.   He made unsuccessful application to Congress for certain claims due him, and

Samuel Thompson

finally died in poverty, on the 31st of August, 1818, aged eighty-four years.

At the first session of the Court of Quarter Sessions held in the newly erected county of Westmoreland at the house of Robert Hanna, Judge William Crawford presiding, an act was passed dividing the county into townships, by which the two townships of Pitt and Springhill retained the same boundaries as those previously quoted. Upon the petition of inhabitants of Springhill Township, which embraced Greene County, the court appointed the following named persons, John Moore, Thomas Scott, Henry Beason, Thomas Brownfield, James McClean and Phillip Shute viewers to lay out a road: "To begin at or near the mouth of a run, known by the name of Fish Pot Run, about two miles below the mouth of Ten Mile Creek, on the west side of the Monongahela River, (it being a convenient place for a ferry, as also a good direction for a leading road to the most western parts of the settlements), thence the nearest and best way to the forks of Dunlap's path, and General Braddock's road on the top of Laurel Hill."

This road, thus early authorized to be laid out and constructed, became a very important thoroughfare to the West. A strong current of emigration was setting from the east to the Ohio country, and this was the nearest and best overland course, whether by the Braddock (the Virginia) or the Forbes (the Pennsylvania) military roads, and was long traveled by settlers seeking the Western country. Though early opened, and probably by a route judiciously selected, it was undoubtedly a very rough thoroughfare, especially in early spring-time when farmers were hurrying forward to commence the season's work. John S Williams, in the *American Pioneer*, as quoted by Crumrine, describes the trip of his family from North Carolina to Marietta in 1802: "The mountain roads, if roads they could be called, for pack-horses were still on them, were of the most dangerous and difficult character. I have heard an old mountain tavern-keeper say that, although the taverns were less than two miles apart in years after we came, he has known many emigrant families that stopped a night at every tavern on the mountains."

The records of the county court for the succeeding three years show a number of roads were laid out in the townships of Pitt and Springhill, a few cases of larceny, of riot, of misdemeanor, a number of cases against the noted Baltzer Shilling, and in the year 1775 that Elizabeth Smith was arraigned for felony, for which offence she plead guilty and received the following sentence of the court: "Judgment that the said Elizabeth Smith be taken this afternoon, being the 11th instant, between the hours of three and five, and there to receive fifteen lashes on her bare back well laid on; that she pay a fine of eighteen shillings and five pence to his Honor the Governor;

that she make restitution of the goods stolen; that she pay the costs of prosecution and stand committed till complied with."

In April, 1776, the county court was held for the last time under the authority of the King. The Revolution had now been fairly inaugurated, and there were no further sessions held until January 6, 1778, when the supreme authority of the Continental Congress was recognized.

On the 23d of January, 1775, a convention of delegates from the several counties of the Province met at Philadelphia, in which resolutions were passed expressing a strong desire that the ancient harmony might be restored between the King and the colonies; but if the attempt should be made to force the colonies to submission then we hold it our indispensable duty to resist such force, and at every hazard to defend the rights and liberties of America. Recognizing the dependent condition of the colonies upon the mother country for cloths and military supplies the people were recommended "on no account to sell to the butchers or kill for the market any sheep under four years old. And where there is a necessity for using any mutton in their families, it is recommended to them to kill such as are the least profitable to keep." It was also recommended to cultivate hemp, and engage in the manufacture of madder, saltpetre and gun powder, and a large number of articles of prime necessity in building and in housekeeping, which had previously been imported The convention adjourned subject to the call of the Philadelphia delegates, who were constituted a committee of safety

By a resolution of the Continental Congress of the 15th of May, 1776, it was recommended that all dependence upon the government of Great Britain cease, and that such governments in the several colonies be adopted, as the exigencies of the situation demanded. Accordingly, delegates from the several counties assembled on the 18th of June, 1776, in Carpenter's Hall, Philadelphia, Edward Cook and James Perry representing Westmoreland County, and proceeded to " Resolve, 1. That the said resolution of Congress of the 15th of May last is fully approved by this conference 2 That the present government of this province is not competent to the exigences of our affairs. 3. That it is necessary that a provincial convention be called by this conference for the express purpose of forming a new government " It then made provision for the electing of delegates to such convention, fixing eight as the number to be sent up from each county, and the qualifications of electors. As the payment of a tax within one year was one of the qualifications, and as Westmoreland had been exempted by law from the paying of any tax for the space of three years, the electors of this county were exempted from the operation of this item of qualification. When all the qualifications of members to be elected and electors were settled, the convention proceeded to divide the counties into election districts, fix the place of holding elections, and appoint judges of elections. The county of Westmoreland was divided into two election districts, the first all the territory north of the Youghioghany, with voting place at Hanna's Town, and the second all to the south of that stream and voting place at Spark's Fort, now Perry Township, Fayette County. James Barr, John Moore and Clement McGeary were appointed as election officers for the northern district, and George Wilson, John Kile and Robert McConnel for the southern. The day fixed for holding these elections was the 8th of July, 1776, just four days after the passage of the Declaration of Independence by the Continental Congress. As the news traveled very tardily in those days, the probability is that the people of Westmoreland County had not heard of it when the election was held. The eight members elected to the Provincial Convention were John Carmichael, Edward Cook, James Barr, John Moor, James Smith, John McClellan, Christopher Lavingair and James Perry.

Heretofore the primal source of authority in the government had been the King of Great Britain; now it was to emanate from the people, and these back-woodsmen, eight from each county, were to try their hands in the great experiment of self-government—"a government of the people, by the people and for the people."

The convention thus chosen met in Philadelphia on the 15th of July, 1776. As the members were separately to make oath on being qualified to a renunciation of all allegiance to King George III., and as they in their representative capacity spoke for all their constituents, it is evident that by that act the whole legal and governmental machinery of the Province was at an end. There was no King supreme over all, no proprietary, no council, no judges, justices, sheriffs, constables, in short no provincial, county or township officers, but all was theoretically in a state of nature. But the moment this convention was organized it proceeded to take up the wand of authority which had been dropped. The convention thus constituted was organized by the election of Benjamin Franklin, president, and on the 24th of July elected what was designated a Council of Safety, composed of twenty-five members, to which was assigned the executive department of the government—the duties of King and Governor. Of this council Thomas Rittenhouse was chosen chairman, and Jacob S. Howell secretary. By this act the proprietary government was entirely superseded. It may here be observed that John Penn, who had been appointed Governor in August, 1773, was the son of Richard, the second of the three sons of William Penn, viz: John, Richard and Thomas. At the time of his appointment as Governor, his father was proprietor of one-third of the Province, and his uncle, Thomas, two-thirds, the latter having inherited the share of his elder brother, John, who died in 1746 By the assumption of power by the Council of Safety the vast proprietary estates of the Penns reverted, amounting, as is shown by an estimate commenced by Thomas Penn and completed by Franklin, to ten millions of pounds sterling, or $50,000,000. But the new government was not disposed to deal harshly by the proprietors; for, by an act of November 27, 1779, for vesting these estates in the Commonwealth, there was reserved to the proprietors, all their private estates, including the tenths of manors and they were granted one hundred and thirty pounds sterling "in remembrance of the enterprising spirit of the Founder," and "of the expectations and dependence of his descendants " Parliament in 1790, on account of the inability of the British Government to vindicate the authority of the Proprietors as decided in the result of the Revolutionary struggle, and "in consideration of the meritorious services of the said William Penn, and of the losses which his family have sustained," voted an annuity of four thousand pounds per annum to his heirs and descendants. This annuity has been regularly paid to the present time, 1888

On the 6th of August, the Council of Safety was organized by the election of Thomas Wharton, Jr., president, which office was equivalent to that of Governor. A new constitution was framed and finally adopted on the 28th of September unanimously, taking effect from the date of its passage. It provided for an annual Assembly, and for a Supreme Executive Council, to be composed of twelve members elected for a term of three years. Members of Congress were chosen by the Assembly. Assemblymen were eligible for four years in seven, and councilmen but one term in seven years This constitution could not be changed for a period of seven years. At the end of that time a board of censors were to determine whether or not there was need of change If such need existed they were empowered to convene a new convention for that purpose.

The Assembly which convened in January, 1777, passed an act early in the session providing that "each and every one of the laws or acts of General Assembly that were in force and binding on the inhabitants of the said province on the 14th day of May last shall be in force and binding on the inhabitants of this State, from and after the 10th of February next, as fully and effectually to all intents and purposes, as if the said laws, and each of them, had been made and enacted by this General Assembly, and all and every person and persons whosoever are hereby enjoined and required to yield obedience to the said laws, as the case may require, * * * and the common law and such of the statute laws of England as have heretofore been in force in the province, except as is hereafter excepted." This act of the Legislature revived the operation of the former laws in the province as completely as though each one had formally been re-enacted. It was also enacted that all the several courts held in the State should continue to be held at the times and with the same formality as before, " and every officer of all and every of the courts of this State that is or shall be appointed shall have, use, and exercise the same or like powers that such officer or officers of the same title, character and distinction might, could or ought to have had, used and exercised under the charter and laws of Pennsylvania, until displaced. And all constables, overseers of the poor, supervisors of the highways, and the wardens and street commissioners of the city of Philadelphia that were last appointed or elected in the said province are hereby authorized and strictly enjoined, and required to exercise their several and respective powers, and execute, do and perform all the business and duties of their several and respective offices until others are appointed."

It was also further provided "that every action that was in any court in the province of Pennsylvania, at the last term the said court was held, except discontinued or satisfied, shall be and is hereby declared to be in the same state, and on the same rule, and may be prosecuted in the same manner in the courts in each respective county, to be hereafter held and kept, as if the authority of such court had never ceased; and if any recognisance has been taken and not returned and prosecuted as the laws direct, saving the style; and where any person had obtained a judgment before any justice of the peace for any debt or sum of money, and such judgment not discharged, the person in whose favor the judgment is, may (on producing a transcript of such judgment to any justice of the peace in the county where the defendant dwells or can be found) demand and obtain an execution for the money mentioned in such judgment, which shall be of the same force and effect as if the judgment was obtained before the justice that granted the execution."

Thus the thread of authority was taken up by the new peoples' government, where the King's and the Proprietor's government had dropped it, by that notable act of the Continental Congress assembled in Carpenter's Hall, Philadelphia, on the ever memorable 4th of July, 1776, entitled the Declaration of American Independence.

CHAPTER XIV.

Subjects of Contention—Allegiance on the Delaware or on the.
James—Largely Settled by Virginians and Marylanders—
"West and Northwest"—Settlers Innocent—Writ of Quo
Warranto—King's Proclamation—Virginia Only a Royal
Colony—Mason and Dixon's Line Continued—Walpole
Grant Covered an Empire—Correspondence of Governors—
Fry had Ascertained Latitude of Logstown—Build a Fort—
Propose Commissioners—Civil Commotion—Wilson's Letter
—Settlers Oppose Penn's Laws and Ask for a Virginia
Court—Material of Fort Pitt Sold—Governor Dunmore—
Connolly's Proclamation—Connolly Arrested— Sheriff
Proctor Arrested—Correspondence of Governors—Formal
Notice of Penn—Connolly Comes With a Detachment of
Militia—His Position—Court's Answer—Connolly Arrests
Justices—Letter of Mackay Tilghman and Allen Sent to
Virginia—Dunmore Arbitrary—Penn Counseled Peace—
Claims Complicate — Dunmore's War — Needless — Logan's
Revenge on Ten Mile Creek—Settlers Flee—Armies of Lewis
and Dunmore—Proclamation of Dunmore—Penn's Counter
Proclamation—Virginia Court at Pittsburg—Arrests and
Counter—Lexington and Concord—Patriotism—Advice of
Congressmen—Fate of Connolly

BUT the early inhabitants of the southwestern corner of the State
scarcely had one subject of contention settled before another
arose Aside from the great impediments to settlement encountered
in the rugged and mountainous country to be passed in reaching it,
and its great distance from the abodes of civilization, the emigrants
had to meet the counter claims of the English and the French to
this whole Mississippi Valley, which was fought out on this ground;
then, the hostility of the Indians in asserting their claims to this
territory, which resulted in the conspiracy of Pontiac, likewise contended for with great bitterness in this valley, and finally settled by
victories gained on this ground, then the lack of right to settle all
this stretch of country not yet having been acquired from the Indians, and the jeopardy of their necks as the penalty of
the new law unless they quickly removed from their homes,

and gave up their lands; again were they in tribulation in securing legal rights by reason of the great distance of the county seat from their homes; and scarcely was this concluded and the court of record and of justice secured within reasonable distance, when the Revolution came, and although the transfer of authority was reasonably speedy, from the crown to the people; yet for eight long and troublous years the question was in doubt, whether the new government would be successfully vindicated, or the colonies would be compelled to go back under the government of the King of Britain; and now, as if their cup of adversity was not yet full, there came another which threatened to be more bitter and deadly than all the others viz: whether they owed allegiance to Pennsylvania, or Virginia, whether they should secure the patents to their lands and pay for them at the capital on the Delaware, or at that on the James.

It doubtless seems strange to the present generation, when the well defined limits of our good old Commonwealth are examined, as shown by any well drawn map of the State, how any such controversy could ever have occurred. And it will seem even more wonderful when the precise and explicit words of King Charles' charter to William Penn are carefully read. But such a controversy did actually occur, which threatened at one time to bring on a conflict of arms and to interfere with the pacific and friendly relations of the two great Commonwealths As Greene County was in the very heart of the disputed territory, and the point where Mason and Dixon's line was interrupted, at the crossing of Dunkard Creek, near the old Indian war-path, was the scene of threatened hostilities, its history would be incomplete without a brief account of it

There can be no question but that this whole Monongahela country was originally settled by emigrants largely from Virginia and Maryland. Nor can there be any doubt but that the authorities of Virginia honestly entertained the belief that this country was embraced in the chartered limits of that colony. Hence, when the Ohio Company was chartered and was authorized to take up a half million of acres in this valley, in which the Washingtons were largely concerned, it is apparent that the company put implicit confidence in the right of Virginia to grant these lands, or they certainly would never have invested their money in the enterprise and induced pioneers to go with their families and settle upon them. Hence, the original settlers could have had no question but that their true allegiance was due to Virginia, from whose constituted authorities they received their conveyances and paid their fees. Having therefore innocently made their settlement under Virginia law, it is not strange that they clung with great tenacity to citizenship in that Commonwealth.

But by what right did Virginia claim this territory? As we

have already seen Queen Elizabeth, in 1583, a hundred years before the time of Penn, granted to Sir Walter Raleigh an indefinite stretch of country in America which practically embraced the whole continent, to which he gave the name Virginia, in honor of the virgin Queen, that portion to the south of the mouth of the Chesapeake receiving the title of South Virginia, and that to the north of it North Virginia. Raleigh spent a vast fortune, and impoverished himself in attempts to colonize the country, but all in vain, and the title lapsed. In 1606, James I, who had succeeded Elizabeth, granted charters to the Plymouth Company, who were to have the territory to the north, and the London, or Virginia Company, to the south; but the boundaries seem to have been drawn indefinitely, the two grants overlaping each other by three degrees of latitude. In 1609, the London Company secured from the King a new grant in this most remarkable language, probably never before nor since equalled for indefiniteness: "All those lands, countries, and territories situate, lying and being in that part of America called Virginia, from the point of land called cape or point of Comfort, all along the sea-coast northward two hundred miles, and from the same point or Cape Comfort all along the sea-coast to the southward two hundred miles; and all that space and circuit of lands lying from the sea-coast of the precinct aforesaid up into the land throughout from sea to sea west and northwest; and also the islands lying within one hundred miles along the coast of both seas of the precinct aforesaid."

On this wonderful piece of scrivener work, which no doubt taxed the best legal acumen of all England, in its composition, the authorities of Virginia hung all their claims to western Pennsylvania and the entire Northwest territory,—that fatal expression, "all that space and circuit of lands lying from the seacoast of the precinct aforesaid up into the land throughout from sea to sea, west and northwest." It does not say due west from the extremities of the four hundred mile coast line from sea to sea, which would have been intelligible, though preposterous, but it was to be "from sea to sea west and northwest." This word northwest could not have meant to apply to the two extremities of the coast line, for in that case it would have formed a parallelogram having the coast line fixed on the Atlantic and an equal coast line somewhere in Alaska on the Pacific and the frozen ocean. If it meant that the southern boundary should be a due west line from the southern extremity, and the northern boundary should be a line drawn due northwest from the northern extremity of the Atlantic coast line, then the limits of Virginia would have embraced nearly the whole boundless continent, as the coast line of four hundred miles would have embraced more than six degrees of latitude, from the 34° to the 40°, reaching from some point within South Carolina

Eli Long

to the central part of the shore of New Jersey, and the due northwest line would have swallowed Philadelphia, two-thirds of Pennsylvania, a part of New York, all the great lakes except Ontario, and would have emerged somewhere in the Arctic Ocean It may seem strange that the sober minded men who held the reins of government in Virginia should have set up so preposterous a claim. But if this claim was good for anything, and there seems to have been no other authority upon which it was based, save the above quoted grant of 1609, why were not Maryland and Delaware, the half of New Jersey and nearly the whole of Pennsylvania claimed at once? For this grant of 1609 antedated that of Maryland, and was made before the foot of a white man had ever pressed Pennsylvania soil. This extravagant claim was not vindicated when the colonies to the north of it had become seated. But now, after it had been pushed down on the sea-shore from more than two-thirds of its northern claim—having left scarcely fifty miles above Point Comfort instead of two hundred—by the grants to Maryland and Pennsylvania, and been limited to the right bank of the Potomac, it now proposes to commence that northwest line at the head-waters of the Potomac instead of at the coast-line.

*But this whole extravagant claim was settled before either Lord Baltimore or Penn had received their charters On the 10th of November, 1623, a writ of *quo warranto* was issued against the treasurer of the London Company. The grounds of this action were the irregularities in the government of the colony, which had invited the hostility of the Indians, resulting in massacres and burnings, which came near the utter destruction of the settlement, whereby the stockholders of the Company in London saw their investments being annihilated. The party of Virginia made defence; but upon the report of a committee sent out by the King to make examination of the Company's affairs, the King's resolution was taken, and at the Trinity term of 1624, June, "judgment was given against the Company and the patents were cancelled." "Before the end of the same term" says the record, "a judgment was declared by the Lord Chief Justice Ley, against the Company and their charter, only upon a failure or a mistake in pleading" The decree may not have been just, as disturbing vested rights; yet it was nevertheless law and the Company was obliged to bow. The matter was brought before Parliament; but public sentiment was against the Company, and the application came to nothing. Henceforward the Virginia settlement became a royal colony, subject to the will of the monarch.

Soon after the conclusion of the war with France, by which that nation was dispossessed of the Mississippi Valley and Canada, the King issued his royal proclamation, in which, after making some restrictions regarding the newly acquired territories of Quebec, and

East and West Florida, he says: "We do, therefore, with the advice of our privy council declare it to be our royal will and pleasure that no Governor nor Commander-in-chief of our colonies or plantations in America do presume, for the present, and until our further pleasure be known, to grant warrants of survey or pass patents for any lands, beyond the heads or sources of any of the rivers which fall into the Atlantic Ocean, from the west or northwest, or upon any land whatever, which, not having been ceded to or purchased by us, as aforesaid, are reserved unto the said Indians, or any of them "

But it may be said that this order would have applied to Pennsylvania as well as Virginia, and would then have confined the former to the eastern slopes of the Alleghanies as well as the latter. But there was this difference, Virginia, being now only a royal colony, was subject to the absolute will of the Monarch, while Pennsylvania, having been purchased for a price, and confirmed under a Proprietary government, was placed beyond his power to alter or annul. It will be oberved that by the cutting off of West Virginia, which occurred during the war of the Rebellion, Virginia is substantially confined to limits fixed by this royal proclamation

As we have already seen, the charter of William Penn made his southern boundary the beginning of the 40° of north latitude. As this encroached upon the the territory supposed to have been granted to Lord Baltimore, a compromise was effected between Penn and Baltimore, by which Penn gave up a belt of 43' 26" of a degree to Baltimore. But this compromise could only apply to the Colony of Maryland, the western boundary of which is a meridian line drawn from the head spring of the Potomac River, which strikes the southern line of Pennsylvania in the neighborhood of the Laurel Hill Ridge When, therefore, Mason and Dixon arrived at this point in running the dividing line between Maryland and Pennsylvania, they should have stopped, as no agreement had been entered into with Virginia touching the partition line, and there was no reason why at this point the line of Pennsylvania should not have dropped down to the beginning of the 40° parallel, as confirmed by the royal charter, which Pennsylvania subsequently claimed. But the surveyors, Mason and Dixon, kept on with this Maryland line across the Chestnut Ridge and across the Monongahela River to a point on Dunkard Creek, where they were stopped by the Indians at their old war-path What, therefore, was done beyond the Maryland western limit, was *ex parte*, and of no force; though it was open to the construction that the Pennsylvania authorities, at that time, were willing to make the same liberal concession to Virginia, that it had to Maryland, and was damaging, to that extent, to the claim which was subsequently set up to the whole fortieth degree of latitude from the ending of the thirty-ninth degree.

In order to comprehend the nature and origin of the controversy between Pennsylvania and Virginia, it should be observed that the excellence of the lands along the upper Ohio and its tributaries, and indeed of the whole Ohio Valley, excited the cupidity of all who had come to a knowledge of them   As we have seen, the Ohio Company was formed in Virginia, in which the Washingtons were interested, which secured the grant of a half million of acres embracing that portion of Pennsylvania along the Monongahela, the members of this . Company seeming at the outset to take it for granted that the western line of Pennsylvania would correspond with that of Maryland.

But this grant of a half million acres of the Ohio Company was but a drop in the bucket when compared to a project which was to follow.   It appears that Sir William Johnson, the Indian agent of the British government in America, and William Franklin, governor of New Jersey, formed the project of founding a great colony on the Ohio, and wrote to Doctor Franklin the father of William, then in London, to advocate their project at court.   The Doctor entered heartily into the project, and so persuasive were his arguments, that, in opposition to the powerful influence of Lord Hillsborough, on the 14th of August, 1772, he secured the grant of an immense tract   It commenced at the mouth of the Scioto River, three hundred miles below Pittsburg, extended southwardly to the latitude of North Carolina, thence northeastwardly to the Kanawha, at the junction of New River and Green Briar, up the Green Briar to the head of its northeasterly branch, thence easterly to the Alleghany Mountains, thence along these Mountains to the lines of Maryland and Pennsylvania, thence westerly to the Ohio, and down that stream to the point of beginning. Thomas Walpole, Thomas Pownall, Dr. Franklin and Samuel Wharton had the management of securing the grant, and hence it was known as "Walpole's Grant;" but Wharton, in a letter to Sir William Johnson, said, " A society of us, in which some of the first people in England are engaged, have concluded a bargain with the treasury for a large tract of land lying and fronting on the Ohio large enough for a government "

It will be observed that this grant swallowed bodily the grant of the Ohio Company, and it was agreed finally that the latter should be merged in the former.   This action stimulated interest in this vast Ohio country; but the Revolution coming on four years thereafter, the whole project, after an existence of a little more than four years, came suddenly to an end.

It seems that Thomas Lee, who was the first president of the Ohio Company, was a very just minded man, and suspecting that a portion of the lands embraced in the limits of his Company might turn out to be within the boundaries of Pennsylvania, by chartered rights, wrote to Governor Hamilton on this question.   The Governor replied under date of Jan. 2, 1749: "I am induced to desire your opinion, whether it may not be of use that the western bounds of this province be run by commissioners to be appointed by both governments, in order to assure ourselves that none of the lands contained in that grant (Ohio Company) are within the limits of this province." When Governor Hamilton learned that it was the intention of the Ohio Company to erect a fort at the Forks of the Ohio, for protection against the Indians, he again wrote, but now to Governor Dinwiddie, declaring that he had received instructions from the Proprietaries to join in such a work, "only taking your acknowledgment that this settlement, shall not prejudice their right to that country."

Without alluding to the matter of boundary, Dinwiddie wrote that he had already dispatched a person of distinction (young Washington) to the commander of the French, to know upon what grounds he was invading the lands of the English, and that he had sent working parties to erect a fort at the Forks of the Ohio   Though Governor Hamilton had promised conditional aid in defending the country, yet little was ever furnished, partly on account of a wrangle over taxing the Proprietary estates, which prevented the voting much money for any purpose, and partly by reason of the peace principles of a majority of the assembly   The question had also been raised in the course of their assembly discussions, from a very short-sighted motive, whether this Ohio country, which they were asked to defend, was really after all within the limits of Pennsylvania

When at Logstown, as agent of Virginia, securing a treaty with the Indians, Colonel Joshua Fry, who was accounted a good mathematician and geographer, had taken an observation by which it was found that that place, which is nine miles below Pittsburg, was in latitude 40° 29', which showed that this was far to the north of the southern line of Pennsylvania. From calculations made, it was evident to the mind of Governor Hamilton that the Forks of Ohio, as well as the French fort at Venango, were far within the boundaries of Pennsylvania, and this conclusion he communicated to the Pennsylvania assembly and also to Governor Dinwiddie.   The latter subsequently responded. "I am much misled by our surveyors if the forks of the Mohongialo be within the limits of your proprietory's grant   I have for some time wrote home to have the line run, to have the boundaries properly known, that I may be able to keep magistrates if in this government, * * * and I presume soon there will be commissioners appointed for that service. * * * But surely I am from all hands assured that Logstown is far to the west of Mr. Penn's grant."

It would seem from this letter that the Governor of Virginia was contemplating the establishment of local government in this portion

of Pennsylvania. It would appear, also, that after the organization
of Bedford County, which was made to extend over all this southwestern corner of the State, and immediately after the purchase of
these grounds from the Indians by the treaty of Fort Stanwix, in
1768, the settlers were called upon to pay taxes for the support of
the Bedford County Court. Bedford being a hundred miles away,
they did not relish the paying of taxes for the support of a court
which afforded them so little convenience   Besides, being natives
largely of Virginia, and having originally been led to suppose that
this was a part of Virginia, they petitioned that colony for the organization of county governments

Early in this controversy over jurisdiction, Colonel George Wilson, a justice of the peace of Bedford County, the grandfather of
Lawrence L Minor, of Waynesburg, wrote a letter to Arthur St.
Clair, of Bedford, in which he says: " I am sorry that the first letter
I ever undertook to write you should contain a detail of grievance
disagreeable to me   *   *   *   I no sooner returned home from
court, than I found papers containing resolves, as they call them, of
the inhabitants to the westward of the Laurel Hills, were handing
fast about amongst the people, in which amongst the rest was one
that they were resolved to oppose every of Penn's laws, as they
called them, except felonious actions, at the risque of life, and under
the penalty of fifty pounds, to be recovered off the estates of the
failure. The first of them I found hardy enough to offer it in public, I immediately ordered into custody, on which a large number
were assembled as was supposed to rescue the prisoner. I endeavored by all the reason I was capable of, to convince them of the ill
consequences that would attend such a rebellion, and happily gained
on the people to consent to relinquish their resolves and to burn the
paper they signed.   When their foreman saw that the arms of his
country, that as he said he had thrown himself into, would not rescue
him by force, he catched up his gun which was well loaded, jumped
out of doors, and swore if any man came nigh him he would put
what was in his gun through him. The person that had him in
custody called for assistance in ye King's name, and in particular
commanded myself.   I told him I was a subject, and was not fit to
command, if not willing to obey, on which I watched his eye
until I saw a chance, sprang in on him, seized the rifle by the muzzle
and held him, so as he could not shoot me, until more help got into
my assistance, on which I disarmed him, and broke his rifle to
pieces. I received a sore bruise on one of my arms by a punch of
the gun in the struggle. Then I put him under strong guard and
told them the laws of their country were stronger than the hardest
rifle among them." After convincing the discontented party of their
error, and inducing them to burn the resolves they had signed,

the prisouer was discharged on his good behavior. Wilson closes his letter in these words: " I understand great threats are made against me in particular, if possible to intimidate me with fear, and also against the sheriffs and constables and all ministers of justice. But I hope the laws, the bulwarks of our nation, will be supported in spite of those low lived trifling rascals "

From this letter we can gather the spirit which actuated the parties to the controversy, and see the beginning of a bitter contention which vexed the people of this section for many years. The idea that Pennsylvania did not extend west of the Alleghany Mountains was studiously circulated. Michael Cressap, and George Croghan, who were interested in land speculations here, were suspected of being privy to these rumors. A petition signed by over two hundred citizens was presented to the court at Bedford, under date of the 18th of July, 1772, " charging the government and officers with great injustice and oppression, and praying that directions might be given to the sheriffs to serve no more processes in that country, as they apprehended it was not in Pennsylvania " Mr. Wilson answered the allegations of the petition before the court, and showed by documentary evidence that the grounds on which the petition rested were unstable, which had a very quieting effect upon the settlers, and induced the court to reject the petition.

Fort Pitt, which had been garrisoned by a detachment of British soldiers, from the time of its erection in 1759, by General Stanwix, was, by order of General Gage, of date of October, 1772, evacuated, and " all the pickets, bricks, stones, timber and iron which are now in the building or walls of the said fort " were sold for the sum of fifty pounds At about this time, upon the death of Lord Bottetourt, Governor of Virginia, a new Governor was appointed in the person of the Earl of Dunmore, a man of a meddlesome disposition, and disposed to exercise the functions of his office with a high hand In 1773, the year following the erection of Westmoreland County, Dunmore made a visit to Fort Pitt, where he met Dr. John Connolly, a nephew of Colonel Croghan. It appears that the new Governor was determined to act upon the assumption, whatever may have been his motive therefor, that all west of the Alleghanies and the whole boundless northwest belonged to Virginia In Connolly he found a willing tool for asserting this claim, for, soon atter the departure of the Governor, Connolly published the following proclamation: " Whereas, his Excellency John, Earl of Dunmore, Governor-in-chief, and Captain General of the colony and dominion of Virginia, and Vice Admiral of the same, has been pleased to nominate and appoint me Captain, Commandant of the Militia of Pittsburg and its dependencies, with instructions to assure his Majesty's subjects settled on the Western Waters, that having the greatest regard to their prosperity and interest, and convinced from their repeated memorials of the grievances of which they complain, that he proposes moving to the House of Burgesses the necessity of erecting a new county to include Pittsburg, for the redress of your complaints, and to take every other step that may attend to afford you that justice for which you solicit. In order to facilitate this desirable circumstance I hereby require and command all persons in the dependency of Pittsburg to assemble themselves there as a militia on the 25th instant, at which time I shall communicate other matters for the promotion of public utility. Given under my hand the 1st day of January, 1774 "

A copy of this high handed proceeding was immediately communicated to the court at Hannastown, and to Governor Penn at Philadelphia. Before receiving instructions from the Governor, Arthur St. Clair, in his capacity as a justice, deeming that he was authorized by his commission to put a stop to such a procedure as was indicated in this proclamation, issued a warrant for the arrest of Connolly, who was apprehended and placed in confinement. Governor Penn wrote immediately to Lord Dunmore informing him of his advices, quoted the language of the charter, which gave five full degrees of longitude for the east and west extent of the State, which would carry the western limit far beyond Pittsburg, and expressed the belief that the Governor could not have authorized the proclamation of Connolly.

. In the meantime Dr. Connolly had been released from jail on promise of returning in time for his trial. But instead of awaiting the result of the case he proceeded with the organization of the militia and took possession of Fort Pitt. On hearing of this, Sheriff Proctor, with Justices Smith, McFarland and Mackay, proceeded to Fort Pitt, and finding that Connolly still professed the intention of delivering himself up for trial at the appointed time of convening court, though he had dispatches from Dunmore approving his conduct and urging him to go forward in asserting Virginia authority, the Sheriff took no further action in regard to Connolly, but served a writ upon William Christy, one of Connolly's lieutenants Whereupon Connolly arrested Sheriff Proctor upon a King's warrant, and held him in custody. Seeing the commotion incident to these proceedings, and the militia drilling with arms in their hands, the Indians became very much alarmed.

In his reply to Penn, the Governor of Virginia, Lord Dunmore freely assumed responsibility for Connolly's acts declaring them performed by his authority by the advice of his Majesty's council. He also referred to that unfortunate declaration made in the Pennsylvania assembly, when a call was made for troops to serve against the French and Indians at Fort Pitt, that Pittsburg was not embraced in the limits of Pennsylvania. Penn answered this communication at great length, setting forth all the facts and arguments relied upon by the authorities of Pennsylvania to hold this territory, and expressing at the outset with considerable warmth his surprise that Dunmore should authorize these high-handed proceedings, while a county government under Pennsylvania authority had already been established there, and was in full operation, and before the lines between the two colonies had been definitely settled by competent authority. Governor Dinwiddie, the predecessor of Dunmore, had informed Penn, "I have for some time wrote home to have the line run," and suggested that if the territory in question actually was a part of Pennsylvania then the quit rents should be paid to the Proprietaries of that province instead of to the King. Penn informed Dunmore that the declaration of the Assembly, to which he refers, was made at a time when no definite limits of the State had been fixed by actual surveys; besides, even if the declaration had been made by the Assembly in the most positive and formal manner it could not affect the validity of the claims of the Proprietaries secured to them by Royal Charter, in which the payment of a stipulated price was acknowledged.

That he might not be chargeable with dereliction of duty in asserting his claims, Penn served a formal notice upon Lord Dunmore in these words: "I must take this opportunity of notifying to your Lordship, that the Proprietaries do claim, by their said petition, as part of their province of Pennsylvania all the lands lying west of a south line to be drawn from Dixon's and Mason's line as it is commonly called at the westermost part of the province of Maryland to the beginning of the fortieth degree of north latitude to the extent of five degrees of longitude from the river Delaware; and I must request your Lordship will neither grant lands nor exercise the government of Virginia within those limits till his majesties pleasure may be known."

It will be seen by the wording of this proclamation that Penn claimed the full three degrees of latitude granted by his charter, beginning at the end of the 39th degree beyond the western boundary of Maryland, not allowing the compromise with that State to effect the line opposite Virginia.

It will be observed that Connolly had given his word that he would return and give himself up for trial at the time of the setting of the court, provided he was allowed his liberty in the meantime. He did return, but with an armed band of militia of some 180 which he had recruited and had under discipline. The court having notice of his coming with a military force deemed it prudent to adjourn, as their business was nearly concluded. On his arrival he took possession of the court room, and stationed his sentinals, and

F. M. Braddock

then sent word to the court that he wished to wait on them. They received him in a private room, when he read to them the letter of Lord Dunmore to Penn, in which he assumes responsibility for Connolly's action, and the following explanation of his procedures: "I am come here to be the occasion of no disturbances, but to prevent them. As I am countenanced by government, whatever you may say or conceive, some of the justices of this bench are the cause of this appearance and not me. I have done this to prevent myself from being illegally taken to Philadelphia. My orders from the government of Virginia not being explicit; but claiming the country about Pittsburg, I have raised the militia to support the civil authority of that colony vested in me. I have come here to free myself from a promise made to Captain Proctor; but have not conceived myself amenable to this court, by any authority of Pennsylvania, upon which I cannot apprehend that you have any right to remain here as justices of the peace, constituting a court of that province; but in order to prevent confusion I agree that you may continue to act in that capacity, in all such matters as may be submitted to your determination by the acquiescence of the people, until I may have instructions to the contrary from Virginia, or until his Majesty's pleasure be further known on this subject."

It will be perceived that Connolly only reflects the sentiments of Dunmore, who was at the root of all the trouble. The Westmoreland court made a very temperate answer to Connolly. "The jurisdiction of the court and officers of the county of Westmoreland rests on the legislative authority of the province of Pennsylvania, confirmed by his Majesty in council. That jurisdiction has been regularly exercised, and the court and officers will continue to exercise it in the same regular manner. It is far from their intention to occasion or foment disturbances, and they apprehend that no such intention can with propriety be inferred from any part of their conduct; on the contrary they wish and will do all they can to preserve the public tranquility. In order to contribute to this salutary purpose they give information that every step will be taken on the part of the province of Pennsylvania to accommodate any differences that may have arisen between it, and the colony of Virginia, by fixing a temporary line between them."

Connolly now marched away with his militia, having given himself not as he had agreed to do, for trial, but in defiance of the court, at the head of a military band. It was, therefore, as clearly a breaking of his word as though he had not come near the court. Having completed their business the court adjourned, and three of the justices, Mackay, Smith and McFarlane, departed for their homes at Pittsburg. Scarcely were they returned, when these three were served with King's warrants issued by Connolly, for the crime of making the

12

answer they did quoted above, and upon their refusal to give bail
for their appearance at the Staunton court to answer to the charge,
they were sent in custody to the Staunton jail   On the way they
were denied the privilege of writing to the authorities at Philadelphia, by the hand of a person just then going there; but before
reaching Staunton, Mackay was allowed to go to Williamsburg to
lay their case before the Governor. This functionary listened patiently, but made answer that their arrest was only a dose of their own,
administered in the arrest of Connolly   Nevertheless he consented
to release them, and allow them to return home.   In a dispatch to
Governor Penn, after describing the interview with Dunmore,
Mackay says, " We are to set off from this place immediately, but
how to act after our return, is a matter we are at this time unable
to determine "   In a further dispatch of the 14th of June, 1774, he
says, " The deplorable state of affairs in this part of your government
at this time is truly distressing, we are robbed, insulted and dra-
gooned by Connolly and his militia in this place and in its environs,
all ranks share of his oppression and tyranny, but the weight of his
resentment falls heaviest on me, because he imagines I oppose his
unwarrantable measures most.   On the 27th of last May he ordered
a party of his militia to put down and destroy a sheep-house and a
stable of mine, in a violent and outrageous manner, and told me at
the time he would take the house I lived in if he wanted it, and
countenanced a perjured villain, a constable of ours that deserted to
him before he was three months sworn in, to shake a stick at my
nose before his face without reproof."
     From this extract some conception can be formed of the state
of this portion of the colony under the divided authority.   Upon
receiving intelligence of the forcible seizure of his commissioned
magistrates, Governor Penn lost no time in sending commissioners
to Dunmore to secure some temporary settlement, until the boundaries could be fixed by Royal authority.   James Tilghman and
Andrew Allen, members of the Council, were selected to conduct this
embassage.   They were cordially received by Lord Dunmore, who
agreed to unite in a petition to the King for the appointment of a
commission to establish the boundaries, but would not agree that
Virginia should bear half of the expense.   The commissioners then
proposed that a temporary line be fixed at five degrees of longitude
from the Delaware, and that the western line of Pennsylvania should
follow the meanderings of that stream.   Dunmore would not agree
to this, but contended that the charter of Penn authorized five degrees
to be computed from a point on the 42° parallel where the Delaware
cuts it, he believing that the Delaware run from northeast to southwest which would, as he believed, carry the western boundary as far
east as the Alleghany Mountains   The commissioners promptly

rejected this interpretion; but in the interest of peace they would be willing to allow a temporary boundary to follow the Monongahela River from Mason and Dixon's line down to its mouth. This would have left all west of that stream to Virginia. Dunmore now became arbitrary in his manner, charging the commissioners with being unwilling to make any concessions, and ended by declaring his unalterable purpose to hold jurisdiction over Pittsburg and surrounding territory until his Majesty should otherwise order.

Until competent authority should establish the boundaries of the two provinces there was now no hope of temporary agreement, as Lord Dunmore was arbitrary and dictatorial Governor Penn saw but too clearly that civil strife in the disputed district would unavoidably lead to a trial of force for the mastery. Dunmore was destined in a short time to quarrel with the Legislature of Virginia, and for safety betook himself to a British man-of-war. Desiring to avoid a conflict over a dispute which Charter stipulations would eventually settle, Governor Penn decided to bide his time, and accordingly wrote to William Crawford, the presiding justice of Westmoreland County, as follows: "The present alarming situation of our affairs in Westmoreland County, occasioned by the very unaccountable conduct of the Government of Virginia, requires the utmost attention of this government, and therefore I intend, with all possible expedition, to send commissioners to expostulate with my Lord Dunmore upon the behavior of those he has thought proper to invest with such power as hath greatly disturbed the peace of that County As the government of Virginia hath the power of raising militia, and there is not any such in this Province, it will be in vain to contend with them, in the way of force The magistrates, therefore, at the same time that they continue with steadiness to exercise the jurisdiction of Pennsylvania with respect to the distributions of justice and the punishment of vice, must be cautious of entering into any such contests with the officers of my Lord Dunmore as may tend to widen the present unhappy breach; and, therefore, as things are at present circumstanced, I would not advise the magistracy of Westmoreland County to proceed by way of criminal prosecution against them for exercising the government of Virginia."

Though it was humiliating for the legally and formally constituted authorities of Westmoreland County to have their authority defied by a set of officers who received their orders to act from Virginia, backed by a lawless military force called out by direction of another colony, yet it was for the time being judicious not to provoke a contest. As we view it now, with State lines all fixed and all county governments crystalized, it seems strange that any such conflict should have arisen. But it must be remembered that the matter of priority of charter, the impossibility of making the actual surveys conform to the language of the royal grants, and the fact that no accurate astronomical observations had been taken, left this whole subject of western boundary at loose ends   Until something definite was settled, it was better, as Penn advised, that force be not resorted to, as the hot-headed Virginia Governor had done   The policy thus recommended, while it left the court at Hanna's Town in operation, practically yielded all this Monongahela country to the authority of the Virginian

The result of Dunmore's diplomacy was of course communicated to Connolly, and he was strengthened in asserting his authority. He discarded the name "Fort Pitt" and gave the fort the name "Fort Dun-more," in honor of his chief. On the 21st of April, 1774, Connolly wrote to settlers along the Ohio that the Shawnees were not to be trusted, and that the whites ought to be prepared to revenge the wrong done them.   This gave authority to the settlers for the taking the right of punishment into their own hands, and lighted anew the fires of Indian warfare. It was known as Dunmore's war   A boat containing goods was attacked while going down the Ohio by a party of Cherokees and one white man was killed   In retaliation two friendly Indians of another tribe, in no way responsible for this crime, were murdered   This was cause enough for the Indians to take up the hatchet, and terrible was the penalty paid   On the evening of the same day Captain Cressap, who had led in the affair, hearing that a party of Indians were encamped at the mouth of Captina Creek, went stealthily and attacked it, killing several of them and having one of his own party wounded.   A few days later, Daniel Great-house, with a band of thirty-two followers, attacked the natives at Baker's, and by stratagem, in the most dishonorable manner, killed twelve and wounded others.   The murdered Indians were all scalped. Of the number of the slain was the entire family of the noted Indian chief, Logan

The savage instinct of revenge was now aroused.   Logan had been the firm friend of the white man, and had done him many ser-vices; but, left alone, all his family slain, he thirsted for blood.   His vengeance was wreaked upon the inhabitants west of the Mononga-hela, along Ten Mile Creek, and he rested not until he had taken thirteen scalps, the number of his own family who had been slain, when he declared himself satisfied and ready for peace.   The tidings of the hostile acts of Cressap and Greathouse, and the stealthy and midnight deeds of savagery by the red men spread terror and con-sternation on all sides, and the inhabitants west of the Monongahela fled, driving before them their flocks and herds, and bearing away their most easily transportable valuables.   "There were more than one thousand people," writes Crawford to Washington, "crossed the Monongahela in one day at three ferries that are not one mile apart."

"Upon a fresh report of Indians I immediately took horse" writes St. Clair to Governor Penn, "and rode up to inquire, and found it, if not totally groundless, at least very improbable; but it was impossible to persuade the people so, and I am certain I did not meet less than one hundred families, and I think two thousand head of cattle, in twenty miles riding."

The Virginia authorities immediately called out the militia. A force under Col McDonald assembled at Wheeling and marched against Wapatomica, on the Muskingum. But the Indians being unprepared for war, feigned submission, and gave five of their chiefs as hostages. But the troops destroyed their towns and crops and retreated. Sir William Johnson counselled the Indians to keep peace In the meantime Andrew Lewis had organized a force of eleven hundred men in the neighborhood of the since famed White Sulphur Springs, and was marching for the mouth of the Great Kanawha, where he was to meet the force gathered in the northern part of the State under Dunmore in person. Before the arrival of the latter the Indians, Delawares, Iroquois, Wyandots, Shawnees, under Cornstalk, Logan and all their most noted chiefs, gathered in upon Lewis, and attacked him with great fury, the battle raging the entire day, but in the end the Indians were driven across the Ohio, though with a loss of Colonels Lewis (brother of the commandant) and Field killed, Colonel Fleming wounded, and seventy-five men killed and one hundred and forty wounded, a fifth of the entire force. The loss of the Indians could not be ascertained, though thirty-three dead were left behind them Lewis was determined to follow up his advantage, which had been gained at so grievous a loss; but Dunmore, who was now approaching with his division of the army, having been visited by the chiefs, who offered peace, and himself having little stomach for fighting, accepted their terms, and ordered Lewis to desist in his pursuit. Lewis refused to obey and pushed on determined to avenge the slaughter of his men, and it was not until Dunmore came up with him that he could be prevailed upon to give up an attack which he had planned upon the Indian town of Old Chillicothe.

The army now retired, though a detachment of one hundred men was left at the mouth of the Great Kanawha, and small detachments at Wheeling and at Pittsburg Thus ended as causeless a war, known as Dunmore's war, as was ever undertaken, all induced by the meddling policy of Dunmore in a matter which the Crown alone had the authority at that time to decide, and the over officiousness of Connolly, who "dressed in a little brief authority" exercised it in un arbitrary and anger provoking way. It was provoked by the Virginians, and was prosecuted wholly by Virginians, known by the Indians as "Long-Knives."

Having thus cut a large figure in a military way, at the expense of Virginia, Dunmore issued his proclamation.

" *Whereas.* The Province of Pennsylvania have unduly laid claim to a very valuable and extensive quantity of his Majesty's territory, and the executive part of that government in consequence thereof, has most arbitrarily and unwarrantably proceeded to abuse the laudable advancements in this part-of his Majesty's dominions by many oppressive and illegal methods in the discharge of this imaginary authority, and whereas the ancient claim laid to this country by the colony of Virginia, founded in reason upon preoccupancy and the general acquiescence of all persons, together with the instructions I have lately received from his Majesty's servants, ordering me to take this country under my administration, and as the evident injustice manifestly offered to his Majesty by the immediate strides taken by the Proprietaries of Pennsylvania in prosecution of their wild claim to this country demand an immediate remedy, I do hereby in his Majesty's name require and command all his Majesty's subjects west of the Laurel Hill to pay a due respect to this my proclamation, strictly prohibiting the execution of any act of authority on behalf of the Province of Pennsylvania, at their peril in this country; but, on the contrary, that a due regard and entire obedience to the laws of his Majesty's colony of Virginia under my administration be observed, to the end that regularity may ensue, and a due regard to the interest of his Majesty in this quarter, as well as to the subjects in general, may be the consequence."

Quite ready to join in this War of the Proclamations, and not unprepared to wield the ponderous words of authority, Governor John Penn caught up the cudgel and hurled back his claims in the following brave pronunciamento:

" *Whereas,* I have received information that his Excellency, the Earl of Dunmore, in and over his Majesty's colony of Virginia hath lately issued a very extraordinary Proclamation setting forth," here is quoted Dunmore's, given above, "And whereas, although the western limits of the Province of Pennsylvania have not been settled by any authority from the Crown, yet it has been sufficiently demonstrated by lines accurately run by the most skillful artists that not only a great tract of country west of the Laurel Hill, but Fort Pitt also are comprehended within the charter bounds of this Province, a great part of which country has been actually settled, and is now held, under grants from the Proprietaries of Pennsylvania, and the jurisdiction of this government has been peaceably exercised in that quarter of the country, till the late strange claim set up by the Earl of Dumore, in behalf of his Majesty's colony of Virginia, founded as his Lordship is above pleased to say, ' in reason, preoccupancy, and the general acquiessence of all persons,' which claim to lands within the said charter limits must appear still the more extraordinary, as his most gracious Majesty, in an act past the very last session of Parliament, ' for making more effectual provision for the government of the Province of Quebec,' has been pleased in the fullest manner to recognize the Charter of the Province of Pennsylvania by expressly referring to the same, and binding the said Province of Quebec by the northern and western bounds thereof: Wherefore there is the greatest reason to conclude, that any instructions the Governor of Virginia may have received, from his Majesty's servants, to take that country under his administration, must be founded on some misrepresentation to them respecting the western extent of this province. In justice therefore to the Proprietaries of the Province of Pennsylvania, who are only desirous to secure their own undoubted property from the encroachment of others, I have thought fit, with the advice of the Council, to issue this my proclamation, hereby requiring all persons west of the Laurel Hill, to retain their settlements as aforesaid made under this province, and to pay due obedience to the laws of this government; and all magistrates and other officers who hold commissions or offices under this government to proceed as usual in the administration of justice without paying the least regard to the said recited proclamation, until his Majesty's pleasure shall be known in the premises; at the same time strictly charging and enjoining the said inhabitants and magistrates to use their utmost endeavors to preserve peace and good order."

It will be noticed that in the matter of thundering with his Whereases and Wherefores Penn is quite equal to Dunmore, and in that part where some doubt is thrown upon the statement of the latter that he is acting under instructions of the Crown, Penn has decidedly the advantage. It had been the intention of Dunmore to open a court at Pittsburg with Virginia magistrates, and by Virginia authority. But the counter proclamation of Penn had somewhat cooled his taste for controversy, as he might be compelled to defend his usurpations by force. But when he discovered that the Pennsylvania authorities were disposed to have their differences submitted to peaceful abitrament he concluded that he might venture a little farther on his scheme of holding possession of this fine country. He, accordingly, had the court for Augusta County, which had formerly been held at Staunton, adjourn to open its next term on the 21st of February, at Pittsburg, Augusta County being made to embrace all the western part of Virginia and Pennsylvania. On the day appointed the following named persons appeared, took the oath of office and sat as justices of the Virginia court: George Croghan, John Connolly, Thomas Smallman, John Cambell, Dorsey Pentecost, William Goe, John Gibson and George Vallandingham. There were now two organized courts, assessors, tax gatherers, sheriffs and all the machinery for conducting a county government over the same territory, Virginia calling it Augusta, and Pennsylvania Westmoreland. Of course what is now Greene County was embraced under this double-headed authority, and its inhabitants involved in the confusion of yielding obedience to two county governments, and paying taxes to two sets of officials for the same purpose.

Having succeeded in setting up their court the new officials bethought them that they must break up any vestiges of a rival court and accordingly issued warrants for the arrest of Robert Hanna and James Caveat, which were served by the Augusta sheriff, and the two offenders were brought in and incarcerated in the Fort Dunmore jail, where they languished for three months, in vain seeking for release Finally the sheriff of Westmoreland County, assisted by a strong posse, proceeded to Fort Dunmore and released the prisoners, and arrested John Connolly at the suit of Robert Hanna who claimed damages for unlawful imprisonment. Incensed by this treatment of their leader his adherents from Chartiers came in force and seized three of the party who had been engaged in the arrest of Connolly. George Wilson, Joseph Spear and Devereaux Smith

It was probably sometime in June or July before Hanna and Caveat were set at liberty, as the records show they were constantly entering complaints of their hardships, and petitioning for relief In the meantime an event had transpired which overshadowed all the petty strife of contending factions, and united all hearts in a common cause. On the 19th of April, of this year, 1775, the battles of Lexington and Concord had been fought which aroused all hearts with singular unanimity to resistance to the British Crown all over the habitable portion of this broad land, even to the cabins of the frontiersmen, far remote from towns or cities The news of these bloody frays had no sooner reached Hannastown and Pittsburg than public meetings were held at both those places, at which Virginians and Pennsylvanians united in their approval of resistance and pledging support. These resolves are important and curious, as showing the unanimity with which they, laying aside domestic troubles, united in a common cause These meetings were held on the same day, the 16th of May, 1775. The resolves of that at Hannastown representing Westmoreland County, Pennsylvania, were conceived in these temperate words: "*Resolved, unanimously*, that the Parliament of Great Britain, by several late acts, have declared the inhabitants of Massachusetts Bay to be in rebellion, and the ministry, by endeavoring to enforce those acts, have attempted to reduce the said inhabitants to a more wretched state of slavery than ever before existed in any State or country, not content with violating the constitutional and charactered rights of humanity, exposing their lives to

P. M. Grimes

the licentious soldiery, and depriving them of the very means of substance. *Resolved, unanimously*, that there is no reason to doubt but the same system of tyrrany and oppression will (should it meet with success in Massachusetts Bay) be extended to other parts of America; it is therefore become the indispensable duty of every American, of every man who has any public virtue or love for his country, or any bowels for posterity, by every means which God has put in his power, to resist and oppose the execution of it; that for us we will be ready to oppose it with our lives and fortunes. And the better to enable us to accomplish it we will immediately form ourselves into a military body, to consist of companies to be made up of the several townships under the following association which is declared to be the association of Westmoreland County.

At Pittsburg, now called Fort Dunmore, not only the adherents of the Virginia, but the men acknowledging no government but that of Pennsylvania, joined in expressing the sentiment of firm resistance. A committee of some thirty members was appointed in which, not only the names of Connolly and Vallandingham, but also those of Devereaux Smith and George Wilson appear, and they unanimously declare "that they have the highest sense of the spirited behavior of their brethren in New England, and do most cordially approve of their opposing the invaders of American rights and privileges to the utmost extreme." And they proceed to pledge themselves to assist by personal service, to contribute of their means, and use their best endeavors to influence their neighbors to resist this attempt at subjugation. As an earnest of their determination they proposed to contribute half a pound of powder and a pound of lead, flints and cartridge paper, which they estimate will cost two shillings and sixpence, and accordingly advise the collection of this amount from each tithable person. It is indeed surprising that a little skirmish, away in a distant part of New England, should arouse a sentiment so strong and unwavering, and prompt them, laying aside colonial quarrels, to unite as one man in aid of the struggle soon to open, even though they had scarcely a cabin to shelter their defenseless heads, and were exposed on this distant frontier to the sudden incursions of the savages.

Though at the outset, and under the influence of a sudden impulse of patriotism, the people seemed to unite to oppose a common enemy, yet the civil government must go on, patents for lands must be issued, deeds for transfer of property must be put on record, and all the details of civil government must be performed. Virginia having established a court at Pittsburg, and having discovered that Pennsylvania would not use force to prevent the exercise of power, continued to authorize the performance of civil functions, and henceforward, as we shall soon see, monopolized authority west of the

Laurel Hills, and although the court of Westmoreland County had an existence, little business was transacted.

In the meantime, in order to quiet any further local contention, in presence of the greater peril that now confronted the United Colonies, the following named gentlemen, members of the Continental Congress from Pennslyvania and Virginia, viz.: John Dickson, George Ross, B. Franklin, James Wilson, Charles Humphreys, P. Henry, Richard Henry Lee, Benjamin Harrison and Thomas Jefferson, united in the following pacific advice addressed " To the inhabitants of Pennsylvania and Virginia on the west side of the Laurel Hill. Friends and Countrymen: It gives us much concern to find that disturbances have arisen and still continue among you concerning the boundaries of our colonies. In the character in which we now address you, it is unnecessary that we inquire into the origin of these unhappy disputes, and it would be improper for us to express our approbation or censure on either side; but as representatives of two of the Colonies united among many others for the defence of the liberties of America, we think it our duty to remove, as far as lies in our power, every obstacle that may prevent her sons from co-operating as vigorously as they would wish to do towards the attainment of this great and important end. Influenced solely by this motive, our joint and earnest request to you is that all animosities which have heretofore subsisted among you as inhabitants of distinct Colonies may now give place to generous and concurring efforts for the prevention of everything that can make our common country dear to us. We are fully persuaded that you, as well as we, wish to see your differences terminate in this happy issue. For this desirable use we recommend it to you, that all bodies of armed men kept up under either province be dismissed, that all those on either side who are in confinement or under bail for taking part in the contests, be discharged, and that until the dispute be decided every person be permitted to retain his possessions unmolested. By observing these directions the public tranquility will be secured without injury to the titles on either side; the period, we flatter ourselves, will soon arrive when this unfortunate dispute, which has produced much mischief, and as far as we can learn, no good, will be peacably and constitutionally determined."

This document has been quoted here in its entirety, not only because of the ability and commanding influence of its authors—such as Franklin and Dickinson, and Henry and Jefferson, the very " master spirits of this age," but on the account of its timely wisdom, and authoritative suggestions. If the title to their lands were to be valid and secure, as here intimated, from whichever colony secured, a great motive for keeping up the controversy would be removed. This assurance, coming from such eminent men, members of the

Congress that was likely to be supreme over all the colonies, had almost the deciding influence over the minds of the settlers, that a legal enactment would have had and must be regarded as a turning point in this heated controversy that was liable at any moment to have broken out into acts of sanguinary conflict~ It should therefore be considered as a vital morsel in the history of these southwestern counties.

Dunmore had betaken himself on board the British man-of-war, Fowey, lying in Chesapeake Bay, and had taken with him the powder from the Virginia arsenal. This, Patrick Henry, at the head of the militia, just before setting out to take his seat in Congress, had compelled Dunmore to settle for, by the payment of £330 by the hand of Corbin, his Majesty's receiver general.

As the war cloud of the Revolution thickened, and the Virginians had broken with their governor, Connolly, probably listening to the suggestions of Dunmore, fancied he saw an opportunity of cutting a larger figure than contending for the right to act as a justice of the peace where his authority was in question, and might be successfully controverted. He, accordingly, abandoned his throne at Pittsburg, and having received from Dunmore instructions to repair to General Gage, at Boston, commander-in-chief of his Majesty's forces in America, he was to make application for authority to raise "an army to the westward," in the name of the King, to fight against the colonies. He fancied that he could induce a large force to join him from the neighborhood of Pittsburg, and southward, to espouse the royal cause, and by making his headquarters at Detroit or Canada, he could raise an army of disaffected whites and Indians with which to make war from the rear upon the Colonies, and "obstruct communication between the Southern and Northern Governments." Could anything evince the character of a black-hearted traitor more conspicuously than this?" He received authority, as desired, and was furnished with blank commissions which he was to execute and bestow at his own discretion. But, on his way to the field of his exploits, when arrived at Hagerstown, Maryland, he was captured, and, skillfully concealed beneath his saddle, a paper was found disclosing all the details of his traitorous scheme. He was held as a prisoner of war until 1780-1 together with his associates, when he was exchanged. In 1782 he was at the head of a force of British and Indians in the neighborhood of Chatauqua Lake on his way to reduce Fort Pitt, and establish himself there. But probably finding his force too feeble for such an enterprise, he abandoned it. To the honor of the friends and relatives of Connolly it should be stated that while he was concerting measures for the destruction of his country, they were equally earnest in patriotic designs.

CHAPTER XV.

VIRGINIA MILITIA SENT TO PITTSBURG—WEST AUGUSTA COUNTY—
OHIO, YOHOGANIA, MONONGHALIA COUNTIES—VIRGINIA SENDS
AMMUNITION TO PITTSBURG—TROOPS ORGANIZED—GUNS SENT
—GOVERNOR PATRICK HENRY OF VIRGINIA URGES A STOUT
DEFENCE OF FORT PITT—MANY NAMES OF EARLY SETTLERS
AMONG MILITIA OFFICERS—DEFEND TO THE LAST EXTREMITY—
A NEW STATE TO BE CALLED WESTSYLVANIA PETITIONED FOR TO
CONTINENTAL CONGRESS TO BE THE FOURTEENTH—STRONG LAN-
GUAGE OF THE PETITION—BOUNDS OF PROPOSED NEW STATE—
240 MILES IN LENGTH BY 70 TO 80 IN BREADTH, EQUAL IN EXTENT
TO AN EMPIRE—" VANDALIA " AND " WALPOLE " PROPOSED—VIR-
GINIA OPENS LAND OFFICES, FIXES PRICE OF LAND—TITLES TO
THE GREATER PART OF SOUTHWESTERN PENNSYLVANIA HELD BY
PATENTS GRANTED BY VIRGINIA.

WHEN the Virginia convention, on the retirement of Lord Dunmore, took the supreme authority of the colony in its own
hands, measures were adopted for retaining the district of Pittsburg
beyond the Laurel Hills in its control, as though the matter of jurisdiction was already settled in favor of Virginia Captain John Neville
was authorized to raise a company of one hundred men and
march to and take possession of Pittsburg Another company of one hundred and twenty-five men was summoned from the
Monongahela country.   The colony of Virginia was divided into sixteen districts of which West Augusta was one, comprising all the territory drained by the Monongahela, Youghiogheny and Kiskiminitas and
the streams falling into the Ohio.   A proposition was made by certain
commissioners sent out by the Continental Congress, Jasper Yeates
and John Montgomery, for Pennsylvania, and Dr. Thomas Walker
and John Harvey, for Virginia, to Pittsburg to treat with the Indians,
that in order to settle the disputed authority temporarily, county
courts should be held under the authority of Pennsylvania north of
the Youghiogheny River, and of Virginia south of that stream; but
no attention was paid to this advice, probably being equally distasteful
to each party.
      Understanding by the establishment of West Augusta district
that the Virginia colonial convention intended a separate county

court from that held at Stranton, for Augusta County, the Justices proceeded to organize an independent court and fixed the county seat at Augusta town just over the ridge west from Washington But this arrangement was of short duration; for at the session of the Virginia assembly held in 1776, Patrick Henry being Governor, an act was passed for ascertaining the limits of West Augusta, and for dividing that district into three counties, Ohio, Yohogania and Mononghalia; Ohio County to embrace all the territory drained by the streams falling into the Ohio River as far north as Cross Creek, embracing the half of the present Greene County; Yohogania, the territory drained by the Youghiogheny and Kiskiminitas Rivers as far east as the Laurel Hills, and as far south as Dunlap's and Cross Creeks; and Mononghalia east and south of the other two and embracing all the land drained by the Monongalia River, extending far into West Virginia, and embracing the eastern slope of Greene County. It was provided by the same act which authorized the limitations of these counties, " that after the said 8th day of November, courts shall be constantly held every month by the justices of the respective counties upon the days hereinafter specified for each county respectively, that is to say for the county of Ohio on the first Monday, for the county of Monongahela on the second Monday, and for the county of Yohogania on the fourth Monday of every month, in such manner as by the laws of this Commonwealth is provided for other counties, and as shall be by their commission directed   It was provided that all cases pending in the whole of West Augusta district before the division into the three counties, should be tried in the court of Yohogania County. The places fixed for holding the courts in the three counties were the plantation of Andrew Heath for Yohogania, the Plantation of Theopholus Phillips, near New Geneva, for Mononghalia, and Black's Cabin, now West Liberty, for Ohio.

The Revolutionary war was now fairly inaugurated, and as the British were using every endeavor to enlist the Indians in their cause against the colonists, issuing commissions freely to diseffected Americans to lead them, and to fit out expeditions from Canada to attack the settlers from the rear, it became evident near the close of 1776, that the Indians were standing in hostile attitude. Accordingly Patrick Henry, then Governor of Virginia, wrote, under date of December 13th, to Lieutenant Dorsey Pentecost, advising him of the hostile temper of the savages and that he had ordered six tons of lead for the West Augusta district, and counselling that he call a meeting of the militia officers of the district to determine on safe places of deposit. " I am of opinion," he says, " that unless your people wisely improve this winter you may probably be destroyed. Prepare then to make resistance while you have time."

A council of war was accordingly held at Catfish Camp, now Washington County, at which the following officers were present: "Dorsey Pentecost, company lieutenant: John Cannon, colonel; Isaac Cox, lieutenant-colonel; Henry Taylor, major; David Sheperd, company lieutenant; Silas Hedge, colonel; David McClure, lieutenant-colonel; Samuel McCullough, major; Zacheriah Morgan, company lieutenant; John Evins, major. Captains—John Munn, David Andrew, John Wall, Cornelius Thompson, Gabrial Cox, Michael Rawlings, William Scott, Joseph Ogle, William Price, Joseph Tumbleson, Benjamin Fry, Mathew Richey, Samuel Meason, Jacob Lister, Peter Reasoner, James Rogers, David Owings, Henry Hogland, John Pearce Davall, James Brinton, Vinson Colvin, James Buckhannan, Abner Howell, Charles Crecraft, John Mitchell, John Hogland, Reason Virgin, William Harrod, David Williamson, Joseph Cisnesy, Charles Martin, Owin Daviss." In glancing over these names it will be noticed that a considerable number are common to Greene County, and represent the families who were its earliest settlers.

According to the request of Governor Henry these officers designated the points suitable for magazines, and called for three tons of gun-powder, ten thousand flints, and one thousand rifles. On the 28th of February, 1777, Governor Henry again wrote requesting that a detail be made of a hundred men "to escort safely to Pittsburg, the powder purchased by Captain Gibson. I suppose it is at Fort Louis on the Mississippi, under the protection of the Spanish Government. I have ordered four 4-pound cannons to be cast for strengthening Fort Pitt, as I believe an attack will be made there ere long. Let the ammunition be stored there, and let it be defended to the last extremity; give it not up but with the lives of yourself and people. Let the provisions be stored there, and consider it as the bulwark of your country." It will be observed that all this legislation and military preparation is had under authority of the Assembly and Governor of Virginia, for the government and protection of territory rightfully belonging to Pennsylvania, which was at this time, and until 1780, remained a part of Virginia, which the authorities of Pennsylvania determined not to quarrel about, until such time as its charter limits could be fixed and vindicated by competent authority.

We come now to a passage in this early history which shows a phase which might have been realized, that would have changed the whole future not only of Greene County, but of this whole valley,—which is no less than the project for a new State, the capital of which would possibly have been within the limits of Greene County, which was to be designated by the euphonious title of WESTSYLVANIA. A very elaborate petition was drawn which recited the inconveniences on account of distance from the seats of government of Virginia and Pennsylvania, of the necessity of having to cross lofty and interminable ranges of mountains, of claims and counter-claims to land, and the unsettled boundary between the two States. This petition was presented to the Continental Congress, was received and ordered filed; but was never acted on, probably because a life and death struggle for existence demanded all the attention of that body, and for the reason that the Congress had no jurisdiction as yet over territory beyond the United Colonies The language of this petition is unique, and in detailing wrongs, cumulative. In reciting the effect of the authority by the two colonies, it proceeds to point out "the pernicious and destructive effects of discordant and contending jurisdictions, innumerable frauds, impositions, violences, depredations, feuds, animosities, divisions, litigations, disorders, and even with the effusion of human blood to the utter subversion of all laws, human and divine, of justice, order, regularity, and in a great measure even of Liberty itself." It details "the fallacies, violences and fraudulent impositions of Land Jobbers, pretended officers and partisans of both land offices and others under the sanction of the jurisdiction of their respective provinces, the Earl of Dunmore's warrants, officer's and soldier's rights, and an infinity of other pretexts." It gives the details of claims of private parties and companies to fabulous tracts of land, the titles to which rest on the pretended purchase of the Indians. "This is a country," it proceeds, "of at least 240 miles in length, from the Kittanny to opposite the mouth of the Scioto, 70 or 80 miles in breadth, from the Alleghany Mountains to the Ohio, rich, fertile and healthy even beyond a credibility, and peopled by at least 25,000 families since 1768." It concludes by asking that the territory embraced in the limits set below be known as the Province and government of Westsylvania, * * * the inhabitants be invested with every other power, right, privilege and immunity vested, or to be vested, in the other American colonies; be considered as a sister colony, and the fourteenth province of the American Confederacy: "Beginning at the eastern bank of the Ohio opposite the mouth of Scioto and running thence to the top of the Alleghany Mountains, thence with the top of the said mountains to the north limits of the purchase made from the Indians in 1768, at the treaty of Fort Stanwix aforesaid, thence with the said limits to the Allegheny or Ohio River, and thence down the said river as purchased from the said Indians at the aforesaid treaty of Fort Stanwix to the beginning." There were other projects for a new State to be known as "Vandalia," or "Walpole," but none so formal or enforced with such elaborate arguments as in this petition for "Westsylvania."

To satisfy the complaints of settlers, the General Assembly of

Virginia opened land offices, fixed the limits of the districts, and
determined the price of land at ten shillings for a hundred acres.
Commissioners were to be appointed for hearing and determining
disputes and counter-claims, and county surveyors were to be appointed to survey and make formal records of sales.   It will thus be,
perceived that Virginia held formal possession of this whole southwestern stretch of Pennsylvania for a period of contention over
a dozen or more years; and, as a large proportion of the land in
Green County was taken up during these years, it will be seen that
the territory was originally held under Virginia patents.

T. R. McMinn

CHAPTER XVI.

ATTRACTIONS IN THIS SECTION FOR THE SETTLER—VALIDITY OF THE
OHIO AND WALPOLE COMPANY'S TITLES IN DOUBT—CONTINENTAL
CONGRESS—ONE WEAKNESS IN PENNSYLVANIA CHARTER—PENN-
SYLVANIA PUBLICATION—PROPOSITIONS FOR SETTLEMENT—COM-
MISSIONERS MEET AT BALTIMORE—TO THE 41°—TO THE 40°—TO
MASON AND DIXON'S LINE—WESTERN BOUNDARY EXTEND WEST-
WARD INTO OHIO—TO THE 39°, 30', WITH A WESTERN CORRES-
PONDING TO THE MEANDERINGS OF THE DELAWARE RIVER—TO
THE 39°, 30', WITH A MERIDIAN LINE FOR THE WESTERN BOUND-
ARY—MASON AND DIXON'S LINE WITH A MERIDIAN LINE FOR THE
WESTERN BOUNDARY SETTLES THE CONTROVERSY—VIRGINIA
SENDS LAND COMMISSIONERS TO REDSTONE AND ISSUES PATENTS
FOR VAST TRACTS—REMONSTRANCE SENT TO CONGRESS—RECOM-
MENDATION OF CONGRESS UNHEEDED—JOINT ADDRESS OF COUNCIL
AND ASSEMBLY OF PENNSYLVANIA—PENNSYLVANIA BECOMES BEL-
LIGERENT—PROPOSITION OF VIRGINIA ACCEPTED—COMMISSIONERS
APPOINTED TO RUN AND MARK THE LINE—JEFFERSON ADVISES A
TEMPORARY LINE—SETTLERS RISE UP IN ARMS TO OPPOSE RUN-
NING LINE—CRY AGAINST TAXES AND DESIRE FOR A NEW STATE,
FINAL REPORT OF COMMISSIONERS MADE—MERIDIAN LINE FOUND
BY ASTRONOMICAL OBSERVATIONS—THE LONG SOUGHT SOUTHWEST
CORNER OF THE STATE FINALLY FOUND AND MARKED—WESTERN
LINE OF PENNSYLVANIA RUN AND MARKED—THE VEXED QUES-
TION OF THE TRUE LIMITS OF THE STATE FINALLY SETTLED.

THE interest which Virginia manifested for this Monongahela and
Ohio country was first aroused by the reports of the beauty of
the scenery, the fertility of the soil, and the salubrity of its climate.
The desire to obtain vast tracts of this country led to the formation
of the Ohio Company with a grant of a half million acres, which was
subsequently swallowed up by Walpole's grant of fabulous extent.
To defend these grants against the French, Washington's embassy to
Le Boeuf was authorized, and military expeditions of Washington,
Braddock, Forbes, Boquet and Stanwix were undertaken After the
French had been finally expelled, Virginia was more eager than be-
fore to hold these, claims, to justify them, and to establish Virginia
civil polity. But the failure of the British government to vindicate

13

its authority broke the validity of the claims of these companies, and for eight years while the Revolutionary war lasted, it was left in doubt whether these titles would eventually be established or lost. During that period, therefore, Virginia continued anxious to assert its authority. But when the surrender of Cornwallis and the breaking of the military force of Britain upon this continent led to a treaty of peace, which left the Continental Congress in supreme authority, then the titles of the Ohio and Walpole companies which claimed their legal status from British government were left without validity, and were valueless.

When Lord Dunmore assumed the Governorship of Virginia he proposed to assert his authority with a high hand, regardless of the rights of other parties, and Patrick Henry, who succeeded to the Gubernatorial power, seemed disposed to take up the cudgels which Dunmore had dropped. But when the delegates from Virginia to the Continental Congress met those from Pennsylvania, the whole subject of disputed authority and mutual boundary seems to have been fairly and candidly canvassed, and more moderate views entertained. And, as we have seen, the paper drawn up by the combined wisdom of these delegates, was the first word that had a quieting effect. There were very able men in those delegations. John Dickinson, the author of the Farmer's Letters, was an accomplished scholar and statesman, and Benjamin Franklin was possessed of practical sense amounting to genius. Besides, the Congress sat at Philadelphia where a strong influence centered favorable to the claims of Pennsylvania. A sentiment was early manifested on the part of both colonies to have commissioners appointed to settle the dispute.

The terms of the Charter of Pennsylvania were very explicit with one exception. The charter proceeded upon the supposition that the perimiter of the circle drawn with a radius of twelve miles from New Castle, would, at some point, cut the beginning of the 40° of north latitude; whereas this parallel fell far to the south of it. This left the beginning of the boundary unfixed and uncertain, and was the original cause of much wrangling and contention, not only on the part of Virginia, but also of Maryland. But the matter of five degrees of longitude and three of latitude were as definite and unchangeable as the places of the stars in the heavens. Earthquakes might change the surface and the subsidence of the land might yield the place to the empire of the waves, yet the boundaries would remain unchanged, and could be easily identified. Some observations had been made at Logstown, a little below Pittsburg, by which it was evident that this place was considerably within the boundaries of Pennsylvania both from the west and south. On any clear night the altitude of certain stars would give the latitude of the place and a good chronometer would show, by difference in time, the longitude. The Virginia delegates in Congress were scholars enough to understand that. It is probable that they saw at the outset that the Pennsylvania title was good, and would eventually prevail. This accounts for the conciliatory temper manifested in that first communication quoted above, and in subsequent action.

During the past few years the government of Pennsylvania have had commissioners engaged in rectifying the boundary lines of the State, and planting monuments to mark them. By an act approved on the 7th day of May, 1885, the reports and maps of these commissioners, together with the complete journal of Mason and Dixon, from December 7, 1763, to January 29, 1768, have been published. From that volume many facts upon this subject have been drawn.

It appears that as early as the 18th of December, 1776, the assembly of Virginia passed a resolution, agreeing to fix the southern boundary of Pennsylvania from the western limit of Maryland due north to the beginning of the 41° parallel and thence due west to the western limit of the State. This was a concession on the part of Virginia, as it had previously claimed all west of the summits of the Alleghany Mountains to the New York line. This would have made a break northward from the western line of Maryland, and would have left the counties of Fayette, Greene and a portion of Washington in Virginia. Pennsylvania would not agree to this. Propositions and counter propositions continued to pass between the assemblies of the two colonies, resulting in nothing until the session of 1779, when it was determined to submit the whole matter in controversy to the arbitrament of commissioners. In a letter of 27th of May, 1779, Patrick Henry, Governor of Virginia, communicated to the council of Pennsylvania the intelligence that commissioners had been appointed. On the 27th of August, 1779, the commissioners met at Baltimore; James Madison and Robert Andrews on the part of Virginia, and George Bryan, John Ewing and David Rittenhouse for Pennsylvania. Their proceedings were in writing.

The first paper was drawn by the Pennsylvania delegates, in which the points in controversy are fully argued, and this demand made: "For the sake of peace, and to manifest our earnest desire of adjusting the dispute on amicable terms, we are willing to recede from our just rights [the beginning of the 40° north,] and therefore propose, that a meridian be drawn from the head spring of the north branch of the Potomac to the beginning of the 40° of north latitude, and from thence that a parallel of latitude be drawn to the western extremity of the State of Pennsylvania, to continue forever the boundary of the State of Pennsylvania and Virginia." This would have made a break southward at the western extremity of Maryland and would have carried into Pennsylvania a large tract of what is now West Virginia, nearly the whole of the territory drained by the Monongahela and its tributaries, a tract equal to six counties of the size of the county of Greene.

This proposition the Virginia commissioners rejected in an elaborate argument in which all the points made by the Pennsylvanians were considered, and they close with the following counter proposition. "But we trust, on a further consideration of the objections of Virginia to your claim, that you will think it advantageous to your State to continue Mason and Dixon's line to your western limits, which we are willing to establish as a perpetual boundary between Virginia and Pennsylvania on the south side of the last mentioned State. We are induced to make this proposal, as we think that the same principle which effected the compromise between Pennsylvania and Maryland should operate equally as strong in the present case." This proposition was the line which eventually prevailed and is the present boundary.

But the Pennsylvania commissioners were unwilling to give up the territory reaching down to the beginning of the 40°. They accordingly made this compensatory proposition: "That Mason and Dixon's line should be extended so far beyond the western limits of Pennsylvania, as that a meridian drawn from the western extremity of it to the beginning of the 43° of north latitude, shall include as much land as will make the State of Pennsylvania what it was originally intended to be, viz: three degrees in breadth, and five degrees in length, excepting so much as has been heretofore relinquished to Maryland." This would have put on to the western end of the State a narrow patch, embracing the Panhandle and a part of Ohio, stretching up to the lake, which should be equal in area to the block of West Virginia, which Pennsylvania would give up if Mason and Dixon's line should be adopted.

This proposition was promptly rejected, and the following submitted: "Considering how much importance it may be to the future happiness of the United States, that every cause of discord be now removed, we will agree to relinquish even a part of that territory which you before claimed, but which we still think is not included in the charter of Pennsylvania. We, therefore, propose that a line run due west from that point where the meridian of the first fountain of the north branch of the Potomac meets the end of the 30', of the 39° of northern latitude, five degrees of longitude to be computed from that part of the river Delaware which lies in the same parallel, shall forever be the boundary of Pennsylvania and Virginia, on the southern part of the last mentioned State." This gave Pennsylvania a break south into West Virginia, not to the amount of six counties of the size of Greene, but less than two; but it also provided that the western boundary of Pennsylvania should, instead of being a due north and south line, 'conform to the meanderings of the Delaware, being at all points just five degrees from the right bank of that stream.

To this the Pennsylvania commissioners made the following reply: " We will agree to your proposal of the 30th of August, 1779, for running and forever establishing the southern boundary of Pennsylvania in the latitude of thirty-nine degrees, thirty minutes westward of the meridian of the source of the north branch of the Potomac River, upon condition that you consent to allow a meridian line drawn northward from the western extremity thereof as far as Virginia extends, to be the western boundary of Pennsylvania " This would have given the narrow strip of West Virginia, and a due north and south line for the western boundary as at present.

This proposition was rejected by the Virginia representatives; but they submitted in lieu thereof the following: " We will continue Mason and Dixon's line due west five degrees of longitude, to be computed from the river Delaware, for your southern boundary, and will agree that a meridian drawn from the western extremity of this line to your northern limit shall be the western boundary of Pennsylvania."

To this the Pennsylvania commissioners returned the following answer: " We agree to your last proposal of August 31st, 1779, to extend Mason and Dixon's line due west five degrees of longitude, to be computed from the river Delaware, for the southern boundary of Pennsylvania; and that a meridian drawn from the western extremity thereof to the northern limit of the State, be the western boundary of Pennsylvania forever." This ended the conference and forever settled the southwestern boundary of our good old Commonwealth and brought to an end a controversy that at one time threatened to result in internecine war.

So far as it could be done in theory the controversy was now at an end, though the approval of the two governments was yet to be had, and when that was secured, the actual running of the lines and marking the boundaries, which, as the sequel proves, were subject to delays and irritating contentions. The labors of the commissioners, who held their sittings in Baltimore, were concluded on the 31st of August, 1779. The Assembly of Pennsylvania, at the sitting of November 19th, 1779, promptly passed a resolution " to ratify and finally confirm the agreement entered into between the commissioners from the State of Virginia, and the commissioners from this State." In good faith Pennsylvania promptly acted. But the Virginia Assembly delayed, and in the meantime commissioners had been appointed to adjust and settle titles of claimants to unpatented lands. Although the commissioners had come to a settlement of differences on the last day of August, as late as December of this year, Francis

Peyton, Phillip Pendleton, Joseph Holmes, and George Merriweather, land commissioners from Virginia, for the West Augusta district, embracing the counties of Yohogania, Ohio, and Monongalia, Virginia counties, but Westmoreland County, under Pennsylvania authority, came to Redstone on the Monongahela, and held a court at which a large number of patents were granted to Virginia claimants to vast tracts of the choice lands along the Monongahela valley to the prejudice of Pennsylvania claimants, though it was now known that all this country, by the award of the Baltimore conference, was within the limits of Pennsylvania   Though Virginia could claim that the award had not been ratified by the Virginia Assembly, yet high minded statesmanship would have held that all questions of the nature of actual sale of lands should have been held in abeyance, at this stage of the settlement   The surveys of lands thus adjudicated averaged in quantity from 400 to 800 acres to each claimant, and the number of claims passed upon was almost fabulous.

As soon as intelligence of this procedure, on the part of Virginia, reached the council of Pennsylvania, which was communicated by Thomas Scott, as member of the council from the Westmoreland district; the President of the council, Joseph Reed, addressed the Continental Congress upon the subject, in which, after recounting the facts, he says, " We shall make such remonstrance to the State of Virginia as the interest and honor of this State require, it these should be ineffectual, we trust we shall stand justified in the eyes of God and man, if, availing ourselves of the means we possess, we afford that support and aid to the much injured and distressed inhabitants of the frontier counties, which their situation and our duty require "   As soon as the state of affairs was known to Congress, a resolution was passed, on December 27th, recommending to the two parties to this controversy not to grant any part of the disputed land, nor to disturb any in possession of such lands, and on the following day, the President of the council of Pennsylvania, issued his proclamation reciting the fact that a Virginia commission was sitting at Redstone issuing certificates for land, quoting the language of the resolution of Congress upon this subject, and closing by calling on all Pennsylvania officers, civil and military, to obey the recommendation of Congress, and directing all Pennsylvania claimants of land to continue in possession and cultivation of their lands, regardless of the claims set up by Virginia.   Fifty copies of this proclamation were sent for distribution in the disputed district   But the Virginia commissioners sitting at Redstone refused to be governed by the recommendation of Congress, and returned the reply that such objection should be made to the Governor of Virginia, under whose authority they were acting.

The authorities of Pennsylvania were now becoming thoroughly aroused, and on the 24th of March, 1780, a joint address of the Council and Assembly was presented to Congress, setting forth in strong light their grievances, and closing in a belligerent spirit. "If Pennsylvania must arm for her internal defence, instead of recruiting her. Continental line, if her attention and supplies must be diverted in like manner, if the common enemy encouraged by our division should prolong the war, interests of our sister States and the common cause be injured or distressed, we trust we shall stand acquitted before them and the whole world; and if the effusion of human blood is to be the result of this unhappy dispute, we humbly trust that the great Governor of the universe, who delights in peace, equity and justice, will not impute it to us."

But all this had small effect upon the authorities of Virginia; for the Legislature, which met in May, enacted that a further time of eighteen months was allowed to obtain certificates from the commissioners to enter their claims, provided they did not secure such certificates to land north of Mason and Dixon's line, claimed by Pennsylvania, yet her surveyors continued to act under Virginia authority, as late as June, 1782

Finally, on the 23d of June, 1780, the Virginia General Assembly took up the matter of boundary and agreed to the terms adopted by the Baltimore commission, but with this important, and to Pennsylvania, humiliating condition: "On condition that the private property and rights of all persons acquired under, founded on, or recognized by the laws of either country *previous to the date hereof*, be saved and confirmed to them, although they should be found to fall within the other, and that in the decision of disputes thereupon preference shall be given to the elder or prior right whichever of the said States the same shall have been acquired under; such persons paying to that State, within whose boundary their land shall be included, the same purchase or consideration money which would have been due from them to the State under which they claimed the right; and where any such purchase or consideration money hath, since the Declaration of American Independence, been received by either State for lands which, according to the before cited agreement, shall fall within the territory of the other, the same shall be reciprocally refunded and repaid. And that the inhabitants of the disputed territory, now ceded to the State of Pennsylvania, shall not before the first day of December, in the present year, be subject to the payment of any tax, nor at any time to the payment of arrears of taxes, or impositions laid by either State."

Though distasteful and manifestly unjust to Pennsylvania, yet "determining to give to the world the most unequivocal proof of their earnest desire to promote peace and harmony with a sister State, so necessary during this great conflict against the common enemy," it agreed to the terms proposed, and the legal forms of settlement were finally at an end.

Nothing now remained to be done but to have the actual surveys made upon this basis of settlement, and to set up the bounds, in order to close the controversy. On the 21st of February, 1781, John Lukins and Archibald McLean were appointed on the part of Pennsylvania, and on the 17th of April, James Madison and Robert Andrews, on the part of Virginia, to make these surveys. Thomas Jefferson was at this time Governor of Virginia, and he recommended that the five degrees of longitude be determined by astronomical observations, as being the most accurate, though Mason and Dixon had made actual measurement and reduced it to horizontal distance, and offered to send westward the instruments necessary, viz: " a good time-piece, telescopes and a quadrant." That there should be no interruption from disaffected parties, James Marshall was ordered to call out a company of militia to the number of forty to act as a guard. As the careful survey and marking of the line would unavoidably consume considerable time, Governor Jefferson proposed that a temporary line be run from the point where Mason and Dixon stopped on Dunkard Creek, a distance of thirty-six miles, in order that the settlers might know as soon as possible under what State government they were living. Mr. McLean was appointed on this service from Pennsylvania, and the Surveyor-General of Yohogania County for Virginia. In the meantime it was ascertained that there was a party among the settlers who were strongly opposed to the running of the line, preferring to remain under Virginia rule, and gratified to see the question kept open, as thereby escaping the payment of taxes and doing military service.

Benjamin Harrison succeeded Thomas Jefferson as Governor of Virginia, and in a communication of the 26th of April, 1782, he objects to commencing to survey from Dunkard Creek where Mason and Dixon left it; but insists that it shall begin at the point where the west line of Maryland cuts Mason and Dixon's line. But now a new impediment is interposed to the running of the temporary line; for Mr. McLean writes to Governor Moore of Pennsylvania, "We proceeded to the mouth of Dunkard Creek, where our stores were laid in on the 10th day of June, and were preparing to cross the river that night, when a party of about thirty horsemen armed on the opposite side of the river, appeared, damning us to come over, and threatening us to a great degree; and several more were seen by our bullock guard, which we had sent over the river, one of which asked them if they would surrender to be taken as prisoners, with other language of menacing." A conference was proposed, and a committee of the settlers opposing was met, but no arguments were of any avail with them. "The cry," writes Mr.

Thos Adamson

McLean, " against taxes in specie is general; this, together with the idea of a new State, which is artfully and industriously conveyed, are only expedients to prevent the running of the line."

Finally, on the 26th of March, 1783, John Dickinson, who had now become Governor of Pennsylvania, issued his proclamation, commanding all persons within the limits of the commonwealth to take notice of the provisions made by the two States for running the line, and " to pay due obedience to the laws of this commonwealth " On September 11, 1783, the following persons were appointed on the part of Pennsylvania: John Ewing, David Rittenhouse, John Lukens and Thomas Hutchins, and on August 31 the following, James Madison, Robert Andrews, John Page and Andrew Ellicott, on the part of Virginia, were designated to make a final settlement of the bounds. Their joint report is as follows: " We, the underwritten commissioners, together with the gentlemen with whom we are joined in commission, have, by corresponding astronomical observations made near the Delaware and in the western country, ascertained the extent of the said five degrees of longitude; and the underwritten commissioners have continued Mason and Dixon's line to the termination of the said five degrees of longitude, by which work the southern boundary of Pennsylvania is completed. The continuation we have marked by opening vistas over the most remarkable heights which lie in the course, and by planting on many of these heights in the parallel of latitude, the true boundary posts marked with the letters P and V, each letter facing the State of which it is the initial. At the extremity of this line, which is the southwest corner of the State of Pennsylvania, we have planted a squared unlettered white oak post, around whose base we have raised a pile of stones " At the Wilmington observatory the commissioners commenced their observations at the beginning of July, and continued observing the eclipses of Jupiter's satellites till the 20th of September, that they might have a sufficient number of them, both before and after his opposition to the sun, making near sixty observations At the other extremity of the line the observations were commenced about the middle of July, and between forty and fifty notes of the eclipses of Jupiter's satellites, besides innumerable observations of the sun and stars were made, and " completed their observations with so much accuracy as to remove from their minds every degree of doubt concerning their final determination of the southwest corner of the State."

Thus was settled the location of the southwest corner of the State. and consequently of Greene County. But the western boundary was still unmarked, though this, being a 'simple meridian line, was not difficult of adjustment. Accordingly a commission, consisting of David Rittenhouse and Andrew Porter, in behalf of Pennsylvania, Andrew Ellicott, of Maryland, and Joseph Neville, of Virginia, was constituted for this purpose, and on the 23d of August, 1785, made this report: "We have carried on a meridian line from the southwest corner of Pennsylvania, northward to the River Ohio, * * * and we have likewise placed stones duly marked on most of the principal hills, and where the line strikes the Ohio."

From the Ohio River northward the line was surveyed by Alexander McLean and Andrew Porter, Rittenhouse and Ellicott having been put upon the northern line, between New York and Pennsylvania, who made their final report on the 4th of October, 1786, "that we have ascertained and completed said line by astronomical observations as far as Lake Erie, having opened a vista and planted stones in the proper direction, marked on the east side Γ., and that said line extends some distance in the lake" Thus was finally settled amicably the question of boundary, which for the full space of a hundred years had vexed the inhabitants of the border and the governments of three of the original colonies, and which had repeatedly been carried up to the place of last resort, the King in council Considerable space has been given to this subject, that it might here be fully understood in all its bearings, as Greene is the county most nearly touched in this whole difficulty, and as it furnishes one of the most interesting topics of American history.

CHAPTER XVII.

TITLES TO LANDS LARGELY DERIVED FROM VIRGINIA AUTHORITY—
CRUMRINE GIVES ENTRIES—PETITIONS FOR A NEW COUNTY—
WASHINGTON COUNTY ORGANIZED—COUNTY OFFICERS—TRIBULA-
TIONS—GEORGE ROGERS CLARK'S EXPEDITION—TO ADVOCATE
NEW STATE, TREASON—COUNTY OFFICERS—HENRY TAYLOR FIRST
JUDGE—ALLEGHANY COUNTY ERECTED—PORTION TAKEN FROM
WASHINGTON COUNTY—BOUNDARY OF TRACT TAKEN FROM WASH-
INGTON COUNTY, WHICH FORMS THE SOUTHERN PART OF ALLE-
GHANY.

AS we have already seen, that portion of the present State of Pennsylvania west of the Laurel Hills and south of the Alleghany
and Ohio rivers was embraced in three counties under Virginia
authority, and though the County of Westmoreland with county seat
at Hannastown, near the present Greensburg, embraced this same
territory, at which courts were held under Pennsylvania authority,
yet the greater share of the county court and county office record
business in all that territory of Pennsylvania west of the Monongahela and south of the Ohio rivers was transacted in Virginia County
courts, for a period of a dozen or more years, and until the southwest
corner of Pennsylvania was finally discovered, and a bound set to
mark it. That spot which three great States had been searching for
and struggling about, and which was disturbing the quiet even of
the King in council, and rendering his life uneasy, was at last discovered and marked, and from that time forward the minds of the
pioneers became settled, and Assembly, and Governors, and King had
peace. Indeed that white oak post with the cone of stone piled
about it was the great peace-maker, more potent in its authority than
governments and courts. That post, which marks the southwest
corner of Greene County, set up the Pennsylvania authority over
this region, which for the space of more than a hundred years has
been unquestioned and undisturbed.

It will be remembered that the commissioners of the two States
of Pennsylvania and Virginia had agreed upon terms of settlement
of the dispute, as early as the 31st of August, 1779, and had these
terms been approved by the two State governments at once, and the
astronomical observations been promptly ordered, the place of the
corner might have been easily found, and the bound set up before

the opening of the year 1780. But on account of the delay on the part of the Virginia assembly in acting, and then the seeming interminable delays in ordering out the surveying parties, it was the close of 1784 before the reports of the surveyors were adopted and the whole subject legalized and set to rest In all this time, therefore, the courts under Virginia authority were kept busy in making entries and perfecting titles to land. Hence, it will be found that a large proportion of the original titles to lands in the present limits of Greene County were obtained under Virginia authority. The records of these Virginia courts are of interest to the students of legal lore; but would probably fail to engage the attention of the general reader. Mr Crumrine, in his history of Washington County, has made quite an extensive collation of these records, to which work the curious reader is referred

The settlers in the district of Pennsylvania, who were adherents of the Pennsylvania rule, as soon as they learned that the commissioners had agreed upon terms of settlement of the disputed boundary, commenced addressing the Governor upon the propriety of forming a new county of this territory. Among these was Thomas Scott, who had been prominent in Lord Dunmore's time. Governor Reed, who was now at the head of the government in Pennsylvania, regarding the subject favorably, in a message to the council of Nov. 6, 1780, recommended the laying off of "one or more counties so as to introduce law, order, and good government, where they have long been much needed." In compliance with this recommendation, as early as the 28th of March, 1781, the act was passed erecting Washington County, to comprise all of the territory inclosed by the Monongahela and Ohio rivers and the south and west bounds of the State, embracing what are now the counties of Greene, Washington, and parts of Alleghany and Beaver. Authority was given for the election of inspectors of election of members of the Assembly and Council, two sheriffs, two coroners, and three commissioners. By the tenth section it was "made lawful to and for James Edgar, Hugh Scott, Van Swearingen, Daniel Leet, and John Armstrong or any three of them, to take up or purchase, and to take assurance to them and their heirs, of a piece of land situated in some convenient place in the said county, in trust and for the use of the inhabitants of the said county, and thereupon to erect and build a court-house and prison, sufficient to accommodate the public service of the said county." Full provisions were made for the transfer of authority from Westmoreland courts to Washington, and the executive council appointed Thomas Scott to be prothonotary, James Marshall lieutenant, and John Cannon and Daniel Leet to be sub-lieutenants of the new county.

It will be observed that the act creating the County of Washington antedated the final running and marking of the boundary line by several years. During all this period of uncertainty there was constant friction and irritation. Indeed the organization of Washington as well as Westmoreland County, was effected in the midst of great tribulation, and the decision on the part of Pennsylvania, not to resort to force to assert authority, tended to encourage those favoring the Virginia ownership in their lawless procedures. The Indians during the whole period of the Revolution, and until General "Mad" Anthony Wayne, by his victory over the Indians in his campaign in the northwestern territory, put a period to Indian barbarity, there was scarcely a day when the settlers did not live in constant dread of the Indian war whoop.

A commission, consisting of Edgar, Scott, Swaringen, Leet, and Armstrong, proceeded to divide the territory into thirteen townships, the number of the colonies, Amwell, Bethlehem, Cecil, Cumberland, Donegal, Fallowfield, Hopewell, Morgan, Nottingham, Peters, Robinson, Smith and Strabane. Preparations were in progress, under George Rogers Clark, for an expedition against the British and Indians in the northwest, and the Virginia authorities in the three counties of, Ohio, Yohogania, and Monongalia, proceeded to raise troops by drafting, and the irritation incident to enforcing the draft tended to keep up the discontent. Again was the project for a new State revived, as the best panacea for all ills. This latter idea was so much advocated and kept before the settlers, that it was found necessary to pass an act declaring it was treason to longer agitate this question.

At the first general election for Washington, the returns show that Dorsey Pentecost was elected counselor; James Edgar, and John Cannon were elected representatives; Van Swearingen, and Andrew Swearingen, sheriffs; William McFarlane and William McComb, coroners; George Vallandingham, Thomas Crooks, John McDowell, commissioners. Henry Taylor as the first commissioned justice, was president of the court, and was succeeded on the 31st of October, 1783, by Dorsey Pentecost; but on the 29th of November, 1786, Pentecost having removed from the State, his commission was revoked by the council, and Henry Taylor again became president judge, which office he held till he was superceded by the appointment of Alexander Addison, under the constitution of 1790. The limits of Washington County as originally laid out seemed very natural, bounded as it was by two great streams and the State limits. But the town of Pittsburg soon becoming a point of great commercial and manufacturing importance it proved a sore inconvenience for its inhabitants to post off to Hannastown for the transaction of legal business. Accordingly, on the 28th of September, 1788, Alleghany County was erected, by which Washington County gave up all that poition of its noithern territory boidering on the Ohio and Monongahela iivers, and by act of assembly passed on the 17th ot September, 1789, a still further portion bounded as follows: " Beginning at the river Ohio, where the boundary line of the State crosses said river, from thence in a straight line to White's Mill (Murdocksville) on Raccoon Cieek, from thence by a straight line to Armstrong's mill, on Miller's run, and from thence by a straight line to the Monongahela River, opposite the mouth of Perry's run, where it stiikes the present line of the county of Alleghany "

CHAPTER XVIII.

Curtailments of Washington County—County Seat Not Central Act Creating Greene County—Name Given—Notice of General Greene—Where Buried—Acquire Land for County Seat—Land of Thomas Slater—Deed — Named Eden — Streets Named—Cider and Whiskey—Name of the New Town—General Wayne, Notice of—Incident Described by Whitman—Purchasers of Lots—Prices Paid—Commissions Issued to County Officers—Court of Common Pleas, Five Districts—Judge Addison—Notice of his Life—Impeached and Removed—Charges Preferred Against Him—Sentence of Court—Associate Justices—Judge Roberts—Thomas H. Baird Over the New Fourteenth District — Notice of Judge Baird—National Road, Nathaniel Ewing in 1838—Term Ten Years—Notice of Judge Ewing—Samuel A. Gilmore in 1848—Notice of Judge Gilmore—James Lindsey in 1861 —Notice of Judge Lindsey—Minute of Fayette County Court.

BY these curtailments of Washington County on the north, and the farthei one made on the 26th of March, 1800, for the formation of Beaver County, the county seat, which had been established at what is now the town of Washington, was thrown considerably to the north of the centre of the territory, and the inhabitants dwelling in the southern portions of the county became restless, under what they regarded an injustice in being compelled to travel so much farthei to the county seat than those dwelling in the northern portions. Accordingly, in response to a memorial numerously signed, praying for the erection of a new county-out of the southern portions of Washington, the Legislature passed an act on the 9th of February, 1796, as follows: "Section 1. *Be it enacted,* etc., That all that part of Washington County lying within the limits and bounds hereinafter described shall be, and is hereby erected into a separate county, that is to say beginning at the mouth of Ten Mile Creek, on the Monongahela River, thence up Ten Mile Creek, to the junction of the north and south forks of said creek; thence up said north fork to Colonel William Wallace's Mills [West Bethlehem]; thence up a southwesterly direction to the nearest part of the dividing line between the north and south forks of Ten Mile Creek; thence along the top of the said ridge to the ridge which divides the waters of Ten Mile and Wheeling Creeks; thence a straight line to the head of Eulow's branch of the Wheeling; thence down said branch to the western boundary line of the State; thence south along said line to the southern boundary line of the State; thence east along said line to the river Monongahela; and thence down the said river to the place of beginning; to be henceforth known and called by the name of Greene County."

This gave a very compact and well situated body of land for a county, and connected by roads of easy grades for reaching its central portion, wherever the county seat should be erected. But there being some dissatisfaction as to a portion of the northern line, the Legislature, at its session of 1802, made the following emendation, viz: " that the following alteration shall take place in the line between the counties of Washington and Greene, viz: beginning at the present line, on the ridge that divides the waters of Ten Mile and Wheeling creeks, near Jacob Bobbet's; thence a straight line to the head waters of Hunter's fork of Wheeling Creek; and thence down the same to the mouth thereof, where it meets the present county line." This gave back to Washington a small strip of territory, not material to Greene, but desired by Washington.

It will be seen that a patriotic motive swayed the originators of Washington County in giving its name. General Washington was then at the zenith of his military fame, and was approaching that period in his career when he should compel the British General, Cornwallis, to surrender with his whole army, which would practically put a period to the war. This county was the only one erected in the State during the period of the Revolution. What more suitable name could be given it than that of the military leader whose name was on every tongue?

If Washington was an appropriate name for all this stretch of country lying to the west of the Monongahela, what name more proper for the tract, cut from the side of Washington—the rib as it were—than Greene, that one of his Generals above all others, whom Washington loved?

Nathaniel Greene was born of Quaker parents in 1740, at Warwick, Rhode Island. His father was a blacksmith, in which trade the boy was schooled, or rather an anchorsmith; for at this time this was one of the most considerable of all the States in mercantile marine. While yet a youth he learned the Latin language, and became well-read in military history. He was chosen a member of the Rhode Island Legislature when he had scarcely attained his majority. When intelligence reached him of the battle of Lexington, his military ardor, as well as his burning patriotism, was aroused, and he determined to take up arms for the defense of his imperiled country, and was appointed to lead the three regiments raised in his State to the army of Observation then stationed at Roxbury, Massachusetts. This act of the young Quaker cost him his membership in that body. The practiced eye of Washington soon detected his cool judgment and zeal for the cause, and recommended his appointment in the following year as Major-General in the Continental Army, a remarkable promotion from a plain officer of State Militia; but, as events subsequently showed, worthily bestowed. He served with distinction in the battles of Trenton, Princton, Brandywine and Germantown, when he was appointed Quartermaster-General of the American Army, a position of great difficulty and responsibility in view of the straightened circumstances of the colonies, and the absolute necessity that the troops be fed. In 1780 he was assigned to active duty in the field, and was invested with the supreme command of the armies of the South, relieving General Gates. At the conclusion of the war he returned to Rhode Island; but soon after returned to Georgia to look after an estate near Savannah. Not mindful of the intensity of the Southern sun, he was overcome by the heat in what is commonly known as "sun stroke," and died from its effects on the 19th of June, 1786, at the early age of forty-six. His body was placed in a vault in Savannah, but so imperfect was the burial that no name or other means of indentification existed, and when, in 1820, a search was made for his remains, they could not be found, and no one knows the sepulchre of the ablest of Washington's Generals. But the Congress of the new nation was prompt in acknowledging his services, and on the 8th of August of that year passed the following resolution: "That a monument be erected to Nathaniel Greene, Esq., at the seat of the Federal Government, with the following inscription: 'Sacred to the memory of Nathaniel Greene, a native of the State of Rhode Island, who died on the 19th of June, 1786; late Major-General in the service of the United States, and commander of their army in the Southern Department. The United States, in Congress assembled, in honor of his patriotism, valor, and

D. L. Donley

ability, have erected this monument,'" It has been said of him that, "In person General Greene was rather corpulent, and above the common size. His complexion was fair and florid; his countenance serene and mild. His health was generally delicate, but was preserved by temperance and exercise"

By the act erecting the new county it was provided that David Gray, Stephen Gapin, Isaac Jenkinson, William Meetkerke and James Seals be appointed commissioners to procure by grant, bargain, or otherwise any quantity of land not exceeding five hundred acres, within five miles of the center of the county, and survey and lay out the same into town lots; and on due notice given sell lots at public auction, so many lots as to raise a fund sufficient, with certain County taxes, to pay for the purchase of the land and the erection of a court-house and prison Until a court-house was erected the courts were directed to be held at the house of Jacob Kline, on Muddy Creek.

In pursuance of the power thus delegated to the above named commissioners, a site for the county seat was selected in a fine sweep of the South Fork of Ten Mile Creek, on land owned by Thomas Slater, James Seals owning land to the north of it, and John Jones to the south of it. Among the first records in the books of the Prothonotary's office is " Deed of Thomas Slater and Uxor to the Trustees of Greene County. This indenture made the twenty-eighth day of October, in the year 1796, between Thomas Slater and Elenor, his wife on the one part, and David Gray, Stephen Gapin, William Meetkerke, Isaac Jenkinson and James Seals, trustees appointed for the county of Greene, by an act of the general assembly of the State of Pennsylvania, dated the 9th day of February, 1796, entitled an act to erect a part of Washington County into a separate county of the other part. *Whereas*, a certain tract of land called Eden, was granted to the said Thomas Slater by patent dated 7th of March, 1789, and enrolled in the Roll's office of said State in patent book number 14, page 507, etc. Now this Indenture witnesseth that the said Thomas and Elenor his wife, for and in consideration of the sum of $2,376, lawful money of Pennsylvania to them in hand paid by the said [commissioners], for and in behalf of of the county of Greene the receipt of which is hereby acknowledged, and the said Thomas Slater and Elenor his wife, therewith fully satisfied and paid, have granted, bargained and sold, and by these present do grant, bargain and sell unto the said [commissioners] in trust for the use of the county of Greene, and for the purpose of erecting thereon a Court House and Gaol and other public buildings for the use of the said county all the following described and bounded part of the said tract of land that is contained in the following bounds and limits: Beginning at a post and running thence by said Slater's land east

14

218 perches to a post in John Jones' line, thence with the same south 12° ½ east 128 perches to a post, thence by said Slater's land west 188 perches, to a thorn bush on the bank of the South Fork of Ten Mile Creek, thence up the same, and by land of James Seals north 43° and ½ west 17 perches $\frac{5}{10}$ to a white walnut tree, north 41° ½ west 47 perches $\frac{2}{10}$. to a white oak, north 15° west 32 perches to the place of beginning, containing 158 acres ½ strict measure, be the same more or less, together with all and singular, the appurtenance unto the same belonging, or in any ways appurtaining, and the reversions, and remainder rents, issues and profits thereof. To have and to hold the said bounded and sold tract of land and premises with the appurtenances unto the said [commissioners] and their assigns to the only proper use and behoof of the said [commissioners] in trust for the use aforesaid, and according to the true intent and meaning of the above cited act of Assembly,' and the said Thomas Slater and Elenor his wife, for themselves, their heirs, executors, and administrators do hereby covenant, promise and grant to and with the said [commissioners] and their assigns that they the said Thomas Slater and Elenor his wife, the aforesaid tract of land containing 158 acres and ½ strict measure against them and their heirs, and against all and and every other person or persons lawfully claiming the same shall and will warrant and forever defend by these presents. In testimony whereof they have hereunto set their hands and seals the day and year first above written.

Sealed and Delivered in presence of
DAN. McFARLAND,
PHILIP KETCHUM.

Received the day and year within written of
$2,376 being consideration money with in mentioned in full

THOMAS SLATER

Witness
JAN. THOMPSON,
CHRISTIAN FAIR

Acknowledged before
WM. SEATON.
Received 28th October, 1796.
Examined
JOHN BOREMAN, Recorder."

This tract of land thus promptly obtained and secured by deed in trust, then only encumbered by the cabin of its owner, has come to be the home of a numerous and busy population, distinguished for intelligence, and the seat of justice for this beautiful and well settled county. It would seem by reference to the provisions of the above recited deed, that the original owner had given it the name of Eden, a name not inappropriate, when we consider its location, upon this commanding ground, the rich and beautiful valley stretching away, above and below, and the pleasant heights and verdant hillsides across the stream which sweeps around and seems to hold it in its fond embrace.

A draft of the plot of the town accompanies the deed, and is accordingly made of record A street, running north from the extreme south bend of the creek, cuts the tract nearly at its center, and is designated Washington street, and parallel with this to the west are Morris street, Blackberry alley, Rich Hill street and West street, and to the east Cider alley, Morgan street, Whiskey alley, Cumberland street, Findlay alley and East street. Running east and west is High street cutting the tract near its center, and to the north in succession are Strawberry alley, Franklin street, North street, and beyond it the common, fronting on which are the imposing buildings of Waynesburg College and the public school building, and on the summit still further to the north is the reservoir of the waterworks. To the south of High street are Cherry alley, Greene street, South alley, Lincoln street, Walnut alley, Elm street, Locust alley, First street and Water street The railroad follows the valley up the northwest. Between Washington and Morris streets, running north and south, and High and Greene streets extending east and west, in the central and most commanding portion of the tract are located the county buildings,—court-house and jail,—on grounds which now seem contracted, considering that the commissioners could have ap-. propriated as much land and in such location as they chose. The names of the streets are in the main patriotic and descriptive of their location; but the two alleys, Cider and Whiskey, in close proximity to the courts of justice, seem in these days of prohibition to be misnomers, though in the age when given may have afforded the mouth a good flavor when pronounced.

A name for the new town was early considered. It has been already observed that this section of the country had been for a period of over thirty years debatable ground for the savages, as it was in the meantime by the inhabitants of two neighboring States. During the quarter of a century preceding the formation of the town this section had been the scene of more Indian outrages, scalpings and burnings than any other equal area in the country. Though peace had been 'declared between the United States and Great Britain, British troops still occupied forts in the northwestern territory, and encouraged and led the Indians in their warfare against the United States. Two armies, one under Harmer and the other led by St. Claire, had been defeated and sadly cut to pieces by the united strength of British and Indians, and as a consequence the savages were more active than ever in their work of blood. But an army led by General Anthony Wayne had proved more successful, and, having marched into the heart of the Indian country, inflicted so crushing a defeat that the tribes were glad to unite in suing for peace, and in giving hostages for an observance of their treaty stipulations. Nowhere were the happy effects of this triumph more felt than in this territory of Greene County. What name, then, more suitable for the capitol of the new county than the honored one of Wayne, and hence Waynesburgh perpetrates the name of the hero.

Perhaps none of the generals in the American army had so much the character of dash, of sleepless vigilance, of heroic daring in the face of the foe, as Wayne He was born in Chester County in 1745. He was in early life a surveyor, a member of the Assembly of 1774, the friend of Franklin and member of the Committee of Safety of 1775. Seeing war impending, he gave himself earnestly to the study of the military art He was with Sullivan at Three Rivers, Canada, and had charge of the posts at Ticonderoga and Mt Independence. In February, 1777, he was commissioned a Brigadier-General, and participated in the New Jersey and Brandywine campaigns with Washington. On the night of the 20th of September, 1777, while encamped at Paoli, with 1,500 men, the location of his camp was betrayed to the British, when General Gray, with a strong detachment of the enemy, stole upon the camp; and put the occupants to the sword, an exploit in civilized warfare little better than a massacre. At Germantown he led the right wing with gallantry, and received the especial commendation of Washington for his conduct in the battle of Monmouth. His surprise an capture of Stony Point gained for him the thanks of Congress. He was transferred to the South during the last of his service in the Revolution, where, by his ceaseless vigilance and energy, he gained no less renown than at the North In councils of war he always favored the aggressive policy, and won the title of "Mad Anthony Wayne." In 1792 he was called from his farm in Chester County, to which he had retired, and placed in command of an army to operate against the hostile Indians. At Maumee, in August, 1784, after a two year's campaign, he gained so signal a victory as to put an end to Indian barbarities, and give peace to the settlers. The most subtle of the savage chieftains had counseled against risking a battle with him, for "that man never sleeps," he declared. The event showed that he had judged correctly. Wayne was afterwards appointed sole commissioner to treat with the natives, and concluded a treaty in 1795, at Greenville, Ohio, which gave peace and secured the emigrant complete immunity from peril. In the autumn of 1796, having concluded the object of his mission, he embarked on a small vessel at Detroit, bound for Presque Isle, now Erie, on his way home. On the way down the lake he was attacked with the gout, a disease to which he was subject. Upon his arrival he was taken, at his own request, to one of the block houses on the garrison tract, and a messenger was dispatched for Surgeon J. C. Wallace, at Pittsburg, who had attended him on his campaigns, and was familiar with his disease. The Doctor started at once, but on arriving at Franklin, on his way up, he was pained to learn that his old commander was dead, having expired on the 15th of December, 1796. Two days after he was buried, as he had directed, with his uniform and boots on, in a plain coffin, with the letters "A. W." cut upon the lid, and his age, 51, and date of his death marked by means of round brass headed tacks driven into the wood. At the age of thirty-two he was described as "about middle size, with a firm manly countenance, commanding port and eagle eye. His looks corresponded with his character, indicating a soul noble, ardent and daring. In his intercourse with his offices and men he was affable and agreeable, and had the art of communicating to their bosoms the gallant and chivalrous spirit which glowed in his own. His dress was scrupulously neat and elegant, his movements were quick, his manners easy and graceful."

Here we might well put a period to the narrative; but a circumstance connected with the remains occurred, so peculiar, that a brief account will be given of it as recorded by Benjamin Whitman in his History of Erie County. "In the fall of 1808, General Wayne's daughter, Mrs. Atlee, was taken seriously ill. While upon her sick bed she was seized with a strong desire to have her father's remains moved to the family burying ground. Realizing that it was her last sickness, and anxious to console her dying moments, Colonel Isaac Wayne, the General's son, consented to come to Erie for the purpose of complying with her wishes. The journey was made in the spring of 1809, through what was then a wilderness, for much of the distance, with a horse and sulky. On arriving in Erie, Colonel Wayne sent for Dr. Wallace, the same one who had been called to minister to the General. The Doctor agreed to attend to the disinterment and preparation of the remains, and Colonel Wayne gave him entire charge of the operation, declining to witness it on the ground that he preferred to remember his father as he knew him when living. Thirteen years having elapsed, it was supposed that the corpse would be decomposed; but on opening the grave, all present were amazed to find the body petrified, with the exception of one foot and leg, which were partially gone. The boot on the unsound leg had decayed, and most of the clothing was missing. Dr. Wallace separated the body into convenient parts and placed them in a kettle of boiling water until the flesh could be removed from the bones. He then carefully scraped the bones, packed them in a small box and returned the flesh, with the implements used in the operation, to the coffin, which had been left undisturbed, and it was again covered over with earth. The box was secured to Colonel Wayne's sulky and carried to Eastern Pennsylvania, where the contents were deposited in a second grave, among those of the General's deceased relatives In the labor of dissection, which took place on the garrison grounds, Dr. Wallace was assisted by Robert Murray, Robert Irwin, Richard Clement, and others. General Wayne's sound boot was given to James Duncan, who found it fitted him, had a mate made for it, and wore the pair until they could no longer be used At the time of the disinterment' Captain Dobins and family were living on the garrison grounds in a large building erected for the use of the commanding officer Mrs. Dobins was allowed to look at the body, with some of her lady acquaintances, and obtained a lock of the dead hero's hair. She had a vivid recollection of the incident when nearly in her hundredth year The body she said was not hard like stone, but was more of the consistency of soft chalk. The hairs of the head pulled out readily, and the general appearance of the corpse was much like that of a plaster of Paris cast In explanation of Dr. Wallace's course, it is argued that he acted in accordance with what the circumstances of the case seemed to require It was necessary that the remains should be placed in as small a space as possible to accommodate the means of conveyance Colonel Wayne is reported to have said in regard to the affair, 'I always regretted it. Had I known the state the remains were in before separated, I think I should certainly have had them again deposited there and let them rest, and had a monument erected to his memory.' * * * Largely through the efforts of Dr. Germer and Captain Welsh, an appropriation was obtained from the Legislature, with which a substantial log block-house in imitation of the original was built to mark the site, and the grounds were surrounded by a railing with cannon at each of the four corners. The grave has been neatly and substantially built up with stone, and the coffin-lid, with other relics of the early days, is carefully sheltered within the block-house The Wayne family burial ground, where the bones of the gallant General repose, is in the cemetery attached to St. David's Episcopal church, at Radnor, Delaware County, not far from the Chester County line, less than an hour's walk from Wayne Station, on the Pennsylvania Railroad, and fourteen miles west from Philadelphia Not far distant is Paoli, the scene of the massacre, which was so brilliantly avenged at Stony Point The Pennsylvania State Society of the Cincinnati erected a monument over the grave on the 4th of July, 1809."

As soon as it was known that the site of the capital of the county had been determined and the tract acquired, building lots were disposed of rapidly. The records of the county, which were kept with care, the chirography being in a very even legible hand, which puts to shame some of the records made at a later date, show that the following named persons purchased lots of the commissioners, paying the sums set opposite their several names·

1st.	Rev. Robert Davis	$ 25
2d.	John Denny	84
3d.	Phillip Ketchum	75
4th.	John Smith	34
5th.	John Smith	106
6th.	James Hook	59
7th.	Job Smith	12
8th.	Ignatius Ross	15
9th.	John Boreman	68
10th	Samuel Clarke	
11th.	Daniel McFarland	16
12th.	Daniel McFarland	78
13th.	Daniel McFarland	14
14th.	Daniel McFarland	13
15th.	Daniel McFarland	50
16th.	John Wilson	78
17th.	William Hunter	70
18th.	James Brown	65
19th.	Robert Adams & Patrick Moore	51
20th.	Robert Hazlett & Robert Wilson	110
21st.	Isaac Jenkinson	139
22d.	Clement Brooke	50
23d.	Thomas Reinhart	50
24th.	Asa McClelland	40
25th.	William Wood	18
26th.	James Eagan	50
27th.	John Baptist Nuglet	66
28th.	William Caldwell	70
29th.	Jacob Burley	42

The forms and legal authorization of procedure in setting in motion the machinery of government over the new county were promptly observed. The first commission issued was to John Boreman, executed under the hand of Governor Thomas Mifflin, July 13, 1796, which authorized him to administer oaths. The second commission was issued to

John Minor to be Associate Justice under date of July 13, 1796.

John Boreman to be Recorder of Deeds under date of March 17, 1796.

John Boreman, Prothonotary, March 17, 1796

John Boreman, Clerk of the Court of Quarter Sessions, March 17, 1796.

John Boreman, Clerk of the Court of Oyer and Terminer, March 17, 1796.

John Boreman, Clerk of the Orphans' Court, March 17, 1796

John Boreman, Register of Wills, March 17, 1796.

David Gray was commissioned to sit as Associate Judge on March 17, 1796.

As Greene County was a part of the Fifth Judicial District, the President Judge of that district continued to hold the courts for Greene County, as before its erection, for the same territory. By the constitution of 1790, the Court of Common Pleas became the principal court of the Commonwealth for the original hearing of causes. The judges, not fewer than three, nor more than four, in each county, were to be appointed by the Governor At the session of the Legislature for 1791, an act was passed dividing the counties of the State into five judicial districts—Philadelphia, Bucks, Montgomery and Delaware to compose the 1st; Chester, Lancaster, York and Dauphin the 2d, Berks, Northampton, Luzerne and Northumberland the 3d; Cumberland, Franklin, Bedford, Huntingdon and Mifflin the 4th; and Westmoreland, Fayette, Washington and Alleghany the 5th When Greene was erected in 1796, that constituted a part of the fifth. The act provided that for each judicial district " a person of knowledge and integrity, skilled in the laws," shall be appointed and commissioned by the Governor to be President of the courts of Common Pleas Any two of the judges of the Common Pleas Court should constitute a quorum, which should constitute the Court of Quarter Sessions, of the Peace and Orphans' Court, and the Register of Wills

The first President Judge of the Fifth district was Alexander Addison· He was a native of Ireland, where he was born in 1759, and was educated at Edinburgh, Scotland, and licensed to preach by the Presbytery of Aberlow   While yet a youth he emigrated to America, and came to western Pennsylvania.   Having been taken in charge by the Redstone Presbytery, he was given permission to preach and officiated for a while at Washington   He subsequently turned his attention to the law, studying in the office of David Reddick, and was admitted to practice in the courts of Washington County.   He was a man of strict probity, of large understanding, well schooled in the polite learning of the day, and was well fitted by native talent, by culture, and legal acumen to preside in the courts of justice.   In conducting the courts of this district he had a difficult part to perform   It was at a time when the laws of both State and Nation were new and untried; the district was one of opposing factions, composed of sturdy frontiersmen; the tax upon distilled spirits had to be enforced over unwilling subjects, among whom was inaugurated the Whiskey Rebellion.   In the midst of all

James Scott

these trying circumstances, he is acknowledged to have performed the duties of his high office with a strict regard to justice, and with honesty of purpose. But he did not escape the shafts of party strife, and rancor, which finally culminated in his impeachment before the Senate of Pennsylvania. The formal charges were as follows:

"1st. That Judge Addison, after Judge Lucas [an associate judge of Alleghany County], had in his official character and capacity of judge as aforesaid, and as he of right might do, addressed a petit jury, then and there duly impaneled, and sworn or affirmed respectively as jurors in a cause then pending, then and there openly did declare, and say to the said jury, that the address delivered to them by the said John Lucas, had nothing to do with the question before them, and they ought not to pay any attention to it. This question will be better understood by lawyers when informed that a justification was pleaded as a defense in an action of slander, and was unsupported by the testimony, and Judge Lucas' charge was intended to reduce the damages of the plaintiff to a small if not a nominal sum.

"2d. That the said Alexander Addison did under pretense as aforesaid of discharging and performing his official duties then and there in time of open court, illegally, and unconstitutionally stop, threaten, and prevent the said John Lucas, from addressing as he of right might do a grand jury of the said county of Alleghany then and there assembled."

The sentence of the Senate, sitting as a court of impeachment, delivered January 27, 1803, was, "That Alexander Addison, President of the several courts of Common Pleas, in the Fifth district of this State, shall be, and he hereby is removed from his office of president aforesaid, and also is disqualified to hold and exercise the office of judge, in any court of law within the commonwealth of Pennsylvania."

The associate judges during his term of office were Henry Taylor, James Edgar, James Allison, and Matthew Ritchie, commissioned August 17, 1791; William Hoge, commissioned April 6, 1798, and John McDowell, commissioned April 7, 1802. Samuel Roberts was commissioned president judge of the Fifth district on June 2, 1803. He was a native of Philadelphia, where he was born September 10, 1761, read law with William Lewis, and was practicing his profession at Sunbury, when appointed judge.

The judicial districts of the State were readjusted by the act of March 23d, 1818, by which Washington, Fayette, Greene, and Somerset became the Fourteenth district, and Judge Roberts remained over the courts composed of Alleghany, Beaver, and Butler. Whereupon Thomas H Baird, was appointed to preside in the Fourteenth district, his commission dating from October 19, 1818. By an act of the Legislature of March 29, 1824, Somerset County was taken from the Fourteenth district to form with Franklin and Bedford the new Sixteenth district, Greene, Fayette, and Washington remaining the Fourteenth district. Judge Baird was a son of Absalom Baird, M. D., and a grandson of John Baird, a Scotchman, who came with Braddock's army, was engaged in the battle under that ill-fated General, and and was subsequently killed on Grant's Hill, in Major Grant's Highlander column defeated on September 14, 1758 The Judge was born at Washington, November 15, 1787, studied law with Joseph Pentecost, and was admitted to practice July, 1808. With Thomas McGiffin and Parker Campbell he was interested in the construction of the National Road through Washington County, and as early as 1830 secured the survey of a railroad up the Chartiers Valley, at his own expense. He resigned his commission in December, 1837, and died November 22, 1866.

Governor Joseph Ritner, who was then in the gubernatorial chair, appointed as successor to Judge Baird, Nathaniel Ewing, his commission bearing date February 22, 1838 In the same year of his appointment the constitutional convention revised the organic law, so as to make the term of a president judge or any other judge who is required to be learned in the law, ten years, and associate judges, five years By an act of the assembly passed as early as 1806, the number of associate judges was limited to two from each county. By the amended constitution of 1838, sheriffs, coroners, prothonotaries, and clerks were made elective. Judge Ewing was the son of William Ewing, who had emigrated from York County to Fayette, as a surveyor, in 1790, and was born July 18, 1794. He was educated at Washington College, read law with Thomas McGiffin, and was admitted to practice June, 1816 He soon after removed to Uniontown, where he continued to reside till his death in 1874. He had the reputation of being an able jurist and a just judge

Samuel A. Gilmore was appointed at the expiration of the ten years' term of Judge Baird, his commission dating February 28, 1848. By an amendment of the organic law, passed by the Legislature in 1849–'50, and ratified by vote of the people, the judges of the Supreme Court of the State were elected by the qualified voters at large, the president judges, and such as were required to be learned in the law, by the electors of the districts over which they presided, and the associate judges by the voters of the respective counties. Accordingly, at the next general election, on November 6, 1851, Samuel A. Gilmore was elected to be his own successor, and was commissioned to serve for the constitutional period of ten years Judge Gilmore was a son of John Gilmore, a lawyer, who practiced his profession at Butler. The son was a practicing attorney at the bar of that place when appointed judge. He resided during his term of office at Uniontown, where he continued to live till his death in 1837.

James Lindsey was elected president judge at the election in 1861. He was a descendant of the first settlers. "Thomas Hughes, John Swan and Henry Vanmetre were," says Mr. Crumrine, "among the first pioneers on the waters of Muddy Creek, coming thither from the Shenandoah Valley, in 1767–'68. Charles Swan, son of John, married Sarah, daughter of Henry Vanmetre, and their daughter Mary, marrying William Collins, became the mother of Annie Collins who married John Lindsey, and became the mother of James, the young judge. John Lindsey's father was James Lindsey, a Scotchman, who, coming from Lancaster County very early, settled at Jefferson, Greene County, and married Mary, a daughter of Thomas Hughes, Jr., who had married a daughter of John Swan before mentioned. Hughes was Irish, Swan was Scotch, Vanmetre German, Lindsey Scotch—three nationalities well blended into one. John Lindsey, the Judge's father, was educated at Jefferson College, at Cannonsburg, was a leading politician, once sheriff, and twice prothonotary of Greene County."

Judge Lindsey was born November 21, 1827, was educated at Greene Academy, Carmichael's, and was admitted to the bar at Waynesburg in 1849. At the August term of 1864 he presided over the court at Washington, and though suffering from a slight attack of billious fever, he sat through the term, but on his way home was seriously attacked at Prosperity. He, however, reached his home a few miles out of Waynesburg, where he remained indisposed, but not seriously so, until the 1st of September, 1864, when he suffered a relapse that terminated his life suddenly.

An extract from the minute entered upon the records of the Fayette County Court will show the estimation in which he was held by the bar. "By those unacquainted with him misgivings were naturally felt when the judical ermine fell upon one so young. * * * But whatever fears Judge Lindsey's youth occasioned were quickly dissipated by masterly hand with which he laid hold of his official duties, and by the apparent ease with which he carried his great burdens."

Upon the death of Judge Lindsey, Governor Curtin appointed James Watson, of Washington, to fill the vacancy until the next general election; but Mr. Watson feeling himself disposed to decline the honor, J. Kennedy Ewing, son of Nathaniel Ewing, was commissioned on Nov. 19, 1864, to serve until the election of 1865. The choice of the people in that election was Samuel A. Gilmore, who was commissioned for a third term, in that grave and responsible office. By an act of the Legislature, of January 25th, 1866, a new judical district was created, comprising the counties of Washington and Beaver, designated the twenty-seventh judicial district, the fourteenth retaining Fayette and Greene, over which Judge Gilmore continued to preside.

On the 3rd of November, 1873, a new constitution was adopted, which was to take effect on the 1st of January, 1874. By the terms of that instrument the Legislature was to re-district the State. This was done, and forty-three districts were formed, all counties containing forty thousand or more inhabitants to constitute a separate judicial district. The time of the beginning of the judicial term was changed, and instead of the first Monday of December it was to be the first Monday of January next succeeding the election. To fill out the unexpired term the Governor appointed Edward Campbell, who was commissioned May 30, 1873, to serve until the first Monday of December, 1873. At the election held on the 6th of November 1873, Alpheus E. Willson was elected for the term of ten years, Judge Willson was a lawyer of acumen and served with credit to himself and advantage to his constituents. At the general election for 1883 James Inghram was elected. A full biography of the judge will be found among the sketches given further on in this book to which the reader is referred. The business of this judicial district having accumulated beyond the ability of a single judge to transact, it was provided by the act of June 15, 1887, that an additional Judge learned in the law should be elected for this district. Accordingly Nathaniel Ewing was appointed and commissioned on August 25, 1887, to serve until the next general election, when Judge Ewing was elected by the people and commissioned to serve for the full term of ten years. He belonged to the Fayette County bar and is of a judicial ancestry.

A complete list of President and Associate Judges, who have served in Greene County since its formation, has been prepared for my use under the direction of Ex-Lieut. Gov. Stone, now Secretary of the Commonwealth, from the records of his office, which is given below.

GREENE COUNTY—Formed of a part of Washington County, Feb. 9, 1796.

LIST OF PRESIDENT JUDGES.

Fifth District or Circuit—Consisting of the counties of Westmoreland, Washington, Alleghany, Fayette, Greene and Crawford. Alexander Addison, August 17, 1791.

Fifth District—Composed of the counties, Washington, Beaver, Alleghany, Fayette and Greene. Samuel Roberts, April 30, 1803.

Fourteenth District—Composed of the counties of Washington, Fayette, Green and Somerset. Thomas H. Baird, Oct. 19, 1818.

Resigned Dec 31, 1837, resignation accepted by the Governor, Jan. 3, 1838

Fourteenth District—Composed of the counties of Washington, Fayette and Greene. Nathaniel Ewing, Feb. 15, 1838; Samuel A. Gilmore, Feb. 28, 1848; Samuel A. Gilmore, Nov. 6, 1851.

Fourteenth District—Composed of the counties of Fayette and Greene. James Lindsey, Nov. 20, 1861; James Watson, Nov. 9, 1864, until the next general election. In place of Judge Lindsey, deceased, declined and commission returned. John Kennedy Ewing, Nov. 18, 1864, until the next general election; Samuel A. Gilmore, Nov. 7, 1865; Edward Campbell, May, 30, 1873, until 1st Monday in December, 1873 Alpheus E. Willson, Nov. 6, 1873; James Inghram, Dec. 11, 1883.

Additional Law Judge—Authorized by Act June 15, 1887. Nathaniel Ewing, Aug. 25, 1887, until 1st Monday in Jan. 1888; Nathaniel Ewing, Dec. 23, 1887.

GREENE COUNTY—*List of Associate Judges.*

John Minor, March 17, 1796. Some doubt having been entertained by Judge Addison, as to whether the commission issued to Judge Minor on March 17th, 1796, was constitutional, the same was communicated by him to the Governor, who, to remove such doubt, (the Attorney-General being of the same opinion with Mr Addison) issued a new commission to Judge Minor, dated the 28th of February, 1797. John Minor's resignation accepted Oct. 7, 1833. John Flenniken, March 17, 1796; John Badolet, March 17, 1796; David Gray, March 17, 1796; Wm. Crawford, June 13, 1822; Asa McClelland, March 6, 1834; Samuel Black, Feb. 10, 1837; Asa McClelland, Feb. 28, 1842; Thos. Burson, March 3, 1843; Mark Gordon, Feb. 24, 1847; Thos. Burson, Feb. 15, 1848, Commission from March 3 next; Benj. Ross, Nov. 10, 1851; James Crea, Nov. 10, 1851; Jonathan Gerard, Nov. 12, 1856; Isaac Burson, Nov. 12, 1856; Jonathan Gerard, Nov. 23, 1861; Thos. P. Pollock, Nov. 23, 1861; George Haskinson, Nov. 8, 1866; Israel L. Croft, Nov. 8, 1866; Wm. Cotterell, Nov. 17, 1871; Thos. Iams, Nov. 17, 1871; Wm. Braden, Dec. 8, 1876; Geo. Sellers. Jan. 9, 1876, until first Monday of Jan 1878; Thos. Scott, Dec. 26, 1877; Wm. F. Scott, Jan. 8, 1879, until first Monday of Jan. 1880; Silas Barnes, Dec. 4, 1879; Jesse Philips, Dec 8, 1881; John T. Elbin, Dec. 22, 1884; Bazel Gordon, Dec. 13, 1886.

CHAPTER XIX.

Value of Education—"Enoch Flower" First Teacher—Friends' School—College Academy and Charity School—Founding Colleges—Founding Academies—Men and Women Make Their Marks—Retarding Causes—Instruct the "Poor Gratis"—Speech of Stevens—Law of 1834—Opposition of 1835—Law of 1836—Governors Wolf and Ritner—Journey of Burrowes—First School Report—Opposition where Least Expected—Greene County Slow in Adopting—Showing of Greene in 1837—Utilizing School Property—Solicitude for its Safety—1,000 Districts—700 in Operation—Broad Plans of Burrowes—Progress of a Pupil Through the Whole—Defects Shown by Fifteen Years' Trial—Revised Law of 1854—Opposition to County Superintendency—Non-accepting Districts—Honorable Charles A. Black, Superintendent—Independent Districts—True Sphere of, County Superintendent—Circular Letter—Beneficient Influence of Law—Recommends Normal Schools—Normal School Law of 1857—Ten Schools—One at California for the Tenth District—Growth—School Architecture—Edited by T. H. Burrowes—No Retrograde Steps—The Peoples Colleges—Sources of Blessings.

NO subject can be of more vital importance to any people than that of a wise education of their youth In presenting some account of the origin and progress of education in Greene County it will not be out of place to give a brief sketch of education in the State at large. At a meeting of the Council held at Philadelphia ye 26th of ye 10th month, 1683, the following record was entered as shown by the printed Colonial Records, Vol I, p. 91: "Present William Penn Propor. & Gov,—Tho. Homes, Wm. Haigue, Wm. Clayton, Lasse Cock. The Govr. and Provil, Council having taken into their Serious Consideration the great Necessity there is of a Scool Master for ye Instruction & Sober Education of Youth in the towne of Philadelphia, sent for Enock flower, an Inhabitant of the said Towne, who for twenty year past hath been exercised in that care and Imployment in England, to whom having communicated their Minds, he Embraced it upon these following terms: to Learne to read English 4s by ye Quarter, to learne to read and write 6s by ye Quarter, to learne to read and cast accot 8s by ye Quarter; for Boarding a Scholar, that is to say, dyet, Washing, Lodging and Schooling, Tenn pounds for one whole year."

It should be borne in mind that this action was taken before Pennsylvania was in reality a year old, while the conies still burrowed unscared in the river bank, and the virgin forest encumbered the soil where is now the great city. The frame of government adopted provided that "the Legislature shall as soon as may be convenient, provide for the establishment of schools, in such manner that the poor may be taught gratis" Among the most wise and sententious sayings of Penn was this, "That which makes a good constitution must keep it, viz.: men of wisdom and virtue; qualities that, because they descend not with worldly inheritance, must be carefully propagated by a virtuous education of youth." The Society of Friends established a school in Philadelphia in 1689. That was as soon as children born in the new city were old enough to go to school. Franklin, who had become a well-settled adopted citizen, and an acknowledged leader in every enterprise intended to build up the city, encourage progress, and diffuse intelligence, in 1749, with others, applied for and secured a charter for a "College, Academy and Charity school of Philadelphia." This was the beginning of an awakening throughout the State upon the subject of higher education, and for the next half century the enterprise and skill of the people seem to have been directed to the founding and building up of colleges. The University of Pennsylvania, at Philadelphia, was chartered in 1753; Dickinson College, at Carlisle, in 1783; Franklin and Marshall College, at Lancaster, in 1787; Jefferson College, at Cannonsburg, in 1802, and Alleghany College, at Meadville, in 1815. This provision reasonably well accommodated all sections of the vast territory of the Commonwealth. For the support of these institutions the colonial assemblies, and subsequently the legislatures, made large grants of lands, and revenues accruing from public domain.

Commencing near the beginning of the present century and continuing for a period of over thirty years, great activity was shown in establishing county academies. The purpose of these academies was to furnish a school of a higher order than the ordinary common school, where reading, writing and arithmetic were alone taught, in order that a fair English and classical education could be obtained without trenching upon the ground occupied by the colleges. They were, on the other hand, regarded as schools preparatory to the college. During this period charters were obtained for academies in forty-one counties, viz : Armstrong, Beaver, Bradford, Bucks, Butler, Cambria, Center, Chester, Clarion, Clearfield, Clinton, Crawford, Cumberland, Dauphin, Erie, Franklin, Greene, Huntingdon, Indiana, Jefferson, Juniata, Lebanon, Lehigh, Luzerne, McKean, Monroe,

Mifflin, Montgomery, Northumberland, Perry, Pike, Potter, Schuyl-kill, Somerset, Tioga, Union, Venango, Warren, Wayne, Westmore-land and York.

It will be seen that Greene is one of the counties thus provided for. The State granted charters and money in sums, varying from two to six thousand dollars for the purpose of building structures at the county seats suitable for the proposed grade of schools, and in some instances extensive land grants were secured. The affairs of these academies were managed by a board of trustees, elected, as were the other county officers, and teachers were employed as they could be in-duced to teach for such compension as they could derive from the tuition of their pupils, the invested funds yielding little more than enough to keep the buildings and premises in repair.

Up to this time, a period of a hundred and twenty-five years, little attention had been given to the liberal views of the founder to make provision for "the education of the poor gratis," which he had inserted in the original draft of the organic law. As a conse-quence it will be found, by reference to the books in the registers offices throughout the several counties of the Commonwealth, that a large proportion of the men, as well as women, affixed their signa-tures to conveyances by a mark.

There were many causes why the common school idea of the State making public provision for the reasonable education of every child within its broad domain, free of any expense to the child, or its parents or guardians, unless they have property on which taxes are levied as for other purposes, was slow in taking root. The popula-tion was so sparse that in many sections it was impossible to bring enough children together to form a school Diversity of origin and language operated as a strong impediment, as many persisted in speaking their native tongue and in having their children taught the language of the fatherland Antagonisms of religious sects, and the prejudice in favor of having children taught exclusively in schools of their own religious denominations, operated as one of the most in-surmountable barriers, even after the common school system had be-come firmly established

By an act of the Legislature of April 4, 1809, provision was made for the education of the "poor gratis" The assessors in their rounds were required to enroll the names of children of indigent par-ents, and they were to be sent to the nearest or most convenient school, and the tuition paid from the county treasury. This enact-ment proceeded upon the supposition that schools were in existence, established by the voluntary contributions of neighborhoods, to which the indigent could be sent. This was really the case in many sec-tions of the State. This system was continued for a period of about a quarter of a century, and the treasurers' books in the several

James McNary

counties show considerable sums paid for tuition in this way. But the natural pride of a free-born American citizen, rebelled at having his name inscribed on the books of the county as a pauper, too indigent to pay for the schooling of his children, and probably a large proportion of those who were most deserving of help were the ones who scorned to receive it in that way. In a burst of impassioned eloquence, Thaddeus Stevens, in his great speech in favor of a general school law, made on the floor of the House of Representatives in 1834, declared that such a law as that, instead of being called a public school law, ought to be entitled "*an act for branding and marking the poor, so that they may be known from the rich and proud.*"

But this system subserved a purpose, while the country was filling up with population, and the dense forests were being cleared away, and the wild beast subdued. It served to keep before the people that there was such a boon as public school education.   The Governors of the Commonwealth had frequently, during the period that the system of educating the *poor gratis* was in force, from 1809 to '34, called the attention of the Legislature to the necessity of a more efficient system.   Finally, at the session 1834, the struggle came. It is well understood how natural it is for men to cling to established methods, and hence we can well comprehend how a radically new system would provoke fierce opposition.   The new act was prepared by Samuel Brœck, a member from Philadelphia, was passed through both branches without serious opposition, and was signed by that sturdy patriot, Governor Wolf.

But the law, though in the main just, proved in practice crude, and unwieldy, and when Legislature assembled at the session of 1835, the mutterings of discontent were heard on every hand.   The almost universal sentiment seemed to be in favor of repeal, and of going back to the *poor gratis* of 1809   It required the most adroit application of parliamentary rules and strategy of the friends of a common school system to ensure non-action for one year more, when it was proposed that a new bill, more simple and easily operated, should be prepared.

Accordingly, at the session of 1836, the final struggle was to come.   Dr. George Smith, a member of the State Senate, from Delaware, drew an entirely new bill, more simple and better adapted to the wants of the people in all their varied circumstances, and presented it.   So great was the antagonism engendered by the law of '34, that it was with the utmost difficulty that the great body of the members could be induced to listen to the provisions of a common school law; but through the firmness and resolution of Governors Wolf and Ritner, and the sturdy virtue and powerful appeals of such men as Stevens, and Brœck, and Smith and Burrowes, the public school system, free alike to rich and poor, to high and low, was firmly

15

established, and from that day to this has been increasing in power and perfection. To secure its passage it was necessary to adopt the principle of local option. It was left to a vote of the people of the several townships to decide whether they would accept the provisions of the law or not. But this did not injure the efficiency of the system where accepted, and it went rapidly into operation, until finally every vestige of opposition disappeared, and it has steadily grown in favor.

In order to explain the provisions of the new system and introduce it to the people of the State, Dr Thomas H Burrowes, then Secretary of State, and *Ex officio* Superintendent of common schools, made a tour of the Commonwealth delivering addresses at the county seats to large assembles of the people, and commending and enforcing the desirable features of the system and answering objections that were brought against it. This official intercourse had an excellent effect, and caused a more hearty attempt on the part of its friends to establish and improve the schools.

The feature of the law, which allowed the people to decide by popular vote whether they would accept the provisions of the law or reject, while it gave an opportunity to prevent its adoption at once and thus to retard the progress of the system, doubtless proved its salvation. For, while the opponents realized that they had the power, if they were in the majority, of rejecting the system, they were at the same time made to feel that in rejecting it they were assuming a fearful responsibility, and caused them to reflect that they might be guilty of an act that would one day return to plague the inventors

Secretary Burrowes, in his first annual report, and indeed the first common school report ever made in this Commonwealth, read before the House of Representatives on the 18th of February, 1837, in commenting on this phase of the law says, " We encounter results directly opposed to those which the same facts under ordinary circumstances, would produce. Counties among the most intelligent enterprising and devoted to the general interests of education are found to be among the most hostile to the system. Others which from their wealth, density of population, and moral character, might be supposed peculiarly adapted to its beneficial action, are scarcely less averse than the class just named On the other hand, as he advances from the older counties, with a population somewhat of a homogeneous character, he finds the system increase in favor among the new and mixed people of the West and Southwest, while it is unanimously accepted by the recent and thinly inhabited settlements of the whole North "

By reference to the tables of the secretary it will be seen that Greene was one of the counties which was at the first slow in adopting the system. Under the head of amount of tax voted at the meeting held for Greene County on the 2d of May, 1836, the sum is given as $2,315.17.   In a comparative statement showing the relative standing of the schools of the county for three years the following is the showing for Greene: Whole number of school districts 14; for the year 1834 no return.   For 1835 one accepting district, five non-accepting, and eight not represented.   For 1836 ten accepting, none non-accepting and four not represented   When it is considered that for the first few years all the resources were required for getting suitable school rooms in which to hold schools, and consequently very little advantage would be obtained by way of instruction, this showing is highly creditable

In the table for 1837 Greene County has the following school districts entered, Cumberland, Franklin, Jefferson, Marion, Morgan, Morris, Monongahela, and Richhill.   Of these Franklin is credited with 35 males and 15 females; schools kept open for two months, as paying $20 a month to male teachers, and the character and qualification of teachers as "Good."   Jefferson is credited with 6 schools, 6 male teachers, 200 male pupils, and 218 female, as paying $20 a month for male teachers; four teachers qualified to teach reading, writing and arithmetic, and two grammar, geography and mathematics.   Marion is credited with three schools, two male and one female teacher, 60 male pupils and 53 female pupils, schools kept open three months; paying male teachers $20 a month and females $10; qualification of teachers, "Equal to teachers of English schools generally."   Morgan is credited with four schools, 4 male teachers, 110 male pupils, 55 females; schools open 3 months; male teachers $20 a month, females $10.   Monongahela is credited with 4 schools, 3 male teachers, 1 female, 75 male pupils, 50 females, salaries of male teachers $16.50, females $13.   "Character good, qualification various."   Reading, writing and arithmetic taught.   Richhill schools "not yet in operation."

In commenting upon the lessons to be gathered from a view of the tables presented in his report, Dr. Burrowes observes, "In other States, having one language, one people, one origin, and one soil, a system suited to one district, satifies the whole.   Not so here.   No project, however wisely planned, or systematically adapted, can be pronounced sufficient till approved by the test of experience.   Hence, it becomes the policy—nay it is the duty of the Legislature, neither on the one hand, unduly to press any part of the design, no matter how theoretically beautiful it may appear, if it have been condemned in practice, nor on the other, ever to relinquish a point once gained in favor of the system however it may fall short of previous calculation.   It is only by resting on and starting from such mutually admitted points, that success can at all be achieved in any great enterprise."

In the first half dozen counties immediately about Philadelphia were assembled the great body of the Society of Friends, followers of the great founder of the Commonwealth To provide for the education of their children, as well as to make provision for their poor, is a part of the religious faith of these people "Hence," proceeds the report, "in every one of these counties the common school system has not proved acceptable for the plain reason that a system of society schools is already in active operation.   For this reason also, and in the abstract it is difficult to gainsay it, their citizens say that no new system is required by a community, who are already in possession of one sufficient for all their wants.   This disposition is participated in by their immediate fellow-citizens, not members of the society, because they, to a certain extent, also receive the benefits of the society schools."

It was not objected that schools and school property already in existence should be absorbed by the common school system. Indeed Secretary Burrowes laid down in his report the following principles. "In its effects the system should be made, 1. To supply common schools, where no system was before in operation.   2. To improve and make common the defective primary schools that preceded it, and 3, To aid with its funds and render common the good schools which it encounters In a word its duty is to build common schools where there are none, and to open the doors of the schools already built." In some localities in Greene County at this time the inhabitants of a neighborhood had united in building a school-house, or in fitting up a room in some private dwelling, where schools had been supported by the voluntary contributions of the patrons. These were generally turned over to the management and support of the legally constituted directors under the common school law, and the immediate expense of securing school property was avoided; but in most portions of the county provision had to be made for setting up schools *de novo*   Of course the expense of either building school-houses, or of renting rooms was quite sorely felt, as the State gave nothing for buildings, and consequently there was less fund left for instruction. But when the system once got in operation the burden of building was relieved, and the ordinary workings of the system moved on in something like regular order After classifying the several counties of the State according to the peculiar circumstances in which they stood related to the system, and explaining the causes which led to the results shown by the reports, the Secretary proceeds in this his first common school report to sum up the results as follows: 1st. "We now have a system —an admitted, permanent, and well understood starting point. To have attained this is a great advance to success   2d. We have now a class of men set apart to watch over the cause of education in every neighborhood—six school directors They may not yet be qualified for the trust, but they will be."

It may seem strange to us, who see the matter of common school education throughout the broad commonwealth regarded as a necessity, and as much an element to be enjoyed as the air we breathe, the vapor of the clouds and the ceaseless flow of water in the streams, that there should ever have been a time when any fear should have been entertained lest the system should be abandoned, or such legislation should be adopted as would greatly cripple or destroy its usefulness. Yet there was scarcely a moment during the early years of the existence of the system when its friends did not entertain the deepest solicitude for its safety.

Superintendent Burrowes in opening his report for 1838 says: "It is true the system is neither in full operation, nor its machinery perfect. But the momentous question, 'Can education be made as general and as unbought as liberty?' has been determined in the affirmative by the intelligence of Pennsylvania." The occasion of his speaking thus exultingly was an event which he sets forth in these words: " The whole commonwealth is divided into one thousand common school districts. Of these about seven hundred had the system in operation, previous to the first Tuesday of May, 1837, when its continuance or rejection was to be decided by a direct vote of the people. On the day which was thus to determine the fate of the system, so far as information has been received [and it has been carefully sought for], not a single district declared against the cause of free education. All stood firm. And during the same season sixty-five additional districts for the first time came out for the system. Thus the momentous question was forever settled, and at a time, and under circumstances too, the most unpropitious for such a result. The common school system had been in existence for three years, but really had been in operation in a majority of accepting districts, only as a system of taxation, and not of instruction. Its funds from the State were small, and, whether from the State or taxation, were necessarily devoted for the first years to the procuring of school houses. Thus little or nothing was left for teaching."

Feeling now tolerably secure of his ground, and realizing full well that the system was securely established, the Secretary knowing that public school education would not be bound and confined to the bare rudiments of reading, writing, and the casting of accounts, but would gradually advance in facilities until a thorough training would be afforded in its scope, proceeded to sketch the ultimate propositions which it would assume; but which it required a half century to realize

" The question," he says, " which has been settled by the adoption of the common school system, does not merely declare that the people of Pennsylvania will have reading, writing and arithmetic taught at the cheapest possible rate, to all, in, half a dozen comfortable school houses in each township. This, to be sure, is determined, and is of itself a great deal. But greater and better things have been willed by the same vote. In the deep and broad foundations of the primary common school are also found the bases of the more elevated secondary school, the practical institute for the teacher and man of business, the academy for the classical student, the college for his instruction in the higher branches of science and literature, and the towering university from which the richest stores of professional learning will be disseminated.

"In other ages and countries the lower orders might be confined to the rudiments of knowledge, while the higher branches were dispensed to the privileged classes, in distant and expensive seminaries. But here we have no lower orders. Our statesmen, and our highest magistrates, our professional men and our capitalists, our philosophers, and our poets, our merchants and our mechanics, all spring alike from the mass, and principally from the agricultural portion of the community."

In vision he contemplates the results, which he labored so earnestly to establish, and which have actually been substantially realized. "The youth," he says, "enters the primary school at five years of age. In five seasons he is prepared to enter the secondary school. He is then ten. Four years here fits him for the practical institute. He is now fourteen, and is supposed to have hitherto sustained himself by devoting one-third, or even one-half, of each year to the business of his parent or employer. He attends two terms at the institute, occupying portions of two years, and in the interim earns enough to pay for his boarding and clothes. He is now sixteen years of age. He may next enter the academy and pass from it to the second class in college, or if his circumstances will permit this one year spent as teacher or clerk in a store, or in the business of agriculture during the day and close study at night, provides him with means and fits him for entering college without attendance at the academy. This he does at seventeen. The same process carries him through the collegiate course, and at twenty-one he is a graduate, with industry and acquirements, well calculated for the study of any profession."

For a period of fifteen years the law thus inaugurated was kept in operation with varying results, producing rich fruitage where faithfully administered. But it was found after this length of trial that there were defects in the system that needed remedy. There was no competent authority provided for ascertaining and certifying to the qualifications of teachers. The annual reports of boards of directors, showing the operations of the schools and the expenditure of money were not certified by a disinterested party, school vistation by an intelligent examiner was only partially done, or not at all, teachers were not assembled in convention for instruction and stimulation in the work of their calling, and plans for building, seating, warming, ventilating and duly providing with necessary apparatus, were not provided. To remedy these defects a revision of the law was commenced in 1854, by which the office of County Superintendent of Common Schools was engrafted upon it This officer was charged with the duty of examining all teachers who were applicants for schools, and granting certificates setting forth the degree of competency of each in the several branches required to be taught, and of wholly refusing certificates to those deemed incompetent whether by lack of education or moral character. He was also to visit the schools as often as practicable and give such advice and instruction to teachers as seemed proper, to organize teachers' institutes for the instruction and encouragement of teachers, and by lectures and conferences with parents, explain the provisions of the law and remove difficulties in the way of its successful operation, to certify to the correctness of the reports made by boards of directors, of the length of each school term and statistics of attendance. The making of these reports was made obligatory before the district could receive its share of the State appropriation The school department, which had previously been an adjunct of the State department, was separated from it and made independent, with a superintendent of common schools at its head, with a deputy, and the necessary corps of clerks. A School Architecture was published by the State, and a copy deposited with each board of the school directors in the Commonwealth, illustrated with plans of school-houses for all the different grades of schools, and provided with the necessary specifications for the builder. An act for the establishment of normal schools, and their efficient regulation was also passed, by which the State was divided into twelve normal districts in which a normal school might be set up and receive aid from the State under stipulated regulations,—ten acres of ground in one body, a hall capable of seating 1,000 persons, capacity for accommodating 800 pupils. It was also provided that cities of the requisite population should elect a superintendent, independent of the county, and the attendance of teachers upon the annual county institute was made obligatory, and their pay during the time of its session was allowed by the districts employing them.

Vigorous opposition was made to some of these changes, especially to that providing for the election of county superintendent, chiefly on account of the expense incurred by spreading a swarm of new officials over the State, whose services, it was claimed, could be dispensed with. This opposition gradually wore away before the

labors of a competent and faithful officer. The value of his labors
in eliminating from the schools incompetent and unskilled teachers,
and bringing to the front the well qualified, was found to be very
great, and the utility of bringing teachers together in institutes and
stimulating them to the adoption of the best methods of instruction
and government was incomparable.

Strange as it may seem, there were a few districts scattered over
the Commonwealth, which as late as 1863, and perhaps later, persisted in refusing to adopt the free school system, and consequently
failed annually to receive their shares of the State appropriation. In
the process of years these arrearages accumulated until they
amounted to a considerable sum. A statement of these accumulations was annually published in the State report of the superintendent, and the offer to pay them over when the system should be
adopted which the people of the refusing districts could see, until
finally, if for no better nor stronger reason, they all were induced
to accept the bait held out to them.

The first annual report after the adoption of the revised system
was made by the Hon. Charles A. Black, who was then Secretary of
State, and *Ex-officio* Superintendent of Schools, and a citizen of our
own County of Greene. It is with a degree of pride that some extracts from that admirable document, illustrating as it does an intelligent view of its spirit and best methods of administration are here
given. Touching a matter which proved to be of vital importance
in the subsequent operations of the system, he says: "With us the
rule has ever been to adopt the township lines as the proper boundaries, and the exception to this is the independent districts under
special acts of assembly. This evil once commenced it, is easy to
perceive how it might run into excess until every thing like order
or system in the arrangement of school districts would be destroyed."
This evil, thus intelligently characterized, was found in practice to
be all that was here pictured, and proved one of the great disturbing
elements to progress.

The remarks of the secretary upon the adoption of the superintendency are most judicious. The addition, then, of this new
feature of our common school system, was the result of an imperative necessity; and it was commended to the attention of the Legislature, not more by the favorable experience of other States, than
the evident adaptation of the measure to the objects in view. It
was foreseen, however, by the department that in all probability the
institution would be received with some disfavor, and more especially
by the directors, whose actions it might seem designed to control.
Great care was consequently taken to convince them that such was
not the purpose, but was designed to assist them in the performance
of their duties, to relieve them of some of the most irksome of their

Jacob Swart

labors, and to elevate, if possible, the character of the entire system for usefulness and efficiency. In a circular addressed to directors, "it was urged that in making choice of county superintendent 'strict regard should be had to qualifications, habits of morality, industry and previous zealous support of education by common schools. That law requires the person elected to be of literary and scientific acquirements, and skill and experience in the art of teaching.'"

The Secretary, in a circular addressed to County Superintendents, gave very judicious advice, which was well conceived for making successful the labors of this new officer and securing the permanence of the office. The value of the counsel given in this circular, at this juncture, can not be overestimated, and doubtless was the means of saving the repeal of this feature of the law—a calamity which had befallen this provision in the neighboring State of New York. " Its usefulness," says the Secretary, " with us will depend materially upon the manner in which its duties are performed. In their intercourse with directors, who are essentially the vitality of our system, Superintendents should be careful to avoid any assumption of authority not conferred by the law. The jealousy which naturally exists towards the creation of a superior office, apparently intended to control their actions, may be conciliated and entirely removed by a spirit of courtesy and forbearance, and a carefulness to avoid any interference with the rights and duties properly given by law to the directors. Their powers remain undiminished, and in some respects the duties of directors are increased by the new law. It may be proper and useful for a superintendent to give advice and instruction when required, upon many points not prescribed by the law. * * * The intercourse of a county superintendent, with the directors of his county, should be as frequent and familiar as possible. In his visitations he should carry with him a spirit of courtesy, and endeavor upon all such occasions to have the personal presence of the directors. Teachers should always be examined in their presence. This is both the duty of superintendents and the right of the directors. * * * By being present at the examination of teachers and visitations they can better judge of the qualification and worth of a teacher, the progress of the schools, and the ability and devotion of the superintendent to the cause of education, and the manner in which he discharges his duties."

" Whatever opposition has been manifested towards the office of county Superintendent, results more perhaps from opposition to the entire system of popular education than to this or any other particular feature of the law. It is to be regretted that there are still those who are so blind to their own true interests as to oppose any system that would call upon them for taxes, and would be hostile to any system of education unless they were especially exempt from taxation. * * * In the moral and intellectual culture of society, more than in the strong arm of the law, do they find the surest security for the safety and protection of themselves and property. The law never interposes to prevent the perpetration of offence, except by way of example—never exhorts or entreats. Its only mission is to detect and punish, or to reform through punishment But education, moral and intellectual, like an angel of mercy, precedes the action of the law, and enables the young to guard against the temptations that might otherwise beset them through life. Has it ever struck the minds of such that just in proportion as we diffuse, the blessings of education, we lessen the public expenditures for the administration of justice—for the support of jails and penitentiaries "

It would be pleasant and profitable to quote still further from this admirable report of Secretary Black, the first to report under the new law It was fortunate for the State and for the new system that so able and liberal minded a man was at the helm at this critical juncture, that his views were so admirably conceived and expressed, and a great credit to the county of Greene that one of its own sons was the instrument of conserving and perpetuating so great a blessing to the commonwealth.

As we have seen, the feature of the new law which was in greatest danger of failure was the county superintendency. Though this was preserved, and in its sphere was capable of effecting great improvements of the system, yet it was not potent for securing all the increase in efficiency desired. One of the defects which it could not immediately remove was the lack of well instructed and skilled teachers. Upon this head the Secretary observes. "The great scarcity of well qualified teachers is still a source of grave complaint in almost every county of the commonwealth. It is an evil that lies at the very root of our system, and until it is entirely removed our schools cannot attain a permanently flourishing condition. Much has been done during the past summer by means of teachers' institutes and kindred associations to infuse a proper spirit of emulation among the teachers and the examinations by the county superintendents have, doubtless, contributed to the same results. * * * The subject of normal schools for the education of professional teachers, has been so frequently urged upon the attention of the Legislature that it is scarcely necessary on this occasion to repeat the arguments in their favor It cannot be doubted that two Normal Schools, one in the eastern and the other in the western or northern part of the State, properly regulated and sustained by the liberality and bounty of the State, * * * would in a very few years not only supply our schools with competent teachers, but give a tone and character to the entire system that it never before enjoyed."

No one can doubt that this recommendation of the Secretary was one of vital importance at this juncture, striking at the very root of the evils under which the system was groaning. The Legislature was not slow in seeing the reasonableness of his recommendation, and in acting upon it. For, at the session of 1857 a normal school law was enacted which provided for beginning with a single school, and for gradually expanding into that imperial system whereby twelve great Normal Institutions will be established in as many well defined districts, representing equal areas and populations. The tenth district, of which Greene County forms a part, comprises the counties of Washington, Greene, Fayette and Somerset. The school for this district was recognized as a State institution in 1874, and is situated at California, Washington County. The value of its buildings is reported to be $95,000, furniture $7,000, libraries $600, musical instruments $1,000, apparatus $1,350, other property $1,500. The total number of students that have been educated in it males 2,287, females 2,232. The annual attendance males 255, females 286. Schools have been established in ten districts, leaving only two still to be provided for. In these schools up to the present time have been educated males 36,950, females 25,591 a total of 62,541, and the value of property in all the ten is $1,566,813.32. From the modest recommendation of Secretary Black, in 1854, has all this grown.

Another improvement of vital importance to the system was effected in the administration of Secretary Black, that of publishing and furnishing each board of school directors in the commonwealth with a copy of School Architecture, furnishing improved plans and specifications for school houses, with directions for properly seating, warming, ventilating, and furnishing with suitable apparatus. After quoting the provisions of the law, the Secretary proceeds to say: "It is to be hoped that, ere long, the rude and unsightly buildings which still disfigure so many of our school districts, will be displaced by comfortable houses located upon pleasant and healthy sites, and built not only in reference to convenience and comfort, but to taste and beauty. I have already had occasion to suggest the intimate relation between the physical comfort and intellectual improvement of the pupil, and that it is scarcely possible for a child to make rapid progress in education, whilst confined within the damp walls of a log cabin or a rickety dilapidated frame, without the slightest pretension towards comfort or convenience. How can he forbear turning with loathing and disgust from his studies, in such a place, to the more pleasing thoughts of home and its genial comforts. It is indeed a matter of surprise how parents themselves can be so insensible to the mental training of their children as to overlook this important fact."

The law authorizing the publication of a school architecture, contemplated the furnishing plans for schools from the humblest pattern required in the rural district to the most ample and best appointed in the crowded cities. The secretary accordingly secured the services of Messrs. Sloan and Stewart, architects of Philadelphia, to make the required drawings and entrusted the superintending of the engraving and furnishing the necessary descriptive matter to Thomas H. Burrowes, who had been the first secretary under the common school law, and whose life had been largely devoted to subjects of education. The book thus produced has been of vast advantage in securing suitable school buildings.

In concluding his report at this critical period in the history of school education in the Commonwealth, Secretary Black takes a hopeful and reassuring view. "Never before," he says, "were the entire body of the people so deeply interested in the results and successful operation of the law; and although some unfortunately, will ever complain, and I confess that all have perhaps had cause to murmur at the unsatisfactory results of former years, still I am firmly persuaded that the great mass of our citizens are ardently devoted to the cause of education by common schools, and would deplore any retrograde action at this time by the Legislature as a great calamity. The people of Pennsylvania are far too sagacious and patriotic to be insensible to the overshadowing importance of popular education to every relation in life. * * * The character, habits and pursuits of the people of Pennsylvania above all others demand the elevating and enlightening agency of popular education. Nowhere else is labor more emphatically the active element of greatness and prosperity; and it should be a matter of intense gratification, that none are more devotedly enlisted in the cause of education by common schools than the industrial interests of the State. The agricultural, mechanical and laboring classes, the true stamina of a commonwealth, find in the common schools a surer source of power than wealth itself. For, whatever influence the higher institutions of learning have had, or shall have in the diffusion of human knowledge, it is to the common schools, the peoples' colleges, that the great mass of the people must look for the advantages and blessings of education. In these humble though mighty agencies labor will find the secret of its power and the means of elevating itself to that just and honorable position intended by the Creator."

CHAPTER XX.

REPORTS OF COUNTY SUPERINTENDENTS—JOHN A. GORDON—OPPOSITION TO COMMON SCHOOLS—ASSISTANCE OF MESSENGER AND EAGLE— REV. G. W. BAKER—WAYNESBURG AND CARMICHALLS GRADED SCHOOLS—NEW HOUSES AND INCREASED ATTENDANCE—A. G. McGLUMPHY—INSTITUTE ORGANIZED—JOHN A. GORDON—NORMAL SCHOOL AT GREENE ACADEMY— GORDON A SOLDIER—PROF. A. B. MILLER—PROF. T. J. TEAL FOR 12 YEARS—NEW BUILDING AT WAYNESBURG—COUNTY INSTITUTE UNDER THE NEW LAW—IN 1870, 113 FRAME, 23 BRICK, 2 STONE, 29 LOG—ARRAY OF TALENT AT COUNTY INSTITUTE—MT. MORRIS GRADED SCHOOL— DR. A. B. MILLER, REV. J. B. SOLOMON, PROF. LAKIN, REV. SAMUEL GRAHAM—JACKSONVILLE GRADED—CENTENNIAL REPORT —EARLIEST SCHOOLS — QUALIFICATIONS OF EARLY TEACHERS MEAGER—TEACH TO DOUBLE RULE OF THREE—NAMES OF EARLY TEACHERS—STONE SCHOOL HOUSE IN WHITLEY TOWNSHIP.

FROM the annual reports of the County Superintendents of schools may be traced the complete history of the origin and progress of common school education in this county. We have seen that by the report of 1837 and 1838 only the townships of Cumberland, Franklin, Jefferson, Marion, Morgan, Morris, Monongahela and Richhill reported, and these but very meager results. In the report of 1854, John A. Gordon, who was the County Superintendent, reports the schools 154 in number, presided over by 147 male teachers, and 20 females, to be in a prosperous condition, the people everywhere manifesting a spirit of co-operation in his labors. In his subsequent reports he mentions opposition not so much to himself or to the office which he filled, as to the taxation which the support of the schools and building of the school houses necessitated. Public meetings were held and resolutions passed; but beyond this it took no more definite form. In the Western townships great difficulties were experienced on account of the sparseness of settlement, great blocks of land having been held back by speculators, which rendered it difficult to secure scholars enough for a school within convenient distance. It is pleasant to note, amidst the difficulties he had to labor under, the hearty manner in which he recognizes the prompt assistance rendered him by the Waynesburg *Messenger*, and Waynesburg *Eagle*; and also the aid and encouragement from the Revs. Jeffries, Collins, Laughlin and Henderson, and from J Laughran, president of the *Waynesburg College*, and Prof. Miller   *   *   * " But to none am I so much indebted as to Rev. G. W. Baker, principal of the Union school at Waynesburg No sacrifice of time or money appears too great for him to make in the cause of common schools. He is always ready at the shortest warning to go wherever the interest of the cause calls him. Neither rain nor frost can deter him " In this early day much unrequited labor was performed in clearing the way for the complete success of the common school system, and it is only simple justice that testimony be borne to these earnest and self-sacrificing toils

One of the first and most important improvements wrought by the revised school law of 1854, was the grading of schools effected, and classification secured in ungraded schools and the uniformity of school books as a necessary concomitant In Mr Gordon's report of 1856 he says, " There are two graded schools in the county, 147 in which a successful attempt has been made at classification, and none in which there is neither grading nor classification One of the graded schools is the Union school at Waynesburg. It is taught by Rev G. W. Baker, principal, and Miss McFerran and Miss Alison assistants I have had frequent occasion to speak of this school in terms of commendation The other graded school is in the borough of Carmichaels. This school has only had the experience of a graded school of two sessions. It was taught by Mr. Poundstone and Miss Wilkins "

Some estimate can be formed of the personel of the teachers employed during this year from the following statement. "There are 27 teachers between 17 and 21 years of age; 40 between 21 and 25; 34 between 25 and 30; 32 between 30 and 40, 4 between 40 and 50, and 14 over 50 years; 135 were born in Pennsylvania, and 16 out of it " In his concluding report for the year 1857 Mr. Gordon reports two school houses as having been built after plans obtained from the new School Architecture furnished by the State Of the materials employed, 70 are reported as of frame, 16 brick, 4 stone and 67 log " Over 30 schools houses," he says, " have been erected during my term of office (3 years) one-fifth of the whole number. These houses, for the most part, are better located, are larger and better adapted to the purpose for which they are intended, than the first ones " In summing up the condition of the schools he says, " The first year of my term the number of pupils exceeded any former year by more than one thousand. This year judging from my notes, the attendance will exceed the first year by several hundreds." In making up his schedule of wants of the system he places at the head a larger State appropriation. This would relieve in a measure the burdensome taxation necessitated by sparseness of population. A second is a more uniform and systematic visitation of schools; a third the sympathy and co-operation of parents; and finally a host of thoroughly qualified teachers.

The transition state from the inefficiency which had prevailed under the old law, to the well regulated system under the new law of 1854 did not come until the second term of the county superintendency. In the attempt to build school houses and keep the schools open four months in the year, as was necessary to secure the State appropriation, some of the districts incurred indebtedness beyond their means, and consequently several of the townships were obliged to levy and collect taxes to pay debts, and therefore had no schools except such as were provided by voluntary contributions. A. J. McGlumphy was elected superintendent for the second term. In his first report he mentions three districts as having no schools open during the school year, at public expense, for the reasons given above.

One of his early official acts was to issue a call " through the county papers for a meeting of teachers, directors, and other friends of education, to convene in the college hall at Waynesburg, to organize a teachers' institute for the county. At the time appointed a few teachers appeared, and an organization was effected. Several practical and interesting lectures were delivered by the teachers present. A number of the citizens of Waynesburg attended every meeting and manifested a deep interest in the proceedings The institute met again in January At this meeting there were more teachers present than at the first. Upon both occasions we had the assistance of Rev. J. P. Weethee, President of Waynesburg College, Professor A. B. Miller, of the same institute, and a number of the students " Provision was made for semi-annual meetings, and it is to the credit of Mr. McGlumphy's administration that the county institute was successfully organized. He retired at the end of the second year and was succeeded by G. W. Baker. In the report of the latter for 1860 he says in six of the districts there were no schools during the last year for lack of funds. He records very much to his credit and his interest in the schools: " I held some seven or eight teachers' institutes, during the fall and winter. They were all but one well attended. Judging from the interest manifested by both teachers and people, they were of great service I lectured nearly every week once or twice of evenings, while performing my school visitations. These were largely attended, and very frequently the schools I visited were crowded with spectators, eager to hear the performances of the children and the lectures given them The increasing interest manifested by the teachers and people of this county augurs favorably for the future." These are the most encouraging words found in any of the reports hitherto made.

At the election, which occurred for the third term of the superintendency, John A. Gordon was chosen, entering upon his duties with the experience of his former service, and the old time zeal, which manifested itself in the plan for work which he immediately laid out. " I have made arrangements," he says, "with the principal of the Greene Academy, to hold a Normal school. It will open on the 26th of August and continue in session four weeks. At the close of the Normal school I shall commence a series of institutes, extending to the 1st of November, when the schools will open." This has the ring of the true metal, and such untiring energy as is here prefigured is sure of its reward.

But now the horrors of our civil war were upon the nation, which overshadowed every other interest. On the 1st of November, 1861, Mr. Gordon resigned to take his place in the ranks of the Union army, and his companions in arms recognized his worth by electing him Captain. Professor A. B. Miller, A. M., was appointed to complete the term. In his report for 1863 Superintendent Miller says, "The war has taken from the county several of its best teachers, several of whom have discharged the debt of patriotism with their lives; still the schools are supplied, and there is a gradual improvement in the general or aggregate qualifications." Though in the midst of war times he reports a good school-house erected in each of the following districts: Cumberland, Perry, Centre, Franklin, Whitely, and Morris; and a Union school building in Waynesburg.

Among the agencies which have exerted a potent influence for good over the common schools of Greene County is Waynesburg College. The superintendent says of it, " Waynesburg College is now in a prosperous condition. This institution is exerting a decided and beneficial influence upon the school interests of the county. It has educated many teachers, and its professors have ever manifested a most cordial co-operation with those who have had supervision of the public schools. Greene Academy has been, for a long time, a 'light shining in a dark place,' and to it the county is greatly indebted."

For the next four terms, embracing a period of twelve years, from 1864 to 1876, Professor T. J. Teal held the office of superintendent. During this long period, the formative period of common school instruction in the county, the reports show a steady improvement in the erection of new and better school-houses, in qualification of teachers, in intelligent interest of parents, and the greater efficiency of directors in managing the business of the districts. In these several reports there are from six to ten new school-houses reported as having been built each year. In the report of 1864 a good Union

James Hughes

school building is reported as having been built in Waynesburg on a commodious and commanding site on a line with the Waynesburg College building, at a cost of $5,000, from plan No. 5 of the State School Architecture The Rev. Dr. Sloan, of the Presbyterian Church, was the first principal, assisted by Miss Mattie H. Parker, Miss Mary Hedge, Miss McCormick, and Miss Annie Allison. The nation was still in the throes of civil war. "The great conflict," he says, "which has been raging for the last three years, has had a deleterious effect upon the cause of education. Many of the ablest and most successful teachers have been called from their peaceful profession to fields of carnage and strife Some fill soldiers' graves on distant fields; others are still in the ranks of war." In many respects the Superintendent of Greene County could do more efficient work, and his labors were more satisfactory to himself and useful to the county, than in the larger and more thickly peopled counties of the State. With reasonable diligence the officer could visit all the schools each year once and some a second time. His examinations of teachers could be held in three weeks, which left him a fair amount of time for holding institutes and educational meetings. Since the first reports a great change had been made in the teaching force in the schools. Whereas in the first years the teachers were almost without exception males, now they stand 89 males to 74 females. The whole number of visits to schools this year, 1864, was 172, varying in length from an hour and a half to two and a half, and all visited except two.

In the report of 1866 an appeal was made for more ample school grounds, better locations, for fencing and ornamentation of lots. It is a sign of encouragement that fourteen of the eighteen districts of the county were supplied with globes and Mitchell's outline maps. This manifests a step in advance, and a sign of progress scarcely anticipated In the report of 1867 the gratifying intelligence is given that Springhill, which, on account of sparseness of settlement and delays in taking up the lands had been retarded in organizing schools, this year had all its schools in operation, and consequently was enabled to draw its share of the State appropriation, and certain arrearages which had been accumulating. All the schools of the district were now in full operation.

The Superintendent's report for 1868 shows a more encouraging and hopeful spirit than has previously been manifested since the passage of the revised school law. "Teachers," he says, "have a more thorough knowledge of the branches to be taught, and better methods of imparting their knowledge. They read more books on the science of education and the art of teaching. They attend more educational meetings and teacher's institutes. These are the teachers who display superior skill and ability in managing schools."

16

The labors of the superintendent during this year appear to have been more energetic and fruitful of good results than in any previous one. Twelve special institutes were held in different parts of the county with an aggregate attendance of one hundred and sixty teachers. In December, 1867, the county institute was organized under the provisions of the new act regulating these meetings. One hundred and three teachers, and a good number of citizens were in attendance. Professors A B Miller, J C. Gilchrist, S S. Jack, and J. M. Moore assisted the Superintendent. " In the number attending, in the interest manifested, and in the practical workings of the institute, it far surpassed any educational meeting ever held in the county " But though great improvements are thus joyfully recorded the Superintendent's Report is not without a tinge of sadness in view of some of the obstacles which still were encountered " Irregular attendance is one of the great opposing elements in the way of progress It destroys the classification of the schools, and obstructs the progress of the pupils. It discourages the teacher, and makes his work inefficient It deprives many of a practical education, and throws them upon the bosom of society without those essential characteristics which constitute good citizenship " By a provision of law which went into operation this year school directors were empowered, if they were unable to obtain suitable ground in a desirable location for school-houses, to appropriate such and so much as was desired and pay for it by appraisement as in the case of land taken for roads.

In opening his report for the year 1870 the Superintendent gives some statistics, which, compared with those given at the first adoption of the system, are gratifying The whole number of school-houses is reported at 167, of these 113 are frame; 23 brick, 2 stone; 29 log. The county institute was reported from year to year as being successfully conducted and growing in interest. Able educators are reported as having been employed to give instruction and lecture Among these were Hon B G Northrop, Superintendent of the Schools of Connecticut; Hon J P. Wickersham, Superintendent in Pennsylvania; Andrew Burtt, author of Grammars; A. B. Miller, D. D., President of Waynesburg College; Prof J A Cooper, President of the State Normal School of the Twelfth district; J. Jackson Purman, of Waynesburg; Prof. F. A. Allen, President of the Normal School in the Fifth district; W. W. Woodruff, Superintendent of Chester County; Prof C. L Ehrenfeld, President of the Normal School in the Tenth district; Prof. J. B. Solomon, President of the Monongahela College. Such an array of talent as this in the special line of institute work, embracing some of the most distinguished educators and authors in the nation, rarely falls to the lot of any one county to have employed, and it could not but exert an important influence over the body of teachers assembled. A free acknowledgment of the progress and improvement of teachers is made in the report of this year. "The enterprising and progressive teachers are making sacrifices to meet the constantly increasing demand of a higher order of qualification; these noble workers in the cause of human progress, deserve the approbation of a grateful people; their meritorious work is seen in the order, neatness, and cleanliness of the school-room; it is read in the happy faces and thoughtful countenances of their pupils "

The report of 1872 shows the erection of a suitable school edifice and the grading of the schools at Mt. Morris   The near completion of the Monongahela College edifice is also mentioned, and the successful opening of the institution.   Special arrangements for the training of teachers were at this time made in Waynesburg College, under the charge of Dr. A. B. Miller; Monongahela College, under Rev J. B. Solomon; Greene Academy, under Prof Lakin; and an Academy at Jacksonville, under Rev. Samuel Graham   While great improvement is annually reported in the qualifications of teachers, the lamentable fact is mentioned that many of the most experienced remain but a short time in the profession.   They either go into other business or seek employment in other localities, where the compensation is more remunerative.   To remedy this crying evil directors are implored to give better remuneration, and the almost annual recommendation is made that the Legislature make a larger State appropriation, so that better wages can be paid worthy teachers without making local taxation too burdensome   The very commendable practice of directors and citizens attending the institutes and the annual examinations of teachers in the several districts is reported, thus evincing a growing interest in the progress of common-school education.

In the report of 1874, the superintendent records fifteen local institutes as having been held, all well attended by directors, teachers and citizens, and the annual county institute as having been attended by 147 teachers.   The institute was held in the court-house, and " a more than usual interest was manifested by the citizens of the place." In 1875 the schools in Jacksonville were graded and put in successful operation.   With this report, Superintendent Teal, after twelve years of faithful, laborious, intelligent and efficient service, closed his official labors.   The schools of Greene County owe much to his skillful work during this protracted period   .

At the election of County Superintendents in 1875, Prof. A. F. Silvius was elected Superintendent of Greene County.   In his first report he records the gratifying fact that eighty-three of the schools during the year were supplied with good school globes, and that directors are beginning to grade the wages of teachers according to the degree of qualification, as shown by the certificate, and success and experience in teaching. Local institutes were held in fifteen districts, and the county institute was conducted by Hon. John H. French, of Burlington, Vermont, and Dr. Miller, of Waynesburg, for three successive sessions

In the year succeeding the Centennial year of American Independance, the State Superintendent of Common Schools called for special reports from the county and city superintendents embracing a history of education in their districts for the past hundred years, with the design of publishing a Centennial volume. From the report of Superintendent Silvius some interesting facts are gleaned. Of the state of education in the territory previous to 1796, when the county was organized, the information is traditional.

"Of the early emigrants, but few could read and write. * * *
They procured some unoccupied cabin, made a few uncomfortable seats, and selected one of their number, who could read and write best, to teach the school In some cases a room was fitted up in one of their cabins, and the woman of the house took in a few of the neighbors' children, and taught them with her own The teachers of that day were very meagerly qualified Of arithmetic, many knew little. To others who attempted to teach it, division was a mystery. The ability to solve examples by the rule of three was considered quite a scholarly attainment, and it was often inserted in articles of agreement, between patrons and teachers, that they would teach arithmetic only to the 'Double rule of Three' The teachers who accomplished most were men of liberal education who had emigrated to this country from east of the mountains, and from foreign countries, and who from misfortune, habits of life, or other causes, had failed to follow the profession for which they were educated, and engaged in teaching as a necessity Many of them were men of doubtful integrity, and irregular lives Though their example was bad, they accomplished much good, and our oldest citizens remember them with gratitude

"The earliest teachers of note were Kennedy, Van Emon, Ely, Denny, Wheelock, Webb, Duffy, Van Meter, Felix Hughes, Frank Fraser, and Mrs. Arnold, followed by Hale, Strowsnider, Foley, Mc-Courtney, Wood, Crawford, Kent, Rinehart, Johnson, Henry, Francis Braddock, Thomas Leasure, Moses Dinsmore, Stephen Uncles, James Tane, W B Teagarden, Robert Cathers and wife and Amos Stanberry. Of the few school-houses built at the early period before the inauguration of the free school system of 1834, by the voluntary subscriptions of neighbors, the most notable now standing is the stone structure in Whiteley Township, a monument of devotion to education at a time when money was scarce and little was being done. It should be ever kept in the best of repair and cherished as a link between that early period and the present. Few such monuments exist within the borders of the Commonwealth.

"Upon the adoption of the common school system of 1834, some opposition was manifested in Greene County, and as the adoption or rejection of the system was left to a vote of the people, many districts chose not to accept its advantages. But the accumulations in the State treasury of monies which would have been paid to non-accepting districts, finally became so great, money freely offered for the building new school-houses, that all accepted and organized under the provisions of the law. It was much in favor of the law that some of the most influential citizens freely gave time and influence in favor of the system by serving as school directors, and pleading the cause of free school education."

In his report of 1878, Superintendent Silvius publishes the report of a committee of teachers, before which he had submitted some recommendations upon the subject of gradation and promotion in the schools, which was adopted at the county institute. The following is the report: 1. Resolved, that we believe that the best interests of education demand a thorough classification of all the schools of the county, and to this end we favor the adoption of a graded course of studies that provides for instruction in proper order in all the common school branches, and that we will use our influence and efforts to secure a course of studies and classification of all the schools of this county at the earliest practicable day. 2. That the County Superintendent, with the aid and co-operation of the school directors and teachers, hold examinations in each township for the purpose of giving those pupils, found worthy of the same, a certificate signed by the county superintendent, the board of directors and the teachers constituting the examining committee, stating that the holder is a person of good moral character, and has completed the common school course of study

"In accordance with this report" the superintendent continues "I suggested a course of study, and near the close of the schools, held examinations at Garrard's Fort, Taylortown, Mt. Morris, Newtown, Rogersville, Bridgeport, Carmichaels, Knisley school-houses, and Jolleytown, at which eighty-three pupils passed satisfactory examinations, and were granted diplomas. Literary exercises were connected with the examinations, and the meetings gave universal satisfaction. I know of no better means to arouse emulation among pupils, schools and districts, and to give an impulse to education, than perfecting the system now introduced."

At the election of county superintendents held in May, 1878, S. F. Hoge, Esq., of Jefferson, was elected for Greene. In his first report he mentions a "wide-spread indifference" among the people to the best interests of the schools; and complains of incompetency on the part of teachers, the complaint being general among them that the wages paid are insufficient. He reports great improvement in the interiors of school-houses, and in the enlargement, planting, and fencing of school grounds.

In 1881 William M. Nickerson, of Carmichaels, was elected superintendent. A passage in his first report affords a fair index to the *personel* of teachers employed at this period: "Number of male teachers employed was 136; females, 59. One hundred and twenty held provisional certificates, forty-nine professional, twenty-one permanent, and five are graduates of Normal schools. Average age of teachers was twenty-four years. Forty have had no experience in teaching * * * Twenty-one public examinations were held at which there were eighty directors and quite a number of citizens present. I examined 206 applicants. I issued 176 certificates, 2 professional, and rejected 30. * * * The method of examination was the written and oral combined." In addition to the county institute, which was unusually well attended, there were forty district institutes held, usually beginning on Friday evening and closing on Saturday evening. In his report of 1884, the superintendent mentions with commendable pride the opening of the new school building in Waynesburg, which occurred on the 15th of October, 1883. "The house," he says, "erected in Waynesburg deserves special notice. It is a three-story brick building, containing eight school-rooms, a room for the principal of the school, and a hall or lecture room which can be used for school rooms. The building is heated with hot air, and is pretty well ventilated. The building will compare favorably with any in the western part of the State."

At the triennial election, held in 1884, James S. Herrington, of Kirby, was chosen superintendent. In his report of 1886 he bears testimony to the steady improvement in school-houses, furniture, enlargement and improvement of school grounds, and the planting of shade trees. But one paragraph in his report shows still a great lack of system in the conducting of the schools. "I observed," he says, "that the greatest need of our schools was system and purpose in the school work. In many schools pupils were pursuing no definite course of study. They studied those books only which they happened to bring with them. Many were receiving no instruction in language or grammar; but few studying or receiving instruction in all the branches. I at once prepared a course of study in five grades, together with a blank report, and got two published for each teacher in the county. These reports enrolled the name of each pupil in the school, showing in what grade he was placed and his standing in the grade; also the teacher's programme, and many other things necessary for a successful school. After being filled out by the teacher, one was sent to the superintendent, and the other placed in the teacher's report book for the inspection of the directors. This did very much for the bettering the condition of the schools."

At the triennial convention of directors held in May, 1887, A. J. Waychoff was elected superintendent, who is the present incumbent.

That a comparative view of the progress of education in Greene County by semi-decades may be seen at a glance, the main statistical items, drawn from the tables printed in the annual reports, are given below. The first entry is taken from Superintendent Burrowes' report, published in 1837, when the operations of the first common school law had been recorded. From that time until 1854, when the revised law went into effect, no itemized tables of statistics seem to have been published. In that year the report of the Hon. Charles A. Black records the complete statistics, and from that time forward they have been regularly inserted in the annual volume. This table will possess interest, as illustrating the changes which have occurred in the half of a century.

Year.	Number of Schools.	Number of Months Schools Open.	Number of Male Teachers.	Number of Female Teachers.	Salaries of Males per month.	Salaries of Females per month.	Average Number of Pupils in Attendance.	Amount of Direct Tax Levied.	Received from State Appropriation.
1837....	5	4	4	1	$20 00	$17 00	287	$215 00	$635 70
1854....	154	4	141	26	22 11	16 40	4,840	14,999 89	1,933 75
1859....	151	4.2	131	37	24 13	18 64	4,223	19,794 75	2,039 08
1864....	161	4.10	105	71	20 22	18 83	4,373	20,287 82	2,212 86
1869....	173	4.4	119	55	35 44	31 66	5,488	36,699 62	3,061 00
1874....	179	5.04	129	52	33 56	29 85	4,720	36,826 10	4,188 61
1879....	178	5.07	135	51	27 87	28 25	5,296	32,683 14	5,499 19
1884....	192	5.14	119	78	33 87	30 25	5,124	44,382 85	6,256 95
1888....	198	5.17	125	77	33 93	31 48	5,500	45,729, 92	6,928 99

CHAPTER XXI.

CHARTER FOR GREENE COUNTY ACADEMY—$2,000 FROM THE STATE—
PRINCIPALS SERVED A USEFUL PURPOSE—PENNSYLVANIA ACAD-
EMIES UNSATISFACTORY—LAW TO TRANSFER PROPERTY TO COM-
MON SCHOOL—SELECT SCHOOLS—WAYNESBURG COLLEGE—ORIGIN
—VALUE OF THE SMALL COLLEGES—MADISON AND BEVERLY—
NEED OF SUCH AN INSTITUTION—PENNSYLVANIA PRESBYTERY OF
CUMBERLAND PRESBYTERIAN CHURCH—WAYNESBURG SELECTED—
REV J LOUGHRAN OPENED A SCHOOL—CHARTER OBTAINED—
SUPPLEMENTS—MARGARET K BELL OPENS SCHOOL IN BAPTIST
CHURCH FOR FEMALES—NEW BUILDING OPENED—FIRST CLASSES
GRADUATE—TAKEN UNDER PENNSYLVANIA SYNOD—RELATIONS
OF THE CHURCH TO THE COLLEGE—MILLER SUCCEEDS FISH—REV.
J P WETHEE, PRESIDENT—INSISTS ON CLASSIFICATION OF MALES
AND FEMALES ALIKE—SETTLED AFTER INVESTIGATION—JOHN C.
FLENNIKEN—REV. ALFRED B MILLER, PRESIDENT, IN 1859—
HIS DEVOTED LABORS—DEBT OF $3,000—STRUGGLES—HAD
UNDERTAKEN TOO MUCH—CHURCH TO SUPPORT THREE PROFES-
SORS—UNSELFISH DEVOTION OF DR. MILLER—MRS. M. K. B.
MILLER—UNTIMELY DEATH—RESOLUTIONS OF TRUSTEES—
MONONGAHELA COLLEGE—REV JOSEPH SMITH—REV. H. K.
CRAIG—REV. J. B SOLOMON—SCOPE OF THE COLLEGE.

AS we have already seen early attention was given to founding
county academies A charter for the Greene County Academy
was secured in 1810. Hugh Barclay at this time represented the
county in the Legislature, and secured the passage of the act granting the charter. The school was located at Carmichaels. The following six named persons were appointed its first trustees: Charles
Swan, James Flenniken, George Evans, Robert Lewis, Robert
Witchell and Hugh Barclay. The first building was the Episcopal
church, and was under the charge of this denomination. An appropriation was made by the Legislature of $2,000, to be used for
building purposes and for teaching poor children gratis under the
law of 1809 Subscriptions of citizens helped to swell the endowment fund But for some reason the school was not established for
several years after obtaining the charter. The following are the
principals who have presided over the institution from its original
opening: Ely, Wakefield, Loughran, Whipple, George W. Miller,

William Lippencott

Craig

Joseph Horner, Ross, Martin, Long, Baker, Craig, Orr, Lakin and W. M Nickerson. It was for many years the chief educational centre in the county. Many of those who afterwards rose to eminence received their early instruction in this institution, and a large proportion of the common school teachers either directly or indirectly received their training here. Dr Miller, president of Waynesburg College, and Prof. G W. Scott, the eminent mathematician, received their early instruction in Greene Academy.

When Dr. Thomas H. Burrowes came to the head of the school department in 1860 he instituted searching inquiries into the condition of the county academies which had received aid from the State. Previous to this time these institutions had not been considered within the purview of the State department. He found the condition of these institutions in the main unsatisfactory. In the counties of Adams, Alleghany, Cumberland, Fayette, Lancaster, Lycoming, Philadelphia and Washington, the academy properties had been conveyed to or disposed of for the benefit of colleges or other institutions in those counties. In others they had been sold for debt. In a number of counties, by special acts of the Legislature, these properties had been sold, and the funds paid over to the common school boards of directors for the benefit of the common school fund. In a considerable number of counties they were not in operation, and only in twelve, Greene being one, was any degree of vigor exhibited. Over a hundred thousand dollars had been appropriated by the State, exclusive of lands donated, to these county academies. The condition of these schools as a whole was anything but encouraging, and "the question," says Dr. Burrowes, "arises as to the best mode of bringing this amount of educational capital into effective employment. * * * The enactment of a general law, authorizing the conveyance of academy property by the trustees to the common school district within which it is situated, is accordingly recommended. Such a course would gradually lead to the establishment of efficient high common schools in the county and other large towns, and thus effect the generous views, in favor of the advanced branches of learning, which led to these numerous grants during the first portion of the present century."

In compliance with this recommendation the Legislature passed a general law authorizing such transfer of property, and in most of the counties where such properties existed the transfers were made, and among them the building and endowment funds of Greene County Academy were turned over to the school board of Carmichaels, and a public high school took its place.

Aside from this academy there have been select schools held at various points in the county, some of which have attained to considerable importance. Nineteen years ago, in 1869, the Rev Samuel

Graham established the Jacksonville Academy, which, during the first three years attained a membership of eighty-three, and maintained a high grade of scholarship. At the present time, 1888, Mr. Graham has a select school at Graysville, which is of a high order, and quite liberally attended. At the Centennial church, near the borders of Aleppo and Springhill townships, Prof. David O. Compson has at intervals taught a school at which students from a considerable distance around, even as far away as Freeport, are in attendance. These are but examples of the methods of education beyond the common-schools in operation throughout the county.

But by far the most important educational agency in the county is that of Waynesburg College. It is not only an institution in which every citizen may justly cherish a pride, affording as it does the highest grade of academic culture at his own door, but is a source of prosperity to the town, and indeed to the whole county, even to its remotest borders. Though not so numerously attended, nor so liberally endowed, nor so widely celebrated on account of age and a long line of illustrious *alumnorum*, yet the elements of all liberal studies may as successfully be acquired here, as in the older and more noted institutions; for, after all, it is not what is put into a student by costly and elaborate appliances, but what can be developed in his inner consciousness, and made to grow and strengthen with use, that is the main end of education, and it is a question which challenges consideration whether the smaller and more secluded institutions are not more favorable for the development of the mental faculties, than those where crowds are gathered, where students must spend large sums of money, and squander much valuable time by night and by day to preserve their social standing. Of the eminent men, who have, by their talents, acquired national and even cosmopolitan prominence, the majority are the children of the minor institutions, and in the coming years the men who shall wield the healthiest influence in church and State, and win for themselves imperishable fame, will come from the institutions which bend all their forces to the strengthening of the individuality of the student.

Waynesburg College originated in a long-felt want on the part of the membership of the Cumberland Presbyterian Church of Pennsylvania for an institution of learning in their midst of a high order. Madison College, at Uniontown, Fayette County, Pennsylvania, and Beverly College, at Beverly, Ohio, had been subjects of their patronage, and confident hopes had been entertained that these institutions would afford all needed facilities. But for reasons not necessary here to be set forth, these anticipations had not been realized. " A sense of the need," says Dr. Miller, in his history of the college, from which this sketch is chiefly drawn, "of better educational facilities must have pervaded the entire Synod.

The number of candidates for the ministry was small, and the Presbyteries felt that provision must be made to meet a demand so vital to the interests of the church. In this state of things the Pennsylvania Presbytery, at its meeting in Greenfield, Washington County, Pennsylvania, in April, 1849, passed the following:

WHEREAS, the educational interests of this Presbytery imperiously demand that an institution of learning be established in its bounds; therefore,

Resolved, That a committee of five persons be appointed to receive proposals for the location and establishment of such an institution and report at the next meeting of the Presbytery.

The Reverends John Cary, Phillip Axtell, and J. H. D. Henderson, and Elders Jesse Lazear, and Samuel Murdock, constituted that committee. In the autumn of this year the Synod adopted resolutions upon the subject of education, of which the following is an extract: " Many young men will continue in the ministry with only such preparations as the high-schools afford. But, admitting a sufficient number of institutions, the want of a fund is a serious obstacle. To many young men, such a fund is the only hope. Aided by the church, they can prosecute their studies and the ministry with high prospects of usefulness. Deploring, therefore, the difficulties of obtaining an education within our bounds, your committee are of opinion that the means of correction are in the hands of the Synod, and that no time should be lost in taking measures to that end "

Applications for proposals made by the committee appointed for the purpose were responded to by the people of Waynesburg, the county seat of Greene County, a town at that time of some twelve hundred inhabitants, and of Carmichaels, a town of about half the population, situated in the central part of Cumberland Township, in the valley of the Monongahela River, known as the seat of Greene Academy Neither party offered a very large sum of money; but, as was shown by the report of the committee, the offers of citizens of Waynesburg were more considerable than those of Carmichaels, and it was accordingly adopted as the seat of the proposed college. Failing in the first proposal, the citizens of Carmichaels, in the fall of 1849, proposed " to erect a building sixty feet long and thirty five feet wide, and three stories high, which they would tender to the Pennsylvania Synod, to be held by the Synod and used as a Female Seminary, in consideration of their extending to it their patronage." But the Synod deemed it prudent to reject this offer, and concentrate all their patronage upon one institution.

As yet no school existed at Waynesburg which should form a nucleus for the proposed college. That there might be something on which to build, in the autumn of 1849, the Rev. J. Loughran withdrew from Greene Academy, and opened a school of a high grade, which was merged into the college when the buildings were ready. The citizens of Waynesburg subscribed some five thousand dollars for the erection of a building, the work upon which was begun in the autumn of 1850, and was completed and occupied in the spring of 1851. It was a substantially built three-story brick edifice seventy by fifty feet, and was erected at a cost of $6,000

To give legal validity to its operations, application was made to the Legislature for a charter, which was granted in March, 1850, of which the following are some of its provisions:

SEC. 1. Be it enacted, by the Senate and House of Representatives of the Commonwealth of Pennsylvania, in General Assembly met, and it is hereby enacted by the authority of the same, That there shall be and hereby is established in the borough of Waynesburg, Greene County, State of Pennsylvania, a college or public school for the education of youth, in the English and other languages, literature and the useful arts and sciences, by the name and style of "The Waynesburg College;" the said college to be under the management of seven trustees, a majority of whom shall constitute a quorum for the transaction of business, and which trustees and their successors shall be, and they are hereby declared to be, a body politic and corporate, in deed and in law, by the name, style, and title of "The Waynesburg College," and by such name shall have perpetual succession, and shall be able to sue and be sued, plead and be impleaded, etc

SEC. 3 That Jesse Lazear, Jesse Hook, W. T. E Webb, Bradley Mahanna, John Rodgers, Mark Gordon, R W Downey, William Braden, A. G. Allison, William W. Sayers, A. Shaw, John T. Hook, and John Phelan, are hereby appointed trustees of said corporation, to hold their office until their successors are elected in the manner hereinafter provided. By the further provisions of this section, three of the seven trustees were to be appointed by the stockholders of the building, and four by the Pennsylvania Presbytery of the Cumberland Presbyterian Church, and if the stockholders at any time should fail to elect their part of the trustees, the Presbytery might elect the entire number; provided, that the said Presbytery should establish and maintain at least three professorships in said college within three years after being notified that the building had been completed, otherwise the stockholders were to elect the whole number of trustees after a failure of said Presbytery to establish and maintain said professorships within said period.

SEC. 4. The President and Professors of the said college for the time being, shall have the power to grant and confirm such degrees in the arts and sciences to such students of the college and others, when, by their proficiency in learning, professional eminence or other meritorious distinction, they shall be entitled thereto, as they may see fit or as aie granted in other colleges and universities in the United States, and to grant to graduates on whom such degrees may be conferred, certificates or diplomas as is usual in other colleges and universities.

To this charter two supplements weie procuied: The first in 1852, increasing the number of trustees to twenty-one, the second in 1853, authorizing the Presbytery to elect twelve, and the stockholders nine, of these trustees. In 1854 the stockholders declined to elect trustees, whereupon the Synod elected the whole number, which it has since continued to do. Thus the stockholders, on the one hand, early and cordially gave the college fully into the control of the Synod, while the Synod, on the other hand has ever respected the rights of the stockholdeis in the selection of persons to fill the Board of Trustees.

In the fall of 1850, Miss Margaret K. Bell was employed to take charge of a school of young ladies, with the design of founding a female seminary in connection with the college. A separate building was proposed, but never erected, a seal and diploma were engraved, and several classes of young ladies were graduated, and received diplomas under the seal of Waynesburg Female Seminary. During the summer of 1851 this female school was conducted in the Baptist church, and the college in the Cumberland Piesbyterian church, Rev. P. Axtell assisting Prof. Loughran in the latter. In the autumn following, both schools were conducted in the new building under the management and tuition of the following instructors: Rev. J. Loughran, A. M., President; Rev. R M. Fish, A. B., Piofessor of Mathematics; A. B. Miller and Frank Patteison, Tutors; Miss M. K. Bell, Principal of the Female Seminary. "On the first Tuesday of November, says Dr. Miller, "the college went into formal operation in the new building, and that day marked my own entrance as a student, and also as a tutor, from which date my connection with the institution has been unbroken."

Of the opening of this new institution, Piesident Miller iecalls most pleasant reminiscences. "This first term," he says, "in the new building was a truly pleasant and auspicious beginning. As I now look back upon that winter's woik, it seems to me that no set of students and teachers were ever happier or more intent on the faithful discharge of duty. Unbroken harmony prevailed. * * * Twenty-six years of arduous and unremitting toil lie between the cheerful work of that winter and the grave responsibilities of the present !

"The opening of the spring term, May, 1852, witnessed a large increase of students, the number in all for this first year being one hundred and thirty. The end of the year was marked by the graduation of the first class in the Female Seminary: Elizabeth

Lindsey, Caroline Hook, and Martha Bayard. At the close of the second year, September, 1853, a class of four graduated. At the same date the first class of young men graduated from the college—A. B. Miller, W. E. Gapen, Clark Hackney, and James Rinehart. This commencement day, September 28, 1853, being the first in the college proper, was an occasion of great interest The Pennsylvania Presbytery held a called meeting the day before, in Waynesburg, and the Synod met in the evening of that day, so that nearly all the members of the Synod were on the platform at commencement, as also other distinguished visitors, among them Hon. Andrew Stewart, and Hon. Samuel A. Gilmore. The young men composing the class seemed not to lack in appreciation of the part they were to play, or the pre-eminence due them as the first class Displaying their class motto, *Ducimus*, above them, they spoke to the apparent satisfaction of a crowded audience. "I may be pardoned," says Dr. Miller, "the egotism of saying it was my privilege to lead my own class, by delivering the first graduating performance, and thus to enjoy the distinction of the 'first born,' of the many sons of *Alma Mater*."

Immediately following the commencement, the college was formally received under the control of the Pennsylvania Synod. This action had been delayed from the fact that the Cumberland Presbyterians of Ohio and Pennsylvania had formed one Synod, and it was deemed expedient that the college at Beverly, Ohio, which was already under the charge of the Synod, should be supported before adopting another institution But when, in 1852, the Synod was divided, Beverly College was turned over to the Ohio Synod, and Waynesburg College was fully received under the fostering care of Pennsylvania Synod The Synod set forth the grounds of its action in a long report, the leading points of which may be thus condensed: "(1) No denomination can maintain a respectable standing without institutions of learning. (2). No denomination can discharge its obligations to maintain the purity of the scriptures, and to present their doctrines in an efficient manner, without collegiate institutions. (3). Only institutions of a high grade can give character and efficiency to a church, in order to which an institution must receive liberal patronage. (4) The benefits of a union between churches and colleges are reciprocal. (5). 'It will be better for the interests of the church that Pennsylvania Synod possesses one well established and influential college, than for the church to be burdened with several feeble ones.'" This report was prepared by Revs. John Cary, J. Loughran and J. T. A. Henderson, and was unanimously adopted.

Dr. Miller proceeds to state in the following succinct terms the relations of the Cumberland Presbyterian church to Waynesburg College:

"1. The charter secures to the Synod the perpetual use of the property, provided the Synod sustains therein at least three professors. The charter makes no requirement as to the manner in which the professors are to be supported.

"2. Of the twenty-one trustees, the charter grants to the Synod the appointment of twelve. The Synod has, in fact, for twenty-four years, appointed the whole number of trustees.

"3. By mutual agreement, it is a by-law that the trustees shall elect no person to a professorship until the Synod has first nominated the person for the place.

"4. The endowment fund of the College is held by another Board, styled the Board of Trust of the College Endowment Fund of the Pennsylvania Synod, consisting of five members appointed by the Synod, and acting under a charter securing to this Board all needful powers, and perpetual succession."

After two years of faithful and acceptable service, as instructor in mathematics, Prof. Fish resigned. Whereupon the Synod nominated, and the trustees confirmed the nomination, to make Alfred B. Miller, Professor of Mathematics, to fill the vacancy. The following is the resolution adopted by the trustees on this occasion: "*Resolved*, That Rev. Alfred B. Miller be employed as Professor of Mathematics, at a salary of one hundred and fifty dollars per session." As there were only two sessions a year, it requires no very profound computation to show that the salary voted was not excessive.

The first President of the College, Rev. J. Loughran, was educated at Jefferson College, and though he did not graduate, the college subsequently awarded him the degree of A. M. A man of large attainments and a ready expounder of learning, he was a popular instructor, but was not so successful in managing the financial problems which arise in all institutions, when but meagerly endowed and unprovided with sufficient funds to pay current demands. Doubtless discouraged by the outlook, in August, 1855, he resigned. To fill the vacancy the Synod nominated the Rev. J. P. Weethee, and he was duly elected President. He had previously been President of Madison College, at Uniontown, and later of Beverly College, Ohio. Simultaneously with his election, the Rev. T. J. Simpson was appointed financial agent of the college, and by his earnest labors directed attention to the institution, and while he was not able to largely increase the endowment fund, he succeeded in bringing in a large number of new students, and created a kindly feeling among the members of the denomination towards the college, which bore fruit in subsequent years. Mr. Weethee entered upon his duties as president with much zeal, and a strong desire was manifested on the part of the people to support his administration; but it proved not entirely harmonious, some of his religious views not being fully in accord with those of his supporters, and his management of the college itself not being in harmony with the views of certain members of the faculty.

As has already been seen, there had been, previous to organizing under the College charter, a Female Seminary conducted in the Baptist church, over which Miss Bell, subsequently Mrs. Miller, presided, and some classes in this department had been graduated from it under the title of the Female Seminary, before any graduations took place in the college proper. When the charter had become operative, President Wethee insisted that the college should be conducted and classification should be made without reference to the sex of the pupils. This was not in accord with the existing system, and accordingly provoked some opposition. The President maintained his position in a public address in the college chapel, previously announced, before a large audience of teachers, students and citizens He declared that the Female Seminary was without a charter, and without any title to recognition This opened the way for a protracted investigation before the constituted authorities, and a decision was finally reached that the institution must be regarded as " One College, with male and female departments " By-laws were also adopted, which prescribed the duties and privileges of the president and principal of the female department In the fall of 1858 President Wethee resigned.

In his brief account of the college, Dr Miller says, " Many of the friends of the college thought the prospects gloomy indeed, and feared that this educational effort would terminate in a repetition of the Madison College trouble. The regular meeting of the Synod was held at Carmichaels soon after the resignation, and in the records of that body I find abundant evidence of feelings of discouragement in such expressions as ' the educational enterprise within our bounds is considerably embarrassed,' ' there is but a partial faculty;' ' demand for immediate attention and action,' ' that the institution be conducted on the most economical plan possible.' " During the three years since 1855, a debt had been incurred of over three thousand dollars. The Rev. J. Loughran, who was now at the head of a school in Wisconsin, was addressed with a view of his again becoming President, but without success In this emergency, Hon John'C Flenniken, a member of the board of trustees, lately State Senator, was elected President, *pro tem.*, but exercised only nominal oversight of the institution

In 1859 the Synod was again called on to wrestle with the old problem, viz, how to carry on a college without money. A committee appointed to fill the vacancy in the Presidential office, recommended to the trustees the name of Alfred B. Miller, who, as student,

Emanuel Beall

professor, and during the last year vice-president, since its founding had been connected with the college, and he was duly elected.

In the face of many discouragements, and with a certain prospect of great labors and uncertain reward, he accepted the position. His own account of his experiences in conducting the college and in holding together and paying the salaries of professors, forms one of the most interesting chapters of collegiate history, and would indeed be amusing were it not in reality so sad. "I was made President of the college," he says, "as already noticed, in the autumn of 1859, though my management of its internal affairs began with the preceding year, Mr. Flenniken being only nominally president. As a student or professor I had been in the college from the first, and felt the deepest possible interest in its welfare. If I had any conviction of Providential direction of my life, it is that God has led me in the course I have pursued in regard to our college. The institution was projected under circumstances by no means promising. Preceding efforts had been only failures, and there was even then a dead college on the hands of the Synod. When I spoke to an associate in an academy, a noble young man, then a candidate for the ministry in the Presbyterian church, of my purpose to enter Waynesburg College as a student, he said in response, 'your people cannot sustain a college in Pennsylvania. They failed in Uniontown; they will fail in Waynesburg. Come with me to Washington; that will be better.' I replied, 'I will go to Waynesburg College, and help to make it succeed.' Certainly, if I did not say so to him, I said it in my heart; and then and there was born the resolution on which rest these years of labor for the college. At various times I have earnestly desired to see the way open for me to leave; but as there are obstructions to a river on all its sides but one, so convictions of duty have ever shut me up to the direction in which my life of labor has been running on through all these years. How much better another man could have discharged the duties of the place, I cannot know. It is a source of comfort to have the internal assurance that I have done as well, as was in my power to do, in performing a work to which my Heavenly Father called me, and which I have been able to do only through a sense of his sustaining grace.

"A debt of over three thousand dollars hung upon the college when it came under my control. A piano that had belonged to it had been sold for debt. My salary was very inadequate, and, worse, there was no reasonable ground of hope that it would be paid. Dissensions had turned a portion of the community against the college, and had begotten in the public mind a feeling of distrust in regard to the future. Accepting the position, and going to work under these unpromising circumstances, it seemed to me much more like an effort to make a college, than the honor of presiding over one—nor
17

have I yet outgrown that feeling. My special aims were, first, to get the college out of debt, and to establish confidence in its value and permanence. To accomplish the former, and to keep the necessary teaching force in the college without incurring debt, has been the constant, ever perplexing problem through all these years. After looking in vain for other sources of reliable pecuniary dependence, I found it necessary to assume toward the college, in fact, the relation of president, financial agent and board of trustees. Taught by bitter experience how great are these cares, thus thrown on a college president, and admitting that ordinarily such a course could promise only financial ruin, I must record my profound conviction that in this case, nothing but the unbounded liberty allowed me in the management of the college could have saved it from hopeless failure. The struggle, that has been necessary on my part, would furnish account of personal sacrifices and pecuniary expedients that would put ordinary credence out of the question, some of which, aside from my personal knowledge, are known only to Him from whom there is nothing hidden. I am sure that only the faith which

> Laughs at impossibilities,
> And cries, *It shall be done,*

could have held me to my purpose through the labors, perplexities, and responsibilities crowding these years. And yet these years have been full of pleasant work, full of occasions for devout thankfulness to Him who leads us in the way that is best, full of grand discipline and experiences that enrich the souls of men, and out of which come strength and patience and the noblest service and sympathy in all grand schemes for human well-being.

"For the sake of my fellow educators, I wish to say to my church, from my heartfelt sorrows in that respect, that *an incompetent support is a great hindrance to the usefulness of a college president or professor.* I have been compelled to preach in order to live, sometimes supplying points twenty miles distant; I have been compelled to deny myself books greatly needed; to stay at home when I should have traveled; to walk many miles because I could not afford to pay hack-fare; to be harassed with debts that have eaten up the mind as cancers eat the flesh; in short to do a great many things, and to leave undone a great many things, which doing and not doing greatly hindered my usefulness as a public servant of the church. I once turned superintendent of schools, and walked all over Greene County, in order to save a little money, and still the college went on—while the nation was fighting battles. At another time I edited the Cumberland *Presbyterian,* did all the necessary correspondence of the office and kept the books, at the same time teaching six hours a day in the college, exercising general over-sight of its financial affairs, and often preaching twice on the Sabbath. How imperfectly all these things were done no one is more painfully sensible than the writer, and he sincerely prays that a like apparent necessity of trying to do so many things at the same time may never come again, though he is scarcely less busy to-day. The adage about too many irons in the fire, doubtless conveys a useful lesson in its ordinary application, but Adam Clarke used to say it conveys an abominable lie, and some lives seem to illustrate that there are men who can keep many irons going, and manage all of them reasonably well. If there is a position, however, which demands all the service of head and heart that any man can give, that position is the presidency of a college, which aims at the noble work of training young men and young women, not only in the knowledge of science, but for virtuous lives, and to be consecrated workers for the well-being of society.

"In dismissing this reference to my own efforts to build up the college, perhaps already too long, I desire to state distinctly that it is not my intention to cast any reflection, directly or by implication, on the Pennsylvania Synod, the trustees of the college, or on any other party to whom it might reasonably be supposed I could have looked for pecuniary support. Any man who knows what it requires to establish and sustain a respectable college will certainly agree with me that, considering the pecuniary resources of the community in which the college is located, the inaccessibility and obscurity of the place at the time, and especially that the sole ecclesiastical dependence was a single isolated synod, the prospect of success at the beginning must have been very moderate indeed. As early as the spring of 1855, while Mr. Loughran was yet in the college, even Hon. Jesse Lazear, who had been chiefly instrumental in having the college located at Waynesburg, and who was its patron financially—if it then had any—wrote to myself and Mrs. Miller during the vacation, deploring the fact that he saw no reasonable ground of hope for remuneration for our work if we continued in the college, expressing also the conviction that the church had perhaps undertaken entirely too much in attempting anything beyond an academy. Had we acted upon his suggestion the career of the college must have closed even then. The Synod has ever given the college a large share of its time, and has ever been willing to devise plans for raising funds, however unsatisfactory many of them have proved; and the trustees have ever been willing to carry out any measures proposed either by the Synod or the faculty; but have found an easy relief from feelings of pecuniary responsibility by simply reiterating that the church is to support the professors.

"Finally, for the encouragement of all who may be called to sustain like burdens, and without seeming presumptuous, I desire to reaffirm the sustaining and abiding conviction, that the Lord has signally opened the way for my support and success in this work. Congregations have encouraged and supported me. Many generous friends have helped me and my family, I have been called to marry a great many people who gave me generous sums, and have been called to lecture before teachers' institutes in various parts of the country, which, though hard work, generally brought a liberal compensation, a portion of which has been devoted more than once to pay the salaries of our professors."

The most remarkable example of unselfish devotion to the interests of a public institution in the whole catalogue of our struggling colléges for existence and permanence is contained in these last statements of President Miller. Here is a man occupying the position of president of a college, a position of great responsibility, and entitled to *bonum otium cum dignitate*, but meagerly paid, if paid at all, earning something by marrying people, and devoting time, that should have been given to rest, to lecturing before teachers' institutes, and then giving the money, which was clearly his own, and doubtless much needed by himself and family, to the payment of the salaries of professors and teachers. Such unselfish devotion as this deserves to live on the brightest page in the history of American colleges. Such devotion as this could not fail to make successful the effort to found Waynesburg College.

As has been seen the female department was at the outset conducted as a Female Seminary, the graduates receiving a diploma emblazoned with that title and embossed with its seal. The first principal, Miss M. K. Bell, who subsequently was united by marriage to President Miller, was largely instrumental in giving the college reputation and standing for scholarship, and deserves mention with the presidents of the institution. She was the daughter of Andrew Bell, and was educated at the justly celebrated Washington Female Seminary. She was possessed of good natural abilities, well schooled, and a remarkable gift for teaching. Through all the years of her too brief life she served Waynesburg College with great acceptance, exerting a strong and healthful influence over her pupils. "On the evening," says President Miller, "of February 10, 1874, after a day's ordinary work in the class-room, while she was sitting at her own fireside, paralysis fell on the wearied brain and nerves, and released them from the tension in which they had for years been held by the power of a dauntless will. Ten weeks of helplessness passed, but not weeks of suffering, when the final fatal stroke came, bringing to the exhausted physical powers the unbroken rest of death, and dismissing the noble spirit to its joy and crown in heaven."

On the occasion of her death the Board of Trustees of the college passed the following resolutions: "Mrs. M. K. B. Miller, Principal of the Female Department of Waynesburg College, having departed this life, the trustees of the institution pay this tribute to her memory.

"Many years ago she came to this place, in the bloom of life, and with a noble desire to do good, she applied with industry and zeal all the energy and resources of a vigorous mind, discharging the duties of principal of her department in the college to the entire satisfaction of the Board of Trustees, and of every one under her care. During all these years of unselfish devotion to the cause of education, she filled her position with consummate ability, and with the greatest advantage to the institution. With a mind pure and cultured, she endeared herself to all who knew her, and from the young ladies under her care for instruction she always received the highest proofs of uninterrupted confidence and attachment. We may truly say,

Her life was too pure for the pencil to trace,
And her goodness of heart could be read in her face

"Although a mother, and having the care of a family, her love for the institution she fostered and so nobly had helped to sustain, never slackened, but seemed to grow more intense, until she was stricken by death. Her demise occasions a vacancy in all her relations to the society she so much adorned, and one that will be difficult to fill."

Monongahela College, located at Jefferson, Jefferson Township, Greene County, was chartered by the Legislature in 1867. The affairs of the institution are managed by a Board of Trustees of which the original organization was as follows: Hon. A. A. Purman, president; Rev. R W. Pearson, vice-president, and Rev. C. Tilton, secretary. The buildings are located just outside the borough, on a beautiful plat of ground containing some fourteen acres. It was founded by members of the Baptist denomination of southwestern Pennsylvania, and West Virginia. Though under the management of members of this denomination it is no way sectarian in its practical workings. The Rev Joseph Smith, A. M., was its first president. In 1877 Mr. Silvius' in his centennial report of education in Greene County, says: "Money has been subscribed to liquidate all indebtedness of the college, and it is supported by a permanent endowment of $30,000. The total income of the institution *per annum* is $2,800. The friends of the college are securing philosophical and chemical apparatus, and have begun the collection of books for a library. The faculty of the college is as follows: Rev. H. K. Craig, president; Rev. J. M. Scott, D. D., professor of mathematics and physical science; W P. Kendall, A. B., professor of Latin and Greek; Miss Lizzie Patton, principal of the female department, and Mrs H K Craig, teacher of music." Rev J. B. Solomon, A. M., was afterward made president of the institution, and Mrs. Solomon principal of the female department. Miss Nannie Pollock was appointed assistant teacher and subsequently became principal. The course of study marked out is similar to that pursued in other American colleges granting the degree of A B   It also has a normal department in which large numbers of the common school teachers have been trained. The college has latterly been suspended

---

CHAPTER XXII.

The Waynesburg "Messenger"—The Waynesburg "Republican" —The Waynesburg "Independent"—The Greene County "Democrat."

THE Waynesburg *Messenger*, the oldest newspaper in Greene County, was established in 1813, and has been published continuously under the same name since. It was originally edited and published by Dr. Layton.   He was succeeded by John Baker, and Baker in turn by Thomas Irons   The latter subsequently associated with him his brother, John Irons, who finally became sole proprietor. The changes thus indicated covered some fifteen years of the early existence of the paper.   John Irons was an excellent practical printer. He was of Irish birth, and had served an apprenticeship of fourteen years in the office of the Washington *Reporter*. He was a gentleman of fine ability and high sense of honor. He conducted the paper with marked skill until the spring of 1837, when he sold it to John Phelan, who had learned the business in the office of the *Messenger*.

Mr. Irons removed to St Clairsville, Ohio, where he bought the St Clairsville *Gazette*, and published it for six months, when he sold it, returned to Waynesburg, and at the end of Mr. Phelan's first year, in the spring of 1838, repurchased the *Messenger*. This was the year of the Gubernatorial contest between David Rittenhouse Porter, Democrat, and Joseph Ritner, Whig, or Anti-mason, as the party was designated at that time in Pennsylvania. The contest was a heated one, and the *Messenger* conducted the canvass with great spirit and success, the majority for Porter in the county reaching over 700, nearly double the Democratic majority up to that time.   Mr. Irons retained control of the *Messenger* until the autumn of 1840, when he sold it to Charles A Black, and went to Uniontown, where he became proprietor of the *Genius of Liberty*.

Mr. Black was a polished writer and gained deserved reputation as an editor. But he retained the paper but two years, when he sold it to James W. Hays. At the expiration of two years more Mr Hays sold it to W. T. H. Pauley in the fall of 1844, just prior to the election of James K. Polk to the Presidency of the United States. The Democratic majority in this election reached about 900. Mr. Pauley sold the paper in the spring of 1852 to John M. Stockdale and James S. Jennings, but at the expiration of a year the *Messenger* reverted to Mr. Pauley. In the spring of 1857 Mr. Pauley sold a half interest in the paper to James S. Jennings, and in the spring of 1859, having rented his half interest, retired to a farm where he remained till the spring of 1867, when he again took full control of the *Messenger*. Mr. Pauley conducted it with his usual success until January, 1883, when he leased it for a term of five years to Col. James S. Jennings, who in turn rented it to Messrs. Woodruff and Dinsmore, and before the expiration of the original lease of five years the paper had been transferred to A. E. Patterson.

On the 1st of January 1888, at the expiration of the five years lease, the *Messenger* reverted to its owner, W. T. H. Pauley, who associated with himself his two sons, James J and John F. Pauley, by whom it is now published. With the exception of a period of four years, from 1838 to 1842, Mr. Pauley senior has been closely associated with the *Messenger*, in the various capacities of apprentice, publisher, owner, and editor, for a term of over fifty-five years, —having first entered the office as an apprentice to John Evans, on the 14th day of May, 1833. The *Messenger* has always been a Democratic paper, and radically so while under the editorial control of its present senior editor.

The Waynesburg *Republican* was founded in 1833 by Job Smith Goff, the editor and proprietor. The first number was issued on Tuesday, May 14. of that year, under the title of "The Greene County *Republican*" It was published weekly. After an existence of a year or more the paper lapsed for want of support. In 1838, however, the type and presses were purchased by James W. Moorhead, and the paper was again started under the title of the Greene County *Whig*. A brother of Mr Moorhead afterwards acquired possession of it and it was published until 1841, when it again lapsed.

In 1843 it was revived by S. Sigfried, Jr., who had charge of the paper until 1851, when it passed into the hands of Thomas Porter, a young man of spirit and enterprise, who purchased a new press and type. Young Porter died, and as a consequence the paper was not published for some months. In 1852 the leaders of the Whig party in Greene County purchased it and induced General J. H. Wells to assume charge of it. At the retirement of General Wells the press and outfit of the office were purchased by Joseph Cook, who changed the name of the paper to the Waynesburg *Eagle*. In 1856 E. R. Bartleson became the editor and proprietor. Under his charge the original name, Greene County *Republican*, was again restored. From his hands the paper passed to the charge of L. K Evans, who remained as editor during the period of the civil war 1861-5, though during the period that Mr. Evans was in the army the paper was in charge of George Cook, but with the name of Evans appearing as editor

The paper subsequently became the property of Ridde and Clark, and was placed first in charge of A. Watkins and afterwards was conducted for a short time by G. W. Daugherty. In 1866 it was purchased by James E Sayers, under whose management the paper flourished. He gave it its present name, the Waynesburg *Republican*, making the change in order to identify the paper with the town In 1868 Mr. Sayers disposed of the paper to James N. Miller, who changed its name to the *Repository*, but only retained possession of it for two years, when he sold it to W. G W. Day, who remained in charge of the paper for a longer period of time than any of his predecessors. He again restored the name Waynesburg *Republican*. He proved himself a spirited and able editor, and during his ownership the paper was enlarged and improved He purchased a new press and introduced steam power.

In 1884 Mr Day disposed of a half interest in the paper to I. H. Knox. It was conducted under the charge and editorship of Day and Knox until February, 1885, when Mr. Day disposed of his remaining interest to G. W. Ray and J. P. Teagarden. The firm of Knox, Ray, and Teagarden. now publishing the paper, was then formed with Mr. Knox as editor and manager. The paper is the only organ of the Republican party in Greene County and is one of the foremost country papers in the commonwealth.

The Waynesburg *Independent* was founded in 1872 by two printers, Z. C. Ragan and J W. Axtell, who conceived the idea of establishing a paper untrammelled by partisan interest, and especially devoted to the growth and prosperity of Greene County. Before the first number was issued over 1,100 subscribers had been obtained. At no time has its patronage been less, and at present it has a circulation beyond most county papers of the State—3,100. The enterprise was not, however, without its share of good and ill fortune; but in face of the predictions of failure, and the trials incident to so large an outlay dependent upon the caprice of public patronage, it has attained a firm footing, and in May, 1875, the proprietors introduced the first power steam printing press in Greene County. This was regarded as a remarkable indication of enterprise and skill.

In the fall of 1877 Mr. Axtell disposed of his interest to W. W. Rodehauer, who continued a member of the firm for about three years. In the fall of 1880 he sold his interest to W. W. Evans,

previously of the Moundsville *Reporter*, who is still associated with Mr. Ragan, one of the original founders. As in its inception, the paper continued to meet with opposition. The *Independent* had taken a firm s'and against the liquor traffic, and other sources of evil, which provoked bitter resentment. In November, 1884, the office of the *Independent*, machinery and entire outfit, were utterly destroyed by fire, entailing a loss to its proprietors of nearly $5,000, on which was an insurance of only $2,000. This was a discouraging reverse, and one which swept away at one blow the accumulations of many years, and threatened to stamp the *Independent* out of existence. But the gentlemen who were at the head of the enterprise were of that stuff that knows no such word as fail, and after the lapse of four years, with its rebuffs and struggles, it has been re-established with something more than its pristine strength and vigor, and still maintains unswervingly its original motto.

The Greene County *Democrat*. Through the solicitation of prominent independent democrats, who believed that it would be for the best interests of their party as well as of the people, to have two Democratic papers published in a county where the majority of the dominant party is so large, J. F. Campbell, an experienced newspaper man of Johnstown, Pennsylvania, came to Waynesburg in the fall of 1881, and with the assistance of D. R. P. Hass, an attorney of the Waynesburg bar, established the Greene County *Democrat*. The material with which the paper was first printed had been used in the publication of the Washington (D. C.) *Standard*, a paper that had ended its existence after a brief career, and was purchased at the National Capital by Mr. Hass. The first number of the *Democrat* was issued Saturday, December 17, 1881. Mr. Campbell published the paper with varying success until March, 1882, when he disposed of his interest to a company of Waynesburg capitalists, who held it but a short time until it was sold to Simon R. Hass, Jr.

Mr. Hass entered upon his duties as editor and proprietor April 15, 1882, and under his management the paper prospered in the increase of its circulation and popularity. On the 11th of July, 1884, the entire property was purchased by F. M. Spragg, who conducted the paper with the aid of Mr. Hass, who was retained as associate editor, with credit to himself and satisfaction to its readers. On April 11, 1885, a half interest was sold by Mr. Spragg to Colonel James S. Jennings, whose experience in the newspaper business extended through many years. Messrs. Spragg and Jennings, editors and proprietors, with Mr. Hass as associate editor, published a paper that was generally recognized as an excellent local sheet, and the organ of the party of commanding influence, in Greene County.

James W. Hays, Jr., became sole editor and proprietor on October 3, 1887, and under his able management its circle of readers is daily widening.' The *Democrat* is in the convenient form of a folio, 22x28, and is printed on a large Taylor steam cylinder press. To the old *Standard* outfit much new material has been added from time to time by its successive publishers until the paper now ranks among the best equipped country printing offices in the State. The job department is complete, its facilities for plain and fancy work being unexcelled.

CHAPTER XXIII.

The Cumberland Road—Recommended by Washington—Canal—Ohio Admitted in 1802—Act Authorizing Road in 1806—Albert Gallatin—Refuses to Interfere—President Madison —By Washington—Finished in 1820—Specifications—Appeared Excellent—Material Defective—Traffic Immense—. Speedy Repairs—Delafield and Cass—Limestone Renewal—Ceded to the States—Toll Houses—"Oyster Line"—Monkey Box Line—1852 Pennsylvania Railroad and Baltimore & Ohio Opened— Baltimore & Ohio Pushed Out of Pennsylvania—Cause of Opposition—Washington & Waynesburg Railroad—By the Hills—Circuitous—Novel Experience.

WILLS CREEK, or, as it was subsequently called, Cumberland, Maryland, was regarded as the extreme verge of civilization in the early stages of colonization. It was by this route that the early pioneers from Maryland and Virginia went as they penetrated into the Monongahela and Ohio country. This route Washington followed on his expedition which terminated in the disastrous affair at Fort Necessity, on the 4th of July, 1754, and this Braddock pursued in his unfortunate campaign of the following year. An apology for a road was cut through this rugged country for the passage of artillery and trains, on the occasion of these expeditions, to Redstone on the Monongahela River; but the frosts of winter, and the rains of spring and fall, soon effaced the small improvements made, until there was scarcely a trace left of them. The later military expeditions followed the route of Forbes, which was wholly in Pennsylvania, corresponding to the Pennsylvania Railroad as that by Cumberland did to the Baltimore and Ohio Railroad.

As we have already seen the progress of the earlier settlers was very slow and toilsome in the first years of settlement in reaching the lands upon the Monongahela. The war of the Revolution coming on, for eight years the subject of a great highway to the west, which had begun to be seriously considered, was interrupted. Soon after the close of the war, General Washington, who had come to feel a fatherly care for all that pertained to the welfare of his country, and who had long meditated the necessity of easy communication between the East and the West, made a journey of exploration to the Ohio country. His favorite project was a great water-way from the waters of the Potomac to those of the Ohio. He conceived that a canal might be cut by way of the head-waters of the Potomac to some point on the Monongahela River which could easily waft the vast tonnage and passenger traffic which he clearly forsaw would soon set towards this delectable country, the new Eldorado. In the year 1784 he made the journey. From Cumberland to Redstone was familiar ground; but when arrived at the head-waters of the Youghioghany he took to a canoe, and floated down that stream to the Falls of the Ohio; thence he rode across the country to the Monongahela; thence up that stream into Virginia, and finally across the country to the Ohio River. At convenient points he met the settlers, and made particular inquiries in regard to the feasibility of the several routes. It was while on this journey that he met, for the first time, Albert Gallatin, then a young man, who subsequently became eminent as an American statesman, by whose opinions and testimony Washington was much impressed.

But Washington became convinced, that, in the financial embarrassment of the country, it could not undertake the vast out'ay needed to build a canal over the Alleghanies; but he was strongly impressed with the feasibility of a great national road across the mountains. In his administration of eight years the subject was kept before the people; but was not urged, as debt still rested, like an incubus, on the young nation. In Adams' administration the subject was brought before Congress, but failed of any action. President Jefferson in his first message recommended action, but nothing resulted from it. Finally, in 1802, Ohio was admitted into the Union as a State, and in the act of admission it was provided that one-twentieth of the proceeds of the sale of lands should be devoted to the construction of roads from the Atlantic sea-board to the Ohio country. In 1806 an act was passed authorizing the laying out and making of a road from Cumberland to the State of Ohio, and commissioners were appointed for its survey. If a straight line be drawn from Cumberland to Wheeling, Virginia, the objective point aimed at, it will pass through New Salem and will cut Jefferson, Nineveh and West Finley. It was not, of course, practicable to lay the road on an entirely straight line; yet it was, eventually, laid on almost exactly such a line until it reached the Laurel Ridge, when it was made to veer to the north, passing through Uniontown, and extending to Brownsville or Redstone. To this point the route recommended by the commissioners was officially adopted and proclaimed by President Jefferson. "From thence," he says, "the course to the Ohio and the point within the legal limits at which it shall strike that river is still to be decided."

But the work on the road was slow. It was 1811 before appropriations were made, and Congress made one of the pittance of but $50,000. During the term of office of Mr. Jefferson, the road was only located as far as Brownsville. Great strife was manifested by those living along the line of the proposed routes to secure its location by their own doors. Especially was their solicitude about its terminus on the Ohio River, as it was confidently anticipated that, wherever that terminus should be, a great town would spring up. Albert Gallatin, a man of strong native ability, having taken up a body of land on the right bank of the Monongahela River, about Mt. Moriah or New Geneva, and having been appointed Secretary of the United States Treasury, was supposed to have great influence in locating it. Properly he would have had, by virtue of his office, the right to decide the question finally. But it appears by the terms of a letter which he wrote, in reply to importunities that he would use his authority to secure its location in a particular course, that influenced by a fine sense of honor he could take no part in the controversy. He says, "I thought myself an improper person, from the situation of my property, to take the direction which would naturally have been placed in my hands, and requested the President to undertake the general superintendency himself." Had he used his influence to carry it further south, instead of north of the direct line, as was done, then this great highway would have passed through Greene County, and taken the valley of South Ten Mile and Wheeling Creeks. But having passed through Uniontown and Brownsville it was thought to be necessary to pursue a more northern course.

When James Madison became President in 1809, he approved the course of the road adopted by Mr. Jefferson, and the contracts were given for the completion of the road to Brownsville. It was 1815 before these contracts were completed. In the meantime the war of 1812 had been carried to a successful issue. When peace was concluded in 1815, President Madison ordered the commissioners to complete the surveys from Brownsville on the Monongahela to Wheeling on the Ohio. They surveyed two routes, one by the way of Washington and West Alexander, and the other through the southern portion of the county. In their report they favor the southern route as the most direct and most favorable for building a road. But the influence brought to bear from Washington finally prevailed, and it was located through that place. It was mid-winter of 1820 before the road was completed from Cumberland to Wheeling, and opened for travel. Thus nearly a quarter of a century from the time when Washington began in earnest to advocate its construction was consumed in making this stretch of a little more than a hundred miles. Any good company now would agree to put a railroad around the earth in that time. But the road was a good one, well built, and subserved a great purpose. The following specifications will give an idea of the manner of its construction. " The natural surface of the ground to be cleared of trees, and other wooden growths, and also of logs and brush, the whole width of sixty-six feet, the bed of the road to be made even thirty-two feet in width, the trees and stumps to be grubbed out, the graduation not to exceed five degrees in elevation and depression, and to be straight from point to point, as laid off and directed by the superintendent of the work. Twenty feet in width of the graduated part to be covered with stone, eighteen inches in depth at the centre, tapering to twelve inches at the edges, which are to be supported by good and solid shoulders of earth or curb-stone, the upper six inches of stone to be broken, so as to pass through a ring of three inches in diameter, and the lower stratum of stone to be broken so as to pass through a seven inch ring. The stone part to be well covered with gravel and rolled with an iron-faced roller four feet in length and made to bear three tons weight. The acclivity and declivity of the banks at the side of the road not to exceed thirty degrees."

The passenger, carrying, and freight traffic of the road from the start was immense, and ever increasing until the opening of through lines of railway reduced it to a common local thoroughfare. When first opened it seemed to be thoroughly and substantially built, and it was believed would last a quarter of a century. But it was soon found that in many parts sandstone had been used in its construction, especially in the part over the mountains. It only required a few passages of heavily loaded teams over this material to reduce it to sand, and heavy rains would soon wash it away into the valleys. But a short time elapsed before the whole eighteen inches of stone was cut through and ground to powder, and was found encumbering the the lowland of the farmers, leaving the gullied road-bed next to impassible. At the opening of the road, it seemed a perfect structure, and the passage over it was delightful, the vehicles rolling along as on a Belgian pave. The traffic was beyond all expectation. The tallyho coaches for passengers and mails, the broad-wheeled Conestoga wagons with their enormous tonnage, droves of cattle, and sheep, and hogs, from the valleys of the Wabash and the Scioto, passing in almost continuous clouds, and horsemen making more expeditious journeys, gave this great highway the appearance of a city thoroughfare. To feed such a continuous column, going and coming at the slow rate of travel, was a subject which taxed the ingenuity and resources of the country. Taverns for the accommodation of man and beast sprang up in almost continuous line along either side of the avenue, with yards for teams and pasturage for droves. "It was frequently the case that twenty-five stages, each containing its full complement of nine inside, and a number of outside passengers 'pulled out' at the same time from Wheeling, and the same was true of the eastern terminus at Cumberland. As many as sixteen coaches, fully laden with passengers were sometimes seen in close and continuous procession crossing the Monongahela bridge between West Brownsville and Bridgeport. The lines ran daily each way, and it was sometimes the case that thirty stages, all fully loaded with passengers, stopped at one hotel in a single day."

As we have indicated, the necessity of repairs came speedily, and the Government was called upon for appropriations. These were made. But as traffic increased these calls for repairs were louder and ever multiplying. Not ten years had elapsed before it was found that these demands were becoming burdensome even to the general Government. The United States could not lay tolls, and had from the first left the road entirely free. With the State rights doctrines of Gen. Jackson, who came into power in 1829, arose opposition to further appropriations. It was accordingly proposed to cede the road to the States through which it runs, with the understanding that they would build toll houses along its entire length, and thereby realize enough to make the road self-supporting. But the road was terribly out of repair and the State Governments refused to accept unless the United States Government would first put it in perfect condition. Captain Delafield, of the topographical engineers, with Gen. George W. Cass made a thorough inspection of the road and recommended that it be macadamized throughout its entire length with limestone, the only material that would stand the ceaseless grinding of the steel banded wheels. This at first view seemed utterly impracticable, inasmuch as the lime underlies the sand-stone, and was supposed to be unapproachable except in the deep valleys. But valuable quarries of the best quality of lime were discovered and opened, along the line, which furnished inexhaustable supplies for the road, for building purposes, and as a fertilizer for the soil as well. It was 1833 before the macadamizing was completed, though the acts of the several Legislatures were passed in 1831–2. The toll-gates were, accordingly, erected, and the road finally passed under the control of the several States.

And now the traffic upon the way was greater than ever. In 1835 the Adams Express Company established a line over this road. It was inaugurated by Alvin Adams and Mr. Green, and Maltby and Holt, oyster dealers of Baltimore. It was at first known as the

"Oyster Line," having been originally established to supply the West with fresh oysters. Light four-horse wagons with relays were employed, and soon other packages besides oysters were carried, until finally it grew into the express system of the present day. In 1837 a horse-back express, requiring nine horses at each relay, and three boy riders for carrying short messages, drafts and paper money, was established between St. Louis and Washington. Later an express mail was established, which was provided with light carriages, which held the mail box and seats for three passengers only. From the peculiarity of the wagons it was known along the route as "Monkey Box Line."

In 1852 the Pennsylvania railroad was opened to Pittsburg, and in the same year the Baltimore and Ohio to Wheeling, and the glory of the "Monkey Box" was at an end.

We have seen how the National road veered to the north, out of the direct course, in order to pass through Uniontown and Washington, even though the route further south was more favorable for building. Thus Greene County was left to one side, though it was reached indirectly as was all that entire region.

When the surveys came to be made for the Baltimore and Ohio, railroad lines were examined through the southern section of Greene County, which were found feasible, and it was the earnest desire of the company to adopt one of them, crossing a long stretch of its territory. But now, when the prospect that the county would be opened up by one of the great trunk roads running east and west, and bringing the best markets of the continent to the very doors of its people, the strange spectacle is presented of the very people, whom it would most benefit, opposing its location through their territory. The frivolous excuses were made that the locomotives would set fire to their haystacks, that the flocks and herds which were driven through by the highways, would be carried in the cars, and thus a great source of revenue would be cut off, and that their live-stock would be killed by the locomotives.

But the real cause of the opposition was probably deeper seated. The Pennsylvania railroad company, as we have seen, was also building a trunk line through the heart of the State, which would be the rival of the Baltimore and Ohio, and it was the policy of this company to retain the entire territory of the State to be reached by its own road and its branches. Consequently, it was for the interest of this company to inspire in the minds of the inhabitants along the line of the proposed location of the rival road, opposition to it, so that there would be argument for the Legislature to refuse a charter to the Baltimore company. The tactics of the Pennsylvania company were successful, and this great thoroughfare, one of the most prosperous and powerful in the country, was crowded beyond the limits of the State, the busy traffic circling in almost continuous line around its corner screaming out notes of derision and defiance as it passes.

Greene was, consequently, among the last counties in the State to be penetrated by a railroad, though the stations along the Baltimore road, on the southern and western borders, became convenient avenues for travel and traffic for the inhabitants of that section. But the county seat finally attained to so much importance, as the center and metropolis of a wide farming country, that a railroad had become a necessity, and its citizens determined to build a road on their own account. Surveys were accordingly commenced with the design of locating one by the best route from Waynesburg to Washington, where it could connect with roads leading in all directions. The most natural and feasible route for this was found to be by the Chartiers Creek Valley, through Van Buren and Prosperity, substantially on the line of the old plank-road. But, as is now asserted, the men of means living along this line refused to aid in the construction of the road and accordingly the surveyors took to the hills. The route finally adopted, by West Union and Hopkin's Mills, is by a series of interminable hills, and while picturesque and beautiful to the last degree, it was proportionately unsuited to a railway by the usual straight line reduction. The only alternative, therefore, was to strike for the summits, and wind by the graceful and endless curves which nature has imposed.

In passing over this road into Greene County for the first time there is a constant cloud of uncertainty hovering over one. He pulls away for a while and seems to be leaving Washington behind him, and he feels sure that in the schedule time he will arrive in Waynesburg. But he has not gone many miles before the sun, which was full in his face at setting out, is now at his back, and he is haunted with a suspicion that he has taken the wrong train, and is on his way to Pittsburg. But while he casts an admiring glance at the landscape, changing at every instant and presenting an endless variety of hill, and vale, and winding stream, he suddenly finds himself turned quarter round, and he is making direct for Ohio, and begins to fear that he is on his way to the far West. But that solicitude has scarcely had time to get a lodgement before the train, by a miraculous transformation, is turned completely about, and is rushing on over the steel banded way directly for the Delaware Water Gap, the gate to New York City. In his perplexity he is just upon the point of calling the conductor and inquiring where he is really going to, when the train pulls around, and seems to be making in the direction of his destination, and he feels ashamed of himself for doubting the integrity of his ticket. So he pulls out a book and settles down to a snatch of romance. But all at once he is brought

Dennis Foye

up in the middle of a sentence by the train starting off on a perfect masquerade, circling around as though out on a cruise for pond-lilies, and when it has made the complete circle and he feels sure that he is about to strike the track on which he came, and go back to Washington, the engine by a dexterous jump veers to the left, and with a scream of laughter at the deception it has practiced, it runs joyfully on its way, and before the traveler is aware of his location the spires of the city and the massive front of Waynesburg College break upon his view. The road is indeed a marvel.

> "It wriggles in and wriggles out,
> And leaves the matter still in doubt,
> Whether the snake that made the track,
> Was going out or coming back."

CHAPTER XXIV.

METHODIST EPISCOPAL CHURCH—THE CUMBERLAND PRESBYTERIAN CHURCH—THE BAPTIST CHURCH—THE PRESBYTERIAN CHURCH— THE WAYNESBURG CATHOLIC CHURCH.

WAYNESBURG METHODIST EPISCOPAL CHURCH.

THIS church first appears on the records in 1803 as a part of a mission circuit called Deerfield, with Shadras Bostune as missionary. Its first place of worship was erected about this time in what is now known as the "Old Methodist Graveyard," just east of the present borough limits. In 1843 the society built a large brick edifice near the center of the town and removed thereto. The church was rebuilt in 1876 on the site of the old building, and dedicated the same year by Bishop Peck and Dr. I. C. Pershing. The Legislature of Pennsylvania, by special act passed in 1845, incorporated the church under the name and style of "The Trustees of the Methodist Episcopal Church of Waynesburg," and under this charter the church and parsonage property is held. From 1803 to 1846 the Waynesburg appointment was a part of a circuit embracing about all of the central and southern part of the county, together with several appointments in the State of Virginia. In 1846 the Mt. Morris circuit of seven appointments was taken off the "lower end" of the Waynesburg circuit. For a number of years after this Waynesburg was still a part of a

18

large circuit, but for several years past its position has varied from station to circuit and the reverse. At present it is a station with 155 members and Rev. Nelson Davis is pastor.

The Sabbath School, organized in 1845, has continued in successful operation down to the present time. It has an enrollment of 130 members. W. W. Evans is its present superintendent, and Nellie Donley, secretary. From 1804 to 1846 Waynesburg circuit had for presiding elders: Thortin Fleming, James Hunter, Jacob Gruber, Christopher Frey, Asa Shinn, James Painter, George Brown, William Stevens, David Sharp, Robert Hopkins, James G. Sansom, T. M. Hudson, Samuel Wakefield, William Hunter, John Spencer and S E. Babcock; and for preachers: Thomas Dougherty, Thomas Church, and William G. Lowman, John West, Asa Shinn and James Wilson, James Riley, John Meek and Wesley Webster, Thortin Fleming and Allen Green, William Monroe, Jacob Dowell and Joshua Monroe, James Laws and John Connelly, John Watson, Asby Pool and Jacob Snider, George Irwin, Henry Baker and Nathaniel Mills, Amos Barnes and Thomas Beeks, Thomas Jamison and Elias Brewin, David Stevens, T. M. Hudson, P. G Buckingham and R. Armstrong, John Tacksberry, Henry Furlong and John Moffitt, Simon Lauck, John White, S. E Babcock and Samuel Worthington and Wesley Smith, George McCaskey and James L. Reed, William Tipton, J. K. Miller, John Summerville and F. H. Reed, Jeremiah Phillips and Walter Chaffant, John L W·lliams and Hosea McCall, Heaton Hill, Isaac N. McAbee and M A. Ruter, B F. Sedgwick, Henry Ambler and Thomas McCleary, S. Cheney, J. W. Reger, G. A. Lowman, John Gregg, M. L. Weakely and Dyos Neil

From 1842 to 1846 the circuit was in the Ohio district, Pittsburg conference; prior thereto it was in the Wheeling district. In 1847 it was in the Uniontown district, with J. J. Sweagee as presiding elder, and Thomas Jamison and N. O Worthington as preachers. In 1848 it was in the Morgantown district, Simon Elliott, presiding elder, and P. F. Jones and J. F. Dorsey, preachers.

From 1849 to 1857 it was again in the Wheeling district with C. D. Battell, T M. Hudson, Edward Burkett and C. A Holmes as presiding elders; Louis Janny and A. Deaves, Joseph Woodruff, J. L. Irwin, C. E. Jones, John White and J. D. Turner, L. R. Beacom, Robert Laughlin, James Kenny and E. H. Green, and Daniel Rhodes as preachers.

From 1858 to 1861 the circuit was in the Washington district, Pittsburg Conference; C· A. Holmes and D. L. Dempsey as presiding elders, and J. J. Hays, J. J. Jackson, J. N. Pierce and J. F. Jones as preachers. From 1862 to 1867 it was part of the Uniontown district with C. A. Holmes and A. J. Endsley as presiding elders, and H. H. Fairall, M. B. Pugh, and John McIntire as ministers. It was in the South Pittsburg district from 1868 to 1875; L. R. Beacon and Hiram Miller as presiding elders; Samuel Wakefield, J. L. Stiffey, D. A. Pierce, J. H. Henry and R. J. White, pastors; and for part of 1876 in the West Pittsburg district with J. A. Miller as presiding elder and R. B. Mansell as preacher; from 1876 to 1888 it has been in the Washington district with S. H. Nesbit, J. W. Baker, James Mechem and J. F. Jones as presiding elders, and M. M. Sweeney, W. D. Slease, G. H. Huffman, E. S. White, L. H. Eaton, N. P. Kerr and Nelson Davis as pastors.

PRESENT OFFICIAL BOARD.

Local Preacher—Rev. Charles A. Martin.

Class Leaders—L. W. Jones, Z. W. Phelan, M. H. Hunnill, W. W. Evans.

Board of Stewards—W. W. Evans, R. Calvert, Mrs. M. A. Calvert, Mrs. R. T. Guiher, Z. W. Phelan, M. H. Hunnill, John Anderson, J. B. Donley, S. W. Scott, A. M. Kline, W. S. Pipes.

Board of Trustees—J. B. Donley, president; I. H. Knox, secretary; S. W. Scott, treasurer; Z. W. Phelan, W. W. Evans, F. H. Horner, A. M. Kline, S. R. Sanders, R. Calvert.

THE CUMBERLAND PRESBYTERIAN CHURCH IN GREENE COUNTY.

The first Cumberland Presbyterian church established in Greene County was organized at Jefferson, in the year 1831, with forty members. In November of the same year, at the instance of the Rev. Mr. Loughran, a Presbyterian minister, who subsequently became a Cumberland Presbyterian, a small Cumberland Presbyterian church was organized in Waynesburg, consisting of twenty members. The Revs. John Morgan and A. M. Bryan conducted the services and effected the organization. The occasion of the visit of these truly great and good men was a personal invitation extended to them by Mrs. Mary Campbell, of Waynesburg, who had heard them preach at a camp-meeting in Washington County in the neighborhood of the present village and Church of Old Concord. Messrs. Bryan and Morgan are tenderly and lovingly remembered by many of the old citizens as among the most eloquent and godly ministers who have ever labored in Western Pennsylvania. Mr. Bryan, who afterward settled in Pittsburg, where he organized, and for many years was pastor of the First Cumberland Presbyterian church, was a man of great popularity. He was a man of the finest presence, and gifted with a voice of marvelous sweetness. His oratory was of a high order of merit and popular with the masses. The church in Pittsburg was very prosperous under Mr. Bryan's ministry. He fell in the pulpit at the Bethel church in Washington County. Mr. Morgan was a man of different type. He was of great bodily stature and of most commanding ability. His power with men was remarkable. He died in his thirty-sixth year, while pastor of the church at Uniontown, which flourished under his flaming ministry.

The Church of Carmichaels was organized August 20, 1832, by the Rev. Leroy Woods, who had been sent by the general assembly of the Cumberland Presbyterian church to supply the Greene County churches. Mr. Woods had arrived in the county from the south on July 7, 1832, having made the entire journey on horseback. He died at Waynesburg in the autumn of 1879 while serving the church as pastor for the second time. There are now Cumberland Presbyterian churches in Greene County as follows: Jefferson, Waynesburg, Carmichaels, Clarksville, Muddy Creek, Jacksonville, Nineveh, Ten-Mile, West Union, Clay Lick and Hewitts. With one or two exceptions these churches are prospering. Several of them have elegant houses of worship.

THE WAYNESBURG BAPTIST CHURCH.

The Waynesburg Baptist church was organized, as shown by the church records, in the following manner: " For the purpose of extending the visible kingdom of our Lord and Saviour, Jesus Christ, and securing to ourselves and families the privileges of the gospel, and at the same time bearing our testimony to the truth in our own vicinity, and in the county town, from which an influence for good or evil goes out in every direction, we whose names are annexed to the following proceedings met agreeably to appointment at Hills' school-house near Waynesburg on the 30th day of June, A. D. 1843. 1. After sermon by brother James Woods, he was appointed moderator. 2. *Resolved*, That we be constituted into a regular Baptist church of Waynesburg, on the 10th day of July next. 3. *Resolved*, That we invite brother Samuel Williams, of Pittsburg, and Francis Downey, to assist brother Woods in the services. 4. *Resolved*, That we invite the Smith's Creek, Muddy Creek, Union, Jefferson, Bates' Fork, and South Ten Mile churches, to send one or more delegates to sit in council with us. Signed by the constituents: Anna Moore, Cynthia Ann Stayhorne, Jane McCormick, Rebecca Carpenter, Nancy Hoskinson, Mary Jennings, Sarah Jennings, Ann Dolison, Eliza Zollers, Neal Zollers, Carl Moore, Charles Carpenter, Thomas Hoskinson, J. S. Jennings, Alfred Chawler.

" Waynesburg, July 10th, 1843, after sermon by Elder Samuel Williams, the Waynesburg Baptist church was organized in the usual manner by Elder Williams and James Woods, with the advice and assistance of brethren from sister churches attending by invitation.

Brother James Woods was invited to take charge of the church and preach as often as his other duties would permit. A declaration of faith and church covenant was adopted by the church." And thus was it brought into existence and sent upon its course to bear some part in the current of human events. The pastors who have presided over it are as follows: Rev. James Woods, supply; S Seigfried, four years; Rev. S. H Ruple, one year; Rev. S. Seigfried, one year; Rev. W. Whitehead, one and a half years; Rev. Samuel Morehead, half year; Rev. R. M. Fish, supply; Rev. A. J. Colliers, two years; Rev. Francis Downey, supply; William Wood, one year; Rev. Charles Tilton, two years; Rev. S. Kendal, three years; Rev. H. K. Craig, seven and a half years; James Miller, three quarters of a year; Rev. W. W. Hickman, two years; Rev. W. M. Ryan, the present pastor, eight years. The following are the names of the deacons who have served the church: Carl Moore, Thomas Hoskinson and Neal Zollers, chosen December 23, 1843. Those subsequently elected were the the following: Jesse Hill, Isaac Hooper, A. A. Purman, George Hoskinson and J. M. Hoge. The following brethren have served as church clerks: J. S. Jennings, S. Seigfried, Jr., J. Y. Brown, Jesse Hill, J. J. Purman, L. K. Evans, J. Yoders, J. M. Hoge, W E. Hill.

The members of the church organized were largely from the country. The membership in 1881 was seventy-two. There have been added during the eight years of Mr. Ryan's ministry seventy-three. In that time sixteen have died; sixteen have been given letters to other churches, and nine have been excluded, leaving the present membership one hundred and four. The house of worship, which formerly was a frame structure, in the progress of a hurricane which swept through the valley was seriously wrecked, having been taken up bodily and twisted from its base. It was accordingly decided to tear down and build anew. A neat and commodious brick structure in the gothic style of architecture, with stained-glass windows was erected to take its place The cost of the new church was $6,565.91, all of which was raised and paid, so that the church is wanting in that very common appendage, a church debt.

THE PRESBYTERIAN CHURCH OF GREENE COUNTY.

The Presbyterian church of Waynesburg was organized by the Rev. David Hervey, and Rev. John D. Whitam, a committee from the presbytery of Washington, June 11th, 1842. The ruling elders chosen at the organization, and duly entering upon the duties of that office were Obadiah Van Cleve and William Braden. The last named has continued with the church and held the office ever since, and with R A McConnell and D H. Haines constitute the eldership of the church at the present time.

The church was incorporated by the court of common pleas of Greene County on the 29th day of September, 1848. The first trustees were R D Mickle, Dr E. S. Blackley, Obadiah Van Cleve, William Braden and Matthew Dill, Jr.

A number of worthy ministers have supplied the church at different times, viz.: Rev J. Y. Calhoun, Rev Mr. Ewing, Rev. A R. Day, Rev J. W. Scott, D D, J. B. Graham and Ashabel Bronson, D. D The following served for a longer period, viz: Rev. S. H Jeffrey, who was pastor for a term of six years, ending in 1859 with his death Rev. James Sloan, D D., stated supply from 1862 to 1868; Rev. E P. Lewis, pastor 1873 to 1875; Rev George Frazer, D. D., supply from 1875 to 1881, and present stated supply, who came to the church in 1882, the Rev. J. A. Donahey.

The first church building was erected in 1849. It was situated on Morris street, just north of the Walton House. It was occupied until 1877. The present house of worship was erected in 1878 It is a neat and substantial brick structure, located near the centre of the town The church also has a very substantial brick parsonage, which was erected during the year 1887. It is located at the corner of Richhill and Greene streets, on ground devised by the will of Mrs Margaret Bradford The foundation of the parsonage fund was laid by Mrs Mary Hook, who left to the church twenty shares of Bank stock, one-half of which was to be used in procuring a parsonage when the church should determine so to do.

In Greene County are churches at Greensboro, at Jefferson, and New Providence at Carmichaels in the Redstone Presbytery, and Unity at Harvey's, and Waynesburg in the Washington Presbytery

Waynesburg Catholic Church —In the years 1828–'29 a brick structure was erected on the site of the present Catholic Church edifice, but for some time it remained unfinished Three brothers, John, Joseph and Andrew Friedly, with others, contributed to the completion of the building, and were fortunate in organizing a society and securing the services of a pastor in the person of Father Michael Galagher, of Brownsville, Fayette County, a man of great personal influence, and who had officiated as the agent of the Catholic Church west of the Alleghany Mountains, which office he continued to exercise until 1843, when the Diocese of Pittsburg was formed with Michael O'Conner as its Bishop. At successive periods this church has been ministered to by Fathers Kearney, (Jerome, Dennis and James) Hickey, Farren, Nolan, Scanlon, McHugh, McEnroe, Sheehan, Tahaney and Herman. During the pastorate of Father McHugh the old edifice was torn down, and a more elegant and convenient one was erected in its place.

CHAPTER XXV.

INTRODUCTORY NOTE TO MILITARY HISTORY.

FROM the earliest period the patriotism of the inhabitants of Greene County has never been questioned.   As we have already seen at the very inception of the American Revolution, when the first intelligence came of the battles of Lexington and Concord, the settlers along all the Monongahela valley, though at the time torn and harrassed by bitter strife over the question of State allegiance, vied with each other in expressions of loyalty to the American cause, and pledged their services and contributions of arms, ammunition and flints in a struggle for the rights of the colonies.   The number of officers and men from this section found in the Continental army in its long conflict with British arms was not excelled in proportion to its population by any part of the Commonwealth.

When the war of 1812 came, and the call was made for soldiers to vindicate the imperilled honor of the nation, the ear of the true-hearted denizen of Greene County was not heavy, and the offer of service came from hill-top and valley along all its broad domain. Contentions might be maintained over disputed State authority, and the right or wrong of an excise tax on distilled spirits, as in the whisky rebellion; but when the honor of the Flag was touched there existed but one mind and one heart—that of intense devotion to the national cause.

The war with Mexico found here a like devoted spirit, and the regiment of John W. Geary, which moved with the column of General Taylor, had within its ranks many citizens of this county.

The war for the suppression of the Rebellion is too recent, and the memory of trials endured and hearthstones made desolate is too fresh, to require the telling of how the calls for men were responded to from mansion and cabin in all its borders.

It would be a fitting recognition of the patriotism displayed by the people of the county if the name and record of every man who served in any capacity in the national armies should be given in this History.   But unfortunately this cannot be done.   In a few cases complete company organizations were made by Greene County recruits, and the full records of these are given below.   But it was the misfortune of the smaller and less populous counties that, instead of companies, small squads of a dozen or score would join in compames forming in other counties, and thus their identity would be lost, as there are no means now existing of identifying the citizenship of individual soldiers. A considerable number joined regiments recruited in West Virginia and were accredited to the quota furnished by that State It is now ascertained that there were no less than twenty-seven regiments known to have contained recruits from Greene County, the complete identity of whom cannot now be traced The Fourteenth, Sixteenth and Twenty-second Pennsylvania Cavalry, the Sixty-first Pennsylvania Infantry, Two Hundred and Fifth Pennsylvania Heavy Artillery, and the First, Third, Fourth, Sixth, Seventh, Eleventh, Twelfth, Fourteenth, Fifteenth West Virginia Infantry, and First West Virginia Cavalry contained varying numbers of Greene County volunteers. Those who· thus volunteered, who died and whose graves have been marked, have been identified, and their names and records are given in connection with this compilation.

The date of muster in of the major part of the companies is given at the heading of each organization. Where a different date of muster in from that thus given was found, it is placed after each individual name This will account for the date of muster in not being given with every name. The records have been chiefly drawn from my own "History of Pennsylvania Volunteers," and from a manuscript compilation made by Colonel John M. Kent, of Waynesburg.

CHAPTER XXVI

Company I, Thirty-seventh Regiment of Infantry, Eighth Reserve—Organization—Battle of Mechanicsville—Gaine's Mill—Charles City X Roads—Second Bull Run—South Mountain — Antietam — Fredericksburg — Wilderness — Spottsylvania—Mustered Out—Record of Individual Members of Company.

AT the opening of the civil war so many volunteers responded to the call of the President for 75,000 men to serve for three months from Pennsylvania that all could not be accepted. At a camp of rendezvous twelve miles above Pittsburg, on the Alleghany River, designated Camp Wright, forty-three companies were as-

James Meek

sembled, most of which could not be received. Hence Greene
County had no organized companies in the three months' service,
though many of its citizens were found in organizations in other
counties, and in West Virginia.

The Eighth Regiment of the Pennsylvania Reserve Corps, in
which was Company I from Greene County, was formed from the
companies assembled at Camp Wright for the three months' service,
but could not be accepted. It was commanded by George S. Hays,
subsequently by Silas M. Baily, and was brigaded with the Fifth,
First and Second Reserve Regiments, the brigade being commanded
by that eminent soldier, John F. Reynolds. This Reserve Corps
was composed of fifteen regiments, thirteen of infantry, one of
cavalry and one of artillery, their place in the line being from the
Thirtieth to the Forty-fourth, and was originally commanded by
George A. McCall. It was formed in compliance with an act of the
Legislature, and was originally designed for exclusive State service,
for the defense of the long stretch of exposed border on the Mason and
Dixon's line.

But in the gloomy days succeeding the first battle of Bull Run, .
when fears were entertained for the safety of the capital itself, the
Government, in casting about anxiously for help, found this splendid
corps already organized, and in prompt response to the call for its
services, it was sent forward, was mustered into the service of the
United States, and was never returned for State service.

Company I was originally commanded by Silas M. Bailey, but
upon his promotion to Major, John M. Kent was promoted from
acting Adjutant to succeed him as Captain. In the battle of Mechanicsville, on the 26th of June, 1862, which was the first real fighting
which it saw, with Companies A, D, and F, under Lieutenant-Colonel
Oliphant, Company I was sent forward on the skirmish line, in front
of Easton's Battery, on the margin of the swamp. "A brief artillery
contest, in which the shells burst in rapid succession in the very
midst of the infantry, was followed by the advance of the rebel
columns, and the battle became general. A charge of the enemy
below the swamp, with the design of capturing Easton's Battery,
caused the skirmishers to be recalled, and the regiment moved to its
support But the enemy being repulsed by other troops, it returned
to its former position. Three times the close columns of the enemy
charged down the opposing slope with determined valor, but was as
often repulsed and driven back. At night the men rested upon the
ground where they had fought."

The Reserves having been ordered back, retired during the night
to Gaines' Mill, where the Eighth was posted in the second line of
battle, holding a cut in the road which afforded some protection. But
the solid shot and shell of the enemy tore wildly through the ground,

scattering the earth over the heads of the men   Hill in his book,
"Our Boys," says: "Suddenly I heard an explosion a little to my
right that pierced my very brain.   I naturally turned in the direction, and saw a sight that is before my eyes yet.   Twenty or thirty
feet from me, where the banks were not high enough to afford much
protection, I saw a cloud of dust and smoke in the very midst of
Company A   I saw a man throw his hands wildly above his head
and fall backward, covered with blood, a moment he lay quivering
convulsively, then he lay still—perfectly still   He was dead. Another
stooped and picked up his own arm, which had been torn off by the
shell as it descended, and rushed wildly towards a small hospital
some distance to the rear, flourishing his dismembered limb above
his head and shouting in the broad tongue—'Och, docther, me
airm's off'   A percussion shell had struck fairly among the boys
killing three outright, and wounding four."   The enemy were led
by some of their most trusted leaders, Stonewall Jackson directing
his celebrated corps.   At five o'clock, after a day of desperate
fighting, the enemy grew impatient, and pushed forward dark masses,
determined to win the day.   Finally word came for the Eighth to
push forward.   Colonel Hays gallantly led the charge.   The valor
of those men was unsurpassed, and the enemy was swept back to
a piece of wood where he had cover, and made a partial stand
The firing was now desperate, and a perfect shower of missiles was
poured upon the foe.   Reinforcements were speedily brought up
by the enemy, when the regiment, rent and torn, was forced back,
but retired in good order   Early in the fight Major Bailey was
wounded and borne from the field.   The loss of the regiment was
twenty-four killed and eighteen severely wounded, among the latter
being Captains Johnson, Wishart, Gallupe and Carter.   Elijah Mc-
Clelland, of Company 1, was among the killed.

On the night preceding the battle of Charles City Cross Roads,
the Eighth was sent out on the road leading to Richmond on
picket duty; but was unmolested.   The fighting on the following
day on this field was desperate, and the regiment had its full share
of bloody work.   The Sixth Georgia was on its front, and when the
time came for the regiment to charge, the Georgians were driven
and scattered like the chaff upon the summer's threshing floor
Charge and counter charge were delivered with terrible
effect, until, in the chances of the battle, the regiment
was forced by overpowering numbers, and took its place
in the new line of battle, where it rested for the night.
Hiram H. Lindsey, of Company I, was among the killed, and the
regiment lost sixteen killed and fourteen severely wounded.   The
regiment lost in the entire seven days' fight two hundred and
thirty.   By the time the regiment reached the Second Bull Run

battle-ground it had become reduced to less than a hundred strong, and Company "I" to fifteen men. Its chief duty in this battle was to defend the artillery, which was employed almost constantly on the part of the field where it was placed. In this sanguinary battle the regiment lost five killed and seventeen wounded and thirty missing. James M. Wells, of Company I, was among the killed. At South Mountain, in Maryland, the old enemy was again found ensconced behind rocks and a stone wall, and from his secure hiding place poured into the breasts of the Reserves the deadly missiles. Taken thus at a great disadvantage the losses were grievous. But resolutely charging up the steep acclivity of the mountain, the enemy was finally routed, and the summit was cleared. The loss in this stubborn fight was seventeen killed and thirty-seven wounded. Under the gallant Hooker the Reserves were sent forward to open the battle of Antietam. More sanguinary than any preceding field was this, the enemy fighting with a desperation bred of previous successes. On the morning of the 17th of September the Eighth was ordered to push forward to the verge of the noted cornfield, where it was subjected to murderous fire from the foe, as he rose up from his concealment and poured in a rapid discharge The loss in this battle was twelve killed and forty-three wounded. Among the killed in Company I was Clark Ingraham.

Scarcely was one campaign ended, and the absentees and recruits brought in and drilled, before it was plunged into another desperate encounter. In the battle of Fredericksburg the Reserves performed a conspicuous part, attracting the attention of the whole army, and, indeed, of the whole country, gaining the only decisive advantage on that sanguinary field. "In the heroic advance of this small division, in the face of the concentrated fire of the enemy's intrenched line, in scaling the heights, and in breaking and scattering his well-posted force, the Eighth bore a conspicuous and most gallant part. Never before had it been subjected to so terrible an ordeal, and when, after being repulsed and driven back by overwhelming numbers, it again stood in rank beyond the enemy's guns, scarcely half its number were there. Twenty-eight lay dead upon that devoted field, eighty-six were wounded, and twenty-two were captured. Adj. J. Lindsey Ingraham, Corp, John P. Burk, Samuel Churchill, Wesley S. Crago, George Delaney, George W. Gramlee. Joseph McCullough, Sergt. Joseph C. Minor, F. A. Phillips, M. Dill. Rinehart, Isaac Riggs, Richard Stewart and William Woody were either killed or mortally wounded, and Col. Baily, Captains R. E. Johnston, J. Eichelberger, H C. Dawson, William Lemon, and J. M. Kent, and Lieuts. Samuel McCandless, J. A. Diebold, S. B. Bennington, H. H. Maquilken were wounded.

After this battle, which bore so heavily upon Company I, and indeed upon the whole body, the corps was ordered to the defences of Washington   Since its arrival at the front this celebrated corps had been put upon the advance line and made to bear a brunt of the fighting in nearly every battle, and had fairly won a chance for re- cuperation.   Indeed there was but very little left of it.   Company I, with the regiment, remained here until the opening of the campaign under Grant, in the spring of 1864.   On the 5th of May, the old enemy was found on the Wilderness field and brisk skirmishing en- sued.   On the following morning the regiment was moved up the Gordonsville Pike, where it formed and drove the enemy   Companies D and I were here thrown forward as skirmishes, and moved up with- in seventy-five yards of the enemy's fortified line.   Here for three hours a hot skirmish fire was kept up, Company I losing two killed, John Lockhart and Corp. James Lucas, and ten wounded.   Hastily marching by the flank, the enemy was again met on the 7th, and the fighting was renewed with even more bitterness than ever, and for a week longer the sound of battle scarcely died away.   But now the three years term of service for which the regiment enlisted had ex- pired, and transferring the veterans and recruits to the One-hundred and Ninety-first, the Eighth was relieved at the front on the 17th, and moving to Pittsburg was there mustered out of service on the 24th.

Company I, Thirty-Seventh, Eighth Reserve Infantry.

Recruited at Waynesburg, Greene County, mustered in June 20, 1861.

Silas M. Bailey, Capt., pro to Maj.; wd at Gaines' Mill, June 27, 1862, pro. from Capt. Co I to Maj., June 4, 1862; to Col , March 1, 1863; to brev. Brig.-Gen., March 13, '65, mus out with Reg. May 24, '64.

John M. Kent, Capt pro. fr. 1st Lieut. to Capt , June 16, '62; wd at Wilderness; mus. out with Co. May 24, '64.

A. H. Sellers, 1st Lieut., pr. from Sergt to 1st Sergt., Oct. 10, 1861; to 1st Lieut , Aug 4, 1862; wd. at Wilderness; mus out May 24, '64.

Charles C Lucas, 2d Lieut , detached for duty as Quartermaster, May 1st, '62; not mus , res. Oct. 3, 1862.

J. Lindsey Ingraham, 2d Lieut , mus in June 13, '61; pr. fr. Sergt to 1st Sergt , July 22, '61; to Sergt.-Maj., Oct. 10, '61; to 2d Lieut , Aug 4, '62; to Adj , Oct. 1, '62; not mus ; killed at Fred- ericksburg, Dec. 13, '62.

James A. Wood, 2d Lieut., pr. fr. Cor. to Sergt., Oct. 10, '62; to 2d Lieut , July 1st, '63; wd at Charles City Cross Roads, June 30, '62, and May 22, '64; abs. in hos. at mus. out.

B. M. Blackley, 1st Sergt., tr. to Reg. Band, July 20, '61.

Joseph W. Smith, 1st Sergt., pr .fr. Sergt , July 1st, '62; mus. out with Co. May 24, '64.

Joseph C. Minor, Sergt., killed at Fredericksburg, Dec. 13, '62.

George G. Crow, Sergt., pr. fr. Corp., Feb. 4, '63, mus. out with Co. May 24, '64.

O S. Pratt, Sergt., pr. fr. Corp., Aug. 1, 62; dis. on Surgeon's certificate Feb. 13 '63.

Edwin H. Minor, Sergt., pr. fr. Corp , Dec. 4th, '62, wd. at Gaines' Mill, June 27, '62, mus. out with Co May 24, '64

George W. Scott, Sergt., pr. fr. Corp , July 1st, '63; wd. at Wilderness; mus. out with Co. May 24, '64.

H. J. Bowler, Sergt., pr. to 1st Sergt., tr. to 191st Reg., P. V., May 15, '64; Vet.

William S. Rinehart, Corp., died at Camp Pierpoint, Va., Jan. 4, '62.

John P. Burk, Corp., killed at Fredericksburg, Dec. 13, '62.

Adam Laughlin, Corp., tr. to Vet. Res. Corps, July, '63.

James Lucas, Corp., mus. Sept. 14, '61; wd. at Charles City Cross Roads, June 80, '62; killed at Wilderness, May 6, '64.

A. J. Bisset, mus. in July 15, '61, tr. to 191st Reg., P. V., May 15th, '64, Vet.

Neil Gray, Corp., wd. at Wilderness, mus. out with Co. May 24, '64.

William Laughlin, Corp , mus. out with Co. May 25, '64.

Samuel R. Estle, muc., pr. to prin. muc. July 1st, '62.

Adams, Robert, disch. May 27, '63, for wds., with loss of arm at Fredericksburg, Dec. 13, '62.

Anderson, Samuel, died at Georgetown, D. C., Oct. 22, '61.

Axton, Joseph M., killed at Charles City Cross Roads, June 30, '62.

Boon, Henry, disch. on Surg. Cert. Sept. 30, '61.

Bane, Asa, disch. Jan. 22, '63, for wds. rec'd. at Gaines' Mill, June 27th, '62.

Bell, John, disch. on Surg Cert. July 16, '62.

Baily, William N., mus. in July 15, '61, tr. to Reg. Band July 20, '61.

Bradley, Charles R., mus. in July 15, '61, tr. to Reg. Band July 20, '61.

Burk, Thomas C., tr. to 191st Reg. P. V., May 15, 64; Vet.

Brown, A. B., tr. to 191st Reg P. V , May 15, '64; Vet.

Bulor, Hugh, tr. to 191st Reg P V , May 12, '64; Vet

Batson, Wilbur F., mus. in March 24, '64; wd., tr. to 191st Reg. P. V., May 15, '64.

Bare, Baker, mus in March 29, '64, wd. tr. to 191st Reg P. V., May 16, '64.

Babbitt, Harrison, mus. in March 29, '64, tr. to 191st Reg. P. V., May 16, '64.

Belford, David, mus in April 7, '64, tr. to 191st Reg P. V., May 15, '64.

Batson, Elisha, mus. in Sept. 8 '62, died at Belle Plain, Jan. 13, '63.

Chapman, Silas, mus in July 15, '61, wd , mus. out with Co. May 24th, '64

Curtis, James R, mus. out with Co. May 24, '64.

Casner, Thomas, mus out with Co May 24, '64.

Church, Henry, mus. out with Co May 24, '64

Church, James M , wd. at Charles City Cross Roads June 30, '62, mus. out with Co. May 24, '64.

Carter, Charles W., mus. out with Co. May 24, '64.

Chapman, Joseph, mus. in July 15, '61, disch on Surg. Cert. July 19th, '62.

Carson, J. H., disch. March 6, '63, for wds rec'd. in action.

Coleman, James A , mus. in Sept. 9, '62, disch. on Surg. Cert. Dec 8th, '62.

Chaplin, Albert G., mus in Sept. 8, '62, disch. on Surg. Cert. Sept. 25, '63.

Copeland, Samuel, mus in Sept. 9, '62, disch. on Surg. Cert. March 19, '63.

Conrad, David, mus in July 15, '61, wd. at Wilderness; tr. to 191 st. P. V., May 15, '64; Vet

Clovis, Solomon R , mus. in March 29, '64, tr to 191st P. V., May 15, '64.

Cornhill, William, mus in March 29, '64, tr. to 191st Reg. P. V., May 15, '64.

Chisler, James, mus. in March 24, '64, tr. to 191st Reg. P. V., May 15, '64.

Cooper, Charles W , died at Georgetown, D. C , October 16, 1861; bur. Mil. Asylum Cem. D. C.

Churchill, Samuel, died Dec 17, '62, of wds. recd. in action

Crago, Wesley S , killed at Fredericksburg, Dec. 13, '62

Deems, George R., mus. out with Co , May 24, '64

Daugherty, Solomon, disch March 14, '64, for wds. recd. in action

Dutton, John W., mus. in Dec. 26, '63, tr. to 191st Reg P. V., May 15, '64.

Dean, Henry, mus. Sept. 8, '62, tr. to 191st Reg. P. V., May 15, '64

Delany, James, mus. in Sept. 8, '62, tr. to 191st Reg. P. V., May 15, '64.

Dean, Benjamin F., mus. in March 24, '64, wd., tr. to 191st Reg. P. V., May 15, '64.

Delany, George, mus. in Sept. 8, '62, died Jan. 10, '63, of wds. recd. at Fredericksburg, Dec. 13, '62.

Engle, Joseph, mus. out with Company May 24, '64.

Eisiminger, Abraham, mus. in March 29, '64, tr. to 191st Reg. P. V., May 15, '64.

Eisiminger, Isaac, mus. in Sept. 8, '62, killed at Spottsylvania, May 10, '64.

Fordyce, John G., mus. in Sept. 8, '62, mus. out with Co. May 24, '64.

Fetters, A. J., disch. on surgeon's certificate Aug. 3, '62.

Fordyce, S. R., mus. in Sept. 9, '62, wd., tr. to 191st Reg. P. V., May 15, '64.

Franks, Ely, mus. in June 29, '61, tr. to 191st Reg. P. V., May 15, '64; Vet.

Franks, Wm. M. F., tr. to 191st Reg. P. V., May 15, '64; Vet.

Franks, Job, mus. in Mar. 12, '62, wd. at Gaines' Mill, June 27, '62, tr. to 191st Reg. P. V., May 15, '64, Vet.

Franks, Emanuel, mus. in March 15, '64, tr. to 191st Reg. P. V., May 15, '64.

Funk, William, mus. in July 15, '61, tr. to 191st Reg. P. V., May 15, '64, Vet.

French, James A., mus. in Feb. 27, '64, wd. at Wilderness, tr. to 191st Reg. P. V., May 15, '64.

Grooms, William, mus. in June 20, '61; mus. out with Co., May 24, '64.

Gooden, James, mus. in April 7, '64, tr. to 191st Reg. P. V., May 15, '64.

Gooden, Francis, mus. in April 7, '64, tr. to 191st Reg. P. V., May 15, '64.

Gramlee, John W., killed at Fredericksburg, Dec. 13, '62.

Hays, John W., mus. out with Co., May 24, '64.

Herrington, Allen, mus. out with Co., May 24, '64.

Huston, George A., mus. out with Co., May 24, '64.

Horner, James H., mus. in Sept. 14, '61; disch. by general order War Dept. Jan. 14, '63.

Hager, Abijah, tr. to 191st Reg. P. V., May 15, '64; Vet.

Hager, Benjamin, tr. to 191st Reg. P. V., May 15, '64; Vet.

Hart, John B., tr. to 191st Reg. P. V., May 15, '64; Vet.

Hickman, Perry, mus. in Sept. 8, '62, tr. to 191st Reg. P. V. May 15, '64.

Hoffman, Levi, mus in Sept. 8, '62, tr. to 191st Reg. P. V. May 15, '64

Hains, Elijah, mus. in March 29, '64; wd. with loss of leg at Wilderness; tr. to 191st Reg P. V., May 15, '64.

Hillen, John, mus. in July 15, '61, drowned at Alexandria, Aug. 29, '62, buried at Alexandria, grave 188.

Headley, Erastus, mus. in Sept 8, '62, killed at Spottsylvania, C. H., May 14, '64.

Inghram, Clark, mus. in July 20, '61, killed at Antietam, Sept. 17, '62.

John, James M., mus. in Sept 9, '62, tr. to 191st Reg P V, May 15 '64.

Kees, David, mus in Dec. 12, '63, tr. to 191st Reg. P. V., May 15, '64.

Lawson, Elisha, wd. at Wilderness, mus out with Co, May 24, '64.

Leonard, D P., mus. in July 15, '61, mus. out with Co., May 24, '64.

Laughlin, G. W., mus. out with Co, May 24, '64.

Long, William, mus. in Sept. 8, '62, tr. to 191st Reg. P. V., May 15, '64.

Lemley, G W., mus. in Sept. 8, '62, tr to 191st Reg. P. V, May 15, '64.

Litzenburg, Alexander, tr. to 191st Reg. P V., May 15, '64, Vet.

Lemley, Basil, mus. in July 15, '61, wd. at Wilderness, tr. to 191st Reg P. V., May 15, '64, Vet.

Lockhart, John, mus. in Sept. 8, '62, killed at Wilderness, May 6, '64.

Lemley, Spencer, mus. in July 15, '61; died at Fredericksburg, Dec. 17, '62.

Lindsey, H. H., killed at Charles City Cross-roads, June 30, '62.

Leonard, Asa, mus. in July 15, '61, disch. on Surg. Cert. Nov. 10, '62.

Levi, Philip, disch. on Surg. Cert., March 7, '63.

Mildred, Albert, mus. out with Co, May 24, '64.

McClelland, J H., mus. out with Co., May 24, '64.

Minor, W. F, wd., mus. out with Co, May 24, '64.

Morris, Harrison, mus. in Sept. 8, '62, disch. Feb. 16, '63, for wds. recd. in action

Morris, James B., mus in Sept. 8, '62, wd., tr. to 191st Reg. P. V., May 15, '64.

Morris, Francis M., mus. in March 29, '64, tr. to 191st Reg. P. V., May 15, '64.

Morris, Richard, died Dec. 13, '61, of wds. recd accidentally.

McClelland, Elijah, killed at Gaines' Mill, June 27, '62.

McCullough, Joseph, mus. in July 15, '61, killed at Fredericksburg, Dec. 13, '62.

Nugent, John, mus. out with Co, May 24, '64.

Ogden, Perry, wd. at Wilderness, May 8, '64, ab at mus. out.

Ogden, Marion, pris. from May 9, '64, to March 3, '65; disch. April 1, '65.

Plants, George W., mus. in July 15, '61; mus. out with Co, May 24 '64.

Province, Joseph, mus. in Sept. 9, '62, disch. on Surg. Cert. Feb. 12, '63.

Phillips, Allen, disch. Oct. 27, '62, for wds. at Charles City Cross Roads, June 30, '62.

Phillips, James, mus. in Oct. 4, '61, disch. on Surg. Cert. Nov. 24, '62.

Phillips, G. W., mus. in Sept. 8, '62, tr. to 191st Reg. P. V., May 15, '64.

Pethtel, Richard, mus. in Feb. 27, '64, wd. at Wilderness; tr. to 191st Reg. P. V., May 15, '64.

Phillips, F A., mus. in Sept. 8, '62, killed at Fredericksburg, Dec. 13, '62.

Parkinson, James H, died April 18, '63; buried at Philadelphia

Rush, Silas, pris. from May 9, '64, to March 3; '65; disch. April 1, '65

Rinehart, John, mus. out with Co, May 24, '64.

Riggs, Maxwell, mus. out with Co., May 24, '64

Rose, Edward J., mus. in Sept. 8, '62, disch. March 10, '63, for wds. recd in action.

Rogers, H. J., mus. in Sept. 8, '62, tr. to 191st Reg. P. V., May 15, '64.

Rice, Alfred, tr. to 191st Reg. P. V., May 15, '64, Vet.

Renshaw, J. L., tr. to 191st Reg. P. V., May 15, '64, Vet.

Roberts, Justice G., mus. in March 29, '64, tr. to 191st Reg. P. V., May 15, '64.

Ritter, Joseph, mus. in March 29, '64, tr. to 191st Reg. P. V., May 15, '64.

Rinehart, M. Dill., mus. in July 15, '61, killed at Fredericksburg, Dec. 13, '62.

Riggs, Isaac, mus. in July 15, '61; died July 11, '63, of wds. received in action; buried at Alexandria, grave 676.

Summersgill, Robert, mus. out with Co., May 15, '64.

Seals, James M., tr. to 191st Reg. P. V., May 15, '64; Vet.

Smith, R. H. L., wd., tr. to 191st Reg. P. V., May 15, '64; Vet.

Stewart, A. A., mus. in Sept. 8, '62, tr. to 191st Reg. P. V., May 15, '64.

Sayres, Robert A., mus. Nov 2, '61; wd. at Gaines' Mill, June 27, '62, tr. to 191st Reg P. V., May 15, '64.

Spicer, John H , mus in March 29, '64, wd., tr to 191st Reg. P. V., May 15, '64,

Spicer, William, mus. in March 29, '64; wd., tr. to 191st Reg. P. V., May 15, '64

Shields, John, mus. in March 29, '64, tr. to 191st Reg. P. V, May 15, '64.

Stewart, Richard mus. in Sept. 8, '62; died, Dec. 28, '62, of wds. recd. in action; buried in Mil Asylum Cemetery, D. C.

Sylveus, William, mus. in Sept 8, '62, died at Annapolis, Jan. 12, '63.

Tuttle, Amos, mus. out with Co., May 24, '64.

Tuttle, William A., mus. in Feb. 29, '64, tr. to 191st Reg. P. V , May 15, '64

Turley, John, mus. in April 25, '62, tr. to 191st Reg. P V., May 15, '64.

Woody, William, mus. in Sept. 8, '62, killed at Fredericksburg, Dec 13, 62.

CHAPTER XXVII.

COMPANY F, FORTY-FOURTH REGIMENT, FIRST PENNSYLVANIA CAVALRY, FIFTEENTH RESERVE.

ORGANIZATION OF REGIMENT—CAMP PIERPONT—DRANESVILLE, CROSS KEYS AND PORT REPUBLIC—ROBERTSON'S RIVER—CEDAR MOUNTAIN—SECOND BULL RUN—FREDERICKSBURG—-DEATH OF BAYARD —MUD MARCH—CHANCELLORSVILLE CAMPAIGN—BRANDY STATION—ALDIE AND UPPERVILLE—GETTYSBURG—SHEPHERDSTOWN—MINE RUN CAMPAIGN—WILDERNESS—RAID TO RICHMOND—HAWES' SHOP—BARKER'S MILL—ST. MARY'S CHURCH—REAM'S STATION—WELDON RAILROAD—MUSTERED OUT—RECORD OF MEN.

BY the provisions of the act authorizing the organization of the Reserve Corps, it was to contain one regiment of cavalry. Hence the Fifteenth and last of the corps belonged to that arm of the service. Company F, of this regiment, was formed at Carmichaels, Greene County, and was mustered into service at Camp Curtin, near Harrisburg. Fortunately, this regiment had for its first Colonel one of the most accomplished cavalry officers in the service—George D. Bayard, whose career was too soon ended, at Fredericksburg, on the 13th of December, 1862. But in the establishment of high soldierly qualities at the outset, and in the drill of the regiment, his impress was set upon the organization and was not effaced in its brilliant career of three years. He attended to the minutest details, even to the selection and purchase of the horses and equipments.

At Camp Pierpont, Virginia, the winter of 1861 was passed, where daily a detachment of thirty men was sent on picket duty. On the 27th of November, 1861, Col. Bayard led the regiment on an expedition to Dranesville, where a few prisoners were obtained. On the return, the head of the column was fired on by guerillas, and in the skirmish which ensued, Bayard was wounded and had a horse shot under him, and two of his men were killed and two wounded. In the battle of Dranesville, which occurred on the 19th of December, the regiment was sent in to unmask the position of the enemy, and subsequently supported Easton's battery. In the movement upon Manassas, at the opening of the spring campaign, it was put upon exhausting service, at the conclusion of which it was posted at Falls Church. It accompanied McDowell on his advance upon the Rappahannock, and on the night of the 13th of May had a sharp skirmish with the enemy, in which company F bore a conspicuous part. At this juncture Col. Bayard was promoted to Brigadier-General, and Lieut.-Col. Owen Jones was selected to succeed him, John P. Taylor, Lieut.-Col. Sylvester D. Barrows, and Josiah H. Ray, of Company F, to Majors. Ordered forward to join McClellan on the Peninsula, this regiment took the advance by Fredericksburg, and had arrived within fifteen miles of the right wing of the army of the Potomac, when it was ordered back to the support of Banks and Fremont, operating against Stonewall Jackson in the valley. At Strasburg, Bayard came up with the enemy, and brisk skirmishing ensued. The enemy was driven beyond Woodstock. At Harrisonburg a brisk skirmish occurred. Subsequently the regiment participated in the battle of Cross Keys on the 8th, and finally at Port Republic, closing a month of active campaigning.

Under Pope the regiment opened a new campaign on the Rappahannock, Bayard's brigade of cavalry guarding the crossings of the river, and beating back the foe. At Robertson's River a warm engagement was had with the advance of Stonewall Jackson's corps, in which the regiment lost two killed and two wounded. Contesting the ground as he withdrew his brigade in the face of Jackson's whole army, by skillful maneuvering the enemy's column was delayed until the forces of Banks' reached their position on the Cedar Mountain battle ground. At a crisis in the battle Knapp's battery was in imminent peril of falling into the enemy's hands; but a handsome charge made by Major Falls, with the first battalion, saved the guns and drove back the foe. Of two hundred and sixteen men who entered the conflict, but seventy-one came back mounted. In the retirement of the Union column before the advance of the army of Northern Virginia, Bayard's brigade formed the rear guard.

On the evening of the 28th the regiment had the advance of Sigel's corps in its progress to Thoroughfare Gap, where Longstreet's corp was held in check for six hours. In the two following days, during the desperate fighting on the field of the Second Bull Run, the regiment held a position on the extreme left of the army. At the close of the campaign, with a force of one hundred available horses and two hundred men, it went into camp at Munson's Hill for rest and recruiting.

On the 12th of December, preparations having been made under Burnside for the battle of Fredericksburg, the regiment moved across the river, now under command of Lieut. Col John P. Taylor, and was deployed as skirmishers, and ordered to advance until the enemy was found   A mile from the river, near the railroad track, the enemy was met and a brisk skirmish ensued, until the infantry came to its relief.   On the following day, the day of the great battle, the regiment was deployed as skirmishers on the left wing, where it was under fire of the enemy's artillery.   At three o'clock in the afternoon, at the moment when the battle was raging fiercest, Gen. Bayard, who was now in chief command of the cavalry, was struck by a fragment of a shell and mortally wounded.   " The original commander of the First Cavalry, he had endeared himself to its members not less by his devotion to their instruction and improvement, than by the heroism he displayed in the hour of danger."

Upon the abandonment of Burnside's second campaign, familiarly known as the " Mud march," in January, 1863, Col Jones resigned, and Lieut.-Col. Taylor succeeded him as Colonel.   Major David Gardner became Lieutenant-Colonel, and Captain William T. McEwen, Major.   On the 12th of April the cavalry moved on the Chancellorsville campaign under Hooker   The operations of the cavalry in this whole movement, wearing and exhausting to the last degree, resulted in little effective service, Gen Stoneman, who was in command, studying to shun the enemy rather than to find and fight him.

Scarcely had the regiment rested and remounted, when it was put upon the march for the Gettysburg campaign   At Brandy Station, on the 9th of June, the cavalry fought in one of the warmest engagements hitherto participated in by this arm of the service.   Following up the charge of the First Maryland, " Col Taylor led a desperate charge upon the left and rear of the foe, reaching the Barbour House, where were Gen. Stuart, his staff and body guard, surrounded by cavalry. Here a desperate encounter ensued, the men using the cavalrymen's true weapon, the sabre, with terrible effect. A number of prisoners were brought off, including Stuart's Assistant Adjutant General." It was subsequently engaged at Beverly Ford, under the immediate command of Buford. The loss was three killed and eleven severely wounded. At Aldie and Upperville, on the 21st and 22d of June, Stuart was again met and severe fighting ensued, the regiment being engaged on the 22d in pushing back the enemy, and acted as extreme rear guard to the army on its way to Gettysburg. At 9 o'clock on the 2d of July it arrived upon that sanguinary field, and was detailed for duty at Gen.' Mead's headquarters, where it served to the end of the campaign. At Shepherdstown, after the crossing of the Potomac, in the pursuit from Gettysburg, the regiment was warmly engaged, and in position along the Charlestown pike held its ground against the repeated attacks of the foe.

The enemy was driven beyond the Rapidan by the 17th of September, the regiment being actively engaged in the campaign and suffering some losses. The necessity which caused the withdrawal of Meade's army to Centreville brought the cavalry into severe duty, and at Auburn and New Hope Church its endurance and bravery were severely tried. The campaign ended in the fiasco at Mine Run; but the winter of 1863-4 was one of little rest for the cavalry. Picket duty, scouts, guards, and details through the mud, and frosts, the sleet and rains of that inclement winter kept it actively employed the whole season through.

The spring campaign of 1864 opened on the 4th of May. Grant was now at the head of the army. Crossing the' Rappahannock, at Kelly's Ford, and the Rapidan, at Ely's Ford, the regiment moved with cavalry to the Spottsylvania Court House and thence to Todd's Tavern, and on the 5th was hotly engaged. Asa S. Allfree, of Company I, was among the severely wounded. On the 7th it advanced dismounted in line with the Sixth Ohio, and after a stubborn fight drove the enemy, his dead and wounded being left in the hands of the victors. On the 9th Gen. Sheridan commenced his grand raid upon Richmond. Crossing the Massaponax, Ny, Po, and Ta rivers the enemy's cavalry was met at Childsburg and a severe action occurred in which the First suffered some losses and the foe was roughly handled. Arrived within sight of the spires of Richmond, less than two miles away, near Meadow bridge, the enemy came out in heavy force intent on effecting the rout and utter destruction of Sheridan's forces; but with undaunted bravery every attack was met with courage and gallantry not excelled by troops fighting to save their capital from capture. Pushing forward, the columns reached Haxall's Landing on the James River, and after a rest of three days returned by White House and Aylett's, and rejoined Grant at Chesterfield Station on the 25th, having made a campaign in less than twenty days, which covered the ground of the whole summer's operations.

At Hawe's Shop a sanguinary battle was fought by the cavalry, in which the regiment bore a conspicuous part and suffered heavy losses. Lieut. Samuel Greenlee was killed and George W. Beam, of Company I, was mortally wounded here. Though reduced to scarcely two hundred men, it expended over eighteen thousand rounds of ammunition. It was again hotly engaged at Barker's Mill, where it exhibited unsurpassed gallantry and courage.

The tireless energy of Sheridan gave the cavalry little time for rest, and seizing the first opportunity when he could be spared from the front, he was off on his Trevilian raid. The destruction of the Virginia Central Railroad having been accomplished for many miles, in the face of a vigilant foe, which required incessant activity to defend the working parties, the regiment finally found itself entrapped in a narrow opening of the forest, and only saved itself from utter annihilation by the most conspicuous coolness and gallantry, losing three officers and thirty-five men killed, wounded and prisoners. As the columns of Grant neared Richmond the enemy grew more and more desperate. At St. Mary's church the rebel cavalry was supported by infantry, and Sheridan found himself hard pushed. It was in this battle that Company I suffered grievous loss. Captain Alexander Davidson was killed, and Thomas Crago and George W. Crawford were missing in action. Crossing the James on the 12th of July it was again engaged at Ream's Station, and returning again across the James, it met the enemy at Malvern Hill, where a severe encounter occurred in which Abner Murdock, of Company I, was killed. At Lee's Mills, at Gravel Hill, and finally at Ream's Station, on the Weldon Railroad, the regiment in quick succession met the foe, and at the latter point, after three years of honorable service, fought its last battle. The veterans and recruits, four hundred and one in number, were organized in a battalion under command of Major Falls, which was subsequently consolidated with the Sixth and Seventeenth Pennsylvania Cavalry forming the Second Provisional. Having been relieved at the front, the regiment proceeded to Philadelphia, where, on the 9th of September, 1864, it was mustered out of service.

COMPANY F, FORTY-FOURTH, FIFTEENTH RESERVE, FIRST CAVALRY.

Recruited at Carmichaels, Greene County, mustered in August 16, 1861.

John M. Harper, Capt., resigned Oct. 19, '61.

Josiah H. Ray, Capt., pro. fr. 1st Lieut. to Capt., Nov. 14, '61; to Major, March 1st, '62; resigned Feb. 23, '63.

Alexander Davidson, Capt., pr. fr. 2nd Lieut., Dec. 8, '61; to Capt. March 1, '62; died Aug. 1, '64, of wds. recd. at St. Mary's Church, Va., June 24, '64.

Thomas Lucas, 1st Lieut., pr. fr. Corp. to Sergt., Jan., '62; to 1st Lieut. Aug. 17, '62; wd. at Brandy Station, Va., June 9, '63; mus. out with company Sept. 1, '64.

Lewis K. Evans, 2d Lieut., pr. fr. private to 2d Lieut., Nov. 14, '61; resigned July 11, '62.

Samuel Greenlee, 2d Lieut., pr. fr. private to 1st Sergt., Dec., '61; to 2d Lieut., June 13, '62; wd. June 9, '63; killed at Hawes' Shop, Va., May 28, '64.

Jonas E. Lucas, 1st Sergt., pr. fr. Sergt; captured in action Nov. 17, '63; com. 2d Lieut. June 26, '64; not mus.; mus. out with Co. June 16th, '65; Vet.

V. Worthington, Q. M. Sergt., pr. fr. Corp. to Sergt; to Q. M. Sergt.; tr. to Co. F. Batt., Sept. 9, '64; pr. to 1st Sergt.; to 2d Lieut. Oct. 11, '64; to 1st Lieut. Co. L, Dec. 13, '64; to Capt. Co. A., March 5, '65; mus. out by consolidation, June 20, '65; Vet.

John H. Hoge, Com. Sergt., wd. at Brandy St., Va., June 9, '63, mus. out with Co. Sept. 9, '64.

John H. Black, Sergt., mus. out with Co., Sept. 9, '64.

S. S. Houlsworth, Sergt., died Nov. 27, '61.

James K. Gregg, Sergt., wd. at Auburn, Va., Oct. 14, '63, mus. out with Co. Sept. 9, '64.

George W. Evans, Sergt., pr. fr. Corp. Aug. 17, '62, mus. out with Co. Sept. 9, '64.

John Haver, Sergt., pr. fr. Corp. Sept. 1, '62, mus. out with Co. Sept. 9, '64.

John R. Dunlap, Sergt., pr. fr. Corp. Sept. 1, '62, mus. out with Co. Sept. 9, '64.

W. H. H. Eberhart, Corp., tr. to Battalion Sept. 9, '64.

John Jones, Corp., pr. to Corp. April, '62, mus. out with Co. Sept. 9, '64.

Alvin H. Wilson, Corp., pr. to Corp. June 13, '62, mus. out with Co. Sept. 9, '64.

Thomas F. Reppert, Corp., pr. to Corp. Sept. 1, '62; wd. July 28, '64; abs. at mus. out.

Joseph A. Shaffer, Corp., prisoner from June 24, '64, to April 28, '65; mus. out June 9, 65; Vet.

Jesse Hughes, Corp., wd. Aug. 22, '64; tr. to Batt. Sept. 9, '64; died Sept. 27, '64; buried at Philadelphia; Vet.

Andrew J. Young, Corp. tr. to Batt. Sept. 9, '64; mus. out as Sergt. Co. F., June 20, '65; Vet.

J. M. Worthington, Bugler, mus. out with Co. Sept. 9, '64.

George W. Walters, Bugler, pr. to muc. March 1, '64, mus. out with Co Sept 9, '64

Alton, James E., disch. on Surg. Cert. Sept 22, '62.

Anderson, John, tr to Batt. Sept. 9, '64, Vet.

Allfree, Asa S , wd. and missing at Wilderness May 5, '64

Alexander, Morris, cap Nov. 21, '63; died at Andersonville, July 14, '64, grave 3,317.

Bristel, Omit, mus. out with Co Sept. 9, '64

Birch, Thomas, disch. on Surg. Cert March 14, '63.

Baker, David S., tr. to Batt. Sept. 9, '64, Vet

Brestel, Jacob, mus. in Sept 1, '62; wd. May 28, '64; tr. to Batt. Sept. 9, '64, mus out in Co F, June 6, '65.

Beam, George W , died Sept 16, '63, bur in Mil Asy. Cem. D. C.

Brown, James W., cap Aug., '62, and Nov. 17, '63; mus out June 16, '65

Crayne, Isaac B , mus. out with Co. Sept. 9, '64.

Cree, Henry C., wd at Auburn, Va , Oct 14, '63, mus. out with Co. Sept 9, '64.

Cree, Joseph M , mus. out with Co Sept 9, '64.

Cox, James, absent in hospital at mus. out

Cummins, William, disch. on Surg. Cert. Jan 4, '62

Cree, Hugh D , disch. on Surg Cert Jan. 4, '62

Craft, Benjamin L , disch. on Surg Cert July 28, '62

Crawford, James, P , disch. on Surg Cert Oct. 17, '62,

Cummins, James R , tr to Batt Sept. 9, '64; mus out with Co as Corp. Co. F, June 20, '64; Vet

Cary, Sylvester P., mus. in Sept 25, '62; tr. to Batt Sept. 9, '64; mus out with Co. F, June 9, '65

Cannon, James, mus in March 30, '64, tr to Batt. Sept. 9, '64.

Crago, James, mus. in March 25, '64, died June 1, '64, of wds. rec'd at Hawes' Shop, Va., May 28, '64.

Crawford, George W , missing at St. Mary's Church, Va , June 24, '64.

Crago, Thomas, mus. in March 25, '64, missing in action June 23, '64.

Davis, Winchester, mus out with Co Sept. 9, '64.

Dean, John W , mus. out with Co. Sept. 9, '64.

Dunlap, Samuel R., died Feb 13, '63

Dukate, John, mus in March 30, '64; cap. at St. Mary's Church, Va , June 24, '64; died at Andersonville, Oct 6, '64; grave 10,436.

Evans, Robert, mus out with Co. Sept. 9, '64

Elginfritz, David F., mus in Aug. 25, '62; tr to Batt. Sept. 9, '64, mus. out with Co F, May 27, '65.

A G Fordyce

Eisinminger, James, mus. in Aug. 22, '62; tr. to Batt. Sept 9, '64; mus. out in Co. F June 6, '65.

Ely, Caleb, mus. in Aug. 25, '62; wd. at Auburn, Va., Oct. 14, '63; tr. to Batt Sept. 9, '64.

Evans, William W, died Jan. 29, '62.

Eisinminger, Thomas, mus. in Sept. 17, '64; not on mus. out roll.

Fisher, Franklin, mus. out with Co. Sept. 9, '64.

Fordyce, Justus G, mus. out with Co. Sept. 9, '64.

Fordyce, James H., mus. in Sept. 16, '62, disch. on Surg. Cert March 14, '64.

Frank, Anthony, mus. in July 17, '63, prisoner from June 24, '64 to April 28, '65; mus. out June 21, '65

Gump, Harrison, disch on Surg. Cert. April 29, '63.

Grove, James P., March 1, '62, tr. to Batt. Sept. 9, '64.

Grim, David C, mus. in Aug. 17, '62; tr. to Batt Sept. 9, '64; mus. out with Co. F, May 27, '65

Glassmyer, Albert, mus. in July, '63, tr. to Batt. Sept. 9, '64.

Gresley, Charles, mus in July 21, '63, missing in action Nov. 17, '63.

Grass, Henry, mus. in July 17, '63; capt. May 31, 64; died, date unknown; bur. at Millen, Ga, Sec A, grave 302.

Hight, Peter A., mus out with Co Sept. 9, '64.

Hummel, David, mus. out with Co. Sept. 9, '64.

Hughes, James, mus out with Co. Sept. 9, '64.

Hill, Samuel, mus. out with Co. Sept. 9, '64

Hopkins, John W., disch. on Surg. Cert Dec 4, '62.

Heaton, Smith, mus. in Aug. 17, '62, disch. on Surg. Cert. Dec. 8, '62.

Ham, Richard W, tr. to Batt. Sept. 9, '64, Vet.

Houseman, Samuel S., tr. to Batt. Sept. 9, 64, mus. out as Sergt. Co. F, June 20, '65.

Herene, Edward, mus in July 27, '63, tr. to Batt Sept 9, '64.

Ham, Alfred M., mus. in Feb. 8, '64; wd in action June 21, '64; tr. to Batt. Sept. 9, '64; tr. to V. R. C. June 15, '65; disch. by Gen. Ord. July 17, '65.

Higginbotham, B. K., disch on Surg. Cert. March 15, '63.

Johns, John, not on mus. out roll.

Johns, Oliver, mus. out with Co. Sept. 9, '64.

Jenkins, Henry S., disch. on Surg. Cert. Jan. 19, '62.

Johnston, George W. L., mus. in Sept. 24, '62; tr. to Batt. Sept. 9, '64; mus. out with Co. F, June 6, '65.

Jones, William, died July 16, '62; burial record July 12, '62, at Alexandria, Va., grave 81.

Jones, Oliver, not on mus. out roll.

Kennedy, David, mus. in March 8, '64, Substitute; abs., sick at mus. out.

Kramer, Phillip L , mus in Aug. 24 '61, disch. on Surg. Cert. Jan. 4, '62

Kendall, James R , disch. on Surg. Cert July 28, '62.

Keigley, George, mus. in Sept. 24, '62, disch. by order Sec'y. of War May 26, '63

Keigley, Newton, mus in Sept. 24, '62; tr. to Batt. Sept. 9, '64; mus out with Co. F, May 27, '65.

King, Henry B., tr. to Vet. Res. Corps, 1863

Keener, David L , mus. in Sept 24, '62; died July 13, '63, bur. at Alexandria; grave 883.

Kiebal, Frederick W., mus. in July 17, '03, died Dec. 29, '03.

Kridel, Frederick W , not on mus. out roll

Lucas, Simeon S., disch. on Surg. Cert. Sept. 18, '63.

Long, Milton, mus. in Aug. 24, '61, disch. by Sec'y of War, Sp. Or. No 52, March 8, '64.

Lightner, Josiah, mus. in Dec. 19, '63, tr to Batt Sept 9, '64.

McFarland, John F., mus. out with Co Sept. 9, '64.

Midlam, Enoch W., mus. out with Co. Sept. 9, '64.

Mercer, Martin V. B., mus. out with Co. Sept. 9, '64

McCullough, John F., disch by order of Sec'y. of War Jan. 16, '62

McClelland, Wm. H., disch on Surg. Cert. Feb. 16, '63.

McClelland, George W., disch on Surg Cert. Feb. 16, '63

Mayhorn, Nelson, tr to Batt Sept. 9, '64; Vet

Mitchel, Jacob, mus. in Sept 24, '62; tr. to Batt. Sept. 9, '64; mus. out with Co. F May 27, '65.

Maple, David, mus in Sept. 24, '62, tr to Batt. Sept. 9, '64.

Mayes, Samuel, mus in Oct 20, '63, tr. to Batt. Sept. 9, '64.

McGlumphey, William, mus. in March 25, '64, tr. to Batt. Sept 9, '64

Moulter, Daniel, mus. in Feb 8, '64, tr. to Batt. Sept 9, '64

Murdock, Abner, mus. in March 30, '64, killed in action July, 12, '64

Mairs, Samuel, not on mus. out roll.

Neff, John, mus. out with Co. Sept 9, '64.

Nutt, Thomas H., disch on Surg. Cert. Dec. 16, '62.

Neff, Abraham, tr. to Batt Sept 9, '64; Vet.

Nearhoff, Abner, mus. in Aug 2, '64; tr. to Batt. Sept. 9, '64; mus. out with Co. F May 27, '65.

Phillips, Addison, mus. in Nov. 2, '63; wd May 10, '64; tr. to Batt. Sept. 9, '64.

Phillips, Joseph A., mus. in Dec 14, '63; tr. to Batt Sept. 9, 64; mus. out in Co. F by G. O. July 29, '65

Holeman, Wm. K., mus. in July 21, '63; missing in action near Warrenton, Nov. 17, '63.

Ross, Samuel, mus. out with Co. Sept. 9, '64.

Ross, Ira, mus. in Aug. 24, '61; pris. at Brandy Station, Va., June 9, '63; wd. June 21, 64; mus. out with Co. Sept. 9, '64.

Rinehart, David H., mus. out with Co Sept. 9, '64.

Rush, William, disch. on Surg. Cert Jan. 7, '63.

Rush, William J., mus. in March 15, '64, tr. to Batt. Sept 9, '64.

Rumble, James, mus. in Sept. 24, '62; wd. at Brandy Station June 9, '63; tr. to Batt. Sept. 9, '64.

Shape, Demas J., mus. out with Co. Sept. 9, '64.

Simmons, Richard D., mus. in Aug. 24, '61; disch. on Surg. Cert. June 7, '62.

Shape, John M., disch. on Surg. Cert June 7, '62.

Shape, John M., mus. in Feb 27, '64; tr. to Batt. Sept. 9, '64.

Shawmon, John W., mus. in March 25, '64; tr. to Batt. Sept. 9, '64; mus out in Co. F, June 6, '65.

Sams, George W., mus. in March 30, '64; tr. to Batt. Sept. 9, '64; died Oct. 8, '64, bur. Nat. Cem., Arlington.

Sams, Henry, Jr, mus. in March 30, '64; died July 28, '64.

Seaton, George W, mus. out with Co. Sept. 9, '64.

Shawmon, John F., mus. out with Co. Sept. 9, '64.

Simmars, Stephen D., not on mus. out roll.

Steaton, Smith, disch. on Surg Cert. Dec. 8, '62.

Toomey, Isaiah W, mus. in Aug. 31, '63; tr. to Batt. Sept. 9, '64.

Tiernan, Joshua, mus. in March 30, '64; tr. to Batt. Sept. 9, '64.

Teagarden, George W., killed at Mt. Jackson, Va., June 3, '62.

Walters, John A., mus. out with Co. Sept. 9, '04.

Wood, Henry A, pr. to Com. Sergt. June 22, '62.

Young, John B., mus. in Feb. 27, '64; tr. to Batt. Sept. 9, '64.

Yarkley, William, mus. in July 17, '63; tr. to Batt. Sept. 9, '64.

Zollars, Richard S, mus. in Sept. 24, '62; tr. to. Batt. Sept. 9, '64; mus. out in Co. F, May 27, '65.

CHAPTER XXVIII.

COMPANIES F AND G, OF THE EIGHTY-FIFTH PENNSYLVANIA INFANTRY REGIMENT.

ORGANIZATION—YORKTOWN AND WILLIAMSBURG—FAIR OAKS—NEW-BERN, N. C —WEST CREEK—KINGSTON—WHITE HALL—GOLDS-BORO—FOLLY ISLAND, S. C.—SIEGE OPERATIONS BEFORE FORT WAGNER—DEATH OF COL. PURVIANCE—BEFORE PETERSBURG—DEEP BOTTOM—LOSSES—TRANSFERS—MUSTERED OUT—RECORDS OF THE MEN.

COMPANY F, of the Eighty-fifth Pennsylvania Infantry, and a portion of Company G, were recruited in Greene County. The regiment was organized on the 12th of November, 1861, by the choice of the following officers· Joshua B. Howell, colonel; Norton M'Giffin, lieutenant-colonel; and Absalom Guiler, major During the winter the regiment was engaged in drill and in fatigue duty, across the east branch of the Potomac, in the construction of works for the defense of Washington In the spring of 1862 it moved to Meridian Hill, and was brigaded with the 101st and 103d Pennsylvania regiments, and the 96th New York, under command of General Wessells.

In the Peninsula campaign, under McClellan, the regiment was engaged in the siege of Yorktown, and in the battle of Williamsburg with a loss of two wounded, one mortally. At Fair Oaks, on the 31st of May, while engaged in fortifying the position, it was vigorously attacked by the enemy under General Joseph E Johnston. The regiment occupied the rifle-pits on the right of the main work, a redoubt held by Hart's battery. General Casey, who held the front was vigorously pushed, but made a stout resistance, throwing grape and canister with terrible effect. He was finally obliged to retire to his supports. In the seven days' battles which ensued, which resulted in the change of base by McClellan from the Chickahominy to the James, the regiment was not actively engaged. When McClellan evacuated the Peninsula, and went to the support of Pope before Washington, Keyes' corps, the Fourth, to which the regiment belonged, remained on duty at Fortress Monroe.

On the 5th of December, 1862, Wessell's brigade was ordered to Newberne, North Carolina, to reinforce Foster, and upon its arrival joined in an expedition to destroy a rebel gun-boat on the Neuse, break up the railroad bridge near Goldsboro, and make a diversion in favor of Burnside at Fredericksburg. At West Creek the enemy was found ready to dispute the passage. Wessells had the advance, and throwing the Eigth-fifth to the right of the road, and Ninth New Jersey to the left, crossed the stream and advanced upon the flanks of the enemy's position, compelling a hasty retreat. Two pieces of artillery and a number of prisoners were the fruits of victory. On the following morning the command moved forward, Wessells upon the left, and soon came upon the enemy in the well made fortifications of Kingston. But by pushing through a swamp, thought to be inaccessible, they entered at the side left open, and immediately charged in face of a hot fire, and soon put the enemy to rout. A brisk skirmish was had at White Hall, and on the 17th the defenders of the bridge at Goldsboro were swept back and the destruction of the bridge, the main object of the expedition, was effected.

Towards the close of January, 1863, General Foster was ordered with a part of his army to proceed to South Carolina, to co-operate with General Hunter in his operations against Charleston. Colonel Howell now had command of the brigade, and Lieutenant-Colonel Purviance of the regiment. At the head of Folly Island the troops witnessed the first bombardment of Fort Sumter, by Admiral Dupont In June, 1863, General Hunter was superceded by General Gilmore. To possess Morris Island it was necessary to erect powerful batteries at the north end of Folly Island. While at this work the dense underbrush shielded the working parties from view. In this duty the 85th shared, working by night, and watching by day. When all was ready the obstructions were cleared away, and fire opened from forty-four heavy guns An assault followed by which the enemy's first line of works was cleared, but Fort Wagner, the main work, still held out. Gilmore determined to reduce it by regular siege approaches. "Ground was broken on the 21st of July, and the work, which was terribly exhausting, was pushed forward with the utmost vigor, day and night; neither the heat of a tropical climate, nor the missiles of a vigilant foe, were allowed to interfere with the labor. On the 20th of August the 85th Pennsylvania, 100th New York, and the 3d New Hampshire, were detailed to occupy the advanced trenches, each twenty-four hours in turn. The trenches were shallow, and afforded little protection from the enemy's fire. On the left were his powerful guns on James Island and in Fort Johnson; in front those of Sumter, Gregg and Wagner; and on the right Fort Moultrie. The nights were damp and cold, and during the day the thermometer stood 100° in the shade. The casualties were numerous, and the sick list increased with alarming rapidity. The 85th took its turn in this terrible ordeal, and on the 21st had one killed and twenty wounded, three mortally; on the 24th, one killed and seven wounded, one mortally, on the 27th, two killed and eight wounded, three mortally; on the 30th, four killed and eight wounded, Lieutenant-Colonel Purviance being of the number killed; on the 2d of September, five wounded, one mortally." The 85th with an aggregate strength of 451 on going upon the outer works, could muster but 270 fit for duty when recalled. Two attempts to surprise and capture Fort Gregg proving unsuccessful, General Gilmore determined to again attempt to take it by assault. But the bombardment by sea and land for forty hours induced the enemy to retire, and the island was occupied.

Upon the death of Colonel Purviance, Major Campbell was made Lieutenant-Colonel, and Captain Abraham, Major Active operations were continued until the middle of April, 1864, when the Tenth corps was ordered north to reinforce the Army of the James. The 85th was of the first brigade, Howell's, first division, Terry's. The usual service of fortifying and picket duty continued until the 20th, when Howell's brigade was ordered to charge and drive out the enemy in front This was gallantly and successfully executed, but with a loss of two killed and twenty-one wounded. The rebel General Walker was wounded and taken prisoner.

On the 14th of June, Grant's troops began to cross the James, and the Tenth corps took possession of the works between the James and the Appomattox. The enemy soon pressed heavily in front of Howell, and the fighting was of unusual severity. Finally the Union line was pushed back to the original line of battle. The loss of the 85th was five killed and two wounded. In the expedition to Deep Bottom, which was made on the 13th of August, in which the Second and Tenth corps engaged the corps of Longstreet and Hill, the 85th had two killed and nineteen wounded, five mortally. In the affair of the 16th, Terry's division was hotly engaged, the 85th participating in a charge, in which the enemy, by withholding his fire while protected by works, was able to deliver it in a manner to produce great destruction, the regiment losing nine killed and fifty-four wounded. In the operations on the south side of the Appomattox by Terry's troops the regiment participated, sustaining slight losses, until the 14th of October, when the veterans and recruits were transferred to the 188th, and on the 22d of November it was mustered out of service.

COMPANY F, EIGHTY-FIFTH INFANTRY REGIMENT.

Recruited in Greene County, mustered in October 16, 1861.
John Morris, Capt. mus. in Nov. 11, '61; disch. June 23, '62
Nicholas Hager, Capt pr to 1st Lieut. Jan. 3, '62; to Capt. June 23, '62; disch. March 9, '63

Levi M. Rogers, Capt. pr. from Sergt. to 2d Lieut. June 23, '62; to 1st Lieut. July 7, '63; to Capt. Aug. 8, '64; died Sept. 4, of wds rec'd at Deep Bottom Aug. 16, '64, bur. in Nat. Asy Cem. Sec. B, grave 1.

Rosberry Sellers, 1st Lieut. disch. Nov. 28, '61.

John Remley, 1st Lieut. mus. in Nov. 11, '61; pr. fr. 2d Lieut. June 23, '62; disch. July 6, '63.

Elmore A. Russell, 1st Lieut. mus in Feb 1, '64; pr. fr. 1st Sergt. Aug. 9, '62; com. Capt. July 21, '64; not mus.; wd. Aug 16, '64; disch. Jan. 28, '65; Vet.

James E. Sayers, 1st Sergt.; absent on detached serv. at mus. out.

Zachariah C.Ragan, Sergt; mus. out with Co. Nov. 22, '64.

James B. Lindsey, Sergt.; mus. in Nov. 11, '61; disch. Feb 20, '62.

Joseph Silveus, Sergt.; disch. on Surg. Cert.

Isaac D. Haveley, Sergt.; mus. in Feb. 1, '64; wd. Aug. 16, '64; tr. to Co. H, 188th Regt P. V. June 28, '65; Vet.

Rinehart B. Church, Sergt. mus. in Feb 1, '64; wd. Aug. 15, '64; tr. to Co. H, 188th Regt. P. V. June 28, '65; Vet.

Thomas J. White, Sergt.; mus. in Feb. 4, '64; absent on detached service at mus. out; Vet.

Oliver M. Long, Sergt.; died at White House, Va., June 12, '62

Alonzo Lightner, Sergt.; mus. in Feb. 1, '64; pr. to Sergt. Nov 18, '62; killed at Deep Bottom, Aug. 16, '64; Vet.

Jefferson H. Zane, Corp.; mus. in Nov. 11, '61; absent, sick at mus. out.

Ryerson Kinney, Corp ; absent, on detached service at mus out.

William H. Hoskinson, Corp.; mus. in Nov. 11, '61; mus. out with Co. Nov. 22, '64.

John Morman, Corp.; disch. on Surg. Cert. May 26, '62.

William C. Leonard, Corp.; disch. on Surg. Cert. July 4, '63.

Thomas Hoge, Corp ; disch. on Surg. Cert. May 26, '62.

Hiram Weaver, Corp.; disch. on Surg Cert , date unknown.

James N. Derbins, Corp.; mus. in Feb. 1, '64; wd. Oct. 13, '64; tr. to Co. H, 188th Regt. P V. June 28, '65; Vet.

Thomas M. Sellers, Corp.; mus. in Feb. 1, '64; wd. Aug. 16, '64; tr. to Co. H, 188th Regt. P. V. June 28, '65; Vet.

Thomas P. Rodgers, Corp.; mus. in Aug. 28, '62; pr. to Corp. June 29, '64; killed at Deep Bottom, Va., Aug. 16, '64.

Daniel Swan, musician, mus. out with Co. Nov. 22, '64.

James McCuen, musician; mus. in Dec. 16, '61; mus out with Co. Nov. 22, '64.

Argo, Simeon, died at Morris Island, So. Carolina, Sept. 3, '63.

Arner, Strosnider, des. date unknown.

Bryner, James, mus. in Nov. 11, '61; mus out with Co. Nov. 22, '64.

Burk, Noah, disch. date unknown.

Babbitt, Joseph, mus. in Nov. 11, '61; disch May 12, '63.

Burroughs, John B , mus. in March 26, '64; tr to Co. H, 188th Regt P V , June 28, '65

Bissett, Jeremiah, mus in Jan. 20, '64; died at Hampton, Va , Oct. 21, '64; bur in Nat. Cem., Hampton, Sec C., grave 32, under name of J. Bussull.

Bissett, Albert, mus. in Jan 20, '64; died at Beverly, N J., Aug. 27, of wds., rec'd at Petersburg, Va., June 17, '64.

Chapman, Charles, mus. out with Co. Nov. 22, '64.

Cheney, Jesse, disch for wds. Nov. 23, rec'd June 10, '65.

Church, Franklin, mus in Aug 28, '62; disch by Gen. Ordor, June 10, '65

Church, George, mus. in Feb. 24, '64; tr. to Co H, 188th Regt P. V June 28, '65.

Cree, Alexander D., mus in Aug. 28, '62, wd at Deep Bottom, Va , Aug. 16, '64; disch. by Gen. Order May 13, '65.

Cooper, James E., mus. in Oct. 22, '62; tr. to Co. H , 188th Regt P. V. June 28, '65. ·

Clouse, John, mus. in Jan 20, '64, tr. to Co. H , 188th Regt. P. V. June 28, '65 '

Cartwright, Jesse L , mus in Aug 22, '64; died at Hampton, Va., Oct 4, '64; bur. in Nat Cem , Hampton, Sec. 8, grave 14.

Cowen, John, mus.. in Nov. 11, '61; died at Washington, D. C.; bur. Mil Asylum Cem., D. C.

Crouse, Nathan, mus. in Nov. 11, '61; died, date unknown.

Crouse, William, died June 11, '62; bur. in Mil. Asylum Cem. D. C

Davis, Benjamin, mus out with Co Nov. 22, '64.

Duvall, Elias, died at Beanfort, So. Carolina, Sept 11, '63, of wds. rec'd at Fort Wagner.

Earnest, Jacob, absent on detached service at mus out.

Engle, Solomon, mus in Nov. 4, '61; mus. out with Co. Nov. 22, '64.

Estrep, Cornelius, mus in Nov. 11, '61; died at Philadelphia, Aug 7, of wds rec'd at Fair Oaks, Va., May 31, '62.

Fry, Thomas R., mus out with Co. Nov. 22, '64.

Fordyce, William, mus. out with Co. Nov. 22, '64.

Fordyce, John, disch.; date unknown.

Fry, David, mus. in Jan. 5, '64; tr. to Co. H, 188th P. V. June 28, '65.

Fry, Henry, mus out Feb. 1, '64; wd. Aug 21, '62; killed near Peterburg, Va , June 17, '64; Vet.

Graham, John P., mus in Nov. 11, '61, mus. out with Co. Nov 22, '64.

Gilbert, Eliel, mus. out with Co. Nov. 22, '64.

Garrison, Thomson, absent on detached service at mus. out.

Gladen, William H., disch.; date unknown.

Gray, Isaac, mus. in Feb. 1, '64; wd. Aug. 3, '61; absent, on detached service at mus. out.

Hickman, George F., mus. out with Co. Nov. 22, '64.

Hummel, William, mus. out with Co. Nov. 22, '64.

Hays, George W., mns. in Nov. 11, '61; disch. on Surg. Cert. April 16, '62.

Hoffmann, James, mus. in Feb. 1, '64; tr. to Co. H, 188th P. V. June 28, '64; Vet.

Hoffman, Jacob, mus. in Feb. 1, '64; absent on detached service at mus. out.

Henderson, William, mus. in Jan. 25, '64;- tr. to Co. H, 188th Regt. P. V. June 28, '65.

Hunt, Josephus, mus. in Nov. 11, '65; died at Beaufort, So. Carolina, Oct. 12, '63, of wds. rec'd at Fort Wagner; bur. record Sept. 29, '63.

Hathaway, Adolph, mus. in Feb. '64; killed at Cold Harbor, June 3, '64; bur. in Nat. Cem. City Point, Sec. A, Div. 1, grave 4 or 62; Vet.

Johnston, Francis M., died at White House, Va., June 19, '62.

Johnson, Nicholas, died at N. Y. Oct. 16, '62; bur. in Cypress Hill Cem., L. I.

Knight, James, disch. on Surg. Cert. Sept. 12, '62.

Kimble, Jackson, mus. in Feb. 4, '64; absent on detached service at mus. out.

Leonard, Harvey, mus. in Nov. 11, '61; mus. out with Co. Nov. 22, '64.

Loughman, Henry, absent on detached service at mus. out.

Lewis, George F., disch. Oct. 20, '62.

Longdon, Morgan, disch. on Surg. Cert. Oct. 11, '62.

Leonard, Wm. E., mus. in Feb. 4, '64; absent on detached service at mus. out.

Mitchell, Andrew J., mus. out in Co. Nov. 22, '64.

Martin, Perry W., mus. in Nov. 10, '61; wd. Aug. 16, '64; mus. out with Co. Nov. 22, '64.

Mitchell, Jonathan, disch. date unknown, for wds. rec'd Aug. 15, '64.

Martin, Silas W., mus. in Sept. 9, '62; wd. Aug. 16, '64; disch. by Gen. Order May 13, '65.

Montgomery, John, mns. in Aug. 13, '62; disch. by Gen. Order May 13, '65.

Montgomery, William, mus. in Oct. 22, '62; absent on detached service at mus. out.

20

Moore, Carl, mus. in March 26, '64; tr. to Co. H, 188th Regt P. V. June 28, '65

Moore, Samuel H., mus in March 26, '64; tr. to Co. H, 188th Regt. P V. June 28, '65.

Murdy, John, mus. in Aug. 22, '64; disch. by Gen Order, June 10, '65.

Martin, James M., mus. in Nov. 11, '61; died at Point Look Out, Md., Oct. 6, '62.

Morris, Andrew J, mus. in Jan 5, 64, died at Hilton Head, S. C. April 18, '64; Vet.

McMullin, William, mus. out with Co. Nov 22, '64.

McCracken, Thomas, disch. on Surg. Cert. July 4, '63.

McGlurphy, Harvey, disch. on Surg. Cort., date unknown.

McGary, Spencer, mus. in Nov. 11, '61; disch. on Surg. Cert. Jan. 31, '63

McGumphrey, W., mus. in Nov. 11, '61, disch. on Surg Cert. Oct 30, '62.

McDonald, Alfred, mus. in Feb. 1, '64; died at Hampton, Va. Oct. 10, '64; Vet.; bur. in Nat. Cem Sec. D., grave 22.

Nelson, LaFayette, died May 23, '62; bur. in Mil. Asy. Cem. D. C.

Ott, Ezra, mus. in Jan 20, '64; tr. to Co. H, 188th Regt. P. V. June 28, '65.

Ott, Salem, mus. in March 31, '64; tr. to Co. H, 188th Regt. P. V. June 28, '65.

Pettitt, Henry, mus. in Nov. 11, '61; mus. out with Co. Nov. 12, '64.

Plants, Maxwell, mus. out with Co. Nov. 22, '64.

Packer, Wm. F., disch. on Surg. Cert Aug. 1, '63.

Pettitt, George, mus in Feb 1, '64; wd. Aug. 24, '63, and Aug. 14, '64, tr. to Co H. 188th Regt. P. V. June 28, '65; Vet.

Patterson, Joseph, died at Malvern Hill, Va. July 1, '62.

Riggs, William, mus. out with Co. Nov. 22, '64

Rinehart, Morgan, mus. in Nov. 11, '61, absent, on detached service at mus. out.

Richard, Lewis, missing in action at Fair Oaks, Va , May 31, '62.

Roseberry, Thomas, disch on Surg. Cert. Feb 12, '63.

Riggs, Peter, disch., date unknown.

Roach, George, mus. in Jan 20, '64; disch. June 23, '64.

Rush, John, mus. in Feb 1, '64; tr. to Co H, 188th Regt. P. V. June 28, '65; Vet.

Riger, John, mus. in Feb. 1, '64; tr. to Co. H, 188th Regt P. V. June 28, '65; Vet

Rinehart, Thomas, mus. in Feb. 1, '64, tr. to Co. H, 188th Regt. P V. June 28, '65; Vet.

Rinehart, Meeker, died at Annapolis July 9, of wds. rec'd May 31, '62.

Scott, Abijah M., abs. on detached service at mus. out.

Scott, Liston, mus. in Feb. 1, '64; pris. fr. May 16, '64, to April 21, '65; dischg. July 5, '65; Vet.

Sutton, John, mus. in Nov. 11, '61; dischg. on Surg. Cert. May 26, '62.

Smith, James E., mus. in Mar. 11, '62; dischg on Surg. Cert. Sept 12, '62.

Seabold, William H., mus. in Feb. 1, '64; abs. on detached service at mus. out.

Sellers, John, mus. in Aug. 28, '62; dischg. on Gen. Order, June 10, '65.

Smith, Ezra, mus. in Nov. 11, '61; died May 29, '62; buried in Mil. Asylum Cemetery, D. C.

Smith, Anthony A., mus. in Mar. 6, '62; died at Point Lookout, Oct. 25, '62.

Thompson, Samuel, mus. in Nov 11, '61; mus. out with Co, Nov. 22, '64.

Thomas, William, dischg. date unknown.

Teagarden, Isaac, mus in Nov. 11, '61; dischg. date unknown.

Taylor, Levi, mus. in Feb. Feb. 24, '64; abs. on detached service at mus. out.

Thomas, Samuel, mus. in Apr. 8, '64; died Feb. 18, '65; buried in Nat. Cem., City Point, Va., Sec. A, div. 3, grave 129.

Terrel, George W., mus. in Aug. 22, '64; dischg. by Gen. Order, June 10, '65.

Vandivender, Eli, mus. in Aug. 13, '62; wd. Aug. 24, '63; dischg. by Gen. Order, June 10, '65.

West, Jacob, mus. in Nov. 11,'61; mus. out with Co, Nov. 22,'64.

Wiseman, George, mus. in Jan. 20, '64; missing as Deep Bottom, Va., Aug. 16, '64.

Weaver, Jacob, dischg. on Sur. Cert., July 9, '62.

Winger, John M., mus. in Feb. 24, '64; dischg. on Surg. Cert., Sept. 26, '62

Wiseman, John, mus. in Aug. 22, '64; disch. by Gen. Order, June 10, '65.

West, Samuel, died at Harrison's Landing, Va, July 26, '62.

Wilkinson, A. J., died at Point Lookout, Md, May 26, of wds. recd. May 20, '64.

COMPANY G, EIGHTY-FIFTH INFANTRY REGIMENT.

Recruited in Greene County, mustered in Nov. 6, 1861.

Isaac M. Abraham, Capt. pr. to Major, Apr. 28, '64; wd near Deep Bottom, Va., Aug. 15, '64; mus. out with Reg, Nov. 22, '64.

John A. Gordon, 1st Lieut., com. Capt. Sept. 8, '63; not mus; mus. out with Co. Nov. 22, '64.

John F. Crawford, 2d Lieut., resigned March 10, '64.

Benoni S. Gilmore, 1st Sergt. mus. in Oct. 15, '61; pr. to Sergt. March 1, '63; to 1st Sergt.; mus. out with Co. Nov. 22, '64.

David R. Graham, 1st Sergt., disch. on Surg. Cert. Nov. 22, '62.

Marquis L. Gordon, Sergt., pr. to Corp. March 1, '63; to Sergt. Nov. 1, '63; mus. out with Co. Nov. 22, '64.

Hiram Gordon, Sergt.; pr. to Sergt. Nov. 1, '64; abs. on detached Serv., at mus. out.

Jesse E. Jones, Sergt.; mus. in Oct. 20, '61; wd. Aug. 14, '64; pr. to Sergt. Nov. 1, '64; mus. out with Co. Nov. 22, '64.

Robert H. Ross, mus. in Oct. 22, '61; wd. Aug. 30, '63; disch. on Surg. Cert. May 11, '64.

James R. Core, mus. in Oct. 15, '61; disch. on Surg. Cert. Feb. 6, '63.

Benj. F. Campbell, mus. in March 17, '62; pr. to Corp. Nov. 1, '63, to Sergt. Sept. 1, '64; abs. on detached service at mus. out.

Francis M. Rush, Sergt., died at Hampton, Va., Aug. 19, of wds. recd. Aug. 16, '64.

Myers P. Titus, Sergt., mus. in Oct. 15, '61; died at Hampton, Va., Oct., '64, of wds. recd. in action.

William Pitcock, Corp., disch. on Surg. Cert. Nov. 21, '62.

George A. Burchinal, Corp, mus. in Oct. 15, '61, died at Yorktown, Va., June 10, '62.

James Sturgis, Corp., died at Beverly, N. J., Nov. 6, of wds. recd. Aug. 16, '64.

Harrison H. Hoge, Corp., died Aug. '62; bur. record Sept. 25, '62; bur. in Cypress Hill Cem. L. I., grave 437.

Thomas S. Knisely, Corp., died at Suffolk, Va., Nov. 4, '62.

George W. Kenny, Corp., Nov. 1, '63, killed at Bermuda Hundred Va., May 20, '64; bur. in Nat. Cem., City Point, Sec. A, Div. 1; Vet.

Adam M'Gill, musician, mus. out with Co. Nov. 22, '64.

Hiram Hickman, musician, died at Crany Island, Va., Sept. 13, '62.

Atchison, Henry K., absent, wounded at mus. out.

Bare, Baker, mus. in Nov. 6, '61; disch. on Surg. Cert. Dec. 29, '62.

Black, Lindsay, mus. in Jan. 5, '64; wd. Aug. 16, '64; tr. to Co. G, 188th Regt. P. V., June 25, '65; Vet.

Bovid, William, mus. in Feb. 12, '62; absent on detached ser. at mus. out.

Bowers, William H., died at Beaufort, S. C., Sept. 4, '63, of wds. recd. in action.

Barnes, Jesse, died May 12, '62; buried in Nat. Cem., York-town, Va., Sec C, grave 206.

Beard, George C, mus. in Oct. 24, '61; died April 9, '62; bu. in Nat. Cem., Yorktown, Va., Sec B, grave 231

Cline, John L., wd. Sept. 2, '63; mustered out with Co. Nov. 22, '64.

Cumley, John G., disch on Surg Cert. May 9, '63.

Conrad, Alexander, disch. Oct. 22, '64, expiration of term.

Cole, Jacob, died near Richmond, Va!, June 6, '62.

Dean, William, mus. in Oct. 24, '64; mus. out with Co. Nov. 22, '64.

David, Wells E., mus. in Oct. 15, '61; died at White Oak Swamp, Va., June 23, '62

Dickson, Philans E., mus. in Oct. 25, '61; died at Washington, D. C., May 25, '62; bur. in Military Cem.

Eberhart, Martin L, mus. out with Co. Nov. 22, '64.

Enrix, Charles M. B., mus. in Oct. 15, '61; absent, sick at mus. out.

Eberhart, William, mus. in Feb. 11, '62; abs. on detached serv. at mus. out.

French, Isaac, mus. in Oct. 15, '61; disch. on Surg. Cert. Feb. 20, '62.

Greene, William P., mus. in Oct. 15, '61; mus. out with Co. Nov. 22, '64

Graham, William A., wd. Aug. 16, '64; mus. out with Co. Nov. 22, '64.

Goodwin, David S, mus. in Oct. 15, '61; disch. on Surg. Cert. 1862.

Gray, James, mus. in Oct. 15, '61; disch. Nov. 17, '64; exp. term.

Gabler, Philarus E., disch. on Surg. Cert. Aug. 5, '63.

Graham, John, disch. on Surg. Cert. Aug. 18, '62.

Griffin, Charles A., mus. in Oct. 15, '61; tr. to Sig. Corps. Sept. 7, '63.

Gooden, David, mus. in Feb 12, '64; tr. to Co. G, 188th Regt. P. V., June 28, '65.

Gehoe, Benjamin, died at Hampton, Va, June 14, '64, of wds. recd. in action.

Gregg, John, des. Nov, 1861.

Grove, David L., mus. in Oct. 25, '61; absent on furlough at mus. out.

Hayden, Caleb F., absent, sick at mus. out.

Honsacker, Nicholas, mus. in Oct. 15, '61; mus. out with Co. Nov 22, '64.

Harden, John P., mus. out with Co. Nov. 22, '64.

Hunter, Isaac, mus. in Oct. 25, '61; absent, sick at mus. out.

Hayden, Henry M., mus in Oct. 15, '61; disch on Surg. Ceit. 1862.

Haney, Wm. H., mus. in March 4, '62; disch. on Suig. Cert. 1862.

Husk, Frederick, mus. in Oct 15, '61; died at Baltimore, Md., July 16, '62

Huss, James, mus. in Oct 15, '61; des. June 30, '62

Hoffman, George, des Nov '61.

Jacobs, Josephus, mus. out with Co. Nov 22, '65.

Jenkins, Andrew J., mus. in Oct. 22, '61; mus. out with Co. Nov 22, '61.

Kent, John R., mus out with Co. Nov. 22, '64

Kniseley, George W., disch on Surg Cert. July, '63.

Kennedy, Van B. mus. in Oct. 15, '61; died at Camp Scott, Va, April 25, '62

Lloyd, George, mus. in Oct. 15, '61; disch on Suig Cert. Aug 21, '62.

Lyon, James F., mus in Oct 15, '61; died at Harrison's Landing, July 2, '62

Lytle, Rodandus, mus in Oct 15, '61; died at Foitress Monroe, Aug 14; '62

Martin, David W, absent on detached service at mus. out.

Meredith, Enrix, mus. in Oct. 15, '61; disch on Surg. Cert Dec. 22, '62.

Mitchell, Allen W., mus in Oct 24, '61; disch. on Surg. Cert. Aug., '62.

Moser, John P., tr. to Co. G, 188th Regt. P. V, June 28, '65; Vet

Murdock, J. H L, died at White Oak Swamp, Va, June 28, '62.

Moore, John, died at Washington, D. C., Dec. 6, '61; bui. in Mil Asy Cem.

Moser, Silas L, des. Nov. 18, '61.

McDonald, John, mus. in Oct. 15, '61; wd., with loss of right arm and left hand, July 29, '63; disch. on Surg Cert. May 7, '64.

McGill, William, mus in Oct. 15, '61, disch. on Surg. Cert. March 6, '63.

McMasters, James, died at Camp Scott, May 16, '62

Nicholson, J. W., mus. in July 16, '62; died at Folly Island, Nov 1, '62.

O'Neal, Henry, mus. in Oct. 15, '61; disch on Surg. Cert. Aug. 5, '63.

Pratt, Joseph S., mus. in Oct. 15, '61; abs. on detached duty at mus out.

Patton, Henry B., mus. in Oct. 15, '61; mus. out with Co. Nov. 22, '64.

Patterson, W. II., mus. in Oct. 15, '61; disch. on Surg. Cert. Nov. 13, '62.

Pratt, Ashabel F, mus. in Oct. 15, '61; disch on Surg. Cert. Aug. 5, '63,

Pitcock, Owen, mus. in Nov. 1, '61; tr. to Vet. Res. Corps., Sept. 16, '63.

Patton, Caleb A., mus. in Oct. 15, '61; died at Philadelphia, Pa., July 10, '62.

Phillips, Ashberry, died at Chesapeake Hospital, Va., June 10, '62, of wds. received in action.

Rush, John W., mus. out with Co. Nov. 22, '64.

Ramor, Minor A., mus. in Oct. 15, '61; disch. on Surg. Cert. May 9, '63.

Rush, John D., disch. on Surg. Cert. Nov. '61.

Reid, Joel, mus. in Oct. 15, '61; died Sept. 22, '62; bur. in Cyp. Hill Cem. L. I.

Sutton, William A., mus. in Oct. 23, '61; absent in ar. at mus. out

Strickler, John, mus. in Oct. 15, '61; abs, sick at mus. out.

Shultz, Israel, disch. Nov. '61.

Strosnider, Reason, disch. on Surg. Cert. Nov. '61.

Spicer, John, disch. on Surg. Cert. Jan. 6, '63.

Sturgis, Phineas W., mus. in Oct. 15, '61; died at Yorktown, Va, June 2, '62; buried in Nat. Cem. Sec. D, grave 167.

Sturgis, David R., mus. in Oct. 15, '61; died at Baltimore, Md., May 29, '62.

Titus, Benjamin, mus. in Oct. 15, '61; absent, sick at mus. out

Thomas, Joshua R., wd. Aug. 9, '63; disch. Nov. 11, '64; exp. of term.

Tell, William, mus. in July 30, '62; disch. by Gen. Order, June 8, '65,

Tannehill, Joseph, mus. in Oct. 15, '61; died at Morris Island, S. C, August 23, '63.

Utt, William II, mus in Oct. 15, '61; disch. on Surg Cert. November 27, '62.

Wilcox, Moses, mus. in Oct. 15. '61; died at Baltimore, Md., May 20, '62.

CHAPTER XXIX.

COMPANY A, ONE HUNDRED AND FORTIETH PENNSYLVANIA INFANTRY REGIMENT

ORGANIZATION—NORTH CENTRAL RAILWAY — CHANCELLORSVILLE— WHITE HOUSE—GETTYSBURG—THE WHEAT FIELD—MINE RUN CAMPAIGN—THE WILDERNESS — CORBIN'S BRIDGE—SPOTTSYL- VANIA—TOLOPOTOMY CREEK—DEATH OF CAPTAIN McCULLOUGH —COLD HARBOR—BEFORE PETERSBURG — JERUSALEM PLANK ROAD—DEEP BOTTOM—REAM'S STATION—HATCHER'S RUN— SOUTHERLAND STATION—SAILOR'S CREEK—FARMVILLE—APPO- MATTOX COURT HOUSE—SURRENDER OF LEE—MUSTER OUT— RECORD OF INDIVIDUAL SOLDIERS

COMPANY A, of the One Hundred and Fortieth Regiment, was recruited in Greene County, and was originally officered by John F McCullough, Captain; J Jackson Purman, First Lieuten- ant; David Taylor, Second Lieutenant   The regiment was organized at Camp Curtin on the 8th of September, 1862, with Richard P. Roberts, of Beaver County, Colonel, John Frazer, of Washington County, Lieutenant-Colonel; Thomas B. Rodgers, of Mercer County, Major.   During the period of Lee's invasion of Maryland, which culminated in the battles of South Mountain and Antietam, the regiment was posted along the line of the North Central Railway to keep open that great thoroughfare.   Having been thoroughly drilled, it was ordered to the front, and arrived as the troops were returning from the disastrous battle of Fredericksburg.   It became a part of the Third Brigade, General Zook, First Division, Second Corps.   In the battle of Chancellorsville it was engaged in front of the Chancel- lor House on the old turnpike leading to Fredericksburg, where General Hancock held an advanced position, and where the enemy made frequent and determined attacks.   With Colonel Miles it was upon the picket line during the nervous and uneasy night of the 2d, when the least movement of troops drew the fire of whole divisions of the army.   During the morning of the 3d, while the One Hundred and Fortieth was supporting the Fifth Maine Bat- tery, the White House, which was situated at the apex of the new line of battle, took fire and was utterly destroyed.   Thirty-three wounded men, and three women, who had taken refuge in the cellar,

Andrew Jackson Young

were brought forth from the burning wreck. When the army retired to the new line the One Hundred and Fortieth occupied a position to the left of the White House, where it remained, subjected to occasional artillery fire, until the 6th, when it retired across the river.

The battle of Gettysburg followed close upon Chancellorsville. The First and Eleventh Corps met a full half of the rebel army on the heights beyond the town to the northwest, and were driven back, through its streets to the ridge to the south, in the centre of which was the quiet little Evergreen Cemetery. On the morning of the 2d the Second Corps, now under the gallant Hancock, came upon the field, and was posted along the left centre of the line, stretching from the cemetery along the Emmettsburg Pike towards the Peach Orchard. About four o'clock Sickles, who, with the Third Corps, occupied the extreme left, stretching from the pike along the Peach Orchard to Little Round Top, was fiercely attacked. His line was thin and weak; but right gallantly did he hold his ground, and hurl back the foe. Again and again he came. In the midst of the fray Sickles was grievously wounded with the loss of a leg. His weakened columns were gradually forced back. "Portions of the Fifth Corps were sent to his relief, but shared a like fate. Finally Hancock sent Caldwell's Division, of his own corps, to check the enemy's mad advance, and repair the threatened disaster. Moving rapidly across the little wooded knoll to the right and front of Round Top, he first sent the brigades of Cross and Kelly to penetrate the Wheat Field and the wood beyond, where the fiercest fighting had been. Colonel Cross was killed, and his command was terribly torn, as it advanced upon that fatal Wheat Field, on three sides of which the enemy in heavy numbers was concealed. And now, as a forlorn hope, the brigades of Zook and Brooke were sent forward. Zook was killed while leading his troops into the fight, and before he had hardly got into action. The command of his brigade then fell upon Colonel Roberts of the One Hundred and Fortieth. Gallantly did these two small brigades push forward over this devoted ground in the face of a severe fire. The enemy was swept back from the cover of the woods, and the rocky ridge beyond the Wheat Field, a position of great natural strength, was carried. But this advantage, gained at a fearful cost, was of no avail. The angle in Sickle's line at the Peach Orchard, the weak point in his formation, had been hopelessly broken, and through this opening the enemy swarmed and turned the right of Caldwell's position, compelling him to withdraw. He rested at night on the low ground on the left centre of the line, where he remained during the heavy cannonade of the succeeding day, and until the close of the battle." The loss in Company A in the battle was severe. Sergeant Brown and Corporal

Eddy were killed, Private Loar was mortally wounded, Lieutenant Purman was wounded with loss of a leg, Captain McCullough, Sergeant Zimmers and Private Eddy were severely wounded, Colonel Roberts, Captain Acheson and Lieutenant Wilson of the regiment were killed.

The One Hundred and Fortieth now became a part of the First Brigade, to the command of which Colonel Nelson A Miles, of the Sixty-first New York, was assigned. Lieutenant-Colonel Frazer was made Colonel, Major Rodgers, Lieutenant-Colonel, and Captain Thomas Henry, Major. "In the advance of the army to the Rapidan, and the retrograde to Centreville, and subsequent advance to Mine Run, where the campaign ended without coming to a decisive battle, the regiment shared the fortunes of the corps, participating in the action of Bristoe Station on the 14th of October, 1863, and the skirmishing in front of the enemy's position at Mine Run, sustaining some loss in wounded "

By midnight of the 3d of May, 1864, the regiment was on the march for the Wilderness campaign. General Grant was now in supreme command. By noon of the fifth, the regiment had arrived upon the Brock road, where it threw up breast-works, the enemy in front. The scenes on that gory field, pen cannot portray. The regiment shared in the fiery conflict. At three on the morning of the 6th, it was aroused, the brigade holding the left of the line where substantial breast-works were erected. On the morning of the 8th the regiment joined in the general movement of the army, and had an encounter with the enemy at Corbin's bridge. On the 9th the Po River was crossed, and the regiment was placed upon the skirmish line and met the pickets of the enemy. A line of rifle pits was thrown up along the Po River. Early on the morning of the 12th the regiment joined in the grand movement of Hancock's corps, which resulted in the movement upon the rebel intrenchments, and large captures of men and material at Spottsylvania. The movement was commenced at the first breaking of the day, and was shielded somewhat from view by a dense fog which prevailed on that morning. The advantage gained was securely held, though the enemy made repeated attacks to regain his lost ground, and atone for his discomfiture. The loss in the regiment in this affair was over one hundred, and in Company A, Benjamin Dunston, John W. Peden, Thomas Doty and Judson W. Paden, were killed. Andrew J. Walders was mortally wounded, John Henry was wounded, and David Frays and Job Smith, Jr., were missing in action.

Starting on another grand flanking movement on the 20th, the North Anna was crossed on the 23d, but finding the enemy advantageously posted, Grant determined not to attack; but, withdrawing, he encountered the enemy at Tolopotomy Creek, and severe fighting occurred, Hancock occupying the centre and successfully carrying the enemy's first line and holding it against every fierce attack of the foe. Here Company A lost its brave leader, Captain John F. McCullough, who was killed, and Norval Troy, who was mortally wounded.

Without loss of time the army moved on to the old battle ground of Gaines' Mill, only with the two opposing columns reversed, Lee having the ground of McClellan, and Grant that of Stonewall Jackson. Grant here boldly attacked along the whole line, Hancock holding the left. But the ground was now found to be completely fortified, and the attack, though successful in parts, was not in the main design fruitful, and was finally abandoned with grievous loss. In Company A, John R. M. Greene, and John Gray, were killed, and Michael Roope was mortally wounded. By the middle of June the army was across the James, and an attack upon the enemy at Petersburg was promptly delivered. But finding, as usual in this campaign, that the enemy had placed himself behind elaborately planned and strongly fortified works, the attempt to carry the place by direct assault was abandoned, and the army sat down before the town and commenced the more tardy operations of the siege. In this first attack before Petersburg, John Acklin, of Company A, was killed. In the movement on the Jerusalem Plank Road, on the 21st of June, the One Hundred and Fortieth participated with the Second and Sixth Corps, but only a partial success was achieved; though a position was taken and fortified, which the enemy found himself unable to break through. On the 26th of July a demonstration was made to the north side of the James, where, in connection with the Nineteenth corps, the brigade gallantly charged the enemy's works, on the 28th, and captured prisoners and four Parrott guns, and on the 30th returned to the Petersburg front. The mine explosion resulted in no advantage to the Union army. On the 14th of August the corps again crossed the James, and at Deep Bottom the rebel works were carried by Birney's division, which was advanced within sound of the rebel capital. Returning to the Petersburg front the corps took up the line of march on the 21st, and at Ream's Station had a desperate encounter with the enemy, who appeared in superior force.

"In the subsequent operations of the corps during the fall and winter, the regiment bore a part, being hotly engaged in front of Petersburg, on the 9th of September, in the general movement of the 27th of October; suffering much from inclemency of the weather in the expedition to Hatcher's Run, from the 8th to the 10th of December, and in that to Dabney's Mills from the 5th to the 17th of February, 1865. Apart from these it remained undisturbed in winter quarters until the opening of the spring campaign on the

25th of March. On that day the Second Corps made an advance upon the rebel lines at Hatcher's Run, and a portion of his works, designed to cover the South Side Railroad, was carried. For four days the fighting was continued on this part of the line, the corps making daily some substantial advance, Miles' Division executing a brilliant move at Southerland's Station on the 3d of April, whereby extensive captures of men and materials were made The corps was again engaged on the 6th at Sailor's Creek, and on the 7th at Farmville fought its last battle. In this engagement an assaulting column led by General Miles was bloodily repulsed. Night put an end to the contest, and under cover of the darkness the enemy withdrew. Two days later Lee surrendered. Hostile operations were soon after concluded, and returning · to the neighborhood of Washington, the regiment, on the 31st of May, was mustered out of service "

COMPANY A, ONE HUNDRED AND FORTIETH REGIMENT

Recruited in Green County, mustered into service Sept. 4, 1862

John F. McCullough, Capt, wd. at Gettysburg, July 2, '63; Com Col. 183d Reg P V, May 28, '64; not mus, killed at Tolopotomy, Va, May 31, '64

James M Pipes, Capt., pro. fr 1st Serg to 2d Lieut, Jan. 2, '64; to Capt, June 27, '64; wd., with loss of arm, at Reame's Station, Va, Aug. 25, '64, disch. on Surg. Cert Feb 17, '65.

John A. Burns, Capt; pr fr. Sergt to 1st Sergt., Jan. 2, '64; to 1st Lieut, June 27, '64, to Capt, March 4, '65; mus out with Co. May 31, '65.

J Jackson Purman, 1st Lieut, wd with loss of leg at Gettysburg, July 2, '63; disch. on Surg Cert, May 20, '64.

Mark G. Spragg, 1st Lieut, pr. fr Corp to Sergt., March 1, '64; to 2d Lieut, June 27, '64; to 1st Lieut, March 4, '65; mus. out with Co May 31, '65.

David Taylor, 2d Lieut., resigned July 31, '63

Charles T. Hedge, 1st Sergt, pr. fr. Corp. July 1, '64; com. 2d Lieut, Dec. 18, '64; not mus.; mus out with Co May 31, '65.

Daniel B. Waychaft, Sergt, pr. to Sergt, July 1, '64; disch. by Gen. Order, July 5, '65.

Nathaniel N Purman, Sergt, wd 'at Chancellorsville, May 3, '63; tr to 105th Co 2d Battl V R C., Jan. 30, '65, disch. Sept. 4, '65; exp. term.

Henry Zimmers, Sergt ; wd at Gettysburg, July 2, '63: abs. at mus out.

John C. Coen, Sergt., pr. to Corp. July 1, '64; to Sergt., May 1, '65; mus. out with Co. May 31, '65.

Cornelius J. Burk, Sergt., pr. fr. Corp, Nov. 1, '63; disch. on Surg. Cert. March 16, '65.

Wiliam A. Brown, Sergt, killed at Gettysburg, July 2, '63

J. S. Herrington' Corp., pr to Corp. July 1, '64; tr. to V. R C.; disch. by Gen. Order, July 20, '65

Alpheus Crawford, Corp., disch. by Gen. Order, June 6, '65.

Carey M. Fulton, Corp., mus. out with Co. May 31, '65

Thomas J. Kent, Corp., pr. to Corp. July 1, '64; mus. out with Co. May 31, '65.

James B. Reinhart, Corp, pr. to Corp July 1, '64; mus. out with Co. May 31, '55.

Joseph Bane, Corp., pr. to Corp. July 1, 64; mus. out with Co. May 31, '65.

Kramer Gabler, Corp., mus. out with Co. May 31, '65.

Spencer Stephens, Corp., pr. to Corp. May 1, '65; mus. out with Co. May 31, '65.

Leroy S. Greenlee, Corp., killed at Gettysburg, July 2, '63; bur. in Evergreen Cemetery.

John W. Peden, Corp., killed in action, May 15, '64.

James Woods, musician, mus. out with Co May 31, '65.

Morgan Dunn, musician, mus. out with Co. May 31, '65.

Anderson, Harrison, mus. out with Co. May 31, '65.

Acklin, Samuel, mus. in Feb. 27, '64; tr. to V. R. C.; disch. by Gen. Order, Feb. 24, '65.

Armstrong, Oliver, tr. to Co. F, 18th Reg. V. R. C., Aug. 10, '64; disch. by Gen. Order, June 27, '65.

Anderson, James, tr. to 114th Co. 2d Battl. V. R. C , March 13, '64; disch. by Gen. Order, July 18, '65.

Acklin, John, killed at Petersburg. Va., June 17, '64.

Burson, Oliver, H. P., mus. out with Co. May 31, '65.

Bennett, John, mus. out with Co. May 31, '65.

Barney, Peter, tr. to 51st Co 2d Battl. V. R. Corps. Nov. 6, '63; disch. Sept. 4, '65; exp. term.

Clutter, Samuel, mus. out with Co. May 31, '65.

Cox, John, Jr., mus. out with Co. May 31, '65.

Clutter, Noah D., mus. in April 13, '64; tr to Co K, 1st Reg. V. R. C, Sept 1, '63; disch. by Gen. Order, July, '65.

Cowan, Joseph, des. Dec. 10, '63.

Doman, George N , mus. out with Co. May 31, '65

Dunstan, Benjamin, killed at Spottsylvania, Va., May 12, '64.

Eddy, Michael, tr. to Vet. R. Corps. Jan. 6, '65.

Eddy, John W., wd. and cap. at Gettysburg, July 2, '63; died at Richmond, Va., Jan. 27, '64.

Freeland, George, disch. on Surg. Cert. Jan. 16, '65.

Fisher, John, mus in Nov 29, '62, tr. to Co. H, 53d Reg. P V., May 30, '65.

Frays, David, missing in action at Spottyslvania, C. H Va, May 12, '64.

Freeland, Charles A , died Nov. 17, '62.

Garber, Thornton, disch. by Gen Order, July 10, '65

Gray, George, mus out with Co. May 31, '65

Geary, Simon, wd. at Tolopotomy, Va , March 31, '65; absent at mus. out.

Green, John R M , killed at Cold Harbor, Va., June 6, '64

Green, Isaac P., died at Falmouth, Va., Jan 8, '63.

Gray, John, killed at Cold Harbor, Va , June 2, '64.

Henry, John, wd at Spottsylvania, C. II., May 12, '64; disch. by Gen Order, June 8, '65

Hopkins, Daniel S. mus in Feb. 29, '64; tr. to Co. H, 53d Reg. P V, May 30, '65

Harris, Stephen C., tr. to Ind. Batty. C, Pa Artillery, Feb 15, '64.

Hoge, David R , died at Washington, D C., Jan. 10, '65; bur. in Nat. Cem Arlington

Jones, John C , mus. out with Co May 31, '65

Jones, George, mus. in Feb. 27, '64; tr. to Co H, 53d Reg P. V., May 31, '65.

Kent, Regin S , wd. at Bristoe Station, Va. Oct. 14, '63; absent at mus. out.

Kener, Oliver, mus. out with Co. May 31, '65.

King, Daniel, disch on Surg Cert Jan 17, '65

Kent, James F disch by Special Order, March 13, '63

King, Daniel, mus in March 22, '64; tr. to Co H. 53d Reg. P. V , May 30, '65; disch by Gen Order, June 3, '65

Loar, Benjamin F., died at Philadelphia, Aug 1, of wds. recd. at Gettysburg. July 2, '63

Meighen, John, mus. out with Co May 31, '65.

Miller, John H., disch on Surg Cert. Jan 20, '63.

Mariner, George W , tr. to 114th Co. 2d Battl. V. R. C., March 13, '65; disch by Gen Order, July 18, '65.

Miller, Abraham, tr. to Vet Res. Cor. Dec. 1, '63

Morris, Franklin R., missing in action at Chancellorsville, Va., May 3, '63

Morris, Lindsay, died at Washington, D. C, Dec. 22, 64; bur. in Nat. Cem. Arlington.

McCullough, L G., disch. by Gen Order, June 6, '65.

McCullough, Hiram, missing in action at Ream's Station, Aug. 25, '64.

Ogden, William, absent, sick at mus. out.

Pipes, Abner, disch by Gen. Order, June 26, '65.

Pettit, Joseph, died July 7, '64, at Alexandria, Va ; grave 2,346.

Rush, John A., mus. out with Co. May 31, '65.

Roop, John E., mus out with Co. May 31, '65.

Roop, William, disch. on Surg. Cert. Jan. 16, '63.

Roop, Lindsay, mus. in March 26, '64; tr to Co II, 53d Reg. P. V., May 30, 65.

Roop, Henry, mus. in March 26, '64; tr. to Co H. 53d Reg. P. V., May 30, '65.

Robinson, Alex. D., mus. in Feb. 29, 64; tr. to Co. II, 53d Reg. P V, May 3, '65.

Ridgway, Samuel, died at Parkton, Md., Nov. 25, '62.

Roope, Michael, mus. in March 26, '64; died July 29, of wds. recd. at Cold Harbor, June 2, '64; bur. in Nat. Cem , Arlington.

Steel, Nicholas, disch. by Gen. Order, July 15, '65.

Steel, Ehud, mus out with Co. May 31, '65

Swart, James M., mus. out with Co. May 31, '65.

Scott, Simon P., mus. out with Co. May 31, '65.

Scott, Henry, mus. out with Co. May 31, '65.

Sprowls, Jesse, wd. at Spottsylvania, C. II., May 12, '64; absent at mus. out.

Strosnider, Caleb, disch. by Gen. Order, July 12, '65.

Sergeant, Richard, disch. March 10, '63.

Strosnider, Kener L., tr. to 169th Co., 2d Battl , V. R. C., Jan. 9, '65; disch by Gen. Order, July 3, '65.

Sanders, Harvey, tr. to Vet. Res. Corps. Sept. 1, '63.

Smith, Job, Jr., mus. in March 9, '64; missing in action at Spottsylvania, May 12, '64.

Simpson, John, mus in Feb. 27, 64; died Sept. 17 of wds. recd. in action, Aug 14, '64; bur. in Nat. Cem., Arlington, Va.

Steward, Jesse, died at Philadelphia, April 9, '65

Spragg, John M., killed at Mine Run, Nov. 29, '63.

Smith, Job, Sr., des. July 2, '63.

Taylor, Abner W., mus. out with Co. May 31, '65.

Taylor, Levi, tr. to Vet. Res. Corps. March 13, '65.

Troy, Norval L , mus. in Nov. 29, '62; died June 27 of wds. recd. at Tolopotomy, May 31, '64; bur. at Alexandria, grave 2,234.

Wilson, John R. H., mus. out with Co. May 31, '65.

Wilson, George W., mus out with Co. May 31, '65.

Wallace, Benjamin F., tr. to 51st Co. 2d Battl. V. R. C., Jan. 18, '65; disch. Sept 4, '65.

Walters, Brezan T. mus out with Co. May 31, '65.

Woolum, Harrison, disch. by Gen. Order, May 15, '65.

Wallace, Francis A., disch. on Surg. Cert. Oct. 12, '63.

West, Simon S , tr. to Independent Battery C, Pa., Art date
unknown.

Walters, Andrew J , mus. in Feb. 27, '64; died at Philadelphia,
July 4, of wds. recd. at Spottsylvania, C. H., May 12, '64.

Welsh, Morris, mus. in April 3, '65, des. May 15, '65.

CHAPTER XXX.

COMPANY K, FIFTEENTH CAVALRY, ONE HUNDRED AND SIXTIETH OF THE LINE.

BATTLE OF ANTIETAM—DISORGANIZED—SENT TO KENTUCKY—STONE
RIVER—REFUSAL TO ADVANCE—COLONEL PALMER RELEASED—
ORGANIZATION COMPLETED—BATTLE OF CHICKAMAUGA—ROSE-
CRANS SHUT UP BY BRAGG AT CHATTANOOGA—GRANT IN COMMAND
—VICTORY—ARMY RELIEVED—VALLEY OF THE FRENCH BROAD
—ORDERED TO NASHVILLE TO RECRUIT—NASHVILLE—PURSUIT OF
HOOD—PURSUIT OF DAVIS—CAPTURE OF BRAGG AND VAST SUMS
OF MONEY—MUSTERED OUT—INDIVIDUAL RECORD.

COMPANY K, of the 15th Cavalry, 160th of the line, was in part
recruited in Greene County. It was partially organized at Carlisle, in September, 1862; but before it was completed, and before the
company officers were selected, the regiment was ordered to the front
and participated in the Antietam campaign then in progress. Unfortunately, Colonel Palmer, who was looked to by the men to see
that suitable officers should be selected, was taken prisoner, and before further company organization was effected, the regiment was
ordered west to the army of Rosecrans, in Kentucky, and arrived
upon the eve of the battle of Stone River. Well knowing that the
regiment was in no condition to go into battle in its disorganized
state, without company officers, and wholly wanting in drill and discipline, all but three companies stacked arms and refused to obey the
order to advance. Majors Rosengarten and Ward, with about three
hundred men, went into the battle. The former officer was killed,
and the latter mortally wounded, and thirteen men were killed and
sixty-nine wounded and missing.

On the 7th of February, Colonel Palmer, having been released
from captivity, returned to the regiment and a complete organization

Isaac A. Morris

of the entire command was effected. On the 24th of June the army moved forward on the Chickamauga campaign, Companies B, H and K being detailed as escorts to General Rosecrans, and the balance of the regiment performing courier duty between the right and left wings of the army. By the disaster to the right wing, and the escape of Rosecrans to Chattanooga, and the final retreat of the army, it became hemmed in, and the animals, as well as men, were brought to a state bordering on starvation. Colonel Palmer was, accordingly, sent into the Sequatchie Valley, thirty miles away, where corn and provisions were found in abundance, and whence supplies were forwarded to Chattanooga. The arrival of Grant, and the battle of the 25th of November, wrought a marvelous change in the condition of the army, Bragg having been swept from before the place. Palmer was now sent with the Fifteenth to join Sherman in his relief of Knoxville, where Burnside was held by Longstreet. Upon its arrival it was sent against a party of whites and Indians approaching from North Carolina, and by skillful dispositions gained a complete triumph. In the active operations in the valley of the French Broad which succeeded, the regiment participated with credit. After Longstreet had put his army in winter quarters, brisk skirmishing ensued on the part of both armies, while engaged in foraging and gathering supplies, in which the Fifteenth gained much credit for its skillful operations, and its midnight descents upon the foe.

In May, 1864, the regiment was ordered to Nashville to recruit and remount. It was August before this was accomplished, and, on approaching the front, was kept busy in defending the communications of Sherman, now well on his way in the Atlanta campaign. After the fall of Atlanta, and Sherman had cut loose for his March to the Sea, the Fifteenth was ordered to the support of Thomas, at Nashville, in his operations against Hood, and when the latter had been routed and put to flight, the Fifteenth was put upon his track, and in the race which ensued, hung upon the rear and flanks of the retreating foe, despoiling him of material and trains so that his army was made powerless for further mischief. The operations were now largely confined, in the Western armies, to daring exploits of the cavalry, in which kind of warfare the men and officers of the Fifteenth had acquired great skill, and were very successful.

With fresh horses the cavalry started on the spring campaign of 1865, under General Stoneman. Its operations extended over portions of east Tennessee, western North Carolina, and northern Georgia, and finally when the news came of the surrender of Lee and Johnston, the Fifteenth was put upon the track of Jeff Davis. "On the morning of the 8th inst.," says General Palmer in his official report, "while searching for Davis near the fork of Appalachee and Oconee Rivers, Colonel Bett's Fifteenth Pennsylvania Cavalry captured

21

seven wagons in the woods, which contained $188,000 in coin, $1,-580,000 in bank notes, bonds, and securities and about $4,000,000 of Confederate money, besides considerable specie, plate, and other valuables belonging to private citizens of Macon. The wagons contained also the private baggage, maps and official papers of Generals Beauregard and Pillow. Two days after, Company G, Captain Samuel Phillips, captured General Bragg, his wife, staff officers and three wagons. On the 15th news was received of the capture of Davis and party by Colonel Pritchard, of the Fourth Michigan Cavalry, detachments from Colonel Bett's command being close upon his trail. The campaigning of the regiment was now at an end, and returning to Nashville on the 21st of June, it mustered out of service.

COMPANY K, ONE HUNDRED AND SIXTIETH REGIMENT, FIFTEENTH CAVALRY.

Recruited in Greene County, mustered in Aug. 30, 1862.

Jacob R. Hewitt, Capt., mus. in Nov. 31. '60; pr. fr. private Anderson Troop, Oct. 10, '62; resigned Feb. 27, '63.

Abraham B. Garner, Capt., mus. in Oct. 3, '62; pr. fr. 1st Sergt. May 8, '63, to Maj., March 13, '65; mus. out with Regt. June 21, '65.

Charles E. Scheide, Capt., mus. in Oct. 3, '62; pr. fr. Adj. March 13, '65; mus. out with Co. June 21, '65.

Frank E. Remont, 1st Lieut., mus. in Aug. 22, '62; pr. fr. Sergt. Co. C, May 8, '63; to Capt., Co. I, Aug. 15, '64; mus. out with Co. June 21, '65.

Nathaniel M. Sample, 1st Lieut., mus. in Oct. 3, '62; pr. fr. private to Q. M. Sergt. March 1, '63; to 1st Sergt. March 16, '64; to 1st Lieut. Nov. 8, '64; mus. out with Co. June 21, '65.

Michael M. Musser, 1st Sergt., mus. in Oct. 3, '62; pr. to Corp. March 1, '63; to Sergt. May 16, '63; to 1st Sergt. Jan. 1, '65; com. 2d Lieut. May 20, '65; not mus.; mus. out June 21, '65.

W. W. Blackmar, 1st Sergt. mus. in Aug. 30, '62; pr. fr. Corp. to Sergt. March 1, '63; to 1st Sergt. May 5, '63; to Lieut. 1st Regt. W. Va. Cav. March 18, '64; disch. as Capt. July 8, '65.

Theophilus H. Smith, Q. M. Sergt., pr. to Corp. Jan. 4, '63; to Q. M. Sergt. March 16, '64; mus. out with Co. June 21, '65.

J. Lingerfield, Jr., Com. Sergt., mus. in Oct. 3, '62; pr. fr. private March 1, '63; mus. out June 21, '65.

John C. Wilson, Sergt., mus. in Oct. 3, '62; pr. to Corp. Oct. 30, '62; to Sergt. March 1, '63; mus. out June 21, '65.

James Agnew, Sergt., mus. in Oct. 3, '62; pr. to Corp. March 1, '63; to Sergt. May 15, '63; mus. out June 21, '65.

Jacob H. Isett, Sergt., mus. in Oct. 3, '62; pr. to Corp. Oct. 30, '62; to Sergt. Feb. 5, '65; mus. out June 21, '65.

James H. Shertz, Sergt., mus. in Oct. 3, '62; pr. to Corp. May 15, '63; to Sergt. Feb 5, '65; mus. out June 21, '65.

Jacob Wentzler, Sergt , pr. to Corp. Nov. 29, '64; to Sergt. March 16, '65; mus. out June 21, '65.

Henry C. Potts, Sergt., mus. in Oct. 3, '62; pr. fr. Corp. Co. L, March 1, '63; disch. March 15, '63.

Sealy S. Byard, Sergt., pr. fr. Sergt. Oct 30, '62; disch. on Surg. Cert Feb. 27, '63.

William H Small, Corp , pr. to Corp. April 1, '64; mus out June 21, '65.

James A. Kenney, Corp , mus. in Sept. 6, '62; pr. to Corp. Feb. 5, '64; mus. out June 21, '65.

Alexander H. Robinson, Corp , mus. in Oct. 3, '62; pr to Corp. Feb. 5, '65; mus. out June 21, '65.

Benjamin Bartram, Corp., mus. in Oct. 3, '62; pr. to Corp. Feb. 5, '65; mus. out June 21, '65

Joseph Copeland, Corp., mus. in Sept. 6, '62; pr. to Corp. March 15, '65; mus. out June 21, '65.

Jacob W. Miller, Corp., mus in Oct. 10, '62; pr. to Corp. March 15, '65; mus. out June 21, '65.

Nathaniel B. Briggs, Corp., pr. to Corp. March 15, '65; mus. out June 21, '65.

John P. Gemmill, Corp., pr. to Corp. May 15, '65; died at Chattanooga Dec. 24, '63.

William M. Murdock, Bugler, mus. in Oct 3, '62; mus. out June 21, '65

George W. Wright, Bugler, mus. in Oct. 3, '62; mus. out June 21, '65.

Jere. K. Parshall, Blacksmith, mus in Oct. '62; disch. on Surg Cert. Jan 15, '63.

William McGee, Saddler, pr. to regimental saddler, March 1, '63

Askwith, John D , mus. in Sept. 28, '64; mus. out with Co. June 21, '65

Adamson, John, tr. to Co. I, date unknown.

Arvecost, Joseph, mus. in Oct. 3, '62; tr. to Co. C., date unknown.

Burke, Joseph R., mus in Oct 3, '62; mus. out with Co. June 21, '65.

Beck, Henry L , mus in Aug 30, '62; tr. to U. S Army Oct 30, '62

Burson, David F , mus. in Aug. 30, '62; disch. on Surg. Cert. Feb 23, '63.

Burchinell, Wm K., mus in Oct 3, '62; tr. to Signal Corps Oct 27, '63.

Burns, Andrew S , mus. in Aug. 18, '64; tr. to Co. A, June 21, '65.

Barnett, James P., died at Carlisle, Pa., Nov. 18, '62.

Brooks, William, died at Lavergne, Tenn , Jan. 5, '63, of wds rec'd in action.

Bell, Joseph, tr. to Co B, date unknown.

Bell, John H., tr to Co. I, date unknown.

Brown, John E., mus in Oct. 3, 62; tr to Co. F, date unknown.

Bond, Edward, mus in Oct. 10, '62; tr to Co H, date unknown

Beitz, Augustus O , mus. in Aug. 6, '64, not on mus. out roll

Campbell, William P , mus in Oct 3, '62; mus. out with Co. June 21, '65

Cleverstone, Daniel, mus. in Sept 24, '64; mus. out with Co. June 21, '65

Clark, Adrian S., mus out with Co. June 21, '65

Carr, Charles, mus. in Oct. 10, '62; disch on Surg Cert. Aug. 6, '63.

Clark, Edward B , disch. on Surg. Cert. March 3, '63.

Cholette, Cor. M., tr to U. S Army Oct 30, '62.

Cover, Michael, mus. in June 4, '64; tr. to Co. A June 21, '65.

Crawford, Edwin E., died in Nashville, Tenn., Feb. 12, '63; bur. in Nat. Cem.

Conner, William B , died in Nashville, Tenn., Feb. 3, '63; bur Nat. Cem Sec B , grave 1,177.

Cotterel, William, mus. in Oct. 3, '62; tr. to Co. G, date unknown.

Cumston, John, mus. in Oct. 10, '62; tr to Co. E, date unknown.

Chambers, William H , mus. in Oct. 10, '62, tr. to Co H., date unknown

Cotterel, Jonas, mus. in Aug. 30, '62; tr to Co. M.

Duer, Florence, mus. in Sept. 23, '64; disch by Gen. Order, June 24, '65

Dye, William L, disch. by Gen. Order, June 24, '65.

Denney, Clark, mus. in Oct. 3, '62; tr. to Co. I, date unknown.

Drake, Alexander S., mus. in Oct. 10, '62; died at Nashville, Tenn , Dec. 31, '62; bur in Nat. Cem., Sec. B, grave 88:

Evaus, Benjamin B., tr to Co. F, date unknown.

Estle, Daniel L , tr. to Co. I, date unknown

Farrer, John G , mus. out with Co. June 21, '65.

Faas, John, mus. in Sept. 10, '64; mus. out with Co June 21, '65

Fisher, David F , mus. in Sept. 19, '64, mus out with Co. I, June 21, '65.

Fullerton, Bryam M , mus in Aug. 20, '64; mus out with Co. June 21, '65

Frankenberry, A. D., tr. to Signal Corps Oct. 27, '63.

Filbey, Barton E., mus. in Oct. 3, '62; des. Dec. 8, '62.

Goshline, Nelson, mus. out with Co. June 21, '65.

Gibbons, Anthony J., mus. in Sept. 25, '64; prisoner from April 12 to 30, '65; disch. June 20, '65; to date May 18, '65.

Grim, David, mus. in Sept. 19, '64; mus. out with Co. June 21, '65.

Griffin, Samuel C., mus. in Jan. 27, '64; tr. to Co. A, June 21, '65.

Gass, Samuel W , mus. in Oct. 3, '62; tr. to Co. F, date unknown.

Grim, William, mus. in Oct. 3, '62; tr. to Co D, date unknown.

Grim, Lycurgus, mus in Aug. 30, '62; tr. to Co. E, date unknown.

Househalter, Philip, mus. in Sept. 22, 64; mus. out with Co. June 21, '65.

Himes, John, mus. in Oct. 3, '63; mus. out with Co. June 21, '65.

Howard, George W., mus. in Sept 6, '62; pr. to 2d Lieut., 4th Regt. U. S. Col. Art., April 5, 65; mus. out Feb. 25, '66.

Heiter, Joseph J., mus. in March 24, '64; tr. to Co. A, June 21, '65.

Hoke, George N., mus. in Sept. 6, '62; died at Murfreesboro, Tenn., April 2, '63; bur. in Nat. Cem. Stone River.

Hawkins, A. LeRoy, mus. in Aug. 30, '62; tr. Co. I, date unknown.

Hewitt, Jacob, mus. in. Aug. 30, '62; tr. to Co F, date unknown.

Hewitt, Eli, mus. in Oct. 3, '62; tr. to Co. B, date unknown.

Hewitt, Samuel, mus. in Oct. 10, '62; tr. to Co. H, date unknown.

Houlsworth, James, mus. in Oct. 3, '62; tr. to Co G, date unknown.

Houston, Samuel, mus. in Oct 3, '62; tr. to Co H, date unknown.

Houston, Joseph, mus. in Oct. 3, '62; tr. to Co. H, date unknown.

Hartzell, Edwin, mus. in Aug. 30, '62; tr. to Co. I, date unknown.

Hartley, John M., mus. in Aug. 30, '62; tr. to Co. D, date unknown.

Hughes, James, mus. in Oct. 29, '64; not on mus out roll.

Johns, Albert M., mus. in Aug. 30, '62; disch. on Surg. Cert. Oct. 12, '63.

Johnstone, Valentine, mus. in Aug. 8, '64; tr. to Co. A, June 21, '65

Jamison, Wilbur T., mus. in Oct. 3, '62; tr. to Co. H, date unknown.

Jameson, John A., mus. in Oct. 3, '62; tr. to Co. F, date unknown

Jordan, Robert H., mus. in Oct. 3, '62; tr. to Co H, date unknown.

Kimmel, Jacob, mus. in Oct. 10, '62; mus. out with Co. June 21, '65.

Kinney, Eaton, mus. in Oct. 3, '62; dis. on Surg Cert. Feb. 23, '63.

Ketchem, John, mus. in Aug. 30, '62; tr. to Co. F, date unknown.

Keys, Cory M , mus. in Oct. 3, '62; tr. to Co. G, date unknown.

Kincaid, Robert, mus. in Oct. 3, '62; tr. to Co. H, date unknown.

Kent, James, mus. in Oct. 10, '62; tr. to Co. E, date unknown.

Krouse, Enos, mus. in Oct. 3, '62; not on mus. out roll.

Lamoreux, E. B., mus. in Aug. 8, '64; mus. out with Co. June 21, '65.

Leas, William H., mus in Sept. 22, '64; disch. by Gen Order, June 9, '65

Lippincott, W. H., mus in Sept 27, '64; mus. out with Co. June 21, '65.

Lundy, William, mus. in Aug. 30, '64; tr to Co. D, date unknown.

Lewis, Josiah, mus. in Oct. 3, '64; tr to Co. G, date unknown.

Mehl, Edwin M., mus. in Aug. 22, '64; mus. out with Co June 21, '65.

Metzler, John C., mus. in Aug. 22, '64; mus. out with Co. June 21, '65.

Miller, C. G. Jr., mus. in Aug. 22, '64; mus. out with Co. June 21, '65.

Mills, Edward L., mus. in Oct. 19, '62; mus. out with Co. June 21, '65.

Moyer, James H., mus. in Oct 3, '62; mus. out with Co. June 21, 62.

Morrow, William H., mus. in Oct. 3, '62; disch on Serg. Cert. April 28, '63.

Myers, Alpheus, mus. in Aug. 30, '62; disch on Surg Cert. Feb. 25, '63

Moore, Jacob B , mus in Oct. 3, '62; tr to Signal Corps, Oct 27, '63.

Marcus, William, mus. in March 21, '64, tr to Co. A, June 21, '65

Morony, Matthew, mus. in March 11, '64; tr to Co. A, June 21, '65.

Minor, Andrew J., mus. in Aug. 30, '62; tr. to Co. H, date unknown.

Murdock, Wm. B., mus in Oct 3, '62; tr. to Co. G, date unknown

Milligan Samuel, mus. in Oct. 3, 62; tr. to Co. G, date unknown

Milligan, James H , mus. in Oct 3, '62; tr. to Co. G, date unknown.

Milligan, Jonas, mus. in Oct. 3, '62; tr to Co. I, date unknown

Milligan, Edward, mus. in Oct. 3, '62; tr to Co. I, date unknown

Messenger, James, mus. in Oct 10, '62; tr. to Co. B, date unknown.

Murdock, John, mus. in Aug. 30, '62; mus. out with Co. June 21, '65.

McNay, Jasper P., mus. in Aug. 30, '62; mus. out with Co. June 21, '65.

McClain, William, mus. in ——— ——— tr. to Co. A, June 21, '65.

McGovern, Thomas, mus. in Aug. 30, '62; died at Nashville, Tenn., Jan. 22, '63; bur. in Nat. Cem. section E, grave 2,089.

McNay, Newton B., mus. in Aug. 30, '62; tr. to Co. H, date unknown.

McCormick, James, mus. in Oct. 3, '62; tr. to Co. F, date unknown.

McCarty, Boyd J., mus. in Oct. 10, '62; tr. to Co. G, date unknown.

McGlumphey, J. B., mus. in Oct. 3, '62; tr. to Co. D, date unknown.

Newman, Wm. H., mus. in Sept. 6, '62; prisoner from May 2 to May 16, '65; disch. June 16, to date, May 21, '65.

Norman, S. H., mus. in Aug. 22, '62; pr. to 2d Lieut. Co. B, 184th Regt. P. V. April 29, '64.

Nichols, Thomas M., mus. in Oct. 3, '62; disch. on Surg. Cert. Feb. 8, '63.

Newbecker, P. C., mus. in Aug 22, '62; tr. to Vet. Res. Corps Aug. 1, '63; disch. by Gen. Order July 5, '65.

Nichols, Erasmus, mus. in Oct. 3, '62; des. Dec. 8, '62.

Pierce, Joseph K., mus. in Aug. 22, '62; disch. by Gen. Order May 29, '65.

Pratt, Ingram, mus. in Aug. 30, '62; died at Nashville, Tenn., Feb. 8, '63; bur. in Nat. Cem., section B, grave 1,104.

Pyles, James M., mus. in Aug. 30, '62; tr. to Co. H, date unknown.

Phillips, John W., mus in Oct. 2, '62; tr. to Co. G, date unknown.

Robertson, John, mus. in Sept. 6, '62; mus. out with Co. June 21, '65.

Rull, William, mus. in Aug. 22, '62; mus. out with Co. June 21, '65.

Ross, Jacob, mus. in Aug. 22, '62; disch. on Surg. Cert. April 4, '65.

Reynolds, Jacob A., mus. in Aug. 30, '62; disch. March 10, '63.

Ransom, George P., mus in Aug. 8, '64; died at Nashville, Tenn., May 26, '65; bur. in Nat. Cem., section 1, grave 1,126.

Riggle, Amos, mus. in Aug. 30, '62; des. Feb. 19, '63

Reynolds, John B., mus. in Sept. 6, '62; des. March 1, '63.

Ross, David D., mus in Oct. 3, '62; tr. to Co F, date unknown.

Richey, James L., mus. in Aug. 30, '62; tr. to Co H, date unknown.

Rex, John, mus. in Aug. 30, '62; tr. to Co. C, date unknown.

Rinehart, Bennett, mus. in Oct. 3, '62; tr. to Co B, date unknown.

Ritchie, Clement, mus. in Aug 30, '62; tr. to Co. B, date unknown.

Sawyers, John W., mus. in Sept. 15, '64; mus. out with Co. June 21, '65.

Schrader, Anthony, mus. in Sept. 12, '64, mus. out with Co. June 21, '65

Shoaf, Daniel, mus. in Aug. 19, '64; mus. out with Co. June 21, '65.

Sullivan, William, mus. in Aug. 21, '64; mus. out with Co. June 21, '65.

Sunday, John, mus. in Oct. 10, '62; mus. out. with Co. June 21, '65.

Struble, Lot J , mus. in Aug. 30, '62; mus. out with Co. June 21, '65.

Sharps, Charles T., mus in Oct 3, '62; disch on Surg. Cert. April 29, '63.

Steel, William, mus. in Aug. 30, '62; tr. to U. S. Army, Oct. 30, '62.

Shaffer, William G., mus. in Aug. 22, '62; tr. to Vet. Res. Corps, Sept. 30, '63.

Supplee, Henderson, mus. in Aug 22, '62; tr. to Vet Res. Corps, April 30, '64.

Smith, John, mus. in Oct 17, '64; tr. to Co. A, June 21, '65.

Smith, William, mus. in June 18, '64; tr. to Co. A, June 21, '65,

Stees, Thomas W., mus. in Oct. 10, 62; died at Murfreesboro. Tenn., June 2, '63

Stevenson, Alfred, mus. in Aug. 30, '62; tr. to Co. F; date unknown

Stone, George E., mus. in Aug 30, '62; tr. to Co.; I date unknown.

Sproat, Timothy R., mus. in Aug 30, '62; tr. to Co B; date unknown.

Smith, William P., mus. in Aug. 30, '62; tr. to Co. F; date unknown.

Sayers, Harry E., mus. in Aug. 30, '62; tr. to Co. G; date unknown.

Shirk, Michael M., mus. in Aug. 30, '62; tr. to Co G; date unknown.

Shope, Milton S., mus in Oct. 3, 62; tr. to Co. G, date unknown.

Strosnider, William M., mus. in Aug. 30, '62; not on mus. out roll.

Thornlee, James W., mus. in Aug. 22, '62; des. March 1, 63

Thomas, Joshua, mus. in Aug. 30, '62; died at Nashville, Tenn., March 4, '63; bur. in Nat Cem., Section E, grave 816.

Turner, Abel, mus. in Aug. 30, '62, tr. to Co. II; date unknown.

Turner, Josiah P., mus. in Aug. 30, '62; tr. to Co. D; date unknown.

Thomas, Francis M., mus. in Aug. 30, '62; tr. to Co. M; date unknown.

Walter, John, mus. in Aug. 30, '62; disch by Gen. Order, July 5, '65

Watts, Wilbur, mus. in Oct. 10, '62; mus. out with Co. June 21, '65.

Weatherby, J. C., Jr., mus. in Aug. 22, 62; mus. out with Co. June 21, '65.

Wagner, Augustus D., mus. in Oct. 10, 62; disch. on Surg. Cert. Oct. 31, '63.

Wilson, Charles T., mus. in Oct. 3, '62; disch on Surg. Cert. July 30, '63

Wilson, William, mus. in Aug. 22, '62; disch. for promotion Feb 28, '65.

Williams, Edward P., mus. in Oct. 10, '62; disch. by Gen. Order, May 31, '65.

Wood, Edward W., mus. in Aug. 30, '62; tr. to Co. C; date unknown.

Waychuff, John D , mus. in Oct. 3, '62; tr. to Co. F; date unknown. .

White, David C , mus. in Aug. 30, '62; tr. to Co. F; date unknown.

Wiser, Angelo, mus. in Aug. 30, '62; tr. to Co. II, date unknown.

Worthington, R., mus. in Aug. 30, '62; tr, to Co. F; date unknown.

Wiley, James M., mus. in Aug. 22, '62; tr. to Co M; date unknown.

Zell, John M., mus. in Aug. 22, '62; mus. out with Co. June 21, '65.

21*

CHAPTER XXXI.

COMPANIES A, C, AND G, EIGHTEENTH CAVALRY, ONE HUNDRED AND
SIXTY-THIRD OF THE LINE.

ORGANIZATION — MOSBY'S GUERRILLAS — HANOVER — GETTYSBURG —
ROUND TOP—PURSUIT OF TRAINS—BRANDY STATION AND UPPER-
VILLE—RAID TO RICHMOND—WILDERNESS—YELLOW TAVERN—.
HANOVER COURT HOUSE—ASHLAND—ST. MARY'S CHURCH—
WELDON RAILROAD—SPENCER RIFLES—WINCHESTER—CEDAR
CREEK—MUSTERED OUT—INDIVIDUAL RECORDS.

THE One Hundred and Sixty-third regiment, of which Companies A,
C, and G, were recruited in Greene County, was organized early
in February, 1862, at camp near Fairfax Court House, with the following field officers, viz.: Timothy M. Bryan, Jr., Colonel; James
Gowan, Lieutenant-Colonel; Joseph Gilmore, William B. Darlington
and Henry B. Van Voorhis, Majors; and was brigaded with Fifth
New York and First Vermont Cavalry, under command of Col. Percy
Wyndham. Here the regiment was pitted against Mosby's guerrillas,
citizens by day and soldiers by night. Being indifferently armed,
the duty was anything but pride-exciting to a soldier. Early in the
spring of 1862 William P. Brinton was made Lieutenant-Colonel in
place of Lieut. Col. Gowan, who was honorably discharged, and the
brigade was associated with a brigade of Michigan troops under
Gen. Custer, the division being in command of Gen. Julius Stahel.
Before entering upon the Gettysburg campaign Gen. Stahel was
superceded by Gen. Kilpatrick, and the division became the Third of
the Cavalry corps of the army of the Potomac.

Proceeding northward, Kilpatrick was sent in search of the rebel
Gen. Stuart, who, since his defeat at Upperville, had been separated
from the main body of Lee's army, and was known to be pushing on
through Pennsylvania, while Lee himself was moving up the Cumberland Valley, the South Mountain intervening. Kilpatrick's
column had already passed Hanover, and the Eighteenth Pennsylvania, which was of the rear guard, was resting in the streets of that
village, when the head of Stuart's column came up and immediately
attacked. Kilpatrick formed on the hills to the south of the town,
while the enemy ranged along the heights to the north. Artillery
firing and skirmishing was kept up until nightfall, when Stuart with-

drew and pursued his journey northward, being thus prevented, by the stubborn front presented by Kilpatrick, from joining Lee at Gettysburg, where he was so much needed in the progress of the battle. The division came up with the enemy's extreme left, at Gettysburg, on the 2d of July, where some skirmishing occurred, and at evening moved to the extreme left of the Union Line, beyond Round Top. Towards evening of the 3d, the First Brigade, led by Col. Farnsworth, was ordered to charge, and gallantly drove the enemy in upon his fortified line behind stone-walls and rocky-wooded heights. The commander, Col. Farnsworth, was killed and several men in the Eighteenth were wounded.

Scarcely was the rebel army withdrawn from the Gettysburg field, before Kilpatrick was upon its track, and struck Ewell's wagon train near Monterey Springs, on its way across South Mountain. Kilpatrick promptly charged, and having scattered the train guard, captured two pieces of artillery, a thousand prisoners, and two hundred wagons and ambulances. At break-neck speed he drove down the mountain, to escape the head of Lee's infantry, which was making a forced march for a crossing of the Potomac. At Smithfield the captured wagons were burned, and the prisoners delivered to the column of Gen. French, at Boonesboro. At Hagerstown, where the rebel infantry had arrived, two batallions of the Eighteenth, led by Captains William C. Lindsey and John W. Phillips, under command of Lieut. Col. Brinton, charged. From shelter in the narrow streets and alleys the enemy kept up a hot fire, even the women joining in the fusilade, while the cavalry only used their sabres, and consequently suffered severely. Capt. Lindsey was killed, as was also the color-bearer, Thomas Eagon, and Benal Jewel, of Company G.

After the escape of Lee across the Potomac, the Union army leisurely followed, "and during the fall and early winter the regiment was actively engaged in scouting and skirmishing, meeting the enemy at Brandy Station and at Culpepper on the 18th of September; on the 11th of October, again near Brandy Station, where the Eighteenth charged a force of the enemy following from Culpepper, and lost its commander, Major Van Voorhis, three lieutenants and fifty men, by capture; on the 13th at Buckland Mills and New Baltimore; on the 18th of November, in a scout across the Rapidan, where the camp equipage, regimental colors, and camp guard, including a number of officers and men, were captured, and Lieut. Roseberry Sellers was killed; and on the 6th of December went into winter quarters near Stevensburg." On the 28th of February the Eighteenth started with Kilpatrick on his raid upon Richmond, for the delivery of Union prisoners. Though unsuccessful in the main object of the campaign, the troops behaved with gallantry, and Dahlgreen, who led a division, was killed. Gen. Wilson now succeeded

Kilpatrick in command of the division, and Col. McIntosh was placed over the brigade.

On the opening of the spring campaign of 1864, now under Grant, The Eighteenth encountered the head of Longstreet's corps on the Plank Road. Brisk fighting immediately commenced, and in the progress the Eighteenth was cut off and apparently surrounded; but by a desperate break at an unguarded point, at a dense pine thicket and swamp supposed to be impenetrable, the command was brought off, though reported captured. The loss was one officer and thirty-nine men in killed, wounded and captured.

On the 9th of May the regiment, with the main body of Sheridan's command, moved around the right of the flank of Lee's army and struck boldly out towards Richmond. In this exciting and difficult march, where the enemy sprang up on all sides, and greatly harrassed and impeded its course, the regiment participated, being engaged on the 11th at Yellow Tavern, on the 12th at Richmond, and, finally, on the 16th, reached Haxall's landing on the James. After a few days rest, Sheridan returned and rejoined Grant near the South Anna. At Hanover Court House the Eighteenth Pennsylvania, supported by the Second Ohio, was ordered to charge and clear the town. At twilight the charge was made, dismounted, and though opposed by vastly superior numbers, well covered with breastworks, was driven in utter rout and confusion, and many prisoners were taken. Lieut.-Col. Brinton and Major Phillips, who led the charge, were both slightly, and Captains M. S. Kingsland and David Hamilton, severely wounded. The enemy was again met at Ashland, and severe fighting ensued. At St. Mary's Church the enemy's infantry was again met, and for five hours was held at bay, the regiment losing thirty-three in killed, wounded and missing, Lieuts. Tresonthick and McCormick being mortally wounded.

In conjunction with the Third New Jersey, the regiment was detached from the division and ordered to duty with Gen. Wright, of the Sixth Corps, and was employed in picketing a line of nearly five miles, on his left flank. On the 23rd of June, the regiment, supported by a few sharpshooters, drove the enemy from the Weldon Railroad, at Yellow House.

In August Sheridan was sent to the Shenandoah Valley, with two divisions of cavalry, to confront the rebel general Early, the Eighteenth being included. At Washington the regiment was armed with Spencer repeating rifles. At Winchester, and Summit Station, at Charlestown, and Leetown, it was actively employed in holding the rebel column in check, and on the 19th of September occurred the memorable battle of Winchester. "With the Fifth and Second New York deployed as skirmishers, the Eighteenth was ordered to charge. The Third Battalion had the advance, and dashing forward, drove the enemy from his works and into a wood beyond, from which it was in turn repulsed by a rapid fire. But at this juncture the main body of the regiment came up, led by Colonel Brinton, and drove the enemy for half a mile, and, aided by the rest of the brigade, held this commanding position until Sheridan's infantry came to his relief. Colonel Brinton, after having his horse twice shot, and his clothing riddled with bullets, finally fell into the enemy's hands" In the general assault, which was delivered in the afternoon, it participated and shared in the glories of the decisive triumph. In the pursuit of the enemy up the valley frequent heavy skirmishing ensued. On the 8th of October the command moved towards Cedar Creek, the Eighteenth acting as rear guard and suffering from frequent and severe attacks of the enemy. On the following day the division assumed the offensive, and swept forward with resistless power, driving the enemy, under Rosser, in confusion, capturing all his artillery, six pieces, and his entire ambulance and wagon train.

In the battle of Cedar Creek the regiment was engaged from early dawn until evening, when it participated with the brigade in a brilliant charge, which closed the struggle and swept from the enemy's grasp his guns and trains. This single brigade was accredited with the capture of forty-five pieces. At Cedar Creek, on the 12th of November, the division again met the enemy and drove him three miles, and soon after went into winter quarters near Harper's Ferry. The regiment subsequently participated in the descent upon Waynesboro, whereby the remnants of Early's army were captured, and with the Fifth New York Cavalry was detailed to conduct the prisoners taken, amounting to fifteen hundred, back to Winchester. On the way General Rosser repeatedly attacked, counting confidently on the release of the prisoners, but was foiled in every attempt, and the prisoners were all safely delivered to the commanders at Winchester. This virtually closed the active campaigning of the regiment, and after consolidation with the Twenty-second Cavalry was finally mustered out on the 31st of October, 1865.

COMPANY A, ONE HUNDRED AND SIXTY-THIRD REGIMENT, EIGHTEENTH CAVALRY.

Recruited in Greene County, mustered in November 21, 1862.

William C. Lindsey, Captain, killed at Hagerstown, Maryland, July 6, '63.

Guy Brian, Jr., mus. in June 12, '63; pr. fr. Adj. May 18, '65; mus. out with Co. B, 3d Reg. Prov. Cav., Oct 31, '65.

James P. Cosgrey, 1st Lieut, resigned May 1, '63

Benjamin F. Campbell, 1st Lieut., pr fr 2d Lieut. May 9, '63; disch Feb. 10, '64

George E Newlin, 1st Lieut. mus in April 7, '64; mus. out with Co. B, 3d Reg. Prov. Cav, Oct. 31, '65

Roseberry Sellers, 2d Lieut, mus. in Aug. 29, '62; pr fr. 1st Sergt. May 9, '63; killed at Germania Ford, Nov 18, '63.

William Scott, 2d Lieut., pr. fr. Sergt Co. G, Jan. 2, '65, mus. out with Co. B, 3d Reg Prov. Cav., Oct. 31, '65

Benj W. Yoders, 1st Sergt, disch by Gen. Order, July 11, '65.

John B Gordon, 1st Sergt., died at Washington, D C, Dec. 5, '64; bur in Mil. Asylum Cemetery

John C White, Com. Sgt, mus. in Feb 23, '64; mus. out with Co B, 3d Reg. Prov. Cav, Oct 31, '65

Joseph Cooke, Com. Sgt, prisoner from June 10 to Dec. 31, '64 disch. by Gen Order, July 11, '65.

Benjamin F. Herrington, Com Sgt., mus. in Aug. 23, '62; pr. to 2d Lieut Co. G, Dec. 8, '62

George W. Kent, Sergt., mus out with Co. B, 3d Reg, Prov. Cav. Oct. 31, '65

Edward Francke, Sergt, mus. in Feb 17, 64; mus. out with Co. B, 3d Reg, Prov Cav. Oct 31, '65.

William J. Holt, Sergt., mus. in Feb 29, '64; wd. near Petersburg, June 27, '64, mus. out with Co. B, 3d Reg, Prov Cav. Oct. 31, '65.

John R Smith, Sergt., disch. by Gen. Order, July 10, '65,

James Graham, Sergt., mus. in Sept. 22, '62, wd. at Spottsylvania, May 8, '64; disch on Surg. Cert May 18, '65.

Jacob Whipkey, Sergt, mus. in Aug. 23, '62, tr. date and org. unknown

William D Smith, Sergt. Nov. 21, '62; died Sept. 29, '64

Cyrus C. Elms, Sergt, mus in April 6, '65; des. Sept. 10, '65

Thomas L. Dagg, Corp mus in March 11, '64; mus. out with Co. B, 3d Regt, Prov Cav. Oct 31, '65.

James Seals, Corp., mus in March 9, '64; mus. out with Co. B, 3d Regt. Prov Cav, Oct 31, '65

Kendal Brant, Corp., mus. in Sept. 10, '62; disch. March 26, '63.

Jonas Whipkey, Corp., mus. in Aug 23, '62; disch by Gen. Order, June 12, '65

Robert M Yates, Corp, mus in Nov. 23, '62; disch., date unknown.

Robert J. Tukesberry, Corp, disch by Gen. Order, July 11, '65.

John Evans, Corp., prisoner fr June 30 to Oct. 9, '63; disch by Gen Order, July 11, '65.

Salatial Murphy, Corp, disch. by Gen. Order, July 11, '65.

George K. Wiscarver, Corp., mus. in Oct. 27, '62; tr , date and org. unknown.

John T. Morris, Corp ; cap ; died at Andersonville, Ga , June 26, '64; grave 2,508.

Henry Cook, Corp., killed at Opequan, Va., Sept 19, '64.

John Boylan, Corp., March 31, '65, des. Sept 10, '65

Samuel S. Rhinehart, Corp., mus in Aug. 23, '62; died March 10, '65; bur. in U. S. Gen. Hosp Cem , No. 2, Annapolis, Md.

Andrew Wilson, Jr., Bugler, died at Washington, D. C., April 1, of wds. rec'd in action Jan. 18, '64; bur. in Mil. Asylum Cem.

Charles White, Bugler, mus. in Feb. 25, '64; mus. out with Co. H, 3d Reg., Prov. Cav. Oct. 31, '65.

Frederick Ramer, blacksmith, disch by Gen. Order, July 11, '65.

Everly L. Dow, blacksmith, disch. by Gen. Order, July 11, '65.

Warren Kneel, blacksmith, disch by Gen. Order, July 11, '65.

Lewis Perry, saddler, disch. by Gen. Order, July, '65.

Adams, Elijah, mus. in Feb 29, '64; mus. out with Co B, 3d Reg , Prov. Cav , Oct. 31, '65.

Adams, Richard L., mus. in Feb. 23, '64; disch. by Gen. Order, Sept. 16, '65.

Ammonds, John, absent at mus. out.

Adams, Jacob, mus in Feb. 23, '64; died Oct. 6, '64.

Anderson, William, mus. in March 31, '65; not acct for.

Boyers, George W., disch. by Gen. Order, July 11, '65.

Bryner, William A., pris. fr. July 6, '63, to Dec. 8, '64; disch by Gen. Order, July 11, '65.

Bryner, George W., mus. in Oct. 27, '62; disch by Gen. Order, June 5, '65. .

Brandymore, Mort., mus. in March 31, '65; disch. by Gen. Order, July 12, '65

Courtright, James, mus. out with Co B, 3d Reg., Pro. Cav., Oct. 31, '65.

Campbell, W T. H., mus. in April 1, '65; mus. out with Co. B, 3d Reg., Pro. Cav., Oct. 31, '65.

Concklin, S. M., abst. at mus. out.

Cole, William, disch by Gen. Order, July 11, '65.

Cooley, Joseph B , mus. Sept. 9, 64; disch. by Gen. Order, June 13, '65.

Church, William, mus. in March 29, '65; disch by Gen. Order, June 10, '65.

Chapman, George, cap., died at Andersonville, Ga., Sept. 9, '64; grave 8,260.

Chapman, Charles, mus. in April 22, '64; not acct. for.'

Champ, Charles, mus in April 20, '64; not acct. for.

Dickinson, William, mus Sept. 8, '62; tr , org. unknown; Jan 21, '65.

Davis, Henry, mus. in April 22, '64; not acct for.

Eckoff, Charles V., mus. in Feb. 29, '64; disch., dis. Oct. 13, '66.

Evans, Azariah, disch. by Gen. Order, July 11, '65

Eagon, Solomon, disch. by Gen Order, July 11, '65.

Evans, Caleb, pris. from Nov 18, '63, to April 11, '64; disch. by Gen. Order, July 11, '65.

Eagon, Thomas, killed at Hagerstown, Md., July 6, '63.

Edwards, Thomas W , mus. in March 21, '65, disch. by Gen. Order, Sept 20, '65

Fox, James F., mus. in March 31, '65; mus. out with Co B, 3d Regt., Prov. Cav , Oct. 21, '65

Finnegan, John, disch by Gen Order, July 11, '65.

Fry, John, disch by Gen. Order, July 11, '65.

Friend, Michael, mus in March 30, '65, not acct for.

Grey, Elijah, mus in March 31, '65, mus. out with Co. B, 3d Reg., Prov. Cav , Oct 31, '65

Goodwin, Frank, mus in May 21, '63; pr to Hospt. Steward U. S. Army, March 28, '64

Gallatin, Joseph R , mus in Nov. 11, '62; disch by Gen. Order, July 11, '65

Gardner, Freeman, mus in Nov. 11, '62, disch. by Gen. Order July 11, '65.

Goff, Mott W., mus in March 31, '64; disch by Gen. Order, May 13, '65.

Gumph, John, disch. by Gen Order, July 18, '65

Gribben, Peter, mus. in Aug. 23, '62, wd. at Old Church, Va , June 11, '64; disch by Gen Order, July 5, '65

Galloway, Nicholas, mus in July 19,,'63; des Oct. '65

Gribben, Elias K , mus in Aug. 23, '63, not on mus out roll.

Hacket, William, mus in Feb. 29, '64, absent at mus. out.

Hendershot, Thomas F , mus in Aug 29, '64, captured at Fisher's Hill, Va., Oct. 8, '64; bur. rec., J Hendershot died at Richmond, Va , Feb. 3, '65

Harrison, Moses, disch. by Gen Order, July 11, '65.

Huffman, James, dischg by Gen. Order, July 11, '65

Hughes, David, mus. in March 23, '64; dischg. by Gen. Order, June 19, '65.

Hedge, Samuel, mus. in Sept. 16, '64; dischg by Gen. Order, June 13, '65.

Hinerman, Henry, mus in Sept 4, '62; died, date unknown

Johns, Ellis J , wd. at Opequan, Va , Sept. 19, '64; dischg. by Gen. Order, July 11, '65.

Jeffries, Elisha, dischg by Gen. Order, July 11, '65

Johns, Hiram M,, mus. in Feb. 23, '64; captured at Old Ch., Va., June 11, '64; died, date unknown.

Knox, William, absent at mus. out.

Kent, Nicholas J., wd. at Opequan, Va., Sept. 19, '64; dischg. by Gen. Order, July 11, '65.

Knight, S. W., mus. in Oct. 29, '62; died, date unknown.

Leonard, Asa, mus. in Feb. 5, '64; mns. out with Co. B, 3d Regt. Prov. Cav., Oct. 31, '65.

Lincoln, Andrew, dischg. by Gen. Order, July 11, '65.

Lindsay, Francis, mus. in March 29, '65; dischg. by Gen. Order, June 27, '65.

Longstreth, William, mus. in Nov. 23, '62; died at Washington, D. C., Aug. 19, '63; buried in Mil. Asylum Cemetery.

Lindsey, James, mus. in Nov. 23, '62; died at Washington, D. C., Aug. 6, '63; bur. rec., July 13, '63; buried in Mil. Asylum Cemetery.

Lapping, John, killed at Hanover Court House, Va., May 30, '64.

Lasnire, Henry, died, date unknown.

Lieb, John A., mus. in Feb. 26, '64; pr. to Capt. 127th Regt., U. S. C. T.; dischg. Sept. 10, '65.

Morris, John P., mus. in Feb. 23, '64; mus. out with Co. B, 3d Regt. Prov. Cav., Oct. 31, '65.

Monroe, Thomas J., mus. in April 4, '65; mus. out with Co. B, 3d Regt. Prov. Cav., Oct. 31, '65.

Minor, Calvin, mus. in March 29, '65; mus. out with Co. B, 3d Regt. Prov. Cav., Oct. 31, '65.

Millaneer, Lemuel H., dischg. by Gen. Order, July 11, '65.

Martin, Wm. H., disch. by Gen. Order, July 11, '65.

Martin, Philip C., disch. by Gen. Order, July 11, '65.

Mankey, Henry C., pris. from June 30 to Nov. 1, '63; dischg. by Gen. Order, July 11, '65.

Martin, Joseph W., mus. in Oct. 8, '64; des. Jan. 14; ret. May 5, '65; dischg. by Gen. Order, May 6, '65.

Morris, Joseph C., captured; died at Richmond, Va., Feb. 26, '64.

Meeks, Eli, captured; died at Richmond, Va., Dec. 22, '63, of wds. recd. in action.

Miller, John D., mus. in Feb. 5, '64; absent at mus. out.

Murphy, John, mus. in April 6, '65; des. Sept. 10, '65.

Martin, Matthias, dischg. by Gen. Order, July 1, '65.

Murphy, Jeremiah, mus. in Sept. 7, '64; dischg. by Gen. Order, June 13, '65.

Madigan, Dennis, mus. in April 5, '65; drafted; dischg. by Gen. Order, June 21, '65.

May, James, mus in March 25, '64; not accounted for.

McGrady, Robert, absent at mus out.

McClellan, Asa S, dischg March 28, '63.

McCullough, Joses, burial record L C. McCough; died at Andersonville, Ga, Aug. 14, '64; grave 5,642.

O'Dwyer, Thos J., mus in April 4, '65; dischg. by Gen Order, Aug. 25, '65

Poland, John W, prisoner from Nov 18, '63, to June 7, '65; dischg by Gen. Order, July 1, '65

Poland, Cavalier, wd. at Spottsylvania, May 8, '64; tr. to Vet. R C.; dischg by Gen Order, Sept 12, '65

Phelan, Wm., mus in April 20, '64; not accounted for

Rinehart, John T., mus in Feb 23, '64; mus. out with Co B, 3d Reg, Prov Cav, Oct. 31, '65

Reese, David, dischg by Gen Order, Aug. 18, '65.

Radlinghafer, M, pris from Nov 30, '63, to Dec. 8, '64; dischg. by Gen. Order, July 11, '65

Rex, Harper, dischg by Gen Order, July 11, '65

Rush, Levi, dischg by Gen Order, July 11, '65.

Rhoade, William P. dischg by Gen Order, July 11, '65

Rush, Peter, dischg. March 28, '63.

Rogers, Alexander W, dischg Aug 25, '63

Rush, Isaiah, dischg on Surg. Cert Nov. 10, '64.

Richie, Samuel, mus. in Sept. 9, '64; dischg. by Gen. Order, June 13, '65.

Rex, George, mus in Feb. 29, '64; capt at Old Ch., Va, June 11, '64; died at Andersonville, Ga, Sept. 17, '64; grave 9,019.

Rhinehart, Arthur J., mus in March 26, '64, died at Philadelphia, Oct. 6, '64, of wds. recd. at Opequan, Va, Sept 19, '64

Syphers, Peter M, mus in Feb 23, '64; mus out with Co. B, 3d Regt Prov Cav., Oct 31, '65.

Smith, Dennis, absent at mus out.

Smith, Francis, mus in Dec. 1, '64; drowned near Racine, O, Oct. 20, '65

Stull, Lewis W, mus in Aug. 23, '62; dischg. May 14, '63

Stickles, Amos, dischg Jan. 22, '63.

Sherrick, Isaac W, wd at Opequan, Va, Sept 19, '64; dischg. on Surg. Cert ; date unknown.

Straight, Henry, dischg by Gen. Order, June 12, '65

Shape, Frederick, captured; died at Andersonville, Ga., Aug. 13, '64; grave 5,494.

Smith, William, des. Nov 22, '62.

Smith, Cowperthwait C, des. June, 5, '65.

Sullivan, Cornelius, mus in Sept. 16, '64; not accounted for

Tukesbury, John, dischg. by Gen Order, July 11, '65

Lindsey. Hinerman

Thomas, John, killed at Fisher's Hill, Va., Oct. 8, '64.

Tukesbury, William, wd. in action, Sept. 1, '64; not on mus. out roll.

Ulum, Henry, captured; died, date unknown.

Valentine, John, mus. in April 10, '65; dischg. by Gen. Order, May 23, '65

White, James D., wd. at Old Church, Va., June 11, '64; absent at mus. out.

Whales, Alexander, abs. at mus. out.

White, Francis M., wd. at Hanover, C. H. Va., May 31, '64; dischg. by Gen. Order, July 11, '65.

Wagner, George W., mus. in Sept 6, '64; dischg. by Gen. Order, June 13, '65.

West, Thomas, died at Fairfax Court House, Va., May 7, '63.

Whipkey, Silas, mus. in March 23, '62; died at Fairfax C. H., June 20, '63.

Wilson, John W., mus. in April 4, '65; des. Sept 10, '65.

Welte, Rudolph, mus. in Aug. 15, '64; not accounted for.

Yates, Hazlet M., wd. at Opequan, Va., Sept 19, '64; dischg. by Gen. Order, July 11, '65.

Yoders, Joseph C., wd. at Opequan, Va, Sept. 19, '64; dischg. by Gen. Order, July 11, '65.

Yates, Alexander, died at Frederick, Md., Aug 6, '63, of wds. recd. in action; bur. rec. July 25, '63; bur. in Nat. Cem., Antietam, Section 26, lot E, grave 501.

Yoders, John J., mus. in March 11, '64; died at City Point, Va., Aug. 9, '64; bur. in Nat. Cem, Section E, division 4, grave 107.

Young, Harrison, mus. in March 30, '65; des. Sept. 10, '65.

Yoders, Wm. H., dischg. by Gen. Order, June 22, '65.

COMPANY C, ONE HUNDRED AND SIXTY-THIRD REGIMENT, EIGHTEENTH CAVALRY.

Recruited in Greene County, mustered in Nov. 23, 1862.

James Hughes, Capt., mus. in Nov. 27, '62; resigned Feb. 14, '63.

Frederick Zarracher, Capt., mus. in April 23, '64; mus. out with Co. C, 3d Regt. Prov. Cav. Oct. 31, '65.

Samuel Montgomery, 1st Lieut., mus. in Dec. 3, '62; resigned Oct. 23, '63.

Francis A. J. Grey, 2d Lieut., mus. in Nov. 29, '62; resigned May 14, '63.

James R. Weaver, 2d Lieut., mus. in Nov. 15, '62; pr. fr. Sergt. to Major, June 18, '63; com. 1st Lieut. April 1, '64; not mus.; Bv. 1st Lieut., Capt., Major and Lieut.-Col. March 13, '65; disch. May 15, '65.

Charles Edwards, 2d Lieut., pr. fr. Sergt. May 16, '65; com 1st Lieut. May 16, '65; not mus ; mus out with Co. 3d Regt. Prov. Cav. Oct 31, '65

James Burns, 1st Sergt , disch. by Gen. Order, July 10, '65.

Eli J. White, 1st Sergt , killed at Opequan, Va , Sept. 19, '64.

Jonathan Gregory, 1st Sergt., captured; died at Richmond, Va , Jan 5, '64; bur. in Nat. Cem., Sec C, div 1, grave 187.

John M. Ashbrook, 1st Sergt., captured at Mine Run, Va., May 5, '64, died at Florence, North Carolina, Nov. 18, '64.

Benjamin H. James, 1st Sergt., not on mus. out roll

W. H. McGlumphey, Q. M. Sergt., dis. by Gen. Order, July 10, '65.

George W Love, Q M. Sergt , mus. in Feb. 27, '64; mus. out with Co 3d Regt Prov. Cav , Oct. 31, '65

Samuel C. Oliver, Q. M Sergt., not on mus. out roll.

John S. Ackley, Com. Sergt., disch. by Gen Order, July 10, '65

Reuben Sanders, Sergt , prisoner fr. Oct 11, '63, to April 16, '64, disch. by Gen Order, July 10, '65.

James L Hughes, Sergt., pr fr Corp. May 1, '65; disch by Gen. Order, July 10, '65.

William M Smith, mus. in Feb. 27, '64; mus. out with Co. C, 3d Regt. Prov Cav Oct 31, '65, Vet

Frederick Filleman, Sergt., mus. in Feb 27, '64; pr. fr Corp. May 1, '65; mus. out with Co C, 3d Regt., Prov. Cav., Oct. 31, '65, Vet

Martin Supler, Sergt.; not on mus. out roll

A. L Montgomery, Sergt , not on mus. out roll

John Hulings, Sergt ; mus. in Oct. 18, '62; tr. to V. R Co., disch. Oct 18, '65; exp term

Maxwell Bayles, Corp., mus. out with Co. C 3d Prov. Cav., Oct. 3, '65.

Thomas Miller, Corp , mus in Feb. 25, '64; wd. at St Mary's Church, Va., June 15, '64; mus out with Co C, 3d Regt. Prov. Cav., Oct. 31, '65

Edward E. Newlin, Corp , mus. in March 8, '64; wd at Opequan, Sept. 19, '64; mus out with Co. C, 3d Regt. Prov Cav. Oct. 31, '65.

William Hofford, Corp , mus. in March 10, '64, mus out with Co C, 3d Regt. Prov. Cav. Oct. 31, '65

William Filby, Corp , disch. by Gen Order, July 10, '65.

Elisha Dailey, Corp., mus. in Dec. 7, '62; wd at St. Mary's Church, Va., June 15, '64; pr. to Corp , May 1, '65; disch by Gen. Order, July 10, '65.

Daniel W. Vanata, Corp., mus in Dec. 7, '62; disch. on Surg. Cert. Jan. 16, '65.

Dennis Murphy, tr. to Vet. Res. Corps, Sept. 3, '64

Francis Clutter, Corp., captured; died at Andersonville, Ga., May 31, '64.

Joseph Eidle, Corp., mus. in March 15, '64; killed at Opequan, Sept. 19, '64; bur. in Nat. Cem., Winchester, Va., lot 18.

John B. Moorse, Corp., not on mus. out roll.

Joseph Spilman, Corp, not on mus. out roll.

Wilson Morford, Corp, not on mus. out roll.

James Hagerty, Corp, not on mus. out roll.

John Anderson, blacksmith, disch. by Gen. Order, July 10, '65.

George Elms, blacksmith, disch by Gen. Order, July 10, '65.

William Henninger, saddler, mus. in March 12, '64; mus. out with Co. C, 3d Regt. Prov. Cav., Oct. 31, '65.

Thomas Vanata, saddler, mus. in March 12, '64; mus. out with Co. C, 3d Regt. Prov. Cav., Oct. 31, '65.

Allums, Porter, disch. by Gen. Order, June 16, '65.

Allen, James, mus in Dec. 7, '63; died at Wilmington, N. C., March 9, '65.

Burns, Harvey, mus out with Co. C, 3d Regt. Prov. Cav., Oct. 31, '65.

Barnhart, Wilson, mus. in Dec. 7, '62; disch. date unknown.

Barger, A. J., not on mus out roll.

Barnhart, Thomas, not on mus out roll.

Barnhart, Benjamin, not on mus. out roll.

Clutter, Seeley B., mus. in Dec. 7, '62; disch. date unkown

Clutter, Addison, mus. in Dec. 7, '62; disch. date unknown.

Carter, Daniel, mus. in Dec. 7, '62; disch. by Gen. Order, July 10, '65.

Crate, Joseph, mus. in March 3, '64; disch June 6, '65.

Clank, Samuel, mus. in Dec. 19, '62; mus. out with Co. C, 3d Regt. Prov. Cav., Oct. 31, '65.

Cuthberson, William, mus. in March 11, '64; mus out with Co. C, 3d Regt. Prov Cav, Oct. 31, '65.

Canavan, John, mus. in Feb. 15, '64; mus out with Co. C, 3d Regt. Prov. Cav., Oct. 31, 65

Curry, William, mus. in April 29, '64; mus. out with Co. C, 3d Regt. Prov. Cav, Oct. 31, '65.

Crooks, John, mus. in March 4, '64; des. Sept. 9, '65.

Crawford, William, died; bur. in Nat. Cem., Gettysburg, Sec. E, grave 12.

Cartwright, James H, tr. to Vet. Res Corps; disch. by Gen. Order, July 14.

Clark, James, not on mus. out roll.

Campbell, Daniel, mus. in March 31, '64; disch. by Gen. Order, June 20, '65.

Conner, Michael, mus. in March 28, '64; not accounted for.

Cox, William, mus in March 19, '64; not accounted for.

Durbin, John, mus. in Dec 7, '62; disch. on Surg. Cert. June 6, '65

Douglass, Andrew J, mus. in Dec. 7, '62, disch. by Gen. Order, July 10, '65.

Dille, Abraham V., mus. in Nov. 23, '62; disch. by Gen Order, July 10, '65.

Durbin, Andrew J, captured; died at Salsbury, N. C., Dec 8, '64

Day, William B., captured; died at Richmond, Va, Feb. 21, '64

Davis, Thomas, mus. in Feb. 26, '64; wd. at Kearneyeville, Va., Aug 26, '64; mus. out with Co. C, 3d Regt. Prov. Cav, Oct. 31, '65.

Davis, Daniel, wd. at St. Mary's Church, Va., June 15, '64; disch by Gen. Order, July 1, '65.

Davis, William, mus. in March 19, '64; captured; died at Salisbury, N. C., Dec. 4, '64

Dunlap, James B., mus. in Aug. 16, '63; des July 20, '65.

Denny, John H., not on mus. out roll

Duncan, John, mus. in March 8, '64; not accounted for

Doyle, Cornelius, mus. in March 22, '64; not accounted for.

Elder, Joshua A. R, mus. in April 7, '64; disch by Gen. Order, July 14, '65.

Elder, Abraham, mus. in March 16, '64; mus. out with Co. C, 3d Regt. Prov. Cav, Oct. 31, '65.

Elliott, George, mus. in Dec 7, '62; captured; died at Richmond, Va, Feb. 20, '64.

Founer, David, disch by Gen. Order, July 10, '65.

Founer, Charles, mus. in March 28, '64; mus out with Co. C, 3d Regt. Prov. Cav, Oct. 31, '65

Fleming, Henry S, mus in March 8, '64; mus. out with Co. C, 3d Regt. Prov Cav, Oct 31, '65.

Filby, Thomas, tr. to Vet. 'Res. Corps, Sept. 20, 64; disch by Gen. Order, Aug. 2, '65.

Fox, Henry, not on mus. out roll

Grandon, Isaac M., disch. by Gen Order, July 10, '65.

Gump, Philip, mus. in Dec. 7, '62; disch May 22, '65, for wds, rec'd at Cedar Creek, Va, Oct. 19, '64.

Gump, George W., died at Baltimore, Md., Feb. 19, '65; burial rec. Feb. 10, '65; bur. in Nat. Cem., Loudon Park.

Gray, William, mus. in Feb 28, '64; mus out with Co. C, 3d Regt. Prov. Cav., Oct. 31, '65; Vet.

Gump, David, not on mus. out roll.

Gump, Peter, not on mus. out roll.

Gaessler, Frederick, mus. in March 17, '64; not accounted for.

Hickman, Morgan, disch. by Gen. Order, July 10, '65.

Humbertson, William, mus. in April 7, '64; mus. out with Co. C, 3d Regt. Prov. Cav., Oct. 31, '65

Hughes, William P., disch. by Gen. Order, May 15, '65.

Hartranft, Levi W, mus. in Feb. 26, '64; des. Sept 17, '65.

Huss, James C, not on mus. out roll.

Harris, Edward, mus. in March 25, '64; not accounted for.

James, John, disch. by Gen. Order, July 10, '65.

Johnson, John D., tr. to Vet. Res. Corps, Sept. 20, '64; disch. on Surg. Cert., July 27, '65

Kemble, James, captured; died at Richmond, Va., Feb. 5, '64.

Kline, Adam, mus. in Feb. 25, '64; mus. out with Co. C., 3d Regt Prov. Cav., Oct. 31, '65.

Klinger, George, mus. in Feb. 25, '64; mus. out with Co. C, 3d Regt. Prov. Cav , Oct. 31, '65

Kerr, Jonathan, mus. in Feb. 25, '64; died at Philadelphia. Jan. 17, '65

Kenney, Henry, mus. in March 2, '64; des. June 1, '65.

Kemble, John R , not on mus. out roll.

Keller, A. J., not on mus. out roll.

Leonard, Richard J., died at Harper's Ferry, Va., Jan. 4, '65.

Lynn, Robert H., mus. in Feb. 25, '64; mus. out with Co C, 3d Regt. Prov. Cav., Oct. 31, '65.

Mauger, Andrew J., mus. in March 2, '64; mus. out with Co. C, 3d Regt. Prov. Cav., Oct. 31, '65.

Masters, Joseph, disch. by Gen Order, July 10, '65.

Meloy, James H., disch by Gen. Order, May 15, '65.

Moser, Nathan, mus. in March 8, '64; mus out with Co. C, 3d Regt. Prov. Cav., Oct. 31, '65

Morris, Randall, mus. in April 7, '64; disch. by Gen. Order, May 23, '65.

Miller, Washington F., mus. in Feb. 2, '64; captured; died at Andersonville, Ga , Oct. 7, '64; grave 10,486.

Murphy, John, mus. in March 16, '64; captured; died at Danville, March 8, '65.

Morse, Jonathan B., captured; died at Richmond, Va., Feb. 20, '64; burial record Dec. 6, '63.

Matthews, Samuel L , mus. in March 15, '64; des. July 7, '63.

Montgomery, Levi, not on mus. out roll.

McNutt, Joel, Dec. 7, '62; mus. out with Co. C, 3d Regt Prov. Cav , Oct. 31, '65.

McDonald, James, disch. by Gen. Order, July 10, '65.

McKean, John, disch. by Gen. Order, July 10, '65.

McKann, John, tr. to Vet. Res. Corps, Sept. 20, '64; disch. by Gen. Order, Aug. 2, '65.

McLaughlin, Thomas, mus in March 23, '64; wd. in action Sept. 1, '64; mus out with Co C, 3d Regt Prov Cav , Oct 31, '65.

McLaughlin, Edward, mus. in March 23, '64;' mus out with Co. C, 3d Regt. Pro Cav. Oct. 31, '65.

McCloskey, F P , mus in March 23, '64; mus. out with Co C, 3d Regt. Prov. Cav., Oct 31, '65

McKean, Alexander, not on mus. out roll.

McCabe, James, mus. in March 25, '64; not accounted for

Pitcock, Andrew, mus. in Dec. 7, '62; prisoner from May 5, '64 to June 8, '65; disch. by Gen. Order, July 1, '65

Pettit, R L , died at Winchester, Va , Nov. 21, of wds rec'd Sept. 28, '64.

Poland, Thomas, died; date unknown

Pettit, Levi, mus. in March 15, '64; mus out with Co C, 3d Regt. Prov. Cav., Oct. 31, '65.

Peel, George W , mus. in Feb 25, '64; mus. out with Co C, 3d Regt. Prov. Cav , Oct 31, '65.

Porter, James M. A., mus. in March 22, '64, mus out with Co C, 3d Regt Prov. Cav., Oct. 31, '65.

Poland, Cavalier, tr.,to Co. A , date unknown

Rum, William, disch by Gen Order, July 19, '65

Roach, Samuel H., tr. to 9th Regt Res Corps, Sept 20, '64; disch by Gen, Order, Aug. 2, '65.

Reese, Abednego, mus. in March 4, '64, mus. out with Co C, 3d Regt Prov Cav , Oct 31, '65

Ray, Joseph, mus in Feb 25, '64; wd in action March 9, '65, mus out with Co C, 3d Regt. Prov Cav , Oct 31, '65

Ray, William, mus in Feb. 25, '64; mus out with Co C, 3d Regt. Prov. Cav , Oct 31, '65.

Richards, John, mus. in Feb 25, '64, mus. out with Co. C, 3d Regt. Prov. Cav., Oct. 31, '65

Rauch, Levi, mus in Feb. 25, '64; mus out with Co C, 3d Regt. Prov Cav , Oct. 31, '65

Rich, Jacob, mus. in March 7, '64: mus out with Co C, 3d Regt. Prov Cav , Oct. 31, '65.

Roberts, Lemuel, tr. to Vet. Res Corps, Jan 21, '65, disch. on Surg. Cert. June 16, '65.

Reaves, James S , mus. in March 17, '64; not accounted for.

Steward, Isaac, mus. in Dec. 7, '62, absent, sick at mus out.

Stall, John, disch on Surg Cert , July 13, '65.

Sloan, James, mus. in Dec 7, '62; disch. on Surg. Cert., Feb. 8, '65.

Shultz, Jacob, disch by Special Order, July 10, '65.

Staggers, John P , disch. by Special Order, July 10, '65.

Snyder, David, disch. by Special Order, July 10, '65

Snyder, Philip, disch. by Special Order, July 11, '65.

Sollers, Levi, tr. to Vet Res Corps; date unknown.

Stewart, John W., des.; date unknown.

Snyder, Gotlieb G., mus. in April 15, '64; mus. out with Co. C, 3d Regt. Prov. Cav., Oct. 31, '65.

Stanley, William J, mus. in March 28, '64; mus. out with Co. C, 3d Regt. Prov. Cav., Oct. 31, '65.

Simmons, Samuel, mus. in Feb 25, '64; disch. by Gen. Order, June 20, '65.

Smith, Peter, mus. in March 18, '64; not accounted for.

Thompson, Stephen B., mus. out with Co C, 3d Regt. Prov. Cav., Oct. 31' '65.

Toppin, John, mus in Feb. 29, '64; mus out with Co C, 3d Regt. Prov. Cav., Oct. 31, '65.

Tatterson, Marshall, mus. in Feb. 29, '64; mus. out with Co. C, 3d Regt. Prov. Cav, Oct. 31, '65.

Vanatta, Clark, not on mus. out roll.

Wright, John M., disch by Gen. Order, July 10, '65.

Whipkey, Noah, mus. in Dec. 7, '62; disch. by Gen. Order, June 21, '65

Winters, Samuel, mus. in March 15, '64; mus. out with Co. C, 3d Prov. Cav. Oct. 31, '65.

Walley, Peter, mus. in March 23, '64; mus. out with Co. C, 3d Regt. Prov. Cav., Oct. 31, '65.

Walker, Edward, mus. in April 6, '64; mus. out with Co. C, 3d Regt. Prov. Cav, Oct. 31, '65.

Wingert, David, mus in March 9, '64; killed at Opequan, Va., Sept. 19, '64

Wingert, Moses, not on mus. out roll.

Wortman, Andrew, not on mus. out roll.

Williamson, Charles, mus. in March 28, '64; not accounted for.

Williams, Thomas, mus. in March 28, '64; not accounted for

Wicks, John, mus. in March 19, '64; not accounted for.

Zeiser, Philip J., mus. in March 4, '64; des. June 1, '65.

COMPANY G., ONE HUNDRED AND SIXTY-THIRD REGIMENT, EIGHTEENTH CAVALRY.

Recruited in Greene County; mustered in Nov. 19, 1862.

M. S. Kingsland, Capt., mus. in Dec. 8, '62; wd. at Germania Ford, Va., Nov. 18, '63, and at Hanover C. H. May 31, '64; disch. Aug. 17, '64.

Benjamin F. Herrington, Capt., mus. in Aug. 23, '62; pr. fr. Com. Sergt, Co. A, to 2d Lieut., Dec. 8, '62, to Capt., May 13, '65; disch. by Special Order, July 21, '65.

22

Thomas P. Shields, 1st Lieut., mus in Nov 23, '62;' disch Oct 22, '63.

James A Irwin, 1st Lieut., pr. to 1st Lieut, Nov. 1, '64, com. Capt. Aug 18, '64; not mus , resigned April 8, '65

John Rodgers, 1st Lieut., pr. fr. Sergt, May 14; '65; mus. out with Co. C, 3d Regt. Prov Cav., Oct. 31, '65.

· William H. Webster, 1st Sergt., mus. out with Co. C, 3d Regt. Prov Cav , Oct 31, '65

Charles H. Hook, 1st Sergt., prisoner from June 10, '64, to June 10, '65; disch. by Gen. Order, June 30, '65.

Isaac Buckingham, Com Sergt., mus. out with Co. C, 3d Regt , Prov Cav , Oct. 31, '65

Wm G. Miliken, Sergt., mus. in Dec. 8, '62, mus. out with Co. C, 3d Regt. Prov. Cav., Oct 31, '65

Theophilus L. Bunzo, Sergt., captured; mus. out with Co C, 3d Regt Prov Cav , Oct. 31, '65

Shudrack M. Sellers, Sergt., mus in Dec 7, '62; dischg by Gen. Order; date unknown

John Coe, Sergt , mus in Dec. 7, '62, dischg. by Gen. Order; date unknown

Samuel Dodd, Sergt , mus in Dec. 7, '62, pro. to Veterinary Surg. March 3, 1863

Nicholas J. Headlee, Sergt.; tr. to Vet Res. Corps, Feb. 2, '63

Lorenzo D. Headlee, Sergt , killed at Chantilly, Va., Feb. 2, '63.

Zenas Jewell, Sergt , killed at Hagerstown, Md , July 6, '63; bur. in Nat Cem , Antietam, Sec. 26, lot D, grave 392.

Thomas Thompson, Sergt., captured at Mine Run, May 5, '64; died at Andersonville, Ga , July 28, '64; grave 4,116

William Scott, Sergt., pro. to 2d Lieut., Co. A, Jan 2, '65.

John Wells, Corp., mus in Feb. 29, '64, mus. out with Co C, 3d Regt Prov Cav., Oct. 31, '65.

Charles T. Webster, Corp , mus. out with Co C, 3d Regt. Prov. Cav., Oct. 31, '65

William Milliken, Corp., mus in Dec 9, '62; dischg. by Gen. Order, date unknown.

James H Miller, Corp., dischg. by Gen Order; date unknown

Amos P. Ryan, Corp , dischg. by Gen. Order; date unknown.

Roseberry, Hughes, Corp , wd. at Hagerstown, Md , July 6, '63, and at Winchester, Va., Aug 17, '64; dischg by Gen Order, July 21, '65

John C. Shields, Corp , dischg.; date unknown

David Thorp., Corp , captured at Mine Run, Va., May, 5, '64; died at Andersonville, Ga , Sept. 19, '64; grave 9,212.

John Yoders, Bugler, mus. in Dec 9, '62; mus. out with Co C, 3d Regt. Prov Cav., Oct. 31, '65.

Anderson, Isaac, mus. in Oct. 9, '62; killed at Hagerstown, Md., July 6, '63.

Burke, Silas, mus. in July 6, '64; drafted; mus. out with Co C, 3d Regt. Prov. Cav., Oct. 31, '65.

Bennett, Isaac, dischg. by Gen. Order; date unknown.

Behey, Henry, mus. in Sept. 19, '64; drafted; dischg. by Gen. Order; date unknown.

Barren, Dalles, mus. in Feb. 29, '64; tr. to V. R C.; dischg. by Gen. Order; date unknown.

Church, John C., mus. in Dec 7, '62; absent, sick at muster out.

Cumley, Henry, absent, sick at mus. out.

Campbell, Duncan, mus. in April 15, '65; dischg. by Gen. Order, Aug. 18, '65.

Cathers, Orin C., mus in Dec. 7, '62; dischg. by Gen. Order; date unknown.

Conner, Calvin, mus. in Dec. 7, '62, dischg. on Surg. Cert.; date unknown.

Church, Rinehart B., mus. in Dec. 7, '62; dischg. by Gen. Order; date unknown.

Cooper, John B., dischg. by Gen. Order; date unknown.

Caster, Porter, drafted; dischg by Gen. Order, June 22, '65

Castlow, James, mus. in Sept 20, '64; drafted; dischg. by Gen. Order, June 22, '65.

Carter, George W., mus. in Sept. 3, '64; dischg. by Gen. Order; date unknown.

Cox, James, mus. in March 18, '65; dischg. by Gen. Order, June 20, '65.

Cunningham, Isaac, died at Washington, D. C., Oct. 17, '63; bur. in Mil. Asylum Cem.

Clayton, James W., mus. in June 25, '64; never joined company.

Cisney, James W., mus. in Sept. 2, '64; never joined Co.

Carroll, Andrew, mus in March 30, '64; not accounted for.

Davis, Lewis, mus. in June 19, 64; drafted; mus. out with Co. C, 3d Regt. Prov. Cav., Oct. 31, '65.

Dunn, Francis, dischg. by Gen. Order; date unknown.

Davis, Simeon, mus. in Feb. 18, '64; dischg. by Gen. Order, June 16, '65.

Davis, John, mus. in Feb. 17, '64; wd. at Cedar Creek, Va., Oct. 19, '64; dischg. on Surg. Cert. June 21, '65.

Debolt, Isaac, wd. at Glendale, Va., May 12, '64; died at Hanover Junc. June 28, '64.

Dunston, Daniel, captured; died at Richmond, Va., April 14, '64.

Edgar, Reuben, dischg by Gen. Order; date unknown

Fordice, Silas, mus. in Feb. 28, '64; mus. out with Co. C, 3d Regt. Prov. Cav., Oct 31, '65.

Grim, Lawrence C., mus. in Sept. 3, '64; disch. by Gen Order; date unknown

George, William, mus. in Sept. 19, '64; drafted; dischg. by Gen. Order, June 22, '65

Gump, David, missing in action at St. Mary's Church, Va., June 15, '64

Gray, Benjamin, des. July 25, '63.

Garrison, Levi, mus. in Feb. 27, '64; died at Alexandria, Va., March 29, '64.

Hoffman, Milton, mus. in Feb 24, '64; mus out with Co. C, 3d Regt. Prov. Cav., Oct 31, '65.

Huffman, Abraham, mus in Sept 24, '62, absent, sick at mus. out.

Headlee, John T, mus. in Dec 9, '62; dischg. to date Oct. 31, '65

Hart, George W., dischg. by Gen. Order, June 17, '65.

Henderson, Abner, wd. at Glendale, Va., May 12, '64; dischg. by Gen Order; date unknown.

Headlee, Epraim, dischg on Surg. Cert.; date unknown

Headlee, Jonas D, captured; died at Andersonville, Ga, March 15, '65; grave 12,883

Ishart, Nicholas, mus in Dec. 9, '62; captured; died at Andersonville, Ga., March 23, '64; grave 124.

Kinney, John H., mus in Feb. 29, '64; mus. out with Co. C, 3d Regt Prov. Cav., Oct 31, '65.

Keyner, Elisha, dischg by Gen. Order, Aug. 18, '65.

Kinney, Hiram, mus in Sept 3, '64; dischg by Gen Order, date unknown.

Kintyhtt, Leroy W., mus in Dec. 7, '62; dischg by Gen. Order; date unknown.

Killian, John, mus. in April 6, '65; never joined Co

Lewis, George T, mus. in Feb 29, '64; wd. in action, Sept. 1, '64, mus out with Co. C, 3d Regt. Prov. Cav, Oct. 31, '65.

Lyons, Henry, mus. in Dec. 7, '62; dischg. by Gen. Order; date unknown.

Lewis, Constantine, mus in April 12, '65; dischg. by Gen. Order, June 14, '65.

Love, Thomas J., mus in Sept. 2, '64; never joined company.

Leely, Ansel, mus in April 15, '65; drafted; dischg. by Gen. Order, July 19, '65

Miller, Samuel, mus. in Sept. 21, '64; absent, sick at mus. out.

Martin, Robert, mus in April 14, '65; drafted, abs., sick at mus. out

Mahon, James, wd. at Cedar Creek, Va, Oct 19, '64; disch. by Gen Order, July 17, '65

Martin, Samuel, mus. in Dec. 7, '62; disch by Gen. Order; date unknown.

Martin, Thomas, mus in April 14, '65; disch. by Gen. Order, June 21, '65.

Milliken, Thomas, mus. in Sept. 21, '64; disch. by Gen. Order, date unknown.

Morris, Joseph, died at Fairfax Court House, Va., June 10, '63.

Morris, James, died at Fairfax Court House, Va , June 23, '63

Malson, Andrew C., mus. in Dec. 9, '62; died at Fairfax, Ct. H., June 23, '63.

Michaels, Ellis E , des.; date unknown.

McGlone, James, mus. in Feb. 24, '64; absent, sick at mus. out.

McKeever, John, died July 23, '64; bur. in Nat. Cem., Arlington, Va.

Phillips, John, Jr., mus. in Dec. 9, '62; died at Annapolis, Md., Oct. 30, '63.

Phillips, John, Sr., mus. in Dec. 7, '62; died at Fairfax, Ct. H., May 19, '63

Piles, William, des ; date unknown.

Roades, John, mus. in Feb 24, '64; mus. out with Co. C, 3d Reg., Prov. Cav. Oct. 31, '65.

Rorick, William J., mus. in Aug. 1, '64; mus. out with Co. C, 3d Reg., Prov. Cav., Oct. 31, '65.

Ryan, Harvey, absent in ar. action at mus. out.

Roupe, Silas, mus. in Dec. 7, '62; disch by Gen. Order, date unknown,

Rush, John, disch. by Gen. Order, date unknown.

Rhone, Jacob P , mus in April 12, '65; sub., disch. by Gen. Order, June 15, '65.

Rush, Stephen, cap., died at Andersonville. June 14, '64; grave, 1,922.

Reynor, Elisha, mus. in Dec. 7, '62; wd. at St. Mary's Church, June 15, and at Kearnysville, Aug. 25, '64; disch. by Gen. Order, Aug. 31, '65.

Seckman, Henry C., mus. in Feb. 29, '64; mus out with Co. C, 3dReg, Prov. Cav., Oct 31, '65

Schofield, Joseph M., wd at Charlestown, Va., Aug 22, '64; absent, sick at mus. out.

Strosnider, Jordan, disch by Gen Order, July 5, '65.

Staggers, James, disch. by Gen. Order, date unknown.

Sterner, Jacob F., disch. by Gen. Order, date unknown.

Stall, John J., killed at Cedar Creek, Va., Oct. 19, '64.

Stiles, Isaac, mus. in Dec. 7, '62; captured, died at Richmond, Va , Dec. 25, '63.

Six, William H., des. Oct. 1, '63,

Thompson, Henry, mus. in Feb. 27, '64, missing in action at Mine Run, Va , May 5, '64.

Thomas, Eli, mus. in Feb 27, '64; died at Alexandria,Va., March 26, '61, grave 1,639.

Vandaver, Donnelly, April 1, '65; mus. out with Co C, 3d Reg. Prov. Cav. Oct. 31, '65.

Watson, Robert, mus. in Feb. 24, '64; mus. out with Co. C, 3d Reg Prov Cav., Oct 31, '65

Wilt, Ephraim, mus in June 18, '64; drft, mus. out with Co. C, 3d Reg. Prov. Cav., Oct 31, '65.

White, Hazlett, mus. in Feb. 29, '64; disch. by Gen. Order, date unknown

Weller, John, disch. by Gen Order, date unknown.

Wells, Thomas, mus. in Feb. 29, '64; disch by Gen. Order, June 17, '65.

Whitlatch, George, captured; died at Andersonville, Ga , '65; burial record, Raleigh, N. C., March 10, '64; bur. in Nat. Cem., Sec. 20, grave 19.

Wise, Isaac, captured; died at Andersonville, Ga , March 27, '64, grave 192.

Yeager, Jesse, disch by Gen. Order; date unknown.

Zimmerman, Joseph, captured; died March 18, '64; bur. in Marietta and Atlanta Nat. Cemetery, Marietta, Ga , Sec. F., grave 1,017.

RECORDS OF SOLDIERS WHO ENTERED OTHER ORGANIZATIONS THAN THOSE GIVEN ABOVE AND WHO DIED IN THE SERVICE.

James Burwell, Sergt Co. A, 168th Pa. Inf., died at Washington, N C , June 22, '63.

John Kennei, Seigt. Co. A, 168th Pa. Inf., died at Washington, N. C , June 29, '63

Joseph Minor, Sergt. Co. A, 168th Pa Inf., died at Hampton, Va., June 2, '63

William Burgess, Seigt Co I, 32d U. S , Colored, died on transport returning from Texas, '65

Monroe Lewis, Sergt. Co I, 32d U. S , Colored, died date unknown.

Emanuel Patterson, Sergt Co. D, 6th U. S , Colored, killed at New Market Heights, Va., Sept. 29, '64.

Kane Richardson, died date unknown.

William Armstrong, Co. D, 1st W. Va Cav , died at Harper's Ferry, Va

James Ushbur, Co. B, 7th W. Va. Inf , died at Beverly, W. Va., Oct. 20, '64.

William Ashber, Co. B, 7th W. Va. Inf, died at Alexandria, July 8, '65.

Maison, Applegate, Co. B, 1st W. Va. Cav., died March 2, '64.

William H. Bland, Co. K, 14th W. Va. Inf., killed at Cloyd, Mt., Va., Oct. 24, '64.

Isaac H. Beach, Co K, 14th W. Va. Inf., died at Andersonville, Ga.

Eli Brant, Sergt., Co. F, 7th W. Va. Int., died at Front Royal, Va., June '62.

Joseph J. Cline, Co. A, 3d W. Va. Inf., date unknown.

John L. Clutter, Co. I, 4th W. Va Inf., died at Danville, Va., March 10, '65.

Jonathan Campbell, Co. B, 7th W. Va. Inf, died at Philadelphia, bur. at Wind Ridge.

George A. Conner, Co F, 7th W. Va. Inf., died at Washington, D. C, of wds recd. at Ream's Station, Va, bur. at Taylorstown, Greene County.

John Degerman, Co. F, 7th W. Va. Inf., died at camp in Md., Feb. '62; bur. at Grafton, W. Va

John A Doty, Co. A, 3d W. Va. Inf, date unknown.

David Durbin, Co. F, 7th W. Va. Inf., date unknown.

Thomas Fonner, Co I, 15th W. Va. Inf., died at Cumberland, Md., '64.

William Gillett, Co. A, 12th W. Va. Inf., died at Point of Rocks, Feb. '65.

Henry Gould, Co. F, 7th W. Va Inf., died March 11, '62.

Doctor Gould, Co. F, 7thW.Va. Inf., prisoner; died at Salisbury, N. C, Oct 30, '64

Andrew Guinip, Co. F, 7th W. Va. Inf., died at Ft. Monroe, Aug. 29, '62.

Isaac Herrington, 7th W. Va. Inf, date unknown.

James Herrington, Co. F, 7th W. Va. Inf, died at City Point, Va, July 30, '64, of wds. at Deep Bottom, July 28, '64; bur. at City Point, Va.

Thomas Herrington, Co. A, 8th W. Va. Inf, died June 15, '62, of wds. recd. at Cross Keys, Va.; bur. at Mapletown.

John W. Hannan, Co. F, 7th W. Va. Inf., died in Hospital, Md., Nov. 29, '62.

Henry Henderson, Co. N, 6th W. Va. Inf., died; bur. at Windy Gap Church.

William Hoffman, Co. F, 7th W. Va Inf, died, date unknown.

George Hoffman, Co. F, 7th W. Va. Inf., died at Baltimore, Feb, 8, '65.

Josiah Holmes, Co. D, 1st W. Va. Inf., killed at Piedmont.

John Jones, Co. F, W. Va Inf, died in Camp in Maryland, Feb. 28, '62; bur in Nat. Cem. Grafton, W. Va

Thomas King, Co. F, 7th W. Va Inf, died March 28, '62; bur. in Nat. Cem., Grafton, W. Va

John Kennedy, Co F, W. Va. Inf., died at Alexandria, Va ; bur. near Mount Morris, Greene County, Pa.

George W. Kent, Co. F, 7th W. Va Inf., died Nov. 18, '63, of wds. recd. at Antietam, Md., Sept. 17, '62.

Daniel Kimball, Co. A, 11th W. Va Inf, date unknown.

John Kimball, Co K, 14th W. Va Inf., Pris. from Jan. 4, '64; died at Andersonville, Ga.

Asa Kimball, Co K, 14th W. Va Inf., Pris. from Jan. 4, '64; died at Andersonville, Ga.

· Mathew Masters, Co. B, 7th W. Va Inf, killed at Wilderness, May 9, '64.

George Masters, Co K, 14th W Va. Inf, killed at Cloyd Mountain, Va., Oct. 24, '64

James Meighen, Co. K, 14th W. Va Inf., died at New Creek, Va., '63.

Andrew Miller, Co. D. 1st W Va. Inf., killed by explosion on board vessel at sea.

Simon Main, Co. F, 7th W. Va. Inf., died at Gettysburg, July 3, '63, of wds. recd. in battle; bur in Nat Cem

George P 'Moore, Co. F, 7th W. Va. Inf, died, date unknown.

Isaac A Moore, Co. F, 7th W Va. Inf, died Dec 18, '62; bur at Mt 'Harmon

Thomas Noon, Co. D, 1st W. Va Inf, died at Cumberland, Md.

James Newman, Co. D, 1st W. Va. Cav., killed at Hagerstown, Md, July 6, '63

Henry Pethtel, Co F, 7th W Va. Inf., died at Camp Maryland, Jan. 10, '62; bur. in Nat Cem, Grafton, W. Va.

John Rogers, Co. F, 6th W. Va Inf., Pris. from March '64; died at Millen, Ga., Aug. '64.

Jacob F. Rainer, Co F, 7th W. Va Inf., Pris., died at Salisbury, N. C; Nov. 15, '64.

Martin Riley, Co B, 1st W. Va. Cav., died 1861; bur. at Hopewell Church, Greene Co, Pa.

Thomas H. Shanes, Co. K, 14th W. Va Inf, killed at Cloyd Mt, Va., Oct. 24, '64.

C. A. Shibler, Co. F, 6th W. Va Inf, died at Andersonville while a prisoner

Jesse Taylor, Co. F, 7th W Va. Inf., killed at Romney, W. Va, Oct 26, '61; bur. at home; first soldier from Greene Co. who lost his life in battle.

John Mc Conkbin

James Tuttle, Co. K, 14th W. Va. Inf., died at New Creek, W. Va., '63; bur. at home, Springhill Township.

Elliot E. Tuttle, Co. I, 2d Col. Cav., died at Ft. Leavenworth, Kansas, Sept. 24, '65.

William Weaver, Co. I, 78th Ill. Inf., killed at Atlanta, Ga., Sept. 17, '64

Wm. F. Ballan, Co. E, 14th Pa. Cav, died from surg. operation; bur. at Greensboro.

Wm. F. Boulton, Co. E, 14th Pa. Cav., died at Beverly, W. Va., Oct. 13, '63.

Elijah Coleman, Co. E, 14th Pa. Cav., killed at Rocky Gap, Va., Aug. 27, '63.

Phillip G. Hughes, Co. E, 14th Pa. Cav., died at Annapolis, Md., March 19, '65.

Adrian Johnston, Co. E, 14th Pa. Cav., drowned at Jackson River, Va., Dec. 20, '63.

Robert L. Keener, Co. E, 14th Pa. Cav, died at Annapolis, Md, Nov. 25, '63.

Charles A. Mestragatt, Co E, 14th Pa. Cav, prisoner, died at Andersonville, Ga.; bur. rec. died at Richmond, Va., March 7, '64.

Wm M Stone, Co. E, 14th Pa. Cav., killed at Bunker Hill, Va., March 19, '64.

Samuel Whetsler, Co. E, 14th Pa. Cav., prisoner, died; bur. rec. S. Nitzler, Richmond, Feb. 13, '64.

Benjamin Woody, Co. E, 14th Pa. Cav, killed accidentally by cars near Grafton, W. Va., 1864.

James W. Yeager, Co. E, 14th Pa. Cav., died at Martinsburg, Aug. 24, '63; bur. at Greensboro, Pa.

Adam H. Hewitt, Co. K, 16th Pa. Cav., died at Philadelphia, Oct. 23, '63.

Mattox, Elias H., Co. K, 16th Pa. Cav, died Aug. 19, '63, of wds. recd. at Shepherdstown, Va., July 16, '63.

Zenas C Riley, Co. K, 16th Pa. Cav., died; date unknown.

Isaac Saunters, Co. K, 16th Pa. Cav., died at Harrisburg, Dec. 4, '62.

John B. Sheets, Co. K, 16th Pa. Cav., died at Dumfries, Va, May 25, '63.

Judson Throckmorton, Co. K, 16th Pa. Cav., died at Harrisburg, Nov. 1, '62.

Abraham C. Teagarden, Co. K, 16th Pa. Cav., died July 20, '63, of wds. recd. at Shepherdstown, Va, July 16, '63.

Early in the summer of 1861, Union mass meetings were held along the border line between Greene County, Pennsylvania, and Monongalia County, Virginia, (now West Virginia) which were largely attended by citizens living on each side of the State line, notably among which was one at Rosedale at which Hon. Jonathan Gerard presided, and an other on the farm of Adam Brown, at which more than one thousand people were present. At these mass-meetings the situation was fully and freely discussed. The people of Western Virginia were encouraged to remain loyal to the government of the United States, with the promise that Pennsylvania would render them all the assistance possible.

West Virginia refused to secede. Delegates were elected who met in convention at Wheeling on the 11th day of June, 1861. Forty.(40) counties were represented and on the 20th of June gave a unanimous vote in favor of separation Francis H. Peirpoint, of Marion County, was chosen Governor. The legislature which soon met at Wheeling was a legislature of Virginia, elected on the regular appointed day of election, eastern as well as western counties being represented therein. This legislature, as well as the convention, heartily assented to the formation of the State of West Virginia. In the meantime a company was recruited along the border on the Greene County side of the State line, all of whom were citizens of Greene County, and on the 18th day of September, 1861, were mustered into the service of the United States as Company F, Seventh Regiment, Virginia Infantry Volunteers.

The following is a complete roster of said company at date of muster into the United States service:

OFFICERS.

James B Morris, Capt., pro. to Major.	Thos. H. B. Fox, Corporal.
Ambrose A. Stout, 1st Lieut.	William Gidley, "
Bayles W. Thompson, 2d Lieut.	John G. Fordyce, "
Eli Brant, 1st Sergeant.	Wm. H. Meighen, "
Henry W. Taylor, Sergeant.	George W Shough, "
James L. Garrison, "	George W. Kent, "
John Fordyce, "	James A. Rice, "
Vincent Stephens, "	Abraham Taylor, "

PRIVATES.

James D. Burns,	William B. Fogg,
Benson Bayers,	William Fox,
William Bosworth,	John Flowers,
Norval Brown,	William Gibbons,
Lewis Chesler,	Noah Guthrie,
George A Conner,	Doctor Gould,
John Coss,	Daniel Gregg,
Abraham Cummans,	William Gehs,
Solomon Calvert,	Andrew J. Gump,
John Deyarman,	Henry Gould,

Jefferson Dye,
David Durbin,
Leonard Gooden,
Samuel Gregg,
Thomas J. Huffman,
James Herrington,
William Hardesty,
Washington Hardesty,
George Hoffman,
William Hoffman,
John M. Hennon,
Isaac Husk,
John Jackson,
Andrew L. Jones,
George Jones,
John Jones,
Nathaniel Jones,
George Kendall,
Sanford Kendall,
James Kendle,
Thomas King,
James A. King,
Alexander King,
John Kennedy,
Coleman Lewellen,
Thomas Longstreet,
John Lightner,
Robert Laughlin,
Francis Taylor, Jr.,
Francis Taylor, Sr.,
Samuel N. Conner,

Samuel Griffith,
David Gibbons,
Dennis R. Meighen,
Simon Main,
Thomas H. Meighen,
James Jones,
John McLelland,
George P. Moore,
Isaac A. Moore,
Morris Pethtel,
Henry Pethtel,
Thomas Phillips,
David Phillips,
Joseph Phillips,
Robert W. Phillips,
John T. Pouge,
Joshua Rice,
Benjamin F. Ramer,
Jacob F. Ramer,
Jacob Rush,
Timothy W. Ross,
Arthur B. Smith,
Manassas Shaw,
Abner Six,
Nathan Starkey,
William Shanks,
Jesse Taylor,
Thomas Taylor,
Zadoc Whitehill,
Hezekiah Walls.
Robert Wears,

DIED WHILE IN THE SERVICE.

Jesse Taylor, the first soldier from the county killed in the war.

John Deyarman,
John Jones,
David Durban,
Henry Gould,
Doctor Gould,
John Kennedy,
Andrew J. Gump,
John M. Hennon,
George W. Kent,
Isaac A. Moore,

Henry Pethtel,
Thomas King,
George Hoffman,
James Herrington,
George P. Moore,
Jacob F. Ramer,
Eli Brant,
George A. Conner,
William Hoffman,
Simon Main.

DISCHARGED FOR WOUNDS OR DISABILITY

William Fox,
Thomas Longstreth,
Benson Boyers,
Lewis Chisler,
John Flowers,
William Shanks,
Washington Hardesty,
A. L. Jones,
James Jones,
James Kendle,
Thomas H. Meigher,
John McLelland,

Robert Wears,
John G. Fordyce,
Manassas Shaw,
John Coss,
Samuel Griffith,
Thomas Taylor,
Isaac Hask,
Nathaniel Jones,
Francis Taylor,
Robert Laughlin,
Dennis R Meigher,
Hezekiah Walls.

RECAPITULATION.

Summary of Losses by Death of Soldiers from Greene County, Penn., while in the Service of the United States during the War of the Rebellion, 1861–'65.

Company.	Regiment.	Date of Organization.	Term of Enlistment.	Number killed, missing, or died of wounds received in action.	Number died of disease or accidents.	Number died in rebel prisons.	Total loss by death in each Company.
F*	1st Penn. Cav.	July, 1861	3 years	10	9	4	23
I*	8th Penn. Res. Inft.	May, 1861	3 "	25	12	8	45
G	8th Penn. Res. Inft.	May, 1861	3 "	1	..	..	1
A	11th Penn. Inft.	Sept. 1861	3 "	..	1	..	1
E	14th Penn. Cav.	Nov. 1862	3 "	2	7	2	11
K*	15th " "	Oct. 1862	3 "	2	17	..	19
K	16th " "	Oct. 1862	3 "	2	5	..	7
A*	18th " "	Nov. 1862	3 "	9	11	11	31
C*	18th " "	Nov. 1862	3 "	7	8	14	29
G*	18th " "	Nov. 1862	3 "	7	10	10	27
D	22d " "	Sept. 1862	3 "	1	..	..	1
C	61st Penn. Inft.	Aug. 1861	3 "	..	..	1	1
D	61st " "	Aug. 1861	3 "	2	..	..	2
I	61st " "	Aug. 1861	3 "	2	..	..	2
A	85th " "	Oct. 1861	3 "	..	1	..	1
B	85th " "	Oct. 1861	3 "	2	1	..	3
D	85th " "	Oct. 1861	3 "	1	2	1	4
F*	85th " "	Oct. 1861	3 "	13	18	..	31
G	85th " "	Oct. 1861	3 "	4	13	..	17
I	116th " "	July 1862	3 "	..	1	..	1
H	123d " "	Aug. 1862	9 mo.	2	1	..	3
A*	140th " "	Sept. 1862	3 "	19	8	..	27
D	140th " "	Sept. 1862	3 "	3	1	1	5
		Drafted Militia					
A*	168th " "	Oct. 1862	9 mo.	..	3	..	3
	U. S. Col'd "	1863	3 years	1	3	..	4
Total in Pennsylvania Regiments				115	132	52	299
D	1st W. Va. Inft.			1	2	..	3
B	1st " Cav.			..	1	..	1
D	1st " Cav.			1	1	..	2
A	3d " Inft.			1	2	..	3
I	4th " "			..	..	1	1
F	6th " "			..	..	2	2
N	6th " "		Three years.	..	1	..	1
B	7th " "			1	3	..	4
F*	7th " "			6	15	2	23
A	11th " "			..	1	..	1
A	12th " "			..	1	..	1
K	14th " "			3	2	3	8
I	15th " "			..	1	..	1
I	2d Colorado Cav.			..	1	..	1
I	78th Illinois Inft.			1	..	..	1
Total in West Virginia and other State Regiments				14	31	8	53
Aggregate loss by death of Greene County Soldiers				129	163	60	352

NOTE.—The Companies marked with a Star (*) were each known as Greene County Companies, having been wholy recruited in and officered by men from the county.

Besides the above the county was represented in the service, during the war, by many of her citizens serving in several other commands, but no losses by death of such are reported to have occurred therein.

CHAPTER XXXII.

County Offices

Sheriffs—County Treasurers—Clerks of Courts—Registers—
Prothonotaries—Recorders—Coroners—Sealers of Weights
and Measures—Notaries Public—County Surveyors—Justices of the Peace—School Superintendents.

SHERIFFS

James Hook, Nov. 8, 1796.
Robert Cather, March 3, 1800
Jacob Burley, Nov. 4, 1802
Samuel Harper, Oct. 25, 1805.
Barnet Reinhart, Oct. 21, 1808
Thomas Mitchel, Nov. 12, 1811.
Thomas Wood, Dec 1, 1814
Adam Hays, Oct 1, 1817.
Isaac Teagarden, Nov. 23, 1820
James Hughes, Oct 13, 1821
Joseph Moms, Oct. 28, 1824
Mark Gordon, Oct. 26, 1827.
Jacob Barnes, Nov 1, 1830.
Benjamin Smith, Oct. 28, 1833.
Benj. Woodruff, Nov 21, 1836.
R H. Lindsay, Oct 25, 1839.
John Barnes, Oct. 27, 1842

Silas Barnes, June 3, 1845.
Nelson Thomas, Nov. 10, 1845.
Isaac Thomas, May 25, 1846.
John Lindsey, Oct. 26, 1846.
R K. Campbell, Oct. 24, 1849.
David A. Worley, Nov. 17, 1852.
Elijah Adams, Oct 29, 1855.
George Wright, Oct. 28, 1858.
Thomas Lucas, Nov. 23, 1861.
Heath Johns, Nov. 10, 1864.
Henry B. Silvius, Oct. 13, 1867.
Abner Ross, Nov. 4, 1870
Jas P Cosgray, Nov 5, 1873.
John G. Dinsmore, Dec. 8, 1876.
Jos. F. Randolph, Dec. 4, 1879.
David A Spragg, Dec. 11, 1882
John S. Lemley, Dec. 14, 1885.

COUNTY TREASURERS.

William Seals, Jan 4, 1821.
William Seals, Jan. 18, 1822
Asa McClelland, Jan. 6, 1825
John Inghram, July 12, 1829.
Benj Campbell, March 18, 1834.
Benj. Campbell, Jan. 8, 1835.
Jesse Rinehart, Jan 6, 1836
Jesse Rinehart, July 3, 1837.
Jesse Rinehart, Jan. 3, 1838.
Robert Adams, Jan. 11, 1839
Robert Adams, Jan. 27, 1840

A. G. Cross, Dec 17, 1851.
Obediah Vancleve, Dec. 21, 1853.
Jacob Lemley, Dec 17, 1855.
Silas Barnes, Nov. 2, 1857.
S H Adamson, Nov. 7, 1859.
Jos. F. Randolph, Nov 12, 1861.
James S. Jennings, Nov. 24, 1863.
Thomas Iams, Oct. 18, 1865.
Abner M. Baily, Oct. 18. 1867.
James Meek, Oct. 19, 1869.
Thomas Goodwin, Dec. 19, 1871.

James Golden, Oct. 31, 1840.
James Golden, Jan 7, 1842
William Cotteral, Oct. 26, 1843.
Elijah Adams, Dec. 11, 1845
W. T. II. Pauley, Dec. 24, 1847.
Hiram C. Wood, Nov 13, 1849.

Samuel Bayard, Nov 10, 1873.
John Hunt, Nov 7, 1875
John South, Dec. 27, 1878.
Furman South, Jan. 1, 1882
William Jacobs, Jan. 5, 1885.
Robert Smith, Jan. 2, 1888.

CLERKS OF COURT.

John Boreman, March 17, 1796.
John Boreman, March 3, 1800.
John Boreman, March 25, 1809
Wm. T. Hays, Oct. 17, 1814.
Wm. T. Hays, Jan. 15, 1818.
Wm. T. Hays, Feb. 8, 1821.
Wm. T. Hays, Feb. 28, 1824.
Wm. T. Hays, Jan. 13, 1827.
Wm. T. Hays, Jan. 20, 1830.
Enos Hook, Dec. 31, 1832.
John Hook, Dec. 23, 1835.
John Phelan, Jan. 25, 1839.
John Phelan, Nov. 14, 1839.
John Phelan, Nov. 12, 1842.
II. L. Pennock, Nov. 17, 1845.

II. L. Pennock, Nov 25, 1848.
John Lindsey, Nov. 22, 1851.
John Lindsey, Nov. 21, 1854.
David A. Worley, Nov. 19, 1857.
David A. Worley, Nov. 19, 1860.
Justus F. Temple, Nov. 23, 1863.
Justus F. Temple, Nov. 8, 1866.
S. Montgomery, Nov. 20, 1869.
H. C. Pollock, Nov. 12, 1872.
II C. Pollock, December 8, 1875.
James C. Garard, Dec. 11, 1878.
James C. Garard, Dec. 28, 1881.
John R. Pipes, Dec 22, 1884.
John R. Pipes, Dec. 24, 1887.

REGISTERS.

John Boreman, March 17, 1796.
John Boreman, March 3, 1800.
John Boreman, March 25, 1809.
William T. Hays, Oct. 17, 1814.
William T. Hays, Jan. 15, 1818.
William T. Hays, Feb. 8, 1821.
K. S. Boreman, Feb. 28, 1824.
Levi Rienhart, Jan. 13, 1827.
Jesse Lazear, Jan. 20, 1830.
Jesse Lazear, Dec. 31, 1832.
A. N. Johnson, Dec. 23, 1835.
George Hoskinson, Jan. 25, 1839.
George Hoskinson, Nov. 14, 1839.
Wm W. Sayers, Nov 12, 1842.
Wm. W. Sayers, Nov. 17, 1845.

Reuben D. Mickle, Nov. 25, 1848.
William A. Porter, Nov. 22, 1851.
Absalom Hedge, Nov. 21, 1854.
Justus F. Temple, Nov. 12, 1857.
Justus F. Temple, Nov. 19, 1860.
Peter Brown, Nov. 23, 1863.
Peter Brown, Nov. 8, 1866.
Thos. Hoskinson, Nov. 20, 1869.
Thos. Hoskinson, Nov. 12, 1872.
James L. Yoders, Dec. 14, 1875.
James L. Yoders, Dec. 11, 1878.
W W. Patterson, Dec. 8, 1881.
W. W Patterson, Dec. 22, 1884.
Wm. II. Sutton, Dec. 24, 1887.

PROTHONOTARIES

John Boreman, March 17, 1796.
John Boreman, March 3, 1800.
John Boreman, March 25, 1809
William T. Hays, Oct. 17, 1814.

John Lindsey, Nov. 22, 1851.
John Lindsey, Nov 21, 1854.
David A. Worley, Nov. 19, 1857.
David A. Worley, Nov. 19, 1860.

William T Hays, Feb. 28, 1824. Justus F. Temple, Nov. 23, 1863 .
William T Hays, Jan. 13, 1827 Justus F. Temple, Nov. 8, 1866
William T. Hays, Jan. 20, 1830 Hiram H. Lindsey, Nov. 13, 1869.
Enos Hook, Dec 31, 1832 Hiram H. Lindsey, Nov. 12, 1872.
John Hook, Dec 23, 1835. George W. Ullom, Dec 8, 1875
John Phelan, Jan. 25, 1839. George W. Ullom, Dec 11, 1878.
John Phelan, Nov. 14, 1839 J. L. Yoders, Dec. 28, 1881.
John Phelan, Nov 12, 1842 James M. Hoge, Jan 4, 1884.
Henry L Pennock, Nov. 17, 1845. J. C. Garard, Dec 22, 1884.
Henry L Pennock, Nov. 25, 1848 J C. Garard, Dec 24, 1887

RECORDERS.

John Boreman, March 17, 1796. Reuben D. Mickle, Nov. 25, 1848.
John Boreman, March 3, 1800. William A. Porter, Nov. 22, 1851
John Boreman, March 25, 1809. Absalom Hedge, Nov. 21, 1854.
Wm. T. Hays, Oct. 17, 1814. Justus F. Temple, Nov 12, 1857.
Wm. T Hays, Jan. 15, 1818. Justus F. Temple, Nov. 19, 1860.
Wm. T Hays, Feb 8, 1821. Peter Brown, Nov 20, 1863.
K. S Boreman, Feb 28, 1824 Peter Brown, Nov 8, 1866.
Levi Rinehart, Jan 13, 1827 Thomas Hoskinson, Nov. 20, 1869.
Jesse Lazear, Jan. 20, 1830. Thomas Hoskinson, Nov 12, 1872.
Abijah N. Johnson, Dec 23, 1835 James L. Yoders, Dec 14, 1875.
Geo. Hoskinson, Jan. 25, 1839 James L Yoders, Dec 10, 1878
George Hoskinson, Nov 14, 1839 W. W. Patterson, Dec. 8, 1881
William W. Sayers, Nov 12, 1842 W W Patterson, Dec 22, 1884.
William W Sayers, Nov 17, 1845 William H Sutton, Dec 24, 1887.

CORONERS.

James Boone, Nov. 8, 1796. Wm. G W. Day, July 11, 1857.
Samuel Harper, Nov. 4, 1802 James Acklin, Feb. 15, 1864.
Samuel Huston, Oct. 25, 1805. Wm. B. Stewart, Jan 4, 1868.
Samuel Harper, Oct 31, 1817. Joel A. Harris, Jan. 6, 1871.
Lot Lantz, Feb. 26, 1821. Lewis N Johnson, Nov. 5, 1873
Robert Maple, March 21, 1822. Robert Dougherty, Dec 8, 1876.
George Morris, Dec. 24, 1833. William H. Rose, Dec. 11, 1878.
Daniel Smith, Feb. 25, 1840 Leroy W Carrel, Dec. 28, 1881.
William Campbell, Nov. 9, 1846. George Frazier, Dec 22, 1885.

SEALERS OF WEIGHTS AND MEASURES

Thomas Hill, April 24, 1857. Isaac Teagarden, Jan 13, 1874.
Samuel Braden, Aug. 4, 1858. Isaac Teagarden, Jan. 25, 1877.
Daniel Owen, April 6, 1864 Isaac Teagarden, Feb. 9, 1880.
James Acklin, Dec 12, 1867 Isaac Teagarden, Feb 15, 1881
James Coates, March 14, 1870.

NOTARIES PUBLIC.

John Phelan, Dec. 17, 1835.
John Strawn, Dec. 2, 1839
John C. Flenniken, March 27, 1848.
John Straun, Dec. 1, 1842.
John C. Flenniken, Sept. 1, 1851, Borough of Waynesburg.
Amos Clevenger, Jan. 6, 1855, Borough of Waynesburg.
John H. Wells, Jan. 13, 1858, Borough of Waynesburg.
Absalom Hedge, Dec. 17, 1860, Borough of Waynesburg.
George E. Minor, Nov. 17, 1863, Borough of Waynesburg.
George S. Geffrey, Dec 27, 1866, Borough of Waynesburg.
George S. Geffrey, Feb. 3, 1870, Borough of Waynesburg.
George W. Dougherty, Sept. 12, 1872, Borough of Carmichaels.
George S. Geffrey, Feb 17, 1873, Greene County.
J. P. Mitchener, Oct. 6, 1875, Greene County.
James E. Sayers, March 11, 1876, Borough of Waynesburg.
J. P. Mitchner, March 31, 1876, Borough of Carmichaels.
James G. Patterson, April 17, 1878, Borough of Carmichaels.
James E. Sayers, March 10, 1879, Borough of Waynesburg.
James E. Sayers, March 1, 1882, Borough of Waynesburg.
James E. Sayers, Feb. 3, 1883, Borough of Waynesburg.
James M. Hoge, March 3, 1885, Borough of Waynesburg.
James E Sayers, March 21, 1885, Borough of Waynesburg.
John F. Thompson, Aug. 19, 1885, Borough of Greensboro.
John F. Thompson, Jan. 29, 1887, Borough of Greensboro.
Samuel M. Smith, Aug. 16, 1887, Borough of Jefferson.
Jesse H. Wise, Nov. 25, 1887, Borough of Waynesburg.
Ira L. Nickeson, March 5, 1888, Richhill, Township.
W. R. Hoge, March 15, 1888, Borough of Waynesburg.

COUNTY SURVEYORS.

George F. Wolf, Dec. 15, 1856.   George Hoge, Dec. 19, 1871.
George F. Wolf, Dec. 26, 1859.   C. C. Brock, Dec. 14, 1874.
George Hoge, Dec. 19, 1865.   C. C. Brock, Jan. 5, 1878.
George Hoge, Feb 17, 1869.   James B. Smith, Dec. 31, 1880.

George Hoge was elected county surveyor in 1883, but died before entering office. James B. Smith was appointed, and held office until 1886, when he was re-elected, and is present incumbent.

JUSTICES OF THE PEACE.

John Minor, July 13, 1796   Thomas Lucas, Oct. 12, 1819.
Wm. Ingraham, Dec. 28, 1797.   Richard Herwood, Feb. 21, 1820.
William Paul, Jan. 12, 1798.   Jonathan Parkinson, Feb. 21, 1820.
Robert Ross, Jan. 12, 1798.   David Gray, Jr., Feb. 21, 1820.
Joseph Gibbons, Jan. 12, 1798. Jeremiah Glasgow, March 20, 1820.

23

Eleazer Luce, Feb. 9, 1799.
Jonathan Johnson, Feb. 9, 1799.
John McKee, Feb. 9, 1799.
Jared Brush, Feb. 9, 1799.
John Glasgow, Feb. 9, 1799.
John Corbly, Jan. 15, 1801.
Thomas Patterson, Feb. 27, 1801.
Jacob Black, April 2, 1802.
Thomas Lazear, April 1, 1803.
John Hair, Jan. 1, 1806.
H. Postlethwaite, April 22, 1807.
David Worley, March 29, 1808.
James Dye, Oct. 20, 1808.
Thomas Hersey, Jan. 21, 1809.
Rees Hill, March 15, 1809.
James Clark, May 2, 1809.
Samuel Hill, Jan. 14, 1811.
Robert Milliken, Jan. 14, 1811.
Ephraim Coleman, July 4, 1811.
Jacob Baily, July 4, 1811.
Robert Lewis, July 4, 1811.
John Morrison, Dec. 15, 1812.
William Heaton, Feb. 13, 1813.
Jacob Rickey, Feb. 3, 1814.
David Taylor, April 28, 1815.
Thomas Burson, Dec. 1, 1815.
Joshua Cobb, Dec. 24, 1816.
William Baily, March 20, 1817.
James Tuttle, Feb. 15, 1819.
Carey McLelland, Feb. 15, 1819.

John Crawford, March 14, 1822.
Corbly Garrard, Jan. 25, 1823.
Matthew Dill, March 24, 1823.
John Pettit, March 16, 1824.
Levi Monis, March 16, 1824.
Nicholas Hagar, Feb. 5, 1825.
Nathaniel Campbell, Feb. 5, 1825.
Ed. McGlumphey, June 23, 1827.
William Burge, May 2, 1828.
Hiram Heaton, May 12, 1828
John T. Rinehart, March 31, 1829.
John Hiller, April 29, 1829.
Joseph Johnson, May 22, 1829.
Abia Minor, Jan. 28, 1830.
Benjamin Miller, April 21, 1831.
James Mustard, Jan. 21, 1832.
John Lindsey, Oct. 29, 1832.
William Seals, March 18, 1833.
Wm. McCallester, March 10, 1833.
Lewis Headlee, March 18, 1833.
John McMay, April 22, 1833.
Joseph Adamson, Dec. 27, 1833.
George Haner, Feb. 14, 1834.
Vincent Smith, May 27, 1834.
Jesse Kent, June 9, 1834.
James Cree, June 9, 1834.
G. B. Goodrich, June 9, 1834.
Benjamin Jennings, June 9, 1834.
Robert Boyd, Dec. 2, 1834.
John Parkinson, Aug. 31, 1835.

District No. 2 is composed of the Township of Morgan and town of Clarksville.

District No. 3 is composed of the Townships of Cumberland and Jefferson.

District No. 4 is composed of the Townships of Greene, Dunkard and Monongahela.

District No. 5 is composed of the Townships of Whitely, Wayne, and part of Aleppo.

District No. 6 is composed of the Townships of Richhill, Centre, and part of Aleppo.

Benjamin F. Black, March 1, '36, District No. 4.

Ralph Drake, March 13, '36, District No. 3.

Henry Neil, March 13, '36, District No. 3.

Ralph Drake, May 15, '37, District No. 2.

Samuel D. McCarl, Jan. 10, '38, District No. 5.

William Phillips, Jan. 10, '38, District No. 6.
Abner Garrison, March 8, '38, District No. 5.
Justus Garard, June 19, '38, District No. 4.
George Strope, March 18, '39, District No. 6.
James Walton, May 10, '39, District No. 2.
Joseph Debolt, April 14, '40, Township of Aleppo.
William Hoge, April 14, '40, Morgan.
Thomas Horner, April 14, '40, Cumberland.
Caleb Kimble, April 14, '40, Aleppo.
Abraham Tustin, April 14, '40, Wayne.
Alexander Stephenson, April 14, '40, Greene.
Asa Sellers, April 14, '40, Centre.
Silas Rush, April 14, '40, Morris.
John Reynolds, April 14, '40, Borough of Jefferson.
James Walton, April 14, '40, Morgan.
Lewis Headlee, April 14, '40, Whitely.
Benjamin Long, April 14, '40, Dunkard.
Benjamin F. Black, April 14, '40, Monongahela.
Edward Barker, April 14, '40, Morris.
James Garrison, April 14, '40, Dunkard.
George Haver, April 14, '40, Cumberland.
Jesse Kent, April 14, '40, Centre.
Justus Garard, 14, '40, Monongahela.
William Kincaid, April 14, '40, Jefferson.
Henry Neel, April 14, '40, Borough of Jefferson.
Vincent Smith, April 14, '40, Franklin.
Jacob Barnes, April 14, '40, Washington.
Michael Strosnider, April 14, '40, Jefferson.
David Gray, April 14, '40, Richhill.
Robert Boyd, April 14, '40, Washington.
Corbly Garard, April 14, '40, Greene.
Fletcher Brock, April 14, '40, Wayne.
John Clark, April 14, '40, Franklin.
Daniel Hook, April 14, '40, Marion.
Thomas Lazear, April 14, '40, Richhill.
Benjamin Jennings, April 14, '40, Marion.
Joseph B. Johnson, April 14, '40, Jackson.
Abner Garrison, April 14, '40, Jackson.
John Fonner, April 14, '40, Aleppo.
Boaz Boydston, April 14, '40, Perry.
Levi Anderson, April 14, '40, Perry.
Samuel Vanatta, April 11, '43, Richhill.
Moses Coen, April 11, '43, Franklin.
Joseph Adamson, April 11, '43, Morgan.
William Phillips, April 11, '43, Aleppo.

William Boone, April 9, '44, Monongahela
James Kincaid, April 9, '44, Jefferson.
Matthew Dill, April 9, '44, Morgan.
George Davis, April 15, '45, Cumberland
William Wiley, April 15, '45, Cumberland.
Samuel C. Orr, April 15, '45, Dunkard
Simon Strosnider, April 15, 45, Wayne.
Abner Hoge, April 15, '45, Centre.
Jacob Loar, April 15, '45, Richhill.
Michael Strosnider, April 15, '45, Jefferson.
Benjamin Maple, April 15, 45, Monongahela.
Alexander Stephenson, April 15, '45, Greene.
Elijah Chalfan, April 15, '45, Whitely.
Benjamin L. Wells, April 15, '45, Wayne
Daniel Fuller, April 15, '45, Whitely.
Benjamin Long, April 15, '45, Dunkard.
James H. Fordyce, April 15, '45, Greene.
Edward Barker, April 15, '45, Morris
John McClelland, April 15, '45, Jackson
James McElroy, April 15, '45, Borough of Jefferson.
Henry Neel, April 15, '45, Borough of Jefferson
Benjamin Miller, April 15, '45, Morris.
Daniel Hook, April 15, '45, Marion
Thomas W. Taylor, April 15, '45, Washington
John Clark, April 15, '45, Franklin
Benjamin Jennings, April 15, '45, Marion.
Robert Boyd, April 15, '45, Washington.
Jesse Kent, April 15, '45, Centre.
Abner Garrison, April 15, '45, Jackson.
Henry Loughman, April 14, '46, Morris.
Silas Ayers, April 14, '46, Aleppo.
John B. Minor, April 13, '47, Perry.
Jesse Headlee, April 13, '47, Perry.
Henry Moore, April 11, '48, Aleppo.
Samuel Vanatta, April 11, '48, Richhill.
David Crawford, April 11, '48, Franklin.
John Lewis, April 11, '48, Morgan.
James McElroy, April 9, '50, Jefferson.
Jacob Loar, April 9, '50, Richhill.
Alexander Stephenson, April 9, '50, Greene.
Samuel P. Bayard, April 9, '50, Jackson.
Johnston T. Smith, April 9, '50, Jackson.
Robert Boyd, April 9, '50, Washington.
William Wily, April 9, '50, Cumberland.
Simon Strosnider, April.9, '50, Wayne.

Samuel C. Orr, April 9, '50, Dunkard.
James Murdock, April 9, '50, Cumberland.
Elijah Chalfant, April 9, '50, Whitely,
Edward Barker, April 9, '50, Morris.
James Garrison, April 9, '50, Dunkard.
Jeremiah Stewart, April 9, '50, Greene.
Henry Shriver, April 9, '50, Wayne.
Samuel Ferguson, April 9, '50, Centre.
Samuel Garner, April 9, '50, Washington.
Benjamin Maple, April 9, '50, Monongahela.
Henry Neel, April 9, '50, Jefferson.
George John, April 9, '50, Whitely.
George Sellers, April 9, '50, Centre.
John Barnes, April 9, '50, Franklin.
Michael Strosnider, April 9, '50, Jefferson.
Daniel Hook, May 21, '50, Marion.
Wm. T. E. Webb, May 21, '50, Marion.
John Bogard, April 15, '51, Aleppo
Joshua C. Phillips, April 15, '51, Borough of Waynesburg.
John Booze, April 15, '51, Morgan.
Abraham Stout, April 15, '51, Jefferson.
Henry Loughman, April 15, 51, Morris.
Wm. T. E Webb, May 9, '51, Borough of Waynesburg.
William F. Bradley, April 15, '51, Borough of Jefferson.
Enas Headlee, May 5, '52, Perry.
John B. Minor, May 5, '52, Perry.
Thomas Hill, June 11, '52, Franklin.
Justice Garrard, April 13, '53, Monongahela.
Jacob Guthrie, April 13, '53, Whitely.
William Fox, April 13, '53, Aleppo.
Samuel Vanata, April 13, '53, Richhill.
Thomas W. Taylor, April 13, '53, Washington.
John Billingsly, April 13, '53, Perry.
James Pipes, April 13, '53, Franklin.
John Lewis, April 13, '53, Morgan.
Daniel Hook, April 11, '54, Borough of Waynesburg.
Azariah Stephens, April 11, '54, Greene
John B. Litzinburg, July 6, '54, Borough of Jefferson.
Johnston L. Smith, April 10, '55, Jackson.
John B. Seckman, April 10, '55, Centre
Peter M. Grimes, April 10, '55, Jackson
Jesse K. Baily, April 10, '55, Cumberland.
Nicholas Shanes, April 10, '55, Wayne.
Jeremiah Stewart, April 10, '55, Greene.
Robert Ross, April 10, '55, Monongahela.

John E. Parkinson, April 10, '55, Aleppo.
Henry Bebout, April 10, '55, Morris.
Joseph Kniseley, April 10, '55, Wayne.
Jacob Loar, April 10, '55, Richhill.
Elijah Chalfan, April 10, '55, Whitely.
George Sellers, April 10, '55, Centre.
Robert Boyd, April 10, '55, Washington.
Thomas Horner, August 8, '55, Borough of Carmichaels.
William Wily, August 8, '55, Borough of Carmichaels.
Thomas Lucas, April 10, '55, Cumberland.
William T. E. Webb, April 19, '56, Borough of Waynesburg.
Robert Wallace, April 16, '56, Borough of Jefferson.
John Booze, April 16, '56, Morgan.
William King, April 28, '56, Wayne.
Edward Barker, April 28, '56, Morris.
William P. Scott, April 16, '56, Jefferson.
James Garrison, May 17, '56, Dunkard.
Thomas H. Meighen, October 1, '56, Gilmore.
John P. Morris, October 1, '56, Gilmore.
Jesse Headlee, April 14, '57, Perry.
Enoch H. Denny, July 14, '57, Borough of Jefferson.
John D. Wood, April 14, '57, Franklin.
John Bradley, July 14, '57, Borough of Jefferson.
Jacob Guthrie, April 13, '58, Whitely.
Justus Garrard, April 13, '58, Monongahela.
James Pipes, April 13, '58, Franklin.
John A. Billingsly, April 13, '58, Perry.
Jonah R. Wood, April 13, '58, Borough of Carmichaels.
Samuel Vanatta, April 13, '58, Richhill.
James A. Black, April 13, '58' Monongahela.
Thomas W. Taylor, April 13, '58, Washington.
John Lewis, April 13, '58, Morgan.
Enoch Estle, July 13, '58, Borough of Jefferson.
William Fox, Nov. 2, '58, Aleppo.
Simon Rinehart, April 12, '59, Marion.
George Howard, April 12, '59, Dunkard.
Jesse Craig, April 12, '59, Washington.
John Stephenson, April 12, '59, Greene.
Jeramiah Stewart, April 10, '60, Greene.
Johnson T. Smith, April 4, '60, Jackson.
John I. Worley, April 10, '60, Wayne.
Peter M. Grimes, April 10, '60, Jackson.
James Hughes, April 10, '60, Richhill.
George W. Bell, April 10, '60, Wayne.
John B. Seckman, April 10, '60, Centre.

John Elbin, April 10, '60, Aleppo.
William Rogers, April 10, '60, Centre.
William Hartman, April 10, '60, Carmichaels Borough.
Morgan Young, April 10, '60, Cumberland.
Jesse K. Bailey, April 10, '60, Cumberland.
Elijah Chalfan, April 10, '60 Whitely.
Norman Powers, April 10, '60, Morris
Michael Strosnider, April 10, '69, Perry.
Stephen White, April 10, '60, Springhill.
·William T. E. Webb, May 28, '61, Marion.
Edward Barker, May 28, '61, Morris.
John Mitchner, May 28, '61, Morgan.
Jackson Hinerman, June 3, '61, Aleppo.
Henry Maskil, June 3, '61, Jefferson
Jacob Rush, June 3, '61, Jefferson.
James Call, June 3, '61, Centre.
Samuel Dodd, June 17, '61, Franklin.
John P. Morris, April 15, '62, Gilmore
Abraham Ammons, April 29, '62, Perry.
John Lantz, April 29, '62, Gilmore.
Elias Scott, April 29, '62, Centre.
Lewis Dowlin, April 29, '62, Dunkard.
Enoch H. Denny, April 29, '62, Jefferson Borough.
Thomas Horner, May 15, '62, Jefferson.
Isaac Clark, May 5, '63, Franklin.
Thomas W. Taylor, May 15, '63, Washington.
James Burdine, May 5, '63, Springhill.
Miller Iams, May 5, '63, Morgan.
Eli Rose, May 5, '63, Whitely.
William L. Pogue, May 5, '63, Jefferson.
James A. Black, May 5, '63, Monongahela
Joseph Connor, May 5, '63, Perry.
Andrew Dunlap, May 5, '63, Monongahela.
Francis Drake, May 5, '63, Richhill.
Jonah R. Wood, July 13, '63, Carmichaels Borough.
Simon Rinehart, April 5, '64, Marion.
Michael McClelland, April 5, '64, Washington.
John Stephenson, April 5, '64, Greene.
George Howard, April 5, '64, Dunkard.
Elijah Chalfan, April 10, '65, Whiteley.
Simon A. Huston, April 10, '65, Richhill.
Stephen White. April 10, '65, Springhill.
Peter M. Grimes, April 10, '65, Jackson.
William Wily, June 29, '65, Borough of Carmichaels.
Johnson L. Smith, April 10, '65, Jackson.

George W. Bell, April 10, '65, Wayne.
John R. Lygard, April 10, '65, Wayne.
Jesse K. Bailey, April 10, '65, Cumberland.
Jeremiah Stewart, April 10, '65, Greene.
Norman Powers, April 10, '65, Morris.
John T. Elbin, April 10, '65, Aleppo.
Morgan Young, April 10, '65, Cumberland.
Henry Lantz, April 10, '65, Greene.
James Coates, July 17, '65, Jacksonville Borough.
William T. E. Webb, April 5, '66, Marion.
James Pipes, April 5, '66, Franklin.
Vincent Lewis, April 5, '66, Morris.
James Call, April 5, '66, Centre.
A. J. Hinerman, April 5, '66, Aleppo.
William Hoskinson, April 5, '66, Springhill.
Thomas B. Ross, April 5, '66, Morgan.
Jacob Rush, April 5, '66, Jefferson.
Wreenbury Wade, April 3, '67, Perry.
George W. Ullom, April 3, '67, Centre.
Lewis Dowlin, April 3, '67, Dunkard.
John Lantz, April 3, '67, Gilmore.
Samuel Bayard, April 3, '67, Jefferson.
Enoch Estle, April 3, '67, Borough of Jefferson.
Salem Lemmons, April 3, '67, Gilmore.
Corbly Ornduff, April 18, '67, Whitely.
Joseph Clutter, April 18, '67, Morris.
Samuel Sharpneck, April 17, '68, Jefferson.
Jesse Headlee, April 7, '68, Perry.
Francis Drake, April 7, '68, Richhill.
Miller Iams, April 7, '68, Morgan.
Jonah R. Wood, April 7, '68, Borough of Carmichaels.
Workman Hickman, April 7, '68, Whitely.
Stephen Day, April 7, '68, Morris.
Isaac Clark, April 7, '68, Franklin.
Andrew Dunlap, April 7, '68, Monongahela.
John P. Williams, April 8, '68, Monongahela.
Wm. L. Pogue, April 7, '68, Borough of Jefferson.
Franklin Seaton, April 7, '68, Greene.
Jacob Johns, May 26, '68, Washington.
Simon Rinehart, April 6, '69, Marion.
Cephas Craig, April 6, '69, Washington.
George Howard, April 6, '69, Dunkard.
William Estle, March 16, '70, Jackson.
William Pollock, March 16, '70, Wayne.
Isaac Hewitt, March 16, '70, Cumberland.

Walter L. Batson, March 16, '70, Morris.
Peter M. Grimes, March 16, '70, Jackson.
Solomon Hoge, March 16, '70, Wayne.
Stephen Knight, March 16, '70, Richhill.
John T. Elbin, March 16, '70, Aleppo.
William Wily, March 16, '70, Borough of Carmichaels.
Stephen White, March 16, '70, Springhill.
J. K. Baily, March 16, '70, Cumberland.
Henry Lantz, March 16, '70, Greene.
Moredock Silveus, Nov. 22, Whitely.
William T. E. Webb, April 1, '71, Marion.
John Mitchiner, April 1, '71, Marion.
Jacob S. Rush, April 1, '71, Jefferson.
J. Monroe White, April 1, '71, Aleppo.
Wm. P. Hoskinson, April 1, '71, Springhill.
Zadock Gordon, April 1, '71, Centre.
Henry Jacobs, April 9, '72, Franklin.
George W. Ullom, April 9, '72, Centre.
Andrew Lantz, April 9, '72, Greene.
James M. Shroyer, April 9, '72, Perry.
Corbly Ornduff, April 9, '72, Whitely.
David H. Paul, April 9, '72, Dunkard.
William Clovis, April 9, '72, Gilmore.
Salem Lemmons, April 22, '72, Gilmore.
John P. Williams, April 15, '73, Monongahela.
Benjamin Mapel, April 15, '73, Monongahela.
Isaac C. Booher, April 15, '73, Richhill.
Stephen J. Day, April 15, '73, Morris.
Samuel Felton, April 15, '73, Franklin.
Jacob John, April 15, '73, Washington.
Greenberry Wade, April 15, '73, Perry.
Franklin Seaton, April 15, '73, Greene.
James G. Patterson, April 15, '73, Borough of Carmichaels.
John B. Johnson, April 15, '73, Centre.
Enoch H. Denny, April 15, '73, Borough of Jefferson.
Solomon B. Wise, April 15, '73, Morgan.
Enoch Estle, April 15, '73, Borough of Jefferson.
Hiram C. Cloud, April 15, '73, Jefferson.
Simon Rinehart, March 17, '74, Marion.
Cephas Craig, March 17, '74, Washington.
George Howard, March 17, '74, Dunkard.
Hiram L. Granlee, March 13, '75, Wayne.
William Estle, March 13, '75, Jackson.
William Johnson, March 13, '75, Wayne.
George W. Daugherty, March 13, '75, Borough of Carmichaels.

John T. Elvin, March 13, '75, Aleppo.
Peter M. Grimes, March 13, '75, Jackson.
J. K. Bailey, March 13, '75, Cumberland.
Norman Powers, March 13, '75, Morris.
James Stiles, March 13, '75, Springhill.
Archibald Kerr, March 13, '75, Cumberland.
Stephen Knight, April 3, '75, Richhill.
Peter A. Myers, May 31, '75, Greene.
D. M. Silveus, March 13, '75, Whitely.
John Munnel, March 9, '76, Marion.
James Hoge, March 11, '76, Centre.
J. Monroe White, March 11, '76, Aleppo.
Thomas H. Meighen, March 11, '76, Springhill.
William Burson, March 11, '76, Morgan.
A. F. Ammons, March 11, '76, Jefferson.
A. C. Pennington, March 11, '76, Monongahela.
John Munnel, March 17, '77, Marion.
Minor L. Carpenter, March 17, '77, Gilmore.
Milton Worley, March 17, '77, Franklin.
James Murdock, March 17, '77, Borough of Carmichaels.
William Clovis, March 17, '77, Gilmore.
Corbly Ornduff, March 17, '77, Whitely.
Manassa Wildman, March 17, '77, Dunkard.
Andrew Lantz, March 17, '77, Greene.
John Blair, March 17, '77, Perry.
Lester Kughn, April 4, '77, Jackson.
Thomas L. Lincoln, March 25, '78, Borough of Carmichaels.
Thomas Tuttle, March 25, '78, Washington.
William Kincaid, March 25, '78, Jefferson.
Henry Bell, March 25, '78, Morgan.
Andrew Dunlap, March 25, '78, Monongahela.
Enoch Estle, March 25, '78, Borough of Jefferson.
Warren Mankey, March 25, '78, Morris.
James M. Scott, March 25, '78, Franklin.
Isaac C. Booher, March 25, '78, Richhill.
E. H. Denny, March 25, '78, Borough of Jefferson.
John B. Johnson, March 25, '78, Centre.
John A. Billingsly, March 25, '78, Perry.
Simon Rinehart, March 4, '79, Borough of Waynesburg.
Cephas Craig, March 27, '79, Washington.
James A. Black, March 27, '79, Borough of Greensboro.
Alfred Maple, March 27, '79, Dunkard.
John Fox, March 27, '79, Whitely.
Simon Rinehart, Jr., March 27, '79, Borough of Waynesburg.
John H. Carson, March 27, '79, Marion.

John Munnel, March 27, '79, Borough of Waynesburg.
Allen J. Neel, May 13, '79, Monongahela.
Peter M. Grimes, March 30, '80, Jackson.
Archibald Kerr, March 30, '80, Cumberland.
David H. Brewer, March 30, '80, Richhill.
James Stiles, March 30, '80, Springhill.
H. S. Granlee, March 30, '80, Wayne.
William H. Johnson, March 30, '80, Wayne.
Norman Powers, March 30, '80, Morris.
Daniel Rich, March 30, '80, Cumberland.
Jesse S. Hinerman, March 30, '80, Aleppo.
P. A. Myers, March 30, '80, Greene.
Jesse Ullom, April 19, '81, Centre.
Thomas H. Meighen, April 19, '81, Springhill.
A. F. Ammons, April 19, '81, Jefferson.
J. M. White, April 19, '81, Aleppo.
John Matthews, April 19, '81, Morgan.
W. H. Laning, April 19, '81, Borough of Greensboro.
Manassa Wildman, April 8, '82, Dunkard.
John Lemley, April 8, '82, Whitely.
Milton Worley, April 8, '82, Franklin.
George W. Lantz, April 8, '82, Greene.
William Knox, April 8, '82, Borough of Carmichaels.
Jefferson Dye, April 8, '82, Gilmore.
Thomas Pennington, April 8, '82, Borough of Greensboro.
John Lantz, April 8, '82, Gilmore.
Hiram Hatfield, April 8, '82, Perry.
George Rinehart, April 8, '82, Jackson.
James Hoge, April 6, '83, Centre.
Thomas Tuttle, April 6, '83, Washington.
James M. Scott, April 6, '83, Franklin.
Thomas L. Lincoln, April 6, '83, Borough of Carmichaels.
William Kincaid, April 6, '83, Jefferson.
Warren Mankey, April 6, '83, Morris.
Andrew Dunlap, April 6, '83, Monongahela.
Michael C. Monroe, April 6, '83, Perry.
Isaac C. Booher, April 6, '83, Richhill.
William Pollock, April 6, '83, Borough of Jefferson.
James L. Corbett, April 6, '83, Morgan.
James A. Black, April 7, 84, Borough of Greensboro.
Alfred Maple, April 7, '84, Dunkard.
Hamilton Kuhn, April 7, '84, Whitely.
W. T. Webb, April 7, '84, Borough of Waynesburg.
Ingram Rush, April 7, '84, Washington.
M. M. McClelland, April 7, '84, Washington.

Simon Rinehart, April 7, '84, Borough of Waynesburg.
A. J. Neil, April 7, '84, Monongahela.
W. H. Laning, April 7, '84, Borough of Greensboro.
Enoch Estle, May 15, '84, Borough of Jefferson.
Archibald Kerr, April 16, '85, Cumberland.
Peter M. Grimes, April 16, '85, Jackson.
Enoch Mapel, April 16, '85, Wayne.
Daniel Rich, April 16, '85, Cumberland.
Jesse S. Hinerman, April 16, '85, Aleppo.
David H. Brewer, April 16, '85, Richhill.
H. L. Granlee, April 16, '85, Wayne.
James Stiles, April 16, '85, Springhill.
P. A. Myers, April 16, '85, Greene.
Elias C. Stone, April 16, '85, Borough of Greensboro.
William Clevenger, April 16, '85, Monongahela.
John H. Carson, October 30, '85, Borough of Waynesburg.
J. M. White, April 17, '86, Aleppo.
A. F. Ammons, April 17, '86, Jefferson.
John H. Smith, April 17, '86, Morris.
Perry Teagarden, April 17, '86, Jefferson.
John L. Matthews, April 17, '86, Morgan.
Francis Barger, April 17, '86, Springhill.
Jesse Ullom, April 17, '86, Centre.
Wm. M. Nickerson, April 17, '86, Borough of Carmichaels.
A. L. Montgomery, April 17, '86, Franklin.
J. H. Carson, April 17, '86, Borough of Waynesburg.
Robinson John, April 17, '86, Whitely.
James F. Morris, April 25, '87, Jackson.
George W. Lantz, April 25, '87, Greene.
Hiram Hatfield, April 25, '87, Perry.
Jefferson Dye, April 25, '87, Gilmore.
J. W. Rinehart, April 25, '87, Franklin.
Salem Lemmon, April 25, '87, Franklin.
Benjamin Stone, April 25, '87, Dunkard.
L. F. Stentz, April 25, '87, Borough of Greensboro.
Thomas Montgomery, April 25, '87, Morgan.
John W. Hays, November 29, '87, Borough of Waynesburg.
Warren Mankey, April 5, '88, Morris.
Thomas L. Lincoln, April 5, '88, Borough of Carmichaels.
W. H. Faddis, April 5, '88, Jefferson.
J. C. Booher, April 5, '88, Richhill.
Jesse McNeeley, April 5, '88, Centre.
William Pollock, April 5, '88, Borough of Jefferson.
George Frazier, April 5, '88, Borough of Waynesburg.

John Milliken, April 5, '88, Perry.
J. O. Kennedy, April 5, '88, Gilmore.

COUNTY SUPERINTENDENTS OF SCHOOLS.

John A. Gordon, May, '54.
A. J. McGlumphy, May, '57.
G. W. Baker, May, '59.
John A. Gordon, May, '60.
A. B. Miller, May, '61.
T. J. Teal, May, '63.
T. J. Teal, May, '66.
T. J. Teal, May '69.
T. J. Teal, May, '72.
A. F. Silvius, May, '75.
S. F. Hoge, May, '78.
William M. Nickerson, May, '81.
James S. Herrington, May, '84.
A. J. Waychoff, May, '87.

DISTRICT ATTORNEYS.

Cornelius Darrah, 1850.
Wm. H. Babbit, 1850 to 1855, two terms.
A. A. Purman, 1855 to 1861, two terms.
R. A. McConnell, 1861 to 1864.
G. G. Ritchie, 1864 to 1866.
D. R. P. Huss, 1866 to 1870.
Geo. W. Ingraham, 1870 to 1873.
W. A. Hook, 1873 to 1879, two terms.
B. W. Carpenter, 1879 to 1882.
W. H. Barb, 1882 to 1885.
D. R. P. Huss, 1885 to 1888.
D. R. P. Huss, 1888.

COMMISSIONERS.

Geo. Estle, January, 1871, to January, 1873.
Stephenson Garard, January, 1872, to January, 1875.
Wm. P. Cosgray, January, 1873, to January, 1876.
Robert Smith, January, 1874, to January, 1876.
Wm. L. Pogue, January, 1875, to January, 1876.

Wm. L. Pogue,
J. P. Morris,   } January, 1876, to January, 1879.
John Morris,

Jacob Coll,
Stephen M. Knotts,   } January, 1879, to January, 1882.
Thomas Lucas,

William Hickman,
Thomas Ross,   } January, 1882, to January, 1885.
S. H. Adamson,

Stephen Acklin,
Corbly Ornduff,   } January, 1885, to January, 1888.
Hiram White,

William Blair,
Thomas Courtwright, } January, 1888.
William Clovis,

AUDITORS.

David A. Spragg, January, 1871, to January, 1874.
Samuel Montgomery, January, 1872, to January, 1875.
Lester Kughn, January, 1873, to January, 1876.
Corbly Ornduff, January, 1874, to January, 1876.
John R. Bell, January, 1875, to January, 1876.
Edward W. Wood,
John R. Bell,   } January, 1876, to January, 1879.
W. C. Leonard,

F. M. Shriver,
Eli Titus,   } January, 1879, to January, 1882.
Richard Zollars,

John A. Knisely,
J. M. White,   } January, 1882, to January, 1885.
J. W. Gregg,

C. H. Fraker,
Jesse Courtwright, } January, 1885, to January, 1888.
Harvey Day,

M. M. Shirk,
Isaac I. Ferrel,   } January, 1888, present board.
John C. Hampson,

POOR HOUSE DIRECTORS.

Richard Iams, January, 1871, to 1874.
Valentine Nichols, January, 1872, to 1875.
Thomas M. Ross, January, 1873, to 1876.
Isaac Mitchell, January, 1874, to 1877.
John Scott, January, 1875, to 1878.
James M. Adamson, January, 1876, to 1879.
Thomas Smith, 1878 to 1881.
George McVay, 1879 to 1882.
James Kelley, elected 1879. . Resigned.
Joseph Webster, 1881 to 1884.
Isaac Mitchell, 1881 to 1883. Short term.
Samuel Braden, 1882 to 1885.
C. W. Scott, 1883 to 1886.

Isaac J. Hupp, 1884 to 1887.
H. P. Rinehart, 1885 to 1888.
Stephen U. McNeely, 1886,
Cephas Grimes, 1887, } Present Board.
Emanuel Beall, 1888,

JURY COMMISSIONERS.

George W. Connor, Jacob Greenlee—1871 to 1874.
Thomas McClenathan, Isaac Teagarden—1874 to 1877.
William P. Scott, Josiah Gwynn, 1877 to 1880.
A. M. Temble, Cephas Guthrie—1880 to 1883.
Samuel Roberts, John L. Ray—1883 to 1886.
J. P. Allum, W. H. Virgin—1886 to 1889.

BURGESSES OF WAYNESBURG.

A. G. Cross, 1862.
G. W. G. Waddell, 1868.
A. G. Cross, 1869.
W. T. E. Webb, 1872.
G. W. G. Waddell, 1873–1874
R. F. Downey, 1876.
J. W. Ray.
D. S. Walton.
John Guiher.
W. E. Miner.
T. R. Purman.
Robt. A. Sayers, 1887–1888.

CHAPTER XXXIII.

ALEPPO TOWNSHIP.

SPECULATORS—BOUNDARIES—OUTLOOK ON THE HIGHLANDS—LEWIS
   WETZEL—HAVE A SCALP OR LOSE MY OWN—NOTE OF THE TUR-
   KEY GOBLER—A PRICE SET ON HIS HEAD—PUT IN IRONS—
   AGILITY IN RUNNING—"CONRAD MAER"—SCHOOLS—DIRECTORS.

ALEPPO was organized as a township in 1821, and formerly
   embraced Springhill. It was, however, late in becoming generally peopled, from the fact that speculators had bought up large
blocks of land and prevented their being opened to settlement except
at high prices. The surface is broken, and though it has no large
streams it is well watered, the copious springs along its highlands forming the source of water-ways that flow to almost every
point of the compass, the South Fork of Wheeling Creek and its
tributaries flowing to the north and east, and those of Fishing Creek
to the south and west. It is bounded on the north by Richhill, on
the east by Jackson, on the south by Springhill, and on the west by
the State line, which separates it from West Virginia.

Tenants are found here, as they are found spread all over the
southwestern corner of the county. The Fletchers, the Hinermans,
the Mitchells, and Gullenstines, and the population generally are industrious, enterprising and prosperous, the farms being under a good
state of cultivation, the highways well kept, and the houses and out-
buildings in good condition. In the western part of this township,
on the highlands which divide the head waters of Long Run from
those of Herod's Run, is one of the most beautiful and picturesque
views that gladdens the eye of the traveler in any part of the world.
The road winds along the very summit of the ridge, past the pleasant seat of the Centennial Church, the outlook from the entrance to
which commands a wide view of all this delectable country. For grandeur, and quiet serene loveliness, not the hills of the Rhine, nor the
valleys of the Arno can match it. On a clear autumnal day, when
all the forests are painted in their matchless colors, and the roseate
tints of the morning are softening into the golden light of noon, the
traveler pauses to revel on the enchanting view and is loth to quit
this bewitching region. It was in the month of May that one
who had trod the highlands of Scotland, and the margins of her

lakes renowned in story, the green lanes of merry England, the goodly heritage of France, tilled like a garden, the towering mountains of Switzerland, and the classic shores of Italy, paused upon this elevation to brush from his brow the dust of travel, and inhale the refreshing breeze beneath the ample shade. The forest, now in full leaf, sweeps down through the deep valley and up the opposing hills, interspersed with patches of wheat and long stretches of green meadow. Soft wooled flocks gladden the hills, and foals with their dams lay stretched at full broadside after their morning feed upon the fresh pasturage. The bird sings his gladsome note, and from far away in the valley comes the monotonous call of the quail, and the quickened drumming of the partridge. On the far distant height of the well rounded hill at the very summit is left a single tree, tall and stately, rejoicing in dense foliage, around which the kine gather to chew the quid of content. And here he thought is the delectable spot, more charming than any that has ever greeted his eye before.

From the fact that the land in this township was held back from settlement, it was for many years the favorite haunt of game and the chosen tramping ground, in the proper season, of huntsmen, both whites and Indians. A celebrated hunter, Lewis Wetzel, though his home was on Wheeling Creek, outside of the township, spent much of his time in roaming up and down its spacious forests. A notice, therefore, of some of his exploits may not inappropriately be given here. His own experience with the cold blooded massacres of the red men had taught him swift revenge, and he lived to be the avenger of their cruelty.

In the summer of 1786 the Indians became very troublesome in the neighborhood of Wheeling. A purse of $100 was offered to the man who would bring in the first Indian scalp. The families of Wetzel and Bonnet dwelt at this time on Wheeling Creek, and the two youths, Lewis Wetzel and Lewis Bonnet, joined the company which volunteered to hunt the savages. Having trailed them across the Ohio into the Indian country, and come upon an encampment greatly outnumbering the volunteers, it was decided to return without attacking. When the return march had commenced, Wetzel was observed to be sullen, and on being asked by the commander, Major McMahan, if he was not going back, "No," was the response, "I have come to hunt Indians, and I shall have a scalp, or lose my own." Moving stealthily through the forest he came upon a hunting camp occupied by two Indians. After cooking their supper they sat down to amuse themselves by telling stories and indulging in boisterous laughter. Finally one of them started out with a torch, as if to watch at a deer lick. When the other had sunk to profound slumber, young Wetzel entered the camp, plunged his knife to the

24

heart of the savage, and departed with his victim's scalp. He reached home on the following day and claimed the prize.

A favorite method practiced by the Indians to decoy the settlers to their death, was to go near a settlement and imitate, at early dawn, the gobble of a wild turkey. This was almost sure to draw forth the settler with his rifle to secure the bird. There was a cave on the hill-side overlooking the creek, and from the neighborhood of this cave Wetzel had heard the familiar call and suspected it to be the decoy of an Indian. Crawling from his cot before the dawn, he went by a circuitous route out of view of the mouth of the cave, until he had reached an opening from which he could observe it without attracting attention. He had not been long in position—the gray dawn now breaking—before the top-knot of an Indian emerged from the cavern, and a very good imitation of a turkey gobbler's note was uttered, when the wily savage slunk back into his secure hiding place, to watch for the approach of some luckless hunter. Soon the polished head of the savage was again seen issuing from the cave. But now Wetzel was prepared for him and taking deliberate aim sent a bullet through the brain of the cunning denizen of the woods. The song of that turkey lured no more huntsmen to their doom.

When bloody massacres had been perpetrated, Wetzel never hesitated to follow single-handed and attack the savages wherever found. On one occasion, having pursued across the Ohio into the Muskingum country, he came upon a camp occupied by four braves. Waiting till they were all in profound slumber, he leaned his rifle against a tree, and seizing his tomahawk in one hand and his long knife in the other, crept noiselessly into their midst and buried his hatchet in the skull of one, and quick as thought hewed down another, accompanying his movements with unearthly yells. A third shared a like fate. The fourth, seized with a mortal terror, rushed wildly into the forest and escaped. With three Indian scalps to grace his belt he returned home.

On another occasion, while out hunting, he entered a deserted cabin and crawling up into the rafters, laid down to sleep. He had not been long there before six marauding Indians entered to pass the night. Waiting till all were asleep he noiselessly descended, and placed himself on guard for the morning. Early one of the Indians came out, yawned, stretched, and at that instant a ball from Wetzel's rifle pierced his heart. Not trusting to further adventure Wetzel lost no time in placing himself at a safe distance from the rest of the party.

Having shot an Indian after terms of peace had been concluded with General Harmer, he was seized and placed in irons; but having excited the pity of Harmer, the shackles were struck from his feet, and he amused his guards by showing his fleetness of foot. One day he ran so swiftly that he forgot to return. He was fired upon, but escaped unharmed to the river bank, where he was ferried across by his old friend, Isaac Wiseman, when the handcuffs were knocked from his hands and he returned to his home. Harmer subsequently offered a reward for his apprehension, and while on a visit to Kentucky he was again captured and put in irons, but was released on bail. Judge Foster describes him in 1789, "as a man 26 years old, five feet ten, full-breasted, very broad-shouldered, long arms, dark-skinned, black eyes, face pitted deep with small-pox, and hair, of which he was very careful, when combed, reaching to the calves of his legs."

Having lived for some time in Kentucky he returned to Wheeling Creek, and having been invited by a young friend and relative to accompany him to Dunkard Creek, he went. Arrived at his friend's cabin, what was their surprise to find a mass of smoking ruins, the work of a party of savages. Examining the trail, Wetzel decided that it was a party of three Indians, a renegade white, and a girl whom they were carrying away captive, and whom they rightly guessed was the affianced of his friend. The young men were not long in preparing to follow the trail. The Indians had crossed the Ohio before they were come up with, and had their camp near the mouth of Captina Creek. Swimming the stream at evening they reconnoitered the camp, but prudently decided to await the dawn. As soon as day broke, Wetzel singled out the largest Indian, and his friend the white man, and fired simultaneously, both bringing down their victims. The two Indians took to the woods, and the friend rescued the maiden dear to his heart. Wetzel pursued the savages, and to draw them from their hiding place, fired at random. With uplifted tomahawk they rushed from their concealment after him. Reloading as he ran, he suddenly turned and shot the foremost Indian. The remaining savage, thinking that his gun was now empty, rushed after him; but by dodging from tree to tree Wetzel foiled his antagonist till he had another charge in his gun, when the remaining foeman fell an easy prey to his trusty rifle. This incident has been made the subject of a thrilling romance entitled "Conrad Maer."

In intelligence and sobriety the people of Aleppo Township hold a commendable rank. The school report of 1855 credits it with nine schools with 149 pupils, and the report of 1887 with ten schools and 448 pupils. Superintendent McGlumphy in his report of 1859 says "This district is poor, the land being but recently disposed of in parcels and consequently not much improved. It is hoped that better times are coming." Twenty years have wrought a marvelous change. The school directors for the present year are: Samuel Evans, President; Frederick Wise, Secretary; George Murray, Blair Michel, J. M. Houston and William B. King.

CHAPTER XXXIV.

CENTRE TOWNSHIP.

LOCATION—HOW WATERED—PRODUCTIONS—OSAGE ORANGE HEDGE—
ROGERSVILLE—BUSINESS—CHURCHES—CLINTON MARKED FOR
COUNTY SEAT—HUNTER'S CAVE—THE HARVEYS—DANIEL THROCK-
MORTON—SOUTH TEN-MILE BAPTIST CHURCH—RUTAN—OAK FOR-
EST—SCHOOLS—THOMAS PURSLEY—MOLLY SELLERS—ATTACKED
BY INDIANS—THOMAS HOGE.

CENTRE, the largest in territory of any township in the county, is
situated in the western central part, and is almost exclusively devoted to agricultural pursuits. It was organized in 1824. It is
bounded on the north by Morris, on the east by Franklin, on the
south by Wayne and Jackson, and on the west by Jackson and Richhill. The surface is very broken, or rather heavily rolling, but the
soil is deep and very fertile. It is well watered by South Ten-Mile
Creek, and Pursley, one of its tributaries. The waters are pure and
sparkling, the springs everywhere copious, and the farms in a high
state of cultivation. In no part of Pennsylvania is there seen greater
evidence of thrift. Grain and hay are produced in great abundance,
fine-wooled sheep are pastured on all the hillsides, the finest blooded
horses are bred, and cattle and swine of the best stock are brought to
perfection here. Sugar maples formerly grew luxuriously in all the
valleys and up the deep ravines; but, influenced by a mistaken policy,
the sugar orchards have nearly all been swept away. Along the highways in some parts are seen hedges of the Osage orange. This also
is probably a mistaken policy. Of all the kinds of fences which the
husbandman employs to hem in his fields, this is one of the most expensive and unphilosophic. It must be planted and fenced several
years before it can be relied on to stop flocks and herds, and when
grown the beast if determined to do so will find a place to break
through. It must be annually pruned, which is anything but an
agreeable occupation, and hence is one of the most expensive fences
to keep in repair that is in use. Besides, it is a nursing place for
every foul weed, bush and bramble, sucks the fertility from the soil
for a considerable distance into the field, and is an ugly barrier for a
human being to cross, especially when chased by a mad bull, an infuriated ram, or a cunning horse.

Rogersville is a thriving village situated at the confluence of Lightner's Run with Ten-Mile Creek, on the great trail from Waynesburg to Wheeling. Archer and Tinens originally owned the tract where the village is now located, but it was subsequently acquired by Henry Church. Fifty years ago he had a large distillery here. John Rogers, who died eight years ago, and for whom the place was named, once owned most of the land. Mrs. Nancy Sellers, wife of George Sellers, a former justice of the peace, resides here and has a remarkably retentive memory of everything pertaining to the history of the town for a long period. A Methodist Church was organized at an early day, but for several years had no house of worship, holding services in the school-house and in barns. Mr. Church once had a protracted meeting in his barn Wilson Braddock was one of the early pastors. James Turner, who died at a great age during the year 1887, also ministered. In 1874 a new house of worship was built. The first store opened here was kept by Cephas Coe, an orphan boy who was in delicate health and unfit to endure the hardships of frontier life. It is now owned by Jesse Uhlom, the present justice of the peace. A fort for protection against the Indians had an existence here at an early day. Clinton, a small place a short distance down the creek, was originally owned by the grandfather of Mrs. Jesse Uhlom, and here it was understood that the county seat was to have been located, quite as central and even more suitable than that chosen; but by some chance it missed that fortune. Hopewell, now known as Hunter's Cave, a small village in the northern part of the township, also has a Methodist Church and a Christian Church.

One of the early families in this township was that of Thomas Harvey. The head of the family originally emigrated from France to Ireland, thence to England, and finally to Philadelphia On the 1st of January, 1807, the family left Philadelphia for the Monongahela country, and were three months in getting through. William, an elder brother, had come on before, and had located in this valley, where he taught school and had pupils from a distance of six and seven miles around. There were three sons, Thomas, Joseph and Samuel. They built a camp or shed the first season, and made maple sugar, and here they lived until fall, when they built a log house. Afterwards they erected a more pretentious house, two stories in height, of hewed logs, where they kept a hotel. The mail carrier from Morgantown to Wheeling made this one of his points, and frequently had not a single letter in his pouch. The family was originally Presbyterian, but became Baptist Daniel Throckmorton and wife were the first Baptists in that section. They were very devout, and were accustomed to go once a month to attend service at Goshen Baptist Church, the oldest in the county, twenty miles away. Tiring of these long journeys to worship, which he was accustomed to take with his' wife on horseback, and moved with the desire to proselyte, he joined with his neighbors in organizing a church in that neighborhood, which was known as the South Ten-Mile Baptist Church. The church was organized and the first services were held in a barn. In 1841 a comfortable frame house was erected, and. in 1883 a fine new edifice. Rutan, a small village, named for State Senator and Congressman James S. Rutan, is located in the Ten-Mile Creek valley, and from its favorable location where leading thoroughfares meet, is likely to become a place of considerable business importance. In 1872 William Hendershot opened a small store here. In the following year W. T. Hays bought the establishment and built up a prosperous trade. In 1887 he sold the store and good will to the Goodwin Brothers. On Pursley Creek, in the southeast corner of the township, there has sprung up a highly prosperous village known by the suggestive name of Oak Forest. It has a flouring mill provided with machinery for reducing the grain by the improved roller process, two stores, and the usual concomitants of a country town. By the official statement in 1855, Centre Township is reported to have fifteen schools and 576 pupils. Great improvement in the qualifications of teachers, grade of school-houses, and devotion of directors and parents to the best interests of the schools, is perceptible since that day. The board of directors is constituted as follows: William Arndoff, President; Jesse Patterson, Secretary; Joseph Mc-Neely, Thomas Scott, S. B. Huffman and Henry Church.

About the year 1775, three German families emigrated and settled near the mouth of Pursley Creek. Two of these, by the name of Sellers, appropriated the lands since owned by John Buchanan and Fordyce Thomas. The other family bore the name of Povator, and improved the tract where Edward Wood and Doc. Huffman live. A year later came Benjamin Pursley, and located the land now owned by George Hoge, Jr., and from him Pursley Creek was named. The family of the elder Sellers consisted of himself, wife, and four sons, Leonard, Jacob, George and John, the latter being demented. They lived in a cabin built for defense, located near a spring below the house of Mr. Buchanan, still standing. Leonard Sellers married Mary, the only child of Gasper Povator, with whom the young couple lived. One afternoon in the fall of 1780, or thereabouts, Leonard shouldered his gun, and journeyed into the forest for game. Molly, the wife, with her twin children, and her sister-in-law, went out to gather grapes. Molly spread her apron upon the ground, and sat the two children upon it, and while busily engaged gathering clusters, Indians, creeping stealthily, fired or rushed suddenly upon them. Molly instinctively and instantly bounded away, oblivious to everything except the terrible vision of the inhuman savages rushing upon her, and firing after her. Having escaped their deadly clutch, she ran at her utmost speed, not halting till she had reached her own cabin, when some one exclaimed, "Why, Molly, where are your children?" This was the first thought that the terror-stricken mother had, that her babes had been with her in the woods. With a shriek and a bound she flew back over the ground by which she had come, to meet death if she must, only intent on rescuing her little ones. When she reached the spot, she found the children sitting upon the apron as she had left them, but horrible to behold, both scalped. Fearing pursuit the Indians had fled. On approaching the children, one of them looked up and smiled, when it recognized its mother. Folding them to her bosom in the apron as they sat, she hurried home, and upon her arrival, found a huge butcher knife in the folds of the apron, that the savage had dropped. One of the children died, and the other lived to become the wife of Joseph Aukram, and the mother of a family. The sister-in-law, who was with her, was carried away, and was never heard of more.

During the first run home the mother saw the bark knocked off a sapling before her by the ball from the Indian's gun, which passed between her body and her arm, but fortunately did not harm her, and when she jumped off the creek bank into the sand she made a greater leap than any man in the settlement was able to do. But the powerful exertion required for the leap, and the running back and forth, together with the shock produced by seeing her poor scalped babes, proved nearly fatal. She was completely broken down, and for over a year was in a very feeble and critical condition, never regaining her natural vigor. So violent was her hatred of the savages ever after, that she not only became much excited whenever she related these incidents, but usually added, "If ever I should see an Indian, no difference where he was, or who, or how friendly he pretended to be, I know I should try to kill him—I know I could not help it." The husband returned at evening, but so horror and grief stricken that he soon sickened and died. Thomas Hoge, who furnishes many of the particulars related above, says: "My parents when first married, sixty years ago, settled on Pursley, where John Hoge now lives, on the improvement made by Ben Pursley, from whom both the creek and Ben's Run took their names. Old Molly was a practicing midwife, and my mother thinks she was a daughter of old Molly Hoffman who lived about the mouth of Pursley Creek, and was also a midwife. She also adds that when they settled on Pursley there were but two or three families above them on all the waters of that stream. There were in places two miles or more together of solid woods, without a stick amiss, where deer, wolves and wild turkeys were very plenty, with a sprinkling of bears and rattle-snakes. The deer were very troublesome in pasturing off the young wheat in winter and early spring, and wolves were so bold that it was difficult to raise poultry, lambs, or pigs."

CHAPTER XXXV.

CUMBERLAND TOWNSHIP.

Boundaries—Fort Swan and Vanmeter—Rattle Snake Meat—
John Swan—Watered—Wife Loads Guns—Carmichaels—
John McMillan—Schools

CUMBERLAND TOWNSHIP was probably one of the first settled townships in Greene County. John Swan, as early as 1767, looked upon the stately forests that encumbered all the valley of Pumpkin Run with an eye of satisfaction, and to give notice that he had chosen this location for himself proceeded to put his mark upon it by blazing the trees around a goodly circuit, a warning to all intruders to stand clear of this tract This method of marking a tract was called a tomahawk improvement, and though it secured no legal right either from the State or the Indians, yet it gave title which it was not safe for a rival settler to disturb, and many a bloody fight was the result when a daring pioneer was bold enough to intrude upon selected lands thus blazed. In 1768–'69 he returned and made here a fixed habitation. He was accompanied by Thomas Hughes and Jesse Vanmeter, who united their strengths for mutual protection. As the treacherous savages were stealing upon their victims by night and by day, and murdering and scalping those whom they had perhaps never seen before, sparing neither age, sex, nor condition, these early pioneers determined to provide for the safety of their families, and accordingly built a strong stockade, which has ever since been known as old Fort Swan and Vanmeter. It was situated near the border of Cumberland Township, on the spot where the house of Andrew J. Young stands, and was a noted rallying point in its day for the venturesome pioneers and their families. This fort was erected in the years 1770–'71. John Swan was the great-grandfather of Mrs. Young, whose home is on this ground, originally inclosed by the strong stockade, and which was hallowed by many sighs and tears of the early pioneers These were the very earliest permanent settlements within the limits of Greene County.

This was one of the original townships and embraced all the southwestern portion of the county. It possessed the most fertile soil and most attractive natural scenery of any part of this beautiful stretch of country bordering on the Ohio and its tributaries The

Dr. W. M. Parry

farms here are under a high state of cultivation, the residences and out-buildings are commodious and in good repair, and the whole section breathes an air of prosperity, contentment and happiness. This imperial township has been despoiled, as slice after slice has been taken from it to form other townships, until it is now reduced to little more than the valley of Muddy Creek, which is among the best improved parts of the county. Pumpkin Run drains a portion of it on the north, and little Whiteley on the south. It has a goodly frontage upon the Monongahela River, and is crossed by five ferries, Davidson's lower ferry, Flenniken's, near the mouth of Muddy Creek, Brown's, which meets the road from Carmichaels and the Green woolen mills, Parker's Landing and McCann's ferry, a little below the mouth of the Little Whiteley Creek. Its present limits are formed by the Monongahela on the east, Jefferson Township on the north and west, and Greene and Monongahela townships on the south.

In the year 1768 John Swan, Jacob Vanmeter, Thomas Hughes and Thomas Guesse, came from the neighborhood of Redstone Fork, which seems to have been the first stopping place of the immigrants to this new country, and charmed by the rich bottom lands along Muddy Creek settled in the neighborhood of Carmichaels, in Cumberland Township, and opened the forest and let in the sunlight for the first time in the vicinity of this ancient village, destined to be the seat of the oldest institution of learning in Greene County.

Mr. Evans in his thirty-first article gives an amusing account of the origin of the name of Muddy Creek. On one occasion when Swan and Hughes, who were among the first settlers, were crossing this stream, Swan's horse stumbled and threw its rider into the water. Gathering himself up and shaking the turbid water from his garments, he remarked in some temper, " its a *muddy* little brook anyhow." He was often rallied upon this adventure, and the name Muddy Creek has stuck to this stream ever since and is likely to as long as it continues to flow. In 1768 these two men brought their families, Swan taking his negro slaves, a goodly number, which were probably the first human chattels brought into the county. Subsequently a number of families from Maryland and Virginia brought thither slaves. Along with these two came also Henry and Jacob Vanmeter, with wagons and pack-horses, altogether a train of over fifty persons. They followed Braddock's road in the main. Henry Vanmeter occupied the tract now known as the Randolph settlement. Old trees near the house of Michael Price mark the spot where his first cabin stood. An Indian burying ground was on the crest of the high bluff overlooking Pumpkin Run upon the south. Until the massacre by Logan and his band, in 1774, there was no trouble with the Indians. Though for safety it had become necessary to have a place of refuge, and a fort was built on John Swan's farm, known as Swan and Vanmeter's fort.

"My informant," says Evans, "spent much of her time in the family of her grandfather, with whom her great-grandmother, Martha Vanmeter, lived. Being twelve years old when the great-grandmother died, she has a very distinct recollection of many incidents related to her of the early settlers. Their flour, salt, and ammunition, and all farming and household utensils were transported on pack-horses from Cumberland, Md. Their corn was ground on hand mills. Granny Vanmeter told of a young girl, her niece, who was captured by the Indians, and who, after being carried many miles away managed to make her escape; that while wandering in the woods alone she subsisted on roots and wild berries; how when she had found a dead rattlesnake, she cooked and ate it, and ever afterwards persisted in pronouncing it the sweetest bit she ever tasted; and how she finally made her way home and made glad the hearts of her friends."

An oath of allegiance to the State by Henry Vanmeter, a warrant to Charles Swan for a thousand acres of land on the payment of £400, a receipt for $1 subscription to the Pittsburg *Gazette*, dated July 15, 1795, to Charles Swan, notification to Col. Charles Swan, dated 1810, of the passage of an act granting $2,000 for Greensburg Academy, at Carmichaels, provided that the Episcopal Church, of which Swan was an active member, would allow the use of its church edifice, are all given by Evans entire, copied from the original papers. The son of John Swan emigrated to Kentucky with his family, and while lying asleep on the craft that was taking him down the Ohio, with his little daughter in his arms, was shot and instantly killed by the Indians. "So fatal was the shot that those on the boat were not aware that anything serious had happened till the little girl exclaimed, 'Oh, papa is shot, for I feel his warm blood running down over me!' There was now but one man, Hughes, left on the boat, whilst the Indians, several in number, kept up a continuous fire. The dead man's wife bravely aided in the defense of the craft by loading the guns and handing them to Hughes."

Colonel Charles Swan married Sarah, daughter of Henry Vanmeter, who, as a girl of ten, had ridden all the way from Maryland, on horseback, with Swan. He built a cabin in 1772 near the creek in the Carmichaels Valley, now owned by John Hathaway.

Carmichaels, a village of some thousand inhabitants, is situated on Muddy Creek, at nearly the centre of the township. At an early day it became the favored location of the County Academy, which attained a well merited reputation for excellence. An Episcopal church was early established here, and in its place of worship the County Academy for many years held its sessions. The New Providence Presbyterian Church is located near the village. The Rev. John McMillan preached here as early as August, 1775. The Rev. John McClintock commenced his ministry here in 1838, and for a period of full fifty years he has been pastor of this flock,—the semi-centennial of his settlement having recently been celebrated,—a venerable service scarcely matched in the history of churches The usual business and manufacturing establishments are found here, and from its favored location in the midst of a rich farming country it is destined to hold an important place as the second town in the county. It is about thirteen miles east of Waynesburg, and four from the Monongahela River. The ferries of Davidson, Fleniken, Brown, Parker and McCann connect the township with Fayette County. By the earliest records under the revised school law Cumberland is shown to have twelve schools and 581 pupils. A good graded school has taken the place of the Academy in Carmichaels, which, as an incorporated borough, is independent of the township, having three schools with 120 pupils. The report of 1859 credits this township with "quite a number of right minded school men." The progress in common school education for the past few years has been commendable. The board of directors for Carmichaels for the current year is J. A. Gilbert, President; L B. Laidley, Secretary; F. W. Rodgers. J. F. Gwynn, James Clawson and Ed. Stillwell, and for the township A. J. Young, President; T. H. Hawkins, Secretary; G. W. Daugherty, W. H. Barclay, Arch Grooms, and George Kerr.

CHAPTER XXXVI.

DUNKARD TOWNSHIP.

EARLY VISITANTS—DUNKARD RELIGION—ECKERLIN BROTHERS—
FATE OF CHRISTINA SYCKS—ENIX—DOGS EXCITED—TWENTY-
TWO AND A HALF YEARS A CAPTIVE—SATISFIED WITH THE RED
MEN—DR. W. GREENE—MARTIN'S FORT—ATTACK ON HARRI
SON'S FORT—MASSACRE—SCHOOLS.

THE valley of Dunkard Creek, embracing the townships of Dunkard, Monongahela and Perry, was the earliest occupied of any
part of Greene County, and was the scene of some of the most exciting events in its history. As early as 1754 Wendell Brown and his
two sons and Frederick Waltzer took up their abode in this neighborhood. At about the same time David Tygart and one Files got
a foothold in Tygart's Valley; but the Files family having fallen a
prey to Indian savagery, Files himself and the Tygarts left the
country. At about this time Dr. Thomas Eckerlin and two brothers
made a lodgment near the mouth of Dunkard Creek, which took its
name from the designation of the religion they professed. Whether
from a desire to insure themselves greater safety, or a wish to obtain
better lands, they removed to what have been known as the Dunkard
Bottoms, on Cheat River, West Virginia. They are reported to
have applied to the chiefs of the Six Nations in May, 1771, at Logstown, for permission to settle on the Youghiogheny, but were
refused. Their supply of ammunition, and other necessaries, having become exhausted, Dr. Eckerlin, with a stock of rich furs, went
to Winchester to barter them for the articles which they most needed.
On his way back he stopped over night at Fort Pleasant, where he
was detained on suspicion of being a spy in collusion with the
savages. Asserting his innocence so strongly, he was permitted to
go under guard to his home, on condition that he would return with
them if his assertions should prove untrue. To his grief and
amazement, on arriving at his home he found his cabin burned, and
his two brothers inhumanly murdered and scalped. His truthful-
ness was acknowledged by his captors, and, touched with pity, they
assisted at the burial. Thus ended, in sadness, the first attempt at
permanent settlement in this valley.

In the year 1760 Conrad Sycks emigrated from Germany, and

in process of time made his way to what is now Monongahela
Township, Greene County, and built a cabin on Rocky Run, some
two miles from the mouth of Dunkard Creek, on land now owned
by Mathew Green and Daniel Sycks. Here he took to wife Miss
Bonnet, a niece of the famous Indian fighter, Lewis Wetzel, and
were blessed with a family of ten children, among them Henry and
Christina When Henry had grown to man's estate, Enoch Enix
lived a mile north of the Syckses A half mile westward was Leonard
Garrison. Lane Robinson lived to the south of Dunkard Creek,
and the Selsors, at Selsor Fort. Sweaiengen's Fort across the
Monongahela was the only real stronghold in the neighborhood.
Rumors of hostile savages in the vicinity induced Garrison
to move his family to a place of security; but as the Syckses were
to remain, Garrison engaged Christina Sycks, then a maiden of
ten, to milk his cows. One evening she was reluctant to go to her
task, manifesting a presentiment of impending evil; but at the
prompting of her mother, bravely went. While driving the cows
homeward through the sugar grove she was suddenly overtaken by
two stalwart savages, the one hideous in black paint, the other red.
The one in black hurled his tomahawk at the innocent girl with
deadly aim; but something in the countenance of the maiden touched
the heart of the other, and at the opportune instant he dashed the
weapon aside, only cutting her tresses, and seizing her in his arms
bore her away into captivity.

Not returning, the household was disturbed, and when darkness
began to deepen and still she did not come, grasping his rifle the
father started for the cabin of Enix for assistance; but the latter
seemed unwilling to go until morning. The father, now with distracted mind, started alone, when the neighbor relented, and mount-
ing his horse, joined in the search. As they approached the cabin
of Sycks two shots were fired by the lurking foe, and Enix tumbled
from his horse mortally wounded. Aroused by the shots, the son,
Henry, and a companion, George Selsor, who were in the cabin, were
eager to rush out, but were held back by the mother, and the father
returning, on the following morning the entire family set out for
the strong fort across the Monongahela In their consternation a
sleeping infant was forgotten; but the boys turning back soon
brought off the treasure. Again these boys returned to reconnoitre
and warn the settlers. At Robinson's the wife with an infant was
prevailed on to escape to the fort, which she did, and was saved.
But Robinson could not be persuaded to abandon his home. At
Fort Selsor, where a number of the settlers had gathered, it was
determined to leave all and escape across the river to Fort Sweai-
ingen. On the way the dogs became terribly excited, and soon
started an Indian from his covert, who dashed away; but tripping,

fell. The dogs were upon him, but could not be induced to grapple him, and he finally made his escape, the party reaching the fort without casuality On returning to the scene of the massacre Enix was found, scalped, and in a dying condition. Robinson was found murdered and scalped, and his body stripped naked. Even the hoop was picked upon which the scalp of Enix had been stretched to dry.

The captive maiden, Christina, was hurried onward, and when tired out her captor would carry her on his shoulders A piece of a gray colt's leg was given her to eat, which she pretended to do; but she could not bring herself to swallow the unsavory dish. For their next meal a lusty warrior brought in a large fat hog, which he had slit open, and placing himself within the beast, marched in, with its head surmounting his own, and the sides of the hog completely enveloping him. The style of butchering and cooking was still not sufficiently appetizing to tempt her to partake. But on the third day they brought her a nice piece of well cooked wild turkey, and this she devoured with a relish For twenty-two years and six months she was a captive, when, in obedience to treaty engagements, she was released at Detroit and returned. Having lived so long with the savages, she could with difficulty be brought back to civilized customs, being satisfied with her life with the red men, and ever ready to defend them when abused She lived to a good old age, and was buried near Clarksburg, West Virginia. Captain Enoch Enix, who died a few years since, near Mount Morris, was the babe of four weeks left with the mother on the fatal night when the father was murdered The only son of Leonard Garrison married Mary Sycks, the babe which was left sleeping in the cradle at the time of the flight of the family, but was rescued by its brother Henry, who subsequently married Barbary Selser, who had been one of the escaping party when the dogs started the lone Indian. She bore him twelve children, and by a second wife he had twelve more. Daniel Sycks, the latest surviving child, through a nephew, Dr. W. Green, of New Geneva, has detailed the above facts which Mr. L. K Evans has recorded with particularity in his fourth Centennial article.

Near the intersection of the Morgantown State road and Crooked Run, just across the Virginia line, Martin's Fort was located in the immediate vicinity of the present site of Martin's Church. It was in the midst of a table land of several thousand acres. This is probably one of the earliest tracts settled in this part of the Monongahela country. Being in the midst of a considerable population, when the Indians became troublesome, it was probably thought necessary to build this fort for mutual protection. Lying near one of the great Indian war-paths, the settlement was particularly exposed to savage depredations One morning in June, 1779, whilst the women were engaged in milking the cows, and the men were weeding the garden patch, and preparing to go to their days work, all unsuspicious of danger, thirteen burly Indians, who had been lying in ambush, suddenly burst upon the settlers, bewildered and helpless, and mercilessly slaughtering James Stuart, James Smalley and Peter Crouse, and took captive John Shriver and his wife, two sons of Stuart, two sons of Smalley and a son of Crouse.'

Lurking about the fort till night-fall, they shut up their captives in a neighboring cabin, and placing two of their number on guard, the remainder returned for the purpose of effecting a lodgment in the fort. But the settlers had now strengthened their defences, and the savages despairing of making further captures, disappeared with their victims. It is reported that the first grave ever made in Martin's graveyard was for the body of an Indian, killed in the neighborhood of the fort. There is a tradition that the Indians were accustomed to torture their captives, and the stump of a hickory tree is still visible here to which they lashed their victims in order to practice upon them their devilish arts.

Harrison's Fort was also located on Crooked Run on land now owned by Josiah Ross, in this general neighborhood. This was probably a minor stockade for a single family, or a few neighbors, and was not a common rendezvous, as was Martin's Fort. At the time of a general alarm, in 1782, when the neighbors had gathered at the fort, Thomas Pindall came in, and induced three young men, Harrison, Crawford and Wright to accompany him to his cabin, alleging that there was no danger. In the night the females in the family awakened Mr. Pindall, saying that they were sure they heard a whistle, as of an Indian upon a charger. Pindall endeavored to allay their excitement, and all remained quiet until morning. In the morning while Pindall had gone out to catch his horse, and the three young men were at the spring, a volley was fired by lurking savages, and two of the young men, Crawford and Wright, fell dead. The women, terrified by the report of fire-arms, sprang out of bed and ran wildly for the fort, but Mrs. Pindall was overtaken, slain and scalped. The others, Mrs. Rachael Pindall and the young man Harrison, made good their escape to the fort.

Dunkard Township in its present reduced territory, is situated in the southeast corner of the county, and is bounded on the north by Greene and Monongahela Townships; on the east by Monongahela Township, and the Monongahela River, which separates it from Fayette County; on the south by Mason and Dixon's line, which separates it from West Virginia, and on the west by Perry and Whiteley Townships. The surface is greatly rolling, the soil fertile, and under a good state of cultivation. Dunkard Creek and its tributaries, and the Monongahela River drain its surface and furnish ample means

of waterpower and navigation.   From its being early settled the
country presents the appearance of greater cultivation than many
other parts of the county, the meadows are smooth and carefully
seeded, the houses and outbuildings in good state of repair, and the
highways kept in excellent condition.   The best breeds of cattle,
horses, sheep and swine, are reared in great numbers, and abundant
crops of corn, wheat rye and oats reward the hand of the diligent
Davistown, in the north central portion of the township, is a thriving
village, and being located in the midst of a rich farming population
is likely to become a place of considerable importance.   Tayloitown,
or Fairview, situated on Dunkard Creek in the southwestern part of
the township, is likewise in the midst of an excellent farming country
and bids fair to make substantial growth.   The post-office here is
known as Dunkard.   It has intercourse with Fayette County by Dilliner's upper and lower ferries   The township is credited in the
earliest report under the revised school law with eight schools and
360 pupils.   The school directors for the current year are: Isaac
Vanvoorhis, President; E S. Taylor, Secretary; W. Knotts, John.
Caigy, David Donley, Eli Russell.

CHAPTER XXXVII

FRANKLIN TOWNSHIP

CENTRAL LOCATION—SURFACE—SUGAR MAPLE—DRAINAGE—WAYNES-
BURG—CEMETERY—ROBERT WHITEHILL—COURT HOUSE—SITE
PURCHASED—ORIGINAL SETTLERS—JACKSON'S FORT—HOW AR-
RANGED—STORY OF JACKSON—SLATER FRIENDLY WITH INDIANS—
FATE OF MATHEW GRAY—NOTES OF ROBERT MORRIS—THREE
BROTHERS RINEHART—BROWN MASSACRE—SCHOOLS—DIRECTORS

FRANKLIN TOWNSHIP, from the fact that the county seat is
comprised within its limits, and that it holds a central location in
the county, possesses an importance beyond that of any of the others.
Franklin was organized as a township in 1787, by act of the Supreme
Executive council with less circumscribed boundaries than at present.
It is now limited as follows: on the north by Washington, on the east
by Morgan Jefferson and Whiteley, on the south by Whiteley and
Wayne, and on the west by Centre.   It bears the name of one of the

early patriots, more honored in foreign lands than any other American citizen. Its surface is diversified by hill and dale, and, though the hills rise to an elevation which may with some propriety be termed mountains, the soil is everywhere productive, copious fountains bursting forth on every hand, even to the loftiest summits. Originally the sugar maple made luxurious growth here, but, as in nearly every other part of the county, the groves of these trees have been swept away, and thus a source of great profit to the husbandman has been cut off. The hay crop in this township is very abundant.

Franklin is principally drained by South Ten Mile Creek and its tributaries. Smith creek drains all the south western section even to its farthest limits. A marked peculiarity of the highways is that they almost exclusively run from north to south, following the valleys, the few connecting roads from east to west forming the exception. The farms in this township are in a high state of cultivation, and exhibit evidences of careful and intelligent tillage. The farm houses are commodious, and those recently built, exhibit evidences of tasteful architecture. Many of the barns are models, and admirably planned to meet the requirements of the husbandman. Waynesburg, the county seat, a place of some 3,400 inhabitants, with Perryville and Morrisville a little to the east and lower down the stream, are the only places of importance. The Washington and Waynesburg railroad enters the township by the Ten Mile Creek valley. On a commanding eminence to the north of the town a beautiful cemetery has been laid out and planted with evergreens and shrubs, and to it many who had been buried in the old burying-ground to the east of the town, and from a burying place on the public common, have been removed. In the latter place Robert Whitehill, one of the earliest lawyers in the county, and his son were buried. Their graves were not marked, and in time all recollection of the place where they were interred was lost, so that the grave of him who in life was one of the profoundest lawyers, and brightest ornaments of the Waynesburg bar, is unknown. Further to the west upon a more commanding elevation is the reservoir of the water works, which supplies the town with water, which is pumped from the creek. The original court house was of logs, and was occupied for four years. The brick structure was built in 1800 and stood just fifty years. The present structure was built in 1850, and the addition, of a more modern style of architecture, has but recently been made.

Thomas Slater, from whom, as we have seen, the present site of Waynesburg was purchased, got the land, a 400 acre tract, originally from a party who had made some "tomahawk improvement" on it, by the payment of "one 2-year old heifer calf, one flint-lock rifle, and some other trifling articles, which the fellow carried away

25

with him." On this tract Slater proceeded to build his cabin, "on a knoll just above the Smith Creek road, and a little southeast of Thomas W. Sayers old barn, which stands directly east of William Johnson's new brick residence in the Sayers' addition to the borough." One Jones occupied the Jesse Hook property, just east of town, and Hathway's mill stood near the site of Hook's distillery. William Brown owned the tract familiarly known as the Jenning's property, since owned by J. A. J. Buchanan, and on which was a mill in the early days. "An ill-fated family by the name of McClelland lived at the mouth of the ravine just below the double bridge. The Archer family resided in the vicinity of Dotysburg. Uriah White first settled somewhere between the mouths of the two Whiteley creeks to which he gave his name and afterwards occupied the Gordon Rich Hills, on the divide between the Ten Mile slope and the head waters of Big Whiteley creek. In like manner, Thomas Smith perpetuated his name to all succeeding generations by lending it to the then poverty stricken stream which now bears it. William Inghram possessed himself of Laurel Run from the camp ground to the Rich Hills, and erected his cabin on the Hiram Kent farm. Simon Thomas and Samuel Rinehart acquired lands on Coal Lick Run, including the Poor House farm. Thomas Smith, Thomas Kent, Arthur Inghram, James Porter, and Billy Lafferty raised a crop of corn on the farms owned by Uriah and Josiah Inghram, on Smith Creek, before the outbreak of the Revolutionary war."

As we have previously seen the massacre of the Spicer family by the band led by the infuriated Logan, brought to the relief of the settlers, the company of Captain McClure, and his forty men, said to be on their way to join Connoly in 1774, and who came up with the Indians on the Reese farm, about one mile and a quarter west of Waynesburg, when a sanguinary skirmish ensued, known as the battle of Ten Mile Creek, in which the leader, Captain Francis McClure, and James Flenniken, a brother of Judge John Flenniken, were killed, and Lieutenant Samuel Kincaid was severely wounded. The Indians were but few in number, variously reported from four to eight; but, by the cunning so common to their savage instincts, they lured the soldiers to their destruction, and then skulked and escaped though the thickets of the forest, which were familiar to them as the streets of a city to men who inhabit it. "After crossing the creek at the site of the Ely bridge," says Evans, "the trail passed up the deep gulch past where W. P. Reese now resides, and about the route of the old road, and whilst toiling up the steep ascent to the table land beyond, I imagine the Indians who were concealed on the top of the hill; amid the thick forest and foliage that then prevailed, attacked them with the result already set forth."

Admonished, by this sanguinary affray, precautions were taken to prepare a place of safety to which the scattered settlers could betake themselves on the intimations of danger. Jackson's fort was commenced in the same year, 1774, on the Jesse Hook property, then owned by a man by the name of Jackson. His cabin, which was the nucleous of the fort, stood near the bluff of the creek, directly south of Hook's town. Remains of the structure are still visible. At first it was but a single cabin, but subsequently consisted of a regular system of cabins, arranged in the form of a hollow square, and enclosed an acre or more of ground. Between the cabins were palisades ten or twelve feet high, supplied with port holes. Each of the neighboring settlers owned one of these cabins, to which he could flee for refuge in times of danger, in addition to the home on his own tract of land. The doors of these cabins opened within the inclosure, the outside having neither windows nor doors, except some look-out in the upper part of each. There was but one entrance, and when once within, each family controlled its own cabin, the inclosed square being common to all. "Such is a very brief description" says Evans, "of an institution once regarded the hope and salvation of its people. Around this devoted spot cluster a myriad of reminiscences, which, if they could be intelligently unravelled, and woven into narrative, would make volumes of interesting·matter. The traditions of Jackson's Fort are exceedingly numerous, but are very vague, contradictory, and unsatisfactory" As an example, the story runs that Jackson was once out beyond the site of Jonas Ely's stone house, (Buchanan) when he discovered a party of Indians coming down the Indian trail. They were almost upon him before he saw them. Being unarmed, and seeing no possibility of escape, he seized a club and brandishing it above his head, cried out, "Hurry up boys! Here they are! Come quick and we'll have them!" when the savages thinking they were about to be attacked, took to their heels and soon disappeared in the ample folds of the forest.

Thomas Slater, in the early years of his settlement here, was on terms of intimacy with the Indians, and was accustomed to receive and entertain them in the most friendly manner, pitching quoits, running, leaping, shooting at mark with them. But when the massacres became frequent, he in common with his neighbors, was accustomed to flee, on the approach of savages, to the friendly folds of the fort. On one occasion when the intimation of lurking savages was received he fled hastily for the fort; but recollecting when near the spring on Mrs D. Owens' lot that he had left his gun, he called to his girls Sallie and Nellie, from ten to fifteen years old, to run back for it. The gun was secured and brought·off with the fleetness of the wind, and one tradition says they were greeted with a flight of arrows from the heights of Duvall's Hill. One of those girls has been known to say that it seemed to her that she not only ran but that she flew. Sarah Slater married Israel White, on the occasion of one of these Indian scares, when the families of all the surrounding country were assembled, who seized the occasion of fright for a genuine merry-making. The Rev. David White of Oak Forest, was one of the numerous issue of this marriage. Nellie Slater, the other daughter, mentioned above, married a Mr. Pipes, and was the mother of James Pipes, a former justice of the peace of Franklin Township. Isaac Slater inherited his father's estate and married Mary Workman, who survived her husband and lived to an advanced age in Waynesburg.

On the occasion of one of these general alarms, when the families for a long circuit had gathered in, Matthew Gray, brother of Judge David Gray, who lived on the creek some three miles west of the fort, determined to venture out to see if his house still stood, and to feed and water his stock. Having gone early in the morning, and not returning at night, his brother David leaped upon a colt and started in search of him. On arriving upon the rising ground beyond the creek, above William Reese's residence, he was horrified to behold the body of his brother lying dead in the path, stripped of his clothing, scalped and mutilated, and stiff with cold, it being winter time and the earth covered with snow. Lifting the body upon the colt, he mounted, and thus carried it back to the fort, where it was given decent burial.

Robert Morris says, that Mr. J. A. Gray, of Ten-Mile, Washington County, who is a grandson of Matthew Gray, writes him that his grandmother told him that Matthew had been to his farm at the brick tavern in 1780, or early in 1781, and while returning to the fort he was shot through the knee and his horse killed, that he hobbled on one leg forty or fifty yards west of R. Seales', where he was overtaken, killed, and his body was terribly mutilated. His wife and two sons—William, four years old, and another ten months old —were in the fort. William could remember seeing his father brought in, dead. He was born in the fort on the 20th of September, 1776. His mother lived with him in Richhill Township, and died on the 20th of September, 1837, in her eighty-first year. She gave her grandson a small iron pot, which she used in the fort, which he still keeps and prizes. William died in 1854, and was about seventy-eight years old. Matthew Gray, Jr., died in Ohio.

Cotemporary with the Grays were Joseph and James Seals. The latter lived near the site of the toll-gate, west of the town, and built the old stone house still standing. He was one of the commissioners for locating the county seat, was appointed "wood ranger," served as Captain of volunteers, and was for a time stationed at Ryerson's fort. He served with Wayne in his heroic campaign against the Indians.

"Three brothers, Simon, Thomas and John Rinehart, Germans, fresh from the Rhine Valley of Faderland, occupied the Coal Lick Run region, and held it by priority of right. They seemed to be on the very verge of the settlement, Jackson fort being the grand center. John, who was the father of the well-known John T. Rinehart, now deceased, occupied the farm above the Poor-House farm, now owned by J. A. J. Buchanan, Esq. At a time when John T. was but a little babe, his father was lured away from his cabin by what he took to be the bawl of a calf, and was killed and scalped by prowling savages. At a time when an alarm of Indians sent the Rineharts with hurried feet flying towards the fort, one of them, a young man who lived on the Jenny Rinehart property, a little way above Mr. Buchanan's, after proceeding some distance, remembered that his cattle were penned up in the cow-yard. Reflecting that it might be some days before they could venture back to their homes, and considering that if the cattle should be fortunate enough to escape the rapine of the savages they would perish for lack of sustenance, he determined to return and let them out. He did so, but that young man never again was heard of by his friends. Blood-stains and some locks of auburn hair corresponding to his, and other evidences of a death struggle were discovered near the site of the cattle-pen, but no other vestiges of his remains could ever be found, though the most thorough search was instituted. The theory was that he was murdered and his body so effectually disposed of as to baffle all efforts to reclaim it.

"Simon Rinehart owned the lands well known as the 'Peggy Porter' and the 'Whitlatch' farms, and William Brown owned the Jennings, more recently known as the Ely farm, west of town, now owned by Mr. Buchanan. In the spring of 1779 these two men traded situations, and in the month of April were actually engaged in moving, when they were attacked by Indians and both killed. After this the contract was annulled, so that none of the older Rineharts ever acquired any possessions west of the fort.

"William Brown and his son Vincent, then an athletic young man, had proceeded with a sled-load of their household goods as far down as the site of the old graveyard at the new brick church in Morrisville, where, meeting some friends, they stopped to chat. Whilst thus engaged they were fired upon by Indians who were lying in ambush hard by. William Brown and two others fell dead on the spot, but Vincent, not being hurt, ran like a deer, hotly pursued by one or more of the fleetest savages. He was so hemmed in by the assailants as to be compelled to shape his course in the direction of a perpendicular precipice of about twenty feet on the brink of Ten-Mile Creek, just in the rear of the village. There was no alternative but to fall into the hands of the infuriated savages or make the fearful plunge over the cliff into the waters below. It was no time for indecision, and without hesitation he took the flying leap and lit in the middle of the stream, many feet from the base of the cliff The Indians paused, awe-stricken and overwhelmed with astonishment; and while they gazed with bewilderment and contemplated the wonderful feat, Brown emerged from' the water unhurt and undaunted, and continued his flight across the bottom land beyond. Ere his pursuers recovered from their amazement he had so lengthened the distance between him and them that they gave up the chase.

"A short distance below the old saw-mill on Laurel Run, between Morrisville and the Camp Ground, still stands a tree with its trunk inclined and peculiarly curved across the stream By this the original pathway led. On this an Indian lay concealed, waiting for the approach of Simon Rinehart, who was known to be coming with some of his household effects, transferring them to his newly acquired home. The skulking assassin had not long to wait till his victim appeared, and taking deliberate aim he shattered his arm Rinehart beat a hasty retreat and endeavored thus to escape; but becoming faint from loss of blood, was overtaken near his home, and tomahawked and scalped. In the meantime Matthew Brown, a lad of about seventeen years, who was riding along on horseback, carrying a load of stuff, and had fortunately loitered some distance behind his father's sled, upon seeing the Indians attack the movers, dashed down his load and rode at the top of his speed to the fort; but was so overcome with fright and horror that he could give no intelligible information, and his mother, Molly Brown, bled him in the arm with a penknife, 'to bring him to,' as she said. It seems that all the women and children had been gathered into the fort, but most of the men were at their farms, preparing ground for corn and potatoes. All the men in the fort, except two old men, immediately armed and started for the scene of conflict; but when they arrived the Indians had departed with their scalps and plunder. The scene at the fort had now assumed a comical as well as tragical aspect. The two old men left in charge of the women and children were Thomas Slater and a man named Clifford. They had but one gun. Clifford shouldered the gun, and Slater secured the wiping-stick. The women became terribly excited, and cried and screamed at a fearful rate. Growing desperate and impatient, they would unbar the gate and rush out, whilst Slater, who was a very hasty man, would run after them, and, brandishing his wiping-stick, would command them to return, and remonstrate with them that the Indians would pounce upon them and murder the whole batch of them. Thus by dint of almost superhuman effort he would prevail on them to return; but no sooner would he turn his back upon the gate till it would be again thrown open, and the distracted crowd rush recklessly out; and thus the excitement continued till the scouting party came in with the four dead men, when the scene became frantic, beggaring all attempts at description. We can but faintly imagine how frightfully heart-rending must have been the spectacle. Barnet Rinehart, who was father of our fellow-townsman, Simon Rinehart, Sr., and of Judge James Rinehart, of Oscaloosa, Iowa, and who was one of Greene County's early sheriffs, was then a little boy, but he maintained a very vivid recollection of seeing his dead father brought into the fort, dangling across the bare back of a horse."

As a quite extensive notice of the town of Waynesburg was given in connection with the organization of the county, it is unnecessary to give a more extended notice here The schools of Franklin Township have always maintained a high standard. By the earliest report the township is credited with eleven schools, with 452 pupils. In the report of 1859 it is reported as having "considerable wealth and some enterprising citizens; one very good school, one good school, the rest of the third class." Great improvement has been made in the thirty years that have elapsed, and it now holds a highly creditable rank. The present board of school directors is as follows: John Lapping, President; Jonas Ely, Secretary; T. J. Morris, George Taylor, Daniel Pratt and Inghram Cummins. The board of Waynesburg is constituted as follows: H. A. Rinehart, J. E. Sayers, W. W. Patterson, A. C. Smalley, P. A. Knox and W. H. Barb.

CHAPTER XXXVIII.

GILMORE TOWNSHIP.

Titles to Land—Boundaries—Well Watered—Fertile—Jolleytown—Conditions of Sale—Mason and Dixon Monument Schools—Dr. Smith's Building the Cabin.

THIS township, like all the southeastern section of the county, was largely settled by pioneers from Maryland and Virginia, with the belief that all the territory west of the Alleghany Mountains was under the jurisdiction of the latter State It was a claim with a very indefinite boundary, stretching away to the northwest, even to the frozen ocean. As the limits of Pennsylvania were for a long time undefined, most of the territory embraced in this township was acquired and titles perfected under Virginia courts as it was held under jurisdiction of Ohio County—one of the counties of Virginia from 1768 till the boundary line known as Mason and Dixon's line was finally settled in 1785 It was natural, therefore, that the inhabitants should cling to the State authority which had been regarded in the early days as possessing rightful authority.

The territory embraced in the limits of Gilmore Township is bounded on the north by Jackson Township, on the east by Wayne, on the south by Mason and Dixon's line which separates it from West Virginia, and on the west by Springhill Dunkard Creek, celebrated in the history of the border controversy and in the early Indian warfare, has its sources in the highlands to the north and west of this township, and here too, across the watershed, several of the tributaries of Wheeling Creek rise. Tom's Run and its numerous tributaries drain the north and eastern portions, and Fordyce Run, Block-house Run, Wildman's Run, and Fish Creek water all parts of its broad territory. The surface being in every part heavily rolling, the waters are pure and sparkling, copious springs gushing forth on every hilltop and along every valley. The soil is fertile even to the summits of the highest hills, and heavy crops of corn and the smaller grains reward the toil of the husbandman It is well adapted to sheep culture, and flocks of the finest breeds gladden all the hills. Many herds of fine dairy cows are also kept, and blooded stock for beef, the short-horn Durham seemingly the favorite In many parts of the township special attention is given to the raising of swine, a cross between the Berkshire and Poland China being the favorite. It is not uncommon to see as many as fifty hogs in a single field. In no part of the county are the inhabitants more sober and industrious than in Gilmore.

Among the earliest inhabitants we notice the names of the Roberts, the Fordyces, the Dyes, the Whites and Hannans The only village of importance is Jolleytown At an early day Titus Jolley acquired the tract where the village is now located Perceiving that this seemed to be a suitable point for business on account of the water power and the centering of roads here, in 1835 having surveyed and staked off the plot of the town he issued the following conditions of sale: "The conditions of this present sale are as follows: the highest bidder is to be the buyer. Any person buying a lot shall have a credit of six months by giving his note with approved security Any person buying and not complying shall forfeit and pay twenty-five cents on each dollar to the amount of what he buys, and the subscriber reserves the right to one bid on each lot if necessary, and further the subscriber doth agree to make a good and lawful deed at the expiration

of six months, or whenever said money is paid. Due attendance by me. Sept. 9, 1835. TITUS JOLLEY.

" N. B. All rails and buildings excepted."

In close proximity to Jolleytown is one of the stone monuments which mark Mason and Dixon's line. Gilmore has six schools and an average attendance of 194 pupils. The following are the names of the present board of School Directors: E L. Wade, President; T. M. Hennen, Secretary; J. O. Kennedy, Joseph Roberts, G. W. Shough, M. J. Clovis.

In our time, when curiously invented machinery turns out everything that a human being can crave for his comfort, or that can gratify his desires, it is interesting to turn back and regard the manner in which the early settlers supplied their wants. Dr Smith, in his secular history of this section, gives us a vivid picture of the building the cabin and supplying it with furniture.

"On an appointed day," he says, "a company of choppers met, felled trees, cut them off at proper lengths; a man with a team hauled them to the place; this, while a carpenter was in search of a straight-grained tree, for making clapboards for the roof. The boards were split four feet long, with a large prow, and as wide as the timber would allow; they were used without shaving. Some were employed in getting puncheons for the floor of the cabin. This was done by splitting trees about eighteen inches in diameter, and hewing the faces of them with a broad-axe. They were half the length of the floor they were intended to make. These were the usual preparations for the first day. The second day the neighbors collected around and finished the house. The third day's work generally consisted in 'furnituring' the house—supplying it with a clapboard table, made of a split slab, and supported by four round legs, set in augur holes. Some three-legged stools were made in the same manner. Some pins stuck in the logs at the back of the house, supported some clapboards which served for shelves for the table furniture, consisting of a few pewter dishes, plates and spoons; but mostly of wooden bowls, trenchers and noggins. If these last were scarce, gourds and hard-shelled squashes made up the deficiency. The iron pots, knives and forks, were brought from the east side of the mountains, along with salt and iron, on pack-horses."

CHAPTER XXXIX.

GREENE TOWNSHIP.

ORIGINAL EXTENT—PRESENT — GARARD'S FORT—GOSHEN BAPTIST CHURCH—JOHN CORBLY—CORBLY MASSACRE—MINUTES OF RED-STONE BAPTIST ASSOCIATION—CURIOUS QUESTIONS—SPICER MAS-SACRE—LOGAN'S REVENGE—CAPTIVITY—BOY NEVER RETURNED—SCHOOLS—DIRECTORS.

GREENE TOWNSHIP, originally one of the six townships of the county, embraced all the southwestern portion of its territory, stretching from Little Whiteley Creek to Mason and Dixon's line, and from the Monongahela River to the dividing ridge between Big Whiteley Creek and Muddy Creek. It was organized in 1782. But it has been shorn of its ample proportions for the making of other townships until it is now one of the smallest in the county, appearing quite diminutive beside several of its grown up daughters. It is bounded on the north by Jefferson and Cumberland, on the east by Monongahela, on the south by Dunkard, and on the west by Whiteley The fertility of its soil was such as to attract the eye of the early explorer and here were the first lodgments. It is well watered by Whiteley Creek which carries a large volume of water and is ample for mill purposes. Few sections of the county present a more inviting appearance than the valley of this stream. In the central portion of this township on the left bank of the creek was located Garard's Fort, a place of great importance at that period when Indian massacres were frequent, as a place of refuge and safety for the settlers, and around it has grown the principal village in the township.

Our ancestors who came by single families and settled far from each other with no convenient roads for communication, were not so circumstanced as to favor assembling themselves together for religious worship. Yet they did not neglect this pious duty, and it was not uncommon for worshipers to travel from twelve to fifteen miles with this reverent intent. It was in the neighborhood of this fort that the first religious worship was held, and here was organized in 1776, on the 7th day of October, the first church in the county. It has subsequently been known as Goshen Baptist Church. It was ministered to by the Sutton brothers, and it is probable that it had no settled pastors during the early part of its existence The Rev. John Corbly was at an early day installed pastor, and ministered to the congregation at the time when the savages were seeking their vengeance upon the helpless and defenceless settlers. In May, 1782, his family was attacked on Sunday morning while on the way to church. In a letter written by Mr Corbly dated 1785, to Rev. William Rogers, of Philadelphia, he gives the following graphic account of the heart-rendering circumstance:

"On the second Sabbath in May, in the year 1782, being my appointment at one of my meeting-houses, about a mile from my dwelling-house, I set out with my dear wife and five children for public worship. Not suspecting any danger, I walked behind 200 yards, with my bible in my hand, meditating. As I was thus employed, all on a sudden, I was greatly alarmed with the frightful shrieks of my dear family before me. I immediately ran with all the speed I could, vainly hunting a club as I ran, till I got within 40 yards of them; my poor wife seeing me, cried to me to make my escape; an Indian ran up to shoot me; I then fled, and by so doing out-ran him. My wife had a suckling child in her arms; this little infant they killed and scalped. They then struck my wife several times, but not getting her down, the Indian who aimed to shoot me, ran to her, shot her through the body, and scalped her; my little boy, an only son, about six years old, they sunk the hatchet into his brain, and thus dispatched him. A daughter, besides the infant, they also killed and scalped. My eldest daughter, who is yet alive, was hid in a tree, about 20 yards from the place where the rest were killed, and saw the whole proceedings. She, seeing the Indians all go off, as she thought, got up, and deliberately crept out from the hollow trunk; but one of them espying her, ran hastily up, knocked her down and scalped her; also her only surviving sister, on whose head they did not leave more than an inch round, either of flesh or skin, besides taking a piece of her skull. She, and the before-mentioned one, are still miraculously preserved, though, as you must think, I have had, and still have, a great deal of trouble and expense with them, besides anxiety about them, insomuch that I am, as to worldly circumstances, almost ruined. I am yet in hopes of seeing them cured; they still, blessed be God, retain their senses, notwithstanding the painful operations they have already and must yet pass through."

As a degree of interest gathers about the church that was first established in this section, the minutes are given below of the Redstone Baptist Association for 1800:

Minutes of Redstone Baptist Association, held at Simpson's Creek, September 26,7,8, 1800:

1. Introductory Sermon by Benjamin Stone, from 2d Corinthians, v. 20.

JOHN CORBLY, Moderator,
BENJAMIN JONES, Clerk.

CHURCHES.	MINISTERS AND MESSENGERS.
Great Bethel,	Benjamin Stone, Simeon Gard.
Goshen,	John Corbly, Benjamin Jones, Robert Jones, Levi Harrad, George Morris, Jonathan Morris.
Turkey Foot,	Robert Cobcorn, Jacob Rush.
Forks of Cheat,	William John, Samuel Bowan, John Patterson.
Mount Moriah,	Joseph Thomas.
Mount Pleasant,	No Report.
Simpson's Creek,	Ephraim Smith, Moses Husted, John Thomas.
Clarksburgh,	John Loofborrow, Moses Sutton, John Gifford, John Kelly, John Pharis.
Pricket's Creek,	William Wood, Joshua Hickman.
Indian Creek,	John Baiker, John Smith, Thomas Dewees, Gilbert Butler.
Buchanan,	John Cozard, John Hiars, David Smith, Jacob Cozard.
Enon,	No Representative.
Philadelphia,	No Representative.
Bethlehem,	Letter, but no messenger.
Connellsville,	Letter, but no messenger.
Roating Creek,	No Representative.
Glady Creek,	Phineas Wells, John Carney, Abraham Wells, John Phillips.
Sandy Creek,	Samuel Dewees, John Jenkins.

3   Query from Glady Creek.   Whether washing of the saints
be an ordinance of the New Testament?   Decided in the
negative.

4.   Query from Indian Creek.   Whether it be legal to receive
a Baptist minister who observes the seventh day Sabbath
as a member of the First day Baptist Church, and to take
the pastoral care of said church?   Decision reserved until
next association.

7.   Next association to be held at Great Whiteley, Greene County,
on first Friday in September.   Brother Corbly to preach
the sermon.   Brother Stone alternate

9.   Brother Isaac Edwards from Kentucky preached out of doors
to the people.

The interest that centers about the Spicer massacre, the result of
the cruel revenge of the celebrated Indian Chieftain Logan, will
never cease to be felt.   The location of Spicer's cabin is not exactly
known, though it was somewhere upon the heights separating the
waters of Dunkard from Big Whiteley Creek.   "Some traditions,"
says Evans, "locate it in the head of Deep Run, which flows into
Dunkard Creek a short distance above Bob Town   Some would have
it on the old Dave Keener farm, on the head waters of a branch of
Meadow Run.   Others place it on the old Eberhart farm, now belonging to Stephenson Garard, I believe, which lies in a cove at the
head of a considerable run which flows into Big Whiteley on Sebastian Keener's farm, nearly a mile below the Willow Tree postoffice.
However these three streams have their source so very close together
that the locality is defined with sufficient accuracy by either or all
of them.   Indeed it is said that there were two cabins, which was
probably the fact, one at the source of Deep Run, and the other on
the Eberhart farm."

Spicer was living with a wife and seven children, in June, 1774,
when Logan, who had been despoiled of eight members of his family
in cold blood, and was out upon his hunt for an equal number of
white scalps, which, according to Indian theology must be had to
satisfy his pious revenge, approached, with his accomplices, the lone
cabin of the Spicers.   It was in the very midst of the primeval
forest.   Not another white inhabitant was living in a circuit of miles
in extent.   Spicer himself was engaged in chopping, all unsuspecting
of danger, and not conscious of an enemy among all the sons of the
forest.   Logan had no cause of quarrel with him.   But the savage
must have the scalps of a certain number of the pale faces.   It was
immaterial to him who they were.   When Spicer discovered the red
men approaching, thinking they were on a friendly errand, and desiring to suitably entertain them, he stuck his axe into the log and
went into his cabin.   Scarcely had he entered when one of the sav-

ages, having seized the axe, came stealthily behind, and with one blow struck him dead. His wife and two children shared a like fate. Three other children were found and speedily dispatched Elizabeth, who was engaged in ironing, seeing the bloody work, ran for her life with her smoothing iron still grasped in her hand, being too excited to think of dropping it. In her attempt to clear the fence, with her brother William, whom she was assisting to escape, they were overtaken and carried away into captivity The murdered were scalped and horribly mutilated, so much so that one of the party under Capt. Crawford who went to bury the bodies, was so horrified by the awful spectacle that he could not endure the sight, and begged to be led away Logan, with a war chief, Snake, proceeded over to Big Whiteley Creek, where they murdered and scalped an old man by the name of Keener, whose body was undiscovered until the circling of the buzzards above his decomposing corpse disclosed its location. It was buried in the famous meadow of John Lantz. The captives, Betty and William, were hurried away beyond the Ohio, and separated, the boy being placed in a more distant tribe than the girl, that they might not be plotting to escape. Subsequently these tribes were compelled by treaty to give up their captives, and the girl was returned in the holidays of the same year of her abduction. Though but a few months in captivity she learned the Indian language, and the medicinal properties of many roots and herbs as practiced in Indian pharmacy, so that her services were much in demand during all her life in cases of sickness peculiar to the climate. She married a man by the name of Bowen, and lived to the advanced age of eighty-four, many of the earlier settlers having cause to remember with gratitude the kind attentions of "Granny Bowen."

"After Betsy returned," says Evans, "to her friends, she visited the sight of the awful tragedy where she was rendered an orphan child, and remembering that one of the Indians finding himself overloaded with plunder, had concealed some things under a log, she repaired to the spot and among other articles found her father's scalp, which she religiously preserved all her life, with the intention of having it enclosed in her own coffin, when she should be called away. She also remembered where she had thrown her smoothing iron and found it, and it is yet preserved by her descendants. Mrs Bowen was the mother of a large family of children, one of whom, Mrs Nancy Steel, is still living at the age of seventy-four. A daughter of Mrs. Steel, Mrs. Azariah Stephens, living near Garard's Fort has furnished the particulars of this narrative."

The boy William became unalterably attached to Indian life, married an Indian squaw and was made a chief. He was induced to return on one occasion to give testimony in the disposition of some property in favor of his sister; but could not be prevailed upon to quit his wild life in the woods.

Greene Township, by the report of Mr. Black, 1854, is credited with five schools and 177 pupils By the report of Mr. McGlumphy it is shown "that the houses in this district are all good, and well furnished. In the latter respect they surpass any in the county." The following is a list of the present board of directors: J. M. Morris, President; P. A. Myers, Secretary; J. B. Roberts, Stephen Garard, Isaac Barclay, George Russell.

CHAPTER XL.

JACKSON TOWNSHIP.

AGRICULTURE—BALTIMORE AND OHIO ROAD—TIMBER—WHITE COTTAGE—SCHOOLS—DIRECTORS—HABITS OF SETTLERS—DR. DODDRIDGE'S REMINISCENSES—DRESS—MOCCASINS — CLOTHING HUNG ON PEGS—OCCUPATIONS OF THE WOMEN—OF THE BOYS—THROWING THE TOMAHAWK.

THIS township was one of the later settled, but is at present under a good state of cultivation. The surface is broken and highly picturesque, but the soil is deep and very fertile Large flocks of sheep are kept in the upper end of the township, nearly all of fine wool. Some years ago a few sheep died from one disease peculiar to the flock, since which more attention has been given to the cultivation of cattle. The short-horn Durham breed is most in demand though some Holsteins are kept The forests of this township were the favorite gathering place of wild turkeys, and the inhabitants raise large flocks of these birds. A few years ago a disease seized upon the flocks of turkeys and many died, which has had the effect to greatly decrease the interest felt in breeding them. Winter wheat is largely cultivated, rarely or never spring wheat. Dent corn is cultivated, yellow, rarely white. Lime is found in abundance, and is used for fertilizing. Formerly large quantities of poultry, eggs, beef, pork and grain were shipped by the Baltimore and Ohio railroad; but latterly by Washington and Waynesburg road, which is more convenient for the Pittsburg market. Hay is also an important article and is sold in large quantities, movable hay-presses being employ ed to prepare it for transportation. Oak, chestnut, poplar, sugar maple, locust, are the home product used in building and fencing, the coarse lumber for timber, joists, studding and roof is commonly of the different oaks. The red oak, which is now coming into use for fine work for expensive finishing, and takes a polish in carved work that rivals mahogany and satin wood, is common here. Timothy, blue grass and clover are abundant on hill and valley, and though the hills are everywhere and of enormous proportions, the mower and reaper is almost exclusively used, and the strain of human muscle avoided. There is in every part a clay and lime subsoil and springs of pure water are copious and abundant. Swine are largely bred, Chester white, Poland-China, and Berkshire being the most numerously kept, though a cross between the Poland and Chester is considered in all respects the best.

There are no considerable villages, though White Cottage, near the center of the township, is the location of the principal postoffice, and will probably in time develop into a thriving place of business. The intelligence and morality of the people are conspicuous, and an air of thrift and contentment is everywhere observable The dwellings are commodious and kept in a good state of repair, and the highways in most parts well wrought. A road machine, very simple of construction, is used to great advantage Nine schools are reported in 1854 by Mr. Black, who was then Secretary of State, with 404 pupils. In 1850 the Superintendent says: " This district is much behind the times in point of education." But a quarter of a century has wrought great changes here The present board of directors is thus constituted: J. F. Morris, President; M. C Hull, Secretary; James Meeks, R. Hughes, A. J. Mitchell, Homer Fordyce.

Of the condition and habits of the people among the earliest settlers little can now be recalled. It would be interesting, if any were now living whose mature lives reached back to those early times, to listen to their recital. As a matter of historical record, in these days when the whirl and excitement of life is so rapidly obliterating every trace of the old time, nothing could be more important. Dr. Doddridge, who has left many interesting details of the early settlers in this section, gives the following graphic account of the habits and peculiarities of our ancestors:

" A pair of moccasins answered much better for the feet than shoes. These were made of dressed deerskins They were mostly made of a single piece, with gathered seams along the top of the foot, and another from the bottom of the heel, without gathers, as high as the ankle joint, or a little higher. Flaps were left on each side, to reach some distance up the legs These were nicely adapted to the ankles, and lower part of the leg by thongs of deerskin, so that no dust, gravel nor snow could get within the moccasin. The moccasins in ordinary use cost but a few hours labor to make them. In cold weather the moccasins were stuffed with deer's hair, or dry leaves, so as to keep the feet comfortably warm. * .* * The linsey-woolsey petticoat and bedgown, which were the universal dress of the women in early times, would make a very singular figure in our days. They went barefooted in warm weather, and in cold, their feet were covered with moccasins, overshoes or shoe-packs. * * * The coats and bedgowns of the women, as well as the hunting-shirts of the men, were hung in full display on wooden pegs round the walls of their cabins; so that while they answered, in some degree, the place of paper hangings or tapestry, they announced to the stranger, as well as neighbor, the wealth or poverty of the family in the articles of clothing. This practice prevailed for a long time.

"The ladies handled the distaff, shuttle, sickle, weeding-hoe, scutching-knife, hackle, and were contented if they could obtain their linsey-woolsey clothing, and covered their heads with sunbonnets made of 600 or 700 linen. * * * Flax was universally culti- vated. When ripe, it was usually pulled by the women and boys, as this operation always occurred in harvest, when the men were occu- pied with their grain or hay. And those who 'pulled' it, after the seed was threshed out of it, perhaps towards the heels of harvest, by the men, then spread it out ' to rot' for some weeks, on some green pasture fields; and after a number of weeks it was taken up, ready for the application of the ' brake' and ' swingling-knife.' The for- mer instrument required the muscular arms of stout men   The latter was often, perhaps most generally, wielded by the women. ' Scutching frolics,' or gatherings of neighbors to scutch or swingle flax, were very common, and afforded much innocent amusement and recreation to the young people, blended with pretty hard work. The old ladies generally took charge of the 'hackling' of the flax. Hack- ling and goose-picking days required much patient toil. * * * One important pastime of our boys was that of imitating the notes or noise of every bird and beast in the woods. This faculty was not merely a pastime, but a very necessary part of education, on account of its utility in certain circumstances. The imitations of the gob- lers, and other sounds of wild turkeys, often brought the keen-eyed and ever-watchful tenants of the forest within the reach of the rifle. The bleating of the fawn brought its dam to her death in the same way. The hunter often collected a company of mopish owls on the trees about his camp, and amused himself with their hoarse scream- ing; his howl would raise and obtain responses from a pack of wolves, so as to inform him of their neighborhood, as well as guard him against their depredations   This imitative faculty was some- times requisite as a measure of precaution in war. The Indians, when scattered about in a neighborhood, often collected together by imitating turkeys by day, and wolves or owls by night. In similar situations, our people did the same. I have often witnessed the consternation of a whole neighborhood in consequence of a few screeches of owls.

"Throwing the tomahawk was another boyish sport, in which many acquired considerable skill. The tomahawk, with its handle of a certain length, will make a given number of turns in a given distance. Say in five steps, it will strike with the edge, with the handle downward, at the distance of seven and a half, it will strike with the edge, the handle upwards, and so on. A little experience enabled the boy to measure the distance with his eye, when walking through the woods, and strike a tree with his tomahawk in any way he chose."

CHAPTER XLI.

JEFFERSON TOWNSHIP.

SWAN AND HUGHES—LINDSEY FAMILY—HEATON'S MILL—JEFFERSON AND HAMILTON—COLLEGE— RICE'S LANDING — BOUNDARIES— SCHOOLS—DIRECTORS—TEAGARDEN FIGHTS FOR HIS CLAIM— MANUMISSION.

THOMAS HUGHES, JR., son of the original settler Thomas, married a daughter of John Swan in 1771 and settled in the Carmichaels Valley on the site of the present brick residence of John Hathaway, and was a neighbor of Colonel Charles Swan. He was a man of undaunted courage, and when all his neighbors would flee to the forts for safety he would stand by his cabin and defend his family there. On one occasion his wife dreamed of Indian massacres, and so vivid was her dream that she prevailed on her husband to escape into the ryefield, where they laid down and slept beneath the shelter of the tall grain. In the morning she crept steathily from her hiding place to the summit of the field, and was horrified to behold their cabin in flames and the Indians dancing around a feather bed which they had ripped open, and amusing themselves by tossing the feathers into the air, tickled beyond measure to see them carried upwards by the currents engendered by the ascending flames

In 1776 he moved to where the town of Jefferson now stands and built a home near the old stone house of the widow Stephens.

All this stretch of country was then a dense pine forest, the lurking place of bears and wolves and deer. In December of this year his third child, Mary, was born, who became the mother progenitor of the Lindsey family of this county.

A little to the west of Hughes came Colonel Heaton and built a cabin on the site of the present village of Jefferson. He built a mill, soon after coming, near the site of that now known as Horn's Mill. Hughes is said to have been implicated as being one of the blackened party which attacked the house of Captain Faulkner, in consequence of which he was required to give bail in the sum of $3,000 for his appearance to answer. Faulkner was an officer of the government, and the opposition to him was his disposition to collect the excise tax on distilled spirits. The county at this early day was so universally devoted to distilling that the county records for 1788 show seventy registered distilleries. So enormous was the cost of transporting the grain, the products of their fields to a market, that the income from produce was all eaten up. Hence the husbandmen resorted to distillation, as a horse could barely carry six bushels of rye to market; whereas after it had been converted into whisky the same beast could transport twenty-four bushels.

Up to the year 1795 the village was known as Jefferson, though there were but two or three cabins on its whole domain. At about this time a violent contention arose about the name which the new town should bear; for already streets had been opened and town lots sold. The point of demarkation on either side was Colonel Joseph Parkinson's store, Hughes owning all to the east, and Heaton all to the west. Heaton being a bold Federalist insisted that the town should be called Hamilton. But the Hughes party claimed just as pertenaciously that it should be called Jefferson. For some time the controversy waxed hot. It was finally agreed about the year 1800 that the eastern half should be called Hamilton and the western half Jefferson. In 1827 the town was incorporated as a borough by an act of the Legislature under the name of Jefferson. It has a population of some 700, and is a place of considerable activity. The buildings of Monongahela College stand on a well selected site just outside the borough limits. It has four churches—Baptist, Presbyterian, Methodist and Cumberland Presbyterian. Few towns in the county are more pleasantly located than this. Rice's Landing, a village of some 350 inhabitants, is situated at Lock No. 6 of the Monongahela slackwater. Previous to the construction of the Washington & Waynesburg Railroad this was of considerable importance, being the shipping point for a large portion of the county. It still distributes many goods to villages in the immediate neighborhood. The part of the town below the run was laid out by Abijah McLean, and was called Newport, and the part above the run was originally owned by John Rice, from whom the place takes its name   Rice's patent bears date of 1786.

Jefferson is the most irregular in form of any of the townships of the county, being a long narrow strip of land, hemmed in between South Ten Mile Creek and Pumpkin Run, scarcely more than two miles in width and fifteen in length. It is bounded on the north by Morgan,' on the east by Cumberland, on the south by Cumberland, Greene and Whiteley, and on the west by Franklin and Morgan. By the report of 1855 Jefferson is given eight schools with 391 pupils The report of 1859 says of this district: "The houses are neat, comfortable, well arranged and admirably fitted to be the training places of youth. The requirements of the law are well enforced by the directors The schools are visited, but not as frequently as would be advantageous by parents and directors " The present board of directors of the township is constituted as follows: J C. Burson, President; H. Waychoff, Secretary; John Dulancy, A. W. Greenlee, Jacob Crayne and J. Randolph Bayard That of the borough as follows: R. H. Jordon, President; S. R Hill, Secretary; T H. Sharpneck, John Cottorell, John Sloneker and Frank Bradley.

Abraham Teagarden, who had settled at Redstone, had a considerable family, which he had transferred to this new land. Indeed Abraham, father of Isaac, was born in Redstone Fort. His sons, as they had come to marriageable age, had taken themselves wives. David married Miss Treble, by whom he reared a family of ten children; William married Miss Craig, by whom he had twelve children About the year 1770 these two, David and William, anxious to secure a homestead while it could be got for the taking, crossed over into what is now Greene County.

The manner in which George Teagarden, who had married a young and blooming maiden, and was ambitious of securing a comfortable habitation for her, maintained his claim to the tract of land he had chosen, is romantic, and illustrates the customs which prevailed among the early settlers. Along the valley of Ten Mile Creek were many excellent and valuable tracts. One of these George had appropriated by making the usual tomahawk improvement. He had selected the site for his house and had called in his neighbors to assist in rearing it. When the work was about to begin, a raw-boned denizen of the forest made his appearance and claimed the ground which Teagarden had selected as his own, and no further progress could be made in building until the question of ownership was settled. As no legal tribunal had yet been established over this territory, the only method of deciding was by personal combat, and it was accordingly agreed that who ever proved himself the better man should be entitled to his claim. The contest was long and bloody, but the youthful vigor of Teagarden was in the end triumphant, and he was acknowledged the rightful claimant. His antagonist, after having washed and dressed his wounds, in which the young wife of Teagarden is said to have assisted, remained and helped build the cabin, subsequently acquired a tract adjoining, and ever after the families were on friendly terms. Such were the ideas of justice and government which prevailed among our hardy ancestors.

Many of the early settlers brought with them from Virginia and Maryland their house servants. In the records of the Recorder's office are several manumission papers. Below is one executed by a citizen of Jefferson:

MANUMISSION.

Jefferson, May 20, 1823.—Know all men by these presents: That I, William Fletcher, of the town of Jefferson, Greene County, Penn., from motives of humanity and benevolence, have this day manumitted, and do hereby manumit and set free from slavery during his natural life my negro boy, Jarrot Rhoads, he being now of the age of twenty-one years and over, and I do hereby relinquish forever all my right, claim, title and interest in the aforesaid Jarrot Rhoads, and any claim that I ever had or could have had to his labor or services in any wise whatever. In testimony whereof I have hereunto set my hand and affixed my seal, the day and year first above written.

WILLIAM FLETCHER.

EDWARD FLETCHER.
THOMAS FLETCHER.

Greene County, ss. Personally came William Fletcher before me, a justice of the peace in and for said county, and acknowledged the above manumission to Jarrot Rhoads to be his act, deed, and desired the same might everywhere be received as such, and that the said Jarrott may pass and repass as a free man of color should he demean himself well. Acknowledged by me the 26th day of June, 1823. Witness my hand and seal.

WILLIAM KINCAID, JR.
KENNOR S. BOREMAN, Rec.

Deed Book E, page 371.

CHAPTER XLII.

MONONGAHELA TOWNSHIP.

JOHN MINOR—MAPLETOWN—FIRST FLOURING-MILL—MORGAN BUILT
FORTS — CLARK'S FLOTILLA — GREENSBORO—NEW GENEVA—
GALLATIN—GLASS WORKS—STONECASTLE—SCHOOLS DIRECTORS
—WHITE SAVAGES.

AS early as 1764, John Minor, a native of London County, Virginia, came to the neighborhood of where is now Mapletown, on Whiteley Creek, Monongahela Township, where he acquired, by tomahawk·improvement, a tract for himself, and likewise one adjoining, now owned by the heirs of Moak Minor, for his brother William, and another contiguous for his friend, Zachary Gapen. Mr. Evans, in his Tenth Centennial article, says, Minor "having built for himself a snug and cosy cabin and made other necessary improvements, went back to the land of Conococheaque the next year, and having married the sister of General Otho Williams, of Revolutionary renown, returned with his bride on horse-back to the land of his adoption Perched up behind her all that long and rugged way sat George, the little negro servant lad. Otho, his first born babe, was ·ocked by George in a sugar trough, the rude cradle of the primitive life."

Minor was a man of thrift, and soon had the largest estate of any one along the river, and built the first flouring-mill west of the Monongahela. It was located about one-hundred yards above the present mill and was driven by the waters of the creek. He held a commission as Colonel from the Governor of Virginia, and under the direction of General Morgan superintended the erection of forts at various points where rangers were stationed to watch the movements of hostile parties and apprise the settlers The boats which transported the expedition of Colonel George Rogers Clarke against the Indians in 1778 were built by Colonel Minor near the mouth of Dunkard Creek on the Monongahela. Whenever the Indians would make a raid, Minor would organize a force of daring militia and hotly pursue the savages, an enterprise requiring the greatest vigilance to prevent ambuscade by day and surprise by night. The cabins of both William and John were fortified, and in John's was kept the huge conch shell, still preserved, from which a furious blast was blown as a note of alarm in times of danger. John Minor was elected to the Legislature in 1791 and immediately commenced to agitate the forming of a new county. His bill was twice defeated and he himself lost his election once; but in 1796, having been triumphantly elected, his bill for the erection of Greene County was passed and became a law. Colonel Minor died in 1833 in his ninetieth year. _

Monongahela is one of the two smallest townships in the county, but from the fact that it has a long stretch of frontage on the Monongahela River, it has a special importance. It is bounded on the north by Cumberland, on the east a distance of fifteen or more miles by the Monongahela River, on the south by Dunkard, and on the west by Dunkard, Greene and Cumberland. Dunkard Creek flows along its southern border, Whiteley Creek flows by a tortuous course through its central part, bending northward in its lower part, and emptying into the Monongahela within two or three miles of its northern boundary, and the Little Whiteley Creek forms its northern boundary. This township has, therefore, the best water facilities of any in the county, and is connected to Fayette County by the ferries of McKann, Matfield, Ross and Greensboro.

The village of Greensboro, the rival of Carmichaels in population and commercial importance, is situated on the Monongahela River at the head of slackwater No. 6. It is opposite New Geneva in Fayette County, the home of Albert Gallatin, and was laid out in 1781 by Elias Stone on a tract which had received the suggestive and appropriate title of "Delight." The original plat contained eighty-six lots of half an acre each. The one-hundred and six lots laid out by Dr. P. L. Kramer, and the site of the old glass works have since been added to it. It has a population at present variously estimated at from 800 to 1,000. It has three churches—Presbyterian, Methodist and Catholic.

Two manufactories of pottery are located here, the products of which are transported by barge down the river and find a market at towns along the Ohio and Mississippi, a cargo sometimes running as far as New Orleans. The Star Pottery works manufacture tile roofing. In 1807 glass works were established here which produced an excellent quality of window-glass and were for a long time very prosperous. It is related that Albert Gallatin, the eminent statesman, who had purchased a plantation near New Geneva, while on his way on horse-back to Washington, stopped over night at Tomlinson's in the mountains, and having his attention attracted by a party singing German hymns in an adjoining room, sought them out and found it was a little company of German glass-blowers, on their way to Maysville, Kentucky, to establish their business. Mr. Gallatin spoke their language, and finally induced them to stop at New Geneva, where they finally established themselves, he taking a share in the

stock of the company.   It was this interest which was finally transferred to Greensboro and became the nucleous of the company mentioned above, and was the earliest manufactory in this section—the
forerunner of the vast business at Pittsburg and vicinity

Mr. Gallatin was born in Geneva, Switzerland, January 29, 1761,
was instructor of French in Harvard University in 1782, married
a beautiful young woman in Richmond, Va., in 1783, in 1785 bought
his plantation at New Geneva, where he lived several years in a log
cabin; but eventually built a quaint stone castle on a commanding
eminence which he named Friendship Hill   Here he was visited by
LaFayette in 1824.   On the death of his wife she was buried here and
her grave never marked, which caused among busy bodies unfavor-
able comments   But on one occasion while out hunting he paused
near her grave and was lost in deep meditation   Finally he said,
"There lies one of the best and purest women ever God made.   I
would have erected a monument to her memory, only she requested
me not to do so, preferring that her grave should not be so marked.
She said I would know where she was laid, and as to the rest of the
world, it was of little importance."   The stone edifice where he lived
still remains, though much changed   He attained eminence as a
member of the Pennsylvania Legislature, member of Congress—the
first representative of Greene County, as Secretary of the United
States Treasury, and as Minister Plenipotentiary to Russia, to Ghent
and to London.   In 1816 he was made Minister to France, and in
the meantime was sent on extraordinary missions to the Netherlands
in 1817, and to England in 1818.   In 1826 he was appointed envoy
extraordinary to England   He died August 12, 1849, at New York.
He was probably the most eminent of the adopted citizens with whose
services the nation has been favored.

Monongahela Township from the earliest times has been noted
for the prosperity which has marked its progress.   Its home markets
have been good and the facility with which from every part it could
reach transportation practically brought the markets beyond the
bounds of the county to its own doors   Near the center of the
township on Whiteley Creek is located the pleasant little village of
Mapletown, named probably from the ancestors of Robert and
Thomas Maple.   The intelligence and culture of the people is marked
The earliest school report under the present system gives the
township seven schools and 250 pupils, and Greensboro with two
schools and 101 pupils   The report of 1859 says " There are a few
active and zealous friends of education in this township who evince
a deep interest in the schools by frequent visitations "   The present
school board is constituted as follows: W H. Cummins, President; N M. Hartley, Secretary; Silas Rose, William Ramsey,
Stephen Maple, Lee Gabler; of Greensboro: W. L. Hamilton, Pres-

ident; C. A. Wolverton, Secretary; David Garrison, James Hamilton, John C. Blake, James Atchison.

As Monongahela was among the earliest portions of the county settled, it doubtless suffered as much from Indian depredations as any other section. If the record of these midnight massacres and burnings could be veritably gathered up and set in order it would form one of the most thrilling pages in American history. But having given accounts of these in connection with the early history of many of the other townships of the county we propose to omit all mention of Indian horrors in this, and show instead the other side of the picture which may serve as a key to the blood-thirsty disposition of the savage. Mr. Evans in his Eighth Centennial article gives several very striking incidents under the title of " White Savages," and from this are given below copious extracts.

" Genuine settlers were seeking homes for themselves and posterity. Feeling that in a certain sense they were intruders upon the territory and hunting grounds of the red man, they chose to court his friendship and cultivate a spirit of amity with him. But in their train followed a class of desperate and despicable outlaws—cormorants upon the peace and well-being of the settlements—who preyed upon the Indians as upon wolves and bears, and improved every opportunity to commit gross insults, rapine, and murder upon them. Deceived by these bad men, and maddened to frenzy by their frequent and brutal atrocities, these uncultivated children of the forest would give unrestrained vent to rankling vengeance, and would visit indiscriminately tortures the most fiendish and murders the most appalling that savage genius could invent. I shudder for civilization when I chronicle the revolting crimes perpetrated in its name. But the truth of history demands the shocking revelation, that no uncertain light may be shed on the pathway of succeeding generations.

" Between the years 1765 and 1774 there was comparative peace and harmony between the frontiersman and the neighboring tribes. They were dwelling together in unity, and a social intimacy was being cultivated by the chiefs and encouraged by the whites. Indian and white man mingled and commingled with perfect freedom and confiding security. But this period of good feeling was from time to time interrupted, and eventually altogether destroyed by the dastardly and reckless piracies of the wicked outlaws above described.

" A fiend in human shape, John Ryan by name, killed at different times three friendly and influential Indians. One of these was Owishtogah, the 'Captain Peter' of our region, to whom many of our forefathers owed a debt of gratitude for his hospitalities and friendly warnings, and judicious advice. Though sadly consternated at the damnable perfidy of these monster crimes, retaliation was not attempted. Gov. Dunmore, of Virginia, offered a reward for the apprehension of the murderer, which caused him to leave the country, and the Indians smothered their just indignation and forebore redress.

"On the south branch of the Monongahela a most wanton and unprovoked massacre was committed on some peaceable Indians on a friendly visit there, by Henry Judah and Nicholas Harpold. The former was arrested for the crime, but the excited and inconsiderate populace rescued him, and he was permitted to go unhung. Bald Eagle was a chieftain of great celebrity, who was known and highly esteemed by all the well-disposed settlers along the Monongahela. He was on familiar and confidential terms with the inmates of every cabin His visits were frequent, and his presence always welcome. Yet this universal favorite was inhumanly murdered by the three dastardly wretches, Jacob Scott, William Hacker and Elijah Runner. They met him all alone in his canoe somewhere near the mouth of the Cheat, and committed the cowardly deed. Not content with the horrible crime of cold-blooded murder, they proceeded to add insult to injury by thrusting a johnny-cake in his mouth, propping him up in the stern of his canoe and setting him afloat on the river In this condition he was discovered by a Mrs. Province, about the mouth of Big Whiteley Creek, who had his remains brought ashore and decently buried. Soon after the death of Bald Eagle, one William White waylaid and assassinated a peaceable Indian, for which he was apprehended and committed to Winchester jail for trial. But the prejudiced and infuriated populace forced the prison doors, knocked off his shackles and set him at liberty.

"About the close of the year of 1772, I think, a most atrocious butchery occurred on a branch of Dunkard Creek A semi-civilized Indian family, by name of Jacob, lived there by hunting and cultivating a patch of Indian corn. He would frequently supply the settlers along the creek with meat and skins But his peaceful wigwam was invaded, and his whole household slain, with the exception of two children, who escaped, half frozen and nearly starved, to tell the story of their wrongs to the kindred tribes beyond the Ohio. The miscreants who perpetrated this deed are now unknown About this time also Bulltown, an Indian village consisting of five families, on the Little Kanawha, was ruthlessly invaded by five demons, among whom were White and Hacker, before mentioned All the villagers, men, women and children, on the frivolous pretext of a mere suspicion, were put to death, and their bodies sunk in the river In the spring of 1774, Capt Cræsop and a party of land sharks first waylaid and murdered a couple of peaceable Indians crossing the Ohio in a canoe, and afterward fired upon a harmless encampment of Indians at the mouth of Captina Creek, killing and wounding several.

"But perhaps of all the black catalogue of unprovoked crimes, the affair a few days later, at the mouth of Yellow Creek, was the most infamous. Here the family of Logan, who up to that time was known as 'the white man's friend,' was killed. One Daniel Great-house led a party of bushwhackers to the scene, ostensibly to protect a family named Baker, who resided at the mouth of the creek, and subsisted chiefly from the miserable occupation of selling the Indians rum. Secreting his men, he crossed the creek in the guise of friend-ship to the Indian camp Being advised by a friendly squaw that the Indians were getting in liquor and were somewhat exasperated on account of the trouble at the mouth of Captina, he returned to Baker's and told him if any of the Indians should come over, to give them all the rum they wanted. The hypocritical scheme succeeded. Lured by his treacherous representations, a party of Indians with two females crossed over to Baker's, and when sufficiently intoxicated were set upon by Greathouse and his minions, and the whole party slaughtered. Another party ventured over, and shared a like fate. By this time, suspecting foul play, a large detachment attempted to cross, but they too were fired upon from the deadly ambuscade, and many of them slain and the rest driven back. The perpetration of this act of fiendish perfidy was fittingly closed by the savage cere-mony of scalping all the victims. These were a few specimens of the treatment the Indians, when disposed to be peaceable, received at the hands of the whites. The soul sickens in contemplation of these revolting scenes! The blood curdles to believe mankind guilty of such nameless horrors! What marvel that speedy retribution was visited upon the settlements? What marvel that swift destruction overtook them at noonday? What marvel that the terrible war-whoop of the blood-thirsty savage pervaded the whole land; that the toma-hawk and the scalping-knife on every hand were reeking with the blood of the innocent; that fire and rapine and general desolation ruled the hour?

"From this time forth Logan was transformed into an avenging demon. His name became a terror. At his beck settlements dis-appeared as with 'a besom of destruction.' The soil of Greene County drank the blood of almost numberless victims to his power. Well could reeking scalps, vacant hearths and smouldering ruins attest his boast: 'I have sought revenge. I have killed many. I have fully glutted my vengeance.'"

CHAPTER XLIII.

MORGAN TOWNSHIP.

Everhart Hupp—Indian Training—Only Fear—Mrs. Hupp, First
White Woman—Cooking—Boundary—Schools—Directors—
Recollections of an Old Settler—School-House—Shoemaker
—Frozen to Death

MORGAN TOWNSHIP was one of the earliest settled in the
county. Everhart Hupp, who lived to be one hundred and
nine years old, married Margarett Thomas, who lived to the age
of one hundred and five years, and purchased of the Indians
a large tract of land on Ten Mile Creek, for which he paid one black
mare and one rifle gun. On running the lines agreed upon with the
Indians, he found it contained 1,400 acres, and embraced lands north
of Ten-Mile Creek and stretching across the North Fork, and consequently overlapping a portion of Morgan Township, where some of
his descendants live to this day. The Hupps were always on good
terms with the Indians, for the reason that they were always made
welcome and given whatever the cabin afforded   Mr. Hupp used to
declare that a feeling of fear of the Indians was never excited in his
mind but once. On that occasion he had gone out upon the creek to
do some work in a grove where he was shielded from view of his
cabin, but where he could himself observe it   Going to the only
point of observation, he was startled to see several stalwart Indians,
tricked out in his own militia trappings, marching around the house
and pretending to go through the evolutions of a squad of soldiers.
At this sight his heart was in his mouth, fearing that his wife had
been murdered and that the savages were bent on mischief   His
agony for the moment was indescribable; but to his great joy he
soon saw his wife coming from the spring-house, bearing a pan of milk,
evidently preparing something for the red men to eat.   He soon returned to his dwelling and had a friendly chat, while they partook of
the *table d' hote* set for them by Madame Hupp, when they departed,
highly elated by their entertainment.

Mr Evans, in his thirty-first Centennial sketch, says: " At this
time, 1767, there was but one white woman west of the Monongahela River known to the settlers   She was the wife of George Hupp
[probably Everhart Hupp] who located a large body of land on the

north bank of Ten-Mile, and erected a cabin near the creek and about two miles from its mouth   Her frugal repast consisted of johnny cake [journey-cake] shortened with bear's fat, dried venison and Adam's ale.   Their hospitality soon became proverbial with the sparse inhabitants, who were else all males, and the Hupp cabin became the Sunday morning rendezvous for all the men in the settlement.   Nauseated with their own unpalatable cooking, they would carry their choice game and fish to her, and enjoy a toothsome meal prepared and served by the veriest lady in the land."

On account of its contiguity to Redstone fort, which was a rallying point in time of danger, and the point at which the new comer tarried until he could find a tract on which to blaze his title, that pleased his fancy, the lands of this township were early appropriated.   This was one of the original townships at the time of the organization of Washington County, and was at that time much larger than at present.   It is bounded on the north by Washington County, on the east by Jefferson, on the south by Jefferson and Franklin, and on the west by Washington.   The surface is very broken but the soil is fertile, and the farms well improved.   It is well watered by North and South Ten-Mile Creek and their tributaries.   Clarksville, the only village in the township, a place of some 350 inhabitants, is situated on a peninsula formed by the two forks of Ten-Mile Creek at their junction, at the head of the creek proper.   It has three churches and the usual business of a centre of a fine farming country.   In the report of Secretary Burrowes, in 1836, Morgan is credited with four schools and 155 pupils, that of Secretary Black in 1854, with six schools and 360 pupils.   The report of 1859 says: "The directors of this district are a philanthropic band, who have the interest of the rising generation at heart.   They have increased the school fund, and have paid their teachers liberally.   Therefore, the cause of education has advanced very rapidly in this township within the past three or four years.   All the school-houses are furnished with blackboards and maps."   The good report thus early won has been maintained and it still holds a foremost rank.   The directors for the current year are: J. M Thistlethwait, President; Joseph Adamson, Secretary; Edward Van Kirk, George Hughes, Solomon Cumrine, and Robert Buckingham.

Below we give some reminiscences of the olden time related by an aged citizen and published some years ago in the Waynesburg Republican:

"The first school-houses were built of logs, with dirt floors and greased paper for windows.   The seats were made of sticks driven into walls and slabs laid on them.   The first teachers I remember were Francis Lazear and John McGuire.   The books used were U. S. speller and the New Testament.   The schools then, as now, were only open in the winter season, and the little folks had often to go several miles through the woods, with the snow two feet or more deep; and as there was no such thing as boots then, it was a very cold operation.

"There were shoemakers in that day, but they did not have shops as they have now, but went around from house to house, shoeing the whole family before leaving. We never got but one pair of shoes in a year. Often times little children had no shoes at all, wearing nothing but stockings.

"I will tell you a story of one of these traveling shoemakers. His name I have forgotten, but I remember he came to my father's and made us all shoes. He was a jolly good fellow, but loved his drink. After he got through at our house, he got his money and started for home. The weather was very cold and as he had to pass a still-house, he stopped and got a jug. As he journeyed on towards home, he frequently imbibed, until he had reached within about one hundred yards of home—that haven of rest where a wife and several children awaited his coming—when he succumbed to the influence of the liquor and got down, where he was found a short time after frozen to death. It created a great deal of excitement in the neighborhood, but like such things to-day, had no influence, as whisky continued to be made and drunk just the same "

CHAPTER XLIV.

MORRIS TOWNSHIP.

MILLIKEN — FIRST COURT HOUSE — NINEVEH — BEULAH CHURCH — METHODIST CHURCH — UNITY CHURCH — CARL BROTHERS MURDERED.

ROBERT MILLIKEN was born in Ireland in 1772, and died in 1865. He was one of the early commissioners of Greene County, and was the first Justice of the Peace of Morris Township. He built a house on the site of Waynesburg, where John Buchanan's house stands, about the year 1798. He was a brick moulder by trade, and built the first brick Court House in Greene County in the year 1800. To this time courts had been held in the house since occupied by Charles S. Hickey. He married Mary, a daughter of

David Gray. He afterwards owned the farm on Brown's Fork, Morris Township, now owned by his son, James Milliken. Mrs. Mary Milliken was one of two children that made the midnight flight to Jackson's fort, elsewhere mentioned.

The principal village in this township bears the bible name of Nineveh, pleasantly located on Brown's Fork of Ten-Mile Creek. William Day purchased a small plot of ground on which the village is located as late as 1845, and having erected a small house, his son Francis opened a store therein. Mr. Day laid out streets through his plot of ground and soon a number of dwellings were erected. In 1850 a Cumberland Presbyterian Church was built, which was thoroughly repaired and modernized in 1881. The place has become of considerable importance as a business center, being in the midst of a fine agricultural section. A wagon shop is reputed to turn out excellent work. It has a substantial brick school building.

The Bates' Fork Baptist Church is located near Sycamore Station on the Waynesburg railroad close to the border of Washington Township. It was organized on the 29th of December, 1842, by Revs. Isaac Pettit, Levi Griffith, William Woods and Thomas Richards. Fifty-one members were received by letter. Lewis Ketchum, Thomas Taylor and John Pettit were chosen deacons. The following named persons have officiated as pastors, as shown by its records: Elders Pettit, Sigfried, Pool, Ellis, Richards, Camonson, Charles Tilton, Parcell, Rossell, Scott, Morgan and Tilton.

The Beulah Baptist Church is located on the water-shed which divides the basins of Ten-Mile and Wheeling creeks, near the Washington County line. The meetings were first held at the house of Lewis Ketchum as early as 1823. Elder Isaac Pettit was one of the early laborers, though for several years preaching was had only occasionally, and sometimes at long intervals. In 1843 Elder Trevor Richards commenced preaching once a month at the school-house near by. Soon afterwards a church organization was effected, Elders Pettit, Brown and Richards officiating on the occasion, and a house of worship was built. The following named persons have officiated as pastors or supply: Elders Trevor Richards, John Thomas, William Whitehead, Charles Tilton, Caleb Rossel, S. L. Parcell, Job Rossel, H. K. Craig, W. F. Burwell, Patton, C. Haven. The church has been weakened from time to time by withdrawals to found other churches and to unite with other organizations.

The Methodist Episcopal Church of Nineveh, Greene County, Pa., was organized January 31, 1881, with five members, viz.: W. S. Throckmorton M D., and wife; John Vancleve and wife, and Edward McVey. During the preceding summer the first church building was erected. The society then organized was in the Waynesburg circuit, Pittsburg Conference, Rev. W. D. Sleas, pastor, with Rev. Geo. H. Huffman as his colleague.

The society at once began to exercise a marked influence on the community, so that at the close of the first year a membership of sixty-five had been gathered into the church.

Rev. E. S. White succeeded to the pastorate, and during his term a new charge was formed, composed of Nineveh and Hopewell, a society that had been organized perhaps sixty years before.

On December 29, 1883, the beautiful little church building at Nineveh was entirely consumed by fire, and but for the faith, courage and liberality of Dr. Throckmorton and his devoted wife this grow-ing and promising society must have been blotted out. On the next day, Sunday Dec. 80, the Quarterly Conference was reconvened and resolved to rebuild. The same building committee was reappointed and the work began at once.

On Monday the smoking debris was cleared away and preparatory work for rebuilding was vigorously begun.

On Sunday Sept. 21, 1884, the new church building, superior in every respect to the one it has replaced, was dedicated.

During the time of its erection, one of the most commodious, convenient and comfortable parsonages, within the bounds of the conference, was also erected by the charge on a beautiful lot adjoin-ing the church.

Rev. R. S. Ross succeeded to the pastorate, and during his term of three years, provision was made for the liquidation of all debts against the church and parsonage, and the membership grew to one hundred and twenty. In all departments of church work the society has prospered while it has gained proportionately in temporal things. At present (1888) the charge is under the pastoral care of Rev. N. P. Kerr.

The Unity Presbyterian Church at Harvey's, Greene County, was organized in 1814. In the spring of that year the Presbytery ap-pointed a committee consisting of Rev. John Anderson and Rev. Joseph Stevenson to organize a church here. Among those of Presby-terian faith who had settled in this neighborhood was Francis Brad-dock who came in 1805 and occupied the farm now held by his son, J. H. Braddock. In 1812 Moses and Thomas Dinsmore came and secured lands where their descendants now live.

The committee appointed by the Presbytery met on August 27, 1814, at the house of David Gray, now occupied by Mrs. McClelland, where after holding religious service the Church of Unity was formed. The ruling elders ordained and installed were David Gray, Jacob Rickey, Francis Braddock and Moses Dinsmore. The families of Messrs. Dodd, Holden and Kent were also represented in the organ-ization. Supplies were appointed by Presbytery who came about six times a year and received from two to five dollars per Sabbath for their services.   The Sacrament of the Lord's supper was usually administered in autumn when the roads were good.   The names of some of those who came as supplies were Rev. John Anderson, Joseph Stevenson, James Hervey, David Hervey, Reed, Marquis, Dodd, McCurdy, Mercer, Moore, Wylie and Patterson.

,   In 1828 the churches of Wolf Run and Unity united in calling Rev. A. Leonard as stated supply, and he was succeeded in 1831 by Rev. W. D Smith, in 1834 by Rev. Samuel Moody, and in 1835 by the unfortunate Rev. John Knox.   Several young men licensed by the Presbytery of Washington supplied for limited periods   Rev. James Fleming preached for a time in 1839, and afterwards occasional supplies until 1842 when the congregations of Unity and Wolf Run settled and installed Rev. John Whittim, who was succeeded in 1844 by Rev. Alexander McCarrell.   Upon the establishment of a Presbyterian Church at Waynesburg, the two churches united in calling pastors who served half time at each place, Messrs. McCarrell, Rosborough, Calhoun and Miller in succession having charge of these flocks.   In 1854 Rev. Samuel Jeffrey became pastor and served faithfully till his death in 1859.   The Rev. J. A. Ewing, Rev. William Jeffrey, Rev. William Hanna and Rev. William S. Vancleve served in succession from 1860 to 1867.   At this time the church at Waynesburg engaged the entire time of a pastor and Unity was without a stated supply.   The Rev. Samuel Graham became pastor in December, 1869, conducting a select school at the same time at Jacksonville.   In 1872 Rev. J. B. Stevenson supplied it until 1875.   Rev. Robert P Farrar in the following year served Unity in connection with the church of Cameron.   He was succeeded by the Rev. Samuel Graham, who in addition to the pastoral work has a select school at Graysville, and is still officiating (1888).

For many years the congregation worshipped in a log schoolhouse which stood below the old grave-yard.   A frame structure 45x50 was erected at a cost of $700.   Francis Braddock, senior, donated the ground and contributed liberally to the building fund. In 1880, after forty years of service, this house was destroyed by fire, and a new edifice was erected at Graysville to take its place.   It is 34x54 feet and 17 feet to ceiling and was built at a cost of $2,250. It was dedicated on the 20th of June, 1880, the Rev Joseph S. Braddock preaching the dedicatory sermon.   The Sabbath-school connected with this church was established in the days of the old log school-house, and Francis Braddock, senior, was the first Superintendant.   It has done efficient work ever since.

The church has been the nursery whence has gone forth a number of able heralds of the cross.   Of the family of Francis Braddock, senior, three—Francis, Cyrus and Joseph, became ministers, and of

27

the sons of Moses Dinsmore, six—Robert S., Francis B , Thomas H , John, Moses and William, studied for the ministry. The Session having been reduced in 1837 to one member, the congregation elected four additional members, A. C. Rickey, Francis Braddock, Jr , Obadiah Vancleve and Thomas Dinsmore. By removals and death the Session had again become weakened, Francis Braddock, senior, after a long and devoted life having been called home, and in 1856 the following were elected· William Loughridge, David Braddock, John Carter and John Reed. Thomas Dinsmore, at the age of eighty-six, William Loughridge, at the age of ninety-five, and Abraham C. Rickey, at the age of seventy-seven, fathers in Israel, were removed by death On the 7th of July, J. H Braddock, Hamilton Teagarden and Daniel Clutter were chosen, and subsequently Thomas Henderson. The church has enjoyed many seasons of refreshing from the Lord

In the early days Robert Carl, his wife and two small children, and his two brothers, John and Hamilton, dwelt in a cabin on a branch of Wheeling Creek not far from Beulah Baptist Church. One night whilst Robert was away from home an alarm of Indians came and the inmates prepared to flee to Lindley's Fort. At dawn the two brothers went out to gather dry sticks with which to cook their breakfast when they were both shot dead by Indians lying in wait. The mother with a two-year-old child in her arms and leading the other four-years-old by the hand, escaped from the house into a dense field of corn and succeeded in eluding the wily savages In attempting to enter the cabin the Indians were met by a furious bitch which had a litter of pups under the bed and so much time elapsed before she could be put out of the way that the mother with her precious charge escaped The murdered brothers were scalped, the cabin pillaged even to the destruction of the feather-beds The mother made her way to Lindley's Fort some ten miles away, where not many days after she gave birth to another child.

"There is another tradition," says Evans, "that on Crab Apple Run there lived in the troublous days, on lands now owned by David G. Braddock, a family by the name of Hume. This family consisted of father, mother and five or six children. The murderous savages came one day, and without a moment's warning massacred in cold blood the entire family, a deed of horror that could not be surpassed. In this same general neighborhood at various times Indians slaughtered a family by the name of McIntyre, one by the name of Beeham, one by the name of Link, another by the name of McIntosh, a Mrs. Nancy Ross, and tomahawked and scalped two Beekman boys, and committed many other depredations, the traditions of which have become so dim by the erasure of time that I have been unable to elicit sufficient particulars to justify an attempt at relating them."

CHAPTER XLV.

PERRY TOWNSHIP.

SURFACE—SOIL—PRODUCTIONS—BOUNDARIES—MOUNT MORRIS—IN-
TELLIGENCE—SCHOOLS—DIRECTORS—JEREMIAH GLASSGOW—PER-
SONAL CONTEST—FIRST SETTLER—WAR PATHS.

THIS township is situated in the southern part of the county. Its surface is broken, and along the streams precipitous, the rocky strata that underlies the soil being exposed to view, piled in massive layers one above another, often overhanging the foliage below, along which the road winds in seeming dangerous proximity to the cliff. But notwithstanding the immensity of the hills, the soil is fertile and produces abundant crops of corn, wheat, rye, oats, potatoes, and roots on which sheep and cattle are fed. The broken and untillable portions are covered with heavy growths of fine timber, thus covering up the deformities of nature and making every part picturesque and beautiful. The township is well watered by Dunkard Creek and its numerous tributaries. There are portions of the territory which have never been improved, being still covered by forest; but the greater portion is under a good state of cultivation, and fine breeds of sheep, cattle, horses and swine are everywhere noticeable. The township is bounded on the north by Whiteley, on the east by Dunkard, on the south by Mason and Dixon's line, and west by Wayne.

At the southeast corner of the township, on the right bank of Dunkard Creek, bordered by towering hills, is the pleasant village of Mount Morris. It is regularly laid out, and has an air of prosperity, though its growth has for some time been impeded by a number of causes which now fortunately seem to be passing away, and an era of prosperity appears to be opening before it. The village has always been noted for the intelligence and public spirit of its people, and here was established one of the earliest graded schools in the county. Secretary Black's report in 1854 gives this township eight schools with 220 pupils, and Mount Morris one school with seventy-five pupils. The report of 1887 gives the township ten schools with 336 pupils, and Mount Morris two schools and ninety-two pupils, thus showing a marked increase The report of 1859 says: "Mount Morris has one school. The directors of this district manifest a determination and active zeal in the work of educational reform worthy the noble cause in which they are engaged. This school stands number one." The directors of the township for the current year are: Perry Fox, President; Z. T. Shultz, Secretary; G. W. Headley, David Fox, Isaac Cowell, J. K. Headley; and of Mount Morris, Dr. M. N. Reamer, President; D. L. Donley, Secretary; J. H. Barrack, Dr. Hatfield, John W. Maxim, M. C. Monroe.

About the year 1765, Jeremiah Glassgow, who had been the companion of John Minor in settling at Redstone, hoping to better his condition, crossed the Monongahela and traveled through the forests and thickets which cumbered all the valley of this placid stream, until he came to the neighborhood of Mount Morris, in what is now Perry Township. On the goodly lands which here border Dunkard Creek he selected as pleased his fancy, and toilsomely blazed his tract. At winter time he returned to his former home in Maryland. On returning in the spring he found that a giant of the forest by the name of Scott had, in his absence, taken possession of his tract, and would not be persuaded to give it up to the rightful, or rather original, claimant. Who was the rightful owner was yet to be determined, not by the Marquis of Queensbury rules, but by those of the backwoodsman. It was accordingly agreed that the two should fight for possession, and he who proved himself the better man should have it. Accordingly Glassgow chose his friend John Minor, who had accompanied him from Redstone and had taken lands at Mapletown, as his second, or best friend, and the contestants stripped for the trial. Glassgow was much the smaller man, though well built. In the first encounters Glassgow was worsted; but practicing wily tactics, in which he seems to have been skilled, he grappled with his antagonist and threw him heavily to the ground. The giant was soon up, but no sooner up than he was again tripped and came heavily to the ground. This was repeatedly practiced until the big man found himself so bruised and exhausted that he could not shake off his assailant. Glassgow was now easily able to give him all the punishment he desired, and when he called for a cessation of the battle, the two arose, shook hands and agreed that the land belonged to Glassgow. Thus in true Horatian and Curatian style was the dispute settled, and Glassgow held the ground which his blood had moistened. Disputes like these were not unusual in those early days of settlement, and we may learn by this example how the land was originally acquired.

Glassgow was undoubtedly one of the earliest settlers who came to stay and cultivate his lands, in the county, and it was the grit displayed in this contest which enabled him to face all the difficulties and dangers which were the lot of the pioneers after the defeat of Braddock. As the great war-path of the natives passed through this township, the inhabitants were exposed to their cruelties.

"The great Catawba war-path," says Mr. Evans, "entered Fayette County from the south at the mouth of Grassy Run, thence northward to Ashcroft, on Mrs. Evans Wilson's land, by Rev. William Brownfield's, through Uniontown, through Col. Samuel Evans' highlands, past Pearse's fort, a little west of Mt. Braddock house, to Opossnm Run, down it to the Youghiogheny, crossing where Braddock's army crossed, thence by the Pennsville Baptist Church, thence by Tintsmon's mill on Jacob's Cieek, thence on through Westmoreland and Armstrong counties, and on up the Alleghany to its source, and over on the headwaters of the Susquehanna into western New York, the grand realm of the mighty Six Nations.

"The warrior branch of this vast trail left the Ohio River at the mouth of Fish Creek, up which it followed to its very source. It then crossed over on to the waters of Dunkard Creek, and followed this water-course to its confluence with the Monongahela, making an intersection with the Catawba line in Springhill Township, Fayette County. But the warrior branch was not absorbed, but kept on by Crow's mill, and bearing towards the mouth of Redstone Creek, joined the old Redstone trail near Grace Church, on the national pike." Mason and Dixon were stopped in their survey in November, 1767, at a point in Wayne Township, where these two paths cross.

CHAPTER XLVI.

RICHHILL TOWNSHIP.

NAME SIGNIFICANT—GRAYSVILLE—JACKSONVILLE—THOMAS LEEPER—
CAMERON STATION—RYERSON'S FORT—OLD SEA CAPTAIN
SEARCHES FOR HIS TOWN—FORT—THE DAVIS MASSACRE—DAVID
GRAY—BRADDOCKS—ABNER BRADDOCK DROWNED—THE TEA-
GARDENS—JACOB CROW—HEADLESS HUNTER—MASSACRE OF
THREE SISTERS—RETURN OF THE MURDERER—SCHOOLS—DI-
RECTORS.

THIS township undoubtedly takes its name from the characteristics of its surface, for it is one stretch of hills throughout its broad domain, and the soil is everywhere deep and rich. This section early assumed importance from its being on the direct trail from Wheeling to the Muskingum country, down Ten Mile Creek to

Braddock's road, and was frequented from the earliest times by the savages, and later by droves of cattle, sheep and swine on their way eastward. Graysville is quite a thriving little village situated on the Waynesburg and Wheeling road thirteen miles from Waynesburg and three and a half miles from Jacksonville. James McLellan built a brick store here, which was occupied by Garret Garrison, subsequently by James W. Hays, and at present by Smith Brothers. Jacobs and Hardy are just opening a place of business here, April, 1888. The United Presbyterians have a fine church edifice, where the Rev. Samuel Graham ministers, and has a school of high grade. The postoffice is known as Harvey's. Jacksonville, near the center of the township, is located on a pleasant elevation known as Elk Ridge, the postoffice having the suggestive name of Windridge. The tract was originally acquired by Thomas Leeper, his patent bearing date of February 15, 1798, issued by the State of Pennsylvania. Robert Brister bought the land where the village is now located and surveyed and laid out the plot of the town. William Super had a hotel here forty-four years ago, and Bryan and Tupper have succeeded in business. Daniel Walton, Garret Garrison and Charles Pettit have carried on trade at successive periods. Sowers and Drake and A. J. Goodman now do a prosperous business. The Cumberland Presbyterian and Methodist Episcopal churches have commodious places of worship. Masonic Hall and Odd Fellows Hall are pretentious structures, the former bearing the name of George Connell, once a leader in the Pennsylvania Senate, conspicuously displayed upon its front. Merchandise is largely brought to this town from a station on the Baltimore & Ohio Railroad.

Ryerson Station, once the site of an important rallying point in times of danger known as Ryerson's Fort, is situated on the great Indian war-path leading across from the Ohio River to the Monongahela, at the confluence of the north and south forks of Dunkard branch of Wheeling Creek—a fine stretch of valley with lines of interminable hills sweeping up on all sides in graceful curves, and covered with luxuriant foliage. So suitable did it appear for a town that the original owner, Thomas Ryerson, bethought him to make the drawing of such a place as he pictured in his imagination would be a suitable concomitant to such a location, and taking it to Philadelphia, sold out his would-be city for a reality, to an old sea captain by the name of Connell, father of the late George Connell. Great was the astonishment of the purchaser of this city on paper to find only a few huts at the forks of two wild streams, the ground not even cleared of the trees and bushes, and the dense, primeval forest resting on all the hills.

It was recognized from the very first as an important strategic point of defence for the settlers against the incursion of hostile Indians from their villages across the Ohio Here the authorities of Virginia had a fort built, to the defence of which Captain James Seals was sent, having in his company the grandfather, father and uncles of Isaac Teagarden, and Thomas Lazear, father of Hon. Isaac Lazear.

"About the year 1790," says Evans, "a family by name of Davis resided on the north branch of Dunkard Wheeling Creek, about three miles above Ryerson Station, and a short distance below Stall's or Kinkaid's mill. The family, with the exception of one fortunate lad who had been sent to drive up the horses, were seated around the breakfast table, partaking of an humble but substantial repast. Suddenly a party of warrior savages appeared at the cabin door. The old man and his two sons sprang up as by instinct to reach for their guns which hung on convenient pegs by the cabin wall; but the design was detected by the Indians, who instantly shot the three dead on the spot. After scalping the victims, despatching the breakfast and pillaging the premises, they made captive the mother and only daughter, and departed on their way up the creek. The boy managed to elude them, and escaped unharmed. It appears that they captured a horse. One of the Indians mounted it, and taking the girl before him, and the woman behind him, was traveling gayly along. However, they had not proceeded far when a shot from the rifle of John Henderson, who lay concealed in an adjoining thicket, knocked the jolly savage off. But whether the wound was fatal or not, Henderson did not remain to find out. He had to provide himself safety from the infuriated savages." Some time after the decaying body of the daughter was found, but no trace of the mother was ever discovered. The mutilated bodies of the slain were buried near the cabin, and their graves are still marked. The skeleton remains of an Indian were afterwards found, supposed to have been the savage shot by Henderson.

David Gray settled on the Ephraim McClelland farm, a short distance east of what is now known as the Brick Tavern at Graysville. Upon one occasion the dreaded savage having made his appearance in that vicinity, Mr. Gray with his wife, each with a child to carry, abandoned their home in the night and fled, the wife and two children on horseback, himself on foot, all the way to Jackson's fort, a distance of about fifteen miles. He was one of the commissioners to locate and plat the town of Waynesburg for a county seat, and was appointed one of the first associate judges. He was appointed a justice of the peace for Richhill in April, 1792, while yet a part of Washington County.

Anna Gray, one of the daughters of Judge David Gray, married Frank Braddock and had a family of five sons—Harvey, David, Frank,

Joseph and Green, the three last becoming quite eminent Presbyterian ministers. Abner Braddock, a brother of Francis, was an Indian scout, and settled on Crabapple Run, where David Braddock now lives. He went on an expedition against the Indians beyond the Ohio River. On returning his comrades arrived at the right bank of the river, and began the construction of a raft on which to cross Being an expert swimmer and not desiring to wait for its completion, he placed his clothes and gun on a slight support, and plunged in, pushing it before him. Near the middle of the stream he was seen to leave his raft and pass on down the current; soon he disappeared beneath the surface and was seen no more Among the scouts who witnessed his death were Shadrach Mitchel, James Brownlee and William Gaston John Gray was a brother of Judge David Gray, and Matthew was one of the scouts with Abner Braddock, and one of Capt. James Seals' soldiers. He had two sons, William and John. The latter is still living in Richhill Township.

William Teagarden sold his possessions on the Monongahela, but receiving his price in Continental scrip (the inflation currency of that day), it fell as flat on his hands as Confederate legal-tenders after Sherman's march to the sea Financially he was ruined. His home was gone, his money of no value, but his spirit was undaunted, and he began life anew by again braving the untried forest. Exploring the country inland, he made another tomahawk improvement on Wheeling waters, near Ryerson Station, to which he removed. Here he remained the remnant of his many days, and reared his large and thrifty family. Here he experienced many a hardship, witnessed many a sad scene in murdered friends, and made many a hair-breadth escape. Here he and two of his boys, Abraham and Isaac, enlisted in Capt. James Seals' company, and served honorably under Gen Anthony Wayne in his eventful but successful campaigns against the hostile tribes Capt Seals and his brave company rendezvoused for some time at Ryerson Station, and afforded security to the much harrassed settlements in that vicinity.

The entire life of that generation of Teagardens was a continual warfare. They were soldiers from the cradle to the grave. Constantly on the frontier, which was either in a state of defence or engaged in actual vigorous warfare in repelling a most blood-thirsty invader, they lived at a time that tried men's souls, and endured hardships and braved dangers almost beyond belief Isaac Teagarden inherited the spirit of his forefathers, and though superannuated long ere the war of the Rebellion broke out, he enlisted in the Eighty-fifth regiment and served honorably throughout the long and terrible years of that civil war.

In 1769 Jacob Crow, a German, settled near where subsequently Crow's Mill was built, some five miles below Ryerson

Station. Michael, his youngest son, was but three weeks old when he came, but Martin, Fred and John, older boys, were also of the family. He was a thrifty farmer, and gradually added tract after tract until he owned a beautiful and valuable domain. While the Crow family was thus living in the seclusion of this delectable valley, two men, whose names have not been preserved, came in and established a hunting camp two and a half miles below Crow's cabin, on lands now owned by the Harshes. Here the two were surprised by the Indians and one of them killed. The other made his escape and roused the settlers. On returning to the camp, they were horrified to find that the head of the murdered man had been cut off, and the most diligent search failed to disclose the place of its concealment. On the following winter while Jacob Crow was drawing wood in this vicinity, what was his astonishment and horror to find, when arrived at his destination, that a man's head was caught fast in the hook of his log chain. The chain left dragging through the leaves had caught firmly in the under jaw—a ghastly spectacle. In this visit to the camp for the burial of the dead, and pursuit of the Indians, two of the sons of Jacob Crow, Fred and Martin, joined, leading their little brother Michael Thinking the tramp too long for him they left him at a vacant cabin intending soon to return. But for three days he was left alone, a faithful dog keeping him company.

On the first day of May, 1791, four daughters of Jacob Crow, Elizabeth, Susanna, Katharine and Christina, from ten to sixteen years of age, started out on a pleasure excursion to visit the family of Thomas Lazear, then living on lands now owned by Thomas Gray. Proceeding leisurely along the creek, they discovered a shad-bellied snake, which, having disabled, they were teasing. While thus engaged their brother Michael came riding down the creek, and called to the youngest to mount behind him and ride home; but this she declined to do, and he rode away. Scarcely had he gone, when two hideous savages, and a heartless renegade white man, by the name of Spicer, darted out from their covert, and motioned the girls to silence. Hurrying them away up the rugged hillside to a dark ravine they were made to be seated upon a fallen tree. After making inquiries about their home and its means of defense, a powerful savage seized a hand of each of the younger girls in one of his, and with uplifted tomahawk prepared to deal the blow of death. Christina, by a sudden movement, released herself and dashed away. The Indian pursued, and gave her such a thrust with his gun as sent her headlong down the declivity. Thinking that she was dispatched, he returned to have a hand in the slaughter of the other three. But Christina still lived, and recovering herself, she saw one of the Indians deal repeated blows upon Elizabeth, felling her to the earth.

Crazed by the appalling sight, she darted away to seek for help. Taking the alarm, the families of the settlers were hurried off to Lindley's fort, and Isaac Teagarden, a lad of ten years, was mounted upon a fleet horse and sent to Inlow's block house for help.

"Next morning," says Evans, "a company was organized, and repairing to the place of death, beheld a spectacle, the like of which only frenzied demons could have produced. There lay Betsy and Susan literally butchered, mangled, dead, scalped. But Katharine was not there. Soon, however, traced by stains of blood, she was discovered near the water's edge, whither she had crept to slake her feverish thirst She, too, had been hewn down by the fierce and infuriated savages, her scalp torn off, and left for dead. Weltering in her gore she lay all that dreary, terrible night, unconscious of her wretched state. Next morning, awakened to consciousness by the gobbling of the wild turkeys, she found herself writhing beneath the scorching rays of a clouldless sun, and almost perishing of thirst. She was tenderly removed to the shadow of a large rock, which, but little changed, yet remains in a patch in a bottom land a few rods down the creek. Here she revived somewhat, and faintly related what little she remembered of the terrible affair, and gently chided her brother Michael, saying, 'I thought you would have come to me sooner'" Her scalp was hitched on a haw bush but a few steps from the rock, supposed to have been drawn from the Indian's belt as he dashed through in pursuit of Christina The scalp was fitted into the place from whence it had been torn, but the wound had become so irritated that it would not again adhere Katharine survived in torment for three days, when she was relieved by death, and the three sisters were buried side by side. John, a favorite son, afterwards shared a like fate at the hands of the savages, and Jacob's hearthstone became desolate indeed Christina lived and became the wife of John Mc-Bride She preserved her scalp, and carried the print of the muzzle of the Indian's gun between her shoulders to her dying day.

Years after at a log-rolling at Jacob Crow's, two strangers, one an Indian, called at the house, and asked for food. Christina recognized the Indian as one of the murderers of her sisters Scarcely had they left when her brother Michael and a trusty friend pursued. They were tracked to the neighborhood of Jackson's fort, where the trail was lost. The young men encamped for the night, and in the morning started to return. They had not gone far before they discovered the trail of their game, leading up a dark ravine. Following it up, their forsaken camp was soon found. Finding that the culprits had escaped and were far out of the way, Crow and his companion returned to their homes. This was after a treaty of peace had been concluded with the Indians. Michael Crow was afterwards apprehended, on suspicion of having murdered these travelers. But on proof that the men had subsequently been seen, he was released, though his neighbors were wont to darkly hint that the hunt of Michael was not gameless.

Martin and Frederick Crow were noted hunters, and fearless Indian scouts. Michael married Nancy Johnson, and was the father of ten children—William, John, Jacob, Michael, Nancy, Mary, Elizabeth, Margaret, Susan and Charlotte. About the year 1845, he and his son Michael built the popular mills known as "Crow's" mills. He died in 1852, at the age of eighty-three. His sons, Michael and Jacob, now old men, still inherit portions of the original Crow lands Michael owns the home farm, upon which the mill now stands. Michael married Sarah Jane Lucas, and has nine children, among whom is John M. Crow, professor of languages of Waynesburg College, who has given much of the information detailed above.

The soil of all this section is well watered and very fertile. The farm houses are commodious and comfortable, and the barns are among the largest and best planned of any in the county. The township is bounded on the north by Washington County, on the east by Morris, Jackson and Center, on the south by Aleppo, and west by West Virginia. The principal streams are the several tributaries of the Dunkard fork of Wheeling Creek By the report of 1855 Richhill is credited with eighteen schools and 900 pupils. In the report of 1859 the superintendent says, "The directors of this district manifest an interest in the general cause of education, highly commendable. They have also taken considerable care in selecting competent teachers." The directors for the current year are: Stephen Knight, President; N. H. Braddock, Secretary; Elias Gribbin, George McCullough, Abner Phillips and William Carpenter.

CHAPTER XLVII

SPRINGHILL TOWNSHIP

CORNER STONE—SURFACE AND SOIL—NEW FREEPORT—ISAAC J. HUPP—DEEP VALLEY—THE CROWS—MASSACRED BY INDIANS SCHOOLS—DIRECTORS.

SPRINGHILL TOWNSHIP is located in the extreme southwest corner of Greene County and consequently of the State of Pennsylvania. At its southwest extremity is that corner bound of the State that was so long sought and contended over by the authorities of Virginia and Pennsylvania, and was finally discovered by erecting an observatory and finding by repeated astronomical observations the true longitude of the place. This method was adopted upon the recommendation of Thomas Jefferson, then Governor of Virginia. Mason and Dixon had attempted to find it by reducing the distance over mountains and down the valleys to horizontal measurement after having found the length of a degree of longitude at the parallel of their line. The two methods, however, substantially agreed.

The surface of this township is seamed by the Pennsylvania fork of Fish Creek and its tributaries, which drain every part and afford ample power for mill purposes and for its numerous flocks and herds. The soil is fertile and the yields of grain are abundant. Though the country is very broken, and the hills rise almost to the proportions of mountains, springs of pure water are found even to their very summits, and there is scarcely a foot of sterile land throughout all its borders. Cattle, sheep and hogs are the most profitable products, though dairying is carried on to some extent. Quantities of hay from its rich bottom lands and timber from the hills are shipped away and afford a good income.

This township was not organized until 1860, and was taken from Aleppo and a part of Gilmore townships. It is almost the only township in the county that has a regular outline, being in the form of a parallelogram. It is bounded on the north by Aleppo, on the east by Gilmore, on the south by Mason and Dixon's line which separates from West Virginia, and on the west by the State line which separates it from the Pan Handle of West Virginia. New Freeport is the most considerable village in the township, and is a

place of business and rapidly growing.   Isaac J. Hupp, son of Everhart Hupp, one of the earliest settlers on Ten Mile Creek, came to
this place in 1854, when there were only three houses here, one of
which he occupied, and kept a hotel.   William Elder had a small
store.   Judge Thompson resided at Wheeling, and was accustomed
to pass through here on his way to Morgantown on his circuit   His
was the only buggy seen in these parts for many years.   He was
accustomed to stop over night at Hupp's.   William P. Hoskinson
came after an interval and succeeded Elder in mercantile business.
James Berdine, Jackson Barker, Edward Fence, James Styles and
Solomon White have from time to time been engaged in business
here.   Peter Bradley & Co. are still engaged in business here   This
valley was once a sugar camp, the sugar maple being very prolific.
A Baptist church edifice was built here in 1856, and the church was
ministered to by Rev. G. W. Archer.   A new edifice is to take the
place of the old one this season.   The Rev. Joseph Clark, an Englishman, preceded Archer in ministrations to this church, and Rev.
Morgan Tilton succeeded.   Deep Valley, a few miles below on Fish
Creek, has a postoffice, and is a place of considerable business, the
steam mills located there giving it an air of importance.

The quiet hills and valleys along this stream at an early day
were the favorite tramping grounds of the whites as well as the
Indians.

Sometime in the year 1780 John, Frederick and Martin Crow,
sons of Jacob, who had settled at Crow's Mill, together with one
Dickson, went out on the waters of Fish Creek and established a
camp for the purpose of hunting elk.   Going out by twos or singly
they separated during the day and returned at evening.   Fred and
Martin came in late, and Fred having shot a duck, and observing a
bright fire in the camp, thought to surprise his comrades by throwing the duck into their midst.   At the instant, they were fired on by
savages concealed near by.   Martin had his ear shot away, and
Frederick was shot through the shoulder.   Dropping forward, his
comrade supposed him killed, and fled for safety.   Thinking the
way was now clear, Fred pulled some sassafras leaves and was chew-
ing them in order to make a decoction to apply to his wound, when,
looking up, he saw an Indian levelling his gun at him.   As if by
instinct he fell to the ground just at the instant that the bullet passed
harmless over him.   Both guns being empty, Fred escaped across
the creek and the savage did not follow.   In the meantime John,
hearing the firing, ran up to ascertain the cause, and was pierced by
seven bullets aimed at his heart by the lurking red skins, and so
accurate was the aim that they entered his body so as not
to make a wound larger than a man's hand.   The wounded Fred
signaled long for his comrades to come to his assistance, using the

call of a wolf which had been agreed on; but, fearful of Indian treachery, they dared not for a long time to come. Returning cautiously they found Fred, whom they supposed to have been dead, still alive. Organizing a party to search for John, his body was found where it had fallen, scalped and mutilated in true Indian fashion The body was buried at the foot of a beech tree, which was duly marked and lettered, and was visible for many years; but was finally girdled and destroyed.

Springhill was among the latest of the townships settled, and even now there are large tracts of forest which have never been cleared away This township has eleven schools with an average attendance of 378 pupils The following are the school directors: John Sellers, President, Peter Bradley, Secretary; John Minor, Lindsay Caseman, Wilson Miller, Owen Chancy.

CHAPTER XLVIII.

WAYNE TOWNSHIP.

LOCATION — BOUNDARIES—WELL WATERED — DYE'S MILL—SCHOOLS —FURNITURE FOR A CABIN—DRESS OF PIONEERS—MASSACRE AT STATTLER'S FORT—BURIAL OF AN INFANT

THIS township is located in the southern portion of the county, and it was here on Dunkard Creek that Mason and Dixon were stopped in running their line, at a point where the great Indian war path crosses it. It is one of the largest townships in the county, and is bounded on the north by Center and Franklin, on the east by Whiteley and Perry, on the south by West Virginia, and on the west by Gilmore and Jackson The water shed in the northern part sends its waters to nearly all points of the compass; by Pursley Creek and Smith's Run to the north, by the Whiteley to the east, by Randolph's, Robert's, Shepherd's, Hoover's and Tom's runs to the south, and by the tributaries of Wheeling Creek to the west. It is, however, substantially in the valley of Dunkard Creek which touches lightly its southern border and receives the numerous tributaries. It has no villages, though Blacksville, a thriving little town, is located just across the line in West Virginia, the northern tier of lots reaching into Pennsylvania. Nearly a century ago James Dye built a flouring-mill here, the remains of which are still visible, which was frequented by the early settlers. Caleb Spragg, John McGee, Uriah Spragg, John Roberts, John Piles, Lences Jackson and John Lantz are mentioned as the pioneer settlers in the township. The surface is broken, as is nearly every part of the county, but is under a good state of cultivation, and the farms present an air of prosperity. The earliest report of the schools gives this township nine with 352 pupils. The report of 1887 credits it twelve schools and 522 pupils, a marked increase. The directors for the current year are J. Morris, President; John King, Secretary; Richard Thralls, Marion Minor, Thomas Hoge and Mathias Brant.

The early settlers had many hardships to endure and were accustomed to privations. Dr. Smith in his secular history of this section gives the following amusing account of the furniture of a pioneer cabin:

"A single fork, placed with its lower end in a hole in the floor and the upper end fastened to the joist, served for a bedstead, by placing a pole in the fork with one end through a crack, between the logs in the wall. This front pole was crossed by a shorter one within the fork, with its outer end through another crack. From the first pole through a crack between the logs of the end of the house the boards were put on, which formed the bottom of the bed. Sometimes other poles were pinned to the fork, a little distance above these, for the purpose of supporting the front and foot of the bed, while the walls were the support of its back and its head. A few pegs around the walls for a display of the coats of the women and hunting-shirts of the men, and two small forks or buck's horns to a joist for the rifle and shot-pouch, completed the carpenter work."

"Their dress was partly Indian and partly that of civilized nations. The hunting-shirt was universally worn. This was a kind of loose frock, reaching half way down the thighs, with large sleeves, open before, and so wide as to lap over a foot or more when belted. The cape was large, and sometimes handsomely fringed with a ravelled piece of cloth of a different color from that of the hunting-shirt itself."

The valley of Dunkard Creek was doubtless one of the most attractive and hence among the first tarrying places for white men in Greene County. The ease with which the Monongahela River could be reached was probably one of its inviting features. In 1778 a considerable settlement had gathered in the neighborhood of where Blacksville now is. A short distance below, on the Virginia side, the settlers had built Stattler's Fort—a place of refuge in time of danger. In 1778 the Indians were known to be on the war path, and for greater security the settlers went forth to their labor in bands, helping each other, and while some worked, others stood guard. One evening after a good day's work they butchered some hogs, and set out with their precious burden for the fort, all unsuspicious of any danger. But, doubtless attracted by the piercing squeals of the swine, a band of over one hundred Indians were on the watch for them, ambushing the path which the pioneers would follow. Toilsomely moving on with their burdens, they had approached within sight of the fort, and were doubtless thinking of the delicious porksteaks they would enjoy for their suppers, when all of a sudden the forest was ablaze with the fire from the Indians' guns. Several were killed by the first volley; but the survivors rallied and returned the fire, fighting their way through to the fort, but leaving eighteen of their number dead, scattered along the path. So weakened were they that it was some days before the survivors ventured forth to bury the dead, whom they found stripped, scalped and shockingly mangled This massacre occurred near the State line, on the Warrior Branch of the great Indian war path, and it is supposed that this was a war party on its way home. The bones of Jacob Stattler, who was killed and buried here, were washed out by the rains, and were reinterred not many years ago Brice Worley, grandfather of John I. Worley, of Wayne Township, settled on a tract of land a half mile below Blacksville in 1778. Brice Worley's first born babe died in infancy, and there is a well preserved tradition that the brave mother stood a faithful sentinel whilst the father nailed up a rude box, prepared the grave, and committed the darling baby to the earth. The little mound is still well preserved Brice Worley's house was stockaded and was known as Worley's Fort. Nathan Worley, his brother, was killed by the Indians.

CHAPTER XLIX.

WASHINGTON TOWNSHIP.

COMMERCIALLY SITUATED — RAIL-ROAD — 800 SUBSCRIBERS — COST $6,500 PER MILE—IN 1877 IS HEARD THE FIRST SCREAM OF THE LOCOMOTIVE—SURFACE—BOUNDARIES — EARLY SETTLERS — RELIGIONS—FIRST SACRAMENT IN 1783—SERVICES IN A BARN—SCHOOLS—DIRECTORS.

COMMERCIALLY, Washington Township is perhaps more favorably located than any other in the county. A highway of an easy grade leads down the valley of Ruff's Run, through the central portion, and connects at Jefferson with good roads leading to Rice's Landing, on the Monongahela River. It was also easily accessible to Waynesburg, so that it had the Pittsburg and home markets at its command from an early day. But latterly it has become especially favored by the opening of the Washington & Waynesburg Railroad, which by the several stations along its course gives easy outlet to Waynesburg and Pittsburg for the immense produce of all this fertile region.

The rail-road, though but narrow guage, is of great importance, not only to this township, but to the entire county. The project had been for a long time agitated; but seeing no prospect of having one built by foreign capital, the citizens of the county put their own money into the enterprise, and soon saw their wishes gratified.

In the fall of 1874 the matter took definite form, and during the winter and spring succeeding, preliminary surveys were made, and experimental lines run. Stock books were opened, and about eight hundred citizens, principally in Greene County, subscribed An aggregate subscription of $130,000 having been obtained, the company was organized in May, 1875, with the choice of the following officers: J. G. Ritchie, of Waynesburg, President; Chief Engineer O. Barrett, Jr, of Allegheny, and the following named eleven gentlemen directors: Simon Rinehart, Henry Sayers, J. T. Hook, A. A. Purman, W. C. Condit, Henry Swart, Jacob Swart, Ephraim Conger, James Dunn, Thomas Iames, John Munnel. The length of the road is twenty-nine miles. The guage is three feet, and with two engines and cars complete, ready to operate, cost $6,500 per mile. By the first of September, 1877, fourteen miles from Washington were completed,

28

and the cars began to run. By the 17th the track-layers had crossed the county line, and the locomotive, " General Greene," entered the limits of Greene, and for the first time in all its borders, screamed out its note of triumph. Early in October the road was completed, and trains commenced running regularly over its entire length. Hon. Justus Fordyce Temple, formerly Auditor-General of the State, was for several years at the head of the company, and his annual reports show that the passenger traffic, and tonnage of the road, had steadily increased under his faithful management. Recently the road has passed under the control of the Pennsylvania Company, and is operated as a part of its great network of *chemin de fer.*

Washington, like all the townships on the northern border of the county, is very rugged, though under a good state of cultivation. The roads, generally following the courses of the streams, run from north to south. It is well watered by a series of runs, Craig's, Crayne's, Boyd's, Ruff's, Overflowing and Hopkins'. It is bounded on the north by Washington County, on the east by Morgan Township, on the south by Franklin and on the west by Morris. There is no village of any importance in the township, though at the almost exact center of its territory, on Ruff's Run, is a mill, store, school-house and dwellings, which will probably in time become a place of some importance. This township was not organized till 1838, and was taken from Morris, Morgan and Franklin.

A number of English and Scotch emigrants, who had come over and settled in New England, subsequently removed to New Jersey, Pennsylvania, Maryland and Virginia. Still not satisfied they crossed the mountains, and some found their way to this and the neighboring township of Amwell, in Washington County, and brought with them a love of religious liberty, first promulgated and acted upon by Roger Williams. Among those who thus early settled here was Demas Lindley, who acquired property just across the county line, on whose land a fort, known as Lindley's Fort, was erected, which was a rallying point and a place of refuge for the inhabitants for a wide circuit in the two counties. He also built a mill, known as Lindley's Mill, which stood upon the site of the present structure which still bears his name. He was accompanied by some fifteen or twenty families, most of whom emigrated with the Pilgrims, who spread abroad in this section, and whose descendants still dwell along this stretch of highlands. Following the example of their New England associates they early established churches, the Baptists in 1772, and the Presbyterians in 1781, known as the upper and lower Ten-Mile. A tract of land was donated by Demas Lindley, which was to be held in perpetuity " for the occupancy and use of a Presbyterian Church and for no other purpose whatsoever." The entry in the church book for Wednesday, April 30, 1783, was " Present, Thaddeus Dodd, V. D. M.; Demas Lindley, Joseph Coe, Jacob Cooke, Daniel Axtell, elders.   At this session twenty-two persons joined." The sacrament was first administered on the third Sabbath in May, 1783, by Rev. Thaddeus Dodd, assisted by Rev. John McMillan. The meeting was held in Daniel Axtell's barn.

The earliest report of the schools of this township, made in 1854, credits it with seven, and an attendance of 436 pupils, which is a remarkable number for a rural population.   In the report of 1887, while the number of schools remains the same, the number of scholars in attendance is only 237, which would seem to indicate that the families are less numerous now than in that earlier day.   The directors for the current year are, T. M. Ross, President; J. B. Cox, Secretary; Benjamin Shirk, Silas Johnson, G. W. Huffman and George Durbin.

CHAPTER L.

WHITELEY TOWNSHIP.

COMMERCIAL ADVANTAGES—SURFACE—BOUNDARIES—EXPERIENCE OF DR. McMILLAN—MR. EVANS' ACCOUNT OF MRS. BOZARTH—HE- ROIC DEFENSE OF HERSELF—RELIEF.

THE northern part of this township reaches up within a few miles of the county seat, and has highways of easy grade that lead by the valleys of Whiteley Creek to the navigable waters of the Mononga- hela River.   It has, consequently, had access to good markets from its earliest settlement.   This advantage is shown by the stimulus it has given to agricultural pursuits, throughout all its borders.   Few townships in the county can show farms under better tillage, the stock more intelligently bred, and the homes of the inhabitants more tasteful and comfortable.

The surface is rolling and well watered by Whiteley Creek and Dyer's Fork.   It is bounded on the north by Franklin and Jefferson, on the east by Greene, on the south by Perry, and on the west by Wayne and Franklin.   In the southern portion of the township, at the forks of Whiteley Creek, is the village of Newtown, which is supplied with mills and the usual places of business, and a Method- ist Episcopal Church is located here.   Secretary Black's report of 1854 shows this township to have eight schools and 274 pupils; by the report of 1887 it is seen to have nine schools and 255 pupils, which would seem to indicate that the families are more diminutive in size now than a third of a century ago. The board of directors for the current year is constituted as follows: Dr. O. C. Conway, President; M. C. Brant, Secretary; John Meighen, James Hatfield, John Cowell, and Thomas Mooney.

The early settlers of this township endured the privations of frontier life, and the terror inspired by Indian savagery. When Dr. McMillan, the eminent Presbyterian divine, came to this section, there was little comfort in the home life of the people, and he began life among them in as simple a way as the humblest to whom he ministered. He says: " When I came to this country, the cabin in which I was to live was raised, but there was no roof on it, nor any chimney nor floor. The people, however, were very kind, and assisted me in preparing my house, and on the 16th of December I removed into it. But we had neither bedstead nor tables, nor stool, nor chair, nor bucket. All these things we had to leave behind us; as there was no wagon road at that time over the mountains, we could bring nothing but what was carried on pack-horses. We placed two boxes on each other, which served us for a table, and two kegs answered for seats, and having committed ourselves to God in family worship, we spread a bed on the floor, and slept soundly till morning. The next day a neighbor came to my assistance. We made a table and a stool, and in a little time had everything comfortable about us."

One of the most thrilling incidents in early pioneer life was that of Experience Bozarth. Mr. Evans gives the following description of it in his Centennial papers:

" In the spring of 1779 we find her living in a cabin in the lower part of the valley of Dunkard Creek. That it was on Dunkard Creek, and in Greene County there is no historic event more positive. But the exact locality, which did we know, would add much to the interest of the story, is not recorded, nor is there any tradition to my knowledge on the subject at all. All accounts speak of her as a lone woman. She is designated as Mrs. Experience Bozarth only.

" About the middle of March there was an alarm of Indians. Besides hers, there were but two or three cabins in the neighborhood. For some reason, either because her cabin afforded the best wall of defence, or because she was such a fearless creature, the neighbors fearing to stay at home all assembled at her house, and were abiding there presuming that in union there was strength.

" After the lapse of some days, when the fears of an attack had begun to subside and a feeling of comparative security was being restored, and the vigilance against surprise had consequently been relaxed, at a moment when there were but two men in the house, some of the children of the various families ran in from their play in much alarm, crying, 'Ugly red men! Ugly red men?' Upon one of the men stepping to the door he received a ball in the side of the breast, which caused him to fall back on the floor. The Indian who shot him sprang in over his prostrate body, and grappled with the remaining white man. The white man threw him on the bed and called for a knife with which to despatch him, and Experience answered that call by seizing an axe and splitting out the brains of the intruding savage. At the same instant another Indian entered the door and shot dead the man who was engaged with the Indian on the bed Weilding again the fatal axe, Experience Bozarth disemboweled that Indian on the spot, who bawled, 'Murder! murder!' Immediately several others of the party who had been engaged in slaughtering children in the yard came to his relief, and one of them thrusting his head in at the door had it cleft in twain by a murderous stroke of Mrs Bozarth's axe. At the same time another having caught hold of the disemboweled Indian, and drawn him out of the way, Mrs. Bozarth, with the aid of the man who had somewhat recovered from his wound in the breast, shut the door and fastened it against the besieging savages. Repeated attempts were made by the Indians to break into the house, but our heroine and her companion by their bold determination and vigilant, heroic exertions, held fast the door and defended every entrance for several days, till a party came from the neighboring settlements and drove the Indians away.

CHAPTER LI.

MISCELLANEOUS.

EXCISE LAW—HELD UNCONSTITUTIONAL—TRANSPORTATION DIFFICULT —WHISKY EASY—LAW RESISTED—OFFICERS ABUSED—LAW MODIFIED—STILL RESISTED—MACFARLANE KILLED—MILITIA CALLED —GEN. LEE IN COMMAND—WASHINGTON MOVES WITH THE ARMY —REVIEWS IT AT CUMBERLAND—SUBMIT—HONEST WHISKY—NO LICENSE—THREE STILLS LEFT—RELIGIOUS EXCITEMENT—SECTS— SLAVERY—GEOLOGY—OIL—HONORED LIST.

AN outbreak which occurred in 1794, previous to the organization of the county, commonly called the Whisky Rebellion, which was confined to the southwestern section of the State, is entitled to mention, though in its bearing upon the history of these parts it has little significance. At that early day the chief sources of wealth to

the inhabitants were the production of grain. So remote from market were they, however, that transportation cost what the produce
would sell for. To put their grain in a more concentrated form, the
farmers erected stills and converted their grain into whisky, which
could more readily be transported to market and would command
ready sale When the Revolutionary war was over, the new nation,
being burdened with a great debt, laid a tax on whisky of four pence
per gallon The passage of this act was vigorously opposed in Congress, on the ground that the .constitution provides that taxation
shall be uniform, and the act would impose a tax on those producing
whisky, from which those not producing it would be relieved.

Adopting this argument, the inhabitants of the southwestern corner of the State, chiefly the counties of Westmoreland, Alleghany,
Washington and Fayette, resolved that they would not pay the tax.
Revenue inspectors and collectors were warned, threatened and
abused. The pipes of a still-house were cut, the proprietor of which
had paid his tax, so that "Tom the Tinker," or the ironical mender
of stills, became the title by which anonymous notices, threats and
calls were signed. As early as 1791, Robert Johnson, collector, was
tarred and feathered, his hair cut off, and his horse taken. The man
sent to serve process upon the offenders, was whipped, tarred and
feathered, his money and horse taken from him, blindfolded and left
tied in the woods Later in the same year, one Wilson was taken
out of his bed, carried several miles to a blacksmith's shop, his
clothing stripped off and burned, branded in several places with a
hot iron, tarred and feathered, and left, naked and wounded, to his
fate. The law was amended in 1792, and again in 1794; but all to
no purpose, and "Tom the Tinker" men, the name by which opposers
of the law were universally known, were only encouraged by these
modifications to more determined resistance. On the 15th of September President Washington issued his proclamation, commanding
all persons to submit to the operations of the law; but it had not the
desired effect Altercations continued to occur, public meetings were
held, resolutions asserting the determination not to pay the tax were
passed, and finally the malcontents called out their adherents, armed
and equipped as militia Assaults were made upon the dwellings of
United States officers, and some burnings occurred. Officers defended
themselves, and in the melee which resulted a number were wounded
with the small shot used Among others the house of Gen. Neville,
the inspector, was attacked. The malcontents were led by Maj. Macfarlane, an officer of the Revolution. Maj. Kirkpatrick, with ten or
twelve United States soldiers, were within the house. Neville himself had left, and when a call was made on Kirkpatrick to surrender,
he made answer that he would defend the house. The firing commenced and continued for some time. Finally it ceased from the

house, and Macfarlane, supposing a surrender was intended, stepped forward, when he was shot and instantly killed. This act enraged the opposers of the tax, and a general rendezvous of their party was called for Braddock's field, armed and equipped, with four days' rations in haversacks.

To such a pass had the opposition to the law now come that both State and national authorities deemed it necessary to take decisive action. On the 6th of August, 1794, Gov. Mifflin sent Chief Justice McKean and Gen. William Irvine to inquire into the facts, and endeavor to allay excitement. On the following day President Washington, who had now entered upon his second term, issued his proclamation commanding all persons to disperse on or before the 1st of September. At the same time he called out the militia of neighboring States, as follows:

	Infantry.	Cavalry.	Artillery.	Total.
Pennsylvania, - - -	4,500	500	200	5,200
New Jersey, - - -	1,500	500	100	2,100
Maryland, - - -	2,000	200	150	2,350
Virginia - - -	3,000	300		3,300
	11,000	1,500	450	12,950

On the 8th of August President Washington appointed James Ross, Jasper Yates and William Bradford to go to the disturbed section, and endeavor "to quiet or extinguish the insurrection," and the Governor called together the Assembly in extra session. A congress of the insurgents, composed of 260 delegates, was convened at Parkinson's Ferry on the 14th of August. But news of the determined stand taken by Washington had been received, and the action of the delegates was considerably modified. A committee of sixty, one from each township in the disaffected district, was appointed, and from these a standing committee of twelve, who were directed to confer with the national commissioners. Conferences were held, at which Gallatin and Brackenridge urged submission, while Bradford, in fiery terms, opposed. But when the vote was taken, and showed thirty-four to twenty-three in favor of submission, he yielded, declaring that if his associates would not stand by him, he was for submission. It was proposed to take the sense of the people throughout the district by having each individual citizen answer, over his own signature, this question: "Will the people submit to the laws of the United States, upon the terms proposed by the commissioners of the United States?" Until the 11th day of September was given to signify their intention. The result of this test was so unsatisfactory, that President Washington gave the order for the army to march, and with banners spread to the breeze, to the music of fife and drum, the column moved forward. Henry Lee—

"Light Horse Harry"—was given command. President Washington, accompanied by Gen. Knox, Secretary of War, Alexander Hamilton, Secretary of the Treasury, and Richard Peters, of the District Court, set out on the 1st of October for the scene of the disturbance. On Friday the President reached Harrisburg, on Saturday Carlisle. The committee of the insurgents held a meeting on the 2d of October at Parkinson's Ferry, when, learning that a well organized army with Washington at its head was on the march to enforce obedience, they delegated two of their number, William Findley and David Roddick, to meet the President and assure him of their readiness to submit They were received at Carlisle; but Washington said that as the troops had been called out, he should not countermand the order to march. Proceeding forward, the President reached Chambersburg on the 11th, Williamsport on the 13th,, and Fort Cumberland on the 14th, where he reviewed the Maryland and Virginia troops This was old tramping ground for Washington, and must have revived many early recollections He was now near the end of his life, dying five years thereafter. On the 19th the President reached Bedford, where he became satisfied that the temper of the people had changed, and that they were now willing to obey the laws; and after tarrying a few days, determined to return to Philadelphia, where he arrived on the 28th, leaving Gen. Lee to meet the commissioners and make such terms of pacification as should be just. A meeting of the committee of sixty was held at Parkinson's on the 24th, and a sub-committee was ordered to repair to the headquarters of the army, and give assurances of submission. This subcommittee did not arrive till after the departure of Washington; but at Uniontown they met Gen Lee, with whom it was agreed that books should be opened in every part of the disaffected district, by justices of the peace, when every citizen should be required to subscribe to an oath to support the Constitution of the United States, and obey the laws At the same time Gen Neville issued an order for all stills to be entered according to law, which was promptly complied with. Having issued a judicious address to the people of the disaffected district, and being convinced that there was a sincere disposition to obey the laws, Gen. Lee, on the 17th of November, gave orders for the immediate return of the troops to Philadelphia, except a small detachment under Gen. Morgan, which was left at Pittsburgh for the winter defence. Thus ended the campaign. Some arrests were made, and a few convictions were had, but all were eventually pardoned.

By the records of the inspector's office, it is shown that, as early as 1788, there were seventy registered distilleries in the district now covered by Greene County. Besides these there were numerous private distilleries, in which small quantities were made, the result at each amounting to little more than was considered necessary for the use of the family, whiskey being regarded as necessary as any article of diet.   Until within a very few years large quantities of whiskey were produced in this county, and a high reputation was maintained for making an honest article   But as other sources of wealth from the produce of the farm were multiplied, stills were gradually abandoned, until now there are only three in the entire borders, Gilpin South's, at Bald Hill, with a daily capacity of thirty-three bushels; James R. Gray's at, Gray's Landing, of 130 bushels; and U E. Lippincott's, at Lippincott, of ninety bushels.   Some eight or ten years ago, Will McConnell, a noted temperence lecturer, came into the county and commenced his work.   He was received with great favor, and a great revival of the temperance sentiment was the result.   Local option was submitted to a vote of the people and was decided in favor of no license, so that now intoxicating liquors are not sold except at drug-stores, and the store-houses of distillers, in quantities, according to law.   This action of the people makes Greene County the paradise of the total abstinence reformers.

On several occasions in the history of the county, great waves of religious excitement have swept over this section, like a whirlwind seeming to carry all before it   Several preachers would combine their efforts, and hold special services.   Vast congregations would be so swayed, that individuals in all parts would get down upon their knees, in the midst of the preaching, while others would come forward and bow at the altar.   Indeed the cradle of Presbyterianism, and Cumberland Presbyterianism, the Baptist faith, and Methodism, west of the Alleghany mountains, may be said to have been rocked here.   The Suttons, and the Corblys, the McMillans and the McClintocks, the Morgans and the Millers, the Hopkinses and the Sansoms, have lead in a great religious work.   As a consequence of deep religious conviction, as was evinced in the great revivals which occurred at the beginning of the present century, several new sects sprang into existence.

From 1800 to 1807, were years remarkable for the rapid growth of the church in Western Pennsylvania.   But as in the days of the primitive church degeneracy and heresy crept in, so now followed delusion and false doctrine   In the northern part of Greene County, and the adjoining portion of Washington County arose a sect called Halconites.   Their leader, Sergeant, claimed to have had a revilation from heaven, denying that there was any hell, either as a locality or as a state of existence.   He gathered many followers, and his fame reached to neighboring States.   He was invited to speak at Wheeling, Va., and at Cumberland, Md.   While at the latter place, as if to illustrate his creed by his conduct, he committed fogery and was imprisoned.   This ended his career as a preacher.   A woman, Rhoda Fordyce by name, was his successor.   She proclaimed "that if a person would abstain from all animal food, live on parched corn and sassafras buds for a given length of time, his body would become so etherial that he would be translated to Heaven without passing through the gates of death." The experiment was tried by a man named Parker, but instead of being translated, he starved to death. Rhoda would not allow the body to be buried until after the third day, insisting that it would then ascend to heaven, but at the expiration of that time the neighbors interposed and buried it. After this we hear no more of the Rhodianites. But a new sect arose in the same locality called "New Lights," whose ranks were swelled by converts from the Halconites and Rhodianites. They denied the divinity of Christ, believed in immersion as the only mode of baptism, and practiced the rite of "washing one another's feet" . These were in turn absorbed by another sect known as Campbellites, founded by Thomas Campbell and Alexander, his son, who came here from Scotland in 1807 They were originally Presbyterians, but their belief not being in entire accord with that body, they resolved to found a new denomination They discarded all creeds and confessions as human inventions, and insisted on immersion as the only Christian baptism. Two churches were established in 1811, one at Cross Roads, six miles northwest of Washington, and the other on Brush Run. Alexander Campbell, the son, was a man of brilliant talents, and superior genius, and one of the most eloquent and forcible public speakers of his day He came at a time when infidelity and fanaticism were rampant, and they fell before the power of his preaching like grass before the scythe of the mower. In some cases, whole congregations of New Lights adopted the views of Mr Campbell Many of his disciples in turn afterward united with orthodox Baptist Churches.

As has been previously observed, slavery existed in this county in the early days, pioneers from Virginia and Maryland, where slavery was legalized, bringing their slaves and household servants with them, the idea prevailing, as late as 1784, that this was a part of the former State The records of the register's office of the county during the first dozen or more year contain numerous entries of manumissions like the following:

"Manumission —Thomas H. and James Hughes to James Butler:

"Know all men by these presents, Whereas, it has been alleged that Felix Hughes, our late father, was entitled to the service of James Butler, a black man, and whereas the said Felix Hughes did promise and agree that the said James Butler should be free from and after the death of the said Felix Hughes, and whereas the said James Butler has conducted and behaved himself well, and conformed to all his engagements with his said master, yet his said master did without giving the said James Butler any written evidence of his said manumission, now know ye that we, Thomas H. and James Hughes, sons of the said Felix Hughes, do hereby, so far as we are interested, renounce all claim to said James Butler and to his services. Given under our hands and seals, A. D. 1805."

But in the year 1780, Pennsylvania, the first of all the States, passed an act for the registration of all slaves, and their gradual emancipation, which worked its complete extinction from among us.

The geological structure of Greene and Washington counties has been the subject of Prof. Stevenson's report made by State authority. Five folds, or waves cross this territory from northeast to southwest, parallel with the Chestnut Ridge. The Waynesburg anticlinal, the second of these folds is about eight miles wide, and its axis dips to the southwest at the rate of twenty feet per mile. Along the synclinal trough of this fold on the eastern side, known as the Lisbon Synclinal, flows the Monongahela River. From the summit of this fold to the bottom of this synclinal is an average dip of about seventy feet per mile in an east southest direction. The Pin-hook Anticlinal is the third marked fold, parallel to the Waynesburg, leaving the Waynesburg synclinal to the east of it. The Washington Anticlinal lies next, and the Ninevah Synclinal is included between it and the Pin-hook. Five miles west of this is the Clayville Anticlinal, having the Mansfield Synclinal between it and the Washington fold.

The stratified rocks of this whole region have been subdivided by geologists into lower productive, lower barren, upper productive and upper barren. The lower productive contain several valuable seams of coal, but they lie about six hundred feet below the Pittsburg coal seam. The lower barren, reaching from the Mahoning sandstone to the base of the Pittsburg coal seam, contains the Morgantown sandstone, several thin seams of coal, but little limestone. It includes the green crinoidal limestone, 250 feet below Pittsburg coal, is four feet thick and is lightly fossiliferous. At the top of the Morgantown stone is the little Pittsburg coal seam a foot in thickness, of little value. Thirty-feet higher is the Pittsburg limestone, from four to six feet thick, useful as a flux in the manufacture of iron. The Pittsburg coal seam lies next, is from nine to ten feet thick, five of which are merchantable coal, and is excellent for fuel and gas purposes. The Redstone coal seam is some sixty feet above the Pittsburg, is four feet in thickness, and also good for fuel. The great limestone strata is about 120 feet above the Pittsburg coal, is eighty feet in thickness, and is largely used in the manufacture of iron, for mortar and for fertilizing. At twenty feet above the great limestone, is the Uniontown coal seam, which is quarried for fuel. Upon this coal seam rests the Uniontown sandstone, forty feet in thickness, which is largely used for building purposes. One hundred feet above the Uniontown coal seam rest the Waynesburg coal seam, six feet in thickness, largely used for fuel locally, but too soft for transportation It will thus be seen that beneath the surface of this county are inexhaustable supplies of valuable minerals, and should the mines lying near the surface ever become exhausted, here would be found a vast magazine of wealth,

Oil has been found in several parts of the county at a depth of less than 1,000 feet The Tanner well has produced for the last twenty years, at the rate of ten barrels a day, lubricating oil. In 1886 the Mt. Morris district was opened and many paying wells are being found. There are doubtless oil and gas underlying this territory that will gladden the hand of the explorer.

In addition to the names of those who have been mentioned in other parts of this work the following may be named who served as representatives in the National Congress. Albert Gallatin, William Hoge, John L Dawson, Jonathan Knight, William Montgomery, Jesse Lazear, George V. Lawrence, J B Donley, Morgan R Wise, Jacob Teemer, Charles E Boyle.   Of the State Senate are the following: Isaac Weaver, William G. Hawkins, Charles A. Black, John C Fleniken, Andrew Lantz, A. Patton, M. D.; Morgan R Wise. Of the House of Representatives of the State: John Minor, John Fleniken, Maxwell McCaslin, James W Hays, Rees Hill, Adam Hays, W. T Hays, Thomas Burson, W S Harvey, Joseph Sedgwick, Thomas Ross, John Phelan, Fletcher Brock, D. W Gray, M. D.; John Hogan, Thomas Laidley, William Kincaid, Patrick Donley. It is a notable circumstance that Isaac Weaver was speaker of the Senate, at the same time that Rees Hill was speaker of the House, both representing Greene County

❊BIOGRAPHICAL SKETCHES.❊

BIOGRAPHICAL SKETCHES.

ALEPPO TOWNSHIP.

ASBURY ANTILL, farmer and stock-grower, son of John and Isabella (Chenith) Antill, was born in this county March 24, 1836. His mother was born in Ohio. His father, who was a farmer and miller, was born and died in Greene County, Penn. The subject of this sketch was the fourth in a family of nine children, all of whom grew to be men and women. He was reared on the farm and has been an industrious farmer all his life. He is the owner of 243 acres of well-improved land where he resides in Aleppo Township. In 1857 Mr. Antill married Sarah, daughter of Moses and Hannah (Whipkey) King. Mrs. Antill is of Dutch extraction, and a member of the Methodist Episcopal Church. Their children are—William, Harvey, Maggie, wife of Benjamin Chambers, Jr., Louis, John and Asbury K. Mr. Antill is a Democrat in politics.

BENJAMIN CHAMBERS, farmer and stock-grower, was born in Marshall County, West Virginia, October 13, 1840, is the son of J. A. and Susan (Kerr) Chambers, natives of West Virginia, and of German ancestry. His father, who spent all his life as a farmer in his native State, reared a family of seven children, of whom the subject of this sketch is the oldest son. He was reared on the home farm, attended the district school and has made farming and stock-growing his chief pursuit. He came to this county in 1865 and settled on his present farm in Aleppo Township, consisting of 324 acres of well improved land. In 1866 Mr. Chambers was united in marriage with M. J., daughter of A. J. and Lucinda (Ayers) Hinerman. Her parents were of German origin. Mr. and Mrs. Chambers' children are C. T., G A., Ward, Lucinda, John A., Olive Dillie, Leota, Elizabeth and Pearl. Mr. Chambers is a Republican. Mrs. Chambers is a member of the Christian Church.

W. W. CLENDENNING, farmer and stock-grower, was born in Marshall County, West Virginia, October 28, 1838. He is a son of Archibald and Jane (Cooper) Clendenning, who were natives of Ireland. They came to America and settled in Greene County, where

Mr. Clendenning was a farmer for many years and died in 1877. Of a family of four children, the subject of this sketch is the youngest. He was reared on the farm and received a common school education. He has made farming his main occupation, and is the owner of 133 acres of land, all of which he has accumulated through his own efforts. Mr. Clendenning was united in marriage August 26, 1862, with Miss Sarah, daughter of James and Jane (McCaslin) Kincaid, and sister of Colonel Maxwell McCaslin Mr. and Mrs. Clendenning have eight children, viz.: Robert Maxwell, William N, Milton L, Anna F., John, Mary, Nellie Grant and Jessie K. Mr. Clendenning and wife are members of the Church of God.

J. T. ELBIN, Associate Judge of Greene County, and one of the earliest settlers of Aleppo Township, now living, was born in Allegheny County, Maryland, March 18, 1824 He was left an orphan when a small child and was reared by his grandfather, John Elbin, who was a prominent farmer of Greene County, and died intestate in 1845. Judge Elbin was thrown out in the world without a dollar, but was ambitious to be independent and worked as a farm hand by the day and month until he succeeded in accumulating enough to invest in land. He has been engaged in farming and stock-growing in this county since 1848, and has been very successful in all his business ventures. In 1847 he was united in marriage with Hannah, daughter of John and Hannah (Sidwell) McVay, and they are the parents of six children, viz : Lucinda, wife of L. Sammons, Rachel, wife of George Grim; Henry, who is an undertaker; John W, a farmer; Belle, wife of George Ullom, and Mary Ann, deceased. Mrs. Elbin belongs to the Cumberland Presbyterian Church, and the Judge is a member of the Church of God, in which he takes an active interest, and has served as superintendent of the Sabbath-school He is a Democrat, and was elected Associate Judge in 1884. He is a member of the I. O O. F., and has served as Justice of the Peace for a period of twenty years; elected in 1860, and held the office until 1880.

AZARIAH EVANS, farmer and stock-grower, was born in Washington County, Penn., August 29, 1828, and is a son of Caleb and Anna (Smalley) Evans His father was a native of Fayette County, and his mother was born in Washington County. They were of Welsh extraction His father, a farmer by occupation, came to Greene County in 1839, and in 1841 he settled in Aleppo Township, where he died in 1860. He reared a family of fourteen children, twelve of whom grew to be men and women, and eight of the family are still alive and in active life. The subject of this sketch is next to the oldest of those now living and was reared on the home farm, receiving a common school education. Mr. Evans has spent his life as a farmer, having lived in Greene County since he was thirteen years of age. He has been very successful, and owns at present a fine farm of 274 acres. He was united in marriage September 3, 1848, with Miss Mary, daughter of William and Elizabeth (Courtwright) Griffith, who were of Irish origin. Mr. and Mrs. Evans have two children living—Elizabeth A., wife of William B. King, and Samuel L., a farmer and stock-grower, who married Lucinda, daughter of James and Julianna (Chess) Parson. Mr. and Mrs. Evans have met with well deserved success. Both have been very hard workers and noted for their liberality. Mr. Evans' name often appears on the church subscription papers, and he has given liberally to both the church and the Sabbath school. Though not a member of any church, he is ever anxious for the success of any church or moral enterprise. His wife is a member of the Church of God. Mr. Evans is a Republican. In 1862 he enlisted in Company A, Eighteenth Pennsylvania Cavalry, and served until the close of the war, being discharged by general order. Among the engagements in which he took part was the famous battle of Gettysburg. He was at one time an active member of the Patrons of Husbandry.

CHRISTIAN GRIM, farmer and stock-grower, son of Jacob and Keziah (Courtwright) Grim, was born in Greene County, Penn., April 12, 1859. His parents were also natives of this county, and of German origin. His father was a farmer during his lifetime. Christian Grim is the eldest of three children, and was reared on the home farm, receiving his education in the common schools. He is a successful farmer, and has the management of his own and Mrs. Grim's farm, amounting in all to 250 acres. His wife was the widow of the late Madison, son of Peter Ullom, a native of Aleppo Township. Mr. and Mrs. Ullom were the parents of five children, viz.—Eliza, wife of Isaac McCracken; Isaac B., a student of Delaware College, Ohio; Clara, Lantz H. and Thomas H. Mrs. Grim's maiden name was Melissa Hupp. She is a daughter of Isaac Hupp, and of German and English lineage. Mr. and Mrs. Grim were married September 7, 1881. They are members of the Church of God. They have three children—Flora, John C. and Ella. Mr. Grim is a deacon in the church. In politics he is a Democrat.

JOHN HENRY, farmer and stock-grower, was born in Somerset County, Penn., July 25, 1827. He is a son of John and Elizabeth (Imell) Henry, who were, respectively, natives of Pennsylvania and Maryland, and of German origin. His father was a farmer all his life. He also learned the blacksmith's trade, and was well known in Somerset County for many years as a hotel-keeper. Of his ten children the subject of this sketch is the ninth. He was reared on the farm in Turkey Foot Township, where he attended the district school. Mr. Henry has been a successful farmer, and

29

owns 165 acres of well improved land. He was married in Somer-set County, February 11, 1847, to Hannah (Garey) Miller, daughter of Peter Garey and widow of Michael Miller. Mrs. Henry is of Dutch descent. Their children are—Amanda, wife of Samuel Pletcher, Mary, wife of J. Matheny; Rebecca, wife of H. Jacobs; Christiana, wife of W. Showalter; William H., Elizabeth, wife of J. McCracken, Peter, Susannah, wife of N. Miller, and Nancy, wife of J. Elbin. Mr. and Mrs. Henry are members of the German Baptist church. Mr. Henry is a Republican In 1862 he enlisted in the One Hundred and Fortieth Pennsylvania Volunteer Infantry. He was in several engagements, and was wounded at the battle of Spottsylvania On account of this wound he is now receiving a small pension Mr Henry's grandfather was in the Revolutionary war,' and his uncle, Peter Henry, was in the war of 1812 under General Harrison.

ANDERSON HINERMAN, farmer and stock-grower, was born May 10, 1832, in Aleppo Township, this county, on the farm where Christian Grim now resides He is a son of Jesse and Sarah (Shutterly) Hinerman. His mother was born in the State of Dela-ware, and his father in Millsboro, Washington County, Penn Both his grandfathers came from Germany, and his grandmothers were of American origin. Mr. Hinerman, the third in a family of ten children, received his early education in the subscription school. Having been reared as a farmer, he has made this occupation his life work, and has met with success, being the owner of a fine farm of 170 acres well stocked and improved On November 4, 1856, Mr. Hinerman was united in marriage with a daughter of Silas and Jane (Rickey) Ayers, who were of American ancestry. Mr. and Mrs. Hinerman's children are Solomon, Stanton, Tillie M , Clara Dell, Blanche A., Walter F , Rosa Balton and Sarah J. (deceased). Mr. Hinerman is a Republican and a member of the I. O. O. F. He and wife are members of the Church of God, in which Mr. Hinerman is superintendent of the Sabbath-school and has been elder for eighteen years.

J. S HINERMAN, farmer and stock-grower, was born in Alep-po Township, October 21, 1845 His parents were Jesse and Sarah (Shutterly) Hinerman, the former born in Washington County, Penn , and the latter in Wilmington, Del They were of German origin, Mr. Hinerman's father, who was a farmer through life, died April 3, 1877 His family consisted of ten children, of whom the subject of our sketch is the youngest He was reared on the home farm and acquired a common school education. From his youth he has been engaged in agricultural pursuits and has been quite successful. He is the owner of a fine residence and eighty-seven acres of well cultivated land Mr. Hinerman was married in 1866 to Rebecca, daughter of Leonard Straight. Her parents were natives of Pennsylvania, and of Dutch extraction. Mr and Mrs. Hinerman are the parents of the following named children—Ida, Alta, Sarah E, Luther W., Mary J., Curtis, Clida, Charles B. and John. Mr. Hinerman, who is a Republican, was elected justice of the peace in 1880 and re-elected in 1885. He and his wife are members of the Church of God.

LINDSEY HINERMAN, farmer and stock-grower, was born June 16, 1828, on the farm he now owns in Aleppo Township, Greene County, Penn. He is a son of George and Mary (McConnell) Hinerman, who were of German and Irish ancestry. His grandfather, George Hinerman, was a British soldier, but remained in this country. He was, like many other members of the family, a farmer. Mr. Hinerman's father came from Millsborough, Washington County, Penn., to Greene County in 1823, where he spent his life as a farmer and died in 1876. Lindsey is the fifth in a family of eight children He was reared on the farm and attended the subscription schools. He has made farming his main pursuit and owns 467 acres of valuable land, well stocked and improved. Our subject was employed on the Baltimore & Ohio Railroad from 1848 to 1853. In May, 1853, Mr. Hinerman married Miss Elizabeth, daughter of Jacob and Mary (Whipkey) Slonaker. Their children are M. S., Martha J., wife of John Tasker; Sarah, wife of H. Wise; Emeline, wife of Sherman W. S. McCracken; David, Mary, J. W. H. and Ellsworth Mr. Hinerman is a Republican.

WILLIAM HOUSTON, deceased, who was a farmer and stock-grower by occupation, was born in Ireland in 1791. When twelve years of age he came to America and settled in Washington County, Penn., where he learned the shoemaker's trade and followed it as a business until he came to Greene County in 1836, and bought the farm in Aleppo Township which is still in possession of the family. Here he died in 1854. In 1820 Mr. Houston married Esther, daughter of Captain James Dickey, of Washington County, Penn. Their family consisted of seven children, three of whom are living. They are W. D., a carpenter and contractor; Samuel, a carpenter and farmer; and Joseph. The last two mentioned were soldiers of the late war, in Company II, Fifteenth Pennsylvania Volunteer Cavalry. The family are highly respected in the community in which they live.

HIRAM P. MOSS, farmer and stock-grower, son of Jacob and Eleanor (Winnett) Moss, was born in Richhill Township, this county, March 22, 1844. His parents were of English and Irish lineage. His mother was a native of Washington County, Penn. His father, who was a cabinet-maker and carpenter during his lifetime, was born in Fayette County, and died in 1878 in Greene County His family numbered eight children, Hiram Porter being the youngest. In 1868 the subject of our sketch was united in marriage with Miss Emma Jane Courtwright. Their children are Maggie, Clara, Mettie, May, Mary Addie, Arthur and Emmett Earl Mr. Moss learned cabinet-making and the carpenter's trade with his father, but has devoted his time chiefly to farming and the raising of stock, and is the owner of ninety-three acres of valuable land He and his wife are members of the Presbyterian Church.

REV. JACOB M. MURRAY, minister and school teacher, was born in Fayette County, Penn, May 25, 1857. He is a son of James A. and Mary (Miller) Murray, who were natives of Fayette County and of German and Irish lineage. His father, who is a minister in The Brethren Church, also engages in farming to some extent and now resides in Aleppo Township, where he settled in 1860. Of his family of nine children six are still living. The subject of this sketch is the eighth in the family and was reared on his father's farm in Aleppo Township. He acquired his education in common and select schools and in Monongahela College at Jefferson, Penn. He began teaching when only seventeen years of age and is now considered one of the most prominent educators in Greene County. At the age of twenty he united with the Church of The Brethren, and was ordained as a minister of that denomination when he was twenty-six Since 1887 he has had charge of a congregation at Aleppo, Penn. Mr. Murray is a frequent contributor to the religious journals. He is held in high esteem by all who know him He was united in marriage, March 17, 1877, with Miss Julia A, daughter of Henry and Elizabeth (Evans) Riggle, who were of German origin. Mr. and Mrs. Murray have four children, three of whom are living—Harry Y., Oscar C and Vernie. Mr. Murray is a Democrat. His wife is a member of The Brethren Church and is held in the highest esteem by all who know her.

JOSEPH McCRACKEN, P. O. Cameron, Marshall County, West Va, was born in Washington County, Penn, February 13, 1827 He is a son of Daniel and Mary (Crall) McCracken, natives of Pennsylvania, and of Irish and Dutch descent. His father, who died in West Virginia, was a farmer all his life. His family consisted of eight children, of whom the subject of this sketch is the oldest. He was reared on the farm and received his education in the common school He has been a very successful farmer and stock-grower, having at one time owned over six hundred acres of land On February 20, 1853, Mr McCracken married Miss Mary E., daughter of Jennings J. Moss, and they have nine children, viz.: Joseph, a farmer, J. C, a physician; George and J. M. B, farmers; Mary, wife of H. T Winnett; S. W. S. and Samuel E Two of the children are deceased. Mr. McCracken is a Republican He and his wife and children are members of the Methodist Episcopal Church.

S. W. S. McCRACKEN, farmer, son of Joseph and Elizabeth (Moss) McCracken, was born in this county, where he was reared on a farm and attended the district school. He is one of the industrious and successful young farmers of his township. In 1888 Mr. Mc-Cracken was united in marriage with Miss Emma, daughter of Lindsey Hinerman, one of the wealthy and influential citizens of the county. Mr. McCracken is a Republican.

JAMES McVAY, farmer and wool-grower, and breeder of short-horn cattle, is among the most prominent, influential and successful farmers of Greene County. He was born in Morris Township, this county, March 21, 1824, and is a son of John and Hannah (Sidwell) McVay, and are natives of Pennsylvania, and of German and Irish descent. His father was a farmer all his life and died in Greene County. His family consisted of ten children, eight of whom grew to maturity. The subject of this sketch is the second and was reared on the farm, attending the subscription schools. Mr. McVay started in the world with little else than a determination to succeed. He commenced to buy stock when he was still a young man, buying for other parties a short time, but soon engaging in the business for himself. He has succeeded in accumulating a handsome fortune. In 1865 Mr. McVay bought 244,000 pounds of wool His land in Greene County amounts to 540 acres, in a high state of cultivation. In 1840 Mr. McVay married Susan, daughter of Henry and Mary (Williams) Neel, and they are the parents of the following children: Mary M., wife of H. H. Parry; Warren, R. M., William I and Hannah M., wife of H C. Snyder; D. L is deceased Mr. McVay is a Democrat. His wife is a member of the Cumberland Presbyterian Church.

GEORGE McVAY, farmer and stock-grower, was born in Aleppo Township, Greene County, Penn, August 11, 1832. He is a son of John and Hannah (Sidwell) McVay, natives of Washington and Greene counties, respectively. Mr. McVay is a member of a family of twelve children. He is the sixth, and was reared in his native township, where he attended the common schools. He has made farming and stock-dealing his business through life and has been greatly prospered, being at present the owner of 300 acres of valuable land in this county. In 1852 Mr McVay was united in marriage with Miss Maria Smith, now deceased. They were the parents of four children, viz.: Elizabeth, Anthony, Sarah and Hannah. Mr. McVay's present wife was Miss Elizabeth Long. They have two children—Samuel Patrick and Clara. Mr. McVay is a Democrat. He has served five years as constable and one term as director of the poor in Greene County.

LEWIS PARRY, farmer and stock-grower, was born in South Wales, Great Britain, February 11, 1838, and is a son of Roger L. and Elizabeth (Pugh) Parry, natives of Wales. They came to America in 1842, first settling in Pittsburgh. They subsequently moved to Washington County, Penn., and settled in Aleppo Township, Greene County, in 1858. Mr. Parry's father was a farmer and blacksmith. Six members of his family grew to maturity, Lewis being the oldest. He was reared in Washington County, where he also received his education. Mr. Parry began life as a poor boy, working by the day or month, but by industry and economy he has made himself a nice and comfortable home. He now owns 116 acres of good land in Greene County. In November, 1859, Mr. Parry married Mary C., daughter of John and Sarah (Hunt) Wood. Her parents, who were of Dutch and Irish descent, were natives of Greene County. Mr. and Mrs. Parry's children are—Sarah, wife of Morgan B. Lewis; John R., William W., Lou, Emma and Mertie. Mr. Parry is a Cumberland Presbyterian, and his wife is a member of the Disciple Church. In 1862 he enlisted in Company A, Eighteenth Pennsylvania Cavalry, and was a non-commissioned officer. He was taken prisoner in Adams County, Penn., June 30, 1863. He subsequently joined the regiment in Virginia, serving in all two years and ten months, and was honorably discharged July 12, 1865. Mr. Parry is a Republican, and a prominent member of the I. O. O. F.

WILLIAM M. PARRY, physician and surgeon, was born in Westmoreland County, Penn., May 12, 1843, and is a son of Roger L. and Elizabeth (Pugh) Parry, natives of Wales. His father was a blacksmith by trade, but engaged in farming after coming to America. The subject of this sketch is the third in a family of six children. He was reared on a farm, received a common-school education, and subsequently took a course in the Academy at West Liberty, Ohio County, W. Va., where he remained for several years and studied medicine with Dr. Cooper of that place. Dr. Parry began the practice of his profession at Jacksonville, Penn., remaining there for a period of two years. In 1870 he located in Aleppo, where he has since been in active practice. Dr. Parry has been very successful. He owns 200 acres of valuable land where he resides, and has a lucrative practice. He was united in marriage, September 13, 1871, with Mary A., daughter of Rev. Lewis Sammons. Mrs. Parry is of Welsh and German extraction. Their children are Edith, Jessie, Jane, Roger and Burdette. Dr. Parry is a Presbyterian, and his wife is a member of the Baptist Church. She is also an ardent prohibitionist and a strong advocate of woman's suffrage. He is a Republican, and takes great interest in educational matters, having for eight years served as school director. He is a member of the Greene County Medical Society. August 12, 1862, Dr. Parry enlisted in Co. D, Twelfth

West Virginia Volunteer Infantry, and served till the close of the war. He is a member of the I. O. O. F., and is Past Master of the Masonic fraternity.

B. F. PHILLIPS, farmer and stock-grower, was born in Washington County, Penn , July 10, 1833, and is a son of Levi and Sarah (McCracken) Phillips, natives of Pennsylvania, and of Irish origin. His father was a farmer all his life. The subject of our sketch, the youngest of eight children, was reared on the farm, where he received a common-school education. Mr. Phillips has made farming and stock-growing his employment through life, and owns 340 acres of land, which he has procured entirely by his own exertions. He was united in marriage, in 1871, with Miss Sarah, daughter of Matthias and Sarah (McClain) Roseberry, natives of Greene County. Mr. and Mrs. Phillips are the parents of four children—Joseph M., Arthur Lee, Maggie R and Levi N. Mr. Phillips is a Republican in politics.

REV. LEWIS SAMMONS, deceased, a minister of the Baptist Church, was born January 22, 1815, and was a son of John and Mary (Jones) Sammons. His parents were of Welsh and Irish descent. His father was a ship captain, and in early life ran on the Ohio and Mississippi rivers. After leaving the river he followed the carpenter trade and auctioneering. Rev. Mr. Sammons was an only child. He was born in Monongahela Township, this county, but was reared in Fayette County, Penn. He received his education in the common schools, and early in life learned the cooper's trade, at which he worked until 1836. It was in that year he accepted his first charge as a minister, and he engaged in ministerial work during the remainder of his life. He was united in marriage, November 18, 1841, with Miss Elizabeth, daughter of Jacob and Susannah (Gans) Rumble, who were of German ancestry. To Mr and Mrs Sammons were born six children, viz: Lebbeus, who is a farmer; Mary, wife of Dr. Parry; Rossell, a prominent farmer, James J., a surveyor and teacher, who has taught for many terms in Ohio, West Virginia, Pennsylvania and Nebraska; J. L , a physician of West Virginia, and Sarah E , a teacher of music. Mrs. Sammons is still living, and is a member of the Baptist Church. Rev. Sammons was the minister in charge at Enon Baptist Church in 1851, and was ordained in 1853 He came to Greene County in 1857, settling in Aleppo Township nine years later. He was ever an active temperance worker and Republican. He was successful in all his business pursuits, owning at the time of his death a well-improved farm where his family reside in Aleppo Township. The family are Republicans, and highly educated, four of them having taught ten terms of school.

ROSSELL SAMMONS, farmer and stock-grower, was born in Fayette County, Penn., July 12, 1852 His father was Rev. Lewis

Sammons, a well-known Baptist minister and active temperance advocate, who died in this county in 1879. He has written many articles against intemperance, and always preached against the great evil. Of his family of six children, Rossell is the third He lived in Center Township until he was thirteen years old, when he came to Aleppo Township His means for an education were limited to the common schools. In 1872, in company with his brother, Mr Sammons established a saw-mill in Greene County, where they were very successful. Mr Sammons bought a small farm and has since added to it other purchases until at present he owns 360 acres of fine land, well stocked and improved In 1881 he was united in marriage with, Miss Sarah, daughter of Joseph and Eliza (Lemmons) Evans Mr and Mrs. Sammons' children are Lewis E., Joseph Wiley, Olive G. and Osceola. Mr. Sammons is a Republican in politics.

LUTHER A. SMITH, farmer and stock-grower, was born in Richhill Township, Greene County, November 21, 1852 His parents were Andrew and Ellen (Little) Smith. His father was born in Scotland, and came to America when a young man He settled in Greene County, where he died in 1880. His mother was a native of Washington County. Of a family of six children, Luther Smith is the fifth who grew to maturity. He was brought up on his father's farm and received a common-school education. He has been a successful farmer, and owns 103 acres of excellent land where he resides in Aleppo Township. Mr. Smith has been twice married, his first wife being Mary, daughter of John and Ellen (Cox) Edgar, whom he married in 1871 They were the parents of three children—Alonzo D., William B and Harry. Mrs Smith died in this county. Mr Smith's present wife is Hannah, daughter of Lewis and Jane Pettit. They were married in 1885, and have one child—John C. Mr. Smith is a member of the I. O. O. F.

WILLIAM TEDROW, farmer and stock-grower, was born in Somerset County, Penn., June 17, 1823, and is a son of Henry and Elizabeth (Johnson) Tedrow, who were of German and English origin. His father, who was a farmer, died in Aleppo Township in 1876. Of his family of nine children, the subject of this sketch is the second He was reared on the home farm and received a limited education in the old log school-house of the district He has made a success of his farming and stock-growing, and now owns 326 acres of well improved land. Mr Tedrow was married in Somerset County, November 17, 1844, to Sarah A , daughter of Leonard and Elizabeth (Whipkey) Straight, who were of German and English extraction Mrs. Tedrow died January 29, 1888 Their children are Josiah, William H., Mariah, Mary E , wife of E. B. Moos; Catharine A., wife of James Whipkey; Minerva J., wife of M. Bayles.

Mr. Tedrow is a Democrat. He belongs to the Church of God, of which his deceased wife was also a member.

DAVID ULLOM, farmer and stock-grower and dealer in wool, was born in Aleppo Township, this county, December 11, 1845, and is a son of Peter and Matilda (Kinney) Ullom, natives of Pennsylvania. His father has spent a long life as a farmer, being now eighty years of age Mr David Ullom is the youngest in a family of six children and was reared on the farm with his parents, receiving a common school education. He has spent his life as a farmer and has given a good deal of attention to the raising of fine stock. He has engaged in wool buying extensively and has been very successful. Mr. Ullom owns a fine farm of 200 acres, and is one of Aleppo's most prominent citizens. On October 14, 1869, he married Marry Ellen, daughter of Jacob and Catharine (Huffman) King. Her parents were of English and German origin. Mr King is a farmer by occupation. Mr. and Mrs. Ullom have one child—Frankie D. The family are members of the Church of God. Mr. Ullom is a trustee in the church and secretary and treasurer of the Sabbath-school In politics he is a Democrat.

J. M. WHITE, farmer and stock-grower, who was born in Somerset County, Penn., July 14, 1826, is a son of Edward and Nancy (Rush) White. His parents were natives of Somerset County, and of English lineage. His father, who came to Aleppo Township in 1828, was a farmer. He died December 13, 1853. His mother lived until 1872. The subject of this sketch is the second in a family of six children, and was reared on the farm, receiving his education in the common schools. He chose farming as his occupation, has made his own way in the world, and is the owner of a well improved farm where he resides in Aleppo Township. Mr. White was united in marriage, February 13, 1848, with Rebecca, daughter of Henry and Elizabeth (Simons) Hemett, and they are parents of three children, viz—Perry J., Stephen and Sarah Esther (deceased). Mrs. White is a member of the Friends' Church. Mr. White is a Democrat, has been for seventeen years justice of the peace, and has served as school director in his township. He is a prominent member of the I. O. O. F.

JOSHUA WOOD, farmer and stock-grower, was born in Tyler County, W. Va., October 8, 1842. He is a son of John and Sarah (Hunt) Wood, who were, respectively, of Scotch and German and English origin. His father was born in Greene County, where he spent all his life as a farmer and died in 1868. His family numbered ten children, of whom Joshua Wood is the ninth. He was reared in Richhill Township, and attended the common schools. Early in life he learned the carpenter's trade, at which he worked till 1878, when he began farming. He is the owner of a well stocked and improved farm of 180 acres. In 1861 Mr Wood enlisted in Company H, Twentieth Volunteer Infantry, where he served three months, then re-enlisted in Company B, Seventh West Virginia Volunteer Infantry and served till 1862, when he was discharged for disability, having had two of his fingers shot off. He subsequently spent some time in Great Salt Lake City. In 1874 Mr. Wood married a widow lady of Parkersburg, W. Va. Her first husband was John Milton Parker, a railroad engineer on the Baltimore & Ohio Roilroad, who was killed in 1871 by the explosion of his engine Mr. and Mrs Parker were the parents of two children Mertie and Kate Parker. Mrs Wood's maiden name was Emma A Barrett, a daughter of Caleb and Jemima (Goucher) Barrett, who were of German origin. Mr. and Mrs Wood have three children— Earl, Herald and Iona Mr. Wood is a Democrat. He and wife are members of the Christian Church.

GEORGE WOODRUFF, farmer and stock-grower, who was born in Jefferson Township, September 18, 1832, is a son of Benjamin and Sarah (Tuttle) Woodruff, who were of Dutch and Irish descent Mr Benjamin Woodruff was a farmer and stock dealer through life. The subject of this sketch is an only child. He was reared as a farmer and has made a success of his business In 1880 he settled in Aleppo Township where he still resides. Mr. Woodruff learned the blacksmith's trade, but has devoted all his time to agricultural pursuits, and owns a good farm of 200 acres. He was married in 1851, to Elizabeth, daughter of James and Rhoda (Lewis) Nuss. Their children are Susan, wife of W. Balden, Alice, wife of F Drake; Benjamin, George, Andrew, David, William, James and Elizabeth The deceased is John Y. Mr. and Mrs. Woodruff are industrious and economical, and have acquired their present possessions entirely by their own efforts.

CENTER TOWNSHIP.

S. H. ADAMSON, retired farmer, Rogersville, Penn.—The subject of this sketch is one of the pioneers of Greene County, Penn. He was born in Morgan Township, May 2, 1822, and is a son of Charles and Sarah (Hatfield) Adamson, natives of Pennsylvania. They were the parents of nine children, of whom only four are living. Charles and Sarah Adamson departed this life in Greene County S H. Adamson was twice married, first, September 17, 1843, with Lucy Knight, who was born in this county March 7,

1825. Mrs. Adamson was a daughter of James and Cassandra Knight, who were natives of Greene County, where they remained through life By this marriage Mr. Adamson is the father of six children, of whom only two are living—James K. and Charles. Mrs. Adamson departed this life November 17, 1868 Mr. Adamson was united in marriage the second time, with Mary (Hipert) Crouse, February 7, 1869. She is a daughter of Peter Hipert, and was born in Richland County, Ohio, June 26, 1837. Mr. Adamson was reared on a farm and has been engaged in farming almost all his life. He was in the mercantile business at Rogersville for a period of two years, and in 1849 was elected auditor of the county and served three years In 1859 he was elected county treasurer and served in that position two years. He was elected county commissioner in 1881 and filled that office three years. Mr. Adamson owns about 450 acres of land. He is one of the enthusiastic Democrats of the county.

GEORGE A. BAYARD, merchant, Rogersville, Penn., was born in this county, April 11, 1832 He is a son of Samuel P. and Hannah Bayard (nee Mitchell) who were natives of Greene County, where they resided until Mr. Bayard's death, which occurred July 17, 1885. His widow survives him. George was united in marriage, October 6, 1859, with Martha Morris, who was born in this county, August 19, 1837. She is a daughter of Ephraim and Martha Morris, deceased. At a very early age Mr Bayard learned the trade of a tanner, which he followed until he was twenty-five years old He then engaged in farming until 1878, when he began merchandising in Rogersville, where he owns a general store. He received the appointment of postmaster at Rogersville in 1880, and has been filling that position ever since.

HENRY BOWLER, retired farmer, Rogersville, Penn.—The gentleman whose name heads this sketch is well known in Center Township, having lived on his present farm since the date of his birth, May 27, 1818. His parents were John and Mary Bowler, the former a native of Maryland and the latter of Greene County, Penn., where they resided until their death. Mrs. Bowler died in 1819, and her husband in 1845. On June 5, 1849, Henry Bowler married Penelope Stewart, who was born in this county in 1815. Her parents were William and Naoma Stewart, natives of Pennsylvania, who departed this life in Monroe County, Ohio. To Mr. and Mrs. Bowler were born two children—Elizabeth S., wife of Stephen Knight; and William, who married Ruth Seckman. Mrs. Bowler departed this life December 31, 1880. Mr. Bowler was reared on a farm and engaged very successfully in farming during the more active part of his life. He is the owner of about 237 acres of land in Center Township. In politics he is a Republican.

THOMAS T. BURROUGHS, farmer, P. O. Rutan, was born in Washington County, Penn., September 20, 1827. His parents were Samuel and Tempeiance (Reeves) Burroughs, also natives of Washington County They lived in Greene County for a short time after their marriage, then moved to Washington County, Iowa, and remained until their death. Thomas was united in marriage January 1, 1852, with Eliza J Scott She was born March 3, 1829, on the farm where she lives in Center Township Mrs. Burroughs is a daughter of John and Susannah Scott (nee Nicehongei), who were natives of Greene County, where they were married and remained through life. Mr. and Mrs Burroughs have a family of nine children—Hamilton S, Arabella, wife ot P F Headley; Charlotte A., wife of Leroy Marsh; Elmira, wife of T. N. Millikin; John M., James H., William E., Bertha V. and Thomas B Mr. Burroughs has spent his whole life as a farmer, and owns 165 acres of land, constituting his home farm

H. S BURROUGHS, physician, Rutan, Penn., was born in Center Township, this county, December 28, 1852 His parents, Thomas T. and Eliza J. Burroughs (nee Scott), are natives of Greene County and residents in Center Township. The Doctor was united in marriage June 28, 1882, with Maggie A. Hopkins, born October 1, 1859 Her parents are Samuel and Martha Hopkins (nee Millikin), who are natives of this county and reside in Morris Township. Dr. Burroughs began reading medicine May 1, 1875, with Dr. John T. Iams, of Waynesburg, Penn He graduated from the Jefferson Medical College of Philadelphia, Penn, March 12, 1879, and in the following April commenced the practice of his profession at Rutan, Penn., where he still resides with his family. The Doctor is well qualified for the duties of his profession and has a good practice. He is a Baptist, and his wife is a member of the Methodist Church.

JAMES CALL, retired farmer, P. O. Rogersville, was born in Center Township, Greene County, Penn, September 17, 1825 His father and mother, James and Sarah (Hoge) Call, were natives of Greene County, where they were married and spent the remainder of their lives. They departed this life at the home of their son James Mrs. Call March 7, 1862, and her husband June 13, 1868. In October 22, 1849, James Call married Martha Vanwey, who was born in Perry County, Ohio, December 31, 1833 Her parents, John and Anna (Mains) Vanwey, were natives of New Jersey, and after marriage resided in Perry County, Ohio, until their death To Mr. and Mrs. Call have been born seven children, of whom six are living Harvey L, Robert H., Zadok G., Mary E., wife of Asa W. Morris; Ida M, wife of Thomas R. Knight and Martha A William is deceased. Mr. Call was reared on a farm, and has engaged in farming as a business through life. He owns about 140 acres of land, where he and family reside. He engaged in merchandising in Oak Forest about nine years. In 1860 he was elected justice of the peace of Center Township, and served ten years. He and family are representative citizens of Center Township, Greene County, Penn.

THOMAS J. CARPENTER, farmer, P. O. Rutan, was born in Gilmore Township, this county, January 1, 1858. He is a son of Joseph and Elizabeth Carpenter (*nee* Stewart). His father was born in New York and his mother in Greene County, Penn., where they were married and have since made their home. Thomas J. Carpenter was twice married; first, January 11, 1879, to Belle Grove, who was born in Center Township, June 14, 1860, and is a daughter of William and Rebecca (Shaw) Grove. By this marriage Mr. Carpenter is the father of one child—W. E. Carpenter. Mrs. Carpenter departed this life October 7, 1883. Mr. Carpenter's second wife was Jessie L. Supler, whom he married September 23, 1885. She was born September 16, 1865, and is a daughter of Martin and Lizzie R. (Goodwin) Supler, who reside in Richhill Township. Mr. and Mrs. Carpenter have one child—Floyd M. Mr. Carpenter was engaged in merchandising until twenty-two years of age, at which time he began farming, in which he has engaged as a business ever since. He owns 112 acres of land, where he lives with his family. He and wife are members of the Methodist Episcopal Church. His deceased wife was a member of the Christian Church.

R. B. CHURCH, farmer, Holbrook, Penn., was born in Center Township, Greene County, Penn., June 17, 1842. His parents are Elijah and Anna Church (*nee* Moore), who are natives of Greene County, where they now reside. The subject of this sketch was united in marriage July 13, 1867, with Sarah Thomas, who was born in Center Township April 18, 1851. She is a daughter of John and Mary Thomas (*nee* Wood), the former deceased. Mr. and Mrs. Church are the parents of four children, two of whom are living—George W. and Hamilton. The deceased are Fannie and Asa C. Mr. Church has followed the occupation of farming through life, and owns 166 acres of land where he and family live. During the late Rebellion he entered the service of his country in Company F, Eighty-fifth Volunteers, serving four years and four months. He was in a number of serious engagements, in one of which, in 1863, he was severely wounded. Mr. and Mrs. Church are consistent members of the Christian church, and are among the leading families of Center Township.

G. M. CHURCH, cabinet-maker, Rogersville, Penn., was born in Greene County, Penn., February 13, 1845, and is a son of Elijah and Anna Church, who were natives of this county, where they now reside. Mr. Church was united in the holy bonds of matrimony July 31, 1870, with Nancy L., daughter of William and Sarah

Sharpnack. Mrs. Church was born at Rice's Landing, Penn , October 11, 1845 She and her husband have a family of three children, two of whom are living, viz , William E and Anna S. Mr Church is a cabinet-maker by trade, which he followed the most of his life He owns a nice furniture store and good property in Rogersville, where he and family reside When the war broke out he enlisted in the service of his county in Company F, Eighty-fifth Pennsylvania Volunteers, and served two years, during which time he passed through a number of serious engagements. In politics Mr. Church is a Republican. He and family are among the leading citizens in the village where they reside

CEPHAS CLUTTER, a retired farmer of Hunter's Cave, Penn., was born in Washington County, Penn , January 6, 1804, and is a son of William and Sarah Clutter (*nee* Rutan). His parents, who were natives of New Jersey, were married in Washington County, Penn , and remained there until their death. The subject of our sketch was united in the holy bonds of matrimony August 25, 1827, with Laura Day, who was born in Greene County July 25, 1809. Mrs. Clutter is a daughter of William and Mary Day (*nee* Sutton), who were also natives of New Jersey, and after marriage settled in Greene County, Penn , where they remained until their death To Mr and Mrs. Clutter were born seven children, five now living, viz —William, Zebulon, John M , Mary J., wife of Lewis Baltzell; and Spencer B. The deceased are Franklin and Robinson Mr. Clutter has always lived on a farm, and has been engaged in farming . and stock-raising all his life. He owned at one time over 640 acres of land in this county. About 400 acres of this he has given to his children, and owns 240 acres where he resides. Mrs. Clutter, who was a devoted member of the Methodist Episcopal Church, died July 19, 1885 She and her husband made their home in Center Township for nearly half a century

J. M. CLUTTER, farmer, Harvey's, Penn., was born in Greene County, Penn., February 29, 1832. His father and mother are Cephas and Laura (Day) Clutter, natives of Washington and Greene Counties, respectively. They were united in marriage August 25, 1827, and settled in Greene County, where they have since resided. Mrs. Clutter departed this life July 19, 1885. Her husband is still living, having reached the advanced age of eighty-four years. The subject of our sketch was united in marriage January 1, 1856, with Elizabeth Ullom, who was born in this county November 14, 1834. Mrs. Clutter is a daughter of Daniel T. and Anna (Johnson) Ullom, who were residents of this county until Mr. Ullom's death His widow is still living at the old homestead. Mr. Clutter was reared on a farm, and has been a successful farmer through life. He owns 146 acres of good land, where he and family reside. He is considered one of the most substantial farmers and among the leading citizens of Center Township.

W. H. COOK, retired farmer, Harvey's, Penn., was born in Norwich, Connecticut, May 7, 1817. He is a son of William and Margaret (Harvey) Cook, the former a native of Scotland and the latter of England. They were married in New York City, where they remained sometime, then moved to Connecticut, and in 1818 moved to Greene County, Penn. Soon after their arrival in the county, Mr. Cook took a trip on a keal boat down the Ohio River, and was never heard of after he left Wheeling, W. Va. His widow remained in Greene County until her death, which occurred in 1875. W. H. Cook was their only child, and was united in marriage, November 2, 1847, with Elizabeth Rinehart, who was born in Waynesburg in 1825. Mrs. Cook is a daughter of Jesse and Lucy (Workman) Rinehart, natives of Greene County, where they remained until their death. Mr. and Mrs. Cook are the parents of seven children, viz.: Jesse R., Margaret, wife of Jacob Braddock; Maria H., wife of Abner Phillips; Samuel H., Lora, Francis L., wife of Hiram Smith; and Thomas H. Mr. Cook is a house-joiner by trade, which he has followed almost all his life. In later years he engaged extensively in farming, and owns 350 acres of land in this county. Mr. Cook has served as school director, and belongs to the Methodist Episcopal Church, of which his wife, who died May 16, 1885, was also a faithful member.

LAYTON CROUSE, farmer, Rogersville, Penn —The gentleman whose name heads this sketch is one of the prosperous farmers of Center Township, where he was born August 23, 1827. He is a son of Samuel and Rebecca Crouse, also natives of this county and residents therein until their death. They were the parents of nine children, five living. Layton was united in marriage, January 5, 1861, with Catharine M Thomas. Mrs. Crouse was born in Greene County, June 28, 1839, and is a daughter of Eli and Sarah Thomas (nee Knight), also natives of this county. Mr. and Mrs. Crouse are the parents of ten children, five of whom are living, viz.: Mary B., Janette, Elizabeth, Campbell and Sherman. The deceased are Lucy, Sarah J., Franklin, Eli and Walter S. Mr. Couse was raised on a farm and has been engaged in farming all his life He owns 140 acres of land where he and his family live. In politics he is a Republican.

S. B. EAGON, farmer, Rogersville, Penn., was born in Center Township November 25, 1831. His father and mother, Uriah and Cassandra (Adamson) Eagon, were natives of Pennsylvania. The former was born August 21, 1802, and the latter March 21, 1804. They were married October 10, 1822, and were the parents of nine children, of whom six are living. The subject of our sketch was united in marriage, September 8, 1853, with Sarah A. Thomas, who was born in Center Township January 23, 1832. Her parents were Eli and Sarah Thomas, natives of Pennsylvania, who departed this life in Center Township. To Mr. and Mrs. Eagon have been born three children, of whom two are living—Jesse R. and Sarah J.,— Uriah is deceased. Mr. Eagon has been engaged in farming the greater part of his life, and owns about 156 acres of land where he and his family reside. During the rebellion he entered the service of his country, enlisting in Company A., Eighteenth Pennsylvania Cavalry, and served two years and ten months. In politics he is a Republican and is a member of the G. A. R.

A. G. FORDYCE, retired farmer, White Cottage, Penn.—The subject of this sketch is one of the pioneer citizens of Greene County. He was born December 4, 1807. His father and mother were Jacob and Elizabeth Fordyce, the former a native of New Jersey and the latter of Fayette County, Pennsylvania. They settled in Greene County and remained until their death. A. G. Fordyce was united in marriage the first time, March 11, 1827, with Nancy Leonard, who was born in this county March 2, 1809. Her parents were William and Elizabeth Leonard, both now deceased. By this marriage Mr. Fordyce is the father of twelve children, of whom eight are living, viz.: Jacob, Elizabeth, wife of LaFayette Eagon; Maria, wife of Jesse Wood; Sarah, wife of Edward Wood; William, Silas, Barnet, and Clarinda, wife of A. R. White. Mrs. Fordyce departed this life October 22, 1855. On October 30, 1856, Mr. Fordyce was again united in marriage with Elizabeth Simmons, who was born in Washington County, Penn., May 28, 1823. Mr. Fordyce's parents were Spencer and Mary Simmons, who settled in Greene County and remained until their death. By the second marriage Mr. and Mrs. Fordyce have three children, only one of whom is living—Albert G. Mr Fordyce was reared on a farm, has been engaged in farming all his life, and owns a farm of 280 acres. In politics he is a Republican. Mr. and Mrs. Fordyce are faithful members of the Christian Church, of which his deceased wife was also a devoted member. Mr. Fordyce has fifty-three grand-children, twenty-eight great-grandchildren and some of them are married.

SILAS FORDYCE, a farmer of Holbrook, Penn., was born June 20, 1842, on the old Fordyce homestead in Center Township, Greene County, Penn. His parents were Archibald G. and Nancy Fordyce (nee Leonard), who were born in this county—Mr. Fordyce Dec. 4, 1807, and his wife March 2, 1809. They were married March 11, 1827 and remained in the county until Mrs. Fordyce's death, which occurred October 22, 1855. After her death Mr. Fordyce was united in marriage with Elizabeth Simmons, a native of Washington County, Penn. On January 23, 1862, Silas Fordyce married Mary J. Orndurf, who was born in Whiteley Township, October 1, 1842. She is a daughter of Jesse and Isabella Orndurf, the latter deceased. Mr. Fordyce and wife are the parents of ten children, of whom nine are living—Nancy B., William L., Jesse, Louella E., Susan, Archibald, Nevada, Garfield, Frank,—and Lillie (deceased). The subject of this sketch was raised on a farm, and has been engaged in farming and stock-raising almost all his life. He owns 300 acres of land where he resides with his family. In politics Mr. Fordyce is a Republican. When the war broke out he enlisted in the Eighteenth Pennsylvania Cavalry and served his country one year and eight months, during which time he was in a number of serious engagements. He and his wife are consistent members of the Christian Church.

JESSE FORDYCE, deceased, was a resident of Center Township, Greene County, Penn., where he was born May 28, 1831. He was a son of Jacob and Martha Fordyce, natives of Greene County, now deceased. Jesse was united in marriage, November 10, 1859, with Rachel Orndoff. Mrs. Fordyce was born in Center Township, this county, September 19, 1829, and is a daughter of William and Salome Orndoff (nee Wisecarver). Mr. and Mrs. Fordyce are the parents of one child—Ardella, born April 5, 1861. Mr. Fordyce was reared on a farm and engaged in farming through life. At the time of his death he was the owner of ninety-six acres of land, where his widow and daughter now reside. He belonged to the Methodist Protestant Church, of which Mrs. Fordyce is also a devoted member. In politics Mr. Fordyce was a Republican. He departed this life April 14, 1885, and by his death the township lost a good citizen, and his family a kind father and husband.

S. R. FORDYCE, farmer, Rogersville, Penn., was born in Center Township August 7, 1841. He is a son of Jacob and Martha Fordyce, who were natives of Greene County and now deceased. On June 22, 1867, S. R. Fordyce married Elizabeth Ornduff, who was born in Greene County March 13, 1850. She is a daughter of Jesse and Susan Orndurf (nee Wear). Mr. Orndurf was born in Franklin Township May 20, 1816, and Mrs. Orndurf in West Virginia November 21, 1826, and they reside in Center Township. Mr. and Mrs. Fordyce are the parents of two children—Archibald and Edison. Mr. Fordyce was born and reared on his present farm, and has been engaged in farming the most of his life. He owns about 111 acres of land where he and family reside. In politics he is a Republican. During the late rebellion he enlisted in the service of his country in Company I, Eighth P. R. V. C., and was in the service almost three years, passing through many serious engagements. Mr. and Mrs. Fordyce are faithful members of the M. P. Church.

D. W. FRY, Waynesburg, Penn., was born in Wayne Township, Greene County, Penn., February 26, 1838, and is a son of George and Elizabeth Fry. His parents were born in Greene County—his

30

father in 1813, and his mother in 1818. She died November 16, 1883. They were the parents of seven children, five of whom are living. The subject of this sketch was united in marriage, March 10, 1859, with Sarah, daughter of John Simington. She departed this life April 18, 1860., Mr. Fry was a second time married, July 14, 1861, with Mary M. Eagon, a native of Greene County, where she was born May 13, 1843. Her parents, Uriah and Cassandra Eagon, are both deceased. Mr. and Mrs. Fry are the parents of three children—Elizabeth S., wife of Joseph Huffman; George W. and Louie. Mr. Fry was reared on a farm and has devoted all his time to farming. He owns 230 acres of land, on which are substantial buildings. He also engaged in the mercantile business at Rogersville for a period of eighteen months. In politics Mr. Fry is a Republican, and he and his wife are prominent members of the Christian Church.

W. C. FRY, farmer, Waynesburg, Greene County, Penn.—The subject of this sketch was born in June, 1847, on the farm where he resides in Center Township, Greene County, Penn. He is a son of William and Susannah (Strosnider) Fry, pioneers of the county. William Fry, Sr., was born June 9, 1808, and his wife in 1812. They were united in marriage in 1832 and have resided in this county all their lives. They are the parents of eleven children, nine of whom are living. W. C. is the sixth. He was united in marriage in April, 1878, with Lizzie R., daughter of Abnor M. Bailey. She was a native of Greene County, born in 1857. To Mr. and Mrs. Fry were born two children—Alonzo B. and Lida B. Mrs. Fry, who was a kind and affectionate wife and mother, departed this life August 1, 1884. Mr. Fry was reared on a farm, and owns 120 acres of land in Center Township. In politics he is a Democrat, and belongs to the Christian Church.

JOHN S. FUNK, farmer, Rutan, Penn., was born in Jefferson Township, this county, November 7, 1827. His parents, Henry and Levina (Smith) Funk, who were natives of Pennsylvania, were united in marriage in Greene County, where they resided until their death. The subject of this sketch was united in the holy bonds of matrimony, June 4, 1854, with Margaret Craft, who was born in Fayette County November 6, 1832. Mrs. Funk is a daughter of Benjamin and Mary Craft, who were natives of Fayette County, and after marriage moved to Greene County, and remained until Mr. Craft's death. His widow is still living. Mr. Funk and wife are the parents of four children—George, Elizabeth, James and Wellington. Mr. Funk taught school for fifteen years in the earlier part of his life, and has since devoted his time exclusively to farming. He still takes an active interest in the educational affairs of his township, and has served as school director. He is the owner of a good farm of 105 acres, where he and family reside.

EAGON GOODEN, a retired farmer of Rutan, Penn, was born in Wayne Township, this county, February 22, 1823. He is a son of William F. and Mary (Shields) Gooden, who were natives of Greene County, where they were married. Mrs Gooden is deceased. Her husband is now a resident of Guernsey County, Ohio. The subject of this sketch was united in marriage September 19, 1850, with Elizabeth Wells. Mrs. Gooden was born in Greene County August 20, 1829, and is a daughter of James and Rhoda (Orndoff) Wells, also natives of this county, where they were married and remained until the death of Mrs Wells. Mr. Wells is still living and resides in Center Township. Mr. Gooden and wife are the parents of eleven children, of whom ten are living—William T., Margaret J., wife of Reasin Davis; Mary, wife of James Morris; James B., John J., Rhoda, wife of Henry Luellen; Eliza A., wife of Thomas L. McKerrian; Sarah A., wife of Charles N. Marsh; Harriet F., Flora B, and Jesse (deceased). In early life Mr. Gooden taught school for about nineteen years; he would teach in the winter and work as a farm hand through the summer. His first purchase of land was in Wayne Township. It consisted of eighty-two acres which he sold, and in 1869 bought his present farm of 162 acres. In politics Mr. Gooden is a Democrat. He has served as judge and inspector of elections, and has been school director of his township.

SETH GOODWIN, farmer, Rutan, Penn., was born in Washington County, Penn., February 6, 1828, and is a son of John and Sarah A. (Gardner) Goodwin, natives of Pennsylvania. His parents were married in Washington County and remained there until about the year 1832, at which time they moved to Greene County and spent the remainder of their days. The subject of our sketch was united in marriage April 4, 1854, with Mary Hill, who was born in Greene County March 16, 1832. Her parents were Dan and Matilda Hill (nee Penn), who were also natives of Pennsylvania, and after their marriage settled in this county and remained until 1854. They then moved West and remained for twenty-eight years, returning in 1882 to their native county in Pennsylvania, where Mr. Hill departed this life. His widow survives him. Mr. and Mrs. Goodwin are the parents of twelve children, the following are living—John W., Daniel H., Sarah M., wife of J. L. Hays; Thomas C , Mary F., Harry B. S., Elizabeth, Nan, and Nettie. Mr. Goodwin has been a tiller of the soil most of his life, and owns 200 acres of valuable land where he and family live. He and wife are prominent members of the Baptist Church.

JOHN T. GOODWIN, farmer, Rutan, Penn., is one of the prosperous citizens of Center Township. He was born in Greene

County, July 31, 1840   His parents were John and Sarah A Goodwin (*nee* Gardner)   They were natives of Pennsylvania, where they were married in Washington County, and about the year 1832 moved to Greene County and remained until their death. John T. was united in marriage, August 18, 1861, with Margaret A. Smith. Mrs. Goodwin was born in Center Township, February, 1842, and is a daughter of Edmund and Elizabeth (Adamson) Smith, who were natives of Greene County, where they were married and resided until Mr. Smith's death in 1887   His widow is still living   To Mr. and Mrs. Goodwin have been born four children—Edmund S, Thomas R, Emma J. and Flossie E   Mr. Goodwin makes quite a success of his farming, and owns about 186 acres of excellent land, where he and family reside.   Mr. and Mrs. Goodwin are leading members of the South Ten-Mile Baptist Church.

SAMUEL J. GRAHAM, farmer, Waynesburg, Penn., was born in Center Township, this county, November 22, 1837.   His parents, George and Sarah B (Mason) Graham, were natives of Greene County and residents therein until their death   Samuel was united in marriage, October 5, 1861, with Lizzie E. Boyd.   She was born in Washington Township, this county, October 6, 1842, and is a daughter of James and Martha Boyd.   Her parents are also natives of this county; her father is now deceased.   By this marriage Mr. Graham is the father of three children, two of whom are living—Sarah A. and James B.—and Florence E. is deceased.   Mrs. Graham, who was a faithful Christian wife and mother, departed this life April 12, 1871.   After her death, November 1, 1875, Mr. Graham was united in marriage a second time, with Sarah A. Price, who was born in Marion County, West Virginia, May 21, 1851.   Her parents are Eli T and Amanda Price (*nee* Troy), natives of West Virginia, where they were married and spent their lives.   Mrs. Price is now deceased.   By the last marriage Mr Graham is the father of two children—Charles W. and George E. P.   Mr. Graham was reared on a farm and devotes his time wholly to agricultural pursuits   He is the owner of about 163 acres of valuable land.   He and wife are prominent members of the M. E. Church.

JAMES HOGE, miller, Oak Forest, Penn, a descendant of one of the pioneer families of the county, was born in Center Township, September 23, 1834   His father and mother were George and Sarah Hoge, who died in this county   James was united in the holy bonds of matrimony, December 23, 1855, with Margaret Kent, a native of Greene County, born September 2, 1835   Mrs Hoge is a daughter of John and Keziah Kent, who reside in Wayne Township, this county.   Mr Hoge and wife are the parents of eight children, of whom five are living, viz: Elizabeth, Maryetta, Lucy B, Jesse B. and Flora M.   The deceased are Albert W., Rinehart K. and Margaretta.

Mr. Hoge is a carpenter by trade, which he followed for many years. He engaged in farming for some time, but for the last fifteen years has been operating a grist-mill. He owns land in the county, a number of houses and lots, one-half interest in mill property at Oak Forest, also one-half interest in the Hoge & Hoge Clothing Store at Waynesburg, Penn. Mr. Hoge has filled the office of justice of the peace for ten years, and is one of the most enterprising and industrious men of the county, and has carried on the undertaking business for thirty years and is still in the same business. He is also in the wagon-making and repairing business.

WILLIAM HOGE, farmer, Rogersville, Penn., was born in Greene County, Penn., December 31, 1830. His father and mother were Morgan and Elizabeth Hoge (nee Lippencott), who were natives of this county, where they made their home through life. William Hoge was twice united in marriage, the first time February 20, 1867, with Eliza A. McQuay. By this marriage Mr. Hoge is the father of four children—Samuel M., William McKinley, Elizabeth N. and David J. Mrs. Hoge died August 17, 1875. November 10, 1878, Mr. Hoge married for his second wife Esther M. Carter, born in Greene County in 1859. Her father and mother were James and Martha Carter, the latter deceased. Mr. and Mrs. Hoge are the parents of five children, viz: Mary J., Cinderella, Levi L., Martha and Jesse. Mr. Hoge is a successful farmer, and owns 250 acres of land—his home farm. He and wife are zealous members of the Baptist Church.

LEVI HOGE, farmer, Holbrook, Penn., was born June 24, 1833. His parents were Morgan and Elizabeth Hoge, who were born in Greene County, Penn., and resided there through life. Levi, the subject of our sketch, was united in the holy bonds of matrimony, October 12, 1868, with Susannah Orndoff. Mrs. Hoge was born in Center Township, April 22, 1840, and is a daughter of William and Salome Orndoff, who, like Mr. Hoge's people, were natives of Greene County, where they remained until their death. Mr. and Mrs. Hoge are the parents of one child—Mary J. Mr. Hoge was raised on a farm, and following out the careful instructions there received, he has, by his industry and economy, proven himself one of the most substantial farmers in his township. He owns a nice farm of 236 acres in Center Township, where he and family live. Mr. Hoge and family are prominent members in the Christian Church.

JOSEPH HOGE, retired farmer. P.O. Oak Forest, Penn., is one of the pioneers of the county, and was born in Franklin Township, November 16, 1806. His parents, Solomon and Mary Hoge, were natives of Virginia, and when first married moved to Greene County, Penn., and remained until their death. Joseph was three times married, first December 4, 1828, to Mary Coen, a native of Greene

County. By this marriage Mr Hoge is the father of ten children, five of whom are living. Mrs. Hoge, who was a faithful Christian wife and mother, died in 1842. In 1843 Mr. Hoge married for his second wife Miss Jane Blair, who was born in this county February 17, 1817 By this marriage there were seven children, four now living Mrs. Jane Hoge departed this life August 22, 1856 Mr. Hoge subsequently married Mrs. Jane M. (Wood) Watson, June 22, 1857. She was born in Washington County, Penn , November 16, 1812 Mr and Mrs. Hoge have one child. Mr. Hoge was reared on a farm, and has been engaged in farming all his life. He has resided on his present farm about sixty-four years. In politics he is a Republican He and wife are members of the Baptist Church, in which he has been deacon for nearly fifty years.

WILLIAM HOGE, farmer, P. O. Holbrook, Penn , was born in Center Township, December 15, 1830 He is a son of Joseph and Mary (Coen) Hoge, who are natives of Greene County. Mrs. Hoge is deceased October 4, 1855, William Hoge was united in marriage with Mary A. Graham, who was born in Franklin Township, Greene County, December 30, 1824. Her parents were William and Margaret (Muckle) Graham, the former a native of this county, and the latter of New Jersey. They were married in Greene County, Penn , where they settled and remained until their death To Mr and Mrs Hoge have been born three children, of whom two are living—William G , and Margaret M , who is the wife of John M. Scott. The deceased is Henry H William G. was born July 28, 1855, and was married July 20, 1878, to Mary A Moore. Mrs. Mary A. Hoge, wife of William G , died August 24, 1883. He was married again June 11, 1885, to Miss Alice M. Orndoff. Margaret M was born July 5, 1859, and married January 29, 1885, to John M. Scott Mr. Hoge has been engaged in farming the most of his life, and owns 241 acres of land in Center Township He and Mrs Hoge are zealous members of the Baptist Church, and are among the leading families of the township

T. J. HUFFMAN, farmer, Oak Forest, Penn.—The subject of this sketch was born in Center Township, Greene County, Penn., August 30, 1829. He is a son of Joseph and Sarah (Hunt) Huffman. On December 27, 1855, Mr. Huffman was united in marriage with Caroline Hathaway, who was born in Washington County, Penn., and is a daughter of Jacob and Jane Hathaway, residents of Washington County, Penn. Mr. and Mrs. Huffman have a family of nine children, eight of whom are living, viz· Joseph, Jacob, Robert, Daniel, Charlie W., Lizzie, Belle and Dora, and Jennie (deceased) Mr. Huffman was reared on a farm, and has been engaged in farming throughout his life. He owns about 240 acres of land in Greene County.

Mr and Mrs. Huffman are prominent members of the Christian Church, and highly respected by all who know them.

REASIN HUFFMAN, farmer, Waynesburg, Penn., is one of the industrious farmers of Center Township, Greene County, Penn , where he was born June 24, 1831. His parents were Joseph and Sarah Huffman (nee Hunt), who were natives and residents of this county until their death. On October 15, 1859, Mr. Huffman was united in the holy bonds of matrimony with Sidney Stewart (nee Thomas). Her father was a native of Ohio, and her mother of Greene County, Penn They now reside in Monroe County, Ohio. To Mr. Huffman, and wife have been born nine children, eight of whom are living—Joseph L., William R , Albert L., Emma F., Biddie E., Alexander C. J , John F., Isa O., and Nancy (deceased). The subject, like his brothers, was reared on a farm and has devoted his life principally to agriculture pursuits. He owns about 200 acres of land. In politics Mr Huffman is a Democrat, has filled the office of school director in his township, and he and wife are devoted members of the Christian Church.

S. B. HUFFMAN, farmer, Waynesburg, Penn , was born on the Huffman homestead in Center Township, this county, September 26, 1847. He is a son of Joseph and Sarah (Hunt) Huffman, who were natives of Pennsylvania, residing in Greene County until their death. Mr. Huffman was united in marriage, May 11, 1872, with Ella Neel, a native of Greene County, born March 21, 1853 She is a daughter of Remembrance and Nellie Neel (nee Thomas), natives of Pennsylvania, the latter deceased. Mr. Huffman and wife are the parents of six children, five of whom are living—Harry, Charlie, Josie, Ray and Roy. Remembrance (deceased) Mr. Huffman has been engaged in farming all his life, and owns 160 acres of land where he and family reside. In politics Mr. Huffman is a Democrat, and is school director in his township He and wife are active members of the Christian Church.

SAMUEL IAMS, retired farmer, Harvey's, Penn., was born in Washington County, Penn , April 8, 1817 His parents, John and Anna (Coulson) Iams, were natives of Washington County, where they were married and remained through life Mr. Iams died in December, 1866, and Mrs Iams in November, 1886. They were the parents of five children, of whom three are living. Samuel was united in marriage, October 29, 1840, with Nancy Grimes, who was born in Greene County, August 15, 1817. Her parents were Peter and Mary (Sherwin) Grimes, deceased. The former was a native of this county, and the latter of Baltimore, Maryland .Mr. and Mrs. Samuel Iams are the parents of seven children, of whom five are living—Dr. John T., of Waynesburg, Penn ; G. P.; Ida, wife of Byron Braddock; Carrie, wife of James B Throckmorton; and Samuel S. The deceased are

Mary A and Cordelia   Mr. Iams is a mill-wright by trade, which he followed for many years.   He subsequently engaged in farming and stock raising, and owns about 420 acres of land in Greene County. Mrs. Iams and family are members of the Methodist Episcopal Church.

F. G JACOBS, farmer, P O , Rutan, was born in Greene County, Penn , November 25, 1832   His father, Daniel Jacobs, was born in New Jersey   His mother, whose maiden name was Hannah Rayle, is a native of Maryland.   They were married in Greene County, Penn , where they still reside.   The subject of this sketch was united in marriage, June 24, 1858, with Catharine Nelson, who was born in this county February 14, 1832.   She is a daughter of Samuel and Barbaia (Ranner) Nelson.   The former was born in Virginia and the latter in Greene County, Penn , where they were married and spent the remainder of their lives   Mr and Mrs. Jacobs have seven chlidren —Daniel, Hannah, wife of Melvin Headley; William R , Baibara E , Mary B., Henry and Delia M   In early life Mr. Jacobs taught school for a few years, but subsequently devoted his time to farming. He owns about 225 acres of land where he and family live.   Mr. and Mrs Jacobs are zealous members of the Methodist Protestant Church.

A J. JOHNSTON, farmer, Hunter's Cave, Penn , was born in Washington County, Penn , Januaiy 18, 1816.   His parents were Andrew and Climena (Conklin) Johnston the former a native of New Jersey, and the latter of Pennsylvania   After marriage they settled in Washington County, and in 1820 moved to Greene County and, remained until their death.   The subject of our sketch was united in holy bonds of matrimony, December 9, 1847, with Phoebe McCullough, who was born in Washington County, April 3, 1817.   Mrs. Johnston is a daughter of Thomas and Sarah (Dunn) McCullongh.   They were also natives of Washington County, wheie they remained two years after their marriage, then moved to Greene County and spent the remainder of their lives.   Mr. and Mrs. Johnston have four children   Sarah A., wife of William Heaton; George W , Andrew J , and Eliza A   Mr. Johnston has been engaged in farming and stock raising all his life, and owns about 400 acres of land—his home farm   Mrs. Johnston and the children are members of the Methodist Episcopal Chuich

COLUMBUS JOHNSTON, farmer, P. O. Rogersville, was born in Center Township, Greene County Penn , June 4, 1831.   He is a son of Andrew and Climena (Conklin) Johnston who were natives of Washington County, but after mairiage resided in Center Township, Greene County, until their death.   Columbus was united in maniage March 5, 1855, with Emeline Bane, who was born in Washington County, June 17, 1838.   Mrs. Johnston is a daughter of Nathan and Hannah Bane (*nee* Caiter), who were also natives of Washington

County, and moved to Greene County about 1844, remaining until Mr. Bane's death. His widow is still living and resides in West Virginia. Mr. Johnston and wife are the parents of four children—Nathan B., Lizzie A., Dora M., and Lewis B. (deceased). Mr. Johnston was reared on a farm and has made farming his business through life, and by strict honesty and industry has procured a nice home, consisting of 108 acres of land, where he and family reside. He and Mrs. Johnston are active members of the South Ten Mile Baptist Church. In politics he is a Republican.

DAVID KNIGHT, retired farmer, P. O. Oak Forest, Penn., was born in Greene County, Penn., October 24, 1818. His parents, James and Cassandra Knight, were natives of Greene County, where they were married and remained until their death. David was united in marriage June 6, 1839, with Mary A. Fry. Mrs. Knight was born in this county February 26, 1819, and is a daughter of John and Mary Fry. They were also natives of Greene County, but moved to West Virginia and resided until their death. To Mr. Knight and wife have been born nine children, seven of whom are living—Mary, Joshua, Cassie J., Thomas J., Lucy A., Jemima and Harriet. The deceased are Catharine and Eli. Mr. Knight has been successfully engaged in farming all his life, and owns about 134 acres of land. In politics he is a Democrat. The Knight family are pioneers of the county, and among its most highly respected citizens.

THOMAS KNIGHT, farmer, P. O. Rogersville, Penn., was born in Franklin Township, Greene County, Penn., November 27, 1820. His father and mother, James and Cassandra Knight, were natives of this county, where they resided until their death. Thomas Knight was united in marriage November 18, 1841, with Nancy Wood, who was born in Jackson Township, October 13, 1822. Mrs. Knight was a daughter of Micajah and Jane Wood, the former a native of Pennsylvania, and the latter of Ireland. Both died in Greene County. Mr. Knight by this marriage is the father of eight children, of whom five are living. Mrs. Knight died March 3, 1863. On December 24, 1863, Mr. Knight married for his second wife Miss Edna Sellers, who was born in Center Township, October 30, 1829. Her parents were Christopher and Nancy (Johnson) Sellers, both natives of Pennsylvania, who departed this life in Greene County. Mr. Knight and wife have two children, one living. Mr. Knight is a cabinet-maker by trade, but has been engaged in farming for many years. He owns 212 acres of good land.

LEVI H. MARTIN, P. O. Rogersville, Penn., is one of the substantial farmers of Center Township, this county, where he was born March 1, 1843. His parents, Daniel and Rachel (Rush) Martin, were natives of Greene County, where they were married and remained until Mr. Martin's death, April 6, 1879. His widow is still living. Levi was united in marriage, December 24, 1867, with Rachel Eddy, who was born July 24, 1842, in this county, and is a daughter of John and Elizabeth (Kughu) Eddy. Her parents are natives of Greene County and reside in Wayne Township. Mr. and Mrs. Martin have a family of three children, two of whom are living—Belle and Levi E. Mr. Martin was reared on a farm, and has engaged in farming as his occupation through life. He is the owner of 150 acres of good land in Greene County. He and Mrs. Martin are active members of the Christian Church, and the family are highly respected in the community.

A. B. McCLELLAND, merchant, Oak Forest, Penn.—The subject of this sketch is one of the leading merchants of Center Township. He was born in Waynesburg, Penn., February 25, 1840. His parents were Dawson and Sarah (Hughes) McClelland, who were natives and residents of this county through life. Asa B. was united in marriage March 10, 1861, with Nancy Donahoe. She was born in Greene County, November 30, 1841, and is a daughter of William and Nancy Donahoe, both deceased. Mr. McClelland is a blacksmith by trade, which he followed about twenty-five years, then engaged in farming and merchandising. He owns a general store at Oak Forest, Penn. In politics he is a Republican, and served as postmaster for five years at Oak Forest under the Republican administration. He and wife are faithful members of the Baptist Church.

J. P. McGLUMPHY, farmer, P. O. Rutan, was born in Center Township, Greene County, Pennsylvania, July 16, 1822. He is a son of Edward and Magaret (Haines) McGlumphy. His father was a native of Ireland, and his mother of Maryland. They were the parents of seven children, of whom four are living. Mr. McGlumphy was united in marriage February 11, 1847, with Lida A. Thomas. Mrs. McGlumphy was born in this county March 12, 1831, and is a daughter of James and Elizabeth Thomas. Mr. and Mrs. McGlumphy are the parents of four children—Maria S., wife of Henry Scott; Hiram R.; Elizabeth M., wife of F. M. Carpenter, and Lucy J., wife of W. H. Throckmorton. Mr. McGlumphy has been a farmer all his life, and owns a nice home where he and family reside. He and wife are prominent members of the Cumberland Presbyterian Church, and are highly respected by all who know them.

JESSE McNEELY, farmer, P. O. Rutan, Penn., was born in Wayne Township, Greene County, Pennsylvania, April 11, 1851. He is a son of John and Elizabeth McNeely, who were natives of Pennsylvania and settled after marriage in Greene County, where Mrs. McNeely departed this life in Wayne Township. Mr. Mc-

Neely afterward married a Mrs. Coen, whose maiden name was Stockdale. They moved to Center Township and remained until Mr. McNeely's death. His widow came to her death June 13, 1888, by the falling of a porch roof. She was standing on the porch when the roof fell in and killed her instantly. Jesse was united in marriage November 6, 1875, with Melissa VanCleve, who was born in Center Township, August 7, 1852. Her parents were John and Ursula (Throckmorton) VanCleve, also natives of this county and and residents of Center Township. Mr. and Mrs. McNeely have two children—James A. and John H. In connection with his farming Mr. McNeeley has been engaged extensively in the lumber business. He is the owner of seventy-six acres of land, where he and family reside. He has served as school director of his township and was elected justice of the peace February, 1888, for a term of five years. Mrs. McNeely is a devoted member of the Methodist Episcopal Church.

JOHN MEEK, a successful farmer, P. O. Rutan, Penn., was born in Washington Township, this county, May 29, 1833. His parents, John and Elizabeth (Boyd) Meek, were also natives of this county, where they remained until their death. On October 15, 1859, John Meek was united in marriage with Jane Simpson. Mrs Meek was born in Greene County, February 7, 1840, and is a daughter of John and Mary (Auld) Simpson, Her father was born in Greene County, Penn., and her mother was a native of Ireland Both died in this county. Mr. and Mrs Meek have three children—Miles, John W. and Ottowa A. Mr. Meek has been engaged in farming all his life, and owns 224 of land where he and family reside. Mr. and Mrs. Meek are leading members in the Methodist Protestant Church.

WILLIAM MILLIKIN, farmer, P. O. Rutan, was born in Morris Township, this county, April 3, 1832. His parents, David and Lida (Rogers) Millikin, were natives of Greene County, the former of Irish and the latter of English descent. They were united in marriage in Greene County, where they remained through life. William was united in marriage, September 1, 1852, with Rebecca Simpson, who is a native of this county, born March 9, 1835. Her parents were John and Mary Simpson, the former a native of Pennsylvania, and the latter of Ireland. They were residents of Greene County, Penn., for the greater part of their lives. To Mr. and Mrs. Millikin have been born eight children, of whom six are living— John W., Robert I., Thomas N, Harry B., Maggie J. and Sadie M. The deceased are Lida A and Cora V. Mr. Millikin is one of the substantial farmers of Center Township, and by his industry and good management has made a comfortable home for himself and family. His farm consists of about 300 acres of land, on which are good buildings Mr. and Mrs. Millikin are consistent members of the Methodist Protestant Church.

JOHN MORRIS, farmer, Rogersville, Penn., was born in Center Township, this county, March 28, 1832. His parents, Ephraim and Martha (Roseberry) Morris, were natives of Greene County, where they were married and spent all their lives. John Morris was twice united in marriage, first November 11, 1854, with Sarah Church, a native of Center Township, and daughter of Elijah and Anna Church (nee Moore). Her parents are natives and residents of this county. By this marriage Mr. Morris is the father of six children, viz: Martha A., wife of Harvey Call; James M., Asa W., John J., Arta M., wife of Goodwin Hunt, and Elijah. Mrs. Morris departed this life March 10, 1878. November 30, 1879, Mr Morris married for his second wife Elizabeth Phillips, a native of Marshall County, W. Va. Her parents were Joseph and Anna (Inghram) Phillips, natives of West Virginia, both now deceased Mr and Mrs. Morris are the parents of two children—Joseph G and Sarah A Mr. Morris is quite a genius, and has learned several different trades. He is a carpenter, stone-mason and blacksmith, and succeeds in almost any kind of work. He has been engaged in farming for several years, and owns about 300 acres of land where he and family reside During the Rebellion he entered the service of his country in Company F, Eighty-fifth Pennsylvania Volunteers, and served over a year, receiving a wound at Williamsburg from a piece of a shell. Mr. Morris was elected commissioner of Greene County and served three years, being one of the few Republicans who ever held that office in the county.

ELI ORNDURF, farmer, P. O., Rogersville, Penn, one of the substantial citizens of Center Township, was born in Greene County, Penn., February 25, 1828. He is a son of William and Salome (Wisecarver) Orndurf, the former a native of Virginia, and the latter of Pennsylvania. They departed this life in Greene County, in 1885. They were the parents of twelve children, of whom eleven are living Eli Orndurf was united in the holy bonds of matrimony, March 23, 1854, with Martha A Wyly, who was born in Greene County, September 6, 1834. Mrs. Orndurf is a daughter of James and Mary Wyly (nee Neel), natives of this county. Mrs. Wyly died February 14, 1876 Mr. Wyly is still living To Mr Orndurf and wife have been born seven children—William H, Mary S, wife of Edmund Scott; James L., Susan, Joseph S, Barney and Mattie I. Mr Orndurf has been a farmer all his life, and owns 365 acres of land where he and family reside. In politics he is a Republican.

W B. ORNDOFF, farmer and stock-raiser, Oak Forest, Penn, one of the substantial and industrious farmers of Center Township, was born in this county, January 15, 1837. He is a son of William and Salome (Wisecarver) Orndoff, who departed this life in 1885. William B. was united in marriage, September 12, 1868, with Mary E Scott, who was born in Greene County, September 22, 1844. She is a daughter of John and Charlotte Scott (nee Mason), both natives of this county and residents of Jackson Township. Mr. and Mrs. Orndoff are the parents of five children—Bertha, Orvil D., Judson H , John D. and Hersey. Mr. Orndoff has been engaged in farming for many years, and owns 338 acres of land in Center Township. In politics he is a Republican, and has served on the school board in his township.

ISAAC ORNDOFF, farmer, Rogersville, Penn., is a descendant of the old pioneer family of Orndoffs. He was born in Center Township, April 4, 1846, and is a son of William and Salome (Wisecarver) Orndoff, the former a native of Virginia, and the latter of Pennsylvania   They were married in Greene County, and remained there through life   Isaac Orndoff was twice married, the first time April 4, 1869, to Margaret R. Seckman, who was born in Rogersville, May 18, 1848. Mrs. Orndoff was a daughter of John W. and Lila Seckman, the former deceased. By this marriage Mr Orndoff is the father of three children—Emma E , John S. and Lora M. Mis. Orndoff departed this life October 25, 1874. Mr. Orndoff's second wife, whom he married in 1877, was Harriet Headley, who was born in Gilmore Township, this county, May 3, 1848   She is a daughter of John and Eliza Headley. Mr. and Mis. Orndoff are the parents of six children—Jesse F., Eddie G., Sweet, Isaac B., Charlie W. and Georgie A. Mr. Orndoff has been a farmer all his life, and owns eighty-five acres of land where he and family reside in Center Township, Greene County, Penn.

D S. ORNDOFF, farmer, Oak Forest, Penn , was born in Virginia, March 29, 1854. His father and mother are William and Margaret Orndoff, natives of Virginia, where they still reside   On November 20, 1875, D. S Orndoff married Mary S. Orndoff, who was born in Greene County, Penn., March 25, 1851. Mis. Orndoff is a daughter of William and Salome Orndoff (nee Wisecarver). The former was born in Virginia, and the latter in Pennsylvania. They settled in Greene County and remained until their death. To Mr. and Mrs. Orndoff have been born four children—Maggie B., Lizzie M., Edsa S and Effa A. Mr. Orndoff came from Virginia in 1875, and has remained in Greene County ever since. He is engaged in farming, and owns 220 acres of land in Center Township   He and wife are consistent members of the Christian Church, and are highly respected throughout the community.

JESSE ORNDURF, retired farmer, White Cottage, Penn , was born in Franklin Township, this county, May 20, 1816. His father and mother were Jesse and Catharine Orndurf, who were natives of

Virginia, but came to Greene County, Penn., and spent their later life. Mr. Orndurf departed this life in 1816, and after his death Mrs. Orndurf was united in marriage with John Gordon. Both are now deceased. Jesse Orndurf was united in marriage the first time with Isabella Mooney, who was a daughter of Thomas and Cassandra Mooney, the former a native of Ireland, and the latter of Pennsylvania. By this marriage Mr. Orndurf is the father of four children, only one of whom is living—Mary J., wife of Silas Fordyce. Mrs. Orndurf departed this life in 1851. In 1853 Mr. Orndurf married for his second wife Susan Wear, born in West Virginia, November 21, 1826. Mrs. Orndurf is a daughter of William and Sarah Wear. Her father died in Portsmouth, Ohio, and her mother in West Virginia. By the second marriage Mr. and Mrs. Orndurf have six children—Elizabeth, wife of S. R. Fordyce; William, who married Eliza Mitchell; Inghram, the husband of Sidney White; Jesse B., who married Mollie L. Hughes; Sarah A, wife of C. V. Smith, and Sidney, wife of Thomas Stewart. Mr. Orndurf has been engaged in farming all his life, and has given his children a great deal of property. He owns at present 400 acres of land in Greene County. He and wife are zealous members of the Methodist Protestant Church. In politics he is a Democrat.

S. B. OWEN, physician, Oak Forest, Penn.—Among the successful young physicians of Greene County, Pennsylvania, we take pleasure in mentioning the name of Dr. S. B. Owen, who was born in Greene County, January 4, 1857. He is a son of Isaac N. and Anna Owen (nee Rush), who are natives of this county, where they have spent most of their lives. Doctor Owen was united in marriage August 28, 1879, with Laura K. Donley, who was born at Mt. Morris, Penn., August 28, 1862. She is a daughter of David L. and Louisa Donley (nee Evans). Her father is a native of this county, and her mother of West Virginia. They have resided in this county since their marriage. To Dr. S. B. Owen and wife have been born two children—Mabel D. and Edward I. The Doctor commenced reading medicine with his father in 1879, and graduated from the Starling Medical College of Columbus, Ohio, March 6, 1884. He began the practice of his profession at Oak Forest, Penn., the same year, where he receives a large patronage and meets with good success.

JOHN PATTERSON, farmer, P. O., Hunter's Cave, Penn., was born in Washington County, Penn., August 18, 1819, and is a son of John and Mary (Enlow) Patterson. His father is a native of Adams County. Mrs. Patterson was born in Washington County, Penn., where they were married and remained until their death. On September 15, 1846, John married Mahala Patterson, a native of Morris Township, Greene County, Penn., born January 15, 1828. Her parents, John and Elizabeth (Shriver) Patterson, were natives of Greene County and resided therein through life. Mr. and Mrs Patterson are the parents of six children, three of whom are living— James E., Samantha, wife of Jacob Schrode; and Ida B. The deceased are Nancy E., Mahalia S and John W. Mr. Patterson was raised on a farm and has made farming the occupation of his life. He is the owner of 220 acres of good land where he and his family reside. Mr. and Mrs. Patterson are leading members of the Methodist Episcopal Church.

JESSE C. PATTERSON, farmer, Waynesburg, Penn., is one of the industrious young farmers of Center Township, where he was born September 22, 1854. He is a son of James and Mary J (Parshall) Patterson, natives of Washington and Fayette counties, respectively They were married in Greene County and remained there until their death. Mrs. Patterson departed this life March 7, 1884, and her husband July 16, 1885. Jesse C. was united in marriage January 18, 1883, with Rebecca Wade, who was born in this county December 4, 1862. Her father and mother are Greenberry and Mary (McCormick) Wade, natives of West Virginia, where they lived for many years. They subsequently moved to Greene County, Penn., and reside in Mt. Morris. Mr. and Mrs. Patterson are the parents of two children, one living, James E., and Wade (deceased). Mr. Patterson has been engaged in farming through life, and owns 102 acres of land which constitutes his home farm. In politics he is a Democrat; he has held the office of school director in his township, and he and Mrs. Patterson are consistent members of the Baptist Church.

O. S. PHILLIPS, farmer, P. O. Hunter's Cave, was born in Washington County, Penn , August 21, 1829. He is a son of John and Lida (Rutan) Phillips, the former a native of Greene and the latter of Washington County, where they were married and remained until about the year 1844. They then moved to Greene County and remained until Mr. Phillips death, which occurred at Fairfax Court House during the rebellion. After his death his widow lived with her son O. S, with whom she made her home until her death Mr. O. S. Phillips was united in marriage, August 1, 1850, with Charity Graham, who was born on the farm where she resides, August 16, 1833. Her parents were George and Sarah B. (Mason) Graham, natives of this county and residents of Center Township until their death. To Mr. and Mrs. Phillips have been born the following named children—George W., Margaret J., wife of Simon Moore; Samuel O., Belle L , wife of W. McCullough; Benjamin F., Sadie L , Dora M., Birdie W., Olive C. and Guy C. The deceased are Rhoda A. and Willis B. Mr. Phillips was raised on a farm and has been engaged in farming and stock-growing all his life. He owns about

440 acres of land in Greene County. In politics he is a Democrat, has filled the office of school director in his township, and he and his wife are active members in the Methodist Episcopal Church.

LEVI PORTER, Harvey's, Penn., was born in Franklin Township this county, June 5, 1845. His parents, John and Hannah (Rinehart) Porter, were natives of Greene County, where they were married and remained until their death. Levi was united in marriage September 3, 1873, with Lizzie, daughter of David and Elizabeth Kent. Her father was a native of Pennsylvania, and her mother of New Jersey. Both are now deceased Mrs Porter was born in Franklin Township. She and Mr. Porter had a family of four children—Linnie L, Mattie M., Alma E. and Florence A. Their mother died October 3, 1883 Mr. Porter was afterwards united in marriage, March 30, 1885, with Linnie Bradford, who was also a native of Franklin Township, born October 20, 1856 She is a daughter of Robert and Sarah J Bradford (nee Kent), also natives of Pennsylvania and residents of Greene County until Mrs. Bradford's death. Mr Bradford is still living. By his last marriage Mr. Porter is the father of two children—Goldie M and Viola E Mr Porter has been engaged in different lines of business during his life, but at present devotes his time principally to farming, and owns one-hundred and thirty-eight acres of land where he and his family reside. Mr. and Mrs Porter belong to the Methodist Episcopal Church, of which his deceased wife was also a devoted member.

W. P. REESE, miller, Rogersville, Penn.—Among the stirring business men of Rogersville we take pleasure in mentioning the name of William P Reese, who is a native of Greene County and was born November 28, 1884. He is a son of John D. and Catharine Reese, who were pioneers of Greene County, and remained in it until their death. William was united in marriage September 11, 1869, with Maria Fry, who was born in this county, March 21, 1847. Mrs. Reese is a daughter of George and Elizabeth Fry, who were born in Greene County. Mr. Fry in 1813, and his wife in 1818 Mr. Fry is still living. Mr Reese and wife are the parents of seven children—John L, Cora B, George C, Catharine E, William A., Alice M. and Allen T. Mr. Reese is a miller by occupation, owns a grist and planing-mill in Rogersville, also 225 acres of land in Greene County He is a member of the Masonic Order and his political views are Democratic. He has been a citizen of Rogersville for nine years.

PHILLIP RUSH, farmer, Rogersville, Penn., was born in Morris Township, Greene County, Pennsylvania, October 17, 1834 He is a son of Abraham and Lida Rush (nee Bottomfield), the former a native of New Jersey, and the latter of Pennsylvania. They were married in Greene County and resided there until their death. In

1857 Phillip Rush married Catharine M. Huffman, who was born in Center Township, this county, in 1837. Her parents, Joseph and Sarah (Hunt) Huffman, were natives of Pennsylvania, and resided in Greene County until their death. To Mr. and Mrs. Rush have been born eleven children, ten of whom are living—Stephen B., Joseph L., Francis M., Nancy E., Clarinda, Timothy R., John, Vada, Lucy, May and Ora. Thomas J. is deceased. Mr. Rush has been a farmer all his life, and owns 123 acres of valuable land where he and his family reside. Mrs. Rush is a devoted member of the Baptist Church.

C. W. SCOTT, farmer, Rutan, Penn, was born December 16, 1837, on the farm where he and family reside in Center Township. He is a son of John and Mary A. Scott (*nee* Teagarden), who were natives of Pennsylvania and residents of Greene County until their death. Mrs. Scott departed this life in 1856, and her husband lost his life in a collision on the Baltimore & Ohio Railroad, near Columbus, Ohio, October 6, 1860. They were the parents of four children. On October 6, 1859, C. W. Scott was united in marriage with Rachel Webster, who was born in this county November 30, 1839. Her parents were John and Elizabeth (Cowell) Webster, also natives of this county. Mr. Webster died in 1871 and Mrs. Webster in 1874. To Mr. and Mrs. Scott have been born five children, four living—William H., George M., John, Flora, and Mary E. (deceased). Mr. Scott was raised on a farm, has spent his life in farming, and is the owner of 124 acres of land. He has served as director of the poor in Greene County for three years. Mrs. Scott is a faithful member of the Baptist Church.

THOMAS SCOTT, farmer, P. O. Rutan, Penn., was born in Center Township, Greene County, December 24, 1834. His parents, Elias and Harriet (Kent) Scott, were natives of this county, where they were married and remained through life. Mr. Scott died August 20, 1884, and his wife June 14, of the same year. On September 13, 1855, Thomas Scott married Elizabeth A. Turner. Mrs. Scott was born in Greene County, June 12, 1838, and is a daughter of Rev. James L and Nancy (Patterson) Turner. Her father was a native of New York and her mother of Greene County, Penn. Both are now deceased. By this marriage Mr. Scott is the father of eight children—Wesley S, Walter P., Elias, Harriet N., Ida L., Albert F., Carrie E. and James E. Mrs Scott died July 16, 1876. Mr. Scott was subsequently united in marriage December 20, 1879, with Anna B. Drake, who was born in Greene County, October 5, 1849. Her parents, Francis and Eliza Drake, were natives of this county. Mr. Drake is deceased. By the second marriage Mr. Scott is the father of three children—Harry R, Leah N. and William. Mr. Scott has been a farmer all his life, and owns 133 acres

31

of land where he and family live, besides property in West Virginia. He has been a member of the school board of his township. He and Mrs Scott belong to the Methodist Protestant Church, of which his deceased wife was also a devout member.

GEORGE W. SCOTT, farmer, Rutan, Penn., was born in Center Township, this county, April 30, 1837 His parents are James and Charlotte (Strawn) Scott, natives of Greene County, where they were married and remained until Mr. Scott's death in 1884 His widow is still living George W. was united in marriage July 4, 1864, with Amanda J. Woods, who was born in Waynesburg, Penn, October 25, 1843, and is a daughter of Samuel and Leah Woods (*nee* Divers) Mrs. Scott's mother was born in Baltimore, Md., and her father was a native of Washington County, Penn, where they were married. They settled in Waynesburg and remained until their death—Mrs Woods dying June 6, 1885, and her husband June 21, 1886. To Mr. and Mrs. Scott have been born six children, viz—Emma L, wife of George B. McNeely, M D.; Mary C., Cora, Nellie L., Reynolds and Claude. Mr. Scott has devoted his life chiefly to farming, and owns 131 acres of land where he and family reside When the war broke out Mr Scott entered the service of his country in Company I, Eighth Pennsylvania Reserves, and served three years. He passed through many serious engagements, and was wounded three times. He has filled the office of auditor of his township. Mrs. Scott is a consistent member of the Methodist Episcopal Church

HENRY A. SCOTT, farmer, P. O. Rutan, was born in Greene County, Penn, April 11, 1842. He is a son of James and Charlotte (Strawn) Scott, who were natives of Greene County, where they resided until Mr. Scott's death, which occurred April 9, 1884. His widow is still living. Henry was united in marriage January 28, 1864, with Catharine Morris. Mrs. Scott was born in this county July 7, 1848, and is a daughter of Ephraim and Martha (Roseberry) Morris Her parents were also natives of Greene County, and residents therein through life. To Mr. and Mrs Scott have been born six children, of whom four are living—James F, Lucy J., Asa and Sarah. Mr Scott has been engaged in farming through life, and owns 184 acres of land where he and family live. Mrs Scott is a devoted member of the Methodist Episcopal Church.

JOSHUA SCOTT, farmer, P. O Rutan, is one of the pioneers of Greene County, Penn. He was born December 20, 1824, and is a son of James and Mary Scott (*nee* Sellers). His parents were natives of Greene County, where they resided until their death. On October 10, 1843, Joshua Scott married Nancy J. Rinehart. She was born in this county in 1826, and is a daughter of Samuel and Mary Rinehart, both deceased. To Mr. Joshua Scott and wife were born four children, of whom three are living—Mary E, Christopher and Samuel. James is the deceased   Mr. Scott has engaged in farming throughout his life, and owns 160 acres of land where he and family reside. He belongs to the Methodist Protestant church, of which his wife, who died January 1, 1866, was also a faithful member. By her death the family were bereft of a faithful and devoted wife and mother

ASA M. SELLERS, farmer, Rogersville, Penn —The gentleman whose name heads this sketch is a descendant of one of the pioneer families of Greene County, Penn., where he was born July 8, 1828. His father and mother were David and Elizabeth Sellers, who were also natives of this county, and remained here until their death. Asa Sellers was united in marriage March 31, 1855, with Jane Orndoff. Mrs. Sellers was born in Center Township March 23, 1832. Her parents were William and Salome Orndoff (nee Wisecarver). To Mr. and Mrs. Sellers have been born six children, of whom four are living—Elizabeth S., wife of Carey Grimes; William L., Atkinson H. and David R. The deceased are Mary A. and Adda M. Mr. Sellers has been engaged in farming and raising stock all his life, and owns about 200 acres of land where he and family reside. In politics he is a Republican.

THOMAS SMITH, farmer, Rutan, Penn , was born in Center Township January 6, 1836. He is a son of Edmund and Elizabeth (Adamson) Smith, who were natives of Greene County, where they were married and remained until Mr. Smith's death, February 11, 1887. Mrs. Smith is still living. Thomas is their oldest child, and was united in marriage April 19, 1855, with Susannah Scott, who was born in Center Township, September 24, 1836. Her parents, Elias and Harriet (Kent) Scott, were natives of Greene County and residents there until their death. Mr. and Mrs. Smith are the parents of eight children, seven living—James L., Hiram R., Laura A., wife of Lindsey D. Grove; William L , Emerson B., Fannie A., Elzie and Harriet E. (deceased). Mr. Smith's life has been devoted to farming and the raising of stock. His farm in Center Township consists of 289 acres of land, on which are fine substantial buildings. Mr. Smith has filled the office of director of the poor, and has been a member of the school board   He and wife are members of the Baptist Church.

JOB C. SMITH, farmer, Rutan, Penn., was born in Center Township December 1, 1848. He is a son of Edmund and Elizabeth Smith (nee Adamson), natives of Greene County, Penn., where they resided until Mr. Smith's death in 1887. His widow is still living.   Job C. was united in the holy bonds of matrimony August 1, 1875, with Christie A Slusher, who was born in Washington County, Penn., November 11, 1846, and is a daughter of David and

Elizabeth Slusher (*nee* Moore). Her parents are also natives of Washington County, and moved to Greene County in 1872. In 1880 they went to Iowa, where they still reside. Mr. and Mrs. Smith have six children—Bessie E., Hattie E., Guy B., Clyde D., Loyd L. and Goldie Z. Mr. Smith is an industrious farmer, and is the owner of 106 acres of land where he and family live. He and wife are zealous members of the Baptist Church

J. C. SMITH, retired farmer, Rutan, Penn., was born in Morgan Township, Greene County, Penn., May 11, 1814. His parents, Job and Mary (Cravan) Smith, were natives of Pennsylvania, settled after marriage in Morgan Township, and remained during life They were the parents of three children. J C. is their only child living, and was united in marriage July 4, 1839, with Elizabeth Scott. She was born in Center Township March 20, 1821, and is a daughter of John and Susannah Scott (*nee* Niceswunger). Her parents, who were natives of Greene County, are both deceased M.. and Mrs. Smith are the parents of eleven children, of whom ten are living—William, Sarah A., wife of William Cowen; John, Maria J., wife of James Wells; Mary, Thomas J., Hiram S., Samuel H., Lydia, wife of George Grimes, and Emma A., wife of Samuel Showalter. The deceased is Job, who died in the Andersonville prison. Mr Smith has been a farmer all his life, and owns a nice home where he and family reside He and wife are active members of the Methodist Protestant Church.

STEPHEN STRAWN a retired farmer residing near Waynesburg, Penn., was born in Franklin Township September 5, 1817. He is a son of Abner and Juda (Grant) Strawn, who were natives of Pennsylvania and died in Washington County. Stephen was united in the holy bonds of matrimony July 15, 1841, with Margaret J. Jewell. Mrs. Strawn was also a native of Franklin Township, born November 3, 1823, and is a daughter of Samuel and Margaret (Mason) Jewell, the former a native of New Jersey and the latter of Ireland. They are now deceased. To Mr. and Mrs Strawn have been born eight children, seven of whom are living—John, Eliza, wife of Jacob Wilson; Samuel, William, Abner, Mason and Morton T. The deceased is Elizabeth, who was the wife of J. B. Smith Mr Strawn has been a farmer all his life, and is the owner of ninety-seven acres of land where he and family reside. He has served as school director and inspector of elections in his township.

SAMUEL THOMPSON, P O. Rogersville, Penn., was born in Center Township, Greene County, Pennsylvania, January 1, 1839. He is a son of Joseph and Margaret (Bowler) Thompson. The former is a native of West Virginia, and the latter of Greene County, Penn., where they were married and made their home until Mr. Thompson's death, which occurred July 7, 1867. Mrs. Thompson is still living. She resides with her son Samuel, who was united in marriage March 4, 1865, with Sarah E. Call. Mrs. Thompson was born in Center Township in 1840, and is a daughter of James and Sarah E. Call who were natives of Pennsylvania, and departed this life in Greene County. Mr. and Mrs. Thompson are the parents of nine children, of whom eight are living—Thomas, Harry, Mary B., Maggie, James, Lindsey, Essa and Coral. Henry is deceased. Mr. Thompson was reared on a farm and has devoted almost all his life to farming He owns about 320 acres of land. When needed in the surface of his country he enlisted in Company F, Eighty-fifth Pennsylvania Volunteers, served for three years, and was in a number of serious engagements. He and wife are faithful members of the Christian Church.

JAMES THROCKMORTON, retired farmer, P. O. Harvey's, Penn., is one of the pioneer farmers of Center Township. He was born in Franklin Township, this county, February 22, 1816. His father and mother were Joseph and Catharine (Hulsart) Throckmorton, natives of Monmouth County, New Jersey, where they were united in marriage in 1809. Soon after marriage they moved to Franklin Township, Greene County, Penn., and remained until Mrs. Throckmorton's death in March, 1853. After her death Mr. Throckmorton was united in marriage the second time in Morrow County, Ohio, with Laura Gilbert, and remained in that county until her death. He then returned to Greene County, Penn., and made his home with his children until his death, September 15, 1881. James, the subject of our sketch, was united in marriage January 9, 1840, with Mary M., daughter of William S. and Jane (Gettys) Harvey. Mrs. Throckmorton was born in Center Township, May 3, 1821. Her father was a native of Philadelphia, Penn , and represented Greene County in the State Legislature. Her mother was born in Fayette County, Penn. After marriage they settled and remained in Center Township until their death. To Mr. and Mrs. Throckmorton have been born nine children, of whom eight are living— Joseph G., Catharine C., wife of Daniel Hopkins; Mary E., wife of Andrew Frantz; William H.; Maggie C., wife of Robert Dinsmore; Sadie A.; Carrie L., wife of George C Davis, and Emma F., wife of John M. Burroughs. Mr. Throckmorton is a millwright by trade, which he followed for fifteen years. He has since engaged in farming, and owns 120 acres of land where he and family live. Mr. and Mrs. Throckmorton are active members of the Methodist Episcopal Church, and the entire family are highly respected by all who know them.

SAMUEL THROCKMORTON, deceased, who was a farmer of Rogersville, Penn., was born in Franklin Township, May 21, 1818. He was a son of Morford and Margaret (Hill) Throckmorton. His father came from New Jersey, and his mother was a native of Greene County, Penn, where they were married and spent all their lives. Samuel was united in marriage July 24, 1844, with Nancy Reese, who was born near Waynesburg, Penn, January 31, 1825 Mrs. Throckmorton is the only daughter of John and Elizabeth (Drips) Reese, also natives of Greene County, where they remained until their death. To Mr. and Mrs. Throckmorton were born eight children, of whom seven are living, viz, Elizabeth M, wife of James B. Smith; William S, John R., James B, Thomas M., Albert B. and Charlie The deceased is Margaret, who was the wife of Morgan Ross, and departed this life February 6, 1883. Mr. Throckmorton was a farmer and wool-grower in his life-time. At the time of his death he owned about 980 acres of land, and his wife about 200 acres He was a member of the M. E Church, and during the last half of his life he held at various times the position of trustee and leader in his chosen denomination Mrs Throckmorton is a faithful member of the Presbyterian Church Mr Throckmorton was killed by lightning, July 28, 1881, while at work in the field with four of his sons. By his death the county lost a good citizen and his family a kind husband and father.

JESSE ULLOM, merchant, Rogersville, Penn. — Among the substantial business men of Rogersville, we take pleasure in mentioning Jesse Ullom, who was born in Greene County June 20, 1836. He is a son of Daniel T. and Anna (Johnson) Ullom, who were natives of Greene County, where they resided until Mr. Ullom's death, in October, 1881. His widow survives him This union was blessed with twelve children, nine of whom are living—three sons and six daughters. On March 29, 1861, Jesse was united in marriage with Phœbe Morris, who was born in this county November 11, 1843. She is a daughter of Ephraim and Martha Morris, both deceased. Mr and Mrs Morris were the parents of ten children, of whom eight are living. Mr and Mrs. Ullom have a family of seven children, four living, viz, Thomas M, Mattie A, John T. and Jesse F. The deceased are Fannie L and two infants. Mr Ullom has been engaged in farming and merchandising all his life He owns forty-seven acres of land, nice property in Rogersville, also a general country store. In 1881 he was elected to the office of justice of the peace in Center Township, and has been serving in that capacity ever since He and wife are active members of the Methodist Protestant Church.

ROBERT WATSON, farmer and stock-dealer, Holbrook, Penn., was born in West Bethlehem Township, Washington County, April 12, 1847 He is a son of John and Anna Watson. His father was a native of Ireland, and came with his parents to America when ten years of age. His mother is a native of Pennsylvania, where she and Mr. Watson were married in Washington County, and remained there until their death. Mr. John Watson departed this life in 1856, and Mrs. Watson in 1869. They are buried on the farm at the head of Castile, where the family settled when they first came to this country. In 1870 Robert Watson married Kate Anderson, who was a native of Amwell Township, Washington County, and born in 1848. Her parents were John and Anna (Howshow) Anderson, natives of Pennsylvania and residents in Greene County through life. Mr. and Mrs. Watson have seven children—Samuel, John I., Smith, Anna F., George W., Maggie and Lizzie. Mr. Watson was reared on a farm and has made farming and stock-dealing his business through life. He owns about 112 acres of land where he resides with his family. During the late Rebellion he went into the service of his country in Company D, Sixth Pennsylvania Cavalry, and served until the close of the war. He and wife are consistent members of the Christian Church, and are highly respected by all who know them.

SAMUEL WEBSTER, a successful farmer and stock dealer, Rutan, Penn., was born in Jefferson Township, this county, November 23, 1833. He is a son of John and Elizabeth (Cowell) Webster. The former was a native of New Jersey, and the latter of Greene County, Penn., where they were married and remained until about the year 1868, at which time they moved to Iowa, where Mr. Webster departed this life, November 9, 1871. His widow then returned to Greene County, and died May 11, 1874. They were the parents of twelve children, eleven of whom are living. In September, 1856, Samuel Webster married Lucinda Goodwin, a native of Center Township, and daughter of John Goodwin, now deceased By this marriage Mr. Webster is the father of two children, one living, Mary E., wife of Andrew Johnson, and John, deceased Mrs. Webster departed this life in 1860. Mr. Webster was afterwards married, September 29, 1863, to Nancy Higinbotham, who was born in West Virginia, October 7, 1834. Her parents were Thomas and Lucretia Higinbotham, who departed this life in West Virginia. Mr. and Mrs. Webster are the parents of eight children—Lucinda J., wife of Daniel W. Jacobs; William W., Anna M., Samuel H., Bertha B, Maggie A., John I. and Adolphus S Having been reared on a farm, Mr. Webster has devoted his whole attention to farming and stock-dealing, and owns about 425 acres of land in Greene County, besides hotel property at Ryerson's Station, Penn. He is one of the enterprising and industrious business men of Center Township. Mr. and Mrs Webster are leading members in the Baptist Church.

BENJAMIN L. WOODRUFF, physician, Holbrook, Penn, was born in Washington County, Penn., August 3, 1822, and is a son of Jesse and Rebecca (Wilson) Woodruff. His father was born in Elizabeth, N. J., June 15, 1784. His mother was born August 27, 1788, in Washington County, Penn., where they made their home for a number of years. Jesse Woodruff departed this life March 3, 1862, and his wife April 8, 1870 The Doctor was united in marriage the first time March 31, 1847, with Martha, daughter of Samuel Barnett. Mrs Woodruff was a native of Washington County, Penn. By this marriage Dr Woodruff is the father of three children—William B., Emily, and Dr Samuel W. (deceased). Mrs Woodruff departed this life January 25, 1854 The Doctor was afterwards united in marriage, September 13, 1855, with Acinda Lough, who was born in West Virginia, April 10, 1836. Her parents, John and Sarah (Basnett) Lough, were natives of West Virginia, and remained there until their death. By his second marriage Dr. Woodruff is the father of seven children, six living—Newton C (late editor Waynesburg *Messenger*), Dora, Lillie, Bessie, Acinda, Benjamin L, and Flora (deceased). Dr. Woodruff began reading medicine about 1844, with Dr. W. G. Barnett, and graduated in 1848. He first engaged in the practice of his profession in Rogersville, Penn., and from there went to West Virginia and remained until 1861 He then moved to his present location, and has been in active practice ever since. He owns 420 acres of land where he and family reside. He and wife are members of the Christian Church

E W. WOOD, farmer, Oak Forest, Penn, is among the representative farmers and wool dealers of Greene County. He was born in Franklin Township, October 28, 1837 His parents were John D. and Nancy (Crichfield) Wood, also natives of this county, where they were married and remained until their death Mr Wood departed this life September 26, 1876, and his wife October 12, 1849 They had a family of seven children, of whom five are now living E. W. Wood was united in marriage, October 17, 1867, with Mary J Patterson, who was born in Whiteley Township, this county, September 11, 1844. She was a daughter of William and Rhoda Patterson, also natives of Greene County, and residents therein through life. To Mr. and Mrs Wood were born five children, of whom four are living, viz: C. Endsley, Norman, Edward, Mary, and Charles B. (deceased). Mr. Wood is a tanner by trade, in which he engaged until twenty-five years of age He then enlisted in Company K, Fifteenth Pennsylvania Cavalry, and served his country three years. He is a member of McCullough Post, No 367, G. A. R. When the war was over he engaged in the wool and stock business, and also farmed extensively. He is the owner of 160 acres of land where he and family live. Mr. Wood is a member of the M E. Church, of which his deceased wife was also a devoted member. She departed this life January 30, 1881, and by her death the family was bereft of a kind and affectionate wife and mother.

CARMICHAELS BOROUGH AND CUMBERLAND TOWNSHIP.

WILLIAM A. AILES, farmer and stock-grower, P. O. Carmichaels, was born in Washington County, December 25, 1835. He is a son of James and Elizabeth (Nixon) Ailes, who were also natives of Washington County, Penn., and were of English and Irish descent. His grandfather was Amos Ailes, also a native of Washington County. William is the youngest of a family of seven children. He has remained on the farm with his parents, where he received his education, and wisely chose farming as his business. His farm consists of 300 acres of land, well stocked and improved. Mr. Ailes was united in marriage, March 1, 1858, with Miss Lucinda, daughter of Thomas and Dorcas (Bell) Patterson. Mrs. Ailes' parents were of Irish descent. Mr. and Mrs. Ailes' only child, Mary Bell, was born in 1880, and died in 1886. In politics Mr. Ailes is a Republican; in religion they are both Cumberland Presbyterians

WILLIAM ARMSTRONG, deceased, who was a farmer and stock-grower, was a son of Abraham and Ruth (Conwell) Armstrong, and was born in Greene County in October, 1805. His parents were natives of Pennsylvania, and of English descent. His father was a farmer by occupation, and among the early settlers of the county. William was the oldest of a large family, and was reared on the farm in Cumberland Township, where he attended the subscription schools. He was united in marriage with Miss Mary Williams, of English descent. She was born in 1807. They were the parents of nine children—Maggie, wife of Archibald Grooms; George W., a farmer; Emma, wife of William M. Murdock; Elizabeth, wife of Josiah L. Minor; Sarah, wife of Oliver Griffeth; Alice, wife of James K. Gregg; Cinthy, wife of Richard Gwynn; Lyda, wife of N. H. Biddle, and James, a farmer. Mr. Armstrong made farming the business of his life, met with great success, and at the time of his death was the owner of a well-improved farm in Cumberland Township, where he died in 1849. In politics he was a Democrat; in religion a Cumberland Presbyterian, of which church his widow is also a faithful member.

ALFRED T. ARMSTRONG, deceased, who was a farmer and stock-grower, was born in Greene County, Penn., February 1, 1807. He was a son of William and Elizabeth (Russell) Armstrong. His mother's parents were of Scotch-Irish origin. Alfred was the oldest in a family of seven children; he was reared in this county and attended the subscription schools. He engaged in farming as a business, and met with more than ordinary success He was united in marriage, February 22, 1837, with Miss Helen M , daughter of Jeremiah and Anna (Alexander) Davidson Mrs. Armstrong's father was a native of this county, and her mother of Mercer County, Penn. They were of English descent Mr and Mrs. Armstrong had a family of ten children, of whom six are living—Russell, Barclay, Elizabeth, wife of Jesse Benner; John, Neri, and Maggie, wife of William Elliott Mr Armstrong was a Democrat, and a devoted Presbyterian, of which church his widow is also a zealous member. He died in 1878.

JOSEPH H. ARMSTRONG, deceased, was a farmer and stock-grower. He was born in Cumberland Township, Greene County, Penn , July 25, 1819, and died July 4, 1887, in his sixty-seventh year His father, William Armstrong, also his grandfather were among the earliest Scotch-Irish settlers of this county. They were all farmers. Joseph was the sixth in the family, and was reared on the farm where he died. His education was obtained in the township and the old Greene Academy at Carmichaels. He was industrious, frugal and a good financier, owning at the time of his death 225 acres of well improved land. He was united in marriage November 23, 1843, with Mary A , daughter of James and Mary (McClelland) Flenniken. Her ancestors were also farmers, and among the earliest settlers of the county They were of Scotch-Irish descent Mr and Mrs Armstrong were the parents of three children—Lizzie, wife of Daniel Thompson, of Uniontown, Penn.; Mary Louisa, wife of Robert Denham, and William W., who is a farmer and has charge of the home place In politics Mr Armstrong was a Democrat

NERI ARMSTRONG, merchant, Carmichaels, Penn , was born in Cumberland Township, December 27, 1855 He is a son of Alfred and Helen M. (Davidson) Armstrong, natives of Fayette and Greene counties respectively, and of Irish descent Mr. Armstrong's father was a farmer, and reared a family of ten children, of whom Neri is the ninth He received a common-school education, remaining on the farm with his parents until 1884, when he went to Carmichaels to engage in business for himself. He there opened a grocery and drug store which he still retains He is a man of good business qualifications, industrious, prompt and obliging, has a great many friends and a fair patronage. In 1876 Mr. Armstrong married Frances, daughter of I. L. Craft Mrs. Armstrong is a native of Greene County, and of German descent. They have two children— Myrtle and Alfred. Mr Armstrong is a Democrat and a member of the town council. He and Mrs Armstrong are prominent members of the Presbyterian Church.

J. K. BAILEY, farmer and stock-grower, was born in Cumberland Township, Greene County, Penn., August 30, 1814. He is a son of William and Zillah (Johnson) Bailey, the oldest in their family of seven children. His parents were natives of Pennsylvania, were members of the Society of Friends, and of English origin. His father was twice married, his first wife being Miss Sarah Miers. By this marriage he was the father of one child, a daughter, who is now the wife of Miller Haines, and resides in Columbiana County, Ohio. J. K. Bailey's sisters and brothers were: Amanda, wife of James Murdock; Rev. E. E, now a missionary to the Indians; Ruth Ann, wife of Samuel Rea; William, Zillah, the widow of R. Richardson, and L M. (deceased). Mr. Bailey was reared in Cumberland Township, and has made farming his business, in which he has met with great success. In 1835 he was married to Miss Delilah, daughter of John and Phœbe (Hibbs) Craft, who were natives of Pennsylvania, and of English ancestry. Mrs. Bailey was born in Cumberland Township, August 10, 1812. Her mother was a member of the Society of Friends. Mr. and Mrs. Bailey's children are —Zillah, wife of N. H Biddle; John Milton; Phœbe, wife of R. S. Long; W. Calvin; Clarinda, wife of Joseph Hawkins, Lydia B., wife of Corbly Fordyce; Almira is the wife of John Rinehart, and J. K. Jr. The family are all members of the Cumberland Presbyterian Church, in which Mr. Bailey has served for many years as elder and Sabbath-school superintendent. In politics Mr. Bailey is a Republican, and has served for twenty-five years as justice of the peace, in which office both his father and grandfather preceded him.

REV. E E. BAILEY, missionary, was born in Greene County, Penn., August 6, 1817, a son of William and Zillah (Johnson) Bailey, also natives of this State His parents were of Quaker origin and of English ancestry. His father came to Greene County when he was about nine years old with his parents, Eli and Ruth Bailey, from Chester County, Penn.; he died at the advanced age of eighty-two years. He was twice married, and the Rev. E. E. is a child of his second wife, and grew up on the farm with his parents, receiving his early education in a log cabin school-house, afterwards attended school at Greene Academy and at Waynesburg, Penn. At the age of sixteen he joined the Cumberland Presbyterian Church in Greene County. He was licensed to preach and ordained by the Union Presbytery of the Cumberland Presbyterian Church. He labored some in West Virginia, six miles west of Morgantown, but mostly in Fayette County, Penn., where he was engaged in the ministry for a term of years. Having had a desire for missionary work he then went West, where he engaged in missionary work among the Indians, and met with good success. In 1887 he was sent to his present position among the Cherokee Indians by the board of missions of the Cumberland Presbyterian Church. In 1839 Mr. Bailey was united in marriage with Miss Mary, daughter of John and Mat-garet (Dowlin) Rea. Mrs. Bailey is of Irish descent. They have five children—Harvey M., John F., Hannah J., Margaret E and William R. Mr. Bailey is a Prohibitionist.

JOSEPH TAYLOR BAILEY, farmer and stock-grower, Carmichaels, Penn., was born in Dunkard Township, Greene County, June 10, 1820, and is a son of Joseph and Hannah (Johnson) Bailey, natives of Pennsylvania. His father, who was a farmer and miller, came when a young man to this county, where he was married and reared a family of six children Of these Joseph Taylor is the youngest, and was reared in Greene and Fayette counties. Early in life he learned the miller's trade with his father, and followed it for forty years He erected and operated a grist-mill for nearly twenty-eight years He is a successful farmer and at the present time the owner 320 acres of valuable land in Cumberland Township. He was married in Fayette County, Penn., November 16, 1854, to Miss Martha Jane, daughter of Francis and Martha (Morehouse) Lee Mrs Bailey is of English descent. Her father was a blacksmith and farmer. Mr. and Mrs. Bailey have two children—Eli and Frances In politics Mr. Bailey has ever been a strong Democrat He and his wife are prominent members of the M. E Church.

ELLIS B BAILEY, farmer and stock-grower, was born in Greene County, Penn., November 21, 1824, and is a son of Eli and Peria (Gregg) Bailey. His parents were natives of Chester County, Penn., were members of the Society of Friends, and of English descent His father was a farmer. Mr Bailey's ancestors were among the earliest settlers in Greene County, and often had to flee to the forts for protection His father died in 1854, in Fayette County, where he had resided since 1837. His family consisted of ten children, eight of whom grew to maturity. Of these Ellis B. was the sixth. He was reared in Fayette County, attended Madison College and had entered the senior year, when he left school and commenced farming and stock-growing. He has made his own way in the world, and is among the wealthiest men of Greene County, owning over 1,000 acres of well improved land. He is a man possessed of more than ordinary energy, his success in life having been due largely to his strong determination to succeed, coupled with a willing disposition to work. His business life has not, however, all been sunshine. He lost $23,000 by the failure of the Exchange Bank of Waynesburg, and $2,000 by the destruction of his wool in a big fire at Boston But every reverse in business seemed only to make him more determined, and to add new strength to his ambition. He has devoted his time to farming, stock-dealing and buying land, and he has dealt considerably in wool He was never given much to speculating; but gave his business close attention and careful oversight, and has succeeded in accumulating a handsome fortune. He was married in Fayette County, Penn., March 7, 1850, to Harriet, daughter of John and Sarah (Barton) Gaddis. Her parents were Quakers, and of English descent. Mr. and Mrs Bailey have six sons and two daughters—William H., John E., Joseph E., George E, Eli F., Richard L., Sarah F., wife of Thomas H. Hawkins, and Anna R., wife of George F. Luse. The two daughters and three sons are married; all are intelligent business men and good citizens. In politics Mr. Bailey has been a Whig and a Republican. He has served nine years as school director in Cumberland Township All the family are members of the Presbyterian Church, in which Mr. Bailey has been elder and superintendent of the Sabbath-school.

J. E BAILEY, farmer and stock-grower, was born in Cumberland Township, Greene County, May 22, 1858. He is a son of Ellis B. Bailey, whose biography appears in this volume. He is the fourth in a family of eight children. He received a common-school education, and also attended Greene Academy at Carmichaels, Pennsylvania. Mr. Bailey married Miss Ella, daughter of J. M. and Charlotte (Rinehart) Morris. They have one child, Earl, an interseting little fellow of four years. Mrs. Bailey's father, Morris Morris, is a prominent farmer and stock-grower of Greene Township, and one of its most influential citizens. He is an ardent Democrat and has taken an active part in the politics of the county. Mr. Bailey is a representative young man of his township, is a Republican in politics, and a member of the Presbyterian Church.

GEORGE E. BAILEY, farmer and stock-grower, son of Ellis B. and Harriet (Gaddis) Bailey, was born in Cumberland Township, Greene County, Penn, December 8, 1860. His father is a prominent farmer, and resides in this township. George E is the fifth in a family of eight children. After attending the district school, he entered Greene Academy at Carmichaels, and subsequently attended Monongahela College at Jefferson, Pennsylvania He is an industrious, energetic young man, and has made farming and the raising of fine stock a decided success. He spent the summer of 1883 in the South and West, as the general agent of a large book publishing establishment of Philadelphia. In politics Mr Bailey is a Republican; and he is a zealous, active member of the Presbyterian Church

W. H. BARCLAY, farmer and stock-grower, Khedive, Penn, was born March 6, 1836, where he now resides on a farm of one hundred and seventy-eight acres. He is a son of Hugh and Phœbe (Craft) Barclay, the oldest of their five children. His grandfather, Hon. Hugh Barclay, was of Scotch-Irish descent. He was a representative of the Pennsylvania State Legislature, and during his term introduced the bill establishing the Greene Academy at Carmichaels, Penn. W. H. Barclay's father was a farmer all his life. His family consisted of five children, all of whom are married. Mr. Barclay was reared on the farm, received his education in Greene Academy, and has made farming the business of his life. In 1856 he was married to Sarah E , daughter of John P. Minor. She died in 1862. In 1866 Mr. Barclay was again united in marriage with Martha J., daughter of Henry and Mary (McCann) Arford Mr and Mrs. Barclay are the parents of seven children—Sarah Ellen, George P , W. H , Myrtle V., Phœbe E., Norval L and Harry S. Mr. Barclay is a Republican, and he and his wife are members of the Cumberland Presbyterian Church, in which he is a trustee.

G. A BARCLAY, merchant-miller, was born in Cumberland Township, this county, February 25, 1850 He is a son of Hugh and Phœbe (Craft) Barclay, and grandson of Hon Hugh Barclay. His father and grandfather were prominent among the early farmers of the county. Mr Barclay is the youngest of a family of six children. He was reared on the farm, receiving his education in the common school and in Waynesburg College. Early in life he learned the miller's trade and operated a mill for a period of four years. In 1882 he engaged in the same business at Carmichaels where he has met with good success. In 1870 Mr. Barclay was united in marriage with Rhoda, daughter of Samuel Kendall, deceased. Mrs Barclay is a native of this county. Her father was a Baptist minister. To Mr. and Mrs. Barclay have been born six children—Ida. L , Stephen H , John F , Ettie, Gertrude and Clarence. Their mother is a devoted member of the Baptist Church Mr. Barclay is a Republican in politics. He is a school director and member of the town council of Carmichaels Borough.

JAMES BARNS, the subject of this sketch, was born June 24, 1790, and died March 12, 1883. He was the youngest son of Thomas and Sarah Barns, who were among the pioneer settlers of West Virginia. They settled in the woods near where the thriving town of Fairmont now stands. His parents were among the first Methodists in West Virginia, his father being a class leader many years, and his father's house a preaching place for a long time. At the age of fifteen, Mr Barns left his home to learn the trade of a millwright, and served an apprenticeship of five years. In 1811 he had an attack of fever, the only sickness that ever caused him to be in bed one day, during a period of nearly ninety-three years. He was badly injured in 1870, by the running away of a team of horses, from the effect of which he was confined to his room for six weeks. On December 10, 1812, he was united in marriage with Miss Rhoda Davidson, of Fayette County, Penn.—a worthy companion of a worthy man Their union was blessed with nine children, five of whom were living, also present when he died. This worthy couple were converted at a camp-meeting held in 1819, near Browns-ville, Penn., and their habitation became emphatically a house of prayer as long as they lived. In 1824 he became dissatisfied with the government of the Methodist Episcopal Church, of which he and his companion were devoted members. He took a deep interest in the controversy that agitated the church, and culminated in the organization of the Methodist Protestant Church, and identified himself with the new organization in 1830. He was elected as a lay representative from the Pittsburgh Annual Conference to the first General Conference of the Methodist Protestant Church, which held its session in Georgetown, D C, in May, 1834. He was also a member of the General Conference of 1838, which held its session in Pittsburgh, Penn. In February, 1868, God took his beloved companion from him. Her loss was painfully felt by him and his children, though assured of her future and eternal happiness in heaven. On March 1, 1870, he married Mrs. Mary Lantz, with whom he lived in the enjoyment of great domestic happiness until February 12, 1880—the date of her death. Two years later, he sold his farm and the old homestead, in which he had lived sixty-seven years, to his son-in-law, Isaac B. Patterson, who married his youngest daughter, Mary Ellen. This was very agreeable to all his children, as it keeps in possession of the family the dear old homestead where they were born and raised. Mr. Barns had a good constitution, and he took good care of it. His habits were exemplary; he was strictly temperate and regular in his manner of life. He always cultivated a cheerful disposition; lived in communion and fellowship with God; was always usefully and honorably employed, and to these things owed his long life, at the close of which he makes this note: " Have had great enjoyment all through life, and also health. Have not laid in bed one day from sickness since 1811 " Thus after a sojourn longer than that usually allotted to man, James Barns peacefully passed away; the last of as good a family as Virginia ever produced, consisting of four brothers—William Barns, M. D.; John S Barns, Esq.; Thomas Barns and James Barns. There were three sisters— Sarah Willie, Phœbe Shinn and Mary A. Thrapp. These all lived and died in the faith, and left behind them families that revere their memories and imitate their virtues. " Children of parents passed into the skies."

ISAAC T. BIDDLE, deceased, who was a farmer and stockgrower, was born in New Jersey, in the year 1799. He was a son of Timothy and Mary (Taylor) Biddle, natives of New Jersey and of English and German origin. His father, who was a shoemaker in early life, came to Washington County, Penn., in 1802, and carried on farming for twenty-eight years. In 1840 I. T. Biddle came to Greene County and bought a farm in Cumberland Township, and one year later his father, Timothy Biddle, came to the same farm. I. T. took charge of the farm and continued his father's business of farming and stock-growing, devoting his time principally to the raising of fine sheep. · He succeeded in accumulating a handsome fortune, but in later years met with serious reverses by the failure of three banks in which he lost about $40,000.   This proved a serious disarrangement in his financial affairs, but he was a good business man and died in fair circumstances after reaching a good old age. His widow, whom he married in Washington County, still survives him. Her maiden name was Jane Kerney, daughter of William and Elizabeth (Montgomery) Kerney. Mrs. Biddle was born in Washington County, September 16, 1804, and is of Irish lineage.   Mr and Mrs Biddle had a family of eleven children, Seven now living—Eliza, wife of Edward Carson; Mary, wife of Lewis Jennings; Morgan, who married Eunice Patterson; Nathan H , married Zillah Bailey and lives on the old homestead; John, married Mary Barclay, Amanda, wife of Dis South; and Edith F , wife of Walter Richey.   Mr. and Mrs Biddle have been faithful members of the Cumberland Presby-terian Church, in which he served as elder for many years   Mrs Biddle has property in Carmichaels, where she still resides, an active and remarkably well preserved woman for her age, and loved and respected by all who know her.

N. H. BIDDLE, farmer and stock-dealer, P. O. Carmichaels, was born in Washington County, Penn , August 25, 1829.   His father was Isaac T. Biddle, now deceased. His mother's maiden name was Jane Kerney; she was born in 1804 and is still living. Harvey came with his parents from Washington County to Cumberland Township in 1840, and has made it his home till the present time   He is the fourth in a family of eleven children, seven of whom are living.   He was reared on a farm and has been engaged in farm-·ing and stock-dealing all his life, owning at present over seven hundred acres of valuable land in Greene County.   Mr. Biddle was united in marriage, December 25, 1856, with Zillah, daughter of J. K. Bailey.   Their family consists of four sons and two daughters—Newton M , Flora, wife of Thomas Patterson; William C , Richard L , Jesse T and Virtue C· Mr. and Mrs. Biddle are zealous members of the Cumberland Presbyterian Church at Carmichaels, Penn., in which he is one of the elders   Mr. Biddle takes an active interest in the educational affairs of the county, served as school director for twelve years, and has been a member of the board of trustees of Waynesburg College for a number of years and is still a member

SAMUEL BUNTING —Among the representative men of Cumberland Township we mention Samuel Bunting, a· farmer and stock-grower, who was born in Fayette County, Penn., April 28, 1836. He is a son of Samuel and Nancy (Butler) Bunting, natives of Pennsylvania, and of German and English origin   Mr. Bunting's father, who has made milling the business of his life, has now reached the advanced age of eighty-four years. Samuel was the fourth in his family of eleven children, and was brought up in Fayette and Greene counties, having lived in the latter since he was eight years old. Early in life he learned the miller's trade with his father, continued in the business until 1885, and has since been engaged in farming where he now resides near Carmichaels, Penn. He was united in marriage February 22, 1859, with Agnes, oldest daughter of Samuel and Mary (Cree) Horner. Mrs. Bunting is of English descent. Her father was a wealthy miller, and also engaged somewhat extensively in farming. In politics Mr. Bunting is a Prohibitionist. He and his wife are zealous and active members of the Presbyterian Church, in which he is an elder, and is also serving as assistant superintendent of the Sabbath-school.

S. S. BAYARD, farmer and stock-grower, was born near Waynesburg, Penn., December 27, 1839, and is a son of Perry A. and Nancy (Sayers) Bayard. His parents were natives of Greene County, descendants of the early pioneers, and of French and English origin. Mr. Bayard's father was a farmer and mechanic; in early life he was a stone-mason in Whiteley Township. S. S. is the fifth in a family of seven children; he was reared in Greene County, attended the schools in Whiteley Township, and afterwards entered Waynesburg College. He is a farmer by occupation, and owns 200 acres of well improved land where he resides in Cumberland Township. He has about twenty acres of his farm in choice fruit trees. In 1866 he married Miss Jane, daughter of W. T. E. Webb, Esq., of Waynesburg. Her mother's maiden name was Mary Stull; she was of French origin and a native of Kentucky. Her father was born in Virginia and was of English descent. Mr. and Mrs. Bayard are the parents of four children, two of whom are living. In politics Mr. Bayard is a Republican. In 1862 he enlisted in Company K, Fifteenth Pennsylvania Volunteer Cavalry, and was Sergeant of the company. He was in several prominent engagements of the late war—among others the battles of Antietam and Stone River, and was discharged for disability in 1863. Both his grandfathers were in the Revolutionary war. Mr. and Mrs. Bayard are active members of the Cumberland Presbyterian Church, and both are prominent teachers in the Sabbath-school.

JEREMIAH CLOUD, retired miller and distiller, Carmichaels, Penn., was born in Cumberland Township, Greene County, September 3, 1797. He is a son of Joel and Susannah (Carrington) Cloud, being the oldest in a family of twelve children. His father was of English-German descent, a native of Chester County, Penn., and was both a farmer and a cooper. His mother was of Welsh origin. He received a common school education, and at an early age learned the hatter's trade, which he followed until he attained his majority. He was married by Rev. William Barley October 3, 1822, to Jane, daughter of John and Sarah (Wright) Morgan, who were of English descent. Three of his seven children are now living—Thomas, a farmer; Marion, a millwright; and Sarah Ellen, wife of Joseph Everly. At the age of twenty-one Mr. Cloud engaged with his father in the distillery business, in which he continued for a period of twenty years. By reason of the meagre facilities of that early day, the distilling art being then in its most primitive state, they could make but slow progress, one barrel a day being considered a big day's work. A grist-mill was erected by him in 1846, which for many years was a great convenience and benefit to the people of his neighborhood. He retired from the cares of an active business life at an advanced age. Mr. Cloud is the owner of 203 acres of valuable farming land in Cumberland Township. He is a self-made man, his success in life being due largely to his strong will and remarkable energy. He has been an enthusiastic Republican ever since the party was organized; and so steadfast was he in the support of Republican principles that he was never prevailed upon but once to vote for a Democrat. He was an active politician, but neither desired nor held an office. His thorough knowledge of politics, however, made him a very popular leader of his party. Mr. Cloud was reared a Quaker, and although he never joined any religious denomination, his sympathies were with the Society of Friends, of whose doctrines he has ever been an earnest advocate. Mrs. Cloud, deceased, was a zealous member of the Baptist Church.

CAPTAIN HIRAM H. CREE, farmer and stock-grower, was born May 21, 1819, where he now resides on the farm of 160 acres, which has been in the possession of the family since 1785. He is a son of Hamilton and Agnes (Hughes) Cree, natives of Pennsylvania, which has been the home of the Crees for many generations. The Captain's father was a farmer, who, in 1848, died at the age of seventy-eight, on the farm where Hiram H. now resides. His family consisted of ten children. Hiram, one of the youngest, was reared on the farm, and attended the common school in Cumberland Township. He engaged in farming until 1847, when he went to Cincinnati, Ohio, and was employed as salesman in a large wholesale dry-goods house. After five months spent in that business, he resumed his farming until 1862, when he went into the army, enlisting in Company A, One Hundred and Sixty-eighth Pennsylvania Infantry. When the company was organized he was unanimously elected its Captain, in which capacity he served most faithfully throughout his term. He was ever a gallant soldier, highly esteemed by all his company. In 1864 he married Miss Elizabeth, daughter of James S. Kerr, and they are the parents of two children—Ellen Agnes and Rose Allena. In politics the Captain is a Republican, in religion a Methodist, and his wife is a member of the Cumberland Presbyterian Church.

JOHN CRAGO, a retired farmer of Cumberland Township, was born February 15, 1814, and is a descendant of one of the pioneer families of Greene County. He is a son of John Crago. He owns 330 acres of well improved land, where his great-grandfather settled and was afterwards killed by the Indians. The Cragos all came of industrious and energetic ancestors, and are noted for their morality and patriotism; they were represented in the Revolutionary war. John Crago, of whom we now write, received his education in the subscription schools of his township, where he was married in 1840 to Eleanor, daughter of John and Mary Flenniken, both natives of Greene County, and of Irish and English descent. They have two children—Caroline, wife of M. L. McMeans; and William H., a farmer, who was born in Cumberland Township April 5, 1843. He grew up on the farm, attended the district school, and has made farming his chosen occupation. In 1862 Mr. Crago enlisted in a cavalry company, which was afterwards consolidated and became Company D, Twenty-second Pennsylvania Cavalry. He was discharged for disability March 22, 1864. Mr. Crago has been blind for a number of years; but is possessed of such a wonderful memory that he can go all over his farm and attend to almost any kind of work. He transacts his own business affairs, in which he has been greatly prospered, having at present a competence sufficient to keep him in comfort the rest of his days.

J. N. CRAGO, teacher and carriage manufacturer, Carmichaels, Penn., was born in Cumberland Township October 10, 1832. He is a son of Thomas and Cassandra Crago. His ancestors, who were of English descent, were among the early pioneers of this county. His father, who died in 1884, spent his life in farming. Mr. Crago is the oldest of five children, all of whom were born and reared in Cumberland township. He attended the common schools and Greene Academy. He learned the cabinet-maker's trade, serving the regular apprenticeship. Early in life he began to teach school, and has been identified with the teachers of Greene County for thirty years. About the close of the war he began the manufacture of carriages at Carmichaels, and has devoted much of the time since to that business, in which he has made a reputation for good style and fine workmanship. In 1861 he married Permelia, daughter of William Spencer. Mrs. Crago is of English descent. They have a family of five children—Richard, Thomas, Samuel, Bertie and Mary. Mr. and Mrs. Crago are zealous members of the Carmichaels Cumberland Presbyterian Church. Mr. Crago is trustee of the church, and served for many years as superintendent of the Sabbath-school. He is a Republican and is a member of the I. O. O. F.

T. J. CRAGO, surveyor and school teacher, was born near Carmichaels, this county, July 16, 1843. His ancestors were among the pioneer farmers of the county. His parents, Thomas and Cassandra (Hughes) Crago, were of Irish and English descent. His father, who was a farmer and teacher, died in 1884. Mr. Crago is the fourth in a family of five children. He was reared in this county, attended Greene Academy, and became a teacher early in life: In 1862 he enlisted in Company C, in what was known as the Ringold Cavalry, which was consolidated with the Twenty-second Pennsylvania Cavalry in 1864, his company then being Company D. He was in many engagements—among others the battles of Winchester and Lynchburg. He was discharged May 28, 1865, at the close of the war, and has since taught school in Greene County, with the exception of two winters. He has also engaged to some extent in farming and surveying. Mr. Crago was united in marriage June 23, 1868, with Fannie J., daughter of James Wright, and is the father of three children—Mary, Albert and James. Mrs. Crago's parents were natives of Westmoreland County, and of Irish and Dutch descent. She died March 26, 1887, a faithful member of the Cumberland Presbyterian Church. Mr. Crago is also one of the leading members of that denomination. In politics he is a Republican; he is a member of the G. A. R., and commander of Post 265 of Cumberland Township.

THOMAS J. CRAGO, boat builder, was born in Cumberland Township, Greene County, Penn., June 30, 1847. He is a son of Joseph and Maria L. (Thomas) Crago, and grandson of Thomas and Priscilla (Thurman) Crago, who were of English descent. His grandfather was a farmer, and one of the early settlers of the county. He was the father of fifteen children, of whom Thomas Crago's father, Joseph, was the youngest. Joseph was born in Cumberland Township, August 7, 1811. He had two older brothers in the war of 1812, and his grandfather, Archibald Crago, was killed in this township by the Indians. Thomas, the oldest in a family of seven children, received a common-school education, and early in life engaged in the saw-mill business. He has also paid considerable attention to boat-building, having built a number of boats and started them out from his place of business. In addition to his saw-mill, he owns a nice little farm of thirty-eight acres, which he has secured through his own industry and a strong determination to succeed. In 1866 he was united in marriage with Mary E., daughter of John Ridge. They have eight children—Amos A., W. L., Lorenzo, Susannah, Louella, Bertha, Grover Cleveland and Tina M. In politics

Mr. Crago is a Democrat, and he and wife are members of the M. E. Church, in which he is a trustee.

GEORGE G. CROW, dentist, Carmichaels, Penn., was born in Fayette County, Penn., January 1, 1837. He is a son of Michael and Sarah (Gant) Crow, also natives of Fayette County, and of German origin. His father was a miller and farmer. Dr. Crow is the third in a family of thirteen children, five of whom reached maturity. He was reared on the farm and attended the common schools of Fayette County. Early in life he began the study of dentistry at Smithfield, Penn. In 1859 he came to Greene County and located at Carmichaels, where he has practiced ever since. He has made a thorough study of his profession, and bears the well-deserved reputation of being a first-class dentist. He has many friends in Greene County, and has had several students in dentistry who have since become successful practitioners. Dr. Crow was the first dentist to locate in Greene County May 1, 1861, he married Sarah, daughter of Daniel Darling. Mrs. Crow is of English descent. They have three children—G. W., Ella and Frank. At the breaking out of the Rebellion the Doctor promptly enlisted in the Eighth Pennsylvania Volunteers, and was afterwards a member of Company I, Thirty-seventh Regiment of U. S Infantry. This company was made up of men from Waynesburg and Carmichaels. Dr. Crow was Third Sergeant, and was in eleven general engagements, among others the battles of Malvern Hill, Harrison's Landing, second Bull Run, Antietam, Fredericksburg, the Wilderness and Spottsylvania. At the close of his term he returned to Carmichaels, and continued his practice in dentistry. He was instrumental in organizing the Dental Society of Greene County, and served five years as its president. The Doctor's family are members of the M. E. Church, in which he takes an active interest, being a trustee and superintendent of the Sabbath-school. In politics he is a Republican.

JERRY DAVIDSON, owner and proprietor of the Davidson Hotel, Carmichaels, Penn., was born in Cumberland Township, May 26, 1834 His parents, Alexander and Elizabeth (Gallaher) Davidson, were natives of Fayette County, Penn., and of Irish descent. His father was a farmer, and reared a family of eight children, of whom Jerry is the fifth. He was reared on the farm and received a common-school education. He followed farming as a business until 1875, when he engaged in the hotel business in Carmichaels. Mr. Davidson keeps an excellent table, and always has first-class horses and carriages for the accommodation of commercial travelers and the traveling public. Mr. Davidson has been twice married, first in 1856 to Miss Selanta Flenniken. Of their three children two are living—J. Calvin, a blacksmith, and Frank F., a tinner. They are both married and doing well in their business at Carmichaels, where they reside. Their mother died in 1872. Mr. Davidson's present wife's maiden name was Harriet Stone She was the widow of Ira J Hatfield They have two children—Henry Alexander and George S Mr. Davidson is a member of the I. O. O. F. In politics he is a Democrat, in religion a Presbyterian. Mrs. Davidson is a member of the Cumberland Presbyterian Church.

JOHN M. DOWLIN, farmer and stock-grower, was born in Jefferson Township, Greene County, Penn., October 16, 1855, and is a son of John and Elma (Bell) Dowlin. His father, who is a native of Cumberland Township, is also a farmer and stock-dealer, and resides in Jefferson Township. He is a Democrat, and was United States Revenue Collector for a number of years. John M Dowlin's grandfather was Paul Dowlin, a farmer of English descent. Mr. Dowlin is the only son in a family of six children. He was reared on the farm and attended the common school. He makes a business of farming and raising fine cattle and sheep, and superintends the home farm, consisting of 400 acres of most valuable land. He was married in Washington County, Penn., February 1, 1875, to Miss Rebecca J., daughter of Simon and Mary (Reynolds) Moredock Their children are—Dessie L., Albert L (deceased), John, Gertrude, Simon E. and Charles B. In politics Mr. Dowlin is a Democrat. He and Mrs. Dowlin are prominent members of the Cumberland Presbyterian Church

J. F. EICHER, who was born in Fayette County, Penn., February 23, 1820, is a foundryman and manufacturer and dealer in farming implements His parents, Abraham and Mary (Freeman) Eicher, were natives of Pennsylvania, and of Irish and English descent. His father's family consisted of twelve children, of whom Mr. Eicher was the ninth. When eighteen years of age he went to Pittsburgh to school. He learned the moulder's trade at Connellsville, Penn.. serving an apprenticeship of three years He then lived for seven years at Uniontown, Fayette County, and in 1850 came to Carmichaels, where he has since been engaged in his present business, and has met with unusual success. Mr Eicher was married at Connellsville, February 14, 1842, to Miss Rosa A , daughter of William Glendenning They are the parents of ten children, six of whom are living, viz: George, Emma, Wallace B., Robert, Sarepta and Anna M. Mr. Eicher has been an ardent Republican ever since the organization of the party. Mr. and Mrs. Eicher are faithful members of the M E. Church.

WILLIAM C. ELLIOTT, blacksmith, was born in Washington County, Penn , April 26, 1848, and is a son of Samuel and Susannah (Bane) Elliott. His mother was born in Virginia, and his father, who was a veterinary surgeon, was a native of Washington County, Penn. William C. is the seventh of a family of nine children. He was reared in his native county, where he owns a fine farm. He attended the graded schools, and early in life learned the blacksmith trade, which he has followed ever since. In 1882 he married Miss Margaret Armstrong, and they have one child—Anna Mary. Mr. Elliott came to Greene County in 1883. In politics he is a Democrat, and he is a member of the I. O. O. F. Mr. and Mrs. Elliott are leading members of the Presbyterian Church.

WILLIAM FLENNIKEN, farmer and stock grower, was born March 25, 1808, on the farm where he now resides in Cumberland Township. He is a son of John, and grandson of James Flenniken, who came from east of the mountains to Greene County, and engaged in farming in Cumberland Township. William's mother's maiden name was Mary McClelland; her parents were of the Scotch-Irish descent. His father was born in Cumberland Township in 1774, and died in 1855. Of his nine children William is the fourth, and was reared on the farm with his parents. He attended subscription school taught in one of the old log school houses of that day, and afterwards engaged in farming as his life work. He has met with unusual success, and now owns the fine farm of 140 acres where he resides. His wife was Miss Isabella, daughter of George C. and Isabella (McClelland) Seaton, natives of Virginia. Mr. and Mrs. Flenniken have four children—George C., a farmer in the West; Mary A., William F., who is at present on the home farm; and Laura J., wife of Oscar Hartley. In politics Mr. Flenniken is a Republican; his wife is a faithful member of the Presbyterian Church.

WILLIAM FLENNIKEN, meat merchant, who was born in Cumberland Township, July 30, 1838, is a son of John W. and Hettie (Wright) Flenniken. His mother was born in Bucks County, Penn., and his father was a native of Greene County. They were of Scotch-Irish descent. Mr. Flenniken's ancestors were among the early settlers of Pennsylvania, coming to Greene County as early as 1767. His father was a farmer, his family consisted of seven children—four sons and three daughters. William was fifth in the family, and was reared on the farm in Greene County, where he remained until 1886. He then came to Carmichaels, where he has since resided. In 1863 he married Eliza A., daughter of William and Achsah (Smith) Hartman. Mr. and Mrs. Flenniken are prominent members of the Presbyterian Church, in which Mr. Flenniken has served as trustee.

ALFRED FROST, deceased, was among the most prominent merchants of Greene County, and was born in Pennsylvania, April 5, 1802. He was a son of William and Mary (Murphey) Frost, natives of Washington County. Mr. Frost was reared on the farm and attended the common schools. He chose farming as his vocation; but after his father's death he was obliged to work as a hired farm hand until he accumulated enough to begin business for himself. By dint of industry and economy he succeeded in acquiring a very fair share of this world's goods. In early manhood he engaged in the mercantile business, and for years owned a store in Carmichaels   He was united in marriage, January 23, 1830, with Mary, daughter of Henry and Elizabeth (Stairs) Sharpnack, of German origin. Mr. and Mrs. Frost were the parents of three children—Mary E, now living in Carmichael's at the old home; William H. (deceased), late of Kansas City, Missouri, who married Caroline Fair, of Leavenworth City Kansas; Elizabeth, who is the wife of George D. D Mustard, and the mother of the following children—John, Mary S., Charles, William D., James A. and George D.   Mr and Mrs. Frost were prominent members of the Methodist Episcopal Church

GEORGE T. GREGG, farmer and stock grower, was born in Cumberland Township, Greene County, July 12, 1852   He is a son of Joseph and Rebecca (Minor) Gregg, natives of this county, where they were married in 1844.   Mr. Gregg's grandfather, Joseph Gregg, was born in Delaware, and was one of the early settlers of Greene County, Penn   He was a farmer and miller by trade.   Mrs. Gregg's ancestors were of English descent, and also among the early settlers of the county.   George T. Gregg's father, also of English descent, was born in Greene Township, and was a farmer and stock dealer until the time of his death.   George's grandfather, John P Minor, was a soldier in the war of 1812   Mr. Gregg is the third in a family of six children, three of whom are now living.   He was reared in this county, attending the common schools and Greene Academy at Carmichaels, Penn. He was united in marriage, September 30, 1870, to Miss Pratt, daughter of James and Milly (Mt. Joy) Pratt, who were natives of Fayette County, Penn , and of English descent.   Mr. and Mrs Gregg have four children—Flora B., Joseph Charles, Myrta Rebecca and Orpha Ethel.   Their mother is a faithful member of the Baptist Church.   In politics Mr. Gregg is a Republican.   Financially, he has been very successful, having 300 acres of land under his present control, and owing a fine farm of 114 acres where he now resides.

GENEALOGY OF THE MINOR FAMILY IN AMERICA.— The following genealogical record will be of interest to all the Minor family: The first member of the family who came to America was Thomas Minor, who was born in England in 1608, and came to this country in 1630   In 1634, he married Frances Palmer Clement, son of Thomas and Frances Minor, married Frances Wiley in 1662. Their son William, who represents the third generation of the Minor family in America, married Anna Lyle in 1691.   Stephen, son of William and Anna Minor, who married Ohalia Updike, was born in 1705, and was the eight son of the fourth generation.   Samuel Minor was the fourth son in the fifth generation.   He was married, and his oldest son was Abia Minor. Abia was the father of John P. Minor, who married Huldah McClelland. Rebecca is the fourth of nine children and is the fourth of the eight generation. She is the wife of Joseph Gregg, of Greene County, Pennsylvania, who is the father of the subject of the preceeding sketch.

WILLIAM GROOMS, retired blacksmith, was born in Carmichaels, Penn., August 14, 1828. His parents were Benjamin and Isabella (Kerr) Grooms, natives of Maryland and Pennsylvania respectively, and of English and Scotch descent His grandfather, William Grooms, was one of the early settlers of Greene County. His father was a farmer and carpenter, and had a family of six children, of whom William is the second of the three living. He was reared in Carmichaels, attended the common schools and Greene Academy, and in early life learned the blacksmith trade, in which he engaged for a number of years. In 1846 Mr. Grooms married Malinda, daughter of Moses and Susan (Vankirk) McIlvaine. They have six children—Susan, wife of James Lincoln; Elizabeth, wife of George Demain; Arabella, wife of Levi Taylor; William and B. F., blacksmiths; and Eliza Jane, a teacher. In politics Mr. Grooms is a Republican. In 1861 he enlisted in Company I, Eight Pennsylvania Volunteers and served three years He re-enlisted in Company B, Fifty-seventh Volunteer Infantry and served till the close of the war. He has been road commissioner, and was postmaster at Carmichaels for a number of years. Mr. and Mrs. Grooms are members of the Methodist Episcopal Church, and he is a member of the G. A. R. Post.

JOSIAH GWYNN, farmer and stock-grower, who was born near where he resides, October 20, 1812, is a son of Joseph and Martha (Dowlin) Gwynn. His grandparents on the maternal side were natives of Montgomery County, Penn , and were of Welsh origin Mr Gwynn's grandfather, Joseph Gwynn, came from London, England, to what is now Greene County, and was among the early settlers in this part of Pennsylvania. His grandfather Gwynn came to this county before the Revolutionary war, and settled on the farm which Josiah now occupies. This was then an Indian settlement— or rather, an Indian neighborhood, and he took what was then called " tomahawk claim." He left this country with the intention of returning to London, but got no farther than the Island of Cuba, and there he engaged in a sugar plantation, and on his return he found other parties had settled on two of his claims. He served as county commissioner in what is now Washington and Greene counties Josiah Gwynn's father farmed on the home place throughout his life. He was drafted in the war of 1812, and died in 1864, at the age of seventy-five. Josiah is the oldest of a family of eight children. He attended school on his own farm, in the old-fashioned log school-house, which he has since seen replaced by one of hewn logs, that by a frame building, and the frame ready to be superseded by a substantial brick. Mr. Gwynn has made farming the business of his life, and owns 200 acres of the original entry made by his grandfather. He was married March 28, 1841, to Lydia, daughter of George W. and Susannah (Myers) Phillips. Mrs. Gwynn was born in Chester County, Penn., in 1824. Her father was a farmer and butcher, of English descent. Mr. and Mrs. Gwynn have eight children, six living—Martha L., wife of Wilson Huston; Joseph C., George W., E. E., wife of Lacy Craft; John R. and J. F. All are members of the Cumberland Presbyterian Church, in which Mr. Gwynn is elder and superintendent of the Sabbath-school. He has always been a liberal high-minded gentleman, and highly respected in the community.

J. F. GWYNN, merchant, who was born in Cumberland Township, September 2, 1842, is a son of John Gwynn. His great-grandfather, Joseph Gwynn, Sr., came from London, England, settled in Greene County, and served in the Revolutionary war. Mr. Gwynn's father was born December 25, 1818, on the farm taken up by Joseph Gwynn, Sr., when he first came to this county. He was married in the fall of 1840 to Elizabeth, daughter of Jesse and Mary (Wright) Rea, who were of English descent. J. F. Gwynn is the elder of two children. He received his education in Greene Academy and Waynesburg College. In 1862 he enlisted in Company F, Fifteenth Pennsylvania Cavalry, but was transferred to the U. S. Signal Corps, where he served till the close of the war. He was in many engagements, among others, Stone River, Chickamauga, Mission Ridge and around Atlanta, etc. At the close of the war he returned to his native town and engaged in the mercantile business in which he has met with success. Mr. Gwynn was united in marriage January 24, 1868, with Elizabeth, daughter of William Hartman. They have three children—William, John and Anna. Mr. Gwynn is a Republican. He has served as school director, is a member of the G. A. R., and is adjutant of Carmichaels Post 265. He and his wife are zealous members of the Cumberland Presbyterian Church.

WILLIAM HARTMAN, born in Jefferson, Greene County, Penn., February 14, 1817, is a son of Adam and Elizabeth (Stickels) Hartman. His parents were of German descent, his mother being a native of Pennsylvania and his father of Ohio. His father's family consisted of eight children, of whom William is the fifth. He attended the schools of Greene County and learned the cabinet-maker's trade, in connection with which he has devoted considerable time to contracting and building. He was united in marriage November 8, 1838, with Acsah, daughter of Daniel Smith. Their children are— Ann, wife of William F. Flenniken; and Elizabeth, wife of J. F.

Gwynn. Mr. Hartman is a Republican, and was elected justice of the peace in 1858. He has also been a member of the town council and burgess of Carmichaels. Mr. and Mrs. Hartman are members of the Cumberland Presbyterian Church, in which he has been superintendent of the Sabbath-school and served as elder for many years.

J. W HATHAWAY, deceased, who was a merchant in Carmichaels for many years, was born in Jefferson Township, this county, May 19, 1821, and was a son of Samuel and Elizabeth (Estel) Hathaway. His mother was born in New Jersey and his father in Pennsylvania, and they were of English and Dutch descent When Mr. Hathaway was only one year old his father died, and he was reared by his grandfather, Matthias Estel, who sent him to school and induced him to learn a trade. He chose the chair-maker's trade, served a regular apprenticeship, and worked at the business for a time at Newtown. There he began business as a clerk in a store at the age of sixteen. At nineteen years of age he went to Carmichaels as clerk. He was for many years junior member in the firm of Carson & Hathaway, merchants; afterwards buying his partner's interest he became sole owner of the large merchandising establishment there He was an energetic, careful and thrifty manager of business, always exercising the keenest tact in his ventures and investments, yet conducting the same with a motive of honesty and fair dealing toward all, bearing the respect of everybody. Years ago when Carmichaels was the business center of Greene County Mr. Hathaway—added to a continued large retail trade—did considerable business at wholesale. He also dealt quite extensively in stock and real estate, and at the time of his death was the owner of 550 acres of valuable land. He was united in marriage January 1, 1846, with Miss Ary, daughter of William and Keziah (Wiley) Anderson, who were of Scotch-Irish descent. Her father was a millwright, and she had two brothers in the war of 1812. To Mr. and Mrs. Hathaway a family of ten children were born, six of whom, together with Mrs. Hathaway, survive the deceased The children are— Charles, Samuel, William, Jacob and Lawrence, of Carmichaels; and Mrs. Mary McGinnis, of Lincoln, Ill. Mr. Hathaway was well known and was regarded as a man of great business ability, sound judgment and sterling integrity. He had been a member of the Cumberland Presbyterian Church for over forty-five years, and was a ruling elder in that church for thirty-two years. He was without question a true Christian.

JOSEPH HAMILTON, deceased, was a farmer and stock-grower and a successful business man He was a self-made man, and by reason of his industry, economy and business ability, succeeded in accumulating a goodly share of this world's possessions.

He died in 1871, leaving to his wife and children over 400 acres of valuable farming land near Carmichaels, Penn. Mr. Hamilton was born in the State of Pennsylvania in 1808, was a son of Joseph Hamilton, and was of Scotch-Irish origin. His father was a manufacturer of boots and shoes   Mr. Hamilton received a common school education; he came to Greene County in 1859 and settled in Cumberland Township   His wife, whom he married in Fayette County, Penn., was Miss Catharine Coursin. Of their eight children, seven are now living—William, Elizabeth, wife of Richard Moffett; Mary, Sarah, Catharine Noah and Nancy J. Mr. Hamilton was known throughout his life as a staunch Democrat and a strict adherent of the Presbyterian Church

I. R. JACKSON, retired carpenter and contractor, was born in Cumberland Township, Greene County, Penn., April 19, 1824. He is a son of Stephen and Hannah (Miller) Jackson, natives of this county   His grandfather, a pioneer farmer, was born in Maryland. Mr Jackson, whose father was a millwright and carpenter, was the third in a family of five children. He learned the carpenter trade, in which he engaged in Cumberland Township for a period of thirty-five years. He was united in marriage April 12, 1846, with Mary A., daughter of B. M. and Martha (Murdock) Horner. Mrs. Jackson's parents were among the early settlers of the county   Of the seven children born to Mr. and Mrs. Jackson, only one survives—Emma C. The deceased are· James J , Mary Ann, Louisa J , Alice L , Stephen T. and Margaret A., who was the wife of William Grooms and mother of two children, one of which, James A. Grooms, is still living. Mr. Jackson is a Democrat, and has served as burgess of Carmichaels Borough. He and his wife are devoted members of the Methodist Episcopal Church.

WILLIAM KERR, manufacturer of saddle-trees, was born in Washington County, Penn , September 12, 1803, and is a son of James and Elizabeth (Boke) Kerr, also natives of Washington County, and of Irish descent   His father was a blacksmith, and reared a family of eight children. William was the third and received a common school education. He learned the saddle-tree trade, and has made it the business of his life, most of which he has spent in Cumberland Township, where he was married in January, 1824 His wife was Elizabeth, daughter of James Curl   Mr and Mrs. Kerr are the parents of ten children, eight of whom are living. They are: Mary A., wife of Elias Flenniken, of Greensboro, Penn , Rachel, wife of James Flenniken; John C , of Carmichaels; Lettie J., wife of Thomas Lucas; Elizabeth M., wife of William H Sharpnack; Sarah E., wife of Thomas Nutt; Hiram A. and William W. Mrs. Kerr died August 29, 1874, a consistent member of the

Methodist Episcopal Church, to which Mr. Kerr also belongs, and has been steward and class-leader. In politics he is a Democrat.

JAMES KERR, farmer and stock-grower, Carmichaels, Penn., was born in Washington, Washington County, Penn., March 31, 1808, and is a son of Archibald and Mary (Huston) Kerr, who were of Irish and English descent. His mother was a native of Washington County, and departed this life in Greene County, Penn., in her eighty seventh year, and his father, a farmer and hotel-keeper, was born in Ireland and died in Virginia in his eighty-fourth year. He had a family of eight children, of whom James was the fourth, and was reared on the farm in Cumberland Township. He attended the common school and chose farming as a business, working by the day and month to get his start in life. He drove hogs from Greene County to Baltimore for twenty-five cents and two meals a day. He has ever practiced the most careful economy and strict integrity in all his dealings, and is now the owner of a valuable farm of 375 acres. Mr. Kerr was united in marriage August 29, 1833, with Miss Ellen, daughter of George and Betsey (Lowery) Davis. Mrs. Kerr was born in Greene County, April 1, 1813. Her parents were natives of Pennsylvania and of German descent. Mr. and Mrs. Kerr have eight children, five living—David, Elizabeth, wife of Captain H. H. Cree; Alexander, Huston and Archibald. The deceased are George, James and Willie. In politics Mr. Kerr is a Democrat. He has served as school director in the township. They are prominent members of the Presbyterian Church.

JOHN C. KERR, manufacturer of saddle-trees, was born in Carmichaels, Penn., December 28, 1832. He is a son of William and Elizabeth (Curl) Kerr, being the third in their family of eight children. He was reared in Greene County, and early in life learned his trade with his father, who still resides near Carmichaels, where John C. has worked for many years. In 1859 Mr. Kerr married Caroline, daughter of Amos Horner. They were the parents of two children—Mary Ellen, wife of John Bell, and Margaret, wife of John Mossburg. Their mother died in 1865. Mr. Kerr was a second time united in marriage, February 9, 1869, with Elizabeth, daughter of Henry and Elizabeth (Rice) Sharpnack. Her parents were of Welsh and English descent. Mr. and Mrs. Kerr have four children, all boys—William Henry, George S., Robert O. and Jesse F. Mr. and Mrs. Kerr are devoted members of the Cumberland Presbyterian Church. In politics Mr. Kerr is a Republican, and has been a member of the town council of Carmichaels, where he has resided for over twenty-five years.

ARCHIBALD KERR, of the firm of Kerr Brothers, furniture dealers and funeral directors, Carmichaels, Penn., was born in Cumberland Township, September 22, 1851. He is a son of James and

Eleanor (Davis) Kerr, natives of Greene County, and of Irish descent. His father is one of the prominent farmers of Cumberland Township. Archibald is the seventh in a family of eight children. He received a common-school education, and early in life learned the cabinet-maker's trade. He worked by the day and job for eight years in Virginia and Pennsylvania, and in 1876 engaged in his present business at Garard's Fort, Penn., where he remained for two years. He then came to Carmichaels, where he has always had the reputation of doing first-class work. In 1873 Mr. Kerr married Frances, daughter of James Clawson. Mrs. Kerr is of English descent. They have a family of five children—Charles Edward, Lida E., Jesse, Alexander and Harry. Mr. Kerr is a leading member of the M. E. Church, and his wife is a Cumberland Presbyterian. In politics Mr. Kerr is a Democrat. He is a member of the town council, and belongs to the I. O. O. F. Lodge at Carmichaels, Penn.

NORVAL LAIDLEY was born in Cumberland Township, this county, May 4, 1829. He is a son of T. H. and Sarah (Barclay) Laidley, being the oldest in their family of twelve children. He was reared in Carmichaels, receiving his education in the old Greene Academy. Early in life he learned the saddler's trade, serving an apprenticeship at Carmichaels, where he soon engaged in the business for himself and continued therein for twelve years. He afterwards started a general store in company with his younger brother, A. D. Laidley, to whom he sold his interest in 1876 and left him sole proprietor of their merchandising establishment.

J. B. LAIDLEY, physician and surgeon, Carmichaels, Penn.— Among the best known physicians in Greene County is the gentleman whose name heads this sketch. He is a son of Dr. Thomas H. and Sarah (Barclay) Laidley, and was born in Carmichaels, August 21, 1830. The Doctor's father was also a prominent physician, and practiced in Carmichaels and vicinity for over half a century. His grandfather, Thomas Laidley, was a soldier in the Revolutionary war, and his maternal grandfather, Hon. Hugh Barclay, was a member of the Pennsylvania State Legislature in 1804. The Doctor is the second in a family of twelve children, ten of whom are now living. He received his education at Greene Academy, and subsequently studied medicine at the medical department of the University of Wooster, at Cleveland, Ohio, where he graduated March 1, 1856. He then returned to Carmichaels, where he has practiced continuously except during a part of the years 1861–'62, when he served as Surgeon of the Eighty-fifth Regiment Pennsylvania Volunteers. In 1859 he was united in marriage with Mary E., daughter of William Galbraith, who was for many years a prominent physician of Jefferson, in this county, where Mrs. Laidley was born. They have three living children—William Galbraith, Edmund Wirt and John Collier.

Dr. and Mrs. Laidley are members of the M. E. Church, in which he has been an official member since he united with the church. He has been school director for thirty years, and has been known as a friend ef education. He is a member of the G. A. R., Post No 265, of Carmichaels, Penn.

HON. T. H. LAIDLEY was born in Carmichaels, Penn He is a son of Dr. T. H. Laidley, who was among the most prominent physicians of Greene County. Mr. Laidley was the seventh in a family of eleven children. He was reared in Carmichaels, attending the Greene Academy. He learned the trade of a tinner and followed it as an occupation for eight years He subsequently clerked on a boat on the Monongahela River for a period of eight years. He married Sarah W., daughter of John W. Flenniken. Her father was a descendant of the early pioneers of this county. Mr. Laidley is the father of three children—Hettie, Thomas II, Jr., and Albert. Mr. Laidley is a Democrat, and has taken considerable interest in the politics of his county. He served as county auditor for several terms. He also represented his county in the State Legislature two terms, at the close of which he engaged in the mercantile business. He is a Presbyterian, of which church his deceased wife was also a member. She died in 1885.

R. S. LONG, stock dealer, farmer and stock grower.—The subject of this sketch was born in Greene County, Penn, October 24, 1835. He is a son of Jerry and Lucretia (Stephens) Long, who were natives of this county and of English origin. His father was reared on a farm where he spent the early part of his life. He afterwards made a specialty of stock-growing, in which he dealt quite extensively in the West, and succeeded in accumulating a handsome fortune, being at the time of his death, in 1863, the owner of 1,300 acres of well-improved land in Greene County, and extensive stock interests in the West. He was married in his native county, and all of his six children were born in Cumberland Township. They are as follows: Milton, Elizabeth, wife of Corbly Garard; Mary, R. S, W. S., Sarah A., wife of James Stephens, and Nancy V., wife of Wallace Eicher. Richard was reared on the farm and attended the common school. In business he has very closely followed the example of his father, and has met with about the same success. At the age of twenty-two he went west and engaged in buying stock, of which he made heavy shipments from Iowa to Chicago. He deals principally in sheep and cattle, and of the latter owns at present 900 head, in company with others in the West. His home farm consists of 261 acres of land, well stocked and improved. He was married, December 4, 1861, to Miss Phœbe C., daughter of J. K. Bailey, and they are the parents of three children—J. C., D 'Annie Laurie and Lucretia V. Nellie. In politics Mr. Long is a Republican, and he and wife are members of the Cumberland Presbyterian Church, in which he is one of the leading officers.

MILTON LONG, farmer and stock-grower, P O. Khedive, was born in Cumberland Township, January 29, 1838.   He is a son of Jerry and Lucretia (Stephens) Long, also natives of this county   He comes of a long line of farmers, of whom his father was one of the most prominent, and also eminently successful as a cattle-dealer in the West.   Mr. Long is the third in a family of six children; he attended the common school of his district, remaining on the farm until 1861, when he enlisted in Company F, First Pennsylvania Cavalry and served his country three years.   He passed through the engagements of Gettysburg and Fredericksburg, and was also in the battle of the Wilderness.   When he came home from the army he went to Page County, Iowa, and engaged in buying and shipping stock to Chicago, Illinois   After remaining there for a period of eight years, he returned to Cumberland Township, where he has since been engaged in his present occupation, and owns 330 acres of well improved land. In 1872 he married Mary E., daughter of Robert McClelland, who died in 1859.   Her mother's maiden name was Elizabeth Weaver; she was of German and English descent.   Mr. and Mrs. Long have one child—Mabel   In politics Mr Long is a Republican, he is a member of the G A. R , and he and his wife are members of the Cumberland Presbyterian Church.

JAMES MURDOCK, retired tailor, was born in Cumberland Township, this county, August 3, 1811, and is a son of Charles and Ann (Campbell) Murdock   Mr. Murdock's grandfather was one of the earliest settlers of Greene County, coming here among the Indians.   His mother was born in Ireland.   His father, who was of Scotch origin, was born in Greene County, Penn, in 1789.   His family consisted of eight children—six sons and two daughters, of whom James was the oldest   He was united in marriage in 1838 with Amanda, daughter of William Bailey.   Mrs. Murdock was born in this county in 1816, and is of English descent   To Mr. and Mrs. Murdock were born six children—Zillah, Anna E , William M , Mary (deceased), Ellis B and Ellen   Mr Murdock is a Republican. He has been school director, was for two years burgess of Carmichaels, and served as justice of the peace for a period of ten years Both are faithful members of the Cumberland Presbyterian Church. They are among the oldest and most highly respected citizens of Carmichaels.

WILLIAM M. MURDOCK, merchant-tailor, was born in Carmichaels, August 28, 1844, and is a son of James and Amanda (Bailey) Murdock, natives of Greene County.   Mr. Murdock is the third of a family of six children.   He was reared in Carmichaels and learned the tailor's trade with his father.   His first work was for the

Government   In 1862, when eighteen years of age, he enlisted as a soldier in Company K, Fifteenth Pennsylvania Volunteer Cavalry, and served until 1865.   He was at the battle of Stone River and in several other engagements and skirmishes   At the close of the war he came home and worked at his trade with his father.   In 1870 he engaged with his brother in the merchant tailoring. business, in which they have continued quite successfully ever since.   In 1866 he married Emma, daughter of William and Mary (Williams) Armstrong.   They have four children—Augustus L., Mary, wife of F. Davidson; Louise and Lottie.   Mr. Murdock is a member of the G. A. R. Post; and both are leading members in the Cumberland Presbyterian Church.

SIMON MOREDOCK, retired farmer and stock-grower, born in Jefferson Township, Greene.County, Penn., is a son of George and Priscilla (Anderson) Moredock. His grandfather, James Anderson, was of Irish descent. Mr. Moredock's father, who was a farmer, had a family of twelve children, ten of whom grew to maturity. Simon is the fourth child, was reared in Jefferson Township, and received his education in the old stone school-house of the district. Early in life he engaged in the distillery business which he followed for ten years. He then bought a farm and has since devoted himself wholly to agricultural pursuits. In 1848 he was united in marriage with Mary J., daughter of John and Jane (Kincaid) Reynolds, who were of Welsh and Dutch descent. Mr. and Mrs. Moredock have six children—Sarah, wife of B. Sharpnack; George W , M. A., Rebecca J., Daniel and Minerva. Mr. Moredock is a Democrat; and both are members of the Cumberland Presbyterian Church, in which he has served as elder.

REV. JOHN McCLINTOCK, pastor of the New Providence Presbyterian Church, in Cumberland Township, Greene County, Penn., was born in Washington, Penn., November 10, 1808, and is a son of William and Mary (McGowan) McClintock. His mother was a native of Pennsylvania and of Scotch-Irish descent. His father was born in County Donegal, Ireland; but when quite a young man, came with his two brothers, to America and settled in Washington, Penn., where they spent the rest of their lives, all dying within nine months   Mr. McClintock is one of five children. He received his early education in the subscription school; then learned the weaver's trade, serving a regular apprenticeship of five years. When he reached his majority he entered Washington College, Penn., and graduated in the regular classical course with the class of 1836, Having chosen the ministry as his profession, he subsequently entered the Western Theological Seminary, at Allegheny, Penn., and was licensed to preach in April, 1837. He seized every opportunity of preparing himself for the high calling which he had chosen, and

33

accepted as his first work the cause of missions, the field being Smyrna,-in Asia.   In July, 1839, he came to Greene County and accepted his present charge, in which capacity he still continues, having outlived all but three members of his original congregation. By reason of his most earnest, efficient work, Rev. McClintock's is among the largest congregations in Greene County.   He has also been instrumental in doing great good outside of his own church, having baptized 261 persons and performed 207 marriage ceremonies. He was married, in Washington, Penn., April 17, 1834, to Miss Mary, daughter of James and Margaret (Hawkins) Orr.   Mrs. McClintock was also a native of Washington, Penn., born December 11, 1803, and of Scotch-Irish descent.   Her grandparents came from Ireland; her father was a magistrate for many years, and among the prominent men of Washington County, where he settled in 1800. Mrs. McClintock is a lady of great piety and motherly kindness, and is most highly respected by those who know her best.   Few have as many friends as this aged couple who have worked side by side in the vineyard of the Lord for more than fifty years.   Their union has been blessed with six children—Margaret E., Mary, John C., a minister; and Ann, living; and James and William, deceased.   Their family is highly respected, and they have a prosperous, happy home near Carmichaels, Penn., where they now reside.

REV. DR. JOHN McMILLAN was born at Fagg's Manor, Chester County, Penn., November 11, 1752.   His parents, William and Margaret (Rea) McMillan, emigrated to America in 1742. They were Scotch-Irish, and devout Presbyterians.   They had eighteen children. Their three sons who attained maturity were Thomas, William, and John, the youngest, whose name heads this sketch. It was his father's wish that John should be a minister of the gospel. He received a classical education at Princeton College, was first licensed to preach October 26, 1774, and was among the pioneer preachers of Washington and Greene counties. He was a strong man, and engaged in physical as well as mental labor.   Early in life he formed the habit of writing and committing all his sermons. He was always greatly interested in his work, and has given account of revival meetings in which he frequently labored through a whole night.   Soon after the Revolutionary war, about the year 1778, he removed with his family to Washington County, Penn., where he was the founder of Jefferson College, now known as Washington and Jefferson College, and was president of the institution at the time of his death.   He was married by the Rev. Mr. Carmichaels, August 6, 1777, to Miss Catharine, daughter of William Brown.   Seven children were born to them, viz: William, John, Samuel, Jane, Margaret, Mary and Catharine.   Jane, the oldest daughter, was twice married, her first husband being the Rev. Mr. Morehead.   She was

afterwards united in marriage with Samuel Harper, a merchant and
farmer, who was born and raised near Philadelphia. He spent most
of his business life in Greene County, Penn., and was one of its
most prominent citizens. He was an elder in the Presbyterian Church
for many years, and served one term as sheriff of the county. Samuel
Harper was twice married and had ten children, the youngest of
whom is H. Harper, now a prominent citizen of Carmichaels, Penn.
He was born in Cumberland Township, this county, September 29,
1819, was reared on the farm and attended school at Greene Academy,
but devoted himself principally to farming, and met with great success. In 1862 Mr Harper married Rebecca M., daughter of William and Rebecca (Norris) Johnson. Her parents were natives of
Chester County, Penn., and of English descent. They were members of the Society of Friends. Mr. Harper is Republican in politics. He and Mrs. Harper are prominent members of the M. E.
Church. Having retired from the more active duties of life, they
now reside in Carmichaels, where they have a neat, substantial residence. Mr. Harper's brother, John McMillan Harper, was born in
1812, in Greene County, where he grew to manhood He was educated at Greene Academy His vocation · was that of farming, for
which he seemed especially adapted, being a powerful man, six feet
and two inches in height, always strong and robust and in the enjoyment of excellent health. He was married in Jefferson Township,
this county, to Miss Isabella Hughes, and they had one child, Margaret Jane, who is the wife of E C. Stone, of Brownsville, Penn.
During the late war Mrs. Stone's father, John Harper, raised a company of cavalry, of which he was soon elected Major, but by some
means was defrauded out of his command. While at home, buying
horses for the regiment, at which time he succeeded in getting 600,
another was installed Major in his place. He then resigned and returned home, spending the remainder of his life on the farm, where
he died in 1878, honored and respected by all who knew him.

PROF. W. M. NICKESON, principal of the Carmichaels High
School, was born in Washington, Washington County, Penn., August
28, 1839. His parents, Solomon and Phœbe (Watson) Nickeson,
were also natives of Washington County, and of Scotch and German
origin His father, who is a farmer and stock-grower, worked at the
cooper's trade in early life. The Professor is a member of a family
of thirteen children—five girls and eight boys He was with his
parents on the farm until eighteen years of age, and attended the
public schools of Washington County. He subsequently entered
Waynesburg College, where he completed the regular course of
study and afterwards received the degree of Master of Arts. After
teaching in Greene and Washington counties for ten years, he returned to Washington, studied law, and was admitted to practice in

1867. He resumed his teaching, however, and had been engaged therein for twenty-four years, when he was elected superintendent of schools in Greene County in 1881, and served a term of three years. Since then he has been principal of the schools of Carmichaels, making in all thirty-one years that he has been connected with the schools of this and Washington counties. In 1866 Mr. Nickeson married Anna S., daughter of William Gass, who is of Irish and German descent, and a resident of Clarksville, Penn. Mr. and Mrs. Nickeson have two children—Frances M. and William Edmon. Mr. Nickeson has served as burgess of Carmichaels; also as justice of the peace for one term. He is a prominent member of the I. O. O. F., and he and wife are active members of the Methodist Episcopal Church, in which he is trustee, and superintendent of the Sabbath-school.

I. B. PATTERSON, farmer and stock-grower, P. O. Carmichaels, Penn., was born on Ruff's Creek, in Greene County, September 28, 1834. His parents, Thomas and Dorcas (Bell) Patterson, were natives of Pennsylvania. His father was a farmer and drover, and often sold stock in the Baltimore market on commission for the citizens of Greene County. He was the father of eight children, of whom I. B. is next to the youngest. He was educated in the common schools of the county, chose farming and stock-growing for his business, and owns 355 acres of valuable land in the county. In 1858 he married Mary E., daughter of James Barns, whose portrait appears in this volume. It is said that Mr. Barns brought the first steam engine into Greene County, and was also founder of its first woolen-mill. He departed this life in 1883, at the advanced age of ninety-three years. Mr. and Mrs. Patterson are the parents of seven children—William B., Thomas, James L., Isaac N., John L., Minnie and Franklin M. Mr. Patterson is a Democrat. Mr. and Mrs. Patterson are prominent members of the Carmichaels Cumberland Presbyterian Church, in which they have ever been faithful, earnest workers.

J. G. PATTERSON was born in Franklin Township, Fayette County, Penn., August 23, 1830. He is a son of James and Jane (Smith) Patterson, who were born near Philadelphia, and of Scotch-Irish descent. Mr. Patterson's father was a farmer, his family consisting of nine children, of whom J. G. is the seventh. He was reared in Fayette County, Penn., attending Madison College at Uniontown, and Greene Academy at Carmichaels, Penn. He studied medicine with Dr. W. L. Lafferty, of Brownsville, Penn., and practiced one year at Havana, Mason County, Illinois. He then engaged in the drug business in Pittsburgh, Penn., for a period of eleven years. In 1854 he married Miss Nancy J., daughter of John McAllister; and they are the parents of two children—Julian S., who is a physician at Carlisle, Penn., and Anna, wife of George L. Denney, of Fayette County, Penn. In 1862 Mr Patterson enlisted in the One Hundred and Sixty-eighth Pennsylvania Volunteer Infantry. When the company was organized he was elected First Lieutenant. In 1863 he resigned on account of ill-health, returned to Greene County and engaged in the oil business, and subsequently in mechanical pursuits. In politics Mr. Patterson is a Democrat, in religion a Presbyterian. His wife is a devoted member of the M. E. Church.

J. H REA, farmer and stock-grower, P. O. Carmichaels, was born in Cumberland Township, August 26, 1831, and is a son of John and Margaret (Dowlin) Rea, who were of Scotch-Irish descent. His mother was a native of Pennsylvania, and his father, who was a blacksmith, was born in New Jersey and came to Greene County in 1803, and died November 25, 1847. Of their ten children, nine grew to maturity, the youngest of whom is the subject of this sketch. He has lived all his life on a farm, with the exception of two years spent in the army. He owns the farm of 106 acres where he now resides He was united in marriage, August 26, 1852, with Miss Orpha, daughter of Benjamin and Mary (Long) Worthington. Mrs. Rea is of English origin. Their family consists of seven children— Calvin B., Margaret Alice, wife of James Craig; Frank L., a stock-dealer in the West; Mary M., Walter G., Anna V. and John Linn. They are all members of the Presbyterian Church, in which Mr. Rea has been elder, trustee, and superintendent of the Sabbath-school. Mr. Rea takes a great interest in educational matters, has served as school director, and filled most of the important offices of his township. In 1861 he enlisted as a private in Company F, First Pennsylvania Cavalry. At the regular organization of this company at Harrisburgh, August 17, 1861, he was elected Captain, and was promoted to the office of Major, November 14, of the same year. He was discharged for disability, January 12, 1863, and was carried home on a stretcher, in what was then thought to be a dying condition. He is a member of the G. A. R Post.

SAMUEL W. REA, farmer and stock-grower, Carmichaels, Penn., was born in the township where he resides, February 2, 1829. He is a son of Jesse and Mary (Wright) Rea, natives of Montgomery County, Penn. His parents were of Scotch-Irish origin, and came to Greene County in May, 1828, where Mr Rea, who was a farmer all his life, died in 1870. Samuel W. was the only son in a family of four children He was with his parents on the farm until he attained his majority, and attended the district school in the township and Greene Academy at Carmichaels He has devoted his time to farming and the growing of fine stock, and has met with more than average success. He owns a fine farm of 360 acres in Cumberland Township Mr. Rea was united in marriage, in 1848, to Miss

Ruth Ann, daughter of William and Zillah (Johnson) Bailey. Their children are—Jesse L., Amanda Jane, wife of H. Kerr, has one daughter, Ruth E. Kerr; L. M., who married Josephine Hewitt, and is the father of one child, Anna Mary; John M, M. Zillah, E. F., C. Albert and Calvin W. William B., Hannah Frances, James W. and Nettie are deceased. In politics Mr Rea is a Republican He has been school director in his township, and filled important offices in Carmichael's Cumberland Presbyterian Church, of which his family are all members.

JOSEPH .REEVES, farmer and stock-grower, was born in Cumberland Township, Greene County, Penn, November 23, 1816, and is a son of John B. and Sarah (Luse) Reeves, natives of Pennsylvania. His father was a farmer, and lived to be eighty- five years of age. His family consisted of twelve children—six sons and six daughters. Joseph was the sixth in the family, received his education in the common schools, and chose farming as his business, which he has followed all his life. He started out in the world with nothing but a willing mind and strong muscle, first working by the day and month. He has met with marked success, and is now the owner of 550 acres of well improved land where he resides. In 1840 he married Miss Rebecca, daughter of Phineas and Hannah (Ross) Clawson, who were of English descent. Mr. and Mrs Reeves were the parents of six children, five living—Hannah J., wife of Wesley Evans, Sarah Ellen, wife of J. B. Sharp; Eliza M., wife of James Chafen; Phineas C. and John L. Their mother was a faithful member of the Baptist Church Mr. Reeves' first son, Phineas C., is a farmer and at present resides with his parents. He was born in Greene Township, January 9, 1850, and received a common school education. In 1875 he was united in marriage with Miss Anna Davis. They have five children—Charles R, Rosa Pearl, Ernest J, Joseph B. and F. A. In politics their father is a Republican, and is a leading member in the Methodist Episcopal Church.

DANIEL RICH, farmer and stock-grower, Khedive, Penn., was born in Cumberland Township, Greene County, April 25, 1830, and is a son of David and Margaret (Morrison) Rich. His parents were also natives of Greene County, and of German and English ancestry. His father and grandfather were both farmers and among the early settlers of the county. Daniel is the ninth in a family of thirteen children, twelve of whom grew to maturity. He was reared on the farm, attending school in the township, and also graded school in Virginia. He chose farming as his occupation and is now the owner of 360 acres of valuable land in Cumberland Township, where he resides and is regarded as one of the leading men of Greene County. He lived four years in Monroe County, Ohio, where he was united in marriage, October 8, 1858, with Miss Lany, daughter of Levi

Stephens, a native of Greene County, Penn., and of German origin. They have two children—A. L., born in Monroe County, Ohio, August 13, 1859, and Phœbe C., who is the wife of Columbus Scott Their son, A. L., was reared on their present farm, in Cumberland. Township, to which his parents returned soon after his birth. He was married, October 8, 1882, to Miss Kate, daughter of C. C. Harry; and they have one child—Stephen Harry, an interesting boy of five years. In politics Mr. Daniel Rich is a Republican, and was elected justice of the peace in 1880, also in 1885. He is energetic and successful in his business, and has always held the confidence of his neighbors. He has settled up fifteen estates for heirs in the neighborhood, to the entire satisfaction of the parties concerned. His family are all members of the Cumberland Presbyterian Church, in which he has served as trustee and superintendent of the Sabbath-school.

ALBERT M. RICHEY, now a resident of Iowa, was born in Fayette County, Penn., February 10, 1810. His parents were Samuel and Elizabeth (Humbert) Richey, natives of Pennsylvania and of German and English ancestry. His father was a soldier in the war of 1812. Leaving his native county at the age of twenty-one, Albert came to Greene County, after having learned cabinet-making, in Fayette County, Penn., and carried on business until 1878. At that time he went West and engaged in the same business at Indianola, Iowa, where he still resides. His family consists of seven children. His oldest and only child in Greene County is Miss Emeline Richey, of Carmichaels, Penn., where she is owner and proprietor of a large dry-goods and dress emporium. Miss Richey is deserving of special mention, her life having been so much out of the range of most of her sex. She was reared in Carmichaels and attended Greene Academy until 1854, when she was employed by J. W. Hathaway, as clerk in his store. Here she displayed such excellent taste and good judgment in the selection and purchase of goods, and such business ability, that Mr. Hathaway soon trusted her to do all the buying in the East, and gave her complete control of the store during the last few years she remained with him. In the fifteen years she was with him Mr. Hathaway's business was far more prosperous than ever before. Miss Richey has met with the same success in her own store, which she opened in 1869. She has a good trade in dry-goods and millinery, and also makes a specialty of fine dress-making, receiving the patronage of many prominent ladies for miles around Carmichaels. She is always prompt and obliging, conducts her business in a business-like way and has met with marked success in all her undertakings.

THOMAS RINEHART, retired farmer and stock-grower, Ceylon, Penn., was born in Greene County, February 14, 1802. His parents, John and Peggy (Inghram) Rinehart, were of Irish and German descent. His ancestors were among the earliest settlers of the county, in which many descendants of both families now reside, some of them having held prominent positions therein. The present President Judge of Greene County is a nephew of Thomas Rinehart, the the subject of our sketch. Mr. Rinehart's father was a farmer all his life. Thomas was his second son and was reared in Greene County, attending the subscription schools. He manifested excellent business proclivities early in life, and was untiring in his zeal to make the best of every opportunity, as a result of which he now owns a fine farm of 200 acres, where he lives in Cumberland Township. Here he was married and is the father of two children— Thomas Franklin and Margaret Ann. Mr. Rinehart is a Democrat, and he and his wife are consistent members of church.

THOMAS W. ROGERS, photographer, who was born in Beallsville, Washington County, Penn., July 17, 1846, is a son of James R. and Sarah (McLean) Rogers, also natives of Washington County. Mrs. Sarah Rogers died in 1854. Mr. Rogers, who is a carpenter and contractor, now resides in the State of Indiana. His family consists of seven children now living—five sons and two daughters (five dead). Thomas, who is the third son, was reared in Washington County on the farm, and attended school at Beallsville. In 1861 he learned photography, at which he worked for over three years before he opened his establishment in Carmichaels, where he has been a very popular and successful photographer. In 1869 Mr. Rogers married Miss Belle, daughter of Joseph Daugherty. They are the parents of five children, viz.—Olly, Velma, Wilber, Ina and Fred. Mr. Rogers is modest and unassuming but industrious and energetic in his business, and has always had the respect and confidence of the community, from which he has received a liberal patronage. In politics he is a Republican; and he and Mrs. Rogers are among the most faithful and prominent members of the Methodist Episcopal Church.

A. J. SHARPNACK, farmer and stock-grower, of Cumberland Township, Greene County, Penn., was born August 25, 1847, on the farm where he now resides. He is a son of Henry and Elizabeth (Rice) Sharpnack. Mr. Sharpnack's father, who died in 1879, made farming the business of his life. Mr. Sharpnack is the youngest of nine children, five of whom are living. He was reared in Cumberland Township on the farm with his parents, where he attended the district school. He wisely chose his father's occupation—that of stock-growing and farming. He owns an improved and well stocked farm. In 1868 he married Caroline M. Rinehart. They have two sons—Levi and Henry. Their mother died and Mr. Sharpnack was again united in marriage with Martha, daughter of David Bowser.

Their children are—Lora, Malinda, Chester A. Arthur, Elizabeth Ann, Lilian Dell, and James G. Blaine. - Mrs. Sharpnack is a devoted member of the Baptist Church.

LEVI A. SHARPNACK, farmer and stock-raiser, Carmichaels, Penn., was born in Cumberland Township, Greene County, December 24, 1850. He is a son of John and Sarah (Autram) Sharpnack, who were natives of Pennsylvania, and of German and English origin. His father was an industrious and energetic farmer and stock-raiser until his death, April 8, 1858. His family consisted of eleven children, seven living, of whom Levi is the youngest and the only son. He was reared on the farm and received a common school education; has made choice of farming as his occupation through life, and meets with great success. He owns ninety-two acres of valuable land where he now resides. In 1874 he married Elizabeth, daughter of William and Susan (Curl) Armstrong. Mr. Sharpnack is of Irish descent. Their children are: Linton, Chauncey, Ora, Charles and Launa. Mr. Sharpnack is a strong Democrat, and one of the most influential citizens of his township.

THOMAS L. STEWART, deceased, was born in Dunkard Township, Greene County, in the year 1813. His parents, Leonard and Elizabeth (Ferrell) Stewart, were of English descent, and among the early settlers of the county. His father was a farmer: Thomas L. was reared in Dunkard Township, and followed farming as his occupation. In 1842 he married Miss Eliza, daughter of John and Elizabeth (Hopton) Johnson. They are the parents of three children: Joseph, Mary E. and Johnson, who married Sarah Durr, and is the father of two children—Charles and G. Pearl. Joseph, their oldest son, was born in Cumberland Township, Greene County, October 24, 1844, and received a common school education. In 1882 he married Miss Amanda, daughter of E. Y. Cowell. Mrs. Joseph Stewart was a member of the Baptist Church. She died in 1884, leaving one child, Mary. Mr. Stewart and his sons are strict adherents to the Republican party.

ELIAS STONE, deceased, who was a farmer and stock grower, was born in Greensboro, Greene County, Penn., September 22, 1808. He was a son of James and Nancy (Sedgewick) Stone, who were natives of Greene County, and descended from its earliest settlers. The history of the family on both sides shows them to have been farmers usually, and of Irish descent. Mr. Stone was the second in a family of eight children. He was reared in Monongahela Township, this county, where he attended the subscription schools. He devoted his business life to farming and the growing of fine stock. In 1833 he married Mary, daughter of Samuel and Nancy (Lackey) Huston. Her parents were natives of Pennsylvania and of Irish descent. Mr. and Mrs. Stone were the parents of three children. Lizzie, Nan and

Fannie   Their mother died in 1843   Mr Stone was Republican in
politics, and a member of the Methodist Episcopal Church.   He was '
twice married, and his widow and two children, Frank and Amanda,
survive him.   He died in 1872

D C STEPHENSON, farmer and stock grower, was born in
Greene Township, Greene County, Penn , June 5, 1826.   His parents, Alexander and Rachel (Jones) Stephenson, were natives of this
county, and of Welsh and Scotch-Irish descent.   His grandfather
and great-grandfather were Hugh and Daniel Stephenson, who were
farmers and soldiers in the Revolutionary war;, they came to Greene
County soon after its close.   His father served as justice of the
peace in Greene County for a period of fifteen years   The history
of the Stephenson family gives farming as their usual occupation.
Mr Stephenson's grandfather was born in Greene County, where he
spent all his life.   He died in 1857 in his eighty-second year.   Mr.
Stephenson is the oldest in a family of four children—two sons and
two daughters.   He was reared on the farm in this county, where he
attended the district school   In 1861 he came to Cumberland Township and engaged in farming until 1869, when he came to Ceylon
and kept store for a period of sixteen years.   He was united in marriage, in Henry County, Iowa, with Miss Martha, daughter of Isaac
and Mary (Barclay) Johnson   Mrs. Stephenson is a great grand
daughter of the Hon. Hugh Barclay.   Her grandfather was also
Hugh Barclay, and her grandfather Johnson's name was William.
Mr and Mrs Stephenson have eight children—Mary E., wife of
Noah M. Hartley; Alexander M., a farmer; Fannie, Hugh C., of
Iowa; J W., a teacher, Anna M , Flora M. and I T. (deceased)   In politics Mr. Stephenson is a Democrat, and has served
as postmaster in Greene County for fifteen years.   He has made his
own way in the world, and by means of his energy and untiring zeal
in his business has become one of the most prosperous farmers in
the county and highly respected by all who know him.

JOHNSON TOPPIN, retired farmer, Carmichaels, Penn., was
born in Maryland February 25, 1808, and is a son of John and Rebecca (Johnson) Toppin   They were members of the Society of
Friends, and of English descent   His father was a farmer and carpenter through life   Johnson was one of three sons and three daughters, and spent most of his life in Greene County, Penn., where he
also attended school   He learned the gunsmith trade, in which he
engaged for a time, then followed ship carpentering as a business.
He also ran on the river as captain on a keel boat for nineteen
years   He afterwards bought a farm in Cumberland Township,
where he lived until 1885—the date of his retirement   In 1833 he
was united in marriage with Miss Harriet, daughter of John and
Jane Dalby.   Mrs. Toppin was born in 1813 and is also a native of

Pennsylvania. Of their five children, three are living—two in Iowa. They are all married: Matilda, wife of William Gass; Rebecca Ann, wife of J. K. Parshall, and Almira, wife of Thomas W. Linch. Mr. Toppin is a Democrat; and his wife is a faithful member of the Methodist Church.

T. P. WARNE, farmer and stock-grower, Carmichaels, Penn., was born in Carroll Township, Washington County, Penn., January 26, 1847. He is a son of Joseph and Elizabeth (Irwin) Warne. His father and mother were natives of Washington and Chester counties respectively, and were of English and Irish descent. His father, who has met with marked success as a farmer, still resides on the old home farm in Carroll Township, Washington County, and also owns a fine farm of 250 acres in Cumberland Township, Greene County. Mr. T. P. Warne, who is the second in a family of seven children, attended school at Monongahela City, where he started in business as a coal merchant and remained there for a period of nine years. In 1882 he sold out his coal interests, and came to this county in 1885 and has since been engaged in farming in Cumberland Township. Mr. Warne was united in marriage, April 21, 1887, with Anna E. Long. Her parents were James and Mary (McClelland) Long, of English and Irish ancestry. Mrs. Warne is third in their family of six children; and is a faithful member of the Presbyterian Church. Mr. Warne is a Democrat, and one of the leading citizens of his community.

LEM H. WILEY, musician, Peoria Ill., was born in Greene County, Penn., April 17, 1844. He acquired a common school education, and worked at the blacksmiths trade with his father. In 1862 he went to Peoria County, Ill., and in the fall he enlisted in the Seventy-seventh Regiment Illinois Volunteers, as chief musician, being then only eighteen years of age. This position he filled faithfully until the regiment was mustered out of service at the close of the war. Upon returning home, Mr. Wiley became a member of the celebrated Light Guards Band of Peoria, with which he remained nine years, during which time he also opened a music business. In 1872 he was one of the twenty-four cornetists at P. S. Gilmore's World's Peace Jubilee at Boston; and has been a member and leader of a number of the noted bands in the United States. He was married, August 17, 1872, to Miss Alta, daughter of Levi Wilson, of Peoria, Ill. In 1880 he became a leader in Haverly's Original Mastodon Minstrels, organized in Chicago, and remained with them five years, during which time he played in all the large cities in the United States and most of the principal cities in the old world. In January, 1885, he became manager of the new Grand Opera House in Peoria, Ill., a position he still holds. Mr. Wiley is considered by the world a thorough musician and remarkable cornetist.

A. J. YOUNG, farmer and stock grower, Rice's Landing, Penn., was born in Washington County, February 7, 1831, and is a son of Abraham and Hannah (Rose) Young His parents were natives of Washington and Greene counties, respectively, and of German and English ancestry. Mr. Young is the seventh in a family of ten children. He was reared in West Bethlehem Township, Washington County, and acquired his education from the common schools of his neighborhood He chose farming as his occupation, and owns 165 acres of well improved land in Cumberland Township, Greene County, where he took up his abode in 1854.   In the same year he was united in marriage with Miss Rachel, daughter of Joseph and Sarah (Swan) Ailes.   The former was a native of Washington County, and the latter of Greene County, and a descendant of one of its earliests settlers Mrs. Young's great-grandfather, John Swan, settled on the farm now owned by A. J. Young, in 1767, and had to build a fort to protect himself from the Indians. Mr and Mrs. Young are devoted members of the Cumberland Presbyterian Church, the former ruling elder of the church Mr. and Mrs. Young are the parents of two children— Amy H., who died when four years old, and William A , a carpenter and farmer. residing on the home farm. He was united in marriage in 1884 with Miss Maggie M , daughter of Jacob and Rachel Braden, and they have one child, Walter B.

MORGAN YOUNG, farmer and stock grower, Rice's Landing, Penn , was born in Washington County, February 8, 1829, and is a son of Abraham and Hannah (Rose) Young His parents were of Scotch-Irish and Dutch descent. His mother was a native of Greene County and his father, who was a farmer and stock raiser during his life-time, was born in Washington County, Penn Both died on the same day in January, 1853, his wife surviving him just four hours They had a family of ten children.   Morgan, who was the sixth, was reared on the farm, attended the common school, and has made farming the business of his life. He is the owner of a well improved farm consisting of two hundred and seventeen acres well stocked and kept in good condition Mr. Young has been twice married; first, in 1850, to Harriet, daughter of Thomas M. and Maria (Phillps) Norris Mrs. Young was of Dutch descent. They had four children—A. L , a teacher and farmer in Ohio; Amy M., wife of T O Bradbury; Mary Ellen and James E   Their mother died in June, 1876. Mr. Young's second wife was Miss Emma, daughter of Aaron and Sarah (McCullough) Bradbury, who were of English descent. Mrs. Young's father, now a farmer of this county, was for many years a farmer and tanner of Washington County, Penn. Mr. and Mrs. Young have one child, Harry H B. In politics Mr Young was a Democrat until 1884, since which time he has been a strong Prohibitionist, and has filled various important offices in his township.

He was justice of the peace for a period of ten years. They were both members of the Shepherds Methodist Episcopal Church, in which both were stewards, and Mr. Young has been trustee, superintendent of the Sabbath-school, and class leader for thirty years, until two years ago, when they united with the Methodist Episcopal Church at Rice's Landing.

DUNKARD TOWNSHIP.

EMANUEL BEALL, overseer of the poor of Greene County, Penn., was born in Monongahela Township, this county, December 31, 1819, and is a son of Thomas and Marian (Engales) Beall. His father was a native of Loudoun County, Va., and his mother was born in Greene County, Penn. They were of English and German extraction. Emanuel's grandfather, William Beall, was a pioneer settler of Greene County, and his maternal grandfather was a soldier in the Revolutionary war. The subject of this sketch is next to the oldest in a family of eleven children. He remained on the farm with his parents until he was near twenty-four years of age, then located in Monongalia County, W. Va., where he engaged in farming and stock-raising. Mr. Beall has made his own way in the world, and at present is the owner of 500 acres of land. He owned at one time over 900 acres. Mr. Beall is a Democrat in politics, and at present is overseer of the poor of this county. He takes an active interest in the public schools, and has served a number of years as school director. In 1869 he returned to his native county and settled in Dunkard Township, where he still resides. He has made the raising of fine sheep a specialty, and has met with great success in his business. Mr. Beall has been three times married, and is the father of eleven children, viz: John T., Bertha J., wife of Daniel Morris; William J., Charlotte, Martha, Barnet, Nancy, George W., Andrew J., Miriam and Columbus. Mr. Beall is a faithful member of the Baptist Church, of which he is clerk.

THORNTON COALBANK, a farmer and stock-grower, born in West Virginia in 1821, is a son of Samuel and Elizabeth (Everly) Coalbank, who were also natives of West Virginia, and of Welsh and English extraction. His father was a farmer all his life. Thornton, the fifth in a family of eleven children, remained on the farm with his parents until he reached his majority. He received his education in the district schools of West Virginia, and Greene County,

Penn., where he has resided since 1842. Early in life he learned the shoemaker's trade, which, in connection with farming, he has followed through life, and has met with financial success, being at present the owner of a valuable farm lying along the Monongahela River. Mr. Coalbank has been twice married, first in Greene County in 1846, to Miss Sarah Hartly, who died in 1875. By this marriage Mr. Coalbank was the father of eleven children, most of whom grew to maturity. Ten years later he married Miss Agnes, daughter of John and Susannah (Bright) Davis. Mr. and Mrs. Coalbank are leading members in the Baptist Church.

AMBROSE DILLINER, retired farmer and stock-grower, was born in Dunkard Township, Greene County, Penn., September 14, 1815. He is a son of George and Sarah (Ramsey) Dilliner, who were natives of this county, and of Irish and German origin. His grandfather, Augustine Dilliner, came to Greene County more than a hundred years ago, and settled above the mouth of Dunkard Creek, in Dunkard Township, where he spent the remaining portion of his life. George Dilliner died in 1824, leaving a family of twelve children, of whom Ambrose is the youngest son. He was reared on his father's farm and received a common-school education. Mr. Dilliner learned the millwright business in early life, and engaged therein for ten years. He owned and operated a saw-mill in this township from 1867 till 1881. He has been quite an extensive lumber dealer, but has made farming his chief occupation, and owns a farm of 130 acres lying along the Monongahela River. Mr. Dilliner was united in marriage, March 23, 1857, with Miss Elizabeth, daughter of William and Sarah (McKee) Griffin. Her parents were natives of Delaware, but have resided in Dunkard Township, this county, for about three-quarters of a century. To Mr. and Mrs. Dilliner have been born seven children, only three of whom are living—Sarah, wife of Jacob Kemp; Lydia F., wife of J. E. Sturgis, and W. L. The deceased are Caroline, Elizabeth, George S. and Walter. W. L., the youngest child living, has charge of the home farm, where he was born April 27, 1850. In 1877 he married Miss M., daughter of David and Jemima (Evans) Rich, and they have three children—Emma, Mamie and Walter S. Mr. and Mrs. Dilliner are members of the Methodist Episcopal Church, in which he has been an official member for forty-six years, and has served as Sabbath-school superintendent. Mr. Dilliner is a Republican, and a member of the Masonic fraternity.

IRA D. KNOTTS, physician and surgeon, was born in Dunkard Township, this county, March 9, 1857. He is a son of William and Ruth (South) Knotts, who were also natives of this county, and of German and Scotch descent. His father is a farmer and stock-grower by occupation, and resides in Dunkard Township, where the Doctor is in successful practice. The Doctor is a grandson of Jonathan

Knotts, who was born in this county in 1797, and was a soldier in the war of 1812. He died in Fayette County, Penn., having lived to the advanced age of ninety years. Dr. Knotts is the fourth in a family of seven children. He was reared on a farm in Perry Township, and his early education was obtained in the district school and Monongahela College at Jefferson, Penn. He subsequently went to Mount Union College, Ohio, and took the regular course up to the senior year, when he left for the purpose of studying medicine. He took the regular medical course in the University of Philadelphia, graduating with high honors in 1887. The Doctor was a diligent student, ambitious to acquire all possible knowledge in his profession. He pursued his studies with unabated zeal, and was awarded the $75 prize offered to his class for the best examination in hygiene. This trophy of honor is a fine microscope, which he finds of great value in his practice. He is a man of more than ordinary energy, and his professional skill and gentlemanly demeanor have won for him a liberal patronage where he is located, in Dunkard, Greene County, Penn. The Doctor, September 15, 1884, in a competitive examination in Latin Physics and English Composition, passed the best examination, and obtained as his reward for the same a scholarship for three years in the University of Philadelphia, Penn.

JOHN B. MASON, farmer and stock-grower, who was born in Perry Township, Greene County, Penn., July 22, 1816, is a son of Peter and Naomi (Jones) Mason. His father, who was born in Cumberland County in 1793, was the son of John E. Mason, one of the first shoemakers in Dunkard Township. Peter Mason was a farmer by occupation, and died January 1, 1888, leaving a family of eleven children. Mrs. Naomi Mason was a confirmed invalid for twenty-one years, and died August 28, 1870. John B., the second son, was reared in Whiteley Township, where he attended the district schools. He has spent a long life in his chosen occupation, and is one of the most successful and best known citizens in his township. He is the owner of a well-improved farm where he resides, near Davistown, Penn. After his mother's death Mr. Mason took care of his aged father until his death. In 1840 John B. Mason married Miss Hannah, daughter of John and Margaret (Wilson) Phillips. They are faithful members of the Methodist Episcopal Church, in which Mr. Mason has served as class-leader for over forty years. He is also actively interested in the Sabbath-school, and has been superintendent for many years.

GEORGE G. MILLER, farmer and and stock-grower, was born in Dunkard Township, this county, December 30, 1836, and is a son of Daniel and Rebecca (Garrison) Miller, who were natives of Pennsylvania, and of German and Irish extraction. Mr. Miller's father and Jonathan Miller, his grandfather, were farmers and millers by occupation. The farm where the subject of this sketch now resides is a part of a 700-acre tract of land purchased by his grandfather in 1808. Mr. Miller's grandfather died in 1849, and his father in 1887, in his seventy-seventh year. George G. was an only child. He was reared on the home faim and received a common-school education He also attended Greene Academy, and Allegheny and Waynesburg Colleges, and subsequently taught school for several years. On September 22, 1862, Mr Miller enlisted in Company E, Fourteenth Pennsylvania Volunteer Cavalry. He was orderly sergeant of the company, and passed through many severe battles. He was with General Aveiill on his famous raids to White Sulphur Springs, Lewisburg, and Salem. The U. S. Government showed its appreciation of the services rendered by the latter expedition by issuing to every man who returned from Salem a complete outfit of clothing free of cost. Returning home at the close of the war, he again engaged in teaching for a time, and always took an active interest in the teachers' institute of the county. For the past few years Mr. Miller has devoted his time and talent wholly to farming and stock-growing, and his farm consists of 230 acres of well improved land Mr. Miller has been twice married: First, in Washington County, to Miss Margery, daughter of John and Jane (Gregg) Hopkins She was of Irish lineage, and died in 1874 Their children were—Laura, Ellen (deceased), Estelle and Charles. In 1877 Mr. Miller married Miss Elizabeth McCormick, daughter of Joseph and Mary (Watson) McCormick, of Dunkard Township, and they are the parents of four children, viz , Wayne, Warren D , Peri and James Clifton. Mrs Miller is a member of the Methodist Protestant Church. Mr. Miller is a Republican, and a prominent member of the G A R.

ASA MILLER, retired miller, farmer and wool-carder, was born in Dunkard Township, this county, May 24, 1812. His parents were of German ancestry and natives of Frederick County, Maryland. His father, Jonathan Miller, was born February 10, 1774, and his mother, Susannah (Tombs) Miller, was born January 7, 1773 They were united in marriage August 8, 1799, and came to Greene County, Penn., in 1802, where he bought a large tract of land and watermill on Crooks Run He immediately put in steam power, by bringing the first engine into the county. The old mill burned in 1856, and was rebuilt by our subject in 1858, and he is now using the engine he first purchased for the old mill. Jonathan and wife were the parents of eight children, five sons and three daughters, and their home was a welcome to the poor and needy. Both were members of the Dunkard Church. He died in December, 1849, and she in August, 1852. The Millers are remarkable for longevity, sagacity and uprightness of character. Of the eight children the youngest was seventy-one before any died. Jacob, the oldest, died in 1885, aged eighty-five years. Asa Miller, our subject, received a good education, attended Washington and Jefferson Colleges in Washington, Penn. He spent his early life as miller, a business he has been connected with through life. He has had success as a farmer and general business man, and owns a mill and over 200 acres of land within one mile of his birth-place in Dunkard Township. He was united in marriage in Monongalia County, West Virginia, September 21, 1837, with Mary, daughter of Owen and Elizabeth (McVicker) John. The former was of English and the latter of German descent. Mr. and Mrs. Miller are the parents of the following children —Susan E., wife of E. McElroy; William L., Jesse F, Amanda K., wife of John Keener; Henry J., an eminent surgeon and physician of Tennessee. The deceased are: J. Q. and Mary V. Mrs. Miller is a devoted member of the Dunkard Church.

I. A MORRIS, retired farmer and stock-grower, was born September 22, 1811, on a farm near Uniontown, Fayette County, Penn., and is a son of Griffith and Hannah (Springer) Morris. His parents were natives of Pennsylvania, and of Welsh and Irish origin. His father came to Greene County in 1824, locating in Dunkard Township, where he spent the remaining portion of his life. His family consisted of eight children, of whom the subject of this sketch is the second. He was reared on the farm and received his early education in the district schools. He very naturally chose farming as an occupation, and engaged therein successfully until he retired from the cares of his more active life. His farm is well improved and consists of 200 acres, where he resides in Dunkard Township. Mr. Morris was united in marriage May 4, 1837, with Miss Nancy, daughter of Samuel and Retilda (Bright) Everly. Her father was born in Virginia, and her mother was a native of Delaware. They were of Irish lineage. Mr. and Mrs. Morris have a family of eight children—Martha J., wife of Josiah Hall; Clarinda, wife of William Hord; Clark, a stonemason, George W., a farmer; Loranda, wife of Isaac Courtwright; Samuel, a merchant at Uniontown, Penn.; Delia, wife of James Sargent, and Single. Mr. and Mrs. Morris are members of the Methodist Episcopal Church, in which he has been a class-leader and superintendent of the Sabbath-school.

JAMES McCLURE, deceased, was born in Perry Township, Greene County, Pennsylvania, February 24, 1816, and was the son of William and Jane (King) McClure. His father was born in Ireland, and his mother in Perry Township, this county. James McClure was a farmer and stock-grower during his lifetime and at the time of his death, in 1886, was the owner of 400 acres of valuable land in Greene County. He was a self-made man, having no educational advantages except such as were afforded by the subscription schools. His success in life was due largely to his great industry and unfailing determination to succeed. In politics Mr. McClure was a Demo-

34

crat, and served as assessor and school director in his township. He was united in the holy bonds of matrimony, February 22, 1838, with Miss Susan, daughter of Reuben and Rebecca (Johns) Brown. Her father was of Irish and English origin. Her mother was of Welsh extraction. To Mr. and Mrs. McClure were born twelve children, eleven of whom are living, viz: Owen, a farmer; Mary J., wife of William Hatfield, of Morgan Township; William L., a gold miner in California; Reuben M, a farmer in Iowa; Anna, Emma, Isabella, wife of Charles Haver; Miranda, Minerva, Josephine, James M., and Rebecca (deceased), who was the wife of Alfred Jamison. Their mother is a faithful member of the Goshen Baptist Church.

THOMAS B. ROBERTS, a farmer and stock-grower, who was born in Dunkard Township, this county, July 9, 1840, is a son of David and Mary (Jamison) Roberts. His parents were also natives of this township, and of Irish and English extraction His father was a farmer, drover and stock-grower, and spent his life in Dunkard Township. Thomas B is the youngest of a family of four children, and attended the district schools of the neighborhood He has diligently followed his occupation of farming and stock-growing, and owns sixty acres of good land where he resides, near Davistown, Penn. Mr. Roberts was united in marriage in this county, November 17, 1863, with Miss Lucretia, daughter of Hiram and Elizabeth (Hunt) Stephens, and they have a family of seven children, viz: Louisa, wife of M. Donley; Mary A., Lucretia B., William Albert, Jesse Jamison, Pleasant E. and John M. Mr Roberts is a Republican, and has served as school director of his township. He and Mrs. Roberts are prominent members of the Methodist Episcopal Church.

DAVID STEELE.—Among the representative farmers of Dunkard Township we mention David Steele, who was born October 16, 1838. His parents, Jesse and Rachel (Zook) Steele, were natives of Greene County, and of Dutch and Irish extraction. They were descendants of the earliest settlers of the county David's father was a farmer in Dunkard Township, and for many years resided on the farm which David now owns. He reared a family of eight children, of whom David is the fourth. He was reared on the farm with his parents, and attended the district schools. He wisely chose his father's occupation, and has met with moderate success In 1870 David Steele married Melissa, daughter of George Stoops. Their children are: George Lee, Edward W, Dora E., Alfred Moss and Jesse. Mr Steele is a Democrat in politics, and one of the most highly respected citizens in the township.

THOMAS B. STEELE, of Dunkard Township, Greene County, Penn, was born March 1, 1841, on the farm where he now resides He is the son of John and Nancy (Bowen) Steele, who were natives of Pennsylvania, and of Irish and English ancestry. His grandfather, John Steele, who was a farmer and drover, died in 1862, having reached the advanced age of ninety-four years. Thomas Steele's father was born in 1797 and lived to be eighty-two years of age. He was a farmer and stock-grower, and spent most of his life in Dunkard Township. His family consisted of eleven children, who all grew to maturity. Thomas, the tenth child, was reared on the home farm, attended the district school and has been an industrious farmer all his life. He was united in marriage, January 13, 1864, with Miss Rebecca, daughter of John Stevenson. Mrs. Steele is a native of Greene County, and of English and German descent. They are the parents of five children, viz.: John M., Artie B., Sadie L., R. B. and Nannie. In politics Mr. Steele is a Democrat. He and wife are leading members of the Baptist Church.

ABRAHAM STERLING, farmer and stock-grower, P. O. Greensboro, Penn., was born in Fayette County, Penn., March 12, 1837. His parents, Andrew and Julia Ann (Mosier) Sterling, were also natives of Fayette County, and of German ancestry. His father spent his life as a farmer and stock-grower in Fayette County, and reared a family of six children. Abraham is the second in the family. He chose farming as his occupation and has engaged therein all his life, with the exception of the time spent in building roads and bridges. Mr. Sterling is a natural mechanic. He has taken several contracts for building roads and bridges, and has always completed his work satisfactorily. Mr. Sterling was united in marriage in Greene County with Miss Jemima, daughter of Asa Miller, and they had one son—Asa. Mrs. Sterling died in 1869. In politics Mr. Sterling is a Democrat. He and his brother own a fine farm of 280 acres situated in Dunkard Township.

JOSEPH SOUTH, farmer and stock-grower, who was born September 5, 1822, is a son of Elijah and Nancy (Johnson) South, who were natives of Greene County, and descendants of its early settlers. Joseph South's grandfather, Elijah South, Sr., came from New Jersey to Greene County, Penn., in the spring of 1796. He took up a tract of several hundred acres of land, a part of which is the farm now owned by the subject of this sketch. It contains 108 acres of valuable land. The Souths have usually been farmers. In 1852 Mr. South married Miss Melissa, daughter of Amos Wright, who was of English lineage. Mr. and Mrs. South have three children, viz.: John C., principal of Schools at Wichita, Kan.; Rachel M. and Dora Alice. The family are all members of the Baptist Church, in which Mr. South takes an active interest, and has served as deacon and superintendent of the Sabbath-school.

REV. FRANK SOUTH, Wiley, Penn., was born in Dunkard Township, Greene County, Penn., August 22, 1858. He is a son of Nicholas and Margaret (Lucas) South, who were also natives of this county.' His ancestors were among the earliest English and Dutch settlers in this part of the State, and the history of the family shows them to have been farmers, usually, and enterprising people The subject of this sketch was reared on the farm in Dunkard Township, and received his early education in the district schools. In 1877 he united with the Methodist Episcopal Church, and was licensed to preach in 1884. He now has charge of the Methodist Episcopal Churches at Davistown and New Geneva, Penn Mr. South was on the farm with his parents until he reached his majority, and has since been in the employ of an oil company in Dunkard Township, and has proven himself faithful to the duties he has assumed In 1886 Mr. South was united in the holy bonds of matrimony with Miss Ellen, daughter of Lewis Dowlin, who was born in Cumberland Township, this county, December 1, 1818. He was 'the son of John and Elizabeth (Gwynn) Dowlin, who came from Bucks County, and were of Scotch and English ancestry. Ellen was the tenth in their family, and is a devoted member of the Baptist Church

L. G VANVOORHIS, a farmer and stock-grower, born in Washington County, Penn., June 2, 1810, is a son of Daniel and Mary (Fry) Vanvoorhis. They were born and reared in Washington County, and were of German origin His father, who was a contractor and builder, also dealt largely in live stock, and was at one time owner of a grist-mill, oil-mill and saw-mill. He died in Washington County, Penn., leaving a family of eleven children, of whom ten are living. The subject of this sketch is the second child, and was reared on the home farm, where he attended the common schools. He has been a farmer most of his life, and has resided in Greene County since 1838. Mr. Vanvoorhis has met with marked success in his business. His present farm consists of 170 acres of good land, and he has given 400 acres to his children. He was united in marriage in Washington County, November 15, 1832, with Essie, daughter of Luke and Mary (West) Fry. Her parents were natives of Washington County, and of Dutch extraction Mr and Mrs. Vanvoorhis are the parents of eight children: Jane, wife of Joseph Ross; Isaac, a wealthy farmer and drover of this 'county; Mary, wife of E. S. Taylor; Minerva C., widow of John Long; G. Jerome, Daniel F , Laura, and Dora, wife of Joseph Call. Mr. and Mrs Vanvoorhis are members of the Baptist Church, in which he has served as deacon for a number of years. He has taken an active interest in the educational affairs of his township, and has been a member of the school board

ISAAC VANVOORHIS, a farmer and stock-grower of Dunkard township, was born in Washington country, Pennsylvania, January 15, 1836. He is the oldest son of L G. and Essie (Fry) Vanvoorhis who were also natives of Washington County, and of German extraction. His father, who for many years has been a prominent farmer, is now a resident of Greene County. Isaac Vanvoorhis was reared on the farm in Dunkard Township, where he attended the district school. During his early life he remained with his parents on the farm, where he commenced dealing in stock and has since spent most of his time in that business He buys large lots of cattle in the Chicago markets, ships them to Greene County for pasture and sells numbers of them to the citizens of the county. Mr. Vanvoorhis has met with great financial success in the stock business, and also owns one of the most valuable farms in Greene County It consists of about 500 acres of land, on which are good buildings and improvements. In 1858 Mr. Vanvoorhis married Miss Ross, a daughter of Bowen and Ann (Gantz) Ross. Mrs Vanvoorhis is a native of this county, and is of German and Irish origin. Their children are—Anna, wife of E. J. Moore; Martin, Cora, Charles R. and A. L. (deceased). Mrs. Vanvoorhis is a faithful member of the Baptist Church Her husband is a Republican in politics, and has served on the school board of his township.

FRANKLIN TOWNSHIP AND WAYNES-BURG BOROUGH

THOMAS ADAMSON, retired farmer and stock-grower, was born in Morgan Township, Greene County, Penn., November 9, 1819. His parents were Charles and Sarah (Hatfield) Adamson, natives of this county, and of Irish and English extraction. The Adamson family came to America many years ago, and four brothers settled in Bucks County, Penn., where they engaged in farming. They were all members of the Society of Friends One of these brothers was the grandfather of Thomas Adamson, also named Thomas, who came to Greene County among the early settlers. He died on the farm where Charles Adamson, who died in 1868, was born and raised Thomas is one of a family of eight children, only four of whom are now living Early in life he learned the carpenter's trade, which he followed for six years, then engaged in farming In 1845 Mr. Adamson had saved enough money, through industry and economy, to enable him to buy the farm of 120 acres where he and family reside. He has at different times added to that purchase until he now owns 220 acres of well-improved land. He was united in marriage, in 1843, with Sarah, daughter of John Hoge, and they are the parents of four children—Caroline, wife of Freeman Smith; Mary, wife of B. F. Bell; Stephen C. and John H. Mrs. Adamson died in 1874. The following year Mr. Adamson married Elizabeth Hoge, a cousin of his first wife. In politics Mr. Adamson is a Democrat.

CYRUS ADAMSON, farmer and stock-grower, who was born in Greene County, Penn., April 19, 1826, is a son of James and Margaret (Smith) Adamson. His parents were natives of this county, and of English lineage. His father was an industrious and successful farmer through life. Of his ten children, Cyrus is the eighth. Having been reared on the farm, he naturally took to the occupation of farming, in which he has met with success. His farm near Waynesburg, Penn., contains 224 acres of valuable land. Mr. Adamson was united in the holy bonds of matrimony, in February of 1851, with Esther, daughter of John Hoge. Her ancestors were among the earliest settlers of the county. To Mr. and Mrs. Adamson have been born four children—Margaret M., John F., James M. and Albert T. John F., the oldest son, married Margaret, daughter of Neal Zollars, and they have two children—Harry N. and Howard C. Cyrus Adamson is a Democrat. His wife is a zealous member of the Baptist Church.

J. P. ALLUM, proprietor of the Allum House, Waynesburg, Penn., was born in Richhill Township, this county, February 2, 1842, and is a son of James and Eveline (Gregory) Allum. His father, who was a farmer, was killed by a threshing machine, February 14, 1850. Of a family of ten children, Mr. J. P. Allum was the fifth. He was reared on the farm in Richhill Township, where he attended the common schools. In 1861 he enlisted in Company B, First West Virginia Cavalry, as a private. He was promoted to Second Lieutenant and served during the whole of the war, being enlisted a part of the time under the famous Gen. Custer. Mr. Allum was present at the surrender of Gen. Lee to Gen. Grant, April 9, 1865. In 1877 he came to Waynesburg, where he opened a hotel. He is a man well qualified for the business he has chosen. He was married in 1866 to Miss Jennie R., daughter of William Carroll. Mrs. Allum is a native of Greene County, and of German extraction. They have but one child living—Anna. Mr. and Mrs. Allum are members of the Disciple Church. Mr. Allum, who is a Democrat, served as jury commissioner from 1886 to 1888, and served in the council of Waynesburg one term. He is a member of the I. O. O. F.

A. I. ANKROM, farmer and stock-grower, Waynesburg, Penn., was born on the farm where he resides, April 21, 1833, and is a son of Joseph and Charlotte (Rinehart) Ankrom. His father was born in this county in 1807, and is now a resident of Franklin Township.

The subject of this sketch is the oldest of a family of four children. He received a good English education in his native township, and was a successful teacher for a number of years. In later life Mr Ankrom devoted his time wholly to farming and stock-growing, and is one of the prosperous citizens of his township. In 1856 he married Miss Margaret, daughter of Abner and Eliza (Murdock) Fordyce, who is a devoted member of the Methodist Protestant Church. Her parents were natives of Greene County, and of Scotch-Irish extraction. To Mr. and Mrs. Ankrom have been born four daughters, viz: R. Anna, Charlotte E, Emma L. and Jennie Leona. In politics Mr. Ankrom is a Republican, and has served one term as United States Store-keeper. In early life he was an active member of the I. O. O. F.

H. B. AXTELL, attorney at law, Waynesburg, Penn., was born in Morris Township, Washington County, May 28, 1844. His parents, Zenas and Asenath (Patterson) Axtell, were also natives of Washington County, where they were married. On April 1, 1852, they moved to Morris Township, Greene County, where Mr. Axtell, who was born May 25, 1812, departed this life May 25, 1844. Mrs Axtell, who was born June 4, 1818, resides on the old homestead in Morris Township They were the parents of six children, five of whom are living, and all reside in this county. H. B. Axtell, Esq., the second in the family, was united in marriage, April 2, 1879, with Miss Maggie Worley, who was born in Wayne Township, this county. Her parents were David A. and Minerva (Inghram) Worley, both deceased. H. B Axtell acquired his education in the common schools and Waynesburg College. He remained on the farm with his parents until twenty-one years of age, then engaged in teaching for a period of ten years In 1874 he began the study of law with Messrs. Donley and Inghram, and was admitted to the bar in October, 1876. He commenced the practice of his chosen profession at Waynesburg in 1877, and since 1878 has been in partnership with J. W. Ray, Esq In politics he is a Republican.

WILLIAM H. BARB, attorney at law, was born in Monongalia County, W. Va., September 28, 1850, and is a son of Gideon and Sarah (Webb) Barb His parents were natives of Virginia, and of German and English extraction. His father was a farmer all his life, and died February 5, 1885. Of his family of nine children, W. H Barb is the sixth. He was reared on the farm, where he attended the district school. In 1866 his parents moved to Greene County, and Mr. Barb entered Waynesburg College. At the age of eighteen he began teaching, and thus was enabled to pay his own expenses through school. He began the study of law with Messrs. Wyly and Buchanan, and completed his studies in the office of Messrs. Donley and Inghram. Mr Barb was admitted to the bar October 1,

1877, and has since devoted his entire time to the practice of his profession. He is a Democrat in politics, and was elected District Attorney in 1881, holding the office for a period of three years. He has also been for several years an efficient member of the school board of Waynesburg. On May 9, 1877, Mr. Barb married Miss Buena Vista, daughter of P. A. Myers, Esq., of Greene Township, this county, where Mrs. Barb was born. They have two children—James A. and Frank.

JASON M. BELL, farmer and stock-grower, Waynesburg, Penn., was born in Morris Township, Greene County, Pennsylvania, May 21, 1807. He is a son of Jason and Sallie (Noel) Bell, who were natives of Winchester, Virginia, and of English descent. His father, who was a farmer, came to Greene County in 1795 and settled in Franklin Township. He reared a family of eight children—four sons and four daughters. Jason was reared on the home farm in Morris Township. He has successfully followed the occupation of farming through life. Mr. Bell was united in marriage, in 1833, with Cassandra, daughter of William Inghram, and they are the parents of five children—Thomas, Eliza, Maria, Alice and Harriet. In politics Mr. Bell is a Republican. He is one of the oldest and most highly respected citizens of this township.

DR. STEPHEN L. BLACHLY, so remarkable for his medical qualifications, was born in Sparta, Washington County, Penn., December 11, 1815, and has spent all his professional life in the locality where his father so long wore the wreath of medical honor. Having completed his preparatory education in Washington College, in his native county, he read medicine under the direction of his father, and afterwards entered Jefferson Medical College, at Philadelphia, from which he received his degree. He was associated with his father in the practice of his profession until the death of the latter, in 1849, practiced alone until 1877, and since that time has associated with him his son, Dr. Oliver L. Blachly. Dr. S. L. Blachly is one of the oldest practitioners in the county, and one of the oldest members of the Washington County Medical Society, of which he has been President at various times. He is a member of the State Medical Society of Pennsylvania, of which he was elected first Vice-President in 1873, and by which he was appointed Censor for the eighth district in 1874, which position he has held by annual appointment ever since. His intelligent discharge of his professional duties has secured for him the confidence of his neighbors and good will of his professional brethren. He has been a member of the Upper Ten-Mile Presbyterian Church for over forty years, and has been an elder for twenty-five years. Dr. Blachly was married, January 9, 1840, to Sarah, daughter of Benjamin Lindley, a descendant of Francis Lindley who came with his Puritan brethren from Holland in the Mayflower. By this marriage there were five children, two of whom died in infancy. Those living are—Mary Minerva, wife of Stephen Day, a merchant in Sparta, Penn.; Dr Oliver L. and Henry Spencer, a druggist of Waynesburg, who was born in Washington County, Penn., July 7, 1850. There he was reared and attended school, and subsequently attended Waynesburg College. When in the senior year of his college studies he abandoned his study and embarked in the drug business, in 1870, in Waynesburg, where he is one of the leading business men. He was united in marriage, in 1885, with Helena, daughter of Samuel Melvin (deceased), and they have one child, Stephen S. Blachly.

HON. C. A. BLACK, attorney and counsellor at law, was born in Greene County, Penn., February 6, 1808. His parents, Jacob and Margaret (Grinstaff) Black, were natives of Virginia, of English and German ancestry, and among the first settlers of Greene County, Penn. They reared a family of twelve children. The subject of our sketch was reared on a farm and acquired his education in the common schools of the county. Very early in life he commenced reading law in the office of Enos Hook, and completed his study in the office of Samuel Cleavenger, after which he engaged in the practice of his chosen profession. In 1842 he was elected State senator and served six years. He filled the office of secretary of the commonwealth under Governor Bigler, and served as the first State superintendent of public schools of Pennsylvania. Mr. Black has been a successful practitioner and has enjoyed an extensive practice In 1872 he was elected a member of the constitutional convention at Philadelphia, Penn. In 1844, Mr. Black married Miss Maria, daughter of William Allison. Their union was blessed with two children—Mary, wife of Hon James Inghram, and Albert of Washington, D C. Mrs. Black departed this life in 1871. She was the idol of her family; and a general favorite among a large circle of acquaintances. She was a Christian of deep and earnest religious convictions, and a member of the Cumberland Presbyterian Church.

WILLIAM BLAIR, county commissioner of Greene County, Penn., was born in Franklin Township, March 7, 1839. He is a son of John and Margaret (Orndoff) Blair, who were natives of this county, and of English descent. The Blairs, who were among the earliest settlers of the county, came from New Jersey and settled in Franklin Township. William Blair's father engaged in the business of stone-masonry for many years. His grandfather, W. J. Orndoff, was a soldier in the revolutionary war. The farm of 125 acres, where William resides, has been in the possession of the family for more than a quarter of a century. In 1861 Mr. Blair married Catharine, daughter of John T. Hook, and sister of W. A. Hook, an attorney at Waynesburg   Mr. and Mrs Blair are the parents of seven children—F L , Jesse, Agnes, Lizzie, John C , Maggie and Ida H. Three of their children belong to the Disciple Church, of which Mr. and Mrs. Blair are prominent members.   He has served as deacon for fifteen years and as Sabbath-school superintendent for twenty years.   Mr Blair is a Democrat and a member of the 1 O O. F.   He takes an active interest in the education of his children, and has served two terms as school director.

JAMES BOYD, farmer and stock-grower, Waynesburg, Penn , was born on Ruff's Creek, March 12, 1850.   His parents, James and Martha (Camp) Boyd, were natives of this county, and of German origin. James is the fifth in a family of nine children, eight of whom grew to maturity.   He was reared on the home farm, attending the district school, and has engaged in farming as his chief occupation. He is the owner of a fine farm of 120 acres where he resides in Franklin Township. In 1874 Mr. Boyd was united in marriage with Miss Anna, daughter of Abraham and Harriet (Watson) Arnold, and they have an interesting family of five children—Gertrude, Wilbert, Seymour, Emery and Martha.   Mr. and Mrs. Boyd are prominent members of the Baptist Church

R E. BROCK, M D , read medicine with his cousins, Drs Hugh W. and Luther S Brock, at Morgantown, W Va. Graduated at Jefferson Medical College, Philadelphia, March 3, '79.   Has been engaged in continuous practice at Waynesburg, Penn., since that time.

C E BOWER, superintendent of the W & W. Railroad, was born at Fredericktown, Washington County, Penn., April 11, 1849. He is a son of Charles W. and Charlotte (Hook) Bower, natives of Pennsylvania, and of German descent   His father was a steam engineer, and died in Waynesburg in 1885.   The subject of our sketch was reared in Waynesburg, where he attended the college.   During the war he and his father were engineers on a United States steamer in the Government service on the Tennessee River.   At the close of the war C E went into the oil business in Dunkard Township. He subsequently engaged in the iron business at Waynesburg, where he still owns one-half interest in the foundry.   In 1872 Mr Bower was united in marriage with Miss Josephine, daughter of Godfrey Gordon, and they are the parents of two children—Gerome and Oliver.   He has been superintendent of the W & W R R. since 1881

JAMES A. J. BUCHANAN, attorney at law, was born in Greene County, Penn., February 8, 1824, and is a son of Andrew and Rhoda (Stephenson) Buchanan.   His mother was born in New Jersey and his father in Chester County, Penn   They were of Scotch-Irish extraction.   His father, who was a prominent attorney, came to

Waynesburg in 1803, where he practiced law until his death in 1848. In 1832 and '33 he was a member of the State Legislature; and from 1836 to 1839 he served as a member of Congress. He served as county commissioner of Greene County when he received fifteen dollars for his services. The subject of this sketch was next to the youngest in a family of eleven children. He was educated in the Greene Academy at Carmichaels and at Washington College. At the age of twenty he commenced the study of law in his father's office, and in 1845 was admitted to the Greene County bar. In 1855 he was admitted to practice in the Supreme Courts of Pennsylvania. Mr. Buchanan, who is a Democrat, is a member of the I. O. O. F., and a Sir Knight Templar in the Masonic fraternity. He was married in this county to Miss Mary A., daughter of Daniel Borror. Mrs. Buchanan is of Scotch origin. Of their six children only two are living—Harriet, wife of William T. Lantz, cashier of the Farmers' and Drovers' Bank of Waynesburg; and Mary A., wife of Daniel S. Walton, Esq., attorney at law of Waynesburg.

HARVEY CALL, merchant, Waynesburg, Penn., was born in Oak Forest, Center Township, and is the son of James and Martha Call. His mother was born in Ohio and his father in Pennsylvania. They were of German and Irish descent. His father was a farmer and merchant in early life, and kept a general store at Oak Forest. Mr. Call is the oldest in a family of six children. He was reared on the farm, attended the district schools, and farmed until he was twenty-one years old. In 1872 he began clerking in a store, and in 1873 went to Fairbury, Ill., where he was employed as a salesman until 1875. He then returned to his native county and was again employed as a clerk in Waynesburg for a short time, and then engaged in the mercantile business for himself in the year 1876, and has since been very successful. In 1875 Mr. Call married Martha A., daughter of Captain John Morris, of Rogersville, Penn. They have one child—Clyde Morris Call. Mr. Call is a Republican. His wife is a member of the Disciple Church.

JOHN CALL, agent for mill works, was born in Oak Forest, Greene County, Penn., September 21, 1833. He is a son of James and Sarah (Hoge) Call, also natives of this county, and of Scotch lineage. His father was a farmer and miller. He owned and operated a mill at Oak Forest for over forty years. He died in 1872. His family consisted of eight children, of whom the subject of our sketch is next to the youngest. He was reared at Oak Forest, attended the common school, and early in life learned the miller's trade with his father; in 1851 commenced working at millwrighting; in 1875 commenced contracting and building in Waynesburg, followed that business for eight years, during which time built the jail and sheriff's house. He afterwards learned the new milling process, and contracts for and builds roller mills. He also takes contracts for other buildings Since 1884 he has been engaged with the Roller Mill Company of Waynesburg. In 1855 Mr Call married Miss Elizabeth, daughter of William Fry Mrs. Call was born in Center Township, this county, and is of German origin. They have four children, viz. William W., Mattie E. (deceased), Emma S. and Lafayette G Mr. and Mrs Call are members of the Baptist Church He moved to Waynesburg in the year 1871

G. W CHAPMAN, of the firm of Lemley & Chapman, liverymen, Waynesburg, Penn., was born in Greene County, Penn., July 15, 1851, and is a son of John and Sarah (Lemley) Chapman. His parents were also natives of this county, and of English lineage. His father was a farmer and engineer by occupation. The subject of our sketch is the oldest in a family of four children. 'He was reared in his native county and received his education in the district schools He started out in life working by the month as a farm hand, and subsequently worked at the blacksmith's trade in Waynesburg for a time Mr. Chapman then bought a team and engaged in hauling and farming until 1887, when he began the livery business in partnership with his uncle. He was united in marriage in 1880 with Lucinda, daughter of James Bradford. Mrs. Chapman is a native of Greene County and of English extraction Their children are—Hattie E. and Emma L Mr. Chapman is a Democrat. He and wife are members of the Methodist Episcopal Church.

A. I. COOKE, agent for the Adams Express Company, was born in Waynesburg May 7, 1853. He is a son of Joseph and Sarah (Bowman) Cooke, the former a native of New Jersey and the latter of Pennsylvania His father, a journalist by profession, was engaged in the newspaper business in New Jersey, and after coming to Pennsylvania was an editor until the breaking out of the war.. He was the owner of the *Commonwealth*, a paper published at Washington, Penn. In 1853 he came to Waynesburg, where he edited and published the *Eagle*, which paper subsequently merged into the *Republican*. At the breaking out of the Rebellion Mr. Cooke promptly enlisted in Company A, Eighteenth Pennsylvania Cavalry, and was elected Commissary Sergeant of his company. He was wounded three times, was taken prisoner, and suffered all the horrors of Andersonville and Libby prisons At the close of the war he was discharged and returned to Waynesburg, where he was appointed postmaster, and held the position for twenty years. He is now living a retired life in Waynesburg His family consists of six children, four of whom are now living. They are George A. B., an editor at Three Rivers, Mich.; Mary A., widow of Charles B. Bradley; Henry, a soldier killed in the battle of Winchester; Winfield Scott, Leslie (deceased), and A. I. All the sons, except A. I. and

Leslie, served as privates in the Union army. The subject of this sketch, Mr. A. I. Cooke, was assistant postmaster in Waynesburg for twenty-one years. Since 1874 he has been express agent, and is now running a freight and omnibus line at Waynesburg. He was married in 1875 to Arabella Blackmore Adams, a daughter of Major Dawson Adams. Mrs Cooke was born in Waynesburg. Her father was a tanner by trade, and was of English extraction. Mr. and Mrs. Cooke's children are Sallie A., Robert A. and Jessie B. Mr. Cooke Cooke is a Republican, and is a prominent member of the I. O. O. F., in which order he has taken many degrees He is also a member of Encampment No. 119.

JACOB COLE, ex-county commissioner, farmer and stock-grower, was born in Morris Township, Greene County, Penn., October 28, 1823. He is a son of John T. and Mary (Crodinger) Cole, who were of English and Dutch extraction. They came to Greene County and settled in Morris Township in 1815, on a farm near Nineveh, resided there until 1835, then removed to Wayne Township, and spent the balance of their lives. Five of their eight children grew to maturity, and all reside in this county. Jacob, the fourth member of the family, was from his youth engaged in agricultural pursuits. He attended the common school, and subsequently bought a farm in Wayne Township and engaged in farming and stock-raising. His farm in Franklin Township contains 100 acres. In 1879 Mr. Cole retired from the active work of the farm, and has since resided in Waynesburg. The same year he was elected county commissioner and served one term. In 1845 he was united in marriage with Frances, daughter of Abraham and Mary (Hamilton) Tustin. The marriage of Mr. and Mrs. Cole has been blessed with eight children, seven of whom grew to maturity—Mary J., deceased, who was the wife of Israel Shriver; Isaac S., a farmer; Elizabeth, wife of Jesse Knight; Caroline, wife of Miner Carpenter; J T., Abijah and William. In politics Mr. Cole is a Democrat. He is ever interested in school affairs, and has been school director in his township. He took an active interest in the Granger movement, and served as treasurer of the society for several years in Wayne Township

DAVID CRAWFORD, deceased, was one of the prominent attorneys of Waynesburg, where he practiced his chosen profession for many years. He was born in Greensboro, Greene County, Penn., June 18, 1825, and was a son of David Crawford, one of the early settlers of the county. Mr. Crawford was the only son in a large family, and at the time of his death, which occurred in March, 1886, he had but three sisters living, viz., Mrs. Margaret Hager, of Rockford, Illinois; Mrs. Mary Barrickman, of Virginia; and Mrs Dr. James Way, of Waynesburg. Mr. Crawford's earlier education was acquired in the rude log school-houses of Greene County. When twelve years of age he was employed to carry the Waynesburg *Messenger*, and in 1841 he walked to Wheeling, W. Va. After arriving in that city he worked in a chair factory for some time, then returned to Waynesburg and went to work in a saddle and harness shop kept by Amos Cleavenger. He improved all his leisure hours in study and his industry attracted the attention of Hon. Jesse Lazear, who was one of the prominent men of Waynesburg and cashier of the Farmers' and Drovers' Bank. Mr. Lazear gave him a position as clerk in the bank, and as all his time was not taken up with his duties there, he was enabled to attend Waynesburg College at the same time. He took an active interest in the literary society of which he was a member, and was debater for the Union society in its first contest with the Philomathean, in 1852. His opponent in this contest was Lorenzo Danford, who was afterwards elected member of Congress from Ohio. After Mr. Crawford had finished his education he read law in the office of John C. Flenniken, and was admitted to practice in 1853. He practiced law until he received the appointment of chief clerk of the Indian Bureau at Washington, D. C., which office he held during the administration of Pierce and Buchanan. He was a member of the Board of Commission and was sent to conclude a treaty with the Chippewas. He succeeded in settling without war, and so attracted the fancy of an Indian chief that he presented him with a saddle and bridle handsomely ornamented with beads and trinkets. After the expiration of his term of office, Mr. Crawford resumed his law practice and succeeded in accumulating a fair share of this world's goods. He served as cashier of the Farmers' and Drovers' Bank for a period of twelve years. Mr. Crawford took an active interest in the Democratic party in Pennsylvania and other States. He was a useful member in the Cumberland Presbyterian Church, and a strong advocate of temperance. He was united in marriage, February 5, 1857, with Miss Elizabeth, daughter of Major Remembrance H. Lindsey.

A. G. CROSS, physician and surgeon, was born at Waynesburg, Greene County, Penn., July 23, 1823. He is a son of Robert and Mary (Syphers) Cross, natives of this State. His father was among the early settlers of this county. Dr. Cross was the youngest in a family of thirteen children. He was reared on the farm near Waynesburg and received his literary education in Waynesburg College. He studied medicine under Dr. Inghram of Waynesburg, and began the practice of his profession in 1857. The Doctor has had quite an extensive practice and is one of the oldest physicians in Waynesburg. He has also written considerably for the press. His writings, which have been mostly on theological subjects and open letters to Robert G. Ingersoll, have been widely read and extensively copied. In 1848 Dr. Cross married Miss Harriet, daughter of Jesse Rinehart, and they have a family of five children—Wilber F., Robert I., Jesse R., Marietta and Walter L. The Doctor and wife are members of the Methodist Episcopal Church, in which he has served as local preacher, class leader, steward, trustee and superintendant of the Sabbath school. He is a Democrat, and served one term as county treasurer. He is a Sir Knight Templar in the Masonic Fraternity.

WILLIAM G. W. DAY was born in Waynesburg, this county, the 28th day of January, 1828, in a log house that stood on the lot adjoining the ground on which the Cumberland Presbyterian Church now stands. His father was Aaron D. Day, once well known in the county. He was a brick-maker by trade, carried on the business for many years, and many buildings, public and private, stand as monuments to his skill and industry. He was born in New Jersey and came to Pennsylvania, with his father, when a small boy and settled with the family in Morris Township, Washington County, and died in Waynesburg in June, 1863, aged seventy-five years. The paternal grandfather of the subject of this sketch, whose name was Moses Day, was born in Wales, and was a soldier in the Revolutionary war, serving seven years, lacking three months, when at home on a furlough on account of a wound received at the battle of Bunker Hill. The subject of this notice spent his early life in the country home, where he attended the subscription school three months in the year; and later on was a student at Waynesburg College a part of two sessions; but bad health compelled him to abandon study and gave up his purpose of a college course and pursue a different life for the time. His first active business in life was in riding as constable for over two years, being re-elected to the office. He was among the first officers appointed under the Internal Revenue law, holding the position of storekeeper and gauger for about three years, having received his appointment in the winter of 1866. After this he was twice elected a member of the Town Council of the borough of Waynesburg, and for a number of years was a member of the board of trustees of Waynesburg College and one of the building committee of the new building. In 1870 he purchased the Waynesburg Republican newspaper, organ of the Republican party of Greene County, and was editor and proprietor of the same for fifteen successive years thereafter, making a success in his new venture, and publishing, as admitted by all parties, the best newspaper ever before edited in the county. It was his paper that introduced the propriety and said the first word in favor of building a narrow-gauge railroad to Waynesburg; and alone, without encouragement and through much ridicule, he persisted for months in writing up the enterprise, and in personal efforts, until finally friends enlisted in the cause and the road was built. Mr. Day married Jane M., daughter of L. L. Miner, Esq., once one of the leading attorneys at the Waynesburg bar, and three children was the result of this union—a daughter, Marguerite, and two sons, Lawrence Minor and Lewis Edwin Mr. Day is a member of the Cumberland Presbyterian Church, and a trustee of the church property at Waynesburg.

HARVEY DAY, a farmer and stock-grower of Franklin Township, was born in Greene County, Penn., June 17, 1831 He is a son of Benjamin and Sarah (Tharp) Day, who were natives of New Jersey, and of German origin. His father, who was a successful farmer, came among the early settlers to this county, where he spent the remaining portion of his life. He died in 1861. Harvey is the sixth in a family of eight children Having been reared on a farm, he naturally engaged in farming as his life work, and is now the owner of a well improved farm of 275 acres Mr. Day is a self-made man, having started out in life with very little means. He at one time met with a heavy loss by fire, in which his house and other buildings were completely destroyed He did not yield to this discouragement, however, but soon replaced them with neat substantial buildings In 1852 Mr. Day married Miss Louise, daughter of Nathan and Hannah (Carter) Bane, who were natives of Washington County, Penn Mr and Mrs Day's children are: Sarah E, wife of J. A. Maple; Hannah J., wife of E. C Kelsey, Nancy A, wife of Elias Piatt; May E and Charles Benton. Their parents are members of the Baptist Church at Ruff's Creek, Penn Mr. Day is a Democrat, and has served as county auditor and school director of his township. He takes a great interest in thoroughbred stock and has done much to improve the stock in Greene County. He is a man of strong will power and unusual energy, to which his success in life may be largely attributed.

B. B. W. DENNY, hardware merchant, was born four miles west of Waynesburg, October 29, 1852. He is a son of M W. and Jane (Luse) Denny, natives of Pennsylvania, and of English extraction His grandparents came from England to Ohio, then moved to Pennsylvania and were among the early settlers of Greene County. Mr. Denny's father, who died in 1875, was the owner of 800 acres of land, and was an extensive dealer in stock. His family consisted of four children, B. B. W. being the second. He was reared on a farm in Center and Jefferson townships, and received his education in Waynesburg College. He has been engaged in farming and stock-growing, and, in partnership with his brother, owns a hardware store in Waynesburg. He was united in marriage January 3, 1882, with Miss Alice, daughter of Samuel Melvin.

HON. J. B. DONLEY, an attorney of Waynesburg, Penn., was born at Mount Morris, this county, October 10, 1838. He is a son of Hon. Patrick and Margaret (Morris) Donley also natives of this county. His ancestors were among the earliest settlers of Greene County, and have usually been farmers. Mr. Donley's great-grand-father was a captain in the Revolutionary war, and his grandfather Morris was a soldier in the war of 1812. His father was a farmer and merchant, and was a member of the State Legislature in 1861 and 1862, serving two terms. At the age of eighty-four years he still resides at Mount Morris, where he has spent many years of his life. Of his family of eight children Hon. J. B. Donley is the fourth. He graduated at Waynesburg College in 1859, when he went West and located in Abingdon, Illinois, having obtained a position as principal of schools. In 1860 he became professor in Abingdon College. When the war broke out Prof. Donley promptly enlisted under the first call of President Lincoln, but on account of the large number offering the company was not received into the service and disbanded, and Prof. Donley continued teaching until the summer of 1862, when he again enlisted and helped raise Company I of the Eighty-third Volunteer Infantry. When the company was organized he was elected captain, being the youngest captain in the regiment. It was the Eighty-third Illinois Infantry that fought the rebels alone at the second battle of Fort Donnelson. This regiment was distinguished for the great number of large men within its ranks, and was among the best regiments organized in the State. Captain Donley was discharged in July, 1865, when he returned to his native county, and went to Albany, New York, and in 1866 graduated from the law department of the Albany University. In 1867 he was admitted to practice at the Waynesburg bar, and was appointed register in bankruptcy during the same year, holding the position until 1869, when he became a member of the Forty-first Congress, having been elected thereto in 1868. He votes the Republican ticket, casting his first vote for President for Abraham Lincoln in 1860. He is president of the board of trustees of the Methodist Episcopal Church, of which he is a member. He is also assistant superintendent in the Sabbath-school. Captain Donley is president of the Waynesburg Park Company. He is a prominent member of the Knights of Honor, and a Master Mason in the Masonic fraternity. He also belongs to the G. A. R. Post of Waynesburg. Captain Donley was married in this county, in 1871, to Miss Ellen W., daughter of Col. John H. Wells, a retired attorney of Waynesburg. They have three children—Nellie W., Grace E. and Patrick. The family are members of the Methodist Episcopal Church.

THOMAS E. DOUGAL, farmer, stock-grower and speculator, Waynesburg, Penn., was born in Washington County, Penn., May 23, 1845, and is a son of David and Elizabeth (Porter) Dougal. His

35

mother was a native of Pennsylvania. His father, who was born in England, was a teacher by profession, to which he devoted most of his life, engaging a short time in farming and merchandising Thomas was the oldest son in a family of eleven children, and enjoyed the advantages of a good education. He attended the schools in his native county, also the high school at Uniontown, Penn. He very naturally took up his father's profession, and engaged in teaching for ten years. He then engaged in farming and stock dealing; has made a success of the business and owns 178 acres of land. Mr. Dougal has been a resident of Greene County since 1865—the year he was married His wife's maiden name was Clarissa Wanee Her parents were Thomas and Elizabeth Wanee, natives of Pennsylvania. Mr. and Mrs. Dougal were the parents of ten children—Elizabeth E , Isabella I , Thomas A., John S , David W., Anna L , Dora B., Archibald and Mary, twins, and Viola. Mr Dougal is a Republican in politics, in religion a Presbyterian Mrs. Dougal is a zealous member of the Methodist Church.

R. F. DOWNEY, attorney and counsellor at law, was born in Waynesburg, Penn , May 18, 1849. He is a son of Robinson and Catharine (Inghram) Downey, who were of Scotch-Irish descent His father came to Waynesburg in 1837 and studied law. He was admitted to the bar in 1839, and was a successful practitioner and business man. He dealt largely in real estate, having erected many of the best buildings in Waynesburg He died in 1874 Mr. Downey was a member of the Baptist Church, of which he was a liberal supporter. For many years he edited a paper in Waynesburg He was one of the earliest and strongest friends of Waynesburg College, never neglecting an opportunity to further the interests of that institution His children were all students in the college and, with one exception, are graduates of the school Mr. Downey was one of the most respected and best beloved of Greene County's citizens His children are R F., John J , who died in the army, Emma (deceased), F. W and Kate. R F. Downey, the subject of this sketch, was reared in Waynesburg and educated in the college, where he graduated in 1867. He then studied law with his father, and was admitted to the bar in 1871 He has been a successful practitioner, devoting his entire time to his profession

J. W ELY, physician, Waynesburg, Penn , was born in Whiteley Township, this county, September 24, 1855. He is a son of George and Mary (Warrick) Ely, who were natives of Washington County and moved to Greene County in 1840. Mrs. Ely departed this life December 30, 1887. Dr. Ely remained on the farm with his parents until he was eighteen years of age, at which time he began teaching school through the winter, and going to school during the summer months. He acquired his education in the select schools and

Waynesburg College. The Doctor was married, June 23, 1878, to Lucy, daughter of Godfrey Gordon, of Waynesburg. Mrs. Ely was born August 9, 1857 They have one child, Mary R., born August 11, 1880. In August, 1878, Dr. Ely opened a store at Garard's Fort, and in April of the next year he moved his store to Newtown, Penn , where he received a large patronage. On June 22, 1879, his store and entire property was destroyed by fire; but not being easily discouraged, he began the study of medicine with Dr. Sherbino, of Waynesburg, and graduated at the Medical College of Cincinnati, Ohio, in 1882 with high honors. He then returned to Waynesburg, and took Dr. Sherbino's place in the practice and has secured a liberal patronage in the county, being its only homœopathic physician. He is a Republican, and a member of the Methodist Episcopal Church.

JONAS ELY, farmer and stock-grower, Waynesburg, Penn., was born in Washington County, Penn., August 28, 1823. He is a son of Jonas and Euphen (Wilson) Ely, who were of German and Scotch extraction. His mother was also a native of Washington County. His father, who was a farmer and. stock-grower, was born in Berks County, Penn , and came to Greene County in 1843. He settled near Waynesburg on the farm now owned by J. A. J. Buchanan, Esq. Mr. Ely reared a family seven children, of whom Jonas is the sixth. He received a common school education in Washington County, where he remained on the farm with his parents until their death. His father died in 1863 and his mother in 1860. Mr. Ely has been successful as a farmer, and is the owner of 384 acres of land. In 1870 he bought his present farm, to which he moved in 1875. The following year he erected one of the finest houses in Franklin Township, where he now resides. Mr. Ely was united in marriage in Greene County, in 1845, with Miss Elizabeth, daughter of William and Margaret (Milligan) Hill, who were of English and Irish origin. Mrs Ely's father was born in Franklin Township in 1798. To Mr. and Mrs. Ely have been born three children—William and Jonas, farmers; and Belle, who is the wife of Jonathan Funk, Esq., of Waynesburg, Penn. Their mother is a consistent member of the Cumberland Presbyterian Church. Mr. Ely takes great interest in the schools of the county, and has served seventeen years as school director. He has also been for several years secretary of the Green County Agricultural Society. In politics he is a Republican. Jonas, his second son, was born October 15, 1848, and is a successful farmer. In 1878 he married Miss Alice, daughter of Madison Saunders, of Waynesburg, Penn.

W. W. EVANS, of the firm of Ragan & Evans, editors and proprietors of the *Waynesburg Independent*, was born in Marshall

County, W. Va., February 8, 1851. His parents were Walter and
Sarah (Roberts) Evans.   His father was of Welsh extraction and
born in Baltimore, Maryland.   Mr. and Mrs. Evans were married
in Marshall County, where they remained a short time and then
moved to Iowa   Here Mrs. Evans' health began to fail and they returned to Virginia, where she died in 1854   When an infant Mr.
Evans was carried on horseback by his parents from Baltimore to
Marshall County, W. Va. · Mr. Evans' second wife was Susannah
Hutchinson (*nee* Francis).· She is still living   Mr. Evans died
January 3, 1882   He was the father of fourteen children, twelve of
whom are living.   W. W Evans, the subject of our sketch, was uni-
ted in marriage, April 29, 1874, with Miss Mary, daughter of W. T.
E. and Mary (Stull) Webb.   Her father was a native of Wheeling,
W Va , and her mother of Louisville, Ky.   To Mr. and Mrs.
Evans have been born three children—Wilbert W , Erma, and Jesse
(deceased).   Mr. Evans remained on a farm until twelve years of
age, when he went with his parents to Moundsville, W Va , his
father having been elected to ·the office of recorder of Marshall
County.   At the age of fifteen he began learning the printer's trade
and has since been engaged in that business.   In 1872 he purchased
the *Moundsville Reporter*, which he owned for a period of seven
years. He came to Waynesburg in 1880, and purchased a half interest in the newspaper of which he is now associate editor and proprietor.   Mr Evans is a member of the Knights of Honor and the
Royal Arcanum.   When sixteen years of age he united with the M.
E. Church, of which his wife is also a member

    J. M FUNK, lumber dealer, Waynesburg, Penn., was born in
Richhill Township, this county, February 5, 1846. He is a son
of Jacob and Mary (McGlumphy) Funk, of German and Irish descent, the former a native of Maryland and the latter of Greene
County, Penn.   His father was a farmer, and died in Waynesburg
in 1884.   J. M. Funk is one of a family of three children—all boys.
He grew to manhood in Waynesburg, and chose farming as his chief
pursuit. When twenty years of age, however, he learned the carpenter's trade, serving the regular apprenticeship of three years.   In
1872 he established himself in business in Waynesburg and, although
he met with a serious loss by fire, May 25, 1881, which amounted to
some ten thousand dollars, he immediately rebuilt and is now owner
and proprietor of a planing-mill, in which a large number of men are
employed the year round. He does contracting and building, and
has a number of substantial residences in Waynesburg In 1878 Mr.
Funk married Miss Belle, daughter of Jonas Ely, a prominent
farmer of Franklin Township   Mr. and Mrs. Funk are members of
the Cumberland Presbyterian Church   He is a Democrat, and has

served as a member of the town council and of the school board in the borough. He is also a member of the I. O. O. F.

J. C. GARARD, Esq., prothonotary, Waynesburg, Penn., was born in Greene County. He is a son of Justus and Emeline (Mestrezat) Garard, also natives of this county, and of French and English descent. The family were among the earliest settlers of the county, Mr. Garard's great-grandfather being the Rev. John Corbly, one of the pioneer Baptist ministers His grandfather Garard was a farmer, and Justus Garard, his father, was a cabinet-maker and engaged in that business for years at Mapletown, Penn. The subject of our sketch was reared in Monongahela Township, where he received his early education in the common schools. He afterwards spent some time in the State Normal School at California, Penn., and Wayesburg College. After leaving college he taught school until 1878, when he was elected clerk of the courts of Greene County and served six years. Mr. Garard was elected prothonotary in 1884 and re-elected in 1887, and has filled that office very acceptably. In politics he is a Democrat. He was married in Fayette County, Penn., in 1879, to Miss A. B. Schroyer, at Masontown, Penn.

CAPTAIN JOHN ADAM GORDON, farmer and stock grower, Waynesburg, Penn., was born in Whiteley Township, Greene County, June 16, 1816. His parents were Mark and Susan (Shriver) Gordon, who were of Irish and German extraction His father, who was a farmer all his life, was a native of West Virginia, came to Greene County, Penn., in 1796 and settled in Whiteley Township. His family consisted of ten children John Adam was reared on the home farm where he received his early education, and subsequently attended Greene Academy at Carmichaels, Penn. He devoted four years of his life exclusively to teaching and also taught about twenty winter terms, spending the summer months in farming, which he has made his chief pursuit. In 1880 he bought his present farm and moved to Franklin Township, where he built a neat and substantial residence in 1887. Mr. Gordon has been twice married; first, in 1842, to Miss Rebecca, daughter of John Crawford, of Carmichaels, Greene County. Mrs Gordon died in 1853. Of their five children only two are living—Rebecca, and Rev. M L. Gordon, D. D., now a missionary in Japan. The deceased are B. Jennings, who died when a child; John Crawford, who was a prominent physician at Waynesburg; and William Lynn, a teacher, who died in Michigan in 1886, he taught in Pennsylvania and Wisconsin and Charleston, S. C., and was principal of a college in Austin, Texas at his death. Mr. Gordon's second wife was Miss Margaret, daughter of Ephraim Crawford, of Fayette County, Penn. They are the parents of five sons: Thomas J, a farmer; Solomon, Robert who died in childhood; Edgar C. and James R. Mr. Gordon has the distinction of being the first superintendent of public schools in Greene County, to which position he was elected in 1856, and was re-elected in 1860. When the war of the Rebellion broke out he resigned and assisted in raising a company, which formed part of the Eighty-fifth Regiment Pennsylvania Volunteers (Col Howell's). It was Company G, of that organization Mr. Gordon was elected First Lieutenant of said company, and served in that capacity until Capt I. M. Abraham was promoted to Major of the regiment; was then commissioned Captain by Gov. A. I. Curtin, of Pennsylvania, serving in all three.

SOLOMON GORDON, a retired farmer and-stock grower who was born in Whiteley Township, April 2, 1801, is a son of John A and Cassandra (Holland) Gordon. The former was a native of Maryland and the latter of West Virginia, where they were married. They were the parents of seven children, the youngest of whom is Solomon His father, who was a farmer, came to Greene County in 1795 and located in Whiteley Township, where Solomon grew to manhood. The subject of this sketch has been for many years a successful farmer in Franklin Township. He was united in marriage the first time, in 1824, with Sarah Inghram, who was a descendent of one of the pioneer families in this county, and died in 1858. They were the parents of five children—Elizabeth, wife of R Huss; William I., a farmer who owns two hundred acres of land; Adam, superintendent of the poor farm; James, and John who was a soldier in the war of 1861 and died in the army Mr. Gordon married for his second wife the widow of George B Willison. Her maiden name was Sarah Mannell In politics Mr. Gordon is a Democrat.

HON. BASIL GORDON, Associate Judge of Greene County, Penn, was born in Whiteley Township, this county, December 27, 1822 He is a son of Mark and Susan (Shriver) Gordon.' His mother was born in Greene County and his father in Virginia. Both were of German extraction. His father came to Greene County when a child, and was a farmer by occupation. Basil was the fourth in a family of ten children. He was reared on a farm in this county, and educated in Greene Academy at Carmichaels, Penn. Mr. Gordon has made farming his occupation and has been very successful. He was united in the holy bonds of matrimony, May 20, 1847, with Mariar, daughter of Arthur Inghram, and they are the parents of five children, viz., John A, a farmer; Susan, Virginia, wife of Thomas Montgomery, Josiah and Alice The Judge is trustee in the M. P. Church He has served as township auditor, superintendent of the poor and school director.

HON. JOHN B GORDON, deceased, was born in Whiteley Township, Greene County, Penn, December 4, 1798 He was a son of John A and Cassandra (Holland) Gordon, natives of Virginia, where their marriage ceremony was performed. They moved to Greene County, Penn., about 1795, and remained until their demise. Mrs. Gordon departed this life in 1805 and her husband in 1816. John B. Gordon, the subject of this sketch, was the fifth of a family of seven children, of whom only one, Solomon, survives. July 12, 1847, Mr. Gordon was united in marriage with Miss Delilah Inghram, a native of Franklin Township, this county, where she was born April 23, 1821. Mrs. Gordon is a daughter of William and Elizabeth (Rinehart) Inghram, who were also natives of this county. Mr. Inghram died in 1845 and Mrs. Inghram in 1864. To Mr. and Mrs. Gordon were born five children, four of whom are living, viz., Lizzie I., George W., Lucy E. and John B. The deceased is Carrie L. George W. was united in marriage with Helen Scott, and they are the parents of two children—Lucy D. and Carrie L. Hon. John B. Gordon was reared on a farm and received instructions from his father in the art of husbandry, which honorable occupation—in connection with raising stock for the markets—he followed until his death. At that time he owned one thousand acres of land in Greene County. He, in common with many of the inhabitants of middle and western Pennsylvania, had a passion for military life. He was elected Major of the Forty-sixth Regiment of militia, held the office for seven years and took much pride in discharging its duties. Mr. Gordon served his fellow citizens in civil as well as in a military capacity. Having been elected to the office of county commissioner in 1825, he served two terms; and was a member of the House of Representatives in 1847 and 1848. Mr. Gordon departed this life December 28, 1876, and by his death the county lost a good citizen, and his family a kind father and husband.

THOMAS GOODWIN, ex-treasurer of Greene County, is at present a farmer, and was born in Franklin Township, this county, September 25, 1807. He is a son of Moses and Elizabeth (Hagan) Goodwin, natives of Maryland. His father, who lived to an old age, was born in 1790 and spent most of his life on a farm in Greene County. Of their eight children, only two are living. Thomas was the fourth in the family. He was reared on the home farm, attended the subscription schools, and has made farming his main occupation. He started out in the world with but little means, but by his great energy and patient endeavor was enabled to purchase his present farm in 1877. Mr. Goodwin is a Democrat in politics. He was elected treasurer of the county in 1873, and served one term. In 1832 he married Miss Catharine, daughter of Jesse Orndoff. Her mother's maiden name was Catharine Strosnider. Her father was a soldier in the war of 1812.

H. M. GRIMES.—Among the descendants of the pioneers of Greene County we mention H. M. Grimes, an enterprising farmer of

Franklin Township, who now owns and resides on the farm where he was born, January 26, 1837   His mother's maiden name was Margaret Muckle   She was a native of this county.   His father, William Grimes, was born in New Jersey.   Of his six children, the subject of this sketch is the youngest.   He was reared in Franklin Township, where he received his education in the district schools   Mr. Grimes has been very successful in his chosen pursuit, and is the owner of 338 acres of land.   In 1861 he married Harriet, daughter of Arthur Rinehart   Their children are—William A , J. W , Lucy, Mary E , Albert R and H. C   Mrs Grimes is a zealous member of the Methodist Episcopal Church   In politics Mr. Grimes is a Democrat

D. H HAINER, freight and ticket agent for the Waynesburg and Washington Railroad, at Waynesburg, Penn., was born in Washington County, Penn., October 9, 1845, and is a son of Henry and Elizabeth (Riggle) Hainer.   His father, who has all his life been a farmer, was born in Germany, and came to Washington County, Penn., in 1832, where he lived until he moved to Richland County, Ohio, where he now resides   Mr Hainer is the oldest in a family of eight children   He was reared on the farm, attended the common schools, and was later a student in the Academy at Savannah, Ohio, and Lexington, Ohio, Male and Female Seminary.   Early in life he taught school for a time.   He was then employed as a salesman in Lexington, Ohio, for five years, when he was accepted as a full partner with his former employer.   He continued in the mercantile trade with him for five years, when he sold out and returned to Washington County, and engaged in farming from 1875 until 1879.   He then came to Waynesburg, where he engaged in business with his uncle until 1883, when he was appointed to his present position   Mr. Hainer was married in Washington County in 1873, to Alice, daughter of David S. Walker, and they have one child, a daughter—Adda E   The entire family are members of the Presbyterian Church, in which he is an elder and also superintendent of the Sabbath-school.

SAMUEL HARVEY was born in Center Township, Greene County, March 2, 1820, and is a son of Thomas and Anna (Higinbotham) Harvey   His mother was born in Fayette County, and his father in Philadelphia.   They were of English and French descent.   His father, a farmer by occupation, came to this county in 1807, and settled on a tract of land eleven miles west of Waynesburg, known as the "Old Harvey Farm," and resided there until his death in 1876, in the eighty-seventh year of his age.   Of his three sons, Samuel is the oldest, and was reared on said farm in Center Township, where he received an education of the rural district, and chose farming as his occupation, at the same time dealing in wool, livestock and real estate.   Mr Harvey has been a successful business man, and is one of Greene County's self-made men, his success being entirely due to his own efforts and business ability. In 1881 he moved to Waynesburg, and is still engaged in the wool trade. In 1846 Mr. Harvey married Sarah I. Throckmorton. Their children are—William C., who enlisted, at the age of seventeen years, in Company I, One Hundred and Sixteenth Pennsylvania Volunteers, and took part, under Gen. Hancock, in the famous "Battle of the Wilderness," and died of typhoid fever in 1864; Anna M., wife of the late Dr. J. S. Barmore, of Chicago; Kate E., wife of Dr. J. T. Iams, of Waynesburg; Alice I., and Charles T., a farmer and stock-dealer, who still resides on the old Harvey farm in Center Township. Mr. and Mrs Harvey are members of the South Ten-Mile Baptist Church, where he has served as deacon and trustee for many years.

WILLIAM THOMPSON HAYS—Among the early settlers of Waynesburg as the county seat of Greene, was William Thompson Hays, who was born in Adams County, Penn., April 8, 1775, and who died in Waynesburg, June 29, 1846. He was married in Newville, Cumberland County, Penn., to Mary McKibben, and in 1804 removed to Waynesburg, embarking in the mercantile business on Main street, on the corner now known as the "Fisher Building," opposite the present F. & D. National Bank. Afterwards, losing his wife by death, he married Sarah Wilson, daughter of James Wilson, Esq , the first post-master of Waynesburg, who lived and kept the post-office opposite the court-house on the site occupied by the Messenger building. Mr. Hays was one of the early representatives of his adopted county in the State Legislature, he and his brother, Adam Hays, who was a bachelor and came with him and made his home in Waynesburg, both having served the people of Greene in that capacity. Adam Hays was also at one time sheriff of the county, and died February 28, 1848, aged about sixty-six. W. T. Hays was also, for a period of about twenty years, phrothonotary of Greene County, he being successor of John Boreman, Esq., who was the first protho-notary of the county. In 1813, while in the mercantile business, Mr. Hays brought on to Waynesburg, and was instrumental in establishing the *Messenger* newspaper, with John Baker as editor and publisher. The paper was first printed about where the tele-graph office now is, just west of the Walton House, Mr. Hays own-ing the premises and living in the house adjoining, occupying the present site of the Walton House. He had four children who lived to reach maturity—two by each wife By the first, George W , who was educated at Cannonsburg College, Penn , studied medicine with Dr. Hays, of Sharpsburg, Md., and died with the cholera while in the practice of his profession, at that place, in 1834 Maria C., the daughter, was married to Laurence L Minor, a prominent attorney of Waynesburg, who died in that place in 1883, she still surviving.

By his second wife were born James W. and Henrietta She was married to William Campbell, son of Benjamin Campbell, one of the early and prominent merchants of Waynesburg, and both her husband and herself, with a large family of children, still live in that place. James Wilson Hays was born in Waynesburg, on December 21, 1817, and received such education as was attainable in his youth in the subscription schools of the town.   The first business engaged in on his own account was as editor and proprietor of the Waynesburg *Messenger* in about 1842, as successor to Hon C. A Black. His editorial career at this time included the presidential canvas of Polk against Clay, and that of Francis R. Shunk for Governor.   At a later period Mr. Hays was associated with Col James S Jennings as co-editor of the *Messenger*, including the presidential canvas of 1860, in which Lincoln was elected President In 1853, during the presidency of Pierce, Mr Hays received an appointment as clerk in the post-office department at Washington City.   This position he occupied some three years, resigning on account of failing health. He held a position, in 1849–50, on the Pennsylvania Canal at Pittsburg, under appointment by canal commissioners of the State. Mr. Hays was married in 1842 to Hannah Minor, daughter of Abia Minor, Esq., and grand-daughter of Hon John Minor, who was one of the original, or first associate judges of Greene County at its formation   Mrs Hays died in 1862   Seven children were born to them, who lived to reach maturity, viz.—William Thompson, married to Jennie Jewell; Sarah Sophia, to Ira L Nickeson; James W , to Emma Smith; Frances Henrietta, to James M. Ferrell; Abia Minor, to Nannie Huston; Hannah Maria, to James L. Smith, and Jesse Lazear, to Sadie Goodwin—all living at this date (1888) except Mrs. Nickeson, who died May 4, 1888   In 1867 Mr Hays removed from Waynesburg, where he had been connected with his brother-in-law, Hon William Cotterel, in the tanning and leather business, to Graysville, Richhill Township, and engaged in merchandising, from which place his children were all married, and where he continued to reside until October, 1887, when he returned to his native town, Waynesburg   In 1875 he was elected, on the Democratic ticket, to the senate of Pennsylvania, for the fourtieth district, embracing the counties of Greene and Fayette, and re-elected to a second term on the expiration of the first

JOSEPH S. HERTIG, dentist, was born in Fayette County, Penn , November 28, 1834, and is a son of John G. and Elizabeth (Showalter) Hertig   His mother, who was of German extraction, was born in Fayette County   His father was a native of France, and a farmer and school teacher by occupation   Dr. Hertig, the oldest of eleven children, was reared on his father's farm, attending the district school.   He spent his early life as a teacher, having taught five terms in Fayette County, Ohio, and subsequently in this county.   In 1858 he commenced the study of dentistry at Smithfield, Penn., and began practicing in 1868 in New Holland, Ohio. He subsequently located at Delphos, Allen County, Ohio.   Returning to Fayette County in 1862, he remained for four years, then came to Waynesburg, where his skill and gentlemanly demeanor soon won for him a large and lucrative practice among the influential families of the town and vicinity.   The Doctor is thoroughly posted in all the details of his profession, and devotes his time diligently to study. He was married in Fayette County, in 1864, to Miss Nancy, daughter of William Scott.   Their children are—Horace and Owen, the latter a graduate of Waynesburg College, and at present a student in the Dental College at Philadelphia, Penn.   Dr. Hertig is a prominent member of the Odontological Society of Western Pennsylvania.

MAJOR B. F. HERRINGTON, a farmer and stock-grower, of Franklin Township, was born in Greene County, Penn., November 18, 1843, and is a son of Thomas and Caroline (Kramer) Herrington. His father was a manufacturer of boots and shoes and carried on his business for many years in the southern part of Greene County. His family consisted of ten children, of whom B. F. is the sixth.   He received his early education in the common schools of his native county, and subsequently attended Duff's Commercial College at Pittsburg, Penn.   Mr. Herrington was employed as a clerk in a store for a number years, and engaged in the mercantile trade at Morrisville, Penn., in 1861.   The year following he enlisted, as a private, in Company A, Eighteenth Pennsylvania Cavalry.   When the regiment was organized, he was elected Second Lieutenant of Company G., and was subsequently promoted to the position of First Lieutenant and then Captain.   He was taken captive and suffered the horror of prison life for sixteen months in Libby, Macon, Ga. and Columbia, S. C.   Major Herrington was one of the six hundred officers who were placed under the fire of the Union gun when the Union men bombarded Charlestown, S. C.   Soon after his return home he was commissioned Major of the eighth division of the National Guards of Pennsylvania and served five years, was commissioned again with same rank and assigned to duty on the staff of Gen. Gallagher as commissary of division.   He again engaged in the mercantile business in Waynesburg, where he had a good trade and liberal patronage. The Major was united in marriage, in 1860, with Miss Maggie Johns. She died in 1877, leaving a family of three children—Ella, Herman and Daisy.   In 1887 he began farming, and was united in marriage, the same year, with Nannie (Wisecarver) Worley.   Major Herrington is a Republican, and a member of the I. O. O. F.   He was the first Commander of the McCullough G. A. R. Post, No. 367.

JESSE HILL, retired farmer and stock grower, Waynesburg, Penn, was born November 23, 1814, on the farm he now owns. His parents, Samuel and Elizabeth (Cather) Hill, were natives of Greene County, and of Irish and English extraction His father was a farmer all his life; his family consisted of eleven children. Jesse is the youngest son. He was reared on his father's farm, educated in the old-fashioned log school-house and has made farming the business of his life. He owns 150 acres of good farming land, and valuable town property in the borough of Waynesburg. In 1841 Mr. Hill married Maria, daughter of Thomas Hoskinson. Of their six children five are living—Carrie, wife of Dr. W S Throckmorton, of Nineveh, Penn.; Thomas B, a physician at Ruff's Creek, Penn ; Elizabeth, wife of J D Nulton; Willie E and Jesse F., who was born March 11, 1853, and has charge of the home farm. He was married in 1881, to Philena, daughter of Thomas Ross, and they have two children—Frank and Willie R Mr and Mrs. Jesse Hill, Sr , are members of the Baptist Church Mr. Hill was for fifteen years clerk of the county commissioners.

NORVAL HOGE, by occupation an organ builder, was born in Waynesburg, March 8, 1835. He is a son of John and Rebecca (Oakes) Hoge, natives of Pennsylvania, and of Scotch-Irish descent. His grandfather was a carpenter and came from Winchester, Va. The history of the family shows them to have been farmers and mechanics, and many of the family have succeeded in accumulating a fair share of this world's goods. Mr Hoge, unlike his ancestors, has turned his attention to study rather than to making money. He has given most of his time to organ building, and has also engaged in repairing all kinds of machinery, making sun dials, building flying shuttle looms, etc. Mr. Hoge has made twelve organs, and his knowledge of almost any kind of complicated machinery gives evidence of unusual mechanical genius The greater part of his life has been spent in Waynesburg He attended the common-school and college, and early in life began to develop a taste for mechanics, being able to repair clocks and watches when a mere boy. For several years he was engaged with a Pittsburgh firm, in tuning pianos and organs, and from some of the most celebrated musicians of the United States his work has received the highest endorsements, among which is the following·

" MR. NORVAL HOGE—My Dear Sir: " Allow me to compliment you upon the magnificent manner in which you tuned the piano for our use. I have never, outside of Boston and New York, met with an instrument that stood so splendidly to pitch throughout our entire programme. It certainly shows the work of an artist Accept my own and company's thanks for your care. Yours,
" LEM H. WILEY, WALTER EMERSON."

Mr. Hoge also repairs and runs steam engines, and since 1886 has run the engine at the roller mills at Waynesburg. In 1856 he married Catharine M., daughter of Reasin Huffman, and they have four children, viz.: Mary Elizabeth, Almira Jane, Minnie May and Thomas J. The family are members of the Waynesburg Baptist Church.

ASA B. HOGE, commercial traveler, was born in Morgan Township, Greene County, Penn., September 23, 1841, and is a son of Solomon and Rachel (Huss) Hoge, natives of this State. His father, who was a miller and grain speculator, was born in this county in 1803, and died in Waynesburg in 1878. Mr. Hoge's grandparents, who were natives of Virginia, and of Scotch-Irish extraction, were members of the Society of Friends. His father's family consisted of eight children, of whom Asa B. is the fifth , He was reared in his native county and received his education in the old Greene Academy at Carmichaels, Penn. Mr. Hoge remained with his parents until eighteen years of age, when he went to Baltimore, Md., and was for two years employed as a clerk in a store He then went to Pittsburgh, Penn , and was salesman in a large jobbing house for a period of twelve years. In 1876 he went to Philadelphia and accepted his present position as traveling salesman, visiting the larger towns and cities throughout Pennsylvania and Virginia. Mr. Hoge has made his own way in the world. • He meets with success in his business, and is the owner of valuable property on Main street in Waynesburg. He was united in marriage in 1877 with Miss Mary, daughter of John and Jane (Walker) Phelan, and sister to Richard Phelan, a prominent attorney of the Waynesburg bar. Mr. and Mrs. Hoge have a bright and interesting family of two little daughters—Jane P. and Mary Frances.

JAMES M. HOGE, attorney at law, was born in this county June 16, 1853. He is a son of Solomon and Sarah (Overturff) Hoge, natives of Pennsylvania, and of Scotch-Irish extraction. His father was a farmer and also justice of the peace for many years, and died December 6, 1874. James M. is the second son in a family of twelve children, all but one of whom grew to maturity. His paternal ancestors were Quakers and among the pioneer settlers of this county. Mr. Hoge received his education in Waynesburg College. He made a special study of surveying, and has devoted much of his time to that business. He studied law with Hon C. A. Black, at Waynesburg, and was admitted to the bar in 1882. In 1883 he clerked in the prothonary's office, and on the death of prothonotary, was appointed by Governor Pattison to fill unexpired term, and in 1885 was appointed notary public, at the same time engaging in the practice of law. He was married in 1878 to Martha M., daughter of John McNeely. Mrs Hoge is of Irish descent.

They have one child—Owen Solomon. Mr. and Mrs. Hoge are members of the Baptist Church. He is a Democrat, and has passed all the degrees in subordinate Lodge of I. O. O. F.

ISAAC HOOPER, tobacconist, Waynesburg, Penn., was born in Washington County, Penn., March 19, 1819, is a son of Isaac and Mary (Steen) Hooper, natives of Pennsylvania, and of Scotch extraction. His father was a farmer of Washington County. His family consisted of six children, of whom Isaac is the youngest. He was reared in the borough of Washington, where he attended school and early in life learned the cigar maker's trade. In 1842 he came to Waynesburg, where he has since engaged in his present business, selling most of his cigars in Greene County. Mr. Hooper was married in 1842 to Miss Rebecca, daughter of Samuel Prigg She was born in Washington County, and is of German origin. They have six children, viz.: Melvina, wife of A. J. Sowers, a prominent merchant of Waynesburg; Saumuel P., a tobacconist; Mary (deceased), Virginia, wife of John Campbell; Margaret, wife of Robert Adams; and Dora. Mr. and Mrs. Hooper are members of the Baptist Church, in which he is deacon. He is a Republican, and a member of the I. O. O. F.

W. A. HOOK, Esq., Waynesburg, Penn., was born October 13, 1838, and is a son of John T. and Eliza (Inghram) Hook. His parents were descendants of the earliest settlers of Greene County, and of Scotch-Irish origin. Mr. Hook's father was a saddler by trade, and died November 3, 1883, at Waynesburg, where he had spent his life. William A., the oldest son, was reared and educated in Waynesburg. He reached his senior year in college, when on account of sickness he was compelled to give up school. He chose the law as his profession, and studied in the office of Wyly & Buchanan, in Waynesburg. Mr. Hook was admitted to the bar of this county in 1871, and in 1872 was elected district attorney, in which capacity he served for six years He is an active member of the Democratic party, and a successful lawyer.

THOMAS HOOK, farmer, was born in Waynesburg, Penn., on the 27th day of September, 1840. He is a son of John T. and Eliza (Inghram) Hook, also natives of this county. His ancestors were among the early settlers of the county. His father, who was a soldier in the war of 1812, was a harness-maker for many years, and in later life engaged in farming. Thomas was reared in Waynesburg where he remained until twelve years of age, then moved with his parents to a farm in Franklin Township where he still resides. He attended the common school, and early in life chose farming as his chief occupation. Mr. Hook has been twice united in marriage— first, in 1863, with Miss Sarah, daughter of William Patterson, a prominent farmer of Whiteley Township Their children are—Ida, wife of William Ely, and Lucy, a student in Waynesburg College. Mrs Hook died in 1887. Her husband afterwards married, in 1885, Miss Susan, daughter of Uriah Inghram. She is a member of the M. E. Church. Mr. Hook is a Democrat, and has been school director in his district.

THOMAS HOSKINSON, who was born in Waynesburg, Penn., July 9, 1834, is a son of George and Sophia (Adams) Hoskinson, who were natives of Pennsylvania and of English origin. His father, who was a farmer and merchant, died in 1884 His family consisted of eight children, of whom Thomas is the oldest He was reared in Waynesburg, and obtained his education in the graded schools and Waynesburg College. When he was twelve years old his father moved on a farm, where Thomas remained with his parents until he was twenty years of age. He then came to Waynesburg and clerked in a general store. The main part of his business career has been spent in the mercantile trade. He was engaged in business in Waynesburg from 1864 to 1878, when he closed out his business and has since met with success as a salesman. Mr. Hoskinson was married in Waynesburg, in 1860, to Sarah A., daughter of George F. Wolfe. Mrs. Hoskinson is also a native of this county, and of German descent, and a graduate of Waynesburg College. Their children are—George Ellsworth, a printer by trade in Pittsburgh, Penn.; Lida, a teacher in Topeka, Kansas; Louise T, Franklin, and Charles W., who died at the age of four in 1877. Mr. and Mrs. Hoskinson are prominent members of the Cumberland Presbyterian Church. He is a leading member in the organization of Odd Fellows and Knights of Honor.

WILLIAM R. HUGHES, farmer and stock-raiser, was born August 18, 1851, on the farm where he resides near Waynesburg, Penn. He is a son of Hiram and Sarah A. (Burks) Hughes, who were of English extraction. His mother was a native of Virginia. His father, who was a farmer all his life, was born in Greene County, and had a family of four children, two of whom are living He died in 1854. His oldest daughter was the wife of A. J. Lippencott, a son of William Lippencott, who is a prominent farmer in Franklin Township. William R. was reared on the farm and attended the district schools and the College at Waynesburg. He taught school for a number of years, but has made farming his chief occupation. His home farm contains 106 acres of valuable land. Mr. Hughes was united in marriage April 23, 1878, with Miss Anna, daughter of Caleb and Sarah (Greene) Rigdon. Her parents were English and natives of Maryland. Mr. and Mrs. Hughes are the parents of three children—Bertha, Clarence L and Arthur E Their mother is a devoted member of the Methodist Episcopal Church. In politics Mr. Hughes is a Democrat.

JOHN T. IAMS, M. D., of the firm of Iams & Ullom, physicians and surgeons, Waynesburg, Penn., was born at Mt Morris, this county, March 25, 1846. He is a son of Samuel and Nancy (Grimes) Iams. His parents are natives of Pennsylvania, and of English extraction. His father was a millwright in early life and afterward a farmer. He now resides in Center Township, and is over seventy years of age Dr. Iams is the second in a family of seven children. He lived with his parents on the farm until he reached his eighteenth year, when he entered Waynesburg College, remaining two years. He then taught for three years In 1868 he began the study of medicine in the office of Dr. Gray, of Jacksonville, remaining with him for one year. He then entered Bellvue Medical College at New York, where he took the regular course and graduated in 1871. He practiced at Jacksonville until 1879, when he moved to Waynesburg, where he has since resided. Dr Iams is a member of the State and county medical societies, and was elected a member of the American Medical Association which met in Chicago in 1886. He was United States examining surgeon for pensions from 1880 to 1885. He was commissioned first assistant surgeon to the Tenth Regiment, N. G. P, May, 1888. Dr. Iams was married May 16, 1874, to Kate E., daughter of Samuel Harvey, of Waynesburg. Their children are Annette and Samuel Harvey.

FREDERICK ILLIG, farmer and general dealer, Waynesburg, Penn, was born in Germany November 7, 1835. His father, Charles Illig, was a brewer, and of his five children Fred is the oldest. He was the first member of the family to come to America. In 1854 he crossed the ocean and settled in Pittsburgh, Penn., where he obtained a position as clerk in a store. He has since made four trips across the water. Some years later he settled in Washington, Washington County, Penn., where he soon became an active dealer in grain and cattle In 1879 he located at Waynesburg, where he has since carried on a large business, a principal feature of which is his creamery. Mr. Illig succeeded in accumulating a handsome competence for himself and family. He owns valuable town property in Waynesburg and a good farm adjoining the borough. He also has two farms in Washington County, containing 260 acres. Mr. Illig received a liberal education in Germany. His success in this country has been due mainly to his own industry and untiring energy. He is a Republican in politics. He was united in marriage in Germany, in 1854, with Miss Caroline Claser, also a native of Germany. Their children are—Charles, Lucy, George, Carrie and William.

WILLIAM INGHRAM, a retired farmer and stock-grower, was born in Franklin Township, Greene County, Penn , July 31, 1822. He is a son of William and Elizabeth (Rinehart) Inghram, natives of this county, and of Irish and Dutch extraction. His father, who was a farmer, had a family of seven children, four daughters and three sons, of whom William is the youngest. He was reared in his native township, received his education in the old log school-house, and has been a successful farmer all his life. He owns a fine farm of 400 acres. In 1851 Mr. Inghram married Martha, daughter of Solomon Hoge, and they were the parents of the following children— Frank, Alice, James, a farmer; Elizabeth, wife of John Murdock; Emma, Maggie, Jessie and Olive. Their mother died in 1885, a faithful member of the Methodist Church. Frank, the oldest of the family, was born June 14, 1853. He was reared in Franklin Township, and received his education in Waynesburg College. He started in life as a school teacher, but subsequently began farming and dealing in cattle, and has been successful in that business. In 1876 he married Rebecca, daughter of Uriah Inghram, and they have two interesting children—Mark and Alice.

JAMES INGHRAM, President Judge of the Fourteenth Judicial District, was born in Waynesburg, Greene County, Penn., September 12, 1842. He is a son of Arthur and Elizabeth (Cather) Inghram, who were natives of this State and of English ancestry. His father read medicine and graduated at Jefferson Medical College, after which he practiced in Greene County for many years. Dr. Arthur Inghram and wife were the parents of five children, of whom the subject of this sketch is the fourth, and was reared in Waynesburg He acquired his education in the common schools and Waynesburg College, graduating in the classical course in 1859. He then commenced the study of law in the office of Lindsey & Buchanan, was admitted to the bar in 1863, and continued in active practice until 1883, when he was elected president judge. Judge Inghram was united in marriage in 1871 with Miss Mary, daughter of the Hon. C. A. Black, a prominent attorney of Waynesburg. The Judge is a member of the Masonic fraternity and I. O. O. F. Mrs. Inghram is a consistent member of the Presbyterian Church.

COL. JAMES S. JENNINGS was born in Waynesburg, Greene County, Penn., August 22, 1829. His father, Benjamin Jennings, was a native of New Jersey, born in 1779; in his youth removed and located near Carmichaels, Greene County, Penn.; in the year 1800 removed to and settled in Waynesburg, where he remained until his death, which occurred in the year 1861. Benjamin Jennings was a carpenter by trade, and many of the early erected buildings in Waynesburg and near by were the results of his industry and skill. He was for many years a justice of the peace in

36

Waynesburg, and served one term as county commissioner. He was twice married, his last wife being Elizabeth Stockdale, mother to the subject of this notice. Col. Jennings received his education in his native place at the public schools and Waynesburg College He learned the printing business in the Waynesburg *Messenger* office, and was subsequently for many years co-editor and proprietor of that paper In 1858 he was married to Laura E. Weethee, of Athens County, Ohio, a native of that State and a graduate of Waynesburg College. They have three children—William C., now a citizen of Kansas; Charles B., a printer by trade, but at present deputy post-master at Waynesburg; and Mary L, who is also an assistant in Waynesburg postoffice. In 1863, while connected with the *Messenger* office, Colonel J. was elected to, and served one term as treasurer of Greene County. During the Gubernatorial term of Governor Pollock, of Pennsylvania, Colonel J. was honored by appointment of aid on the Governor's staff as Colonel, and the same honor conferred on him by Governor Packer. In 1867 Colonel Jennings removed to a farm in Athens County, Ohio, where he remained for about twelve years. He was there for a time engaged in the land and mineral business, with a view to develop the mineral resources of his neighborhood, and was, with this view, connected with the construction of the Ohio Central Railroad. But the panic of 1873 coming on, the enterprise that had been so promising failed to materialize in time, and his pecuniary interests, as well as those of all concerned, severely suffered While in Ohio his Democratic friends nominated him as their candidate for the State Legislature, but being in a district hopelessly Republican, without success He was urged by his Democratic friends in his Congressional District, and by the Democratic newspapers therein, to allow his name to be used as the Democratic candidate for Congress, but the Colonel persistently declined the nomination. His name was also prominent before the State Convention in Ohio as candidate for Governor at the time Bishop was nominated and elected In the year 1879 Colonel J. removed from Ohio to the State of Kansas to take a fresh start and recover from the money losses sustained in his Ohio mineral enterprises. But his love for his native county had such hold on him that he concluded to return to Waynesburg, and in January, 1883, he again took charge of the *Messenger* on a lease On the election of Cleveland to the Presidency, in 1886, he was by him appointed postmaster of Waynesburg, which position he holds at the present time, with his family around him as assistants, except the son, who is "growing up with the West."

WILLIAM R JOHNSON, contractor and builder, was born in Cumberland Township, this county, November 30, 1834, and is a son of Richard and Mary (Smith) Johnson His parents were natives of this State. Jonathan Johnson, his grandfather, was born in Chester County, Penn, in 1796, and came with his parents to Greene County when Richard Johnson was but a small boy. Richard was a brick-layer, and worked at his trade until his death in 1885. His family consisted of nine children, of whom six are living William R. is the fifth, and was reared in Cumberland Township, on the farm with his parents. At the age of fifteen he learned the brick-layer's trade with his father, and has done considerable business as a contractor and builder, having erected most of the fine buildings in Waynesburg. Mr. Johnson was united in marriage, in 1855, with Miss Minerva, daughter of Reuben and Susan (Hayes) Fleming. Her parents were natives of Virginia, and of Irish descent. Their children are—Ida, widow of E. P. Lantz (deceased), and Emma, wife of J. A. F. Randolph, Esq. Mr. Johnson is a member of the Masonic fraternity.

REV. C. P. JORDAN, retired minister of the Methodist Protestant Church, was born in Greene County, Penn., January 22, 1827, and is a son of John and Rebecca (West) Jordan His parents were natives of eastern Pennsylvania, and of English and German lineage. His father was a mill-wright by occupation. He was among the early settlers of this county, and died in 1834. His family consisted of nine children, of whom five grew to be men and women. Rev. C. P. Jordan is the only surviving member of the family. He was reared in Jefferson Township, and in Waynesburg, where he attended school Early in life he learned the boot and shoemakers trade, which he followed as a business for five years. He then learned the carpenter's trade, at which he worked until he was licensed to preach and admitted to the Pittsburgh Conference. In 1856 he accepted his first charge, and for years has devoted his time to the ministry in Pennsylvania, West Virginia and Ohio. The greater part of his ministerial work has been in Pennsylvania, and largely in his own county. He has been an active member of the order of Odd Fellows, and was a charter member of the Sons of Temperance society in this county. He has been actively engaged in the mission work of the church, and has organized fifteen Methodist Protestant churches during his ministry. He was a revivalist in the true sense of the word. In 1861 Rev. Jordan married Mrs. Maria Cunningham. His first wife, whom he married in 1850, was Mary, daughter of Nicholas Johnson. She and her two children died in 1854, all within four days.

HIRAM KENT, of the firm of Kent & Driscoll, carriage manufacturers, Waynesburg, Penn., was born in Center Township, this county, July 27, 1847, and is a son of John and Keziah (Shields) Kent His ancestors were among the early settlers of Greene County. His father, a farmer, had a family of thirteen children, of whom Hiram is the eighth, and was reared in his native township. He attended the common schools, and in early life learned the wagon-maker's trade, at which he worked until 1880, when he began his present business. In 1871 Mr. Kent married Miss Lucy A., daughter of Dawson McClelland, and they have three children—Minnie R., Nancy Maria and Z Wilber Mr. Kent is a Democrat, and a prominent member of the I. O. O. F. He is now Noble Grand of the Lodge, No 469, in Waynesburg.

COL JOHN M. KENT, born in Waynesburg, Penn., February 29, 1836, is a son of Peter M. and Mary (Hook) Kent, who were of English and Irish origin. His father, who was a native of Ohio, came to Greene County, Penn, when he was a young man, taught school for a number of years, and later in life worked at the stone-mason's trade. He died in 1852 Col. Kent, the third in a family of eight children, was reared in Greene County, and received his early education in the common schools He was a plasterer by trade, also engaged in contracting and building until the war broke out. He enlisted in Company I, Eighth Pennsylvania Reserves, was elected First Lieutenant and served in that capacity one year. He was then elected Captain for the remainder of his term of service He returned home and raised a company, and was elected Captain of the Fifth Pennsylvania Heavy Artillery, in Company K, in which position he served until the close of the war. Col. Kent was twice wounded, first at the battle of Fredericksburg, Va, in December, 1862, when he was reported as among the killed, having been pro-nounced by the physician mortally wounded. The second time he was wounded at Spottsylvania. He participated in many skirmishes and ten regular battles, among which were the Seven Days' battle in front of Richmond, Bull Run, South Mountain and Antietam, in 1862, and the Wilderness and Spottsylvania battles in 1864. At the close of the war Col. Kent returned to Waynesburg, where for five years he engaged in his former business of contracting and building In 1869 he was appointed United States Store-keeper and Gauger, which position he held for sixteen years In 1874 he enlisted in the Pennsylvania National Guards, in Company K of the Tenth Regiment; was elected Captain, and soon after elected Major. He was subsequently elected to the position of Lieutenant-Colonel, in which capacity he served until he resigned in 1887 In 1886 he took charge of the Hotel Walton, of which he was proprietor for nearly two years, when he removed with his family to Pittsburgh, Penn. The Colonel was married September 21, 1871, to Nanna A. Wallace, a native of Pittsburgh, Penn, and of Scotch-Irish descent. They are the parents of two children—William H. and James W. Mrs. Kent is a member of the Presbyterian Church The Colonel is a Republican in politics. He has served as a member of the town council, and as Quartermaster of the G. A. R. Post at Waynesburg. He was always noted for his energy and zeal in organizing and conducting military and civic parades and demonstrations in his native town.

CAPT. W. C. KIMBER, fire insurance agent, was born in Fayette County, Penn, April 11, 1821 He is a son of Benedict and Mary S. (Vernon) Kimber, natives of Pennsylvania, and of English descent. His father was a glass-blower in early life, but later was engaged in boat-making He owned and operated a number of boats, and was for many years Captain of a steamboat. The subject of our sketch was the oldest of a family of six children, and was reared in Brownsville, Penn., where he attended school When quite a young man he went on the river with his father. He subsequently became Captain of the steamboat "Empire," one of his father's boats running on the Ohio and Mississippi rivers. Capt. Kimber was on the river from 1838 to 1885, with the exception of fifteen years A part of that time he was engaged in transporting freight across the plains, and part of the time in the milling business. In 1859 he was elected to the Legislature of Kansas from Doniphan County, serving the first term after the organization of the State. He was married at Brownsville, Penn., in 1846, to Miss Dorotha Ann, daughter of Dr Henry W. Stoy. They were the parents of three children, viz: Lewis E., book-keeper for the National Transit Company at Oil City, Penn.; Charles E., a miner in Colorado, and Laura D., who died in Waynesburg in 1878 Mrs. Kimber died at Oil City in 1883.

I. H. KNOX, editor of the Waynesburg *Republican*, was born at East Finley, Washington County, Penn., April 23, 1862. He is a son of John S. Knox, who has been a merchant and postmaster at East Finley for thirty-five years. His parents were of English and Scotch descent. Mr Knox is one of a family of eight children, four of whom are now living. He was reared in Washington County, and attended Waynesburg College. When he left Waynesburg College he was a member of the senior class. During a period of three years he was a clerk in his father's store at East Finley, and was also for some time a salesman in a dry goods store at Pittsburgh; but on leaving college turned his attention to journalistic work. In 1884 he bought one-half interest in the Waynesburg *Republican*, in company with W. G. W. Day. Mr Day retired in 1885, since which time Mr. Knox has edited and had charge of the paper. He is a Republican, and edits the only Republican newspaper in the county. On September 15, 1886, he was married to Miss Theodosia B., daughter of G. W. G. and Carrie (Throckmorton) Waddell. Mrs. Knox is a graduate of Waynesburg College, in the class of 1884. She is of English descent, and a member of the Cumberland Presbyterian

Church. Mr. Knox is a member of the Methodist Episcopal Church, in which he is secretary of the board of trustees.

P. A. KNOX, attorney, Waynesburg, Penn., was born in Bentleysville, Washington County, November 17, 1842 He is a son of William and Rosannah (Clark) Knox His parents, who were natives of Washington County, Penn., were of Scotch and Irish origin. His father was a carpenter and mill-wright by occupation, and spent most of his life in Washington, Allegheny and Greene counties. In 1848 he went to Allegheny County, and in 1849 removed to Greene County and settled in Carmichaels, where he resided until his death, June 4, 1884. He was the father of three children, of whom P A Knox is the second. Mr. Knox received his earliest education at the public schools and at Greene Academy, and subsequently attended Waynesburg College, where he graduated in 1864 in the regular classical course. He began teaching school in 1858, when not quite sixteen years of age, and taught almost every winter until 1868. In 1866 he began the study of law with Messrs. Wyly and Buchanan. He was admitted to the bar in 1868, and commenced the practice of law in Waynesburg the following year. In March, 1869, he was appointed to succeed Hon. J B Donley as register in bankruptcy for the twenty-fourth district, which was then composed of Greene, Washington, Beaver and Lawrence counties Mr. Knox, who is a Republican, holds the office of United States Commissioner by appointment. He was married in 1868 to Miss Martha H , daughter of James P Parker Their children are—Luella, William Parker, James Albert and John Clark Knox

W. T. LANTZ, cashier of the Farmers and Drovers National Bank of Waynesburg, is one of the substantial and enterprising citizens of Greene County. He was born in Blacksville, West Virginia, October 25, 1842 His parents, William and Sarah (Thomas) Lantz, were also natives of West Virginia Their family consisted of nine children, of whom four are living. Mr. W. T. Lantz is the sixth and was reared in Blacksville where he obtained his early education, and afterward attended the college in Waynesburg. In 1872 he opened a store in Waynesburg, and began taking an active interest in the enterprises of the county—among which was the building of the Waynesburg & Washington Railroad Mr. Lantz was a member of the building committee with S W Scott, Jacob Swart and others, and was also a director of the road. These gentlemen are deserving of credit for the active interest they manifested in that enterprise. Again we find Mr. Lantz and others taking an active interest in building the Waynesburg Roller Mills. In 1876 he was elected president of the Waynesburg Agricultural Association, and in 1878 he was elected to his present position in the Farmers and Drovers Bank. He is one of the trustees of the college, and a member of the I. O. O. F. Mr. Lantz was united in marriage in Waynesburg with Miss Harriet, daughter of James A. Buchanan, a prominent attorney of the Greene County bar. They have one son, an intelligent and promising young man, named James for his grandfather. Mrs. Lantz is a consistent member of the Presbyterian Church.

J. S. LEMLEY, sheriff of Greene County, Penn., was born in Springhill Township, this county, March 22, 1845. He is a son of Israel and Mazy (White) Lemley, natives of this county, who were of German origin. His father was a farmer, and died at the early age of thirty-three. Mr. Lemley was the youngest in a family of four children—two boys and two girls. His ancestors were among the early farmers of Springhill Township He was reared on the farm, attended the common school, and was a farmer by occupation. Mr. Lemley is a Democrat, and was elected sheriff of the county in 1885 He was justice of the peace while a resident of Whitely Township In 1867 Mr. Lemley married Jane, daughter of David Lapping. Mrs. Lemley is of Irish descent They have one child, a daughter, Lizzie. Mr. and Mrs. Lemley and their daughter are members of the Methodist Episcopal Church.

MORRIS LEVINO, merchant, of the firm of Levino Brothers, was born in Germany, June 20, 1863. His parents, Alexander and Fannie (Helburn) Levino, were also natives of Germany. Mr. Levino's father was a teacher in Germany, spending his life in that profession in which he was very successful. Mr. Morris Levino, the youngest in the family of four children, came to America in 1877, and clerked for three months in New York City. He then went to Lewisburg, Penn., where he was employed as a salesman for a period of two years. In 1880 he became the junior member of the firm of A. Levino & Brother, of Waynesburg In 1882 they established a branch store at Mercer, Penn., and have been very successful in the business. The subject of our sketch has charge of the Waynesburg store, where may be found everything usually found in a first-class clothing house. Mr. Levino was united in marriage, January 18, 1888, with Miss Sophie Stern. She was born in New York City, February 17, 1868, and is the daughter of Herman Stern, of Allegheny, Penn.

HON. JAMES LINDSEY, deceased, was an attorney and counselor at law. He was born near Jefferson Borough, November 21, 1827, and was a son of John and Anne (Collins) Lindsey, who were natives of Greene County, and of Scotch-Irish extraction. His father was a farmer and subsequently sheriff and prothonotary and spent his life in this county. Judge Lindsey was the oldest in a family of eleven children, and was reared on a farm in Jefferson Township. He was educated at the Greene Academy in Cumberland Township, and studied law in Waynesburg, where he practiced his chosen profession until 1863, when he was elected President Judge of the fourteenth judicial district, then composed of Washington, Fayette and Greene Counties.   He was a Democrat and a successful business man and was noted for his honesty and integrity as well as for his scholarly attainments   In 1855 Judge Lindsey was united in marriage with Miss Sarah, daughter of Dr. Arthur Inghram, and a sister to the President Judge of the fourteenth judicial district, Hon James Inghram.   He died at the early age of thirty-seven years.   To Mr. and Mrs Lindsey were born four children   Arthur I, the oldest, was born at Waynesburg, July 10, 1856.   He was educated in Waynesburg College, and in 1874 began clerking in the F. & D. National Bank of Waynesburg, in which he is now assistant cashier   He is a Democrat, and is among the most prominent young men of the county.   The three remaining children are William W. and John H., who are in the West, and Annie L   Judge Lindsey was a Presbyterian, and his widow is a member of the Methodist Episcopal Church

II. H. LINDSEY, merchant, who was born in Jefferson, Borough, this county, October 27, 1823, is a son of James and Catharine (Shroyer) Lindsey.   His parents were also natives of Greene County, and of Scotch-Irish descent   Mr. Lindsey's grandfather, James Lindsey, built the first brick hotel in Jefferson Borough, where he spent the remainder of his life   Mr. Hiram Lindsey was the second in a family of three children and was reared in Jefferson where he attended school.   At the age of sixteen he began to clerk in a store and was engaged as a salesman till 1850, when he opened a general store and continued in that business for twenty-five years.   In 1869 Mr Lindsey was elected prothonotary of the county, served one term and was re-elected in 1872.   In 1876 he removed to Chicago, Illinois.   Returning to Waynesburg in 1881, he has since been engaged in the mercantile business.   In 1847 Mr Lindsey married Miss Sarah, daughter of Philip Minor   Mrs. Lindsey is a native of Greene County, and of Welsh origin   Their children are—William L., for the last twenty-one years with J. V. Farwell & Co, Chicago, Ill   James M. who is a clerk in the United States revenue office at Pittsburgh, Penn, Laura, wife of Robert D. Myers, of Chicago; Margaret, wife of L L. Minor, Esq, of Uniontown, Penn., Anna, and George B, who is with Farwell & Co, of Chicago   The deceased are Helen, wife of W. A. Bane, and Jessie.   Mr. Lindsey is a member of the I. O. O. F. and A Y. M., and his wife is a faithful member of the Presbyterian Church.   They are among the representative citizens of Waynesburg, Penn

WILLIAM LIPPENCOTT, Sr, farmer, Waynesburg, Penn., was born in Franklin Township, this county, October 14, 1812.   He is a son of Uriah and Nancy Lippencott, natives of New Jersey, and of English descent. Mr. William Lippencott's grandfather was among the earliest settlers of Greene County, and engaged in farming and stock growing. He gave his son Uriah instructions in the art of husbandry—a business he followed all his life, except the time he spent in teaching school. His death occurred in 1855. William Lippencott is the fifth in a family of eight children, and was reared on the farm where he and his family reside. Like his ancestors, he chose farming and stock growing as a business and has been very successful. His home farm contains 400 acres of valuable land. Mr. Lippencott was united in marriage, in 1832, with Rachel, daughter of George and Margaret (Bowen) Ullom, and they are the parents of five children, viz., Uriah, Margaret, Melissa, Martha and Maria. Mrs. Lippencott died in 1848. In 1849 Mr. Lippencott married Rebecca, daughter of Sylvanus and Rachel (Pew) Smith, natives of New Jersey, and of English lineage. Their children are—Smith, A. J., Elisha, Rachel A., B. F. and Sylvanus I. Mr. Lippencott has filled the offices of assessor, director of the poor and school director. Mrs. Lippencott is a consistent member of the Methodist Protestant Church.

H. C. LUCAS, druggist, was born at Hopewell, Greene County, Penn., August 23, 1859, and is a son of Samuel and Maria (Nicely) Lucas. His parents were born in Pennsylvania—the former in Washington County, and the latter in Greene. They were of Scotch-Irish origin. His father was a merchant and carried on business in this county for several years. He conducted a general mercantile business in Waynesburg, died at Kenton, Ohio in 1863. Of his family of six children, Harry C., is the fifth. But three of the children are now living. Mr. Lucas, the subject of this sketch, spent most of his early life with his grandparents in Ross County, Ohio, on the farm where he attended the district schools. He was afterwards a student in Waynesburg College for three years. In 1876 he went into a store to learn his present business, and was a faithful student. In 1882 he accepted a position as prescription clerk in a large drug store at Pittsburg, Penn., and remained there for two years, closely confining himself to his work. He returned to Waynesburg in 1884 and opened a drug store on Main street. As a business man Mr. Lucas is spoken of, by those who know him best, as a high-minded, honorable gentleman. He is a Republican, and an active member of the Presbyterian Church.

A. B. MILLER, D. D., LL. D., now president of Waynesburg College, was born near Brownsville, Fayette County, Penn., October 16, 1829. His parents, Moses and Mary (Knight) Miller, were respectively of German and English descent. The subject of this sketch was the fourth of ten children, eight of whom grew up, seven being still alive and in active life. His school opportunities in boyhood were very meagre, because of a dissension which closed the district school for several years, during which his youth was spent on a farm where his parents resided until his father's death in 1859. In 1847 he entered Greene Academy, at Carmichaels, Penn., spending there three summers, and teaching in the winters, his first effort being near Greenfield, Washington County, Penn., which proved so successful as to place at his option four terms in the school of his home district. A few months before twenty-one he was licensed to preach by Union Presbytery of the Cumberland Presbyterian Church, his first field being Masontown, Penn., where, within a few months he secured the erection of a house of worship, his first preaching being in a school-house. In the autumn of 1851, by earnest entreaty, he gained the consent of his presbytery for his return to school, and entered Waynesburg College at the very opening of the institution in the first building. At his graduation in 1853 he was elected Professor of Mathematics in his Alma Mater, and in 1858 was advanced to the position of President, which he has occupied continuously. It is perhaps within the bounds of truth and justice to say that, all things considered, the success of Waynesburg College has been so remarkable as to present few parallels. It has now property and endowment fund valued at considerably over $100,000, all acquired little by little through persistent effort covering many years. The new college edifice is capacious, substantial, and a marvel of architectural beauty, of which the St. Louis *Observer* perhaps justly says, in referring to Dr. Miller's recent call to a University in Illinois, that "all who are acquainted with the facts will agree that this building would not have been there but for the untiring labors of Dr. Miller." The alumni of the college now number hundreds, many of them being men and women of distinction in their spheres of useful work. In connection with his college work Dr. Miller preached regularly to the Waynesburg Cumberland Presbyterian Church for ten years, and for several years owned and published the *Cumberland Presbyterian* while preaching twice of Sundays and teaching daily six hours in the college, and supplementing all this, while largely managing the financial affairs of the college, with an immense amount of lecturing for teachers' institutes, on temperance, etc., and with all this maintaining such health as to be spoken of as "the man who is never sick." In 1855 he married Margaret K. Bell, then principal of the female department of Waynesburg College, a position she held until her death, in April, 1874, her labors being so efficient, and her life so noble, as to leave among the people who knew her an admiration that is little short of worship. From this marriage came eight children, of whom seven still survive, the death of one resulting from an accident in infancy. The oldest is the well known Mrs. Lide Simpson, wife of Dr. Theodore P. Simpson, of Beaver Falls, Penn. The second daughter, Lucy, is the wife of Prof. W. M Beach, late president of Odessa College, Missouri, now a student in Jefferson Medical College. The oldest son, Lieut Albert B. Miller, is pursuing medical studies, and will enter Jefferson College in the autumn; and the younger children, Miss Haddie, Miss Jessie, Howard B. and Alfred Tennyson are at home with their father, the home management being now in the hands of Mrs. Jennie (Wilson) Miller, wife of Albert B. If success and, perseverance are evidence of ability, it cannot be doubted that Dr. Miller is a man of marked endowment in all his lines of effort, to which he adds that of almost boundless capacity to work, which someone has declared to be itself genius. While he has certainly not earned the reputation of having enriched himself, his long continued and arduous labors have enriched many with high qualifications for success and useful ness, and will leave the people of Waynesburg and Greene County the legacy of Waynesburg College.

ISAAC MITCHELL, retired farmer and resident of Waynesburg, was born in Washington Township, Greene County, Penn., September 9, 1816. His parents were Shadrick and Margaret (Rinehart) Mitchell. The former was a native of Maryland and the latter of Greene County, Penn. They were of English and German ancestry. Mr. Shadrick Mitchell was a farmer and stone-mason, and in early life followed his trade. He purchased land in what is now Washington Township in 1799, and settled and remained there until his death, which occurred in 1863. He was then ninety-seven years old. The farm he purchased is still in the possession of the family. He was the father of five daughters and five sons, of whom Mr Isaac Mitchell is the youngest. He was reared in Washington Township, on the farm that has been in possession of the family for eighty-nine years. He made farming his business and has been very successful, owning at present 300 acres of fine land besides other property. He moved to Waynesburg in 1877, since which time he has been living a retired life. Mr. Mitchell's political views are Democratic, and he served two terms as overseer of the poor of Greene County. Mr. Mitchell was united in marriage October 4, 1838, with Elizabeth Barnes, whose parents were Jacob and Phœbe (Crayne) Barnes. Mr. and Mrs. Mitchell are the parents of six children—Margaret P., Mary E., Lucy, Thomas, George and Ross. Mrs. Mitchell is a consistent member of the Cumberland Presbyterian Church.

T. P. MOFFETT, merchant tailor, Waynesburg, Penn , was born at Carmichaels, Penn , December 8, 1854. He is a son of Richard and Rebecca (Jackson) Moffett, who were of Scotch and English extraction. His mother was a native of this county. His father, a native of Maryland, was a merchant tailor, and for many years carried on a successful business at Carmichaels. His family consisted of four children—all boys—of whom the subject of this sketch is the second. He was reared in Carmichaels and educated in Greene Academy. He very naturally learned to be a tailor with his father, serving a regular apprenticeship He afterwards learned cutting with the well known J B. West, of New York City Mr. Moffett engaged in business in West Elizabeth for a period of three years In 1877 he commenced business in Waynesburg, where he does first-class work, keeps good materials and always guarantees satisfaction to his many customers Mr Moffett was united in marriage in 1877 with Emma R , daughter of Abner W. Beddell. Mrs. Moffett is a native of Allegheny County, Penn., and a member of the Cumberland Presbyterian Church at Waynesburg. They have two children —Edwin Richard and Fannie Blanche Mr Moffett is a Republican, and a member of the Knights of Honor.

JOHN A. MOORE, liveryman, of the firm of Moore & Hill, was born in Whiteley Township, this county, June 9, 1848, and is a son of Thomas and Rachel (Maple) Moore His mother was born in Maryland and was of English extraction. His father, who was a farmer all his life, was of Irish lineage, and a native of Greene County. His family consisted of ten children, eight of whom grew to maturity. Mr. Moore attended the district schools of Whiteley Township, and worked on a farm until he became of age, then taught school. He then began clerking in a general store, and remained there three years. Mr. Moore subsequently engaged in selling buggies and continued that business for a period of eight years. In 1885, in company with F. M. Patterson, he engaged in his present business in Waynesburg, where they keep a first-class livery stable and have a fair share of the patronage Mr. Patterson, in 1888, sold his interest to Mr. S M. Hill. Mr. Moore was united in marriage, October 6, 1872, with Miss Eliza M , daughter of Eaton Rose, and they have one child—Golda Myrtle. Mr. and Mrs Moore are members of the Methodist Episcopal Church South He is a Democrat, and a member of the I O. O. F

WILLIAM H. MORRIS, farmer and stock-dealer, Waynesburg, Penn., was born in this county April 23, 1847, and is a son of Jacob and Nancy (Jewel) Morris. His father is an active, energetic business man and prominent farmer of Greene County, and has succeeded in accumulating a fair share of this world's goods His family consists of nine children, of whom William H. is next to the oldest He was reared on the farm with his parents, and after receiving a limited education in the district schools started out in life as a huckster. He subsequently started a general store at Holbrook, Penn , where he continued in business until 1878, then bought his present farm where he resides in Franklin Township. In 1873 Mr. Morris married Miss Sallie, daughter of Benjamin Huffman, and they have seven children, viz. Milton, Emanuel, Jacob, Anna, Frank, Guy and Nannie. Mr. Morris is a Republican. His wife is a devoted member of the Baptist Church.

HON. ROBERT A. McCONNELL, attorney at law, Waynesburg, Greene County, Penn., was born October 29, 1826, at New London, ten miles south of Lynchburg, Virginia. He is the son of James and Elizabeth (Luckey) McConnell, who were natives of Franklin County, Penn., and of Scotch-Irish lineage. The subject of our sketch came from the pure Celtic stock, his great-grandfather, Robert McConnell, being a native of County Antrim, Ireland, and born in 1695. His ancestors went from Scotland to the Green Isle in the Sixteenth century. Robert McConnell and wife emigrated to the American colonies, settling in Franklin County, Penn., where he died in 1770. The members of the family have occupied many exalted positions and offices of trust. They have participated in all the wars of America. James McConnell, grandfather of Robert A., served as a captain through the Revolutionary war. After the close of the war he returned to Franklin County, where he served as justice of the peace and as county commissioner for several years. From 1804 to 1806 he was a member of the State Legislature of Pennsylvania. Robert A. McConnell's father, James McConnell, was born in Franklin County, Penn., October 9, 1784, being the fourth son in a family of twelve children. In 1808 he was united in marriage with Elizabeth Luckey, who was born near Winchester, Virginia, April 5, 1785. Their children numbered eleven, of whom Hon. Robert McConnell is the tenth. The family have usually been Presbyterians. James McConnell graduated at Jefferson College, in 1805, and was admitted to the bar in 1810. On account of failing health he had to abandon his profession and subsequently engaged in teaching. Having come to Greene County in 1828 and resided on a farm in Morris Township, where Robert A., the subject of our sketch was reared. He attended the common schools and in 1845 entered the West Alexander Academy. He subsequently attended Washington College where he graduated in 1851. He then began the study of law at Waynesburg, in the office of Hon. C. A. Black and John Phelan. He was admitted to the practice in 1854 and was elected district attorney in 1858, serving six years. In 1870 he was elected to the State Legislature, where he introduced a number of important bills and was a strong advocate of local option. In 1872, when the members of the Legislature made the Speaker a present of $500 worth of silverware, Mr. McConnell was selected to make the presentation speech. On January 5, 1888, he was united in marriage with Miss Sallie E. Arrison, of Waynesburg, Penn. Mr. McConnell is a Democrat, and an elder and useful member of the Presbyterian Church. He is a member of the board of trustees of Waynesburg College Since the death of his brother, Joseph L McConnell, he has been employed in settling up the estate.

JOSEPH L. McCONNELL (deceased), surveyor and civil engineer, who was born in Virginia, August 25, 1814, was a son of James and Elizabeth (Luckey) McConnell, being the fourth in their family of eleven children. His early childhood was spent in Virginia, but at the age of fourteen years he came with his parents to Greene County, Penn He received a good English education and devoted much of his time to the study of surveying He first began surveying in 1836 and followed that as a business for many years He also made a map of the county which is very correct Mr. McConnell was a very clever and genial man and had a large acquaintance throughout the county. He was married, May 11, 1859, to Miss Anna Luckey, and died January 31, 1875. He was a Democrat and he and his wife were members of the Presbyterian Church

SAMUEL J. McNAY —Among the prominent and wealthy farmers of Greene County we mention the name of Samuel J. McNay. Mr. McNay was born December 11, 1821, on the farm in Franklin Township where he now resides. His parents, James and Anna (Dickenson) McNay, were natives of Pennsylvania and were among the pioneers of the State Mr McNay is the second of a family of eleven children—eight sons and three daughters He was reared on the farm and attended the common schools. Early in life he chose farming as his business, in which he has met with marked success.and is the owner of 1,329 acres of land For a number of years he has operated a saw-mill, and has done most of his own work. In 1845 Mr. McNay married Miss Priscilla Mofford and they were the parents of six children, only two of whom are living--Melissa, wife of John Baldwin, and Lucy, wife of George Knox. Mrs McNay died in 1875, a faithful, loving wife and devoted mother Mr McNay was again united in marriage, in 1882. with Miss Mary J , daughter of Jesse Adams, a Cumberland Presbyterian minister. They are the parents of two children—Luella G. and Jessie Mr. and Mrs. McNay are members of the Cumberland Presbyterian Church, in which he has been elder for many years He is a Democrat, and has served as school director in his township.

.JESSE B. ORNDOFF, farmer and stock-grower, Waynesburg, Penn , was born in Greene County, Pennsylvania, October 6, 1857, and is a son of Jesse and Susan (Wear) Orndoff His father was also a native of this county, and his mother was born in Virginia. His father is a prominent farmer of Center Township, where Jesse was reared and received his early education. Mr. Orndoff is one of the most industrious farmers of Franklin Township, where he owns a well improved farm. He was united in marriage, in 1886, with

Miss Mary L , daughter of Thomas and Susannah (Loar) Hughes Mrs Orndoff is of Dutch and Irish ancestry. They have one child Mr. Orndoff is a Democrat, and one of the representative young men of the county.

NATHANIEL PARSHALL deceased, was born in Fayette County, Penn , February 12, 1824, and died in 1881 He was a son of James and Hannah (Coldren) Parshall His father was a farmer by occupation, and reared a family of eleven children. Nathaniel was the second and was reared in Fayette County, where he attended the district schools When twenty years of age (1844), he came to Greene County and worked at the cooper's trade, in connection with farming, for a time, but subsequently worked at the carpenter's trade. In 1858 Mr. Parshall married Miss Priscilla Delaney, and they were the parents of five children—three boys and two girls— Charles T , Hannah, wife of Elmer Keenan; Sarah, wife of Joseph Mason; Alpheus and Isaac S. Mr. and Mrs. Parshall were members of the Baptist Church, in which he served as deacon for thirty years. He was a highly respected citizen and his death was mourned by all who knew him.

W. W. PATTERSON, register and recorder of Greene County, Penn., was born in Whiteley Township, this county, September 17, 1855. He is a son of James and Susan (Groves) Patterson, who were of Scotch-Irish descent His ancestors were among the pioneer settlers of Whiteley Township, and were usually farmers. Mr. Patterson was reared on the farm, attending the common schools in the county, and also Waynesburg College. For a few years he devoted himself to teaching, having taught seven terms in this county. He has held his present position in the county for seven years. He is a Democrat, and has served on the school board of Waynesburg. In 1885 Mr. Patterson married Miss Edith N. Meek, a consistent member of the Baptist's Church. Mrs. Patterson's father served one term as county treasurer, and is a prominent farmer of Jackson Township.

REV. ALBERT E. PATTERSON, of the firm of Rinehart & Patterson, owners of the Keystone Marble Works at Waynesburg, Penn , was born in Center Township, Greene County, Penn , March 14, 1860. He is a son of James and Mary J. (Parshall) Patterson, who were natives of Pennsylvania, and of Scotch and French origin. His father, who was a farmer all his life, was twice married. His first wife's maiden name was Julia Ann Quick. Of his six children, four are children of the first wife and two of the second. Rev. Albert E is the youngest. He was reared on the farm and received his education at Monongahela College, with a view of entering the ministry. He received a license in 1884, and was for some time a supply for the Bates Fork Baptist Church. In 1886 Rev. Patterson was married, near Uniontown, West Virginia, to Miss Elvira

Glover. Mr Patterson expects to devote his life to the ministry, but will for a time engage in his present business, in which he is very successful.

HON. ALEXANDER PATTON, deceased, was born in Washington County, Penn , in 1819, and was the son of Joseph Patton, a native of Ireland. His education was limited, but by energy and pluck he was enabled to begin the study of medicine at Cannonsburg, where he finally completed his studies = He began the practice of his chosen profession at Waynesburg, remaining there only a few years. He then removed to Clarksville, Penn , where his genial and gentlemanly demeanor and professional skill soon won for him an extensive practice He remained in Clarksville until 1865, when he moved to Auburn, near Jefferson, where he died in 1884 He was a successful physician, and had many friends in Greene County. For many years he was an acknowledged leader in the Democratic party in Greene County, and in 1863 and 1864 he was elected to represent the county in the assembly. In 1882 he was elected State Senator. He was an active politician, and able to carry almost every vote in his township. He was married in Greene County in 1845 to Miss Ann, daughter of Abraham and Mary (Carter) Burson. Mrs. Patton's parents were of Scotch-Irish descent and natives of Bucks County, Penn. Mr. and Mrs Patton's family consisted of nine children. Two of their sons are now residents of Waynesburg, one, Joseph, is an attorney and counselor at law; and the other, A. B., is a physician and surgeon. Hon. Mr Patton was one of Greene County's most highly esteemed citizens.

JOSEPH PATTON, attorney and counselor at law, was born in Clarksville, Penn , August 4, 1855 He is a son of Hon. Alexander and Ann (Burson) Patton. His mother was a native of this county, and his father was born in Washington, Penn. Mr Patton, the sixth in a family of nine children, was reared on a farm in Jefferson Township and attended the Monongahela College. He studied law at Waynesburg, where he was admitted to the bar in April, 1880 He has met with more than average success in the practice of law. He was married in January, 1884, to Miss Ellen, daughter of W T. Webb, justice of the peace at Waynesburg. Mr Patton's father was born in Waynesburg February 21, 1840, and is the son of W T. E Webb, Esq , deceased. Mr. and Mrs. Patton have one child— William A. Mr Patton is a Democrat in politics.

WILLIAM THOMPSON HAYS PAULEY, editor and proprietor of the Waynesburg *Messenger*, was born in Youngstown, Ohio, February 6, 1820, and is a son of Thomas and Sarah (Hays) Pauley, who were of Irish and English descent. His father, who was a farmer, was born in Pennsylvania, as was his mother also. Mr. Pauley is the second in a family of three sons. He lived in Youngstown,

Ohio, until he was twelve years old. His father died in 1830, and two years later he came to Waynesburg and learned the printer's trade. He has been in the newspaper business ever since he was thirteen years of age, except while at school, and the greater part of that time he spent in the Waynesburg *Messenger* office, where he learned his trade He went to Oxford, Ohio, to school in 1838, and remained four years. In 1842 he was employed by Major Hays to publish the Waynesburg *Messenger* until 1844, when he purchased the paper, which had been established in 1813, by Dr. Duston. Mr. Pauley is a Democrat, and his paper has been the supporter of all regularly nominated Democratic candidates in the county, state and nation. In 1847 he was elected county treasurer and served one term He was married in 1845 to Miss Mary Jennings, who died September 2, 1887. Their children are—Sarah E., wife of Isaac Bell; James J, of the *Messenger;* Benjamin J., a farmer; John F., a printer, and Thomas C. (deceased). Mr. Pauley is a member of the Masonic fraternity and a Sir Knight Templar. He has been connected with the *Messenger* in some capacity, with the exception of the four years spent in Oxford, ever since the 14th day of May, 1833.

ZADOCK WALKER PHELAN, manufacturer, foundryman and machinist, is a member of the firm of Bower & Phelan, Waynesburg, Penn., where he was born June 21, 1838. He is a son of John and Jane (Walker) Phelan. His mother was born in Fayette County, Penn. His father, a native of Greene County, was an attorney by profession, practiced in Waynesburg for many years and represented his county in the State Legislature His family consists of five sons and one daughter. Z. W., the third in the family, was reared in Waynesburg and educated in the college. He learned the cabinetmaker's trade and carried on the furniture business in Waynesburg; then went to Kansas and shared the struggles of that young State, and in 1884 he began his present business Mr. Phelan's wife was Miss Harriet, daughter of J Wesley Chambers of Washington County, Penn They have three children—Anna W., John Charles and Zadock Walker Mr. and Mrs. Phelan are members of the Methodist Episcopal Church, in which he has held many important positions. He is a strong advocate of the temperance cause and votes the Prohibition ticket. He was the first county chairman of the party, and a candidate on the first ticket issued by the party.

R H. PHELAN, attorney and counsellor at law, was born at Waynesburg, February 21, 1836, and is a son of Hon. John and Jane (Walker) Phelan. His mother was a native of Maryland, and was of English and Irish descent. His father, who was an attorney, was born in this county, of which he was prothonotary for about twelve years He was elected a member of the State Legislature in 1867, and served two terms He died August 31, 1874. R H.

37

Phelan is the second in a family of six children. He was reared in Waynesburg and attended the common school and college He went to the territory of Kansas in 1854 and remained until 1861, when he returned to Waynesburg and subsequently studied law in the office of his father and Hon. C. A. Black. He was admitted to the bar in 1867, and has been in active practice ever since Mr. Phelan is a Democrat. He has been a member of the town council, and is a trustee of the Presbyterian Church. His grandfather, Richard H Phelan, was born in Ireland, and case to Greene County, Penn, at an early date. He served on the first grand jury in 1796 R H Phelan is president of Green Mount Cemetery Company, treasurer of the Waynesburg Park Company, and a director in the Farmers' and Drovers' National Bank of Waynesburg.

JOHN R. PIPES, clerk of the courts of Greene County, Penn., was born in Morrisville, Penn, March 25, 1855, and is a son of James and Elvira (Rinehart) Pipes. His parents were natives of Franklin Township, and of English extraction. His father, who was a farmer all his life, died September 5, 1881. The subject of our sketch was reared in Franklin Township, attended the common school and the Monongahela College at Jefferson, Penn. He first engaged in teaching as an occupation, teaching in the winter for five years and mining coal in the summer. Mr. Pipes is a Democrat, and was elected to his present position in 1884. In 1882 he was united in marriage with Miss Melinda, daughter of William Pitcock, one of the early pioneers of the county. Mr. and Mrs. Pipes have two children—Mary Emma and Daisy Mr. and Mrs Pipes are members of the Methodist Protestant Church, in which he has held many offices, and also served as superintendent of the Sabbath-school He is a member of the I. O. O. F. His father was born in 1800 and his mother in 1818. She is still living, making her home with John R. in Waynesburg, Penn

D. B. PRATT, farmer and stock-grower, Waynesburg, Penn., was born in Franklin Township, Greene County, Penn, December 25, 1838. He is a son of William Pratt, also a prominent farmer in this township, who was born in Fayette County, Penn, October 13, 1814 His parents were James and Sallie (Boner) Pratt, also natives of Fayette County, and of English lineage William Pratt owned a well improved farm of 200 acres in Franklin Township, where he died in 1874. He was a blacksmith by trade, in which he engaged until 1854 when he began farming He spent most of his life in Greene County, where he was united in marriage, in 1838, with Miss Harriet, daughter of Joshua and Catharine (Livengood) Thomas. Her father was born near Philadelphia, Penn., and was of Dutch ancestry. Mrs. Pratt was born in Center Township, this county, June 2, 1820, and was the seventh in a family of fifteen children D.

B. Pratt, the subject of this sketch, is a man of tireless zeal and unusual energy, by means of which he has been very successful in his chosen pursuit, and owns a well improved farm of 175 acres. On August 25, 1870, he married Margaret, daughter of William and Sarah (Bodkin) Smith, who were of English and Irish lineage. Her mother was a native of Pennsylvania. Her father was born in New Jersey, and died in 1874. They were the parents of sixteen children, of whom Mrs. Pratt is the youngest. To Mr. and Mrs. Pratt have been born two sons—William Harvey and Lindsley Inghram. Their mother is a member of the Baptist Church. Mr. Pratt is a Democrat and a member of the I. O. O. F. He has served as school director and auditor of his township.

ANDREW ARMSTRONG PURMAN, attorney and counselor at law, was born on Short Creek, in Ohio County, Virginia (now West Virginia), April 8, 1823. He is a son of John and Barbara (Burns) Purman. His parents were natives of Pennsylvania, and of German and Scotch extraction. His father was a farmer and came to Greene County in 1833, settling on a farm in Richhill Township. Later in life he moved to Shelby County, Indiana, where he died in 1838. His family consisted of nine children, of whom the subject of this sketch is the third son. A. A. Purman, Esq., the subject of our sketch, spent his early life with his parents on the farm, where he first went to subscription school. He was afterwards a student in a select school in Waynesburg, and at the founding of Waynesburg College he entered it as one of its first students. He began the study of law in Waynesburg in 1847, in the office of Hon. Samuel Cleavenger, and at the death of Mr. Cleavenger, 1848, finished the course with Lewis Roberts, Esq., and was admitted to the bar in May, 1849. He has devoted his life to the practice of his chosen profession. In 1856 Mr. Purman was elected district attorney, serving three years. In 1869 he was elected State Senator from Greene, Fayette and Westmoreland counties, and served in the session of 1871 as chairman of the finance committee. He was elected in the year 1872, on the Democratic ticket, a delegate at large to the constitutional convention of 1872-1873, and served on the committee on legislation and corporation. Mr. Purman was a school director for fifteen years, and served for several years as a member of the borough council. He is a Democrat, and commenced public speaking for the party in 1844, for Polk and Dallas, has spoken in every presidential campaign since, and was offered the nomination for Lieutenant-Governor of Pennsylvania in 1874. In 1865 he came within one vote of being nominated President Judge of the Fourteenth Judicial District. Mr. Purman was united in marriage June 26, 1856, with Miss Mary Ann, daughter of Thomas and Elizabeth (Morris) Russell. Of their nine children seven are now living. They are Thamas R., John, a physician and surgeon; Lida, wife of B. R. Williams, of Sharon, Penn.; James J., a law student; Alexander E., Elizabeth M. and A. A. Jr. Mr. Purman's grandfather, James Burns, was a soldier in the Revolutionary war. Mr. and Mrs. Purman are members of the Baptist Church, in which he has held many official positions. He is and has been president of the board of trustees of Monongahela College at Jefferson ever since its organization in 1867.

Z. C. RAGAN, of the firm of Ragan & Evans, editors and proprietors of the Waynesburg *Independent*, was born in Zanesville, Ohio, July 14, 1833, and is a son of Joab and Mary (Stull) Ragan. His mother was born in Kentucky, and his father in Beaver County, Penn. They were of Scotch-Irish descent. His father, who died at the early age of thirty-three, was a minister of the Methodist Protestant Church, and served as president of the conference. He was a self-made man and an able linguist, speaking and writing four languages. Z. C. Ragan is an only child. He was brought to Waynesburg in 1840, where he was reared, and partially educated in Waynesburg College. Early in life he learned the printing business, a calling he has followed the greater part of his life. He started a paper in Waynesburg in 1872, in company with J. W. Axtell, called the Waynesburg *Independent*, which has a circulation of over 3,000 copies per week. The financial success of the paper has been largely due to Mr. Ragan's untiring efforts. He was for seven years a member of the board of trustees in Waynesburg College, and is a prominent member of the Knights of Honor. In 1861 he enlisted in Company F, Eighty-fifth Pennsylvania Volunteer Infantry, and was discharged in 1864. He served as Sergeant, and had charge of his company when it was mustered out. Mr. Ragan was united in marriage, in 1858, with Miss Anna M., daughter of Thomas Hill, a farmer of Greene County. Their children are—Emma L., a graduate of Waynesburg College, and wife of W. S. Pipes; and Minnie E., a student in the college. Mrs. Pipes was for three years a teacher in Enfield College, Illinois. The family are members of the Cumberland Presbyterian Church, in which Mr. Ragan is an elder, and was superintendent of the Sabbath-school over eight years.

JAMES F. RANDOLPH, a farmer and stock-grower of Franklin Township, was born in Jefferson Borough, Greene County, Penn., April 23, 1832. He is a son of Isaac and Sarah (Adamson) Randolph, who came from New Jersey, their native State, and settled in Greene County, Penn., in 1795, on a farm where they spent the remainder of their lives. They reared a family of ten children, eight of whom grew to maturity. James F., the third in the family, was reared on the farm with his parents, and attended the district school. He has successfully engaged in farming as a business, and is the owner of some fine land in this county. In 1855 Mr. Randolph married Elizabeth, daughter of William Braden, who is an ex-associate judge, and a prominent citizen of this county. To M. and Mrs. Randolph were born eight children—Sarah M., wife of Smith Adamson; Mary, wife of Isaiah Gordon; Rachel, wife of Jackson Pratt; Lucy, Isaac L., William, Lizzie and Thomas. Mr. Randolph is a Democrat. He and wife are prominent members of the Cumberland Presbyterian Church.

J. A. F. RANDOLPH, insurance and real estate agent, Waynesburg, Penn., was born in Jefferson Township, this county, March 18, 1851, and is a son of Abraham F. and Emily A. (Adamson) Randolph, also natives of this county. Abraham F. Randolph was a son of James F. Randolph, a native of Middlesex County, N. J., and member of the Society of Friends. He came to Greene County, Penn., in 1795, and remained all his life on the farm where Abraham F. was born. The farm is still in possession of the family. Abraham F. and Emily A. Randolph were married in this county, June 18, 1833, where they died, the former December 8, 1866, and the latter March 9, 1885. They were the parents of four children, two of whom are living—William H. F. and James A. F. The deceased are an infant, and Sarah L., wife of C. C. Strawn. The subject of our sketch was united in marriage, January 9, 1888, with Miss Emma F. Johnson, who was born September 26, 1859. She is a daughter of William R. and Minerva E. (Fleming) Johnson, the former a native of this county, and the latter of West Virginia. Mr. Randolph acquired his education in the common schools and Waynesburg College. He remained at home until twenty-one years of age, then taught school for a period of five years. He first engaged in his present business in 1880. He represents some of the best insurance companies of the United States, and also deals extensively in real estate. Mr. Randolph is a member of the board of trust of the Pennsylvania Synod of the Cumberland Presbyterian Church, and treasurer of the endowment fund for support of Waynesburg College. He and his wife are members of the Cumberland Presbyterian Church. He is at present city clerk.

JOSEPH W. RAY.—The subject of this sketch, Joseph W. Ray, is the eldest son of James E. and Margaret (Leonard) Ray, and was born May 25, 1849, in Morris Township, Greene County. His father, who is now (July, 1888) in his eightieth year, was born in Morris County, N. J., and his mother in Trumbull County, Ohio. His parents, immediately upon their marriage, settled in Washington County, Penn., but removed therefrom April 1, 1849, to a farm in Greene County, where they have ever since resided. They gave him the advantage of such educational facilities as the common schools of that time and section afforded. At nineteen years of age he secured employment as a teacher, a calling to which he devoted several years In 1871 he became a student of Waynesburg.College, and was graduated by that institution in the class of 1874. About this time he commenced the study of law, and was admitted to the bar of his native county in June, 1876. Two years later, or April 1, 1878, having associated himself with H. B Axtell, Esq., they opened an office in Waynesburg, under the firm name of Ray & Axtell, since which time he has been actively engaged in the practice of his profession. He was admitted to practice in the Supreme Court of the State in 1883. In politics Mr. Ray is a Republican. He was chairman, for three years, of the Republican County Committee of Greene County He has represented the county in a State Convention, and was an alternate delegate to the Republican National Convention of 1880 He has twice been the nominee of his party for office. In 1884 he ran for Congress against Hon. Charles E. Boyle, the Democratic candidate, in what was then the twenty-first district, composed of the counties of Fayette, Greene and Westmoreland. Although defeated by 2,500 votes, this was much the smallest Democratic majority the district ever gave, up to that time. In 1886 he was nominated for the State Senate, in the fortieth senatorial district, composed of Fayette and Greene counties, having for his Democratic competitor Hon. Thomas B Schnatterly The official returns gave Mr. Schnatterly 8,438 votes, and Mr. Ray 8,256 votes, a reduction of the usual Democratic majority of more than 2,000 in the district to 182. Mr. Ray was married May 18, 1878, to Miss Henrietta Iams, a daughter of the late Thomas Iams, of Morris Township, Greene County. Since their marriage they have resided in Waynesburg, and have four children, two girls and two boys.

WILLIAM RHODES, farmer, Waynesburg, Penn, who was born in Franklin Township, July 12, 1818, is a son of William and Nancy (Rinehart) Rhodes, who were of German extraction. His father was a native of this county, and a farmer all his life. The Rhodes family have usually been farmers William Rhodes is an only child He was born in a house where the poor-house now stands. The subject of this sketch received his early education in the district schools of Franklin Township. He has been a successful farmer, and owns 300 acres of good farming land. He remained on the farm with his parents until 1852, when he married Miss Jane, daughter of William and Elizabeth (Shull) Shriver. Her parents were natives of this county, and of Dutch and Irish lineage. To Mr. and Mrs. Rhodes were born seven children—Lizzie, Rettie J., wife of Rinehart Gwynn; George F., Belle H., Ida D, Willie B. and Charley. Mr. Rhodes is steward in the Methodist Church, is a member of the Masonic fraternity and the I. O. O. F The following sketch of William Rhodes' grandfather will be of interest to many readers· William Rhodes was born at Newport, R. I., about 1759. He went to sea at sixteen and remained a sailor for sixteen years. With many vicissitudes his career seems checkered. From his manuscript journals we find him a prisoner in the French prison from 1778 to 1780, and on his very next voyage from London in May was recaptured, but liberated through the influence of American friends, as an American citizen. In October of 1780 he sailed for Barbadoes with a large fleet of merchant ships, convoyed by ten line of battle ships. The next year he was once more captured by the French and again liberated. Again he was a prisoner in New York, being captured by the English, and exchanged after five months' confinement. In 1784 he was wrecked off Cape Cod, and the following year (1785) he heard for the first time of the Ohio settlement. About 1787, his father dying, William Rhodes' attention was directed to the settlements west of the Alleghany Mountains, and on the 18th of January, 1788, reached the old Redstone Fort (now Brownsville) in Fayette County. After peddling, and keeping store at Jackson's Fort (then Washington County), he bought, in 1791, a plantation (where his son, James R. Rhodes, now resides), married and began farming. In his own words: "Settled for life, I hope. Here I began jogging for life and family, not in the least discouraged in my new profession." The manuscript is rather amusing and interesting, illustrated by drawings of his own, of ships, scenery, women, men, birds, fishes and animals, according to the fancy of this backwoods artist.

S. S RINEHART, merchant, Waynesburg, Penn., son of Samuel and Mary (Zook) Rinehart, was born in this county February 16, 1848. His mother was also a native of this county, and his father was born in Ohio They were of German and Irish extraction. His father was a farmer and coal miner, and reared a family of nine children, of whom the subject of this sketch is the fourth. He was reared in Franklin Township, attended the common schools, and in early life learned the harness maker's trade. He engaged in that business in Waynesburg until 1872, when he commenced clerking in a store. He was employed as a salesman until 1878, when he began business for himself at Morrisville, Penn., and has met with success. Mr. Rinehart was united in marriage October 7, 1872, with Mary Ella Lippencott, a native of this county Their children are—Mattie, Nettie, Eddie H. and Hermon. Mr. Rinehart is a Democrat in politics.

JAMES R. RINEHART, Professor of Languages in Waynesburg College, was born at Woodsfield, Monroe County, Ohio, in October, 1832, and is a son of Simon and Hannah (Morris) Rinehart, natives of Greene County, Penn. His father was of German and Irish extraction. Prof. Rinehart's great-grandfather, who was a farmer, was among the early settlers of this county, and was killed by the Indians. His grandfather, Barnett Rinehart, was born September 8, 1777, in this county. His maternal grandparents were natives of Mon-. mouth County, New Jersey, and were of Scotch and German descent. The Rinehart family have, as a rule, been farmers and very successful in business　Several members of the family have entered the professions and have met with unusual success　Prof Rinehart's father was a blacksmith by trade. He was clerk for the county commissioners for several years, and also served as justice of the peace. He reared a family of four children, of whom the Professor is the third. He was educated in Greene County, graduating in the regular classical course at Waynesburg College. He then took up the study of law and was admitted to the bar in 1857. He began the practice of his profession in Clinton, Illinois, and after a short time went to St Louis, Missouri, where he remained until 1860, then returning to Greene County, Penn　In 1887 he accepted his present position as instructor in Waynesburg College, and has filled the same continuously since that time　Prof. Rinehart was married in 1873 to Miss Ida, daughter of Hon Patrick Donley, of Mt. Morris, Penn. Their children are—Patrick Donley and Margaret Morris　The Professor is a member of the, Masonic Fraternity.

PROF. A. I P. RINEHART, superintendent of the public schools of Waynesburg, Penn., is among the prominent instructors of the county, and a man of marked ability as a teacher. He was born in Franklin Township, this county, April 17, 1860, and is the son of William and Elizabeth (Porter) Rinehart, who were of English and German descent　His parents were natives of Greene County, and descendants of its early settlers. His father was a farmer, and of his family of nine children Prof. Rinehart is the oldest　He received his early education in the common schools and afterwards took a regular course in the Edinboro State Normal School, graduating in 1883. He has since engaged in teaching as a profession, and his work has been confined to Greene County, with the exception of two years that he was principal in the High School at Freeport, Armstrong County, Penn　In 1885 he was elected to his present position of principal of schools in Waynesburg　During vacation he has frequently instructed other teachers of the county. In 1888 he taught a very successful term in Jackson Township, his pupils being principally those who had themselves been teachers. Prof. Rinehart is a genial, pleasant gentleman, and is held in high esteem by the teachers of Greene County.

J. G. RITCHIE, Chicago, Illinois, was born in Cumberland Township, Greene County, Penn, June 27, 1834. His parents were Col. Newton J. and Anna (Gwynn) Ritchie, natives of Pennsylvania, both now deceased. They were the parents of four children, of whom two are living—Mrs William Smith and the subject of this sketch. He was united in marriage February 10, 1876, with Miss Philinda

Andrew, who was born in Richland County, Ohio, April 18, 1847. Her parents were William and Mary J. (McConnell) Andrew, the former a native of Washington County, Penn, and the latter of Virginia. Mr. Andrew departed this life in 1850, and his widow in 1863 They were the parents of five children, four of whom are living, viz : Elizabeth, wife of Samuel Bonar; Louisa, wife of John Chambers; Mary J., widow of Di. F. M. Denny, and Mrs. J. G. Ritchie. The deceased was James A., who was killed in the late war. Mr. and Mrs. Ritchie are the parents of one daughter—Anna M., born in Waynesburg, Penn, February 19, 1878. Mr. Ritchie acquired his education in the common schools and Greene Academy at Carmichaels, Penn. He subsequently taught for a number of years, then read law with E M. Sayers. After his admission to the bar he practiced in partnership with A. A. Purman, Esq. Mr. Ritchie served as District Attorney for Greene County, after which he engaged in the hardware business for five years with his brother-in-law, William P. Smith, in Waynesburg. He next turned his attention to the W. & W. R. R. enterprise, in which he took an active interest and was one of those most instrumental in procuring the road to Waynesburg. He served as first president of the road, was also superintendent, and is still one of the directors. In 1887 he went to Chicago, and in company with J. S Wolf, has been engaged in the real estate business. He and his wife own property in Greene County, Penn., Richland County, Ohio, and in Chicago. They are consistent members of the Presbyterian Church,

MORGAN ROSS, dealer in wagons, carriages and harness, Waynesburg, Penn., was born in Center Township, this county, February 22, 1844. He is a son of Peabody Atkinson and Maria (Matthews) Ross. His parents were natives of Pennsylvania, and of Scotch-Irish origin. His father was for some time a manufacturer, but devoted most of his life to farming. His family consisted of eight children, of whom the subject of this sketch is the oldest living. Until he was twenty-one years old Mr. Ross remained on the farm with his parents in Center Township, where he attended the district school. In 1865 he came to Waynesburg and learned the carriage and wagon-maker's trade, subsequently engaging in that business until 1883, the year in which his first wife, Maggie Throckmorton Ross died. Mr. Ross has one child, Charles, born July 4th, 1879. He was married the second time in 1885 Mr Ross is a Democrat, and a member of the I. O O. F.

JOSEPH B. ROSS, manufacturer, of the firm of McGlumphy & Ross, Waynesburg, Penn., was born in Dunkard Township, Greene County, Penn., January 24, 1844. His parents, Thomas and Eliza (Bailey) Ross, were natives of Fayette County, and of German origin. His father was a cabinet-maker by trade, to which he devoted the

early part of his life   In later years he retired to the quiet of the
farm, where he spent the remaining portion of his life   His family
consisted of five children—three daughters and five sons, of whom
Joseph B. is the second.   He was reared in Cumberland Township,
where he attended the common schools and early in life learned the
manufacturing of woolen goods   He was employed in that business
at Clarksville, Penn., until 1873, when he bought land near Waynesburg and engaged in farming from 1876 to 1879.   Mr. Ross was
then proprietor of a grocery and meat-market for two years, when he
bought the old planing-mill and started his present business   In
1873 Mr Ross married Susan, daughter of Samuel Luse, a prominent
and successful farmer of Franklin Township.   They have three
children—Charles L , Walter S and Franklin.   Mr' Ross is a Republican   His grandfather, Thomas Ross, was one of the pioneers
of Greene County.

HON. ABNER ROSS, ex-Senator, is a merchant by occupation
He was born in Washington Township, this county, March 30, 1838,
and is a son of Benjamin and Hannah (Johns) Ross, also natives of
this county   His grandfather, Timothy Ross, was among the early
pioneer farmers of the county   Mr. Ross is the fourth in a family of
twelve children, eight of whom grew to maturity.   He was reared
on the home farm, and his early education was obtained at an Academy
in Fayette County, Penn.   He afterwards spent some time in
Waynesburg College.   Mr Ross chose farming as a business in which
he engaged until he was elected sheriff of the county in 1870.   He
held that office for three years, then engaged in the mercantile business in Waynesburg until 1884, when he was elected State Senator
and served two years, was elected to fill the unexpired time of
Senator Patton.   He has since continued in the boot and shoe business which he established in 1882.   In 1863 Mr. Ross married
Margaret P., daughter of Isaac Mitchell.   Mrs. Ross is also a
native of this county, to which her grandfather came at an early
date and lived to the advanced age of ninety-six years   Mr and
Mrs. Ross are the parents of four children—Albert Lee, Benjamin
F and Isaac Wilbert   Jennie E. died July 14, 1885, aged fifteen
years   Mr. Ross is a Democrat.   He and his wife are members of the
Baptist Church.

J. H. ROGERS, photographer, was born December 11, 1831,
near the place where the Union depot now stands in the city of Pittsburgh, Penn.   His parents are James R. Rogers, born in 1805, and
Sarah O. Rogers, born in 1812.   They were both natives of Pennsylvania   They were married in 1830, afterward settling in Pittsburgh where they remained for six years.   Mr. James Rogers was a
carpenter and contractor and resided in several different towns after
leaving Pittsburgh.   He resided for a time in Bealsville, Penn,

where Mrs. Sarah O. Rogers died.   Mr. Rogers afterwards married Mary Price and moved to Clover Hill, and from there to Brownsville, Penn. He then moved near Mount Pleasant, Ohio, and finally to Indiana, where they reside at the present   By the first marriage there were ten children, of whom Mr. J. H. Rogers is the oldest Of these five are living.   The subject of our sketch was united in marriage, October 31, 1854, with Charlotte V. Rearhard, who was born in Uniontown, Fayette County, Penn., January 3, 1833, and is a daughter of Conrad and Elizabeth Rearhard, natives of Pennsylvania   Her father was born in 1787, and departed this life December 5, 1870   Mrs Rearhard was born in 1792, and died May 24, 1888.   Mr. and Mrs. Rogers have six children, five of whom are living; viz, Sarah E., Emma J., Anna V., Craig S and James H. Frank is deceased.   Mr. Rogers acquired his education in the common schools, after which he learned the carpenter's trade with his father and worked at that business till 1861.   He then began studying photography with J. S. Young, of Washington, Penn.   He finished the study in two years and opened a gallery in Bealsville. After remaining there about nine months he carried on a successful business at Brownsville for a period of eight years.   He then returned to Washington and purchased the gallery owned by J. S Young.   He remained there for eight years, then purchased a farm in Amwell Township, Washington County, on the W. & W. Railroad, consisting of one hundred acres.   He remained on his farm three years, then moved to Waynesburg, opened a gallery and has been very successful in his business. He makes photographs of all kinds and sizes, making a specialty of copying and enlarging pictures.   Mr. Rogers is a member of the Knights of Honor, and both he and his wife are members of the C. P. Church.

REV. W. M. RYAN was born March 7, 1848 near West Alexander, Washington County, Pennsylvania. His parents, Joseph and Isabella Ryan, still reside in Washington County.   His father has been a farmer all his life, hence the subject of this sketch was reared on a farm.   He enjoyed the advantages of the public schools of his native county, and also a term or two in the Academy at West Alexander.   After this he became a teacher, teaching for five years.   In December, 1868, he made a profession of religion, and became a member of the Pleasant Grove Baptist Church.   In 1871 he entered Waynesburg College, graduating in the class '74, in the classical course, after which he took a three year's course in Crozer Theological Seminary, at Chester, Pennsylvania.   He was ordained as a gospel minister in September, 1877, since which time he has been engaged in the active duties of his profession. His first pastorate was with the Beulah and Bates Fork Baptist Churches of this County.   From these churches he was called to the charge of the

Waynesburg Baptist Church, where he is now in the ninth year of pastorate. His labors in all these fields have been eminently success-ful. Mr. Ryan has been twice married; first, to Miss Nantie, daughter of Jesse Hill, August 24, 1876   She died June 21, 1880. He was again married May 17, 1883, to Miss Lizzie, daughter of Calvin Rush, of Morris Township, this County. Mr. Ryan's family now consists of himself, wife and four children; viz., Gertrude M., and Nantie Belle, by his first wife; and Isa Lee and Jessie J., by his second marriage.

E. M. SAYERS, attorney at law, Waynesburg, Penn., is one of the first and most active business men of the county. He was born in Waynesburg May 30, 1812   His father Ephraim Sayers, was a native of Loudon County, Virginia, and his mother, Mary (Wood) Sayers, was born in Hartford County, Maryland   Both were of English ancestry. Ehpriam Sayers was a pioneer of Greene County, having in 1786 settled two miles east of the present site of Waynes-burg borough, where he led an industrious life, and reared a family of four children—three sons and one daughter   The subject of this sketch was reared on a farm in Franklin Township, this county, and completed his education in Washington College,   He read law in Waynesburg with the Hon. Samuel Cleavenger, and commenced the practice of his profession in his native town in 1835.   He has met with marked success, which may be attributed.to his more than ordi-nary business qualifications.   He is the owner of a number of farms in Greene County, large tracts of land in the South and West, and considerable real estate in Waynesburg.   He has been a member of the Republican party since its organization.   Mr Sayers was united in marriage with Miss Jane Adams, a daughter of Robert Adams, in 1839, she died in 1847.   Their children are Henry C., a farmer and business man of Waynesburg ; James E., a member of the Greene County bar—Thomas and Ezra, deceased.   Mr Sayers was united in marriage the second time, in 1852, with Miss Harriet W. Tan-ner, a native of Massachusetts   They are the parents of six chil-dren : Norman, a farmer of Franklin Township ; Florence A., wife of Charles A. Martin; Mary, D. L., and two children who were burned to death when quite young   Mr. Sayers has given his children the advantages of a liberal education.   His sons Henry C. and James E., were soldiers in the late war ; and his uncle, Josiah Sayers, and his grandfather, William Sayers, were in the Revolutionary war, be-ing present when Lord Cornwallis surrendered his army at York-town, Virginia.   The farm settled by William Sayers the ancestor is still in possession of the family, and has been for about a hundred years

JAMES E SAYERS attorney at law of Waynesburg, Penn., where he was born May 30, 1845, is a son of E. M. and Jane

(Adams) Sayers, also natives of Waynesburg. His father is an attorney and counsellor at law. James E. was reared in Waynesburg, where he attended the common school and college. He was afterwards a student in the Ohio State University, and learned the printing trade when a boy. July 15, 1862, he enlisted in Co. F, 85th Penn. Vol. Infantry, as a private, was discharged at Richmond, Va., with the rank of Orderly Sergent on May 13, 1865. He was "in at the death," having fired his last gun at Appomattox C. H. Va., and having participated in twenty-two battles and skirmishes and three seiges—Charlestown, S. C., Petersburg and Richmond, Va. Returning from the army, his first business venture was as an editor. In 1866 he bought the Waynesburg *Republican*, of which paper he was editor and proprietor for nearly three years, when he again entered school and graduated, in 1870, in the law course in the Indiana State University. For four years thereafter he continued in journalistic work. In 1874 he began the practice of law in Waynesburg, where he has since remained. Politically Mr Sayers is an earnest Republican He was a delegate in the National Republican Convention of 1884, and was once the nominee of his party for Congress in the Twenty-first District. On June 16, 1868, Mr. Sayers married Anna A., daughter of Albert Allison, One of the first merchants of Waynesburg. Mr. and Mrs. Sayers are the parents of two children—Albert H. and Jane

ROBERT A SAYERS, chief burgess of Waynesburg, Penn., born May 27, 1841, is a son of William W. and Rebecca (Adams) Sayers, natives of this county. His father was born August 12, 1805, and died May 22, 1886. He was a brother of E. M. Sayers, Esq., and they were for years associated in the real estate business in Waynesburg. William's main occupation was the stone and marble business, in which he was a partner with Simon Rinehart, Esq., for many years. He was married in Waynesburg to Miss Rebecca, daughter of Robert Adams, who was a Whig and a Republican, and lived to be ninety-six years old He was at one time register and recorder of Greene County. Robert A., the subject of our sketch, was reared in Waynesburg, where he was educated in the college. When the war broke out he left college and enlisted Nov. 4, 1861, in the 8th Penn. Reserves. His military career is worthy of record. He participated in severe battles; was taken prisoner and suffered all the horrors of prison life He was wounded at the battle of Gaines Mill, in left thigh, and left on the battle-field for two weeks receiving no medical aid. He was then sent to Belle Isle, and subsequently to Libby prison, where he was paroled and sent home He only remained until his wound was well enough, and went through a long siege of typhoid and malarial fever, when he again joined his regiment at Upton Hill, Virginia. At the close of his three years' service he returned home and engaged in the coal business for six-teen years. In 1883 he was appointed U. S. Store-keeper and Guager. Mr Sayers was married in Potter County, Penn., January 21, 1869, to Miss Florence Stevens, whose parents were born in Ver-mont. Mr and Mrs Sayers have one child—Fendora, now a student at Oberlin College, Ohio. Mr. and Mis. Sayers and daughter are members of the Presbyterian Church. He is a Republican and a member of the G. A. R. Post, No. 367, Department of Pennsylvania

HENRY C SAYERS is among the successful busines men of Greene County   He has made farming his chief pursuit and has also dealt extensively in stock and real estate.   He began business early in life, being the oldest son of E M. Sayers, Esq. Mr. Sayers was born in Waynesburg, November 21, 1840. Here he grew to man-hood and was a student at the first session of the college. He went to Iowa in 1859 and engaged in buying and shipping stock to Chicago, Illinois   He returned to Waynesburg in 1861, and August 11, 1862, he enlisted in Company G, Fifteenth Pennsylvania Cavalry. This was an independent regiment which acted as body guard to General Rosecrans   Among the battles in which he engaged were the following: Antietam, Murfreesboro, Chickamauga, Tullahama and Rome, Georgia, pursuit of Longstreet through Tennessee by way of Knoxville to North Carolina, and then had quite a skirmish with the Indians   In 1863 he was captured by General Wheeler's Cavalry and marched with Wheeler's command for some time before being paroled. After joining his regiment he was for a time detailed as a courier to carry despatches to the front facing the enemy. At the close of the war Mr. Sayers returned to Waynesburg, where he has been success-fully engaged in business. He was united in marriage, in 1867, with Miss Clementine, daughter of Samuel Rush. Mrs. Sayers is a native of this county, and of English descent. Their children are—Ella Jane, C E. and Henry C , Jr. Mrs Sayers is a member of the C. P. Church. Mr. Sayers is a Republican, was constable of the county, two terms and has served as a member of the school board of Waynes-burg. He is a member of the Masonic fraternity. Mr. Sayers was formerly a member of the Templeton Post of Washington, Penn., but now belongs to Col J F. McCullough Post, of Waynesburg, of which he has been commander, and was an alternate delegate to the Twenty-first National Encampment at St. Louis, Mo.

J M. SCOTT, farmer and stock-grower, and U S store-keeper and ganger in the twenty-third collective district of Pennsylvania, was born in Jefferson Township, Greene County, Penn , December 10, 1844, and is a son of William P and Sarah (Long) Scott. His father and grandfather were farmers. His grandfather, James Scott, came from Baltimore, Md , to Greene County, Penn., among the early settlers of Jefferson Township   J M Scott's grandmother, Scott, was ninety-eight years of age; her maiden name was Margaret Kincaid, she died April 1, 1888. The subject of our sketch is the oldest in a family of seven children, all of whom are living and married He was reared on the farm, attended the district school in Jefferson Township and Waynesburg College. He taught school in early life, but has made farming his main pursuit, and is a resident of Franklin Township. In 1871 Mr. Scott marrried Miss Margaret, daughter of Hiram Rinehart. Their children are—Harry, Henry and Jésse. Mrs. Scott is a member of the Methodist Episcopal Church. Mr. Scott is a Democrat, and a member of I. O. O. F, and is a member of the encampment He is also a Master Mason.

S. W. SCOTT, wool and grain merchant, was born in Washington County, June 26, 1835, and is a son of William and Abigail (Wood) Scott, natives of Washington County, Penn. His father was Scotch and his mother was of English and Irish origin. His father who was a farmer nearly all his life died in 1878. His family consisted of eight children. The subject of our sketch was reared in Greene County, to which his parents removed in 1839. He attended the public schools and Waynesburg College. He learned the carpenter's trade at which he worked for six years. Mr. Scott then began dealing in wool and has been extensively engaged in that business since 1863 He is prominent among the successful business men of Waynesburg. Mr. Scott, who is a Republican, was appointed Deputy U. S Revenue Collector in 1864, and served until 1866. He was re-appointed in 1869 and served until 1874. Mr. Scott was married in 1865 to Miss Frances, daughter of Thomas Hill. Their children are—Ella B , wife of A. P. Dickey, Esq , of Waynesburg; William E., Nannie, Fannie and Samuel W. Mr. and Mrs. Scott are members of the Methodist Episcopal Church, in which he is a trustee.

W. G. SCOTT, Professor of Mathematics of Waynesburg College, was born in Washington County, Penn., December 11, 1832. His parents were William and Abigail (Wood) Scott, also natives of Washington County, and of Scotch and English ancestry. They were married in Washington County, where they remained until 1839, at which time they removed to Greene County, where they remained until their death. Mr. Scott departed this life in 1878, and his widow in 1880. They were the parents of nine children, eight still living. Prof. W. G. Scott is the oldest and was united in marriage, April 17, 1862, with Miss Mary Sutton, who was born in England, being the daughter of the Rev. R H. and Martha (Cowen) Sutton, now residents of Waynesburg. To Mr. and Mrs. Scott have been born three children—Mattie E., wife of Rev. J. H. Lucas; Minnie M , wife of J. N. Norris, and Gail. Prof. Scott acquired his earliest education in the old-fashioned log school-house and afterwards attended Waynesburg College, where he graduated in the year 1867. After teaching one year in Greene Academy, he was elected to the chair of mathematics of Waynesburg College, and has filed the position ever since. He has also been engaged in the mercantile business since 1867, being now sole proprietor of the store opened by him and his father in that year. It is one of the leading stores in Waynesburg, receiving a large patronage from the town and vicinity.

E H. SHIPLEY, druggist, was born in Uniontown, Fayette County, Pennsylvania, November 3, 1864, and is a son of Julius and Eliza (Hair) Shipley. His parents were also natives of Fayette County, and of English descent His father was a civil engineer, and is now deceased. The subject of our sketch is the second in a family of three children. He was reared in a Uniontown, where he attended school He afterwards clerked in a drug store for a period of three years. Mr. Shipley came to Waynesburg in 1881, clerked in a drug store for two years, then opened up his present business, in which he has been very liberally patronized by the people of Waynesburg and vicinity. He is a Democrat in politics On January 23, 1888, Mr. Shipley married Miss Anna L, daughter of Captain J. R. and Nancy (Bayard) Hewitt. Mrs. Shipley is a native of this county, born July 7, 1865.

A. F SILVEUS, attorney at law, Waynesburg, Penn., was born near Jackson Centre, Mercer County, on the 5th of December, 1851. He is the son of Henry B. and Rachael (Taylor) Silveus, who were natives of Greene County, and were of German and English origin. His father, a farmer and stock-grower, was elected sheriff of Greene County in 1867, and served the term of three years The son was the fourth in a family of eight children, five sons and three daughters. He was reared upon the farm, attended the common schools, and when his father was elected sheriff he served as deputy. He subsequently taught school, and became a student at Waynesburg College, from which he graduated in 1873 He then resumed teaching, and in 1875 was elected superintendent of the schools of Greene County. For two terms he taught in Waynesburg College, giving special attention to the normal classes He read law with Hon. A. A Purman, was admitted to practice in 1878, and opened an office at Waynesburg, where he has practiced since. He has served as a school director. He was married in 1877 to Miss Lida, daughter of John T. Hook. Both are members of the Cumberland Presbyterian Church They have two children—Jessie and John T. In politics Mr. Silveus is a Democrat.

REV. J. L SIMPSON, a retired Methodist minister, was born in Virginia, January 6, 1822 He is a son of William and Mary Ann (Leech) Simpson, who were of English and Irish descent His father was a boot-maker. Rev. J. L. Simpson is the second in a

family of eight children. He received a collegiate course in West
Virginia, and also served a regular apprenticeship at the saddler's
trade. He entered the ministry in his twenty-second year, in which
field he has successfully labored ever since. He was first licensed
in 1844 and was appointed as an assistant in Pittsburgh, Penn. In
1846 he came to Waynesburg and took charge of a circuit, but subsequently went to Virginia, where he engaged in the ministry until
1862. When a large number of the young men in his church and
congregation enlisted in the army and insisted on his going with
them, he enlisted and was elected Captain of their company. They
were assigned to the Fourth Virginia Cavalry. Captain Simpson
was elected chaplin of the regiment and served two years in that
capacity. At the close of the war he again entered the ministry and
went to Wisconsin, where he took charge of the Methodist Protestant
Church at Beliot for two years. In 1854 he was married to Miss
Mary J., daughter of Thomas and Nannie Black. Her parents were
natives of West Virginia, and of Scotch and English descent. Mr.
and Mrs. Simpson have six children, three of whom are living—
Anna May, wife of Harvey Clifford, of Wisconsin; Mary L. and
George B. The deceased are Charles R., Helen V. and Carrie Olive.
The family are members of the Methodist Protestant Church. Mr.
Simpson is a Republican, and has met with more than average suc-
cess as a minister of the gospel.

A. C. SMALLEY, chief of police, was born in Waynesburg,
September 10, 1843. His parents, E. P. and Catherine (Rinehart)
Smalley, were also natives of Waynesburg. His father was born in
1805, and died in 1885. The subject of this sketch is the oldest
in a family of three children—two sons and a daughter. He attended
the public school and Waynesburg College. Mr. Smalley learned
the chairmaker's trade and carried on the business in Waynesburg
for a time. In 1862 he enlisted in Company H, in the One-Hundred
and Twenty-Third Pennsylvania Volunteer Infantry and served his
term of enlistment. On returning home, he resumed chair making
and carried on the business until he embarked in the mercantile
trade. On account of failing health he retired from business in 1883,
sold out in 1887 and was appointed chief of police, which position he
still holds. In 1868 Mr. Smalley was married to Mary E., daughter
of Absalom Hedge. She is also a native of this county, and of English lineage. Mr. and Mrs. Smalley are members of the Baptist
Church, in which he is trustee and treasurer of the Sabbath-school.
He belongs to the G. A. R. Post, No. 367, Department of Pennsylvania, of which he has been quartermaster, and is also a Master
Mason.

J. M. SMITH, saddle and harness manufacturer, was born at
Carmichaels, Penn., November 18, 1845, and is a son of H. A. and
38

Mary E. (McGee) Smith. His grandfather, J. H. McGee, was a wealthy merchant at Carmichaels, where he also engaged extensively in the coal business. Mr. Smith's father was also a saddle and harness manufacturer and carried on a successful business at Carmichaels for many years, was also post-master for sixteen years. The subject of our sketch is the oldest of a family of five children—four sons and one daughter. He was reared in this county, receiving his education in the old Greene Academy at Carmichaels. Mr. Smith earned harness making with his father and has been engaged in that business since 1867. In 1864 he enlisted in the Twenty-Second Regiment of Pennsylvania Cavalry, or Ringold Cavalry, and was with General Sheridan on his famous ride from Winchester. He then went West for eight years, returning to Waynesburg in 1875, when he engaged in his present business and has met with average success. Mr. Smith was united in marriage, September 19, 1876, with Melissa Donley, whose ancestors were among the early Irish settlers of Pennsylvania, and among the first to find a home in Greene County. Mr. and Mrs. Smith have four children—Harry, Joseph R. D., Donley McGee and Catharine D. Mr. Smith is a Republican and has been a member of the town council three terms. He is Captain of the Waynesburg Blues—Company K, Tenth Regiment, N. G. P., and a member of the G. A. R. Post of Waynesburg.

JAMES B. SMITH, county surveyor, was born in Center Township, August 16, 1846, and is a son of Edmund and Elizabeth (Adamson) Smith. They were also natives of this county, and of English origin. His father was a farmer all his life, and died in February, 1887. Of his family of eight children six are now living, of whom James B. is the third. He was reared in Greene County, attending the common school and the Millsboro Normal school. He gave especial attention to the study of surveying and civil engineering and has devoted most of his time to that business, having served as county surveyor for several years. Since 1880 he has been principally engaged in civil engineering. In September, 1868, Mr. Smith married Miss Elizabeth M., daughter of Samuel Throckmorton, and they have one child, Albert Bunyan.

D. A. SPRAGG, U. S. Revenue Collector of the twenty-third district, Greene County, Penn., was born January 28, 1835. He is a son of Jeremiah and Sarah (Shriver) Spragg, natives of this county. His ancestors were among the earliest English farmers of Wayne Township. The original farm is still in possession of the family. Mr. Spragg's father died in 1877. Of his family of three children the subject of our sketch is the second. He was reared on the farm in Wayne Township, attending the district school. He chose farming as an occupation, but followed it only a short time.

At the age of thirty-two he opened a store at Spraggsville. He was elected sheriff of the county in 1882 and held the office three years. In April, 1886, he was appointed to his present position. In 1860 Mr. Spragg married Elizabeth, daughter of John Gibbons. Mrs. Spragg is also a native of this county, and of English extraction. Their children are—Sidney D., wife of C. T. Wise, and Herman. Mr. Spragg is a Democrat, and a member of the I. O. O. F., in which order he has taken all the degrees.

T. ROSS SPROAT, farmer and stock-grower, who was born in West Virginia, January 7, 1842, is a son of James and Susan (Johnson) Sproat. His mother was born in Washington County, Penn. His father, a native of Greene County, and a farmer and carpenter by occupation, settled in Whiteley Township in 1844, and died in 1849. Mr. Sproat's grandfather was David Sproat, a native of Virginia. At his father's death Ross was obliged to make his home among strangers, and received but a limited education in the district schools. He started out in life, however, with a determination to succeed and, by means of his energy and close application to his work, he has secured a good farm of one-hundred and fifty-nine acres, where he resides near Waynesburg, Penn. In 1862 Mr. Sproat enlisted in Company K, Eighteenth Pennsylvania Cavalry. He was discharged in 1863, having taken sick at the battle of Stone River and never again being able for duty In 1869, he married Miss Harriet, daughter of Joseph and Charlotte (Rinehart) Ankron. Her parents were natives of this county—her father was born in 1807 and is still living Mr. and Mrs Sproat are the parents of seven children—Charlotte, Joseph, Susan, Eva V., Wilbert, Jesse and May. Their parents are members of the Methodist Episcopal Church, in which Mr. Sproat has been class-leader, and superintendent of the Sabbath-school.

M. L. STROSNIDER, manufacturer of woolen goods, Waynesburg, Penn, was born in West Virginia, June 11, 1847, and is a son of Moses and Mary (Thompson) Strosnider. They were natives of Greene County, Penn., and of German and Scotch-Irish extraction. His father was a wheelwright by trade. M. L. Strosnider is next to the youngest of ten children, was reared in West Virginia, and received his education in Waynesburg College. He first began manufacturing in Blacksville, W. Va, in 1870, where he continued until 1884. In that year he established the woolen-mills at Waynesburg, where he has since successfully engaged in that business Mr. Strosnider was united in marriage May 19, 1875, with Caroline, daughter of Alexander Wallace, and they have had three children, viz.—James W., Harley L. and Flora, of which two are living. Mr. and Mrs. Strosnider are members of the Methodist Episcopal Church. He is a Democrat, and a member of the Knights of Honor.

CAPT. W. H. STOY was born at Brownsville, Penn., February 12, 1815, and is a son of Henry W. and Catharine (Cook) Stoy. His mother was born at Hagerstown, Maryland, and his father at Lebanon, Penn. They were of Dutch and English descent. His father received a medical education in Germany. His grandfather was a graduate of Heidleberg College, and was sent to this country by the King of Germany as a foreign minister. Captain Stoy's father came to Brownsville in 1807 and practiced medicine for forty-five years. Captain Stoy had a natural inclination for music, which he wisely cultivated, and for fifty years he has been a teacher and composer. He has twenty bands in different towns and cities for which he furnishes music. In 1861 he enlisted and served in the Union army as leader of the band for the Eighth Pennsylvania Reserves. He served until the bands were discharged by general order, when he returned to Waynesburg, where he has since resided. He was married in 1844 to Margaret, daughter of Allen Biggs. Mrs. Stoy was born in Ohio County, W. Va., in 1826. Their children are all married except the youngest. They are—Mary, wife of J. P. Sullivan; Charlotte, wife of George Albertson; Catharine, wife of I. B. Raisor; Henry W., a printer; Gustavus, a drug clerk; Dollie, wife of T. J. Hawkins; Lillie, wife of D. M. Morrison; Jennie, widow of W. F. Clayton; George B., who married Miss Anna Robison, of Bealsville, in 1888; and Frank, a tailor in Pittsburgh, Penn. Captain Stoy is a prominent member of the Masonic fraternity and a Sir Knight Templar. Gustavus, his second son, was born in Washington, Penn., August 26, 1854. He was reared in Waynesburg, where he attended school and also learned telegraphy. At the present time he is salesman and prescription clerk for H. S. Blachly, of Waynesburg. He was married in 1884 to Miss Ruth Robinson, a native of West Moreland County, Penn., and a niece of Hon. R. S. Robinson.

GEORGE TAYLOR, a successful farmer and stock-grower of Franklin Township, was born in Washington Township, this county, February 16, 1832. His parents were William and Jane (Crane) Taylor, also natives of this county. His father's family consisted of three children, of whom George is the oldest. He was reared in Washington Township, where he received his education, and early in life began farming. He is now the owner of 318 acres of good farming land in Greene County. In 1858 Mr. Taylor married Miss Dorcas, daughter of William Grimes. Mrs. Taylor was born in Franklin Township in 1831, and is a sister of H. M. Grimes, a prominent farmer. Mr. and Mrs. Taylor have a family of eight children—Margaret Maria, wife of J. Huffman; Elizabeth Mary, wife of Thomas Robinson; William G., George W., C. F., Daniel C., Ella and Dorcas'Anna. Mr. Taylor is a Democrat, and has served on the school board of his district.

JUSTUS FORDYCE TEMPLE, ex-auditor general of the State of Pennsylvania, was born in this county February 13, 1824, and is a son of John and Elizabeth (Douglas) Temple. His parents were natives of Pennsylvania, and of English extraction. His father, an inn-keeper, was also a drover, and dealt in stock extensively. General Temple was the oldest in a family of four children, and was reared in Greene County, where he attended the common schools. Early in life he learned the cooper's trade, at which he worked for four years. He then taught school and took an active part in the teachers' institutes. In 1854, General Temple, who is a Democrat, was elected county auditor, and in 1857 was elected register and recorder, which office he held for six years. He was then elected prothonotary of the county and served for six years in that office. He then took up the study of law and was admitted to the bar in 1869, remaining in active practice until 1874, when he was elected State auditor general, where he served with honor for three years. He then resumed the practice of law. General Temple was at one time somewhat of a musician, and considered by the boys in blue as an expert fifer. He takes an active interest in the schools, and has served as a member of the school board. He was an active mover in the erection of the new college building at Waynesburg, and gave liberally to the enterprise. General Temple was married in 1851 to Miss Nancy Ann Schroy, who died in 1875. Their children are— Mary, wife of William J. Bayard; Nevada, wife of William G. Osgoodby; James B. and Anna Belle, wife of Joseph O'Neill. In 1877 the General married Katherine, daughter of Michael Salmon. General Temple is a prominent member of the I. O. O. F. He has been Deputy Grand Master, and is also a member of the Masonic fraternity.

JOHN P. TEAGARDEN, attorney at law, was born at the old Teagarden homestead in Richhill Township, Greene County, Penn. His father was Colonel Isaac Teagarden. His mother's maiden name was Sarah A. Parker. The family is of Prussian origin, and the ancestry is traced back many generations. Abraham Teagarden was an educated civil engineer, and came from Prussia to America in 1744, locating first at Philadelphia, Penn., where in 1745 he married Miss Mary Parker, of English birth. Their oldest child, William Teagarden, was born in Philadelphia on the 17th day of January, 1746. Some time after this Abraham Teagarden, with his family, moved to Western Pennsylvania. He was one of the first white men who attempted to make a settlement in this part of the State. Tradition tells of the many thrilling adventures he and his family had with the Indians. William Teagarden was married to Bethia

Craig, of Maryland   Shortly after this Abraham and William Teagarden, and two other families named Hughes and Hupp, made the first settlement attempted in the limits of Greene County, near where Clarksville now stands.   Old Fort Red Stone, near Brownsville, was the nearest fort or place of refuge from the savage maranders.   William Teagarden and his wife, had, one occasion taken refuge in old Fort Redstone, and it was there, on March 6, 1775, that Abraham Teagarden, grandfather of John P. Teagarden, was born   Abraham Teagarden secured a liberal education for those days.   During the Indian wars following, he enlisted as a private soldier in General Wayne's army, and remained in the field until peace was restored. He married Nancy McGuier, and immediately moved to lands he had located in Richhill Township and in West Finley Township, Washington County.   His first house was on the old Teagarden homestead in Richhill Township.   Twelve children were born to them, the third being Isaac, the father of John P. Teagarden   Isaac Teagarden was born April 12, 1807.   He was a mill-wright by occupation, and built many of the mills in this and Washington County When the slavery question arose he was among the first to array himself on the side of liberty and equal rights.   He assisted in the organization of the so-called Abolition party and cast one of the first votes for that party in this county.   He voted for Birney, the Freesoil candidate for President, and continued to act with the party of freedom, voting for all its candidates, until the organization of the Republican party in 1856, when he connected himself with that party, and remained steadfast to its principles till the time of his death, June 20, 1886.   He was elected Colonel of the Forty-sixth Pennsylvania Militia and was commissioned Colonel by Governor Ritner in 1838, for three years.   When the war of the late Rebellion came, he, at the advanced age of fifty-four, enlisted in Company F, Eighty-fifth Pennsylvania Volunteers.   He participated with his regiment in the battles of the Peninsula and before Yorktown. He was a member of the Christian Church.   His family consisted of four children—Phœbe Jane, Charity Louise, John Parker and Thomas L , the latter having died early in childhood   Phœbe Jane Teagarden was one of the prominent teachers of the county, but she abandoned that profession and commenced the study of medicine, which she completed in a three years' course at the Woman's Medical College at Philadelphia, graduating from that institution in the class of 1882. She then immediately commenced the practice of medicine at Waynesburg, where she now has a large and lucrative practice. Charity Louise Teagarden is also a teacher of prominence, and is at present a teacher in the Union school of Waynesburg, a position she has held for the past twelve years   John P. Teagarden commenced life as a teacher   In 1869 he went to Iowa to teach school, and in the fall of that year commenced the study of law under the tutorship of W. W. Haskel, of the Oskaloosa, Mahaska County bar, and was admitted to practice in the several courts of Iowa in 1871. He returned to the home of his parents in Richhill Township, and in 1872 the entire family moved to Waynesburg. He was admitted to practice at the Greene County bar in 1872, and later to the Supreme Court of Pennsylvania and the United States Courts, and has continued in the practice ever since. He is a Republican in politics, and has always taken an active interest in political affairs. In 1878 he was tendered the Republican nomination for State Senate in the Fortieth Senatorial District composed of Greene and Fayette counties; and while he was defeated, yet he materially reduced the large Democratic majority in the district. In 1880 he was elected Presidential elector and cast one of Pennsylvania's votes for General James A. Garfield for President. He served two years as Secretary and three years as Chairman of the Republican County Committee. He was elected burgess of Waynesburg borough two terms, was a member of council two terms, and is a prominent member of the I. O. O. F. of this county. He was married in 1885 to Miss Mary E. Davis, of Waynesburg.

JOB THROCKMORTON, a farmer and stock-grower of Oak Forest, Penn., was born in Greene County December 17, 1809. His father and mother were Joseph and Catharine (Hulsart) Throckmorton, natives of New Jersey, and of English origin. His father, who was a farmer all his life, came to Greene County in 1809, and settled two miles west of Waynesburg, Penn. His family consisted of ten children, five daughters and five sons, of whom Job was the oldest, and was reared on the farm with is parents. Early in life he learned the tailor's trade and engaged in that business for seventeen years. He then bought his first farm, in 1835, and has since devoted his time wholly to farming. His home farm contains 109 acres of valuable land. Mr. Throckmorton was united in marriage with Sarah Fry, who is of German extraction. Her grandparents were among the earliest settlers of this county. Her father was a farmer and lived to be over forty-five years old. Mr. and Mrs. Throckmorton's children are—George, a farmer; Catharine; wife of John Maple; Joseph R., a farmer; and Franklin B., a carpenter. Mrs. Maple, the only daughter, died February 17, 1885, and her husband died February 18th of the same month and year, and both were buried in one grave at the same time. Mr. and Mrs. Throckmorton are members of the M. E. Church, in which he has held various official positions. He has been a life-long Democrat, and has held most of the offices in Franklin Township. Mr. Throckmorton is greatly interested in school matters, and has served as school director for a number of years.

F. B. THROCKMORTON, secretary of the Waynesburg Roller Mill Company, was born in Franklin Township, Greene County, Penn., October 12, 1852. He is a son of Job and Sarah (Fry) Throckmorton, the former a native of Pennsylvania and the latter of New Jersey. They were of English descent. His father was a tailor by trade and followed that business in early life, but later he retired to the farm where he now resides in Franklin Township. F. B. Throckmorton is the youngest in a family of four children and was reared in Franklin Township, where he attended the district schools. Early in life he learned the cooper's trade which he followed until 1885, when he was employed by the roller mill company at Waynesburg. In 1872 Mr. Throckmorton married Sarah A., daughter of William Johnson. Their children are Ada B., Jesse E., George Albert and William. Mr. and Mrs. Throckmorton are members of the Methodist Episcopal Church, of which he is trustee. He is a Democrat and has served as township assessor. He is chaplain of the Royal Arcanum at Waynesburg.

J. T. ULLOM, physician and surgeon, of Waynesburg, Penn., was born in Center Township, Greene County, Penn., April 11, 1847. He is a son of D. T. and Anna (Johnson) Ullom, natives of this county, and of German and Irish lineage. His ancestors were among the earliest settlers of the county. Dr. Ullom is a member of a family of twelve children, nine of whom grew to maturity. He was reared on the farm and attended Waynesburg College. He began the study of medicine in 1866, with Dr. S. L. Blachly, at Sparta, Washington County, Penn. In 1868 he attended lectures at Charity Hospital Medical College at Cleveland, Ohio. In 1869 he entered Jefferson Medical College at Philadelphia, and graduated in 1870. He at once began the practice of his profession in Rogersville, Greene County, where he continued for seventeen years. He came to Waynesburg in 1887 and formed his present partnership with Dr. J. T. Iams. Dr. Ullom was married in Rogersville, January 8, 1875, to Anna, daughter of George Sellers. She is also a native of this county, and of English descent. Their children are—Blanche and Frank S. Dr. and Mrs. Ullom are members of the Methodist Protestant Church. He is a member of the Masonic fraternity. He has been president of the County Medical Society, and in 1887 was elected first vice-president of the State Medical Society.

W. S. VANDRUFF, surveyor, born in Perry Township, this county, May 18, 1852, is a son of John and Rachel (Maple) Vandruff, natives of Greene County. They own a well-improved farm of 119 acres in Perry Township, where Mr. W. S. Vandruff was born. He is the oldest in a family of ten children, and was reared on the farm, attending the common schools of the county. When he reached his majority, he began working by the month on a farm. At the age of twenty-three he learned the carpenter's trade, at which he worked until 1880. While working at his trade he studied surveying, and is now considered a competent surveyor. He also draws maps with great speed and accuracy. In 1887 Mr. Vandruff erected a neat and substantial residence in Waynesburg, where he now lives. He owns a small farm in Perry Township, where he has given considerable attention to bee culture. Mr. Vandruff, who is a man of more than ordinary ability, is a great reader and has a bright future before him. He was married in 1876 to Matilda, daughter of John and Dorotha (Haines) Fox, natives of this county. Mr. and Mrs. Vandruff are the parents of two children—Ross Elliott and Ottly Earl. They are members of the Methodist Episcopal Church.

D. S. WALTON, attorney, and member of the firm of Wyly, Buchanan & Walton, was born at Ryerson's Station, Greene County, Penn., May 17, 1853. His parents were D. M. and Mary M. (Drake) Walton, the former a native of Washington County, Penn., and the latter of Philadelphia. They were married in Clarksville, this county, and settled in the city of Pittsburgh, where they were burned out in 1845. They then returned to Clarksville, and in 1850 moved to Ryerson's Station. Mrs. Walton departed this life in 1859. Nine years after her death Mr. Walton moved with his family to Oskaloosa, Iowa, where he has since resided. The family consisted of ten children, of whom three are living. Mr. D. S. Walton, who is next to the youngest, acquired his education in the common schools and in the colleges at Oskaloosa and Waynesburg. He read law with Wyly and Buchanan, of Waynesburg, and Judge Rinehart, of Oskaloosa. He was admitted to the bar in Iowa, November 17, 1874, practiced one year, and came to Waynesburg, entering the firm of which he is still a member. Mr. Walton is a member of the Masonic fraternity, and has filled several offices of trust in Waynesburg. He has been a member of the borough council, a member of the school board, and in 1884 was burgess of the borough. He has been a trustee of the college for twelve years, and is now president of the board. Mr. Walton was united in marriage, March 18, 1873, with Miss Mary A., daughter of James A. J. Buchanan, and they are the parents of one child, Jimmie B., a bright and interesting son, who was born March 27, 1874, and departed this life April 17, 1888.

GEORGE W. WISECARVER, farmer, Waynesburg, Penn.— Among the representative business men of Greene County, we take pleasure in mentioning the name of George W. Wisecarver, who was born in Whiteley Township, this county, July 22, 1813. His parents were George and Catharine (Orndorf) Wisecarver, natives of Frederick County, Va., and of English and German descent. The former was born in 1756. Mrs. Wisecarver was several years younger.

They came to Greene County in 1800, settled in Whiteley Township and remained until their death   They were the parents of nine children, all of whom lived to be over seventy years of age.   Of these six are living, the youngest now past the seventieth mile-stone. George W. Wisecarver's early life was spent with his parents on the farm in Whiteley Township, and on account of the thinly settled country his opportunities for an education were very limited, and he received but four months' schooling.   His father did not succeed in accumulating very much of this world's goods, and was obliged to have his children raised by strangers.   At the age of sixteen George started out in life for himself, and has succeeded so well that at one time he was the owner of 4,000 acres of good land in Greene County, the most of which he has divided with his family.   It is very interesting to hear Mr. Wisecarver relate the many things that have transpired from the time he did his first day's work in the county for himself, up to the present, when we find him among the wealthiest men of Greene County   The pay for the first day's work was a fish-hook, and we would presume that he did not like work by the day, as he soon found employment by the month at very low wages, and for his first month's work received from his employer, Samuel Nelson, one pair of shoes valued at $1 50.   At that time $4 was considered good pay for a month's work.   Mr. Wisecarver learned the cooper's trade, which he followed in connection with his farming.   Most of the time for twelve years he worked eighteen hours out of every twenty-four, and for seven years he made enough at night at his trade to pay two men for their work through the next day.   In 1843 he bought a farm of 210 acres in Washington Township   In 1849 his shop and coopering tools were destroyed by fire.   Since then he has devoted most of his time to farming, dealing in real estate and raising live stock.   In 1854 Mr. Wisecarver went to Iowa and entered 2,000 acres of land.   In 1857 he bought 330 acres more in Greene County, and in the same year he traded his land in Iowa for 500 acres in Richhill Township, this county, giving the difference in cash   He traded most of his land in Iowa for land in Pennsylvania. By good management and industry he added many acres to these purchases, and has cleared over 1,000 acres in this county   Mr. Wisecarver, like the majority of business men, has had his share of bad luck, and has paid over $45,000 for security and otherwise, from which he derived but little benefit; but being more of a believer in pluck than luck, he has succeeded notwithstanding his losses.   He was united in marriage, May 1, 1843, with Priscilla, daughter of Jacob and Phœbe (Crayne) Barnes.   To Mr. and Mrs. Wisecarver have been born eight children, viz: Nancy, who has been twice married, first to Norman Worley, deceased, her present husband being Maj. Benjamin Herrington; Caroline, wife of Amos A. Allison;

Frank P., of Philadelphia; Timothy J., a large land-owner in this county; Margaret M., wife of Jesse Wise, a young attorney of the Waynesburg bar; and Virginia, a very estimable young lady. The deceased are Phœbe J. and Elizabeth. Mr. Wisecarver's father served as wagon-master under Gen. Washington, and drew a pension until his death. He was present when Lord Cornwallis surrendered·

REV. JOEL J. WOOD, farmer and stock-grower, Waynesburg, Penn.—The subject of this sketch is one of the few Methodist ministers who have been financially successful. He owns over four hundred acres of land in Greene County, and also has land in the State of Iowa. Mr. Wood, who is of English extraction, was born in Whiteley Township this county, in 1814, and is the third son of Edward Wood, also a native of Greene County. Rev. Mr. Wood attended the old Greene Academy at Carmichaels, Penn., and obtained a good English education, together with a fair knowledge of the languages. Early in life he made a profession of religion. He taught school a few months, but subsequently accepted a circuit in the Pittsburg conference, and was actively engaged as a minister over twenty-five years. He was always faithful to his charge and allowed nothing to interfere with his appointments. He has met with marked success in building church houses and has been to a great extent instrumental in building up the Methodist Protestant Church. Since 1866 Mr. Wood has engaged in farming. He has been twice married. His present wife, whom he married in 1864, was Miss Maggie E. Boyd, of Washington County, Penn. He was first married at Fairmount, West Virginia, to Mary Ann, second daughter of Rev. A. A. Shinn, D. D., who was one of the organizers of the Methodist Protestant Church. Mrs. Wood died in 1852. They had two children, one now living—Asa R., a prominent business man of Washington, Penn. By his second marriage Mr. Wood is the father of three children—Mary E., Phœbe A. and Harriet Frances.

HIRAM C. WOOD, wool and stock-dealer, was born in Franklin Township, Greene County, Penn., April 11, 1851. He is a son of John D. and Sevela (Barnes) Wood. His mother was a native of New Jersey. His father, who was born in Greene County, Penn., was an extensive dealer in wool and stock, and died September 26, 1876. He was also a physician of the Eclectic School and had an extensive practice. Mr. Hiram C. Wood is the youngest of six children living. He received his education in the common schools of Greene County. He very naturally took up the business of his father and was his partner in stock-dealing for several years. He owns a fine farm of one hundred and seventy-five acres in Franklin Township. In February, 1873, Mr. Wood was united in marriage with Sarah J., daughter of Corbly Orndoff, ex-county commissioner, and they are the parents of three children—John F., Nora M. and

Mattie C. Mr. and Mrs. Wood are members of the Methodist Episcopal Church. He is a Democrat, and a member of the I. O O. F.
Lodge at Oak Forest, Penn ; also a member of the Waynesburg
Council, No. 550, Royal Arcanum. He was a member of the firm
of John Hesket & Co., commission merchants for the sale of live
stock at the Central Stock Yards, Pittsburg, Penn.

HENRY ZIMMERMAN.—The writer takes great pleasure in
giving a sketch of the life of Henry Zimmerman, of Franklin Township, one of the oldest citizens of Greene County, born November 23,
in the year 1813. He has witnessed great strides in the progress
and improvement of the county. He has seen the wilderness
metamorphosed into highly cultivated and rich farming lands,
covered with pleasant homes and inhabited by a prosperous and
intelligent people His parents, who were of English and German
descent, came to Greene County in 1809, and resided in Whiteley
Township twenty-five years, then they took up five hundred acres of
land in Franklin Township, on which they resided until their death.
Henry was a member of a family of nine children, all boys; and his
father lived to see the day—the proudest of his life—when he and
his nine sons could march to the polls in solid phalanx and cast ten
democratic votes. At present writing (1888), however, but two of
his sons are living—the subject of our sketch and Robert Zimmerman,
of Wayne Township. In his youth Henry Zimmerman learned the
trade of stone masonry, which he has followed through life, together
with farming, being the owner of a fine farm of one hundred and
twenty-five acres in Franklin Township. His California peaches
are the finest ever brought to market in this part of the country,
and he takes great pride in his orchard of over eight hundred
trees Mr. Zimmerman was united in marriage, September 29,
1839, with Mary Ellen, daughter of William and Ellen (Hood)
Seals, who were of Irish and English ancestry Mrs. Zimmerman
is a grand-daughter of James Seals, who was a Colonel in the
Revolutionary war. To Mr. and Mrs. Zimmerman were born two
children—Ellen J. and James B., who was born in 1856, and in
1879 married Jane A , daughter of Robert and Elizabeth Tewksberry.
Their children are W. S , Robert H and Gilbert T. R. Ellen J.
was united in marriage with J. S. Herrington, and they were the
parents of two children—Mary C. (deceased) and Emma A

R S ZOLLARS, farmer and stock-grower, Waynesburg, Penn ,
was born in this county July 4, 1835. He is a son of Neal and
Elizabeth (Spencer) Zollars, natives of Pennsylvania, and of French
and Dutch extraction. His father, a farmer, came to this county
in 1834. Richard, the oldest of his six children, was reared on the
farm, and received his earliest education in the district school. He
subsequently attended Waynesburg College, and for three years

clerked in a dry goods store. In 1862 he enlisted in Company F, First Pennsylvania Cavalry, and served until the close of the war. Returning to his native county, he has since successfully devoted his time to farming. Mr. Zollars was united in marriage in 1882, with Miss Mary, daughter of Caldwell Orr. Mrs. Zollars was born and raised in this county, and is a zealous member of the M. E Church. Her husband is a Republican, and served one term as coroner of the county. He is a prominent member of the I. O. O. F. and the G. A. R. Post.

GILMORE TOWNSHIP.

WILLIAM CLOVIS, a farmer and stock-grower of Greene County, Penn., was born in Monongalia County, West Virginia, September 9, 1825. His parents, Matthias and Nancy (Barr) Clovis, were natives of eastern Pennsylvania, and of German extraction. His father was a shoemaker by trade, and spent most of his life in Greene County. He died in 1861. William is the ninth in a family of twelve children. He received his education in this county, and early in life learned the miller's trade and engaged in that business for sixteen years. He has since been farming and dealing extensively in stock. He has lived in Gilmore Township since 1864. Mr. Clovis has made a success of his business, and has a wide circle of friends in Greene County. He is a Republican in politics, and was elected county commissioner in 1888. His home farm contains two hundred and eighty-seven acres of good land. William Clovis was united in marriage, in West Virginia, with Miss Rebecca, daughter of Robert and Margaret (Hinkens) Chalfant, who were of English and German lineage. Mr. and Mrs. Clovis have a family of twelve children, eleven of whom are living—Jacob C., a farmer and miller; Marion J., a farmer; John H., a merchant; L. B., a stock-dealer; Frances E., widow of Phenix Meighen; A. E., a merchant; Peter, Samuel S. and Robert M., farmers; Dora Belle and Oscar W. Their parents are members of the M. E. Church, in which Mr Clovis is steward, trustee and class-leader. He also takes an active interest in the Sabbath school. He has served as justice of the peace for a period of ten years.

JEFFERSON DYE, hotel-keeper at Jolleytown, Penn., is a descendant of the earliest settlers of this county, and of English and German extraction. His father was a farmer and miller by occupation.

Mr. Dye comes of a large family, of which there are representatives now located in various parts of the United States. He was born November 16, 1844, a son of Minor and Rachel (Caine) Dye. His mother was born in Loudoun County, Virginia, and was of German and English lineage Jefferson was reared in Greene County, Penn., where he attended the common schools. He was with his father in the mill until he went to the war, in 1861. He enlisted in Company F, Seventh West Virginia Infantry, and was a non-commissioned officer. He was in many serious engagements, among others, the battles of Antietam, Chancellorsville and Gettysburg. Mr. Dye was a brave soldier, and at the battle of Antietam when his regiment was relieved by a regiment of Meagher's Irish Brigade, he did not retire from the field with his regiment, but went in with the Irish Brigade. After exhausting all his ammunition he replenished his cartridge box from the box of a wounded comrade of Company H At the close of the war he returned to Jolleytown, where he has been proprietor of a hotel and undertaking shop since 1872, and recently engaged in merchandising He was married in this county, February 9, 1871, to Rebecca A, daughter of Henry Shriver. Mrs. Dye was born in Monongalia County, W. Va. She was appointed postmistress under President Cleveland's administration. To Mr. and Mrs. Dye were born five children, four of whom are living—Eva, Charles, Frank, Fannie and Mary (deceased). Mr. Dye's first wife was Mary J. Mc-Cans. They had one daughter—Harriet. Mr. and Mrs Dye are members of the Methodist, Episcopal Church He was elected justice of the peace in 1882, re-elected in 1887; is a member of the I. O O F. and G. A R. Post No 367, J F. McCullough, Waynesburg, Penn.

JACOB M. EAKIN, who is a farmer and stock-grower of Gilmore Township, was born in Monongalia County, West Virginia, September 1, 1827, and is a son of Justus and Mary (Myers) Eakin, who were of Dutch and Scotch-Irish extraction His mother was born at Garard's Fort, this county. His father, a native of Virginia, was a cooper by trade, came to Greene County in early life, and died in 1870 His grandfather, William Eakin, was a carpenter, and located for many years at the old glass works at Greensboro, Penn. Jacob's grandfather was a soldier in the Revolutionary war, and died in Virginia. Jacob M is the eighth of a family of ten children. He was reared in West Virginia and remained there until August, 1844 He then removed to Greene County, Penn, where he has been a very successful farmer, and is the owner of 600 acres of valuable land in this county. Mr Eakin has been twice married, his first wife being Miss Mary, a daughter of Erastus and Mary (Barnes) Woodruff, Her parents were natives of Delaware, and of English descent To Mr. and Mrs. Eakin were born four children—Phœbe

J , wife of David Staggers; Sarah, wife of Marion Clovis; Athaliah, wife of Jacob Clovis, and J. Pierce, the only son. He was born in Gilmore Township, May 31, 1856, where he spent his early manhood. He was married in West Virginia, near Morgantown, January 29, 1880, to Mattie, daughter of Colonel Reuben Finnell, and they have three children—Jacob Myres, Mary Bodley and Robert Leemoyne. Mrs Jacob Eakin died in 1856. Two years later Mr. Eakin married Miss Fannie, daughter of William and Nancy Lemmon, and they are the parents of one child—Mary E , who is the wife of O. J. Brown, of Mt. Morris, Penn.

JOHN G. FORDYCE. farmer and stock-grower, born in Gilmore Township, February 14, 1841, is a son of Corbly and Jane (Bailey) Fordyce. His parents were also natives of this county, and of English extraction. His father, who was a farmer and stock-grower all his life, was reared in Greene County. He died in 1862, leaving a family of twelve children, of whom John G is the sixth. He was reared in Gilmore Township, on the farm where his brother resides. He received a common-school education, then engaged in farming as an occupation, and is now one of the most successful farmers in the county. He owns 400 acres of valuable land. In 1866 Mr. Fordyce married Jane Huffman, and they were the parents of two children—Dora and Charles. Mrs. Jane Fordyce died in 1877, a faithful member of the Methodist Episcopal Church. Mr. Fordyce was afterwards united in marriage, in 1878, with Miss Anna, daughter of Phillip and Lydia (Kennedy) Phillips, and they have one son— Phillip Corbly. Mr. and Mrs Fordyce are prominent members of the Methodist Episcopal Church.

S W GILMORE, farmer and stock-grower, Jolleytown, Penn., was born in West Virginia May 24, 1842, and is a son of Peter and Ellen (Trowbridge) Gilmore. His parents were also natives of West Virginia, and of German and Irish lineage His father, from whom Gilmore Township took its name, was a farmer during his life time, and died in West Virginia May 19, 1876. The subject of this sketch was the youngest in a family of five children. He was reared in Monongalia County, West Virginia, and received a common-school education. Mr. Gilmore has followed farming as his chief occupation, and is the owner of a good farm of 400 acres. He was first married January 13, 1873, to Hannah Taylor, daughter of George and Marinda (Garrison) Taylor. Of their five children, four are living, viz: William H., Oscar E., Martha M. and Marinda E. Their mother died September 30, 1881. Mr. Gilmore was again united in marriage, in 1883, with Elizabeth, daughter of John and Elizabeth (Sanders) White, and they are the parents of one child—John W. Mr. and Mrs. Gilmore are members of the Methodist Episcopal Church, in which he is class-leader and trustee. He has also been

superintendent of the Sabbath-school. Mr. Gilmore is a Republican.
In 1862 he enlisted as a private in Company K, Fourteenth West
Virginia Infantry, and was promoted to the office of Second Lieu-
tenant He was wounded at the battle of Cloid Mountain. He
served until the close of the war, and is now a member of G. A. R
Post 550

HON. JOHN HAGAN.—Among the most successful business
men of Greene County may be mentioned Hon. John Hagan, deceased. He was born in County Londonderry, Ireland, and came to
America while very young. He located at Pittsburgh, Penn , working at anything that came to hand, and was successful in everything
he undertook He had a taste for the mercantile trade, and when he
came to Greene County—more than half a century ago—he entered
into partnership with Patrick McCullough and carried on a general
store at Jolleytown, Penn. At his death he owned over 700 acres
of land in Greene County His success was due mainly to his industry and a determination to succeed. He died in 1873, shortly after
his election to the Legislature. Mr. Hagan was united in marriage
in this county, in 1859, with Martha, daughter of Abner and Hannah (Morris) Garrison, and they had a family of five children, viz:
John Patrick, Charles L , a prominent attorney of West Virginia;
Clara May, Mary and Catherine The family are all members of the
Catholic Church. Mrs. Hagan is now a resident of Ohio Her
mother was a sister of Major J. B Morris, of Mt Morris, Penn.

T M. HENNEN, wool and stock-dealer and secretary of the
Philadelphia Oil Company, was born in Greene County, Penn., July
27, 1839. He is a son of George and Jane (Munyon) Henner, who
were of Irish and English origin His father was a farmer and
stock-grower by occupation, and died September 13, 1885 His
family consisted of eleven children, of whom the subject of this
sketch is the sixth. He was reared in Gilmore Township and received a good English education Mr. Hennen first engaged in
farming and dealing in wool, in which business he has spent most
of his life. In 1863 he became actively interested in the oil business in Dunkard Township, and when the Philadelphia Oil Company
was formed and commenced operations in Greene County he was
elected secretary. He is the owner of a good farm of 165 acres,
where he now resides in Gilmore Township Mr. Hennen was
united in marriage in 1868 with Rachel, daughter of Thomas W.
Taylor, Esq , of this county, and they are the parents of three children—Frank W., George B. and Tinna A. Mrs. Hennen is a
devoted member of the Baptist Church. Her husband is a Democrat and secretary of the school board in his township.

JOHN LANTZ, farmer and stock-grower, Jolleytown, Penn.,
was born in Wayne Township, Greene County, Penn , May 8, 1829.

He is a son of Jacob and Delilah (Coen) Lantz, natives of this county, and of German and English lineage. His father was a farmer and stock-grower and a great hunter, born in Greene County in 1791. He was a soldier in the war of 1812, and died in 1858. His family consisted of five sons, of whom John is the fourth. He was reared on the home farm in Wayne Township, and has successfully engaged in farming as an occupation. He owns 350 acres of valuable land in Gilmore Township, where he has lived since 1850. Mr. Lantz was married in Greene County September 19, 1850, to Miss Sarah, daughter of Jacob and Charlotte Bradford, natives of this county, and of English descent. Mr. and Mrs. Lantz have a family of eleven children, ten of whom are living, viz.—William H. and M. J., merchants; A. B., a farmer; L. W., S. C., a carpenter; John, Delilah, Martha, Jacob and Alexander. Their mother is a member of the Methodist Episcopal Church. Mr. Lantz is a Republican, and has served as justice of the peace for fifteen years.

SALEM LEMMON, deceased, was born March 20, 1823, and died August 15, 1887. He was a farmer and stock-dealer and a successful business manager, being at the time of his death the owner of over 600 acres of land in Gilmore Township. Mr. Lemmon was the son of William and Nancy Lemmon, of this township. They were of Irish and German lineage. Mr. Lemmon was reared in this township, attended the common schools, and subsequently chose farming and stock dealing as his business through life. He was twice united in marriage; first, with Mary (Babbit) Lemmon, and they were the parents of two children—William Milton, a farmer; and Harry, (deceased). Their mother died February 14, 1853. Mr. Lemmon's second wife, Maria (McCune) Lemmon, is still living. She was born in Dunkard Township, this county, and is a daughter of John and Mary McCune, who were of Irish origin. Mr. and Mrs. Lemmon were married December 25, 1859. Their children are Mary M., owner of a well improved farm in Gilmore Township, and a dressmaker by occupation; Sarah A., wife of Andrew Lantz; and Nancy V., wife of George Strawn. The family are all members of the Methodist Episcopal Church, in which Mr. Lemmon was steward and trustee. He was a Democrat, and served fifteen years as justice of the peace. He had just been re-elected, at the time of his death, to another term of five years.

W. M. LEMMON, farmer and stock-grower, who was born in Gilmore Township May 17, 1850, is a son of Salem and Mary (Babbit) Lemmon. His parents were also natives of this county, and of German and English descent. His father was a prominent farmer and stock-dealer, and was justice of the peace for many years in Gilmore Township. He was twice married. W. M. is the only child by the first marriage. He grew to manhood in this township,

39

attended the common schools, and has engaged extensively in farming and stock growing. Mr. Lemmon is specially interested in fine horses, and is the owner of Diomede No. 1118 in France, and in America No. 2523. Diomede was brought from France and cost $2,000. Mr. Lemmon also owns a good farm of 150 acres. He was married in West Virginia August 30, 1874, to Clarissa J., daughter of Alexander and Rachel (Russell) Hennen. Mrs. Lemmon is a native of Virginia, and of English extraction. Their children are—Jesse Harry, Lydia Ellen, Mary Hally, Owen R. and Emma Alice. Mr. and Mrs. Lemmon are leading members in the Methodist Episcopal Church, in which he is steward and trustee.

SALATHIEL LEMMON, farmer and stock-grower, was born November 2, 1838, on the farm where he resides in Gilmore Township. He is a son of William and Nancy (Lemmon) Lemmon, who were of Irish and German origin. His mother was a native of this county. His father was born in Lancaster County, Penn. He was a farmer all his life, and died in this township in 1868. His family consisted of five children, of whom Salathiel is the youngest. He grew to manhood in this township, where he has been quite successful as a farmer, and is considered one of Greene's most prosperous citizens. He has also devoted some time to milling. Mr. Lemmon owns 450 acres of well improved land. He is a genial, agreeable gentleman, and has a wide circle of friends. He was united in the holy bonds of matrimony May 15, 1860, with Miss Nancy, daughter of B. Renner, and they are the parents of six children—William J., Elizabeth E., wife of Lewis Cumpston; Barney R., Dora M., Charles M. and Rosa M. William, the oldest, was born in 1862, and reared on the farm with his parents. He was married in 1883 to Rosa May, daughter of Abraham Taylor, and they have one child—Abraham Salathiel. Elizabeth E. and Lewis Cumpston were married in 1883, and have three children—Bertie O., Goldie M. and Barney M. Mr. Lemmon votes the straight Democratic ticket. He takes an active interest in school affairs, and has been one of the board of directors for seven years.

PETER MEIGHEN, deceased, who was a pioneer farmer and stock-grower, was born in Wayne Township, Greene County Penn., September 25, 1809. He was the son of William and Elizabeth (Hughes) Meighen, the former a native of Ireland, and the latter of this county. Peter Meighen's grandfather Hughes came to Greene County in 1762, at sixteen years of age, and died in 1836. He was a farmer by occupation, as were most of the Hughes family in America. Some of them have engaged quite successfully in the mercantile business. The subject of our sketch died in 1867. Of his thirteen children ten are still living. Elizabeth, the oldest daughter, died in 1855. William H., the oldest son was born in this township in 1841. In 1861 he enlisted in Company F., Seventh West Virginia, Infantry. Afterwards re-enlisting, he served until close of the war. During his services he was Corporal, afterwards Sergeant, then promoted to First Lieutenant. Catherine, and Belinda are the two oldest daughters. James, deceased 1850. Felix, deceased 1884, was a prominent merchant of Jolleytown this Township. Susan, wife of Peter Bradley, a prominent merchant of New Freeport; Matthias is a partner of the firm of P. Bradley & Co. (New Freeport.) Priscilla, wife of Thomas C. Bradley, clerk in the Farmer's and Drover's National Bank of Waynesburg, Greene County, Penn ; Martha youngest daughter, teacher in the public schools this county. John, William, Dennis and Peter are prominent farmers and stock-raisers, they together, with their mother own seven hundred acres of land. Peter Meighen's widow is still living in Gilmore Township. She is a daughter of James Dye, who was born December 1, 1769. He was a hunter and pioneer farmer, and among the first to find the Corbley family after they had been murdered by the Indians at Garard's Fort

PHILIP SHOUGH, farmer and stock-grower, son of Joseph and Catharine (Chisler) Shough, was born near Uniontown, Fayette County, Penn., August 10, 1809 His mother was a native of Maryland. His father, who was of German extraction, was born in Lancaster County, Penn., July 16, 1761, and died in Fayette County, Ohio. He was a farmer and gunsmith through life. Philip was the youngest of a family of thirteen children, all of whom reached maturity except one, who died at the age of seventeen. Mr. Shough was one of the few persons in Greene County who were so fortunate as to see General LaFayette during his last visit to America. Being a bound boy, he received but a limited education in the common schools. He was bound for five years to learn a trade, but has made farming his chief occupation, in which he has been very successful. At one time his possessions amounted to over seven hundred acres of land, but much of it has been given to his children. He now owns one hundred and fifty acres where he resides in Gilmore Township. He was united in marriage in Dunkard Township, January 15, 1832, with Matilda, daughter of George and Elizabeth (Long) Garrison. Mrs. Shough, who was of German origin, died January 18, 1885. Of their six children, four are living; Rebecca, wife of William Hoskinson; George W., a farmer; Sarah Ann, wife of Hiram Milliken; and Mattie. Josephus and Elizabeth are deceased. Mr. Shough is a Cumberland Presbyterian, of which church his deceased wife was a faithful member. Mr. Shough is a Republican in politics, and was a captain in the old militia. · He takes an active interest in school affairs and has been a member of the board of directors in his township. G. W. Shough, his oldest son now living, was born March 16, 1839, and was reared in Gilmore Township on the old home farm. He has made farming his occupation, and is the owner of three hundred acres of land. He is married and the father of eleven children. He was a student at Waynesburg College when the war broke out in 1861, but enlisted in the Seventh Pennsylvania Volunteer Infantry, and was elected Lieutenant of the company. He was in many hotly contested battles—among others Gettysburg and Antietam.

JACOB L. SHRIVER, physician and surgeon, Jolleytown, Penn., was born in Whiteley Township, January 11, 1828. He is a son of William and Elizabeth (Shull) Shriver, who were also natives of this county, and of Irish and German origin. His father was a farmer all his life and died in 1880. His family consisted of nine children, of whom the Doctor is the oldest. He remained on the farm with his parents until he was eighteen years of age, and attended the district schools. He afterwards spent some time in the old Greene Academy at Carmichaels, and the College at Waynesburg, Penn. He studied medicine with Doctors Arthur Inghram and Alexander Shaw, of Waynesburg. Dr. Shriver first engaged in his chosen profession, in 1851, at Jolleytown, Penn., where he has had a large and lucrative practice, and is now the owner of considerable estate. He has a farm of two hundred and thirty acres in Gilmore Township. The Doctor is a registered member of the Greene County and State Medical Societies. He was united in marriage, December, 4, 1851, with Sarah, daughter of John and Sarah (Gardner) Goodwin, and they are the parents of nine children: Elizabeth Ann, wife of A. E. Clovis, a merchant at Jolleytown; John M., a physician; Josephine, wife of Morris J. Lantz; William G., who is in the real estate business in the West; Isaac N., a farmer; Sadie, wife of John Russell; J. F., Jessie May, and Mary Mattie. The Doctor is a member of the Methodist Episcopal Church, and has served as school director of his Township.

ABRAHAM TAYLOR, farmer and stock-grower, was born in Gilmore Township, this county April 1, 1839. His parents, Francis and Susannah (Baldwin) Taylor, were also natives of this county, and of English extraction. His father, who was a successful farmer, died in 1887. His family consisted of twelve children—four daughters and eight sons—of whom Abraham is the fifth. He was reared on the farm in Gilmore Township, and attended the district schools. He has been engaged as a farmer all his life, and owns seventy acres of good land where he resides. Mr. Taylor was united in marriage, August 20, 1864, with Eliza Ellen, daughter of Alexander and Maria (Clovis) Compston. Mr. and Mrs. Taylor have three children—Rosa May, wife of William Lemmon; Patrick Henry and John H. They are members of the Southern Methodist Church, in which Mr. Taylor is trustee. He is a Democrat in politics, and at the breaking out of the Rebellion, he promptly enlisted in Company F, Seventh West Virginia Infantry and served two years and nine days. He was in many battles and skirmishes, among which were the battles of Fredericksburg, Bull Run, Antietam, Chancellorsville and Gettysburg. He is a member of the G. A. R. Post 550.

GREENE TOWNSHIP.

W. C. BAILEY, farmer and stock-grower, who is descended from the early pioneers of Greene County, was born March 27, 1842, on Muddy Creek, this county, on the farm where his parents reside. He is a son of J. K. and Delilah (Craft) Bailey, who are natives of this county, and of German origin. W. C. is their fourth child. He was reared in Cumberland Township, and attended the common school and Greene Academy at Carmichaels, Penn. Mr. Bailey taught school for several years, but subsequently devoted his time wholly to farming and stock-growing, and owns 236 acres of good land near Whiteley P. O., Greene Township, this county. Mr. Bailey was united in marriage, January 15, 1874, with Miss Maggie, daughter of Richard and Emeline (Wise) Hawkins. She is of German and English origin. Mr. Bailey is a Republican. He and wife are active members of the Cumberland Presbyterian Church.

B. W. DENNY, M. D., was born in Jefferson Borough, Greene County, Penn., September 17, 1836, and is a son of William and Rebecca (Litzenburg) Denny, natives of Pennsylvania. His father and grandfather, John Denny, were farmers. The latter came from England to America, and settled near Jefferson, Penn., where B. W. spent his youthful days and attended the common school. The Doctor attended Waynesburg College until he began the study of medicine in the office of Dr. W. D. Rogers, of Jefferson. In 1859 he entered the Medical College at Cleveland, Ohio, where he graduated in 1862. Then, instead of entering the practice of his profession, he raised a company for the service of his country. He was elected Captain of Company E, of the Ringold Cavalry, which afterwards became Company F, of the Twenty-second Regiment. Capt. Denny remained in command for three years, with the exception of about eight months when he was sent on detached service to Washington, D. C. Dr. and Mrs. Denny were at Washington at the time of the assassination of President Lincoln, and had intended going to Ford's Theatre that night; but fortunately, owing to the Doctor's indisposition, they were not present on that fatal occasion At the close of the war he began the practice of medicine in Greene County, where he has been actively engaged in the profession ever since Financially the Doctor has met with success, and owns a good farm where he resides in Greene Township. He was married October 8, 1862, to Miss Rachel, daughter of Samuel, and grand-daughter of James Braden Her mother's maiden name was Hannah Ross. Mrs. Denny is of English and Irish descent. They have one child—Millie May. The family are faithful members of the Baptist Church, in which the Doctor is one of the trustees.

W. C. FLENNIKEN, merchant at Whiteley, Greene County, Penn., was born in Carmichaels, Penn , February 4, 1853. He is a son of James and Rachel (Kerr) Flenniken, natives of this county. His ancestors were among the earliest settlers of Greene County. Mr Flenniken's father was a merchant and drover, and met with success in his business For nearly half a century he was engaged in merchandising at Rice's Landing, Carmichaels, Jefferson and Ceylon, Penn., where he departed this life in 1886. Of his six children, three are now living, viz: Horace G , Emma J., wife of George Mc-Millan, and W. C , the subject of this sketch. He was reared in this county, and early in life went as a clerk into his father's store, where he remained until he took an interest in the business with his father. They established the present business in 1879, and since his father's death W. C. has been sole proprietor He was united in marriage, in 1873, with Miss Samantha, daughter of John Hughes. Their children are—Walter and Clyde. Mr. and Mrs. Flenniken are leading members of the Baptist Church.

STEPHENSON GARARD, farmer and stock-grower, P. O. Willow Tree, was born at Taylortown, Dunkard Township, Greene County, Penn , May 18, 1828, and is a son of Jonathan and Ann (Gregg) Garard His father, who was a farmer, stock-grower and manufacturer, served ten years on the bench as associate judge of this county, where he died. His family consisted of five children, of whom Stephenson was next to the youngest He was reared in Greene County, where he attended the subscription schools. In 1854 he bought a farm and has since very successfully devoted his time and talent to farming and stock-growing. Mr. Garard is the owner of about 500 acres of valuable land. On his home farm are the Garard oil wells, Nos. 1, 2 and 3, all producing wells. In 1850 Mr. Garard was united in marriage with Mary A , daughter of William Robinson. Mrs Garard is of English descent. Their children are—Elizabeth, wife of John Minor; Emma M , wife of Albert Dowlin; Flora B., wife of G. W. W. Blair; Jesse L., A. Y.,

Anna and Rachel, all of whom, with one exception, are members of the Goshen Baptist Church, in which. Mr. Garard serves as deacon. Mr. and Mrs. Garard come from two of the representative families of the pioneer settlers of Greene County, and are highly respected citizens.

CHARLES KEENER, farmer and stock-grower, P. O. Willow Tree, was born October 8, 1827, on the farm where he resides. He is a son of Robert and Elizabeth (Eberhart) Keener, natives of this county. His father, who is a successful farmer, has reached the advanced age of eighty-five years. He has reared a family of seven children, four of whom are living. Of these, Charles is the oldest. He was reared on the farm and received his education in one of the old-fashioned log school-houses of the district. ' Charles wisely chose his father's occupation, and by industry and economy has increased his father's farm from 180 to 233 acres of well-improved land. Mr. Keener was married October 16, 1857, to Miss Tabitha E., daughter of Charles Stewart. Mrs. Keener is a native of Virginia. Their children are—Robert C., Aaron, L. L., C. E., F. H., James W. and Thorton F. Mr. and Mrs. Keener are faithful members of the Methodist Episcopal Church, in which he is a steward. He is a Democrat in politics, has been school director, supervisor of Greene Township, and inspector of elections.

HON. ANDREW LANTZ, farmer and stock-grower, Whiteley, Penn., was born in Greene Township, this county, May 8, 1839. His parents, John and Jane (Wildman) Lantz, were natives of Greene County, and of English and German descent. His father, who was a farmer and stock-grower, was a man of marked business ability, and at the time of his death, in 1876, was the owner of 2,000 acres of land. Andrew has 1,400 acres. He was reared on the home farm and attended the district schools. Being the only child who grew to maturity, his father carefully instructed him in all kinds of work and the proper transaction of business. In 1860 Mr. Lantz married Miss Lucretia, daughter of George Lemley. Mrs. Lantz is of English descent. Their children are—John F., David E., Charley and Ada Alice. Mr. and Mrs. Lantz are active members, in the Methodist Episcopal Church, in which he is trustee. In politics Mr. Lantz is a Democrat, and has served as justice of the peace for ten years in Greene County. He takes an active interest in educational affairs, and has served as school director for a number of terms. In 1882 he was elected to the Legislature, and was an active member during the two terms he was connected with that body.

JOHN F. LANTZ, farmer and stock-grower, Lone Star, Penn., was born October 10, 1861, in the township where he now resides. He is the oldest son of Hon. Andrew Lantz, of Greene Township, whose biographical sketch appears in this volume. John was reared on the farm and obtained his early education in the district schools. He subsequently took a regular course of instruction at Iron City College, Pittsburg, Penn., where he graduated in 1881. Mr. Lantz has a good farm of 201 acres well adapted to the raising of stock, in which he engages extensively, making fine cattle a specialty In 1882, Mr. Lantz was united in marriage with Sarah, daughter of Imri Taylor, who is a merchant and farmer in Whiteley Township. Mr Lantz is a Democrat in politics. His wife is a faithful member of the Methodist Episcopal Church.

GEORGE W. LANTZ, farmer and stock-grower, was born in Greene Township. March 24, 1844. He attended the district school, and has been engaged in his present occupation from his youth. In 1886 he engaged in the lumber business in company with Abner Munnell, and is owner and proprietor of a large planing and saw-mill, at Greensboro, Penn. Mr. Lantz is a son of Jacob and Cassandra (South) Lantz, natives of this county. His father, who was a success-ful farmer, died in 1861 Mr. Lot Lantz, George's grandfather, was at one time elected brigade inspector of the militia of the county, and was a pioneer of Greene County. He was a wealthy stock-drover and engaged extensively in pork packing, making heavy ship-ments to Baltimore. He also carried on a distillery for years. September 4, 1870, George Lantz married Miss Mary, daughter of Joseph Tannehill, and they were the parents of the following children: Laura V. Chandas, Hughes and James. Lessie being deceased. A remarkable fact exists in the history of these children Lessie, born July 14, 1878, who lived to be two years of age, was born just six-teen days after her brother Hughes, who was born June 29, 1878 Mrs Lantz was a devoted member of the Baptist Church. She de-parted this life August 19, 1888, she and her babe were buried in the same coffin. Mr. Lantz is a Democrat in politics, has served as justice of the peace in Greene Township, and is now postmaster at Willow Tree, Penn.

P. A. MYERS, hotel keeper, Whiteley, Penn., is a descendant of Rev. John Corbly, one of the pioneer settlers of Greene County. He was born near Garard's Fort, Penn., April 2, 1836. His parents are Alfred and Jane J. (Evans) Myers, who were of German and Welsh origin. Mr. Meyers is the oldest in a family of six children, was reared on a farm, received a common school education, and has been a successful business man. His boyhood days were spent with his uncle, an extensive cattle-dealer. When but fourteen years of age would help his uncle drive large droves of cattle, and conduct them overland to the Philadelphia markets, making as many as two or three trips a year. The greater part of his later years has been devoted to farming. While a young man he taught school for sev-eral terms, and has ever manifested an active interest in educational affairs. In politics he is a Republican. He has held various township offices—among others school director and justice of the peace. On November 1, 1857, Mr. Myers married Miss Louisa M., daughter of David and Mary Roberts, who were of Welsh and English descent. Her father, who was a farmer of Dunkard Township, died in 1885, at the advanced age of eighty-five years. Mr. and Mrs. Myers have two children and four grandchildren. Their children are—Buena V., wife of W. H. Bark, Esq., of Waynesburg, Penn.; and Pleasant J., wife of M. E. Garard, of Greene Township. Mr. and Mrs. Myers are prominent members of the Baptist Church.

JACOB REAMER, retired farmer and stock-grower, of Greene Township, was born in Monongahela Township, this county, January 16, 1814. He is a son of Jacob and Margaret (Black) Reamer, who were natives of Pennsylvania, and of German origin. His father, who was a farmer and distiller, spent most of his life in Greene County, and died in 1852. His family consisted of five children, of whom Jacob is the third. He was reared on the home farm, and received his education in the district schools. He has met with average success in his chosen occupation, and at present is the owner of a well improved farm of ninety-four acres, near Garard's Fort, this county. Mr. Reamer was united in marriage, in 1840, with Miss Louisa, daughter of John and Ortha Myers. They were Quakers and of English descent. Mr. Reamer is a Democrat in politics. He manifests great interest in educational matters, and has served as school director in his township. Mr. and Mrs. Reamer are leading members in the Goshen Baptist Church.

J. B. ROBERTS, farmer and stock-grower, Whiteley, Penn., was born in Greene Township, this county, March 18, 1832. His parents, Joseph and Jane (Johnson) Roberts, were natives of Greene County, and of Welsh descent. His father, who was a farmer by occupation, reared a family of eleven children, of whom J. B. is the ninth. He was reared on the farm and attended the subscription schools. He chose farming and stock-growing as his occupation, and has met with average success, owning at present a good farm of 150 acres. Mr. Roberts was united in marriage, December 31, 1879, with Elizabeth, daughter of James and Elizabeth (Clark) Henderson. Mrs. Roberts is a faithful member of the Methodist Episcopal Church. Her parents were natives of Greene County, and of English descent. At the time Mr. and Mrs. Roberts were married, she was the widow of Henry Lantz. Mr. Roberts is an enthusiastic Democrat, and a member of the I. O. O. F.

T. H. SEDGEWICK, M. D., of Whiteley, Greene County, Penn., was born at Rice's Landing, Penn., April 20, 1852, and is the son of Hon. Joseph and Elizabeth (Hawthorne) Sedgewick, who were of English and Irish descent. His mother was born in Washington County. His father, who was a natives of Virginia, served two terms as a member of the Legislature from Greene County. He was a commission merchant by occupation, in which business he engaged for many years at Rice's Landing, Penn., having first come to this county when seventeen years of age. He died in 1882. He was twice married and was the father of eight children. Dr. Sedgewick is the second child by the last marriage, and was reared at Rice's Landing, where he received his early education. He subsequently attended Monongahela College until he began the study of medicine in the office of Dr. T. H. Sharpnack, of Jefferson Borough. He then took a regular course in the Jefferson Medical College at Philadelphia, where he graduated in 1877. He entered the practice of medicine the same year in Greene County, and has since devoted all his time to his profession. In 1880 he settled in Whiteley, where his professional skill and remarkable energy soon won for him a good practice. That he might be better prepared for the practice of his profession, the Doctor took a post graduate course at New York City in 1888. He is a man of large stature and marked physical abilities which, coupled with his great industry and determination, eminently qualify him for the duties he has assumed. He was married at Rice's Landing, December 25, 1873, to Miss Lucinda, daughter of John Dowlin, a wealthy farmer of this county. They have two children—Joseph and John. The Doctor is a Democrat, and he and Mrs. Sedgewick are prominent members of the Baptist Church.

BENJAMIN SOUTH, farmer and stock-grower, P. O. Willow Tree was born in Greene Township, Greene County, Penn., January 16, 1819. He is a son of Enoch and Ruth (Gregg) South, who were of English descent. His mother was a native of Delaware. His father, who was a native of New Jersey, came to Greene County, Penn., in 1794, where he died in 1863. His family consisted of eleven children,—nine girls and two boys, of whom Benjamin was the sixth. He was reared in Dunkard Township, receiving his education in the subscription schools. Mr. South was a stone-mason early in life, and also worked for some time at the blacksmith's trade. In later years he has given his attention to farming, and by means of his untiring zeal and industry, is now the owner of 315 acres of well improved land. In 1842 Mr. South married Matilda Gapen, who is of English descent, and a daughter of Stephen and Rebecca (Snyder) Gapen. Their union has been blessed with seven children, four sons and three daughters—Maria, wife of D. Sikes; Melinda, widow of E. Alexander; Enoch C., a farmer; Stephen, a carpenter; Olive; Ortha, wife of Noah Minor; and Otho M., a school teacher. In politics Mr. south is a Democrat. He takes an active interest in educational affairs, and has served as school director for a number of years.

· JOSEPH VANCE, farmer and stock-grower, was born in Greene County, Penn., January, 28, 1838, and is a son of Joseph and Margeret (Divens) Vance His parents were natives of Pennsylvania, and of Irish and German origin. His father was born in Greene Township, in 1795, and lived to the advanced age of seventy-eight years. He was a farmer, stock-grower and stone-mason His family consisted of ten children, of whom Joseph is the youngest. He has been reared in this township, where he received a common school education. Having chosen farming as his occupation, he has given it all his care and attention, and is the owner of a nice farm of eighty acres where he resides near Willow Tree, this county. The subject of our sketch was married in this township, in 1884, to Miss Martha Ann, daughter of Coverdel Cole, of Virginia. Mr. Vance is a Democrat in politics, and a highly respected citizen.

JEFFERSON TOWNSHIP AND JEFFERSON BOROUGH.

A. F. AMMONS, Khedive, Penn., one of the substantial farmers of Jefferson Township, was born in Perry Township, Greene County, April 20, 1824. He is a son of Abraham and Mary (Frost) Ammons. His mother was a native of Fayette County, Penn., and his father of Greene County, where they were married and spent the greater part of their lives, moving to West Virginia a few years before their death. Mr. Abraham Ammons died in 1833; his widow was afterwards united in marriage with Jerry Wright, now deceased. In 1847, January 21, A. F. Ammons married Rebecca Wade, who was born in West Virginia, January 15, 1828. She is a daughter of Sylva and Catharine (Dusonberry) Wade, and is a consistent member of the Cumberland Presbyterian Church. Her parents were also natives of West Virginia, where they were married and remained until Mr. Wade's death, March 31, 1850; his widow is still living. Mr. and Mrs. Ammons have nine children, six living—Mary, wife of Benjamin Fox; Perry, Douglas, Forney, Frank and Nettie; the deceased are—Jasper, William and Louvernia. Mr. Ammons was raised on a farm and worked by the month until nineteen years of age; then learned the carpenter trade which he followed for sixteen years. He afterwards engaged in farming and stock-dealing and, by great industry and good management, has secured a nice home for himself and family and a fine farm of 315 acres of improved land in Greene County. He filled the office of justice of the peace in Perry Township five years, served as school director eight years, and was assessor one year. Since moving to Jefferson Township, he has filled the office of justice of the peace for twelve years, and has voted the Democratic ticket all the time and still is for Cleveland, Thurman and the Mills bill.

N. M. BANE, retired farmer, P. O. Jefferson, was born in Washington County, Penn., February 27, 1818, a son of Abraham and Elizabeth (Venom) Bane, who were natives of Washington County, where they were married, settled and remained all their lives. Their son, N. M., is the only one of their nine children now living. He was united in marriage, November 21, 1844, with Mary McClenathan, who was born in Washington County, Penn., October 22, 1822, a daughter of William and Mary (Coulson) McClenathan. Her parents were also natives of Washington County, where they were married and remained through life. They were the parents of eleven children, five living. Mr. and Mrs. Bane's family consists of five children, two of whom are living—Jennie, wife of David Crayne, and John L., who married Mary E. Neal. The deceased are—Eveline, Thomas S. and James M. Mr. Bane owns 150 acres of land in Washington County, Penn., also some land and property in Greene County. He and wife are faithful members of the Baptist Church.

SAMUEL BAYARD, farmer, P. O. Rice's Landing, was born in Centre Township, Greene County, Penn., January 4, 1819, a son of William and Nancy Bayard (*nee* Scott). The former was born in Washington County and the latter in Greene County, Penn., where they were married, settling in Centre Township, where they remained until 1826; they then moved to Whiteley Township, where Mrs. Bayard died in 1840. Her husband died in Jefferson Township in 1860. They were the parents of three children—John S., Thomas W., and Samuel. March 3, 1839, Samuel Bayard married Miss Lucinda Randolph, born in Jefferson Township in 1818, a daughter of Jonah F. and Leah Randolph (*nee* Leonard). By this marriage Mr. Bayard is the father of two children—J. Randolph, who married Martha E. Oliver, they are the parents of two living children, Frank and Lon L.; Nancy, who is the wife of Capt. J. R. Hewitt, their children are Anna, who married E. H. Shipley, and William B. Mrs. Bayard departed this life July 3, 1845. August 18, 1846, Mr. Bayard was again united in marriage, with Rebecca A. Randolph, who was born in Jefferson Township, February 24, 1820, a daughter of Jacob and Ruth (Bailey) Randolph, and a faithful member of the Cumberland Presbyterian Church. Her father was a native of New Jersey and her mother of Pennsylvania; both are now deceased. By his second marriage Mr. Bayard is the father of three children—

William J., who married Mary Temple and is the father of J. Temple Bayard; Lucy R. and John A., who married Permelia Lucas and is now the father of two children—Lettie and Samuel. Mr. Bayard is one of the most highly respected farmers in his neighborhood, and owns 200 acres of land where he and family reside.

J. C BURSON, farmer, Clarksville, Penn., was born September 27, 1825, in the house now occupied by himself and family, His father, Abraham Burson, was born on the farm which J. C now owns in Jefferson Township. His mother was born in Washington County, Penn. After marriage they settled in Greene County, and remained until their death; Mrs. Burson died in 1839, July 17. Her husband afterwards married Hannah Crawford, now deceased; and he died in 1886. By the first marriage there are four children, three of whom are living. Mr. J. C. Burson was united in marriage, December 30, 1849, with Rebecca Reynolds, who was born in Jefferson Township, December 24, 1827. Her parents, John and Jane (Kincaid) Reynolds, were natives of Greene County, where they resided till death: Mrs. Reynolds died October 12, 1839. Mr. Reynolds afterwards married Priscilla Gwynn (*nee* Long), deceased. He departed this life February 20, 1882. To Mr. and Mrs. Burson have been born six children, five living—John R., who married Emily Leslie; David M., who married Emma Moredock; Abraham, who married Margaret Greenlee; Alexander P. and James O.; Abraham being deceased. Mr. Burson was raised on his present farm formerly owned by his father and grandfather; it consists of 200 acres. Mr. Burson has filled the offices of school director and overseer of the poor, and has been a member of the Masonic fraternity for about thirty-seven years.

WILLIAM COTTERREL, saddler and harness-maker, was born in New Jersey in 1772; he married Isabela Livingston, also a native of New Jersey. They settled in Jefferson, Greene County, Penn, about 1796, and lived there until the year 1824, when they moved to Waynesburg; he there followed his trade until his death in 1836. His wife died in 1826. They raised four childern—John, William, Isabela and Martha. Isabela died in 1844. Martha married Clark Ely, and died young; left one daughter, Isabel, who married David Babbit, and died without issue; William married Frances Minor, who died and left one daughter, Elizabeth, who married David Taylor. She died and left one daughter, Lee Taylor. William married for his second wife Mrs. Sarah Bane (formerly Sellers). He followed the tanning business for a number of years in Waynesburg, and died January, 1886, aged seventy-four years. His widow still survives at an advanced age John Cotterrel, Sr., was born in Jefferson, Greene County, September 25, 1802. At the age of fifteen years he went to Uniontown, Penn, and learned the tanning trade with John Miller. He came back home and worked for his father until 1824, when he started business for himself. In 1828 he married Permelia, daughter of John and Mary Milliken (natives of Ireland). They raised nine children—Isabela, John, Mary A., Permelia, William, Jonas, Elizabeth, Martha A. and George. Isabela married William Anderson, of Pittsburgh. She died and left one daughter, Laura Bell. Mary A. married Dr. James W. Hancher, of Ohio—are both dead. They raised seven children. Permelia is dead. William married Olive Gorden, of Washington, Penn. Jonas married Anna Short, of Claysville, Penn. Elizabeth married Joseph A. Bell. Martha A. married Jacob Haver. George now lives in Hiawatha, Brown County, Kansas. John Cotterrel, Jr., was born in Jefferson, Penn., November 29, 1832. He learned the tanning trade with his father, and married Priscilla Swan, daughter of Samuel and Priscilla (Crago) Swan; she died June 10, 1861, and left two daughters— Elmyra P. and Margaret A. Elmyra P. now resides in Iowa. Margaret A. married T. Reed McMinn. She died June 11, 1885; left one son, Robert C. John Cotterrel's present wife is Mary H., daughter of William and Harriet (Randolph) Davis, and they have a family of three children—John F., William D. and Joseph R. In politics Mr. Cotterrel is a Republican, and takes an active interest in farming, wool-growing and stock-raising and now owns a farm of 175 acres one mile southeast of Jefferson, Penn.

HUGH D. CREE, plasterer and contractor, was born in Greene County, September 11, 1840. He is a son of William and Ann (DeFrance) Cree, who were natives of Jefferson Township, and of French and Irish origin. Our subject's father, William Cree, was born in Greene County, May 18, 1796. By occupation he was a farmer, and in religion a Presbyterian, in which church he was an elder. Mr. Cree's father was a farmer, who died November 5, 1871. His family consisted of twelve children—eight sons and four daughters. Their mother was born in Greene County in 1802, and died in 1875. Hugh grew up on the farm with his parents, attended the district school, and chose farming as his business; but subsequently learned his present trade, which he has pursued with more than ordinary success. He was married April 26, 1862, to Mary Elizabeth, daughter of Isaiah and Nancy M. (Guseman) Dean, who were of Dutch descent. Mr. and Mrs. Cree have one child, a daughter— Elizabeth Ann, now wife of George B. Waychoff. Mr. Cree and wife are members of the Methodist Episcopal Church. In politics he is a Republican. In 1861 he enlisted as a member of Company F, First Pennsylvania Cavalry, and was discharged the same year for disability. His five brothers were all soldiers in the Union army, three of them being in from the beginning till its close.

JESSE DOWLIN, farmer, P. O. Khedive, was born in Cumberland Township, Greene County, Penn., March 21, 1830. He is a son of John and Elizabeth (Gwynn) Dowlin, natives of Pennsylvania. They were married in Greene County and made it their home until their death. He departed this life November 26, 1874, and she September 30, 1878. Eight of their nine children are now living. Jesse Dowlin was united in marriage, February 22, 1855, with Eliza A. Huston, born in Fayette County, Pennsylvania. Her parents were John and Hannah (Sproat) Huston, both of whom died in Greene County—her father, March 5, 1885, and her mother in 1886. In the earlier part of his life Mr. Dowlin taught school through the winter and worked on the farm in the summer. He has since devoted all his time to farming and, as a result of his faithful labors, now owns a fine farm of 117 acres on which are good buildings. He has served as school director of his township.

WILLIAM GOODWIN, farmer, P. O. Jefferson, was born in Washington County, Penn., June 16, 1822. He is a son of John and Sallie (Gardner) Goodwin, the former born in York County, Penn., and the latter in Washington County, where they were married and remained until 1830, at which time they moved to Center Township, Greene County, and lived there till Mrs. Goodwin's death in 1843. Mr. Goodwin afterwards married Mary Dalripple (nee Bell), now deceased. He died in 1859. William was united in marriage, February 26, 1847, with Nancy Wilson, born in Ireland March 7, 1827. Her parents, James and Martha (Craigmills) Wilson, were both born in Ireland, where they were married and emigrated to America in 1827, living first in Washington County, and then in Westmoreland County, where she died in 1830. Mr. Wilson then married Catharine McKee, now deceased; he died in 1878. Mr. and Mrs. Goodwin are the parents of ten children, eight of whom are living—Sarah E., John T., Mary, wife of R. H. Armstrong; Rachel, wife of W. S. Scott; Margaret J., Nancy A. B., William W. and Jessie M. The deceased are: Martha J. and an infant. Mr. Goodwin was reared on a farm, and is now regarded as one of the most substantial farmers in his township. He owns 350 acres of land in Greene County. He and wife are consistent and earnest Christians.

MARSHALL GWYNN, farmer, Khedive, Penn., a descendant of one of the pioneer families of Greene County, Penn., was born in Jefferson Township, March 9, 1826. His parents, James and Hester (Cree) Gwynn, were natives of Greene County and residents therein through life. They were the parents of five children, two of whom are living, viz: Joseph and Marshall. In 1861, November 29, Marshall married Kate Hill, born in Greene County September 3, 1835, daughter of Thomas and Nancy Hill (nee Roseberry), who were natives of Greene County, where they remained through life. Mr.

Hill died in 1876 and Mrs. Hill in 1880. They were the parents of eleven children, ten now living. Mr. and Mrs Gwynn have seven children—Frank, Frances, Thomas, Jesse, Ida, Remembrance and Albert Mr. Gwynn is a farmer and owns eighty-eight acres of land where he and family reside He is a faithful member of the Cumberland Presbyterian Church.

JOHN HAVER, P. O. Jefferson, is one of the pioneers of the township, where he was born October 12, 1802. He is the son of George and Priscilla Haver (nee Villars); the former was born in New Jersey and the latter in Pennsylvania, where they were married in Greene County and remained all their lives. They were the parents of ten children, of whom four are living. John is the oldest and was united in marriage March 8, 1832, with Jane Rex, born in Jefferson Township March 25, 1815, a daughter of George and Jane (Black) Rex, deceased. Mr. and Mrs. Haver are the parents of eleven children, of these seven are living—George R., Priscilla, Mary E., Hiram, Jacob, Charles and James. The deceased are Sarah, John, Margaret and Emma Their mother departed this life January 9, 1879. Mr. Haver is one of the retired farmers of Jefferson Township, and owns one hundred and fifty acres of land where he and his family reside. He has held a majority of the offices in his township He belongs to the Cumberland Presbyterian Church, of which his deceased wife was also a member.

JACOB HAVER, farmer, P. O Jefferson, son of John and Jane (Rex) Haver, was born in Jefferson Township, Greene County, Penn , September 13, 1846. His father is living, and his mother deceased. His wife was Miss Nettie Cotterel, also born in Jefferson Township, January 17, 1847, a daughter of John and Permelia Cotterel (nee Milliken), deceased. Mr and Mrs. Jacob Haver were married January 30, 1871, and are the parents of six children, of whom five are living— John C., Jane R , Laura B., Joseph B. and Lizzie; William being deceased Mr Haver was raised on a farm and has made farming and stock-dealing his business through life. He owns a good farm in Jefferson Township, containing about two hundred acres, on which are good, substantial buildings.

CHARLES H HAVER, farmer and stock-dealer, P. O. Jefferson, who was born in Jefferson Township January 22, 1820, is a son of John and Jane Haver (nee Rex). The former is living and the latter deceased. Mr. Haver was united in marriage January 22, 1880, with Isabella McClure, who was born in Dunkard Township, Greene County, Penn., in September 1859, a daughter of James and Susan (Brown) McClure Mr. McClure departed this life August 8, 1886; his widow is still living Mr. and Mrs Haver are the parents of two children—James C., born September 28, 1881, and Owen W., born March 27, 1884. Mr. Haver was reared on a farm and has been engaged in farming and stock-dealing all his life. He owns valuable property in the borough of Jefferson.

ISAAC HAYS, farmer, Millsboro, Penn., is one of the pioneer farmers of Greene County, and was born in Morgan Township May 10, 1816, a son of David and Mary Hays, (*nee* Rush). His father was a native of Maryland and his mother of Greene County, Penn., where they were married and remained all their lives. David Hays died in 1827 and his widow in 1870. They were the parents of four children, only two of whom are now living—Jane, and Isaac, the subject of our sketch. His wife was Margaret A Walton, who was born in Washington County, Penn., in 1823, a daughter of John and Sarah (Paul) Walton, deceased. Mr. and Mrs. Hays were married September 22, 1838, and had a family of ten children, four living—Sarah A., wife of Wesley Rinehart; Mary M, widow of Lafayette Vernon; Margaret J, wife of George R. Baker, and Emeline E. Of the deceased Henry C. was born September 27, 1844, and died January 11, 1882, and John W, born November 1847, and died May 25, 1862. Mr. Hays owns a fine farm of one hundred and fifty-five acres on which he and family now reside. Mrs. Hays departed this life February 13, 1872. She was a kind and affectionate mother, and a loving, faithful wife.

CHARLES HUGHES, retired farmer, P. O. Jefferson, is a descendant of one of the first settlers of Greene County, Penn. He was born August 22, 1816, a son of John and Mary (Rex) Hughes. His mother was a native of Lancaster County, and his father of Greene County, where they were. married in Jefferson Township in 1794, lived there seven years, then moved to Morgan Township and spent the remainder of their days. Mr. John Hughes died in 1844, and his wife in 1849. They were the parents of twelve children, only two of whom are living—Maria, the widow of Joseph McNealy, and Charles. He was united in marriage September 21, 1843, with Catharine McEowen, a native of New Jersey, and daughter of George and Permelia (Coleman) McEowen, deceased. By this marriage Mr. Hughes is the father of five children, four living—John S., Mary E., wife of Hamilton Riggle, of Iowa; Permelia, wife of D. A. Bumgarner and Maria C, wife of B F. Kendall. Amy is deceased. Mrs. Catharine Hughes departed this life June 13, 1856; and two years later, May 26, 1858, Mr. Hughes married Elizabeth Hill, who was born in Greene County July 14, 1829, a daughter of Samuel and Hannah Hill, both deceased. Mr. and Mrs. Charles Hughes are the parents of two children—Maggie and Anna M. Mrs. Elizabeth Hughes died November 27, 1887, a faithful member of the Cumberland Presbyterian Church, of which Mr. Hughes' former wife was also a consistent member. Like his ancestors, Mr. Hughes made farming his business through life, and owns 116

40

acres of land—his home farm. He filled the office of assistant assessor under appointment by the Government.

JOHN H. HUGHES, merchant, Jefferson, Penn., is a descendant of the early settlers of Greene County, and of Irish and English descent. His great-grandfather, Thomas Hughes, laid out the borough of Jefferson. His grandfather, John Hughes, was born in Jefferson, where our subject's *great-grandfather settled in 1776; Barnett Hughes was born in 1819, and died in 1882. Two of his children are now living—George, a farmer; and John H., who was reared in Jefferson, attended the schools of Greene County, and early in life went into the dry goods business as salesman. In this capacity he worked for some years at Danville, Illinois, returning to Jefferson in 1871, when he established a general store, in which he has met with deserving success. Mr. John Hughes' wife was Mary, daughter of David and Lettie Bell. Their family consists of one son and one daughter—Barnett and Lettie, both now deceased. Mr. Hughes has served as a member of the town council of Jefferson Borough. In politics he is a Republican; his wife is a member of the Baptist Church.

ROBERT H. JORDAN, farmer, born in Washington Township, Greene County, Penn., is a son of Silas and Sarah (McCormick) Jordan. His parents were natives of Greene County, Penn., and of Irish and English lineage. His grandfather, John Jordan, was a pioneer mill-wright of this county. His father was also a mill-wright and carpenter. His family consisted of eight children, of whom Robert H. was the second. Robert was reared in Jefferson and received a common school education. Early in life he learned the carpenter trade, which occupation he followed for many years. He was twice married, his first wife being Harriet, daughter of John Daniels; she was a native of Ohio. By this union there were three children, all of whom died young. Mrs. Jordan died in 1873. Mr. Jordan was afterwards united in marriage, in 1874, with the widow of Gideon John, of Waynesburg, Penn. Mr. and Mrs. John's children were F. J. John, druggist; R. S., a jeweler at Waynesburg; and Harry J. at home in school. Their father was born in Washington County, Penn., and was of English descent; he died in 1870. Mr. and Mrs. Jordan have one child, James Leroy. Mr. Jordan is the owner of a farm of sixty-eight acres. He is a member of the town council and president of the school board of Jefferson Borough, also was at one time a member of the executive committee of the Monongahela College. He is an upright temperance man and one of the leading members in the Methodist Episcopal Church.

JOHN C. KENDALL, furniture dealer, Jefferson, Penn., was born in Smithfield, Fayette County, Penn., April 26, 1840. His parents were Samuel and Pauline (Custead) Kendall, who were of

German and English origin. His father was a Baptist minister; he died in 1872. His family consisted of twelve children, eleven of whom—nine sons and two daughters—attained the age of maturity. John is the oldest son, and was reared in Fayette County until ten years of age, when he came with his parents to Greene County. He went to school in Fayette County and at Waynesburg College; afterwards returning to Fayette County, where he learned the wagon-maker's trade, and followed it as a business for nine years. He taught school fifteen years, five years of that time in Illinois. In 1861 he married Catharine, daughter of John and Elizabeth Grimm, and by this marriage is the father of two children—Eva and John. The latter is a graduate of the Commercial College, of Springfield, Ill. Mrs. Kendall died in 1866. In 1876 he was next united in marriage with Hannah B., daughter of John and Maria (Loughman) Ross. At the time of her marriage Mrs. Kendall was the widow of the late Thomas Johns, and the mother of one child, Albert Leslie. Mr. and Mrs. Kendall have two children—Paul and Samuel. Mr. Kendall takes quite an active interest in educational matters, and is a member of the board of trustees of Monongahela College. They are both members of the Baptist Church, in which Mr. Kendall is a deacon, and has served as teacher and superintendent in the Sabbath-school.

ELI LONG, deceased, was born April 28, 1821, near Khedive P. O., on the farm now occupied by his heirs. His father and mother were Richard and Mary Long, who were natives of Pennsylvania, were married in the eastern part of the State, and came to Greene County, where they settled and remained until their death. Mr. Eli Long was united in marriage October 25, 1853, with Sarah Pryor, who was born in Belmont County, Ohio, July 27, 1831,—a daughter of Joshua and Susan Pryor, now deceased. To Mr. and Mrs. Long were born four children, of whom two are living—Lizzie L. and Albert C. The deceased are Vincent P. and Della. Mr. Long was reared on a farm, and made a great success of farming and stock dealing, possessing at the time of his death, October 1, 1881, 560 acres of land, which is now owned and managed by his son and daughter. Mrs. Long departed this life August 27, 1886. She and her husband were faithful members of the Cumberland Presbyterian Church, of which the son and daughter are also members.

MARTIN J. LOVE, farmer, P. O. Jefferson, one of the substantial citizens of Jefferson Township, was born in Greene County, Penn., March 11, 1826. His parents were Alfred and Ann Love (nee Piper), who were natives of England, where they were married and emigrated to America in 1819, coming to Greene County, Penn., where they remained until their death. Mrs. Love departed this life in 1853 and her husband in 1863. They were the parents of six children, four of whom are living. Martin J. is the youngest, and was united in marriage November 5, 1857, with Harriet Rinehart, who was born in Greene County November 11, 1829. She is a daughter of Jacob and Abigail (Huss) Rinehart, who were also natives of Greene County and residents therein through life. Mrs. Rinehart died in 1841. Mr. Rinehart afterwards married Elizabeth Hoge, now living; he died in 1874. To Mr. and Mrs. Martin J. Love have been born nine children; of these five are living, viz.— Emma, George, Ruth, wife of Thomas Hughes; Kate, wife of Hugh Hamilton, and Charlie. The deceased are Ella, wife of Dr. C. H. Pollock; Lizzie M., Milton J. R. and Millard F. Mr. Love was raised on a farm, has made farming and stock dealing his business, and owns 300 acres of land where he and family live. He and wife are consistent members of the Cumberland Presbyterian Church.

EWING McCLEARY, merchant, Jefferson, Penn.—Among the prominent business men of Greene County we mention the name of Ewing McCleary. He was born in Fayette County, Penn., February 3, 1840, a son of William and Rebecca McCleary. His parents were also natives of Fayette County. His father was a merchant in early life, in later years a banker. Ewing was the only son in a family of three children, and had the advantages of good schools, having attended both the High School and Academy at Uniontown, Penn. In 1865 he was admitted as a partner in his father's store, in which he had been a salesman for several years. In 1872 he came to Jefferson and established his present business. Here his long experience in the mercantile trade, and his polite and gentlemanly demeanor, soon won for him a good trade. His store is an example of neatness, and in the arrangement and selection of goods he exhibits marked ability and good taste. Mr. McCleary was married in Fayette County, Penn., to Miss Lizzie, daughter of P. G. and Martha (Burchinal) Sturgis. Mrs. McCleary's father was a Baptist minister, and she is a faithful member of the Baptist Church. In politics Mr. McCleary is a Democrat.

MICHAEL McGOVERN, deceased, a man highly respected for his many excellent qualities, was a prominent farmer and stockgrower in Jefferson Township, where he died in 1876 at the advanced age of eighty-four years. He came to Jefferson Township when a young man, and made the tilling of the soil and raising stock the business of his life, which he pursued with more than ordinary energy. As the fruits of his toils, he was the owner of two farms well stocked and improved. He was quite happily married to Miss Lucinda Daken, who was born in Ohio, and of English origin. She has spent most of her life in Greene County, Penn. The union of Mr. and Mrs. McGovern proved a very pleasant one. Their youngest child is J. E., who is now a full-grown man. In politics Mr.

McGovern was a Democrat. He was a zealous member of the Catholic Church.

THOMAS R. McMINN, deceased, who was a saddler and harness-maker, was born in Cumberland Township, Greene County, Penn., April 22, 1820. He was a son of Robert and Rachel (Rice) McMinn, of Irish and English origin. His father was born in Ireland, and was a school teacher by occupation; in later life he engaged in farming. Thomas McMinn was the youngest in a family of four children—Elizabeth, deceased, who was the wife of James Mahanna; Mary, the widow of James Pogue; Sarah, wife of John Curl; and Thomas R, who married Miss Elizabeth V., daughter of William Lee Pollock, of Pittsburgh, Penn. Mrs. McMinn is next to the youngest of a family of twelve children. The marriage of Mr. and Mrs. McMinn has been blessed with seven children, five of whom are living—Mary A, wife of John Rex; W. J, a saddler; Elizabeth L., Thomas Reed, a liveryman at Jefferson; and John C., a minister in the Methodist Episcopal Church. Robert L. and an infant are deceased. Mr. McMinn took great pride in fine horses and cattle, in which he dealt quite extensively during his life. He was a man of more than ordinary intellect, always foremost as a peacemaker, and beloved by everybody who had the pleasure of his acquaintance. In the language of all persons of that section with whom we have been able to converse, "his place can never be filled." Nothing can be said that would not be appropriate to the character of so honored a friend of the people. He started in life a poor boy, and by industry, honesty and integrity, he amassed considerable fortune, leaving every member of his family in comfortable circumstances. His widow is a devoted member of the Methodist Episcopal Church.

DANIEL MOREDOCK, farmer, Jefferson, Penn., was born in Jefferson Township, Greene County, March 29, 1820. His father, George Moredock, a native of Greene County, was three times married, his first wife being Priscilla Anderson, Daniel's mother, who was born January 10, 1798, with whom he lived in Jefferson Township until her death, May 16, 1841. He married for his second wife Mary (Moredock) Worthington, and for the third, Emily A. Randolph, now deceased He departed this life in 1881. He was the father of twelve children, nine of whom are living. Daniel is the second, and was united in marriage, November 25, 1849, with Elizabeth Rex, who was born in Jefferson Township, August 23, 1834, a daughter of Charles and Mary (Hickman) Rex, deceased. By this marriage Mr. Moredock is the father of ten children, eight living, viz: Rex, Margaret, wife of Samuel Cox; Emma, wife of David Burson; Sarah, wife of Anderson Moredock; Anna, wife of William Daugherty; Edda, Elizabeth and Austin L. The deceased are George and James A. Their mother departed this life April 11, 1877.

August 26, 1885, Mr. Moredock married Rosa A. Stephens, who was born in Delaware. Mr. Moredock is an industrious and economical farmer and stock-dealer, and owns a nice home and good farm of 240 acres where he and family now live.

JEREMIAH PRICE, farmer, P. O. Rice's Landing, was born in Monongahela Township, Greene County, Penn., September 7, 1814. His parents, Michael and Mary (Evans) Price, were natives of Wales, where they were married and lived about one year, then emigrated to America, locating in Greene County, Penn., where they remained until Mr. Price's death, July 9, 1853. Mrs. Price died in June, 1870, being one hundred years and thirteen days old. They were the parents of six children, only two of whom are living—Michael, single, and Jeremiah, who was united in marriage, August 14, 1855, with Mary J. Goslin. She was born in Fayette County, Penn., September 17, 1821, and is a consistent member of the Cumberland Presbyterian Church. Her parents were Richard and Jane (Millison) Goslin, who were natives of Fayette County, Penn., and moved from there to Greene County, where they died. Richard Goslin was a soldier of the war of 1814. Mr. and Mrs. Price have three children, two living, viz: Oliver J. and George E. The deceased was Maria J., wife of Simon Sharpnack. Mr. Price is a farmer and quite a genius, having engaged at different times in blacksmithing, malting, and the practice of veterinary surgery. He and his brother Michael own 400 acres of good land in Greene County. Mr. Michael Price filled the office of auditor of the county one term, and has met with success as a farmer and school-teacher. The following is a copy of the naturalization papers of the parents of our subject: "Delaware District, ss. I,—Do Hereby Certify That, Michael Price wife & one child of Radnor, Shire—Himself aged 34 years, a Native of Wales Subject to King of Great, Brittain, and that, he intends residing in Newyork, an is regestered in the Office of the District Court in Testimony whereof, I, have hereunto set my hand and affixed the, Seal, of the District Court of the United, States For the, Delaware District at Wilmington this, 22d day of July—in the year of our Lord—one Thousand Eight Hundred and one. Thomas Stocton, Clerk, Delaware District."

GEORGE REX, farmer, P. O. Jefferson, is a descendant of one of the pioneer families of the township, and was born November 30, 1838, on the farm where he and family now reside. He is a son of Charles and Mary (Hickman) Rex. His father was born on the old Rex homestead in Jefferson Township, Greene County, July 1, 1801, and was a son of George and Margaret (Keppler) Rex, the former a native of England, and the latter of Germany. They emigrated to America, and were married in Pennsylvania, settling in Greene County, which at the time of their settlement was known as Washington County. Here they remained until their death. Mary Rex, George's mother, was born in Fayette County, Penn., January 19, 1801, a daughter of Solomon and Elizabeth Hickman, who were natives of Pennsylvania, and departed this life in Jefferson Borough. Charles and Mary Rex were the parents of seven children, three of whom are living, viz: Margaret, wife of W. F. Hughes, of Mount Pleasant, Iowa; John, a resident of Fairbury, Ill.; and George, the subject of our sketch. George was united in marriage, December 8, 1861, with Mary E Strickler, born in Westmoreland County, January 5, 1843, and is a consistent member of the Presbyterian Church. Her parents are Isaac and Catharine (Heath) Strickler, natives of Fayette County, where they lived a few years, then moved to Westmoreland County, where they now reside. Mr. and Mrs. Rex have a family of ten children, eight living—Charles, Ella J., Edward B., Georgianna, Joseph A., Albert G., Mattie M. and Ernest. The deceased were Catharine and George. Mr. Rex, like his ancestors, has made farming the business of his life, and owns 125 acres of land, known as the old Rex homestead.

H. P. RINEHART, farmer, P. O. Waynesburg, was born in Franklin Township, Greene County, Penn., June 1, 1844. He is a son of Arthur and Rebecca (Roberts) Rinehart, who were natives of this county and residents therein until death. He departed this life April 6, 1872, and she January 5, 1873. They were the parents of thirteen children; seven are living, the youngest of whom is H. P, who was married June 28, 1866, having chosen as the sharer of his fortunes Miss Maria Bowers, who was born in Whiteley Township, February 22, 1844 Her parents were John and Elizabeth (Cowell) Bowers, also natives of Greene County, where they lived until 1869, at which time they moved to Taylor County, Iowa. Mrs. Bowers died February 14, 1877. Mr. Bowers is still living. Mr. and Mrs. Rinehart have had eight children—Charles W., Floe F., Jesse B., Mary L., John R., William W. and Maria K.; Maggie being deceased. Mr. Rinehart owns 123 acres of land where he and family live. He filled the office of director of the poor one term, also served on the school board of his township. He and wife are consistent members of the Methodist Protestant Church.

JAMES SCOTT, deceased, was one of the most successful and enterprising farmers of Jefferson Township. He was born October 6, 1822, on the farm where his family resides. His father and mother were James and Margaret (Kincaid) Scott. His father was a son of Mordecai and Kizzie (Potete) Scott, and came with his parents from Maryland to Greene County, Penn., where he married Margaret Kincaid, who was born in 1790, and departed this life in 1888. James was the fourth in their family of five children. He was united in marriage, May 19, 1853, with Mary A., daughter of William and

Elizabeth (Hedges) Spencer, who were natives of Washington County, Penn. Mr. Spencer came with his parents to Greene County when only two years of age. He was married in Washington County, returned with his wife to Greene County and remained until 1871, then moved to the State of Tennessee, where Mrs. Spencer died April 12, 1883 In the fall of the same year he again returned to Greene County, and has since made his home with his daughter, Mrs. James Scott To Mr and Mrs Scott were born six children, five of whom are living. The oldest of these, Lizzie E., is the widow of I. N. Mc-Nay, the mother of one child, named Newton for his father, the second daughter is Anna S., wife of Dr. J. L. Millikin, of Greensboro, Penn., and the mother of one son, Joe P ; the others are William S., Emma K. and J. Newton Margaret is deceased. Mr. Scott acquired his education in the common schools in Jefferson Township. Like his ancestors, he made farming and stock-raising his business, and owned 400 acres of land He was a member of the Masonic fraternity, and belonged to the Cumberland Presbyterian Church, of which Mrs. Scott is also a devoted member. He remained on the old Scott homestead until his death, September 30, 1878.

MILTON S. SHAPE, farmer, Clarksville, Penn., was born in Greene County, July 29, 1835, a son of Jacob and Joanna Shape (nee Pettit), who were also natives of Greene County, where they were married, settled and remained until Mrs. Shape's death, which occurred in 1859. Her husband afterwards married Elizabeth Black (nee Walters), and they reside in Clarksville, Penn. Mr. Jacob Shape is the father of eight children, six now living Milton S. is the oldest and was united in marriage, August 16, 1878, with Catharine A. Lancaster, who was born in Fayette County, Penn, February 10, 1844. Her parents, Bartholomew and Minerva (Fraley) Lancaster, were natives of Maryland, where they were married and then came to Greene County, Penn, in 1843, removing two years later to Fayette County, Penn., where they died. Mr. and Mrs. Milton Shape are the parents of four children, only one living, Hadashia B , born November 11, 1880. Mr. Shape is a carpenter by trade, which he followed for sixteen years. He then engaged in farming, and owns seventy-two acres of land He enlisted in Company G, Fifteenth Pennsylvania Cavalry and served his country three years He is a member of the Masonic fraternity and Mrs. Shape is a member of the Methodist Episcopal Church

THOMAS SHARPNACK, farmer, Jefferson, Penn., was born in Cumberland Township, Greene County, June 30, 1827. He is a son of Peter and Mary (Alfree) Sharpnack, who were native of Greene County, where they were married and made their home until Mr. Sharpnack's death in 1845. Mrs. Sharpnack died in 1867. They were the parents of nine children, five now living. Of these

Thomas is the oldest and was united in marriage, June 27, 1852, with Elizabeth Craft, who was born in Fayette County, Penn., November 6, 1826. She is a daughter of Benjamin and Mary Craft, also natives of Fayette County. Her father died March 27, 1886; her mother is still living. They were the parents of fifteen children, nine living. To Mr. and Mrs. Sharpnack have been born five children, only one living, Simon. The deceased are George, Adaline, Benjamin and Peter. Mr. Sharpnack is a farmer and owns 166 acres of land where he and his family reside. Mrs. Sharpnack is a faithful member of the Cumberland Presbyterian Church.

T. H. SHARPNACK, M. D., born at Rice's Landing, Penn., November 20, 1843, is a son of William and Sarah (Neel) Sharpnack. His parents were natives of Greene County, Penn., and were of Scotch and German descent. His father is a farmer and stock-grower and resides in Cumberland Township, where he was born in June 9, 1810, a son of Samuel and Nancy (Crago) Sharpnack. The Doctor's grandmother, Nancy Sharpnack, was born in 1776 and lived to be eighty-four years old. His grandfather, Samuel, died in 1852 at the age of sixty-three. The Doctor's grandparents on his mother's side were Barney and Martha (Hughes) Neel. They were natives of Cumberland Township. Eleven of their children grew to maturity. The Doctor is the fourth in a family of nine children. He was reared in Jefferson Township, educated at Waynesburg College, and studied medicine with Dr. Laidley, of Carmichaels. He took the regular course in medicine at Jefferson Medical College, at Philadelphia, and graduated in 1872. He then entered his profession at Jefferson, where he has had a good practice since. The Doctor is a member of the Greene County Medical Society, and was sent as delegate to the State Medical Association. He has served as the physician of the Children's Home in this county, and is examining physician for three life insurance companies. He was married, June 23, 1870, to Cynthia, daughter of James and Hannah Moredock. They have four children—James M., William F., Gertrude H. and Thomas P. (deceased). Mrs. Sharpnack died August 16, 1877. The Doctor is a member of the Baptist Church; in politics he is a Democrat.

STIERS SHARPNACK, farmer, Jefferson, Penn., was born on the farm where he and his family reside, July 2, 1855. His parents were Thomas E. and Catharine (Haver) Sharpnack, who were natives of Greene County, Penn., where they were married, settled and remained until their death. He departed this life October 2, 1876, and she November 8, 1887. They were the parents of three children —Calvin, Andrew S. and Stiers, the subject of this sketch. He was united in marriage, April 14, 1877, with Jennie Hupp, born in Morgan Township, March 4, 1856, a daughter of Uriah and Marinda

Hupp (*nee* Cox)   Mrs. Sharpnack is a consistent member of the Disciple Church.   Her father was a native of Washington County, Penn, and her mother of Greene County, where they reside in Morgan Township   Mr. and Mrs. Sharpnack have four children— John H, Minnie L, William H. and Harry A.   Mr Sharpnack was raised on a farm and makes farming his business   He owns 107 acres of land in Jefferson Township.

.ALVA C. SHAW, merchant and burgess of Jefferson Borough, was born in Canaan Township, Morrow County, Ohio, March 4, 1844, a son of John and Mary A. (Bell) Shaw.   Their parents were of Scotch-Irish origin; they were Quakers and among the early settlers of Pennsylvania.   The Shaws have usually been farmers and mer chants.   Alva's father, J. L. Shaw, was a farmer and stock-grower, born in Morrow County, Ohio, June 6, 1806   He was a son of John and Polly (Luther) Shaw, and was the oldest in a family of six children   He always met with marked success in business   In 1877 he moved from Ohio to Jefferson, Penn., and engaged in selling farm ing implements. He died in Jefferson Borough.   Of his six children, only three reached maturity.   Alva is the youngest and was educated at Delaware College, and Ohio Wesleyan University.   He started in life as a teacher, but was induced by his father to work on the farm till 1874 when he went to Lincoln, Nebraska, and engaged in the coal business till 1879.   He then came to Jefferson and began mer chandising.   He was elected burgess in 1887.   He is a strong temperance man, and in politics is a Prohibitionist   He is a member of the Methodist Episcopal Church, in which he is steward, trustee and teacher in the Sabbath-school

SYLVANUS SMITH, M. D, Jefferson, Penn., was born in Franklin Township, Greene County, November 30, 1832, a son of Samuel and Elizabeth (Huss) Smith, they were natives of Pennsyl vania and of German and English origin   His father was born in Greene County, in 1796.   His grandfather, Sylvanus, a native of. Monmouth County, New Jersey, came to Greene County, Penn., in 1793.   They were all farmers and members of the society of Friends   Dr. Smith's father died in 1879.   Of his four children, the Doctor is the youngest, and was reared on the farm with his parents in Franklin and Morgan townships.   He attended the district schools and studied medicine in Jefferson Borough, with Dr. W D. Rogers. Here he commenced the practice of his chosen profession in 1862, has met with good success, and accumulated quite a competence from his practice.   June 1, 1862, he married Louisa Crayne, who is of English descent, and daughter of Miller Crayne.   Dr. and Mrs. Smith's children are—John S., a physician and druggist; Sam uel M., a law student at Waynesburg; Elizabeth, C. Harry, Albert P. and Lucinda.   In politics the Doctor is a Democrat.   He is a member of the I. O. O. F., and a Sir Knight Templar of the Masonic Fraternity.

REV. CHARLES W. TILTON, pastor of the East Bethlehem Baptist Church in Washington County, was born in Washington County, Penn., November 21, 1815. He is the son of Enoch and Elizabeth (Wheatley) Tilton, natives of New Jersey. They were of Scotch, English and German ancestry. His father was a farmer, and his family consisted of thirteen children, eleven of whom grew to manhood and womanhood. Charles W., the eighth in the family, remained on the farm with his parents until fifteen years of age, and attended the district school. His parents then moved to Beaver County, after which he entered Frankfort Academy. Early in life he taught school as a business. In 1839 he joined the Pleasant Grove Baptist Church in Washington County. In 1840 he came to Jefferson, Penn., and has lived in this vicinity ever since. In 1843 he was ordained as a minister and has been an active worker in the Baptist Church up to the present time, having held over one hundred protracted meetings, resulting in the conversion of fully 2,000 persons, and baptized over 1,500 converts. For many years he has taken a deep interest in education, and labored in the interests of Monongahela College, having served as secretary of the board of trustees from the organization of the college, and as financial agent for several years past. He has been twice married, first to Miss Nancy Hoge, who died in 1858. Again in 1861 to Sarah Elizabeth Davidson, daughter of William Davidson, of Baltimore, and Margarett (Oliver) Davidson. In his last marriage they had four children— Enoch Randolph, Charles Louis, Nannie Clare and John Hunt— three of whom are graduates of Mononghela College. The oldest son, E. R., a graduate of Crozer Theological Seminary, is pastor of a Baptist Church in Evans City, Penn. The second son, C. L., graduated in the Western Reserve University of Cleveland, Ohio, and is a practicing physician in the State of Colorado. The youngest son is still at school.

F. B. WISE, druggist and postmaster, Jefferson, Penn., is a native of Morgan Township, Greene County, where he was born April 24, 1846. His parents, Solomon and Hannah Wise, were natives of Pennsylvania, and of German origin. His father has been a farmer all his life, and at present is in the cattle business in the West. Frank is the oldest in a family of seven children now living, and was educated at Waynesburg College. He taught school and farmed until 1872, when he engaged in the drug business in company with Dr. Sharpnack, of Jefferson, whose interest he bought in 1879 and established his present business. In 1870 he married Miss Lizzie, daughter of H. Johns, ex-sheriff of Greene County, and of English descent. Mr. and Mrs. Wise are members of the Baptist Church, in which he is clerk and superintendent of the Sabbath-school, and clerk of the Ten-Mile Baptist Association. He is a member of the board of trustees and secretary of the executive committee of Monongahela College. In politics Mr. Wise is a Democrat. He is a member of the town council, and was appointed postmaster in 1883.

JACKSON TOWNSHIP.

JAMES CARPENTER, farmer and stock-grower, Nettle Hill, Penn., was born in Franklin Township, Greene County, Penn., March 5, 1838. He is a son of Joseph and Elizabeth (Smith) Carpenter, natives of this county, and of English and German origin. His father is a farmer and now resides in Gilmore Township. Of his family of eleven children James is the third. James was drafted in the three years' draft of 1863, paid his conscript and received his discharge the same year. He was reared on a farm, receiving his education in the common schools of Jackson Township. He makes farming and stock-growing his chief pursuit, and owns 125 acres of well improved land where he resides. Mr. Carpenter was united in marriage, December 12, 1863, with Miss Mazy, daughter of Joseph and Rachel (Shriver) Kniseley, and their children are—J. C., a teacher; Robert E. Lee and John B. Mr. Carpenter is a Democrat. He and his wife are members of the Methodist Protestant Church.

WILLIAM GRAHAM, farmer and stock-grower, was born in Franklin Township, this county, March 29, 1828. He is a son of William and Margaret (Muckel) Graham, who are of Dutch descent. The Grahams are an industrious, energetic family. Some branches of the family spell the name Grimes, but the original name was Graham. William Graham's father was a blacksmith by occupation, but also engaged in farming, spending most of his life in Greene County. His family consisted of six children, of whom William is the third. He was reared on the farm in his native township, and attended the common school. He has made a very successful business man, devoting himself principally to farming and stock-growing. He owns 318 acres of well improved land where he resides, near Holbrook, Penn. He also owns land in other parts of the county, making in all 473 acres. On November 7, 1850, Mr. Graham married Charlotte, daughter of William and Sallie (Bodkin) Smith, who were of English and Dutch extraction. Mr. and Mrs.

Graham's children are—Sarah M., wife of Thomas Henning; James F., a farmer; William S., who is in Kansas; Lydia Ann, Mary Elizabeth, wife of John Morris; Cephas J , who is in Kansas; John A. and Spencer Milton, all farmers, and Japheth E. All the family, with one exception, are members of the Baptist Church. Mr. Graham is a Democrat and a member of the Democratic County Committee.

HARVEY ALLISON GRIMES, a farmer and stock-grower of Jackson Township, this county, was born May 9, 1857, on the farm where his father now resides. His parents, P. M. and Maria (Ridgeway) Grimes, are natives of Greene County, and of English origin. His father is a merchant and farmer, and one of the influential citizens of Jackson Township. Harvey A. Grimes is the fifth in a family of eight children. He was reared on a farm, attended the common schools, and early in life made choice of farming as his chief pursuit. His present farm consists of 120 acres of finely improved land. On January 29, 1876, Mr Grimes was united in marriage with Martha D., daughter of George and Mary (Gump) Loar, of German origin. Her father was a minister in the Methodist Church. Mr. and Mrs. Grimes are the parents of three children—Ada May, Eva Maria and Luta Lena Mr. Grimes is a Republican. He has served as school director in his district. He and wife are members of the Methodist Episcopal Church.

GEORGE W. GRIMES, farmer and stock-grower, who was born in Jackson Township, this county, June 8, 1859, is a son of P. M. and Maria (Ridgeway) Grimes, natives of Greene County. The subject of this sketch is the sixth in a family of eight children. He was reared on a farm and received his education in the common schools. He made choice of farming as his occupation, and has been very successful and is the owner of 108 acres of land where he resides, near White Cottage, Penn. Mr. Grimes was united in marriage, January 10, 1880, with Miss Ella, daughter of William and Nancy (Dunson) Roberts, who are of English descent. Mr. and Mrs. Grimes are the parents of three children—John H., James A. and William E. Mr. Grimes is a Republican. He and wife are members of the Methodist Episcopal Church Mr. Grimes belongs to one of the oldest families in the township, his ancestors having been among the earliest settlers in the county.

P. M. GRIMES, merchant and farmer, was born in Franklin Township, this county, October 16, 1823. He is a a son of William and Margaret (Muckle) Grimes, who were born in New Jersey, and of German descent. His father, who was a successful farmer and mechanic, died in 1877, at the age of seventy-six years. His mother died in 1865, and was sixty-six years of age. Mr. P. M. Grimes was reared on the farm and received his education in the subscription schools. He has resided in Jackson Township since 1846, and at

White Cottage, Penn., since 1851 He opened a dry goods and grocery store there in 1855, and has been very successful in his business. Mr. Grimes'bought 800 acres of land, and has given several hundred acres to his children. He has the reputation of being an honorable, high-minded gentleman, and has a wide circle of friends. Mr. Grimes is a Republican, and has served as justice of the peace for thirty-three years. He has been postmaster at White Cottage for many years, and is a prominent member of the I O O. F and the Masonic fraternity. Mr. Grimes was united in marriage in 1841 with Maria, daughter of David and Lydia (Calahan) Ridgeway Mis Grimes is of English and Irish extraction. Their children are —William, Allison, George, David, James, A L and Margaret, wife of William Millikin, a prominent farmer of Greene County; and Jane, wife of Perry Scott, a prominent farmer and Democrat. Mrs. Grimes is a member of the Methodist Episcopal Church.

JOHN GROVES, farmer and stock-grower, born in Whiteley Township, this county, in 1837, is a son of Jacob and Nancy ('Orndoff) Groves, natives of Pennsylvania, and of German descent. His father was a farmer all his life and died in Greene County, in 1868. He reared a family of twelve children, of whom John is the ninth. He was reared in Whiteley Township near Newton, Penn. Early in life he chose farming as his chief pursuit and has met with marked success. He is the owner of a good farm of one hundred and ninety acres where he resides near Holbrook, Penn. By his own exertions Mr. Groves has succeeded in making himself independent. Mr. Groves married Nancy, daughter of Robert Dunson. She died in 1886—eighteen years after their marriage. They were the parents of three children—William T., Anna Belle, and Flora Viola. Mr. Groves is a Democrat, and has served as school director in his township. He belongs to the Disciple Church, of which his deceased wife was also a member.

WILLIAM HUFFMAN, farmer and stock-grower, White Cottage, Penn , was born December 27, 1850, on the farm which he now owns in Jackson Township, Greene County, Penn. He is a son of Peter and Elizabeth (Stagner) Huffman, who were natives of this county, and of English origin His father died in 1885 at the advanced age of eighty-three years Of his family of nine children William is the seventh. He was reared on his present farm in Jackson Township, and has made. farming his business through life. He has been very successful and owns two hundred and six acres of land well stocked and improved. Mr. Huffman was united in marriage, November 27, 1870, with Miss Jennie, daughter of Corbly and Jane (Bailey) Fordyce. Mrs Huffman's ancestors were among the pioneers of Greene County. They were of English origin. Mr.

Huffman is a Democrat His wife is a member of the Methodist Protestant Church.

N. H. JOHNSON, farmer and stock-grower, was born February 1, 1829. on the Haines farm, east of Waynesburg; he resides near White Cottage, Penn. He is a son of William and Hester (Haines) Johnson, who were born in Pennsylvania and were of German and English origin. His father, who was a tanner by trade, died in Greene County, May 3, 1847. Of his family of six children the subject of this sketch is the second. He was reared on the farm and received a limited education in an old-fashioned log school-house with slab seats and paper windows He has been a successful farmer and owns a fine farm of 230 acres of land in Jackson Township. Mr. Johnson was a poor boy and by industry and patient effort has made himself independent. He has been thrice married. His children now living are—William Henry, who is in the West; N. J., Mary, wife of Ambler Elliot; W. S., J. S. and E. J. His first wife's name was Charlotta Coen, second Elmira Burge, and third Susannah Wagonner.

LINDSEY KEENER, farmer and stock-grower, Pine Bank, Penn., was born April 30, 1836, in Jackson Township He is a son of Peter and Susan (Stewart) Keener. His mother was born in Maryland and his father in Pennsylvania They were of English extraction. His father spent his life in Greene County, and was a farmer by occupation. Mr. Keener is the youngest of nine children. He was reared on the home farm, attended the common schools and chose farming as his life work. He owns a good farm of 110 acres which he has acquired by patient toil and earnest effort being a self-made man, and anxious to succeed in life. In politics Mr. Keener is a Republican, and one of the representative men of the county.

ALEXANDER KIGER, farmer and stock-grower, was born in Whiteley Township, Greene County, Penn., and is a son of John and Sarah (McLaughlin) Kiger, who were of German and Irish descent. His father was a farmer all his life, and died in 1872. Of his family of ten children, the subject of this sketch is the eighth. He was reared on a farm in his native township, and attended the district school Mr. Kiger has made a success of farming and is the owner of 173 acres of valuable land where he resides near Holbrook, in Jackson Township. Mr. Kiger was united in marriage, March 9, 1862, with Catharine, daughter of Isaac and Phoebe (Pope) Higgins, who were of Dutch and English origin. Mr. and Mrs. Kiger's children are—Jerome B, Elizabeth, John L, Newton, Belle and Sadie. Mr. and Mrs· Kiger are members of the Methodist Protestant Church. He is trustee and class-leader in the church and a teacher in the Sabbath-school. In politics he is a Democrat.

JACKSON KUGHN, farmer and stock-grower, was born in Wayne Township, Greene County, Penn. December 22, 1828 He is a son of Abraham and Elizabeth (Huffman) Kughn, who were of German and English ancestry. His mother was born in Maryland and his father in Greene County, Penn, where he died in 1861 Jackson Kughn is the oldest of eight children He was reared in this county and received a good English education in the common schools He chose farming as his occupation through life and is the owner of the farm of 121 acres where he now resides near Pine Bank, Penn. On May 27, 1859, Mr. Kughn married Eliza Jane, daughter of John and Sarah (Stewart) Thomas, who were of English origin. Mr and Mrs. Kughn's children are—John L., Abraham, William Henry, George Morgan, Rachel Ellen and Mary Alice. Mr Kughn is a Democrat. He and wife are members of the Baptist Church.

LESTER KUGHN, merchant and farmer, Pine Bank, Penn, was born in this county, May 12, 1841, and is a son of Abraham and Elizabeth (Huffman) Kughn His father, who was of English and German ancestry, was born in Greene County, Penn, where he spent all his life as a farmer. The subject of our sketch is the fifth in a family of eight children. He was reared on the farm in Jackson Township, and received his education in the common schools. Early in life he learned the carpenter's trade, at which he worked for several years, and also farmed considerably. He owns a good farm where he resides in Jackson Township Since 1884 he has been engaged in the mercantile business. In 1863 Mr. Kughn married Ellen, daughter of John and Mary (King) Cole, and their children are—George, a carpenter; Mary A. and Elizabeth Jane. Mr. and Mrs. Kughn are members of the Baptist Church, in which he is a deacon and has been superintendent of the Sabbath-school. Mr. Kughn is a Democrat, and has served justice of the peace in his township

JAMES MEEK, farmer, and stock-grower, was born in Greene County, Penn., April 3, 1821. He is a son of John and Elizabeth (Boyd) Meek, natives of Greene County, Penn. His father was of French descent and his mother of Scotch ancestry. His father was a farmer and died in 1877. He served his country in the war of 1812 His family consisted of ten children. The subject of this sketch is the oldest of the children. He was reared on the farm, and was a school teacher early in life He has made farming his main occupation, and owns a farm of 225 acres of well improved land. Mr. Meek is a self-made man, having acquired his present possessions entirely through his own industry. He was united in marriage, October 20, 1842, with Miss Mary, daughter of Samuel and Bithiah (Sharp) Smith, who were of Scotch and Irish lineage. Mrs.

Meek was born in Millsboro, Washington County, Penn, July 10, 1824. They have ten children, eight now living, viz., Melinda, wife of George Jewell; Elizabeth, wife of Abner Johns; James R., a farmer; Sarah Jane, wife of S. Lang; Martha, wife of W. Ankrom; C. J., a farmer; Eddie, wife of W. W. Patterson, ex-county register and recorder; and Mary A. Mr. Meek is a member of the Baptist Church. He is a Democrat, and in 1869 was elected county treasurer. He has held most of the offices in his township, and has also served as auditor of the county. He is a member of the I. O. O. F. and the Masonic fraternity

W. E. MILLIKEN, farmer and stock-grower, White Cottage, Penn, was born in Jefferson Borough, January 6, 1845. He is a son of John and Mary (Ketchem) Milliken, natives of Greene County, and of Irish lineage. His grandfather, Thomas Milliken, was one of the early settlers of the county, and a blacksmith by trade. Mr. Milliken's father is a farmer, and now resides in Washington County, Penn. The subject of this sketch was reared on a farm, receiving his education at the common schools. He has always been a farmer and owns a farm of 119 acres where he resides in Jackson Township. In 1866 Mr. Milliken married Margaret M., daughter of P. M. Grimes, one of the prominent farmers of Jackson Township. They are the parents of six children, viz., T. W., Maria Jane, James P., Mary Ellen, Lora Belle and Emma M. Mr. and Mrs. Milliken are members of the Methodist Protestant Church in which he is trustee and treasurer of the Sabbath-school. Mr. Milliken's oldest daughter is one of the stewards in the church and an active Sabbath-school teacher. Mr. Milliken is a Republican In 1862 he enlisted in Company G, Eighteenth Pennsylvania Cavalry and was a non-commissioned officer. He was in the battles of Cedar Creek, Gettysburg, and was at Winchester when Gen. Sheridan made his famous ride. He is a member of the G. A. R. Post.

L. H. MITCHELL, farmer and stock-dealer, was born in Greene County, Penn, June 10, 1846. He is a son of Jackson and Catharine (Lemmon) Mitchell, who were of English and Irish lineage His father, who was a farmer, died in this county in 1858 or 1859. Mr. L. H. Mitchell is one of a family of four children. He was reared on the farm and attended the common schools of the county. Mr. Mitchell has made his own way in the world. In 1867 his only possession was thirty dollars, and he now owns 360 acres of land well stocked and improved. He has engaged extensively in the culture of fish and has two large ponds. His success, which seems indeed wonderful, may be attributed wholly to his great industry and unbounded energy. He is a temperance man and votes the prohibition ticket. In 1867 Mr Mitchell married Miss Julia Ann, daughter of Peter and Elizabeth (Stagnard) Huffman. Their chil-

41

dren are—J. B., E. I. and C. A., aged respectively (in 1888) twenty, fifteen and ten years. Mr. Mitchell and wife were born on the 10th day of June—he being just one year the older. They are members of the Methodist Protestant Church. In connection with his other business projects, Mr Mitchell is one of the managers of the roller flour mill at Oak Forest, Penn He was actively interested in the Granger movement for many years and served as Master of the Order or lecturer for twelve years.

RUFUS C. MITCHELL, farmer and stock grower, who was born in Jackson Township, this county, August 23, 1851, is a son of Jesse and Dorcas (Long) Mitchell, who were of English lineage. His father followed farming as an occupation, and died September 5, 1870. The Mitchells have ever been noted for their energy and industry, and have usually been farmers by occupation Jesse Mitchell was twice married and had in all eight children. The subject of our sketch is the third child by the last marriage. He is a self-made man, and has made a success of his farming and stock-growing, being the owner of 100 acres of well improved land near Holbrook, Penn. Mr. Mitchell was united in marriage, December 24, 1870, with Miss Hettie, daughter of Peter Huffman. Their children are—Cora Belle, Mary Luella, Charles B, Ada, May, Elizabeth and Ross N. Mr. Mitchell is a Democrat. His wife is a member of the Methodist Protestant Church.

A. J. MITCHELL, farmer and stock-grower, was born in Rich-hill Township, Greene County, Penn., April 23, 1837. He is the son of Jesse and Lydia (Kerr) Mitchell His father was born in Allegheny County and his mother in Greene County. They were of Irish and English lineage. His father was a blacksmith in early life and in later years a farmer. Mr. A. J. Mitchell is the second in a family of eight children. He was reared on the farm and received a common school education He has followed farming and stock growing as an occupation, has been very successful in his business, and owns a farm of 248 acres At the breaking out of the war in 1861 he enlisted in Company F, Eighty-fifth Pennsylvania Volunteer Infantry, and served for three years He is a member of the G. A. R. Post No. 552. In 1865 Mr. Mitchell married Harriet, daughter of Bateman and Hannah (Howard) Martin Their children are —Sarah E, Jesse, Eliza M, Jonathan, Thomas Jefferson, James Madison, George McClellan, Martha A. and Clara Belle. Mr. Mitchell, who is a Democrat, has been an efficient member of the school board in his township

JACOB MORRIS, farmer and stock-grower, Holbrook, Penn., was born in Greene County December 17, 1819. He is a son of Robert and Salona (Renner) Morris, natives of Greene County, and of German origin. His father, who was a mechanic and farmer, died in this county. Jacob Morris is the oldest in a family of six children, and is the only one now living. He never had the advantages of a common school education, and as a consequence never learned to read. He grew up on the farm and chose farming and stock-growing as his occupation. Mr. Morris has by industry and good business management succeeded in building a good home. By his own exertions he has come into possession of 450 acres of land, and has also done much for his children. He is careful in all his business transactions, and seldom makes an error. On March 6, 1845, Mr. Morris married Miss Nancy, daughter of William and Mary (Dunn) Jewell, who were natives of this county, and of English descent. Isaac Dunn, grandfather of Mrs. Morris, was a soldier in the Revolutionary war. He died in this county. The children of Mr. and Mrs. Morris are—Rufus, William Henry, Mary Ann, wife of William T. Grimes; Phœbe J., wife of J. McCosh; James M., Hannah, wife of David Grimes; Sarah M., Charity, wife of Samuel Smith; and Jacob J. Mr. and Mrs. Morris are members of the Baptist Church. In politics he is a Republican.

CAPTAIN JOHN SCOTT, retired farmer and stock-grower, was born in Center Township, this county, April 6, 1815. He is a son of John and Susannah (Nicewonger) Scott. His parents were descendants of the Quakers, his mother being a native of West Virginia, and his father of Greene County, Penn. His father died May 21, 1857, at the advanced age of seventy-three years; his mother died December 12, 1870, aged eighty-five. Their family consisted of nine children, of whom the subject of this sketch is the fourth. He was reared on the farm in Center Township and received his education in the common schools. He has met with marked success as a farmer, and owns 252 acres of finely improved land. Captain Scott was an active member of the militia in Greene County many years ago. He has made his own way in the world, starting a poor boy, and has succeeded in acquiring a good home for himself and family. He was united in marriage June 16, 1836, with Miss Charlotte Mason, who was born in this county May 3, 1817, and is the daughter of James and Mary (Sayers) Mason. Her mother was born in New Jersey and was of German descent; she died February 9, 1883, aged ninety-six years. Her father was a native of Ireland, and died June 12, 1869. Mr. and Mrs. Scott are the parents of the following named children; Mason and J. C., farmers; Mary, wife of William Orndoff; Oliver Perry, a farmer; Eliza Jane, wife of A. C Carpenter; Sarah, wife of George Moore; and Matthias, deceased. Mrs. Scott is a member of the Baptist Church. Captain Scott has always taken great interest in school affairs, and has served as school director for many years. He is a member of the I. O. O. F. His children and grandchildren were all present at the fifteenth anniversary of their marriage, which was one of the happiest events transpiring in the neighborhood for many years.

HUGH SMITH, a descendant of the earliest settlers of Greene County, and among its most prominent citizens, was born on Smith Creek in Franklin Township, January 26, 1832. His grandfather, Thomas Smith, was the first settler on the creek which bears his name. Mr. Hugh Smith is a son of Vincent and Elizabeth (Bell) Smith, the former a native of this county and the latter of Virginia. His father, who was of Irish descent, was born in 1791 and died in 1884. His family consisted of ten children, of whom the subject of our sketch is the youngest of those now living. He was reared on the farm, and has made a successful farmer. He is the owner of a fine farm of 400 acres where he now resides. Mr. Smith was married in his native county to Miss Mary E., daughter of John and Jane (Hennen) Lemley. Mrs. Smith's parents were descendants of the early settlers of the county, and of German and English origin. Mr. and Mrs. Smith have two children—Clara and Maggie.

JOHNSON T. SMITH, deceased, who was an attorney and justice of the peace, was born in this county December 8, 1818, and was a son of Thomas and Catharine (Johnson) Smith. His father was a farmer, and Mr. Smith was reared on a farm in his native county, where he attended the common schools. He also engaged in the study of law, and served as justice of the peace for a period of twenty years. He was a successful business man, and at the time of his death, in 1870, he was the owner of 400 acres of land. He was married December 19, 1853, to Martha J., daughter of Silas and Eliza (Huffman) Barnes. Mrs. Smith is of English ancestry. Their children are Thomas H., Eliza, wife of J. W. Phillips; Silas B., Hiram G., John E. and Elizabeth Jane, wife of M. Peththel. In politics Mr. Smith was a Republican. His oldest son, Thomas H., is a farmer and stock-grower, and was born in this county February 8, 1854. He received a good common school education, and has made farming his favorite pursuit. He has the management of his mother's farm, in connection with his own 100 acres of valuable land. Thomas Smith was married in 1875 to Miss Charlotte, daughter of Richard Peththel. Their children are—Maggie, Lawrence, Garfield, Oscar, Gracie and Blanche. Mr. Smith is a Republican in politics.

ABRAHAM STAGGERS, farmer and stock-grower, Bristoria, Penn., was born in this county January 22, 1818. He is a son of Abraham and Catharine (Grim) Staggers, natives of Greene County, and of German descent. His ancestors were all of German extraction and among the first settlers of Greene County. Of a family of eight children, Abraham Staggers is the fourth. He was reared on a farm near Waynesburg, where he was born. He spent a con-

siderable portion of his early life chopping wood and clearing timber. He has made a very successful farmer, and is the owner of
294½ acres of land where he resides. Mr. Staggers was united in
marriage December 27, 1857, with Rebecca, daughter of Robert and
Salona (Renner) Morris. Her parents were natives of Greene County, and of Dutch ancestry. The children of Mr. and Mrs. Staggers
are Hannah, James and Sarah A. Mrs. Staggers, who was a member of the Church of God, died in Jackson Township in 1873. In
politics Mr. Staggers is a Republican.

DAVID WEAVER, farmer and stock-grower, was born in
Washington County, Penn., May 10, 1833. His parents were Jacob
and Julia Ann (Jackman) Weaver, who were natives of Washington
County, and of German and English lineage. Mr. Weaver's father
died in 1886. His family consisted of nine children, of whom
David Weaver is the oldest. From his early youth Mr. Weaver
has been engaged in farming. He is a plasterer and house painter
and takes contracts for mason work on large buildings He has
been successful in all his business affairs, and is the owner of 100
acres of land in Jackson township where he and his family reside.
He was married on the 22d day of April, 1858, to Mary Jane,
daughter of Thompson and Anna (Johnson) Ullom, who are of Dutch
extraction. Mr and Mrs. Weaver are the parents of eight children,
viz.: Amanda, George M., Elizabeth, Thompson, Charles, Henry,
James and Flora. Mr. Weaver is a Republican. In 1863 he enlisted
in the Twenty-second Corps, Fifth Pennsylvania Artillery, and was in
many important engagements. He is a member of the G. A R. Post
and the I. O. O. F.

HIRAM WEAVER, merchant and minister, Holbrook, Penn.,
was born in Jackson Township, this county, April 17, 1839. He is
a son of Jacob and Julia Ann (Jackman) Weaver, natives of Washington County, Penn , and of English and German lineage. His
father, who was a farmer and school-teacher, died in Greene County
April 15, 1886. His family consisted of nine children, of whom
Hiram is the fourth. He was reared on the farm and attended
the common school. He learned plastering and house-painting, at
which he worked until the war broke out. He then enlisted in
Company F, Eighty-fifth Pennsylvania Volunteer Infantry, and was
a non-commissioned officer. He served three years and twenty days
and was in many serious engagements. In 1865 he established a
saw-mill, and in 1871 started a general store in Jackson Township,
where he has been in business ever since. In 1884 Mr. Weaver
married Elizabeth, daughter of Peter Fry, who is of German descent. Mr. and Mrs. Weaver are members of the Christian Church,
in which he has held several important offices. In 1858 he was

licensed to preach, and has since been a local preacher In politics he is a Republican.

JACOB WEAVER, merchant, Nettle Hill, Penn, was born on
Ten Mile Creek, this county, January 26, 1844. He is a son of
Jacob and Julia Ann (Jackman) Weaver, who were of German and
English origin His father was a farmer and school-teacher, and
lived in Greene County for forty years He died in 1886. His
family consisted of nine children, of whom the subject of this sketch
is the seventh. He was reared on the farm in Jackson Township,
receiving his education in the common schools. He learned the
blacksmith's trade near Waynesburg, and followed it as a business
until 1861. He then enlisted in Company F, Eighty-fifty Pennsylvania Volunteer Infantry. He re enlisted in 1864, in the Twenty-
second Pennsylvania Cavalry, Company A, where he served until
the close of the war He was in the battles of Williamsburg, Fair
Oaks, Bolivar Heights and Winchester. He was wounded at Fair
Oaks, losing two fingers. After the war he bought a saw-mill,
operating the latter for a period of five years. He then farmed until
1880, when he established his store at Nettle Hill. He carries a
large stock of dry goods, clothing, groceries, hardware and queens-
ware, and has a good country trade Mr. Weaver has built his present
store and a neat and substantial residence since 1886. He was united
in marriage December 5, 1867, with Miss Elizabeth, a daughter of
Abraham and Margaret (Shields) Hickman, who died in 1882. He
was again married December 3, 1883, to Miss Eliza, a daughter of
J. and Perrie (Headlee) Smith, and they have two children, Roscoe
Conkling and Otta D. S. Mr. Weaver is a member of the G A. R.
Post, and is Quartermaster.

JOSEPH WEBSTER, farmer and stock-grower, Bristoria, Penn,
was born in Greene County, Penn, January 25, 1830, and is a son of
John and Elizabeth (Cowell) Webster His father was born in New
Jersey and his mother in Greene County, Penn They were of English extraction. His father, who was a farmer, moved to Iowa during
the latter part of his life His family consisted of eleven children, of
whom Joseph is the third. He was reared as a farmer and has been
very successful in that occupation, owning 147 acres of land in Jackson Township He also has spent considerable time at the carpenter's
trade. In 1853 Mr Webster was married in Washington County to
Cynthia Ann Keys, who died in 1858. They were the parents of one
child, Alexander Leroy. Mr Webster was again united in marriage
December 16, 1859, with Jane, daughter of John and Sarah (Gardner)
Goodwin, whose parents were of German lineage. She was the widow
of J S. Hunt, deceased, and they were the parents of two children—
a son and daughter. The son, J. G. Hunt, is a farmer and school-
teacher The children of Mr and Mrs. Webster are J. C. and S M.

The family are members of the Baptist Church, and Mr. and Mrs. Webster are teachers in the Sabbath-school. Mr Webster is a prominent member of the I. O. O. F. He has served on the school board of his township.

HIRAM WHITE, farmer and stock-grower, Nettle Hill, Penn., was born in Greene County, May 1, 1840. He is a son of Isaac and Lydia (Tustin) White, who were of English descent. His father, who was a farmer, was a soldier in the late war, serving in the Seventh West Virginia Regiment. He was twice married, and there were three children by the first marriage. By the second marriage there were eight children, of whom Hiram White is the fifth. He was reared in Wayne Township, on the farm, and attended the district school in that township. Mr. White has been a successful farmer and is the owner of a farm of 147 acres of land where he resides in Jackson Township. In 1865 Mr. White married Mary Ann, daughter of Henry and Elizabeth (King) Cole, and their children are John Henry, Elizabeth, wife of Isaac Hughes; George, Thomas, Eliza, James M., Zella and Lucy. Mr. White is a Democrat, and in 1844 was elected county commissioner. In 1861 he enlisted in Company E, Second West Virginia Volunteer Infantry. He was a brave soldier and fought in many battles. In 1884 Mr. White was appointed reporter for the Greene County Agricultural Society. He took an active interest in the Granger movement, and for years was deputy of the county. He is P. C of the G. A. R. Post, No. 552, at Nettle Hill.

DR. T. T. WILLIAMS, Nettle Hill, Penn., was born in Washington County, Penn , July 22, 1826 He is a son of David and Mary (Thomas) Williams, who were natives of Washington and Westmoreland counties. They were of English, Welsh and Irish descent. His father was a farmer, and died in 1859. His family consisted of five children, of whom the Doctor is the third. He was reared on the farm and attended the common schools. He was subsequently a student in the Academy of Monongahela City, Penn., where he studied the classics, sciences and literature, and while still a young man he taught school for several years, aggregating three and a half years of continuous teaching. He studied medicine while engaged in the profession of teaching, and attended a Medical Institute at New York City, where he graduated, and after his return engaged in the practice of his profession. He subsequently took other special courses in medicine and collateral sciences, attended the Jefferson Medical College at Philadelphia, Penn., and afterwards resumed for a brief period his practice at Monongahela City, Penn. In 1857 he came to Greene County and located at Rogersville, where he remained for a period of four years in successful medical practice, the first year practicing with Dr. D. W. Braden, now of Waynesburg, Penn , as partner. Since 1861 he has been in practice at Nettle Hill.

Dr. Williams was married September 7, 1858, to Miss Elizabeth, daughter of Samuel Crouse, near Rogersville. Mrs. Williams is of English, Scotch and German extraction They are the parents of seven living children, viz: Layton B., a farmer, Mary Etta, wife of Prof. T. R. Stockdale; Caroline R, wife of W Scott Johnson; Samuel T., Jennie E, Britta L E. and Leonora Estella Dr Williams is a Democrat in politics, and at this writing holds the commission of postmaster at Nettle Hill, Penn.

JAMES WOOD, farmer and stock-grower, Holbrook, Penn., was born October 14, 1819, on the farm he now owns in Jackson Township, and is a son of Micajah and Jane (Mason) Wood, who were of English origin His ancestors were among the earliest settlers of ·Greene County, where his father spent most of his life as a farmer, having lived to the advanced age of eighty-three years. Of his family of nine children, all grew to maturity. Besides the subject of our sketch, there is but one other member of the family now living—a brother who was born in 1806, and now resides in Morrow County, Ohio. James Wood has spent most of his life in Aleppo and Jackson townships He received a common-school education in his early youth, has been a successful farmer, and owns 204 acres of well-improved land. On March 11, 1844, Mr. Wood married Mary Ann, daughter of Morgan and Elizabeth (Lippencott) Hoge. Their children are L. W. and Thomas, farmers, Elizabeth Jane, wife of Henry Church; L H., a merchant, and Lucinda, wife of Z. G. Call. Mr. Wood is a Republican. He and wife are members of the Christian Church.

MONONGAHELA TOWNSHIP AND GREENSBORO BOROUGH.

H K ATCHISON, a retired potter, who was born in Elizabeth, N J., August 5, 1820, is a son of Robert and Jane (Parshall) Atchison, who were of Irish descent. His father was born on the ocean while his parents were on their way to America. They settled in New Jersey, where Robert grew to manhood. He learned the potter's trade, which he followed in Newark, N. J., for many years. He subsequently moved to Elizabeth, where he died in 1883. The subject of this sketch was the second in a family of eight children, and was reared in Elizabeth, N. J., where he received his early education. He very naturally learned the potter's trade with his father, and was employed as a journeyman for several years. In 1855 he engaged in the business at New Geneva, Fayette County, Penn , and continued therein for six years. On September 20, 1861, he enlisted in the service of his country in Company G, Eighty-fifth Pennsylvania Volunteer Infantry, and was in the following battles: In front of Yorktown and Fair Oaks; Siege of Yorktown, Va.; Williamsburg, Va , May 5, 1862; Savage Station, May 24, 1862; Seven Points, May 31, 1862; Jones' Ford, June 28, 1862; S W. Creek, S. C., December 13, 1863; Kingston, N.C , December 14, 1863; White Hall, N C., December 16, 1863, and others. In 1864 Mr. Atchison was wounded in front of Petersburgh, and lost his right arm Returning to Greensboro at the close of the war, he was appointed United States store-keeper in 1869, and served for a period of twelve years. He was united in marriage, May 14, 1846, with Susan, daughter of Henry and Susan (Billingsley) Stephens. Her mother was born in West Virginia, and her father was a native of Greene County, Penn. . They were of English and Scotch descent. Mr and Mrs Atchison have nine children and fourteen grandchildren, all but three of whom are living. The children are—Anna, wife of John Rumble; James, Henry, Charley, Jane, wife of William Halliday; Mary J. and Joseph. Robert and Clarinda are deceased. Their mother is a faithful member of the Baptist Church.

JOHN W. BARB, farmer and stock-grower, Mapletown, Penn , was born in Monongalia County, W. Va., July 8, 1854. His parents, Gideon and Sarah (Webb) Barb, were natives of Old Virginia, and of German descent In early life his father was a farmer. He subsequently became a manufacturer of boots and shoes, and came to Mapletown in 1866, where he engaged in that business until his death in 1875. John W. is the eleventh in a family of twelve children. He was reared in Mapletown, and attended the district school. He has followed farming as his occupation, and is the owner of a farm of 100 acres in Monongahela Township, where he resides. Mr. Barb was united in marriage, in 1876, with Louisa E., daughter of Alexander and Maria (Debolt) Mestrezat, who were of French descent Mr. and Mrs. Barb's children are—Lilian, Minnie, Charles A., Lamar and William. Mr. Barb is a Democrat. His wife is a zealous member of the Baptist Church.

GEORGE F. BIRCH, M. D., deceased, was born in Washington County, Penn., August 9, 1824 His father, David Birch, who was a farmer and school-teacher, was born in Ireland. His mother, Lucretia Ellen (Vankirk) Birch, was a native of Washington County, Penn., and of English extraction. Dr. Birch was the oldest in a family of six children, and was reared on the farm with his parents. He attended the Washington and Jefferson College, where he graduated in the classical course. He studied medicine with Dr Isaac

Reed, of Jefferson Borough, this county, and subsequently attended
the Western Reserve Medical University at Cleveland, Ohio, where
he graduated in 1852 In 1853 he first engaged in the practice of
his profession in Greene County, where he spent the remainder of
his life in active practice. His practice in Greensboro and vicinity
was quite extensive from 1853 until his death, which occurred September 18, 1884 Dr. Birch took an active interest in education,
and served as school director for twelve years. He was an active
member of the I. O. O. F. and the Masonic fraternity He was married in this county, February 17, 1854, to Miss Adelia, daughter of
Benjamin and Margaret (Kramer) Jones, who were of Welsh and
English origin. Dr. and Mrs Birch were the parents of eight children—two daughters, both deceased, and six sons, four living: William David, a carriage trimmer; B. J., a physician; George F., a
book-keeper, and Samuel B , who is registered as a drug clerk The
Doctor was a member of the Disciple Church, and his wife is a devoted Baptist Their second son, B J , who was born in Greensboro,
attended the University at Morgantown, W. Va., and read medicine
at Cleveland, Ohio, where he graduated in 1883. He also attended
the Medico-Chirurgical College at Philadelphia, graduating in 1887,
and has since been engaged in the drug business and the practice of
his chosen profession, at Greensboro, Penn.

JAMES A BLACK, farmer and stock-grower, who was born in
Greensboro, Penn , May 19. 1822, is a son of Benjamin F. and Sophia
(Gabler) Black. His parents were natives of Greensboro, and of
German and Scotch descent. His father, the brother of Hon. C. A.
Black, a prominent attorney of Waynesburg, Penn , was a merchant
and justice of the peace in Greensboro, and served one term in the
State Legislature. He died in his forty-second year, June 10, 1843,
leaving a family of six children James was the second and was
reared in Greensboro. He has made farming. his chief occupation,
and owns his present farm near Greensboro and other valuable lands.
In 1844 Mr Black married Miss Ann, daughter of James and Sarah
M. (Morris) Steele, and they have a family of eight children, viz.:
Charles E , John S., Emma V., wife of Rev. Mr Patterson, of Meadville, Penn ; Anna, wife of Rev. Mr McGree; James A., B. F ,
Samuel and Asia, five of whom, with their mother, are faithful members of the Methodist Episcopal Church. Mr. Black has served as
justice of the peace at Greensboro for over a quarter of a century,
and was at one time Master in the Masonic lodge

J. S BLACK, farmer and coal merchant, Greensboro, Penn , was
born in Greensboro, March 30, 1852 His parents were James and
Sarah (Steele) Black, the former a native of Virginia and the latter
of Greene County, Penn. The subject of this sketch is the fourth
in a family of eight children. He was reared in Greensboro and

attended the common school. His first occupation was that of farming. He then engaged in the coal business, which he has since carried on quite extensively. Mr. Black was married in Fayette County, Penn, December 12, 1876, to Miss Jessie Nicholson. Her parents were natives of Fayette County, and of English descent Mr. and Mrs. Black have four children—Eunice Aden, Nina May, Bessie N. and Albert Crystie. Mr. Black is a Democrat, and belongs to the Methodist Church. His wife is a Presbyterian.

JAMES E. BLACKSHERE, farmer and stock-grower, Mapletown, Penn., was born in Monongahela Township, Greene County, Penn, April 15, 1832. His parents, Frank and Sarah Blackshere, who were natives of Delaware, came to Pennsylvania early in life and settled in Greene County Mrs. Blackshere is still living, having reached the advanced age of eighty-five years. They had a family of four children, of whom James E. is the youngest. He was reared on the farm and attended the common schools of the township. Mr. Blackshere is a prosperous farmer and owns a fine farm of 450 acres where he now resides. In 1856 Mr. Blackshere married Eliza, daughter of William Gray, who was among the wealthiest men of Greene County. Mr and Mrs. Blackshere's children are six in number.

A. V. BOUGHNER is a merchant and postmaster of Greensboro, Penn., where he was born in 1830. He is a son of Daniel and Mary (Vance) Boughner, being the youngest in their family of six sons and three daughters. Mr. Boughner was reared in Greensboro, where he received a common-school education, and had some advantages above the common schools. He learned the potter's trade, in which business he engaged for almost twenty-five years He also carried on a store during that time, and since 1868 has given all his attention to merchandising In 1857 Mr. Boughner married Perie Minor, who is of English descent Their children are—Alice, wife of Harry C. Lemmon; Mary, Eunice, Sherman and Claude. Mr Boughner is a Democrat in politics, and was appointed to his present position of postmaster in 1885. He and wife were zealous members of the Presbyterian Church, in which he is an official member. His wife died in 1880.

O. P. COOPER, merchant miller, Mapletown, Penn., was born in Preston County, Virginia, April 25, 1836, and is a son of John G. and Elizabeth (Kearns) Cooper, who were natives of Virginia, and of German origin. His father, who was a miller and hatter by occupation, died in 1868, in Fayette County, Penn, where he had resided for many years. His family consisted of eleven children, of whom O. P. is the seventh. He remained in Fayette County till he was ten years of age, then came to Greene County, and received his education from the common schools. Early in life Mr. Cooper learned the miller's trade, and spent most of his life in that business. His long experience and natural mechanical ability, coupled with his universally polite and gentlemanly demeanor, eminently qualify him for his chosen occupation. In 1885 he bought the old Minor mill in Monongahela Township, which he has refitted and greatly improved. Mr. Cooper was married in Greene County to a Miss Hildebrand, who was a native of this county, and of German descent. Their children are—Walter L., principal of schools at Alton, Penn.; John F., telegraph operator and agent on B. & O. R. R.; Joseph M., practical engineer; Jefferson, in government land office in Kansas; Lewis M., a miller; Oliver P., studying medicine; Harry E., at home. Mr. and Mrs. Cooper are prominent members of the Methodist Episcopal Church.

A. B. DONAWAY, a druggist of Greensboro, Penn., was born near Brownsville, Fayette County, Penn., April 3, 1849. He is a son of John and Margaret (Robinson) Donaway, who were of Irish and English descent. His father, who was a teamster, died in 1882. His mother is still living at the advanced age of eighty-seven years. They had a family of three sons and one daughter. A. B., the youngest of the family, was reared in Greensboro, where he learned the potter's trade and followed it as a business until 1872. He then engaged in the drug business, in which he has met with unusual success. In 1878 Mr. Donaway married Elizabeth, daughter of E. O. Ewing, and they have three children—Minor G., Katie and Warren. Mr. Donaway is a Democrat, has been a member of the town council of Greensboro, and served as street commissioner. He also belongs to the Royal Arcanum.

J. H. DULANY, merchant and postmaster, Mapletown, Penn., was born in Cumberland Township, this county, August 13, 1856. He is a son of Dennis and Elizabeth (Seaton) Dulany, natives of Greene County, and of English descent. His father is a tailor by occupation, in which he is now engaged at Garard's Fort, Penn. The subject of this sketch is the sixth in a family of seven children. He was reared in Greene County, where he attended the common schools. While at home he assisted his father in the nursery, of which he was proprietor. Attaining his majority, he engaged in merchandising at Mapletown, where he has the postoffice in connection with his large general store, and meets with success in his business. In 1884 Mr. Dulany married Miss Cecilla B., daughter of Elisha and Cynthia (Coleman) Walters, who were natives of Pennsylvania, and of English descent. Mr. and Mrs. Dulany have one child—Maud E. Mr. Dulany is a Republican in politics, and his wife is a devoted member of the Baptist Church.

SAMUEL DUNLAP, farmer and stock-grower, Mapletown, Pennsylvania, was born in Fayette County, Penn., June 2, 1837, and is a son of Andrew and Mary (Stone) Dunlap. His parents were of Scotch descent, but natives of Pennsylvania. His father came to Greene County in 1844 and settled in Monongahela Township, where Samuel now resides. He was successful through life as a farmer, and had been acting justice of the peace for twenty-five years—at the time of his death in 1888. His family consisted of two children—Elizabeth Ann, wife of H K Barb; and Samuel, the subject of this sketch. He obtained only a common-school education in this county, was reared on a farm and has made farming the business of his life. Mr. Dunlap's wife was Miss Martha A., daughter of William and Elizabeth (Hedge) Spencer, who were of English and German descent. Her father was born in Jefferson Borough, this county, in 1805. Mr. and Mrs. Dunlap have but one child—Harry L. Mr. Dunlap is a Democrat in politics, and his wife is a devoted member of the Presbyterian Church.

E. S. EVANS, farmer and stock-grower, Greensboro, Penn., was born January 27, 1845, and is a son of Evan and Rebecca (South) Evans, who were of Welsh and German origin. His father was a farmer and stock-grower by occupation, and met with marked success throughout his life. He was a deacon in the Greensboro Baptist Church. Enoch S. was reared on the farm and received his education from the common schools and Waynesburg College. His father left him in comfortable circumstances and he follows farming more from choice than necessity. Mr. Evans has resided for many years on his farm in Monongahela Township, where he makes a specialty of raising fine stock. He was united in marriage, in 1871, with Miss Ada Lawson, daughter of A. C. and Martha D. Pennington, who were of English origin. Mr and Mrs. Evans have an interesting family of seven children—Carrie May, Pierre O., Nona O., Evan, A. C. P. Wilson, W. B. and Nellie B. In politics Mr. Evans is a Republican. He and his wife are faithful members of the Baptist Church, of which he is deacon.

ELIAS A. FLENNIKEN, proprietor of the Greensboro hotel and livery stable, was born June 2, 1824, and is a son of J. W. and Hettie A. (Wright) Flenniken, natives of this county. He is the oldest of a family of seven children, and was reared on his father's farm in Cumberland Township, where he received his early education. He afterwards attended school in the old Greene Academy at Carmichaels, Pennsylvania. His ancestors were among the pioneers of Greene County. For many years Mr. Flenniken has bought and sold horses and has been particularly interested in fast horses. For the last twenty years he has dealt extensively in wool. For two years he was captain of a steamer on the Monongahela River. In politics Mr. Flenniken is a Republican. In 1846 he married Mary Ann, daughter of William Kerr of Cumberland Township. Mr. and Mrs.

Flenniken's children are—Joseph D., Sarah J., widow of Byrass Thompson, deceased; Thomas, Belle, wife of George Stemets; John F., James, Elizabeth, wife of Oliver McClain; George N , Mary, and William. Mr. and Mrs. Flenniken have twenty-one grandchildren now living and one dead, being the only member of the family deceased.

A. K. GABLER, a retired farmer of Greensboro, Penn , was born May 29, 1821, at the old glass works near Greensboro, and is a son of Thomas and Wilhelmina (Kramer) Gabler. Mr Gabler's ancestors, who were of German extraction, were pioneers in the glass business in this part of Pennsylvania and established the first glass works in Greene County. Thomas Gabler was born in Maryland in 1798 and died in 1875. His wife died in 1881, having reached the advanced age of eighty.two years. Their family consisted of nine children, six of whom are living—four sons and two daughters Mr. A. K. Gabler is the oldest son. He was reared at the old glass works, received a common school education and chose farming as his occupation through life. In 1852 Mr. Gabler married Miss Maria, daughter of John Jones, of Greensboro, and they are the parents of two children—Benjamin and Thomas C., a prominent young attorney. Mr. and Mrs. Gabler are members of the Presbyterian Church. A. K. Gabler's brother, Kramer, who is also a farmer and stock-grower, was born and raised at the old glass works, where he received his early education, and learned the saddler's trade with his brother, J. W. Gabler, of Greensboro. He worked at the trade until 1882, when he commenced farming and has met with success Mr. Gabler is a Republican in politics. August 31, 1862, he enlisted in Company A, in the One Hundred and Fortieth Regiment, Pennsylvania Volunteer Infantry. He was a non-commissioned officer, and served until the close of the war. He has also served one term as Officer of the Day in Greensboro, G. A. R. Post. The youngest brother is George, born in 1841, who is also a farmer, and like his brothers, a Republican in politics. His farm consists of eighty-six acres of well improved land in Monongahela Township. Mr Gabler comes of a family noted for their energy and industry. They have ever been diligent in business, and have met with financial success.

J. W. GABLER, harness-maker and saddler, Greensboro, Penn. Among the successful business men of Greene County we mention the gentleman whose name heads this sketch. He was born in this county April, 3, 1825, and is a son of Thomas and Wilhelmina (Kramer) Gabler, who were of German and English descent. His mother was born in Fayette County, Penn. His father was born in Frederick City, Md , and was a glass-blower and manufacturer, and came from Pittsburg to Greensboro, where he engaged in that business for many years. He died in 1879 at the age of seventy-seven. The subject of this sketch was the third in a family of nine children. He was reared in Greensboro, where he received his early education. At the age of nineteen he learned the saddler's trade, to which he devotes most of his time He is also a manufacturer of harness, in which he uses good material and does good work. Mr. Gabler has been in business in Greensboro for nearly forty-five years, and by means of his industry and careful investments, has secured a good competence for himself and family. He has a half interest in the Greensboro hotel, and is the owner of 350 acres of land and real estate in Greensboro and elsewhere. Mr. Gabler was married in Greensboro, December 21, 1858, to Amy, daughter of Daniel and Mary (Vance) Boughner. Mrs. Gabler is of Irish and Dutch descent. They have but one child—Myrtilla. Mr. Gabler is a Republican in politics, and in religion a Presbyterian, in which Church he has been teacher and treasurer for a period of twenty years.

J R. GRAY, a farmer and merchant, of Gray's Landing, Penn., was born July 4, 1831, on the farm near Mapletown, in Monongahela Township, this county. He is a son of William and Catharine (Robinson) Gray, who were of English and Irish origin. His father, who was a wealthy farmer and prominent business man, was engaged in the commission business in Baltimore, Md., for several years. He died in 1885, having had a family of six children, two of whom are deceased. The subject of this sketch was the oldest, and was reared on the farm with his parents. He attended the common-school at Mapletown, Penn , and spent two years at Waynesburg College. Mr. Gray was first employed with his father in the distillery, of which he is now proprietor. He has also engaged in farming and owns 500 acres of land, in connection with a general store which they established in 1858. On February 22, 1855, Mr. Gray married Catharine, daughter of James and Catharine Huston. Their children are—L Alice, wife of O. M. Boughner; Selisia and Selena. Their mother is a devoted member of the Presbyterian Church. Mr. Gray is a Republican in politics. He ever manifests great interest in the educational welfare of his township, and has served as school director for twelve years.

DR WILSON GREENE, of New Geneva, Penn., was born in Monongahela Township, Greene County, Penn , December 1, 1829. His parents were Matthew and Rachel (Sycks) Greene. His father was of English origin and his mother was of German origin. His father was born February 17, 1806, in Monongahela Township, Greene County, Penn., where he still resides and now in his old age is often visited by his son who is ever considerate of his happiness. The Doctor's mother, who died in 1869, was a member of the Sycks family who came to Monongahela Township while the Indians were still inhabitants. They with the Seltzers built a fort for protection on, Dunkard Creek, where the first Dunkard oil field is. Daniel Sycks, an elder brother of Rachel, was born, on the farm where she died, December 8, 1788 and died July 16, 1888, and was the oldest man in the township. When Dr. Greene's grandparents, William and Rebecca (Larue) Greene, first came to Greene County they settled on a farm near Willow Tree, on Big Whiteley Creek. They were natives of Bucks County, Penn., and descendants of the pioneer Quakers, who came from England with William Penn. Dr. Greene is the second and only son of a family of four children. He was reared on a farm and at an early age he made choice of the practice of medicine as his profession. His medical education was obtained at the Cleveland Medical College, Cleveland, Ohio. In 1859 he he opened an office at Bristol, Perry County, Ohio, where he soon gained an enviable reputation as a practicing physician. In order to be near his aged parents he returned in 1864 to the scenes of his childhood and settled in Fayette County, on the banks of the Monongahela River, in New Geneva, within three miles of his old home. Here the Doctor soon won a large and lucrative practice in Greene and Fayette counties. He was united in marriage March 23, 1859, with Miss Pleasant M., daughter of Evan and Nancy (Myers) Evans. Mrs. Greene is a sister of L. K. Evans, editor of the "Three Rivers Tribune," Michigan, and is of Welsh descent. Her father was a successful farmer of Greene County and died in 1865. Dr. and Mrs. Greene have two children, who took a course in Monongahela College, Isa D., wife of O. J. Sturgis, editor of the *Republican Standard*, at Uniontown, Penn., and Willie W., who is a graduate of Duff's College, Pittsburg, Penn. Isa, the only daughter, received all the advantages of a good musical education and graduated at Dana's Musical Institute, of Warren, Ohio. Dr. Greene is a Republican in politics. He devotes all his time to his business and profession, in which he has proven himself one of the most prominent in the county. The family are prominent members of the Baptist Church.

JOHN JONES, of the firm of Hamilton & Jones, manufacturers of earthen ware and tile roofing at Greensboro, Penn., was born in Monongahela Township, Greene County, Penn. He is a son of Benjamin and Laura (Kramer) Jones, natives of this county, and of Welsh and German descent. Mr. Jones' father was a glass-blower by occupation. His family consisted of eight children, all of whom reached maturity. Mr. John Jones, the fifth was reared in Greene County, and attended the common schools. Early in life he learned the potter's trade at Greensboro, and engaged in the business until 1866, when he went into partnership with Mr. Hamilton. They employ about twenty-five men, and have contributed much to the improvement of the town. In 1865 Mr. Jones married Miss Mary A., daughter of W L Hamilton, a prominent citizen of Greensboro They are the parents of one child, Asia K. Mrs Jones is a member of the Presbyterian Church. Mr. Jones is a Republican, and a member of the town council, of which he has served as treasurer. He enlisted under Captain Harper, of Carmichaels, Penn., in Company F, First Pennsylvania Cavalry. He was wounded and taken prisoner at the battle of Warrington, Virginia, but managed to escape the first night. . Mr. Jones has been engaged in the pottery business since the close of the war. He is Post Commander of the Alfred Shibler G. A. R. Post No. 119, of Greensboro.

T. P. KRAMER, a retired glass manufacturer of Greensboro, Penn., was born October 20, 1804, and is the son of Baltzer and Sarah (Phillips) Kramer. His mother was the daughter of Hon. T. P. Phillips, who at an early age was a member of the Pennsylvania State Legislature. He was a farmer by occupation and resided in Fayette County, near Greensboro for many years, and in his house was the first court held in Fayette County. T. P. Kramer's grandfather, Baltzer Kramer, came from Germany to Maryland, and subsequently removed to Fayette County, Penn., and settled on a farm near New Geneva He was afterwards one of a party induced by Hon. Albert Gallatin to settle near Greensboro and establish a glass works, Mr. Gallatin taking one-half interest and furnishing the material. The firm consisted of George Reppert, Lewis Reitz, Christian and Baltzer Kramer, Jr., and Adolphus Everhart, one of the men who carried Gen. LaFayette off the battle-field, and was recognized by the General when making his farewell visit to America. Baltzer Kramer's family consisted of seven children, of whom T. P. Kramer's father, Baltzer, Jr., was the oldest. He was born in Maryland in 1777, and in 1808 became a member of the glass company near Greensboro, where he died in 1852, leaving a family of six children. The subject of this sketch is the oldest, and has been a resident of this county the most of his life. He was sent to school at Cannonsburg, Penn., but ran away and refused to go to college, so his father allowed him to learn the glass-blowing trade, and he has followed that as a business for many years. In 1834 Mr. Kramer married Sarah, daughter of George Harter. Mrs Kramer is of German and English extraction. They had a family of ten children—S. E. B., Sarah M., Elizabeth Ann, William, May Ellen, George, Baltzer, John P., and Virtue and Edward R, deceased. Their mother died in 1884 Mr. Kramer has been a member of the Methodist Episcopal Church for nearly sixty years. He has always taken an active interest in the affairs of the church, and has served as class-leader, steward and trustee. His children are all members of the church. Mr. Kramer is a Republican and a strong advocate of

42

the temperance cause. Although in his eighty-fifth year, he is strong and vigorous in mind and body, seldom failing to walk from his home to Greensboro every day—a distance of more than a mile.

JOHN C. KRAMER, Greensboro, Greene County, Penn.—The subject of this sketch is a descendant of the early settlers of Greene County. He was born in Monongahela Township, September 15, 1838, and is a son of George R. and Louisa (Jones) Kramer, also natives of Monongahela Township. Mr. Kramer's mother was born in 1814, and was of German origin. His father, who was a farmer and glass-blower, was born in 1808 and died June 28, 1881. John Jones, Mr. Kramer's grandfather, was a farmer by occupation, and died at the age of forty-two. His grandfather Kramer was a glass-blower, and lived to a good old age. John C is the second in a family of six children; and was reared on his father's farm where he received his early education. At an early age he learned glass-cutting and he is now employed in that business in Pittsburg. Mr. Kramer was married in Camden, New Jersey, May 26, 1870, to Sallie C., daughter of Joseph and Lydia (Caine) Southard. Her parents were natives of New Jersey, and of German extraction. Mrs. Kramer is the third in a family of eight children, and was reared in Camden New Jersey. Mr. and Mrs. Kramer are the parents of four children, viz : William M., Franklin B., Louisa J. and George R. Mr. Kramer is a Republican in politics, and in religion a Presbyterian. He is also a prominent member of the Masonic fraternity.

JOHN P. KRAMER, potter by trade, is the youngest son of T. P. Kramer, was born at the glass-works February 7, 1854. He received a common-school education and learned the potter's trade, which he has followed as a business very successfully. Mr Kramer was united in marriage June 26, 1876, with Miss Josephine, daughter of William and Frances (Black) Wolverton. Mrs. Kramer is of German lineage. They are the parents of six children, viz.: Harry, Estella, Harris, Clarence, Fannie and Sarah. Mr. Kramer is a Republican. He and his wife are zealous members of the Methodist Episcopal Church, in which he has served as steward and superintendent of the Sabbath-school.

PROF. GEORGE F. MARTIN, principal of schools at Greensboro, Penn., was born in the State of Mississippi, June 25, 1846. His parents are Daniel P. and Hannah (Reynolds) Martin, the former a native of Virginia and the latter of Mississippi. They were of English origin. His father was a cotton planter in early life, and subsequently engaged in farming and stock-raising in southern Kansas. His family consisted of six children, of whom George F. was the fourth. He was sent to a private school in Mississippi until his father lost his fortune, which was valued at one million dollars. At his father's suggestion George went North when fourteen years of age, and worked about two years for a sewing machine company at Elizabeth, New Jersey He then spent two years in Yale College. Being obliged to leave the school for lack of funds, he taught for two years, and was given the position of principal of schools at Stoughton, Wisconsin—a place of about two thousand inhabitants. He remained there about four years, afterwards teaching in Wisconsin and Michigan. Returning South, Prof. Martin taught several years in West Virginia, and in 1880 was appointed by the State superintendent of schools to conduct an institute at Morgantown, W. Va. For the past eight years he has been identified with the schools of Greene County, Penn., and has assisted in conducting two summer normals at Waynesburg College. Prof. Martin is one of Greene's most able educators and makes frequent contributions to the leading school journals He was united in marriage in Monongalia County, W. Va., with Miss Anna M., daughter of John Blosser. Mrs. Martin is of English descent. They are the parents of five children—Frank, P., William R., Clara M., Florence M. and Elmer W. The Professor is a Democrat in politics, and a member of the Royal Arcanum.

JEAN LOUIS GUILLAUME (called William) MESTREZAT, retired farmer and stock-grower, was born in Mapletown, this county, May 11, 1809. His parents, Charles Alexander and Louisa (Dufresne) Mestrezat, were natives of France, and came to Greene County, Penn., in 1795, among the earliest settlers. They lived a short time near Carmichaels, in Cumberland Township, then settled in Mapletown and spent the remainder of their lives Mr. Mestrezat died April 1, 1815, and his widow in 1849. They were the parents of eleven children, of whom Jean Louis Guillaume is the eighth. He was reared in Mapletown, and early in life learned the gunsmith trade. He subsequently carried on the mercantile business, and also engaged in farming to some extent. He owns 330 acres of valuable land. In 1843 Mr. Mestrezat married Mary Ann, daughter of Matthias and Hannah (Leslie) Hartley, who were of Irish lineage. Mr. and Mrs Mestrezat have five children—C. A., Harriet M., widow of the late Samuel Hudson; S. L, a prominent attorney at Uniontown, Penn.; Charlotte Amanda, wife of Hon. M. John, of Colorado; and J. L. G., a cattle-dealer in the West. Mr. Mestrezat is a Democrat in politics. He has served as school director for fifteen years.

FREDERIC MESTREZAT, deceased, was born September 25, 1807, and was the son of Charles Alexander and Louisa Elizabeth (Dufrene) Mestrezat, natives of France, who came to America in 1793. Frederic was the sixth child and second son in a family of eleven children. He attended the select schools of Mapletown, which were taught by teachers hired by the parents, by the year and half year. He was one of the foremost men during his short life in securing good educational advantages for the town in which he resided He learned the hatter's trade, and dealt extensively in wool and furs. April 4, 1833, Mr. Mestrezat married Miss Martha Hall, daughter of Lemuel and Sarah (Grove) Hall. Her parents were natives of Delaware, and of Scotch-Irish and German origin To Mr. and Mrs. Mestrezat were born six children, four of whom are living—John A., a carpenter; Mary A , wife of B F. Mercer; Aline A., wife of William W. Shaffer, and Caroline A. Charles Alexander, the oldest son, was educated in Morgantown, W. Va. He enlisted in Company E, Fourteenth Pennsylvania Cavalry, and was captured at the battle of White Sulphur Springs, August 27, 1863, while in active service for his country. He was taken to Belle Isle, Richmond, and from there was removed to Hospital No 21 in Richmond, where he died March 27, 1864. Mr. Frederic Mestrezat was a Republican in politics. He was an earnest and faithful worker in the Sabbath-school and for the church, although he did not unite with the church until a short time before his death, when he became a member of the Presbyterian Church of Greensboro, where his wife had been a faithful member since her youth.

ROBERT MILLIKIN was born in Ireland in 1773, and died in 1869. He came to America in 1794, and took up a tract of about 800 acres of land, situated six miles northwest of Waynesburg, on Brown's Fork of South Ten-Mile Creek. Nearly all of the upper end of Greene County was at that time covered with forests Mr. Millikin was a farmer by occupation, and was one of the substantial citizens among the early settlers of this county. He held the office of county commissioner, and was the master builder of the first brick court-house in Greene County. At the age of twenty-four he married Miss Mary, daughter of Lindsey Gray, of this county, and aunt of the late Dr. D. W. Gray, who for many years was in successful practice at Jacksonville, Richhill Township. At their wedding the principal feature in the marriage feast was a young fat bear which had been caught in the neighborhood. There were born to them six children, and their son David, who married Miss Lydia Rogers, was the father of thirteen children. The youngest of these is Dr J. L. Millikin, of Greensboro, one of the leading physicians of the county. Dr. Millikin was born in Greene County, six miles north of Waynesburg, June 24, 1854 He received his early education in the district schools, and afterwards attended Waynesburg College. He was a successful teacher in the public schools for several years, and began the study of medicine with Dr W. S. Throckmorton at Nineveh, Penn , in 1873, and subsequently took the regular course in the Jefferson Medical College at Philadelphia, graduating at that institution in March, 1878. He then practiced with Dr. Throckmorton for nearly two years, when he located at Carmichaels, Penn., and during one year of his residence there was in equal partnership with Dr. J.

B. Laidley, of that place In 1884 Dr Millikin located at Greensboro, Penn., where his professional skill and genial disposition soon won for him a large practice in the town and surrounding country. The Doctor is an active member of the Greene County Medical Society, and served one term as its president. He is a permanent member of the State Medical Society of Pennsylvania, and belongs to the I. O. O. F. and R. A. He is examining surgeon for three insurance companies and for the Royal Arcanum He has a special fondness for surgery, and has performed several difficult operations. He frequently contributes articles to the medical journals, and is a strong advocate of the temperance cause. November 30, 1883, Dr. Millikin married Miss Anna, daughter of James Scott, of this county. They have one child—Joseph Pancoast

OTHO W. MINOR, farmer and stock-grower, Greensboro, Penn , was born in Greene Township, this county, January 22, 1830. He is a son of John and Melinda (Lantz) Minor, natives of Greene County, and of English descent. His father, who followed the blacksmith's trade in early life, was in later years a farmer and merchant miller, owning and operating a grist-mill for many years in this county. He died in 1881, leaving a family of five children, viz: Frances, Mary, William, Rebecca A , and Otho, who is the second in the family. He was reared on the farm, attended the common schools, and has made farming his occupation through life. In 1859 Mr. Minor married Miss Lucinda, daughter of Hiram and Elizabeth (Hunt) Stephens. Mrs. Minor is of English and Irish descent. They have a family of five children—Sylvanus K , John W., Ellsworth, Sarepta, and Viola (deceased). Mr. Minor is a Democrat, and he and wife are leading members in the Baptist Church.

JOHN S. MINOR, carpenter and contractor, Mapletown, Penn., was born in Monongahela Township, Greene County, Penn., March 5, 1859. His parents, William and Martha (Robinson) Minor, were natives of this county, and of English descent. His father, who was a farmer by occupation, was killed by the falling of a tree, January 5, 1875. John S is the oldest of a family of four children. He was reared on the home farm and received a common-school education. He remained at home with his parents until he was sixteen years of age, when he learned the carpenter's trade and has since followed it as an occupation. He was united in marriage, March 10, 1878, with Miss Flora, daughter of Dissisiway and Maria (Maple) South, who were of English and German origin. Mr. and Mrs. Minor have three children—Myrtie, Walter T. and Willie Ray. Mr. Minor is a Democrat in politics, and in religion a Methodist, of which church his wife is also a devoted member.

T. F. PENNINGTON, merchant, Greensboro, Penn., was born in Brownsville, Penn., June 11, 1853. He is a son of A. C. and

Martha D. (Fall) Pennington, who were natives of Pennsylvania and
of English descent. His father was for several years a silversmith
and justice of the peace in Greensboro, where he located in 1868.
He also served as burgess of the borough. His family consisted of
nine children, eight of whom are living. The subject of this sketch
is the third, and was reared at Brownsville, where he received a good
English education. Early in life he learned the tinner's trade, in
which he engaged at Greensboro. In 1878 he bought the Greensboro
foundry, which he has since operated in connection with a stove and
tin-ware store. In 1887 he procured a patent for a new kind of fire
front, which seems to prove quite a success. Mr. Pennington was
married at Grafton, W. Va., in 1884, to Miss Mattie, daughter of
Nathan and Catharine Means, who are of English descent. Mr.
Pennington is a Democrat, and in 1888 was elected burgess of
Greensboro. He is a member of the Royal Arcanum, and a strong
advocate of the temperance cause. His wife is president of the
Greensboro W. C. T. U. They are both members of the Methodist
Episcopal Church, in which he is steward and Sabbath-school super-
intendent.

J. Y. PROVINS, retired farmer, Greensboro, Penn., was born
in Monongahela Township, this county, in 1813. He is a son of
Benjamin Provins, who was a soldier in the war of 1812 and died
soon after its close. Mr. Provins was reared on the farm by his
grandfather, who was a soldier in the Revolutionary war, and a pioneer farmer of Fayette County, Penn. The Provins family were
strong, courageous and patriotic, and ever ready to respond to the
country's call for help. Mr. Provins' grandfather, James Hartly,
was for many years a prominent citizen of this county. The subject
of this sketch attended school in the old log school-house for a few
months in winter. He chose farming as his occupation and has met
with marked success. He has made his way in the world unaided,
his success being due largely to his business ability. He began as
a farm laborer working by the month or day, but is now the owner
of 300 acres of valuable land. Mr. Provins was united in marriage,
in 1834, with Miss Melinda, daughter of John and Catharine (Knife)
Sterling, of German origin. She died in 1884. Mr. Provins, who is a
Democrat, manifests great interest in the educational affairs of his
township and has served as a member of the school board.

SILAS ROSS, farmer and stock-grower, Greensboro, Penn., was
born in Dunkard Township, this county, June 27, 1843. He is a
son of Bowen and Anna (Gantz) Ross, who were of Scotch-Irish
descent. His father, who was a farmer all his life, was a native of
Fayette County and died in Greene County in 1880. His family
consisted of twelve children, all but two of whom grew to maturity.
Silas was the seventh in the family and was reared in Dunkard Town-

ship, where he attended the common schools. He chose farming as his business, and at present is the owner of 110 acres of well improved land where he resides. In 1868 Mr. Ross married Bunnie V., daughter of Alfred and Jane (Evans) Myers, and they are the parents of two children—Robert C. and Alfred M. Mr. Ross is a Republican. He takes a great interest in educational matters and has served on the school board in his district. Mr. and Mrs. Ross are zealous members of the Baptist Church.

ELI N. TITUS, farmer and stock-grower, Greensboro, Penn., was born in Dunkard Township, Greene County, Penn., January 22, 1844. He is a son of Eli and Sarah (Myers) Titus, natives of this county and among the families most noted in its history. Mr. Titus is the seventh in a family of eleven children. His parents reside in Dunkard Township, on the farm where Eli was reared and attended the district schools. He also took a thorough course of instruction in Iron City College at Pittsburg, Penn., and graduated in 1863. He then enlisted in the Fourteenth Pennsylvania Cavalry and was assigned to Company E of the One Hundred and Sixty-ninth Regiment. During his service with this regiment Mr. Titus was in forty battles and skirmishes, and at different times narrowly escaped death. He served as a non-commissioned officer, quartermaster-sergeant, and was discharged by general order at the close of the war. In 1866 Mr. Titus married Miss Miranda, daughter of John and Leah (Keener) Durr. Her father was a native of Fayette and her mother of Greene County, and they were of German origin. A year after his marriage Mr. Titus went to West Virginia and engaged in farming and stock dealing. In 1870 he returned to Greene County, Penn., and continued in the same business in which he has met with great success. His farm is well stocked and improved and his house is one of the most substantial in the county. He owns 245 acres of land in Dunkard and Monongahela townships. Mr. Titus is a Republican in politics, and was once sent as a senatorial delegate from Greene and Fayette counties to the Republican State Convention. He is also a member of the G. A. R. of Greensboro. The family are members of the Baptist Church, in which Mr. Titus takes an active interest and is one of the trustees of the Greensboro Baptist Church.

E. L. TITUS, farmer and stock-grower, Greensboro, Penn., was born in Dunkard Township, Greene County, Pennsylvania, December 26, 1845, and is a son of Eli and Sarah (Myers) Titus. His grandparents, Peter and Pleasant (Corbly) Myers, were among the earliest settlers of Greene County. His ancestors were of English descent and usually farmers by occupation. Mr. E. L. Titus is the eighth in a family of eleven children. He was reared in Greene County, attending the common schools in Dunkard Township. He afterwards spent some time at the State Normal School at California,

Penn. He made choice of farming and stock-growing as an occupation and has made it the business of his life. In 1875 Mr. Titus married Elizabeth Jane, daughter of Jesse Steele. Mrs. Titus is of English and Irish descent. They have a family of four children, viz., Arcy V., Oscar V., Scott and Charles Eli. In politics Mr. Titus is a Republican.

J. D. WELTNER, a farmer and stock-grower of Monongahela Township, this county, was born February 23, 1824, and is a son of John and Elizabeth (Dunaway) Weltner. His parents were natives of Greene County, Pennsylvania, and of Dutch and English descent. His father, who was also a farmer and stock-dealer, was twice married. J. D. Weltner was the second child by the first marriage and was reared on the home farm, attending the common schools of Greene and Fayette counties. He chose farming as a business and also dealt in stock to some extent. He spent two winters in this business in Pittsburg, Penn., and met with marked success. Mr. Weltner has also proved a success as a farmer and his children own 380 acres of well improved land in Monongahela Township, where he has resided since 1856. Here he always keeps a number of cattle, usually sending fifty or seventy-five head to the markets each year. In 1854 Mr. Weltner was united in marriage with Miss Margaret, daughter of William and Catharine (Robinson) Gray, natives of this county. Her father was a wealthy and influential business man and succeeded in accumulating a handsome fortune. To Mr. and Mrs. Weltner were born seven children, viz., Charles W., Daisie, Minnie, Perlie and Eunice Ann, and two deceased. In politics Mr. Weltner is a Republican. His wife died in 1882, a faithful member of the Presbyterian Church.

BENJAMIN G. WILLIAMS, farmer and stock-grower, Greensboro, Penn., was born March 19, 1863, and is a son of Charles and Melissa (Johnston) Williams, who were of Scotch and English extraction. His father, a farmer and speculator, who was born in 1835, died in 1885 at Greensboro, where he spent the last nineteen years of his life. Mrs. Williams died in 1878. They were the parents of three children—Hattie M., Laura May, wife of George C. Steele, a merchant of Morgantown, W. Va., and Benjamin, the subject of our sketch. He first attended school in Greensboro, and spent some time in the West Virginia University. He is registered as a law student at Waynesburg, Penn., and is pursuing his studies. Early in life Mr. Williams engaged in the drug business—first in Greensboro, then in Dunbar, Fayette County, where he remained three years. At his father's death he was appointed administrator of the estate. He has carefully looked after the farm of 200 acres and valuable coal mines, and is at present engaged in building a railway from the farm to the river, in order to ship the coal more conveniently. Mr. Williams is a Democrat in politics, and one of the most enterprising and successful young men of the county.

MORGAN TOWNSHIP.

JOSEPH ADAMSON, merchant, Lippincott, Penn., was born in Greene County, Penn, August 1, 1843. His parents were Thomas and Mary (Hoge) Adamson, the former deceased. In 1866, March 24, Joseph Adamson married Mary E. Bell, who was born in Morgan Township, July 19, 1849. She is a daughter of Henry and Deborah (Adamson) Bell. Her father is a resident of Washington County. Mrs Bell died April 15, 1886. To Mr. and Mrs. Adamson have been born eight children, four living—Maggie H., wife of J. L. Pyle, of Waynesburg; John B, Henry L. and Letitia D. The deceased are William T., James L. and two infants. Mr. Adamson was reared on a farm and engaged in farming until 1881, at which time he began merchandising in Morgan Township. In addition to his large general store, he owns fifty acres of land where he and his family reside. He and wife are descendants of pioneer families of this county.

SMITH ADAMSON, farmer, P. O. Lippincott, was born in Franklin Township, this county, October 5, 1850, and is a son of Thomas and Mary Adamson (*nee* Hoge). His father was born in Greene County, October 5, 1816, and his mother in Centre Township, September 9, 1818. They were married December 24, 1840, in the same house where the widow resides. Mr. Adamson died February 14, 1856. They were the parents of five children—all of whom are living, except John, the eldest, who died October 23, 1863, in the State of Alabama, while in the service of his country during the Rebellion. The subject of this sketch was united in marriage, October 12, 1875, with Sarah M. Randolph. She was born in Jefferson Township, February 4, 1856, and is a daughter of James and Elizabeth (Braden) Randolph, residents of Franklin Township. Mr. and Mrs. Adamson are the parents of four children—Walter, Laura, and Thomas, living; and Nora, deceased Mr. Adamson, who is an enterprising and successful farmer and stock dealer, owns a good farm of 142 acres Mr. and Mrs. Adamson are faithful members of the Baptist Church.

J R BELL, farmer, Jefferson, Penn , was born in Morgan Township, this county, April 12, 1836. His parents were Morgan and Mary Bell (*nee* Richards). His father was also a native of Morgan Township. He was born December 24, 1808. Mrs Bell was born in Chester County, Penn , March 14, 1804 They were married in Greene County, where they remained until Mrs. Bell's death, April 8, 1878, Her husband died February 5, 1880. They were the parents of eight children, four of whom are living. J R Bell is the fifth, and was united in marriage, September 3, 1863, with Miss Helen Davis, born in Greene Township, this county, August 23, 1839. She is a daughter of Henry J and Amelia (Myers) Davis. Mr Davis was born in Jefferson Township, September 27, 1800, and his wife was born in Greene Township, October 22, 1814. They were married in this county, where they remained until the death of Mr Davis, November 6, 1862. His widow died at the home of her daughter in Morgan Township, April 9, 1871. To Mr and Mrs Davis were born three children, two now living   Mr. and Mrs. Bell have three children Maggie A , wife of W. K Scott; Mary E and Henry D Mr. Bell was raised on a farm and received valuable instructions from his father in the art of husbandry, which he has made his occupation through life. He acquired his education in the common schools and Waynesburg College, and engaged in teaching for a few years He filled the office of auditor of the county one year, under the old constitution; was re-elected and served three years under the new   Mr. Bell and family are consistent members of the Baptist Church.

B F BELL, farmer, Lippincott, Penn., was born in Morgan Township, this county, February 20, 1840, and is a son of Henry and Deborah (Adamson) Bell. His parents were natives of Greene County, where they were married and remained until Mrs Bell's death, April 15, 1886. Mr. Bell subsequently married Marinda Spriggs (*nee* Keys), and they now reside in Washington County. He is the father of four children. B F. is the oldest of the three living He was united in marriage, February 10, 1867, with Mary E. Adamson, who was born in Franklin Township, this county, August 27, 1846. Mrs Bell is a daughter of Thomas and Sarah (Hoge) Adamson, natives of Greene County. Her mother is now deceased. To Mr. and Mrs. Bell have been born three children—Clementine, Samanthia and William. Mr Bell was raised on a farm, and has engaged in farming from the time he first started out in life. He owns ninety-five acres of good land where he and family reside. He served his country in the late Rebellion, in Company B, Pennsylvania Heavy Artillery. Mr. and Mrs. Bell are faithful members of the Baptist Church.

S. H. BRADEN, farmer, P O Lippincott, is a native of Morgan Township, Greene County, Penn., where he was born June 7, 1831. His parents were William and Rachel (House) Braden. His father was born in Washington County, and his mother in Greene, where they were married and made their home until Mrs. Braden's death, in 1838. Her husband afterwards married Nancy Douglas, who died in 1842 Mr. Braden married for his third wife, Miss Margaret Gibson, who departed this life in 1881. Mr. Braden still resides in Franklin Township, this county. In 1856 Samuel H. Braden married Charlotte (Huss) Adamson, who was born in Greene County, May 16, 1826. She is a daughter of David and Delilah (Rinehart) Huss, natives of Washington and Greene counties, respectively After marriage they settled in Greene County and remained until the death of Mr. Huss in 1871. Mrs. Huss then went West on a visit, where she died in 1876. Mr. Braden is the father of four children— Albert, who married Anna Shriver; Eva, Smith and Lizzie. Mr. Braden is one of the substantial and enterprising citizens of Morgan Township. He owns 140 acres of land where he and family reside. Mrs Braden is a consistent member of the Baptist Church.

HENRY BUCKINGHAM, farmer, Clarksville, Penn., was born in Washington County, Penn., December 19, 1809. He is a son of Isaac and Hannah (Heaton) Buckingham. His father was born in Washington County, and his mother in Greene County, where they were married. They settled in Washington County, where they remained until their death. Mr. Buckingham died in 1833 and his widow in 1846. They were the parents of eight children, two living— Hannah, wife of John A. Greenlee; and Henry, the subject of our sketch. He was united in marriage, December 25, 1833, with Mary Morton, who was born in Washington County, October, 18, 1814. Mrs. Buckingham's father, Thomas Morton, was a native of Washington County, and her mother, Mary (Cree) Morton, was born in Greene County, where they died—Mr. Morton December 2, 1869, and his widow, June 6, 1880. To Mr. and Mrs. Buckingham have been born six children, five living—Isaac, Elizabeth, wife of Stephen Morton; Thomas O., Robert, Francis J., and Isabella J. (deceased). Mr. Buckingham was reared on a farm, and has been engaged in farming and stock dealing all his life. He and his son Isaac own 143 acres of land where the family reside. Mr. and Mrs. Buckingham are leading members in the Cumberland Presbyterian Church.

A. S. BURSON, merchant, Clarksville, Penn., is a descendant of one of the pioneers of that village, where he was born November 16, 1837. He is a son of Edward C. and Maria Burson (nee Stewart). The former was born in Columbiana County, Ohio, April 20, 1815, and the latter in Millsboro, Washington County, Penn., April 3, 1815. His parents were married June 7, 1836, in Clarksville, where they settled and remained until their death. Mrs. Burson died July 23, 1874, and her husband January 19, 1880. Of their six children, A. S is the oldest. He was united in marriage Decem-

ber 19, 1866, with Mary A. Greenlee, who was born in Washington
County September 11, 1839. She is a daughter of John and Mary
(Balentine) Greenlee, the latter deceased. Mr. and Mrs. Burson
have three children, two living—Harry L. and May; William S.,
deceased. Mr. Burson was reared in Clarksville, and early in life
began merchandising with his father. He has continued in that
business all his life, with the exception of five years in which he
learned and worked at the carpenter trade. He owns a general store
in Clarksville. He has filled the offices of auditor and school director of his township, and has served as postmaster for about six
years. He has been a member of the Masonic fraternity for twenty-
seven years. Mrs. Burson is a consistent member of the Methodist
Episcopal Church.

CEPHAS CARY, retired farmer, Clarksville, Penn., is one of
the pioneer farmers of Greene County. He was born in Washington Township, August 6, 1812. His parents, Able and Eunice Cary,
(nee Woodruff), were natives of this county, where they were married and resided until their death. Mr. Cary died in 1820. Mrs.
Cary was afterwards united in marriage with John McGinnis. She
departed this life in 1833. Cephas Cary was united in marriage
January 11, 1844, with Mary Mitchener, who was born in Jefferson
Borough October 8, 1820. She is a daughter of Mercena and Mary
(Black) Mitchener, the former a native of West Virginia and the
latter of Maryland. They were married in Greene County, Penn.,
where they spent the remainder of their lives. Mrs. Mitchener died
May 5, 1859, and Mr. Mitchener April 15, 1880. To Mr. and Mrs.
Cary have been born five children, four living—Lizzie M., Sophrona,
wife of Daniel Hoover; Mercena M. and Jesse W., and Sarah J.
(deceased), who was the wife of Hiram Baker. Mr. Cary is a cabinet-
maker by trade, but after marriage he engaged in farming. He
owns 100 acres of land, besides valuable property in Clarksville.
Mr. and Mrs. Cary are consistent members of the Methodist Episcopal Church; also each one of their children. J. W. is a minister
laboring in the Pittsburg Conference.

JOHN CLAYTON, deceased, farmer and stock-dealer, Lippincott, Penn., was born in Morgan Township, Greene County, June
27, 1826. He is a son of William and Sarah Clayton (nee Mickins),
who were natives of this county, where they resided until their
death. William Clayton was born December 30, 1796, and died
February 1, 1851. His wife was born January 15, 1798, and departed this life October 12, 1869. They were the parents of ten
children, three daughters and seven sons, of whom John is the
oldest. He was united in marriage January 20, 1853, with Miss
Elizabeth, daughter of Hugh and Priscilla (Hoge) Montgomery.
Mrs. Clayton was born in Morgan Township, October 14, 1833. Her

father, who was a native of Harford County, Maryland, was one of the early settlers of Morgan Township, Greene County, Penn. He died in June, 1882. His widow is a native of this county, and resides in Waynesburg, Penn. Mr. John Clayton and wife are' the parents of four children, two deceased—Priscilla and Samuel; and two living, Sarah A, wife of Benjamin F. Lippencott; and Maria, wife of J. L. Corbett. Mr. and Mrs. Corbett are the parents of five children. Mr. Clayton was raised on a farm, and owned at the time of his death, which occurred June 23, 1888, 400 acres of land in Morgan Township where the family lived He has served his county as auditor one term, and was a member of the Masonic fraternity and I. O. O. F. Mrs Clayton is a faithful member of the Baptist Church.

JOHN B. COX, farmer and stock-grower, Jefferson, Penn., was born in Morgan Township, this county, August 17, 1824. He is a son of Jesse and Dorcas (Bell) Cox, also natives of Morgan Township, where they were married and remained through life. Mr. Jesse Cox died in Greene County, Maryland, in 1826, and was buried in that State. His widow, who was afterwards married to Thomas Patterson, died in Iowa, while on a visit to her daughters in 1872. Mr. Patterson died near Carmichaels, Penn. John B, the subject of this sketch, was two years old when his father died. He lived with his grandfather, John Bell, until twenty-one years of age. He was then united in marriage April 17, 1845, with Maria Crayne, who was born in Morgan Township, April 29, 1825. Her parents were Samuel and Mary (Huss) Crayne, deceased. Mr. and Mrs. Cox are the parents of eight children, six of whom are living—Mary A, wife of T. C. Buckingham; Samuel C., Dorcas L., widow of Adam Horn; Emeline, wife of Joseph Gordon; Stephen and Frank. The deceased are John B. and Calvin. Mr. Cox was raised on a farm, and has been greatly prospered in his farming and stock-raising for many years. He owns 380 acres of fine land on Castile. He is a member of the I. O. O. F.

MILLER CRAYNE, farmer, Lippincott, Penn., who was born in Morgan Township April 22, 1817, is a son of Samuel and Mary Crayne (nee Huss). His mother was a native of Maryland, and his father was born in Greene County, Penn., where they were married and spent the remainder of their lives Mr. Samuel Crayne departed this life October 27, 1853, and his wife June 14, 1865. They were the parents of ten children, eight living. Miller is the third, and was united in the holy bonds of matrimony May 14, 1840, with Miss Lucinda Bell. Mrs. Crayne was born in Greene County January 18, 1821 She is a daughter of John and Ann (Cox) Bell, also natives of this county, where they departed this life—Mrs. Bell in 1871, and Mr. Bell in 1880 Mr. and Mrs. Crayne are the parents of four children, two of whom are living—Louisa, wife of Dr. Silveus Smith; and John B., who married Martha A. Lippencott. Elmey and an infant are deceased. Mr. Crayne was raised on a farm, and has been an industrious tiller of the soil all his life. He owns eighty acres of improved land where he and family live. Mr. and Mrs. Crayne are consistent members of the Baptist Church.

STEPHEN CRAYNE, farmer, Jefferson, Penn., is one of the pioneer farmers of Greene County, and was born in Washington, Township, January 4, 1813. He is a son of Samuel and Mary (Huss) Crayne, the oldest of their ten children. The subject of our sketch was united in the holy bonds of matrimony, March 18, 1834, with Miss Mary Bell, who was born in Morgan Township, May 26, 1816. Her parents were Isaac and Elizabeth (Herrod) Bell, natives of Greene County, where they remained until their death. Mr. and Mrs. Crayne are the parents of six children, four of whom are living— Isaac B., Rachel, wife of James Fulton; David, Anna M., wife of George Hughes, and Caroline and Martha, deceased. Mr. Crayne was reared on a farm. He is one of the best known and most industrious farmers in the township, and owns a good farm of 157 acres. Mr. and Mrs. Crayne are faithful members of the Baptist Church.

DAVID CRAYNE, farmer, Waynesburg, Penn., was born in Morgan Township, February 2, 1818. His parents were Samuel and Mary (Huss) Crayne. The former was a native of Greene County, and the latter of Maryland. They were the parents of ten children— four boys and six girls—of whom eight are living. David is the fourth in the family, and was united in marriage, December 8, 1841, with Caroline Harry. Mrs. Crayne was born in Morgan Township, March 8, 1825. Her parents, Jacob and Catharine (Buskirk) Harry, were natives of eastern Pennsylvania. They were married in Greene County, where they remained until their death. To Mr. and Mrs. Crayne have been born eight children, six of whom are living— Samuel, Jacob, Emily A., Thomas, Stephen and Joseph. The deceased were Martha and Mary C. Mr. Crayne was reared on a farm, and has been successful as a farmer and stock-dealer through life. He owns 276 acres of land where he and family reside. Mr. and Mrs. Crayne are members of the Methodist Protestant Church. He also belongs to the I. O. O. F.

SAMUEL FULTON, farmer, P. O. Castile, was born January 10, 1818, on the farm where he and family reside in Morgan Township. John Fulton, his father, was a native of Virginia, and his mother, Isabella (Barr) Fulton, was born in Ireland. They were married in Washington County, Penn., afterwards settling in Greene County, on the farm now owned by Samuel, where they remained through life. Only two of their nine children are living. In 1836

Samuel Fulton married Harriet Huss, a native of this county, and daughter of John and Elizabeth (Eaton) Huss. Mrs. Harriet Fulton died in the same year in which she was married. In 1838 Mr. Fulton was again united in marriage, his second wife being Miss Louellen McClelland, who was born in Washington Township, this county, in 1818. Her parents were John and Nancy (Montgomery) McClelland, deceased. Mr Fulton is the father of eleven children, nine of whom are living—Eliza, Isabella, wife of Clark Denney; Cerry, James, Nancy, wife of James Tharp; Evan, Henrietta, wife of George Weaver; L Herrod and William. The deceased are Albert . and John. We take pleasure in mentioning Mr. Fulton among the pioneers of Morgan Township. He was raised on a farm, and after his second marriage moved to Richland County, Ohio. Remaining there about nine years, he returned to Morgan Township, Greene County, Penn., where he owns a nice farm of 245 acres. Mr. and Mrs. Fulton are consistent members of Cumberland Presbyterian Church.

JAMES GREENLEE, farmer, P. O. Castile, Penn., was born in Washington County, Penn., November 11, 1818, and is a son of Samuel and Nancy Greenlee (*nee* Gantz). His parents were natives of Fayette County, Penn., but moved to Washington County, Penn., where they remained until death. On March 25, 1851, Mr. Green-lee married Catharine Bell, a native of Greene County, and daughter of Levi H. and Sarah Bell (*nee* Fulton) By this marriage Mr. Greenlee is the father of five children, four living—James L, Margaret, wife of Abraham Burson; Samuel B. and William—and Levi, (deceased). Their mother died in 1863. In 1865 Mr. Green-lee married Catharine Fulton, a native of Washington County, and daughter of Stephen and Ruth Fulton (*nee* Cary). James and Mrs. Catharine Greenlee are the parents of three children, two living—Lewis and John B —and Stephen, (deceased). Mrs Greenlee died in 1882. On October 6, 1887, Mr. Greenlee married for his third wife, Eliza Armstrong (*nee* Gregg), daughter of Alfred Gregg. Mr. Greenlee was reared on a farm, and has made farming his business through life. He owns 164 acres of land where and family reside. His present wife and both the deceased were devoted members of the church

JAMES GREENLEE, farmer, P. O. Clarksville, was born in Greene County, Penn., November 2, 1841. He is a son of John and Mary Greenlee (*nee* Balentine). His mother was a native of Scotland. His father was born in Washington County, Penn, where they were married. They afterwards settled in Greene County, where Mr. Greenlee has since remained. Mrs. Greenlee died in September, 1855. His second wife was Eliza J. Cain. Mr. James Greenlee was united in the holy bonds of matrimony, January 10,

1871, with Mary E Arnold, who was born in Washington County, December 27; 1847. Mrs. Greenlee is a daughter of Michael and Harriet (Miller) Arnold, who reside in Clarksville. To Mr and Mrs. James Greenlee have been born two children—Ida V., born March 6, 1875; and John C., who was born June 15, 1872, and died December 11 of the same year. Mr. Greenlee was reared on a farm, and has made farming his business through life. He owns sixty acres of land in Morgan Township, and valuable property in Clarksville. He and wife are consistent members of the Cumberland Presbyterian Church

HENRY GRIMES, farmer and stock-dealer, Lippincott, Penn, —Among the representative business men of Greene County, we take pleasure in giving the sketch of Henry Grimes, who was born in Centre Township, this county, September 4, 1820 He is a son of Peter and Mary (Sharon) Grimes The former was born in New Jersey, February 17, 1789, and the latter near Baltimore, Maryland, February 5, 1786. They were married in Greene County where they remained through life Four of their five children are now living. Henry Grimes was united in marriage, March 27, 1846, with Nancy McClelland, born in Washington Township, February 1, 1823, and a daughter of John and Nancy McClelland (nee Montgomery). To Mr. and Mrs Grimes have been born five children, four living—Caleb, Carey, who married Lizzie S Sellers, Samuel, who married Clara Adams; Mary E., wife of Samuel C. Hawkins, and Sarah J. (deceased). Mrs. Grimes departed this life September 18, 1873, a consistent member of the Baptist Church. Mr. Grimes was reared on a farm, and owns about 1,500 acres of land, 812 acres of which are in Greene County. When sixteen years of age, Mr. Grimes received $300, in gold from his father, and by means of industry and careful management in his farming and stock-dealing has accumulated quite a handsome fortune, being considered one of the wealthiest men in Greene County.

C. C. HARRY, farmer, Jefferson, Penn., was born September 13, 1831, in the house where he and his family live in Morgan Township He is a son of Jacob and Catharine Harry (nee Van Buskirk) The former was a native of Chester and the latter of Northampton County, Penn They were married in Greene County, where they departed this life—Mr Harry in 1834, and Mrs. Harry December 1, 1859 They were the parents of five children, of whom C. C. is the youngest. In 1857 Mr Harry married Martha Houlsworth, a native of Greene County, and daughter of Hugh C. and Isabella Houlsworth, deceased By this marriage Mr Harry is the father of four children, two of whom are living—Catharine, wife of Andrew Rich, and Belle The deceased are Emma and James. Their mother died March 4, 1868 Mr. Harry afterwards married

Elizabeth Bayard, October 11, 1877, she was born in Whiteley Township, November 26, 1844, and is a daughter of John S. and Malinda Bayard (nee Leonard) They were natives of this county, where they remained until Mrs. Bayard's death, March 26, 1883. Mr. Bayard is still living Mr. and Mrs. Harry are the parents of two children —Charles C. and John B. Mr Harry has been very successful in his farming and stock-dealing, and owns 325 acres of excellent land. He is a members of the I O. O. F. Mrs Harry belongs to the .Presbyterian Church, of which the deceased wife was also a devoted member.

WILLIAM HATFIELD, farmer, Morgan Township, Penn , was born in Whiteley Township, this county, February 4, 1848 His parents, George W. and Mary (Richie) Hatfield, are both living and reside in Whiteley Township February 8, 1872, William Hatfield married Mary J. McClure, a native of Dunkard Township. Mrs. Hatfield was born September 2. 1843, and is a daughter of James and Susan (Brown) McClure. Mr. McClure died August 8, 1886; his widow is still living. Mr. and Mrs. Hatfield are the parents of two children—Ida L , born March 9, 1873, and Sudie M., born July 24, 1876. Mr. Hatfield was reared on a farm, and has been engaged in farming and stock-dealing through life. He owns about 163 acres of land where he and his family reside Mr. Hatfield has been greatly prospered in his business, and is one of the leading citizens in his community. Mrs. Hatfield is a faithful member of the Baptist Church.

JOHN C. HAWKINS, farmer, Zollarsville, Penn., was born in Greene County, Penn., December 15, 1825, in the house now occupied by himself and family. He is a son of Richard and Cynthia Hawkins (nee Crawford). His father was born in Maryland, and his mother in Fayette County, Penn. They were married in Washington County where they remained until 1814, at which time they moved to Greene County and remained until their death. Mrs. Hawkins departed this life in July 1845, and her husband February 6. 1856. They were the parents of eleven children, four of whom are living. June 7, 1882, John C. Hawkins married Elizabeth McMurray, who was born in Washington County, December 5, 1846 She is a daughter of James and Catharine (Whitely) McMurray. Her father was a native of Ireland, and her mother was born in Allegheny County, Penn., where they remained a few years, then moved to Washington County Here Mrs. McMurray died November 26, 1866, and Mr. McMurray, March 17, 1875. Mr. Hawkins has been engaged in farming and stock-dealing through life. His farm in Morgan Township contains about 289 acres of land in a high state of cultivation. Mr. and Mrs Hawkins are consistent members of the Baptist Church.

43

R. C. HAWKINS, farmer and stock-dealer, Jefferson, Penn, was born in Morgan Township, this county, November 14, 1814 He is a son of Richard and Cynthia (Crawford) Hawkins. The former was born in Maryland and the latter in Fayette County, Penn. They were united in marriage in Washington County, where they remained a few years then moved to Greene County and spent the rest of their lives   Mrs. Cynthia Hawkins departed this life in July 1845, and Mr. Hawkins in February, 1856   The subject of this sketch was united in marriage November 25, 1841, with Emeline Wise, who was born in Washington County, November 28, 1820. Her parents were Frederick and Elizabeth (Burson) Wise, native of Washington and Greene counties, respectively.   They were married in Greene County, remained a short time, then moved to Washington County where Mr. Wise died in 1877, and Mrs. Wise in 1881. Mr. and Mrs Hawkins are the parents of nine children, of whom seven are now living.   Joseph W., Maggie V., wife of William C. Bailey; Thomas, Clara E., wife of William Bodley; William B, Tressa, wife of Charles T. Harvey, and Samuel C.   The deceased are Frederick W. and James F.   Mr. Hawkins was reared on a farm and has been engaged in farming and stock-dealing all his life.   He owns the fine farm of 280 acres where he and his family reside.   Mr. and Mrs. Hawkins are faithful members of the Cumberland Presbyterian Church.

J. F. HAWKINS, deceased, was born in Morgan Township, Greene County, Pennsylvania, April 13, 1845, and died May 1, 1888.   He was a son of Richard C. and Emeline (Wise) Hawkins His father is a native of this county, and his mother of Washington County, Penn, where they were married   They subsequently removed to Morgan Township, Greene County, where they still reside   J. F. is the third of their large family, and was united in marriage, March 3, 1870, with Anna E. Greenlee.   Mrs. Hawkins was born in Morgan Township, September 10, 1846.   She is a daughter of Jacob and Mary (Spencer) Greenlee, natives of Washington and Greene counties, respectively   They were married in Greene County, where they remained until Mr. Greenlee's death, August 20, 1887; his widow survives him   To Mr and Mrs. Hawkins were born seven children, five of whom are living—Walter R, F. Bernice, Wilber J., Emma M. and Edna B.   Warren K. and an infant are deceased   Mr. Hawkins was reared on a farm.   Like his ancestors, he made farming and stock-dealing the business of his life, owning at the time of his death 200 acres of well improved land where his family now reside.   Mrs. Hawkins and W. R. are consistent members of the Baptist Church.

THOMAS J. HOLDER, farmer, P. O Clarksville, was born in Greene County, Penn., July 27, 1827.   He is a son of Abraham and

Jane (Cree) Holder. The former was born in Virginia and the latter in Greene County, Pennsylvania, where they settled after marriage and remained until their death Mr Abraham Holder died January 9, 1846, and his wife in 1866. They were the parents of seven children, four of whom are living In 1851 Thomas J. Holder married Malinda Cox, who was born in Washington County, Penn, in 1831 Her parents, Andrew and Margaret (Hupp) Cox, were natives of Washington County, where they remained until the death of Mr. Cox. His widow is still living. To Mr. and Mrs. Holder have been born twelve children—Lebenas P., Margaret J., Calvin, Josephus, Permelia, Emma, L. Dora, Lizzie, Elmer, Laura, Charlie and William Although a farmer by occupation, Mr. Holder is also quite a genius in his way, and can accomplish almost any kind of work he undertakes. He owns 131 acres of land, on which are good substantial buildings. He has filled the office of auditor of his township, has served as school directors, and is also a member of the Masonic fraternity.

O. C. HORNER, farmer, Clarksville, Penn, was born in Fayette County, Penn, March 15, 1839. He is a son of Hiram and Malinda (Reynolds) Horner, the former a native of Fayette County, and the latter of Greene. They were married in this county, but made their home in Fayette until Mr. Horner's death, which occurred in November, 1874. His widow is still living and resides on the old home farm. They were the parents of five children, of whom O C. is the oldest living. He was united in marriage, October 15, 1864, with Amy Cox, born in Jefferson Township, January 2, 1843. Her parents, Christopher and Mary (Rush) Cox, were natives of this county, where they were married and remained through life. Mrs. Cox died in 1857, and her husband in 1861. Of their ten children, three are now living. Mr. and Mrs. Horner are the parents of eight children —James L., Sarah F., Anna M, Cora B., Hiram C, Emma A, William and Oliver G. Mr. Horner was reared on a farm, and makes a business of farming and stock-raising. He owns 170 acres of land where he and family reside. Mrs Horner is a devoted member of the Disciple Church.

HENRY KEYS, farmer, P O. Castile, was born in Morgan Township, Greene County, Penn, June 10, 1837. His parents were David and Mary Keys (nee McGinnis). The former was a native of Washington County, and the latter of Greene County After marriage they settled in Washington County and remained a few years, afterwards removing to Morgan Township, Greene County, where they spent the remainder of their lives. David Keys departed this life in August, 1872, and his widow in August, 1884. They were the parents of ten children, six of whom are living On January 14, 1875, Henry Keys was united in marriage with Amelia Litzenburg, who was born in Morgan Township November 14, 1854. Mr. and Mrs. Keys have an interesting family of children—John R., Mary O., Wesley H., Priscilla R. and George W. Mr. Keys devotes his time principally to farming, and owns 104 acres of fine land where he and family now reside. He enlisted in behalf of his coun-try's cause, in Company F, One Hundred and Fourth Illinois, and served one year. Mr. and Mrs. Keys are faithful members of the Methodist Episcopal Church.

SAMUEL LEWIS, farmer, Castile, Penn., was born on the farm where he and family reside in Morgan Township, this county. His parents were John and Hannah (Arnold) Lewis, who spent all their lives on the farm now occupied by their son. Seven of their nine children survive them. In 1854 Samuel married Martha Blackledge (nee Sharpnack). Her parents were natives of Greene County. Her father was born October 15, 1797, and her mother February 14, 1801. After marriage they settled in Jefferson Township and remained until their death. Mr. Blackledge died November 5, 1870, and his widow April 11, 1876. To Mr. and Mrs. Lewis have been born six chil-dren, three living—Stiers, Margaret and Levi. The deceased are—Mary M., John and Ellsworth. Their mother departed this life in 1863. Mr. Lewis is a farmer by occupation, and owns 325 acres of excellent land. In addition to the care of his land, he has also de-voted considerable time to the raising of stock, and is one of the most prosperous citizens of his township.

SAMUEL MONTGOMERY, farmer, P. O. Lippincott, Penn., is a descendant of one of the old families of Greene County, and was born in Morgan Township, July 17, 1835. He is a son of Hugh and Priscilla (Hoge) Montgomery. His father was a native of Maryland and when but a child came with his parents to Greene County, Penn., where they were united in marriage. They remained in this county until Mr. Montgomery's death, which occurred in 1882. His widow survives him. Mr. Samuel Montgomery was twice married, his first wife being Mary Stentz, a native of Fayette County, and daughter of Thomas Stentz. By this marriage there are two children—Charles, and Anna, who is the wife of Nelson Goslin. Mrs. Montgomery died September 28, 1869. After her death, March 5, 1870, Mr. Mont-gomery married Cyrene Davis (nee Dales), who was born in Wash-ington County January 16, 1837. They are the parents of five children—Mary E., Priscilla, Lizzie, Hugh and John. Mr. Mont-gomery was raised on a farm and received many instructions from his father in the art of husbandry. He owns 130 acres of land where he and family reside. He filled the office of auditor of the county one term. He is a member of the Masonic fraternity. Mrs. Montgomery belongs to the Baptist Church, of which the deceased wife was also a devoted member.

THOMAS H. MONTGOMERY, farmer and stock-dealer, Lippincott, Penn.; was born in Morgan Township January 24, 1847, and is a descendant of one of the pioneer families of Greene County. His father and mother were Hugh and Priscilla (Hoge) Montgomery. The former was born in Maryland and the latter in Greene County, Penn., where they were united in marriage and remained until the father's death, June 14, 1882. His widow survives him. Thomas H. Montgomery was united in marriage, October 17, 1878, with Virginia E. Gordon, who was born in Franklin Township, April 14, 1853. Mrs. Montgomery is a daughter of Bazil and Maria (Inghram) Gordon, natives and residents of this county. Mr. and Mrs. Montgomery are the parents of four children—Walter C., born September 5, 1879; Bernice L., born May 14, 1881; Florence M., born May 5, 1883; and Pauline E., born August 23, 1886. Mr. Montgomery has always lived on a farm, and owns 185 acres of good land where he and family reside. He is a member of the Masonic fraternity, and is filling the office of justice of the peace in his township. He is a Baptist, and has held the office of deacon since 1879, and his wife is a member of the Methodist Protestant Church. Previous to marriage he was a teacher in the public schools.

SAMUEL MURRAY, farmer, P. O. Jefferson, Penn., was born in Fayette County, Penn., January 28, 1822. His father, Jacob Murray, was also a native of Fayette County; and his mother, whose maiden name was Susannah Aukerman, was born in Westmoreland County, where they were married. After marriage they settled in Fayette County and remained until their death—Mr. Murray dying in 1852, and his widow in 1886. They had twelve children, eleven of whom are living. On August 29, 1843, Samuel Murray married Agnes Fulkerth, who was born in Westmoreland County, Penn., October 31, 1821. Her parents were Joseph and Esther Fulkerth (nee Stauffer), deceased. Mr. Murray and wife are the parents of eleven children, seven living—Cyrus, David, Anna, Jennie, Elias A. F., Joseph H. and Isaac G.—and Susannah, Rachel, Jacob and an infant, deceased. Mr. Murray was raised on a farm, and has devoted his time principally to agricultural pursuits.. He owns ninety acres of land where he and family reside. He and wife are faithful members of the Brethren Church.

ABLE McCULLOUGH, retired merchant, Clarksville, Penn., was born in Washington County, Penn., October 18, 1845. He is a son of Aaron and Naomi McCullough (nee Turner). His father was also a native of Washington County, and his mother was born in Greene County. After their marriage they settled in Washington County and remained until their death. They were the parents of four childern, two living—William and Able, the subject of our sketch. He was united in the holy bonds of matrimony, September

17, 1871, with Leah Craig (*nee* Horn), born in Washington County, April 29, 1841 She is a daughter of John and Mary Horn (*née* Shape), residents of Washington County until their death. To Mr. and Mrs McCullough have been born three children—Olin W., Martha E. and Naomi L. Mrs. McCullough, by her first marriage, is the mother of one child—Mary H , wife of Samuel Teagarden. Mr McCullough has made farming and merchandising his business through life He and wife are faithful members of the Methodist Episcopal Church.

J. C. POLLOCK, farmer, was born in Amwell Township, Washington County, Penn ; September 5, 1824 His parents were Thomas and Cynthia (Carter) Pollock. The former was a native of Waynesburg, and the latter of Washington County, where they were married and remained until 1835. They then moved to Greene County, where Mr. Pollock died January 3, 1876 He served as commissioner of the county three years, representative of the county two terms, in 1841 and 1842, and associate judge one term. He and wife were the parents of eleven children, ten of whom are living—nine in this county On November 8, 1854, J C. Pollock was united in marriage with Miss Malissa Ailes, born in Washington County, Penn., January 27 1833 She is a daughter of Stephen and Mary (Nixon) Ailes, the former a native of Washington County, and the latter of Ireland. To Mr. and Mrs. Pollock have been born six children, three living—James M., William P., David L.—and Mary M., Stephen A and an infant, deceased. Mr. Pollock was raised on a farm, and when twenty-one years of age he began merchandising with his father, in which he continued for three years He afterwards served as a clerk four years, then engaged in purchasing stock and grain for a distillery. He worked in this capacity for six years, then engaged in farming and milling He owns fifty acres of land and a half interest in a large flouring-mill. He belongs to the Masonic order, and he and wife are members of the Cumberland Presbyterian Church.

WILLIAM PYLE, hotel-keeper, Clarksville, Penn., was born in Washington County, Pennsylvania, November 10, 1838. He is a son of Joseph and Albenah (Thornburg) Pyle, natives of Pennsylvania. His parents were married in Washington County, where they remained a number of years and then lived in Morgan Township, Greene County, for a short time. In 1858 they returned to Washington County and remained until their death. Mrs. Joseph Pyle departed this life in 1861 Her husband afterwards married Catharine Kenann, who is still living. Mr. Pyle died in 1873. William is the only one of the family in this county In 1859 he married Sarah Yonker, who was born in Washington County, August 10, 1842. Mrs. Pyle is a daughter of Noah and Elizabeth Yonker (*nee*

Watt). Her father was born in Pennsylvania, and her mother in Maryland. They were married in Washington County, Penn., and remained there until Mr. Yonker's death January 9, 1853. His widow remained in Washington County until 1859, at which time she came to Greene County and lived with her daughter, Mrs. William Pyle, until her death, which occurred December 25, 1872, while she was on a visit to Pittsburg, Penn. William Pyle and wife are the parents of eight children—Joseph, Samuel, Frank, Lizzie, Jesse, Emma and William T., living; and Lucy, deceased. Mr. Pyle was reared on a farm, and has devoted almost all his life to farming. He owns property in Clarksville, where he has been proprietor of a hotel for the past two years. He and Mrs. Pyle are faithful members of the Christian Church

W. H. F. RANDOLPH, farmer, Lippincott, Penn, was born in Jefferson Township, this county, July 14, 1836. His parents Abraham F. and Emily A. (Adamson) Randolph, were natives and residents of Greene County until their death. His father died December 8, 1866, and Mrs. Randolph, March 9, 1885. They were the parents of three children, two living—J. A. F. and W. H. F.—and Sarah L., deceased. The subject of this sketch was united in marriage, November 25, 1855, with Mary A. Heaton, who was born Morgan Township, January 28 1834, and died April 30, 1888. She was a daughter of Daniel and Elizabeth (Woods) Heaton, the second of their six children, three of whom are now living. Mr. Heaton was born in Greene County, and Mrs. Heaton in New Jersey. They were married in Greene County, Penn., where they remained until their death Mr. Heaton died August 21, 1856, and his wife January 26, 1877. To Mr. and Mrs. Randolph was born one daughter— Laura L., October 7, 1856. Mr. Randolph was reared on a farm and is a farmer and stock-grower by occupation. He owns a well improved farm of seventy-five acres where he now resides. The family belong to the Baptist Church, of which his deceased wife was also a devoted member.

W. D. ROGERS, physician, Jefferson Penn., was born near Beallsville, Washington County, Penn., April 5, 1816. His parents, Philip and Mary (Johns) Rogers, who were natives of Maryland, came to Washington County, Pennsylvania, about the year 1806, and remained there the rest of their lives. Mrs. Rogers died in 1838. Her husband subsequently married Mary Borom, who departed this life in 1869. Mr. Rogers died in 1870. He was the father of seven children, four of whom are living. Dr. Rogers is the only one of the family in Greene County. He was united in marriage, January 13, 1847, with Charlotte H. Black. Mrs. Rogers was born in Morgan Township, this county, November 26, 1820, and is a devoted member of the Presbyterian Church. Her parents were Honarale and Charlotte (Heaton) Black, who were among the first settlers of the county Dr. and Mrs. Rogers are the parents of five children —Ellen D., wife of H. A. Russell, of Iowa, William B , who married Cora L. Rogers; John A , Mary L and Norval P. The Doctor acquired his education in the common schools of his county and in the academy at Brownsville, Penn. In 1842 he began leading medicine with W. L Wilson, M. D., of Beallsville, Penn In 1835 he gradu ated from the Medical University of Marlyand, at Baltimore Since that time he has been engaged in the practice of his profession, most of which has been in Greene County, where he and family have resided for many years, and where he owns a fine farm of about one hundred and ninety-five acres. During the late Rebellion, Dr Rogers was examining surgeon of the first drafted men from this county, and afterwards appointed examining surgeon for pensioned soldiers. He was a delegate to the National Convention of 1872, at Philadelphia, Penn , which nominated Grant and Wilson for President and Vice-President of the United States.

JOHN ROSE, farmer, Lippincott, Penn., was born in Cumberland Township, this county, August 29, 1832, and is a son of David and Mary (Hewitt) Rose His mother was a native of Washington County, and his father of Greene County, where they were married and remained until their death. After his wife's death, in 1874, Mr. Rose married Eliza Greenlee, who is still living. Mr Rose died May 14, 1879. He was the father of thirteen children, eleven of whom are living. John, who was their second child, was united in marriage, August 27, 1855, with Priscilla A. Litzenburg. Mrs. Rose was born in Washington County, Penn., January 20, 1836. Her parents, William and Charlotte (Rush) Litzenburg, were natives of Greene County, where they resided a short time, then moved to Washington County and remained until their death. Mr. and Mrs. Rose had one child, W. H., born October 6, 1857, and died September 16, 1858. Mr. Rose is a farmer and owns one hundred and sixteen acres of fine land He and wife are zealous members of the Cumberland Presbyterian Church.

JACOB RUSH, farmer, Jefferson, Penn , was born January 27, 1823, on his present farm in Morgan Township, this county. His father, Matthias Rush, was also born on the same farm now owned by Jacob and his mother, Sarah (Iams) Rush, who was a native of St. Charles County, Maryland. They were married in Greene County, Penn., and resided their until their death. Mr Rush died in 1863, and his widow in 1874. They were the parents of two children—Jacob, and William, who married Martha Hughes, and resides in Clarksville, Penn Jacob Rush was united in marriage, November 11, 1846, with Elizabeth Cox, born in Morgan Township, May 13, 1824. Her parents were William and Abigail (Rush) Cox, natives of Greene County, and residents therein until their death. To Mr. and Mrs. Rush have been born four children, viz: Sarah A., wife of Stephen M. Hill; Isabella, wife of A. C. Myers; Micca and Benjamin F., who married Abigail Cox; now deceased. Mr. Rush was reared on a farm, and has been very successful in farming and stock dealing throughout his life. His home farm contains 200 acres of valuable land. Mrs. Rush at the age of sixteen became a member of the Christian Church, to which she was very devoted until her death, December 17, 1887.

JAMES RUSH, deceased, was born in Virginia, in 1770, and came with his parents to Clarksville, Penn., when he was only four years of age. He remained there until his death in 1842. He married Priscilla Case, who was a native of Greene County, and departed this life in 1825. They were the parents of nine children, eight daughters and one son. Only two of these are living—Priscilla and Sarah A., widow of Fletcher Allman, who was born near Clarksville in 1812. Mr. and Mrs. Allman were the parents of seven children. Mr. Allman departed this life February 10, 1877. James Rush was a farmer during his lifetime, and at one time owned 1,300 acres of land, of which the Allman heirs own 135 acres. Miss Priscilla Rush lives with her nephew Fletcher Allman, in Clarksville, Penn., where she owns nice property. She comes of a highly respected family, and is greatly esteemed by a wide circle of friends.

W. B. STEWART, farmer, Clarksville, Penn., was born in Millsboro, Washington County, Penn., June 26, 1818. His parents, Alexander and Elizabeth (Metzlar) Stewart, were natives of Franklin County, Penn., where they were married. They made their home in Fulton County until 1813, then moved to Washington County, and in 1828 came to Greene County, where they remained until their death. Mrs. Stewart died in 1858, and her husband in 1862. They were the parents of eight children, of whom only three are living, viz.: Eliza L., widow of Francis Drake; Melvina, widow of H. P. Hurst; and W. B., the subject of this sketch. He was united in marriage, October 7, 1849, with Elizabeth Wise, who was born in Washington County, May 28, 1823. Her parents, Joseph and Parmelia (Barnard) Wise, were natives of Washington and residents their until their death. Mrs. Wise died in 1852. Mr. Wise subsequently married Julia Welch, who survives him. Mr. Wise died in 1875. Mr. and Mrs. Stewart are the parents of seven children, five living—Joseph W., Elizabeth, wife of William Orr; Emma, wife of William Hoge; William B., Jr. and John C.—and Alexander and Francis, deceased. Mr. Stewart is a tanner by trade, which he followed until twenty-five years of age. After that his time was variously employed until 1851, when he turned his attention to farming, in which he has successfully engaged ever since. He owns 144 acres of land where he and family reside.

He has belonged to the Masonic fraternity for about twenty years, and he and his wife are devoted members of the Baptist Church.

EDWARD VANKIRK, Sr., retired farmer, Jefferson, Penn., was born in Washington County, Penn , October 14, 1813, and is a son of Arthur and Elizabeth (Parkinson) Vankirk. His father was a native of New Jersey, and his mother was born in Pennsylvania, where they were married, settling in Washington County. They remained there until 1835, lived in Greene County seven years, then returned to Washington County, where they remained until Mrs. Vankirk's death in 1847 Mr. Vankirk died in 1865. They were the parents of eight children, three of whom are living—Edward, Ralph and William. Edward was united in marriage, May 21, 1835, with Jane E. Blake, who was a native of Pennsylvania, and daughter of Samuel and Elizabeth (Carr) Blake. By this marriage Mr. Vankirk is the father of six children, only two of whom are living—Elizabeth, widow of W. H Kline; and Emma, wife of A. J. Barr. The deceased are Samuel, William, George and Anna J., who was the wife of Hugh Montgomery, one of the substantial citizens of Morgan Township. -Mrs Vankirk departed this life July 27, 1852, a devoted member of the Christian Church. After her death, December 13, 1853, Mr. Vankirk married Sarah A. Gantz, who was born in Washington County, Penn., March 20, 1829. Her parents were John and Christina Gantz, deceased. Mr. and Mrs Vankirk are the parents of eight children, seven living—David, Edward, Thomas, Clark, Lucy, James, Bertha,—and John F., deceased. Mr. Vankirk was raised on a farm and met with great success as a farmer during his more active life. He owns 160 acres of land in this county, where he and family reside. Mr. and Mrs. Vankirk belong to the Baptist Church.

W. H. VIRGIN, farmer, Clarksville, Penn , was born in Millsboro, Washington County, Penn , November, 17, 1840 He is a son of Jesse and Ophillipphia (Huntsberry) Virgin, the former a native of Fayette County, Pennsylvania, and the latter of Maryland After marriage his parents settled in Greene County, Penn,, subsequently removing to Millsboro, where they remained until Mrs Virgin's death in 1842 Her husband afterwards married Clarinda Hupp, who is still living. Mr. Virgin died in 1880. He was the father of five children, of whom the subject of this sketch is the second. He was united in marriage, December 13, 1864, with Mary A. Anderson, born in Belmont County, Ohio, September 4, 1837. She is a daughter of John R and Maria (Perry) Anderson, the former a native of Greene County, Penn., and the latter of Guernsey County, Ohio. After marriage, Mrs. Virgin's parents settled in Belmont County, Ohio, and remained until Mrs. Anderson's death, in 1855. Mr. Anderson afterwards married Mary Wildman, and they reside in Harrison County, Ohio. To Mr. and Mrs. Virgin have been born four children—Elizabeth R, Lena M., Hannah V. and Jesse A. Mr. Virgin has always lived on a farm, and has made farming the principal occupation of his life. He owns nice property in Clarksville. He is filling the office of jury commissioner of the county, and has served as assessor and constable of his township. He enlisted in the service of his country, in Company D, Eighty-fifth Pennsylvania Volunteers, November 6, 1861, and served over three years, passing through a number of serious engagements. Mr. Virgin is a member of the G. A. R. Post, No. 205. Mrs. Virgin is a faithful member of the Cumberland Presbyterian Church

AMOS WALTON, retired merchant, P. O. Clarksville, was born in Washington County, Penn., October 12, 1807. He is a son of John and Sarah (Paul) Walton, who were also natives of Washington County, and residents therein until their death. Mr. John Walton died October 6, 1834. His widow was afterwards united in marriage with Levi Burson, who died in 1863. Mrs. Burson departed this life in 1874. On March 11, 1830, Amos Walton married Sarah A. Stephenson, who was born in Clarksville in 1813. She is a daughter of Asa and Priscilla (Gregg) Stephenson. To Mr. and Mrs. Walton were born ten children, five of whom are living—Jesse, Louisa, widow of B F. Swan; Priscilla, wife of Dr. James A Sargent; Ellis B. and Isaac N. The deceased are John M., Joseph R, Amos G, Morgan M. and an infant. Though raised on a farm, Mr. Walton began merchandising when starting out in life for himself, and has continued in the business for fifty years. He owns 300 acres of land, and good property in Clarksville. Mr. Walton is an elder in the Cumberland Presbyterian Church, of which he has been a faithful member for forty-four years. Mrs. Walton died May 14, 1875.

HENRY WATSON, farmer, Lippincott, Penn., was born in West Bethlehem Township, Washington County, July 28, 1845. He is a son of John and Mary A. (Almost) Watson. His father was a native of Ireland. His mother was born in Greene County, Penn., where they were married. They afterwards removed to Washington County, and remained until their death. He died September 3, 1856, and she May 27, 1869. September 6, 1866, Henry Watson was united in marriage with Mary A. Weaver, who was born in Washington County, October 17, 1846. She is a daughter of Jacob and Sarah (Register) Weaver, residents of Morgan Township. To Mr. and Mrs. Watson have been born eight children—Jacob W., William H., Charles F., Clara S, John F., Ida B., Lucy A. and Mary E. Mr Watson was reared on a farm, and owns ninety-six acres of fine land where he and family live. He and wife are prominent members of the Baptist Church.

MORRIS TOWNSHIP.

HUGH AULD, farmer and stock-grower, Nineveh, Penn, was born in Morris Township, Greene County, Penn., October 1, 1824. His parents, Hugh and Sarah (Howard) Auld, were natives of Ireland, and came to Greene County, Penn., in 1815. His father, who was a farmer, reared a family of six children, of whom Hugh is the youngest. He was reared in Morris Township, and has met with success in his chosen occupation. He is the owner of a farm of 283 acres of well-improved land where he now resides. In 1851 Mr. Auld married Mary J. Auld, and they are the parents of seven children—Sadie R., Will M., Howard H., Mattie J., Mary M, Tom B. and Ida B. Mr Auld is a Democrat in politics, and in religion a Presbyterian, of which church his wife is also a devoted member.

JASPER BANE, deceased, was born in Amity, Washington County, Penn., October 27, 1827, and died in Greene County in 1866. Mr Bane was a son of Jacob Bane, the ninth in his family of twelve children. He was reared on the home farm in Washington County, and was a successful farmer through life, owning at the time of his death 111 acres of well-improved land. In 1855 Mr. Bane married Jane, daughter of George Lightner. Mrs. Bane's ancestors were among the early settlers and farmers of Greene County. She is a sister of Henry Lightner, a prominent farmer of Morris Township. Mr. and Mrs Bane are the parents of five children—Sarah J., wife of Otho Iams; George, who is a farmer by occupation and has charge of the home farm; Mary, wife of D. W. Hopkins; Samuel and Frank. George was born in Morris Township, October 28, 1857, and received his education in the district school. In politics Mr. Bane was a Republican, and in religion a Cumberland Presbyterian, of which church Mrs. Bane is also a zealous member.

CYRUS BRADBURY, farmer and stock-grower, was born in Mercer County, Penn., July 24, 1830. He is a son of John and Jane (Tuttle) Bradbury, natives of New Jersey, and of English descent. In early life his father was a tanner, afterwards a farmer. He came from Washington County to Greene in 1838, and settled on the farm where Cyrus resides. He died at the advanced age of eighty-four years. His wife is eighty-four years of age, and makes her home with Cyrus, the only one of the three children living. He grew to manhood on the farm, receiving his education in the district schools. He has made a success of his farming, and owns 132 acres of well-improved land. In 1861 he married Nancy, daughter of Thomas and Rebecca (Hedge) Moore, who were natives of this county and of English descent. Mr. and Mrs. Bradbury have five children —Mary Ann, Emma B., wife of John Penn; Ella R., wife of George B. Iams; Lizzie J, wife of Thomas A. Welsh, and Dora B. They have also an adopted child—William Washington. Mr. Bradbury is a Democrat in politics. He and wife are members of the Cumberland Presbyterian Church, in which he is one of the trustees.

ENOCH BROOKS, farmer and stock-grower, Swart's, Penn., was born in Morris Township, this county, November 24, 1837, and is a son of Enoch and Mary (Russell) Brooks. His father, who was a farmer, spent his whole life in this county, and died in 1838. His family consisted of seven children, all of whom grew to maturity. Enoch is the youngest, was reared on the farm and attended the common school. He made choice of farming as his occupation, in which he has engaged through life. He has made his own way in the world, and is the owner of a well-improved farm containing 137 acres. He was united in marriage, April 3, 1869, with Elizabeth M. Rush, and they are the parents of seven children—Mary Laura, George R., Anna Bell, Maud L, Perry M., William H. and Robert E. Mr. Brooks is a Democrat, and a member of the I. O O. F. In 1861 he enlisted in Company D, Eighty-fifth Pennsylvania Volunteer Infantry. He was taken prisoner and sent to Richmond, Va., where he remained for five weeks. He also passed through many of the principal battles and engagements. Mr. and Mrs. Brooks are prominent members of the Baptist Church.

STEPHEN C. CARY, farmer and stock-grower, Swart's, Penn., was born in Morris Township, January 27, 1846. His parents were Abel and Delilah (Mitchell) Cary, natives of this county and of English origin. His ancestors came among the early settlers from New Jersey to Greene County. They were usually farmers, of whom his father was one of the most successful. He died in 1875. Stephen was the ninth in a family of eleven children, six of whom reached maturity. Mr. Cary was reared on a farm, attended the common-schools, and has followed the occupation of his father. He has met with great success in his business, being the owner of a fine farm of 448 acres well stocked and improved. His success in life has been due largely to his own efforts. He was united in marriage April 27, 1872, with Miss Harriet, daughter of Harrison and Elizabeth (Longdon) Conger. Mrs Cary was born in Washington County, and is of English and Irish descent. Mr. and Mrs. Cary are the parents of six children—William H., Lizzie B., Lawrence G , James W , Fannie D. and Hattie M. In politics Mr. Cary is Republican. His wife is a devoted member of the Cumberland Presbyterian Church.

JOHN M. CONKLIN, farmer and stock-grower, Sycamore, Penn., was born in Washington County, Penn., October 17, 1830, and is a son of Isaac and Lydia (Sayers) Conklin, also natives of Washington County. His father, who was a farmer by occupation, had a family of seven sons and four daughters, all living but one. John was reared on the farm in Washington County, attended the common-schools, and learned the painter's trade. He worked for several years at Claysville, Penn., where he took contracts for painting, and was one of the few who made a financial success of the business. Through his energy, good management and careful investments, he was able, in 1859, to buy a good farm near Beulah Church in Greene County. Ten years later he sold this farm, and in 1872 he again invested in 291 acres of land, where he has since resided. He is a first-class farmer, is the owner of a saw-mill, and is also largely interested in the roller flour-mill at Waynesburg, Penn. Mr. Conklin was united in marriage in Washington County, Penn., in 1855, with Delilah, daughter of Abraham and Elizabeth (Craft) Henkins, natives of Washington County. Mrs. Conklin's father was a farmer by occupation and had a family of seven children. Mr. and Mrs. Conklin have had fourteen children, of these eight are living, viz.: Ida M., wife of James R. Sargent; Lizzie L., Shriver C., Elver D., Charlie T., Annie E., Willie O., Oliver G. and Hollis P. Hollis P. was the oldest son, and met with a very untimely death by falling on a circular saw which cut him almost to pieces. He was one of the promising young men of his neighborhood, and at the time of his death was a consistent member of the Methodist Episcopal Church.

H. DRIER, farmer and stock-grower, Nineveh, Penn.—Among the successful business men of Greene County, we mention the subject of this sketch as one who started out in life in a strange land, with only twenty-four dollars in his pocket, the amount of his earthly possessions when he landed in Pittsburg, in 1865. He was born in Germany February 16, 1844, a son of William and Elizabeth (Barger) Drier. His father, who was a farmer, spent all his life in Germany and reared a family of five children, of whom the subject of our sketch was the third. He received his education in his native country, and also went to school a short time in Allegheny City, Penn., where he learned the carpenter's trade. At the close of his apprenticeship, he had saved sixty-five dollars. Mr. Drier was united in marriage, in 1867, with Sophia, daughter of William Tennemire, and they have a family of five children—William, John, Minnie, Christian and Lizzie. Mr. Drier was a good carpenter, receiving as high as twenty-three dollars for a week's wages. He worked so hard that his health became impaired, and at the suggestion of a physician he went to the country in 1873 and engaged in the huckstering business in Greene County, Penn. The next year he took his family for a visit to his native country. Returning in 1875, he started a creamery at Nineveh, Penn., where he owns a fine farm of 221 acres. Mr. Drier is a Republican. Mr. and Mrs. Drier are devoted members of the Lutheran Church.

JOSEPH DUNN, deceased, who was a farmer and stock-grower, was born in Washington County, Penn., June 2, 1801, and was a son of Samuel and Jemima (McEntyre) Dunn. His mother was a native of Pennsylvania, and his father of New Jersey. They were of English and Irish origin. Joseph was the oldest of a family of six children. He spent the greater part of his active life in Morris Township. In his chosen occupation of farming and stock-growing he met with marked success, being at the time of his death, January 6, 1856, the owner of more than 1,000 acres of land. He was married in Washington County, Penn., October 25, 1827, to Miss Elizabeth, daughter of Richard Montgomery. Her parents were of English and Irish descent. Mrs. Dunn was born in Washington County, June 10, 1807, and now resides with her youngest son in Morris Township. To Mr. and Mrs. Joseph Dunn were born six children, five living— three sons and two daughters, all prosperous and succeeding well in life.

WILLIAM DUNN, of West Union, Penn., is the youngest son of Joseph and Elizabeth (McEntyre) Dunn. He was born in Morris Township, Greene County, Penn., July 4, 1847. His mother, to whom he is greatly attached, resides with him, and although eighty years of age, is still quite bright and active. William was reared on the farm, received a common-school education, and also attended Waynesburg College for some time. He has met with more than average success in his chosen occupation of farming and stock-growing. In 1869 he married Miss Florence, daughter of Jacob Swart. Mr. and Mrs. Dunn are the parents of two children—Dora, wife of John G. Loughman, and Ida. Mr. Dunn is Republican in politics, and one of the influential citizens of his community. Mrs. Dunn is a faithful member of the Methodist Episcopal Church.

JESSE L. HAYS, merchant, Nineveh, Penn., was born at Parkersburgh, West Virginia, October 3, 1857. He is a son of Hon. James W. and Hannah (Minor) Hays, natives of Pennsylvania. His ancestors were among the early settlers of Pennsylvania. His father, who is an editor by profession, served two terms as a member of the State Senate. His family consisted of eight children, of whom Jesse L. is the seventh. Mr. Hays has spent the most of his life in Greene County, and received a good English education. He began clerking in his father's store in early life, and continued in the capacity of a salesman until he engaged in the mercantile trade at Nineveh, Penn., in September, 1882. His long experience as a salesman eminently qualifies him for the business, and he meets with deserving success.

In politics he is a Democrat, and is postmaster at Nineveh. In 1881 Mr. Hays married Sadie, daughter of Seth Goodwin. Mrs. Hays' father was of German origin, and her mother was English, a descendant from William Penn. They have one child, Harold G. Hays, born May 30, 1883.

SAMUEL HOPKINS, farmer and carpenter, Swart's, Penn., was born in Greene County, January 10, 1820, and is a son of Daniel and Esther (Johnson) Hopkins. His mother was a native of Washington County, Penn. His father was born in Maryland near Baltimore, and died in 1828. They were of English descent, the first Hopkins having come to this country in the Mayflower and settled at Plymouth, Mass., where Samuel Hopkins' great-grandfather was a Puritan minister. He was also an author of some note, having written several important works on religious subjects. Samuel was the fifth in a family of eight children. He spent his early life on a farm, and received his education from subscription schools. Early in life he learned the carpenter's trade, which, together with farming, he has followed through life. In 1860 he bought his present farm of 150 acres, which is well stocked and improved. In 1845 he married Miss Martha, daughter of David and Lydia (Rogers) Milliken. Mrs. Hopkins' grandfather, John Rogers, laid out the town of Rogersville, and was a prominent citizen of Greene County, where her parents died. They were among the early Presbyterian settlers. Mr. and Mrs. Samuel Hopkins are the parents of three children—Abigail, wife of John Reese; David, a farmer; and Margaret, wife of Dr. Hamilton Borroughs. In politics Mr. Hopkins is a Republican. Following in the footsteps of his grandfathers, who were both soldiers in the Revolutionary war, he enlisted in 1862 in Company A, One Hundred and Sixty-eighth Pennsylvania Volunteer Infantry, and served one year. He and wife are members of the Methodist Episcopal Church, in which he has served as trustee and superintendent of the Sabbath-school.

D. W. HOPKINS, farmer and stock-grower, Swart's, Penn., was born October 31, 1850, on the farm where he now resides in Morris Township. His parents, William and Ellen (Simpson) Hopkins, were natives of this county, and of English and Irish descent. His father was born April 22, 1816, and was the son of Daniel and Esther (Johnson) Hopkins. He died August 12, 1870, being at that time owner of 148 acres of well improved land. His family consisted of five children, three daughters and two sons, four of whom grew to maturity. D. W. was the third in the family, spent his early life on the home farm, and chose farming as his occupation, in which he has engaged very successfully. On February 3, 1880, he married Miss Mary, daughter of Jasper and Jane (Lightner) Bane. Mr. and Mrs. Hopkins have an interesting family of two children—

Nellie Maud and Sarah Lizzie. Their mother is a devoted member of the Methodist Episcopal Church. Mr. Hopkins is a Republican in politics, and one of the enterprising young men of his township.

JOSEPH HUFFMAN, farmer and stock-grower, Nineveh, Penn., was born in Greene County, Penn., July 7, 1838. His parents, John and Nancy (Johns) Huffman, were of English descent. His father was a farmer all his life. Joseph is next to the youngest of a family of eight children, and was reared on the farm in this county, where he attended the common school. He is quite successful as a farmer, and owns a good farm of 150 acres adjoining the village of Nineveh. He sold the lots on which about half of this village now stands. In 1869 Mr. Huffman married Miss Nancy, daughter of John Reese. Mrs. Huffman is also a native of this county. Their family consists of four children—Lizzie, R. E. Lee, Jessie Blanche and John D. Mr. Huffman is a Democrat, and has served as school director in his township. He and wife are zealous members of the Methodist Episcopal Church, in which Mr. Huffman is assistant superintendent of the Sabbath-school.

OTHO IAMS, farmer and stock-grower, Swart's, Penn., was born on Ruff's Creek, this county, September 4, 1846, and is a son of Thomas and Delilah (Huffman) Iams. His grandfather, Otho Iams, came to Greene County from New Jersey in 1790, and settled in Morris Township, and was one of the most prominent and successful farmers of his day. Thomas Iams, his father, died in 1881, leaving to his three sons about 600 acres of valuable land. Otho is the second in a family of seven children. He was reared in Morris Township, where he has been a successful farmer through life. In June, 1881, he was united in marriage with Miss Sarah, daughter of Jasper Bane, and they are the parents of one child—Allen. Mr. Iams is an enthusiastic Democrat, and one of the most enterprising citizens of the community. His wife is a devoted member of the Methodist Episcopal Church.

J. L. IAMS, Swart's, Penn., is a farmer, stock-grower and school teacher. He was born in Morris Township, this county, January 2, 1857, and is a son of Thomas and Delilah (Huffman) Iams. His parents were natives of Greene County, and of English and German ancestry. His father was a prominent and successful farmer and an influential Democrat during his lifetime. His party elected him to several prominent county offices—among others, that of treasurer. He also served a term on the bench as associate judge. Judge Iams and wife were the parents of eight children, five of whom are living. Benjamin H. enlisted in the Eighteenth Pennsylvania Cavalry, under Captain James Hughes, and died in the service of his country. The five living are all residents of this county, except F. P. Iams, Esq., of Pittsburg, Penn. James L. was reared on the farm in Morris

44

Township, and attended the district school. He also spent some time in Waynesburg College. In 1877 he married Miss Belle S., daughter of Jacob Swart. Mr. Iams is one of the enterprising young men of the county, is an enthusiastic Democrat, and a member of the State Democratic Central Committee.

HENRY LIGHTNER, retired farmer, Nineveh, Penn., was born in Center Township, this county, January 30, 1823, and is the oldest son of George and Sarah (Woods) Lightner. His parents were also natives of Center Township, and among the earliest settlers of the county. His father died in 1867. The family have usually been farmers; some of them, however, have entered the different professions and met with success. Henry's grandfather, Micajah Woods, was an Orderly Sergeant in the Revolutionary war. The subject of our sketch was reared in Center Township until nine years of age. He then came with his parents to Morris Township, where he grew to manhood. He attended the common school and chose farming as a business, in which he has met with marked success. Mr. Lightner's farm consists of 300 acres of well improved land. He was united in marriage in Athens County, Ohio, December 12, 1850, with Eliza J., daughter of Thomas Jefferson and Elizabeth Tewksbury, who were of English descent. Mr. and Mrs. Lightner have a family of nine children—Thomas Jefferson, George M., Samuel, Micajah, William, James, Martha Ellen, Mary Jane and Bertha Ann. Their parents are leading members of the Methodist Episcopal Church.

DANIEL LOUGHMAN, retired farmer and stock-grower, of West Union, Penn., was born June 15, 1813, on the farm where he now resides. His parents, Frederick and Catharine (Hammers) Loughman, came to this county in 1812. They were natives of Maryland, and of German origin. His father was a blacksmith and wagon-maker in early life. He subsequently engaged in farming, and was among the pioneer settlers of Morris Township, where he spent most of his life. He reared a family of thirteen children, of whom Daniel is the twelfth. He was reared on the home farm attending the subscription schools, and has devoted his time principally to agriculture. He owns a well improved farm where he now resides. Mr. Loughman was united in marriage, January 15, 1833, with Rachel, daughter of John and Mary (Red) Stagner, who were of German descent. She was born in Maryland in 1812. Mr. and Mrs. Loughman are the parents of six children—Thaddeus, a farmer; Frederick, a blacksmith; Mary, wife of Oliver McVay; Susan, wife of Warren Conklin; Adaline, wife of S. B. Clutter, and John, (deceased). Mr. Loughman is a Democrat, and he and his wife are prominent members of the West Union Cumberland Presbyterian Church.

WILLIAM LOUGHMAN, West Union, Penn., was born in Morris Township, this county, October 22, 1822, and is a son of David and Christine (Fonner) Loughman. His mother was born in Ireland. His father, who was of German origin and a native of Maryland, spent most of his life as a farmer in Greene County, Penn., where he died in Morris Township. William, the second in a family of seven children, was reared on the home farm, and attended the district schools. He chose farming as an occupation, and when twenty-one years of age he received from his father seventy acres of land which, through industry and a strong determination to succeed, he has increased to 400 acres, well stocked and improved. Mr. Loughman has been twice married: first, in 1846, to Mary J., daughter of William Day, and they were the parents of three children —Lucretia A., Elymus and Irvin. Their mother died in 1852 For his second wife, Mr. Loughman married Elizabeth, daughter of John and Mary (Miller) Longdon, and widow of Harrison Corger. Her parents were natives of Washington County, and of English descent. To Mr. and Mrs. Loughman have been born three children: Hannah C., wife of John Conger; Alice, wife of John Auld, and John G. Mrs. Loughman is a member of the Mount Hermon Baptist Church; and her husband is a Cumberland Presbyterian, in which church he has been an elder for sixteen years, and has also served as superintendent of the Sabbath-school. Mr. Loughman stands high in the community as an enterprising citizen and a sound business man. He never sued or was sued by any one.

DANIEL LOUGHMAN, farmer and stock-grower, Sycamore, Penn., was born in Morris Township, Greene County, Pennsylvania, April 25, 1832. He is a son of Henry and Nancy (Smith) Loughman, also natives of this county, and of Dutch origin. The Loughmans, who are among the prominent citizens of Greene County, have usually been farmers, and were among the early settlers in Morris Township. Mr Daniel Loughman is the second in a family of ten children, and attended the schools of his township. He makes a success of farming, and is the owner of a good farm of 307 acres where he resides. In 1853 Mr. Loughman married Miss Sarah, daughter of Dennis and Matilda (Huffman) Iams, who were of German origin. Her father was born in Greene County, Penn., and met with great success as a farmer. Mr and Mrs. Loughman are the parents of ten children—Dennis, George, Belle, Matilda, Dora, Jackson, Ida, Charley, Mattie and Bertha Their mother is a devoted member of the Baptist Church. In politics Mr. Loughman is a Democrat He is greatly interested in the educational affairs of his township, and has served as school director for several years.

SILAS M. McCULLOUGH, farmer and stock-grower, Nineveh, Penn., was born in Morris Township, November 9, 1852 He is the

only child of John and Caroline (Jennings) McCullough, natives of
Greene County, and of Dutch and English descent.　They were mar-
ried in 1852, and his mother died in 1854.　His father, who was
born October 21, 1832, was a son of Samuel and Elizabeth (Shape)
McCullough, who were of Dutch origin.　Silas grew to manhood in
Morris Township, receiving his education in the district schools.
He is a self-made man, and through great industry and economy has
been prospered in his farming, which he has made his life work.　He
owns a good farm of seventy-three acres　In 1877 he married Miss
Jennie, daughter of Elymas and Mary (Ross) Pettit, who were of
English descent.　To Mr and Mrs. McCullough have been born five
children—Clarence A., Grace M., Oscar Lee, Jessie Blanche and
Elymas.　Mr. and Mrs. McCullough are leading members of the
Methodist Episcopal Church, in which he is a trustee and prominent
worker

OLIVER McVAY, a prominent business man of West Union,
Penn., was born in Morris Township, Greene County, August 7,
1842　His parents, Silas and Dorcas (Jennings) McVay, were natives of Washington County, Penn., and of Scotch-Irish lineage.
His father was a stone-mason by occupation, and later in life he engaged in farming and huckstering for many years.　He died in
Washington County　His family consisted of twelve children,
eleven of whom grew to maturity　Oliver was the fourth in the family, and was reared in Greene and Washington counties, receiving a
common-school education.　In 1870 he engaged in merchandising,
his present business, which he makes a great success.　In 1867
he married Mary, daughter of Daniel Loughman.　Her mother's
maiden name was Rachel Stigner, whose father, Frederick Stigner,
was among the earliest settlers of the county.　Mr and Mrs McVay
have one child, Silas E., who married Elizabeth, daughter of Elias
Conger　They have one child, Pearl.　In politics Mr. McVay is a
Republican.　September 16, 1861, he enlisted in Company D, Eighty-
Fifth Pennsylvania Volunteer Infantry, and was discharged for disability in 1862　He is a member of the G A R. Post　Mr. and
Mrs. McVay are prominent members of the West Union Cumberland
Presbyterian Church.

THOMAS PATTERSON, deceased, was born March 17, 1809,
in Morris Township, Greene County, where he spent his entire life.
His parents, Mark and Nancy (Gregory) Patterson, were natives of
Ireland, and among the early settlers of this county.　His father,
who was a farmer, reared a family of nine children, of whom Thomas
was the third.　He received his education in the district schools.　He
spent all his life on a farm, devoting his time chiefly to farming
and stock-growing, and at the time of his death, 1876, was the owner
of a good farm of 200 acres.　In 1831 he married Miss Margaret

Hopkins, and they were the parents of nine children—Daniel, Levi, Mark, John, Esther, Eliza, Catharine, Mary and Margaret. Mr. and Mrs. Patterson were prominent members of the Methodist Episcopal Church. In politics Mr. Patterson was a Republican.

ELYMAS PETTIT, farmer and stock-grower, Nineveh, Penn., was born March 27, 1834. He is a son of Charles and Keziah (Coe) Pettit, natives of Washington County, Penn. Elymas is the fourth in a family of eight children, seven of whom are still living. He was reared on the farm and attended the district school. He made choice of farming as his life-work, and is now the owner of a well improved farm of 157 acres, and a neat, substantial dwelling. In 1856 he married Mary, daughter of Isaac and Sarah (McGlumphy) Ross. Mrs. Pettit is of Irish descent, and is a faithful member of the Baptist Church. Their union has been blessed with three children—Melissa, wife of Henry Breese; Jennie, wife of Silas McCullough, and Charles F., a student at Delaware College in Ohio. In politics Mr. Pettit is a Democrat. In 1862 he enlisted in the first Ringold battalion, and served two years and ten months, being discharged for disability, at Cumberland, Maryland, in 1865.

MATTHIAS PETTIT, farmer, Swart's, Penn., who was born April 23, 1831, is a prominent farmer and stock-grower of Morris Township. He is a son of Charles and Keziah (Coe) Pettit. His father, who was a farmer by occupation, was born July 2, 1801, and died in 1871. He spent most of his life in Greene County, where he reared a family of eight children—five girls and three boys. Matthias is the oldest in the family, and was reared in Morris Township. He has been engaged in agricultural pursuits from his youth, and is the owner of a well improved farm of 125 acres where he now resides. He was married in this county, December 11, 1868, to Miss Ruth, daughter of Nathan Penn. Mrs. Pettit's father was a farmer, of English descent. Her mother's maiden name was Rachel McCullough, who was of Irish descent. Mr. and Mrs. Pettit have a family of four children—Jennie, Mary, Rachel and Richard. In politics Mr. Pettit is a Democrat. He and wife are leading members of the Baptist Church.

THOMAS M. ROSS, ex-county commissioner, Sycamore, Penn., is a prominent farmer and stock-grower of Morris Township. He was born in Washington Township, Greene County, Penn., March 10, 1831, and is a son of Jacob and Abigail (Ross) Ross. Though of the same name, his parents were not related. They were natives of this county, and of English and German origin. His father, who was a farmer, died in 1856. Thomas M. was the sixth in a family of nine children. He was reared on the farm in Richhill Township, where he attended the district schools and made farming his main occupation. He was united in marriage, March

13, 1856, with Sarah Elizabeth, daughter of Benjamin Franklin and Mary (Goodwin) Rickey, who were of English and Dutch origin Mr and Mrs. Ross are the parents of eleven children, ten living— Celesta Ann, wife of Benjamin F. Oir; Hiram Franklin, who married Dora, daughter of Daniel Loughman, Catharine I. V., wife of John Church, Philena, wife of Jesse F. Hill; Sadie A., Timothy J., Mary, Emma, Arthur, Stella and Thomas L A (deceased). In 1875 Mr. Ross sold his farm and engaged in the business of hucksteiing until 1881, when he was elected commissioner of Greene County. In 1884 he bought his present farm of 155 acres He has served three years as director of the poor He belongs to the Masonic fraternity and the I O. O. F. Mr. Ross took an active interest in the Granger 'movement. He is a public-spirited, progressive citizen. He belongs to the Bates' Fork Baptist Church, of which his wife, who died in 1887, was also a devoted member.

REUBEN SANDERS, farmer and stock-grower, West Union, Penn., was born February 17, 1834, on the farm where he now resides He is a son of Reuben and Fannie F. (Rutan) Sanders. Reuben Sanders, Sr., was an early settler and prominent farmei of Morris Township. His family consisted of thirteen children, ten of whom grew to maturity The subject of our sketch, who was next to the youngest in the family, was reared on the farm he now owns, and attended the district school. He has made farming his occupazion through life, and is the owner of 182 acres of land well stocked and improved. In 1857 he was united in marriage with Miss Margaret, daughter of Charles and Keziah Pettit Mrs. Sandeis is a sister of Matthias and Elymas Pettit, prominent farmers in this township. Mr and Mrs Sanders have one child—Hester Ann, who is the wife of Jonathan Supler. Mrs Sanders is a faithful member of the Baptist Church.

GEORGE SHAPE.—Among the descendants of the early settlers we mention the name of George Shape, one of the representative farmers and stock-growers of Greene County. He was boin in 1842, on the farm wheie he resides in Morris Township, and is a son of John and Elizabeth (Huffman) Shape, the former a native of Maryland. His grandfather, Peter Shape, came from Maryland to Greene County, Penn., in 1814, and settled on a farm. Heie George's father was raised, and spent his life as a farmer He died in 1858, in his sixty-third year. He reared a family of twelve children, eleven of whom are now living. They are—Peter, Katie, Mary, Julia Ann, Elizabeth, Reasin, George, Eliza J., William, Mineiva, Deborah and S B. Their parents were members of the Cumberland Presbyterian Church. George was the seventh in the family. He has made farming his business, owning at present a fine farm of 135 acres. His brothers are all farmers, except Reasin, who is a first-class carpenter; he also owns a farm where he resides in this township George is a member of the Cumberland Presbyterian Church at Nineveh, and has served as elder.

JACOB SHOUP, farmer and stock-grower, Swart's, Penn., was born in Fayette County, Penn., May 24, 1825. His parents, John and Margaret (Miller) Shoup, were also natives of Fayette County, and of English and German origin. His father was a millwright and miller by trade and occupation, and followed his chosen business through life His family consisted of three children. Jacob was the second, and spent the first sixteen years of his life on the home farm in Fayette County He attended the common schools in Greene County, and chose farming as his occupation, in which he has met with more than average success. Through his own enterprise and industry he has secured a fine farm of 117 acres. In 1860 Mr. Shoup was united in marriage with Miss Catharine, daughter of Frederick and Rebecca (Stewart) Hunnell, natives of this county. Mr. and Mrs Shoup have four children—William Spencer, Rebecca Ann, wife of Samuel McCullough; George E. and Ulysses Grant. Mr. Shoup is a Republican in politics, and he and Mrs. Shoup belong to the Methodist Episcopal Church.

HUGH SIMPSON, farmer and stock-grower, Swart's, Penn., was born in Morris Township, this county, February 21, 1833, and is a son of John and Mary (Auld) Simpson. His father, a native of this county, of Irish descent, was a mechanic, and died in 1846. Hugh was the oldest of a family of five children, was reared on a farm and received a common-school education. He chose farming as an occupation, and has engaged therein all his life. He is the owner of a well-stocked and improved farm consisting of 162 acres. He was united in marriage, in 1859, with Esther, daughter of Thomas Patterson, and they are the parents of three children—Waitman T., Annie and Maggie. Mr. and Mrs. Simpson are prominent members of the Methodist Episcopal Church, in which he is trustee, and superintendent of the Sabbath-school. In politics Mr. Simpson is a Republican. He has served as school director in his township.

J. W. SIMPSON, farmer and stock-grower, Swart's, Penn., was born in Morris Township, this county, April 23, 1842, and is a son of William and Ruth (Fulton) Simpson. His mother was a native of Washington County, Penn. His father was born on the farm where J. W. resides. This farm first came into the possession of the family through their grandfather, Rev. John Simpson, who was born in Ireland, March 13, 1758. He landed in America August 12, 1791, and came to Greene County in the fall of 1796. He married Miss Rebecca Gregory, who was born in Farmingah, Ireland, August 12, 1767. In 1816 they opened their dwelling as a place for public worship, and the neighbors held meetings there for near forty years.

J. W Simpson was an only child, was reared on the farm and received a common-school education He has made a business of farming and has met with success. His farm consists of 197 acres of land well stocked and improved. He was married, September 27, 1866, to America Ann, daughter of Jacob and Permina (Allum) Swart, who were of English origin. To Mr. and Mrs Simpson have been born seven children—Carrie, Mary, Ruth, Swart, Flora, John and William Their mother is a zealous member of the Methodist Episcopal Church In politics Mr Simpson is a Republican. In 1864 he enlisted in Company E, Fourteenth Pennsylvania Cavalry, and was discharged May 30, 1865 He belongs to the Masonic fraternity He is a member of the Waynesburg Encampment, No 119, and Waynesburg Lodge, No 467, I. O. O. F, and also of the G A. R, Post No. 367, Department of Pennsylvania.

JACOB SWART, farmer and stock-grower, Swart's, Penn., was born in Washington County, Penn., December 25, 1820. His parents, Phillip and Ascnah (Walton) Swart, were also natives of Washington County, and of Dutch and Irish ancestry. Jacob is the second in a family of nine children He was reared on a farm in Amwell Township, where he received his education in one of the old log school-houses of that day. He chose farming as a business, to which he devoted his entire time until forty years of age He came to Greene County in 1842, and was united in marriage, May 5, with Paulina, daughter of Charles and Jemima (Barnhart) Allum, who were of English descent. Mr. and Mrs. Swart have twenty-seven grandchildren. They have a family of four sons and five daughters— America A., wife of J. W Simpson; Amos O., a farmer; Florence B, wife of William Dunn; Virginia I., wife of James Iams, and Senic Jane, Mary E, John N., Henry Clay and Franklin L., deceased. Mr. Swart bought a farm in Washington Township in 1843, and in 1880 he bought his present farm. In 1861 he purchased an interest in a general store, and they continued in business together for two years, when Mr. Swart became sole proprietor. He continued in the mercantile business for fifteen years, and sold his store in 1877. Mr. Swart is a Republican, but is always willing to vote for a good man for office, independent of party or politics He has been postmaster at Swart's for the past seventeen years. Mr. Swart is a self-made man, his success in life having been due largely to his own enterprise and industry. He is a progressive citizen, ever ready to aid a good enterprise, and was one of those most instrumental in the building of the W. & W. Railroad. He was a member of the building committee and superintendent of the road for two years.

WILLIAM SIMPSON THROCKMORTON, physician and surgeon, Nineveh, Penn, was born March 2, 1838. He is a son of Mofford and Nancy (Simpson) Throckmorton, who were of English and Irish origin. His mother was born in this county, and his father was a native of New Jersey, and among the early settlers of Greene County, Penn., where he died in 1884. The Doctor is the ninth in a family of thirteen children, and was reared on the farm in Center Township, where he obtained his early education. He subsequently attended Allegheny College, but afterwards completed his collegiate studies at Waynesburg College, Penn. He chose the practice of medicine as his profession, and in 1863 entered Jefferson Medical College at Philadelphia, where he graduated in 1865. He then began the practice of his profession at Nineveh, in Greene County, where he has been actively engaged ever since, with the exception of the time spent at the lectures The Doctor has thoroughly prepared himself for his work, having taken a regular course of lecturers in five of the most noted medical colleges in the United States. He has an extensive library and keeps his office well supplied with the leading publications in medical science. He is much attached to his profession, and also takes an active interest in the welfare of his town and community He is a leading member of the State Medical Association, and belongs to the Greene County Medical Society, of which he has been president and corresponding secretrry. He was married in 1866, to Miss Caroline M, daughter of Jesse Hill, of Waynesburg, Penn., and they have four children—Jessie, Charley, Willie and Mofford Doctor Throckmorton and wife are members of the Methodist Episcopal Church, in which he is trustee, steward, superintendent of the Sabbath-school, and has been an official member for thirty years. He has been identified with the Masonic and Odd Fellowship fraternities and is forward in every good word and work, a blessing to his generation and community.

PERRY TOWNSHIP.

HON JOHN BLAIR, the present member of the Legislature from Greene County, Penn., is a farmer and stock-grower by occupation, and was born in Wayne Township, December 25, 1841. He is the only son of Isaac and Elizabeth (Ross) Blair, the former a native of Greene County, and the latter of Crawford County, Penn., and of Dutch and Irish extraction. His father, who was a farmer and stone-mason, was born in 1810 and died August 26, 1846. Mr. Blair was reared on the home farm in this county, and attended the district schools. He has been a successful farmer all his life, and owns a fine farm of 250 acres. In 1861 he was united in marriage, in Monongalia County, W. Va., with Miss Amy, daughter of Jonathan and Charlotte (Bightodah) Brown. Mr. and Mrs. Blair's children are William F., G. W. W., a teacher; Anna, wife of Oliver Lemley; Belle, wife of William Wright; L. L., Olive, O. B. and Ross B. Mr. and Mrs. Blair are members of the Disciple Church. He is a Democrat, and was elected to the House of Representatives in 1886. He had previously held the office of justice of the peace for five years, and was school director for a period of twelve years.

T. W. BOYDSTON, proprietor of the Mount Morris Tannery, was born in West Virginia, November 1, 1844. He is the son of E. L. and Ruhama (Jackson) Boydston, who were of English and Irish origin. They resided in Dunkard Township, this county, where the father died in 1853, leaving a family of six children. Of these the subject of our sketch is the oldest, and was reared in West Virginia, where he received his education in the Military Academy at Morgantown. Early in life he learned the printer's trade, which he followed successfully for some time. He had charge of the printing for the Legislature at Harrisburg, Penn. Since 1877 he has been engaged in his present business at Mount Morris. In 1862 Mr. Boydston enlisted in Company K, Fourteenth West Virginia Infantry, in which he served first as a private, then as Seargeant, and Second Lieutenant. He was united in marriage, in 1877, with Hannah, daughter of James L. Donley. They are the parents of four children—Clara, Sallie, Frederick and Virginia. Mr. and Mrs. Boydston are members of the Methodist Episcopal Church, in which he holds several official positions, and is also greatly interested in the Sabbath-school. He is a Republican, also member of the I. O. O. F., and is Quartermaster of G. A. R. Post, No. 450.

THORNTON E. BOYDSTON, Mount Morris, Penn.—Among the most highly respected citizens of Perry Township is the gentleman whose name heads this sketch. He was born at Mount Morris, October 12, 1833, and is a son of B. and Mary (Wiley) Boydston. His father was also a native of this county, and his mother was born in West Virginia. His father was a farmer all his life, and reared a family of twelve children. The subject of this sketch was next to the youngest in the family, and was reared in his native township. He received his education in the common schools, and engaged in farming as his life work. Mr. Boydston has been successful in his business affairs, and now owns a fine farm of 160 acres. In 1858 he married Susannah, daughter of Joseph R. Donley. Their children are—Emma, wife of L. C. Evans; Sarah A., wife of Lewis Lemley; Mary, Charles B., James and Anna M. Mr. and Mrs. Boydston are consistent members of the Methodist Episcopal Church, in which he serves as trustee. He is a Republican in politics, and has been a member of the school board in his township.

O. J. BROWN, farmer and stock-grower, Mount Morris, Penn., was born in Perry Township, Greene County, Penn., May 21, 1852, and is a son of Reuben and Rebecca (McClure) Brown, also natives of this county. His ancestors were early settlers of Dunkard Township, and of Irish, Welsh and German extraction. His father is a prominent farmer in this county. The subject of our sketch is the youngest in a family of five children. He was reared on the farm and received a good English education. He subsequently attended Jefferson and Waynesburg colleges, and made a special study of surveying and civil engineering. He turned his attention to farming and stock-growing, however, and has a fine little farm of sixty-five acres. In 1884 Mr. Brown married Miss Mary, daughter of Jacob and Fannie (Lemmon) Eakin, and they have one daughter—Hallie May. They are Methodists in religion, and Mr. Brown is superintendent of the Sabbath-school in that church. He is a Democrat in politics, and judge of elections in 1888.

REUBEN BROWN, is a descendant of the early settlers of Greene County, his ancestors having settled near the source of Dunkard Creek in 1801, and removed to Perry Township in 1812. Reuben still owns and resides on the farm where they settled, near Mount Morris, Penn. He was born August 26, 1816, on this farm, where he has spent all his life, except the short time he lived in Monongalia County, W. Va. Here he grew to manhood, receiving his early education in the old log school-house. His father was Reuben Brown, and his mother's maiden name was Rebecca John. They were of Welsh and German origin. His father was born in Loudoun County, Va., was a farmer by occupation; and died in Greene County in 1867, at the advanced age of ninety-seven years. The history of the family shows them to have been farmers and stock-growers, and usually successful in their business affairs. Reuben is one of the prosperous farmers of his township, and owns 200 acres of valuable land. He was married September 20, 1839, to Rebecca McClure, who is a native of Dunkard Township, and the daughter of William and Jane (King) McClure. Her ancestors, who were of Irish extraction, came to Greene County in 1817 and settled in Dunkard Township. Mr. and Mrs. Brown are the parents of five children—James M., who is now engaged in farming and railroading in the West; Susan C., wife of B. Ross; O. J., a farmer in Perry Township; Samantha Jane, who was the wife of L. A. Morris (deceased), and William, who was shot through mistake by a deserter in the late Rebellion. Mr. and Mrs. Brown are active members of the Baptist Church. He takes an active interest in the schools, and has frequently served as school director in his township.

S A. COWELL, farmer and stock-grower, Mount Morris, Penn, was born in Whiteley Township, Greene County, Penn., October 15, 1864. He is a son of Solomon and Eliza (Mike) Cowell, who were of English extraction His mother was a native of West Virginia. His father, who was a farmer and stock drover, was born in Greene County, Penn., where he died, leaving a family of fourteen children. Of these the subject of our sketch is the youngest, and was reared in this county, receiving his education in the common schools. He is one of the industrious and enterprising young farmers of his township, and owns a good farm of ninety-eight acres. In 1885 Mr Cowell was united in marriage with Miss Sarah, daughter of Dennis Fox, a prominent farmer in Perry Township. They have two bright and interesting children—Vincent Earl and Dennis Floyd. Mr. Cowell is a Republican in politics.

D. L. DONLEY, farmer and stock-grower, Mount Morris, Penn. Among the most prominent members of the large family of Donleys in this county, none are more noted for their liberality and progressive spirit than D. L Donley, the subject of our sketch. He was born in Perry Township, Greene County, Penn., June 11, 1836, and is the son of J. R. and Sarah (Lemley) Donley. His mother was the daughter of David and Ruhana (Snider) Lemley, and of German and Irish origin His father is a native of Dunkard Township and is still living at the advanced age of seventy-six years D L. Donley's grandparents, James and Susannah (Robinson) Donley, came from Washington County, to Greene County in 1790, and settled on a farm. The subject of our sketch is a nephew of Hon Patrick Donley, and a cousin of ex-congressman J. B. Donley, of Waynesburg, Penn. He was reared in Perry Township, attended the common schools and early in life was put to work on the farm. He has been successful in his business and is the owner of 500 acres of valuable land. It was through Mr. Donley's influence that the oil field has been opened up in that section, and the largest gas and oil wells are situated on his land near Mount Morris. Mr. Donley was married in West Virginia, August 20, 1861, to Miss Louisa, daughter of Alexander and Sarah (Hague) Evans. Her father was born near Garard's Fort in January, 1806, and is the son of Eleazar and Martha (Vance) Evans. Mrs. Evans is a native of New Jersey and Mr. Evans of Loudoun County, Virginia He is a retired farmer, owning over 400 acres of land Mr. and Mrs. Donley have seven children—Laura, wife of Dr. Owen, of Oak Forest, Penn ; Josephine, wife of D. B Adams, of Waynesburg, Penn.; Evans, Leanna, Meda, Ellsworth J. and Edward G. Mr. and Mrs Donley are prominent members of the Methodist Episcopal Church. He takes great interest in educational matters, and has served as school director at Mount Morris.

DENNIS FOX, who is probably as well known as any private citizen of Greene County, is a successful farmer and stock-grower, and was born April 5, 1827, on the farm where he resides. His parents, Henry and Susan (Dulaney) Fox, were descended from the Dutch, and natives of this county. Peter and Mary (Thomas) Fox, his grandparents, came to this county from New Jersey, and settled on the farm which Dennis now owns. Here Peter Fox planted a little willow sprout which he brought with him, and the tree is now twenty-one feet in circumference, by actual measurement. This tree is to remain standing, as Dennis says, a monument to the memory of him who planted it so many years ago. Mr. Fox has a fine farm of nearly 500 acres, well stocked and improved, his barns being among the best in Perry Township. He was united in marriage, January 18, 1848, with Miss Betsey, daughter of David and Elizabeth (McCann) John. She is of Irish and English extraction. Mr. and Mrs Fox have ten children—Henry, David, Osborn, Kinsey, James, Marion, Susan, wife of Spencer Cowell; Sarah Jane Cowell, and John and Elizabeth, deceased. Mr. Fox is a Republican in politics.

SAMUEL GUTHRIE, a farmer and stock-grower of Perry Township, was born in Greene County, Penn., December 18, 1820, and is a son of Archibald and Elizabeth (Lemley) Guthrie, also natives of Greene County, and of Irish and Dutch origin. His father, who was a farmer and a pioneer settler in Whiteley Township, died in this county in 1845. Samuel is the seventh in a family of ten children and grew to maturity on the home farm, attending the subscription schools. He has successfully followed farming as his chief pursuit, and is the owner of 133 acres of valuable land where he resides near Kirby P. O. Mr. Guthrie's wife was Miss Nancy, daughter of James and Nancy (Stephens) Patterson. Her parents were natives of this county, and of Irish and German descent. Mr. and Mrs. Guthrie's children are—Elizabeth, wife of Alfred Moore, of West Virginia; James P., a farmer; Hannah Martha, wife of Franklin Henderson, and Priscilla, deceased. Mr. Guthrie is a Republican. His wife is a devoted member of the Methodist Episcopal Church.

GEORGE W. GUTHRIE, farmer and stock-grower, Kirby, Penn., was born in Whiteley Township, this county, March 26, 1848. His parents, Solomon and Elizabeth (Fry) Guthrie, are also natives of Greene County, and of English and German origin. His father, for many years a farmer and stock-grower, has now retired from the more active duties of life and resides in Whiteley Township. George is the fifth in a family of six children, and was reared on the farm in Whiteley Township. He is an industrious farmer, paying close attention to his business, and is the owner of a good farm of 123 acres In 1870 he married Adaline, daughter of John and Hannah (Rose) Cowell, natives of Greene County, and of Dutch extraction. Mr and Mrs. Guthrie have one daughter—Ida Estella. They are members of the Southern Methodist Church, in which Mr. Guthrie is trustee, and superintendent of the Sabbath-school. He is a Republican, and has served as assessor in his township.

CYRENIUS HAINES, farmer and stock-grower, was born in Greene County, Penn., April 1, 1823. His parents, George and Jane (McCord) Haines, were natives of New York. His mother was of Scotch and Dutch ancestry. His father, who was of English extraction, was a farmer by occupation, and died in 1850 in his seventy-seventh year. Cyrenius is the eighth in a family of eleven children and was reared on the farm in this county, where he attended the common school. Early in life he spent some time as a bookseller but subsequently turned his attention to farming and stock-growing, and is the owner of a farm of 255 acres, well stocked and improved. Mr. Haines has been twice married. His first wife died in 1851, but a few weeks after her marriage. His second wife, whom he married in Virginia in 1852, was Mary Ann, daughter of Burton and Nancy (Sutton) Pride. She is of English origin. Her father was born in 1800 in Virginia Mr. and Mrs Haines' children are Francis B, George D, William G., Lewis Spencer, D D., a farmer; John J. and Melinda A. They have eleven grandchildren— Lewis E, Emerson, John C and Clarence, children of their oldest son; Franklin, Margaret, Cora Bell and Viola, whose father is George D.; and Ida E, William L., Cyrenius, George and Sarah A., whose father is William G.; Noah L. and D., whose father is Lewis S. Mr and Mrs Haines are Methodists in religion. He has been trustee in the church and superintendent of the Sabbath-school

JACOB HATFIELD, physician and surgeon, Mount Morris, Penn, was born in Monongahela Township, this county, December 19, 1839, and is a son of G W. and Mary (Richey) Hatfield, who are of English descent and natives of Greene and Fayette counties, respectively. Dr Hatfield's father is a farmer by occupation. Of his seven children, six are now living, of whom the Doctor is the oldest. He was reared with his parents on the farm in Whiteley Township, where he attended the district schools. At an early age he manifested an inclination for the study of medicine, and went to Columbiana County, Ohio, where he took a regular course. In 1864 he began his professional career at Mount Morris, Penn., where he has since remained in active practice Dr. Hatfield is very much attached to his profession, and has thoroughly informed himself in its different branches. He has successfully performed several extremely difficult surgical operations On May 12, 1863, Dr Hatfield was united in marriage with Caroline, daughter of Henry Morris, of

Whiteley Township. Mrs. Hatfield is of German origin. They have three children—G. W., Maggie N. and Henry Morris. Their oldest son is a physician and is now in practice with his father. He was born and reared in Mount Morris. He first studied medicine with his father, after which he went to Baltimore and attended the College of Physicians and Surgeons, for two years; subsequently took the regular course at the Western Pennsylvania Medical College, at Pittsburgh, Penn., graduating in 1887. Dr. Hatfield and wife are prominent members of the Methodist Episcopal Church, in which he has held various official offices. He is a Republican, and has served on the school board at Mount Morris, Penn.

G. F. HEADLEY, teacher and surveyor, Brock, Penn., was born in Perry Township, Greene County, Penn., June 27, 1853. His parents, Ephraim and Maria (Haines) Headley, were also natives of this county, and of Scotch and English extraction. His father, a prominent farmer in Perry Township, is a son of Jesse and Maria (Cox) Headley. G. F. Headley's grandfather was born in Greene County, Penn. His great-grandfather, Ephraim Headley, was among the pioneer settlers of New Jersey, and one of the first farmers and hunters who came to Greene County, Penn., while it was still inhabited by the Indians. The family have usually been farmers and drovers. The subject of our sketch grew up on the farm, being the second in a family of three children. He attended the High School at Mount Morris, Penn., and also took a college course. For thirteen years Mr. Headley has been successfully engaged as a teacher. He has also given considerable attention to the study of surveying, and devotes a part of his time to that work. He is also a farmer and stock-grower by occupation and owns a good farm where he resides. In 1879 Mr. Headley married Miss S. A., daughter of John Conner, of Perry Township. Mrs. Headley is of German and Irish origin. Their children are Florence B., Julius B., Fred and Gertrude. Mr. Headley is a Republican. He and his wife are members of the Methodist Episcopal Church. In connection with our subject's sketch, we give a brief sketch of his ancestor's advent into Greene County, Penn.: Sometime prior to the American Revolution, the great-great-great-grandfather, Richard Headlee, who was an English sailor, in the the service of Great Britain, concluded to desert the standard of the Stuarts, and seek an asylum in the wilds of North America. After making his escape from the British service, he settled in New Jersey, where he afterwards married. But according to English law, "Once an Englishman always an Englishman," he was not allowed to enjoy the quiet of his new home very long. The British authorities finding out his whereabouts, had him arrested, which was done by a party of twenty British sailors, not however until he had given them an exhibition of his prowess, and felled several of them to the ground in good old British style. He was overpowered, taken back into service and kept seven years from his family But his long service as a sailor made him familiar with the seaport towns and the American coast, so taking advantage of the situation in the darkness of the night, while near shore, he leaped overboard and swam ashore, and finally united with his family We know little of his family, except that his son John, who was G. F Headley's great-great-grandfather, died while in the Patriot army, he being old enough to have a son engaged in the same struggle. Robert Headlee, a nephew of John, was in the expedition sent against the Indians, who committed the Wyoming massacre. Ephraim, G. F. Headley's great-grandfather, lived during the Revolution in New Jersey, not far from Trenton, being within sound of the battle fought at that place. After the war he emigrated to North Carolina, but disliking the country, he removed to Greene County, Penn, where he reared a large family.

W. O. HEADLEE, farmer and teacher, Mount Morris, Penn, was born January 27, 1858, in Perry Township, where he grew to manhood He was reared on the farm with his parents, receiving a common school education. He also attended the High School at Mount Morris. Mr. Headlee has been for eight years teaching in Perry Township, but engages in farming as his chief pursuit, and owns a well improved farm of 100 acres In 1880 he was united in marriage with Miss Margaret, daughter of Phineas Headley. Mrs. Headlee is of English origin They are the parents of four children, viz: Cora, Ray, James Fay and Effie Mr Headlee is a Democrat. He and wife are prominent members of the Methodist Episcopal Church. He is a self-made man, is industrious and energetic, and has a great many friends throughout the county.

JOSEPH HEADLEE, farmer and stock-grower, is descended from the early setttlers of Greene County. He was born September 9, 1834, and is a son of Jesse and Maria (Cox) Headlee. His mother was a native of New York. His father who was born in this county, was eminently successful as a farmer and owned 400 acres of land at the time of his death, March 15, 1876. Of his ten children, Joseph is the fourth and was reared on the farm in Perry Township. Mr. Headlee is an energetic, industrious farmer and owns ninety-three acres of well improved land where he resides, near Mount Morris, Penn. He was united in marriage in Greene County, in 1869, with Catherine, daughter of Alexander Henderson. Her mother's maiden name was Catharine Lemley. To Mr. and Mrs. Headlee were born four children, viz: Earnest, Clyde, Mark and M. D. Mr. Headlee has been a member of the Methodist Episcopal Church since 1852. He is a member of the board of trustees, and take great interest in the welfare of his chosen denomination. He was drafted in 1863 and served his regular term in the army. Mr. Headlee is a member of the G. A. R., belonging to the Jesse Taylor Post, No. 450, of Mount Morris, Penn.

J. S. HOY, farmer and stock-grower, born in Whiteley Township, this county, January 18, 1843, is a son of James and Isabella (Kuhn) Hoy, also natives of Greene County, and of German origin. His father died in 1880. He was a farmer and stock-grower, and reared a family of eight children, of whom the subject of this sketch is the third. J. S. was reared in Perry Township, where he has lived since he was one year of age. He received his education in the common schools in this township, and has made farming his life work. Mr. Hoy's farm contains 159 and three quarters acres of well improved land. He was married in this county, January 13, 1869, to Melissa, daughter of Isaac and Anna (Myers) Lemley. Her mother was born in Virginia, and her father in Perry Township, this county. Mr. and Mrs. Hoy have an interesting family of four children; viz., Eliza J., James Isaac, David Arthur, and Cassie Ellen. Mrs Hoy died in 1884, a faithful member of the Southern Methodist Episcopal Church. Mr. Hoy is a Democrat. He is a genial, agreeable gentleman, and has a wide circle of friends in the county.

MORRIS LEMLEY, farmer, stock-grower and drover, was born in Perry Township, April 2, 1834. His parents, Samuel and Margaret Lemley, were natives of Greene County, and of German extraction. His father, who was a farmer by occupation, moved to Iowa in the latter part of his life, where he died at the age eighty-six. Morris, the fifth in a family of ten children, was reared on the farm and attended the common school. He made his own way in the world, and is the owner of eight hundred acres of land—360 in his home farm. Mr. Lemley's example is worthy of emulation. He first engaged in farming on rented property, and by his patient toil and unfailing industry has succeeded in accumulating a handsome fortune. In 1854 Mr. Lemley married Miss Martha Jane, daughter of Job and Margaret (Simington) Phillips. Their children are: Margaret A., wife of William Headlee; Samuel, a farmer; Emeline, Elizabeth, Josephus, and Spencer who died at the age of twenty-one years. Mr. Lemley is a Democrat. He and his wife are prominent members of the Methodist Episcopal Church.

CLARK LEMLEY, farmer and stock grower, Brock, Penn, was born in Perry Township, November 20, 1849, and is a son of Isaac and Anna (Myers) Lemley. His mother was born in West Virginia. His father is a native of this county and a prominent farmer of Whiteley Township. Clark is the third in a family of six children. He was reared in this county, where he received a common school education. Mr. Lemley has met with success as a farmer and owns 152 acres of good land where he resides. In 1870 he married Miss

45

Rachel, daughter of Eli and Mary (Dulaney) Headlee. Mr. and Mrs. Lemley's children are Haddie L., William L., and Alva G. Mr. and Mrs. Lemley, with their oldest daughter are members of the Methodist Episcopal Church. He is a Democrat in politics.

ASBERRY LEMLEY, farmer and stock-grower, was born June 20, 1823, on the farm where he now resides in Perry Township. He is a son of David and Ruhana (Snider) Lemley, being the oldest of their eight children. His parents spent the most of their lives on a farm in this county, where Asberry was reared and received his education in the common schools. He has made farming his chief pursuit, and is the owner of 300 acres of well improved land. Mr. Lemley was united in marriage, October 12, 1849, in Greene County, Penn., with Miss Rachel, daughter of John and Lydia Headlee. Mrs. Asberry Lemley is of English and German origin. They have eight children; viz., Ruhana, wife of William Howard; Elizabeth, wife of Thomas Patterson; L. L., David, Lydia, Martha, wife of Jonathan Kennedy; and Mary. Mr. Lemley is one of the most industrious and successful business men in his township.

J. W. LONG, deceased, was born in Perry Township, this county, December 3, 1836, and died October 4, 1885. He was a highly respected citizen and one of Greene County's most successful business men, being at the time of his death the owner of over 800 acres of land. Mr. Long was the son of George and Mary (Berge) Long who were natives of Ohio, and of English descent. They spent most of their lives in Greene County, Penn., where his father made farming and stock-growing his chief pursuit. In 1860 the subject of our sketch married Minerva O., daughter of L. G. Vanvoorhis, a prominent farmer of Dunkard Township. To Mr. and Mrs. Long were born six children—F. G., proprietor of the Commercial Hotel at Oakland, Maryland; Frank W., a farmer; Fannie E., John J., Loyd L. and Lawrence George (deceased.) Mr. Long was a Republican in politics. He took an active interest in the schools of his township, and for many years served as school director.

WILLIAM LONG, a farmer and stock-grower, residing near Mount Morris, Penn., was born near Garard's Fort, this county, December 22, 1831. He is a son of Samuel and Adaline (Mestrezat) Long, who were of French and Irish lineage. His father, who was farmer all his life, was twice married, and reared a family of six children, of whom William is the oldest, by the last marriage. He was reared on the farm in Whiteley Township, receiving his early education in the subscription schools. He made farming his chief pursuit, and has met with success, being at the present the owner of 400 acres of good land in this township. In politics Mr. Long is a Democrat, as is also his son, Merritt Leonard Long, who was born in this township, March 7, 1869. His daughter Fannie E., was born

March 30, 1876, in Perry Township. William Long's father died in 1886, and his mother in 1880.

COLEMAN LUELLEN, carriage and wagon manufacturer at Mount Morris, Greene County, Penn., was born in Monongalia County, West Virginia, February 8, 1840. He is a son of William G. and Mary (Norris) Luellen, also natives of West Virginia, and of Welsh and English extraction. Mr. Luellen was reared on the home farm in West Virginia, where he received his education He worked on the farm until 1861, when he went to Greene County, Penn., to learn the blacksmith trade. He then enlisted under Capt. J. B. Morris, in Company F, Seventh Virginia Volunteer Infantry and served three years and two months. After his return from the war, Mr. Luellen learned the wagon-maker's trade and has successfully engaged in that business at Mount Morris since 1868. He was united in marriage October 5, 1876, with Catharine, daughter of Philip and Rhoda (Dulaney) Hite Their children are: Carrie L., Benjamin F., James W. and Luretta B. Mr. Luellen is a Republican and a member of the G. A R. Post, No. 450. He and wife belong to the Methodist Episcopal Church.

SPENCER MORRIS, M. D., Ph. D, of Greene County, Penn., was born at Garard's Fort, Penn, October 26, 1820. He is a son of Jonathan and Sarah (Clymer) Morris, who were of German and English extraction. His mother was a native of Bucks County, Penn. His father was born in Greene County; was a physician and merchant at Garard's Fort, and died July 19, 1848. Dr. Morris is a grandson of the Rev. John Corbly. The Doctor is the third in a family of four children. He was reared in the place of his nativity, and attended the common schools. He subsequently attended Greene Academy at Carmichaels, Penn, afterwards attended college in Virginia He then began the study of medicine at Cincinnati, Ohio, where he graduated in 1846, and was for some time thereafter in successful practice of his chosen profession in Greene County, Penn. In 1871 he received the degree of Doctor of Medicine from the medical department of the University of Pennsylvania, afterwards the degree of Doctor of Philosophy from the same institution. In 1873 he graduated from the Jefferson Medical College in Philadelphia. For fifteen years he was a popular quiz teacher in that city, having large classes of medical students In the summer of 1886 he was elected to the chair of lecturer on the symptoms of diseases in the Medico-Chirurgical College of Philadelphia In 1851 Dr. Morris was united in marriage, in West Virginia, with Belinda A , daughter of John H. Bowlby, and their summer residence is near the Mason and Dixon Line in Perry Township This has been their quiet retreat for several years. Here the Doctor is sought after for his excellent medical advice by patients for miles around.

LEVI MORRIS, son of George and Margaret Morris, was born on the waters of Whiteley Creek, on the 14th day of April, 1783. His mother was the oldest child of Rev John Corbly, whose second wife and several of their children were massacred by the Indians at Garard's Fort, on the 10th day of May, 1781. Levi Morris was married to Lucretia Stephens in 1809. He bought a farm and went to housekeeping on Dunkard Creek, near the present site of Mount Morris. This farm was all in the woods and the nearest store was at Greensboro, twelve miles distant. There was but little use for a store, however, at that early history of the country, for the clothing worn by both sexes was domestic, or home-made, and coffee was used but once a week—Sunday morning Mr. Morris, with three of his brothers, volunteered and served in Captain Seeley's cavalry company in the war of 1812. Soon after the war he bought another farm and laid out the town of Mount Morris, which bears his name, and resided there until his death. Soon after the war he was appointed justice of the peace, which office he held until near the close of his life Living near the State of Virginia, a State in which a marriage license was required, and none being required in Pennsylvania, his office was the Gretna Green, to which many of the lads and lassies hied to have their nuptials consummated. Mr. Morris kept the first hotel in Mount Morris, and engaged in milling, farming and stock-raising, always keeping the best blooded stock in the county He raised a family of eleven children, seven sons and four daughters, all of whom grew to maturity, each raising a family Margaret married Patrick Donley; Louisa, George Lemley; Hannah, Abner Garrison; Josephus H., Temperance Smith; W. G, Emily Kirby; Jefferson S., Sarah Ingram; Edward F, Elizabeth Smith, and for second wife, Rhetta Roberts; Thomas I, Sarah Way; James B., Keziah Way; Levi A, Samantha Brown; and Lucretia, C C. Hardin. Levi Morris died an honored and respected citizen on the 20th day of January, 1842, his widow and all their children surviving him. Lucretia Morris, his widow, died April 15, 1885, at the ripe old age of ninety-five years and four months Her children, grandchildren, and great-grandchildren number over two hundred, and reside in several States. Their son, Major James B. Morris, is perhaps the best known man in the county. He is respected for his liberality and true manliness, both as a soldier and a citizen. He was reared and educated in Mount Morris, and has been employed in farming, milling and stock-growing. He was married in Monongalia County, W. Va, August 26, 1848, to Keziah, daughter of Gideon and Jane (Sturgis) Way, of English extraction. They were natives of Fayette County, Penn., but spent most of their lives in Monongalia County, W. Va Major Morris and wife have a family of seven children—Mary J, wife of W. F. Lewellen, of West Virginia; Belle M., wife of Jerome Vanvoorhis, of Dunkard Township; Emma L., wife of J. W. Hatfield; George G., a physician at Washington, D. C., and F. K. and S. W., deceased. Their mother is a devoted member of the Baptist Church. Major Morris is a Republican, has been school director at Mount Morris, and was special agent for the U. S. Treasury Department for several years. In 1861 he enlisted in Company F, Seventh West Virginia Volunteer Infantry, and served as Captain until 1862, when he was promoted to the position of Major, in which capacity he served until the expiration of his term, then returned to Mount Morris. The first man killed from Greene County belonged to Captain Morris' Company, and was killed October 26, 1861.

JOSEPH PATTERSON, farmer and stock-grower, Brock, Penn., was born in Whiteley Township, this county, March 29, 1829. He is the oldest son of William and Rhoda (Whitlatch) Patterson, who were natives of Greene County, and of German and Irish ancestry. Like his father, Joseph has been a successful farmer through life. In 1850 he married Elizabeth, daughter of Thomas and Elizabeth Mooney. Mrs. Patterson is of German and English origin. They have eight children, of whom William Franklin is the second. He also is a farmer and stock-grower, and was born in Whiteley Township February 18, 1854. He received a common-school education, and early in life engaged in the mercantile trade at Waynesville for three years. He has since devoted his time to farming and has met with success. He is the owner of 135½ acres of well improved land. Mr. Patterson was united in marriage in Greene County, December 22, 1872, with Elizabeth, daughter of Jacob Whitlatch, and they are the parents of seven children, viz: Ross, David, Enlow, Arthur, Norval, Ada and Harvey. Mr. and Mrs. Patterson are members of the Methodist Episcopal Church, in which he is a trustee. He is a Democrat in politics.

MINOR N. REAMER, dentist, was born in Monongahela Township, Greene County, Penn., February 2, 1846. He is a son of Benjamin and Anna Maria (Minor) Reamer who were of Welsh and German ancestry. His father, a farmer, died in 1866. Minor, the third in a family of four children, was reared in his native township attended the district schools and was subsequently a student in Waynesburg College for one year. Early in life he studied dentistry in Greensboro, where he commenced the practice of his profession in 1871, remaining there three years. He then located at Mount Morris, Penn., where he has since been actively engaged in the practice of dentistry. The Doctor is a Republican. In 1861 he enlisted in Company G., Eighty-Fifth Pennsylvania Volunteer Infantry, and served two years. He is an active member of the G. A. R., belongs to the I. O. O. F. and is officer of the day in Post No. 450, for 1888. In 1871 Dr. Reamer married Miss Fannie, daughter of G. C. Black.

Her mother's maiden name was Rebecca Sowers. They were of German extraction Doctor and Mrs. Reamer are the parents of three children—Harry B , Nellie E. and Emma D. Their mother is a member of the Methodist Episcopal Church.

Z. T. SHULTZ, farmer and stock-grower, Kirby, Penn , was born in Whiteley Township, this county, July 20, 1848, and is a son of Elijah and Ruth A. (Bailey) Shultz, who were of German and English descent. His mother died in 1881 His father, now seventy-four years of age, is a resident of Waynesburg, Penn. The subject of our sketch was reared in Perry Township, where he has engaged in farming most of his life He received a common-school education, also attended Waynesburg College and subsequently taught for five years. His home farm contains one hundred and twenty-seven acres of well improved land Mr. Shultz taught in this county, in Iowa, and West Virginia, but has devoted his time wholly to farming since 1872—the year he was married. His wife was Miss Hettie A., daughter of Justus and Mary (Bowen) Cowell, and their children are Minnie M., Harmon R , Elijah F., Gurney W and Harold L Mr. and Mrs Shultz are members of the Methodist Episcopal Church In politics he is a Republican, and has served as a school director in his township.

A. SNIDER, a retired blacksmith of Mount Morris. Penn , was born in Monongalia County, West Virginia, October 8, 1813 He is a son of Jeremiah and Anna (Rich) Snider who were also natives of West Virginia, and of German lineage. His great-grandfather came from Germany to America and settled in Virginia. Jeremiah Snider was twice married and reared a family of thirteen children The subject of our sketch was the third child by the second marriage. He was reared on a farm and attended the subscription school in his native township. He was employed as a farm laborer early in life and in 1853 learned the blacksmith's trade with Daniel Bowen, in Waynesburg, Penn . He then engaged in that business at Mount Morris and has met with success. Mr. Snider is the owner of valuable town property and one hundred and sixty acres of land in Perry Township In 1838 he married Mary Bowers; they have had a family of six children; viz., Lucretia, wife of James Fox; Elmer, a blacksmith, and Lindsey Jacob Rolla, Mary J. and Eliza, deceased. Mary J. was the wife of Oliver Evans, now deceased. Mr. Snider is a Democrat in politics He has served as school director and three terms as assessor in his township. He and wife are prominent members of the Methodist Protestant Church.

JESSE SPITZNAGEL, farmer and stock-grower, Brock, Penn., was born in Fayette County, Pennsylvania, February 24, 1838. He is a son of Simon and Jemima (Miller), Spitznagel, who were also natives of Fayette County, and of English and German origin. His father was a successful farmer during his life-time. His family consisted of eleven children, of whom Jesse is the fifth. He was reared on the farm, has been successful in his chosen occupation and owns the farm of one hundred and five acres where he now resides. In 1856 Mr. Spitznagel married Miss Dorotha Whitlatch, who was a native of this county and of German extraction. To Mr. and Mrs. Spitznagel were born five children, viz.—Loziella, wife of Alpheus Wade; Simon E., John, Lewis G. and Lucinda. Mr. Spitznagel is a Republican in politics and belongs to the Methodist Episcopal Church, of which his deceased wife was also a devoted member. Mrs. Spitznagel died March 5, 1887, a faithful wife and kind and loving mother.

SPENCER STEPHENS, farmer and stock-grower, Mount Morris, Penn., was born in Greene Township, this county, September 15, 1839. He is a son of Washington and Joan (Steel) Stephens, being the oldest of their eight children. His parents were of English ancestory. His father was a farmer all his life. Spencer was reared on the farm with his parents, where he attended the district school. He has made farming his main occupation and owns the farm where he resides in Perry Township. In 1865 he was united in marriage in Greene County, with Miss Abigail, daughter of Joseph Conner. Mrs. Stephens is of Irish and English extraction. Their children are Rebecca, Albert, S. C., Leroy, Mary Alice, Stacy and Clara. The family belong to the Baptist Church of which Mr. Stephens is an official member. He is a Republican in politics. He takes an active interest in the education of his children, the oldest two of whom are teachers. In 1862 Mr. Stephens enlisted in Company A., One Hundred and Fortieth Pennsylvania Volunteer Infantry. He was a non-commissioned officer and served under Gen. Hancock. Mr. Stephens was in the battles of Gettysburg, Chancellorsville and the Wilderness and served until the close of the war.

LEWIS WHITLATCH, farmer and stock-grower, Brock, Penn., was born in Perry Township, Greene County, Penn., January 10, 1855. His parents, Jacob and Catharine (Headlee) Whitlatch, were also natives of this county and of English extraction. His father, who was a farmer through life, died in 1884, a highly respected citizen. His family consisted of eleven children, ten of whom grew to maturity. Lewis is the ninth and was reared on the farm in his native township, where he attended the common school. Mr. Whitlatch has made farming his chief pursuit, and has also engaged to some extent in the mercantile trade. He has made a success of his business and owns a farm of one hundred and seventy acres. In 1884 Mr. Whitlatch married Hannah, daughter of William Conley. She is of English and German origin. They have one child—Goldie Lee. Mr. and Mrs. Whitlatch are members of the Methodist

Episcopal Church. He has been a steward, class-leader and trustee in the church, and held various important positions in the Sabbath-school. In politics he is a Republican.

RICHHILL TOWNSHIP.

F. W. BALDWIN, farmer and stock-grower, Ryerson's Station, Penn., was born in Richhill Township, this county, July 15, 1846, and is a son of S. W. and Nancy A. (Barnett) Baldwin, who were of English, Irish and Dutch lineage. His mother was a native of Greene County. His father, who was born in Washington County, Penn., was a mechanic and farmer by occupation, and died in 1884. The subject of this sketch is the only member of his father's family who grew to maturity. He was raised on the farm with his parents and chose agricultural pursuits as his business through life He also worked in his father's mill for years until the mill was sold. Mr Baldwin is the owner of three farms, containing in all 271 acres. He has been very successful in his undertakings Mr Baldwin was united in marriage September 14, 1871, with Susan, daughter of George and Elizabeth (Nuss) Woodruff, who are of English and German origin. They have six children, viz.—Eva E., John W, Mary A L., George M, Ira C and Michael, who died in his infancy. Mr. and Mrs Baldwin are members of the Baptist Church, in which he has served as deacon and treasurer

ELLIS BANE.—Among the prominent farmers and stock-growers who spent a long life in Greene County was Ellis Bane, deceased, who was born in Richhill Township, March 6, 1804, and died in 1882. He was a son of Jesse Bane, a pioneer settler of this county. The history of the family shows them to have been farmers, and usually successful. At the time of his death Mr. Bane was the owner of 400 acres of land. His remains lie in Leazure Cemetery; a handsome monument marks the last resting place He was twice married. His second wife was Elizabeth Conkey. Three of their children are now living, the oldest being Ellis Bane, who now resides on the home farm, and owns 237 acres of well improved land. He was born in Richhill Township, received a common-school education, has been an industrious, energetic farmer, and successful in his business. Mr. Bane was married in October, 1886, in West Virginia to Lelia, daughter of Joshua and Rebecca (Fitzgerald) Hipsley. Mrs.

Bane is of English and Irish descent.   They have one child—Clyde.
Mr. Bane is a strict adherent of the Democratic party.   His wife is
a member of the Presbyterian Church.

A. B. BARNETT, teacher, farmer and stock-grower, was born
in Richhill Township, July 11, 1842   He is a son of John and
Margaret (Stoughton) Barnett, natives of Greene County, and of
Irish and Welsh extraction.   His father, who was a farmer, died
June 12, 1859   The gentleman whose name heads this sketch is
the seventh son and the youngest in a family of eleven children.
He was reared on the farm he now owns, and received his education
in the district school.   He subsequently attended the State Normal
School, chose teaching as a profession, and enjoys the well deserved
reputation of being one of the foremost educators in the county.
He also takes an active interest in the teachers' institutes.   Mr.
Barnett owns and manages a farm of 151 acres of land well stocked
and improved.   He was united in marriage February 21, 1873, with
Miss Jennie, daughter of Stephen Durbin.   Mrs. Barnett is of Irish
descent.   Their children are—Leni Clare, Neicie and Bessie B.
Mr and Mrs Barnett are members of the Baptist Church

JOHN BEBOUT, farmer and stock-grower, was born in Morris
Township, Greene County, Penn., January 17, 1845.   His parents
were Moses and Elizabeth (Smalley) Bebout, natives of Pennsylvania,
and of English lineage.   His father was a farmer and stock-dealer,
and at the time of his death resided in Greene County.   He had a
family of eight children; of these, seven are living, John Bebout,
the subject of our sketch, being the youngest.   He received his
education in the common school, and from an early age up to the
present has been engaged in farming.   He owns 337 acres of valuable land where he resides in Richhill Township.   Mr. Bebout was
married in this county in 1863 to Lizzie, a daughter of Joseph
Tilton, a brother of Rev. Charles W. Tilton, a Baptist minister of
Jefferson, Penn.; also a brother of Rev. Morgan Tilton, of Rutan,
Penn   Mr. and Mrs. Bebout's children are—Charles B., John L,
I. Tilton and Willie S. living, and two infant daughters deceased.
Mr. Bebout is a Democrat.   His wife is a consistent member of the
Baptist Church.

I C. BOOHER, justice of the peace, Ryerson's Station, Penn.,
is a native of Washington County, Penn., and of Welsh and German
ancestry.   His father has dealt extensively in horses, and now resides in Richhill Township, Greene County.   His family consists of
five children, of whom the subject of our sketch is the second.   He
was reared on the farm and received his education in the common
schools, and Greene Academy at Carmichaels, Penn.   He remained
at home with his parents until he reached his majority, then clerked
in a general store for two years.   He has, however, devoted his time

principally to farming, stock-growing and milling, and for several years owned and operated a valuable mill at Ryerson's Station. The mill was burned down February 19, 1885, resulting in a loss to Mr. Booher of $7,000. He owns the farm where he now resides, containing 130 acres. In 1854 Mr. Booher married Miss Rebecca' J., daughter of John Barnett. She was of Irish and Welsh extraction. Their children are—Anderson R., James L., S. E., Jesse L., J. Bentley, Mary M., M. Lattie, Wilmetta and Birdie. Mr. and Mrs. Booher are members of the South Wheeling Baptist Church. He is deacon in the church, and takes an active interest in the Sabbath-school. He is serving on his fourth term as justice of the peace.

JAMES H. BRADDOCK, Harvey's, Penn.—Among the descendants of the early settlers of this county we mention the gentleman whose name heads this sketch. He was born on the farm he now owns, September 18, 1819, and is a son of Francis and Ann (Gray) Braddock. His mother was the daughter of Judge Gray, one of the first associate judges in this part of the State. Mr. Braddock's parents were born in the old fort near Washington, Penn., and were of Irish and English origin. His father died in 1856. Mr. James H. Braddock is the seventh in a family of nine children. He has been a very successful farmer, accumulating quite a good deal of property, the greater part of which he has given to his children. In 1845 Mr. Braddock was united in marriage with Miss Jane, daughter of William and Sarah (Cox) Henderson. Their children are— Adda, wife of Thomas Blair; Frank, a clerk in the War Department at Washington, D. C.; and Sadie, wife of Dr. Teagarden, of West Virginia. Mrs. Braddock died in 1876. In 1883 Mr. Braddock married Miss Belle, daughter of Ephraim McClelland. They are members of the Presbyterian Church, in which Mr. Braddock has been an elder for a period of fifteen years. He also takes an active interest in the Sabbath-school, of which he is now assistant superintendent. In politics he is a Republican.

NEWTON H. BRADDOCK, farmer and stock-grower, was born in Richhill Township, June 1, 1834, and is a son of David and Susan (Crow) Braddock. He is a descendant of the pioneer settlers of this county, a brief history of whom is given in the biographical sketch of F. M. Braddock, also a resident of this township. Newton Braddock is the fourth of a family of nine children. He was reared on the farm in Richhill Township, and attended the district school. He has made farming his occupation and owns 160 acres of valuable land, where he now resides. In 1869 Mr. Braddock married Miss Jane, daughter of Alexander Burns. Their children are—Lizzie N. and David G., Jr. In 1864 Mr. Braddock enlisted in Battery B, First Pennsylvania Light Artillery, and was with the army of the Potomac at Lee's surrender. He taught in the schools of Richhill Township each winter from 1856 till 1873, except the time he spent in the army, and has also served as school director, and was secretary of said board. He is a Republican, and a member of the G. A. R. Post.

F. M. BRADDOCK, farmer and stock-grower, born August 14, 1830, is a son of David G. and Susan (Crow) Braddock, who were of English and Irish and German origin. His father was born in Rich-hill Township in 1807, and still resides on the old Braddock farm, which has been in the possession of the family for more than a hundred years. His family now living consists of nine children. Francis Braddock, great-grandfather of F. M Braddock, was one of the pioneer settlers of this county when the western part of it was all a wilderness. He first settled in Richhill Township, he settling on the old Braddock farm which he took from the Government. F. M Braddock's maternal grandfather, Jacob Crow, was also among the first settlers in this part of the county, and his family of two boys and three girls were murdered by the Indians in Richhill Township. In the Braddock family there are many successful farmers and prominent professional men. As a farmer the subject of our sketch has been very successful, and now owns a 150 acre farm which is in a high state of cultivation. Mr. Braddock was united in marriage November 20, 1862, with Maria J., daughter of Dr. W. B. Porter. Mrs. Braddock was of English and Scotch-Irish ancestry. She died in 1880, leaving a family of three children—Eva L., wife of Charles Buckingham; Sherman F., and Mary, now deceased. In politics Mr Braddock is a Republican. He has been an able member of the school board in his township.

D. A. BRADDOCK, the fourth son of David G. and Susanna (Crow) Braddock, was born in Richhill Township in May, 1840. He was raised on the farm, attended the common-schools, and has made farming and stock-growing his business, although he has worked at the carpenter's trade to some extent. He owns a good farm of 106 acres near Harvey's, Penn. Mr. Braddock was married in December 1877, near Marysville, Union County, Ohio. His wife's maiden name was Lucella Henderson, daughter of Thomas and Ethel (McGee) Henderson, She was born in West Virginia. Mr. and Mrs. Braddock have one son—J. H. Braddock. Mrs. Braddock is a member of the Presbyterian Church. Mr. Braddock is a Republican in politics. The Braddocks were originally from Loudoun County, Virginia, and were among the first settlers of Greene County, Penn.

ROBERT BRISTOR, deceased —Among the prominent citizens of Richhill Township, and descendants of the earliest settlers of Greene County, we mention the gentleman whose name heads this sketch. He was born May 31, 1835. His mother's maiden name was Delilah Hixenbaugh. His father was a farmer and surveyor, and one of the most prominent citizens of the county. He was of

German and English ancestry. Robert Bristor, the third in a family of seven children, was reared on a farm in Richhill Township He was a successful farmer and stock-grower during his lifetime, being at the time of his death, in 1873, the owner of a farm of 171 acres, where his family now resides In April, 1856, Mr. Bristor married Eliza, daughter of John and Ann (McNeely) Gillogly, who were of Irish extraction To Mr. and Mrs. Bristor were born the following named children: John F., J. G , J. H , L L , W S., Anna, wife of L. Booher; Lizzie, Robert and William. Mr. Bristor belonged to the Christian Church, of which his widow is also a member. In politics he was a Republican

ABRAHAM CLUTTER, farmer and stock-grower, was born in Morris Township, Washington County, May 18, 1822. He is a son of William and Sarah (McNay) Clutter, also natives of Washington County, and of German extraction. John Clutter, grandfather of Abraham Clutter, was a soldier in the Revolutionary war, serving under General Washington. The subject of this sketch grew to maturity in his native county, attended the district schools and has made farming his chief occupation He was married January 12, 1845, to Jane, daughter of James Meek, ex-treasurer of Greene County, and now a resident of Jackson Township. Mr. and Mrs. Clutter are the parents of eleven children, ten of whom are now living, viz.: John, Luella, wife of Thomas Hare; Andrew J., George W., Sadie, wife of William Conkey; Mary J., wife of B. Temple; Rachel, wife of John F. Donley; A. Judson, Frank and Clarabel. Elizabeth is deceased. Mr. Clutter has given his children the advantages of good schools, and they are highly respected in the community. He is a member of the Disciple Church, in which he is a deacon, and takes great interest in the Sabbath-school. In politics he is a Democrat

WILLIAM CLUTTER, farmer and stock-grower, is a native of Morris Township, Washington County, born March 2, 1828. His parents are Cephas and Laney (Day) Clutter, natives of Pennsylvania, and of German and Irish descent. His father, a farmer of Cen'er Township, is now eighty-five years of age He reared a family of seven children, five of whom are now living The subject of this sketch, having been reared on a farm, has made farming his chief pursuit and has met with success in his business, owning a good farm of 132 acres where he resides in Richhill Township. In 1847 Mr. Clutter married Miss May J. Hunnell. They have nine children— Lana, deceased, who was the wife of F Conger; John M , Jane, wife of S. McVay; Elizabeth, wife of Simon Pettit; Catharine, wife of Thomas Iams, Belle, wife of George Kinney, Ida Ella, and Cephas. Mrs. Clutter died in 1880; she was a member of the Methodist Episcopal Church. In 1881 Mr. Clutter married Mary Shape, of

Morris Township. Mr. Clutter is a Democrat. In 1862 he enlisted in Company A, One Hundred and Sixty-eighth Pennsylvania Volunteer Infantry, and was discharged in 1863, at the expiration of his term of service.

J. M. CONKEY, farmer and stock-grower, was born in Richhill Township, November 9, 1836. His parents, John and Mary (Prong) Conkey, were respectively natives of Virginia and Greene County, Penn., and were of English and Irish and German origin, His father was a plow-maker, and served in the war of 1812. He was also a successful farmer, and accumulated a handsome fortune. He died in 1884. Of his family of nine children, J. M. Conkey is next to the youngest. He was raised on a farm, attended the common-schools and has served three years in the war of 1861; he has been a successful farmer and stock-grower. He owns a well-stocked and improved farm of 137 acres in Richhill Township, and in 1886 purchased the grist-mill at Graysville, which he now operates. In 1866 Mr. Conkey was married to Miss Celestia Moninger, daughter of George and Susan (Biddle) Moninger, who were of English descent. Mr. and Mrs. Conkey's children are Royal, Ada and Jennie. Mr. Conkey is a Democrat. He and his wife are members of the Presbyterian Church.

JAMES HARVEY CONKEY, farmer and stock-grower, born in Richhill Township, August 2, 1840, is a son of John and Mary (Prong) Conkey, who were respectively natives of Pennsylvania and Virginia, and of English, Irish and German origin. His father was a farmer during his lifetime, and died in 1884. His family consisted of seven children, of whom James Harvey is the youngest. He has from his youth been engaged in agricultural pursuits, in which vocation he has met with success and is the owner of 135 acres of well improved land in Richhill Township. In 1867 Mr. Conkey married Anna Eliza Marsh, who is a daughter of Phillip Marsh, and of English descent. Mr. and Mrs. Conkey have seven children—John, Mary, James, Thomas, Emmett, Elsie and Otto. Mr. Conkey is a Democrat. He and wife are members of the Cumberland Presbyterian Church.

HIRAM DAY, retired farmer and stock-grower, was born in Morris Township, this county, December 18, 1814. He is a son of William and Mary (Sutton) Day, who were of English descent. His father, who spent the latter part of his life as a farmer, was a shoemaker in earlier years, and among the first settlers in Morris Township. The subject of this sketch is the fifth in a family of ten children and was raised on the farm, receiving a limited education in the common schools. He came to Richhill Township when he was a young man and opened a farm in the wild woods, where his only possessions were an ax, a maul, iron wedge and a grubbing hoe   He has since accumulated enough to keep himself and family in luxury, and owns 250 acres of well improved land.   Mr. Day was first married November 28, 1839, to Miss May E , daughter of Samuel Thompson.   Mrs. Day was of German origin, she died March 14, 1863.   Their children were Eliza Jane, wife of Warren Burns, and William A.   Mr Day's present wife was the widow of David Dougal.   Her maiden name was Dorcas Blair, a daughter of Alexander Blair, who was of Irish descent.   Mr and Mrs. Day have one son, Harvey.   Mrs. Day is a member of the Presbyterian Church, Mr. Day is the treasurer of the Sabbath-school.   He is a Democrat in politics

W. S DRAKE, merchant and dealer in agricultural implements, Jacksonville, Penn., was born in Morgan Township, February 11, 1838.   He is a son of Francis and Eliza (Stewart) Drake, who were respectively natives of New Jersey and Washington County, Penn., and of English, Scotch and German origin.   His father was a chair maker and painter, and was also skilled in other trades.   He died February 20, 1878.   The subject of this sketch is the oldest of a family of five children, four of whom are living.   He was raised in this county, receiving his education in the common schools of Morgan, Jefferson and Richhill townships.   He taught for several years and, in 1860, being desirous of seeing more of the world, he went to Texas, where he again engaged in school teaching until 1862. He then enlisted in the Twenty-ninth Texas Cavalry. was Orderly Sergeant, and served until 1865.   While his service was in the Confederate army, yet at heart he was a Union man   In 1865, he, with about one-hundred others, started for the Union lines and were captured and returned, and were in prison when the war closed. After the close of the war Mr. Drake again taught school for a year in Denton County, Texas, and in 1866 returned to Richhill Township, for four years engaging in farming and carpenter work.   In 1870 he formed his present partnership with Perry Sowers, dealing in general stock, wool and farming implements   In 1861 Mr. Drake married Miss Julia E , daughter of George C and Julia E. (Ohlhausen) Parker.   Her father was born in Virginia and her mother near Philadelphia, Penn.   They were of English and German origin. Mr and Mrs Drake have six children—Anna, wife of Silas Jennings; May, John, W. C., George and Emma.   Mr. Drake is a Democrat, and a prominent member of the Masonic fraternity.

GEORGE W. FERRELL, a shoemaker by occupation, was born in Center Township, April 16, 1828, and is a son of Peter and Nancy (Huffman) Ferrell who were, respectively, natives of New Jersey and Pennsylvania, and of German extraction.   His father was a farmer and his family consisted of ten children, of whom George W. is the eighth.   He received a common-school education and early in life learned the shoemaker's trade, which he has made his main occupation. Mr. Ferrell has lived in Jacksonville, Penn., since 1848. He has been twice married—first, in 1850, to Sarah Isabella Pettit, and they were the parents of three children—James M., a merchant at New Freeport, Penn.; W. S., a shoemaker, and Clara I., wife of William John. Mrs. Ferrell died in 1858, and in 1859 Mr. Ferrell married Nancy, daughter of James R. Throckmorton. At the time of their marriage she was the widow of Stephen Durbin. Mr. and Mrs. Durbin were the parents of two children—Jennie, wife of A. B. Barnett, and Mary, wife of W. A. Day. To Mr. and Mrs. Ferrell have been born the following named children—Ida May, deceased, who was the wife of John Henderson; Lizzie C., wife of Perry E. Wright; Effie A. and Harvey D. W. Mr. and Mrs. Ferrell are members of the Cumberland Presbyterian Church, in which he is a trustee. In politics he is a Republican. He is a member and present chaplain of the G. A. R. Post, No. 428. In 1864 Mr. Ferrell enlisted in Company F, Eighty-fifth Pennsylvania Volunteer Infantry and served till the close of the war, being present at Lee's surrender.

H. B. FLETCHER, farmer and stock-grower, was born April 12, 1836, on the farm he now owns, and where he has spent all his life, in Richhill Township. He is a son of William and Nancy (Bane) Fletcher, who were of Irish and English descent. His father was born in Ireland in 1803, came to Philadelphia, Penn., in 1821, and soon after came to Jefferson Township, Greene County, and spent the remainder of his life. He died in 1869. The subject of this sketch is his only child who grew to maturity. He received a common-school education, and has made a success of farming, being at present the owner of 200 acres of valuable land. In 1858 Mr. Fletcher married Mary, daughter of Abraham Rickey, and they have a family of seven children—Edward, J. W., William, Frank, W. C., Lydia and Clara B. Mr. Fletcher is a Republican. His wife is a member of the Presbyterian Church.

WILLIAM R. FONNER, retired farmer and stock-grower, was born in Morris Township, Greene County, Penn., September 5, 1824. He is a son of Henry and Abigail (Taylor) Fonner, who were of German and English descent. His father was a teacher in early life, in later years a farmer. He came across the mountains and settled in Greene County in 1801, and died in 1851, at the age of seventy-five years. William R. Fonner is the fourth in a family of seven children, six of whom grew to be men and women. He received his education in the schools of the county. In his business as a farmer he has ever exercised good judgment and practiced economy and now owns a fine farm of 200 acres in Richhill Township, where he now enjoys a life of retirement. In July of 1849 Mr. Fonner married

Eliza, daughter of Samuel and Nancy (Flick) Rail, and they had a family of two son, both now deceased, and two daughters—Mary Ann, wife of Daniel Miller, and Hannah J., wife of Miles Meek. In religion Mr. Fonner is a Baptist, in politics a Republican.

A. J. GOODWIN, merchant, Jacksonville, Penn , was born in Washington County, Penn , February 2, 1817, and is a son of John and Sarah (Gardner) Goodwin, natives of Washington County, and of German origin. His father was a weaver and farmer, and reared a family of ten children. The subject of this sketch is the second child, and lived on the farm with his parents until he was fifteen years of age. The family then came to Greene County, and settled on a farm in Center Township   Mr Goodwin attended school in an old log school-house. He naturally took up his father's occupation, and was engaged therein until he reached his majority. He then began working at the carpenter's trade and stone work, and took contracts for buildings. He was engaged in this business for a period of twelve years or more, and succeeded in gaining a good start in the world. From 1850 to 1874 he devoted his time principally to farming and stock-growing. Since that time he has been in his present business, in the store owned by his son for five years previous to 1874   In 1842 Mr. Goodwin married Miss Eliza, daughter of William and Lydia (Russell) Sargent, and they have four children—Elizabeth, wife of Martin Supler, Lydia, wife of Samuel Grim; J. T , wholesale druggist in Wheeling, W Va., and William (deceased). Mrs. Goodwin was a member of the Baptist Church until her death in 1871. Mr. Goodwin belongs to the Christian Church, in which he has been superintendent of the Sabbath-school. Mr. Goodwin is (1888) the Prohibition candidate for sheriff of Greene County

DANIEL GOODWIN, farmer and stock-grower, Wind Ridge, Penn., was born in Washington County, Penn., April 3, 1820, and is a son of John and Sarah (Gardner) Goodwin, natives of Pennsylvania and of German origin   His father was a weaver and farmer, and reared a family of nine children, the subject of our sketch being the oldest. He was reared on the farm on Ten-Mile Creek in Center Township, where he attended the district school. Mr. Goodwin is a very successful farmer, industrious, economical and prudent in his business. He has succeeded in accumulating a handsome fortune. He started in life a poor boy, his first investment in land being the purchase of thirty acres on time when land was very cheap, and when he did not have money enough to pay for five acres at present prices. But through energy and determination to succeed he has been able to add to his possessions, until now he is the owner of 600 acres of valuable land, well stocked and improved. Mr Goodwin was united in marriage, in 1844, with Miss Julia Ann, daughter of Ezekiel and Catharine (Huffman) Braden, who were of Irish and German origin.

Mr. and Mrs Goodwin were the parents of five children—Eliza J., wife of Richard Supler; Sarah, wife of D. W. Vanatta; John, Mary A. and Daniel Mack. Mrs Goodwin died March 5, 1888. Mr. Goodwin is a member of the Baptist Church, in which he has served as deacon for many years. He takes an active interest in the schools of his district, and has served a number of years as school director.

THOMAS L. GRAY, farmer and stock-grower, was born in Marshall County, W. Va., August 19, 1824, and is a son of Matthew and Sarah (Lazear) Gray. They were natives of Pennsylvania, his mother having been born on the farm where the subject of our sketch now resides. His father, who war a farmer all his life, died in 1884. Thomas L. Gray is a member of a family of nine children. He was reared on the farm where he now resides, and has made farming his main occupation, in connection with which he has engaged in the coal business extensively, having opened a valuable bank on his farm about twenty years ago. Mr. Gray is the owner of 600 acres of land, 170 acres being in his home farm in Richhill Township, and 300 acres in Washington County. In 1859 Mr. Gray married Miss Hannah, daughter of James and Hannah Barnhart Their children are —John W., a farmer; James M., Sarah L., wife of Peter Gibbons; Benjamin Franklin, Margaret, wife of James Braden; Hannah, Jesse L. and Thomas L. Mr. Gray is a member of the Methodist Episcopal Church In politics he is a Democrat, and has served as clerk and inspector of elections

ELIAS K. GRIBBEN, farmer and stock-grower, was born in Richhill Township, Greene County, Penn., September 27, 1843, and is a son of James and Nancy (Kerr) Gribben. His mother was a native of Allegheny County, Penn. His father was born in Ireland and came to America at the age of twenty-one, was a farmer all his life, and died in Greene County, Penn, in 1885. His family consisted of eleven children, nine of whom are still living, Elias K. being the third in the family. He has spent his life in farming, and still continues in that business. He is the owner of a fine farm of 140 acres where he resides in Richhill Township. In 1862 he enlisted in Company A, Eighteenth Pennsylvania Cavalry, was in the battles of Hagerstown, Gettysburg, and Brandy Station, Va., was wounded three times, and was discharged in 1864. In 1869 Mr. Gribben married Hester Jane, daughter of Jacob Loar, a prominent citizen of Richhill Township. Mrs. Gribben is of Dutch lineage. Their children are—Jacob L., James Harvey, Olive M. and Charley T. Mr. and Mrs. Gribben are members of the Methodist Protestant Church, in which he is a trustee and superintendent of the Sabbath-school. In politics he is a Democrat, and has served as school director.

46

CAPT. SAMUEL GRIM, farmer and stock-grower, who was born in Richhill Township, March 24, 1837, is a son of Armstrong and Mary Ann (Scott) Grim, natives of this county, and of German and English origin. His father spent his life as a farmer. Of his family of nine children, all grew to be men and women and are now in active life. Capt. Grim is the third in the family, was reared on his father's farm, and received his education in the common schools and Waynesburg College. When the war broke out he gave up his studies and enlisted in Company B, First West Virginia Cavalry, was elected First Lieutenant and served three years. He was afterwards promoted to the position of Captain, and among other engagements he was in the second battle of Bull Run and the battles of Gettysburg and Winchester. After returning from the war, February 25, 1865, he embarked in the mercantile trade, opening a general store at West Finley, Washington County, Penn. After a period of nine years he returned to Richhill Township, settled on a farm, and has since continued in that occupation. He owns the farm where he now resides, which is well stocked and improved and contains 216 acres. Capt Grim was united in marriage, February 14, 1864, with Lydia J., daughter of A. J. and Eliza (Sargent) Goodwin, natives of Greene County, and of German extraction. Their children are— Francis Sherman, Rosala, wife of James Allison, of Waynesburg, Penn.; Robert Lincoln, Henry Ward Beecher, Edna Blanche, James G. Blaine, Loa Logan and Frances Lydia   In politics Capt. Grim is a Republican. He is Adjutant of the William Smith G. A. R. Post, No 428   '

REV. WILLIAM HANNA, Presbyterian minister, is a native of the Buckeye State, having been born in Trumbull County, Ohio, May 6, 1820. He is a son of Isaac and Martha (Davis) Hanna, who were natives of Pennsylvania, and of Scotch-Irish descent. The subject of this sketch is a descendant of Robert Hanna, the founder of Hannatown, Westmoreland County, Penn. The Hanna family are usually farmers and as a rule have been successful in their business. Rev. Hanna wrote one volume of a history of Greene County, but did not complete the work as it was financially a failure. He has been quite successful in business, and is the owner of a large and well improved farm in Richhill Township, where he resides a part of each year   He also owns two business blocks in Cannonsburg, Penn., and a splendid winter residence at Beck's Mills, Penn., and has considerable personal property. When Mr. Hanna was six years of age his father died. His early life was spent in Fayette County, where he attended the George's Creek Academy. At an early age he became a member of the Presbyterian Church, and was licensed to preach in 1850. His first charge was at Masontown, Fayette County, Penn., where he remained for a period of nine years. He then preached in

Graysville, Richhill Township, Greene County, Penn., six years, and for some time had a charge at West Elizabeth in Allegheny County. He is an earnest temperance man and votes the prohibition ticket. He is a member of the Sons of Temperance. In 1844 Mr. Hanna married Sarah, daughter of Hon. Samuel Nixon, of Fayette County, Penn., who was of Scotch-Irish descent. This union has been blessed with ten children, three of whom are now living, viz: William C., Martha J., and James W. The family are members of the Presbyterian Church.

JAMES HUGHES, farmer and stock-grower, was born near Jefferson, Penn., February 12, 1829. He is the son of James and Margaret (Heller) Hughes, and grandson of Thomas Hughes, founder of Jefferson Borough. His father was a farmer and land speculator, and acted in the capacity of high sheriff of Greene County. He died in 1861. The subject of this sketch is the eighth in a family of ten children. He was reared on a farm near Jefferson, where he acquired his early education. In 1864 he moved from his birthplace to Richhill Township. He owned a general store at Bristoria for twelve years, but has devoted most of his life to farming. He owns over 400 acres of valuable land where he now resides in Richhill Township. Mr. Hughes was united in marriage, October 25, 1854, with Hester, daughter of Valentine Nichols. Her mother's maiden name was Nancy A. Cooper. They were of English origin. Her father was a farmer. He was among the early settlers. Mr. and Mrs. Hughes have four children—Winfield S., whose wife died in 1885, leaving two children—Lulu Z. and Bessie Pearl; Anabel, deceased, who was the wife of J. L. Supler, and mother of one child—Willis W.; George V. and William. Mrs. Hughes is a member of the Cumberland Presbyterian Church. Mr. Hughes is a Republican. He took an active interest in the Granger movement. During the late Rebellion he took an active part in trying to put it down, helping to raise money and men. He also reared his nephew, William G. Milllken, who at the age of seventeen enlisted in Company G, of the Eighteenth Pennsylvania Cavalry. The Hughes, Swans and Vanaters were among the first settlers of Greene County; they settled along the Monono, at or near Jefferson

WILLIAM JACOBS, ex-treasurer of Greene County, was born in Richhill Township, August 18, 1835. He is a son of Daniel B. and Hannah (Rail) Jacobs, natives of Maryland His father is a prominent farmer and resides in Franklin Township. William was reared on the farm, attended the common schools and made farming his main occupation until 1884, when he was elected to the office of treasurer of the county. Mr. Jacobs was an efficient officer and made many friends while in that capacity. He was ably assisted by his son, D. W. Jacobs, a steady, industrious young man and a first-class penman. Mr. Jacobs owns a well improved farm in Richhill Township where he resides. He was united in marriage, January 17, 1856, with Hester J., daughter of John Loar, and they have two children—D. W. and Anna B., wife of Robert R Headley. Mr. and Mrs Jacobs are members of the Methodist Protestant Church. Mr. Jacobs is a Democrat, and has served as school director of his township. He is also a prominent member of the I. O. O. F.

S. KNIGHT, undertaker and furniture dealer, Jacksonville, Penn., was born in Monroe County, Ohio, September 4, 1829. His parents, Stephen and Sarah (Wells) Knight, were natives of Pennsylvania, and of English origin. His father was a farmer by occupation, and died in Ohio. His family consisted of fifteen children, twelve of whom grew to maturity. The subject of our sketch is the ninth in the family. He was reared on his father's farm, received a common school education, and early in life commenced his present business, which he has carried on at Jacksonville, Penn., for nearly half a century. During that time he has been director at twenty-five hundred funerals Mr. Knight has been twice married—first, December 20, 1849, to Lucy L., daughter of John Conkey, and they were the parents of six children, four living—Anna, J M., William and Elizabeth Mrs Lucy Knight died in 1886 In 1887 Mr Knight married Charlotte, daughter of Andrew Smith, and sister of the present county treasurer. She is of Scotch descent. His wife is a member of the Church of God, and Mr. Knight is a Cumberland Presbyterian, of which church he is a trustee He is a Democrat. He has served as school director, and as justice of the peace for ten years. He is a member of the I. O O. F., belongs to the Encampment, and is one of the best and most highly respected citizens of the county.

JESSE LAZEAR was born in Guernsey County, Ohio, June 25, 1825. He is a son of Francis and Mary (Crow) Lazear, natives of Greene County, Penn., and is among the earliest settlers His mother was of German origin. His father was of French descent. He died in 1871, at the advanced age of seventy years Thomas Lazear, grandfather of Jesse Lazear, was apointed magistrate by the Governor, served for years in that capacity. The family have usually been farmers and successful in all their business ventures. Jesse Lazear is the oldest in a family of six children. His parents came to Richhill Township in 1827, where he was raised on the farm and received his education in the common schools. He has made farming and stockgrowing his business through life, and has met with success, being at present the owner of a large, well improved farm where he resides near Ryerson's Station, Penn. His residence is a substantial brick building, beautifully located. Mr. Lazear was united in marriage, March 25, 1856, with Miss Alice, daughter of Morfford and Nancy (Simpson) Throckmorton, who were of Irish and English extraction.

Mr. and Mrs. Lazear are the parents of the following named children—William, Mary, wife of J. C. McCracken, M.D., Cameron, W. Va.; Fannie, wife of Silas Inghiam; and John. In politics Mr. Lazear is a Democrat.

JOHN J. LESLIE, farmer and stock-grower, born in Richhill Township, December 3, 1836, is a son of Samuel and Sarah (Jones) Leslie, who were respectively natives of Ireland and Pennsylvania. His father worked on public-works during his early life, but devoted his time to farming after coming to Greene County in 1834. He settled on a farm in Richhill Township, remaining there until his death in 1869. The gentleman whose name heads this sketch was reared on the farm in his native township, where he attended the district schools. He took up farming as his occupation and has made it a success, owning at present one hundred and fifty-three acres of land, well stocked and improved, where he now resides near Harvey's, Penn. Mr. Leslie was united in marriage, in this county in 1869, with Miss Nancy A., daughter of Spencer Bebout. They were the parents of four children—two now living, Florence and Samuel S Mrs. Leslie died in 1877. In 1879 Mr. Leslie was again united in marriage, his second wife being Mary G., daughter of Munson Post They are the parents of one child—Robert P. Mr. Leslie is a member of the Christian Church. In politics he is a Democrat. He takes an active interest in school affairs, and has served on the school board of the township where he now resides.

JACOB LOAR, farmer and stock-grower, was born in Allegany County, Maryland, February 6, 1817. His parents were John and Hester (Stephens) Loar, natives of New Jersey, and of German lineage. His father, who was born in 1794, was a farmer by occupation. He came to Whiteley Township, Greene County, in 1820, and died in 1873 at the advanced age of eighty-four years. His family consisted of fourteen children, eleven of whom grew to maturity. Three of his sons were physicians and two ministers. Jacob, the second in the family, settled in Richhill Township, in 1837, and has been very successful in business. He owns the valuable farm of of two hundred and twenty acres where he now resides. Mr. Loar is prominent and influential in his community, has been a member of the school board and served as the justice of peace for a period fifteen years. He has been three times married—first, in 1836, to Maria Nelson, and they were the parents of nine children, six of whom are now living, viz., John M., a farmer; Nelson, a physician in Bloomington, Illinois; George, a physician in Munroe, Iowa; Margaret Ann, wife of A. K. Allum; Hester Jane, wife of E. J. Gribben and Anna, wife of Oliver Burns. The deceased are James Apoloe, Jacob H. and Catharine who was the wife of B. F Temple. Mrs. Loar died in 1864. Mr. Loar's second wife was Sarah Williams widow of Morrison Applegate, who died February 11, 1875. They had one son—William C., a medical student in Indianapolis, Ind., and one daghter, Ora who died April 1888. Mr. Loar was again married, in 1881, to Mary Dinsmore, widow of Benjamin Durbin. She was the mother of six children; viz., Mary, Harvey, Elizabeth, Thomas, William and Bothenia. Mr. Loar is a member of the Methodist Protestant Church, of which he has been steward and trustee. He wife is a Presbyterian.

J. K. LOUGHRIDGE, farmer and stock-grower, was born in Wheeling, W. Va., May 21, 1823, is a son of William and Mary (Kettler) Loughridge. His father was of Scotch origin, born in Coleraine, County Derry, Ireland, came to America during the war of 1812, being six weeks in making the passage. Was married in Phildelphia, Penn., in 1814, where he remained for some time. He afterwards came to Pittsburg and next moved to Wheeling, W. Va., where he engaged in the hotel and livery business, these being the first established in the city. He purchased a portion of the farm on which J. K. Loughridge now resides in 1817. Here he removed his family, in 1827, where he remained until his death, in 1867, being ninety-five years of age. He was one of the first school directors under the free-school system in Richhill Township, Greene County, Penn., and elder of the Unity Presbyterian Church. His mother was of German origin, was born in Philadelphia, Penn., in 1787, where she was married to Briton Sollars. Their eldest child, Levi, was married to Elizabeth Burns and resides in Richhill Township. Their daughter Elizabeth married Alexander Burns and is now deceased. They were both educated at Wheeling, W.Va. Elizabeth was the first female school teacher in Richhill Township, and produced some of the finest specimens of penmanship of the day. After the death of her husband, Mrs. Sollars married Mr. Smith, a painter, in Philadelphia, who lost his life in the war of 1812. She next married William Loughridge, by whom she had nine children, of which seven grew to man and womanhood. Margaret married R. S. Dinsmore, a Presbyterian minister, both are now deceased; Mary taught in the high school at New Castle and afterwards in Ohio, where she married Jesse McBride, a Wesleyan Methodist minister, both are now deceased. William A. married Hannah Grey and is now a carpenter and farmer in Keokuk County, Iowa; Alexander W. married Susan Jennings and is how a stock-merchant in Iowa; Dr. J. H. married Candace Power, was a physician and surgeon in the late war and is now located in Rensellaer, Ind., where he has an extensive practice. Emma, the youngest, married John C. Booher, and is now deceased. John K., the fourth in his father's family, married Harriet Campsey, daughter of James and Isabella (Dougherty) Campsey, Claysville, Penn. The family of Mr. and Mrs. Loughridge, are James H., Willmette, wife of Dr. T. B. Hill; William W., John W., Maud I., David G. C. and Hettie M. Mr. Loughridge took an active interest in the Sabbath-schools at an early day; also took a great interest in the progress of the district schools, acting in the capacity of school director for seven years in succession. His education and the greater portion of his property has been acquired principally by his own efforts, his farms are well situated for farming and grazing, well improved, contains nearly 500 acres and has been his place of residence from early childhood. He is a Democrat in politics. A man of good moral principles and was the first chosen on the jury which found George Clark guilty of the murder of William McCauslain near Carmichael's, Penn.

PHILLIP MARSH, deceased, was one of Richhill Township's representative citizens. He was born in New Jersey in 1811. His parents were Joseph P. and Nancy (Minton) Marsh, natives of New Jersey, and of English lineage. His father was a shoemaker by occupation, which vocation he followed for many years. He had eight children, the subject of this sketch being the fifth. Phillip Marsh was raised in Washington County, Penn., where he had removed with his parents about the year 1824. He came to Greene County and engaged in farming until the time of his death in 1877. He was an elder in tne Cumberland Presbyterian Church and superintendent of the Sabbath-school. In politics he was a Republican. Mr. Marsh was married, November 20, 1835, to Martha, daughter of Ephraim and Martha (Elliott) Post, and they were the parents of the following named children—Ann Eliza, wife of Harvey Conkey; Caroline, widow of Samuel Thompson; Eveline, Lucy, wife of George Jennings; Laura F., wife of Cassius Jennings; Leroy, a farmer; and Ellsworth. Mrs. Marsh is a member of the Cumberland Presbyterian Church.

WILLIAM G. MILLIKEN, merchant, of the firm of Milliken & Supler, Bristoria, Penn., was born on Wheeling Creek, in this county, January 21, 1845. His parents, Joseph and Mary (Hughes) Milliken, were of Irish and English origin. His father, who was a cooper and farmer by occupation, died in this county. Of his family of six children, William is the third, and was reared in Jefferson Township, where he received his education. In 1862 he enlisted in Company G, Eighteenth Pennsylvania Cavalry, and was a non-commissioned officer. He was taken prisoner at Hanover, Penn. Mr. Milliken participated in the battles of The Wilderness, Spottsylvania, Cold Harbor, Cedar Creek and Winchester, and many others, and was discharged at the close of the war in 1865. He then returned to Richhill Township and engaged in farming until 1881, when he embarked in his present business, in which he has a liberal patronage and meets with success. In 1866 Mr. Milliken married Margaret, daughter of Valentine Nichols. To Mr. and Mrs. Milliken were born five children—Isadora, Mary F., John W., Mettie, and Loyd (deceased). Mrs. Milliken departed this life in 1885. She was a consistent member of the Cumberland Presbyterian Church. Mr. Milliken is a member of the G. A. R. Post, in which he has served as Quartermaster.

JOHN M. MURRAY, physician and surgeon, Jacksonville, Penn., was born in the State of Iowa, April 23, 1846. He is a son of Joseph and Leah (Larimer) Murray, who were natives of Pennsylvania, and of Scotch-Irish descent. His father was a schoolteacher in early life, in later years a farmer. His family consisted of nine children, Dr. Murray being the sixth. He was reared in this county and received his literary education in the State Normal School of Erie and Waynesburg College. He studied medicine with Dr. J. T. Iams, then a practicing physician of Richhill Township. Dr. Murray afterwards attended Bellevue Medical College at New York City, where he graduated in 1876. He began the practice of his profession at Wind Ridge, Penn., during the same year, and has met with a liberal and successful patronage. He is an active member of the Greene County Medical Society. In 1879 Dr. Murray married Miss Jennie, daughter of Morrison Applegate. Mrs. Murray was of English descent. She died in 1885, leaving two children —Austin and John C. Mrs. Murray was a member of the Methodist Protestant Church, and Mr. Murray is a member of the Presbyterian.

T. J. McCLEARY, farmer, stock-grower and attorney at law, was born February 20, 1837, in Claysville, Washington, County, Penn., and is the son of William and Susan G. (Wilkinson) McCleary. His father was born near Winchester, Virginia, and his mother was a native of Fayette County, Penn. His grandfather, Thomas McCleary, came from Ireland to America in company with his three brothers. They were all in the army of Washington during the Revolutionary war, Thomas being the only one who lived to the close of the war. After peace was declared he settled near Winchester, Virginia, and engaged in farming, T. J. McCleary's father, who died in Washington County in 1881, had a family of eleven children, of whom the subject of our sketch is the oldest son. He was reared on the farm and received his education in the common schools, the academy and normal school. He taught in Greene and Washington counties a number of terms. He afterwards read law, and has given it his particular attention, although he has lived on the farm the greater part of his life. He owns and deals in Western lands. Mr. McCleary was married in Washington County, August 8, 1860, to Martha J. Rossell, daughter of Rev. Job and Mariah L. (Layton) Rossell, and their children are—W. Clarence, Arthur V., Thomas W., Z. Linn; one daughter, Idesta Ethleen. Mr. and Mrs. McCleary are members of the Baptist Church, and he belongs to the I. O. O. F. and Patrons of Husbandry, or the Grange.. He is a Democrat, and accustomed to addressing the public when called upon to do so. The father of Mrs. McCleary, Rev. Job Rossell, is deserving of special mention He was born July 19, 1813, in Fayette County; was licensed to preach by the Flatwoods Baptist Church. For nearly fifty years he labored in the Master's cause. During all these years to the many people who knew him in Westmoreland, Fayette, Washington and Greene counties, the name of Job Rossell was not uttered without bringing to those who heard it a train of thought by which their better natures were more fully developed, and their love for their fellow man strengthened and broadened. He moved to this township in 1861, locating near Ryerson's Station; was for a number of years pastor of South Wheeling Church. He passed to the other shore on September 21, 1884, there to realize more fully the fruits of his labor here. He is the only man, so far as the writer knows, who gave his whole time to the Baptist Churches and missionary work in this region, in which work he was successful. Many organizations by him were started which are to-day prosperous churches; among which is Fork Ridge, West Virginia. I have told you he was the only man, and yet he was not the only one. During these many years to his good wife was left largely the care of the home and family, and she did her part nobly; her sacrifices were many; for many years she was an invalid, but ever cheerful and bright. She passed to her rest November 30, 1887. During the last years of their lives they were tenderly cared for by Mrs. McCleary and her husband, T. J. and children. Eternity alone can reveal the greatness of these lives, in producing fruit for the Master's kingdom. A handsome bronze monument now marks their last resting place.

B. H. McNAY, farmer and stock-grower, was born in Franklin Township, Greene County, Penn , December 20, 1836. His parents, James and Anna (Dickerson) McNay, were natives of Pennsylvania and among the early settlers of this county. They were of Irish and English extraction. His father was a farmer during his lifetime, and died in this county in his eighty-first year. He reared a family of eleven children, ten of whom grew to maturity. The subject of our sketch is the ninth in the family. He was reared on the farm, obtained a common-school education, and afterwards attended Waynesburg College He has since been engaged in agricultural pursuits, and owns 240 acres of land where he resides in Richhill Township. Mr. McNay has been twice united in marriage, his first wife being Frances Carson, and they were the parents of three children—J. W., Anna Maud and Leonora M. Mrs McNay died in 1879. Her husband was afterwards married, in 1882, to Miss Mary, daughter of Thomas Stewart, and they have three children—Mabel

M., H. Earl and Louie Mr McNay is a Republican. He and wife are members of the Cumberland Presbyterian Church.

JOHN ORNDOFF, farmer and stock-grower, born in Greene County April 9, 1839, is a son of William and Salone (Wisecarver) Orndoff His mother was a native of Greene County. His father, who was born in Old Virginia, was a farmer all his life, having over sixty years ago settled in Center Township, where he resided until his death in 1885. His family numbered eleven children, of whom the gentleman whose name heads this sketch is the sixth. He was reared on his father's farm, attended common school in Center Township, and has made farming a success. He is the owner of 435 acres of valuable land and a fine country residence Mr. Orndoff is energetic and industrious, having followed the example of his father who, when he came to this county, was a poor boy with no earthly possessions but his clothing and a horse and saddle; but by economy and a determination to succeed, he owned at the time of his death 900 acres of land. John Orndoff was united in marriage, November 2, 1867, with Minerva, daughter of Matthias Roseberry, and they are the parents of six children; viz., Oscar F., Amanda S, Alice M, John B, Jessie L and Benjamin H In politics Mr. Orndoff is a Republican His wife is a member of the Baptist Church.

H. H. PARRY, blacksmith, Bristoria, Penn., was born in Westmoreland County, Penn , February 16, 1845, and is the son of Royal L., and Elizabeth (Lidea) Parry. His parents were natives of Wales His father was a blacksmith, and followed the trade during his lifetime. He had a family of thirteen children, five of whom are now living. Mr H. H Parry was raised on a farm in Richhill and Washington townships. He received the benefit of a common school education, and learned his trade early in life. In 1863 he enlisted in Company D, Twelfth West Virginia Infantry, and was in several engagements—among which were the battles of Petersburg, Cedar Creek, Hunter's Raid and Winchester. At the close of the war he was discharged by general order. After his return home he opened a blacksmith shop, and worked for four years in Aleppo Township, and since that time has been located at Bristoria. He owns a small farm, in connection with his shop, also a neat and substantial residence. In 1869 Mr. Parry married Miss Mary, daughter of James McVay, Aleppo Township, one of the prominent farmers and stockgrowers in this county. Mr. and Mrs. Parry's children are Charles McVay, M. Jane, Flora B., James M., Harry L. and Mary M. Mr. Parry is a Republican. and a member of the G A R Post

J. E. PATTERSON, physician, was born near Claysville, Washington County, Penn , March 20, 1848. His parents were John and Mahala (Patterson) Patterson, who were of Irish and German extraction His father, who was a farmer all his life, came to Greene County in 1854, and settled in Center Township on the farm where the subject of this sketch was reared   Dr. Patterson acquired a common school education, after which he attended Waynesburg College and the State Normal School. He began the study of medicine with Dr. Gray, of Jacksonville, Penn., and subsequently attended the Medical College at Cleveland, Ohio. He first engaged in his profession, in 1871, in the vicinity of Graysville this county, where he has since been in active practice, with the exception of a short time spent in Nineveh, Pennsylvania.   In 1874 Dr. Patterson married Anna, daughter of Mulford Burroughs, and they are the parents of four children, viz., Charles, John, Alma and Bashie.   In politics Dr Patterson is a Democrat.

MASON SCOTT, farmer and stock-grower, was born in Richhill Township, Greene County, Penn., May 3, 1837, and is a son of Capt. John and Charlotte (Mason) Scott, who were of German and Irish descent.   His father is a farmer and a resident of Jackson Township, this county.   Mr. Mason Scott is the oldest of six children now living.   He grew to maturity on his father's farm and received a good common-school education.   Early in life he taught school for a time, but he made farming and stock-raising his chief pursuit. He is the owner of 252 acres of land well stocked and improved, where he resides near Bristoria, Penn.   Mr. Scott was united in marriage, December 22, 1866, with Sarah, daughter of James and Jane (Sanders) Lemmon.   They were of Dutch and English descent. Mr. and Mrs. Scott's children are Albert, Clara Alice; and Westley, (deceased).   Mr. Scott is a Democrat, and an efficient member of the school board of his township.

HIRAM SCOTT, farmer and stock-grower, who was born in Center Township, Greene County, Penn., May 13, 1841, is a son of Elias and Harriet (Kent) Scott, natives of this county, and of Dutch and Irish extraction.   His father spent all his life as a farmer, and died in Greene County in 1884.   His family consisted of eight children, of whom Hiram Scott is the third.   Having been reared on a farm, he has followed farming as his chief pursuit and is the owner of 180 acres in Richhill Township, where he now resides.   In 1861 Mr. Scott was united in marriage with Miss Mary, daughter of the late Dennis Iams, who was a wealthy and influential farmer. Mrs. Scott is of German lineage.   Their children are Thomas, George B. McClellan, a medical student; Matilda, wife of James Throckmorton; Florence and Charles.   Mr. Scott is a Democrat.   He and his wife are members of the Baptist Church

ROBERT SMITH, county treasurer, was born in Washington County, October 29, 1836, and is a son of Andrew and Ellen (Little) Smith, His mother, who was of English extraction, was born in New Jersey.   His father was a native of Scotland, where he was a farmer and herdsman He died in this county in 1870 at the age of seventy-four years. His family consisted of twelve children, of whom Robert is the oldest. He has spent most of his life in Greene County, having received his education in the schools of Richhill Township He also attended school for some time in Fayette County. Mr. Smith engaged in farming and stock-growing until he was elected to his present position in 1887. He was married in this county, May 26, 1859, to Miss Elizabeth, daughter of Thomas and Elizabeth (Caine) Milliken, and they are the parents of the following children, viz., Mary Ellen, who died at the age of fourteen; Arabella, W D., A. J., T E, R. M. and J. H. P. Mr Smith is actively interested in educational matters In 1872 he was elected county commissioner and served two years and ten months in that position.

JAMES L SMITH.—Among the enterprising young business men of Greene County, few have met with better success than the firm of Smith Bros. Dealers in general merchandise, Graysville, Penn., successors to J. W. Hays James L. Smith. the senior member of the firm, was born in Center Township, this county, March 12, 1856, and is a son of Thomas and Susan (Scott) Smith, natives of Greene County, and of Scotch-Irish extraction. His father, a successful farmer, now resides in Center Township on a finely improved farm of 300 acres The subject of our sketch is the oldest of a family of seven children Early in life he learned the blacksmith and wagon maker's trade, in which he engaged for several years. He was a good mechanic and made a first-class wagon Since 1879 Mr. Smith has been in the mercantile business with his brother at Graysville. He is a Democrat in politics, and is postmaster at Harvey's Penn. He was married in 1879 to Miss May, daughter of Hon. James W Hays, ex-member of the Legislature. They have two children—Jesse F and Nora. Mr and Mrs. Smith are active members of the Baptist Church

MARTIN SUPLER, farmer and stock-grower, was born in Richhill Township, Greene County, Penn., July 29, 1840, and is a son of William and Lucinda (Cummings) Supler, who were natives of this county, and of English lineage His father was a farmer and hotel keeper at Jacksonville. Penn , and died August 20, 1872 His family consisted of seven children, of whom the subject of our sketch is the second. He was reared on the farm, attended the common schools and has made farming and stock-growing his occupation all his life, with the exception of the time he spent in the army and a few years during which he engaged in the mercantile trade at Jacksonville In 1862 he enlisted in Company C, Eighteenth Pennsylvania Cavalry, and served as Sergeant for his company. While on picket duty on one occasion he received a gunshot wound which caused him to lose three and one-half inches of bone from his left arm. He was discharged in 1864, having passed through many serious engagements, among which were the battles of Williamsport, South Mountain and Gettysburg. After his return home Mr. Supler engaged in the mercantile business for two years, and has since devoted his time to farming. He owns 135 acres of land with first-class improvements. He was married in this county in September, 1862, to Elizabeth, daughter of A. J. and Eliza (Sargent) Goodwin. They have four children, viz., Jessie L., wife of T. J. Carpenter; Fannie D., A. J. and John B. Mr. Supler is a Democrat, and a member of Smith's Post, No. 428, G. A. R., Jacksonville, Penn.

JOHN M. WRIGHT, born October 12, 1820, is a son of Reasin and Nancy (McGlumphy) Wright, who were of German and Irish and English ancestry. He is the oldest of six children and was raised on his father's farm. When a young man he learned the trade of a millwright. In 1862 he enlisted in Company C, Eighteenth Pennsylvania Volunteer Cavalry, and was discharged at the close of the war, when he returned to Richhill Township, where he still resides. He was married in this county, in 1844, to Hester Ann, daughter of John and Lydia (Boyd) Caseman. Mrs. Wright is of Dutch extraction. Their children are—George W., a farmer; Sarah M., Perry and Elizabeth. In politics Mr. Wright is a Democrat.

G. W. WRIGHT, farmer and stock-grower, born in Richhill Township, February 22, 1849, is a son of John and Hester Ann (Caseman) Wright. He is the oldest of his father's family was raised on the farm and received his education in the common schools. Early in life he learned the carpenter's trade and followed that as a business until 1879, since which time he has both farmed and worked at his trade. Mr. Wright has made his own way in the world. He now owns a well improved farm of 135 acres near Bristoria, Penn. He was married in Vermilion County, Ill., in January, 1871, to Elizabeth J., daughter of Abraham and Mary (Gardner) Kimball, and their children are—Norton, Mary F., Oliver M., Maud D. and Hester L. In religion Mr. Wright is a Methodist, and his wife was a member of the Baptist Church. He is a Democrat and belongs to the I. O. O. F.

P. J. WHITE, merchant, Ryerson's Station, Penn., was born in Aleppo Township, August 4, 1850. His parents, J. M. and Rebecca (Hewitt) White, were natives of Greene County, and of Dutch and English extraction. His father is a farmer and justice of the peace, and now resides on a farm in Aleppo Township. The subject of this sketch is the only member of the father's family now living. He was reared on the farm, attended the select schools and engaged in farming until 1879, when he embarked in the mercantile trade for two years on Hart's Run, in Aleppo Township. He then located at New

Freeport, and carried on a general store until 1883, when he removed to his present location and established the business in which he is meeting with great success. Mr. White was united in marriage in this county in 1872, with Miss Margaret Ann, daughter of W. J. Moore. Mrs. White is of English and Irish lineage. Their children are Mary Rebecca and Hannah E. In politics Mr White is a Democrat, and was appointed to his present position of postmaster at Ryerson's Station in 1885.

SPRINGHILL TOWNSHIP.

J R. AYERS, the subject of this sketch, was born in Richhill Township, Greene County, Penn., March 12, 1824, and is a son of Silas and Jane (Rickey) Ayers. His parents were natives of New Jersey, from whence they emigrated to Richhill Township, Greene County, Penn., September, 1807, and are of English origin His father was a farmer and soldier in the war of 1812, and was engaged in the battles of Lundy's Lane and New Orleans. Of his father's family of eleven children, J R. is the fourth He grew to manhood in this county, spent his early life in teaching school, and subsequently chose the occupation of farming and stock-dealing, in which occupation he has been very successful. He owns a fine farm of 200 acres where he resides in Springhill Township He was married November 9, 1848, to Miss Caroline Dye, who was born in this county November 9, 1829 They are the parents of the following named children: E. L., deceased; R H , Nanna J., Pennina, Silas and Minor (deceased), Mary M., Ola L., A. D. and J L. R H., the second son, who is a farmer, was born in Springhill Township, November 23, 1852 He was reared on the farm, received his education in the district schools. He was married to Miss Avaline White, April 3, 1874. Pennina, widow of E. B. Darling, deceased, was born in Springhill Township, May 20, 1858, and was married March 12, 1874 Mr and Mrs. Ayers are members of the Baptist Church, in which he is deacon He is a Republican. and has filled the office of school director and auditor in his township.

JOHN BARGER, retired farmer and stock-grower, who was born in Morris Township, this county, May 25, 1827, is a son of Francis and Sarah (Pettit) Barger. His mother, who is of German and Irish origin, is the daughter of Nathaniel Pettit, an early settler of Morris

Township. His father, whose chief occupation was that of farming, was in early life a shoe-maker and school-teacher. He died in this county April 12, 1854. He was twice married, and the subject of this sketch is the oldest of his four children, aged sixty-one years. Mr. John Barger was a resident of Richhill Township until he was ten years of age, when he moved with his parents to Aleppo, now Springhill Township, and has remained there for over half a century. His education was obtained in the common-schools, and while still a young man he was employed as a farmer for some time. He subsequently established a store in New Freeport, Penn, and carried on a successful business for five years, and in that time he made $10,000. Mr. Barger now owns 400 acres of valuable land, besides good town property. He is a self-made man,—his father, Francis Barger, having been bound out by his father to work for Robert Pelleet, of New York, until he should attain his majority. He,—John Barger—however, managed by industry and economy to get a start in the mercantile trade, with what subsequent success we have already noted. Mr. Barger was united in marriage November 2, 1854, with Emily J., daughter of Noah and Elizabeth (Pettit) Lyon, and their children are—David W., a farmer; James P., a silversmith of New Freeport, Penn.; John W., a teacher, and Homer. Mr. Barger is a Republican, and has been postmaster at New Freeport for a period of twenty years He and his wife are members of the Christian Church.

JAMES BURDINE, retired farmer and stock-grower, was born in Perry Township, Greene County, Penn., March 7, 1820, and is the son of Levi and Rebecca (Fox) Burdine, who were of Dutch and Irish lineage. His grandfather, Joseph Fox, was a soldier in the Revolutionary war. At the age of five years the subject of our sketch was left an orphan. Most of his early life was spent on the farm in Monongalia County, W. Va, where he attended the common-schools. He was bound out as a farm laborer until eighteen years old, when he came to Whiteley Township, this county. He soon found work on a farm, and received eight dollars per month. On November 22, 1842, Mr Burdine was united in marriage with Abigail, daughter of Joseph Johnson, of Dunkard Township. Their children are—Dennis, Eliza Jane, Johnson, Mary, wife of J. L. Morford; Harriet A, who was the wife of Lewis Hamilton, and died in 1883; Delila and James Milton. Mr. Burdine's present wife is Fannie, daughter of Rev. John Henderson. They have one child — Orphia. Mrs Burdine is a member of the Christian Church. Mr. Burdine is a Democrat. He is a self-made man, having begun life as a poor boy, and is now the owner of a fine farm of 118 acres in Springhill Township. He at one time owned over 400 acres He has paid out over $4,000 of bail money, and has till been able to give his children a good start in life.

W. L. BURGE, farmer and stock-grower, was born in Whiteley Township, Greene County, Penn., August 25, 1827, and is a son of Henry and Rachel (Wildman) Burge His parents, who were of English and Dutch descent, were natives of this county, and members of the Society of Friends. His father, who died in Virginia in 1866, was a blacksmith, and spent most of his life in that occupation. He was twice married, and his family consisted of fourteen children. The subject of this sketch grew to manhood in Greene County, learned the blacksmith's trade with his father and has followed that as a business for over forty years In 1861 he went to Virginia and worked at his trade until 1866, when he returned to this county. He has since farmed, and now owns a farm consisting of 118 acres of well-stocked and improved land. In 1850 Mr. Burge married Miss Margaret, daughter of John and Sarah Knight. Mrs. Burge is of English and Dutch ancestry. They have a family of ten children, viz.: Plesa Ann, wife of W. H Main; Alfred·J., William L, Melissa, wife of Albert J. Fordyce; Rachel, wife of John L. Main; Maggie, wife of William H. Dye; Mary M., Ella E., John C. and Rosa E. Mr. and Mrs. Burge are members of the Methodist Episcopal Church, where he has served as class-leader for twenty years, and has also served as steward Mr. Burge is a Democrat. He takes an active interest in the public schools, and has been for a number of years a member of the I. O O. F.

THOMAS M. CARPENTER, physician, Deep Valley, Penn, was born in Greene County, January 14, 1843, and is a son of William and Agnes (Derbin) Carpenter. His father, who is a blacksmith by trade, was born in New Jersey, but now resides on a farm in Jackson Township His mother was a native of Morgantown, W. Va. His grandfather, James Carpenter, was among the earliest farmers of Richhill Township, this county. His father was twice married, and Dr. Carpenter is the oldest child of the first wife. He was reared on his father's farm, obtaining his earliest education in the district school. He studied medicine in the College of Physicians and Surgeons, Baltimore, Md., and is now in active practice as a physician Dr. Carpenter is a close student, and endeavors to keep himself posted in matters pertaining to his profession He was united in marriage April 5, 1865, with Miss Margaret J. White, whose parents were of English and Irish origin. Mrs. Carpenter's father, Stephen White, was the first man to build and settle in Deep Valley Dr. and Mrs. Carpenter are the parents of the following named children: Emma, William, Virginia, James, Stephen, Sarah (deceased), Harriet and Jordan. Winfield Burdine, the youngest child was adopted by Mr. and Mrs. Carpenter when only nine days old The Doctor is a Democrat, and a member of the Greene County Medical Society. He and wife belong to the Methodist Protestant Church.

P. C. DINSMORE, M. D., Deep Valley, Penn., was born in Richhill Township, Greene County, Penn., January 9, 1854. He is a son of Thomas and Elizabeth (Dickey) Dinsmore, natives of Greene and Washington counties, respectively. They are of Irish and English ancestry. Dr. Dinsmore's father is a farmer and stock dealer now residing on a farm in Washington County. The Doctor is the oldest in a family of six children, and was reared in his native township. He attended the graded schools of Washington County, and commenced the study of medicine with Dr. Silas McCracken, of Claysville, Penn. He practiced for a year in West Virginia, was a student in the Cleveland Medical College one year, and subsequently attended Baltimore Medical College, where he graduated with the honors of his class in 1887, and ex-graduate of Medico Chirurgical Faculty, Philadelphia. The token of honor bestowed on Dr. Dinsmore on this occasion was a gold medal, which he still retains as a souvenir. Dr. Dinsmore has been very successful in his profession, to which he is greatly attached. He was united in marriage August 10, 1881, with Miss Mary B., daughter of George and Harriet Hunt, and they have two children—Thomas A. and George H. In politics Dr. Dinsmore is a Democrat.

JAMES M. FERRELL, Merchant, New Freeport, Penn.— Among the most prominent business men in this part of Greene Greene County we mention the gentleman whose name heads this sketch. He was born at Jacksonville, Penn., April 13, 1851, and is a son of George W. and Sarah (Pettit) Ferrell. His ancestors were among the early German settlers of the county. His father was a shoe-maker all his life, and was in business in Jacksonville for over forty years. His father was twice married, having three children by the first marriage and eight by the second. Mr. James M. Ferrell attended the common schools and Jacksonville Academy at Jacksonville, Penn. Early in life he taught school for a period of nearly three years. In 1873 he engaged in the mercantile trade at Jacksonville, and in 1876 he was appointed salesman for the Singer Sewing Machine Company, for which he acted as general agent for three years, with Harrisonburg, Va., as headquarters, where he and his family lived during the time. In 1882 Mr. Ferrell located at New Freeport, where he established a general store. He is eminently qualified for his business. His affable manner and obliging disposition, coupled with a determination not to be excelled or undersold, have drawn to his store many of the affluent and influential citizens of Springhill Township and surrounding country. He owns a commodious store building, which enables him to carry an extensive stock. Mr. Ferrell was married October 26, 1876, to Miss Frances Henrietta, daughter of Hon. James W. Hays, of Waynesburg, Penn. Mrs. Ferrell was born in Washington, D. C. Their children are—

47

Russell Hays, Jessie Virginia and James Wilson. They are members of the Cumberland Presbyterian Church. Mr. Ferrell is a Republican, and for a time was postmaster at Jacksonville. He is a member of the I. O. O. F. and the Encampment, and in 1875-'76 was representative to the Grand Lodge at Philadelphia, Penn.

F. H. GRIFFITH, a farmer and stock-dealer, residing in Springhill Township, Greene County, is the oldest son of Samuel and Lydia (Blake) Griffith. He was born in Marshall County, W. Va., October 13, 1858, but has spent most of his life in Greene County, Penn., where he came with his parents at a very early age. He attended the schools of Springhill Township, and while still a young man he began farming as his chief pursuit. He has met with more than average success, and has a valuable farm of 150 acres. In 1881 Mr. Griffith was united in marriage with Miss Joanna, daughter of Edward Dowlin, of West Virginia. Mrs. Griffith is of English ancestry. They have two children—Shannon A. and Caddie A. Mr. and Mrs. Griffith are members of the Church of God. He is superintendent of the Sabbath-school, and his political views are Republican.

SAMUEL GRIFFITH, farmer and stock-grower, who was born in Maryland, August 1, 1835, is a son of Daniel and Mary (Strickler) Griffith, who were, respectively, natives of West Virginia and Maryland, and of English origin. His father, who was a farmer and stock-grower, died in this county in 1848. The subject of this sketch is the second in a family of nine children. He was reared on the home farm and attended the district school. Early in life he made choice of farming as his occupation, and has met with great success. He started in life as a poor boy, working for twenty-five cents per day, and has succeeded in accumulating a handsome fortune. His farm, which lies in West Virginia and Greene County, Penn., consists of 257 acres of well improved land, and he has a neat and substantial residence in Springhill Township, where he has lived for twenty-six years. In 1857 Mr. Griffith was united in marriage with Miss Lydia J., daughter of Nathan and Susannah (Richardson) Blake, and they have a family of nine children, viz.—F. H., Susan Mary, wife of John Earnest; Sarah E., J. J., Thomas J., Clarabel, Margaret, Bruce and Martha. Mr. Griffith is a Republican. He and wife are members of the Disciples Church.

LEWIS W. HAMILTON, farmer and stock-grower, was born in Whiteley Township, Greene County, Penn., September 19, 1848, and is a son of William and Margaret (Maple) Hamilton. His mother was a native of this county, and died October 29, 1869, and his father was born in Greene County, Penn., where he spent most of his life. He was a farmer by occupation, and died April 3, 1879. He reared a family of fifteen children, of whom Lewis W. is the youngest. He was reared on the farm, receiving a common-school education. He has made farming his chief pursuit, and has followed it very successfully. On March 10, 1872, Mr. Hamilton married Miss Harriet A., daughter of James Burdine, of Springhill Township. Mrs. Hamilton died in 1883. Their children are— George W., Mary Ellen, Thomas J., Eliza Jane and James W. (deceased). On October 20, 1884, he was again united in marriage, his present wife being Maria M., daughter of John C. Church, of Isabella County, Mich. They have one child—Calva E. Mr. Hamilton is a Democrat; his wife is a member of the Methodist Episcopal Church.

ENOCH HAMILTON, farmer and stock-grower, was born in Whiteley Township, this county, September 20, 1844, and is a son of William and Margaret (Mapel) Hamilton. His parents were of English and German origin, and were natives of this county. His father, who was a farmer and stock-grower, died in 1879. He was reared in Springhill Township, where he attended the common schools. Here he has spent much of his life as a farmer, and has met with marked success. He owns 118 acres of well improved land where he lives near New Freeport, Penn. Mr. Hamilton was united in marriage in 1871 with Elizabeth, daughter of John and Mary (Philson) Tustin. Her parents were of German and English descent. Mr. and Mrs. Hamilton are the parents of the following named children· Delilah Ann, John W., William C., Elizabeth E, Fannie H., Cora L, Festus C. and Lewis W. In politics Mr. Hamilton is a Democrat

W. P. HOSKINSON, farmer and stock-grower, who was born in this county, December 28, 1838, is a son of George and Sophia (Adams) Hoskinson. His parents were natives of Waynesburg, Penn., and his ancestors, who were of English extraction, were among the pioneer settlers of Greene County. Mr. Hoskinson's great-grandfather, Adams, was killed by the Indians. His grandfather, Robert Adams, built one of the first brick houses in Waynesburg—the house now occupied by Henry C. Sayers, Esq. Mr. Hoskinson's father was a saddler by trade, and among the prominent citizens of the county, in which he served as associate judge, and also as register and recorder. He died in Waynesburg, July 24, 1884. He was twice married, and by the first marriage there were eight children, of whom the subject of this sketch is the third. W P. Hopkinson was reared in Waynesburg, where he received his early education. Most of his early life was spent as clerk in a store, and he was given the management of his father's business. In 1860 he bought a half interest in the store, and bought his father's interest in 1861 and carried on a successful business for a period of twenty years. He has since devoted his time to farming and owns 200 acres of valuable land near New Freeport Mr Hoskinson was married June 21, 1860, to Rebecca, daughter of Phillip and Matilda (Garrison) Shough. Her father is a prominent farmer of Gilmore Township, having at one time owned over seven hundred acres of land. Mr and Mrs. Hoskinson are the parents of four children—Phillip D , a clerk and salesman, George W , a farmer; Mary S and Robert L., who is a student at Waynesburg College. Squire Hoskinson is an active members of the Baptist Church, in which he is a trustee and deacon. He belongs to the I. O. O. F. and the Masonic fraternity.

JOSEPHUS ISIMINGER —The history of the Isiminger family commences in Greene County with Abraham Isiminger, who came from New Jersey to this county and was among the pioneer German settlers. His descendants have been usually farmers. The subject of this sketch, Josephus Isiminger, was born in this county November 3, 1839, and is a son of Andrew and Sarah (Kughn) Isiminger, who were of German and English extraction. His father was a farmer and reared his son to that occupation. Josephus Isiminger, is the sixth in a family of twelve children; attended the district school in Whiteley Township. He owns a good farm where he resides, and has also spent some time at the carpenter's trade, in connection with his agricultural pursuits In 1861 Mr. Isiminger married Miss Maria Lemley, and they had five children—Nicholas, Eliza J , Elizabeth, R., John and William. Mrs Isiminger died in 1873 She was a member of the Baptist Church Mr. Isiminger's second wife was Miss A. M. Dollison, to whom he was married in 1879. They have two children—Elias and Eva. Mrs Isiminger is not a member of the Baptist Church, but she is of Baptist faith

JACOB ISIMINGER, farmer and stock-grower, was born in Greene County, Penn , February 17, 1830. He is a son of Andrew and Sarah (Kughn) Isiminger, who were also natives of this county, and of German extraction. His father's family consisted of five sons and four daughters, all of whom grew to maturity. Jacob Isiminger was the oldest and was reared in Whiteley Township, on the farm where his father now resides. He attended the common schools and chose farming as an occupation. He is the owner of 100 acres of fine land where he resides, near Deep Valley Postoffice, in Springhill Township. Mr. Isiminger was united in marriage, June 1, 1859, with Hannah, daughter of William and Elizabeth (Hinerman) Miller, and they are the parents of four children, viz: McClelland, Stanton, Henry and Willie Mr and Mrs. Isiminger are members of the Baptist Church, and Mr. Isiminger has been superintendent of the Sabbath-school for years. He is a Democrat in politics

JOHN H. MILLER, M. D , Deep Valley, Penn., was born in Springhill Township, Greene County, October 6, 1858, and is a son of Hiel and Mary (Warrick) Miller. His parents were also natives of this county, and of Irish and English lineage. His father who was a farmer all his life died in 1864. Mr. Miller was then in his sixth year and was the eldest of four children He received his education in the district schools, and at the age of fifteen obtained a certificate and taught his first school. He was for sometime thereafter engaged in teaching the country schools of the county. He then worked for a time in the glass works at Martin's Ferry, Ohio, in which place he was appointed policeman by the town council. He had previous to this time begun the study of medicine, but was obliged to abandon it for the lack of funds. In 1885 he entered the College of Physicians and Surgeons, at Baltimore, Maryland, and in 1886 he became a student in the Western Pennsylvania Medical College, graduating with high honors. He was a diligent and successful student, and was elected president of his class. Dr. Miller returned to Greene County, where his genial manner and professional skill soon won for him a good practice. He has had unusual success in surgery. He was married in Deep Valley to Miss Charlotte, daughter of Joseph and Elizabeth (Geary) Nuss. Her parents were of German origin. Dr. and Mrs. Miller have four children, three now living—Leon, Furman and Floyd. The Doctor and wife are members of the Methodist Episcopal Church. He is a Democrat, and a member of the Greene County Medical Society.

JOHN MILLER, farmer and stock-grower, was born in Springhill Township, Greene County, Penn., June 20, 1845, and is a son of Jacob and Sarah (McConnell) Miller, who were of Irish and German origin. His father was a farmer and stock-grower, and died in this county in 1881. Of his family of eleven children, John Miller is the ninth. He was reared on the farm, attending school in the old log school house of the district. Since his marriage in 1870, he has devoted much of his leisure time to study, and has acquired his education without assistance. He is is now able to read and write and keep his accounts correctly. Mr. Miller owns the farm where he resides, consisting of 123 acres of well improved land. Mr. Miller's wife was Miss Caroline Reeves. She is a daughter of Phineas and Matilda Reeves, and of Irish origin. Her ancestors were among the pioneers of Greene County. In politics Mr. Miller is a Democrat

J. L. MORFORD, farmer and stock-grower, was born in Springhill Township, this county, November 23, 1847, and is a son of Isaac and Elizabeth (Brown) Morford. His parents were of Irish and German ancestry, and were natives of Greene County. Mr Morford's ancestors were among the pioneer settlers of the county. His grandfather, James Morford, was a pioneer farmer. Isaac Morford, his father, who spent his life in this county, was killed at Burton, West Virginia, November, 1864, where he was shot by a man who' opposed him in a political discussion His family consisted of six children, of whom the subject of this sketch is the youngest. He was reared on his father's farm, receiving his education in the common schools. He chose farming as his occupation through life and has been very successful, owning at present a fine farm of 122½ acres near New Freeport, Penn In 1866 Mr. Morford married Miss Mary, daughter of James Burdine. They are the parents of seven children, viz: James B., Mary Ann Eliza, Valma L, Elizabeth A, Samuel M., Lewis Q. and Delilah Harriet. In politics Mr. Morford is a Democrat.

JOHN McNEELY, farmer and stock-grower, New Freeport, Penn., was born in this county March 8, 1842. He is a son of John and Elizabeth (Coen) McNeely, natives of Greene County, and of English extraction His father was a farmer His family numbered eleven children, of whom John is the fifth He spent his early manhood on the farm, receiving his education in the common schools. He has made farming his life work, and his home farm contains 278 acres of valuable land. In 1861 Mr. McNeely was united in marriage with Mary, daughter of Michael and Sarah (Taylor) Roupe Mrs. McNeely is of Dutch origin. Their children are—Jacob, a farmer; Rachel, wife of Himus Null; Nancy, wife of William Roupe; John, Elizabeth and Robert, Mr. McNeely is a Democrat. His wife is a member of the Baptist Church.

J. H. RINEHART, M. D., New Freeport, Penn., was born in Franklin Township, Greene County, Penn , January 28, 1859. He is a son of William H. and Ruth Ann (Bowen) Rinehart, residents of Springhill Township Dr. Rinehart is the third in a family of eight children. He attended the common-school and was later a student of Waynesburg College. He studied medicine with Dr. P. C Dinsmore, of Deep Valley, Penn., and also attended the Starling Medical College at Columbus, Ohio, where he graduated in 1887. He then entered the practice of his chosen profession at New Freeport, Penn , his present location. In 1888 he formed a partnership with Dr I. N. Owen, an old and experienced physician who has been in active practice in Greene County for many years At the early age of seventeen the Doctor began teaching school, spending some time in that employment both in this county and in West Virginia He began the study of medicine at the same time and also paid considerable attention to the study of surveying and civil engineering He has been through life a diligent student and gives promise of a successful career

W. H. RINEHART, farmer and stock-dealer, son of Jacob and Abigail (Huss) Rinehart, was born January 6, 1827. His parents were natives of Greene County, and of German descent. The Rinehart's were among the earliest settlers of the county. Several mem-

bers of the family were killed by the Indians, and others were taken
captive when children growing up among the savages.   They were
almost without exception farmers, but some few a member of the
family were professional men.   Mr. Rinehart's father, who was a
farmer and stock-dealer, died in 1874.   The subject of this sketch
is the oldest of a family of seven children.   He was reared on the
farm, receiving his education in the district school in Franklin
Township   He has made farming and stock-dealing his occupation
and now owns the farm where he resides in Springhill Township.
In 1852 Mr. Rinehart was married to Miss Ruth Ann, daughter of
Corbly and Joanna (Garrison) Bowen, who were of German, English
and French origin.   Mrs. Rinehart's paternal grandmother was a
member of the Corbly family who were murdered by the Indians
near Garard's Fort, this county.   Mr. and Mrs. Rinehart are the
parents of the following children—M. E., a resident of Deep Valley,
Penn.; J. H., a practicing physician; Joanna, wife of Scott Lippencott;
Arabell, wife of J. C. F. Milligan; S. Cora and Maude B.   The family are members of the Methodist Episcopal Church.

JAMES STILES, merchant and justice of the peace, Deep Valley, Penn , was born in Monongalia County, West Virginia, January
4, 1841, and is a son of Thomas and Frances (Cross) Stiles.   His
father, who was a farmer, died in West Virginia in 1852.   The
subject of this sketch, the youngest of seven children, was reared in
his native county, where he received a common-school education.
After his father's death he was apprenticed as a bound boy until
twenty-one years of age.   In 1869 he entered the employ of Hon. H.
S. White, as a salesman, and formed a partnership with him the
same year.   This partnership was dissolved in 1871, and Mr. Stiles
located at Deep Valley, where he established a general store.   In
1883, in company with J. K. Null, he erected the mill at Deep Valley, and later he dissolved partnership with Mr. Null.   Squire Stiles
has met with success in business and is an honorable, high-minded
gentleman.   In politics he is a Republican.   In 1869 he was united
in marriage with Jennie, daughter of Rev. D. Charnock, of Wheeling, W. Va.   They were the parents of one child, James, deceased.
Mrs. Jennie Stiles died in 1871.   In 1873 Mr. Stiles married
Emma J , daughter of George Wright, they are the parents of seven
children—Ora Belle, Lucy H., Minnie P., James G., Nellie A.,
Christie and Goldie.   Mrs Stiles is a member of the Methodist
Episcopal Church.   In 1875 Mr Stiles was elected justice of the
peace, which office he has since held continuously.   In 1864 he enlisted in Company N, Sixth West Virginia Infantry, and served until
the close of the war.   He is an active member of the G. A. R. Post,
No. 550, and is now Adjutant.

THOMAS STROPE, farmer and stock-grower, Deep Valley, Penn., was born November 22, 1823, and is a son of Thomas and Sarah (Elems) Strope. His parents were of English descent. His father, who was a farmer during his lifetime, died in 1848. Mr. Thomas Thrope is the fourth in his father's family and the eldest who grew to maturity. His opportunities for an education were very limited. He is a self-made man and now owns 290 acres of well improved land. When he was a small boy he worked by the month and then worked on a farm as a tenant. He also learned the tanner's trade, at which he was employed until twenty-four years of age. Mr. Strope's first wife was Eliza Mitchell, who lived twenty-five years after their marriage. They had one child, George W. Mrs. Sarah Jane Strope, the present wife, was the daughter Jacob Miller, a prominent farmer of Springhill Township. Mr. and Mrs. Strope are the parents of two children—Park L. and Purman D. Mr. Strope is a Republican. He is a member of the Masonic Fraternity and the Patrons of Husbandry. He and wife are members of the Church of God.

W. T. WHITE, farmer and stock-grower, Deep Valley, Penn., was born in Monongalia County, West Virginia, April 30, 1842. He is a son of Michael and Mary A. (Russell) White, who were also natives of West Virginia, and of German extraction. Mr. White's father was a farmer through life, and died in Monongalia County, W. Va., in 1868. Of his family of four children, W. T. White is the second. He was reared on the home farm and received his education in the common-schools. Having chosen farming as his occupation, Mr. White came to Greene County, Penn., in 1872, and settled on a farm in Springhill Township where he now resides. His farm consisting of 185 acres, is well stocked and improved. In 1868 he was married to Miss Harriet, daughter of William and Elizabeth (Odenbaugh) Kent. Mrs. White is of English descent. They have four children—Luella, a school teacher; Guy W., Nettie E. and Charles F. Mrs. White died March 13, 1888. The family are members of the Methodist Episcopal Church, in which Mr. White takes an active interest. He is also greatly interested in school affairs and has been one of the most efficient members of the school board in his township. In 1861 he enlisted in the Sixth West Virginia Volunteer Infantry in Company N., where he served until the close of the war, being a non-commissioned officer.

JOSEPH WHITLATCH, farmer and stock-grower, was born in Whiteley Township, this county, November 22, 1821, and is a son of Joseph and Barbara (Hostetler) Whitlatch. His mother was born in Fayette County, and his father in Greene, and they were of English and Dutch extraction. His father was a farmer and distiller by occupation. His grandfather, Thomas Whitlatch, who was an energetic and industrious farmer through life, was born in England and emigrated to America, coming to Greene County among the earliest settlers. The subject of this sketch, who is the sixth in a family of ten children, resided in Whiteley Township until he was twenty-four years of age. He has followed his father's occupation and has been very successful, being now the owner of 220 acres of well-improved land. Mr Whitlatch was united in marriage, December 11, 1845, with Miss Jane, daughter of Thomas Owen, who came from Wales. They are the parents of thirteen children—Elizabeth, wife of George Plantz; Benson, who died July 5, 1888, aged thirty-eight years; Barbara J, wife of George Murphy; Sarah Ann, wife of John Springer; Susan Caroline, wife of William Patterson; Mary Ellen, wife of John Nicholas; John W, Peter O., Belle, wife of James Brewer; Viola, William, Isaac N., and David (deceased), who was their oldest child, died April 12, 1880, aged thirty-three years. Mr. Whitlatch is a member of the Baptist Church, in which he has been a deacon for twenty-three years, and also superintendent of the Sabbath-school. The other members of the family are members of the Church of God. Mr. Whitlatch is a Republican, and has been school director in his township. He went into the army as a private in 1864, and served until the close of the war.

WILLIAM WILDMAN, farmer and stock-grower, was born in Gilmore Township, Greene County, Penn., October 31, 1847, and is a son of Joseph and Frances (Cumpston) Wildman His parents were born in Dunkard Township, and were of English descent. His father spent his life as a farmer. His family consisted of nine children, of whom William is the seventh. He was reared on the home farm, receiving his education in the common schools. Since early life he has made farming his chief pursuit, and has met with unusual success. Mr. Wildman has made his own way in the world, and is now the owner of 175 acres of well-improved land. In 1868 he married Miss Ruth, daughter of Alexander Compston. Mrs. Wildman is of German origin. Their children are—-Anna C., wife of Jacob Tustin; Fannie, Eliza Ellen, Harriet, Charles W, and Rebecca (deceased). Mrs Wildman is a member of the Methodist Episcopal Church. In politics Mr. Wildman is a Democrat.

WASHINGTON TOWNSHIP.

SILAS BARNES, retired farmer, P. O. Ruff's Creek, was born on the farm where he now resides in Washington Township, Greene

County, Penn., August 22, 1810 His parents were Jacob and
Phœbe (Crayn) Barnes, who were natives of Pennsylvania They
were the parents of nine children, of whom six are living. The
subject sf our sketch is the second of these children, and was united
in marriage, in 1832, with Catharine Johns She was born in Washington Township, this county, in 1816, a daughter of Jacob and
Elizabeth (Smith) Johns, who were pioneers of Greene County. Mr.
and Mrs Barnes are the parents of three children—Maria, Elizabeth
and John. Mr. Barnes was reared on a farm and has been engaged
in farming through life. He owns 300 acres of land. He served as
sheriff of the county by appointment, was elected treasurrr in 1847,
and in 1878 was elected associate judge and served one term. Mrs.
Barnes died in November, 1886.

JAMES BOYD, farmer (deceased), was born in Greene County,
Penn , September 10, 1813. His parents, Richard and Mary (Pitney)
Boyd, were natives of Maryland, but settled in Greene County, Penn.,
and remained until their death. James Boyd was united in marriage,
April 14, 1839, with Martha Decamp, who was born in Washington
County, November 2, 1816. She was a daughter of Runion and
Hannah (Winget) Decamp, who departed this life in Iowa To Mr
and Mrs Boyd were born eight children, six of whom are living—
Permelia, Minerva, wife of George W Johnson, James, Martha J.,
Mary S., wife of B. R. Bell, and Hannah J., wife of James C. Bell;
the deceased being Elizabeth E., who was the wife of Samuel J Graham, and Emeline Mr. Boyd was a farmer, and at the time of his
death owned 176 acres of land where his widow and family reside,
at Hope P O., Greene County. He was a consistent member of the
Baptist Church, of which Mrs. Boyd is also a member. Mr Boyd's
death occurred August 2, 1885, and he was much mourned, not only
by his own family and immediate friends, but as a good citizen
throughout the township and county.

ROBERT BRISTOR, farmer, P. O. Hackney Penn , was born
in Washington Township, Greene County, August 11, 1818, a son
of James and Catharine (Sibert) Bristor, the former a native of
Pennsylvania and the latter of Virginia. They settled and remained
in Greene County until their death. Robert Bristor was united in
marriage, June 15, 1841, with Margaret Oliver, who was born in
Washington Township, November 18, 1821. Her parents were
Samuel and Elizabeth (Holingsworth) Oliver, the one a native of
New Jersey and the other of Pennsylvania. They also settled in
Greene County and remained until their death. Mr. and Mrs.
Robert Bristor have ten children—Mary J., widow of Shadrach
Mitchell; James N., Melinda, wife of Samuel Kelley; Caroline, wife
of Joseph Smith; Timothy J , Hannah M., wife of Joseph Martin;
Rachel E., Oliver D , John W., and George W. (deceased). Mr.

Bristor has always lived on a farm, and has devoted himself to stock-raising and the care of his land of which he owns 200 acres where, with his family, he now resides. He and his wife are consistent members of the Bethlehem Baptist Church..

SYLVESTER CARY, farmer, deceased, was born in Washington Township, Greene County, Penn., May 6, 1819. His father and mother were Daniel and Mary Cary (*nee* Cooper), who were natives of Washington County, where they were married, then settled in Greene County, remaining till their death. Sylvester Cary was twice married, his first wife being Miss Hannah Cooper, born August 14, 1820, a daughter of Zebulon Cooper. By this marriage Mr. Cary was the father of nine children, only one of whom—Elmas W. —is now living. Mrs. Cary died in 1858. Her husband then married, March 10, 1859, Sarah J. Cooper; she was the widow of Nathaniel Cooper, and was born March 29, 1833. Her father and mother were John and Martha Cooper (*nee* Atkinson), who were natives of Pennsylvania, and after marriage residents of Washington County until death. By his second marriage Mr. Cary was the father of five children—Laura B., wife of Oscar Day; Thomas S., Alice S., wife of John M. Simpson, John C.; and Hannah M., deceased. Mrs. Cary by her first marriage is the mother of one child— Flora S., wife of John Andrew. Sylvester Cary, deceased, was one of the substantial citizens of Washington Township, In connection with the farming he made quite a success of stock-dealing during his life, and at his death was the possessor of a fine farm containing about 600 acres. He belonged to the Methodist Protestant Church, of which his widow is also a member. Mr. Cary's death occurred January 3, 1886, and it proved a great loss not only to his family but also throughout the community in which he lived.

JAMES W. CLOSSER, farmer, grain and stock-dealer, Waynesburg, Penn.—Among the stirring and prosperous business men of Greene County, we take pleasure in mentioning the name that heads this biographical sketch. He was born in Amwell Township, Washington County, October 15, 1852, and is a son of Andrew J. and Sarah (Totton) Closser, who were natives of Pennsylvania, married and settled in Bethlehem Township, Washington County, where they remained through life. On September 24, 1882, James W. Closser married Miss Elazan Garner, who was born in Washington Township, April 4, 1858, and is a member of the Baptist Church. Her parents were Matthew and Sarah (Huffman)Garner, the latter of whom is deceased. Mr. and Mrs. Closser's family consists of three children—Daniel, Hallie J. and James I. Although reared on a farm, Mr. Closser has been engaged in various pursuits since starting out in life for himself. He is at present dealing in grain, stock and agricultural implements, besides managing his farms which consist of about 600 acres, owned in partnership with his brother Henry.

JESSE CRAIG, deceased, was born in Virginia, October 20, 1799; and following in the footsteps of the early pioneers, while still a boy, came to Pennsylvania and settled in Greene County, on March 12, 1829, he married Miss Hannah Evans, who was born in Washington County, April 27, 1803, a daughter of David and Elizabeth Evans, both deceased. By this marriage Mr. Craig was the father of one child, David, who married Nancy Matthews. Mr. Craig lost his wife by death, January 27, 1831; but realizing that it was not good for man to be alone, on April 22, 1832, he was married to Miss Sophrona Cary, who was born on the farm where she and family reside, March 5, 1815, a daughter of Abel and Eunice Cary (*nee* Woodruff). Her parents were natives of New Jersey, and early in life settled in Greene County, Penn., remaining until their death. By the last marriage Mr. Craig was the father of thirteen children, of whom nine survive him—Cephas, married Eunice Bigler; Daniel, married Malinda Bane; Sarah, wife of Abel Turner; Abel, married Sarah J. Rejester; Eunice, wife of John G. Barr; Hannah, Eleanor, wife of Silas Hoover; Margaret, wife of George Stilwell, and Sophrona, wife of William Taylor. Thomas (married Leah Horn), Mary, Elizabeth and Jesse, being deceased. Mr. Craig was a successful farmer, and stock-raiser through life, owning at the time of his death a farm of 150 acres. He was a member of the Baptist Church, of which his widow is also a member. He filled in his lifetime the office of justice of the peace of Washington Township. He departed this life, April 26, 1882; and by his death the township lost a good citizen and his family a kind husband and father.

ENOCH DURBIN, retired farmer, Swart's Station, Penn., was born in Richhill Township, Greene County, July 24, 1820, a son of Stephen and Mary Durbin (*nee* McDonell), the former a native of Maryland. After marriage they resided in Richhill Township until their death. Enoch Durbin was united in marriage the first time in 1845, with Mary M. Stagner, born in Morris Township in 1819, a daughter of John and Mary Stagner. By this marriage Mr. Durbin is the father of four children—Peter H., George W., Eliza J., wife of Thomas Iams; and John (deceased). Mrs. Durbin died May 27, 1866. Four years after her death, December 7, 1870, Mr. Durbin took for a second wife Eliza Hopkins, born January 27, 1818, on what was known as the old Hopkins farm, where she and family still reside. Her parents were Daniel and Esther Hopkins (*nee* Johnson). The former was born in eastern Pennsylvania, November 27, 1782, and his wife in Washington County, November 8, 1787. They were married November 15, 1811, and settled in Maryland, then lived in Washington County, Penn., one year and moved to Greene County in 1816, remaining until their death. Mr. Hopkins died October 10,

1828, and his widow October 5, 1866. They were the parents of eight children, of whom six are living—Margaret, Levi, Eliza, the wife of subject of this sketch, Samuel, Abigail, the wife of Rev. J. T. Riley, and Aranna. The deceased are William S. and John J. Enoch Durbin has been a farmer all through life, and he, wife and sister-in-law are all members of the Methodist Episcopal Church.

G. W. DURBIN, farmer, Sycamore, Penn., was born in Morris Township, Greene County, December 20, 1849, a son of Enoch and Mary Durbin (*nee* Stagner). His father and mother were natives of Richhill and Morris townships respectively. They remained in this county after their marriage, Mrs. Durbin departing this life in 1866. Sometime after her death Mr. Durbin contracted a second marriage with Miss Eliza Hopkins, and now resides in Washington Township. George W. Durbin chose as his life partner, September 11, 1875, Miss Jennie L. Fonner, who was born in Morris Township, November 4, 1854, a daughter of James and Eliza Fonner (*nee* Taylor). Her parents were natives of Greene County, where they were married and lived until Mr. Fonner's death, March 16, 1883. His widow is still living. To Mr. and Mrs. Durbin have been born five children—James R., Lizzie B., Albert F., Charlie B. and Maggie E. Mr. Durbin is a farmer by occupation and has made that his life work. He is the possessor of a 100-acre farm on which he and family reside. Both he and wife are consistent members of the Bates' Fork Baptist Church; and he is a leading director of the school board, taking great interest in the educational affairs of the township.

JOHN EDGAR, farmer, Castile, Penn., is one of the substantial farmers and stock-dealers of Washington Township, Greene County, where he was born May 2, 1845. His parents were Isaac and Margaret Edgar, the former a native of New Jersey, and the latter of Washington County, Pennsylvania. After marriage they settled in Greene County and remained until 1868, then lived in Washington County till 1874—the year of Mrs. Edgar's death. Her husband died in 1875. John Edgar was united in the holy bonds of matrimony February 9, 1869, with Mary A. Keys, born in Washington County, September 24, 1850. Her parents, Daniel and Ruth (Bane) Keys, are natives of Washington County where they still reside. Mr. and Mrs. John Edgar are the parents of nine children—Daniel A., Ida R., Maggie M., Lucy L., William K., John, Anna M., Minnie and Clarence. Mr. Edgar has been engaged in farming and stock-dealing all his life. He owns 228 acres of land in one tract, on which he and his family reside. They are consistent members of the Baptist Church, in which he has served as deacon for three years. He has also been a member of the school board of his township.

STEPHEN FULTON, farmer, Castile, Penn., was born in West Bethlehem Township, Washington County, August 16, 1818, a son of Stephen and Jerusha Fulton (*nee* Cary). His mother was a native of Greene and his father of Washington County, where they settled after their marriage and remained through life, Mr. Fulton's death occurring in 1847 and his widow in 1858. September 16, 1847, Stephen Fulton wedded Miss Mary Greenlee, who was born in Washington County, December 26, 1822. She is a daughter of Samuel and Nancy Greenlee (*nee* Gantz), the one a native of Maryland and the other of Fayette County, Penn. After marriage they resided in Washington County until the death of Mrs. Gantz in 1863. Her husband died in 1876. Stephen Fulton and wife are the parents of eight children, five of whom are living Emma, wife of Zephaniah Johnson; Samuel G., Henry H., Eliza, wife of Amos Shirk, and Albert G.; Nancy, Margaret and Ruth, are deceased. Mr. Fulton has always lived in the country and engaged in farming throughout his life, which has been one of usefulness and activity, and he has acquired for himself and family a farm of 120 acres, where he now lives. They are both members of the Mount Zion Baptist Church.

SPENCER B. GARNER, farmer, P. O. Waynesburg, was born in Greene County, Penn., March 10, 1851. His father, Matthew—son of Samuel and Catharine (Miller) Garner—was born in Washington Township, August 9, 1820; and September 29, 1844, wedded Sarah, daughter of Amos Masters. She was a native of Greene County, and died August 5, 1851. After her death Matthew married Sarah, daughter of John Huffman, December 24, 1854. She was also a native of Washington Township, and died August 23, 1871. Her husband then married, October 3 1872, Miss Maria Keigley, his present wife, a native of the same township and a daughter of George and Anna Keigley, both deceased. Spencer B., the subject of this sketch, was united in marriage, September 16, 1875, with Ella Huss, who was born in Greene County, Penn., August 7, 1854, a daughter of William H. and Maria Huss (*nee* Keys), the former a native of Greene and the latter of Washington County. Mr. Huss is deceased and his widow is now living with her daughter, Mrs. S. B. Garner. To Mr. and Mrs. S. B. Garner have been born two children—Weatha and Isa G. Mr. Garner has been a farmer, stock-dealer and miller through life, and owns 184 acres of land in Washington Township. He and wife are members of the Bates' Fork Baptist Church.

T. J. HUFFMAN, farmer and stock-dealer, Ruff's Creek, Penn., was born in Washington Township, December 17, 1849. His parents, George and Susannah (Stagner) Huffman, are natives of Greene County, where they reside at present. Mr. Huffman, the subject of this sketch, was united in marriage, May 25, 1871, with Eliza M. Mattox, who was born in Morris Township, this county, October 12, 1852, a daughter of John and Clarissa Mattox (*nee* Rial). Her mother was a native of New Jersey and her father of Greene County,

Penn., where they settled after marriage and remained till the death of Mr. Mattox; his widow survives him. Mr. and Mrs. Huffman are the parents of four children, one living—George E., born May 24, 1880; and Lonny, Ida and an infant, deceased. Mr. Huffman is a member of the Baptist and his wife of the Cumberland Presbyterian Church. Mr. Huffman was raised on the farm where he now resides with his family and parents, and in connection with his farming, has dealt in all kinds of stock, making the raising of fast horses a specialty; of these the principal ones are "Slow-Go," and two that Vanderbilt bought. Mr. Huffman has always been known as one of the most successful and enterprising farmers of his township.

G. W. HUFFMAN, farmer and stock dealer, P. O. Ruff's Creek, was born in Washington Township, Greene County, Penn., January 17, 1845. He is a son of George and Susannah (Stagner) Huffman, who are natives of Greene County, where they were married and have resided all their lives. Mr. Huffman was united in marriage, September 20, 1866, with Phœbe J. Baldwin, who was born in Washington County, March 27, 1846. Her parents, Amos and Sarah (Lindley) Baldwin, were natives of Washington County, but moved to Iowa where they both died. Mr. and Mrs. Huffman are the parents of two interesting daughters—Cora B. and Sadie A. Mr. Huffman was brought up on a farm, and in connection with his farming interests has made the raising of fine stock a specialty. He owns 380 acres of land where he and family live, and a fifth interest in 700 acres in Kansas. The whole family are consistent and leading members in the Bethlehem Baptist Church.

ANDREW HUGHES, retired farmer, Ruff's Creek, Penn., is one of the old pioneers of Greene County, having been born in Washington Township, November 1, 1810, a son of Nathan and Nancy (Sharon) Hughes. Mrs. Hughes was a native of England, and her husband was born in Greene County, Penn., where they resided from the time of their marriage until their death. Andrew Hughes was united in marriage, September 25, 1834, with Hannah Crayne, born in Washington Township, April 4, 1815, a daughter of Daniel and Hannah (Clawson) Crayne, the one a native of Greene County, Penn., and the other of New Jersey. After marriage they made their home in Mr. Hughes' native county until their death. Mr. Andrew Hughes and wife are the parents of two children—Asa and Samuel. Mr. Hughes was raised on a farm and has been a tiller of the soil all his life. He owns the 200-acre farm where he now lives with his family. He and wife are members of the Bethlehem Baptist Church, in which they have ever been regarded as among the most prominent and faithful workers.

ZEPHANIAH JOHNSON, retired farmer, Castile, Penn.—The subject of this sketch is one of the substantial pioneer farmers of

Greene County, having been born in Morgan Township, December 21, 1812. His parents were Zenas and Phœbe (Wolf) Johnson, who were natives of New Jersey, and after marriage moved to Greene County, Penn., and spent the remainder of their lives. March 6, 1837, Zephaniah Johnson took unto himself a wife in the person of Miss Rachael Ulery, born in Greene County, February 24, 1819. Her parents were Stephen and Jane (Crayn) Ulery, who were natives of Washington County, Penn., but moved to Knox County, Ohio, remaining until their death. By this marriage Mr. Johnson is the father of the following children—Phœbe J., wife of Isaac Keys; Stephen, Zenos, Daniel and Sarah. Mrs. Johnson departed this life July 21, 1853. After her death Mr. Johnson was united in marriage, in 1857, with Mrs. Mary Horn (*nee* Moore), a daughter of Joseph and Mary Moore, both deceased. By the last marriage Mr. Johnson is the father of one daughter—Ellen. Her mother departed this life May 21, 1872. Mr. Johnson has always lived on a farm, to which, in connection with stock-raising, he has given his care and attention through life. His farm consists of 234 acres. He is named among the prominent citizens of his township, and is a leading member in the Mount Zion Baptist Church.

GEORGE W. JOHNSON, farmer, P. O. Ten-Mile, was born in Morgan Township, Greene County, Penn., May 21, 1818. His parents were Zenas and Phœbe (Wolf) Johnson, who were natives of New Jersey, where they were married, then moved to Greene County, Penn., remaining till Mrs. Johnson's death, which occurred in 1819. Her husband then married Sarah Crayn. Both died in Greene County. The subject of our notice was united in marriage, November 4, 1841, with Eunice Smith, born in Amwell Township, Washington County, April 16, 1821. She is the daughter of Peter and Priscilla (Cooper) Smith, the former a native of Germany, and the latter of Washington County, Penn., where they were married, and after settling for a short time in Greene County, returned and died there. Mr. G. W. Johnson and wife are the parents of five children —Smith, I. B., Phœbe J., wife of Othaniel Rhoads; Zephaniah and George A. Having been reared on a farm, Mr. Johnson has been a tiller of the soil all his life, and owns the farm of 170 acres where he now lives with his family. He has served as a member of the school board of his township, and both he and wife are members of the Baptist Church.

ZENAS JOHNSON, farmer, P. O. Ruff's Creek, born in Greene County, Penn., April 12, 1827, is a son of Zenas and Sarah Johnson, the former a native of New Jersey, and the latter of Greene County, Penn., who after marriage settled and remained in this county until their death. Our subject was united in marriage, October 28, 1862, with Sarah J. Watson, born in Washington County, Penn., October

28, 1839, who is still living and is a consistent member of the Methodist Episcopal Church. Her parents were John and Mary A. (Almost) Watson, the former a native of Ireland, and the latter of Greene County, Penn., who settled in Washington County after marriage, where they remained until their death. To Mr. and Mrs. Johnson have been born eight children—George B., Daniel D., Silas C., Sadie, Emma, Maggie, Jennie and Cora. Having been raised on a farm, Mr. Johnson has made farming his business through life, and through industry and economy has secured for himself one of the best farms in Washington Township, consisting of 257 acres.

D. W. JOHNS, farmer, P. O. Ruff's Creek, is a descendant of one of the Pioneer families of Greene County, Penn. He was born in Washington Township, May 21, 1838, a son of Jacob and Elizabeth Johns (*nee* Ross), who are natives of Greene County, the former of Washington Township and the latter of Morgan. They have resided in Washington Township ever since they were married. The subject of this sketch was united in marriage, February 24, 1870, with Rachael Meek, who was born in Washington Township, November 17, 1842, a daughter of John and Elizabeth Meek (*nee* Boyd), who were natives of Greene County, where they remained until their death, Mr. and Mrs. Johns have two children—Thomas S., born June 5, 1871; and John F., born February 8, 1873. Mr. Johns was raised on a farm and has been engaged in farming and dealing in stock all his life. He owns 345 acres of land where he and family live. He and wife are members of the Bethlehm Baptist Church.

JACOB JOHNS, a retired farmer of Ruff's Creek, Penn., is one one of the pioneers of Washington Township, Greene County. He was born on the farm where he and family reside, December 3, 1806, and is a son of Jacob and Elizabeth (Smith) Johns, the former a native of Delaware and the latter of Washington County, Penn., who settled in Greene County after marriage and remained until their death. Jacob Johns was united in marriage March 27, 1834, with Elizabeth Ross, born in Morgan Township, Greene County, May 29, 1816. Her parents, John and Phœbe (Eaton) Ross, were natives of Greene County and residents therein until their death. Mr. and Mrs. Johns are the parents of eight children, four of whom are living and married, as follows: J. R., to Mary J. Huffman; D. W., to Rachael Meek; Abner, to Elizabeth Meek; and Jacob, Jr., first to Lourinza R. McClelland, then to Josephine V. Hickman. The deceased are—Phœbe, Timothy, Thomas, and Elizabeth, who was the wife of Jacob Hoge. Mr. Johns has been engaged in farming all his life and owns about 500 acres of land in Greene County. He held the office of justice of the peace of Washington Township for ten years, and filled the positions of assessor, auditor, inspector and tax collector of his township.

48

GEORGE KEIGLEY, farmer, Waynesburg, Penn., was born in Washington Township, Greene County, April 8, 1831, a son of George and Anna Keigley (nee McCaslin). They were natives of Pennsylvania, where they were married and remained in Greene County until their death. Both departed this life where the subject of this notice now resides. March 21, 1869, George Keigley married Similda J. Rose, who was born in Guernsey County, Ohio, March 27, 1845, a daughter of Thomas and Elizabeth Rose (nee Haines). They were natives of Pennsylvania but lived in Ohio until about 1850, when they returned to Fayette County, Penn., where Mrs. Rose died in 1852. Mr. Rose married again and moved to Greene County, Penn., then to Fulton County, Penn., where he died November 10, 1887. To Mr. and Mrs. Keigley have been born eight children— Laura V., Homer L., Mary M., Jessie L., Sadie E., Louie, Anna P. and Thomas H. Mr. Keigley is a saddle and harness-maker by trade, which he followed about fifteen years, after which he engaged in the service of his country in Company F, Pennsylvania Cavalry, and served nine months. He and his wife are faithful members of the Baptist Church.

JOHN M. MARTIN, farmer and stock-dealer, P. O. Ten Mile, was born in Morgan Township, Greene County, August 12, 1823. His parents were Thomas and Mary (Bradbury) Martin, natives of New Jersey. They were married in Washington County, Penn., and made their home in Greene County, where Mr. Martin died. Mrs. Martin died in Missouri. After her husband's death, she lived with her children, who were—John M., the eldest and the subject of this sketch; Thomas and David C. John M. was united in marriage January 18, 1848, with Miss Martha Moore, born in Washington County, Penn., in 1819. Her parents were Joseph and Mary (Shackleton) Moore, both deceased. By this union Mr. Martin is the father of four children—Joseph T., Martha A. and James J., living; and Mary E., deceased. Mrs. Martin departed this life in 1880. February 8, 1881, Mr. Martin was again united in marriage with Isabella (Barr) Montgomery. She was born in Washington County, and is a daughter of Samuel and Sarah Barr, the former deceased. By his last marriage Mr. Martin is the father of two sons—Charles A. and Ira H. He was raised on a farm and made farming his business through life, having also delt somewhat in stock. He owns about 200 acres of land in Greene County, and is one of the industrious and substantial citizens of Washington Township.

L. W. MEEK, farmer, P. O. Swart's, was born on the farm where he and his family reside in Washington Township, December 26, 1858. He is a son of Cary and Jane Meek (nee Milliken), who were natives of Greene County, Pennsylvania, where they were married, settled and remained until their death. He died in

October, 1873, and his widow in November of the same year. They were the parents of four children—L. W., A. W., Josie and Lillie. L. W. Meek was united in marriage with Sena Buchanan, born in Waynesburg, March 18, 1859, a daughter of David and Cassie Buchanan (*nee* Swart), the former a native of Greene and the latter of Washington County, Penn. They reside in Morris Township, Greene County. Mr. and Mrs. Meek are the parents of two children—Cassie J. and David B. Mr. Meek was raised on a farm and has given considerable attention to stock-dealing in connection with the care of his farm which consists of 140 acres. He has also taken much interest in the educational affairs of his township and has served as a members of the school board. His wife is a member of the Cumberland Presbyterian Church.

CEPHAS MEEK, farmer, Ruff's Creek, Penn., is a descendant of one of the pioneer families of Greene County. He was born in Washington Township, January 24, 1832, a son of John and Elizabeth (Boyd) Meek, who were natives of Greene County, where they were married, settled and remained until their death. She died December 24, 1869, and her husband February 3, 1878. They were the parents of eleven children, eight of whom are living. Cephas Meek was united in marriage April 2, 1868, with Phœbe J. Conklin. She was born in Washington County, Penn., December 2, 1838, a daughter of William and Catharine (Ross) Conklin, natives of Washington and Greene counties respectively. They were married in Greene and settled in Washington County. He departed this life June 25, 1880; his widow is still living. Mr. and Mrs. Meek are the parents of one child, William R., born January 11, 1869. Mr. Meek has been engaged in farming all his life and owns a farm of 145 acres. He was a member of the school board of his township for six years, and also served as judge and inspector of elections. Mrs. Meek is a member in the Cumberland Presbyterian Church.

ASA MITCHELL, a retired farmer of Ruff's Creek, Penn., was born in Washington Township, Greene County, October 6, 1811. He is a son of Shadrach and Margaret (Rinehart) Mitchell, the former a native of Maryland and the latter of Greene County, Penn., where they were married and remained until their death. January 25, 1835, Asa Mitchell married Miss Rachel Johns, born in Washington Township, December 1, 1815. She is a daughter of Jacob and Elizabeth (Smith) Johns who, after marriage, settled and remained in Greene County until their death. To Mr and Mrs Asa Mitchell have been born eight children, of whom four are living—Jacob J., John, Maria and Catharine, who is the wife of George V. Shirk; and Shadrach, Thomas, Delilah and Mary J. (deceased). Mr. Mitchell was raised on a farm and has been engaged in farming all his life He owns 227 acres of land where he now lives with his family and he is one of the most substantial and highly respected citizens of Washington Township.

M. M. McCLELLAND, retired farmer, Ruff's Creek, Penn., was born on the farm where he and his family reside in Washington Township, Greene County, December 22, 1824, a son of John and Nancy McClelland (*nee* Montgomery) His father was a native of Pennsylvania and his mother of Harford County, Md. They were married in Greene County, Penn. Mr. McClelland departed this life in 1840, and his widow May 5, 1862. The subject of our sketch was united in marriage February 27, 1848, with Elizabeth Mettler, born in Columbia County, Penn, May 6, 1826, a daughter of Daniel and Waty Mettler, (*nee* Baker). They were natives of Pennsylvania, married there, and in 1831 moved to Knox County, Ohio; from there they moved to Williams County, in 1860, and in 1866 went to Iowa, where he died December 13, 1884. His widow survives him, making her home with her children. Mr. and Mrs McClelland have ten children, of whom five are living—Sarah F., wife of J. D. Iams; Cary, Elmira, wife of Stephen Cox; Emma J and Ettie. The deceased are Melvin T., Waty A., Marinda, Mary and Lourinza. She was married October 30, 1878, to Jacob Johns, and died September 7, 1879. Mr. McClelland was raised on a farm and has been engaged in farming almost all his life. He owns 345 acres of land, constituting one of the finest farms in Washington Township. He was elected to the office of county auditor in 1856 and served the term of three years In 1868 he was elected county commissioner, and served three years. He is now serving a second term as justice of the peace of Washington Township, having at different times successfully filled almost all the township offices He has also been a member of the Masonic order for twenty years. His wife is a faithful member of the Bethlehem Baptist Church

JOHN PETTIT, farmer, Swart's was born in Washington Township, Greene County, Penn., January 22, 1831, a son of Isaac and Cynthia Pettit (*nee* Hathaway), who were natives of Greene County and residents there until their death. In 1860 Mr. Pettitt was united in marriage with Rachel Pettit, who was born in Morris Township January 2, 1840, a daughter of Charlie and Keziah Pettit, natives of Greene County and residents there until their death. To Mr. and Mrs. John Pettit have been born seven children—Eliza, wife of G H. Loughman, who is the mother of two children—Ohie M. and Stanley J; Isaac, Mary A., wife of George Fry; Kizzie, Charlie, Frank and Nora Mr. Pettitt was raised on a farm and has been engaged in farming all his life He owns 325 acres of land, all in Washington Township. He and wife are consistent members of the Baptist Church.

JOSEPH H. PETTIT, farmer, Swart's, Penn., was born in Washington Township, Greene County, May 6, 1837, a son of Isaac and Cynthia Pettit (*nee* Hathaway), who were natives of Greene County, where they remained until their death. She departed this life in 1873, and her husband in 1881. December 13, 1862, Joseph H. Pettit was united in marriage with Elizabeth Hedge, born in Greene County, February 2, 1846. She is a daughter of Aaron and Eva Hedge (*nee* Fonner), natives of the same county, both deceased The latter departed this life April, 1888. Mr. and Mrs Pettit are the parents of eight children, six of whom are living—Laura, Jessie, Cynthia, Martha, George and Bert; and Eva and Mary, deceased. Having been reared on a farm, Mr. Pettit has made farming his occupation through life, and owns 148 acres of land where and his family live. Mrs. Pettit is one of the faithful members of the Baptist Church.

JOHN ROSS, retired farmer, Dunn's Station, Penn.—The subject of this biographical sketch is one of the pioneer citizens of Washington Township, Greene County, born on his present farm, November 3, 1820. He was the oldest child of Thomas Ross, a native of this county, who died in 1832. His mother's maiden name was Hannah Denney, a native of Jefferson Township, who after marriage resided in Washington Township until her death in 1847. They were the parents of seven children, of whom three are living. John Ross married Miss Maria Loughman, October 7, 1847. She was born September 20, 1825, in Morris Township, of which her parents, David and Christina (Fonner) Loughman, were also natives and residents therein until their death. Mr. and Mrs. John Ross have eight children—Hannah B, wife of John Kendall; David, Mary J., Lydia, wife of John W. Kelley; Timothy, Christina A, Maria I. and William, (deceased). Mr. Ross was born and raised on the farm on which he now resides, and like his ancestors, has made farming and stock-raising his business through life. His home farm consists of 237 acres of excellent land. He has most acceptably filled the offices of auditor and assessor of his township, and served as member of the school board for fourteen years. He and his wife are among the most prominent members of the Baptist Church.

THOMAS ROSS, farmer and stock-dealer, P O Ruff's Creek, was born in Washington County, Penn., October 8, 1833. He is the son of Benjamin and Hannah Ross (*nee* Johns,) both natives of Washington Township, Greene County, where they were married and where they returned after a few years spent in Washington County, and remained until their death, which occurred in the house where the subject of this sketch and his family now reside—his father having departed this life in 1863, and his mother in 1868. Six of their twelve children still survive them. Thomas Ross was united in marriage May 11, 1870, with Helen M. Lindley, born in Washington County, January 10, 1844, a daughter of Zebulon and Julia Lindley (*nee* Parkinson), natives of the same county, and residents therein during their whole life, with the exception of a short time spent in Ohio immediately subsequent to their marriage. They were the parents of three children, all now living. Mrs. Lindley died in 1873 and her husband in 1887. To Mr. and Mrs. Ross have been born two daughters—Estella J., born May 26, 1872; and Clara H., born February, 23, 1871, died September 29, 1878. Mr. Ross was reared on a farm. In 1859, at the age of twenty-six, he went to California and engaged in the mining business. Returning to his native county ·in 1863, after an absence of four years, he has since devoted himself to stock-dealing and the care of his farm of 290 acres in Washington Township. He and his family are members of the Baptist Church, and for the consistency of their Christian character are highly respected throughout the community.

BENJAMIN SHIRK, retired farmer, Ruff's Creek, Penn., born in Lancaster County, Penn., July 23, 1815, is a son of Michael and Barbara (Alobough) Shirk, also natives of Lancaster County. They were married and lived there until about 1830, when they moved to Coshocton County, Ohio, and remained until Mrs. Shirk's death. Mr. Shirk again married and moved to Illinois, where he died. On September 5, 1839, Benjamin Shirk first married Margaret Martin, born in Washington Township, Greene County, June 13, 1818, a daughter of Amos and Ruth Martin, both deceased. To Mr. and Mrs. Shirk were born seven children, five of whom are living—Michael M., Daniel, George V., Joel and Amos; and John and Benjamin F., deceased. Mrs. Shirk died February 20, 1859. In 1860 Mr. Shirk married Elizabeth (Turner) Ullom. She was born in Greene County, February 6, 1827, a daughter of Za and Elizabeth Turner, who departed this life in Greene County. By his last marriage Mr. Shirk is the father of three children—Charles, Maggie and Benjamin F. Mr. Shirk has been a tiller of the soil all his life, and at one time owned 700 acres of land. He has given this all to his children, except the farm of 325 acres where he and his family reside. He and. his wife are consistent members of the Baptist Church, of which his deceased wife was also a member. Mr. Shirk has been a member of the school board, and judge of the election at different times. He is one of Greene County's oldest and best known citizens, having lived in Washington Township for fifty years.

J. H. SMITH, farmer, P. O. Sycamore, was born in Washington Township, Greene County, Penn., January 17, 1841. His parents, Jacob and Nancy Smith (nee Hill), were natives of Greene County, where they have always resided. His death occurred in 1887, and her death May 2, 1888. Mr. J. H. Smith was united in marriage June 6, 1861, with Martha Armstrong, who was born in Washington County, Pennsylvania, September 24, 1842. Mrs. Smith is a daughter of James and Elizabeth Armstrong (nee Richie), the former a native of New York, the latter of Ohio, who after marriage settled in Washington County, Pennsylvania, and from there moved to Marshall County, West Virginia where she died in 1853. After her death he married again and moved to Richhill Township, this county, and died in 1881. The widow is still living. To Mr and Mrs. Smith have been born five children: Anna, wife of G. M. Fordyce; Mary L, Maria B., Ida M. and Jacob H. Mr. Smith has been engaged in farming through his life, and owns 112 acres of land where he and family reside. He and wife are consistent members of the Baptist Church.

JOHN WALKER, farmer, Ruff's Creek Penn, was born in Center Township, Greene County, January 6, 1818. His parents were Joseph and Rebecca (Higinbotham) Walker, the former a native of New Jersey, and the latter of Fayette County, Pennsylvania. They were married in Greene County where they remained for several years, when they moved first to St. Clairsville, Ohio, then to Moundsville, West Virginia. From that point Mr. Walker commenced running on the Ohio River. About this time he disappeared very mysteriously, and his family never knew what became of him. His widow, with her family, moved to Centre Township, Greene County, and married George Williams They lived first in Washington, County Penn, then moved to Wellsburgh, West Virginia. Mr. Williams died in Ohio County, West Virginia. His widow then moved to Washington County, Penn., then to Greene County where she was first married, and made her home with her son until her death. The subject of this sketch was united in marriage, November 7, 1839, with Rachael Supler. She was born in Richhill Township, Greene County, September 12, 1820, a daughter of John and Mary (Sargent) Supler, natives of Pennsylvania They were married and settled in Richhill Township, where they remained until their death, To Mr. and Mrs. Walker have been born twelve children: John L, Minerva, George S., William W., David L, Rebecca, Nancy, Jackson V., and Fannie M., living; and Joseph L., Samuel H. and Mary M. deceased. Mr. Walker is a farmer and owns about 367 acres of land where he and family reside in Washington Township, Greene County Pennsylvania.

WAYNE TOWNSHIP.

GEORGE W BELL, P O Hoover's Run, one of the oldest residents of Greene County, Penn, was born in Virginia, September 30, 1809   His parents were Jason and Sarah (Noll) Bell, natives of Virginia, where they married and settled, afterwards removing to Washington County, Penn, then to Greene County, where his father died in 1873 and his mother in 1840   George W. was the seventh of their nine children, and was joined in the holy bonds of wedlock, February, 8, 1844, with Clementine, daughter of William and Sarah Tygart (*nee* Eagon).   Mr Tygart was a native of Virginia, and his wife of Greene County, Penn., where they spent their married life   He departed this life in Guernsey County, Ohio, in the year 1846, and his wife in April, 1857.   Mr. Bell and wife are the parents of nine children: Sarah J., Felix, Julia A., wife of David Stoneking, Maria, wife of J. Harvey Stewart; Mary, wife of Eli Pethtell; Josephine, wife of William Cole; Susan R, William H. and Eliza abeth M. deceased.   Mr. Bell has always lived on a farm, and his life has been characterized by great industry and economy, as a result of which he owns a fine farm of 500 acres in Greene County, also 100 in West Virginia, and 7,000 at interest.   He has served as justice of the peace for ten years; has been a member of the school board, and was at one time assessor of Jackson Township.

HON. MATTHIAS BRANT, Spragg's, Penn., is one the most successful farmers and stock-raisers of Greene County, and owns 300 acres of land.   He was born in Wayne Township, December 29, 1828, a son of Christopher and Susan Brant (*nee* Meighen)   His father was a native of Maryland, and his mother of Greene County, Pennsylvania, where they were married and lived until 1863, when Mrs Brant died   Mr. Brant then moved to Fillmore County, Minnesota, where he died in November, 1857   They were the parents of thirteen children, of whom Matthias was the oldest, and was united in marriage, June 28, 1868, with Mary Shaw, who was a native of Greene County, where she remained through life.   By this marriage Mr. Brant is the father of six children, of whom four are living.— Susan M, Gertrude M, William H. and Fanny; Emma being deceased   Mrs Brant departed this life in August, 1880.   Mr. Brant married for his second wife, October 25, 1883, Elizabeth, daughter of John and Mary (Varlow) Fitzgerald, natives of County Carey, Ireland, where they were married.   They soon after emigrated to America, settling in West Virginia where they now reside.   Mr.

Brant taught school for sixteen years, beginning when sixteen years of age. He was elected member of the State Legislature in 1878 and re-elected in 1880. He has been a member of the school board for about thirteen years. In politics he is a Democrat. He and his wife are honored members of the Catholic Church at Waynesburg.

KENDALL J. BRANT, Spragg's Penn., was born in Gilmore Township, September 23, 1839, a son of Christopher and Susannah Brant (*nee* Meighen). The father was a native of Maryland, and the mother of Greene County, Penn., where they were married and resided until Mrs. Brant's death, which occurred in May, 1863. Her husband died in November, 1857, in Fillmore County, Minnesota. They were the parents of thirteen children, of whom Kendall J. was the twelfth. He was twice married, his first wife being Minerva, daughter of John and Margaret (Hamilton) Spragg, who are natives and residents of this county. Mr. and Mrs. Brant were married December 16, 1860, and were the parents of two children—Margaret C., wife of William E. Spragg, and Matthias L. Mrs. Brant departed this life February 15, 1865. Mr. Brant was afterwards united in marriage, December 17, 1871, with Maria, daughter of James and Eliza (Rush) Stewart, natives of Greene County, living in Franklin Township. By this marriage Mr. and Mrs. Brant have seven children—Susannah G., Lida A., Priscilla, Lydia, Minerva, James D. and William E. Mr. Brant was reared on a farm and is now one of the most successful farmers in this township. He has also been much interested in the raising of fine, stock in which he has dealt quite extensively. His farm consists of about 200 acres.

RICHARD T. CALVERT, Blacksville, West Virginia, was born in Wayne Township, Greene County, Penn., April 16, 1836. He is a son of John and Eleanor Calvert (*nee* Thralls). His father was born in Mapletown. After marriage they lived in this county until his mother's death which occurred in 1857. His father then married Margaret, daughter of James Marshall. She died February 9, 1888; her husband is still living. Richard Calvert's wife was Sarah J. Conklin, born in this county December 1, 1832. They were married October 19, 1859. Mrs. Calvert's parents were Josiah and Cassandra (Brown) Conklin, deceased. Mr. and Mrs. Calvert have five children, three living—Cassie A., Thomas and John; Martha E. and an infant being deceased. Mr. Calvert is a farmer, and by industry and good management has made a good home for himself and family where he now lives, on a 228 acre farm in Wayne Township.

JOHN F. COEN, merchant and postmaster, Dent, Penn., born in Wayne Township, Greene County, March 8, 1844, was the only son of Francis and Barbara (Cumberledge) Coen, natives of Pennsylvania, who were married in Greene County and resided there until Mr. Coen's death in December, 1843. His widow was afterwards married to Isaac Stiles and now lives in West Virginia. John F. Coen's wife was Miss Mary Kent, born in Greene County, February 18, 1841, and married May 1, 1866. She is a daughter of William and Elizabeth (Odenbaugh) Kent. Her mother is deceased. Mr. and Mrs. Coen have no family of their own but have adopted two sons, William H. and Benjamin T. Mr. Coen was raised on the farm which he now owns consisting of ninety acres. When eighteen years of age he went into the army, enlisting in Company A, One-hundred and Fortieth Pennsylvania Volunteers, and remained three years, during which time he was in a number of hotly contested battles. He has filled the offices of assessor and auditor of his township; has been engaged in merchandising since 1880. He and wife are members of the Methodist Episcopal Church.

EPHRAIM COLE, farmer, Hoover's Run, Penn., was born June 11, 1842. His parents, Jeremiah and Delilah (Filson) Cole, were natives of Maryland, they were married in Greene County, Pennsylvania, where he died March 14, 1870, and she February 6, 1871. Jeremiah's first wife was Christener Crotinger, a native of Maryland, but died in Greene County, Penn. Ephraim was the youngest of eight children, and was united in marriage July 12, 1862, with Missouri, daughter of Adam and Sabia Geho (*nee* Garrison). Mr. Geho was a native of Ohio and his wife of Maryland. They were married in Washington County, Penn., then moved to Greene County in 1889, where they resided until Mr. Geho's death, May, 1871. Mrs. Geho is still living. Mr. and Mrs. Cole have seven children—Benjamin T., Simon T., James C., Albert M., Everett P., Mary E. and William G. Mr. Cole's farm contains 105 acres. He has served as school director two terms. He and wife are member of the Patrons of Husbandry Lodge at Kughntown; and the whole family except the two youngest children are consistent members of the Bethel Baptist Church.

JAMES L. COLE, farmer, Hoover's Run, Penn., was born March 30, 1840. He is a son of Jeremiah and Delilah (Filson) Cole, who were natives of Maryland. Subsequently they removed to Greene County, Pennsylvania, where Mr. Cole, Sr., departed this life March 14, 1870 and his wife February 6, 1871. They were the parents of eight children, James L. was the seventh and was united in marriage November 26, 1865, with Maria, daughter of Adam and Sabia (Garrison) Geho. Mr. Geho was a native of Ohio; they were married in Washington County, Pennsylvania, settling in Greene County in 1839. The former departed this life May, 1871; his widow is still living. Mr. and Mrs. Cole have three children—Sarah C. and Elizabeth J., both born May 26, 1867, and Edward L., born November 13, 1870. Mr. Cole devotes all his time to stock-raising and the care of his farm containing 102 acres. He has served as inspector of elections of Wayne Township; he and his wife are members of the Patrons of Husbandry Lodge at Kughntown.

HENRY COLE, deceased, was one of the most prosperous farmers of Greene County, owning at the time of his death a fine farm of 858 acres. He was born April 25, 1819 and died March 15, 1882. His parents were John and Mary Cole (nee Crotinger), who were natives of Maryland, came to Greene County, Penn., early in life, where they made their home until Mr. Cole's death in May, 1862. His wife died in November, 1868. Henry was the second of their nine children and April 2, 1840, married Elizabeth, daughter of George and Ellen King (nee Stewart). Mrs. Cole's parents were native of Pennsylvania and residents in this county until their death. Her mother departed this life January 24, 1843, and her father in 1863. Mr. and Mrs. Cole were the parents of nine children—Mary A., wife of Hiram White; Sarah, wife of William D. Phillips; George W., Frances E., wife of Abram Tustin; John L., James H., Josephus; and Jacob and Peter, (deceased). Mrs. Cole is still living and resides on the old homestead in Wayne Township.

HENRY CONKLIN, Brock, Penn., born in Greene County, November 17, 1834, is a son of Josiah and Cassandra Conklin (nee Brown), who were also natives of this county, where they were married and remained through life. His father died in September, 1856, and his mother August 13, 1884. Of their ten children, eight are now living. Henry is the third child and was united in marriage November 22, 1857, with Eleanor Hoy, born in this county January 16, 1839. She is a daughter of James and Isabella (Kuhn) Hoy, also natives of Greene County. Mr. Hoy died November 8, 1878; his widow is still living. Mr. and Mrs. Conklin are the parents of eleven children—James H., Sarah E., wife of Richard Stewart; Sanford M., Israel, Ruie, William A., Lissie J., Clara B., Emma L., Lewis H.; and John S., (deceased). Mr. Conklin is one of the most substantial farmers and stock-dealers of Wayne Township, and owns 400 acres of land. He has served as school director in his township. He and wife belong to the Methodist Episcopal Church.

A. J. CUMBERLEDGE, P. O. Dent, was born in Monongalia County, W. Va., August 24, 1838. His parents were George and Elizabeth (Lantz) Cumberledge, the one a native of Maryland and the other of Greene County, Penn., where they were married, then moved to Monongalia County, W. Va., and remained until their death. His father died November 17, 1881, and his mother October 23, 1884. They were the parents of sixteen children, nine living, and were united in marriage August 14, 1818, by James Dye, Esq. A. J. Cumberledge was united in marriage August 14, 1856, with Martha J. Grim, born in Greene County, September 30, 1841, a daughter of Christian and Dorcas E Grim (*nee* Carpenter), both deceased; the latter died May 28, 1888. Mr. and Mrs. Cumberledge have six children—Harriet, wife of William L. Harker; George, Samuel L., Dorcas E , Martie; and Emma (deceased). Mr Cumberledge is a shoe-maker by trade, but has engaged in farming all his life His present farm comprises 140 acres. He enlisted in the service of his country in Company N, Sixth Virginia Volunteers, remaining in the war three years and two months. He belongs to the Masonic order, and his wife is a member of the Methodist Episcopal Church.

JOHN FREELAND, Pine Bank, Penn., was born in Monongahela Township, Greene County, May 15, 1814. His parents were George and Nancy (Fitch) Freeland, also natives of this county, where they were married and remained until Mrs. Freeland's death, December 23, 1863. Her husband died May 16, 1873. Of their four children, two are living—Sarah, and John, the subject of this sketch, who was united in marriage September 20, 1840, with Minerva Cleavenger, born in Greene County in 1823 She is a daughter of Edward and Mary (Kline) Cleavenger (deceased) To Mr. and Mrs. John Freeland were born nine children, six now living, viz.—George, who married Eliza E. Jolley; Cyrus F , who married Nancy E. Owen; Mary A , wife of W J. Bell; David L , who married Sarah J. Kiger; Elizabeth J., wife of W Lowther; and Martha A. The deceased are Edward A., Charles A. and William L. Mrs. Freeland died January 26, 1877, a faithful member of the Methodist Episcopal Church. Mr. Freeland afterwards, May 16,.1879, married Agnes Wright, born in Greene County, February 28, 1838 Her parents were John F and Agnes (Vance) Wright, also natives of this county and residents therein until their death Her mother died in 1874 and her father in 1880 Mr. Freeland was raised in Mapletown. He began teaching school when twenty-one years of age, and taught until 1876 He has since given all his time to the management of his farm, which consists of 122 acres. Mr Freeland is a member of the Methodist Episcopal and his wife of the Baptist Church.

SAM. H HEADLEY, merchant at Pine Bank is a descendant of the Headleys, who emigrated from the north of England in 1689 and settled in East Jersey Francis Headley, his great-grandfather, was born in 1731, and who remained in Essex County, N. J , until after the close of the war of the Revolution, and in 1790 traded his farm in New Jersey for 1,400 acres in Randolph County, Va. (now West Virginia). He had one brother, Joseph Headley, who settled on North Ten Mile, Washington County, Penn. Francis Headley died in Randolph County, Va , in 1805. He had several children Samuel Headley, his grandfather, was born in the year

1765, and was married to Abigail Trace in the year 1788; he and his wife moved from Essex County, N J, in 1790 with his father, Francis. Samuel Headley (his grandfather), had a family of eight children. An older claim or title was established for the land in Randolph County, Va., so all was lost and the family moved to other parts. Samuel Headley moved to Jefferson Township, Greene County, where John Headley, his father, was born in the year 1809. He learned the blacksmith trade with John Young during the years 1828 and 1829, and in 1833 commenced business in Washington Township He was married to Eliza Hoffman during that year, and in 1843 moved to Tom's Run in Gilmore Township, where he is now living. His first wife died in 1875, and in the same year he was married to the widow Silveous, who died in 1888. He had a family of eight children by his first wife, Sam. II. Headley being the third child. He was born in Washington Township in 1838. In 1856 he left home to attend school, working nights and mornings for his board, and for several years he taught school during the winter and attended school during the summer. In 1868 he commenced the mercantile business with T. J. Hoffman as a partner, and in 1872 set up for himself at Pine Bank. He was married to C. J. Fletcher, of Blacksville, W. Va., in the year 1870. They have one child—Robert B Headley, who was born in 1871. Sam. II. Headley and son religiously are Friends

WILLIAM H. JOHNSON, farmer, P. O. Blacksville, W. Va, was born in Wayne Township, Greene County, Penn., November 4, 1840, a son of William and Nancy Johnson (nee Lantz). Mrs. Johnson was born in Monongalia County, W. Va., and her husband was a native of Greene County, Penn., where they lived until his death, November 16, 1857. Mrs. Johnson was afterwards united in marriage with Henry Stephens, who died June 8, 1877; the widow is still living. William H Johnson's wife was Sarah A. McDougal, born in Wayne Township, October 24, 1843, and married January 30, 1862 She is a daughter of Alexander and Sallie (Franks) Mc Dougal, the former deceased. Mr. and Mrs. Johnson have three children, viz.—Nancy A., wife of John McPhillips; Minerva J., wife of Josephus Thomas; and John W. Mr. Johnson is one of the enterprising farmers of Wayne Township, where he owns 115 acres of land. He filled the office of justice of the peace in his township two terms, has served as school director six terms, and held the position of assessor and inspector of elections. He and his wife are members of the Southern Methodist Church.

J. S. KENT, farmer, Dent, Penn., was born in Centre Township, Greene County, January 31, 1835. His parents, William and Elizabeth (Odenbaugh) Kent, were natives of this county and residents therein until Mrs. Kent's death, May 4, 1868. Her husband afterwards married Jane White, widow of Rev. Michael White, of West Virginia; they live in Wayne Township. William Kent is the father of eleven children, seven boys and four girls, of whom nine are living. In 1858 J. S. Kent was united in marriage with Rebecca Morris, born in West Virginia in 1837, a daughter of James and Sarah Morris, the former deceased. By this marriage Mr. Kent is the father of one child—William J. Mrs. Kent departed this life September 25, 1860. Mr. Kent was a second time united in marriage, August 20, 1861, with Catharine Eddy, born in Wayne Township, January 5, 1830, a daughter of John and Sophia Eddy (nee Steel). Mr. and Mrs. Kent have a family of three boys and three girls, five living—Elizabeth, wife of Jesse Coen; Minerva, wife of Thomas Hoy; John R., Hiram W. and Michael I.; and Nancy J. (deceased). Mr. Kent is one of the most enterprising citizens of Wayne Township, and owns 237 acres of land where he now lives with his family. His wife is a member of the Methodist Episcopal Church.

JAMES KNIGHT, Oak Forest, Penn., one of the enterprising young farmers of Wayne Township, was born January 27, 1848, and is a son of David and Mary Knight (nee Fry), who are natives of Greene County, Penn., where they were married and now reside in Centre Township. They are the parents of nine children, seven of whom are living. James Knight's wife was Elizabeth S., daughter of Jacob and Frances (Tustin) Cole, natives of Greene County and now residents of Waynesburg. Mr. and Mrs. Knight were married August 29, 1868. Their children are—John H., Frances A., William M. and Mary C. As noticed in the beginning of this sketch, Mr. Knight is a farmer by occupation, and has also given much attention to the raising of fine stock. His farm contains 156 acres.

WILLIAM LANTZ, Dent, Penn., was born April 27, 1835, on the farm where he and family reside in Wayne Township. His parents, Jacob and Delilah (Coen) Lantz, were natives of Greene County and residents therein through life. His father died in 1858 and his mother in 1866. They were the parents of five children, three living. William is the youngest, and was united in marriage May 22, 1856, with Minerva, daughter of William and Elizabeth (Odenbaugh) Kent, the latter deceased. Mrs. Lantz was born in this county November 24, 1837, and is a consistent member of the Methodist Episcopal Church. Mr. William Lantz and wife are the parents of seven children—Mary, wife of William Wiley; William, who married Belle Phillips; Ulysses and Emma; Harriet, Delilah, and an infant (deceased). Mr. Lantz has been eminently successful as a farmer and stock-dealer, and owns 480 acres of good land in Greene County.

GEORGE W. MOORE, Spragg's, Penn., was born in Whiteley Township, Greene County, January 3, 1834. His parents, James and Matilda (Franks) Moore, were also natives of this county, where after marriage they settled and remained all their lives. After Matilda's death, Mr. Moore married Elizabeth (Brown) Provence, who is still living. Mr. Moore is deceased. He was the father of eleven children, six living. George W. is the third child, and was united in marriage, July 26, 1859, with Louisa R. Phillips, born in Cumberland Township, September 26, 1840, a daughter of Job and Margaret (Simington) Phillips, natives of Greene County, where they remained until Mrs. Phillips' death, after which he married Mary Mason. To Mr. and Mrs. Moore have been born seven children— James E., Thomas L., Job, Peter C., Elizabeth L., Lafy E. and Matilda M. Mr. Moore's occupation is that of farming and stock-dealing, and he owns 275 acres of land in Wayne Township. He and wife are among the most prominent members of the Methodist Episcopal Church.

HON. JESSE PHILLIPS, Spragg's, Penn., born in Whiteley Township, February 10, 1824, is a son of Richard and Abigail (Starkey) Phillips. His parents were natives of Greene County, where they spent their whole life. His father died in the year 1877, and his mother in 1879. They were the parents of eleven children, of whom our subject is the second, and was united in marriage, December 22, 1845, with Mary, daughter of David and Nancy (Gorden) Spragg. They were also natives of this county, where they remained till Mr. Spragg's death in 1877. His wife died in 1886. By this marriage Mr. Phillips is the father of twelve children—William D., Richard, Caleb, Levi, Adam F., Thomas E., Jesse L., Deborah F., James L., John W.; and Otho and Nancy E. (deceased). Their mother departed this life in 1871. She was a faithful member of the Methodist Episcopal Church. Mr. Phillips' second wife was Deborah, daughter of David and Nancy (Gorden) Spragg, now deceased. By this marriage Mr. and Mrs. Phillips have three children—George Daniel, and Clemmie (deceased). Although raised on a farm and devoting much of his time to agricultural interests and stock-raising, Mr. Phillips has also been actively engaged in political affairs. He is a Democrat, and in 1881 was elected associate judge, having polled nearly as many votes as his three competitors. In April, 1888, he sat on the jury which found George Clark guilty of murder in the first degree, for the killing of William McCausland. This was the first verdict of murder in the first degree ever found by a jury in Greene County. Mr. Phillips has a fine farm of 500 acres, and he and wife are members of the Patrons of Husbandry Lodge of Kughntown. The whole family are members of the Methodist Episcopal Church.

WILLIAM D. PHILLIPS, Hoover's Run, Penn., is one of the most successful of the younger farmers of Greene County. He was born in Wayne Township, December 22, 1846, a son of Jesse and Mary (Spragg) Phillips, natives of Greene County, where Mr. Phillips still resides. Mrs. Phillips died in the year 1871. William D. is the oldest of twelve children, and was united in marriage, August 4, 1866, with Sarah, daughter of Henry and Elizabeth (King) Cole, also natives of Greene County, where Mrs. Phillips' mother still resides. Her father departed this life March 15, 1882. Mr. and Mrs. Phillips have eight children—Mary E., Justice, Henry O., James P., Adam P., Frances A., Walter S. and Sarah E. The subject of our sketch was reared on a farm and is greatly interested in all matters pertaining to agriculture and stock-raising. He owns 200 acres of land in Wayne Township. He and wife are members of the Patrons of Husbandry Lodge of Kughntown, and are also communicants in the Methodist Episcopal Church of that place.

JOHN Mc. PHILLIPS, P. O. Spragg's, is one of the substantial young farmers and stock-dealers of Wayne Township, where he was born August 26, 1862. He is a son of Armstrong and Eleanor (Spragg) Phillips, also natives of Wayne Township, and residents therein all their lives. His father died August 13, 1870, aged thirty years and four months; and his mother died December 25, 1870, aged thirty-three years, seven months and twenty days. John Mc. is their only child. He was united in marriage, December 17, 1882, with Nancy A. Johnson, a daughter of William H. and Sarah A. (McDougal) Johnson, whose sketch appears in this history. Mr. and Mrs. Phillips have two children—William A., born February 7, 1884, and Ora A., born November 10, 1887. Mr. Phillips owns 219 acres of good land where he resides with his family. In religion Mr. and Mrs. Phillips are members of the Methodist Protestant Church.

DAVID SPRAGG (deceased) was born May 2, 1806, in Wayne Township, Greene County, Penn., on the farm now owned by the heirs of Otho Spragg. He was a son of Caleb and Deborah (McClure) Spragg, who were married November 6, 1798. The former was born September 22, 1778, and died April 20, 1854. The latter was born August 1, 1780, and departed this life September 22, 1860. They emigrated from Trenton, N. J., to what is now Wayne Township, Greene County, Penn., where they reared a family of twelve children, six sons and six daughters. Eleven of these grew to be men and women, one daughter dying in infancy. The oldest daughter, Amy, was born April, 1800, and was united in marriage with Joseph Wells. They were the parents of a large family. John was born June 30, 1801, and was married to Margaret Hamilton in 1820. To this union was born eleven children. He departed this life February, 1888. Sarah was born December 30, 1802. She remained single through life, and died in 1865 Uriah was born October 7, 1804, and was married to Susannah McLaughlin in 1820. He was the father of seven children, and departed this life in 1875. William was born February 28, 1808, and married Nancy Maple in 1833. They were the parents of four children. He died in 1872. Jeremiah was born September 26, 1809, and was married in 1832 to Sarah Shriver. This union was blessed with three children. He died March 3, 1878. Otho was born October 5, 1811, and was united in marriage in 1833 with Lydia Shul. They were the parents of two children. He departed this life March, 1882. Elizabeth was born July 4, 1814, and was married to Simon Strosnider in 1833. She was the mother of eight children, and departed this life February, 1884. Rebecca was born May 17, 1817, and was married to W. J. Casgray, December 15, 1842. To them were born seven children. She died May 6, 1881. Deborah was born November 9, 1820, and was united in marriage, in 1848, with Thomas Hoge. She was the mother of one child, and departed this life in 1849. David (deceased), who is the subject of this sketch, was the fifth in the family, and was united in marriage, at the age of twenty-one, with Nancy A. Gordon, who was born November 3, 1806, and died March, 1886. She was a daughter of William Gordon, and was reared in Whiteley Township, Greene County, Penn. Her parents, with all their children except herself, moved to Perry County, Ohio, in 1836. To Mr. David Spragg and wife were born five children. The oldest, Mary, was born in 1827, and was married to Hon. Jesse Phillips in 1845. She was the mother of twelve children, and departed this life September 29, 1872. Caleb A. was born December 18, 1829, and is one of Greene County's most substantial citizens. He was united in marriage, November 6, 1851, with Sarah Johnson, a daughter of William and Nancy (Lantz) Johnson. The former is deceased, and the latter is living. By this marriage Mr. Caleb A Spragg is the father of five children—Sylvenus L, a prominent physician of Pittsburgh, Penn.; Francis M. and David G., of Harrison County, Mo.; William E., proprietor of the marble works at Waynesburg, and Clara N., wife of Corbly K. Spragg. Mrs. Spragg departed this life December 21, 1882. After her death Mr. Spragg was again united in marriage, April 6, 1884, with Matilda Porter, a daughter of John and Hannah (Rinehart) Porter. This union has been blessed with one child— Porter M. In connection with the raising of stock and the management of his farm of 125 acres, upon which he has bestowed much care and attention, Mr Spragg has filled various offices in his township, and served as a member of the school board two terms William, the second son of David and Nancy Spragg, was born November 14, 1832, and was married to Sarah A. Brock, October, 1859. They

49

were the parents of six children. He departed this life October 10, 1872. Adam, the third son, was united in marriage with Lydia Pettit, December 3, 1858. To this union was born four children. He died September 10, 1872. Debbie, the youngest daughter, was born May 14, 1839, and was married to Joel Strawn in 1858. They were the parents of six children. Mr. Strawn died in 1871. David, our subject, died February 7, 1877, on the farm known as the Spragg homestead, in Wayne Township. He was from his early youth engaged in land speculations and farming. He obtained but a limited education, but being a great philanthropist he proved a blesings to the community in which he lived. At the age of thirty-five he became a member of the Methodist Protestant Church. He possessed good social qualities. His wife was of a kind disposition, and their home was one of the most attractive in the neighborhood. He and his wife lived a long and happy life together, and were known to every one in that neighborhood as "Uncle Dave" and "Aunt Nancy Spragg."

HENRY M. SPRAGG, postmaster, Spragg's, Penn., is one of the most successful farmers of Greene County, and owns about 300 acres of land. He was born August 8, 1837, a son of Jeremiah and Sarah Spragg (*nee* Shriver), who were natives of this county, where they were married and resided until his father's death, March 10, 1878; his mother is still living. Henry M., the youngest of their three children, was united in marriage, March 19, 1862, with Eliza, daughter of John and Kezia Kent (*nee* Shields), natives and residents of this county. Mr. and Mrs. Spragg are the parents of five children—McClelland, Lazear, Simon T., Laura S. and Harriet E. Mr. Spragg has served his township as constable, assessor and school director; and is a member of the Independent Order of Odd Fellows Lodge, of Blacksville, West Virginia.

ISRAEL STEWART, deceased, was born in Greene County, Penn., May 17, 1830, a son of James and Mary Stewart (*nee* Blair), (deceased). Mr. Stewart was united in marriage, March 24, 1853, with Rebecca Phillips, born in Wayne Township, December 18, 1827, a daughter of Richard and Abigail (Starkey) Phillips, natives of Greene County, and now deceased. Mr. and Mrs. Stewart were the parents of ten children—Thomas L., Richard, James, Elizabeth M., wife of Kenney Strosnider; Jesse H., Spencer M., Mary J., wife of Thomas Calvert, Abigail F. and Sarah R.; and George W., (deceased). Mr. Stewart was a stone-mason by trade, but in later years devoted his time to farming, and owned 300 acres of land near Blacksville, West Virginia. He was a deacon in the Baptist Church, of which his widow and family are also members. He died October 29, 1887.

ABRAHAM, TUSTIN, farmer, P. O. Hoover's Run, Penn., was born in Wayne Township in 1848, a son of John and Mary (Bumgarner) Tustin, natives of Greene County, where his father died in the year 1882, and his mother in 1850. They were the parents of five children, of whom Abraham is the third. On September 2, 1862, he chose for his life companion Miss Frances E., daughter of Henry and Elizabeth (King) Cole, who were natives and residents of this county, where Mr. Cole died March 15, 1882; Mrs. Cole is still living. Mr. and Mrs. Tustin's children are—John L , Elizabeth M., Jacob H., Sarah C., Lucy J., Margaret E. and Osa E.; Fanny M. and Rachel A. being deceased. Mr. Tustin was reared on a farm, and although comparatively a young man, he has been greatly prospered in his farming and stock dealing, and owns 191 acres of land in Wayne Township. He and wife and two of their children are members of the Patrons of Husbandry Lodge of Kughntown, and belong to the Oak Shade Methodist Episcopal Church.

REASIN WHITE, farmer, Oak Forest, Penn., was born in Franklin Township, January 13, 1833. His father is the Rev David White, founder of what is known as "White's Church," near Waynesburg. He is now over ninety years of age and still quite active in mind and body. His mother's maiden name was Leah Strosnider; both were natives of Greene County. Mrs. White departed this life in 1867. On June 3, 1854, Mr. Reasin White married Miss Elizabeth, daughter of Daniel and Jemima Rogers (nee Pettit), also natives of this county, where they were married and first settled. They afterwards removed to Ohio, where Mr. Rogers died in 1883. Mrs. Rogers departed this life January 21, 1886, in Wayne Township, Greene County, Penn. Mr. and Mrs. White have five children, two of whom are living—Judge D. and Samuel K. The deceased are: Mary E., David W. and Israel. Mr. White is one of the most industrious and highly respected farmers in his community, and owns 200 acres of excellent land. He and family are faithful members of the Pursley Baptist Church.

JOHN I. WORLEY, farmer and stock-dealer, Blacksville, West Virginia, is a descendant of one of the first settlers of Wayne Township, Greene County, Penn. He was born December 1, 1823, on the farm where he and family reside in Wayne Township His father, David Worley, was born in Wayne Township, May 8, 1775, on the farm now owned by John I. His mother, Margaret Cather, was a native of Franklin Township, born May 20, 1780 They were married December 30, 1799. Three of their ten children are living, viz.: William C , of West Virginia; Dr. Asberry, of Fayette County, Ohio, and John I. Their father died September 10, 1851, and the mother December 5, 1853. Mr. John I Worley was twice married, his first wife being Miss Maria Gordon, with whom he shared his fortunes, December 21, 1843. Mrs. Worley was born in Franklin Township, January 6, 1824, a daughter of Bazil and Sarah (Shriver)

Gordon (deceased). By this marriage Mr. Worley is the father of seven children—Sarah, wife of R. W Dougan; William G , David R., Jesse L., Alpheus B and Lizzie, wife of Rev. James E. Mercer; and Maggie, (deceased) Their mother departed this life February 7, 1877, a consistent member of the Methodist Protestant Church. On June 17, 1879, Mr. Worley chose for his second wife Mrs Delilah Higgins, born in Whiteley Township September 15, 1830, a daughter of Mark and Susan Gordon (deceased). Mr. Worley was brought up on a farm and has always followed his present occupation He owns 600 acres of land in Greene County He has served as justice of the peace in Wayne Township, an office which his father held for forty years. He has held almost all the important offices of his township, having ever been one of its most highly respected citizens. He and Mrs. Worley are consistent members of the Methodist Episcopal Church.

ROBERT ZIMMERMAN, farmer, Spragg's, Penn., was born in Greene County, December 19, 1819 His parents, Henry and Elizabeth (Mitchell) Zimmerman, were natives of Maryland, where they were married, then moved to Greene County, Penn , near Waynesburg, and remained until their death. Robert and his brother Henry are their only children living. On December 17, 1840, Robert married Mary Flick, a native of Greene County and daughter of Daniel Flick . To Mr. and Mrs Zimmerman were born six children, four living—Elizabeth, wife of Lot Rose; Susan, wife of Solomon Lemley; Eliza, wife of Hudson Kiger; and Henry, who married Caroline Headley. The deceased are Daniel and William. Mrs. Zimmerman died August 5, 1852 February 1, 1855, Mr. Zimmerman married Catharine, daughter of John Cree, also a native of this county. By this second marriage he is the father of one child—Ruth, wife of Bowen Stephens. Mrs. Catharine Zimmerman died September 2, 1860. Robert Zimmerman afterwards married Dorcas Rinehart, January 5, 1862. She was born in Franklin Township, November 8, 1819, a daughter of John T. and Susannah Rinehart. Mr. Zimmerman owns 204 acres of land where he and family reside in Wayne Township.

WHITELEY TOWNSHIP.

A. M. BAILEY, retired farmer, Kirby, Penn., is one of the pioneers of Whiteley Township, where he was born on his present farm
April 30, 1814. His father, Joab Bailey, was a native of Chester
County, Penn., and when only twelve years of age came with his
parents to Greene County, where he married Miss Jane Mundell, a
native of Greene Township, this county. They lived on Muddy
Creek a few years and then purchased the farm on Pleasant Hill in
Whiteley Township, now owned by Abner M., and remained on that
farm until their death. They were the parents of nine children, of
whom only three are living, viz.: Abner M. and two sisters, Jaen
and Eliza A. Mr. A. M. Bailey was united in marriage the first
time, in 1838, with Elizabeth South, born in Dunkard Township in
1816, a daughter of Enoch and Ruth South (*nee* Gregg). By this
marriage he is the father of six children, four living—Benjamin,
Presley, Ruth, wife of William Patterson, and Jane, wife of Jasper
Morris; and Ellis and Joab E. (deceased). Mrs. Bailey died in 1849.
In 1855 Mr. Bailey took unto himself a helpmate in the person of
Mrs. Mary Cowell, who was born in Dunkard Township, this county,
in 1824, a daughter of Thomas and Rachael Bowen (*nee* Fordyce).
By this union Mr. Bailey is the father of four children, two living,
viz.: Abner J. and Elvador; and Elizabeth and Susan A., (deceased).
Mrs. Mary Bailey died in 1874. In 1877 Mr. Bailey was united in
the holy bonds of matrimony with Miss Margaret Taylor, who was
born in Washington Township in 1825, a daughter of Thomas and
Angeline Taylor (*nee* McCaslin). Mrs. Margaret Bailey departed
this life in 1885. Then Mr. Bailey was married the fourth time,
November 24, 1885, to Mrs. Ruth A. Hoover, born in Jefferson
Township, December 10, 1840, a daughter of Thomas and Elizabeth
Wickersham (*nee* Randolph). During the early years of his life
Mr. Bailey was actively engaged in farming and stock-dealing, from
which he has secured enough of this world's goods to keep him in
comfortable circumstances the remainder of his days. In 1867 he
was elected to the office of county treasurer and served one term very
creditably. He and his wife are members of the Methodist
Protestant Church.

DAVID BARE, Kirby, Penn., is one of the pioneers of Whiteley
Township, Greene County, where he was born September 29, 1818,
a son of David and Susannah (Rittenour) Bare. His father was a

native of Bedford County, Penn., and his mother of Washington County, Maryland, where they were married and remained till 1810, at which time they moved to Fayette County, Pennsylvania. In 1812 he enlisted in the service of his country, and the same year his wife moved with the family to Greene County. She departed this life in 1845; her husband died in 1862. They had a family of fourteen children, nine of whom are living. Mr. David Bare was united in marriage May 13, 1840, with Lucinda Hickman, who was born in Greene County in 1822, a daughter of Abraham and Mary (Nelson) Hickman. By this marriage Mr. Bare is the father of six children —Martin B., Eliza, wife of John M. Bradford; Mary A., wife of Andrew Pitcock, and John; the deceased are James and Emily. Mrs. Bare died in 1853. Then in 1860 Mr. Bare married Rebecca Lemley, born in Whiteley Township, November 5, 1822, a daughter of Ezekiel and Sarah (Bowers) Lemley. By this marriage Mr. and Mrs. Bare have four children—Benjamin F., living; and Sophrona, Emma and an infant, (deceased). Mr. Bare is a blacksmith by trade, which he followed about forty-eight years; since that time he has been engaged in farming, and owns eighty acres of land in Whiteley Township. He filled the office of assessor of his township. In religion he and his wife are Methodists.

HENRY BOWERS, farmer, Lone Star, Penn., was born in Virginia, January 1, 1826. He is a son of Solomon and Peggy Cowers (nee Bradford), who were natives of Whiteley Township, Greene County, Penn., where they were married, then moved to Virginia and remained until their death. They had twelve children, eight of whom are now living. Henry is the oldest son and was united in marriage October 21, 1847, with Catharine Barockman, born in Virginia, July 27, 1824. She is a daughter of John and Barbara Barockman (nee Franks), natives of Pennsylvania, who after marriage moved to Virginia and remained until their death. Mr. and Mrs. Henry Bowers are the parents of seven children, four dead—Lucinda, Elizabeth, Clark and Marion; and three living— Morgan, Sarah E. and Josephus, who married Josephine Fuller, and is the father of two children—Charlie E. and Lizzie M. Mr. Bowers is a farmer, as we learn from the heading of this sketch, and is the owner of a fine farm of 170 acres. He and his family are members of the Methodist Protestant Church, in which he has been one of the trustees for about ten years.

M. C. BRANT, P. O. Kirby, is one of the leading business men of Newton, Pennsylvania. He was born in Cameron, West Virginia, September 29, 1858, a son of Eli and Sarah Brant (nee Spragg), natives of Wayne Township, Greene County, where they lived until about 1856, at which time they moved to Cameron, W. Va., and remained till 1859, then returned to Wayne Township. When the war commenced, Mr. Brant enlisted in behalf of his country's cause, and while in service contracted the disease of diphtheria from which he died. After his death his widow was united in marriage with Abraham Gump, whose sketch appears in this work. M. C. Brant was united in marriage February 14, 1885, with Edna Thompson, born in Center Township, Greene County, August 22, 1859. Her parents, Elijah and Sarah Thompson (*nee* Hoge), were natives of Center Township, and residents there until Mr. Thompson's death which occurred in 1861. Sometime afterwards his widow was united in marriage with Lisbon Staggers, whose sketch also appears in this book. Mr M C. Brant and wife are the parents of one child, Jay F., born February 22, 1886. Mr. Brant was raised on a farm, and acquired a good common-school education. In 1884 he opened a general store in Newton, where he has a large and liberal patronage. His wife is a consistent member of the Baptist Church.

DAVID L. COWELL, farmer, Kirby, Penn., was born in Dunkard Township, Greene County, November 5, 1829, a son of Daniel and Susannah Cowell (*nee* Bowers). The former was also a native of Dunkard, and the latter of Whiteley Township, where they were married They then settled in Dunkard Township and remained until their death. They were the parents of twelve children, only four of whom are living. September 15, 1864, David L Cowell married Miss Harriet Long. She was born in Whiteley Township October 15, 1843, and is a consistent member of the Methodist Episcopal Church. Her parents, Samuel and Adeline Long, were natives Greene County and residents therein until their death, which occurred in Perry Township. Of the five children born to Mr. and Mrs Cowell, three are living—William L., Ellsworth and Amanda. Throughout his life Mr. Cowell has been engaged in stock-dealing and farming, in which he has been eminently successful, owing at present a fine farm of 400 acres of land in Whiteley Township.

JOHN M. COWELL, Lone Star, Penn., is a descendant of one of the pioneer families of Greene County He was born in Whiteley Township, January 1, 1851, on the farm where he and his family now live. His parents were Solomon and Eliza Cowell (*nee* Michael). The former was born in Greene County and the latter in West Virginia where they were married, settled in Whiteley Township on the farm now owned by John M., and remained until Mr. Cowell's death which took place in 1879. Mrs. Cowell is still living in Newton. They were the parents of thirteen children, five living. September 23, 1873, John M. Cowell married Mary J. Norton, born in Butler County, Penn, December 29, 1855. Her parents were Martin K. and Rebecca Norton, also natives of Butler County, who now

live in the State of Iowa   To Mr. Cowell and wife have been born
seven children—Minnie L , Wesley A., William S , Charles N., John
E., Sadie R. and Cleveland.   Mr. Cowell's farm consists of 246
acres, and on it can be found fine horses, cattle and sheep, the raising
of which has formed an important part of his business.   He is a
public spirited citizen, and has held the office of school director in
his district.   Mrs Cowell is a consistent member of the Methodist
Episcopal Church.

   JOHN A. CUMMINS, Waynesburg, Penn , is one of the most
industrious farmers of Whiteley Township, where he was born September 14, 1840.   His parents, William and Catharine Cummins,
are natives of Greene County and reside in Whiteley Township.   They
have a family of ten children, of whom nine are living.   September
14, 1878, John A. Cummins married Miss Hannah Rush, a native of
Franklin Township.   To them have been born four children—William A , Lona O., Catharine E , and John B.   Having been raised on
a farm, Mr. Cummins has made a business of farming and stock-
dealing all through his life, and as a result of his faithful and persistent labors is now in possession of an excellent farm of about 230
acres in Whiteley Township, where he and family live.   His wife is
among the most consistent and prominent members of the Methodits
Protestant Church.

   JOHN FOX, Kirby, Penn., one of the substantial citizens of
Whiteley Township, Greene County, was born in Perry Township,
April 25, 1830. His parents were Henry and Susannah (Delany)
Fox, who were natives of Greene County, where they were married
and remained till death.   He departed this life October 29, 1882, and
she December 25, 1875.   They were the parents of ten children, of
whom six are living   Mr. John Fox was united in marriage December 13, 1849, with Dorothy Hains, who was born in Whiteley Township October 15, 1830, a daughter of John and Jane Hains (*nee* John),
who were natives of Greene County, lived in Whiteley Township until
1857, then moved to West Virginia where Mr. Hains died in 1887.
His widow is still living.   They had a family of eleven children—
Eli, Christopher C , Matilda, wife of Winfield S. Vandruff; Jane, wife
of John L. Walters; Taylor, Daily, Luther, Maggie, wife of George
Patterson; William and Nancy; and Walter, (deceased)   Mr. Fox is
quite a genius in his way, and successful in almost every undertaking
His principal business is farming, and he owns 475 acres of land in
Greene County.   He filled the office of justice of the peace of his
township for five years; and at different times has held the positions
of auditor, constable, assessor, trustee and member of the school
board.   He and his wife belong to the Methodist Episcopal
Church.

JOHN S. FULLER, farmer and stock-dealer, P. O. Lone Star, was born in Whiteley Township, Greene County, Penn., April 24, 1833. His parents are Daniel and Nancy (Whitlatch) Fuller, the one born in Fayette and the other in Greene County, where they were married in Whiteley Township and remained through life. He departed this life April 22, 1874, and she December 14, 1876. They were the parents of eight children, all but one living. Subject's grandparents were natives of Ireland. The grandfather was born in the city of Dublin, and the grandmother in the county of Tyrone. They were married after emigrating to America. Mr. John S. Fuller was united in marriage August 13, 1852, with Emily Phillips, born in Greene County September 28, 1837. She is a daughter of Elmer and Elizabeth Phillips (nee Vandruff), natives of this county, the latter deceased. Mr. Fuller and wife are the parents of seven children, five living—Nancy, wife of Henry Zimmerman; Josephine, wife of Josephus Bowers; Smith, Bowman and Ida M.; Elizabeth and Daniel L. being deceased. Mr. Fuller owns 700 acres of land where he and his family reside, and has taken considerable interest in the raising of fine stock, being the first to bring a herd of thorough-bred short-horned cattle into Whiteley Township, in 1883. He was a member of the school board two terms; served as assessor three terms and as assistant assessor for many years. Both he and his wife are members of the Methodist Protestant Church.

ABRAHAM GUMP, farmer and stock-dealer, is a descendant of one of the pioneer families of Greene County, Penn. He was born in Whiteley Township, December 15, 1832, a son of John and Dorcas Gump (nee Whitlatch). His father was a native of Virginia, and his mother of New Jersey. They were married in Whiteley Township, Greene County, Penn., residing there until their death; she departed this life in 1840 and her husband in 1863. They were the parents of thirteen children, of whom only two are living, viz.: Cassandra, now the widow of Jacob Lemley, and Abraham, the subject of our notice, who was united in marriage the first time March 4, 1852, with Maria Adamson. She was born in Waynesburg, a daughter of Cyrus and Elizabeth Adamson, now deceased. By this union Mr. Gump is the father of two children, one living—John C; and Samantha A., deceased. In the spring of 1857, Mr. Gump and family moved to Warren County, Illinois, and about two months later Mrs. Gump met with a sad accident resulting in her death. While alone in the house with her little family, in passing too near the grate her clothes took fire and were burned off before any assistance could reach her and she died in about sixteen hours from the effect of the burns. This occurred May 16, 1857. Mr. Gump afterwards returned with his family to Whiteley Township, Penn., and was united in marriage

June 16, 1867, with Sarah Brant, (*nee* Spragg). She has two children—Otho and Matthias. Her parents, Otho and Lida (Shull) Spragg, were natives of Greene County, and residents of Wayne Township until Mrs Sragg's death March 23, 1874. Her husband died April 12, 1882 By his last marriage Mr. Gump is the father of three children—George M., Corbly and Debbie Mr Gump has been a farmer and stock-dealer all his life, and he and his wife own about 650 acres of land in Greene County. They are consistent members of the Methodist Episcopal Church, and his deceased wife also

SOLOMON GUTHRIE, a retired farmer of Kirby, Penn, was born in the house where he and his family reside in Whiteley Township, Greene County, April 7, 1816. He is a son of Archibald and Elizabeth (Lemley) Guthrie, who were natives of Pennsylvania. They were married in Greene County, afterwards settling in Whiteley Township, where Mrs Guthrie died. After her death, Archibald married Mary Scott, who is still living. He died August 23, 1845. He was the father of twelve children, of whom eight are living Solomon Guthrie was united in marriage January 31, 1839, with Elizabeth Fry, born in Centre Township, November 20, 1818. Mrs Guthrie's parents were George and Elizabeth Fry (*nee* Beckingbaugh), who were natives of Greene County To Mr. and Mrs Guthrie have been born ten children, of whom seven are living—Susan, wife of Robinson John, Elizabeth S, wife of Benona John, George W, Lucinda, wife of Abraham Shull; Solomon E., Jessie L. and William F.; Job, Maria and Archibald B. being deceased. Mr. Guthrie has been engaged in farming all his life, and owns 120 acres of land where he and his family reside He and Mrs. Guthrie are consistent members of the Methodist Church

G W. HATFIELD, farmer, P. O Lone Star, was born in Whiteley Township, Greene County, Penn., July 30, 1816 His parents were Jacob and Rebecca (Mundle) Hatfield, the former a native of New Jersey and the latter of Greene County, Penn., where they were married and remained through life. In 1839, G. W. Hatfield married Miss Mary Richie, born in Fayette County, Penn., in 1806, daughter of James Richie. Mr and Mrs. Hatfield have seven children, six living—Jacob, James, Hiram, William, Elizabeth, wife of Lindsey Stephens and Madison, and Frank, (deceased) Mr. Hatfield has always lived on a farm, and has been one of the most enterprising and successful farmers and stock-dealers in the county, where he owns 900 acres of land He served his district on the school board for about twelve years Mr. and Mrs. Hatfield are exemplary members of the Methodist Protestant Church.

CHRISTOPHER JOHN, deceased, was born May 26, 1820, on the farm where the family reside in Whiteley Township. His father and mother were James and Margaret (Robinson) John, natives of eastern Pennsylvania. They were married in Greene County and settled on the farm now owned by the heirs of Christopher John, (deceased), and remained until their death. His father died January 16, 1874, and his mother July 20, 1852. They were the parents of eleven children, five now living Christopher John was united in marriage in 1839 with Nancy Fox, born in Greene County, March 23, 1823, a daughter of Henry and Susannah (Delany) Fox, natives of Greene County, now deceased. Mr. and Mrs. John's family consists of eleven children, seven living—Barbara, wife of David Lockhart; Sarah J , widow of George Connor; Margaret, wife of R Fox; Kinsey, Reasin, Elizabeth, wife of I. N. Kiger; and Sidonia, wife of William Vandruff. Henry, Susannah, Franklin and William, are deceased. Notwithstanding the fact that Mr. John, like the rest of the early settlers, received but a limited education, he was quite a successful farmer through life, and owned 550 acres of good land in Greene County at the time of his death, which occurred August 11, 1888.

DR. G. W. MOSS, deceased, was born in Washington County, Penn., May 5, 1836. His parents were Jennings J. and Ellen (Winnet) Moss. After marriage they resided in Washington County until 1844, at which time they moved to Richhill Township, Greene County, for a few years, then returned to Washington County, and remained until their seven children grew to maturity. They again retraced their steps to Greene County, and remained until their death. Only four of their children survive them. Dr. Moss was the third, and acquired his education in the common schools of Greene and Washington counties. He graduated in the Jefferson Medical College at Philadelphia in 1870, and afterwards took a course of lectures at Bellevue, N. Y. He began the practice of medicine at Jefferson, Penn., and in 1856 located at Newtown, where he was actively engaged in the profession until his death, January 16, 1888. The Doctor was united in marriage February 15, 1863, with Sarah J. Hudson, who was born in Newton, Penn., November 17, 1846. Mrs. Moss is a daughter of John and Sarah J. (Morris) Hudson, the former a native of West Moreland and the latter of Greene County, where they were married. They settled in Newtown, where Mr Hudson departed this life in August, 1884. His widow still resides at Newtown. They were the parents of nine children, of whom five are living. Dr. and Mrs. Moss were the parents of one daughter— Ethel H., born March 4, 1882. The Doctor was a member of the I. O. O. F., was a Knight Templar in the Masonic order, and belonged to the Methodist Episcopal Church, of which his widow is also a faithful and devoted member.

HENRY MORRIS, farmer, Fordyce, Penn , was born in Jefferson Township, Greene County, February 25, 1824. . His parents, Peter and Elizabeth (Renner) Morris, are natives of this county, where they were married and remained until Mrs Morris' death Her husband is still living and resides in Whiteley Township. They were the parents of seven children, of whom three are living.   Henry is the oldest child, and was united in marriage May 31, 1846, with Eliza Morris, who was born in Franklin Township, December 7, 1828.   She is a daughter of John and Jemima (Pipes) Morris, now deceased   Mr. Henry Morris and wife have seven children—Caroline, wife of Dr. Jacob Hatfield; Lindsey, John, George W., Andrew J. and Milton R; Franklin being deceased.   Mr Morris is one of the progressive business men of his township, in which he has been engaged in farming and stock dealing all his life.   He owns a fine farm of 370 acres   He served one term as director of the poor. His wife is a consistent member of the Methodist Church

ELIJAH MORRIS, farmer, Fordyce, Penn., was born in Jefferson Township, Greene County, January 7, 1809, a son of Henry and Edie (Hickman) Morris   They were natives of this county, where they were married and lived a number of years, then moved to Noble County, Ohio, where they died.   Their son, Elijah, was united in marriage October 10, 1830, with Nancy Morris, a native of Ohio and daughter of Isaac and Mary Morris.   By this marriage Mr. Morris is the father of ten children, seven are living—Peter, Mary, wife of John Morris; David, Abner, Richard, Simon and Sarah J., wife of Eli Stoops, and Andrew J., Elizabeth and Selah (deceased). Mrs. Morris died in 1850, and in 1864 Mr Morris married Nancy Ketcham (*nee* Mofford), a native of Greene County and daughter of William and Susan Mofford.   By this second marriage Mr. Morris has one child—Emma E., wife of Johnson Stickels.   Mrs. Morris died December 23, 1867.   Mr Morris is a farmer, and owns 152 acres of land in Whiteley Township, where he and family reside.

RUFUS PATTERSON, Kirby, Penn., is one of the substantial young farmers of Whiteley Township, where he was born August 11, 1861.   His father, William Patterson, a native of the same township, was united in marriage the first time with Rhoda Whitlatch, born in Perry Township, this county.   By this marriage Mr. William Patterson was the father of fourteen children, of whom ten are living.   His wife departed this life in 1852, and November 6, 1856, Mr. Patterson was again united in marriage with Sophia Kuhn, the mother of Rufus, the subject of this sketch.   She was born in Whiteley Township, October 29, 1815, a daughter of Abraham and Eleanor Kuhn (*nee* Mooney), the one a native of Germany and the other of Ireland, who after marriage settled in Greene County, Penn., remaining until their death By his last marriage Mr. William Patterson is the father of two children, of whom only Rufus is living. Mr. Patterson died May 13, 1887. March 2, 1887, Rufus married Emma Connor, who was born in Perry Township, this county, February 12, 1861, a daughter of Simon and Nancy Connor (*nee* Herrington), who resides in Whiteley Township. Like his father, Mr. Patterson was raised on a farm, and makes farming the business of his life. He owns 160 acres of land (the old Patterson home), where he and family reside.

ARTHUR SHRIVER, farmer, Kirby, Pennsylvania. Among the younger class of farmers and stock dealers of Whiteley Township, we mention the name that heads this sketch. He was born in Whiteley, April 26, 1845, his parents being Jacob and Elizabeth (Inghram) Shriver, who were pioneers of Greene County where they were married, July 5, 1831, and remained through life. He departed this life February 1, 1885, and she February 22, 1855. They were were the parents of ten children, nine living. The subject of our sketch is the youngest son. 1873, on October 2, he married Miss Ella Hickman, who was born in Whiteley, January 7, 1848. She is a daughter of Gilmon and Phœbe (Cloves) Hickman, natives of Greene County and residents of Whiteley Township. To Mr. and Mrs. Shriver have been born three children, two living, Minnie M. and Lizzie P. Mr. Shriver was reared on a farm and has been a successful farmer and stock-dealer through life, owning at present 200 hundred acres of excellent land where he lives with his family. Mr. Shriver is a member of the Methodist Episcopal Church.

A. J. SMITH, farmer, Kirby, Penn., born in Washington Township, December 14, 1833, is one of the pioneers of Greene County. His parents were Dennis and Sarah Smith, who were natives of this county and residents therein till death. His father died in Missouri. In 1855, A. J. Smith married Miss Phœbe J. Estle, born in Jefferson Township in 1828, a daughter of Matthias and Mary Estle (*nee* Stewart) who were natives of this county, both now deceased. Mr. and Mrs. Smith's family consists of six children, of whom four are living: Leroy W., Mary A., wife of Frank Johnson; Sarah M. and Elizabeth E.; Abraham and Matthias being deceased. Mr. Smith was reared on a farm and, following in the footsteps of many of his ancestors, he has made the tilling of the soil the pursuit of his life. He owns ninety-seven acres of good land where he resides with his family. Mr. and Mrs. Smith are faithful membess of the Methodist Protestant Church.

LISBON STAGGERS, retired farmer and stock-dealer, Kirby, Penn., was born in Franklin Township, Greene County, December 17, 1820, a son of John and Catharine Staggers (*nee* Maple). His parents were natives of Franklin Township and residents there until their death. His mother died in 1851, and his father, December 16, 1882. They were the parents of fifteen children, of whom seven are living. Lisbon, the subject of this sketch, is the fifth, and was first united in marriage, December 16, 1843, with Eliza J. Mooney, born in Franklin Township November 20, 1820, a daughter of Thomas and Cassandra Mooney (nee Inghram), now deceased. To Mr. and Mrs. Staggers were born nine children, four living—Cassandra, wife of Albert Rice; Arthur, Catherine M., wife of Sebastian Bowlby and James M. The deceased are Thomas J., William F, John, Martha E. and Harvey. Their mother died May 31, 1864. After her death, Mr. Staggers was again united in marriage, September 16, 1866, with Sarah Thompson (nee Hoge), who was a native of Centre Township, this county. She was born July 14, 1835, a daughter of Joseph and Mary Hoge (nee Cowen) the latter deceased. By the last marriage Mr. Staggers is the father of six children, five living—Hamon, Alice, Ida, Lisbon C., and Elva; and Selah, (deceased.) Mr. Staggers was reared on a farm and has made the care and management of his farm his life work. He owns 300 acres of good land where he and his family now live. Both he and his wife are communicants of the Baptist Church.

LINDSEY STEPHENS, Kirby, Penn, was born in Greene Township, June 23, 1836, a son of Barzilla and Margaret (Lantz) Stephens, who were natives of Greene County, where they were married and have since resided. Mr. Barzilla Stephens departed this life, April 24, 1884; his widow survives him and resides with her children, of whom three are living. Lindsey is the second of their five children, and was united in marriage, September 26, 1861, with Margaret Fordyce, born in Whiteley Township, December 30, 1843, a daughter of Benson and Maria (Nicholas) Fordyce, the latter deceased. By this marriage Mr. Stephens is the father of one daughter, Amanda. On October 27, 1863, Mrs. Stephens died, leaving to her daughter the example of her christian character and consistent life, On February 23, 1865, Mr. Stephens married Elizabeth J. Hatfield, who was born in Whiteley Township, September 4, 1846, a daughter of George W. and Mary (Richie) Hatfield, residents of the same township. Mr. and Mrs. Stephens have a family of seven children, of whom four are living—Nora, John, James and Harry; the deceased being Lafayette, Ida and Salina. Mr. Stephens has always lived on a farm and has been an industrious farmer and stock-dealer all his life. He and his wife own 975 acres of land in Whiteley Township. He has been a member of the Masonic Order for about thirty years; and he and wife are members of the Methodist Episcopal Church.

SIMON R. STROSNIDER, farmer, Waynesburg, Penn, was born in Whitley Township, Greene County, March 9, 1834, a son of Peter and Charlotte Strosnider (*nee* Gordon). His father was born in Whiteley and his mother in Franklin Township. They were married and lived in Greene County until 1850, after which time they moved to Perry County, Ohio, where they died. They had a family of eight children, of whom seven are living. Simon R., their son, was united in marriage, October 12, 1862, with Sarah A. Inghram, who was born in Waynesburg, January 11, 1843. Her parents were Arthur and Susannah Inghram (*nee* Eagon), natives of Greene County, both now deceased. To Mr. and Mrs. Strosnider have been born four daughters, Dolly, Lillie A., Laura V. and Lucy O. Mr. Strosnider was reared on a farm and has carried on the business of farming quite successfully all his life, at present owning 120 acres of land constituting his home farm. He filled the office of auditor of his township with credit to himself and his constituents. Dolly, the oldest of the four daughters was born August 26, 1864, united with the congregation at Mount Pleasant Church, March 13, 1881, she departed this life at the home of her parents, February 4, 1888, she was loved and respected by all who knew her.

A. M. TEMPLE, farmer, Fordyce, Penn, is a pioneer of Whiteley Township, Greene County. He was born October 11, 1825, a son of John and Elizabeth Temple (*nee* Douglass), the former of Greene and the latter of Fayette County, Penn, where they were married. They lived at Garard's Fort, Greene County, until 1831, when they moved to the farm where the subject of this sketch now resides. Mr. John Temple died three weeks later; his widow survived him until 1873. They had a family of four children, three living. Mr. A M. Temple was united in marriage, in July, 1846, with Lucy Greene, born in Franklin Township, September 13, 1829, a daughter of Morris and Sarah (Grooms) Greene. By this marriage Mr. Temple is the father of three children—Benjamin, living, and Elizabeth and Rebecca, deceased. Mrs. Temple died, June 17, 1881, having been a faithful member of the Methodist Episcopal Church. April 20, 1882, Mr. Temple married Mrs. Anna M. Burwell, who was born in Jefferson Township, June 13, 1832, a daughter of Jacob and Nancy Waychoff, the former a native of New Jersey and the latter of Greene County, Penn. Mr. Temple is a cooper by trade, which he followed about twenty-five years. He has since engaged in farming and stock raising, and owns a good farm of 300 acres. He has filled the offices of director of the poor and jury commissioner. He is a member of the Methodist Episcopal and his wife of the Baptist Church.

JAMES R. ZIMMERMAN, farmer, P. O. Delight, was born in Franklin Township, Greene County, Penn., September 15, 1840. His parents were William and Eliza A. Zimmerman (*nee* Seals), natives of the same township, where they were married, settled and remained until their death. He departed this life, January 21, 1852, and she, in October of the same year. They were the parents of seven children, of whom six are living, viz: William H., James R., Caroline, wife of Robert McGlumphy; Enos, Anna E, wife of Perry Cummins, and Vanamburg; Maria, deceased. Like his ancestors, the subject of our sketch was raised on a farm, and has always been engaged in farming and stock-dealing. Through industry and good management he has succeeded in getting a good farm, consisting of 225 acres, where he resides.

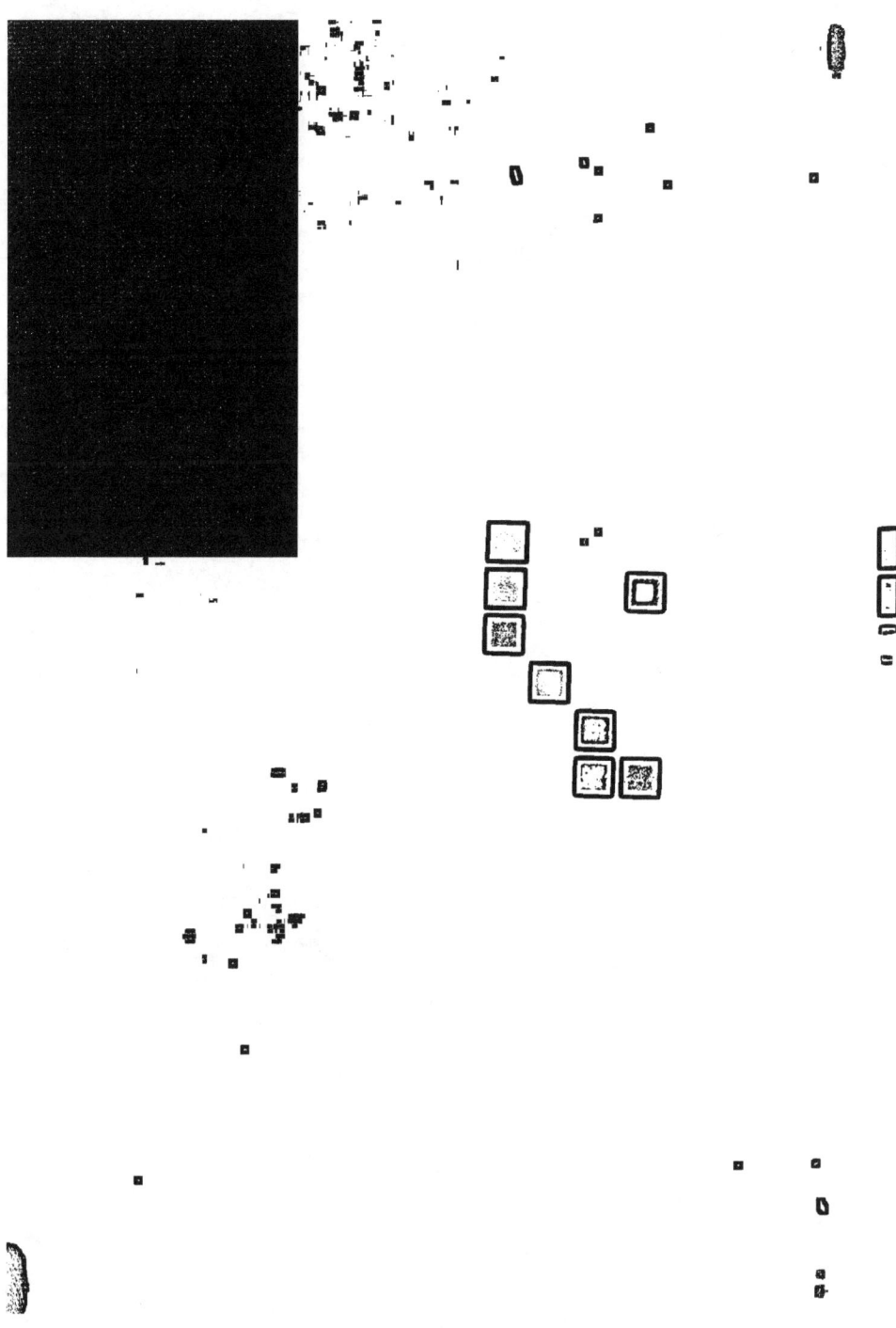

CPSIA information can be obtained
at www.ICGtesting.com
Printed in the USA
LVHW080759050121
675712LV00025B/968